INTERNATIONAL FINANCIAL ACCOUNTING AND REPORTING

4th Edition

By

Ciaran Connolly

Chartered
Accountants
Ireland

Published in 2013 by
Chartered Accountants Ireland
Chartered Accountants House
47–49 Pearse Street
Dublin 2
www.charteredaccountants.ie

ISBN: 978-1-908199-71-3

Typeset by Datapage
Printed and bound by CPI Group (UK) Ltd, Croydon, CRO 4YY

Contents

Introduction

This 4th Edition of *International Financial Accounting and Reporting* is designed to meet the continued and growing demand for up-to-date coverage of International Accounting Standards (IASs) and International Financial Reporting Standards (IFRSs). Accordingly, it has been fully revised to reflect the requirements of all extant IASs and IFRSs as at 31 December 2012.

It is important to note that in June 2011 the International Accounting Standards Board (IASB) issued amendments to IAS 1 *Presentation of Financial Statements*. While these changes are addressed in detail in **Chapter 2** (and elsewhere throughout the text, where relevant), they included the adoption of the title 'Statement of Profit or Loss and Other Comprehensive Income' (SPLOCI). However, while IAS 1 still permits the use of other titles (for example, SCI), this text applies the designation SPLOCI. In broad terms, regardless of the title adopted, the statement is divided into two components: a statement of profit or loss; and other comprehensive income (OCI). The former section shows the revenues from operations, expenses of operating and the resulting net profit or loss over a specific period of time; while OCI includes items such as changes in revaluation surplus, actuarial gains and losses on defined benefit plans recognised in accordance with IAS 19 *Employee Benefits* (see **Chapter 17**) and gains and losses arising from translating the financial statements of a foreign operation (IAS 21 *The Effects of Changes in Foreign Exchange Rates* – see **Chapter 31**). Reporting entities have the option of presenting profit or loss and OCI either in a single continuous statement or in two separate, but consecutive, statements (see **Chapter 2**).

In addition to the *Conceptual Framework for Financial Reporting 2010*, the IASs and IFRSs that are covered in detail in this textbook are listed below, together with a reference to the primary chapter where the accounting standard is explained, illustrated with examples and relevant questions provided.

	Primary Chapter
Conceptual Framework for Financial Reporting 2010	Chapter 1
IFRS 1 *First-time Adoption of International Financial Reporting Standards*	Chapter 3
IFRS 2 *Share-based Payment*	Chapter 34
IFRS 3 *Business Combinations*	Chapter 26
IFRS 4 *Insurance Contracts*	Chapter 34
IFRS 5 *Non-current Assets Held for Sale and Discontinued Operations*	Chapter 20
IFRS 6 *Exploration for and Evaluation of Mineral Resources*	Chapter 34
IFRS 7 *Financial Instruments: Disclosures*	Chapter 25

This 4th Edition of *International Financial Accounting and Reporting* provides students with the knowledge and skills to enable them to appraise underlying accounting concepts and apply extant IASs and IFRSs. It is particularly suitable for the intermediate and advanced levels of undergraduate accounting degree programmes, together with postgraduate and professional accounting courses. The format and presentation of the text is designed to inform and teach the reader about the application of IASs and IFRSs in an understandable and structured manner. Each chapter includes:

- clearly defined learning outcomes;
- the separate explanation of key terms and definitions used in the chapter;
- additional worked examples designed to lead the reader through the text; and
- an extensive range of *review* and *challenging* questions, together with full solutions.

The text is structured as follows:

Part I: Accounting in Context addresses the theoretical underpinnings of financial reporting and illustrates the presentation of financial statements in the following chapters:

Chapter 1   Framework for Financial Reporting
Chapter 2   Presentation of Financial Statements
Chapter 3   First-time Adoption of International Financial Reporting Standards

Part II: Preparation of Statement of Profit or Loss and Other Comprehensive Income and Statement of Financial Position covers the core IASs and IFRSs associated with the preparation of a statement of profit or loss and other comprehensive income and statement of financial position, namely:

Chapter 4   Revenue Recognition
Chapter 5   Investment Property
Chapter 6   Property, Plant and Equipment
Chapter 7   Borrowing Costs
Chapter 8   Leases
Chapter 9   Intangible Assets
Chapter 10   Impairment
Chapter 11   Inventories
Chapter 12   Construction Contracts
Chapter 13   Income Taxes
Chapter 14   Provisions, Contingent Liabilities and Contingent Assets
Chapter 15   Events after the Reporting Period
Chapter 16   Accounting for Government Grants and Disclosure of Government Assistance
Chapter 17   Employee Benefits
Chapter 18   Distribution of Profits and Assets

Part III: Preparation of Statement of Cash Flows explains the preparation of a statement of cash flows for single entities:

Chapter 19   Statement of Cash Flows – Single Company

Part IV: Disclosures concentrates on disclosure-related issues:

Chapter 20   Non-current Assets Held for Sale and Discontinued Operations
Chapter 21   Accounting Policies, Changes in Accounting Estimates and Errors
Chapter 22   Related Party Disclosures

Part V: Accounting for Business Combinations deals in depth with the preparation of consolidated financial statements, including subsidiaries, associates, joint arrangements, foreign operations and the consolidated statement of cash flows as follows:

Part VI: Further Issues, together with completing the coverage of extant IASs and IFRSs, concludes the text by dealing with the analysis and interpretation of financial information and partnerships:

The term 'IFRS' has both a narrow and a broad meaning: narrowly, IFRS refers to the new numbered series of pronouncements issued by the IASB, as distinct from the IASs issued by its predecessor, the International Accounting Standards Committee (IASC); and, more broadly, IFRSs refer to the entire body of pronouncements, including standards and interpretations approved by the IASB and IASs and SIC interpretations approved by the IASC. The broader definition is applied throughout this text. In addition, while IASs and IFRSs have international application, the examples and questions included in this text are denominated in the 'Euro'/'€' for convenience. Furthermore, with the exception of Chapter 36, IFRS terminology is applied throughout this text, for example, statement of financial position (previously balance sheet); statement of profit or loss and other comprehensive income (previously statement of comprehensive income or income statement); and statement of cash flows (previously cash flow statement).

This **Introduction** finishes by considering the issue of ethics in accounting as knowledge of ethics can help accountants (and auditors) to overcome ethical dilemmas. Ethics is of utmost importance to accountants, whether in practice or/and in business, as those who rely on their services expect accountants (and auditors) to be highly competent, reliable and objective. Those who work in the field of accounting must not only be well qualified but must also possess a high degree of integrity. An accountant's good reputation is one of his/her most important possessions.

Finally, before considering ethics, I hope that you find this text useful and informative. If you are a student, I wish you the very best of luck with your studies and examinations. Remember, practice makes perfect, so attempt as many questions as you can as often as possible. I sincerely hope that, like me, you find that it is worth it in the end.

ACCOUNTING AND ETHICS

Introduction

While the focus of this text is the application of extant IASs/IFRSs, it is important not to view the role of the professional accountant as 'simply' being the application of accounting standards. The nature of a professional accountant's work places him/her in a special position of trust in relation to his/her clients, employer and the general public, all of whom rely on the judgement and advice of professional accountants when making decisions which impact upon *inter alia* employment, personal wealth and resource allocation. Professional accountants are trusted and relied upon because of their professional status and ethical codes; thus, the key to maintaining the confidence of clients and the public in the profession is for accountants to behave in a professional and ethical manner. Therefore, before addressing the application of IASs/IFRSs in the subsequent chapters, this section considers the concept of ethics and its implications for the role of the professional accountant.

Ethics concern an individual's moral judgements about right and wrong. It is likely that throughout our careers we will be faced with deciding what we believe to be the right (moral) course of action, and this may involve rejecting the path that promises the biggest short-term gain (or profit). Many of these dilemmas are simple and easy to resolve, but some are complex and the solutions are not always obvious. Ethics are important for professional accountants because history suggests that accounting (at least partially) reflects the broader moral values of society. The significance of ethics in accountancy (or lack thereof) has been illustrated by recent accounting scandals, including Enron and WorldCom, which have damaged the reputation of the profession and placed in doubt the effectiveness of contemporary accounting, auditing and governance practices. As mentioned above, the role of the modern professional accountant involves more than dealing with technical accounting issues; professional accountants must always be sensitive to potential ethical dilemmas and maintain the highest ethical standards.

However, basic questions such as 'is this right or wrong?' or 'what should I do?' cannot always be answered by simply complying with accounting standards. Technical competence is usually insufficient when dealing with ethical decisions. Moreover, pressures to 'bend the rules', 'play the game' or 'just ignore it' can be considerable. Sometimes, doing things for the 'good of the firm' or 'because that's the way it has always been done' may be at odds with your own moral compass. In addition, deciding what course of action to take can be complicated by time, job, client, personal and peer pressures. Indeed, regardless of such pressures, acting in an ethical manner can be difficult and there may not always be a 'right' answer.

If you and a friend decide to split the cost of a pizza, the fair outcome is easy; you each get half to eat! In many business situations, however, the fair outcome may not always be easy to determine. In the financial world, people invest money in companies by buying shares and they expect a fair return on their money, just as we expect a fair return when we buy a pizza. In simple terms, there are two ways a company can reward investors: one is through dividends;

and the other is through an increase in share price. A company will typically distribute some of its profits to shareholders and, in addition to giving its shareholders a monetary return, the dividend announcement may increase the company's share price, thus giving the shareholders a double reward. But even so, what constitutes a fair return for investors?

The answer to this question of fairness is not as easy to determine as in the case of sharing a pizza. A company's financial statements, for example, heavily influence share price. If the reported results are good, this can increase the share price. However, inaccurate results that overstate performance disrupt this process, since those unaware of the inaccuracies may drive up the share price by buying more shares based upon the false information being reported, only to lose money when the inaccuracies come to light. In contrast, those who know the reported results are false will sell their shares when the price is high, obtaining an unfair reward before the shares (likely) lose their value.

Two processes designed to protect against such corrupt practices and ensure that published financial information is accurate, and that no one gains unfairly, are corporate governance (the oversight of management decisions and company actions by Boards of Directors that are supposed to represent the interests of shareholders) and auditing (an external assessment by independent, certified accounting firms designed to guarantee the accuracy of financial reports). While past experience and recent scandals suggest that these processes can break down, this arguably should not have happened as professional accountants do have a code of ethics to help guide their actions and decisions.

Code of Ethics

Whether employed in business or in practice, professional accountants have a responsibility to take into consideration the public interest and to maintain the reputation of the accountancy profession. Personal self-interest must not prevail over those duties and professional accountants are required to adhere to a code of ethics. The *Code of Ethics*, published by Chartered Accountants Ireland, helps professional accountants to meet their ethical obligations by providing them with guidance. In broad terms, the *Code of Ethics*:
- establishes the **fundamental principles** of professional ethics for professional accountants; and
- provides a conceptual framework that professional accountants should apply in order to:
  - identify **threats** to compliance with the fundamental principles,
  - evaluate the significance of the threats identified, and
  - apply **safeguards**, when necessary, to eliminate the threats or reduce them to an acceptable level.

The **fundamental principles** are:
- *Integrity* – to be straightforward and honest in all professional and business relationships;
- *Objectivity* – not to allow bias, conflict of interest or undue influence of others to override professional or business judgements;
- *Professional competence and due care* – to maintain professional knowledge and skill at a level required to ensure that clients or employers receive competent professional service;
- *Confidentiality* – to respect the confidentiality of information acquired as a result of professional and business relationships and, therefore, not disclose any such information to third parties without proper and specific authority, unless there is a legal or professional right or

duty to disclose, nor use the information for the personal advantage of the professional accountant or third parties; and

- *Professional behaviour* – to comply with relevant laws and regulations and avoid any action that discredits the profession.

The **threats** to compliance with the fundamental principles include:

- *Self-interest* – for example, inappropriate use of company assets;
- *Self-review* – for example, determining the appropriate accounting treatment for a business combination after performing the feasibility study that supported the acquisition decision;
- *Advocacy* – for example, promoting the organisation's position using statements that may be false or misleading;
- *Familiarity* – for example, accepting gifts or preferential treatment the values of which are not trivial or inconsequential; and
- *Intimidation* – for example, a dominant personality attempting to influence the application of an accounting principle to achieve a preferred accounting outcome.

The **safeguards** to eliminate or reduce threats to an acceptable level include those created by the profession, legislation or regulation and those implemented in the work environment by the organisation.

There may be times when a professional accountant's responsibilities to an employing organisation and professional obligations to comply with the fundamental principles are in conflict. For example, a professional accountant may be under pressure to act or behave in ways that could create threats to compliance with the fundamental principles. Such pressure may be explicit or implicit; it may come from a supervisor, manager, director or another individual within the employing organisation. Safeguards to counter such conflicts include: obtaining advice, where appropriate, from within the organisation, from an independent professional advisor or from Chartered Accountants Ireland; using a formal dispute resolution process within the employing organisation; and seeking legal advice.

Professional accountants are often involved in the preparation and reporting of information that may either be made public or used by others inside or outside the employing organisation. Accordingly, professional accountants should not be associated with reports, returns, communications or other information where they believe that the information: contains a materially false or misleading statement; contains statements or information furnished recklessly; or omits or obscures information required to be included where such omission or obscuration would be misleading.

With regard to professional competence, an accountant should only undertake significant tasks for which the accountant has sufficient experience. An accountant should not intentionally mislead as to the level of expertise or experience possessed nor should an accountant fail to seek appropriate expert advice and assistance when required.

Self-interest threats to objectivity or confidentiality may be created through the existence of the motive and opportunity to manipulate price-sensitive information in order to gain financially. An accountant should not manipulate information nor use confidential information for personal gain. Offers of inducements may create threats to compliance with the fundamental principles. When an accountant (or an immediate or close family member) is offered an inducement, the situation should be evaluated. Self-interest threats to objectivity or confidentiality are created when an inducement is made in an attempt to unduly influence actions or decisions, encourage illegal or dishonest behaviour, or obtain confidential information. Intimidation threats to objectivity or confidentiality are created if such an inducement is accepted and it is followed by threats to make that offer public and damage the reputation of the accountant.

However, it is impossible to define every situation that creates threats to compliance with the fundamental principles of professional ethics and specify the appropriate course of action. Consequently, it is necessary to exercise professional judgement when applying the conceptual framework. As judgement by definition is subjective, some guiding steps are now outlined to assist with this.

Guiding Steps

Stakeholder analysis in decision-making

Stakeholder analysis is a commonly applied approach to analysing ethical issues in business. Using stakeholder analysis, management applies its consideration to stakeholders and not just shareholders in the decision-making process. 'Stakeholders' encompasses shareholders, employees, suppliers, customers, etc. and any other party that may be affected by the decision. This involves encouraging management to reflect on both the moral and social implications of its decisions – taking into consideration how those decisions may affect all stakeholders of the company – rather than only focusing on shareholders and the maximising of shareholder wealth.

Considering stakeholders

Taking into account this broader set of stakeholders helps create a more complete understanding of the decision to be made, not just the repercussions beyond the initial impact to the immediate parties.

There are a number of actions in stakeholder analysis that will benefit the ethical decision-making process. These include:
1. Recognising that an ethical issue has arisen in the first instance. It is important to know when you have an ethical dilemma to resolve. This requires developing awareness of ethical practice and of the potential problems that may arise. Being aware of the potential harm – or benefit – of your decisions to others is an important first step in resolving ethical dilemmas.
2. Identifying and considering all available details of the dilemma, for instance asking:
    (a) What parties (stakeholders) may be affected (i.e., who may be harmed, and who may benefit)?
    (b) Will the rights or claims of any party be affected by the outcome of the decision-making?
    (c) Are there conflicts of interest? What are they?
3. Assessing what your responsibilities and obligations are. This is achieved by identifying the likely outcomes of the decision-making process and evaluating the potential effect of each one on different stakeholders, to determine which stakeholders are harmed or benefited the most.
4. Decide on the solution that, considering all the circumstances and the consequences for stakeholders, is the most ethical.

As noted above, it is not possible to identify every situation that poses a threat to compliance with the fundamental principles of the *Code of Ethics* and specify the appropriate course of action. Consequently, the following six **Ethical Dilemmas** merely provide a flavour of the types of issue that may arise. Moreover, while some arguably have one 'right answer', others require an evaluation of the options and the selection of the best or most ethical alternative. For *each* **Ethical Dilemma**, please read the background information and think about what you would do before reading the feedback provided.

In *The Power of Ethics Management*, Blanchard and Peale offer an ethics check that might be useful to consider:

"1. Is it legal? Does it violate either civil law or company policy?
 2. Is it balanced? Is it fair to all concerned in the short-term as well as the long-term? Does it promote win-win relationships?
 3. How will it make me feel about myself? Will it make me feel proud? Would I feel good if my decision was published in the newspaper? Would I feel good if my family knew about it?"

If the answer to any of the three questions is 'negative', it is very likely the decision should be the same.[1]

ETHICAL DILEMMA 1: CLIENT CONFIDENTIALITY

Mr Ryan calls you to his office and asks you what you would do if two police officers came to the office and asked to see the files of one of your clients who own a newsagent's shop.

Requirement What should you do?

Feedback on Ethical Dilemma 1
(Leaving aside that you may be a trainee accountant and, in reality, should simply refer the matter to your manager/partner, the principles involved are important.) The issue is one of confidentiality. While you should always be polite and courteous to the police, you also have a duty to your client. You should therefore ascertain under what authority they are requesting the information. If a search warrant is produced or they are acting under other statutory or court authority, you must comply. If you are in any doubt, you should seek your own independent legal advice.

If you are unfamiliar with the legal documentation and/or you are unable to obtain your client's authority, you may wish to obtain your own legal advice as to the legal effect of such documentation and your own position before taking any further action.

In all other situations, you should explain to the police that under the rules of your professional body you are not in a position to discuss your client's affairs without their authority or appropriate statutory or court authority.

The only times you can divulge information about a client without their authority is:
• when those requesting the information have statutory authority;
• it is in the public interest; and
• to protect your own interests in certain circumstances.

In addition to the police, examples of other appropriately empowered authorities could include taxation authorities, fire authorities, health and safety, and those empowered under local jurisdictions.

---

[1] Blanchard, N. and Peale K. (1988), *The Power of Ethical Management*, HarperCollins, London. See also http://ebeni.wordpress.com/decisions/frameworks/favourite/

Ethical Dilemma 2: Potential Conflict of Interest

Another of your firm's audit clients is a jewellery designer who sells her products from her own store. One day, after a meeting, you mention that you have to find a special present for your mother's 60th birthday. Your client shows you a pair of diamond earrings set in white gold and says that she can sell them to you for a 'good price'.

Requirement What should you do?

Feedback on Ethical Dilemma 2

This is an issue of potential conflict of interest. Would a reasonable and informed third party, having knowledge of all the relevant information, reasonably conclude that your independence was compromised? Have you actually been influenced in your professional judgement as a result of your client's offer?

It is necessary to establish the facts of the case. For example, is the client offering a discount greater than that currently being offered? Is it greater than the discount to which her members of staff are entitled on a regular basis? Indeed, is it a 'good price' merely by reference to other retailers and is it in fact her 'normal' list price?

Even if the offer made by the client is specific to you, her accountant, the quantum of the benefit is likely to be relevant. If the effective discount is a flat rate 10%, whatever the list price of the jewellery bought, then it is unlikely that an informed third party would regard that your independence was compromised. In addition to the ethical guidance of Chartered Accountants Ireland, you should also refer to your employer's internal policies and contractual obligations. Moreover, common sense should dictate that it would be sensible to clarify your position with your employer.

Independence of mind is the state of mind that permits the provision of an opinion without being affected by influences that compromise professional judgement, allowing an individual to act with integrity and exercise objectivity and professional scepticism. Independence in appearance requires you to avoid facts and circumstances that are so significant that a reasonable and informed third party, having knowledge of all relevant information, including safeguards applied, would reasonably conclude that integrity, objectivity and professional scepticism had been compromised. Thus, it can be seen that there are circumstances when your client's offer may not compromise your integrity, especially as you are a trainee accountant.

However, there are others where your integrity could be called into doubt: and the more senior your position in the firm, the greater the risk of this occurring. It may, however, be possible to ensure that safeguards are put in place to protect your independence. These might include an independent review of any work undertaken, the work to be undertaken by qualified staff within your firm and not directly under your influence, rotation of the partner in charge and the senior staff. The appropriate safeguards will depend on: your position within the firm; the size and circumstances of the practice and the client; and the perceived threat to your independence.

Variation on the Issue

If you were working for a department store and your supplier, the owner of the jewellery store, made you the same offer, there might still be a conflict of interest. As an employee of the department store, you could be in a situation to influence and repay the favour, perhaps by ensuring that the department store gave her a favourable contract. The significance of such a threat would depend on the nature and value of the offer and the intent behind it. In addition to the ethical guidance of Chartered Accountants Ireland, you should also refer to your employer's internal policies and contractual obligations.

ETHICAL DILEMMA 3: CLIENT IDENTIFICATION

Your firm has been approached by a prospective new client, a small subsidiary of an overseas company involved in import/export in a country where your firm has no business contacts.

Requirement What should your firm do?

Feedback on Ethical Dilemma 3
This is a client identification matter. Your firm must carry out the same identification procedures it would with any new client. Your firm will need to identify the parent company to the extent that it knows who runs the company and verify that they are authorised to instruct your client.

If your firm is unable to do this itself, then it will need to instruct an appropriately qualified firm, such as a member of Chartered Accountants Ireland in that country, or ask them to suggest a lawyer who can undertake the verification on its behalf. They will need to send your firm certified copies of all original documentation seen by them. The verification will include: the structure of the parent company, letters of incorporation filed with the government, lists of board members, and other publicly available material.

If your firm cannot verify the ownership, ultimate control or significant influence over the business and its assets, it is likely to result in your firm not accepting the appointment.

Your firm should also be aware of relevant guidance on money laundering.

ETHICAL DILEMMA 4: DUTY OF CARE

Your firm holds a practicing certificate with audit qualification from Chartered Accountants Ireland. It has joined a network arrangement with other accountants because it promised clients and support, as well as discounted professional indemnity insurance, group advertising and full technical back-up. Your firm paid a joining fee and pays an annual charge based on turnover. Your firm also has to meet the network's conditions to undertake all work for a fixed fee and be available 24/7. The network advertises as a one-stop shop, able to undertake a full range of accounting and auditing services. The director of the network has approached your firm and asked that your firm, for the good of the network, sign off the audit report on a set of accounts prepared by another member of the network who does not hold an audit qualification certificate. He has assured the firm that "it's only a matter of putting your signature to the report, because the client is well-known to the network".

Requirement What should your firm do?

Feedback on Ethical Dilemma 4
In all circumstances, the membership regulations of Chartered Accountants Ireland and the standards of the jurisdiction in which you practice take precedence over the requirements of any network your firm may be a member of. Your firm must therefore comply in full with all the relevant Auditing and Ethical Standards and the membership rules of Chartered Accountants Ireland. The firm cannot rely on the fact that "the client is well-known to the network". If your firm agrees to do the work, it will need to undertake a full audit, as it would do if the client had been referred from any other source. Only then can your firm put its signature to the report.

Ethical Dilemma 5: Potential Threat to Objectivity or Confidentiality

Your firm has recently taken on new clients: a partnership and the tax affairs of the two individual partners who are otherwise unconnected. You have become closely involved in their affairs, and as your firm was completing the partnership accounts, it was informed that one of the partners is intending to leave the partnership. The two partners have agreed the figure to be paid for the goodwill of the business (which is all internally generated and off balance sheet). It has been further agreed between the two partners that the outgoing partner will be paid the balance on his capital account.

A property, which is owned jointly by the two partners, has been included in the partnership accounts at its written down historic cost of €75,000. In preparation for buying out the partner who is leaving, the property has been transferred into the name of the remaining partner, who has taken out a mortgage on the property. For the purposes of the new mortgage, the property has been valued at €150,000. The partnership is a very profitable one, and the work will continue to be carried out by the remaining partner, who will trade as a sole trader. Her partner had undertaken the administration and book-keeping for the partnership.

You are uncomfortable about this position as your firm acts as accountant/tax advisor to all three parties and you are also concerned that the partner who is leaving does not appear to be getting anything for his share of the increase in the value of the property.

Requirement What should you do?

Feedback on Ethical Dilemma 5

As advisor to the partnership, and both the individual partners, your firm has a responsibility to provide balanced advice and avoid any conflict of interest. The key issues to be addressed are:
* What is the real issue?
* Are there threats to compliance with fundamental principles?
* Are the threats clearly significant?
* Are there safeguards that will eliminate the threats or reduce them to an acceptable level? and
* Can you face yourself in the mirror?

What is the real issue?

The partners relying on the accounts to determine the amount due to the outgoing partner when there are assets which are not reflected at their current value in the statement of financial position is not in itself unfair to the outgoing partner. Your firm should take the following steps to establish whether or not there is any reason to be uneasy:
* look to the partnership agreement, if one exists, to determine the basis on which the partnership should be dissolved. This may also contain details of the basis on which the factory was brought into the partnership accounts;
* if there is no partnership agreement, it will be necessary to look to any partnership law, for the jurisdiction in which the partnership falls, to see if this sets out how the assets are to be distributed on the dissolution of the partnership;
* in many jurisdictions, interests in land are held outside the partnership. It might therefore be necessary to look to the title deeds and any ancillary agreement relating thereto; and
* it should also be noted that individuals are free to enter into such arrangements as they see fit; after all, one partner could gift their share of the partnership to the other. You need to establish if the partners have arrived at this basis for dissolving the partnership because of

specific circumstances. For example, the partners may have agreed when they first went into partnership that, although they held the property in joint names, the continuing partner would be entitled to any increase in value in the property because he/she had provided all the original capital.

Are there threats to compliance with fundamental principles?
A threat to objectivity or confidentiality may be created when members perform services for clients whose interests are in conflict or the clients are in dispute with each other in relation to the matter (or transaction) in question. Therefore, if after considering all of the above, your firm believes that the partner who is leaving has not made an informed decision to accept the balance standing to his credit in the statement of financial position, there may be a conflict of interest between the two partners with regard to the basis on which the partnership should be dissolved.

Where such a situation arises, all reasonable steps should be taken to ascertain whether any conflict of interest exists, or is likely to arise in the future, both in regard to new engagements and to the changing circumstances of existing clients, and including any implications arising from the possession of confidential information. There is, on the face of it, nothing improper in firms having two or more clients whose interests may be in conflict, provided that the work the firm undertakes is not in itself likely to be the subject of dispute between those clients.

Are the threats clearly significant?
If, after following the previous steps, it is clear that there is a conflict of interest, then this will be significant because the accounts that your firm has prepared are likely to form the basis of agreement between the partners. It is important to remember that perceived threats are as relevant as actual threats. The underlying test is whether a reasonable and informed third party, having knowledge of all relevant information, including the safeguards applied, would conclude a firm's integrity, objectivity or professional scepticism had been compromised.

Are there safeguards that will eliminate the threats or reduce them to an acceptable level?
If you are in a large practice, it might be possible to put safeguards in place by ensuring that different partners acted for the different parties. However, a sole practitioner, for example, if it is established that there is a conflict of interest between the partners, would no longer be able to act for all three parties (the two partners and the business) since the accounts prepared by him are likely to become drawn into any dispute between the partners as to their rights on the dissolution.

If a sole practitioner (or small practice) were to continue to act for both of the individual partners, it could be forced into a position where it had to choose between the interests of different clients. Ideally, a meeting should be arranged at which both partners are present so that the position can be explained to them, one or both being advised to take independent professional advice on the dissolution of the partnership. If this is not possible, your firm should write to both partners setting out the position.

Can you face yourself in the mirror?
Having followed these steps, it is likely that your unease will have been resolved and you can indeed 'face yourself in the mirror'. It may be, however, that there are circumstances which still leave you feeling uneasy. In that case, you may have no alternative but to cease to act for any of the parties

ETHICAL DILEMMA 6: FIDUCIARY RESPONSIBILITIES AND INDUCEMENTS

The directors of Magic Limited have been involved in negotiations with the official representatives of a foreign government about the feasibility of Magic Limited supplying a range of generic medicines for their country's health service. The negotiations began in early 2012 and are now at an advanced stage. The award of the contract would help secure the long-term future of Magic Limited and could lead to further similar business opportunities. The next major round of negotiations is due to take place at Magic Limited's Irish head office and Magic Limited's directors are considering presenting the foreign government's representatives with some gifts in recognition of the good relations that have developed during the negotiations and also to help conclude the deal.

Requirement
(a) Discuss the ethical issues surrounding the implementation of a policy that utilises lower-paid contract staff rather than higher-paid salaried employees.
(b) Advise the directors on the ethical considerations associated with their proposal to offer gifts to the foreign government's representatives.

Feedback on Ethical Dilemma 6
(a) The ethical issues surrounding the implementation of a policy that utilises lower-paid contract staff rather than higher-paid salaried employees.
Points might include:
- Directors have a fiduciary responsibility to act in the best interests of shareholders.
- While a business has to ensure effective operations, it also must consider various ethical obligations or demands (legal and constructive):
  - macro level – political, legal, cultural pressures;
  - organisational level – corporate social responsibilities of the organisation; and
  - individual level.
- There are different views on a business's responsibilities. For example:
  - separatist view – profit maximisation for the benefit of shareholders; and
  - integration view – while a business has to respond to market forces, it also has wider social responsibilities, i.e. it should consider the long-term societal implications of its decisions.
- Employment practices and the treatment of employees is a major concern for businesses and the public, more so in certain countries and in certain industries.
- There is pressure on management to balance the interests of investors, employees, customers and the wider public. While at one level it can be argued that the company is clearly justified in implementing such a policy, wider considerations, including the 'cost' of negative publicity, may outweigh the more tangible benefits.

(b) The ethical considerations associated with their proposal to offer gifts to the foreign government's representatives.
Points might include:
- The practice of giving and receiving gifts has always been a very fine ethical question. Ideally gifts should not be seen as an inducement to promote business in a manner that is not open and honest.
- Although gifts might be a sign of goodwill and respect, it is important to bear in mind:
  - the scale of the gifts – small, low value items are unlikely to be perceived as inducement and therefore not considered unethical (e.g. diaries, inexpensive pens, etc.);

° the payment of 'bribes' to encourage business is unacceptable in the view of most people, although it could be common practice in some countries and industries; and
° organisations should have a precise code for dealing with both giving and receiving gifts, including where government officials are involved.
• Social, environmental and ethical reporting is experiencing an increasing role and prominence. The professional accountancy bodies, including Chartered Accountants Ireland, have issued codes of professional conduct, with the key themes being: integrity; objectivity; professional competence; and confidentiality.

SUGGESTED READING

CCAB (2011), *Ethical Dilemmas: Case Studies for Professional Accountants in Public Practice*, November. Available at: http://www.icaew.com/~/media/Files/Technical/Ethics/ethical-case-studies/ccabeg-case-studies-accountants-public-practice.pdf.
CCAB (2011), *Ethical Dilemmas: Case Studies for Professional Accountants in Business*, December. Available at: http://www.ccab.org.uk/documents/CCABEG_Case_Studies_Professional_Accountants_in_Business.pdf.
Chartered Accountants Ireland, *Code of Ethics*.
Fisher, C. and Lovell, A. (2009), *Business Ethics and Values*, FT Prentice Hall, London.
Hines, R. (1998), "Financial Accounting: In Communicating Reality, We Construct Reality", *Accounting Organizations and Society*, Vol. 13, No. 3, pp.251–261.
Molyneaux, D. (2008), *What do you do now? Ethical Issues Encountered by Chartered Accountants*, The Institute of Chartered Accountants of Scotland. Available at: http://icas.org.uk/home/technical-and-research/research-centre/research-publications/what-do-you-do-now--ethical-issues-encountered-by-chartered-accountants/.

QUESTIONS

Review Questions

(See **Appendix One** for Suggested Solutions to Review Questions.)

Question Intro. 1

Tim Lambe, the Financial Controller of ABC Limited, is worried that the company's operating profit this year may be lower than that reported last year and he is concerned that the directors will therefore seek to reduce costs by laying-off accounting staff. The depreciation of non-current assets is a major expense for ABC Limited and Tim is considering increasing the estimated useful lives and residual values of the company's non-current assets in order to reduce the annual depreciation expense and therefore increase operating profit. While the change is not necessarily justified, Tim believes it could be just enough to save his job and those of some of his staff.

Requirement What would you recommend to Tim?

Question Intro. 2

DEF Limited has several trade receivable balances reported as current assets in its statement of financial position. While the company is confident that the amounts due will be received in full, this will extend beyond one year. Consequently, the accountant wishes to reclassify these trade receivables as non-current. However, the finance director does not support reclassification because this will reduce the company's current ratio from 1.6:1 to 0.7:1 and this will be detrimental to the company's prospects of securing new major debt finance.

Requirement Should the accountant reclassify the trade receivables and does the finance director's position pose an ethical dilemma for the accountant?

Question Intro. 3

GHI Limited has a bonus arrangement that grants the directors a €20,000 bonus if the company's profit before tax exceeds the previous year's figure by €1,000,000. The draft financial statements show an increase of €950,000 in profit before tax compared to the previous year and the managing director has suggested that the finance director reduce the estimate of warranty expense by €60,000. The current estimate of the warranty expense is €600,000 and it is accepted by the directors that this is a fairly 'soft' amount.

Requirement Is it ethical for the finance director to reduce the warranty expense by €60,000 as suggested?

Question Intro. 4

You are the financial accountant of JKL Limited, a company that specialises in the installation of heating, ventilation and air-conditioning in large venues such as airports, shopping centres and sports stadiums. Such contracts normally take two to three years to complete and, at any reporting date, the percentage of work completed represents a sizable percentage of the company's assets. The compensation of the company's senior management team is based largely on reported profit before tax. This year has not been as successful or as active as previous ones, and you know that the project managers' estimates of project completion are fluid. Consequently, you are contemplating revising the project managers' estimates of project completion so as to increase the compensation due to senior management to a figure that you believe more fairly reflects their efforts during the year.

Requirement Is it ethical for you to adjust the project managers' estimates of project completion so as to increase the compensation due to senior management to a figure that you believe more fairly reflects their efforts during the year?

Question Intro. 5

You are a trainee chartered accountant with D. Turpin & Company. One of your firm's clients is Russell Group plc (Russell), a large, divisionalised Irish company engaged in a wide range of activities. One morning, while having a coffee with the Financial Accountant of Russell, you mention that you are having difficulty finding a suitable second-hand car that is within your budget. That afternoon, the Financial Accountant provides you with the contact details for the manager of one of the group's companies that trades in second-hand vehicles and informs you that he has told the manager to 'do you a good deal'.

Requirement Discuss what you should do.

Challenging Questions

(Suggested Solutions to Challenging Questions are available to lecturers.)

Background

You are an advisor to Sorp Limited, a large, well-known charity dedicated to improving treatment for those suffering from curable diseases prevalent in underdeveloped countries where basic sanitation is often lacking. A donation of €10 million has recently been received by Sorp Limited and the donor has requested that it be used in the treatment of either R Fever or Y Fever or both, as the charity sees fit.

The estimated cost of successfully treating one R Fever patient is €100, and the estimated cost of successfully treating one Y Fever patient is €20. Each treatment has an equally high chance of success and increasing or decreasing the amount of money spent on one condition has proportional benefits (i.e. doubling the funds allocated to R Fever will always double the number of patients treated successfully).

In response to each of the questions in the scenarios given below, state how much of the €10 million you would advise Sorp Limited to spend on R Fever (with the remainder being spent on Y Fever). Please answer each question separately and do not go back and change your answer to previous questions.

Question Intro. 1

Based on the costs of courses of treatment given above, €10 million would cure 100,000 people of R Fever or 500,000 people of Y Fever.

Requirement How much do you spend on R Fever?

Question Intro. 2

R Fever tends to be contracted in crowded buildings, such as schools and hospitals, because it is transmitted very easily via air; it can be caught by anybody irrespective of age and lifestyle. However, Y Fever is only transmitted via direct contact and is strongly associated with people who have chosen certain lifestyles and habits, specifically promiscuity and poor personal hygiene.

Requirement How much do you spend on R Fever now?

Question Intro. 3

There is an increased awareness of R Fever. Internationally influential pressure groups are campaigning to increase the amount spent on R Fever, and a review commissioned for the World Health Organisation recently recommended increased resources be allocated to R Fever by health charities. The higher profile of R Fever means that more facilities are available for aftercare and follow-up advice on how to prevent recurrences.

Requirement How much do you spend on R Fever now?

PART I

ACCOUNTING IN CONTEXT

CHAPTER

FRAMEWORK FOR FINANCIAL REPORTING

LEARNING OBJECTIVES

Having studied this chapter on the framework for financial reporting, you should be able to:
1. describe the main aspects of the regulatory framework;
2. define what is meant by the term 'conceptual framework for financial reporting';
3. explain the need and purpose for such a framework;
4. discuss the key components of the *Conceptual Framework for Financial Reporting 2010;* and
5. explain the key issues with respect to fair value measurement.

KEY TERMS AND DEFINITIONS FOR THIS CHAPTER

Accruals Accounting Under this basis of accounting the effects of transactions are recognised when they occur and are recorded and reported in the accounting periods to which they relate, irrespective of cash flows arising from transactions.

Assets Assets are rights or other access to future economic benefits controlled by an entity as a result of past transactions or events.

Going Concern Basis Financial statements are prepared on the basis that the entity will continue to operate without the threat of liquidation for the foreseeable future, usually regarded as at least one year.

Liability An obligation to transfer future economic benefits as a result of past transactions or events.

Materiality This is an expression of the relative significance of a particular matter in the context of the financial statements as a whole. A matter is material if its omission or misstatement could reasonably be expected to influence the decisions of users of financial statements.

Statement of Cash Flows (often referred to as a 'cash flow statement') This statement reports on an entity's cash flow activities, particularly its operating, investing and financing activities.

Statement of Changes in Equity This statement shows the changes in an entity's equity throughout the reporting period.

Statement of Profit or Loss and Other Comprehensive Income (often referred to as an 'income statement', 'profit and loss account' or 'statement of comprehensive income' (SCI)). In June 2011 the IASB issued amendments to IAS 1 *Presentation of Financial Statements*. These included the adoption of the title 'Statement of Profit or Loss and Other Comprehensive Income' (SPLOCI). However, while IAS 1 still permits the use of other titles (for example, SCI), this text applies the designation SPLOCI. In broad terms, regardless of the title adopted, the statement is divided into two components: a statement of profit or loss; and other comprehensive income (OCI). The former section shows the revenues from operations, expenses of operating and the resulting net profit or loss over a specific period of time; while OCI includes items such as changes in revaluation surplus, actuarial gains and losses on defined benefit plans recognised in accordance with IAS 19 *Employee Benefits* (see **Chapter 17**) and gains and losses arising from translating the financial statements of a foreign operation (IAS 21 *The Effects of Changes in Foreign Exchange Rates* – see **Chapter 31**). Reporting entities have the option of presenting profit or loss and OCI either in a single continuous statement or in two separate, but consecutive statements (see **Chapter 2**).

Statement of Financial Position (often referred to as a 'balance sheet') This financial statement reports an entity's assets, liabilities and equity at a given point in time.

Note: some additional definitions are included separately in **Section 1.4** as they relate specifically to that section.

1.1 INTRODUCTION

Financial reporting is the communication of financial information – it is an information system. A company's directors are responsible for the preparation of its annual report and financial statements, which together are generally recognised as the key documents in the discharge of financial accountability to external users.

The fundamental objective of financial reporting is to communicate economic measurements of and information about the resources and performance of the reporting entity, which is useful to those having reasonable rights to such information.[1] Moreover, the annu-

---

[1] *The Corporate Report* (Accounting Standards Steering Committee (ASSC, 1975)), which was the first major initiative in Britain and Ireland to examine the purpose of financial reporting.

al report and financial statements "are the primary means by which the management of an entity is able to fulfil its reporting responsibility".[2]

It is generally accepted (see **Section 1.3** below) that financial reports consist of:
- the financial statements –
  - a **statement of financial position**,
  - a **statement of profit or loss and other comprehensive income**,
  - a **statement of changes in equity**,
  - a **statement of cash flows**;
- notes to the financial statements, comprising a summary of significant accounting policies and other explanatory notes supporting information contained in the financial statements; and
- narrative information (often non-statutory), such as a chairman's report, directors' report or discussion and analysis statement.

Key to this Chapter

The purpose of this chapter is to explain both the regulatory and the conceptual frameworks that govern the preparation and presentation of financial statements prepared in accordance with International Accounting Standards (IASs) and International Financial Reporting Standards (IFRSs). It begins with a review of the regulatory framework within which financial reports are prepared, including consideration of why there is a need for regulation and the principal forms that it takes (**Section 1.2**). In recognition of its importance to financial reporting, the conceptual framework for financial reporting is then considered in detail, including its purpose, historical development, scope and content (**Section 1.3**). The chapter concludes by explaining the concept of fair value measurement (**Section 1.4**).

1.2 REGULATORY FRAMEWORK

Introduction

Financial reporting is regulated through a combination of company law, the regulations of relevant stock exchanges and accounting standards. The purpose of this regulatory framework is to standardise the principles on which financial statements and reports are prepared, together with their format and content, in order to assist investors and analysts in their understanding and interpretation of financial information. A lack of comparability in financial reporting can affect the credibility of a company's reporting and analysts' reports thereon, and can have a detrimental effect on financial investment. The increasing levels of cross-border financing transactions, securities trading and direct foreign investment has increased the need for a single set of rules by which **assets, liabilities, equity, income and expenses** are recognised and measured. Thus, regulation can help to:
- protect the users of financial reports;
- ensure consistency in financial reporting;
- ensure comparability between the financial reports of different companies; and
- ensure that financial reports give a true and fair view of a company's financial performance and position.

---

[2] *The Corporate Report* (ASSC, 1975), p. 16.

Company Law

In June 2002 the European Union (EU) Council of Ministers adopted the EU Regulation requiring all EU *listed* companies (i.e. those listed on an EU-regulated stock exchange) to prepare their *consolidated financial statements* in accordance with international accounting standards by 1 January 2005 at the latest. The term 'international accounting standards' refers to IFRSs, IASs and related interpretations issued by the IASB and endorsed by the EU. Consequently, the legal framework under which companies prepare their financial statements changed significantly in 2004/2005.

Companies and groups that are not directly impacted by the EU Regulation (for example, non-listed companies) have a choice as to the financial reporting framework that they apply in preparing their individual and group financial statements. As a result, two financial reporting frameworks are available for accounting periods beginning on or after 1 January 2005. These are:
• company law-based financial statements prepared in accordance with the formats and accounting rules of company law and accounting standards. For example, the applicable Statements of Standard Accounting Practice and Financial Reporting Standards adopted/issued by the Accounting Standards Board in the UK; and
• financial statements prepared in accordance with IASs/IFRSs adopted/issued by the IASB (and endorsed by the EU) and certain mandatory disclosures carried forward from company law.

Generally speaking, the move from company law-based financial statements to IAS/IFRS-based financial statements is a one-way street, and only with 'relevant changes in circumstances' can a company revert to preparing company law-based financial statements. It should be noted that the parts of company law that do not deal with the preparation of financial statements still continue to apply to all companies in the Republic of Ireland and the UK regardless of which financial reporting framework they adopt. Therefore, current requirements regarding the filing and signing of financial statements, the rules regarding redemption and purchase of own shares or financial assistance for the purchase of own shares and the rules regarding distributions still continue to apply to IAS/IFRS-based financial statements.

Stock Exchange Regulations

The securing of a stock exchange listing binds a company to the requirements or 'listing rules' of that stock exchange; for example, the 'Yellow Book', issued by the London Stock Exchange (2012), or the Listing Rules of the Irish Stock Exchange (2011). This requires a company to observe certain rules and procedures regarding its status as a listed company. Some of these concern its behaviour; whilst others concern the disclosure of accounting information, which is more extensive than the disclosure requirements of companies' legislation. The reason for the additional disclosure requirements for listed companies is that their shares are available in the open market and the stock exchange wants to ensure that all potential investors have access to all available information about the company. Many stock exchange requirements do not have the backing of law, but the ultimate sanction that can be imposed on a listed company that fails to abide by them is the withdrawal of its securities from that stock exchange's list (i.e. the company's shares would no longer be traded on the market).

The US Securities and Exchange Commission ruled in December 2007 that international accounting standards should be accepted for cross-border listings without reconciliation to US GAAP (Generally Accepted Accounting Principles).

Accounting Standards

An **accounting standard** is a rule or set of rules that prescribes the method by which financial statements should be prepared and presented. They are issued by a national or international body of the accountancy profession and are intended to apply to all financial statements, which are intended to give a true and fair view of the financial position and profit/loss. Accounting standards are detailed working regulations within the framework of government legislation and they cover areas in which the law is silent.

In an international context, from 1973 and until a comprehensive reorganisation in 2000, IASs were set and published by the International Accounting Standards Committee (IASC). In 2001 the International Accounting Standards Board (IASB) was formed to replace the IASC, with this new body taking over the responsibility for setting accounting standards, albeit calling them IFRSs. The IASB operates under the oversight of the IFRS Foundation.

Objectives of the IASB

Since its formation in 2001, the IASB has amended some IASs, replaced some IASs with new IFRSs and adopted or proposed certain new IFRSs on topics for which there were no previous IASs. The formal objectives of the IASB are to:
(a) develop, in the public interest, a single set of high quality, understandable and enforceable global accounting standards that require high quality, transparent and comparable information in the financial statements and other financial reporting to help participants in the world's capital markets, and other users who make economic decisions;
(b) promote the use and rigorous application of those standards;
(c) in fulfilling the objectives associated with (a) and (b), take account of, as appropriate, the special needs of small- and medium-sized entities and emerging economies; and
(d) bring about convergence of national accounting standards and IASs/IFRSs to high quality solutions.

IASB's Process for the Development of Standards

Typically, the process for the development of a standard involves the following steps.
• During the early stages of a project, the IASB establishes an Advisory Committee to advise on the issues arising in the project. Consultation with this committee and the Standards Advisory Council (SAC) occurs throughout the project.
• The IASB then develops and publishes discussion documents for public comment.
• Following receipt and review of comments, the IASB then develops and publishes an Exposure Draft for public comment.
• Following the receipt and review of comments, the IASB issues a final IFRS.

Given the primary function of the IASB is to develop and publish IFRSs, it is important to recognise that the term 'IFRS' has both a narrow and a broad meaning.

- In its narrow meaning, 'IFRS' refers to the numbered series of pronouncements issued by the IASB, as distinct from the IASs issued by its predecessor (the IASC).
- More broadly, the term 'IFRS' refers to the entire body of pronouncements, including the standards approved by the IASB and IASC, and Interpretations of IASs and IFRSs are developed by the IFRS Interpretations Committee (see below).

The principles underlying both the narrow and broad definitions of IFRS are embraced in the *Preface to the International Financial Reporting Standards*, which sets out the IASB's objectives (see above), the scope of IFRSs, due process for developing IFRSs and Interpretations and policies on effective dates, format and language for IFRSs. When the IASB publishes a standard, it also publishes a Basis of Conclusions to explain publicly how it reached its conclusions and to promote background information that may help users apply the standard in practice.

IFRS Interpretations Committee

Interpretations of IASs and IFRSs are developed by the IFRS Interpretations Committee, which was previously known as the International Financial Reporting Interpretations Committee (IFRIC) (until January 2010) and the Standing Interpretations Committee (SIC) (until March 2002). Despite the various name changes, the role of the IFRS Interpretations Committee remains to:

- interpret existing IASs/IFRSs in light of the *Conceptual Framework for Financial Reporting 2010* (*IFRS Framework*) (see below) in order to prevent confusion; and
- provide authoritative guidance on issues not specifically addressed in IASs/IFRSs that would otherwise lead to differing practices. Financial statements may not be described as complying with IASs/IFRSs unless they comply with all of the requirements of every applicable standard and every applicable interpretation. In developing interpretations, the IFRS Interpretations Committee works closely with similar national committees.

The IFRS Framework

While not a standard, the *IFRS Framework* (see **Section 1.3** below) serves as a guide to resolving accounting issues that are not addressed directly in a standard. Moreover, IAS 8 *Accounting Policies, Changes in Accounting Estimates and Errors* requires that, in the absence of a standard or an interpretation that specifically applies to a transaction, an entity must use its judgement in developing and applying an accounting policy that results in information that is relevant and reliable. In making that judgement, IAS 8 requires management to consider the definitions, recognition criteria and measurement concepts for assets, liabilities, income and expenses in the *IFRS Framework*. In short, this means that, in the absence of a standard dealing with a specific issue, management are expected to base their accounting treatment on the principles contained in the IFRS *Framework*.

IASs and IFRSs Extant at 31 December 2012

In addition to the *IFRS Framework* and the *Preface to International Financial Reporting Standards*, extant IASs and IFRSs as at 31 December 2012 are listed in TABLE 1.1, together with a reference to the primary chapter where the accounting standard is explained and relevant questions provided.

TABLE 1.1: EXTANT ACCOUNTING STANDARDS

Accounting Standard	Primary Chapter
IFRS 1 *First-time Adoption of International Financial Reporting Standards*	Chapter 3
IFRS 2 *Share-based Payment*	Chapter 34
IFRS 3 *Business Combinations*	Chapter 26
IFRS 4 *Insurance Contracts*	Chapter 34
IFRS 5 *Non-current Assets Held for Sale and Discontinued Operations*	Chapter 20
IFRS 6 *Exploration for and Evaluation of Mineral Resources*	Chapter 34
IFRS 7 *Financial Instruments: Disclosures*	Chapter 25
IFRS 8 *Operating Segments*	Chapter 24
IFRS 9 *Financial Instruments* (applicable for annual periods beginning 1 January 2013, with early adoption from 2009)	Chapter 25
IFRS 10 *Consolidated Financial Statements* (applicable to annual reporting periods beginning on or after 1 January 2013)	Chapter 26
IFRS 11 *Joint Arrangements* (applicable to annual reporting periods beginning on or after 1 January 2013)	Chapter 30
IFRS 12 *Disclosure of Interests in Other Entities* (applicable to annual reporting periods beginning on or after 1 January 2013)	Chapter 26
IFRS 13 *Fair Value Measurement* (applicable to annual reporting periods beginning on or after 1 January 2013)	Chapter 1
IAS 1 *Presentation of Financial Statements*	Chapter 2
IAS 2 *Inventories*	Chapter 11
IAS 7 *Statement of Cash Flows*	Chapters 19 & 33
IAS 8 *Accounting Policies, Changes in Accounting Estimates and Errors*	Chapter 21
IAS 10 *Events after the Reporting Period*	Chapter 15
IAS 11 *Construction Contracts*	Chapter 12
IAS 12 *Income Taxes*	Chapter 13
IAS 16 *Property, Plant and Equipment*	Chapter 6
IAS 17 *Leases*	Chapter 8
IAS 18 *Revenue*	Chapter 4
IAS 19 *Employee Benefits*	Chapter 17
IAS 20 *Accounting for Government Grants and Disclosure of Government Assistance*	Chapter 16
IAS 21 *The Effects of Changes in Foreign Exchange Rates*	Chapter 31
IAS 23 *Borrowing Costs*	Chapter 7
IAS 24 *Related Party Disclosures*	Chapter 22
IAS 26 *Accounting and Reporting by Retirement Benefit Plans*	Chapter 34
IAS 27 *Consolidated and Separate Financial Statements* (superseded by IAS 27 (2011), IFRS 10 and IFRS 12, which are effective for annual reporting periods beginning on or after 1 January 2013)	Chapter 26
IAS 27 *Separate Financial Statements* (issued in May 2011 and effective for annual reporting periods beginning on or after 1 January 2013)	Chapter 26

IAS 28 *Investments in Associates* (superseded by IAS 28 (2011) and IFRS 12, which are effective for annual reporting periods beginning on or after 1 January 2013)	Chapter 29
IAS 28 *Investments in Associates and Joint Ventures* (issued in May 2011 and effective for annual reporting periods beginning on or after 1 January 2013)	Chapter 29
IAS 29 *Financial Reporting in Hyperinflationary Economies*	Chapter 31
IAS 31 *Interests in Joint Ventures* (superseded by IFRS 11 and IFRS 12, which are effective for annual reporting periods beginning on or after 1 January 2013)	Chapter 30
IAS 32 *Financial Instruments: Presentation* (superseded by IFRS 9, which is applicable for annual periods beginning 1 January 2013, with early adoption from 2009)	Chapter 25
IAS 33 *Earnings per Share*	Chapter 23
IAS 34 *Interim Financial Reporting*	Chapter 34
IAS 36 *Impairment of Assets*	Chapter 10
IAS 37 *Provisions, Contingent Liabilities and Contingent Assets*	Chapter 14
IAS 38 *Intangible Assets*	Chapter 9
IAS 39 *Financial Instruments: Recognition and Measurement*	Chapter 25
IAS 40 *Investment Property*	Chapter 5
IAS 41 *Agriculture*	Chapter 34

1.3 THE CONCEPTUAL FRAMEWORK FOR FINANCIAL REPORTING

Having discussed the regulation of financial reporting in the previous section, the fundamental principles that inform the development of new accounting standards and the assessment of extant standards, together with providing the foundation for said regulations, are now explained.

Definition of a 'Conceptual Framework'

A 'conceptual framework' is a coherent system of interrelated objectives and fundamentals that can lead to consistent standards that prescribe the nature, functions and limits of financial reporting. It is a statement of generally accepted theoretical principles, which form the frame of reference for financial reporting and provide the basis for the development of new accounting standards and the evaluation of those already in existence.

Purpose of a Conceptual Framework

One of the major challenges in communicating financial information is facilitating the needs of the numerous and disparate users of that information. It is difficult to assess its ultimate usefulness when you are unsure how the information is being used and by whom, and it is almost impossible to address all technical issues in a business context that would meet the needs of every user.

It is therefore important that all users appreciate the general principles of financial reporting. A conceptual framework goes some way to providing this as it gives guidance on the broad principles of how items should be recorded and how they should be presented. Where there are no standards specifically covering an issue, a conceptual framework provides a point of reference for preparers of financial information. For example, the framework can provide guidance on how like items are treated and give definitions and criteria that can be used in deciding the recognition and measurement of the item.

Accounting standards deal with a variety of specific technical issues, and the existence of a conceptual framework can remove the need to address the underlying issues over and over again, for example, by providing definitions of assets and liabilities that must be met for items to be included in financial statements. This is an underlying principle and, as accounting standards are based on the principles within the framework, they need not be dealt with fully in each individual standard. The process of creating a new accounting standard can be a long one, but where a conceptual framework exists, the issue can be dealt with temporarily by providing a short-term solution until a specific standard is developed.

Historical Development

As referred to above, *The Corporate Report* (Accounting Standards Steering Committee, 1975) was a comprehensive review of the users, purposes and measurement bases for financial reporting. Unfortunately, its immediate impact was limited because many believed that it went too far in:
- the identification of the user groups beyond the shareholders and creditors;
- the demand for additional statements; and
- wishing to discard historical cost as the measurement base.

As time has progressed, however, *The Corporate Report* has come to be regarded as a seminal document. Indeed, its impact can be clearly traced to the *Framework for the Presentation and Preparation of Financial Statements* by the IASC in 1988 ('the *Framework*') and then the *Conceptual Framework for Financial Reporting 2010* ('the *IFRS Framework*'), as discussed below.

In October 2004 the IASB and the US national standards-setting body, the Financial Accounting Standards Board (FASB), decided to add to their respective agendas a joint project to develop a common conceptual framework that would be based upon the *Framework for the Presentation and Preparation of Financial Statements* (IASC, 1988) and that would be used by both Boards as the basis for developing and revising accounting standards. The objective of the project was and is to create a sound foundation for future accounting standards that are principles-based, internally consistent and internationally converged. It was agreed that the joint project should focus initially on concepts applicable to business entities in the private sector and that it should be divided into phases, with the initial focus being on dealing with objectives, qualitative characteristics, elements, recognition and measurement. Furthermore, it was agreed that priority should be given to addressing issues that are likely to yield benefits in the short term, that is, cross-cutting issues that affect projects for new or revised standards.

However, during late 2010 it was decided to defer further work on this joint project until after other, more urgent convergence projects were finalised. Subsequently, in December 2012, as a result of the IASB's Agenda Consultation project (public consultation on the IASB's future plan of work), the IASB decided to reactivate the *IFRS Framework* project as an IASB-only project and that:

- it should focus on elements of financial statements, measurement, reporting entity, presentation and disclosure; and
- the aim should be to work towards a single discussion paper covering all these areas, rather than a separate discussion paper for each.

A discussion paper is expected in 2013, with the intention being to complete the project in 2015.

Before being suspended, the joint IASB–FASB Conceptual Framework project was being conducted in a number of phases. **TABLE 1.2** summarises the progress of each phase, and the IASB's future plans for that phase.

TABLE 1.2: PHASES AND STATUS OF THE *IFRS Framework*

Phase	Status at 31 December 2012
Phase A – objectives and qualitative characteristics	Completed, with the *Conceptual Framework for Financial Reporting 2010* ('the *IFRS Framework*') being issued in September 2010.
Phase B – elements and recognition Phase C – measurement	To be further considered as part of the IASB-only project.
Phase D – reporting entity	Exposure Draft *Conceptual Framework for Financial Reporting: The Reporting Entity* published in March 2010 is to be further considered as part of the IASB-only project.
Phase E – presentation and disclosure	To be further considered as part of the IASB-only project. However, it will not be extended to other areas within the original scope of Phase E, such as preliminary announcements and press releases.
Phase F – purpose and status	Work on this phase is to be discontinued as one of the objectives was to reach a converged IASB–FASB view on the secondary purpose of the framework to assist preparers in preparing financial statements.
Phase G – application to not-for-profit entities	Work on this phase is to be discontinued as the current focus of the IASB-only project is on business entities in the private sector.
Phase H – remaining issues	This phase is no longer needed as the remaining topics to be considered as part of the IASB-only project are intended to be developed and issued together.

The *IFRS Framework* is a conceptual accounting framework that sets out the principles that underlie the preparation and presentation of financial statements for external users. It can assist with:
- the development of future IFRSs and in its review of existing accounting standards; and
- promoting the harmonisation of regulations, financial reporting standards and procedures relating to the presentation of financial statements by providing a basis for reducing the number of alternative accounting treatments permitted by IASs/IFRSs.

In addition, the *IFRS Framework* may support:
- national standard-setting bodies in developing national standards;
- preparers of financial statements in applying IASs/IFRSs and in dealing with topics that have yet to form the subject of an IFRS;
- auditors in forming an opinion as to whether financial statements conform with IASs/IFRSs;
- users of financial statements in interpreting the information contained in financial statements prepared in conformity with IASs/IFRSs; and
- those who are interested in the work of the IASB, providing them with information about its approach to the formulation of IASs/IFRSs.

Given that the *IFRS Framework* underpins the work of the IASB, it is not surprising that its various uses referred to above are consistent with the IASB objectives discussed in **Section 1.2** above.

As explained above, the *IFRS Framework* is not an accounting standard and does not define standards for any particular measurement or disclosure issue. If there is a conflict between the *IFRS Framework* and the requirement of an IAS/IFRS, the requirements of the IAS/IFRS prevail.

Scope of the *IFRS Framework*

The *IFRS Framework* applies to general-purpose financial reports, which are those intended to serve users who are not in a position to require financial reports tailored to their particular information needs. As indicated in **Section 1.1** above, it is generally accepted (see **Section 1.3** below) that financial reports consist of:
- the financial statements –
  - a statement of financial position,
  - a statement of profit or loss and other comprehensive income,
  - a statement of changes in equity,
  - a statement of cash flows,
- notes to the financial statements, comprising a summary of significant accounting policies and other explanatory notes supporting information contained in the financial statements; and
- narrative information (often non-statutory), such as a chairman's report, directors' report or discussion and analysis statement.

The *IFRS Framework* acknowledges that the primary users of general-purpose financial statements are present and potential investors, lenders and other creditors who use the information to make decisions about buying, selling or holding equity or debt instruments and providing or settling loans or other forms of credit. The *IFRS Framework* also notes that other parties, including market regulators, may find general-purpose financial reports useful. However, the IASB concluded that the objectives of general-purpose financial reports and financial regulation may not be consistent and thus regulators were not considered to be primary users.

Users of Financial Reports

Notwithstanding the primary users of general-purpose financial statements referred to above, the following is a generally accepted list of users, together with their information needs.

- **Investors**, who are mentioned explicitly in the *IFRS Framework*, are concerned about the risk and return provided by their investments. They need information to help make decisions about: buying or selling shares; the company's ability to pay dividends; whether the management has been running the company efficiently; the liquidity position of the company; the company's future prospects; and how the company's shares compare with those of its competitors. In broader terms, this group also includes analysts and advisers (for example, financial analysts, financial journalists, economists, statisticians, researchers and stockbrokers) who require information to pass on to clients and other interested parties.

- **Employees** are interested in the stability and profitability of their employer. They require information to help assess: their employment security and future job prospects; the company's ability to pay salaries and wages, pensions and other benefits; and their position in collective pay bargaining.

- **Lenders**, who are referred to specifically in the *IFRS Framework*, wish to assess whether their loans and interest can be repaid at the appropriate time. They also need to verify that the value of any security remains adequate and that any financial restrictions (such as maximum debt/equity ratios) have not been breached. In acquisition situations, all parties will want information about each other.

- **Suppliers and other trade creditors**, who are mentioned expressly in the IFRS *Framework*, need to know whether the company will be a good customer and pay its debts when they fall due.

- **Customers** are interested in whether the company will be able to continue producing and supplying goods.

- **The government**, which includes the tax authorities, regulatory departments and local authorities, are concerned with tax and company law compliance, the ability to pay tax and the general contribution of the company to the economy. This group falls under the category of 'market regulators' referred to in the *IFRS Framework*, and their interest in a company may be one of creditor or customer.

- **The public**, which includes taxpayers, ratepayers, consumers and special interest groups (for example, consumer and environmental organisations), is interested in the (local) economy, numbers employed and environmental issues.

The *IFRS Framework* concedes that general-purpose financial reports cannot provide all the information that users may need to make economic decisions and that they will also need to consider pertinent information from other sources.

Content of the *IFRS Framework*

As explained above, the *IFRS Framework* project is now an IASB-only project. The current status of the project is summarised in **TABLE 1.2**. The *IFRS Framework* addresses the following topics:
- the objective of financial reporting;
- the qualitative characteristics of useful financial information;
- the reporting entity;
- the definition, recognition and measurement of the elements from which financial statements are constructed; and
- the concepts of capital and capital maintenance.

The September 2010 version of the *IFRS Framework* consists of four chapters (Phase A, **TABLE 1.2**), although this may change as the IASB progresses the project (see above). Each of the four (current) chapters is now discussed in turn.

IFRS Framework Chapter 1: The Objective of General Purpose Financial Reporting

The objective of general purpose financial reports is to provide information about a reporting entity's economic resources, claims and changes in resources and claims. This includes information about:
- *economic resources and claims*, which assists users to assess an entity's financial strengths and weaknesses. It incorporates the resources the entity controls, its financial structure, liquidity and solvency, the information for which is normally provided in the *statement of financial position*;
- *changes in resources and claims*, which can primarily be found in the *statement of profit or loss and other comprehensive income*. These result from an entity's performance and from other events or transactions, such as issuing debt or equity instruments. Performance measures, particularly profitability, are required to help assess the entity's ability to generate future cash flows from trading and other activities. It also helps users evaluate how effective the entity is at using its resources;
- *financial performance reflected by past cash flows* which is held primarily in the *statement of cash flows*. This can help explain the entity's investing, financing and operational activities and how these activities have affected the financial position over the reporting period; and
- *changes in economic resources and claims not resulting from financial performance*, such as the issue of equity instruments or distributions to shareholders. Such information is typically presented in the statement of changes in equity.

The component parts of the financial statements are interrelated since they reflect different aspects of the same transactions. Each depends on the other. A statement of profit or loss and other comprehensive income, for instance, provides an incomplete picture unless it is used in conjunction with the statement of financial position and the statement of cash flows. For example, users can make better informed economic decisions if they are provided with information that focuses on an entity's ability to generate cash and to meet its cash repayments. This requires details about the current financial position, the performance for the period and changes in its financial position. Liquidity and solvency information is useful in predicting the ability of an entity to meet its financial commitments as they fall due, with the former addressing short-term needs and the latter the long-term availability of cash to meet financial commitments. Profitability information and its variability are important in assessing potential changes in economic resources, while information on financial position is useful in assessing investing, financing and operating activities during the reporting period.

IFRS Framework Chapter 2: The Reporting Entity

This chapter will be added once the IASB-only project has further considered Phase D.

IFRS Framework Chapter 3: Qualitative Characteristics of Useful Financial Information

Qualitative characteristics are the attributes that make the information useful to users. The *IFRS Framework* states that the two fundamental qualitative characteristics of relevance and faithful representation are enhanced by a further four qualitative characteristics so that there are six qualitative characteristics altogether.

- **Relevance** To be useful, information must be relevant to the decision-making needs of users; such needs will vary between user groups (for example, see information needs of users above) and over time (for example, as employees get older, information on the performance of their company pension may be of greater interest). Information is relevant when it influences the economic decisions of users by helping them to evaluate past, present or future economic events or confirming or correcting their past evaluations (i.e. it has predictive and/ or confirmatory value). Financial statements do not normally contain information about future activities. However, historical information can be used as the basis for predicting future financial position and performance; users then have to use their predictions as the basis for their decision-making. An example of this could be where the financial statements show the profitability of a division that has been sold during the year. Users then know to eliminate that division's resources and profitability in evaluating the performance of the entity for the following year.

Information that helps users assess the future performance and financial position of an entity is likely to be relevant. An item is likely to be relevant by virtue of its nature (for example, high-profile litigation) and **materiality**. Information is material if its omission or misstatement could influence the decision-making of users; materiality is therefore an entity-specific aspect of relevance. Information can be relevant because of its nature, irrespective of materiality. For example, if an entity has commenced operating activities in a country with an unstable economy, this could change the users' assessment of the overall risk that the entity is exposed to and as a result change the users' assessment of the entity's future results. Consequently, irrespective of the materiality of that segment's results, the information may be disclosed. Information should be released on a timely basis to be relevant to users.

- **Faithful Representation** To be useful, financial information must not only be relevant, it must faithfully represent the transactions it is intended to represent. This fundamental characteristic seeks to maximise the underlying characteristics of:
  - completeness – reports should present a rounded picture of the economic activities of the reporting entity and, to be reliable, the information must be complete. An omission can cause information to be false or misleading and therefore unreliable;

- ○ neutrality – to be reliable, the information must be neutral, that is, free from bias. This will be enhanced by the application of accounting standards, which are neutral as between competing interests; and
- ○ freedom from error.
- **Comparability** This involves consistency in the application of accounting concepts and policies, and is vital to users in their decision-making. The ability to identify trends in performance and financial position and compare those both from year to year and against other entities assists users in their assessments and decision-making. It is important that users are able to understand the application of accounting policies in order to compare financial information. To achieve comparability, users must be able to identify where an entity has changed its policy from one year to the next and where other entities have used different accounting policies for similar transactions. The requirement of IASs/IFRSs to disclose accounting policies adopted and the inclusion of prior periods' comparative figures helps promote comparability.
- **Verifiability** This helps to assure users that the information is a faithful representation of the underlying transactions and events. This will be enhanced in the case of financial reports that are independently verified and implies:
  - ○ substance over form – transactions must be accounted for and presented on the basis of their commercial or economic reality rather than their legal form. Only by applying substance over form will users see the effects of the commercial or economic reality of the transactions; and
  - ○ prudence – many estimates are made in the preparation of financial statements (for example, inventory valuation, estimated useful lives of assets, recoverability of debts). Being cautious when exercising judgement in arriving at these estimates is known as prudence. While this is a generally accepted concept in the preparation of financial statements, the concept does not extend to including excess provisions, overstating liabilities or understating income or assets. This would bias the information and make it unreliable to users. Consequently, it is important to note that Chapter 3 of the *IFRS Framework* does not include prudence as an aspect of faithful representation as doing so would be inconsistent with neutrality.
- **Timeliness** The usefulness of information is diminished the later it is produced after the time to which it relates, and also if the intervals at which it is produced are unreasonably long.
- **Understandability** An essential quality of financial information is that it is readily understandable by users. For this purpose, users are assumed to have a reasonable knowledge of business, economic activities and accounting, together with a willingness to study the information with reasonable diligence. Information on complex issues should be included if relevant and should not be excluded on the grounds that it is too difficult for the average user to understand. However, in certain circumstances, too much detail is as much a defect as too little.

In practice, a trade-off between the qualitative characteristics must take place and the aim is to achieve an appropriate balance across them. For example, information that is produced on a timely basis may be less reliable. In achieving a balance between relevance, faithful representation and timeliness, the overriding consideration is how best to satisfy the decision-making needs of users. The relative importance of the characteristics will be a matter of judgement. Moreover, the benefits derived from providing information should exceed the cost of providing it. The process of evaluating benefits and costs, however, is judgemental.

IFRS Framework Chapter 4: The Framework

Chapter 4 of the *IFRS Framework* contains the remaining text of the 1988 *Framework* document; it will be updated as the IASB-only project to revise the *Framework* progresses. Notwithstanding that the form, but not necessarily the underlying content, of this chapter is likely to change as the *IFRS Framework* project progresses, its importance cannot be overstated as it is the bedrock on which financial accounting is based. Consequently, an understanding of the key components of this chapter, each of which is explained below, is imperative:

• underlying assumptions of financial reporting;
• the elements of financial statements;
• recognition of the elements of financial statements;
• measurement of the elements of financial statements; and
• concepts of capital and capital maintenance.

Underlying Assumptions of Financial Reporting Two assumptions that underlie the preparation of financial statements are:

• *going concern* This assumption, which is specifically referred to in Chapter 4 of the *IFRS Framework*, states that financial statements are normally prepared on the assumption that an entity is a **going concern** and will continue in operation for the foreseeable future, which is usually regarded as being at least one year. Consequently, any intention to liquidate or significantly reduce the scale of an entity's operations would place this assumption in doubt and require the financial statements to be prepared on a different basis and this basis must be disclosed; and

• *accruals accounting* This assumption, which is included in IAS 1 *Presentation of Financial Statements* (not the *IFRS Framework*) along with going concern, states that financial statements should be prepared on an **accruals accounting** basis, whereby the effects of transactions are recognised when they occur and are recorded and reported in the accounting periods to which they relate, irrespective of cash flows arising from transactions. Under cash accounting, expenses are recorded in the financial accounts when the cash is actually paid and revenue is recognised when the cash is actually received. For example, an accountant who prepares his financial statements to 31 December each year on a cash basis and who completed an engagement in December 2012, but did not get paid by the client until February 2013, would reflect this in the financial statements for the year ended 31 December 2013. Under accruals accounting, revenue is recorded when the actual work is completed (such as the completion of work specified in a letter of engagement between an accountant and client), not when the cash is received. In the above example, the revenue and related expenses would be reflected in the 2010 financial statements.

The Elements of Financial Statements Financial statements portray the financial effects of transactions and other events by grouping them into broad classes according to their economic characteristics. These *five* broad classes are termed the *elements of financial statements* and are explained below.

• **Asset** – this is a resource controlled by the entity as a result of past events and from which future economic benefits are expected to flow to the entity. Future economic benefits represent the potential to contribute to the cash flow of the entity. Future economic benefits embodied in an asset may flow to the entity in a variety of ways. For example: the asset may be used singly or in combination with others to produce goods/services to be sold by the entity; the asset may be exchanged for other assets; the asset may be used to settle a **liability**; or the asset may be distributed to the owners of the entity. Many assets have a physical form (for example, property, plant and equipment), but others do not (for example, goodwill or patents). In addition, many assets are associated with legal rights (for example, receivables), but others are not (for example, finance leases or know-how). Past events are normally signified by the purchase or production of assets (for example, the payment of cash to acquire equipment), but not necessarily (for example, government grants may be received in advance or as the result of the passage of time). Intentions to purchase or produce assets are not assets; they are merely future intentions. Expenditure is normally required to receive an asset, but it is not necessary (for example, donated assets).

- *Liability* – this is a present obligation of the entity arising from past events, the settlement of which is expected to result in an outflow of resources from the entity. A liability can be legally enforceable (for example, a binding contract), but can also arise from normal business practice or custom (for example, company policy to rectify faults even after warranty has expired). It is important to make a clear distinction between a present obligation and a future commitment. A management decision, by itself, is not sufficient; it requires an asset to be delivered or the entity to be put into a position of having very little discretion to avoid an outflow of resources. Settlement usually involves the entity giving up resources to satisfy the claim of the other party. Settlement may occur in a number of ways: payment of cash; transfer of other assets; provision of services; replacement of an obligation by another obligation; or conversion of the obligation into equity. It could also be extinguished by other means, for example, a creditor waiving or forfeiting its rights. In addition, a liability must be the result of a past transaction. For example, under new legislation a company is required to fit filters to its factories by 31 December 2012 in order to reduce emissions, but has not done so by this date. At 31 December 2012 there is still no obligation for the cost of fitting the filters because no obligating event has occurred (i.e. the fitting of the filters). However, there is an obligation for any fines or penalties that may arise under the legislation because the obligating event has occurred (i.e. the non-compliance with the legislation). Moreover, as some liabilities require considerable estimation (for example, provisions), they therefore can be broader than a legal obligation.

- *Equity* – this represents the residual interest in the assets of an entity after deducting all its liabilities. It may be sub-classified into different components that reflect differing rights or show restrictions on the ability of the entity to distribute certain reserves. The creation of reserves is sometimes required by statute or law to protect creditors from losses, and the existence and size of these reserves, together with transfers during the accounting period, is important information for users. It is important to note that the equity figure in the financial statements is unlikely to correspond with the market value of the entity or the sum that could be raised by disposing of the assets either on a piecemeal or going concern basis. While there are different types of business entity (for example, sole trader, partnership, limited company), each of which is subject to different regulations, the definition of equity is appropriate for all such entities. In assessing whether an item meets the definition of an asset, liability or equity, attention should be paid to the substance and economic reality of the item and not merely its legal form (for example, items held under finance leases are recorded as assets in the lessee's books).

- *Income* – this is defined as increases in economic benefits during the accounting period in the form of inflows or enhancements of assets or decreases of liabilities that result in increases in equity, other than those relating to contributions from equity participants. Income includes both revenues and gains. The former arises in the ordinary course of business (for example, sales, royalties, rents, fees and interest), while the latter represent other items of income that may not normally arise in the ordinary course of business (for example, a gain arising on the disposal of non-current assets). Both types of income are, however, treated the same for accounting purposes. In addition, income may also include unrealised gains (for example, the revaluation of marketable securities or non-current assets). Gains are often reported net of related expenses.

- **Expenses** – these are decreases in economic benefits during the accounting period in the form of outflows or depletions of assets that result in decreases in equity, other than those relating to distributions to equity participants. This includes losses (for example, those arising on the disposal of non-current assets) as well as expenses incurred in the ordinary course of business (for example, wages, depreciation and heat and light). Expenses also include unrealised losses (for example, those arising on foreign currency transactions), and they are often reported net of any related income. Income and expenses are presented in the statement of profit or loss and other comprehensive income in different ways and under different headings, so as to provide relevant information for making economic decisions. Distinguishing between items of income and expense and combining them in different ways also permits several measures of performance to be displayed (for example, gross margin, profit before taxation and profit after taxation).

After having explained the elements of financial statements (asset, liability, equity, income and expenses), the next section considers how these elements are recognised in the financial statements.

Recognition of the Elements of Financial Statements While an item must meet one of the definitions referred to above in order to be recognised (i.e. reported or recorded), two further criteria must be met before an item can be recognised.
1. It is probable that any future economic benefit associated with the item will flow to or from the entity.
2. The item has a cost or value that can be measured with reliability.

For the *first criterion*, the idea of *probability* is used regularly in the preparation of financial statements (for example, the probability that credit customers will pay in order that receivables can reliably be included in the statement of financial position). The assessment of the degree of certainty that an event will take place must be completed using the evidence available when the financial statements are prepared. Where economic benefits are estimated to arise over time, any related expenses should be systematically recognised over the same periods and matched with the income. If no future benefits are anticipated, expenses should be recognised immediately.

The *second criterion* requires that a *monetary value* be attached to the item. While for some transactions this is straightforward, often the value attached to an item has to be estimated. This is acceptable provided that it is a reasonable estimate and does not undermine reliability (one of the qualitative characteristics referred to above). Where information is relevant to users, it should not be excluded from the financial statements because it fails to meet the recognition criteria. For example, where a contingent liability exists at the end of the reporting period but cannot be measured with any degree of certainty, it fails the second recognition criterion; however, due to its nature and existence, it should be disclosed to users on the grounds that it is relevant. An item that initially fails the reliability test may qualify later as a result of subsequent events.

Materiality must always be considered when assessing recognition. Moreover, it is important to remember that the recognition of one element (for example, an asset) will affect another element (for example, an increase in a liability or creation of income). Recognition should be made as follows:

- *Assets* should be recognised in the statement of financial position when it is probable that future economic benefits will flow to the entity (i.e. they will help to generate positive cash flows) and the asset has a cost or value that can be measured reliably (for example, its purchase price or market value). If expenditure incurred is seen to be improbable in terms of future benefits, it should be expensed immediately. Even though the intention may be to improve future benefits, the uncertainty means an asset may not be recorded (for example, market changes suggest that the predicted demand for a product manufactured by a particular machine will decline significantly);
- *Liabilities* should be recognised in the statement of financial position when it is probable that an outflow of resources will result from the settlement of a present obligation and the amount can be measured reliably (for example, a claim against the company is likely to be successful and the amount of damages can be reasonably estimated). While orders for inventory may be liabilities if the recognition criteria are met, despite the fact that the contracts are unperformed, these would usually not pass the recognition criteria;
- *Income* occurs simultaneously with the recognition of assets and liabilities (for example, a sale leads to the recognition of either 'cash' or a 'receivable', both of which are assets). Income recognition is restricted to those items that can both be measured reliably and provided with a sufficient degree of certainty (i.e. following a credit sale, the amount due is known and the expectation is that the customer will pay for the goods in accordance with the credit terms); and
- *Expenses* occur simultaneously with the recognition of an increase in liabilities or a decrease in assets (for example, the purchase of goods on credit will result in the recognition of a liability to pay for those goods, while the purchase of goods for cash will result in a reduction of the asset of money in the bank).

Note: Equity is omitted from this list since, as defined previously, it is the residual interest in the assets of the entity after deducting all its liabilities.

Where benefits are expected to arise over several accounting periods, and the link between income and expenses can only be loosely determined, expenses should be recognised in the statement of profit or loss and other comprehensive income on the basis of systematic and rational allocation procedures (for example, with respect to depreciation or amortisation). An expense should be recognised immediately in the statement of profit or loss and other comprehensive income when no future economic benefit exists or the item ceases to qualify for recognition as an asset (for example, rent relates to a particular time period and should be expensed when that time period expires). An expense is also recognised in the statement of profit or loss and other comprehensive income when a liability is incurred (for example, a company may provide for future warranty claims (a liability) in respect of current sales. The cost of the expected warranty claims will be recognised as an expense 'now').

Measurement of the Elements of Financial Statements Once it is determined that an item should be recognised in the financial statements, it is then necessary to decide on what basis it is to be measured. To be included in the financial statements, the item must have a monetary value attached to it. Four measurement bases that are often used in financial reporting are historical cost, current cost, realisable value and present value. While historical cost is the most commonly adopted measurement base, arguably because of its relative simplicity, it is often applied together with a combination of bases (for example, valuing inventory at the lower of cost and net realisable value, marketable securities at market value and pension liabilities at present value). The key aspects of the four bases are as follows.

(a) **Historical cost** Assets are recorded at the cash paid at date of acquisition. Liabilities are recorded at the amount of proceeds received in exchange for the obligation or the amount of cash expected to be paid to satisfy the liability (for example, taxation). Historical cost has many advantages. It is familiar and, in many circumstances, has a high degree of objectivity. It also reflects the transactions actually engaged in by the entity, rather than hypothetical alternatives. The most notable drawback of historical cost, however, arises not on initial recognition but at later times. Historical cost does not reflect price changes, and hence will not necessarily reflect the value of the asset at any time after initial recognition.

(b) **Current cost** Assets are recorded at the cash that would have to be paid to acquire the same or equivalent assets. Liabilities are carried at the undiscounted amount of cash required to settle the obligation. Some entities adopt current cost accounting to cope with the inability of historical cost accounting to deal with the effects of changing prices. Current cost could be used as a possible alternative to historical cost, with the advantage being that it focuses on the services the asset will provide rather than the precise physical asset. However, the main flaw with this model is where the cost has to be estimated, which has to be carried out after reviewing the asset, the market and an assessment of whether an identical asset is still being traded in the market. Moreover, the current cost is not based on an actual transaction.

(c) **Realisable value** Assets are recorded at the cash that would be obtained by selling the assets in an orderly disposal. Liabilities are carried at their settlement values, which is typically the undiscounted amounts of cash expected to be paid to satisfy the liabilities in the normal course of business. Realisable value adopts a selling price view, or the amount that the entity would obtain through sale. There are several advantages to the use of realisable value: it is easy to understand; and it indicates the amount of cash resources at the entity's command. Selling prices are relevant to management decision-making and a decision to continue holding an asset (presumably for its potential economic benefits) entails a decision to forego the receipts from its sale. However, the general adoption of a realisable value approach is not without problems. For example, with respect to non-current assets held for use in the business, where there is no necessity (or intention) to sell them in the short term, it is arguable that the relevance of realisable value is peripheral; what is most relevant is the value of the asset to the business. Despite objections to realisable value, there seems to be a strong case that it is the most relevant and useful basis for assets where sale is the most profitable opportunity open to the entity. For example, for assets that are surplus to the requirements of the business.

(d) **Present value** Assets are recorded at the present value of future net cash inflows that they are expected to generate in the normal course of business. Liabilities are carried at the present value of the future net cash outflows that are expected to be required to settle the liabilities in the normal course of business. Present value can be viewed as the value in use of an asset in terms of the value of the returns expected from the asset, reduced to present value using a discount rate that is appropriate to the risks involved. From a capital budgeting perspective, this is arguably the most relevant value of an asset as it may be reasoned that, on acquisition, the returns expected from an asset will be greater than its cost. Therefore, if present value were to be generally used for financial reporting, it might be expected that the acquisition of an asset would typically lead to reported gains. However, given that future returns must be based on forecasts, the use of present value gives rise to the use of subjective, and often impractical, forecasts.

The issue of measurement is developed further in **Section 1.4** below.

This section has considered alternative ways of recognising or measuring items in financial statements. Depending on which method is adopted, this will impact upon the reported equity or capital of the business. The two most common approaches to measuring income are the transaction approach (see historical cost accounting above) and the capital maintenance approach. Under the transaction approach, income is calculated by analysing the effects of revenue and expense transactions during a period. Any change in the value of the entity that is not a result of a transaction is not reflected in the entity's net income. Under the capital maintenance approach, however, net income is defined as the difference between the net assets (assets minus liabilities) at the beginning of a period and net assets at the end of the period, excluding owners' contributions and distributions during the period. The capital maintenance approach captures all changes in the value of the entity during a period, regardless of whether the change resulted from a transaction. The next section considers two different views on capital.

Concepts of Capital Maintenance There are two concepts or models of capital maintenance:
• the *financial concept* of capital maintenance; and
• the *physical concept* of capital maintenance.

The principle of capital maintenance is fundamental to protection of creditors of limited liability companies since shareholders may deplete the equity or capital of a company by withdrawing excessive dividends. In general terms, an entity has maintained its capital if it has as much capital at the end of the period as it had at the beginning of the period. The key in capital maintenance is deciding which concept is being adopted, because this then defines the basis on which profit is calculated. The choice of model will depend on the different degrees of relevance and reliability available and management must seek an appropriate balance between the two. At present, the IASB does not prescribe a particular model, except in exceptional circumstances (for example, in the case of hyperinflationary economies (IAS 29 *Financial Reporting in Hyperinflationary Economies* (see **Chapter 31**)).

Under the *financial concept of capital maintenance*, the capital of a company is only maintained if the financial or monetary amount of its net assets at the end of a financial period is equal to or exceeds the financial or monetary amount of its net assets at the beginning of the period, excluding any distributions to, or contributions from, the owners. Under this concept, profit is earned if the financial amount of the net assets at the end of the period is greater than that at the beginning of the period, after deducting any distributions to and contributions from owners. Financial capital maintenance is measured in either nominal monetary units (i.e. historical amount) or units of constant purchasing power (i.e. in real terms, taking account of inflation).

Under the *physical concept of capital maintenance*, the physical capital is only maintained if the physical productive or operating capacity, or the funds or resources required to achieve this capacity, is equal to or exceeds the physical productive capacity at the beginning of the period, after excluding any distributions to, or contributions from, owners during the financial period. Under this concept, profit is earned if the physical productive capacity (or operating capacity) of the entity (or the resources or funds needed to achieve that capacity) at the end of the period is greater than that at the beginning of the period, after deducting any distributions to and contributions from owners. Physical capital maintenance requires the adoption of the current cost basis of measurement (i.e. an appreciation of what it would cost to replace assets at current prices).

The main difference between the two concepts of capital maintenance is on the effects of changes in the prices of assets and liabilities of the entity. Generally, capital is maintained if an entity has as much capital at the end of the period as at the start, with any amount over and above that representing profit. Under financial capital maintenance, if capital is defined in nominal terms, profit is the increase in nominal money capital over the period. Holding gains (losses), which are generally defined as increases (decreases) in the replacement costs of the assets held during a given period, are therefore included in profit. Alternatively, if current purchasing power is applied, profit represents the increase in purchasing power over the period. Thus, only that part of the increase in prices of assets that exceeds the increase in the general level of prices is regarded as profit, with the rest being a capital maintenance adjustment and therefore part of equity. Under physical capital maintenance, where capital is defined in terms of productive capacity, profit represents the increase in that capital over the period.

Most entities adopt the financial concept of capital maintenance, which deals with the net assets or equity of the entity. If, instead of being primarily concerned with the invested capital of the entity, the users are concerned with, for example, the operating capability of the entity, then the physical concept of capital should be used. The selection of the most appropriate basis to adopt should be based on user needs.

1.4 FAIR VALUE MEASUREMENT

Chapter 4 of the *IFRS Framework* (see above) states that **The Elements of Financial Statements** (asset, liability, equity, income and expenses) portray the financial effects of transactions and other events by grouping them into broad classes according to their economic characteristics. Then, once it is determined that an item should be recognised in the financial statements, it is necessary to decide on what basis it is to be measured. Four measurement bases that are often used in financial reporting are historical cost, current cost, realisable value and present value. The issue of measurement is now discussed.

Background

The IASB began a joint project in 2005 with the US national standard-setting body, FASB, to create a common set of high quality global accounting standards, part of which involved standardising the definition and meaning of fair value in order to reduce diversity in application and improve the comparability of financial statements. The global financial crisis emphasised the importance of having common fair value measurement and disclosures. The IASB's objectives with respect to fair value measurement were to:

(a) establish a single source of guidance for all fair value measurements required or permitted by existing IFRSs to reduce complexity and improve consistency in their application;

(b) clarify the definition of fair value and related guidance to communicate the measurement objective more clearly; and

(c) enhance disclosures about fair value to enable users of financial statements to assess the extent to which fair value is used to measure assets and liabilities and to provide them with information about the inputs used to derive those fair values.

These objectives were based on the belief that the:

- purpose of fair value measurement is to determine the price that would be received for an asset or paid to transfer a liability in a transaction between market participants at the measurement date;
- fair value measurement should reflect market views of the attributes of the asset or liability being measured;
- fair value measurement should consider the location and the condition of the asset or liability at its measurement date.

In May 2011 the IASB issued IFRS 13 *Fair Value Measurement*.

Why is a Single Accounting Standard on Fair Value Measurement Important?

IFRSs require some assets, liabilities and equity instruments to be measured at fair value. However, guidance on measuring fair value has been added to IFRSs piecemeal over many years as the IASB or its predecessor (IASC) decided that fair value was the appropriate measurement basis in a particular situation. As a result, guidance on measuring fair value is dispersed across many IFRSs and it is not always consistent. Furthermore, the current guidance is incomplete, in that it provides neither a clear measurement objective nor a robust measurement framework and thus adds unnecessary complexity to IFRSs and contributes to diversity in practice. Consequently, as evidenced by the piecemeal manner in which fair value measurement is currently addressed in different standards, IFRS 13 is long overdue.

For example, standards that require fair value measurement in certain circumstances include:
- IAS 16 *Property, Plant and Equipment* (see **Chapter 6**);
- IAS 17 *Leases* (see **Chapter 8**);
- IAS 18 *Revenue* (see **Chapter 4**);
- IAS 19 *Employee Benefits* (see **Chapter 17**);
- IAS 36 *Impairment of Assets* (see **Chapter 10**);
- IAS 38 *Intangible Assets* (see **Chapter 9**);
- IAS 40 *Investment Property* (see **Chapter 5**); and
- IFRS 5 *Non-current Assets Held for Sale and Discontinued Operations* (see **Chapter 20**).

For example, standards that require fair value measurement by reference to another standard include:
- IAS 2 *Inventory* (see **Chapter 11**);
- IAS 21 *The Effects of Changes in Foreign Exchange Rates* (see **Chapter 31**);
- IAS 28 *Investments in Associates and Joint Ventures* (see **Chapter 29**); and
- IFRS 7 *Financial Instruments: Disclosures* (see **Chapter 25**).

Standards that do not require fair value measurement:
- IAS 7 *Statement of Cash Flows* (see **Chapters 19** and **33**);
- IAS 8 *Accounting Policies, Changes in Accounting Estimates and Errors* (see **Chapter 21**);
- IAS 12 *Income Taxes* (see **Chapter 13**); and
- IAS 24 *Related Party Disclosures* (see **Chapter 22**).

IFRS 13 *Fair Value Measurement*

Scope of the Standard

IFRS 13 applies when another IFRS requires or permits fair value measurements or disclosures about fair value measurements (and measurements, such as fair value less costs to sell, based on fair value or disclosures about those measurements), except for:
- share-based payment transactions within the scope of IFRS 2 *Share-based Payment* (see **Chapter 34**);
- leasing transactions within the scope of IAS 17 *Leases*; and
- measurements that have some similarities to fair value but that are not fair value, such as net realisable value in IAS 2 *Inventories* or value in use in IAS 36 *Impairment of Assets*.

IFRS 13, therefore, does not mandate when fair value measurements should be used; this is addressed in other IFRSs. IFRS 13 is applicable to annual reporting periods beginning on or after 1 January 2013. An entity may apply IFRS 13 to an earlier accounting period, but if doing so, it must disclose the fact.

Key Definitions

(**Note:** while a number of key definitions are included at the beginning of this chapter, the following definitions are included separately here as they relate specifically to this section.)

Active Market A market in which transactions for the asset or liability take place with sufficient frequency and volume to provide pricing information on an ongoing basis.

Exit Price This is an estimate of the price that would be received to sell an asset or paid to transfer a liability. It is not the price to buy the asset or to incur the liability.

Fair Value The price that would be received to sell an asset or paid to transfer a liability in an orderly transaction between market participants at the measurement date. This is sometimes referred to as an 'exit price'.

It is important to clarify a number of issues that may arise with respect to the above definitions.
1. Is there a difference between 'price' and 'value'?
   'Price' is the amount agreed on in a transaction while 'value' is the outcome of a valuation. In practice, most valuations assume a transaction but, depending on the purpose of the valuation exercise, a value could also be entity-specific. In many cases price and value will result in (nearly) the same number.

---

2. Is there a valuation difference between an entry and an exit price?
   For non-entity-specific values, entry and exit price for the same market should be the same. Often a perceived difference results because entry price is determined on a different market than the exit price.
3. What makes the market?
   While there is an opinion that fair values can only be made where an active market exists, the IASB believes that this is not the case. The valuation profession assumes as long as there is enough evidence to establish a valuation, it is assumed that a market exists, even if the degree of reliability is lower than that for a market with frequent transactions.

Determining Fair Value

The first step is to identify the relevant asset or liability. This may be a stand-alone asset or liability, a group of assets *or* liabilities or a group of assets *and* liabilities (for example, a cash-generating unit). In addition, it is important to note that the level at which fair value is measured may depend upon the level at which the asset or liability is aggregated for recognition. Moreover, when determining the fair value, the characteristics of the asset or liability should be taken into account if market participants would take those characteristics into account when pricing the asset or liability. Such characteristics include the condition and location of the asset and/or any restrictions on the sale or use of the asset.

Fair value measurement assumes that the transaction takes place in either: the principal market for the asset or liability or, in the absence of a principal market, in the most advantageous market for the asset or liability. The principal market is deemed to be the market with the greatest volume and level of activity for that asset or liability, while the most advantageous market is the market in which the entity could achieve the most beneficial price.

The fair value of an asset or liability should be measured using the assumptions that market participants would use when pricing the asset or liability. For this purpose, it is assumed that market participants are independent of each other, knowledgeable about the asset or liability and able and willing to enter into the transaction. In addition, fair value measurement assumes that the asset or liability is exchanged in an orderly transaction (i.e. not a forced transaction, such as a liquidation or distress sale) under current market conditions at the measurement date.

With respect to a non-financial asset, fair value measurement takes into account a market participant's ability to generate economic benefits by using the asset in its highest and best use. This is the highest and best use that is:
- physically possible (for example, given the location or size of a property);
- legally permissible (for example, based on planning regulations); and
- financially feasible (i.e. it generates an adequate return for market participants).

In the case of a liability or an entity's own equity instrument, fair value measurement assumes that the liability or equity instrument is transferred to a market participant and would remain outstanding (i.e. it is a transfer value, not an extinguishment or settlement value).

Fair Value Hierarchy

IFRS 13 seeks to increase consistency and comparability in **fair value** measurements and related disclosures through a 'fair value hierarchy'. The hierarchy categorises the inputs used in valuation techniques into three levels. The hierarchy gives the highest priority to quoted prices in active markets for identical assets or liabilities and the lowest priority to unobservable inputs. The three-level hierarchy is summarised as follows.

Level 1 Inputs are quoted prices in active markets for identical assets or liabilities that the entity can access at the measurement date. A quoted market price in an active market provides the most reliable evidence of fair value and is used without adjustment to measure fair value whenever available, with limited exceptions.

Level 2 Inputs are observable inputs other than quoted prices for identical assets or liabilities in active markets at the measurement date.

Level 3 Inputs are unobservable inputs, e.g. inputs derived through extrapolation or interpolation that cannot be corroborated by observable data. However, the fair value measurement objective remains the same. Therefore, unobservable inputs should be adjusted for entity information that is inconsistent with market expectations. Unobservable inputs should also consider the risk premium a market participant (buyer) would demand to assume the inherent uncertainty in the unobservable input.

Fair Value Measurement Techniques

The objective of fair value measurement is to estimate the price at which an orderly transaction to sell the asset or to transfer the liability would take place between market participants at the measurement date under current market conditions. When transactions are directly observable in a market, the determination of fair value is relatively straightforward. In other circumstances, a valuation technique should be used. IFRS 13 sets out three approaches for determining fair value using a valuation technique:
- a market approach – which uses prices and other relevant information generated by market transactions involving identical or comparable assets or liabilities (or businesses);
- an income approach – which converts future amounts (for example, cash flows or income and expenses) to a single discounted present value amount; or
- a cost approach – which reflects the amount that would currently be required to replace the service capacity of an asset (often referred to as 'current replacement cost').

IFRS 13 acknowledges that, in some cases, a single valuation technique will be appropriate, whereas in others multiple valuation techniques will be appropriate. The valuation techniques used should maximise the use of relevant, observable inputs and minimise the use of unobservable inputs (see above).

Disclosure

The purpose of the IFRS 13 disclosures is to require an entity to disclose information that helps users of its financial statements assess both of the following:
- for assets and liabilities that are measured at fair value on a recurring or non-recurring basis in the statement of financial position after initial recognition, the valuation techniques and inputs used to develop those measurements;
- for fair value measurements using significant unobservable inputs (i.e. Level 3), the effect of the measurements on profit or loss or other comprehensive income for the period.

The main disclosures required for each class of asset and liability measured at fair value are:
- the fair value measurement at the end of the reporting period;
- the reasons for the measurement;
- the level of the fair value hierarchy within which the fair value measurements are categorised (Level 1, 2 or 3);
- the amounts of any transfers between Level 1 and Level 2, the reasons for those transfers and the entity's policy for determining when transfers between levels are deemed to have occurred;
- for fair value measurements categorised within Level 2 and Level 3, a description of the valuation technique(s) and the inputs used in the fair value measurement, any change in the valuation techniques and the reason(s) for making such change; and
- for fair value measurements categorised within Level 3, quantitative information about the significant unobservable inputs used in the fair value measurement and a description of the valuation processes used by the entity.

Recommended Reading (Fair Value)

Accounting & Business Research (2007), Special Issue, International Accounting Policy Forum.
Barth, M.E. (2000), 'Valuation-based research: implications for financial reporting and opportunities for future research', *Accounting and Finance*, Issue 40, pp. 7–31.
Hitz, J.M. (2007), 'The decision usefulness of fair value accounting–a theoretical perspective', *European Accounting Review*, Vol. 16, No. 2, pp. 323–362.
Rayman, R.A. (2007), 'Fair value accounting and the present value fallacy: the need for an alternative conceptual framework', *British Accounting Review*, Vol. 39, September, pp. 211–225.
Wyatt, A. (1991), 'The SEC says: mark to market!', *Accounting Horizons*, Vol. 5, No. 1, pp. 80–84.
van Zijl, A. and Whittington, G. (2006), 'Deprival Value and Fair Value: A Reinterpretation and A Reconciliation', *Accounting and Business Research*, Issue 36, July, pp. 121–130.

1.5 CONCLUSION

Financial reporting is concerned with the communication of information, and the main purpose of accounting is to provide users with relevant, reliable, comparable and understandable information about an entity's financial position, performance and changes in financial position. The *IFRS Framework* presents a set of definitions and fundamental principles that underpin financial reporting, with one of its main functions being to reduce or eliminate variations in accounting practices and to introduce a degree of uniformity into financial reporting. In addition, it seeks to assist in the review and development of accounting standards.

Consistent with the objectives of the *IFRS Framework*, the regulatory framework comprises the statutory regulations created to regulate the format and content of financial statements and reports. It consists of a combination of legislation, stock exchange regulations (if applicable) and accounting standards. Company legislation typically sets out broad rules with which companies must comply when preparing their financial statements, while the stock exchange regulations offer more detailed guidance for public limited companies. Accounting standards provide rules and policies to assist with the accounting treatment of transactions and balances.

Summary of Learning Objectives

After having studied this chapter on the framework for financial reporting, you should be able to:

Learning Objective 1 Describe the main aspects of the regulatory framework.

A lack of comparability in financial information could affect the credibility of financial reporting and have a detrimental effect on financial investment. The global nature of trade, finance and investment has resulted in the need for a single set of rules by which assets, liabilities and income are recognised and measured. Financial reporting is regulated through a combination of company law, the stock exchange regulations and accounting standards.

Learning Objective 2 Define what is meant by the term 'conceptual framework for financial reporting'.

In broad terms, this is a coherent system of interrelated objectives and fundamentals that form the frame of reference for financial reporting and provide the basis for the development of new accounting standards and the evaluation of those already in existence.

Learning Objective 3 Explain the need and purpose for such a framework.

One of the major challenges for financial reporting is facilitating the needs of the numerous and disparate users of that information. As it is important that financial reports are prepared on a consistent and comparable basis, a conceptual framework seeks to achieve this by providing guidance on the broad principles on how items should be recorded and how they should be presented. It provides a point of reference for preparers of financial information. For example, the framework can provide guidance on how like items are treated and give definitions and criteria that can be used in deciding the recognition and measurement of the item.

Learning Objective 4 Discuss the key components of the *Conceptual Framework for Financial Reporting 2010*.

The *IFRS Framework* addresses: the objective of financial reporting; the qualitative characteristics of useful financial information; the reporting entity; the definition, recognition and measurement of the elements from which financial statements are constructed; and the concepts of capital and capital maintenance. The September 2010 version of the

IFRS Framework consists of four chapters: Chapter 1 – The Objective of General Purpose Financial Reporting; Chapter 2 – The Reporting Entity (which will be further considered as the IASB-only conceptual framework project progresses); Chapter 3 – Qualitative Characteristics of Useful Financial Information; and Chapter 4 – The Framework (which contains the remaining text of the 1988 *Framework* document and will be updated as the IASB-only conceptual framework project progresses).

Learning Objective 5 Explain the key issues with respect to fair value measurement.

IFRS 13 establishes a single framework for measuring fair value where this is required by other standards. Fair value is defined as the price that would be received to sell an asset or paid to transfer a liability in an orderly transaction between market participants at the measurement date. IFRS 13 categorises the inputs used in valuation techniques into three levels and sets out three approaches for determining fair value using a valuation technique (market, income and cost).

QUESTIONS

Self-test Questions

1. What is relevance?
2. What is meant by the term 'faithful representation'?
3. What is a conceptual framework?
4. Outline the contents of the chapters that comprise the *IFRS Framework*.
5. Describe the three levels in the fair value hierarchy and the three different approaches to determining fair value.

Review Questions

(See **Appendix One** for Suggested Solutions to Review Questions.)

Question 1.1

(a) Who are considered to be the potential users of financial reports?
(b) What do you consider to be their information needs?
(c) How would you expect a consideration of user needs to influence financial reporting?

Question 1.2

The Technical Committee of the International Organisation of Securities Commissions (IOSCO) and the IASB agree that there is a compelling need for high-quality, comprehensive, international accounting standards.

Requirement Discuss briefly why the development of international accounting standards is considered to be important.

Question 1.3

The *IFRS Framework* has a number of purposes, including assisting:
- the IASB in the development of future accounting standards and in its review of existing IASs/IFRSs;
- the IASB in promoting harmonisation of regulations, accounting standards and procedures relating to the presentation of financial statements by providing a basis for reducing the number of alternative treatments permitted by IASs/IFRSs; and
- preparers of financial statements in applying IASs/IFRSs and in dealing with topics that have yet to be covered in an accounting standard.

Requirement Discuss how a conceptual framework can help the IASB achieve these objectives.

Challenging Questions

(Suggested Solutions to Challenging Questions are available to lecturers.)

Question 1.1

The *IFRS Framework* includes the following definition:

"An asset is a resource controlled by the entity as a result of past events and from which future economic benefits are expected to flow to the entity."

Requirement Explain this definition, using the example of a trade receivable.

Question 1.2

The *IFRS Framework* states that relevance and faithful representation are the two fundamental qualitative characteristics of financial information.

Requirement

(a) Briefly discuss what is meant by these terms; and
(b) Give an example of when these two attributes could come into conflict and what the outcome is likely to be.

Question 1.3

In 1988 the IASC issued the *Framework for the Preparation and Presentation of Financial Statements*. Then, in October 2004, the IASB and the US FASB decided to add to their respective agendas a joint project to develop a common conceptual framework. However, during late 2010, it was decided to defer further work on this joint project until after other, more urgent convergence projects were finalised. Subsequently, in December 2012, as a result of the IASB's Agenda Consultation project (public consultation on the IASB's future plan of work), the IASB decided to reactivate the *IFRS Framework* project as an IASB-only project.

Requirement Evaluate the relationship between a conceptual framework and the standard-setting process.

Question 1.4

The *Conceptual Framework for Financial Reporting (2010)* (*IFRS Framework*) states that accounting information should be decision-useful for the principal classes of users.

Requirement With reference to the *IFRS Framework* document, identify these principal classes of users and explain what is meant by the expression 'accounting information should be decision-useful'.

Question 1.5

Calls for action to prevent a repeat of the global financial crisis have touched upon accounting standard-setting and the way in which accounting information (or lack thereof) contributed to the global financial crisis.

Requirement Drawing on relevant academic literature, discuss:
(a) whether financial reporting, particularly with respect to fair values, in contrast to accounting regulation, contributed to the Global Financial Crisis;
(b) the usefulness of the information standard-setters require companies to provide to enable the capital markets to assess the financial position of a company; and
(c) suggestions for potential changes in financial reporting to improve the transparency of information provided to the capital markets.

Question 1.6

A number of major corporate scandals, together with the current global financial crisis, have all been linked directly or indirectly to false, misleading or untruthful accounting. Thus, in a pragmatic sense, the question of the veracity of accounting or what it could mean for accounting to be true seems to exist. Moreover, the assertion of a false or misleading financial report implies some belief that there could exist a true or not-misleading report.

Requirement Drawing on relevant academic literature, discuss the role of accounting in a democratic society and whether reporting truth represents a genuine problem for the accounting profession and for financial statement preparers and users.

Question 1.7

The *Conceptual Framework for Financial Reporting (2010)* (*IFRS Framework*) sets out the concepts that underlie the preparation and presentation of financial statements for external users.

Requirement Prepare a report for an investor with no prior knowledge of accounting that explains the:
(a) qualitative characteristics of financial information as detailed in the *IFRS Framework*; and
(b) objective of a statement of financial position and its major limitations as a source of information for general users of financial statements.

REFERENCES

Accounting Standards Steering Committee (ASSC) (1975), *The Corporate Report*, London, ASSC.

International Accounting Standards Committee (IASC) (1988), *Framework for the Presentation and Preparation of Financial Statements*, London: IASC.

Irish Stock Exchange (2011), *Main Securities Market Listing Rules and Admissions to Trading Rules*, December, Dublin: Irish Stock Exchange. (http://www.ise.ie/ISE_Regulation/Equity_Rules_Listing_Rules/Listing_Rules.pdf)

London Stock Exchange (2012), *Rules of the London Stock Exchange*, November, London: London Stock Exchange. (http://www.londonstockexchange.com/traders-and-brokers/rules-regulations/rules-lse.pdf)

PRESENTATION OF FINANCIAL STATEMENTS

Having studied this chapter on the presentation of financial statements, you should be able to:
- discuss the principles that govern the presentation of financial statements;
- identify the components of a set of financial statements;
- describe the structure and content of each component of a set of financial statements; and
- explain the detailed disclosure requirements of IAS 1 *Presentation of Financial Statements*.

Key Terms and Definitions for this Chapter

In order to aid your understanding of the concepts and issues covered in this chapter, it is important to understand and be familiar with the following key terms and definitions. As you study this chapter, you should refer back to the key terms and definitions listed below.

Associate An entity in which the investor has significant influence, which is deemed to be the power to participate in the financial and operating policy decisions of the investee but not control those policies. If an investor holds, directly or indirectly, 20% or more of the voting power of the investee, it is presumed that it has significant influence, unless it can be clearly demonstrated that this is not the case. Conversely, if less than 20%, the presumption is that the investor does not have significant influence. A majority shareholding by another investor does not preclude an investor

having significant influence. Its existence is usually evidenced in one or more of the following ways:
- representation on the board of directors;
- participation in policy-making processes;
- material transactions between the investor and the investee;
- interchange of managerial personnel; or
- provision of essential technical information.

Cash This refers to cash-in-hand and deposits repayable on demand.

Cash Equivalents These are short-term, highly liquid investments that are readily convertible to known amounts of cash and which are subject to an insignificant risk of changes in value. Cash equivalents are not held for investment or other long-term purposes, but rather to meet short-term cash commitments. Therefore their maturity date should normally be no more than three months from their acquisition date.

Consolidation In the context of financial accounting, consolidation refers to the aggregation of the financial statements of more than one company into a single set of financial statements as if they were one separate entity.

Current Assets Current assets include cash or other assets that can reasonably be expected to be converted to cash in the normal course of business (usually within 12 months), including inventories, receivables and prepayments.

Current Liabilities Liabilities incurred in the normal course of business that fall due within one year and include payables and accruals.

Depreciation This is defined as a measure of the wearing out, consumption or other reduction in the useful life of a non-current asset whether arising from use, passage of time or obsolescence through technological or market changes. For intangible assets, the term amortisation is used instead of depreciation.

Intangible Assets Non-current assets that do not have physical substance but are identifiable, are controlled by the entity and have estimated useful lives of more than one year. Examples include patents and copyrights.

Inventory This includes consumable stores, goods or other assets purchased for use or resale by the business in the provision of its services.

Non-controlling Interest (NCI) This is the portion of equity ownership in a subsidiary not attributable to the **parent** company (i.e. the party that has a controlling interest (greater than 50% but less than 100%)). For example, suppose company Alpha acquires 80% of the equity of company Beta. Because Alpha owns more than 50% of Beta, Alpha **consolidates** Beta's financial results with its own. The 20% of Beta's equity that Alpha does not own is known as the non-controlling interest.

Non-current Assets Assets with an expected life of more than one year held for use on a continuous basis, for example land and buildings, patents. Non-current assets usually comprise tangible and intangible non-current assets.

Parent In the context of consolidation, a parent is an entity that holds more than 50% of the equity of another entity and is therefore deemed to control that entity. Control in this context is defined as ability to direct policies and management. In this type of relationship the controlling company is the parent and the controlled company is referred to as the subsidiary. The parent company prepares and publishes consolidated financial statements at the end of the year to reflect this relationship.

Prepayments Amounts paid in a period which relate to charges of a subsequent period.

Provision This is a liability of uncertain timing or amount. Examples of provisions are restructuring provision, provision for early retirement and pension commitments.

Short-term Investment This is an item in the current assets section of a statement of financial position and represents any investments that a company has made that will expire within one year. For the most part, these will consist of shares and bonds that can be liquidated fairly quickly.

Trade and Other Payables Monies owed to another entity by the business as a result of the normal course of activities of a business.

Trade and Other Receivables Monies owed by another entity to the business as a result of the normal course of activities of a business.

2.1 INTRODUCTION

In **Chapter 1** we addressed the legal and conceptual frameworks that govern financial reporting. This chapter focuses on the requirements of IAS 1 *Presentation of Financial Statements*, which prescribes the basis for the presentation of general purpose financial statements that are prepared in accordance with International Accounting Standards (IASs) and International Financial Reporting Standards (IFRSs). When considering the presentation of information in financial statements, it is important to remember that their objective is to provide information about the financial position, financial performance and cash flows of an entity that is useful to a wide range of users in making economic decisions.

Key to this Chapter

This chapter builds upon the accounting concepts explained in **Chapter 1**. It begins by briefly reviewing the principles of financial reporting that govern the manner in which financial statements are presented, including going concern, the accruals basis of accounting and materiality (**Section 2.2**). After that, the structure and content of each of the components of a set of financial statements is described and illustrated (i.e. statement of financial position, statement of profit or loss and other comprehensive income, statement of changes in equity and statement of cash flows) (**Section 2.3**). In particular, the criteria that determine whether assets and liabilities should be classified as current or non-current are explained in this section, and the distinction between the 'nature of expense' method and the 'function of expense' method of classifying expenses in the statement of profit or loss and other comprehensive income is described.

2.2 PRINCIPLES OF FINANCIAL REPORTING

IAS 1 sets out a number of principles that govern the presentation of general purpose financial statements, many of which are driven by the *Conceptual Framework for Financial Reporting 2010* (*IFRS Framework*) (see **Chapter 1, Section 1.3**) to ensure comparability both with the entity's financial statements of previous periods and with the financial statements of other entities. As explained in **Chapter 1**, general-purpose financial statements are those intended to serve users who are not in a position to require financial reports that are tailored to their particular information needs. For example, an individual trade supplier is unlikely to be able to obtain the detailed cash flow information necessary to properly assess the likelihood of prompt payment. The main principles addressed in IAS 1 are discussed below.

Fair Presentation and Compliance with IFRS

Financial statements should present fairly:
* the financial position,
* financial performance and
* cash flows

of an entity. It is likely that financial statements that comply with all relevant IASs/IFRSs will almost always achieve this objective of fair presentation and therefore, consistent with the objective stated in the *IFRS Framework*, be useful to a wide range of users in making economic decisions.

Fair presentation requires faithful representation of the effects of transactions, events and conditions, in accordance with the definitions and recognition criteria for assets, liabilities, income and expenses set out in the *IFRS Framework*. The application of IASs/IFRSs, with additional disclosure when necessary, is presumed to result in financial statements that achieve a fair presentation. An entity must make an explicit and unreserved statement of compliance with IFRS in the **notes to the financial statements** (see **Section 2.3** below), and such a statement should only be made on compliance with *all* of the requirements of IFRS. This compliance statement is often included in the accounting policies note and is usually the first stated policy.

In the (*unlikely*) event that the directors of a business, who are the ones legally responsible for the preparation of the financial statements, decide that compliance with a particular requirement of an IAS/IFRS would result in misleading information and conflict with providing information useful to users in making economic decisions, the entity can depart from that requirement in order to achieve fair presentation (for example, a decision not to provide **depreciation** on **non-current assets** in accordance with accounting standards). In this event, the entity should disclose, normally by way of a note to the financial statements:
* that management has concluded that the financial statements are a fair presentation of the entity's financial position, performance and cash flows;
* that it has complied with all relevant IASs/IFRSs and has departed from a standard to achieve fair presentation;
* the specific IAS/IFRS it has departed from, details of why the departure was necessary and the alternative treatment that has been adopted; and
* the financial impact of the departure.

Going Concern

Financial statements should be prepared on a **going concern** basis (see **Chapter 1, Section 1.3**), unless there are plans to liquidate the entity or to cease trading, or there is no realistic alternative but to do so. When financial statements are not prepared on a going-concern basis, that fact must be disclosed, normally by way of a note to the financial statements, together with the basis on which the financial statements are prepared and the reason why the entity is not regarded as a going concern.

Accruals Basis of Accounting

Financial statements prepared in accordance with IASs/IFRSs should be prepared under the **accruals basis of accounting** (see **Chapter 1, Section 1.3**), with the exception of the statement of cash flows.

Consistency of Presentation

Financial statements should retain a consistent approach to the presentation and classification of items in each accounting period (which is normally one year) unless:
• it is apparent, following a significant change in the nature of the entity's operations or a review of its financial statements, that another presentation or classification would be more appropriate having regard to the criteria for the selection and application of accounting policies in IAS 8 *Accounting Policies, Changes in Accounting Estimates and Errors* (see **Chapter 21, Section 21.2**); or
• an IAS/IFRS requires a change in presentation.

Materiality and Aggregation

IAS 1 requires that each **material** (see **Chapter 1, Section 1.3**) class (i.e. type or category) of similar items must be presented separately in the financial statements. Items of a dissimilar nature or function may be aggregated only if they are individually immaterial. (Remember, as stated in **Chapter 1**, omissions or misstatements are *material* if they could influence the economic decisions of users.)

Offsetting

Assets and liabilities, and income and expenses, should not be offset (i.e. netted against each other – for example, money in a bank deposit account with an overdraft) unless required or permitted by a standard.

Comparative Information

With respect to numerical information, the financial statements must disclose this information not only for the 'current' accounting period being reported but also for the previous accounting period (i.e. comparative information should be disclosed for the previous period for all numerical information). In order to assist users in their understanding and assessment of the information, it is important that it is presented in a similar manner and calculated on a similar basis for each of the accounting periods presented. Consequently, if the presentation or classification of an item has changed (for example, a particular expense may have been disclosed as part of administrative expenses in the past and is now included under cost

of sales), the comparative figures should be restated using the new treatment, if possible. When comparative figures can be restated, the entity should disclose the:
- nature of the reclassification;
- amount of each item or class of items that is reclassified; and
- reason for the reclassification.

If it is impracticable to reclassify comparative figures, the entity should state the:
- reason for not reclassifying the amounts; and
- nature of the adjustments that would have been made if the amounts had been reclassified.

In order to clarify the difference between voluntary additional comparative information and the minimum required comparative information, the IASB, in May 2012, issued an amendment to IAS 1. Generally, the minimum required comparative period is the previous period. When an entity voluntarily provides comparative information beyond the minimum required comparative period, this must be included in the related notes to the financial statements. However, the additional comparative period does not need to contain a complete set of financial statements. Although the opening statement of financial position (known as the third balance sheet) must be presented in the following circumstances: when an entity changes its accounting policies; and/or makes retrospective restatements or makes reclassifications, and that change has a material effect on the statement of financial position. The opening statement would be at the beginning of the preceding period. For example, the beginning of the preceding period for a 31 December 2014 year-end would be 1 January 2013. However, unlike the voluntary comparative information, the related notes are not required to accompany the third balance sheet. This amendment is applicable for annual periods beginning on or after 1 January 2013.

2.3 STRUCTURE AND CONTENT OF FINANCIAL STATEMENTS

IAS 1 sets out overall requirements for the presentation of financial statements, guidelines for their structure and minimum requirements for their content. The standard applies to all general purpose financial statements prepared and presented in accordance with IFRS.

> **Note:** it does not apply to interim financial statements prepared in accordance with IAS 34 *Interim Financial Reporting*, for which see **Chapter 34**.

In order to fully understand the structure and content of financial statements, it is important to remember that they are a structured representation of the financial position and financial performance of an entity. Their objective is to provide information about the financial position, financial performance and cash flows of an entity that is useful to a wide range of users in making economic decisions. To do this, financial statements provide information about an entity's:
- assets;
- liabilities;
- equity;
- income and expenses, including gains and losses;
- other changes in equity; and
- cash flows.

This information, along with other information in the notes to the financial statements, assists users of financial statements in predicting the entity's future cash flows and, in particular, their timing and certainty. This is important because, while financial statements report what has happened in the past, users (for example, existing or potential investors) will be interested in the future performance and prospects of the entity. Financial statements, which also show the results of management's stewardship of the resources entrusted to it and therefore the assets available to potentially generate future profits, should be presented at least annually and issued on a timely basis to be useful to users. As stated in **Chapter 1, Section 1.1**, it is generally accepted that financial reports consist of:

- the financial statements –
  - ○ a statement of financial position,
  - ○ a statement of profit or loss and other comprehensive income,
  - ○ a statement of changes in equity,
  - ○ a statement of cash flows; and
- notes to the financial statements, comprising a summary of significant accounting policies and other explanatory notes supporting information contained in the financial statements; and
- narrative information (often non-statutory), such as a chairman's report, directors' report or discussion and analysis statement.

IAS 1 focuses on the financial statements and their related notes, and each of these are now addressed in turn.

The Statement of Financial Position

A statement of financial position reports an entity's assets, liabilities and equity at a given point in time. IAS 1 stipulates that, as a minimum, certain line items or key headings must appear on the face of the statement of financial position where there are amounts to be classified within these categories (i.e. where values against an item in either the current or comparative period are more than zero). These 'minimum' line items ((a) to (r)) are listed below, and a suggested format for a statement of financial position that fulfils these minimum disclosures is presented in **Figure 2.1**. In order to be able to prepare a statement of financial position in a form suitable for publication, it is important to learn these minimum headings (together with the suggested format shown in **Figure 2.1**):

(a) Property, plant and equipment;
(b) Investment property;
(c) Intangible assets;
(d) Financial assets (non-current);
(e) Investments in associates (accounted for using equity accounting)*;
(f) Biological assets;
(g) Inventories;
(h) Trade and other receivables;
(i) Cash and cash equivalents;
(j) Trade and other payables;
(k) Provisions;
(l) Financial liabilities;
(m) Current tax assets/liabilities;
(n) Deferred tax assets/liabilities**;

(o) Non-controlling interests*;
(p) Issued capital and reserves;
(q) Total of assets 'held for sale' under IFRS 5 *Non-current Assets Held for Sale and Discontinued Operations*; and
(r) Liabilities held 'for sale'.

*   These items relate to group accounts (see **Part V**).
**   Deferred tax assets/liabilities must not be classified as current (IAS 12 *Income Taxes* – see **Chapter 13**).

Further Guidance from IAS 1

Notwithstanding the importance of learning the minimum headings presented above (together with the suggested format shown in **Figure 2.1**), there are a number of other key points that must be borne in mind with respect to the disclosure and presentation of items in the statement of financial position. The key matters identified in IAS 1 are now discussed.

FIGURE 2.1: X LIMITED – CONSOLIDATED STATEMENT OF FINANCIAL POSITION
AS AT 31 DECEMBER 2012

	2012 €000	2011 €000
ASSETS		
Non-current Assets		
Property, plant and equipment	520,500	485,400
Investment property	200,400	184,600
Intangible assets	45,700	41,100
Financial assets	67,900	59,700
Investments in associates *(accounted for using the equity method)*	58,200	56,800
Biological assets	22,100	19,900
	914,800	847,500
Current Assets		
Inventories	18,850	16,500
Trade and other receivables	14,550	13,860
Cash and cash equivalents	10,400	9,740
	43,800	40,100
Assets held for sale	12,300	10,200
Total Assets	970,900	897,800
EQUITY AND LIABILITIES		
Equity Attributable to Owners of the Parent		
Issued share capital	400,000	380,000
Reserves	140,600	127,800
Non-controlling interests *(group financial statements only)*	82,000	78,600
	622,600	586,400
Non-current Liabilities		
Financial liabilities	123,400	109,600
Deferred tax	88,700	81,900
Provisions	76,300	69,100
	288,400	260,600

Current Liabilities		
Trade and other payables	16,200	15,500
Short-term borrowings	8,700	7,300
Current portion of long-term borrowings	18,100	16,200
Current tax payable	10,000	9,000
	53,000	48,000
Liabilities classified as held for sale	6,900	2,800
Total Equity and Liabilities	970,900	897,800

1. **Format of the Statement of Financial Position** It is important to note that IAS 1 does *not* prescribe the format of the statement of financial position. Assets can be presented as current, then non-current, or vice versa. Similarly, liabilities can be presented as current, then non-current then equity, or vice versa. A net asset presentation (assets less liabilities) is allowed, as is a long-term financing approach (non-current assets plus current assets less current liabilities). In judging the most suitable presentation, management should consider the usefulness of the information they are providing.

   Regardless of the format adopted, however, all assets should be classified as either **non-current** or **current** and all liabilities should be classified as either current or non-current. An exception to this is when a presentation based on liquidity provides information that is reliable and more relevant. In such circumstances, all assets and liabilities should be presented broadly in order of liquidity. For example, this might apply when the going-concern basis is no longer considered appropriate. As information about the financial position of an entity is often used to predict expected future cash flows, details about the expected date of recovery and settlement of items is likely to be useful and therefore worth disclosing.

2. **Classification of Assets as 'Current'** An asset should be classified as a *current* asset when it is:
   - expected to be realised in the normal course of business (**trade receivable**) or is held for sale in the normal course of business (**inventory**);
   - held primarily for trading purposes (inventory) or for the short term and expected to be realised within 12 months of the end of the reporting period (**short-term investment**); or
   - **cash or cash equivalent** (IAS 7 *Statement of Cash Flows* – see **Chapter 19**).

   All other assets should be classified as non-current assets. IAS 1 uses the term '*non-current*' (i.e. rather than 'fixed') to include tangible, intangible and financial assets of a long-term nature.

3. **Classification of Liabilities as 'Current'** Current liabilities are those which satisfy any one of the following four criteria. They are:
   - (i) expected to be settled in the normal operating cycle (typically 12 months) (**trade payable**);
   - (ii) held primarily for the purpose of being traded (derivatives – see **Chapter 25**);
   - (iii) due to be settled within 12 months of the end of the reporting period (tax liability); or
   - (iv) the entity does not have the right to defer settlement for at least 12 months after the end of the reporting period (bank overdraft (which technically is repayable on demand)).

   All other liabilities should be classified as non-current liabilities. While an overdraft would normally be classified as current, one with the ability to be rolled-over can be presented as non-current.

4. **Different Measurement Bases** Assets and liabilities that have a different nature or function within an entity are sometimes subject to different measurement bases. For example, property may be carried at cost or held at a revalued amount (in accordance with IAS 16 *Property, Plant and Equipment* – see **Chapter 6**). A company that has a chain of hotels may decide to record its administrative offices at historical cost and its hotels at market value. These two categories of property should therefore be presented separately since the use of these different measurement bases for 'like' items suggests separate presentation is necessary for users to fully understand the accounts.

5. **Sub-classifications** The minimum line items ((a) to (r)) listed above, and the suggested format for a statement of financial position presented in **Figure 2.1**, represent those headings that must be presented on the face of the statement of financial position. However, in order for the user to fully understand the information, further sub-classifications of these minimum line items may have to be presented. This is a matter of judgement for the directors, and the additional information may be presented either in the statement of financial position or in the notes to the financial statements. The size, nature and function of the amounts involved or the requirements of another IAS/IFRS will normally determine whether the disclosure is on the face of the statement of financial position or in the notes. The disclosures will vary with each item, but examples include:
   * non-current assets analysed by class of asset (for example, separate presentation of property, plant and equipment);
   * receivables analysed between amounts receivable from trade customers, related parties and **prepayments**;
   * inventories sub-classified into production supplies, materials, work-in-progress and finished goods; and
   * provisions analysed to show provisions for employee benefit costs separate from any other provisions.

   In deciding whether additional items should be presented separately, consideration should be given to:
   * the nature and liquidity of assets and their materiality (for example, the separate disclosure of monetary and non-monetary amounts and current and non-current assets);
   * their function within the entity (for example, the separate disclosure of operating assets and financial assets, inventories and cash); and
   * the amounts, nature and timing of liabilities (for example, the separate disclosure of interest-bearing and non-interest-bearing liabilities and provisions and current and non-current liabilities).

6. **Equity** IAS 1 requires that the following information on share capital and reserves (i.e. equity section of the statement of financial position) is provided, either on the face of the statement of financial position or in the notes:
   (a) for each class of share capital –
      (i) number of shares authorised, issued and fully paid, and issued but not fully paid;
      (ii) par value;
      (iii) reconciliation of the number of shares outstanding (i.e. unissued) at the beginning and at the end of the period;
      (iv) description of rights, preferences and restrictions;
      (v) treasury shares, including shares held by subsidiaries or associates; and
      (vi) shares reserved for issuance under options and sales contracts;

(b) a description of the nature and purpose of each reserve within equity (for example, the share premium account – which arises when shares are issued for more than their nominal value).

Statement of Profit or Loss and Other Comprehensive Income

In June 2011 the IASB issued amendments to IAS 1 *Presentation of Financial Statements*. In the main, these amendments affected the title of the performance statement and the presentation of other comprehensive income (OCI) within the statement. Each of these is now addressed in turn.

With respect to the name of the statement, it was proposed that the title 'Statement of Profit or Loss and Other Comprehensive Income' (SPLOCI) be adopted. While IAS 1 still permits the use of other titles (for example, 'statement of comprehensive income' (SCI)), this text applies the designation 'statement of profit or loss and other comprehensive income' regardless of whether the reporting entity has 'other comprehensive income' on the basis that IAS 1 states that a complete set of financial statements should include a 'statement of profit or loss and other comprehensive income'. Moreover, this avoids any possible confusion as to whether a two-statement approach has been adopted (see below).

In broad terms, regardless of the title adopted, the statement of profit or loss and other comprehensive income is divided into two components: a statement of profit or loss; and other comprehensive income. The former section shows the revenues from operations, expenses of operating and the resulting net profit or loss over a specific period of time; while the latter includes items such as changes in revaluation surplus, actuarial gains and losses on defined benefit plans recognised in accordance with IAS 19 *Employee Benefits* (see **Chapter 17**) and gains and losses arising from translating the financial statements of a foreign operation (IAS 21 *The Effects of Changes in Foreign Exchange Rates* – see **Chapter 31**). Reporting entities have the option of presenting profit or loss and OCI either in a single continuous statement or in two separate, but consecutive, statements. For clarity in other circumstances (for example, with respect to journal entries), this text distinguishes between the two components of the statement as follows: Statement of Profit or Loss and Other Comprehensive Income – Profit or Loss (SPLOCI – P/L); Statement of Profit or Loss and Other Comprehensive Income – Other Comprehensive Income (SPLOCI – OCI).

Regarding the presentation of OCI, the changes were driven by a desire to address a perceived lack of distinction between different items in OCI, as well as a lack of clarity in the presentation of those items. For example, while some items in OCI could have a considerable effect on the financial performance of an entity if they were to be recycled through profit or loss, this impact was unclear based upon the presentation requirements prior to the amendments. In addition, while previously only a limited number of transactions were recognised in OCI, changes to IFRSs (for example, IAS 19 and IFRS 9 *Financial Instruments* – see **Chapter 25**) have led to increased recognition of items within OCI. As a result, the amendments to IAS 1 change the grouping of items presented in OCI, with items that could be reclassified (or 'recycled') to profit or loss at a future point in time (for example, upon derecognition or settlement) being presented separately from items that will never be reclassified.

Examples of OCI items that can be reclassified into profit or loss include:
- foreign exchange gains and losses arising from translations of financial statements of a foreign operation (on the disposal of a foreign operation) (IAS 21); and
- effective portion of gains and losses on hedging instruments in a cash flow hedge (IAS 39 *Financial Instruments: Recognition and Measurement* – see **Chapter 25**).

Examples of OCI items that cannot be reclassified into profit or loss include:
- changes in revaluation surplus (IAS 16 *Property, Plant and Equipment* – see **Chapter 6** – and IAS 38 *Intangible Assets* – see **Chapter 9**);
- actuarial gains and losses on defined benefit plans (IAS 19);
- gains and losses from investments in equity instruments measured at fair value through OCI (IFRS 9); and
- for those liabilities designated at fair value through profit or loss, changes in fair value attributable to changes in the liability's credit risk (IFRS 9).

Figure 2.2 illustrates the Statement of OCI after the IAS 1 amendments relating to OCI have been applied.

FIGURE 2.2: STATEMENT OF OCI AFTER THE IAS 1 AMENDMENTS ARE APPLIED

Other Comprehensive Income	2012 €000	2011 €000
Items that may be reclassified into profit or loss		
Foreign exchange gains arising from the translation of foreign operations	1,771	1,071
Share of associate's OCI	–	412
Change in value of the effective portion of derivatives designated in qualifying cash flow hedges	73	601
Tax related to OCI items that may be reclassified to profit or loss	(189)	(715)
	1,655	1,369
Items that will not be reclassified into profit or loss		
Revaluation of property, plant and equipment	4,460	(1,154)
Remeasurement of net defined benefit liability	266	157
(Loss)/gain from investments in equity instruments measured at fair value through OCI	(358)	1,542
Fair value through profit or loss – changes in fair value attributable to changes in the liability's credit risk	4	(15)
Tax related to OCI items that will not be reclassified to profit or loss	(1,175)	279
	3,197	809
Total other comprehensive income	4,852	2,178

The amendments to OCI do not change the nature of the items that are recognised in OCI, nor do they impact upon the determination as to whether items in OCI are reclassified through profit or loss in future periods. Furthermore, entities are still permitted to present components of OCI either net of the related tax effects or before tax, with one amount shown for the aggregate amount of income tax relating to those components. However, if an entity presents

OCI items before the related tax effects, then tax is required to be allocated and disclosed separately for each of the two OCI groups (i.e. the total amount of tax is required to be split into two amounts: tax related to items that might be reclassified subsequently to profit or loss, and tax relating to those items that will not be reclassified subsequently to profit or loss).

While the change in presentation of OCI is relatively minor with respect to the overall financial statements, it should allow users of financial statements to more easily identify the potential impact that OCI items may have upon future profit or loss. The IASB acknowledges that the amendments did not address the issue of the lack of clear underlying principles for the recognition of OCI items (as well as for the reclassification of such items to profit or loss) within IFRSs and it accepts that further work is needed to develop a clear principle for measuring performance items such as OCI. This is likely to take considerable time to develop.

The amendments to IAS 1 are effective for annual periods beginning on or after 1 July 2012, with early adoption permitted. If an entity applies the amendments for an earlier period, it is required to disclose that fact. It is important to remember that reporting entities continue to have the option of presenting profit or loss and OCI either in a single continuous statement or in two separate, but consecutive statements.

Information to be Presented on the Face of the Statement of Profit or Loss and Other Comprehensive Income

Similar to the statement of financial position, discussed above, IAS 1 stipulates that, as a minimum, certain line items or key headings must appear on the face of the statement of profit or loss and other comprehensive income where there are amounts to be classified within these categories (i.e. where values against an item in either the current or comparative period are more than zero). These 'minimum' line items ((a) to (i)) are listed below:
  (a) revenue;
  (b) finance costs;
  (c) share of the profit or loss of associates and joint ventures accounted for using the equity method;
  (d) tax expense;
  (e) a single amount comprising the total of –
      (i) the post-tax profit or loss of discontinued operations, and
      (ii) the post-tax gain or loss recognised on the measurement to fair value less costs to sell or on the disposal of the assets or disposal group(s) constituting the discontinued operation;
  (f) profit or loss;
  (g) each component of other comprehensive income classified by nature;
  (h) share of the other comprehensive income of associates and joint ventures accounted for using the equity method; and
  (i) total comprehensive income.

The following must also be shown on the face of the statement of profit or loss and other comprehensive income as allocations for the period:
  (a) profit or loss for the period attributable to non-controlling interests and owners of the parent; and
  (b) total comprehensive income for the period attributable to **non-controlling interests** and owners of the **parent**.

In order to be able to prepare a statement of profit or loss and other comprehensive income in a form suitable for publication, it is important to learn these minimum headings, together with the suggested formats that fulfil these minimum disclosures, shown in **Figure 2.2**, **Figure 2.3**, **Figure 2.4** and **Figure 2.5**.

FIGURE 2.3: Y LIMITED – STATEMENT OF PROFIT OR LOSS AND OTHER COMPREHENSIVE INCOME FOR THE YEAR ENDED 31 DECEMBER 2012
*(Single statement **excluding** discontinued operations)*

	2012 €000	2011 €000
Revenue	390,000	355,000
Cost of sales	(245,000)	(230,000)
Gross profit	145,000	125,000
Other operating income	20,667	11,300
Distribution costs	(9,000)	(8,700)
Administrative expenses	(20,000)	(21,000)
Other expenses	(2,100)	(1,200)
Finance costs	(8,000)	(7,500)
Share of profit of associates	35,100	30,100
Profit before tax	161,667	128,000
Income tax expense	(40,417)	(32,000)
Profit for the year	121,250	96,000
Other comprehensive income:		
Items that may be reclassified into profit or loss		
Exchange differences on translating foreign operations	5,334	10,667
Items that will not be reclassified into profit or loss		
Gain/(loss) on property revaluation	7,933	(7,300)
Other comprehensive income for the year	13,267	3,367
Total comprehensive income for the year	134,517	99,367
Profit/(loss) attributable to:		
Owners of the parent	121,250	99,367
Non-controlling interests *(Group financial statements only)*	–	–
	121,250	99,367
Total comprehensive income/(loss) attributable to:		
Owners of the parent	134,517	99,367
Non-controlling interests *(Group financial statements only)*	–	–
	134,517	99,367
Earnings per share (see **Chapter 23**)	23.1c	14.6c

Format of the Statement of Profit or Loss and Other Comprehensive Income

IAS 1 permits the preparation of a statement of profit or loss and other comprehensive income on either the 'function of expenditure' (or cost of sales format) or the 'nature of expenditure' format. The choice between the two is made according to which most fairly presents the elements of the entity's performance. A pro-forma for each of these two formats is shown in **Figure 2.3** and **Figure 2.5**, respectively.

The 'Function of Expenditure' Format This is sometimes also referred to as the 'by function' or 'cost of sales' format and it classifies expenses according to their function as part of cost of sales, distribution or administrative activities. While this presentation can provide more relevant information to users, the allocation of costs to the different functions can often be arbitrary. **Figure 2.3** illustrates this form of presentation for a single statement of profit or loss and other comprehensive income (excluding the disclosure of discontinued operations, which is shown in **Figure 2.4** and discussed further below).

FIGURE 2.4: Y LIMITED – STATEMENT OF PROFIT OR LOSS AND OTHER COMPREHENSIVE INCOME FOR THE YEAR ENDED 31 DECEMBER 2012
(Single statement including discontinued operations)

	2012 €000	2011 €000
Continuing Operations		
Revenue	360,000	355,000
Cost of sales	(230,000)	(230,000)
Gross profit	130,000	125,000
Other operating income	20,667	11,300
Distribution costs	(9,000)	(8,700)
Administrative expenses	(20,000)	(21,000)
Other expenses	(2,100)	(1,200)
Finance costs	(8,000)	(7,500)
Share of profit/(loss) of associates	35,100	30,100
Profit/(loss) before tax	146,667	128,000
Income tax expense	(40,417)	(32,000)
Profit/(loss) for the year for continuing operations	106,250	96,000
Discontinued Operations		
Profit/(loss) for the year for discontinued operations*	15,000	–
Profit/(loss) for the year	121,250	96,000
Other comprehensive income:		
Items that may be reclassified into profit or loss		
Exchange differences on translating foreign operations	5,334	10,667
Items that will not be reclassified into profit or loss		
Gain/(loss) on property revaluation	933	(3,300)
Gain/(loss) from investments in equity instruments measured at fair value through OCI	7,000	(4,000)
Other comprehensive income for the year	13,267	3,367

Total comprehensive income for the year	<u>134,517</u>	<u>99,367</u>
Profit/(loss) attributable to:		
Owners of the parent	121,250	99,367
Non-controlling interests *(Group financial*		
statements only)	–	–
	<u>121,250</u>	<u>99,367</u>
Total comprehensive income/(loss) attributable to:		
Owners of the parent	134,517	99,367
Non-controlling interests *(Group financial statements only)*	–	–
	<u>134,517</u>	<u>99,367</u>
Earnings per share (see **Chapter 23**)	<u>23.1c</u>	<u>14.6c</u>

*Alternatively, profit from discontinued operations may be analysed in a separate column in the statement of profit or loss and other comprehensive income.

It is important to remember that an entity should choose the format that provides the fairest presentation of its business activities. Entities choosing to classify expenses by function (as illustrated in **Figure 2.3**) must also disclose additional information on the *nature of expenses*, primarily depreciation and staff costs.

Chapter 1 emphasises that the *IFRS Framework* states that financial statements are intended to serve users who are not in a position to require financial reports tailored to their particular information needs and that users need information to help make decisions about, *inter alia*, whether the management has been running the company efficiently and the company's future prospects. A key aspect of this would be information on whether the company intends to curtail or shut down part of its activities. In the context of financial reporting, this is referred to as discontinued operations. Given its potential significance to users, the definition and disclosure of discontinued operations is dealt with in a separate accounting standard, IFRS 5 *Non-current Assets Held for Sale and Discontinued Operations* (see **Chapter 20**). The impact this has on the format of the statement of profit or loss and other comprehensive income is illustrated in **Figure 2.4**.

The 'Nature of Expenditure' Format   An analysis based on the nature of expenses results in classifications for depreciation, purchases, wages and salaries, marketing costs, etc. with the expenses being presented in total for each type of expense. This format is normally adopted for manufacturing entities as, given the nature of their activities, the additional detail provided for raw materials, work-in-progress and finished goods is considered more relevant. This nature of expenditure format is illustrated in **Figure 2.5**.

The first item of expense shown in **Figure 2.5** can be confusing (i.e. changes in inventories of finished goods and work-in-progress). The change represents an adjustment to production expenses to reflect the fact that either:
• production has increased inventory levels, or
• sales exceeds production activity, resulting in a reduction in inventory levels.

FIGURE 2.5: Y LIMITED – STATEMENT OF PROFIT OR LOSS AND OTHER COMPREHENSIVE
INCOME FOR THE YEAR ENDED 31 DECEMBER 2012
*(Single statement **excluding** discontinued operations)*

	2012 €000	2011 €000
Revenue	390,000	355,000
Other operating income	20,667	11,300
Changes in inventories of finished goods and work-in-progress	(115,100)	(107,900)
Work performed by the entity and capitalised	16,000	15,000
Raw materials and consumables used	(96,000)	(92,000)
Staff costs	(45,000)	(43,000)
Depreciation and amortisation expense	(19,000)	(17,000)
Impairment of property, plant and equipment	(4,000)	–
Other operating expenses	(6,000)	(5,500)
Finance costs	(15,000)	(18,000)
Share of profit of associates	35,100	30,100
Profit before tax	161,667	128,000
Income tax expense	(40,417)	(32,000)
Profit/(loss) for the year	121,250	96,000
Other comprehensive income:		
Items that may be reclassified into profit or loss		
Exchange differences on translating foreign operations	5,334	10,667
Items that will not be reclassified into profit or loss		
Gain/(loss) on property revaluation	933	(3,300)
Gain/(loss) from investments in equity instruments measured at fair value through OCI	7,000	(4,000)
Other comprehensive income for the year	13,267	3,367
Total comprehensive income for the year	134,517	99,367
Profit/(loss) attributable to:		
Owners of the parent	121,250	99,367
Non-controlling interests *(Group financial statements only)*	–	–
	121,250	99,367
Total comprehensive income/(loss) attributable to:		
Owners of the parent	134,517	99,367
Non-controlling interests *(Group financial statements only)*	–	–
	134,517	99,367
Earnings per share (see **Chapter 23**)	23.1c	14.6c

It is important to note that changes in raw materials inventories are *not* included in this line item. The change in raw materials inventories is reflected separately in the next expense line. The way in which it is calculated is illustrated in **Figure 2.6**, and would normally be disclosed in the notes to the financial statements in this manner.

FIGURE 2.6: Y LIMITED – RAW MATERIALS AND CONSUMABLES USED

	2012 €000	2011 €000
Opening inventory of raw materials	10,000	8,800
Plus: purchase of raw materials	124,000	93,200
Less: closing inventory of raw materials	(38,000)	(10,000)
Raw materials and consumables used	96,000	92,000

Regardless of which format is adopted, additional line items, headings and subtotals should be shown in the statement of profit or loss and other comprehensive income if another IAS/IFRS requires it or where it is necessary to show a fair presentation. For example, revenue derived from different sources may be shown separately if considered appropriate. Materiality and the nature and function of the item are likely to be the main considerations when deciding whether to include an additional line item in the statement of profit or loss and other comprehensive income. If an item of expense or income is material, then its nature and amount should be disclosed separately, either in the statement of profit or loss and other comprehensive income or in the notes. Examples include:

* write downs of inventories to net realisable value (see **Chapter 11**);
* write downs of property, plant and equipment to recoverable amount (see **Chapter 10**);
* restructuring costs (see **Chapter 14**); and
* disposals of plant, property and equipment (see **Chapter 6**).

Example 2.1 below illustrates the preparation of a statement of profit or loss and other comprehensive income – profit or loss using both the 'function of expenditure' and the 'nature of expenditure' formats.

EXAMPLE 2.1: 'FUNCTION OF EXPENDITURE' AND 'NATURE OF EXPENDITURE' FORMATS

An extract of the balances in the financial statements of Z Limited at 31 December 2012 shows the following:

	€m
Revenue	10.1
Cost of sales	4.6
Distribution costs	1.3
Administrative expenses	2.1
Interest cost	1.4

An analysis of the costs other than interest, i.e. €8.0 million (€4.6m + €1.3m + €2.1m) indicates:

	€m
Raw materials and consumables	3.1
Increase in inventories finished goods and work-in-progress	(0.2)
Depreciation	1.8
Staff costs	2.9
Other operating expenses	0.4
	8.0

A provision for income tax expense has been agreed at €0.2 million.

Based on this information, it is possible to prepare a statement of profit or loss and other comprehensive income – profit or loss under both the 'function' and 'nature' formats.

'By Function' Format:

Z Limited

STATEMENT OF PROFIT OR LOSS AND OTHER COMPREHENSIVE INCOME – PROFIT OR LOSS
for the Year Ended 31 December 2012

	€m	€m
Revenue		10.1
Cost of sales		(4.6)
Gross profit		5.5
Distribution costs	1.3	
Administration expenses	2.1	(3.4)
Profit from operations		2.1
Finance cost		(1.4)
Profit before tax		0.7
Income tax expense		(0.2)
Profit for the year		0.5

'By Nature' Format:

Z Limited

STATEMENT OF PROFIT OR LOSS AND OTHER COMPREHENSIVE INCOME – PROFIT OR LOSS
for the Year Ended 31 December 2012

	€m	€m
Revenue		10.1
Increase in inventories of finished goods and work-in-progress		0.2
		10.3
Raw materials and consumables	3.1	
Staff costs	2.9	
Depreciation	1.8	
Other operating expenses	0.4	(8.2)
Profit from operations		2.1
Finance cost		(1.4)
Profit before tax		0.7
Income tax expense		(0.2)
Profit for the year		0.5

Statement of Changes in Equity

This is the third component of a set of financial statements. It shows the changes in an entity's equity throughout the reporting period, and it is based on the principle that changes in an entity's equity between two reporting periods reflect the increase or decrease in its net assets or wealth during the period. This information is useful to users as such changes – excluding changes resulting from transactions with shareholders (e.g. capital injections and dividends) – represent the total gains and losses generated by the entity in that period.

The components that make up an entity's comprehensive income must not be shown in the statement of changes in equity. While this statement includes the total amount of comprehensive income, its main purpose is to show the amounts of transactions with owners (for example, share issues and dividends) and to provide a reconciliation of the opening and closing balance of each class of equity and reserve. An example is presented in **Figure 2.7**.

FIGURE 2.7: W LIMITED – STATEMENT OF CHANGES IN EQUITY FOR THE YEAR ENDED 31 DECEMBER 2012

	Share Capital	Other Reserves	Retained Earnings	Total
	€m	€m	€m	€m
Opening balance	10,000	4,800	11,200	26,000
Changes in accounting policy	–	–	1,900	1,900
Restated balance	10,000	4,800	13,100	27,900
Changes in equity for the year				
Dividends	–	–	(2,100)	(2,100)
Total comprehensive income	–	600	500	1,100
Issue of share capital	5,000	–	–	5,000
Total changes in equity	5,000	600	(1,600)	4,000
Closing balance	15,000	5,400	11,500	31,900

Statement of Cash Flows

This is the fourth component of financial statements and its form and content is governed by IAS 7 *Statement of Cash Flows*. A statement of cash flows reports on an entity's cash flow activities, particularly its operating, investing and financing activities. Given the extensive nature and importance of IAS 7, the format and preparation of a statement of cash flows is addressed in **Chapters 19** and **33**.

Notes to the Financial Statements

The notes to the financial statements normally include narrative descriptions or more detailed analysis of items in the financial statements, as well as additional information, such as contingent liabilities and commitments. IAS 1 also provides guidance on the structure of the

accompanying notes to financial statements, the accounting policies and other required disclosures. The accounting policies section of the notes to the financial statements should describe:
- the measurement basis (or bases) used in preparing the financial statements; and
- each specific accounting policy that is necessary for a proper understanding of the financial statements.

In addition, as mentioned previously, the notes to the financial statements should also:
- disclose the information required by other IASs/IFRSs that is not presented elsewhere in the financial statements (for example, the detailed disclosures required in respect of operating segments (see **Chapter 24**)); and
- provide additional information that is not presented in the financial statements but that is necessary for a fair presentation (for example, disclosure in relation to related parties (see **Chapter 22**)).

Notes to the financial statements should be presented in a systematic manner and any item on the financial statements should be cross-referenced to any related information in the notes. The notes are normally provided in the following order, in order to assist users in understanding the financial statements and compare them with those of other entities.
1. Statement of compliance with IFRS.
2. Statement of the measurement bases (for example, historical cost) and accounting policies applied.
3. Supporting information for items presented in each financial statement in the order in which each line item and each financial statement is presented.
4. Other disclosures, including contingencies, commitments and other financial disclosures, and non-financial disclosures.

Other Disclosures

Details of the amount of dividends proposed or declared after the end of the reporting period, but before the financial statements were authorised for issue, together with the amount of any cumulative preference dividends not recognised should be provided. In addition, the following disclosures should also be provided:
- the domicile and legal form of the entity, its country of incorporation and the address of the registered office (or principal place of business, if different from the above);
- a description of the nature of the entity's operations and its principal activities;
- the name of the parent entity and the ultimate parent of the group; and
- either the number of the employees at the end of the period or the average for the period.

2.4 CONCLUSION

The objective of financial statements is to provide information about the financial position, financial performance and cash flows of an entity that is useful to a wide range of users in making economic decisions. IAS 1 states that a complete set of financial statements comprises:
- a statement of financial position;
- a statement of profit or loss and other comprehensive income;
- a statement of changes in equity;

- a statement of cash flows; and
- accounting policies and explanatory notes.

Financial statements should be prepared on a going-concern and accruals basis, and the effects of transactions and other items should be faithfully represented in the financial statements. Compliance with IASs/IFRSs should normally ensure that this is the case.

SUMMARY OF LEARNING OBJECTIVES

After having studied this chapter on the presentation of financial statements, you should be able to:

Learning Objective 1 Discuss the principles that govern the presentation of financial statements.

In broad terms, the main principles addressed in IAS 1 are that financial statements should: present fairly the financial position, financial performance and cash flows of an entity; be prepared on a going concern basis; be prepared under the accruals basis of accounting; retain a consistent approach to presentation and classification year on year; present separately each material class of similar items; avoid offsetting assets/liabilities and income/expenses; and disclose comparative information.

Learning Objective 2 Identify the components of a set of financial statements.

A set of financial statements includes a statement of financial position, a statement of profit or loss and other comprehensive income, a statement of changes in equity, a statement of cash flows and accounting policies and explanatory notes.

Learning Objective 3 Describe the structure and content of each component of a set of financial statements.

Statements of financial position, profit or loss and other comprehensive income and changes in equity are illustrated in **Figures 2.1–2.7**. (See **Chapters 19** and **33** for statement of cash flows.)

Learning Objective 4 Explain the detailed disclosure requirements of IAS 1.

As a minimum, certain line items must appear in each of the financial statements. In broad terms, additional line items, headings and subtotals should be shown if another IAS/IFRS requires it, or where it is necessary to show a fair presentation. Materiality and the nature and function of the item are likely to be the main considerations when deciding whether to include an additional line item.

QUESTIONS

Self-test Questions

1. What are the main principles of financial reporting?
2. What are the components of a complete set of financial statements?
3. What criteria determine whether assets should be classified as current or non-current?

4. What criteria determine whether liabilities should be classified as current or non-current?
5. What minimum information should be presented in the statement of profit or loss and other comprehensive income?
6. Distinguish between the function of expenditure and nature of expenditure methods of classifying expenses in the statement of profit or loss and other comprehensive income.

Review Questions

(See **Appendix One** for Suggested Solutions to Review Questions.)

Question 2.1

The following information relates to V Limited, a manufacturing company.

V Limited – Trial Balance as at 30 September 2012

	Notes	€000	€000
Sales revenue			430
Inventory as at 1 October 2011	(a)	10	
Purchases		102	
Advertising		15	
Administration salaries		14	
Manufacturing wages		60	
Interest paid		14	
Dividends received	(e)		12
Audit fees		7	
Irrecoverable debts		10	
Taxation	(d)	10	
Dividends paid	(e)	120	
Grant received	(c)		30
Premises (cost)	(b)	450	
Plant (cost)	(c)	280	
Premises (depreciation)			40
Plant (depreciation)			160
Investments (long-term)		100	
Receivables		23	
Bank		157	
Payables			7
Deferred taxation	(f)		62
Loan notes			140
Share capital			100
Accumulated profit at 1 October 2011			391
		1,372	1,372

Additional Information:
(a) Inventory was worth €13,000 on 30 September 2012.
(b) Premises consist of land costing €250,000 and buildings costing €200,000. The buildings have an expected useful life of 50 years.

(c) Plant includes an item purchased during the year at a cost of €70,000. A government grant of €30,000 was received in respect of this purchase. These were the only transactions involving non-current assets during the year. Depreciation of plant is to be charged at 10% per annum on a straight-line basis.

(d) The balance on the tax account is an under-provision for tax brought forward from the year ended 30 September 2011.

(e) The company paid €48,000 on 27 November 2011 as a final dividend for the year ended 30 September 2011. A dividend of €12,000 was received on 13 January 2012 (record the €12,000 received with no adjustment). The 2012 interim dividend of €72,000 was paid on 15 April 2012.

(f) The provision for deferred tax is to be reduced by €17,000.

(g) The directors have estimated that tax of €57,000 will be due on the profits for this year.

(h) The directors have proposed a final dividend for the year of €50,000.

(i) It is company policy to charge depreciation to cost of sales.

Requirement Prepare a statement of profit or loss and other comprehensive income for V Limited for the year ended 30 September 2012 and a statement of financial position as at that date. These should be in a form suitable for presentation to the shareholders and be accompanied by notes to the accounts insofar as is possible from the information provided.

Question 2.2

Extracts from the statement of financial position of Rose Limited as at 31 December 2011 are as follows:

€1 ordinary shares	€300,000
Share premium account	€50,000
Revaluation reserve	€80,000
Retained earnings	€1,280,000

The following information is relevant with respect to the year ended 31 December 2012.

• 1 April 2012 – company made a bonus issue of 1 for 10 from the share premium account.

• 1 June 2012 – company made a rights issue of 1 for 11 @ €1.50 per share.

• 1 July 2012 – a firm of Chartered Surveyors carried out a valuation of the company's properties, which showed surpluses as follows:

Land	€20,000
Buildings	€50,000

• Profit after tax for year ended 31 December 2012 amounted to €120,000.

• Proposed (and approved by shareholders prior to end of reporting period) dividends for year ended 31 December 2012 amounted to €25,000.

• During 2012, Rose Limited changed its accounting policy for the treatment of expenditure relating to exploration for, and evaluation of, mineral resources. In previous periods, Rose Limited had capitalised such costs. The company now treats these costs as an expense. Management judges that the new policy is preferable because it results in a more transparent treatment of such costs and is consistent with local industry practice, making Rose Limited's financial statements more relevant to the economic decision-making needs of users and no less reliable. The company had capitalised €35,000 research costs to 31 December 2011.

Requirement Prepare the statement of changes in equity for the year ended 31 December 2012 for Rose Limited.

Challenging Questions

(Suggested Solutions to Challenging Questions are available to lecturers.)

Question 2.1 (*Based on Chartered Accountants Ireland, P3 Summer 2006, Question 6*)

ZIPCO Limited (ZIPCO), a company that was incorporated on 23 January 1986, is involved in the production and distribution of electronic games. Prior to 1 January 2012, ZIPCO had issued 100,000 € ordinary shares as follows:
- 90,000 €1 ordinary shares were issued for €2 per share cash on 23 January 1986;
- 5,000 €1 ordinary shares were exchanged on 3 September 1990 for a patent that had a fair value at the date of exchange of €50,000; and
- 5,000 €1 ordinary shares were issued on 14 July 2011 for €20 per share cash.

At 1 January 2012, ZIPCO had a balance in its retained earnings of €500,000, while the general reserve and the revaluation reserve had credit balances of €200,000 and €300,000, respectively. The purpose of the general reserve is to reflect ZIPCO's need to regularly replace certain computer equipment because of technological advances.

During the year ended 31 December 2012, the following transactions occurred:

23 January	ZIPCO paid a €20,000 dividend that had been declared and approved by shareholders in November 2011.
11 April	10,000 €1 ordinary shares at €25 per share were offered to the public. The shares were fully subscribed and issued on 14 June 2012. On the same date, a further 10,000 €1 ordinary shares were placed with major investors at €25 per share.
12 July	ZIPCO paid an interim dividend of €20,000.
2 August	ZIPCO revalued land by €100,000 (ignore any deferred tax implications).
4 August	ZIPCO adopted a new international financial reporting standard early. The transitional liability on initial adoption was €100,000 more than the liability recognised under the previous accounting standard, and under the transitional arrangement should be recognised as a movement in retained earnings in 2012.
1 October	ZIPCO declared a one for eight bonus issue to existing shareholders, using the general reserve to create the bonus issue.
1 December	ZIPCO repurchased 1,000 €1 ordinary shares on the open market for €20 per share. The repurchase was accounted for by writing down share capital/share premium and retained earnings by an equal amount.
31 December	ZIPCO calculated that its profit after tax for the year ended 31 December 2012 was €400,000. The directors proposed a final dividend of €25,000 and transferred €100,000 to the general reserve from retained earnings.

Requirement
(a) If a company announces a final dividend at the end of its financial period, discuss whether the dividend payable should be recognised.
(b) Prepare the statement of changes in equity for ZIPCO for the year ended 31 December 2012.

Question 2.2 *(Based on Chartered Accountants Ireland, CAP 2 Summer 2009, Question 2)*

> ***Please note:*** due to the nature of this question (i.e. preparation of financial statements), it addresses a number of different issues, many of which are not covered in this chapter. Consequently, the chapter that deals with the issue is indicated at the end of the relevant note.

FRANKLIN Ltd. ("FRANKLIN") is an Irish company that sells bathroom equipment direct to the public from two large outlets in different areas of Ireland. The company prepares its financial statements to 31 December each year and the following trial balance has been prepared as at 31 December 2012.

TRIAL BALANCE
as at 31 December 2012

	Notes	DR €000	CR €000
Revenue			15,000
Inventory at 1 January 2012	1	1,500	
Purchases		4,500	
Operating expenses		1,800	
Government grant received	2		200
Interest received			50
Interest paid		90	
Property – cost at 1 January 2012	4	40,000	
Property – accumulated depreciation at 1 January 2012	3		10,000
Plant and equipment – cost at 1 January 2012		28,000	
Plant and equipment – accumulated depreciation at 1 January 2012	3		8,000
Plant and equipment – additions during 2012	2	2,000	
Trade receivables	6	6,700	
Trade payables			1,600
Bank and cash			800
€1 ordinary shares			1,000
Retained earnings at 1 January 2012			47,940
		84,590	84,590

Notes

1. Inventory at 31 December 2012 was valued at €1,300,000. (See **Chapter 11**.)
2. A government grant of €200,000 was received during the year ended 31 December 2012 in respect of the additions to plant and equipment. (See **Chapter 16**.)
3. It is company policy to charge a full year's depreciation in the year of acquisition and none in the year of disposal. Property is depreciated on a straight-line basis over 40 years. Plant and equipment is depreciated at 10% per annum on a straight-line basis. Depreciation is charged to operating expenses. (See **Chapter 6**.)
4. Property shown in the trial balance at 31 December 2012 consists of two retail premises purchased on the same date at €20,000,000 each. At 31 December 2012, the directors of

FRANKLIN are committed to a plan to sell one of these properties. This is part of a single co-ordinated plan to dispose of a separate geographical area of the company's operations and the directors have already found a potential buyer. The net sales proceeds are expected to be €23,000,000. As soon as the sale has been agreed, FRANKLIN will vacate the property and transfer it to the new owners. While this process is expected to take a number of months to complete, no unusual delays are anticipated. (See **Chapter 20**.)

5. As part of the decision to sell one of the company's properties referred to in Note 4, the directors of FRANKLIN decided to run down those parts of the company's activities that represented the separate geographical area of operations. These activities were finally discontinued in December 2012 and the contribution to the business of these activities in 2012 was:

	€
Revenue	4,000,000
Cost of sales	1,900,000
Operating expenses	1,000,000

These amounts are included in the corresponding figures shown in the Trial Balance at 31 December 2012. Apart from the figures shown above, all other amounts shown in the Trial Balance at 31 December 2012, and adjustments to FRANKLIN's financial statements for the year ended 31 December 2012 relate to continuing operations. (See **Chapter 20**.)

6. On 1 December 2012 FRANKLIN factored a trade receivable of €500,000 to ARETHA FINANCE Ltd. ("ARETHA"). The terms of the factoring agreement were:
   • ARETHA paid 80% of the factored debt immediately to FRANKLIN;
   • the remaining 20% would be paid to FRANKLIN, less charges, when the receivable is collected in full. Any amount outstanding after three months would be transferred back to FRANKLIN;
   • ARETHA charges 3% per month of the net amount owing at the end of each month.

   On 1 December 2012 FRANKLIN debited the cash received from ARETHA to its bank account, removed the trade receivable from its records and charged the difference to operating expenses. ARETHA had not collected any of the amounts owing at 31 December 2012. (See **Chapter 1**.)

7. The directors of FRANKLIN have estimated that tax of €2,000,000 will be due on profits for the year ended 31 December 2012. This includes €500,000 in respect of the discontinued activities referred to in Note 5. (See **Chapter 13**.)

Requirement Prepare the statement of profit or loss and other comprehensive income of FRANKLIN for the year ended 31 December 2012 and the statement of financial position as at that date.

Question 2.3

The presentation of financial statements is addressed in IAS 1 *Presentation of Financial Statements*. The objective of IAS 1 is to prescribe the basis for presentation of general purpose financial statements, in order to ensure comparability both with the entity's financial statements of previous periods and with the financial statements of other entities. To achieve this objective, IAS 1 sets out the overall requirements for the presentation of financial statements, guidelines for their structure and minimum requirements for their content.

Requirement

(a) What are the objectives of a statement of financial position?

(b) What are the major limitations of a statement of financial position as a source of information for general users of financial statements?

(c) Expenses are required to be classified either on the face of the statement of profit or loss and other comprehensive income or in the notes according to their nature or function, whichever provides the more relevant and reliable information.

    (i) What is meant by classification by nature or function?

    (ii) Identify, and explain why, the types of organisation that would ordinarily adopt each of these classifications.

(d) What is the objective of a statement of changes in equity?

(e) Why is a summary of accounting policies important to ensuring the understandability of financial statements to general users of the statements?

(f) Financial reporting, by its nature, involves a considerable number of judgements by preparers about a range of issues. What are some of the more important judgements made that can lead to estimation uncertainty at the reporting date?

Question 2.4

Alanis Limited compiles its financial statements to 31 December each year. At 31 December 2012, the company's Trial Balance was as follows:

	€000	€000
Land at valuation	27,300	
Buildings: cost	20,800	
Buildings: accumulated depreciation at 1 January 2012		5,538
Plant and equipment: cost	33,280	
Plant and equipment: accumulated depreciation at 1 January 2012		6,448
Trade receivables and payables	10,712	5,824
Cash at bank	416	
Ordinary shares of 50c each: at 1 January 2012		26,000
Ordinary shares of 50c each: issued during 2012		10,400
Share premium account: at 1 January 2012		5,200
Share premium account: arising on shares issued during 2012		5,200
Revaluation reserve as at 1 January 2012		7,800
Retained earnings		8,164
10% loan notes		5,200
Sales		38,480
Purchases	21,528	
Inventory at 1 January 2012	3,614	
Distribution costs	2,808	
Administration expenses	3,796	
	124,254	124,254

2. PRESENTATION OF FINANCIAL STATEMENTS 63

Additional Information
1. Land is to be revalued to €31,200,000. No change is required to the value of the buildings.
2. Depreciation should be provided as follows:
   Buildings   2% per year on cost; and
   Plant and equipment   20% per year on cost.
   Depreciation should be allocated as follows: 80% to cost of sales and 10% each to distribution costs and administrative expenses.
3. Inventory at 31 December 2012 amounted to €2,028,000 at cost. A review of these inventory items revealed the need for some adjustments for two inventory lines.
   (a) Items costing €104,000, and which would normally sell for €156,000, were found to have deteriorated. Remedial work costing €26,000 will be needed to enable the items to be sold for €117,000.
   (b) Some items sent to customers on sale-or-return terms have been omitted from inventory and included as sales in December 2012. The cost of these items was €21,000 and they were included in sales at €32,000. In January 2013 the items were returned in good condition by the customers.
4. Accruals and prepayments at 31 December 2012 were:

	Accruals €000	Prepayments €000
Distribution costs	247	156
Administrative expenses	91	78

5. The 10% loan notes were issued on 1 October 2012, with interest payable 31 March and 30 September each year. They are redeemable in 2020.
   repay all at once.

Requirement
(a) Prepare the statement of profit or loss and other comprehensive income for the year ended 31 December 2012 of Alanis Limited and the statement of financial position as at that date.
(b) Prepare a statement of changes in equity for the year ended 31 December 2012 of Alanis Limited.

3

FIRST-TIME ADOPTION OF INTERNATIONAL FINANCIAL REPORTING STANDARDS

LEARNING OBJECTIVES

Having studied this chapter on the first-time adoption of International Accounting Standards (IASs) and International Financial Reporting Standards (IFRSs), you should understand:
1. the language of IFRS; and
2. an entity's reporting obligations when it adopts IFRS for the first time.

3.1 INTRODUCTION

This is the third and final chapter in **Part I**, which seeks to describe the structures that frame international financial reporting before the technical aspects of the different International Accounting Standards (IASs) and International Financial Reporting Standards (IFRSs) are explained in the remaining Parts of the text. **Chapters 1** and **2** focused on the Framework for Financial Reporting and the Presentation of Financial Statements. This chapter concentrates on the issues facing an entity adopting IFRS for the first time.

The globalisation of capital markets has required a single set of global accounting, reporting and disclosure standards. Due to the high volume of cross-border capital flows and the growing number of foreign direct investments (FDI) via mergers and acquisitions, the need for the harmonisation of different accounting practices and the acceptance of worldwide standards has risen. It is likely that many of those entities, in both the private and public sectors, that have so far avoided the need to adopt IFRS will soon be required to make the transition. Consequently, an entity's reporting obligations when it adopts IFRS for the first time, which is the focus of this chapter, should have growing relevance. However, experience has shown that the transition to IFRS can be both lengthy and complex, with wide-reaching implications across the organisation, particularly for staff training and management information systems.

Indeed, considerable research has been published that highlights the far from seamless transition to IFRS. Much of this research (see **Table 3.1**) has analysed the key differences between IFRS and a particular country's **Generally Accepted Accounting Principles** (**GAAP**).

TABLE 3.1: RESEARCH STUDIES INTO IMPLEMENTATION OF IFRS

Country	Reference
Australia	Brown and Tarca (2001); Collett, Godfrey and Hrasky (2001); Goodwin and Ahmed (2006); and Jones and Higgins (2006).
Finland	Lantto and Sahlström (2009).
France	Standish (2003).
Germany	Weißenberger, Stahl and Vorstius (2004).
New Zealand	Bradbury and van Zijl (2005, 2006 and 2007).
Spain	Callao, Jarne and Lainez (2007).
United Kingdom	Aisbitt (2006); Fearnley and Hines (2007); Christensen, Lee and Walker (2007); and Jeanjean and Stolowy (2008).
United States of America	Daske (2006); and Erchinger and Melcher (2007).

In broad terms, the above research recounts significant changes in the reported financial accounting figures for a number of corporate sectors when reporting under international standards compared to their national accounting standards (or **GAAP**), usually due to more assets being recorded on the statement of financial position and the fair valuing of these assets. In a UK context, Aisbitt (2006) studied the effect on equity of the transition from UK GAAP and concluded that, while there would not be a significant change to the final net assets figure, careful examination of the individual line items in the statement of financial position was required on a company-by-company basis. Christensen, Lee and Walker (2007) also investigated the effect on equity, suggesting that the more willing a company was to adopt international standards the more positive would be the share price reaction. Jeanjean and Stolowy (2008) compared the UK with two other first-time adopters (Australia and France) and concluded that harmonising incentives and institutional factors, rather than harmonising accounting standards, would be a better way of creating a common business language. Fearnley and Hines (2007) believed that a single coherent system of accounting regulations for all companies would be much harder to achieve under international standards than it was under UK GAAP. Moreover, it was considered that the top-down decision-making approach, which was more concerned with satisfying the American market, was partly responsible for this dilemma. Consequently, the evidence suggests that the transition to IFRS may have great practical significance for business sectors and countries that are expected to adopt IFRS in the near future.

Key to this Chapter

IFRS 1 *First-time Adoption of International Financial Reporting Standards* applies to an entity that presents its first IFRS financial statements, setting out ground rules an entity must follow when it adopts IFRS for the first time. In the context of IFRS 1, a **first-time adopter** is an entity that, for the first time, makes an explicit and unreserved statement that its general-purpose financial statements (see **Chapter 1**) comply with IFRSs. This chapter begins by identifying some of the changes in accounting terminology following the adoption of IFRS (**Section 3.2**). Then explains, by posing and subsequently answering a number of questions, an entity's reporting obligations when it adopts IFRS for the first time (**Section 3.3**).

3.2 THE LANGUAGE OF INTERNATIONAL ACCOUNTING STANDARDS

There are a number of potential benefits for users and preparers of financial statements from having one accounting language throughout the world. For example:
- Investors – both individual and corporate – would be able to compare the financial results of different companies internationally as well as nationally when making investment decisions;
- Global/international companies – management control would be improved because harmonisation would aid internal communication of financial information. In addition, in today's global capital and trading markets, the appraisal of foreign companies would be more straightforward and companies would have better access to foreign investor funds;
- International accounting firms – accounting and auditing would be much easier if similar accounting practices existed throughout the world;
- Tax authorities – easier to calculate the tax liability of investors, including multinationals that receive income from overseas sources.

However, achieving a common accounting language is fraught with difficulties, which include:
- different purposes of financial reporting – in some countries the purpose is solely for tax assessment, while in others it is for investor decision-making;
- different legal systems – these prevent the development of certain accounting practices and restrict the options available;
- nationalism – this has resulted in an unwillingness by some countries to accept what are perceived as another country's standards;
- different needs – developing countries are behind in the standard-setting process and they need to develop the basic standards and principles already in place in most developed countries; and
- lack of strong accountancy bodies – many countries do not have a strong independent accountancy profession to press for better standards and greater harmonisation.

Despite these difficulties, international accounting standards are now firmly embedded in the accounting syllabi of most professional accounting bodies, and the differences between IASs/IFRSs and national accounting standards (or GAAP) have diminished greatly in recent years. At the same time, however, in the UK and Ireland, IASs/IFRSs only apply to listed companies; the vast majority of companies (and practitioners) continue to use **Statements of Standard Accounting Practice** (SSAP) and **Financial Reporting Standards** (FRS) (notwithstanding the minimal technical accounting differences). Indeed, many students are likely to use and apply UK GAAP on a daily basis in the workplace rather than IASs/IFRSs. Arguably, one of the main hurdles to be overcome, particularly by those whose background and training is UK GAAP-based, is becoming familiar with the different terminology. Some of the more common differences are outlined in **Table 3.2**.

TABLE 3.2: ACCOUNTING TERMINOLOGY – UK GAAP VS INTERNATIONAL ACCOUNTING STANDARDS

UK and Ireland	International Accounting Standards
Acquisition accounting	Purchase accounting
After the balance sheet date	After the reporting period
Balance sheet	Statement of financial position
Balance sheet date	End of reporting period
Cash flow statement	Statement of cash flows
Creditors	Payables
Debtors	Receivables
Equity-holders	Owners
Fixed assets	Non-current assets
On the face of the profit and loss account	In arriving at profit or loss in the statement of profit or loss and other comprehensive income
Recognised in equity	Recognised in other comprehensive income (for other comprehensive income components, see **Chapter 2**)
Recognised in the income statement	Recognised in profit or loss
Reconciliation of movements in shareholders' funds	Statement of changes in equity
Reporting date	End of reporting period
Shareholders' funds } Capital and reserves }	Equity
Stock	Inventory
Tangible fixed assets	Property, plant and equipment
Taxation	Income tax
Turnover or sales	Revenue

Please note that, as explained in **Chapter 2**, the IASB issued amendments to IAS 1 *Presentation of Financial Statements* in June 2011. These included a *proposal* that the title 'Statement of Profit or Loss and Other Comprehensive Income' (SPLOCI) be adopted (rather than, for example, 'statement of comprehensive income') and a *requirement* to revise the presentation of other comprehensive income (OCI) within the SPLOCI. These amendments are explained in detail in **Chapter 2, Section 2.3**.

3.3 FIRST-TIME ADOPTION OF INTERNATIONAL ACCOUNTING STANDARDS

Introduction

The International Accounting Standards Board (IASB) has sought 'to address the demand of investors to have transparent information that is comparable over all periods presented, while giving reporting entities a suitable starting point for their accounting under IFRSs'.

Consequently, following its initial publication in June 2003, IFRS 1 *First-time Adoption of International Financial Reporting Standards* has been amended on a number of occasions in order to improve its structure and reduce the level of complexity.

The Scope of IFRS 1

IFRS 1 applies when an entity adopts the complete package of IFRSs for the first time, that is, it includes an 'explicit and unreserved statement of compliance with IFRSs'. In May 2012, IFRS 1 was amended to allow an entity that meets the criteria for applying IFRS 1 but has applied IFRSs in previous reporting periods to elect (rather than being required) to make a repeat application of IFRS 1 when re-adopting IFRSs. Prior to this amendment an entity was required to apply IFRS 1 when its most recent previous annual financial statements did not contain an explicit and unreserved statement of compliance with IFRSs, even if the entity had already applied IFRS 1 in a previous reporting period. If an entity does not elect to reapply IFRS 1, it is required to apply IFRSs retrospectively in accordance with IAS 8 *Accounting Policies, Changes in Accounting Estimates and Errors* as if the entity had never stopped applying IFRSs. An entity that reapplies IFRS 1 is required to disclose the reason why it stopped reporting under IFRSs and the reason why it is resuming.

IFRS 1 sets out how an entity should make the transition to IFRSs from another accounting basis. IFRS 1 also applies to each interim financial report, if any, that the entity presents under IAS 34 *Interim Financial Reporting* for part of the period covered by its first IFRS financial statements (see **Chapter 34**).

IFRS 1 requires that the same accounting policies are used in all periods presented. IFRSs effective for an entity's first IFRS period should be applied to all periods reported, regardless of whether an earlier version of the standard existed. For example, IAS 27 *Separate Financial Statements* was revised in May 2011 and is effective for annual reporting periods beginning on or after 1 January 2013. Therefore, an entity applying IFRS for the first time in 2013 should apply the revised IAS 27 for all periods, even though the previous version of IAS 27 was applicable in 2012 (i.e. the prior year comparative). One year of comparative IFRS information is required, and IFRS 1 requires disclosures that explain how the transition from previous GAAP to IFRSs affected the entity's reported financial position, financial performance and cash flows. If historical summaries are presented (i.e. in addition to full financial statements with comparative figures), these do *not* have to be restated from previous GAAP. However, clear labelling is required, together with disclosure of the nature of the main differences. IFRS 1 grants limited exemptions from these requirements in specified areas where the cost of complying would be likely to exceed the benefits to users of financial statements.

Key Questions and Answers

Who is a first-time adopter?

As stated above, a first-time adopter is an entity that, for the first time, makes an explicit and unreserved statement that its general-purpose financial statements comply with IFRSs.

Can an entity be a first-time adopter if, in the preceding year, it has prepared IFRS financial statements for internal management use?

Yes, as long as those IFRS financial statements were not given to owners or external parties, such as investors or creditors. If a set of IFRS statements was, for any reason, given to an external party in the preceding year, then the entity will already be considered to be 'on IFRS' and therefore IFRS 1 does *not* apply.

What if, last year, an entity said it complied with selected, but not all, IFRS, or it included in its previous GAAP financial statements a reconciliation of selected figures to IFRS figures?

It will still qualify as a first-time adopter.

When an entity adopts IFRSs for the first time in its annual financial statements, what is it required to do?

1. The reporting entity must make an explicit and unreserved statement of compliance. For example:

   "These financial statements have been prepared in accordance with all International Accounting Standards and International Financial Reporting Standards approved and/or issued by the International Accounting Standards Board."

2. A reporting entity must use the same accounting policies in its opening IFRS statement of financial position and in all periods presented in the first IFRS financial statements. Typically, the periods involved will be the first reporting period and one comparative period, which will begin with the opening IFRS statement of financial position. For example:

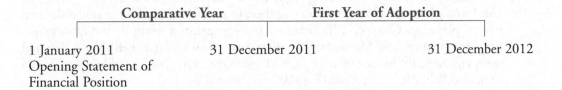

Comparative Year	First Year of Adoption

1 January 2011   31 December 2011   31 December 2012
Opening Statement of
Financial Position

The opening statement of financial position should:
• recognise all assets and liabilities required by IFRS (and only those). Some reclassification of assets, liabilities, income or expenses may be necessary to change from previous GAAP to IFRS if previous accounting treatment was not consistent with IFRS; and
• apply IFRS in measuring the reported assets and liabilities (see **Chapter 1**).

If preparation of the opening IFRS statement of financial position involves adjustments to amounts reported at the same date under previous GAAP, disclosure must be given of the effects of those adjustments on the reporting entity's results, financial position and cash flows. All adjustments should be recognised in retained earnings or other category of equity and not in the statement of profit or loss and other comprehensive income.

What adjustments are required to move from previous GAAP to IFRS?

1. **Derecognition of some previous GAAP assets and liabilities** The entity should eliminate previous GAAP assets and liabilities from the opening statement of financial position if they do not qualify for recognition under IFRS. For example:

    (a) IAS 38 *Intangible Assets* does not permit recognising expenditure on any of the following as an intangible asset (see **Chapter 9**): research; start-up, pre-operating and pre-opening costs; training; advertising and promotion; and moving and relocation. If previous GAAP recognised these as assets, they should be eliminated in the opening IFRS statement of financial position.

    (b) If previous GAAP allowed accrual of liabilities for 'general reserves', restructurings, future operating losses, or major overhauls that do not meet the conditions for recognition as a provision under IAS 37 *Provisions, Contingent Liabilities and Contingent Assets* (see **Chapter 14**), these should be eliminated in the opening IFRS statement of financial position.

    (c) If previous GAAP had allowed recognition of reimbursements or contingent assets that are not virtually certain (see **Chapter 14**), these should be eliminated in the opening IFRS statement of financial position.

2. **Recognition of some assets and liabilities *not* recognised under previous GAAP** Conversely, the entity should recognise all assets and liabilities required to be recognised by IFRS, even if they were never recognised under previous GAAP. For example:

    (a) IFRS 9 *Financial Instruments* requires recognition of all derivative financial assets and liabilities (that are not recognised under many national GAAPs) (see **Chapter 25**). (*Note:* The IASB is partway through a process of replacing IAS 39 *Financial Instruments: Recognition and Measurement* with IFRS 9 *Financial Instruments* (see **Chapter 25**). IFRS 9 is being developed in stages and the standard is not yet complete. The current version of IFRS 9 is mandatory for annual periods beginning on or after 1 January 2015 (with early application being permitted). It is assumed that a first-time adopter will apply IFRS 9; although a first-time adopter could equally apply IAS 39);

    (b) IAS 19 *Employee Benefits* requires an employer to recognise its liabilities under defined benefit plans (see **Chapter 17**). These are not just pension liabilities but also obligations for medical and life insurance, vacations, termination benefits, and deferred compensation. In the case of 'over-funded' plans (i.e. where projected benefits exceed projected liabilities), this would be a defined benefit asset;

    (c) IAS 37 requires recognition of provisions as liabilities (see **Chapter 14**). Examples could include obligations for onerous contracts, restructurings, decommissioning, site restoration, warranties, guarantees, and litigation; and

    (d) Deferred tax assets and liabilities would be recognised in conformity with IAS 12 *Income Taxes* (see **Chapter 13**).

3. **Reclassification** The entity should reclassify previous GAAP opening statement of financial position items into the appropriate IFRS classification. For example:

    • IAS 10 *Events after the Reporting Period* does not permit classifying dividends declared or proposed after the end of the reporting period as a liability at the reporting date (see **Chapter 15**). If such liability were recognised under previous GAAP, it would be reversed in the opening IFRS statement of financial position.

- The reclassification principle would also apply for the purpose of defining reportable segments under IFRS 8 *Operating Segments* (see **Chapter 24**).
- The scope of consolidation might change depending on the consistency of the previous GAAP requirements to those in IFRS 10 *Consolidated Financial Statements* (see **Chapter 26**). In some cases, IFRS will require consolidated financial statements where they were not required before.
- Some offsetting (netting) of assets and liabilities or of income and expense items that had been acceptable under previous GAAP may no longer be acceptable.
- IFRS 7 *Financial Instruments: Presentation* has principles for classifying items as financial liabilities or equity (see **Chapter 25**). For example, mandatorily redeemable preferred shares that may have been classified as equity under previous GAAP would be reclassified as liabilities in the opening IFRS statement of financial position.

4. **Measurement** The general principle is to apply IFRS in measuring all recognised assets and liabilities (i.e. compliance with extant IASs/IFRSs is expected), although there are several significant optional and mandatory exceptions (see below).

What are the exceptions to the basic measurement principle in IFRS 1?

1. **Optional exceptions** There are some important exceptions to the general restatement and measurement principles. For example:

(a) For business combinations that occurred before the start of the reporting period, an entity may retain the original previous GAAP accounting figures and adjustments. However, in all cases the entity must make an initial IAS 36 *Impairment of Assets* (see **Chapter 10**) test of any remaining goodwill in the opening IFRS statement of financial position, after reclassifying, as appropriate, previous GAAP intangibles to goodwill.

(b) For property, plant and equipment, intangible assets, and investment properties carried under the cost model (see **Chapters 5, 6** and **9**):
- these assets may be measured at their fair value at the start of the IFRS reporting period (this option applies to intangible assets only if an active market exists). Fair value becomes the 'deemed cost' going forward under the IFRS cost model. 'Deemed cost' is a surrogate for an actual cost measurement;
- if, before the date of its first IFRS statement of financial position, the entity had revalued any of these assets under its previous GAAP, either to fair value or to a price-index-adjusted cost, that previous GAAP revalued amount at the date of the revaluation can become the deemed cost of the asset under IFRS; and
- if, before the date of its first IFRS statement of financial position, the entity had made a one-time revaluation of assets or liabilities to fair value because of a privatisation or initial public offering, and the revalued amount became deemed cost under the previous GAAP, that amount (adjusted for any subsequent depreciation, amortisation, and impairment) would continue to be deemed cost after the initial adoption of IFRS.

The above rules are also applicable to investment properties (see **Chapter 5**), if an entity wishes to use the cost model under IAS 40 *Investment property*, as well as to intangible assets that meet the revaluation criteria as set out in IAS 38 (see **Chapter 9)**.

(c) An entity may elect to recognise all translation adjustments arising on the translation of the financial statements of foreign entities in accumulated profits or losses at the start of the IFRS reporting period, i.e. reset the translation reserve included in equity under previous GAAP to zero (IAS 21 *The Effects of Changes in Foreign Exchange Rates* – see **Chapter 31**). If the entity elects to apply this exemption, the gain or loss on subsequent disposal of the foreign entity will be adjusted only by those accumulated translation adjustments arising after the start of the IFRS reporting period. If the entity does not elect to apply this exemption, it must restate the translation reserve for all foreign entities since they were acquired or created.

(d) When calculating the cost of an investment, IFRS 1:
- allows first-time adopters to use a 'deemed cost' of either fair value or the carrying amount under previous accounting practice to measure the initial cost of investments in subsidiaries, jointly controlled entities and associates in the separate financial statements;
- adds a requirement to present dividends as income in the separate financial statements of the investor; and
- requires that, when a new parent is formed in a reorganisation, the new parent must measure the cost of its investment in the previous parent at the carrying amount of its share of the equity items of the previous parent at the date of the reorganisation.

(e) In March 2012 IFRS 1 was amended to eliminate the need for those entities to apply, retrospectively, certain requirements in IAS 20 *Government Grants and Disclosure of Government Assistance*. One of the requirements of IAS 20 (para 10A) is for entities with a government loan at a below market rate of interest to be measured at fair value on initial recognition. However, as it may be difficult for a first-time adopter with a government loan to identify a fair value at the earlier date of initial recognition, the amendment provides relief by making an exception to the retrospective application of IFRSs in this case. Hence, if, under previous GAAP, a first-time adopter did not account for government loans at a below market rate of interest at fair value as required by IAS 20, it does not have to adjust its previous GAAP carrying amount for the loan at the date of transition. Therefore, the fair value recognition will only apply on or after the date of transition to IFRSs. Despite this, an entity may retrospectively apply the requirements of IAS 20 in relation to government loans at below market rate of interest as long as the information needed to account for a government loan at fair value was obtained at the time of initially accounting for that loan.

(f) In May 2012, IFRS 1 was amended to clarify that a first-time adopter of IFRS with capitalised borrowing costs under a previous GAAP can carry them forward under IFRS. Additionally, while a first-time adopter is required to account for borrowing costs incurred from the date of transition for qualifying assets under construction at the date of transition under IAS 23 *Borrowing Costs*, it may choose to apply IAS 23 from an earlier date.

2. **Mandatory Exceptions** There are important exceptions to the general restatement and measurement principles set out above that are mandatory, including the following.

(a) IFRS 9 *Financial Instruments* – a first-time adopter must apply the derecognition requirements in IFRS 9 prospectively for transactions occurring on or after the date of transition to IFRS (see **Chapter 25**). However, the entity may apply the derecognition requirements retrospectively provided that the needed information was obtained at the time of initially accounting for those transactions. (*Note:* The IASB is partway through a process of replacing IAS 39 *Financial Instruments: Recognition and Measurement* with IFRS 9 *Financial Instruments* (see **Chapter 25**). IFRS 9 is being developed in stages and the standard is not yet complete. The current version of IFRS 9 is mandatory for annual periods beginning on or after 1 January 2015 (with early application being permitted). It is assumed that a first-time adopter will apply IFRS 9; although a first-time adopter could equally apply IAS 39.

(b) IFRS 9 – the general rule is that the entity shall not reflect in its opening IFRS statement of financial position a hedging relationship of a type that does not qualify for hedge accounting in accordance with IFRS 9. However, if an entity designated a net position as a hedged item in accordance with previous GAAP, it may designate an individual item within that net position as a hedged item in accordance with IFRS, provided that it does so no later than the date of transition to IFRS.

(c) With respect to non-controlling interests, IFRS 1 lists specific requirements that must be applied prospectively.

How will the change to IFRS affect an entity's ongoing disclosures?

For many entities, new areas of disclosure will be added that were not requirements under the previous GAAP (perhaps segment information, earnings per share, discontinuing operations, contingencies and financial instruments), and disclosures that had been required under previous GAAP will be broadened (perhaps related party disclosures).

IAS 1 only requires one year of full comparative financial statements. If a first-time adopter wants to disclose selected financial information for periods before the date of the opening IFRS statement of financial position, is it required to restate that information in accordance with IFRS as well?

No, restating earlier selected financial information to IFRS is optional. If the entity elects to present the earlier selected financial information based on its previous GAAP rather than IFRS, it must prominently label that earlier information as not complying with IFRS. Furthermore, it must disclose the nature of the main adjustments that would make that information comply with IFRS. This latter disclosure is narrative and not necessarily quantified.

What disclosures is a first-time adopter required to make when switching to IFRS?

IFRS 1 requires disclosures that explain how the transition from previous GAAP to IFRS affected the entity's reported financial position, financial performance and cash flows, including the following:
1. Reconciliations of equity reported under previous GAAP to equity under IFRS both: (a) at the date of the opening IFRS statement of financial position; and (b) at the end of the last annual period reported under the previous GAAP (see **Example 3.1**). For an

entity adopting IFRS for the first time in its 31 December 2012 financial statements, the reconciliations would be as of 1 January 2011 and 31 December 2011.

2. Explanation of material adjustments (including error corrections and impairment losses) that were made, in adopting IFRS for the first time, to the statement of financial position, statement of profit or loss and other comprehensive income and statement of cash flows (for example, see Notes 3 and 4 in **Example 3.1**).

EXAMPLE 3.1: RECONCILIATION OF EQUITY

If Tom Limited first adopts IFRS in 2012, and the company's last financial statements under previous GAAP were for the year ended 31 December 2011, then the date of transition to IFRS is 1 January 2011. Consequently, Tom Limited must include the reconciliations of equity at 1 January 2011 and 31 December 2011. Furthermore, the adjustments to the financial statements under previous GAAP should be explained in the Notes.

Reconciliation of Equity at 1 January 2011 (date of transition to IFRS):

Note		Previous GAAP €	Effect of Transition to IFRS €	IFRS €
	ASSETS			
	Non-current Assets			
1	Property, plant and equipment	8,299	100	8,399
2	Financial assets	3,471	420	3,891
		11,770	520	12,290
	Current Assets			
	Trade receivables	3,710	-	3,710
3	Inventories	2,962	400	3,362
4	Other receivables	333	431	764
	Cash and cash equivalents	748	-	748
		7,753	831	8,584
	Total Assets	19,523	1,351	20,874
	EQUITY AND LIABILITIES			
	Capital and Reserves			
	Issued capital	1,500	-	1,500
2	Equity investment reserve	-	294	294
4	Foreign exchange contract reserve	-	302	302
6	Retained earnings	3,882	500	4,382
		5,382	1,096	6,478

	Non-current Liabilities			
	Interest-bearing loans	9,396	–	9,396
5	Deferred tax liability	579	255	834
	Current Liabilities			
	Trade and other payables	4,124	–	4,124
	Current tax liability	42	–	42
		19,523	1,351	20,874

Notes to the Reconciliation of Equity at 1 January 2011:

1. Depreciation was influenced by tax requirements under previous GAAP, but under IFRS reflects the useful lives of the assets. The cumulative adjustment increases the carrying amount of property, plant and equipment by €100.
2. Financial assets are equity investments measured at their fair value of €3,891 in the statement of financial position and Tom Limited has elected to report value changes in 'other comprehensive income'. They were carried at cost under previous GAAP. The resulting gain of €294 (€420 less deferred tax €126) is included in the revaluation reserve.
3. Inventories include fixed and variable production overheads of €400 under IFRS, but this overhead was excluded under previous GAAP.
4. Unrealised gains of €431 on unmatured forward foreign exchange contracts are recognised under IFRSs, but were not recognised under previous GAAP. The resulting gains of €302 (€431 less related deferred tax €129) are included in the foreign exchange contract reserve.
5. The above adjustments increased the deferred tax liability as follows:

	€
Financial assets (Note 2)	126
Forward foreign exchange contracts (Note 4)	129
	255

6. The adjustments to retained earnings are as follows:

	€
Depreciation (Note 1)	100
Inventories (Note 3)	400
	500

3. Reconciliations of total comprehensive income for the last annual period reported under the previous GAAP to total comprehensive income under IFRS for the same period (see **Example 3.2**).
4. Appropriate explanations if the entity has availed itself of any of the specific recognition and measurement exemptions permitted under IFRS 1 (for example, if it used fair values as deemed cost).

EXAMPLE 3.2: RECONCILIATION OF TOTAL COMPREHENSIVE INCOME

An entity first adopted IFRS in 2013, with a date of transition of 1 January 2012. Its last financial statements in accordance with previous GAAP were for the year ended 31 December 2012. A reconciliation of the total comprehensive income reported under previous GAAP for the latest period in the entity's most recent annual financial statements to its total comprehensive income under IFRS for the same period could be presented as follows:

Reconciliation of total comprehensive income for the year ended 31 December 2012:

Notes		Effect of Previous GAAP €	Transition to IFRS €	IFRS €
	Revenue	20,910	–	20,910
1, 2	Cost of sales	(15,283)	(97)	(15,380)
	Gross profit	5,627	(97)	5,530
1	Distribution costs	(1,907)	(30)	(1,937)
1	Administrative expenses	(2,842)	(50)	(2,892)
	Financial income	1,446	–	1,446
	Finance costs	(1,902)	–	(1,902)
	Profit before tax	422	(177)	245
3	Tax expense	(158)	53	(105)
	Profit (loss)	264	(124)	140

Notes to the reconciliation of profit or loss for 2012:
1. A pension liability is recognised under IFRS, but was not recognised under previous GAAP. The pension liability increased by €130 during 2012, which caused increases in cost of sales (€50), distribution costs (€30) and administrative expenses (€50).
2. Cost of sales is higher by €47 under IFRS because inventories include fixed and variable production overheads under IFRS but not under previous GAAP.
3. Adjustments 1 and 2 led to a reduction of €53 in the tax expense.

If an entity is going to adopt IFRS for the first time in its annual financial statements for the year ended 31 December 2012, is any disclosure required in its financial statements prior to the 31 December 2012 statements?

Yes, but only if the entity presents an interim financial report that complies with IAS 34 (see **Chapter 34**). Explanatory information and a reconciliation are required in the interim report that immediately precedes the first set of IFRS annual financial statements. The information includes changes in accounting policies compared to those under previous local GAAP.

A parent or investor may become a first-time adopter earlier than or later than its subsidiary, associate, or joint venture investee. In these cases, how is IFRS 1 applied?

1. If the **subsidiary** has adopted IFRS in its own individual company financial statements before the group to which it belongs adopts IFRS for the **consolidated** financial statements, then the subsidiary's first-time adoption date is still the date at which it adopted

IFRS for the first time, not that of the group. However, the group must use the IFRS measurements of the subsidiary's assets and liabilities when preparing its first IFRS financial statements.

2. If the group adopts IFRS before the subsidiary adopts IFRS in its entity-only financial statements, then the subsidiary has an option either to:
   (a) elect that the group date of IFRS adoption is its transition date; or
   (b) first-time adopt in its entity-only financial statements.

3. If the group adopts IFRS before the parent adopts IFRS in its entity-only financial statements, then the parent's first-time adoption date is the date at which the group adopted IFRS for the first time.

4. If the group adopts IFRS before its associate or joint venture adopts IFRS in its entity-only financial statements, then the associate or joint venture should have the option to elect that either the group date of IFRS adoption is its transition date or the later date at which it adopts IFRS for the first time in its entity-only financial statements.

3.4 CONCLUSION

As explained in **Chapter 1**, the framework under which European Union-listed companies prepare their consolidated financial statements changed significantly in 2004–2005. Over the next five to 10 years, it can be expected that entities in many other jurisdictions across the world will adopt IFRS for the first time. Indeed, within the EU, the requirement to apply IFRS may be extended to cover non-listed companies as well. Consequently, as IFRS 1 applies when an entity presents its first IFRS financial statements, the significance and importance of this accounting standard is likely to continue for the foreseeable future. This chapter commenced by identifying some of the changes in accounting terminology following the adoption of IFRS. Then, by posing and subsequently answering a number of questions, an entity's reporting obligations when it adopts IFRS for the first time were explained.

SUMMARY OF LEARNING OBJECTIVES

Having studied this chapter on the first-time adoption of International Accounting Standards (IASs) and International Financial Reporting Standards (IFRSs), you should understand:

Learning Objective 1 The language of IFRS.

At present in the UK and Ireland, IFRS only applies to listed companies and the vast majority of companies (and practitioners) continue to apply UK GAAP. Arguably, and notwithstanding the minimal technical accounting differences, one of the main issues still to be overcome is the different terminology. Some of the more common differences are outlined in **Table 3.2**.

Learning Objective 2 An entity's reporting obligations when it adopts IFRS for the first time.

IFRS 1, which applies when an entity adopts the complete package of IFRS for the first time, requires that the same accounting policies are used in all periods presented. In addition to one year of comparative IFRS information, IFRS 1 also requires disclosures that explain how the transition from previous GAAP to IFRS affected the entity's reported financial position, financial performance and cash flows.

QUESTIONS

Self-test Questions

1. Explain the main requirements of IFRS 1 that must be satisfied when a company adopts IFRS for the first time.
2. Identify the reconciliations which a company must include in its financial statements when it adopts IFRS for the first time.

Review Questions

(See **Appendix One** for Suggested Solutions to Review Questions.)

Question 3.1

"There can be few who work for multinational companies, with some involvement with their financial reporting systems, who have not thought how good it would be to have one accounting language throughout the world. At present, accounting is far from that objective. Accountants inhabit a kind of Tower of Babel, where we not only speak different languages but also give different interpretations of the same events and transactions." *Sir Bryan Carsberg, Secretary-General of the International Accounting Standards Committee, 1995.*

Requirement Discuss:
(a) the advantages of harmonising accounting standards;
(b) the reasons why global harmonisation has not yet been achieved.

Challenging Questions

(Suggested Solutions to Challenging Questions are available to lecturers.)

Question 3.1 (Based on Chartered Accountants Ireland, P3 Summer 2005, Question 6)

The directors of Emerald plc (Emerald), an Irish listed company, have decided to adopt International Financial Reporting Standards (IFRS) for the first time in the company's financial statements for the year ended 31 December 2012.

Requirement With respect to the financial statements for the year ended 31 December 2012, prepare a *memorandum*, addressed to the directors of Emerald, explaining:

(a) what Emerald will be required to do when it adopts IFRSs for the first time;

(b) in general terms, the type of accounting adjustments that Emerald is likely to have to make when moving from Irish/UK Generally Accepted Accounting Practice to IFRS; and

(c) outline the disclosures that Emerald is likely to have to make as a first-time adopter of IFRS.

REFERENCES

Aisbitt, S. (2006), 'Assessing the Effect of the Transition to IFRS on Equity: The Case of the FTSE 100', *Accounting in Europe*, Vol. 3, No. 1, pp. 117–133.

Bradbury, M.E. and van Zijl, T. (2005), 'Shifting to IFRS', *University of Auckland Business Review*, pp. 77–83.

Bradbury, M.E. and van Zijl, T. (2006), 'Due Process and the Adoption of IFRS in New Zealand', *Australian Accounting Review*, Vol. 816, No. 2, pp. 86–94.

Bradbury, M.E. and van Zijl, T. (2007), 'International Financial Reporting Standards and New Zealand – Loss of Sector Neutrality', *Research in Accounting Regulation*, Vol. 19, pp. 37–54.

Brown, P. and Tarca, A. (2001), 'Politics, Processes and the Future of Australian Accounting Standards', *Abacus*, Vol. 37, No. 3, pp. 267–296.

Callao, S., Jarne, J.I. and Lainez, J.A. (2007), 'Adoption of IFRS in Spain: Effect on the Comparability and Relevance of Financial Reporting', *Journal of International Accounting, Auditing and Taxation*, Vol. 16, No. 2, pp. 148–178.

Christensen, H.B., Lee, E. and Walker, M. (2007), 'Cross-sectional Variation in the Economic Consequences of International Accounting Harmonization: The Case of Mandatory IFRS Adoption in the UK', *The International Journal of Accounting*, Vol. 42, No. 4, pp. 341–379.

Collett, P., Godfrey, J. and Hrasky, S. (2001), 'International Harmonisation: Cautions from the Australian Experience', *Accounting Horizons*, Vol. 15, No. 2, pp. 171–182.

Daske, H. (2006), 'Economic Benefits of Adopting IFRS or US-GAAP – Have the Expected Costs of Equity Capital Really Decreased?', *Journal of Business Finance & Accounting*, Vol. 33, Nos. 3 & 4, pp. 329–373.

Erchinger, H. and Melcher, W. (2007), 'Convergence between US GAAP and IFRS: Acceptance of IFRS by the US Securities and Exchange Commission (SEC)', *Accounting in Europe*, Vol. 4, No. 2, pp. 123–139.

Fearnley, S. and Hines, T. (2007), 'How IFRS has Destabilised Financial Reporting for UK Non-listed Entities', *Journal of Financial Regulation and Compliance*, Vol. 15, No. 4, pp. 394–408.

Goodwin, J. and Ahmed, K. (2006), 'The Impact of International Financial Reporting Standards: Does size matter?', *Managerial Auditing Journal*, Vol. 21, No. 5, pp. 460–475.

Jeanjean, T. and Stolowy, H. (2008), 'Do Accounting Standards Matter? An Exploratory Analysis of Earnings Management Before and After IFRS Adoption', *Journal of Accounting and Public Policy*, Vol. 27, No. 6, pp. 480–494.

Jones, S. and Higgins, A. (2006), 'Australia's Switch to International Financial Reporting Standards: A Perspective from Account Preparers', *Accounting and Finance*, Vol. 46, pp. 629–652.

Lantto, A-M. and Sahlström, P. (2009), 'Impact of International Financial Reporting Standard Adoption on Key Financial Ratios', *Accounting and Finance*, Vol. 49, No. 2, pp. 341–361.

Standish, P. (2003), 'Evaluating National Capacity for Direct Participation in International Accounting Harmonisation: France as a Test Case', *Abacus*, Vol. 39, No. 2, pp. 186–210.

Weißenberger, B.E., Stahl, A.B. and Vorstius, S. (2004), 'Changing from German GAAP to IFRS or US GAAP: A Survey of German Companies, *Accounting in Europe*, Vol. 1, No. 1, pp. 169–189.

PART II

PREPARATION OF STATEMENT OF PROFIT OR LOSS AND OTHER COMPREHENSIVE INCOME AND STATEMENT OF FINANCIAL POSITION

CHAPTER

4

REVENUE RECOGNITION

LEARNING OBJECTIVES

Having studied this chapter on revenue recognition, you should understand:
1. The term 'revenue' and how it applies to the supply of goods, the provision of services and the receipt of rent, interest and dividends;
2. The conditions that must be met before each type of revenue can be recognised in the statement of profit or loss and other comprehensive income;
3. How each type of revenue should be measured; and
4. The disclosure requirements of IAS 18 *Revenue*.

KEY TERMS AND DEFINITIONS FOR THIS CHAPTER

As you study this chapter, it is important to understand and be familiar with the following key terms and definitions. You may find it useful to refer back to them.

> **Fair Value** The price that would be received upon the sale of an asset or paid to transfer a liability in an orderly transaction between market participants at the measurement date (see **Chapter 1, Section 1.4**).
>
> **Fraud** The intentional misstatement or omission of amounts or disclosures designed to deceive financial statement users.
>
> **Revenue** IAS 18 *Revenue* defines revenue as the gross inflow of economic benefits (cash, receivables, other assets) arising from the ordinary operating activities of an entity, such as sales of goods, sales of services, interest, royalties and dividends. Revenue should be measured at the **fair value** of the consideration receivable.

Please note that, as explained in **Chapter 2**, the IASB issued amendments to IAS 1 *Presentation of Financial Statements* in June 2011. These included a *proposal* that the title 'Statement of Profit or Loss and Other Comprehensive Income' (SPLOCI) be adopted (rather than, for example, 'statement of comprehensive income') and a *requirement* to revise the presentation of other comprehensive income (OCI) within the SPLOCI. These amendments are explained in detail in **Chapter 2, Section 2.3**.

4.1 INTRODUCTION

Revenue, and its recognition, is a critical issue in financial reporting since revenue is typically the single largest item reported in an entity's financial statements. Indeed, not only is it significant in money terms but also in the weight and importance that investors place upon revenue when making investment decisions. Trends and growth in revenue are barometers that investors use when assessing past performance and future prospects. While the fundamental revenue recognition principle is that it should not be recognised until realised or realisable and earned by the entity, the practical issues that bear upon how, when and in what amount revenue should be recognised are broad and detailed.

Given the importance of revenue as a performance yardstick, it is often an area that is subject to deliberate misstatement or even **fraud**. Frequently this begins with a 'one-off adjustment just until results improve' in order to mask the impact of performance that was below expectations. For example, the inclusion of a small amount of additional revenue in order to meet expectations may not begin as part of a grand fraudulent scheme and it can often be 'easily' rationalised by those involved. Unfortunately, such policies frequently snowball and become complex schemes that result in material misstatements of financial statements over an extended period. A number of studies have reported that the restatement of financial figures to correct improper revenue recognition has resulted in larger drops in market capitalisation for the companies involved than any other type of restatement. Two of the best-known, and arguably the most extreme, examples of this are Enron and WorldCom.

Some of the most common means used to overstate revenue include:
- sales being recorded that are dependent upon uncertain future events and this uncertainty not being disclosed to management;
- sales being recorded before delivery is completed;
- contract revenue being recognised before services are performed; and
- false sales agreements and documentation being created.

Key to this Chapter

This chapter considers when revenue should be recognised in an entity's financial statements. The principles that guide revenue recognition are contained in IAS 18 *Revenue* and, in order to place these in context, the chapter begins by outlining other guidance associated with revenue recognition that may be more familiar to readers from the UK and Ireland as UK GAAP does not have a separate, dedicated revenue recognition accounting standard (**Section 4.2**). In the same section, IAS 18 is then explained, using a number of examples to illustrate the key issues. This is followed by a discussion on the different points at which revenue may be recognised, depending upon the nature of the goods or services being provided (**Section 4.3**). The chapter concludes with an overview of other guidance that supplements the revenue recognition principles contained in IAS 18 (**Section 4.4**).

4.2 ACCOUNTING FOR REVENUE

Background

As explained in **Chapter 1**, **income**, which encompasses both revenue and gains, is defined in the *Conceptual Framework for Financial Reporting 2010* as increases in economic benefits during the accounting period in the form of inflows or enhancements of assets or decreases of liabilities that result in increases in equity, other than those relating to contributions from equity participants. In practical terms, revenue is typically viewed as income that arises in the course of ordinary activities of an entity and is referred to by a variety of different names including 'sales', 'fees', 'interest', 'dividends' and 'royalties'. The issue of when revenue should be recognised has traditionally been associated with specific accounting procedures that are primarily directed towards determining the timing and measurement of revenue. Accordingly, the revenue recognition debate has taken place in the context of the historical cost double-entry system, with accounting principles focusing on determining when transactions should be recognised in the financial statements, what amounts are involved in each transaction, how these amounts should be classified and how they should be allocated between accounting periods.

Historical cost accounting in its pure form avoids having to take a valuation approach to financial reporting by virtue of the fact that it is transaction-based (i.e. it relies on transactions to determine recognition and measurement of assets, liabilities, revenues and expenses – see **Chapter 1**). Over an entity's life, its total income will be represented by net cash flows generated. However, because of the requirement to prepare periodic financial statements, it is necessary to break up an entity's operating cycle into artificial periods. Therefore, at each reporting date an entity will have entered into a number of incomplete transactions (for example, a product has been delivered or service rendered for which payment has not yet been received). As a result, the important questions to be answered with respect to revenue recognition revolve around how to allocate the effects of incomplete transactions between the periods for reporting purposes, rather than simply letting them fall into the periods in which cash is received or paid.

Under UK GAAP, attempts have been made to address revenue recognition in, for example, SSAP 2 *Disclosure of Accounting Policies*, which has been replaced by FRS 18 *Accounting Policies*, Chapter Five of the *Statement of Principles for Financial Reporting* (the UK GAAP equivalent to the *Conceptual Framework for Financial Reporting 2010*) and FRS 5 *Reporting the Substance of Transactions*. Some of the key points arising out of these documents are that, for example, the *Statement of Principles for Financial Reporting* adopts a 'balance sheet' (statement of financial position) approach and defines gains and losses in terms of changes in assets and liabilities rather than in terms of matching transactions with accounting periods. FRS 5 stipulates that, before revenue can be recognised, the seller needs to have performed its contractual obligations by transferring the principal benefits and risks of the goods to the customer:
- if the substance of the transaction is that the goods represent an asset of the customer, then the seller has a right to be paid and the seller should recognise the related changes in the assets or liabilities and turnover. The amount recognised should be adjusted for the time value of money, where significant, and for risk; or

- if the substance of the transaction is that the goods represent an asset of the seller, they should be retained in the seller's statement of financial position. Any amounts received from the customer should be included within payables.

Arguably the most influential 'UK' guidance is contained in Application Note 'G' to FRS 5, which specifically addresses five types of arrangement that have been subject to differing interpretations in practice:
- long-term contractual performance;
- separation and linking of contractual arrangements;
- bill and hold arrangements;
- sales with right of return; and
- presentation of turnover as principal or as agent.

As an indication of the importance of clear and consistent guidance on revenue recognition, Mary Keegan (the then Chairperson of the Accounting Standards Board) stated the following when introducing the Application Note: 'Many investors focus on revenue growth as an important indicator of a company's performance. Recent reports of questionable practice have highlighted the need for us to set out best practice.' Of particular relevance for those currently applying UK GAAP that may be concerned about its similarity with international practices is her comment: "The standard will also assist those faced with making the transition to International Financial Reporting Standards in 2005, as both its principles and its specific requirements are consistent with the international standard, IAS 18."

IAS 18 *Revenue*

The objective of IAS 18 is to prescribe the accounting treatment for revenue arising from certain types of transaction and event:
1. sale of goods;
2. rendering of services; and
3. use by others of entity assets yielding interest, royalties and dividends.

IAS 18 does *not* deal with revenue arising from transactions covered by other standards (e.g. revenue arising from lease agreements is dealt with in IAS 17 *Leases* (see **Chapter 8**)).

IAS 18 defines **revenue** as the gross inflow of economic benefits (cash, receivables, other assets) arising from the ordinary operating activities of an entity, such as sales of goods, sales of services, interest, royalties and dividends. Revenue should be measured at the **fair value** of the consideration receivable. The consideration is usually cash. If the inflow of cash is significantly deferred and there is no interest or a below market rate of interest, the fair value of the consideration is determined by discounting expected future receipts (i.e. using a discount rate that discounts the nominal amount to the current cash price of the goods and services). This would occur, for instance, if the seller is providing interest-free credit to the buyer or is charging a below-market rate of interest. Interest must be imputed based on market rates. If dissimilar goods or services are exchanged (as in barter transactions), revenue is the fair value of the goods or services received or, if this is not reliably measurable, the fair value of the goods or services given up.

Each of the three types of transaction and event referred to above will now be explained.

1. Accounting Treatment for Revenue arising from Sale of Goods

Revenue arising from the sale of goods should be recognised when *all* of the following four criteria have been satisfied:
- the seller has transferred to the buyer the significant risks and rewards of ownership. This may be evidenced by the transfer of legal title to the goods;
- the seller retains neither continuing managerial involvement to the degree usually associated with ownership nor effective control over the goods sold;
- the amount of revenue can be measured reliably; and
- the costs incurred or to be incurred in respect of the transaction can be measured reliably.

However, even if the above criteria are met but it is considered unlikely that goods or services provided will actually be paid for, then the revenue should *not* be recognised. In most cases, the transfer of legal title coincides with the transfer of risks. However, each transaction must be examined separately because in certain specific industries (for example, harvesting of crops or extraction of mineral ores), the entitlement to revenue may arise before the goods are actually transferred to the buyer.

At a practical level, the test of when revenue can be recognised depends upon whether the 'seller' has satisfied the terms of the sales contract. A common instance of whether the seller has satisfied the performance criteria in a sales contract is illustrated in **Example 4.1**.

EXAMPLE 4.1: CONTRACT PERFORMANCE

Chris Limited (Chris) received and accepted an order for 'widgets' from a regular customer, Toffer Limited (Toffer), on 21 December 2012 for an agreed price of €50,000. However, due to the Christmas holidays, the goods were not despatched until 4 January 2013. Toffer received the goods on the same day, and paid for them on 23 January 2013. The goods are included in Chris's inventory at 31 December 2012 at their cost price of €40,000.

Requirement Explain how this transaction should be accounted for in Chris's financial statements for the year ended 31 December 2012.

Solution
Revenue should only be recognised when a critical event occurs. Normally, this is when 'performance' has been carried out via delivery of an asset to a customer (i.e. this is the point at which the revenue recognition criteria referred to above have been met). As this occurs in 2013, therefore the goods should remain in Chris's inventory at 31 December 2012 at their cost price of €40,000.

As stated above, the transfer of the risks and rewards from the 'seller' to the 'buyer' is central to revenue recognition, and the transfer of legal title is often an indication that these have been transferred (i.e. ownership is linked to legal title and the transfer of risks and rewards is an indication of ownership). This is illustrated in **Example 4.2**.

EXAMPLE 4.2: TRANSFER OF RISKS AND REWARDS

Due to increased competition, particularly from overseas, Caití Limited (Caití) began selling goods on a sale-or-return basis during 2012. Under the terms of the sale, customers are able to return items within 31 days from the date of sale. Payment for goods not returned within this 31-day period is required 28 days thereafter. During 2012 a number of Caití's customers exercised their right of return. Caití typically sells goods on this basis at cost plus 20%. The sales figure in the draft financial statements for the year ended 31 December 2012 is based upon goods supplied to customers by 31 December 2012. Sales on a sale-or-return basis in November and December 2012 were €1,000,000 and €1,200,000 respectively.

Requirement Explain how this transaction should be accounted for in Caití's financial statements for the year ended 31 December 2012.

Solution
IAS 18 states that revenue should not be recognised until the risks and rewards associated with ownership have been transferred to the buyer. In this instance, title does not pass until the end of the return period (i.e. 31 days from the date of sale). The requirement for payment 28 days thereafter is not relevant for determining revenue recognition. Therefore, Caití should not recognise the revenue until the 31-day period has expired (i.e. when the risks and rewards of ownership have passed from Caití to the customer). Thus, the December 2012 sales should not be recognised and these goods should be included in inventory at 31 December 2012 at cost in accordance with IAS 2 *Inventories* (see **Chapter 11**). The December sales of €1,200,000 are included in inventory at their cost of €1,000,000. However, the November sales of €1,000,000 would be recognised in revenue as the risks and rewards have been transferred from Caití to the customer at 31 December 2012.

When assessing whether all of the four criteria referred to above have been met, and therefore whether revenue can be recognised, it is vital to consider the substance of a transaction and not just its legal form. A common instance of this is presented in **Example 4.3**.

EXAMPLE 4.3: SUBSTANCE OF THE TRANSACTION

Ruby Limited (Ruby) is a port manufacturer and the manufacturing process involves maturing wine in stainless steel for two years before bottling. The port is sold at cost plus 200%. On 1 January 2012, the first day of its accounting period, Ruby sold 100,000 litres of one-year-old port to an investment bank at its cost to Ruby of €1,260,000 and agreed to buy it back two years later for €1,524,600.

Requirement Explain how this transaction should be accounted for in Ruby's financial statements for the year ended 31 December 2012 and 2013.

Solution
In accordance with IAS 18, revenue from the sale of goods can only be recognised when all of the following conditions are met:
(a) all risks and rewards associated with the ownership of the wine would have to pass to the investment bank;

(b) the amount of revenue can be measured reliably;

(c) Ruby will obtain economic benefit from the transaction;

(d) costs relating to the transaction can be measured reliably; and

(e) Ruby does not retain any managerial involvement or control over the wine.

From the circumstances outlined, it is clear that the substance of the transaction is not a sale but a means of raising finance. The appropriate accounting entry would be to recognise the loan and charge the interest related to this advance in the financial statements. The interest is calculated as the difference between the cost of the wine and the amount it will cost to buy it back in two years' time.

DR	Bank	€1,260,000	
CR	Loan		€1,260,000

Year ended 31 December 2012:

DR	SPLOCI – P/L – finance charge (€1,260,000 × 10%)	€126,000	
CR	Loan		€126,000

Year ended 31 December 2013:

DR	SPLOCI – P/L – finance charge (€1,386,000 × 10%)	€138,600	
CR	Loan		€138,600

Note:
Finance charge – €1,524,600/€1,260,000 = 1.21
Square Root of 1.21 is 1.1, therefore the interest rate is 10%

2. Accounting Treatment for Revenue arising from Rendering of Services

Revenue arising from the rendering of services should be recognised by reference to the stage of completion of the transaction at the reporting date (e.g. based upon the percentage of work done to date relative to the total amount of work to be done), provided that all of the following criteria are met:

• the amount of revenue can be measured reliably;

• it is probable that economic benefits will flow to the service provider;

• the stage of completion of the transaction can be measured reliably; and

• the costs of the transaction (including future costs) can be measured reliably.

This type of approach is most commonly applied in relation to construction contracts (see **Chapter 12**). When the above criteria are not met, revenue arising from the rendering of services should be recognised only to the extent of the expenses recognised that are recoverable (the cost recovery approach).

Example 4.4 below illustrates how the nature of the relationship between two parties determines whether one party is *selling goods* or *rendering services*, and how the recognition of revenue changes depending upon the nature of that relationship.

Example 4.4 illustrates how a particular transaction could involve *either* the sale of goods or the rendering of a service, depending upon the nature of the relationship between two parties. **Example 4.5** develops this further by showing that it is possible for a 'single' transaction to involve *both* the sale of goods and the provision of a service. This latter scenario is normally assessed with reference to 'performance obligations' and whether the seller is obliged to perform more than one duty as a result of the sale. If so, then the duties have to be identified and separated. The sale of goods that also contains a warranty, guarantee or right of return is likely to involve separate performance obligations. For example, a sale with a warranty involves two distinct performance obligations. First, there is the sale of the goods specified in the contract. Secondly, there is the obligation to do whatever the warranty specifies, and a portion of the total consideration should be allocated and recognised as revenue when the warranty obligation is satisfied (which may not necessarily be evenly over the contract life). This type of transaction is often referred to as 'bundling' and its accounting treatment is illustrated in **Example 4.5**.

EXAMPLE 4.4: NATURE OF RELATIONSHIP

Erin plc (Erin), a company based in Ireland, prepares its financial statements to 31 December each year. Columbus Inc. (Columbus), an American company, has approached Erin to sell Columbus's products in Ireland. Columbus has offered the following alternatives to Erin:

(a) Erin acts as Columbus's agent and sells the products at a fixed price calculated to yield a profit margin of 50%, receiving a commission of 12½% of sales; or

(b) Erin buys the products from Columbus and sells them at a gross profit margin of 25%.

It is estimated that Erin will achieve total sales of €140 million per annum from Columbus's products.

Requirement Explain how the two proposals should be accounted for in Erin's financial statements.

Solution
The two proposals put forward by Columbus are very different.

Under scheme (a) Erin would act as Columbus's agent. Under this arrangement Erin must only record in income the amount of commission it is entitled to under the agreement, amounting to €17.5 million (€140 million × 12½% commission) based on the estimated figures.

Under scheme (b) Erin would buy the goods from Columbus as principal and the sales and cost of sales would be included in Erin's statement of profit or loss and other comprehensive income – profit or loss as normal.

	€million
Sales	140
Cost of sales	(105)
Gross profit	35

EXAMPLE 4.5: BUNDLING

Kitkar Limited (Kitkar) sold a vehicle with a warranty for €30,000. If it sold the vehicle and the warranty separately, it would cost €27,000 for the vehicle and €4,500 for the warranty.

Requirement Explain how Kitkar should account for this transaction in its financial statements.

Solution
The overall transaction price of €30,000 should be allocated pro rata to the two distinct obligations. The sale of the vehicle element is €25,714 ((€27,000/€31,500) × €30,000), and the amount allocated to the warranty element is €4,286 ((€4,500/€31,500) × €30,000). Kitkar can recognise revenue of €25,714 on the sale of the vehicle immediately, with the revenue of €4,286 relating to the warranty being recognised over the life of the warranty.

3. Accounting Treatment for Revenue arising from Interest, Royalties and Dividends

For interest, royalties and dividends, provided that it is probable that the economic benefits will flow to the entity and the amount of revenue can be measured reliably, revenue should be recognised as follows:
- interest – on a time-proportion basis that takes into account the effective yield;
- royalties – on an accruals basis, in accordance with the substance of the relevant royalty agreement; and
- dividends – when the shareholder's right to receive payment is established.

The recognition of interest, royalties or dividends as income from a foreign source may need to be postponed if exchange permission is required and a delay in remittance is expected. Furthermore, if the ultimate receipt of this revenue is doubtful, revenue recognition should be postponed. In such cases, it may be appropriate to recognise the revenue only when the cash is received.

With respect to dividends, the concept of '**right to receive**' is particularly important. This is explained in **Example 4.6**.

EXAMPLE 4.6: RIGHT TO RECEIVE

Seasons Limited (Seasons) is a wholly-owned subsidiary of Vivaldi Limited (Vivaldi), with both companies preparing their financial statements to 31 December each year. On 23 January 2013, after reviewing the draft financial statements for the year ended 31 December 2012, the directors of Seasons proposed an ordinary dividend of 10 cent per ordinary share in respect of the year ended 31 December 2012.

Requirement Explain how this transaction should be accounted for in the financial statements of both Seasons and Vivaldi for the year ended 31 December 2012.

Solution

In accordance with IAS 10 *Events after the Reporting Period* (see **Chapter 15**), equity dividends declared after the end of the reporting period do not meet the definition of a liability at the end of the reporting period and should not be accrued in Seasons' 2012 financial statements (i.e. as the dividends have not been approved at the reporting date, there is no obligation to pay the dividends at 31 December 2012). These dividends should be disclosed in a note to the financial statements of Seasons as a contingent liability. With respect to Vivaldi, the dividends due from Seasons cannot be recognised as investment income in their 2012 financial statements, nor is it likely that they would be disclosed in Vivaldi's financial statements as they would represent a 'contingent asset' and, as explained in **Chapter 15**, the criteria for disclosing contingent assets are more strict than that for contingent liabilities. Vivaldi's right to receive the dividends only arises once they have been approved by the shareholders of Season, which occurred after the end of the reporting period.

Disclosure Requirements

In addition to providing guidance on the recognition of revenue in the financial statements, IAS 18 also stipulates the disclosures that should be provided in the financial statements so that the user can better understand the basis on which revenue has been recognised. The following information must be provided in accordance with IAS 18:

1. the accounting policies adopted for the recognition of revenue; and
2. the amount of each significant category of revenue recognised (for example, figures for sale of goods, rendering of services, interest, royalties and dividends, if material).

This is illustrated in **Example 4.7**.

EXAMPLE 4.7: IAS 18 DISCLOSURE

Notes to the Financial Statements:

Income and expenses for the year are recognised on an accruals basis. Income from the sale of goods and services is recognised when delivery has taken place, transfer of risk has been completed and the amount of future returns can be reasonably estimated.

Product returns are accepted as a matter of contract or as a matter of practice. In the reported periods, product returns were insignificant. Sales rebates and discounts as well as amounts collected on behalf of third parties, such as sales taxes and goods and services taxes, are excluded from net sales.

4.3 THE REVENUE OPERATING CYCLE

The previous section explained revenue recognition by examining each of the three types of transaction and event (sale of goods, rendering of services and assets yielding interest, royalties and dividends) identified in IAS 18. This section examines revenue recognition from a different perspective by considering the different stages in the revenue operating cycle (for example, from where a customer places an order to the delivery of the goods) in order to illustrate that revenue may be recognised at different points along this cycle, depending on the nature of the goods or services being provided.

It is important to remember that the critical event in the operating cycle of a business is that point at which most or all of the uncertainty surrounding a transaction is removed (see **Chapter 1, Section 1.3**). With respect to revenue, the point at which this occurs is *usually* when the goods or services are delivered. However, the critical event could occur at other times, depending on the circumstances. Different points in the revenue operating cycle are illustrated in **Table 4.1**.

TABLE 4.1: THE REVENUE OPERATING CYCLE

Different Points in Revenue Operating Cycle	Criteria for Revenue Recognition	Examples of Practical Application
Placing of an order by a customer, prior to manufacture	Little or no uncertainty regarding the final outcome of the contract. However, in most cases, as there is likely to be uncertainty regarding the final outcome of such contracts, it would generally not be prudent to recognise revenue at this point.	In rare circumstances, revenue may be recognised at this point in the case of long-term construction contracts, depending on the right of the contractor to be paid (see **Chapter 12**).
During production	If revenues accrue over time and no significant uncertainty exists as to measurability or collectability, then revenue may be recognised.	This may apply to interest, dividends and royalties as the right to receive typically accrues on a time basis (even though the actual payment may only occur annually).
	If a contract of sale has been entered into and future costs can be estimated with reasonable certainty, then revenue recognition may be possible.	This may apply to long-term construction contracts where the percentage of completion method is adopted (see **Chapter 12**).
At the completion of production	This is nearing the point where most of the uncertainties in the operating cycle in a business are resolved. For revenue to be recognised, there should be a ready market for the commodity, together with a determinable and stable market price. In addition, the selling and marketing costs involved should be insignificant.	Certain precious metals and commodities.

	In most cases, recognition is usually delayed until delivery.	
At the time of sale (but before delivery)	The goods must have already been acquired or manufactured, and be capable of immediate delivery. The selling price should be established and all material-related expenses, including delivery, ascertained. No significant uncertainties should remain (i.e. cash collection should be reasonably certain, with the likelihood of the goods being returned low).	Certain sales of goods (e.g. bill and hold sales). Property sales where there is an irrevocable contract.
On delivery	In this case, while the criteria for recognition before delivery were not met, no significant uncertainties now remain.	This is the point at which revenue is recognised for most goods and services. Property sales where there is doubt that the sale will be completed.
Subsequent to delivery	This point in the cycle may be appropriate where there was significant uncertainty regarding collectability at the time of delivery or, at the time of sale, it was not possible to value the consideration with sufficient accuracy.	Sales where right of return exist or goods shipped subject to conditions (for example, installation, inspection or maintenance).
On an apportionment basis (revenue allocation approach)	Where the revenue represents the supply of initial and subsequent goods or services.	Franchise fees or the sale of goods with an after-sales service.

4.4 OTHER RELATED GUIDANCE

Additional guidance that addresses specific issues relating to revenue recognition has been published to supplement the more generic principles outlined in IAS 18. Examples of this are IFRIC 13 *Customer Loyalty Programmes* and SIC 31 *Revenue – Barter Transactions Involving Advertising Services*, which are dealt with below.

IFRIC 13 *Customer Loyalty Programmes*

Customer loyalty programmes are now widespread and they typically provide customers with incentives to buy the goods or services of a particular entity. Generally, if a customer buys goods or services, the entity grants the customer 'points' depending on the nature of the scheme. Customers subsequently redeem these points for awards, such as free or discounted goods or services.

IFRIC 13 *Customer Loyalty Programmes* addresses the accounting by the entity that provides its customers with incentives to buy goods or services by providing awards (these are called 'award credits' in IFRIC 13) as part of a sales transaction. Common examples are airline and hotel loyalty schemes and credit card reward schemes.

IFRIC 13 requires the entity that grants the awards to account for the sales transaction that gives rise to the award credits as a 'multiple element revenue transaction' and allocate the fair value of the consideration received or receivable between the award credits granted and the other components of the revenue transaction. This treatment applies irrespective of whether the entity supplies the awards (the discounted goods or services), or whether a third party supplies them. IFRIC 13 explicitly prohibits recognising the full consideration received as revenue, with a separate liability for the cost of supplying the awards. The accounting treatment of customer loyalty programmes is explained further in **Example 4.8**.

EXAMPLE 4.8: CUSTOMER LOYALTY PROGRAMMES

During the year ended 31 December 2012, Patches started giving vouchers to customers who spent more than €200 in a single transaction on qualifying items. The vouchers entitled customers to €20 off a subsequent transaction, within three months, of more than €200 on qualifying items. Past experience indicates that 50% of customers redeem the vouchers. The total sales of qualifying items during the year ended 31 December 2012 amounted to €10,000,000. At 31 December 2012, it is estimated that there are unredeemed vouchers *eligible for discount* amounting to €1,000,000 (i.e. vouchers in respect of sales during the last three months of 2012). No account has been taken of these unredeemed vouchers in Patches' draft financial statements for the year ended 31 December 2012.

Requirement Explain how the vouchers should be accounted for in the financial statements of Patches for the year ended 31 December 2012.

Solution

The revenue of each separate component should be measured at fair value. Where vouchers are issued that are redeemable against future purchases, revenue should be reported at the amount of consideration received less the vouchers' fair value (i.e. customers are purchasing goods/services plus the voucher).

IFRIC 13 does not mandate a specific approach for estimating fair value, but requires that the fair value is based upon the value to the customer, not the cost to the company. Deferred revenue could be estimated using the fair value of the award or the relative fair values of the award and the goods or services sold. IFRIC 13 requires that consideration be given to the proportion of rewards expected to be redeemed.

If the amount allocated to the vouchers is based on the fair value of the vouchers relative to the other components of the sale then, as 50% of customers are expected to redeem the vouchers, Patches has sold goods worth €10,500,000 (i.e. sales €10,000,000 + estimated redemption (50%) €500,000) for consideration of €10,000,000.

Allocating the discount between the two components:

$\frac{€10,000,000}{€10,500,000} \times €10,000,000 = €9,523,809$

i.e. €9,523,809 allocated to sales and €476,191 to vouchers, which is deferred and recognised when obligation is fulfilled (or lapses). Therefore 25% (last three months of the year) of this figure represents deferred income at 31 December 2012.

DR Retained earnings	€119,048	
CR Current liabilities – deferred income		€119,048

4.5 CONCLUSION

This chapter considers when revenue should be recognised in an entity's financial statements. It began by outlining the guidance relating to revenue recognition, in particular IAS 18, before illustrating the different stages in the revenue operating cycle (i.e. from where a customer places an order to the delivery of the goods) in order to illustrate that revenue may be recognised at different points along this cycle, depending on the nature of the goods or services being provided. In recent years there has been a steady growth in the complexity and diversity of business activity and this has resulted in a variety of forms of revenue-earning transactions that could never have been imagined even a decade ago. Consequently, the notion of recognising revenue at the 'point of sale' is no longer appropriate for many business transactions. Indeed, it could be argued that the long-established (and arguably simplistic) principles of accruals and prudence are out of date. This is particularly the case since the statement of profit or loss and other comprehensive income now combines traditional notions of revenue resulting from the success, or otherwise, of selling goods and services with newer concepts of holding gains and losses into a single statement of performance (see **Chapter 2**).

Finally, in November 2011, the International Accounting Standards Board and Financial Accounting Standards Board jointly published, for public comment, a revised Exposure Draft (ED) on *Revenue from Contracts with Customers*. If adopted, this would create a single revenue recognition standard for IFRS and US GAAP that would be applied across various industries and capital markets. The publication of this joint proposal represents a significant step forward toward global convergence in one of the most important and pervasive areas in financial reporting, with the proposed standard replacing IAS 18, IAS 11 *Construction Contracts* and related interpretations. For many companies the new approach will not change the amount or timing of revenue recognition. However, in some cases there could be a significant impact. For example, for mobile telecommunications companies, the standard would require separate upfront recognition of revenue from providing a mobile phone without a separate charge that is bundled as part of a contract for mobile phone services.

Summary of Learning Objectives

After having studied this chapter on revenue recognition, you should understand:

Learning Objective 1 The term 'revenue' and how it applies to the supply of goods, the provision of services and the receipt of rent, interest and dividends.

IAS 18 defines **revenue** as the gross inflow of economic benefits (cash, receivables, other assets) arising from the ordinary operating activities of an entity, such as: (i) sales of goods; (ii) sales of services; and (iii) interest, royalties and dividends.

Learning Objective 2 The conditions that must be met before each type of revenue can be recognised in the statement of profit or loss and other comprehensive income.

These are:
(a) **Sale of goods** should be recognised when:
  - the significant risks and rewards of ownership are transferred to the buyer,
  - the seller retains neither continuing managerial involvement nor effective control over the goods involved;
  - the amount of revenue can be measured reliably;
  - it is probable economic benefits will flow; and
  - the related costs can be measured reliably.
(b) **Sale of services** should be recognised by stage of completion when:
  - the amount of revenue can be measured reliably;
  - it is probable that the economic benefits associated with the transaction will flow to the enterprise, the stage of completion of the transaction at the reporting date can be measured reliably; and
  - the costs incurred and costs to complete the transaction can be measured reliably.
(c) **Interest** on a time-apportioned basis, **Royalties** on an accrual basis per contract, and **Dividends** when the right to receive is established.

Learning Objective 3 How each type of revenue should be measured.

Revenue should be measured at the **fair value** of the consideration receivable. The consideration is usually cash. If the inflow of cash is significantly deferred, and there is no interest or a below market rate of interest, the fair value of the consideration is determined by discounting expected future receipts. This would occur, for instance, if the seller is providing interest-free credit to the buyer or is charging a below market rate of interest.

Learning Objective 4 The disclosure requirements of IAS 18.

The following information must be disclosed: the accounting policies adopted and the amount of each significant category of revenue recognised.

QUESTIONS

Self-test Questions

1. At what value should revenue be measured?
2. What conditions must be met before revenue from the sale of goods can be recognised?
3. What conditions must be met before revenue from the delivery of services can be recognised?

Review Questions

(See **Appendix One** for Suggested Solutions to Review Questions.)

Question 4.1 (Based on Chartered Accountants Ireland, P3 Summer 2006, Question 4)

Issue 1 On 3 September 2012, Mastertickets Limited (Mastertickets), a concert ticket agency, made a number of concert reservations for customers, receiving €5,000 from them. The customers collected the concert tickets from the agency on the same day. Mastertickets remitted €4,500 to the concert promoter on 4 September 2012, retaining €500 as commission. Mastertickets acts purely as an agent for the concert promoter and has no responsibility for the concert, which is taking place in July 2013.

Requirement How should Mastertickets reflect this transaction in its financial statements for the year ended 31 December 2012?

Issue 2 Lagan Limited (Lagan) operates an internet site from which it sells the products of various manufacturers. Customers, using the Internet site, select the products they wish to purchase, provide their credit card details and the address to which the goods are to be delivered. Once the credit card authorisation is received, Lagan passes the order details immediately to the relevant manufacturer. The manufacturer is responsible for delivering the goods directly to the customer, and is also responsible for any disputed credit card charges, product returns or warranty claims. Lagan charges each manufacturer a fee of 8% of the product's selling price. During the year ended 31 December 2012, total product sales through the Internet site amounted to €500,000, earning Lagan commission of €40,000.

Requirement How should Lagan reflect this transaction in its financial statements for the year ended 31 December 2012?

Issue 3 Purple Limited (Purple) provides mobile telephone services. Customers subscribing to Purple initially pay a non-refundable activation fee followed by a quarterly call usage charge. Only nominal costs are incurred by Purple to activate the telephone service, and the quarterly call usage charge is more than adequate to cover operating costs.

Requirement How should Purple reflect this transaction in its financial statements for the year ended 31 December 2012?

Issue 4 Nectar Limited (Nectar), on 1 February 2012, entered into a €15,000,000 contract to build a multistorey car park, with a completion date of 30 June 2013. Nectar has not yet accounted for the contract in its financial statements for the year ended 31 December 2012. It is company policy to adjust cost of sales by the amount of attributable profit or loss to be recognised in the period to arrive at contract revenue. Further details in relation to the contract at 31 December 2012 are as follows:

	€000		€000
Amount invoiced	9,500	Costs incurred	9,250
Amount received	9,000	Costs certified	8,500
		Costs to complete	4,000

Requirement How should Nectar reflect the contract in its financial statements for the year ended 31 December 2012?

(**Note:** knowledge of IAS 11 *Construction Contracts* is required to answer this issue (see **Chapter 12**).)

Challenging Questions

(Suggested Solutions to Challenging Questions are available to lecturers.)

Question 4.1

You are the financial accountant of Incara plc, a company that operates from a number of retail outlets throughout Ireland, selling vehicle entertainment and navigation systems. Incara plc prepares its financial statements to 31 December each year. Incara plc received and accepted an order for car CD changers from a regular customer, CCE Limited, on 21 December 2012 for an agreed price of €50,000. However, due to the Christmas holidays, the goods were not despatched until 4 January 2013. CCE Limited received the goods on the same day, and paid for them on 13 January 2013. The goods are included in Incara plc's inventory at 31 December 2012 at their cost price of €40,000.

During the year ended 31 December 2012, Incara plc began selling a particular model of satellite navigation system with a three-year warranty at no extra cost to the customer. Incara plc sells the navigation systems for €500 and, during the year ended 31 December 2012, 200 of these navigation systems were sold and included in revenue for the year ended 31 December 2012 at €500 each. One of Incara plc's competitors sells an identical navigation system without a warranty for €475, while an unrelated insurer offers an equivalent warranty for €75. The experience of other retailers suggests that the navigation systems have an equal probability of breaking down in each of the three years covered by the warranty.

Requirement Prepare a Memorandum addressed to the board of directors of Incara plc which explains:
(a) how the order from CCE Limited and the income from the sale of the navigation systems, together with the related warranties, have been accounted for in the financial statements of Incara plc for the year ended 31 December 2012; and
(b) the principles underlying revenue recognition and their application to different industries.

Question 4.2

A supermarket awards 100 points to customers for each €100 worth of purchases in a single transaction. The customers may then exchange 1,000 points for goods with a retail value of €60; the cost to the supermarket for these goods is estimated to be €15. The points awarded must be redeemed by customers within three months and past experience indicates that 80% of the points awarded will be redeemed.

In December 2012, total sales eligible for reward points amounted to €1,500,000 and the supermarket issued the points to customers at the end of December.

In January 2013, 55% of the points were redeemed.

In February 2013, 15% of the points were redeemed and the supermarket estimated that a further 10% would be redeemed.

In March 2013, 15% of the points were redeemed.

Requirement Explain and calculate how the reward points should be accounted for in the financial statements of the supermarket for the months December 2012 to March 2013.

Question 4.3

The International Accounting Standards Board and the Financial Accounting Standards Board are currently undertaking a joint project to develop a new revenue model that would replace IAS 11 *Construction Contracts* and IAS 18 *Revenue*.

Requirement With reference to relevant academic literature, discuss:
(a) whether the establishment of revenue recognition criteria is important;
(b) the theoretical problems and practical consequences of revenue recognition criteria;
(c) the conceptually different revenue recognition models that might be adopted to over-
    come these issues; and
(d) the current developments with respect to the revenue recognition debate.

5

INVESTMENT PROPERTY

LEARNING OBJECTIVES

After studying this chapter, you should understand the following:
1. the definition of an *investment property*;
2. how to account for an investment property initially;
3. the two allowable methods of measuring an investment property subsequent to initial recognition;
4. how to account for gains and losses using the fair value model and on the disposal of investment property; and
5. the disclosure requirements of IAS 40 *Investment Property*.

KEY TERMS AND DEFINITIONS FOR THIS CHAPTER

In order to aid your understanding of the concepts and issues covered in this chapter, it is important to understand and be familiar with the following key terms and definitions. As you study this chapter, you should refer back to them.

Arm's Length Transaction This is a transaction when all parties to the transaction are independent and on an equal footing.

Consolidation In the context of financial accounting, *consolidation* refers to the aggregation of the financial statements of more than one company into a single set of financial statements as if they were one separate entity.

Finance Lease This is a lease that transfers substantially all the risks and rewards incidental to the ownership of an asset to the lessee (see **Chapter 8**).

Investment Property This is property (land or a building, or part of a building, or both) held (by the owner or by the lessee under a finance lease) to earn rentals or for capital appreciation or both. It excludes property that is held for:
- use in the production or supply of goods or services or for administrative purposes; or
- sale in the ordinary course of business.

Operating Lease This type of lease does *not* transfer all the risks and rewards incidental to ownership of an asset to the lessee; these are retained by the lessor (see **Chapter 8**). An operating lease typically involves the lessee paying a rental for the hire of an asset for a period of time that is substantially less than its useful economic life.

Subsidiary In the context of **consolidation** (see **Chapter 26**), a subsidiary is an entity in which another entity (the parent) normally holds more than 50% of its ordinary capital and is therefore deemed to control this entity. Control in this context is defined as ability to direct policies and management.

5.1 INTRODUCTION

Investment property is land and/or buildings held to earn rentals or for capital appreciation, or both. It includes properties that are owned and properties that are held on a finance lease by an enterprise. Investment properties have the distinguishing feature that they earn cash flows largely independently of an enterprise's other assets, whereas owner-occupied properties earn revenues in combination with other assets, normally in the production or supply process. Consequently, investment properties are not considered to be like most non-current assets (which are typically accounted for under IAS 16 *Property, Plant and Equipment* – see **Chapter 6**), since they are not acquired for 'use' in an organisation's operations in the traditional sense. As a result, the accounting treatment of investment properties is dealt with in a separate accounting standard, IAS 40 *Investment Property*.

Perhaps until recently, investment in property by both companies and individuals has been viewed as an unfailing means of acquiring wealth. The cliché 'as safe as a house' suggests that property is an investment that never fails. Indeed, it could be argued that history has shown that investment in property is a low-risk investment, as the return from the property services the investment, the net worth grows over time and generates income for further investments in property. Consequently, banks will often lend to a company and use the company's property as collateral. While the events of recent years might have tempered these views, some might contend that it is not the investment in property that is the problem but rather it is the excessive debt that is often associated with it.

Most entities will own and/or use properties in their operations, and it is likely that they will be 'acquired' using a variety of different means (for example, purchased for cash or leased) and used for a variety of different purposes (for example, administrative offices or rental income). Consequently, the accounting treatment of properties may fall under a number of different accounting standards. For example, IAS 40 *Investment Property* (this chapter), IAS 16 *Property, Plant and Equipment* (see **Chapter 6**) or IAS 17 *Leases* (see **Chapter 8**). Unfortunately, from a student's perspective, these standards are interrelated, each has to be learnt and there is no more appropriate or best sequence in which to do this.

Key to this Chapter

This chapter explains how to account for investment properties in accordance with IAS 40 *Investment Property*. It also explains the disclosure requirements for investment properties in accordance with IAS 40. The chapter begins by defining the term **investment property**, before explaining how to account for an investment property both upon initial recognition and then subsequently (see **Section 5.2**); this includes the application of the cost and fair value models, together with the treatment of gains and losses when the fair value model is applied. The disclosure requirements of IAS 40 are also outlined. The chapter concludes by informing the reader that there are key differences between IAS 40 and IAS 16 and that, particularly from an examination perspective, it is important to be aware of these (**Section 5.3**).

5.2 IAS 40 *INVESTMENT PROPERTY*

The Objective of IAS 40

The objective of IAS 40 *Investment Property* is to prescribe the accounting treatment for investment property and related disclosure requirements.

Definitions and Examples

An **investment property** is property (land or a building – or part of a building – or both) held (by the owner or by the lessee under a finance lease) to earn rentals or for capital appreciation or both. An investment property is *not* property held for:
• use in the production or supply of goods or services or for administrative purposes; or
• sale in the ordinary course of business.

Examples of items that are or are not investment properties are given in **Table 5.1**.

TABLE 5.1: WHEN IS PROPERTY *INVESTMENT* PROPERTY?

Investment Property	Not Investment Property
• Land held for long-term capital appreciation rather than for short-term sale in the ordinary course of business.	• Property intended for sale in the ordinary course of business or in the process of construction or development for such sale. In such cases IAS 2 *Inventories* applies (see **Chapter 11**).
• Land held for a currently undetermined future use (this means that if the company has not determined that it will use the land as owner-occupied property or for short-term sale in the ordinary course of business, then that land is regarded as being held for capital appreciation and IAS 40 applies).	• Property being constructed or developed on behalf of third parties. In such cases IAS 11 *Construction Contracts* applies (see **Chapter 12**).
• A building owned by the entity (or held by the entity under a **finance lease**) (see **Chapter 8**) and leased out under one or more **operating leases**.	• Owner-occupied property, which includes property leased or rented to a **subsidiary** company as this is deemed to be 'owner-occupied'. In such cases IAS 16 *Property, Plant and Equipment* applies (see **Chapter 6**).

- A building that is vacant but is held to be leased out under one or more operating leases.

- Property that is being constructed or developed for future use as investment property.

- Property that is leased to another entity under a **finance lease** (see **Chapter 8**) is not an investment property.

Example 5.1 applies a number of the investment property conditions outlined in **Table 5.1**.

EXAMPLE 5.1: APPLICATION OF INVESTMENT PROPERTY CONDITIONS

IP Limited purchased three identical properties (called 'Green', 'White' and 'Gold') and leased a fourth (Star) under a finance lease during the year ended 31 December 2012. The details of each of the properties is as follows:
- Green is currently vacant but is held to be leased out under an operating lease;
- The White property is let to, and occupied by, a subsidiary of IP Limited;
- Gold is used as IP Limited's head office; and
- Star is let to, and occupied by, a company outside the IP Limited Group under an operating lease. The unexpired term on the lease is 12 years.

Requirement Explain which, if any, of the above properties should be classified as *investment property* in accordance with IAS 40 *Investment Property* in the group financial statements of IP Limited.

Solution

Green is currently vacant but is held to be leased out under an operating lease; this type of property is specifically identified as an investment property in IAS 40.

The White property is let to, and occupied by, a subsidiary of IP Limited and is therefore specifically precluded from being treated as an investment property by IAS 40 as it is deemed to be owner-occupied as IP Limited controls the subsidiary. (It should be accounted for under IAS 16 *Property, Plant and Equipment* (see **Chapter 6**).)

Gold is used as IP Limited's head office, and is therefore owner-occupied. Owner-occupied properties are not investment properties and should be accounted for under IAS 16 *Property, Plant and Equipment* (see **Chapter 6**).

The Star property is let to, and occupied by, a company that is outside the IP Limited Group, with an unexpired lease term of 12 years. A property leased to an unconnected company qualifies as an investment property under IAS 40.

Example 5.2 addresses another of the investment property conditions outlined in **Table 5.1**, namely property under construction.

EXAMPLE 5.2: PROPERTY UNDER CONSTRUCTION

Kelly Limited purchased four acres of land on 23 January 2012 and immediately commenced building commercial offices. The construction is expected to be completed by 3 September 2013 when Kelly Limited intends to let the premises. The land cost €3.5 million and the construction work to 31 December 2012 cost €6 million, with a further €4 million estimated to complete it.

Requirement Explain how Kelly Limited should account for this in its financial statements for the year ended 31 December 2012.

Solution

IAS 40 allows the classification of properties under construction that are intended for use as investment properties to be classified as such during their construction. At 31 December 2012, land and buildings would be capitalised at their costs-to-date of €9.5 million and classified as an investment property in the financial statements.

Initial Recognition and Initial Measurement

If a property meets the definition of an investment property outlined above, then a decision has to be made as to whether it can be recognised in the financial statements and, if so, at what amount.

An investment property should be *recognised* as an asset when and only when:
(a) it is probable that the future economic benefits (i.e. rental income and/or capital appreciation) that are associated with the investment property will flow to the entity; and
(b) the cost of the investment property can be measured reliably (see below).

Investment property should initially be measured at cost. *Cost* includes purchase price and any directly attributable expenditure, such as professional fees for legal services, property transfer taxes and other transaction costs for self-constructed investment properties. For property being constructed, *cost* is the cost at the date when the construction or development is complete.

Subsequent expenditure on the property should only be recognised when it is probable that future economic benefits in excess of those originally assessed will flow to the entity. Otherwise the subsequent expenditure should be expensed in the statement of profit or loss and other comprehensive income – profit or loss in the period incurred and not capitalised as part of the cost of the investment property.

Measurement after Initial Recognition

After a property has been initially recognised and measured at cost, an entity should choose as its accounting policy *either* the fair value model *or* the cost model. The selected policy should then be applied to *all* of its investment properties. Each of these two options is now explained.

The Fair Value Model

The fair value of investment property is the price at which property could be exchanged between knowledgeable, willing parties in an **arm's length transaction**. A gain or loss arising from a change in the fair value of investment property should be recognised in profit or loss for the period in which it arises (i.e. charged or credited to the statement of profit or loss and other comprehensive income in arriving at operating profit). When a company chooses the fair value model, it must measure all of its investment properties at fair value on an annual basis.

The determination of fair value is dealt with in detail in **Chapter 1, Section 1.4**. However, in summary, fair value will normally be obtainable by reference to current prices on an active market for similar properties in the same location and conditions as the property under review (i.e. the fair value will generally be the market price for similar properties). In the absence of such an active market (and therefore reliable market price), information from a variety of sources may have to be considered, including:

- current prices on an active market for properties of a different nature, condition or location adjusted to reflect those differences;
- recent prices on less active markets; and
- discounted cash flow projections based on reliable estimates of future cash flows.

Example 5.3 shows the application of the fair value model.

EXAMPLE 5.3: APPLYING THE FAIR VALUE MODEL

Floyd Limited commenced trading on 1 January 2012 and its non-current assets at 31 December 2012 include two investment properties, Gilmore and Waters, that are let on an arm's length basis to a third party. Floyd Limited applies the fair value model in accounting for its investment properties, which were professionally valued for the first time on 31 December 2012. The valuation details are as follows:

Property	Cost	Fair Value	Increase/(Decrease)
	€m	€m	€m
Gilmore	210	345	135
Waters	390	280	(110)

Requirement Explain and set out the journal entries necessary to record the movements between cost and fair value in respect of each of the properties for the period ended 31 December 2012.

Solution

Under the fair value model, changes in valuation are taken to the statement of profit or loss and other comprehensive income – profit or loss:

Gilmore:
    DR   Property   €135m
    CR   SPLOCI – P/L   €135m

Waters:
    DR   SPLOCI – P/L   €110m
    CR   Property   €110m

Note: if an entity wishes to adopt the fair value model but a fair value cannot be reliably determined on a continuing basis, then the cost model (as discussed below) should be used and retained until the property is disposed of.

The Cost Model

If an entity decides to apply the cost model to measure its investment properties after initial recognition, then it should measure *all* of its investment properties at cost less accumulated depreciation and impairment losses. This is consistent with the IAS 16 cost model described in **Chapter 6**.

Note: the exception to this rule is those properties that meet the criteria to be classified as 'held for sale' in accordance with IFRS 5 *Non-Current Assets Held for Sale and Discontinued Operations*. These properties should be measured in accordance with IFRS 5 (i.e. at the lower of depreciated historical cost and fair value less costs to sell – see **Chapter 20**).

Example 5.4 compares the application of the cost and fair value models.

EXAMPLE 5.4: APPLYING THE COST AND FAIR VALUE MODELS

ABC, a manufacturing company, purchases a property for €1 million on 1 January 2012 for its investment potential. The land element of the cost is believed to be €400,000 and the buildings element is expected to have a useful life of 50 years. At 31 December 2012, local property indices suggest that the fair value of the property has risen to €1.1 million.

Requirement Show how the property would be presented in the financial statements as at 31 December 2012 if ABC adopts a:
(a) cost model; and
(b) fair value model.

Solution

(a) Depreciation in the year is €600,000/50 = €12,000
    Therefore:
    1. in the SPLOCI – P/L, there will be a depreciation charge of €12,000; and

> 2. in the statement of financial position, the property will be shown at a net book value of €1 million − €12,000 = €988,000.
> (b) In the statement of financial position, the property will be shown at its fair value of €1.1 million. In the statement of profit or loss and other comprehensive income, there will be a gain of €100,000 credited in arriving at profit or loss for the year ended 31 December 2012; this represents the fair value adjustment.

Other Points

1. As explained above, after a property has been initially recognised and measured at cost, an entity should choose as its accounting policy *either* the fair value model *or* the cost model. The model selected then becomes the 'accounting policy' for investment properties and should be applied to *all* investment properties. While the expectation is that this policy will not be changed, it may be. However IAS 8 *Accounting Policies, Changes in Accounting Estimates and Errors* states that a voluntary change in accounting policy should be made *only* if the change will result in a more appropriate presentation of transactions, other events or conditions in the entity's financial statements.

2. While IAS 40 allows the application of either the fair value or the cost model in the financial statements, the selection of the cost model does not negate the requirement for entities that hold investment properties from obtaining fair value information. This is because IAS 40 requires all entities that hold investment properties to determine the fair value of investment property for the purpose of either measurement (if the entity uses the fair value model) or disclosure (if it uses the cost model). An entity is encouraged, but *not* required, to determine the fair value of investment property on the basis of a valuation by an independent valuer who holds a recognised and relevant professional qualification and has recent experience in the location and category of the investment property being valued.

Transfers

Over the life of a property, its use may change. For example, it may initially be held as an investment property under IAS 40 and then later used as the entity's own head office, meaning it no longer meets the criteria to be held as an investment property and would be accounted for under IAS 16 (see **Chapter 6**). Such changes in use are referred to as transfers to or from investment property. This is explained below and illustrated in **Table 5.2**.

Transfers to Investment Property For example, at the end of construction or development, a property may cease to be accounted for under IAS 16 and change to IAS 40. Any difference between the carrying amount at the date of change and the fair value should be treated as a revaluation under IAS 16 (see **Chapter 6**).

Transfers from Investment Property An example of this would be a transfer from an investment property to owner-occupied property. In this case, the deemed cost for subsequent accounting is the fair value at the date of change in use (i.e. the value of the property at the date the property is transferred).

Different types of transfer, together with the treatment of the gain or loss on transfer, are illustrated in **Table 5.2**.

TABLE 5.2: INVESTMENT PROPERTY TRANSFERS

Type of Transfer	Treatment of Gain or Loss on Transfer
(a) Commencement of owner-occupation (transfer from investment property to owner-occupied).	Cost is fair value at date of transfer.
(b) Commencement of development with a view to sale (transfer from investment property to inventory).	Cost is fair value at date of transfer.
(c) End of owner-occupation (transfer from owner-occupied property to investment property).	IAS 16 applies till date of transfer; any difference is treated as a revaluation under IAS 16 (see **Chapter 6**).
(d) Commencement of an operating lease to another party (transfer from inventory to investment property).	Any difference is treated as a gain/loss and included in arriving at profit/loss in the statement of profit or loss and other comprehensive income for the period.
(e) End of construction or development with property continuing to be held as an investment property.	Any difference to fair value is recognised in arriving at profit/loss in the statement of profit or loss and other comprehensive income for the period.

Disposals

Not only may the way in which an investment property is used change (see above), it may also be disposed of. A gain or loss arising from the disposal of an investment property is the difference between the net disposal proceeds and the carrying amount of the asset at the date of disposal. This difference should be recognised in arriving at operating profit/loss in the statement of profit or loss and other comprehensive income for the period in which the disposal takes place.

Disclosure Requirements

Financial reporting is the communication of financial information. The purpose of accounting disclosure is to inform both current and potential investors of the accounting policies and methods used when preparing published financial statements. Many entities have different types of tangible non-current asset; for example, those held for productive use in the business (see **Chapter 6** – IAS 16 *Property, Plant and Equipment*) and/or those held for capital appreciation and rental income. This section outlines the disclosures required when IAS 40 is applied.

Disclosure Requirements Applicable for Both Cost and Fair Value Models

The following disclosures are required regardless of which measurement model is applied after initial recognition:
(a) Whether the cost model or the fair value model has been applied.
(b) Amounts included in the statement of profit or loss and other comprehensive income for rental income for the period and operating expenses for the period.

(c) Details of any restrictions on the reliability of investment property or the remittance of income and proceeds of disposal.
(d) Contractual obligations to purchase, construct or develop investment properties.

Disclosure Requirements for Fair Value Model

The following disclosures are required if the *fair value model* is adopted after initial recognition:
(a) Methods and assumptions applied in determining the fair value of investment properties.
(b) The extent to which the fair value of investment property has been based on valuations by a qualified independent valuer.
(c) Additions and disposals during the period.
(d) Net gains or losses from fair value adjustments.
(e) Details of any transfers during the period (see above).

Disclosure Requirements for Cost Model

The following disclosures are required if the *cost model* is adopted after initial recognition:
(a) Depreciation methods used.
(b) Useful lives or depreciation rates used.
(c) Gross carrying amount and accumulated depreciation (including impairment losses) at the beginning and end of the period.
(d) A reconciliation of the carrying amount at the beginning and end of the period showing additions, disposals, depreciation, impairment losses recognised or reversed and transfers (see above).
(e) The fair value of the investment property or, if that fair value cannot be determined reliably, a description of the property, an explanation of why fair value cannot be determined reliably and, if possible, the range of estimates within which fair value is likely to be. Disclosures (a) and (b) above with respect to fair value-based investment properties are required in connection with this disclosure by note of the fair value of cost-based investment properties.

5.3 COMPARING IAS 16 AND IAS 40

While this chapter deals specifically with IAS 40, it includes a number of references to, or comparisons with, IAS 16 (see **Chapter 6**) and, to a lesser extent, IAS 17 (see **Chapter 8**). This is unavoidable as each of these accounting standards deals with the accounting treatment of properties, albeit from a different perspective.

From a student's perspective, each of the standards referred to above is equally important and must be studied, However, it is the different accounting treatment required under IAS 16 and IAS 40 that is often the most confusing and difficult to grasp. As stated above, there is probably no appropriate or best sequence in which to study these standards; for example, while IAS 16 is arguably the most prominent, it is arguably the most difficult to fully understand because of its detail; in contrast, IAS 40 is possibly easier to come to terms with, but its use is likely to be less prevalent (especially in exams).

Table 5.3 summarises the key differences between IAS 16 and IAS 40. Even if you have not yet studied IAS 16, just being aware of the differences at this stage is useful. Once you have studied both standards, reviewing Table 5.3 should help you to clarify the key differences between these two important accounting standards.

TABLE 5.3: IAS 16 vs IAS 40

IAS 16 Property, Plant and Equipment	IAS 40 Investment Property
• Apply Cost or *Market Value* models.	• Apply Cost or *Fair Value* models.
• There are different recognition rules for 'first' and 'subsequent' gains and losses.	• All gains and losses are recognised in the statement of profit or loss and other comprehensive income in arriving at operating profit/loss (i.e. not in 'other comprehensive income'). There is no revaluation reserve.
• Depreciation is charged under both the cost and market value models.	• Depreciation is only charged under the cost model.
• If the market value model is adopted, there is an option to transfer a percentage from the revaluation reserve to retained earnings (through the statement of changes in equity, not the statement of profit or loss and other comprehensive income), in order to offset the higher depreciation charge.	• Not applicable since a revaluation reserve is not created under the fair value model and depreciation is not charged.

5.4 CONCLUSION

This chapter explains how to account for investment properties and illustrates the disclosure requirements for investment properties in accordance with IAS 40. Investment properties have the distinguishing feature that they are held to earn rentals and/or for capital appreciation largely independently of an enterprise's other assets, whereas owner-occupied properties earn revenues in combination with other assets normally in the production or supply process. Investment properties include properties that are owned and properties that are held on a finance lease by an enterprise.

An investment property should initially be measured at cost. The two allowable methods of measuring an investment property subsequent to initial recognition are the fair value model and the cost model. The model selected should be applied to *all* investment properties held by the entity. If the fair value model is adopted, gains or losses should be recognised in arriving at operating profit/loss in the statement of profit or loss and other comprehensive income in the period they arise. Different disclosure requirements apply depending on whether the cost or fair value model is applied.

Finally, particularly from an examination perspective, it is important to have a clear understanding of how IAS 40 differs from IAS 16 (see **Table 5.3**).

SUMMARY OF LEARNING OBJECTIVES

After having studied this chapter, you should understand the following:

Learning Objective 1 The definition of an *investment property*.

An *investment property* is defined as a property (land or a building – or part of a building – or both) held (by the owner or by the lessee under a finance lease) to earn rentals or for capital appreciation or both.

Learning Objective 2 How to account for an investment property initially.

An investment property should initially be measured at cost.

Learning Objective 3 The two allowable methods of measuring an investment property subsequent to initial recognition.

An entity should choose as its accounting policy either the fair value model or the cost model and should apply that policy to *all* of its investment properties. When a property interest held under an operating lease is classified as an investment property, there is no choice of accounting policy – the fair value model *must* be applied.

Learning Objective 4 How to account for gains and losses using the fair value model and on the disposal of investment property.

Gains or losses should be recognised in arriving at profit or loss in the statement of profit or loss and other comprehensive income in the period they arise.

Learning Objective 5 The disclosure requirements of IAS 40.

Different disclosure requirements apply depending on whether the cost or fair value models are applied.

QUESTIONS

Self-test Questions

1. What is meant by an investment property?
2. How does one account for investment property?
3. How does one account for gains/losses on disposals of investment property?
4. Are investment properties depreciated?
5. What are the main disclosure requirements of IAS 40?

Review Questions

(See **Appendix One** for Suggested Solutions to Review Questions.)

Question 5.1

Helix Limited (Helix) purchased three identical properties (Right, Left and Up), and leased a fourth (Down) under a finance lease, during the year ended 31 December 2012.

- Right is used as Helix's head office;
- Left is let to, and occupied by, a subsidiary of Helix;
- Up is let to, and occupied by, an associate of Helix; and
- Down is let to, and occupied by, a company outside the Helix Group under an operating lease. The unexpired term on the lease is 12 years.

Requirement Explain how each of the four properties should be treated in the group financial statements of Helix for the year ended 31 December 2012.

Challenging Questions

(Suggested Solutions to Challenging Questions are available to lecturers.)

Question 5.1

United Limited, a company that manufactures sporting equipment and accessories, owns a number of properties, which are listed below:

1. Trafford Lane: a freehold factory and office block used entirely by United Limited for its own manufacturing and administration.
2. Stretford Road: a freehold office block, let at commercial rates to a large insurance company.
3. Red Way: a property held by United Limited under a finance lease and leased out to City Limited under an operating lease.
4. Numbers 2, 4, 6 and 8 Black Street: four freehold cottages which were originally purchased to provide assistance to employees but are now let commercially to tenants who have no other connection with the company.

United Limited had all the above properties valued by an independent professional valuer on 31 December 2012. The following is a summary of the valuations and original costs of the properties:

	Cost		Valuation	
	Land	Buildings	Land	Buildings
Freehold Properties:	€	€	€	€
1. Trafford Lane	10,000	24,000	40,000	90,000
2. Stretford Road	25,000	60,000	30,000	80,000
4. Black Street	4,000	8,000	16,000	24,000

Each of the above properties is estimated to have a further useful life of 40 years.

	Cost	Valuation
Leasehold Properties:	€	€
3. Red Way	72,000	120,000

United Limited adopts a straight-line depreciation policy.

Requirement Prepare the necessary journal entries to incorporate the above revaluations in the books of United Limited as at 31 December 2012.

Question 5.2

Prague Limited commenced trading on 1 April 2012 and the company's non-current assets include two properties (Praha 1 and Praha 2), which are let to tenants who are not connected with the company. Prague Limited has decided to adopt the fair value model in accounting for its investment properties, which were professionally valued for the first time on 31 December 2012. Details of the valuation are as follows:

Property	Cost €000	Fair Value €000
Praha 1	1,000	1,400
Praha 2	1,300	1,100

Requirement Explain and show the journal entries needed to record the change in value of each of the properties for the nine months ended 31 December 2012.

PROPERTY, PLANT AND EQUIPMENT

LEARNING OBJECTIVES

Having studied this chapter on property, plant and equipment, you should be able to:
1. discuss the elements of expenditure that are included in the cost of property, plant and equipment;
2. define depreciation;
3. account for a change in depreciation method;
4. apply the required accounting treatment if the estimated useful economic life of a non-current asset is revised;
5. explain when property, plant and equipment may be revalued;
6. account for revaluation gains and losses with respect to property, plant and equipment;
7. understand and account for the circumstances when an amount may be transferred from the revaluation reserve to the credit of the statement of profit or loss and other comprehensive income; and
8. apply the main disclosure requirements of IAS 16 *Property, Plant and Equipment*, including those required when property, plant and equipment is revalued.

KEY TERMS AND DEFINITIONS FOR THIS CHAPTER

In order to aid your understanding of the concepts and issues covered in this chapter, it is important to understand and be familiar with the following key terms and definitions. As you study this chapter, you should refer back to them.

Accumulated depreciation Non-current assets are recorded in the statement of financial position at their cost less accumulated depreciation, with accumulated depreciation being the depreciation charge made in the first year that the asset is owned and used, plus the depreciation charge made in subsequent years of ownership and use.

Carrying Value This is the amount at which an asset, which includes property, plant and equipment, is recognised in the statement of financial position after deducting any **accumulated depreciation** and accumulated **impairment losses**. This is also referred to as the 'net book value' or 'written down value'.

Cost The amount of cash or cash equivalents paid or the **fair value** of the other consideration given to acquire an asset at the time of its acquisition or construction or, where applicable, the amount attributed to that asset when initially recognised in accordance with the specific requirements of other IFRSs (for example, IFRS 2 *Share-based Payment* (see **Chapter 34**)).

Depreciable Amount The **cost** of an asset, or other amount substituted for cost (for example, market valuation), less the **residual value** of the asset.

Depreciation The systematic allocation of the depreciable amount of an asset over its estimated useful economic life.

Estimated Useful Economic Life is the:
   (a) period over which an asset is expected to be available for use by an entity; or
   (b) number of production or similar units expected to be obtained from the asset by an entity.

Fair Value The amount for which an asset could be exchanged between knowledgeable and willing parties in an arm's length transaction.

Impairment Loss The amount by which the **carrying amount** of an asset exceeds its **recoverable amount**. (Impairment should be recognised in accordance with IAS 36 *Impairment of Assets* (see **Chapter 10**)).

Non-current Asset This is an asset acquired for use within the business, with a view to earning profits from its use. A non-current asset is not acquired for resale and includes property, plant and equipment. Non-current assets are usually held and used by a business for a number of years.

Property, plant and equipment are tangible items that are:
   (a) held for use in the production or supply of goods or services, for rental to others or for administrative purposes; and
   (b) expected to be used during more than one accounting or financial period.

Recoverable Amount The higher of an asset's **net selling price** and its **value in use**.

Residual Value of an Asset This is the estimated amount that an entity would currently obtain from the disposal or sale of the asset, after deducting the estimated costs of disposal, if the asset were already of the age and in the condition expected at the end of its estimated useful economic life.

Value in Use This is the present value of future cash flows expected to be derived from using the asset (i.e. property, plant and equipment in the context of this chapter).

Please note that, as explained in **Chapter 2**, the IASB issued amendments to IAS 1 *Presentation of Financial Statements* in June 2011. These included a *proposal* that the title 'Statement of Profit or Loss and Other Comprehensive Income' (SPLOCI) be adopted (rather than, for example, 'statement of comprehensive income') and a *requirement* to revise the presentation of other comprehensive income (OCI) within the SPLOCI. These amendments are explained in detail in **Chapter 2, Section 2.3**.

6.1 INTRODUCTION

Property, plant and equipment are tangible items that are:
(a) held by companies for use in the production or supply of goods or services, for rental to others or for administrative purposes; and
(b) expected to be used during more than one accounting or financial period.

Property, plant and equipment is vital to business operations, but often cannot be easily liquidated or sold. The figure for property, plant and equipment in a company's financial statements can vary widely, depending on the industry in which the company operates, the size of the company, the age of the assets and the depreciation and valuation methods applied. In broad terms, service companies would be expected to have a relatively low property, plant and equipment figure, while manufacturing companies would be expected to have a much more significant portion of their assets classified as such.

An example of a business with a high amount of property, plant and equipment might be a shipping company, because most of its assets will be tied into its fleet of ships and administrative buildings. On the other hand, an accounting firm is likely to have less property, plant and equipment because it is likely to need only computer equipment and an office in a building to provide its services. The three categories of property, plant and equipment are disclosed separately in financial statements because they are treated differently. This is because improvements, replacements and betterments can pose accounting issues, depending on how the associated costs are recorded.

As emphasised in **Chapter 5, Section 5.3**, it is important to clearly distinguish between properties that fall under IAS 16 *Property, Plant and Equipment* and properties that fall under IAS 40 *Investment Property* (see **Chapter 5**). The accounting treatment prescribed in IAS 16 applies to the majority of property, plant and equipment *unless* another international accounting standard requires or permits an alternative accounting treatment, for example, IFRS 5 *Non-current Assets Held for Sale and Discontinued Operations* (see **Chapter 20**) and IAS 40 *Investment Property* (see **Chapter 5**). With respect to IAS 40, it is vital to have a clear understanding of how it differs from IAS 16. This is summarised in **Table 5.3** in **Chapter 5, Section 5.3**.

Key to this Chapter

The main purpose of this chapter is to explain the accounting treatment of property, plant and equipment that falls under the scope of IAS 16. The chapter begins by explaining the objective and scope of IAS 16, together with how property, plant and equipment should be initially recognised and measured (**Section 6.2**). The application of the cost and revaluation models after initial recognition is also explained, together with the depreciation of property, plant and equipment under both models. Some additional, arguably more specific, aspects of IAS 16 are then explained, together with the accounting standard's disclosure requirements (**Section 6.3**).

6.2 IAS 16 *PROPERTY, PLANT AND EQUIPMENT*

The Objective of IAS 16

The objective of IAS 16 is to prescribe the accounting treatment for property, plant and equipment. It deals primarily with when such assets should be recognised, their **carrying values** at each reporting date and the associated **depreciation**. Property, plant and equipment are classed as **non-current assets** in the statement of financial position. It is important to note that, while the classes of non-current assets referred to in the title of IAS 16 are 'property, plant and equipment', it applies equally to other classes of non-current assets, such as motor vehicles and computers.

> ***Note:*** for ease of reference, the term 'property, plant and equipment' will be used throughout the remainder of this chapter to refer to all classes of non-current assets that fall under the scope of IAS 16.

The Scope of IAS 16

> ***Note:*** from an examination perspective, it is important to consider IAS 16 in association with IAS 23 *Borrowing Costs* (see **Chapter 7**) and IAS 36 *Impairment of Assets* (see **Chapter 10**), and also to have a clear understanding of when IAS 16 or IAS 40 applies, together with the differences in accounting treatment depending on which of these two accounting standards applies. The study of property, plant and equipment should also include the three 'excepted' standards referred to above (i.e. IFRS 5, IAS 17 and IAS 40) as examination questions on property, plant and equipment often require a knowledge of some or all of the standards referred to in this note.

IAS 16 prescribes the accounting treatment for property, plant and equipment unless another standard requires or permits a different accounting treatment. The most common areas where *another* standard applies are:
- property, plant and equipment classified as held for sale in accordance with IFRS 5 *Non-current Assets Held for Sale and Discontinued Operations* (see **Chapter 20**);
- IAS 17 *Leases* (see **Chapter 8**); and
- IAS 40 *Investment Property* (see **Chapter 5**).

Initial Recognition

Before an entity decides the amount of expenditure to capitalise relating to property, plant and equipment (i.e. to record the expenditure as an asset in the statement of financial position rather than as an expense in the statement of profit or loss and other comprehensive income), the first decision is actually whether the expenditure should even be recognised at all in the statement of financial position. Consistent with the principles contained in the *Conceptual Framework for Financial Reporting 2010* (see **Chapter 1**,

Section 1.3), property, plant and equipment should only be recognised as an asset if, and *only* if:
(a) it is probable that future economic benefits associated with the item will flow to the entity; and
(b) the **cost** of the item can be measured reliably.

Measurement at Initial Recognition

If it has been determined that the expenditure on property, plant and equipment can be capitalised, then it has to be determined what amount or value should be placed on the expenditure.

IAS 16 states that all items of property, plant and equipment should be recognised *initially* at **cost**. This includes:
- the purchase price, including import duties and non-refundable purchase taxes, after deducting trade discounts and rebates; and
- any costs *directly attributable* to bringing the asset to the location and condition necessary for it to be capable of operating in the manner intended by management.

The application of this statement is illustrated in **Example 6.1**.

Examples of *directly attributable* costs include:
- costs of site preparation;
- initial delivery and handling costs;
- installation and handling costs;
- costs of testing whether the asset is functioning properly after initial installation. The net proceeds from selling any items produced (e.g. samples) while testing the asset should be deducted from the cost of testing;
- professional fees; and
- the anticipated costs of dismantling and/or removing the asset, together with any costs of restoring the site on which it is located, at the end of its life should be included in the cost of the property, plant and equipment when it is initially recognised.

Some of these costs are included in **Example 6.1**.

EXAMPLE 6.1: MEASUREMENT AT INITIAL RECOGNITION

A manufacturing company commissioned the building of a new factory. The costs associated were as follows:

	€
Site selection	30,000
Site purchase	1,000,000
Architect's fees	50,000
Engineer's fees	150,000
Legal fees	50,000
Construction costs	1,500,000
Testing and checking of machinery (Note 1)	250,000
Administration costs	500,000

The plant was available for use on 31 March 2012 and reached normal production levels by 31 October 2012.

Note 1 Included in testing and checking of machinery costs was €50,000 in connection with a six-monthly diagnostic check of machinery.

Note 2 €50,000 relating to the six-monthly diagnostic check is excluded as it is not a direct cost of purchase since it is not necessary in getting the machinery ready for use.

Note 3 Site selection and administration overheads are not direct costs.

Note 4 Subsequent expenditure on property, plant and equipment is only recognised as an asset when the expenditure *improves* the asset beyond its originally assessed standard of performance. For example:
• modification extending the estimated useful economic life of plant; and
• upgrading a machine.

Requirement Calculate the cost to be recorded as an asset (i.e. capitalised) in the statement of financial position.

Solution

	€
Site cost	1,000,000
Construction cost	1,500,000
Architect's fees	50,000
Legal fees	50,000
Engineer's fees	150,000
Testing costs	200,000
Total cost	2,950,000

IAS 16 states that an entity should *not* recognise in the carrying value of an asset the costs of its day-to-day servicing. These costs should be expensed to the statement of profit or loss and other comprehensive income – profit or loss as incurred. This is illustrated in **Example 6.2.**

EXAMPLE 6.2: DAY-TO-DAY RUNNING COSTS

If an aircraft is repainted, how should this expenditure be treated?

Solution
The repainting costs should be written off to the statement of profit or loss and other comprehensive income – profit or loss (i.e. expensed in the period incurred). The costs are deemed to be part of the day-to-day running or servicing costs which, do not lead to an increase or enhancement in the performance of the aircraft.

Example 6.3 develops the previous example and illustrates when subsequent expenditure would be capitalised (i.e. included in the cost of the asset) because it leads to an enhancement in the performance of the asset.

EXAMPLE 6.3: ENHANCEMENT IN PERFORMANCE

Manders Limited installs a new production process in its factory at a cost of €50,000. This enables a reduction in operating costs (as assessed when the original plant was installed) of €10,000 per year for at least the next 15 years.

Requirement How should the expenditure be treated?

Solution
It should be capitalised and added to the original cost of the plant as it results in enhancement of economic benefits.

Measurement after Initial Recognition

Once property, plant and equipment is initially recognised and measured at cost in the statement of financial position, an entity must choose either the:
1. cost model, or
2. revaluation model
for each class of non-current asset (for example, property, plant, equipment and motor vehicles). The application of these two models is explained below.

Note: the revaluation model under IAS 16 is not the same as the **fair value** model under IAS 40 (see **Chapter 5**). The differences between IAS 16 and IAS 40 are summarised in **Table 5.3** (see **Chapter 5, Section 5.3**).

1. The Cost Model

If this model is adopted, then property, plant and equipment should be carried at cost less **accumulated depreciation** in the statement of financial position. **Example 6.4** addresses the recording of the property at cost. The issue of depreciation is introduced immediately after **Example 6.4**.

EXAMPLE 6.4: RECORDING PROPERTY AT COST

A company records its property, plant and equipment at cost (*less accumulated depreciation*). On 1 January 2012, the company purchased property at a cost of €500,000 for cash.

Requirement How should this transaction be recorded in the company's financial statements on 1 January 2012?

Solution
DR Property   €500,000
CR Cash   €500,000

Depreciation

Each year that a non-current asset is used it will wear it out a little, until it eventually reaches the end of its **estimated useful economic life** (with the exception of freehold land, which is not considered to have a finite useful life). Consequently, as the value of non-current assets will generally be declining over time, it would be inappropriate or misleading to continually include non-current assets in the financial statements at their original cost. The financial statements try to recognise that the cost of non-current assets is gradually consumed as it wears out – this is done by gradually writing off their cost in the statement of profit or loss and other comprehensive income over their estimated useful economic lives. This process is known as **depreciation**. This annual depreciation charge becomes an expense and is included in the statement of profit or loss and other comprehensive income with other operating expenses in arriving at operating profit/loss for the period.

Depreciation can be defined as the measure of the wearing out, consumption or other reduction in the estimated useful economic life of a non-current asset, whether arising from use, passage of time, or obsolescence through technical or market changes. Depreciation should be allocated so as to charge a fair proportion of cost or valuation of the asset to each accounting period expected to benefit from its use. The total amount of depreciation to be charged in the statement of profit or loss and other comprehensive income – profit or loss is usually its cost less any expected **residual value** at the end of the asset's life. Depreciation can be caused by a number of factors.

Causes of Depreciation

1. Physical Depreciation
   (a) wear and tear – when property, plant and equipment are used they eventually wear out;
   (b) erosion – for example, land may be eroded or wasted by wind, rain or sun, motor vehicles will rust and wood will rot.

2. Economic Factors
   (a) obsolescence – non-current assets can become out of date as more advanced models are introduced;
   (b) inadequacy – a non-current asset may no longer be used because of changes in the size of the firm.

   These economic factors do not necessarily mean the asset is destroyed as it may be possible for it to be used by another company.

3. Time Factor
   Some non-current assets have a fixed legal life (e.g. a building lease or a patent).

4. Depletion
   Some assets have a wasting character, perhaps due to the extraction of raw materials from them (e.g. natural resources, such as mines, oil wells and quarries).

Under the cost model, non-current assets are recorded in the statement of financial position at their cost less accumulated depreciation, with accumulated depreciation being the depreciation charge made in the first year that the asset is owned and used, plus the depreciation charge made in subsequent years of ownership.

Depreciation as an Allocation of Cost Depreciation in total over the life of a non-current asset is simply its cost less the amount received when put out of use (i.e. the asset's scrap or secondhand value). Depreciation allocates cost to each accounting period, but there is no 'true' method of performing this task. Cost should be allocated over the life of the non-current asset in such a way as to charge it as equitably as possible to the periods in which the asset is used. But in practice this has considerable difficulties:

1. apart from a few non-current assets (e.g. a lease), it is not possible to accurately assess an asset's useful economic life;
2. as it is difficult to measure usage (especially in advance), then it is difficult to know how the cost should be apportioned; and
3. other expenses may affect the rate/speed of depreciation (e.g. repairs and maintenance).

The calculation of depreciation is not an exact science and is done mainly as an accounting custom.

Choice of Depreciation Method The purpose of depreciation is to spread the total cost of the asset over the periods in which it is available to be used. The method chosen should be that which allocates cost to each period in accordance with the amount of benefit gained from the use of the asset in the period. The two most common methods are:

1. the straight-line method; and
2. the reducing balance method.

Each of these is now explained in turn.

1. The Straight-line Method The total depreciable amount is charged in equal instalments to each accounting period over the estimated useful life of the asset.

This method of depreciation requires three items of information:

1. original cost of asset (**C**);
2. estimated useful life of asset in years (**N**); and
3. estimated scrap or realisable value at end of useful life (**S**).

The annual depreciation charge (D) is given by:

$$D = \frac{(C - S)}{N}$$

The application of the straight-line method is shown in **Example 6.5**.

EXAMPLE 6.5: STRAIGHT-LINE METHOD OF DEPRECIATION

Original cost of asset	€4,200
Estimated useful life	4 years
Estimated scrap value	€200

Requirement Calculate the annual depreciation charge using the straight-line method.

Solution
Annual depreciation charge:

$$= \frac{€4,200 - €200}{4} = €1,000 \text{ p.a.}$$

The application of the straight-line method is further developed in **Example 6.6**, which illustrates its impact over the estimated useful life of the asset.

EXAMPLE 6.6: STRAIGHT-LINE DEPRECIATION OVER ESTIMATED
USEFUL ECONOMIC LIFE

Cost of asset	€15,000
Estimated useful economic life	3 years
Residual value	€nil

$$\text{Depreciation charge per annum} = \frac{€15,000}{3} = €5,000 \text{ per annum}$$

Therefore, €5,000 is charged to the statement of profit or loss and other comprehensive income – profit or loss each year.

Effect on Statement of Financial Position:

	Year 1	Year 2	Year 3
	€	€	€
Cost of asset	15,000	15,000	15,000
Accumulated depreciation	5,000	10,000	15,000
Carrying value	10,000	5,000	-

The straight-line method of depreciation assumes that the business enjoys equal benefits from the use of the asset in every period throughout its life.

2. The Reducing Balance Method The reducing balance method of depreciation calculates the annual depreciation charge as a fixed percentage of the net book value of the asset as at the end of the previous period. This means that, in the year in which the asset is acquired, the percentage is applied to the original or historical cost. In successive periods, the percentage is applied to the asset's written-down value. The aim of this method is to reduce the net book amount to its scrap value at the end of the estimated useful life of the asset. The application of the reducing balance method is shown in **Example 6.7**.

EXAMPLE 6.7: REDUCING BALANCE METHOD OF DEPRECIATION

An asset, with an estimated useful economic life of four years, cost €1,000. It has an expected nil scrap value and the business depreciates at the rate of 50% reducing balance.

Requirement Calculate the annual depreciation charge.

Solution

	Depreciation Charge €	
Year 1	500	(€1,000 × 50%)
Year 2	250	(€500 × 50%)
Year 3	125	(€250 × 50%)
Year 4	62	(€125 × 50%)
	937	

Note Depreciation in the last year could be increased by (€1,000 – €937) €63 to €125 in order to write the net book value down to its nil scrap value at the end of its useful life. One particular feature of the reducing balance method is that the net book value never equals zero.

The application of the reducing balance method is developed in **Example 6.8**, which illustrates its impact over the estimated useful life of the asset.

EXAMPLE 6.8: REDUCING BALANCE METHOD OF DEPRECIATION OVER
ESTIMATED USEFUL ECONOMIC LIFE

Cost of asset:	€10,000
Residual value:	€2,160
Estimated useful economic life (n):	3 years
Rate of depreciation:	40% reducing balance

(The reducing balance rate of depreciation can be calculated using the following formula:

$$1 - \sqrt[n]{\frac{\text{residual value}}{\text{cost of asset}}}$$

$$1 - \sqrt[3]{\frac{2,160}{10,000}}$$
$$= 0.40)$$

The total depreciable amount is: €10,000 – €2,160 = €7,840

	€
Asset at cost	10,000
Depreciation year 1 (40%)	4,000
Net book value at end year 1	6,000
Depreciation year 2 (40%)	2,400
Net book value at end year 2	3,600
Depreciation year 3 (40%)	1,440
Net book value at end year 3	2,160

Effect on Statement of Financial Position:

	Year 1	Year 2	Year 3
	€	€	€
Cost of asset	10,000	10,000	10,000
Accumulated depreciation	4,000	6,400	7,840
Carrying value	6,000	3,600	2,160

The reducing balance method assumes that the benefits obtained by the business from using the asset decline over time.

But which depreciation method should be used? While there is arguably not a right answer, some guiding factors are as follows:

(a) If the main value is to be obtained in early years, reducing balance may be appropriate as it charges more in early years. The advocates of reducing balance argue that it helps to even out the total charged as expenses for the use of the asset each year (i.e. depreciation is not the only cost charged, there are also running costs and repairs and maintenance that increase with the age of the asset).

Early Years:		Later Years:
Higher depreciation	Approximates to	Lower depreciation
+		+
Lower repairs		Higher repairs

(b) If the benefits are to be gained evenly over the years, the straight-line method would be appropriate.

The *expected pattern of consumption*, *useful life* and *residual value* should be reviewed at least annually. If there has been a significant change in the *expected pattern of consumption* of the asset, the depreciation method should be changed to reflect the changed pattern. This is illustrated in **Example 6.9**. Such a change should be accounted for as a change in an accounting estimate in accordance with IAS 8 *Accounting Policies, Changes in Accounting Estimates and Errors* (see **Chapter 21**), with the carrying amount of the asset at the date of the revision being depreciated over the revised remaining useful economic life of the asset.

EXAMPLE 6.9: CHANGE IN PATTERN OF CONSUMPTION

An item of plant cost €600,000 in March 2010 and was depreciated at 12.5% reducing balance. During the year ended 31 December 2012, the directors changed the method to 20% straight-line in order to give a fairer reflection of consumption of benefits (i.e. an estimated useful economic life of five years). It is company policy to charge a full year's depreciation in the year of acquisition and none in the year of disposal.

Requirement Explain how this should be reflected in the financial statements.

Solution
1. Calculate the net book value at the start of the year of change.
   €600,000 × 87½% × 87½% = €459,375 (i.e. to calculate net book value at 31 December 2011).

2. Write off the net book value over the remaining life using the new method of depreciation in accordance with IAS 8.
   Annual depreciation charge for the year ended 31 December 2012 onwards = €459,375/3* = €153,125.
   *change to 20% − 5 years, less 2010 and 2011 results in 3 years remaining.

If a *useful life* is revised, the carrying amount of the asset at the date of revision should be depreciated over the revised remaining useful life (i.e. there is no retrospective application). Such a change should be accounted for as a change in an accounting estimate in accordance with IAS

8 *Accounting Policies, Changes in Accounting Estimates and Errors* (see **Chapter 21**). Frequently the date of revision is the first day of the year of change. This is illustrated in **Example 6.10**.

EXAMPLE 6.10: CHANGE IN USEFUL LIFE

Team Limited purchased a machine for €800,000 in June 2010. It is company policy to depreciate machinery over 10 years on a straight-line basis, charging a full year in the year of purchase and none in the year of sale. During the year ended 31 March 2013 the useful life of this machine was revised to six years in total because of technological advances.

Requirement Calculate the net book value of the asset at the date of revision (i.e. the start of the year of change – 1 April 2012).

Solution
NBV at 1 April 2012: €800,000 × 80% = €640,000
Write off this amount over the remaining revised useful life: €640,000/4 = €160,000 p.a. (i.e. no retrospective application).

As noted above, once property, plant and equipment is initially recognised and measured at cost in the statement of financial position, an entity must choose either the cost model or the revaluation model for each class of non-current asset (e.g. property, plant, equipment and motor vehicles). The application of the second of these models is now explained.

2. The Revaluation Model

If the revaluation model is adopted, then property, plant and equipment should be carried at a revalued amount in the statement of financial position. This is the **fair value** at the date of the revaluation less any subsequent accumulated **depreciation** and subsequent accumulated **impairment losses**. Fair value is usually the market value as determined by professionally qualified valuers, although they do not have to be independent of the entity. The recording of a fair value increase under IAS 16 is illustrated in **Example 6.11**.

EXAMPLE 6.11: RECORDING A VALUATION ADJUSTMENT

X Limited had buildings with a book value of €142,000 at 31 December 2012 (its year end). On 1 January 2013 the property was professionally valued for the first time at €250,000.

Requirement How should this valuation be recorded in the financial statements of X Limited on 1 January 2013?

Solution

	DR	CR
Accounting entry:		
DR Buildings	€108,000	
CR Revaluation reserve in statement of financial position (and reflected in 'other comprehensive income' in the statement of profit or loss and other comprehensive income – see **Chapter 2, Section 2.3**)		€108,000

> **Note:** in the rare case where there is no recognised market (for example, because items are rarely sold), items should be valued at their depreciated replacement cost (i.e. the cost to replace an asset of similar age and type).

Where an item of property, plant and equipment is revalued, all other assets in the same class should also be revalued. Revaluations should be made with sufficient regularity such that the **carrying amount** does not differ materially from that which would be determined using fair value at the reporting date. Examples of separate classes of asset, for which all assets in that class have to be revalued, include:
• land;
• land and buildings;
• machinery;
• motor vehicles;
• fixtures and fittings; and
• office equipment.

Accounting Treatment of Revaluations

If the *first time* that an asset is revalued that revaluation is *downwards*, then the decrease should be recognised as an expense in the statement of profit or loss and other comprehensive income in arriving at profit/loss for the year. If the *first time* that an asset is revalued that revaluation is *upwards*, then the increase should be credited to the revaluation reserve in the equity section of the statement of financial position and taken through 'other comprehensive income' (for example, under the heading of Gain on Property Revaluation[1]). This is illustrated in **Example 6.12**.

EXAMPLE 6.12: FIRST TIME DOWNWARDS REVALUATION

Ben Limited, a company that prepares its financial statements to 31 March each year, purchased a tangible non-current asset for €200,000 on 1 April 2009. Depreciation is charged at 10% straight-line. The carrying value of the asset at 31 March 2011 is therefore €160,000 before taking account of a revaluation on this date, which showed a valuation of €130,000.

Requirement How should this be reflected in the financial statements of Ben Limited for the years ended 31 March 2011 to 2013?

Solution

		DR	CR
Accounting entry:			
DR	Statement of profit or loss and other comprehensive income – profit or loss – expenses	€30,000	
CR	Tangible non-current assets		€30,000

(Being revaluation loss at 31 March 2011 = €160,000 − €130,000 = €30,000.)

---

[1] The components and presentation of other comprehensive income are explained in **Chapter 2, Section 2.3**.

Depreciation charge per annum for the years ending 31 March 2012 and 2013:
= €130,000/8 = €16,250

It is stated above that if the *first time* an asset is revalued that valuation is *upwards*, then the increase is credited to the revaluation reserve through other comprehensive income. However, if the *first time* that an asset is revalued that valuation is *downwards* (see **Example 6.12**), then any subsequent increase should be recognised in the statement of profit or loss and other comprehensive income in arriving at profit/loss for the year to the extent that it reverses a revaluation decrease of the same asset previously recognised in the statement of profit or loss and other comprehensive income in arriving at profit/loss for the year. Using the information for Ben Limited in **Example 6.12**, **Example 6.13** below illustrates this point.

EXAMPLE 6.13: SUBSEQUENT UPWARDS REVALUATION

Example 6.12 Continued: ... On 31 March 2013, the asset was revalued to €120,000.

Solution:
The carrying value at 31 March 2013 (before taking account of the valuation on this date) is:
€130,000 − (2 × €16,250) = €97,500

Therefore the revaluation increase is €22,500 (€120,000 − €97,500), and the previous downwards revaluation was €30,000.

Accounting entry to reflect valuation at 31 March 2013:
DR	Tangible non-current assets	€22,500	
CR	Statement of profit or loss and other comprehensive income (in arriving at profit/loss for year)		€22,500

Note: a further €7,500 of upward revaluations may still be credited to the statement of profit or loss and other comprehensive income – profit or loss, if there are further revaluations upwards of the same asset in the future.

Example 6.12 illustrates that the *first time* that an asset is revalued, if that valuation is *downwards*, then the revaluation deficit is recognised as an expense in arriving at profit or loss in the statement of profit or loss and other comprehensive income. However, if previous revaluations were upwards (i.e. credited to the revaluation reserve through other comprehensive income), then subsequent downward revaluations can be debited to equity to the extent of any previous reserve in respect of the same asset (i.e. not charged as an expense in the statement of profit or loss and other comprehensive income, as is the case when the first revaluation is downwards). This is illustrated in **Example 6.14**, which also includes the depreciation of revalued assets.

Depreciation of Revalued Assets

The depreciation charge on a revalued asset should be calculated on the carrying amount of the asset (i.e. based on the revalued amount) and charged to the statement of profit or loss and other comprehensive income – profit or loss (see **Example 6.14**).

EXAMPLE 6.14: DEPRECIATION AND REVALUATIONS

Ross Limited, a company that prepares its financial statements to 31 July each year, purchased a property for €1 million on 1 August 2011. The property has a useful life of 20 years and no residual value. Depreciation is charged on a straight-line basis and property is revalued annually. Depreciation is calculated on the opening book value. The property was valued as follows:
- 31 July 2012   €1,064,000; and
- 31 July 2013   € 700,000.

Requirement How should this be reflected in the financial statements of Ross Limited?

Solution

	31 July 2012 €	31 July 2013 €
Cash/opening book value	1,000,000	1,064,000
Depreciation	50,000[1]	56,000[2]
Book value	950,000	1,008,000
Revaluation gain/(loss)	114,000	(308,000)
Recognised in 'other comprehensive income'	114,000	(114,000)
Recognised in arriving at profit/loss	0	(194,000)
Closing book value	1,064,000	700,000

[1] €1,000,000 ÷ 20 years
[2] €1,064,000 ÷ 19 years

Treatment of Accumulated Depreciation at Date of Revaluation

When an item of property, plant and equipment is revalued, any accumulated depreciation at the date of revaluation is treated in either of the following ways.

Method 1 The accumulated depreciation is restated proportionately with the gross carrying amount, so that the carrying amount after revaluation equals the revalued amount (see **Example 6.15**).

Method 2 The accumulated depreciation is eliminated against the gross carrying amount and the net amount restated to the revalued amount of the asset (see **Example 6.15**).

EXAMPLE 6.15: ACCUMULATED DEPRECIATION AT DATE OF REVALUATION

Top Limited has a building with the following carrying value at 1 January 2012:

	€
Cost	500,000
Cumulative depreciation	100,000
Carrying value	400,000

The building is revalued on 1 January 2012 to €800,000.

Requirement Show how this should be reflected in the financial statements of Top Limited for the year ended 31 December 2012 using both Method 1 and Method 2.

Solution

Method 1 of treating accumulated depreciation:

	Before Revaluation	After Revaluation
	€	€
Cost/revalued amount	500,000	1,000,000
Cumulative depreciation	100,000	200,000
	400,000	800,000

Accounting Entry
DR   Buildings   €500,000
   CR   Cumulative depreciation   €100,000
   CR   Revaluation reserve   €400,000

Buildings

	€		€
Balance b/d	500,000		
Revaluation reserve	500,000	Balance c/d	1,000,000
	1,000,000		1,000,000

Accumulated Depreciation

	€		€
Balance c/d	200,000	Balance b/d	100,000
		Revaluation reserve	100,000
	200,000		200,000

Method 2 of treating accumulated depreciation:

	Before Revaluation	After Revaluation
	€	€
Cost/revalued amount	500,000	800,000
Cumulative depreciation	100,000	–
Carrying amount	400,000	800,000

Accounting Entries
DR   Cumulative depreciation   €100,000
   CR   Buildings   €100,000
DR   Buildings   €400,000
   CR   Revaluation reserve   €400,000

Buildings			
	€		€
Balance b/d	500,000	Accumulated depreciation	100,000
Revaluation reserve	400,000	Balance c/d	800,000
	900,000		900,000

Accumulated Depreciation			
	€		€
Buildings	100,000	Balance b/d	100,000
	100,000		100,000

Depreciation and the Revaluation Reserve

As explained above, in broad terms, if an asset is revalued upwards, then its carrying value increases and a revaluation reserve is created. Two points should be noted as a result of this:

1. as the depreciation charge is based on a 'higher' revalued amount, then the charge to the statement of profit or loss and other comprehensive income – profit or loss will typically be higher than if the cost model was applied; and
2. as the asset is depreciated its carrying value declines, but the revaluation reserve remains the same.

Consequently, IAS 16 gives companies the *option* of transferring some of the gain/surplus from the revaluation reserve to retained earnings (through the statement of changes in equity) to offset the additional depreciation. The amount of the surplus transferred is the difference between depreciation based on the revalued carrying amount of the asset and depreciation based on the asset's original cost (see **Example 6.17** below).

Derecognition

The carrying amount of an item of property, plant and equipment should be derecognised (i.e. removed from the statement of financial position) under the following circumstances:
(a) when the asset is disposed of (i.e. sold or traded-in); or
(b) when no future economic benefits are expected from its use or disposal (i.e. scrapped).

The gain or loss arising from derecognition of an item of property, plant and equipment should be included in arriving at operating profit in the statement of profit or loss and other comprehensive income. The gain or loss arising from the derecognition of an item of property, plant and equipment should be determined as the difference between the net disposal proceeds, if any, and the carrying amount of the item. These points are illustrated in **Example 6.16**.

EXAMPLE 6.16: DISPOSAL OF AN ASSET

FIXIT Limited is preparing its financial statements for the year ended 31 December 2012. A van, which had cost €5,000 and had a net book value of €2,813 at 1 January 2012, was traded in on 1 March 2012 as a part exchange for the purchase of a new van, which cost €7,800. A cheque for €5,800 was paid by the company to complete the purchase. Depreciation is charged on vans at 25% per annum on a straight-line basis. A full year's depreciation is to be charged in the year of purchase and none in the year of sale.

Requirement Prepare the journal entries necessary to record the above in the company's financial statements for the year ended 31 December 2012.

Solution	DR	CR
	€	€
Vans – Cost of Additions	5,800	
Bank		5,800
Cheque payment for acquisition of new van		
Vans – Cost of Additions	2,000	
Disposal account		2,000
Accumulated depreciation – Vans	2,187	
Disposal account	2,813	
Vans – Cost of disposals		5,000
Depreciation charge – Vans (€ 7,800 × 25%)	1,950	
Accumulated depreciation – Vans		1,950

This results in a loss on disposal of the van of €813 (i.e. €2,813−€2,000).

Any revaluation surplus included in equity in respect of an item of property, plant and equipment that has been revalued upwards should be transferred directly to retained earnings when the asset is disposed of or sold. Transfers from revaluation surplus to retained earnings are not made through profit or loss.

Example 6.17 combines a number of the issues discussed above. It includes the purchase of an asset, together with its subsequent depreciation, revaluation and disposal. It also illustrates the transfer of a portion of the revaluation reserve to retained earnings (through the statement of changes in equity) to offset the higher depreciation charge.

EXAMPLE 6.17: PURCHASE, DEPRECIATION, REVALUATION AND DISPOSAL

JD Limited, a company that prepares its financial statements to 31 December each year, revalues its property every two years. It is company policy to charge a full year's depreciation in the year of acquisition and none in the year of disposal. Before the change on 31 December 2009 (see below), property was depreciated at 20% p.a. using the reducing balance method.

- 1 January 2008: property purchased at a cost of €390,000.
- 31 December 2009: property revalued to €275,000, with remaining useful economic life revised to 4 years from 1 January 2010 and depreciation method being changed to straight line.
- 31 December 2011: property revalued to €112,500, with decline believed to be permanent.
- 30 September 2012: property sold for €125,000.

Requirement How would the property be reflected in the company's financial statements in each of the years ending 31 December 2008 to 2012, assuming that JD Limited opts to transfer a portion of any revaluation surplus from the revaluation reserve to offset the additional depreciation?

Solution

		€
Cost		390,000
Depreciation @ 20% (RB)	(Charged to SPLOCI – P/L)	(78,000)
NBV at 31/12/08		312,000
2009:		
Depreciation @ 20% (RB)	(Charged to SPLOCI – P/L)	(62,400)
		249,600
Revalued at 31/12/09	(Recognised in SPLOCI – OCI and revaluation reserve)	25,400
NBV at 31/12/09		275,000
2010:		
Depreciation @ 25% (SL)	(W1 – see below)	(68,750)
NBV at 31/12/10		206,250
2011:		
Depreciation @ 25%	(Straight-line depreciation)	(68,750)
NBV at 31/12/11		137,500
Revaluation loss	(The revaluation reserve balance of €19,050 is debited to OCI (W2) and the remaining €5,950 is charged to the statement of profit or loss and other comprehensive income in arriving at profit or loss.)	(25,000)
		112,500
2012:		
30/9/12 proceeds		(125,000)
Profit on disposal		12,500

(W1)		€
Depreciation based on historical cost	(€249,600/4 years)	62,400
Depreciation based on valuation		(68,750)
Transfer from revaluation reserve to retained earnings (through the statement of changes in equity)		6,350

(W2)

Revaluation reserve balance = €19,050 (€25,400 less amount transferred in 2009 of €6,350).

This section has covered a substantial volume of material and it is likely that it will have to be read (and re-read) on a number of occasions in order to fully grasp all of the issues covered. While the following example is relatively straightforward, certainly in the context of all that has been covered in this section, part (a) is nonetheless a useful test of whether at least the fundamental principles have been understood. Part (b), which involves basic analysis and interpretation of financial statements (see **Chapter 35**), encourages students to think beyond the pure IAS 16 accounting adjustments and consider their overall impact on the financial statements.

EXAMPLE 6.18: SUMMARY OF BASIC PRINCIPLES

The directors of Tiny Limited are considering recording the three properties that the company owns and uses at valuation. The following information is available with respect to these properties, each of which was deemed to have a useful economic life at its date of acquisition:

	Original Cost €000	Accumulated Depreciation at 31 December 2012 €000	Valuation at 31 December 2012 €000
Property Alpha	640	256	240
Property Beta	480	192	240
Property Gamma	720	288	560

Alpha has fallen into a poor state of repair in recent years. Beta, however, although located in an area that has experienced poor market conditions in recent years, has been well-maintained.

Gamma is in a reasonable state of repair and is located in an area that has experienced rising property prices in recent years.

Requirement
(a) Describe the impact on Tiny Limited's 2012 financial statements if the directors decide to record these properties at valuation.
(b) Explain clearly how the revaluation policy may affect Tiny Limited's key accounting ratios. (While the analysis and interpretation of financial statements is dealt with in detail in **Chapter 35**, after having studied this chapter and **Chapter 2**, students should be able to reflect on the impact of the valuation adjustments on the financial statements of Tiny Limited.)

Solution
Based upon the informatiion provided, all of the properties appear to have been depreciated for 10 years out of an estimated 25-year life.

	NBV €000	Market Value €000	Difference €000
Property Alpha		240	(144)
Property Beta	384	240	(48)
Property Gamma	288	560	128
	432	1,040	
	1,104		

(a)
Property Alpha: a loss on revaluation of €144,000 arises. There is no revaluation reserve to offset the loss, therefore it should be charged to the statement of profit or loss and other comprehensive income in arriving at operating profit/loss.

Property Beta: a loss on revaluation of €48,000 arises. There is no revaluation reserve to offset the loss, therefore it should be charged to the statement of profit or loss and other comprehensive income in arriving at operating profit/loss.

Property Gamma: a gain on revaluation of €128,000 arises. The gain should be credited to other comprehensive income in the statement of profit or loss and other comprehensive income.

(b)
Return on Capital Employed (ROCE) = Net profit/Capital employed

An increase in valuation means an increased depreciation charge and increased capital employed. In Tiny Limited's case, there has been a net decrease in property values and therefore Tiny Limited is likely to experience an increase in ROCE.

Gearing = Non-current debt/(Shareholders' funds + Non-current debt)

As Tiny Limited has experienced a net fall in valuation, the 'bottom line' falls in value without any change to the 'top line', therefore the gearing ratio will increase.

6.3 OTHER ISSUES

Separate Components

Some items of property, plant and equipment comprise separate components with different useful lives. For example, an airplane might itself have a life of 30 years, while the seats and fabric in the interior only have a life of five years. In such situations the separate components should be capitalised as separate assets and each depreciated over its useful life.

Major Inspection or Overhaul Costs

Normally, all inspection and overhaul costs are expensed as they are incurred. However, to the extent that they relate to a separate component of an item of property, plant and equipment, such costs should be capitalised separately as a non-current asset and depreciated over their useful lives. To use the example of the seats and fabric in an airplane from above: every five years the cost of overhauling the interior of the plane should be capitalised as a non-current asset and depreciated over the five-year period before the next overhaul is carried out.

Servicing Equipment

In May 2012, IAS 16 *Property, Plant and Equipment* was amended to allow items such as spare parts, stand-by equipment and servicing equipment to qualify as property, plant and equipment when these items are used during more than one accounting period; otherwise they are classified as inventory. The change is applicable to annual accounting periods beginning on or after 1 January 2013.

Disclosure Requirements

The purpose of accounting disclosure is to inform both current and potential investors of the accounting policies and methods used when preparing published financial statements.

These financial statements include, but are not limited to, the statement of financial position, statement of profit or loss and other comprehensive income, statement of cash flows and the statement of changes in equity. A wide variety of stakeholders (for example, investors, creditors and providers of finance) rely on organisations disclosing complete and accurate accounting information in order to make decisions based upon published financial reports. Answers to important questions can be gleaned from the financial statements; for example, whether the company has adequate capacity to meet demand, whether non-current assets will have to be replaced, and therefore financed, in the near future and whether there is adequate cash on hand to expand current projects. In this regard, IAS 16 has extensive disclosure requirements. These include:

(a) measurement bases used (i.e. cost or valuation);
(b) depreciation methods used;
(c) useful lives or depreciation rates used;
(d) gross carrying amount and accumulated depreciation, at the beginning and end of the period;
(e) reconciliation of opening and closing figures, with details of additions, disposals and depreciation;
(f) details of any pledging of items of property, plant and equipment as security for liabilities;
(g) commitments for future capital expenditure;
(h) if the asset has been revalued:
     (i) basis of valuation;
     (ii) date of valuation;
     (iii) whether an independent valuer was used;
     (iv) the carrying value of the assets if no revaluation had taken place; and
     (v) the revaluation surplus.

6.4 CONCLUSION

The main purpose of this chapter is to explain the accounting treatment of property, plant and equipment that falls under the scope of IAS 16. Given its importance in the context of financial accounting, and the volume of material covered in the chapter, it is worthwhile recapping the issues addressed. The chapter begins by discussing the initial recognition and measurement of property, plant and equipment, including the elements of expenditure that are included in their cost. The cost and revaluation models, which are applicable following initial recognition, are then explained. Issues associated with depreciation are examined, including its definition, purpose and common methods of calculation, together with how to account for a change in depreciation method and useful economic life of property, plant and equipment. The chapter also covers the accounting treatment of revaluation gains and losses with respect to property, plant and equipment, and illustrates the circumstances when an amount may be transferred from the revaluation reserve to retained earnings (through the statement of changes in equity). Finally, the main disclosure requirements of IAS 16 are outlined.

Given the importance of this chapter, it is worthwhile reflecting on the brief summary above and considering whether aspects of this chapter need to be revisited.

SUMMARY OF LEARNING OBJECTIVES

Having studied this chapter on property, plant and equipment, you should be able to:

Learning Objective 1 Discuss the elements of expenditure that are included in the cost of property, plant and equipment.

Property, plant and equipment should be initially recognised at cost. This is the amount of cash or cash equivalents paid or the fair value of the other consideration given to acquire the asset at the time of its acquisition or construction. It typically includes:
- the purchase price, including import duties and non-refundable purchase taxes, after deducting trade discounts and rebates; and
- any costs directly attributable to bringing the asset to the location and condition necessary for it to be capable of operating in the manner intended by management.

Learning Objective 2 Define depreciation.

Depreciation is the measure of the wearing out, consumption, or other reduction in the estimated useful economic life of a non-current asset, whether arising from use, passage of time, or obsolescence through technical or market changes. Depreciation seeks to allocate the cost or valuation of an asset over its estimated useful economic life. The method of depreciation used must reflect the pattern in which the asset's future economic benefits are expected to be consumed.

Learning Objective 3 Account for a change in depreciation method.

Such a change should be accounted for as a change in an accounting estimate in accordance with IAS 8 *Accounting Policies, Changes in Accounting Estimates and Errors* (see **Chapter 21**).

Learning Objective 4 Apply the required accounting treatment if the estimated useful economic life of a non-current asset is revised.

The carrying amount of the asset at the date of revision should be depreciated over the revised remaining useful life (i.e. there is no retrospective application). Such a change should be accounted for as a change in an accounting estimate in accordance with IAS 8 *Accounting Policies, Changes in Accounting Estimates and Errors* (see **Chapter 21**).

Learning Objective 5 Explain when property, plant and equipment may be revalued.

Once property, plant and equipment is initially recognised and measured at cost in the statement of financial position, an entity must choose either the cost model or revaluation model for each class of non-current asset (for example, property, plant, equipment and motor vehicles).

Learning Objective 6 Account for revaluation gains and losses with respect to property, plant and equipment.

If an asset's carrying amount is increased as a result of a revaluation, the increase should be credited to the revaluation reserve in the equity section of the statement of financial position through other comprehensive income in the statement of profit or loss and other comprehensive income. If an asset's carrying amount is decreased as a result of a revaluation, the decrease should be recognised as an expense in the statement of profit or loss and other comprehensive income in arriving at profit/loss for the year. However, an increase should be recognised in the statement of profit or loss and other comprehensive income in arriving at profit/loss for the year to the extent that it reverses a revaluation decrease of the same asset previously recognised in the statement of profit or loss and other comprehensive income in arriving at profit/loss for the year.

Learning Objective 7 Understand and account for the circumstances when an amount may be transferred from the revaluation reserve to retained earnings (through the statement of changes in equity).

IAS 16 gives companies the *option* of transferring some of the gain/surplus from the revaluation reserve to offset the additional depreciation. The amount of the surplus transferred is the difference between depreciation based on the revalued carrying amount of the asset and depreciation based on the asset's original cost.

Learning Objective 8 Apply the main disclosure requirements of IAS 16 *Property, Plant and Equipment*, including those required when property, plant and equipment is revalued.

These include the measurement bases used (e.g. cost or valuation), the depreciation methods used, the useful lives or depreciation rates used and a reconciliation of opening and closing figures with details of additions, disposals and depreciation.

QUESTIONS

Self-test Questions

1. What elements of expenditure are included in the production cost of a non-current asset?
2. What disclosures are required when a non-current asset is revalued?
3. In what circumstances may an amount be transferred from the revaluation reserve to retained earnings?
4. What is depreciation?
5. What accounting treatment is required if the estimated useful life of a fixed asset is revised?

Review Questions

(See **Appendix One** for Suggested Solutions to Review Questions.)

Question 6.1

You have just been given the tangible non-current assets section from the audit file of WELLER Limited (WELLER) in relation to the financial statements for the year ended 31 December 2012, with a note from the partner-in-charge asking you to clear the outstanding review points.

Review point 1 WELLER owns two freehold properties, one in Derry and the other in Cork. The company uses both as regional administrative offices. The properties had an expected useful life of 50 years on their date of acquisition, and the directors believe that this assumption is still appropriate at 31 December 2012. It is company policy to depreciate the properties on a straight-line basis over their estimated useful economic life.

	Derry property	Cork property
Date of acquisition	1 January 2003	1 January 2003
Original cost	€5,000,000	€5,000,000
Net book value at 31 December 2012	€4,000,000	€4,000,000
Market value at 31 December 2012	€3,000,000	€7,000,000

In the financial statements for the year ended 31 December 2012, the directors of WELLER are proposing to show the Cork property at market value and the Derry property at its depreciated historic cost. The directors believe the fall in the market value of the Derry property is only temporary and property values in the Derry area will rise in the next one to two years.

Is the policy put forward by the directors of WELLER acceptable?

Review point 2 On 1 January 2012, WELLER entered into a contract with a building company to build a new manufacturing facility for the company at a cost of €10,000,000. In order to finance the cost of the contract, WELLER entered into a short-term loan agreement with its bankers to borrow €10,000,000 at an interest rate of 6% per annum for the year that the manufacturing facility would take to build. The manufacturing facility was completed on 31 December 2012 and the loan was repaid on the same date. As WELLER's profits for the year ended 31 December 2012 are lower than expected, the directors of WELLER wish to capitalise the loan interest paid.

Is the policy put forward by the directors of WELLER acceptable?

Review point 3 On 1 July 2012, WELLER signed, as tenant, an operating lease of a warehouse, which it intends to use as a distribution depot. However the warehouse needed to be fitted out before it could be used. The monthly rental for the warehouse is €10,000, commencing on 1 July 2012. The fitting was completed on 1 December 2012 and the warehouse became operational on this date. The directors of WELLER wish to capitalise the rent paid during the five-month fitting-out period, together with the cost of the fixtures and fittings.

Is the policy put forward by the directors of WELLER acceptable?

Review point 4 TAYLOR Limited (TAYLOR) is also an audit client of your firm. The company operates in the same business as WELLER and is similar in size. Both companies purchased identical equipment from the same supplier on 1 January 2011 at a cost of €6,000,000. Shown below are extracts from the tangible non-current assets Notes of both companies in respect of this equipment.

	WELLER	TAYLOR
	€	€
Plant and equipment – cost	6,000,000	6,000,000
Plant and equipment – accumulated depreciation	(2,400,000)	(1,500,000)
Net book value at 31 December 2012	3,600,000	4,500,000

What are the possible reasons for the difference in the net book value of the equipment held by the two companies at 31 December 2012 and what problems might this present when reading and comparing financial statements?

Review point 5 In 2000, WELLER purchased freehold land that it carries in its financial statements at its original cost of €1,000,000 without charging depreciation.

Are there valid reasons for the policy of non-depreciation of freehold land?

Requirement Prepare a memorandum addressed to the partner-in-charge of the audit of WELLER addressing the issues raised in each of the review points.

Question 6.2

During 2012, Tiny Limited decided to update and network the company's computer equipment. The details are as follows:

	€
List price of computer hardware	500,000
Additional costs:	
Shipping and handling	20,000
Four-year on-site maintenance contract	80,000
One month testing prior to going live	10,000
Cabling and wiring	30,000
Own staff costs related to preparation of offices prior to installation	16,000

With respect to the computer hardware, Tiny Limited negotiated a 10% trade discount on the list price and took advantage of a 5% early settlement discount for payment within 30 days.

Requirement Calculate the initial cost at which the computer equipment should be included in Tiny Limited's 2012 financial statements.

Challenging Questions

(Suggested Solutions to Challenging Questions are available to lecturers.)

Question 6.1

Seamus plc manufactures and operates a fleet of small aircraft. It draws up its financial statements to 31 March each year.

Seamus plc also owns a small chain of hotels (carrying value of €16 million), which are used in the sale of holidays to the public. It is the policy of the company not to provide depreciation on the hotels as they are maintained to a high standard and the economic lives of the hotels are long (20 years' remaining life). The hotels are periodically revalued and on 31 March 2010, their existing use value was determined to be €20 million, the replacement cost of the hotels was €16 million and the open market value was €19 million. One of the hotels included above is surplus to the company's requirements as at 31 March 2010. This hotel had an existing use value of €3 million, a replacement cost of €2 million and an open market value of €2.5 million, before expected estate agent's and solicitor's fees of €200,000. The company wishes to revalue the hotels as at 31 March 2010.

There is no indication of any impairment in the value of the hotels.

The company has recently finished manufacturing a fleet of five aircraft to a new design. These aircraft are intended for use in its own fleet for domestic carriage purposes. The company commenced construction of the assets on 1 April 2008 and wishes to recognise them as fixed assets as at 31 March 2010, when they were first utilised. The aircraft were completed on 1 January 2010, but their exterior painting was delayed until 31 March 2010.

The costs (excluding finance costs) of manufacturing the aircraft amounted to €28 million and the company has adopted a policy of capitalising the finance costs of manufacturing the aircraft. On 1 April 2008, Seamus plc had taken out a three-year loan of €20 million to finance the aircraft. Interest is payable at 10% per annum, but is to be rolled over and paid at the end of the three-year period, together with the capital outstanding. Corporation tax is 30%.

During the construction of the aircraft, certain computerised components used in the manufacture fell dramatically in price. The company estimated that at 31 March 2010, the net realisable value of the aircraft was €30 million and their value in use was €29 million.

The engines used in the aircraft have a three-year life and the body parts have an eight-year life; Seamus plc has decided to depreciate the engines and the body parts over their different useful lives on the straight-line basis from 1 April 2010. The cost of replacing the engines on 31 March 2013 is estimated to be €15 million. The engine costs represent 30% of the total cost of manufacture.

The company has decided to revalue the aircraft annually on the basis of their market value. On 31 March 2011 the aircraft have a value in use of €28 million, a market value of €27 million and a net realisable value of €26 million. On 31 March 2012 the aircraft have a value in use of €17 million, a market value of €18 million and a net realisable value of €18.5 million. There is no consumption of economic benefits in 2012 other than the depreciation charge. Revaluation surpluses or deficits are apportioned between the engines and the body parts on the basis of their year end carrying values before the revaluation.

Requirement
(a) Explain how the hotels should be valued in the financial statements of Seamus plc on 31 March 2010 and explain whether the current depreciation policy relating to the hotels is acceptable under IAS 16 *Property, Plant and Equipment*.
(b) Show the accounting treatment of the aircraft fleet in the financial statements on the basis of the above scenario for the financial years ending on:
  (i) 31 March 2010;
  (ii) 31 March 2011 and 2012;
  (iii) 31 March 2013, before revaluation.

(c) Discuss the economic consequences of asset revaluations.

Question 6.2 (Based on Chartered Accountants Ireland, CAP 2 Summer 2010, Question 3)

Note: this question covers a number of related issues, some of which are covered more fully in other chapters. Consequently, before attempting this question, you should also study **Chapter 5** and **Chapter 7**.

PROVINCE Limited ("PROVINCE"), an Irish company that prepares its financial statements to 31 December each year, is involved in a range of different leisure-related activities throughout Ireland. At 31 December **2012**, the company owned four properties: Connacht, Leinster, Munster and Ulster. Further information on these properties is provided below.

On 1 January **2011**, PROVINCE acquired Connacht and Leinster, two sites located in out-of-town shopping centres, with the intention of building a multi-screen cinema on each. Construction on each site commenced on 1 January 2011 and was completed on 31 December 2011. Details of the costs associated with the construction are as follows:

	Connacht	Leinster
	€000	€000
Land	1,000	900
Direct materials	800	700
Direct labour	200	150
Direct overheads	130	120
	2,130	1,870

PROVINCE financed the construction of Connacht and Leinster by issuing a €5,000,000 zero coupon bond on 1 January 2011. The bond is redeemable on 31 December 2014 with a one-off payment of €6,802,721. While both properties were brought into use on 1 January 2012, Connacht was retained by PROVINCE for use as a cinema and Leinster was let at a commercial rent to an unrelated company that was able to easily convert the property into a 10-pin bowling alley.

PROVINCE owns two successful four-star country hotels, Munster and Ulster, and the company intends to develop this specialist part of its business. These two properties were professionally valued on 1 January 2012, the details of which are as follows:

	Historical Cost	Historical Cost Net Book Value	Current Use Value	Market Value
	€000	€000	€000	€000
Munster	37,500	22,500	17,500	18,750
Ulster	40,000	24,000	28,000	30,000

The buildings element of Munster and Ulster represents 50% of both the historical cost and revalued amounts, and their remaining useful economic life at 1 January 2012 was 30 years. It was company policy to record all owned properties at historical cost and to depreciate them over their estimated useful economic life of 50 years on a straight-line basis. However, with effect from 1 January 2012, the directors of PROVINCE have decided to record Munster and Ulster at valuation in the financial statements. The directors do not intend to obtain valuations for Connacht and Leinster, or other non-current assets held by the company. It is company policy to include finance costs in the cost of non-current assets, where permitted by extant international accounting standards.

Requirement
(a) Explain whether PROVINCE is permitted to record Munster and Ulster at valuation and other non-current assets, including Connacht and Leinster, at depreciated historical cost.

(b) Based on the information provided, show the amounts that should be included in the statements of profit or loss and other comprehensive income of PROVINCE for the years ended 31 December 2011 and 2012, and the statements of financial position as at those dates, in respect of the four properties.

Question 6.3

You are the management accountant of Psychedelic Limited, a company that makes up its financial statements to 30 September each year. The financial statements for the year ended 30 September 2012 are currently being prepared. The directors have always included non-current assets under the historical cost convention. However, for the current year they are considering revaluing some of the non-current assets. They obtained professional valuations as at 1 October 2011 for the two properties owned by the company. Details of the valuations were as follows:

	Historical cost NBV	Current use value	Market value
	€000	€000	€000
Property One	15,000	16,800	17,500
Property Two	14,000	12,000	12,500

No acquisitions or disposals of properties have taken place since 1 October 2011 and none is expected in the near future. The buildings element of the two properties comprises 50% of both historical cost and the revalued amounts. Each property is believed to have a useful economic life to the company of 40 years from 1 October 2011.

Given the results of the valuations, the directors propose to include Property One at its market value in the financial statements for the year to 30 September 2012. They wish to leave Property Two at its historical cost. They have no plans to revalue the other non-current assets of the company, which are plant and fixtures.

Requirement
(a) Evaluate the directors' proposal to revalue Property One as at 1 October 2011 but to leave all other non-current assets at historical cost.
(b) The directors have decided to revalue the non-current assets of the company in accordance with their original wishes, amended, where necessary, to comply with appropriate IFRSs. Calculate the carrying value of each property as at 30 September 2012. You should clearly explain where any differences on revaluation will be shown in the financial statements.

7

BORROWING COSTS

Learning Objectives

After having studied this chapter on borrowing costs, you should:
1. Be able to discuss the arguments for and against the capitalisation of borrowing costs;
2. Understand and be able to apply the accounting treatment for qualifying borrowing costs;
3. Understand and be able to apply when capitalisation of borrowing costs can begin and when it must end; and
4. Apply the main disclosure requirements of IAS 23 *Borrowing Costs*.

Key Terms and Definitions for this Chapter

In order to aid your understanding of the concepts and issues covered in this chapter, it is important to understand and be familiar with the following key terms and definitions. As you study this chapter, you should refer back to them.

Borrowing Costs Interest and other costs incurred by an entity in connection with the borrowing of funds. Examples of borrowing costs include:
- interest on bank overdrafts and other short-term and long-term borrowings;
- amortisation of discounts and premiums on borrowings;
- finance charges in respect of finance leases (IAS 17 *Leases*); and
- exchange differences arising from foreign currency borrowings when they cause adjustments to interest costs.

Non-current Asset This is an asset acquired for use within the business, with a view to earning profits from its use. A non-current asset is not acquired for resale and includes property, plant and equipment. Non-current assets are usually held and used by a business for a number of years.

Qualifying Asset An asset that necessarily takes a substantial period of time to get ready for its intended use or sale. For example, a property or bridge that has to be constructed.

7.1 INTRODUCTION

The capital structure of a business refers to the way it is financed. In simple terms, there are two types of capital: debt (or borrowing) and equity. Each has its own advantages and disadvantages, and it is the job of management to try to find the perfect debt/equity ratio for the business in terms of the risk/return payoff for shareholders. The term 'debt' refers to borrowed money and while there are different types of debt, each will require some form of interest to be paid (i.e. the return for the lender). Equity is the money put into the business by the shareholders (i.e. owners of the business). Typically, equity consists of two types: first, money given in exchange for shares; and secondly, retained earnings, which represent profits from past years not withdrawn from the business by shareholders in the form of dividends. It is often argued that equity capital is more expensive than debt because the cost of equity is essentially the return that the business must earn in order to get investors to buy shares in the company. Hence, debt financing can be very attractive and, some would argue, cost-effective.

It is argued that **borrowing costs** (i.e. interest) are an inevitable cost of funding the day-to-day activities of an organisation and therefore should prudently be considered an expense in the statement of profit or loss and other comprehensive income, rather than the statement of financial position, on the basis that they do not meet the definition of an asset provided in the *Conceptual Framework for Financial Reporting 2010* (see **Chapter 2**). However, others argue that **non-current assets** often require considerable funds to finance their construction and that borrowing costs incurred during the construction phase can reasonably be considered a necessary cost of bringing a non-current asset to its present location and condition so that it has the ability to generate revenue. It therefore holds that borrowing costs are as much a legitimate cost as materials or labour used in the construction of an asset, the cost of which would be capitalised (i.e. included in the cost of the asset in the statement of financial position and not expensed in the statement of profit or loss and other comprehensive income). One way of justifying the capitalisation of borrowing costs is that if an organisation acquired a completed non-current asset (for example, a property), the construction company is likely to have included its borrowing costs during the construction phase when determining the selling price and the buyer would legitimately capitalise the full acquisition cost. Therefore, if a company constructs a property itself, it seems logical that the interest cost that it incurs in doing so should also be capitalised.

While there is a legitimate argument for capitalising borrowing costs incurred during the construction phase of a non-current asset on the basis that these costs provide future economic benefits consistent with the definition of an asset in the *Conceptual Framework for Financial Reporting 2010* (see **Chapter 2**), clear rules are needed to ensure that on-going borrowing costs related to day-to-day operations do not disappear altogether from the statement of profit or loss and other comprehensive income. Lest we forget, capitalising revenue-related costs was one of the techniques used by WorldCom to lower costs and enhance earnings. In 2002, WorldCom, an American telecommunications company, announced that it had overstated profits in 2001 and the first quarter of 2002 by more than $3.8 billion. This was achieved largely by classifying payments for using other companies' communications networks as capital expenditure (i.e. an asset) rather than an expense. By capitalising part of a current expense, WorldCom increased both its net profit (since expenses were understated) and its assets (since these were capitalised as such in the statement of financial position). Had it not been detected, capitalising expenses would have enabled the company to spread its current expenses into the future through depreciation.

Key to this Chapter

The aim of this chapter is to explain when borrowing costs should be capitalised in the statement of financial position as part of the cost of a qualifying asset. The focus is on explaining when the capitalisation of borrowing costs should begin and when it must end, together with the application of the accounting treatment for qualifying borrowing costs in accordance with IAS 23 *Borrowing Costs*. The main disclosure requirements of IAS 23 are also outlined. The key points to remember when reading the chapter are that:
- the borrowing costs must be directly attributable to the construction of the qualifying asset;
- capitalisation begins when construction work begins;
- capitalisation is suspended when work is interrupted; and
- capitalisation ceases when work on the construction is substantially completed.

7.2 IAS 23 *BORROWING COSTS*

The Objective of IAS 23

The objective of IAS 23 *Borowing Costs* is to prescribe the accounting treatment for borrowing costs. This standard *requires* the capitalisation of borrowing costs that are directly attributable to the acquisition, construction or production of a **qualifying asset**.

Accounting Treatment

IAS 23 states that borrowing costs *must be* capitalised as part of the cost of an asset when:
1. it is probable that the costs will result in future economic benefits and the costs can be reliably measured (in accordance with the definition of an asset provided in the *Conceptual Framework for Financial Reporting 2010* (see **Chapter 2**); and
2. they are directly attributable and they would have been avoided if the asset was not bought, constructed or produced.

This is illustrated in **Example 7.1** below.

Period of Capitalisation of Borrowing Costs

The key points are as follows:
1. capitalisation of borrowing costs should commence when expenditure on the asset and borrowing costs are being incurred;
2. capitalisation of borrowing costs should be suspended during extended periods in which active development is interrupted; and
3. capitalisation should cease when substantially all the activities necessary to prepare the relevant asset for its intended use have been completed.

These points are illustrated in **Example 7.1**.

EXAMPLE 7.1: CAPITALISATION OF BORROWING COSTS

On 1 January 2012, X began to construct a supermarket. It purchased a leasehold interest in the site for €25 million. The construction of the building cost €9 million and the fixtures and fittings cost €6 million. The construction of the supermarket was completed on 30 September 2012 and it was available for use from 1 January 2013.

X borrowed €40 million on 1 January 2012 in order to finance this project. The loan carried interest at 10% per annum. It was repaid on 30 June 2013.

Requirement Calculate the total amount to be included in property, plant and equipment in respect of the development at 31 December 2012.

Solution

The total amount to be included in property, plant and equipment at 31 December 2012 is:

	€m
Lease	25
Building	9
Fittings	6
Interest capitalised ($40 \times 10\% \times 9/12$)	3
Carrying value	43

Only nine months' interest can be capitalised because IAS 23 states that capitalisation of borrowing costs must cease when substantially all of the activity necessary to prepare the asset for its intended use or sale is complete. The interest incurred from the date the construction was completed to the date when the loan is repaid is charged to the statement of profit or loss and other comprehensive income – profit or loss (SPLOCI – P/L). No depreciation is charged in 2012, because the supermarket was not available for use until 1 January 2013.

Where borrowings relate *specifically* to expenditure on an asset, the amount of borrowing costs that should be capitalised are the actual costs less any investment income received from the temporary reinvestment of unutilised borrowings (i.e. borrowings drawn down but not yet spent and therefore available for investment until required). This is illustrated in **Example 7.2**.

EXAMPLE 7.2: REINVESTING SURPLUS FUNDS

Onora Limited prepares its financial statements to 31 December each year. On 1 January 2011, Onora Limited entered into a contract with a construction company to build a new distribution depot for the company at a cost of €15 million. In order to finance the contract, Onora Limited borrowed €15 million at an interest rate of 6% per annum. While the depot was expected to be completed by 31 March 2012, delays were incurred as a result of extremely inclement weather during the period 1 December 2011 to 28 February 2012, during which no construction work was possible. During this period, however, the directors of Onora Limited invested the surplus funds, earning interest of €24,000. The distribution depot was completed on 31 May 2012 and Onora Limited repaid the loan in full on 30 June 2012.

Requirement Illustrate how Onora Limited should reflect the above in its 2011 and 2012 financial statements.

Solution

As noted above, the key points to remember:
- borrowing costs must be directly attributable to the construction of the qualifying asset;
- capitalisation begins when construction work begins;
- capitalisation is suspended when work is interrupted; and
- capitalisation ceases when work on construction is substantially completed.

Commencement date:	1 January 2011
Completion date:	31 May 2012
Construction period:	17 months, but with one month suspended in 2011 and two months in 2012

2011:
Total interest – €15m × 6% = €900,000
Capitalised interest – €15m × 6% × 11/12 = €825,000
Therefore, charge to SPLOCI – P/L = €75,000

2012:
Total interest – €15m × 6% × 6/12 = €450,000
Capitalised interest – €15m × 6% × 3/12 = €225,000
Therefore, charge to SPLOCI – P/L = €225,000

Per Statement of Financial Position at 31 May 2012:

	€
Initial cost of depot	15,000,000
Interest (€825,000 + €225,000)	1,050,000
	16,050,000

The depot will be depreciated from the date it is ready for use (i.e. 1 June 2012).

Note: as the €24,000 interest received was earned during a period when work was suspended and therefore borrowing costs were not eligible for capitalisation, it does not reduce the amount of interest eligible for capitalisation.

When funds are borrowed *generally* (i.e. specific funds are not borrowed for the construction of a qualifying asset and the construction is funded from general borrowings), the amount to be capitalised is calculated as follows:

Asset Cost × Weighted Average Capitalisation Rate

The application of this is shown in **Example 7.3**.

EXAMPLE 7.3: USING GENERAL BORROWINGS

Kelly Limited, a company that prepares its financial statements to 31 December each year, commenced the construction of a property for its own use on 1 March 2012. However, construction was halted in July and August 2012 to enable certain design issues to be resolved. The costs incurred during the year ended 31 December 2012 in relation to the construction of the new property were as follows:

	€
Materials	1,800,000
Labour	1,500,000
Other construction costs	600,000
General allocation of central overheads	500,000
Site preparation costs	300,000
Total	4,700,000

Rather than borrow specifically for this project, Kelly Limited included the financing in the overall funding requirements for the company. During 2012, Kelly Limited was financed as follows:

3-year 8% loan	€5,000,000
5-year 5% loan	€15,000,000

Kelly Limited expects the construction to be completed on schedule in June 2013.

Requirement Explain how Kelly Limited should account for the construction of the property in its financial statements for the year ended 31 December 2012.

Solution

The relevant accounting standards that apply to this issue are IAS 16 *Property, Plant and Equipment* (see **Chapter 6**) and IAS 23 *Borrowing Costs*.

The general allocation of central overheads cannot be included in the construction cost of the property; therefore the cost of the property in accordance with IAS 16 is €4,200,000 (i.e. total costs €4,700,000 less €500,000).

Weighted average cost of borrowings:

8% × €5m / (€5m + €15m)	2.00%
5% × €15m / (€5m + €15m)	3.75%
	5.75%

Therefore:
- capitalise borrowing costs relating to the construction of the property for the period 1 March to 30 June and 1 September to 31 December 2012 = 8 months; and
- expense borrowing costs for the period 1 January to 28 February and 1 July to 31 August 2012 = 4 months.

Total interest cost:	€
€5m × 8%	400,000
€15m × 5%	750,000
	1,150,000
Capitalise €4.2m × 5.75% × 8/12	(161,000)
Charge to SPLOCI – P/L in 2012	989,000

The property should be recognised in the financial statements of Kelly Limited at 31 December 2012 at €4,361,000. This comprises:

	€
Materials	1,800,000
Labour	1,500,000
Expenses	600,000
Site preparation costs	300,000
Borrowing costs	161,000
	4,361,000

Depreciation is not required until the property is ready for use (which is anticipated to be June 2013).

The amount of borrowing costs capitalised in a period cannot exceed the amount incurred in that period (i.e. it is not allowable to capitalise more interest in a period than was actually incurred).

IAS 23 allows exchange differences arising from foreign currency borrowings to be capitalised as borrowing costs to the extent that they are regarded as an adjustment to interest costs. From a practical perspective, this involves determining how much of the exchange difference represents an adjustment to the interest cost of the borrowings. This could involve identifying another local currency loan that could have been taken at the same time for the same purpose and, based on that, calculating how much of the borrowing cost can be capitalised.

Disclosure Requirements

Financial reporting is the communication of financial information and the annual report and financial statements are generally recognised as the key documents in the discharge of financial accountability to external users (for example, investors, creditors and providers of finance). Such reports communicate economic measurements of and information about the resources and performance of the reporting entity, which is useful to those having reasonable rights to such information. As a result, IAS 23 requires that the following information be disclosed in the financial statements:
(a) amount of borrowing costs capitalised during the period; and
(b) capitalisation rate used to determine the amount of borrowing costs eligible for capitalisation.

Using the information in **Example 7.3**:
(a) the amount of borrowing costs capitalised during the period was €161,000; and
(b) the capitalisation rate used to determine the amount of borrowing costs eligible for capitalisation was 5.75%.

Note: from an examination perspective, it is important not to think of accounting standards in individual silos. Just as in practice, businesses have to deal with a number of different accounting standards and some will impact on each other. Arguably, it is not possible to have studied everything before starting to attempt questions; indeed, I believe that it is never too soon to begin practising questions and that this can be a very productive means of studying. After all, an examination consists of questions, elements of which you may not have seen before. Practice makes perfect, even if it is just the practice of learning to think on your feet and applying the knowledge/fundamentals that you have acquired to new circumstances and scenarios.

For example, IAS 16 (see **Chapter 6**) should not be viewed in isolation as it is likely that other related standards will be incorporated into a question. For example, IAS 23 (see **Chapter 7**), IAS 36 (see **Chapter 10**) and IAS 40 (**Chapter 5**) are often included with IAS 16 in a question.

Example 7.4 below is a comprehensive example that integrates a range of issues, with particular emphasis on IAS 40 (**Chapter 5**), IAS 16 (**Chapter 6**) and IAS 23 (**Chapter 7**). There is also an element of IAS 39 *Financial Instruments: Recognition and Measurement*/IFRS 9 *Financial Instruments* (**Chapter 25**), albeit in the context of IAS 23. The IASB is partway through a process of replacing IAS 39 *Financial Instruments: Recognition and Measurement* with IFRS 9 *Financial Instruments* – see **Section 3.3**. The IAS 39/IFRS 9 issue is adequately explained in the solution below so that it is not necessary to study **Chapter 25** at this stage.

EXAMPLE 7.4: APPLYING IAS 16 AND IAS 23

Compass Limited prepares its financial statements to 31 December each year, and at 31 December 2012 the company owned four properties: North, East, South and West.

On 1 January 2011, Compass Limited acquired North and East, two sites located in out-of-town shopping centres, with the intention of building a multi-screen cinema on each. Construction on each site commenced on 1 January 2011 and was completed on 31 December 2011. Details of the costs associated with the construction are as follows:

	North €000	East €000
Land	1,000	900
Direct materials	800	700
Direct labour	200	150
Direct overheads	130	120
	2,130	1,870

Compass Limited financed the construction of North and East by issuing a €5 million zero-coupon bond on 1 January 2011. The bond is redeemable on 31 December 2014 with a one-off payment of €6,802,721. While both properties were brought into use on 1 January 2012, North was retained by Compass Limited for use as a cinema, whereas East was rented commercially to an unrelated company that converted the property to a 10-pin bowling alley.

(***Note:*** this point requires a limited knowledge of IAS 39 *Financial Instruments: Recognition and Measurement*/IFRS 9 *Financial Instruments* (**Chapter 25**). The main point, in the context of IAS 23, is to calculate the interest arising on the debt in order to determine the amount of borrowing costs that can be capitalised. It is quite straightforward and is explained in the solution below so that it is not necessary to study **Chapter 25** at this stage.)

Compass Limited owns two successful four-star country hotels, South and West, and the company intends to develop this specialist part of its business. These two properties were professionally valued on 1 January 2012, the details of which are as follows:

	Historical Cost €000	Historical Cost Net Book Value €000	Current Use Value €000	Market Value €000
South	37,500	22,500	17,500	18,750
West	40,000	24,000	28,000	30,000

The buildings element of South and West represent 50% of both the historical cost and revalued amounts, and their remaining useful economic life at 1 January 2012 was 30 years. It was company policy to record all owned properties at historical cost and to depreciate them over their estimated useful economic life of 50 years on a straight-line basis. However, with effect from 1 January 2012, the directors of Compass Limited have decided to record South and West at valuation in the financial statements. The directors do not intend to obtain valuations for North and East or other non-current assets held by the company.

Requirement

(a) Explain whether Compass Limited is permitted to record South and West at valuation and other non-current assets, including North and East, at depreciated historical cost.

(b) Based on the information provided, show the amounts that should be included in the statements of profit or loss and other comprehensive income of Compass Limited for the years ended 31 December 2011 and 2012 and the statements of financial position as at those dates in respect of the four properties.

(*Note:* ignore deferred tax consequences.)

Solution

(a)
Non-current assets may be included at either depreciated historical cost (subject to impairment test in accordance with IAS 36 – see **Chapter 10**) or at valuation (usually market value) under IAS 16 (see **Chapter 6**).

Revaluations are optional, but if adopted they should be applied to all assets within that class to avoid 'cherry-picking'. It is reasonable to assume that North and East fall into a different class of property than South and West (i.e. the hotels can be treated as specialised).

Therefore, the evidence suggests that Compass Limited would be able to record South and West at valuation (usually market value) and other non-current assets (to which IAS 16 applies, e.g. North) (see (b) below – IAS 40 applies to East – see **Chapter 5**) at depreciated historical cost (subject to impairment test).

(b)
NORTH AND EAST
Year Ended 31 December 2011:

	North €	East €
Cost	2,130,000	1,870,000
Interest (see workings)	170,400	149,600
Book value at 31 December 2011	2,300,400	2,019,600

Year Ended 31 December 2012:

North and East are now in use; therefore the capitalisation of interest should cease in accordance with IAS 23 (see **Chapter 7**).

North is used by Compass Limited, therefore IAS 16 applies. Under IAS 16, non-current assets may be included at either depreciated historical cost (subject to impairment test in accordance with IAS 36) or at valuation (usually market value). As valuation information is not provided, the cost model should be applied.

East is held for its investment potential and let to an unrelated company. It should be classified as an investment property in accordance with IAS 40, and may be recorded using either the cost or fair value model. As no information is provided on fair value, the cost model should be applied (i.e. in accordance with IAS 16's requirements – cost less accumulated depreciated and impairment losses).

	North €	East €
Carrying value	2,300,400	2,019,600
Less land	(1,000,000)	(900,000)
	1,300,400	1,119,600
/50 years = 2012 depreciation charge	26,008	22,392
Therefore, carrying value of land and buildings at 31 December 2012	2,274,392	1,997,208

SOUTH AND WEST

Year Ended 31 December 2011:

	South €	West €
Historical cost at 31 December 2011	37,500,000	40,000,000
Depreciation charge – 50 years × 50% (land/buildings = 50/50)	375,000	400,000

Year Ended 31 December 2012:

Both hotels should be carried at their market value in accordance with IAS 16. As explained in (a) above, other classes of property need not be carried at valuation.

South	€
Historical cost net book value	22,500,000
Market value	18,750,000
Loss	3,750,000

As 2012 is the first year of recording South at valuation, the loss should be charged to the statement of profit or loss and other comprehensive income in arriving at operating profit or loss (i.e. no previous revaluation reserve to set the loss against).

Depreciation charge = €18,750,000/30 × 50%	€312,500
Therefore, net book value at 31 December 2012	€18,437,500

West	€
Historical cost net book value	24,000,000
Market value	30,000,000
Gain (other comprehensive income/revaluation reserve)	6,000,000

Depreciation charge = €30,000,000/30 × 50%	€500,000

Therefore, net book value at 31 December 2012	€29,500,000

Note: Compass Limited may credit a percentage of the revaluation reserve to retained earnings (through the statement of changes in equity) to offset the increased depreciation charge, i.e. €6,000,000/30 × 50% = €100,000.

WORKINGS:

Finance Cost

	€
Redemption cost	6,802,721
Proceeds	(5,000,000)
Finance cost	1,802,721

The finance costs should be spread over the life of the bond (i.e. 4 years from 2011 to 2014) so as to produce a constant return:

€5,000,000/€6,802,721 = 0.735 = 8% (per present value tables where n = 4)

Therefore the finance costs for the year ended 31 December 2011 that can be capitalised are:

€5,000,000 × 8% = €400,000

€400,000 × €4,000,000/€5,000,000 = €320,000

North = €2,130/€4,000 × €320,000 = €170,400

East = €1,870/€4,000 × €320,000 = €149,600

Therefore, the balance of interest, €80,000, should be charged to the SPLOCI – P/L in 2011 (i.e. €400,000 − €320,000).

7.3 CONCLUSION

IAS 23 states that borrowing costs *must be* capitalised as part of the cost of an asset when it is probable that the costs will result in future economic benefits, and the costs can be measured reliably and they are directly attributable to the acquisition, construction or production of a qualifying asset. Borrowing costs include interest and other costs incurred by an entity in connection with the borrowing of funds. Common examples include interest on bank overdrafts and borrowings. The key points to remember with respect to the capitalisation of borrowings are:
1. capitalisation should begin when expenditure on the asset and borrowing costs are being incurred;

2. capitalisation should be suspended during extended periods in which active development is interrupted; and
3. capitalisation should cease when substantially all the activities necessary to prepare the relevant asset for its intended use have been completed.

Finally, where borrowings relate *specifically* to expenditure on an asset, the amount of borrowing costs that should be capitalised are the actual costs less any investment income received from the temporary reinvestment of unutilised borrowings. If funds are borrowed *generally*, the amount to be capitalised is the 'Asset Cost $\times$ Weighted Average Capitalisation Rate'.

SUMMARY OF LEARNING OBJECTIVES

After having studied this chapter on borrowing costs, you should be able to do the following:

Learning Objective 1 Discuss the arguments for and against the capitalisation of borrowing costs.

While prudence might dictate that borrowing costs should be expensed immediately, borrowing costs incurred during the construction phase of a non-current asset can reasonably be considered a necessary cost of bringing the asset to a condition that enables it to generate revenue. It therefore holds that borrowing costs are as much a legitimate cost as materials or labour.

Learning Objective 2 Understand and apply the accounting treatment for qualifying borrowing costs.

Borrowing costs *must be* capitalised as part of the cost of an asset when:
• it is probable that the costs will result in future economic benefits and the costs can be reliably measured; and
• they are directly attributable and they would have been avoided if the asset was not bought, constructed or produced.

Learning Objective 3 Understand and apply when capitalisation of borrowing costs begins and when it must end.

Capitalisation should commence when expenditure on the asset and borrowing costs are being incurred; capitalisation should be suspended during extended periods in which active development is interrupted; and capitalisation should cease when substantially all the activities necessary to prepare the relevant asset for its intended use have been completed.

Learning Objective 4 Apply the main disclosure requirements of IAS 23.

The financial statements must disclose the:
(a) amount of borrowing costs capitalised during the period; and
(b) capitalisation rate used to determine the amount of borrowing costs eligible for capitalisation.

QUESTIONS

Self-test Questions

1. What are the arguments for and against the capitalisation of borrowing costs?
2. What is the accounting treatment for qualifying borrowing costs?
3. When may capitalisation of borrowing costs begin and when must it end?

Review Questions

(See **Appendix One** for Suggested Solutions to Review Questions.)

Question 7.1

On 1 January 2012, Robinson plc (Robinson) entered into a contract with a building company to build a new administrative and visitors' facility for the company at a cost of €10 million. In order to finance the cost of the contract, Robinson entered into a short-term loan agreement with its bankers to borrow €10 million at an interest rate of 6% per annum for the year that it would take to build the facility. The construction of the facility is expected to be completed on 31 December 2012 and the company intends to repay the loan on the same date. As Robinson's profits for the year ended 31 December 2012 are likely to be lower than expected, the directors wish to capitalise the loan interest paid.

Requirement Is the policy put forward by the directors of Robinson acceptable?

Challenging Questions

(Suggested Solutions to Challenging Questions are available to lecturers.)

Question 7.1

Yellow Limited (Yellow), a company that prepares its financial statements to 31 December each year, is involved in the manufacture of made-to-order customised sports cars. The company commenced trading in January 2008 and has gained an excellent reputation within this specialised industry.

In January 2012, Yellow commenced a programme to extend and modernise the company's manufacturing facilities. The programme cost €1,000,000 and Yellow financed the work through a mixture of general and specific debt. The directors estimate that 50% of the programme was financed by general debt and 50% by specific debt. Yellow's current general borrowing rate is 10% per annum, while the specific debt carries an interest rate of 15% per annum. The programme was completed on 31 December 2012.

Requirement Explain how Yellow should account for the borrowing costs in the financial statements for the year ended 31 December 2012.

LEASES

LEARNING OBJECTIVES

After having studied this chapter on leases, you should be able to:
1. Explain the difference between a finance and an operating lease;
2. Account for an operating lease;
3. Account for a finance lease from the lessee's perspective; and
4. Apply the main disclosure requirements for both operating leases and finance leases (lessee only).

KEY TERMS AND DEFINITIONS FOR THIS CHAPTER

In order to aid your understanding of the concepts and issues covered in this chapter, it is important to understand and be familiar with the following key terms and definitions. As you study this chapter, you should refer back to them.

Fair Value Fair value is the amount for which an asset could be exchanged or a liability settled, between knowledgeable and willing parties in an arm's length transaction.

Finance Lease A finance lease is a **lease** that transfers substantially all the risks and rewards associated with the ownership of an asset to the lessee. The risks and rewards of ownership are summarised in **Table 8.1**.

TABLE 8.1: RISKS AND REWARDS OF OWNERSHIP

Risks	Rewards
• Idle capacity	• Generation of profits from use of asset
• Fall in asset value due to obsolescence	• Potential profit arising from future sale of asset
• Cost of maintenance and repair	

A finance lease usually involves payment by a lessee to a lessor at the full cost of the asset, together with a return on the finance provided by the lessor. IAS 17 identifies five situations that would normally lead to a lease being classified as a finance lease:

1. The lease transfers ownership of the asset to the lessee at the end of the **lease term**.
2. The lessee has the option to purchase the asset at a price sufficiently below its **fair value** at the end of the lease term so that it is reasonably certain the option will be exercised.
3. The lease term is for a major part of the asset's economic life, even if title is not transferred (for example, an asset with an estimated economic life of five years is leased for four years).
4. The present value of **minimum lease payments** (see below) amounts to substantially all of the asset's value at the inception of the lease.
5. The leased asset is so specialised that it could only be used by the lessee without major modifications being made (e.g. a machine for high-speed and high-volume sorting of mail is leased by the Post Office).

Other indicators that a lease is a finance lease include when:

- the lessee can cancel the agreement and any losses are borne by the lessee; or
- the lessee has the right to continue the lease for a secondary period at a rent that is much lower than the market rent (which is often referred to as a 'peppercorn' rent).

Lease This is an agreement whereby the lessor conveys to the lessee, in return for a payment or series of payments, the right to use an asset for an agreed period of time. There are two types of lease: a **finance lease** and an **operating lease**.

Lease Term This is the non-cancellable period for which the lessee has contracted to lease the asset, together with any further terms for which the lessee has the option to continue to lease the asset, with or without further payment, when at the inception of the lease it is reasonably certain that the lessee will exercise the option.

Minimum Lease Payments The minimum lease payments are the payments over the **lease term** that the lessee is, or can be, required to make (excluding contingent rent, costs for services and taxes to be paid by and reimbursed to the lessor), together with any amounts guaranteed by the lessee or related party.

Operating Lease This type of lease does *not* transfer all the risks and rewards incidental to ownership of an asset to the lessee; these are retained by the lessor. Indicators that a lease is an operating lease are that:

- at the inception of the lease, the present value of minimum lease payments *does not* amount to substantially all of the **fair value** of the leased asset; and
- the **lease term** is significantly less than the useful life of the asset (for example, an asset with an estimated economic life of five years is leased for two years).

Please note that, as explained in **Chapter 2**, the IASB issued amendments to IAS 1 *Presentation of Financial Statements* in June 2011. These included a *proposal* that the title 'Statement of Profit or Loss and Other Comprehensive Income' (SPLOCI) be adopted (rather than, for example, 'statement of comprehensive income') and a *requirement* to revise the presentation of other comprehensive income (OCI) within the SPLOCI. These amendments are explained in detail in **Chapter 2, Section 2.3**.

8.1 INTRODUCTION

The acquisition of property, plant and equipment may be financed in a number of ways (for example, typically through cash or bank debt), and the attraction of different financing methods will vary according to the entity's requirements. Leasing is another way of purchasing such assets without having to pay the full amount upfront. In essence, a lease is an agreement between the entity (the lessee) and the finance company (the lessor) under which the lessee pays a periodic fee, usually monthly, for the use and possibly ownership of the asset at the end of the lease term. The range of property, plant and equipment that can be bought under a lease is expanding rapidly, partly due to the fact that the number of companies providing leasing services has expanded rapidly. Not only do most banks and a number of specialised leasing companies offer leasing services, but there have also been a growing number of manufacturers entering the market.

How Does Leasing Work?

Using a motor vehicle as an example: the motor vehicle will have a retail price (i.e. the money that would have to be paid if it was purchased outright at that point in time). Under a lease, as the vehicle is not being purchased, another value of the vehicle is determined. This is the 'residual value', which is an estimate of what the vehicle will be worth at the end of the lease, after depreciation is taken into account. The monthly payments are then based on the difference between the retail price and the residual value. Therefore, as the lessee does not pay the full price of the vehicle, the monthly payments should be lower (e.g. compared to financing the entire cost of the vehicle through a bank loan). At the end of the lease term, the vehicle is returned to the leasing company, at which point the lessee will have the option of taking out a lease on another new vehicle or, depending on the nature of the original lease contract, it may be possible to keep the vehicle (usually for a price).

Key to this Chapter

This chapter addresses the accounting treatment of, and the disclosure requirements for, leases in the books and records of lessees and lessors in accordance with *current* recommended practice, which is governed by IAS 17 *Leases*.

Exceptions to IAS 17 are:
(a) property accounted for as an investment property (IAS 40 *Investment Property* – see **Chapter 5**); and
(b) biological assets held by lessees under finance leases or held by lessors under operating leases (IAS 41 *Agriculture* – see **Chapter 34**).

At present, IAS 17 classifies leases into two types, a **finance lease** and an **operating lease**, and prescribes a different accounting treatment for each. However, as explained in **Section 8.7** below, this is likely to change in the next one to two years. **Section 8.2** deals with operating leases, which is arguably the more straightforward of the two, with **Section 8.3** focusing on the accounting treatment for finance leases in the financial statements of the lessee and, to a limited extent, the lessor. Sale and leaseback transactions are explained in **Section 8.4**, while other guidance relating to leases and the IAS 17 disclosure requirements are outlined in **Section 8.5** and **Section 8.6**, respectively.

8.2 ACCOUNTING FOR OPERATING LEASES

As stated above, a **lease** is an agreement whereby the lessor conveys to the lessee, in return for a payment or series of payments, the right to use an asset for an agreed period of time. IAS 17 distinguishes between two types of lease, a **finance lease** and an **operating lease**. This section addresses the accounting treatment of operating leases by both the lessor and lessee.

> **Remember:** in broad terms, an operating lease typically involves the lessee paying a rental for the hire of an asset for a period of time that is substantially less than its useful economic life.

Operating Leases in the Financial Statements of Lessors

In the books and records of the lessor, the asset that forms the basis of the operating lease is capitalised and depreciated in the normal way (see **Chapter 6**). The depreciation policy should be consistent with the lessor's normal depreciation policy for similar assets and accounted for under IAS 16 *Property, Plant and Equipment*. Lease income should be recognised in the statement of profit or loss and other comprehensive income – profit or loss (SPLOCI – P/L) on a straight-line basis over the lease term, unless another systematic basis gives a better representation of the benefits received.

Operating Leases in the Financial Statements of Lessees

The accounting treatment of operating leases is relatively straightforward in the financial statements of lessees because payments by the lessee are charged to the lessee's statement of profit or loss and other comprehensive income – profit or loss (SPLOCI – P/L). Consistent with the treatment of income for operating leases in the financial statements of *lessors* (see above), lease payments by lessees should be charged/debited in the SPLOCI – P/L on a straight-line basis over the lease term, unless another systematic basis gives a better representation of the benefits received from using the asset. (This is illustrated in **Example 8.1**.) An accrual or prepayment may be necessary if the rental payments are uneven or if the timing of the payments does not correspond with the end of the entity's accounting period.

EXAMPLE 8.1: OPERATING LEASE CHARGE

Ben Limited leased a car for its managing director under the following terms:

Cost of car:	€24,000	Term:	2 years
Rental:	€1,040 per month	Implicit rate of interest:	18%

Requirement What is the annual lease charge in Ben Limited's statement of profit or loss and other comprehensive income?

Solution

The rental should be charged to the SPLOCI – P/L on a straight-line basis over two years.

Operating lease rentals per annum (12 × €1,040):

Cash paid: €12,480   SPLOCI – P/L – expense   €12,480

8.3 ACCOUNTING FOR FINANCE LEASES

As noted above, IAS 17 distinguishes between two types of lease, a **finance lease** and an **operating lease**. While the previous section focused on operating leases, this section addresses the accounting treatment of finance leases in the financial statements of both the lessor and lessee. It begins by dealing with lessors before concentrating upon the accounting treatment of finance leases by lessees.

Finance Leases in the Financial Statements of Lessors

With respect to the accounting treatment of finance leases in the financial statements of the lessor, the key points to remember are:
- the leased asset is not included in the statement of financial position of the lessor;
- as the leased asset is not included in the statement of financial position, there is therefore no depreciation charge;
- lessors should recognise assets held under a finance lease in their statement of financial position as a receivable at an amount equal to the net investment in the lease;
- each rental received should be split between interest receivable and a reduction in the receivable (i.e. investment in finance leases); and
- the recognition of finance income (interest) should be based on a pattern reflecting a constant periodic rate of return on the lessor's net investment in the lease. This is likely to involve applying the actuarial method, as in the lessee's books and records.

Assessing whether a lease should be classified as either a finance lease or an operating lease in the books of the lessor is illustrated in **Example 8.2**.

EXAMPLE 8.2: LEASE CLASSIFICATION

Crossbow Limited, a manufacturer of machinery, leased out two machines during the year ended 31 December 2012 as follows:

	Machine A	Machine B
Annual rental	€8,000	€10,000
Cost of manufacturing machinery	€25,000	€30,000
Expected useful life	8 years	8 years
Lease term	2 years	8 years
Normal sales value	€40,000	€45,000

Requirement Based on the information provided above, and in accordance with IAS 17 *Leases*, assess whether the two machines have been leased out by Crossbow Limited on either a finance lease or operating lease.

Solution

Referring to the definitions of a finance lease and an operating lease shown above, Machine A appears to have been leased out on an operating lease as the lease term is two years and the expected useful life of the machine is eight years. In contrast, Machine B appears to have been leased out on a finance lease as the lease term matches the expected life of the machine and the minimum lease payments of €80,000 (€10,000 × 8) are greater than the normal sales value of the asset of €45,000.

Finance Leases in the Financial Statements of Lessees

With respect to the accounting treatment of finance leases in the financial statements of the lessee, IAS 17 requires that the leased asset be capitalised (i.e. shown as a tangible non-current asset under the subheading 'leased assets' – see **Chapter 2**) in the lessee's statement of financial position (see below), despite the fact that the lessee is not the legal owner of the asset. This treatment recognises that, in accordance with the *Conceptual Framework for Financial Reporting 2010* (see **Chapter 1**), transactions must be accounted for and presented on the basis of their commercial or economic reality rather than their legal form, and that only by applying substance over form will users see the effects of the commercial or economic reality of the transactions. The explanatory note to IAS 17 argues that it is not the asset itself but rather the lessee's 'rights in the asset' that are being capitalised.

In addition to capitalising the asset, the obligation of the lessee to make future payments is shown as a liability. Rentals payable should be apportioned between the finance element (see below) and a reduction of the outstanding obligation for future amounts payable. The finance element should be apportioned to accounting periods so as to produce a constant periodic rate of charge on the remaining balance of the obligation for each accounting period.

> *Note:* when classifying a lease that includes **both land and buildings**, the land and the buildings elements of the lease should be treated separately. Land would normally be classified as an operating lease, unless title (ownership) passes at the end of the lease term. The buildings should be classified as either a finance lease or an operating lease, in accordance with IAS 17.

Capitalising the Leased Asset

A finance lease should be included in the statement of financial position of the lessee by recording a non-current asset (e.g. leased plant) and a finance lease liability at the fair value of the asset or the present value of the minimum lease payments, if lower. The discount rate used to calculate the present value of the minimum lease payments is the interest rate implicit in the lease. In simple terms, the double entry required to record this is:

DR Non-current asset
CR Finance lease liability

The amount to be recorded in this way is the capital cost or **fair value** of the asset. This may be taken as the amount the lessee might expect to pay for it in a cash transaction. The amount shown as a liability will be reduced each year by the capital element of payments made each year.

Depreciation for non-current assets held under finance leases must be consistent with that for similar assets that are owned. If there is no reasonable certainty that the lessee will obtain ownership at the end of the lease, the asset should be depreciated over the shorter of the lease term or the life of the asset. The double entry required to record this is:

DR   SPLOCI – P/L – depreciation expense
CR   Non-current assets

As with other non-current assets, and as the asset is recorded in the financial statements of the lessee, **impairment** reviews should be conducted by the lessee in accordance with IAS 36 *Impairment of Assets* (see **Chapter 10**).

Allocating the Finance Element to Accounting Periods

When the lessee makes a rental payment it will comprise two elements:
1. a repayment of part of the capital cost of the asset. In the lessee's books, this proportion of each rental payment must be debited to the lessor's account to reduce the outstanding liability; and
2. interest on the finance provided by the lessor.

The total interest is calculated as follows:

	€
Total lease payments	P
Less fair value of asset (or present value of minimum lease payments if lower)	(FV)
Total interest	I

> *Note:* careful attention must be given to whether payments are in advance or arrears. Interest accrues over time and it is assumed to be included in the repayment if made at the *end* of the period. However, where *instalments are paid in advance*, it is often assumed that the first instalment repays capital only, as no interest has yet accrued. At the end of each accounting period, the year-end liability will therefore include capital and interest accrued to date but not yet paid.

The interest is allocated to each period over the lease term so as to produce a constant periodic rate of interest on the remaining balance of the obligation. This proportion of each payment is charged as a finance cost in the statement of profit or loss and other comprehensive income – profit or loss. The double entry required to record this is:

DR   SPLOCI – P/L – finance charge
DR   Finance lease liability
CR   Bank

The accounting problem is to decide what proportion of each instalment paid by the lessee represents interest, and what proportion represents a repayment of the capital advanced by

the lessor. IAS 17 requires the interest to be allocated to each period to give a constant periodic rate of interest on the outstanding lease obligation. There are three ways in which you may do this:
- the level spread or straight-line method;
- the actuarial method (see **Examples 8.3, 8.4, 8.5, 8.6** and **8.7**); or
- the 'sum of digits method' (see **Examples 8.8** and **8.9**).

The Level Spread (or Straight-line) Method

The level spread (or straight-line) method of allocating interest is based on the assumption that interest charges accrue evenly over the term of the lease agreement.

For example, if an asset with a fair value of €3,000 is being 'acquired' on a finance lease for five payments of €700 each, the total interest is €(3,500 – 3,000) = €500. This is assumed to accrue evenly and, therefore, €100 interest is structured into each rental payment, the €600 balance of each instalment being the capital repayment. The level spread method is unscientific and takes no account of the commercial realities of the transaction. Consequently, while its use is permitted, it is the least preferred method of the three.

The Actuarial Method

The actuarial method of allocating interest, which is recognised as the most accurate of the three, derives from the assumption that the interest charged by the lessor company will equal the rate of return desired by the company, multiplied by the amount of capital it has invested. Therefore:
(a) at the beginning of the lease the capital invested is equal to the fair value of the asset (less any initial deposit paid by the lessee); and
(b) this amount reduces as each instalment is paid. It follows that the interest accruing is greatest in the early part of the lease term, and gradually reduces as capital is repaid.

The breakdown of each rental payment between capital and interest using the actuarial method where payments are in arrears is shown in **Example 8.3**.

EXAMPLE 8.3: CAPITAL AND INTEREST ELEMENTS
(PAYMENTS IN ARREARS)

On 1 January 2012 DEF Limited, a wine merchant, buys a small bottling machine from BAS Limited on hire-purchase terms. The cash price of the machine was €7,710, while the total lease price was €10,000. The lease agreement required the immediate payment of a €2,000 deposit, with the balance being settled in four equal annual instalments commencing on 31 December 2012. The lease charge of €2,290 represents interest of 15% per annum, calculated on the remaining balance of the liability during each accounting period. Depreciation on the plant is to be provided for at the rate of 20% per annum on a straight-line basis, assuming a residual value of nil.

Requirement Show the breakdown of each instalment between interest and capital using the actuarial method.

Solution

Interest is calculated as 15% of the outstanding capital balance at the beginning of each year. The outstanding capital balance reduces each year by the capital element in each instalment. The outstanding capital balance at 1 January 2012 is €5,710 (€7,710 fair value less €2,000 deposit).

	Total €	Capital €	Interest €	
Capital balance at 1 January 2012		5,710		
1st instalment	2,000	1,144	856	(Interest €5,710 × 15%)
Capital balance at 1 January 2013		4,566		
2nd instalment	2,000	1,315	685	(Interest €4,566 × 15%)
Capital balance at 1 January 2014		3,251		
3rd instalment	2,000	1,512	488	(Interest €3,251 × 15%)
Capital balance 1 January 2015		1,739		
4th instalment	2,000	1,739	261	(Interest €1,739 × 15%)
	8,000	–	2,290	

The actuarial method involves applying the interest rate implicit in the lease, which is the discount rate that, at the inception of a lease, causes the aggregate present value of the minimum lease payments and the unguaranteed residual value to be equal to the fair value of the leased asset. **Example 8.4** below shows how to calculate the interest rate implicit in a lease.

EXAMPLE 8.4: CALCULATING THE INTEREST RATE IMPLICIT IN A LEASE

Bow Limited negotiated a four-year lease for a piece of equipment worth €40,000, with the annual lease payments being €12,000 in advance. The cost of borrowing for Bow Limited is 14%.

Requirement What is the implicit rate of interest in the lease?

Solution

Present value: €40,000 = €12,000 + €12,000 (annuity for 3 years as payments are in advance) = €12,000 + €12,000 (2.322)* = €39,864
[*See cumulative present value factor tables − 3 years at 14%]

Therefore, the present value of the lease payments represents substantially all of the fair value of the equipment.

€40,000 = lease payments discounted at implicit interest rate
€40,000 = €12,000 + €12,000 × a_{3i}
€28,000/€12,000 = a_{3i}
Implicit rate = 13.7%

Note: as indicated above, careful attention must be given to whether payments are in advance or arrears.

Accounting for a finance lease in the books of the lessee using the actuarial method for allocating interest where the lease payments are in arrears is illustrated in **Example 8.5**.

EXAMPLE 8.5: ACCOUNTING FOR A FINANCE LEASE
(PAYMENTS IN ARREARS)

X Limited leased an asset under the following terms:
Fair value of asset – €10,000;
Rentals 4 years – €3,000 p.a. in arrears;
Implied rate of interest – 7.72%; and
Useful life of asset – 4 years.

Requirement Show the breakdown of each instalment between interest and capital using the actuarial method, together with the necessary journal entries required to record the transaction.

Solution

Year	Opening Balance €	Rental €	Interest €	Capital €	Closing Balance €
1	10,000	3,000	(a)772	2,228	7,772
2	7,772	3,000	(b)600	2,400	5,372
3	5,372	3,000	415	2,585	2,787
4	2,787	3,000	215	2,787	–

(a) €10,000 × 7.72%
(b) €7,772 × 7.72%

Opening Entry:
DR   Leased assets   €10,000
CR   Obligation under finance lease   €10,000

Obligation under finance lease

	€		€
Cash	3,000	Leased assets	10,000
Bal c/d	7,772	SPLOCI – P/L	772
	10,772		10,772

	€			€
Cash	3,000	Bal b/d		7,772
Bal c/d	5,372	SPLOCI – P/L		600
	8,372			8,372

Extracts from Financial Statements

Statement of profit or loss and other comprehensive income – profit or loss:

Year	1	2	3	4
	€	€	€	€
Depreciation	2,500	2,500	2,500	2,500
Finance charge	772	600	415	215

Statement of financial position:

Non-current assets				
Leased assets at NBV	7,500	5,000	2,500	–
Non-current liabilities				
Obligations under finance lease	5,372	2,787	–	–
Current liabilities				
Obligations under finance lease	2,400	2,585	2,787	–

Year 1 – note to financial statements:

Obligations under finance lease	€
Payable next year	2,400
Payable 2–5 years	5,372
	7,772

Statement of profit or loss and other comprehensive income:
As illustrated above, the SPLOCI – P/L of the lessee will show the finance charge relating to the lease and the depreciation charge of the asset.

Note: it is standard practice that, unless the implicit interest rate is provided, the sum of digits should be used. These two methods are preferred to the straight-line method (which admittedly may often provide a close approximation).

Note: as indicated above, careful attention must be given to whether payments are in advance or arrears. Interest accrues over time and it is assumed to be included in the repayment if made at the *end* of the period. However, where *instalments are paid in advance*, it is often assumed that the first instalment repays capital only as no interest has yet accrued. At the end of each accounting period, the year-end liability will therefore include capital and interest accrued to date but not yet paid.

The breakdown of each rental payment between capital and interest using the actuarial method where payments are in advance and the first payment is assumed to repay capital is shown in **Example 8.6**.

EXAMPLE 8.6: CAPITAL AND INTEREST ELEMENTS
(PAYMENTS IN ADVANCE)

A company has a year end of 31 December. A finance lease commences on 1 January 2012. Lease payments comprise four annual payments of €10,000, commencing on 1 January 2012. The asset would have cost €34,869 to buy outright. The implicit rate of interest is 10%.

Requirement Calculate the interest charge and year-end liability each year using the actuarial method.

Solution

As stated previously, a finance lease should be included in the statement of financial position of the lessee at the fair value of the asset or the present value of the minimum lease payments if lower. Therefore, comparing the fair value and the present value of the minimum lease payments:

Fair value = €34,869
Present value = €10,000 + €10,000 × $a_{10\%3}$ (see **Example 8.4**)
Present value = €10,000 + €10,000 × (2.487) = €34,870

Total finance charge to be allocated:

	€
Total lease payments	40,000
Less initial cost of lease	(34,869)
Total finance charge	5,131

	Balance b/f at 1 January	Rental payment 1 January	Capital balance remaining 1 January	Finance charge at 10%	Capital at 31 December
2012	34,869	(10,000)	24,869	2,487	27,356
2013	27,356	(10,000)	17,356	1,736	19,092
2014	19,092	(10,000)	9,092	909	10,000
2015	10,000	(10,000)	–		
		40,000			

Developing the previous example, accounting for a finance lease in the books of the lessee using the actuarial method for allocating interest where the lease payments are in advance and the first payment is assumed to repay capital is illustrated in **Example 8.7**.

EXAMPLE 8.7: ACCOUNTING FOR A FINANCE LEASE
(PAYMENTS IN ADVANCE)

The terms of a finance lease are as follows:
Cost of asset – €25,000;
Estimated useful life – 5 years;

Lease terms for 5 years at €6,500 per annum in advance; and
Implicit rate of interest – 15.2%.

Requirement Calculate the interest charge and year-end liability each year using the actuarial method, together with the relevant statement of financial position extracts and T accounts for year 1.

Solution

The total finance charge is the total payments less the cost of the asset.

	€
Total payments (€6,500 × 5)	32,500
Cost of asset	(25,000)
Total finance charge	7,500

Calculation of interest charge element and capital element:

Year	Opening Capital Balance €	Rental Payment €	Capital Element €	Accrued Finance Charge at 15.2% €	Closing Capital Balance €
1	25,000	6,500	6,500	(a)2,812	18,500
2	18,500	6,500	3,688	(b)2,251	14,812
3	14,812	6,500	4,249	1,606	10,563
4	10,563	6,500	4,894	862	5,669
5	5,669	6,500	5,638	—	—
			24,969		

(a)(€25,000 − €6,500) × 15.2% = €2,812
(b)(€18,500 − €3,688) × 15.2% = €2,251

Assumption The first payment is in advance and it is deemed to be all capital. Therefore, as the payment in year one was deemed to be a 'capital' advance, an accrual of €2,812 must be made in respect of the finance charge for year one in accordance with the matching concept. The payment on the first day of year two will first go towards clearing this finance charge accrual. The balance is available to reduce the capital outstanding to €14,812 for year two.

STATEMENT OF PROFIT OR LOSS AND OTHER COMPREHENSIVE INCOME – PROFIT OR LOSS:

Year	Finance Charge €	Depreciation Charge €	Total Charge €
1	2,812	5,000	7,812
2	2,251	5,000	7,251
3	1,606	5,000	6,606
4	(862–31*)	5,000	5,831
5	—	5,000	5,000

* Rounding difference due to using finance charge to one decimal place.

There is no finance charge in Year 5 because the full liability is paid off on the first day of the year and so no interest is chargeable.

STATEMENT OF FINANCIAL POSITION (EXTRACT):

	Year 1 €	Year 2 €	Year 3 €	Year 4 €	Year 5 €
Tangible assets held under finance leases					
Cost	25,000	25,000	25,000	25,000	25,000
Accumulated depreciation	5,000	10,000	15,000	20,000	25,000
Net book value	20,000	15,000	10,000	5,000	–
Non-current liabilities					
Net obligations under finance leases	14,812	10,563	5,669	–	–
Current liabilities					
Net obligation under finance lease	3,688	4,249	4,894	5,669	–
Accruals (finance charges due)	2,812	2,251	1,606	831	–
	6,500	6,500	6,500	6,500	Nil

Leased Asset

	Year 1 €		Year 1 €
Finance lease obligation (fair value)	25,000	Balance c/d	25,000

Obligation under Finance Lease

	Year 1 €		Year 1 €
Cash (rental)	6,500		
Balance c/d net obligation	18,500	Leased asset	25,000
Interest accrual (see above)	2,812	SPLOCI – P/L – finance cost	2,812
	27,812		27,812

Depreciation Leased Asset

	Year 1 €		Year 1 €
Balance c/d	5,000	SPLOCI – P/L – depreciation	5,000

Note: while the assumption above is the most common, it could be argued that the first payment (in advance) includes the repayment of both interest and capital for year one. While there would still be an interest expense in the SPLOCI – P/L in year one, there would be no interest accrual in the statement of financial position at the end of year one. This assumption would therefore result in a different Current Liability/Non-current Liability (CL/NCL) split.

The Sum of Digits Method

As noted above, IAS 17 requires the interest included in each finance lease payment to be allocated to each period in order to give a constant periodic rate of interest on the outstanding lease obligation. Two of the three ways in which you may do this (the level spread method (which is the least-favoured of the three) and the actuarial method) are discussed above. The third method, the sum of digits method, is now explained.

IAS 17 states that, in practice, when allocating the finance charge to periods during the term, a lessee may use some form of approximation to simplify the calculation. The sum of digits method (also known as 'the rule of 78') provides such an acceptable approximation. This method approximates to the actuarial method, splitting the total interest in such a way that the greater proportion falls in the earlier years.

The sum of digits method works as follows:
(a) Assign a digit to *each* instalment/payment. The digit 1 should be assigned to the final instalment, 2 to the penultimate instalment, and so on.
(b) Add the digits. For example, if there are 12 instalments, then the sum of the digits will be 78, and so forth.

Note: when lease payments are in advance, use the sum of the digits of the lease term minus 1 (see **Example 8.9** below).

The application of the sum of digits method for allocating interest is shown in **Examples 8.8** and **8.9**.

EXAMPLE 8.8: SUM OF DIGITS (PAYMENTS IN ARREARS)

Requirement Using the information from **Example 8.3**, show the breakdown of each instalment between interest and capital using the sum of digits method.

Solution

Each instalment is allocated a digit as follows:

Instalment	Digit
1st (2012)	4
2nd (2013)	3
3rd (2014)	2
4th (2015)	1
	10

The €2,290 interest charges can then be apportioned:

		€
1st instalment	€2,290 × 4/10	916
2nd instalment	€2,290 × 3/10	687
3rd instalment	€2,290 × 2/10	458
4th instalment	€2,290 × 1/10	229
		2,290

	1st Instalment	2nd Instalment	3rd Instalment	4th Instalment
	€	€	€	€
Interest	916	687	458	229
Capital (bal)	1,084	1,313	1,542	1,771
	2,000	2,000	2,000	2,000

As noted above, when lease payments are in advance, the sum of the digits of the lease term minus 1 should be used. This is illustrated in **Example 8.9**.

EXAMPLE 8.9: SUM OF DIGITS (PAYMENTS IN ADVANCE)

Requirement Using the information from **Example 8.7**, show the breakdown of each instalment between interest and capital using the sum of digits method.

Solution

Number of payments (excluding first payment in advance) = 4
Therefore, sum of digits = 4 + 3 + 2 + 1 = 10
The split of rentals between capital and finance charge would be as follows:

Year	Finance Charge		Rental	Capital Repayment
	€	€	€	€
1	–	–	6,500	6,500
2	4/10 × 7,500	3,000	6,500	3,500
3	3/10 × 7,500	2,250	6,500	4,250
4	2/10 × 7,500	1,500	6,500	5,000
5	1/10 × 7,500	750	6,500	5,750
		7,500	32,500	25,000

The accounting treatment will be as before, only the split between the finance charge and capital repayments has changed, giving a higher finance charge in earlier periods and a lower charge towards the end of the lease.

Note: as before, it could have been assumed that the first payment (in advance) included the repayment of both interest and capital for year one.

As noted previously, IAS 17 requires the interest included in each finance lease payment to be allocated to each period in order to give a constant periodic rate of interest on the outstanding lease obligation. The three ways in which you may do this are: the level spread method (which is the least-favoured of the three), the actuarial method and the sum of digits method. Using the information from **Example 8.7**, the different annual finance charges, and hence the impact on the SPLOCI–P/L each year, are compared in **Example 8.10**.

EXAMPLE 8.10: COMPARISON OF INTEREST ALLOCATION METHODS

Comparison of Finance Charges:

	Actuarial		Sum of Digits (see **Example 8.9**)		Level Spread	
Year	€	%	€	%	€	%
1	2,812	38	3,000	40	1,875	25
2	2,251	30	2,250	30	1,875	25
3	1,606	21	1,500	20	1,875	25
4	831	11	750	10	1,875	25
	7,500	100	7,500	100	7,500	100

The smaller the value of the lease, the less material will be the difference between the level spread (straight-line) method and the more accurate methods; the higher the rate of interest, then the greater the difference between the sum of the digits ('rule of 78') method and the actuarial method.

8.4 SALE AND LEASEBACK TRANSACTIONS

It is not uncommon for a company to sell an asset to a third party, receive the sale proceeds and then lease the asset back, paying a rental for its use. A sale and leaseback allows a company to raise finance from the sale of non-current assets (usually land and property) while retaining the use of them, but at the cost of increasing operational gearing (i.e. the effect of fixed costs on the relationship between sales and operating profit – see **Chapter 35**). While the finance raised from selling the assets may make the company financially stronger, the cost of the leaseback rental payments means that operational gearing will be increased; although the impact of this on earnings may, if the money raised is retained, be softened by a lowering of financial gearing (i.e. the relationship between debt and equity – see **Chapter 35**).

Depending on the substance of the transaction, a sale and leaseback will result in either a finance lease or an operating lease.

1. Where the sale and leaseback results in a finance lease, any excess of sales proceeds over the carrying amount cannot be immediately recognised as income by the seller/lessee. It must be deferred and amortised over the lease term (see **Example 8.11** below).

EXAMPLE 8.11: SALE AND LEASEBACK – FINANCE LEASE

During the year ended 31 December 2012 Funny Limited sold an item of equipment for €200,000 when its net book value, which was the same as its fair value, was €175,000. Funny Limited immediately leased back the equipment under a five-year finance lease.

Requirement Explain how this transaction will be reflected in the 2012 financial statements of Funny Limited.

Solution

The substance of the transaction is not that of a sale. In accordance with IAS 17, a profit on disposal cannot be recognised in full in the SPLOCI – P/L for the year ended 31 December 2012; it should be recognised over the lease term of five years.

Therefore, the equipment should not be derecognised, but should be recorded at its fair value of €175,000. A finance lease obligation must be set up, with the SPLOCI – P/L being charged with the finance cost using the implicit rate of interest in the lease.

The 'gain' of €25,000 should be shown as a provision and released to the SPLOCI – P/L as a credit against the finance lease charge.

2. When a sale and leaseback results in an **operating lease**:
   (a) any profit or loss on sale can be recognised immediately as long as the transaction is at fair value;
   (b) if the sale price is above fair value, the excess must be amortised over the period for which the asset will be used (see **Example 8.12**);
   (c) if the sale price is below fair value, any profit/loss should be recognised immediately, except when a loss is compensated by future lease payments at below fair value, when the loss should be deferred and amortised over the period for which the asset will be used.

EXAMPLE 8.12: SALE AND LEASEBACK – OPERATING LEASE

During the year ended 31 December 2012, Honey Limited sold a warehouse for €195,000 when its carrying value was €100,000 and its fair value was €150,000. The company immediately leased back the warehouse under a three-year operating lease.

Requirement Explain how this transaction will be reflected in the 2012 financial statements of Honey Limited.

Solution

The profit on disposal to be recognised in the SPLOCI – P/L in 2012 is €50,000 (€150,000 – €100,000). The excess to be amortised over the period during which the asset will be used is €45,000 (€195,000 – €150,000), at €15,000 per annum (with the deferred amount of €30,000 being classified between current (€15,000) and non-current (€15,000) liabilities).

8.5 OTHER GUIDANCE

Two other related pieces of guidance that have implications for the accounting treatment of leases are explained briefly below.

SIC 15 Operating Leases – *Incentives*

SIC 15 deals with how incentives (such as rent-free periods or contributions by the lessor to the lessee's relocation costs) in an operating lease should be recognised in the financial statements of both the lessor and the lessee.

SIC 15 requires that lease incentives be recognised as an integral part of the net consideration for the use of the leased asset.

The lessor should recognise the aggregate cost of the incentives as a reduction of rental income over the lease term, in line with the recognition of the rental income (which, as explained above, will usually be on a straight-line basis).

The lessee recognises the aggregate benefit of the incentives as a reduction of rental expense over the lease term, in line with the recognition of the rental expense (which, as explained above, will normally be on a straight-line basis).

SIC 27 *Evaluating the Substance of Transactions Involving the Legal Form of a Lease*

SIC 27 provides guidance on when a series of transactions should be regarded as linked and accounted for as one transaction.

SIC 27 states that when the overall economic effect of a transaction cannot be understood without reference to a series of transactions then the series of transactions should be accounted for as one transaction. This means that all aspects of an arrangement should be evaluated to determine its substance, with weight given to those aspects and implications that have an economic effect.

8.6 DISCLOSURE REQUIREMENTS

The acquisition of property, plant and equipment may be financed in a number of ways (for example, typically through cash or bank debt), and the attraction of different financing methods will vary according to the entity's requirements. Leasing is another way of purchasing such assets without having to pay the full amount upfront. Given that a lease is a legally binding contract between the entity (the lessee) and the finance company (the lessor), under which the lessee agrees to pay a periodic fee, usually monthly, for the use and possibly ownership of the asset at the end of the lease term. Therefore, it is important that adequate information is disclosed to enable users of financial statements to fully understand how an entity has financed its acquisition of non-current assets and the payments that it is committed to making in the future, IAS 17 classifies leases into two types, a finance lease and an operating lease, and prescribes the disclosures required for each by both lessors and lessees. These are summarised below.

Operating Leases (Lessors)

IAS 17 requires lessors to disclose the following information in respect of operating leases:
(a) amounts of minimum lease payments at the reporting date under non-cancellable operating leases in the aggregate and for:

    (i) the next year,
    (ii) years 2 through 5 combined,
    (iii) beyond five years;
(b) contingent rent recognised in income; and
(c) general description of significant leasing arrangements.

Finance Leases (Lessors)

IAS 17 requires lessors to disclose the following information in respect of finance leases:
(a) reconciliation between gross investment in the lease and the present value of minimum lease payments;
(b) gross investment and present value of minimum lease payments receivable for:
    (i) the next year,
    (ii) years 2 through 5 combined,
    (iii) beyond five years;
(c) unearned finance income;
(d) unguaranteed residual values;
(e) accumulated allowance for uncollectible lease payments receivable;
(f) contingent rent recognised in income; and
(g) general description of significant leasing arrangements.

Operating Leases (Lessees)

IAS 17 requires lessees to disclose the following information in respect of operating leases held:
(a) the total of operating lease rentals charged as an expense in the SPLOCI–P/L should be disclosed;
(b) the payments to which the lessee is committed under operating leases, analysed between those in which the commitment expires:
    (i) the next year,
    (ii) years 2 through 5 combined,
    (iii) beyond five years;
(c) the lessee should also provide a description of the lessee's significant arrangements (for example, contingent rent arrangements and renewal or purchase options) and a note on how these have been dealt with in the financial statements.

Finance Leases (Lessees)

IAS 17 requires lessees to disclose the following information in respect of finance leases held:
(a) for each class of asset, the net carrying amount at the reporting date;
(b) reconciliation between the total of minimum lease payments at the reporting date and their present value. In addition, an enterprise should disclose the total of minimum lease payments at the reporting date and their present value for each of the following periods:
    (i) the next year,
    (ii) years 2 through 5 combined,
    (iii) beyond five years; and
(c) any contingent rents charged during the period.

8.7 CONCLUSION

Leasing is an important activity for many organisations, with the amounts involved being potentially substantial. Currently under IAS 17, with respect to finance leases (for example, a lease of equipment for nearly all of its economic life), a lessee recognises lease assets and liabilities on the statement of financial position; in contrast, for operating leases (for example, a lease of office space for 10 years), a lessee does not recognise lease assets or liabilities on the statement of financial position. Consequently, many leases are not reported on a lessee's statement of financial position. As a result, particularly in the wake of the financial crisis, the different accounting treatment of finance and operating leases has given rise to various criticisms and problems, in particular:

- it is claimed that IAS 17 fails to meet the needs of users of financial statements because it does not always provide a faithful representation of leasing transactions (for example, contractual commitments under lease contracts are not recognised in a way that is transparent and useful to users);
- many users of financial statements believe that all lease contracts give rise to assets and liabilities that should be recognised in the financial statements of lessees. Therefore, these users routinely adjust the recognised amounts in the statement of financial position in an attempt to assess the effect of the assets and liabilities resulting from operating lease contracts;
- the split between finance leases and operating leases can result in similar transactions being accounted for very differently, reducing comparability for users of financial statements; and
- the difference in the accounting treatment of finance leases and operating leases provides opportunities to structure transactions so as to achieve a particular lease classification.

In response, the International Accounting Standards Board (IASB) and the Financial Accounting Standards Board (FASB) initiated a joint project in 2006 to improve the financial reporting of leasing activities. Building upon a Discussion Paper issued in March 2009 to gather constituent views on the treatment of leases in the financial statements of lessees and lessors, the IASB and FASB issued a first Exposure Draft (ED) Leases in August 2010. Then, in May 2013, the IASB and FASB published for public comment a revised ED (ED/2013/6 Leases). For leasees, the ED proposes an approach that would require a lessee to recognise assets and liabilities for the rights and obligations created by leases of more than 12 months. For lessors, the model proposed in the ED is similar to current lease accounting under IAS 17, with some nuances for the recognition of revenue and discounting of the residual asset. It is likely, therefore, that from the leasee's perspective, current accounting requirements for leases will change.

SUMMARY OF LEARNING OBJECTIVES

After having studied this chapter on leasing, you should be able to:

Learning Objective 1 Explain the difference between a finance and an operating lease.

A finance lease is a lease that transfers substantially all the risks and rewards incidental to the ownership of an asset to the lessee. An operating lease does not transfer all the risks and rewards incidental to ownership of an asset to the lessee; these are retained by the lessor. Indicators of an operating lease are that: at the inception of the lease, the present value of minimum lease payments *does not* amount to substantially all of the fair value of the leased asset; and the lease term is significantly less than the useful life of the asset.

Learning Objective 2 Account for an operating lease.

To account for an operating lease, payments by the lessee are charged to the lessee's SPLOC–P/L on a straight-line basis over the lease term. Consequently, an accrual or prepayment is necessary if the rental payments are uneven.

Learning Objective 3 Account for a finance lease from the lessee's perspective.

A finance lease is shown as a tangible non-current asset in the lessee's financial statements, despite the fact that the lessee is not the legal owner of the asset. In addition, the obligation of the lessee to make future payments is shown as a liability. Rentals payable are apportioned between the finance element and a reduction of the outstanding obligation for future amounts payable. The finance element is apportioned to accounting periods, preferably to produce a constant periodic rate of charge on the remaining balance of the obligation for each accounting period.

Learning Objective 4 Apply the main disclosure requirements for both operating leases and finance leases (lessee only).

The total of operating lease rentals charged as an expense in the SPLOCI–P/L should be disclosed, together with details of the payments to which the lessee is committed. With respect to finance leases, for each class of asset, IAS 17 requires lessees to disclose the net carrying amount at the reporting date and to reconcile the total of minimum lease payments at the reporting date and their present value.

QUESTIONS

Self-test Questions

1. What is the difference between a finance and an operating lease?
2. With respect to a finance lease, what should you show in the statement of financial position of the lessee?
3. With respect to a finance lease, how do you account for the rental payments from the lessee's point of view?
4. What is the preferred method of apportioning the rental repayments between the interest and capital element?
5. List the disclosure requirements for both operating and finance leases.

Review Questions

(See **Appendix One** for Suggested Solutions to Review Questions.)

Question 8.1

On 1 January 2012, ARIES Limited acquired a machine, under a finance lease, which could have been purchased outright for €64,000. The lease provided for four annual payments of €20,000 in arrears commencing on 31 December 2012. The implicit rate of interest was 10% and the machine is expected to have no residual value at the end of the lease term. ARIES Limited calculates depreciation on a straight-line basis.

Requirement Applying the provisions of IAS 17 *Leases*, calculate the effect of the above lease on the financial statements of ARIES Limited for the year ended 31 December 2012.

Question 8.2

The managing director of LEES Limited is considering a proposal to acquire a new, fully automatic machine to increase production capacity and efficiency. The machine would cost €150,000 to purchase outright but, because the company has insufficient resources, a lease contract has been proposed with the following terms:
1. primary period – four years at an annual rental of €45,690 payable annually in advance. The implicit rate of interest is 15% per annum;
2. secondary period – unlimited and at an annual rental of €1; and
3. cancellation – the lease may not be cancelled by LEES Limited during the primary period, but may be terminated at any time during the secondary period.

The managing director has been advised that the machine will have an effective useful life of six years, after which time its value would be negligible. The company depreciates all machinery on a straight-line basis over their effective useful lives, commencing from the date of acquisition. It is proposed to acquire the machine and enter into the lease on 30 November 2012, and to make the first rental payment on that date.

Requirement You are required to prepare a schedule for the managing director showing, in columnar form:
(a) the effect of the lease on the projected profits for each of the three years ending 31 May 2013, 2014 and 2015; and
(b) extracts from the projected statement of financial position as at 31 May 2013, 2014 and 2015, showing how LEES Limited would be required to reflect the lease and the machine.

Note: calculations should be made to the nearest month and nearest euro.

Question 8.3

Sam Limited has entered into a finance lease in respect of a crane. The terms of the lease are:
1. three-year primary period, with a quarterly rent payable in advance of €2,500, i.e. total payment of €30,000; and
2. ten-year secondary period at a nominal rent (which can be ignored for the purposes of this question).

The cost of a new crane, if purchased outright, would be €25,000. Its estimated useful life is six years with a nil scrap value. Sam Limited uses the straight-line basis of depreciation for plant. It is not reasonably certain that ownership of the asset will transfer to Sam Limited.

Requirement

(a) Compute the charge in the statement of profit or loss and other comprehensive income (SPLOCI), assuming the lease is an operating lease.

(b) Compute the charge in the SPLOCI assuming the leasing commitment is capitalised using the:

  (i) sum of digits approach, spreading the interest charge over 12 quarters; and

  (ii) actuarial approach.

(c) Show the relevant entries in the statement of financial position for the first year, using the actuarial method.

Note: the implicit rate of interest in each lease payment is 3.5%.

Challenging Questions

(Suggested Solutions to Challenging Questions are available to lecturers.)

Question 8.1 (Based on Chartered Accountants Ireland, P3 Summer 2002, Question 6)

JAZZ Limited (JAZZ) is currently preparing its financial statements for the year ended 31 December 2012. A number of issues need to be resolved before the financial statements for the year ended 31 December 2012 can be finalised.

Issue 1 On 1 January 2012, JAZZ leased drilling equipment to SOUL Limited (SOUL). The finance lease, which runs for a period of five years, requires SOUL to make five annual payments of €150,000, with the first payment due on 1 January 2012. The present value of the minimum lease payments is €625,500 and the implicit rate of interest in the lease is 10%. The equipment originally cost JAZZ €500,000.

Issue 2 On 1 April 2012, JAZZ entered into two non-cancellable operating leases. One of the leases relates to equipment and runs for a period of two years, with monthly payments of €10,000; the other lease is in respect of property rental and extends for three years, with quarterly payments of €25,000.

Issue 3 On 1 January 2012, JAZZ sold excavation machinery with a remaining useful life of four years to RAP Limited (RAP). Although the book value of the machinery at the date of disposal was €25,000,000, the machinery was sold for its fair market value of €38,000,000. Immediately after the sale, JAZZ leased back the machinery from RAP for a period of four years on a non-cancellable lease. Rental payments under the lease amount to €10,875,000 per annum for four years, payable in advance. At the end of the four-year term, JAZZ may purchase the machinery from RAP for €1. During the term of the lease, JAZZ is responsible for the upkeep and maintenance of the machinery. Prior to the sale, the machinery was depreciated on a straight-line basis. The implicit rate of interest in the lease is 10% per annum.

Requirement Show how each of the issues should be reflected in the financial statements of JAZZ for the year ended 31 December 2012.

Question 8.2 (Based on Chartered Accountants Ireland, CAP 2 Autumn 2010, Question 2)

> ***Please note*** that this question covers a number of related issues, some of which are covered more fully in other chapters. Consequently, before attempting this question, you should also study **Chapter 14** and **Chapter 35**.

You are the financial accountant of Redflash Limited ("Redflash"), a medium-sized Irish company that makes specialised tents for extreme conditions and that prepares its financial statements to 31 December each year. Upon your return from holidays you learn that your assistant was pressurised by the managing director for draft financial statements for the year ended 31 December 2012 in advance of a meeting with the company's bankers. The draft financial statements for the year ended 31 December 2012 prepared by your assistant indicate:

Redflash

DRAFT STATEMENT OF PROFIT OR LOSS AND OTHER COMPREHENSIVE INCOME
for the Year Ended 31 December 2012

	€
Revenue	38,750,000
Operating profit	16,800,000
Finance costs	(300,000)
	16,500,000
Income tax expense	(5,250,000)
	11,250,000

Redflash

DRAFT STATEMENT OF FINANCIAL POSITION
at 31 December 2012

	€
ASSETS	
Non-current Assets	6,000,000
Current Assets	18,000,000
	24,000,000
EQUITY AND LIABILITIES	
Equity	20,000,000
Non-current Liabilities	2,500,000
Current Liabilities	1,500,000
	24,000,000

While discussing the draft financial statements for the year ended 31 December 2012 with your assistant, the following matters come to your attention:

1. A payment of €1,100,000 made on 1 January 2012 in respect of a hydrostatic fabric cutting machine has been charged to the draft statement of profit or loss and other comprehensive income in arriving at operating profit. This payment was the first of four annual payments due on 1 January each year, under a lease agreement entered into on 1 January 2012. The cost of the hydrostatic fabric-cutting machine if purchased outright on 1 January 2012, which has an estimated useful economic life of five years, was €3,835,000. The implicit interest rate in the lease is 10% per annum.

2. One of the new products introduced to the market by Redflash in 2012 was a two-man tent that is available in three models: standard, advanced and super deluxe. While it is estimated that 20%, 15% and 10% of the standard, advanced and super deluxe models,

respectively, will require repair during their warranty period, the company is uncertain when claims may arise during the warranty period. During the year ended 31 December 2012, REDFLASH spent €52,000 repairing new two-man tents sold during 2012. This has been charged in arriving at operating profit for the year ended 31 December 2012. No other costs are included in the financial statements for the year ended 31 December 2012 in relation to potential future repair costs of the new two-man tents and the following information is available with respect to the new two-man tents:

Model	Warranty Period	Estimated Repair Costs per Tent	Number Sold During Year Ended 31 December 2012
Standard	2 years	€150	5,000
Advanced	3 years	€200	7,500
Super deluxe	4 years	€250	4,000

REDFASH expects future sales of the two-man tent to be similar to those in 2010.

Requirement
(a) Revise Redflash's draft statement of profit or loss and other comprehensive income for the year ended 31 December 2012 and draft statement of financial position at that date in light of the above information.
(b) Prepare a memorandum addressed to the managing director of Redflash that clearly analyses and interprets the impact of the adjustments on the original draft financial statements and illustrates the effect of the adjustments on the company's key accounting ratios.

Note: *you may ignore the tax effect of any adjustments.*

Question 8.3

You are employed as the financial accountant for Denver plc, a company listed on the Stock Exchange. The managing director of Denver plc has heard that you have recently attended a number of training courses on IFRS and that you are in the process of preparing the company's financial statements for the year ended 31 December 2012 in accordance with IFRS. The managing director is confused in relation to the reporting of lease transactions in the financial statements. Denver plc has recently entered into the following finance lease agreements:

Machine A
Denver plc leased the machine for three years from John plc. The machine had a cash price of €38,000. A deposit of €5,000 was payable on 1 January 2012, followed by six half-yearly payments of €6,500, payable in arrears and commencing on 30 June 2012. Finance charges are to be allocated on a sum of digits basis. The machine has a useful life of five years.

Machine B
This machine is being leased over four years from RBT bank, commencing 1 January 2012. Rental payments are €20,000 per annum, payable in advance. The rate of interest implicit in the lease is 10%. The machine has a fair value of €70,000 and a useful life of six years. The present value of minimum lease payments amounted to €69,738. Finance charges are allocated using the actuarial method.

Requirement

(a) Discuss how the accounting treatment of assets acquired under finance leases reflects the definition of elements and the measurement bases as set out in the IASB's *Conceptual Framework for Financial Reporting 2010*.

(b) Calculate the amounts to be included in the financial statements of Denver plc for the year ended 31 December 2012 in relation to both leases. You should include the reconciliation note for plant and equipment, and the analysis of finance lease liabilities note required by IAS 17 *Leases*.

INTANGIBLE ASSETS

9

LEARNING OBJECTIVES

Having studied this chapter, you should be able to:
1. define an intangible asset;
2. explain when expenditure on an intangible asset can be capitalised and demonstrate how such expenditure should be recognised and measured;
3. discuss how to account for internally generated goodwill;
4. explain what conditions must be satisfied before development expenditure can be capitalised; and
5. apply the main disclosure requirements of IAS 38 *Intangible Assets*.

KEY TERMS AND DEFINITIONS FOR THIS CHAPTER

In order to aid your understanding of the concepts and issues covered in this chapter, it is important to understand and be familiar with the following key terms and definitions. As you study this chapter, you should refer back to them.

Amortisation The systematic allocation of the depreciable amount of an **intangible asset** over its useful life.

Carrying Amount/Value This is the amount at which an asset is recognised in the statement of financial position after deducting any accumulated amortisation and any accumulated impairment losses (i.e. it is the amount at which the asset is stated in the financial statements).

Development The application of research findings or other knowledge to plan or design the production of new or substantially improved materials, devices, products, processes, systems or services prior to the commencement of commercial production or use.

Fair Value The amount for which an asset could be exchanged between knowledgeable and willing parties in an arm's length transaction.

Human Capital This is the stock of competences, knowledge and personality attributes embodied in the workforce of the business so as to produce economic value.

Intangible Asset An intangible asset is an identifiable non-monetary asset without physical substance. Examples of such assets include organisational ability, research and development, customer databases, exclusivity within a particular market or geographic area, software, customer satisfaction and the speed at which companies are able to bring new products and services to market.

Research This is an original and planned investigation undertaken with the prospect of gaining new scientific or technical knowledge and understanding.

Residual Value This represents the estimated amount that an organisation would currently expect to obtain from disposal of an asset, after deducting the estimated costs of disposal, if the asset were of the age and in the condition expected at the end of its estimated useful life.

9.1 INTRODUCTION

Most entities have different types of tangible non-current asset, such as property, plant, machinery and computers, which, if necessary, can be exchanged in trade or used to pay off debts. Assets like these normally have established market values and are relatively easy to quantify and include on financial reports. However, many entities also possess **intangible assets**, which have real value but are much harder to measure and quantify than their tangible counterparts. Examples of such assets include organisational ability, research and development, customer databases, exclusivity within a particular market or geographic area, software, customer satisfaction and the speed at which companies are able to bring new products and services to market.

Intangible assets are important to the future success of a business. For example, a strong brand can influence customers' decision-making processes, as well as enabling a premium price to be charged, as it is perceived as a guarantee of quality and, sometimes, even social status. Furthermore, brand recognition can make it easier to enter new geographical markets or sell new products. Intangible assets, therefore, provide potential competitive advantage, but as assets they clearly demand specialist attention given their nature. Consequently, although intangible assets may not be visible to the naked eye in the same way that tangible assets are, it is important for businesses to understand the intangible assets that they have and find ways to capture and preserve them. However, despite widespread acceptance that intangible assets, such as brands, are critical to the future success of a business, they are often not reflected in a business's financial statements. One reason for this is that it can be difficult to obtain reliable information on the value of brands or patents, which, together with the sensitivity of that information, has perhaps resulted in reluctance by businesses to reflect such assets in their statement of financial position.

Notwithstanding the description above, **intangible assets** can be defined as identifiable non-monetary assets that cannot be seen, touched or physically measured, which are created through time and/or effort and that are identifiable as separate assets.

There are two primary forms of 'intangible asset' or 'intangibles':

1. **Legal intangibles**, such as trade secrets (e.g. customer lists), copyrights, patents, fishing licences, import quotas, franchises, trademarks and goodwill. Legal intangibles are known under the generic term **intellectual property** and generate legal property rights defensible in a court of law.
2. **Competitive intangibles**, such as knowledge activities (i.e. know-how and knowledge), collaboration activities, leverage activities (i.e. organisational processes, policies and procedures) and structural activities (i.e. the extent to which an organisation depends on employee interaction and knowledge-sharing) are the source from which the competitive advantage of an organisation derives, or is lost. Competitive intangibles, such as customer loyalty or supplier relationships, while legally non-ownable, directly impact effectiveness, productivity, wastage and opportunity costs within an organisation and consequently costs, revenues, customer service and satisfaction, market value and share price. **Human capital** is the primary source of competitive intangibles for organisations today.

Key to this Chapter

Companies frequently expend resources, or incur liabilities, on the acquisition, development, maintenance or enhancement of intangible resources, such as scientific or technical knowledge, design and implementation of new processes or systems, licences, intellectual property, market knowledge and trademarks. IAS 38 *Intangible Assets* was introduced in order to give guidance as to how to account for intangible assets, including **research** and **development** activities.

IAS 38 is an important accounting standard that impacts upon, and is impacted by, a number of issues in financial reporting, including accounting for business combinations (see **Part V** of this **text**) and impairment (see **Chapter 10**). Consequently, it is important to have a clear understanding of the definition of an intangible asset and how such expenditure should be recognised and initially measured, in particular research and development expenditure.

This chapter begins by explaining the objective and scope of IAS 38, before considering whether expenditure on 'intangibles' should be expensed immediately in the SPLOCI or capitalised as an intangible asset in the statement of financial position. The distinction between internally generated goodwill and internally generated intangible assets is then discussed, followed by the identification of what elements of expenditure should be capitalised/ initially recognised at cost in accordance with IAS 38. The measurement of intangible assets after initial recognition using either the cost or valuation models is explained, together with related issues, such as useful life, the **amortisation** period and the derecognition of intangible assets.

9.2 IAS 38 *INTANGIBLE ASSETS*

Objective and Scope of IAS 38

The objective of IAS 38 *Intangible Assets* is to prescribe the accounting treatment for intangible assets. In simple terms, when an entity incurs expenditure on 'intangibles', there are two options as to how that is treated/recorded in the financial statements:

- either it is expensed immediately in the SPLOCI; or
- it is capitalised as an intangible asset in the statement of financial position.

IAS 38 therefore specifies when expenditure on 'intangibles' can be capitalised (i.e. recognised in the financial statements as an intangible asset), how to measure the **carrying amount** of intangible assets and the disclosures that are required.

IAS 38 prescribes the accounting treatment for intangible assets, *except for*:
- intangible assets covered by another standard, for example, those for sale in the ordinary course of business (see **Chapter 20**), deferred tax assets (see **Chapter 13**), leases under IAS 17 *Leases* (see **Chapter 8**), employee benefits under IAS 19 *Employee Benefits* (see **Chapter 17**) and goodwill, which is addressed in IFRS 3 *Business Combinations* (see **Chapter 26**);
- financial assets as defined per IAS 32 *Financial Instruments: Presentation*, IAS 39 *Financial Instruments: Recognition and Measurement* and IFRS 7 *Financial Instruments: Disclosures* (see **Chapter 25**);
- mineral rights and expenditure on the exploration for, or development and extraction of, minerals, oil, natural gas and similar non-regenerative resources; and
- insurance contracts with policy-holders.

As some intangibles may be contained in a physical asset (e.g. a compact disc), judgement is required to decide if IAS 16 *Property, Plant and Equipment* or IAS 38 should be applied. In broad terms, where software is *not* an integral part of related hardware, it is an intangible asset and therefore IAS 38 applies.

Capitalising Intangible Assets

As mentioned above, in simple terms, when an entity incurs expenditure on 'intangibles', **the key question is whether that expenditure should be expensed immediately in the SPLOCI or capitalised as an intangible asset in the statement of financial position**.

In order for the expenditure to be capitalised, it must meet the IAS 38 definition of an intangible asset. This definition includes the following three criteria, ***all*** of which must be met:
1. identifiability;
2. control over a resource; and
3. the existence of future economic benefits.

If the expenditure fails to meet *all* of the above criteria, then the expenditure must be expensed. Each of the criteria is now discussed in more detail.

1. Identifiability

An intangible asset meets the identifiability criterion when it:
(a) is separable (i.e. capable of being separated or divided from the entity and sold, transferred, licensed, rented or exchanged, either individually or together with a related contract, asset or liability); or
(b) arises from contractual or other legal rights, regardless of whether those rights are transferable or separable from the entity or from other rights and obligations.

2. Control over a Resource

An entity controls an intangible asset if it has the power to obtain future economic benefits and restrict the access of others to those benefits. Capacity to control is usually, but not necessarily, via legal rights. Market and technical knowledge may give rise to future economic benefits if protected by legal rights, such as copyright, a restraint of trade agreement or by a legal duty on employees to maintain confidentiality.

Skilled staff, specific management or technical talent are *unlikely* to meet the definition of an intangible asset unless protected by legal rights and capable of satisfying the other criteria in the definition. An entity has not sufficient control over customer loyalty and customer relationships and thus is also unlikely to meet the definition.

3. Existence of Future Economic Benefits

While future economic benefits can be a number of things, it typically includes revenue from the sale of products or services, cost savings or other benefits resulting from the use of the asset (e.g. the use of intellectual property may reduce future production costs rather than increase future revenues). An entity should assess the probability of future economic benefits using reasonable and supportable assumptions that represent management's best estimate of the economic conditions that will exist over the asset's useful life (see **Example 9.2**). Greater weight should be given to external evidence when using judgement as to the degree of certainty attached to future flows.

Expenditure that meets the three criteria discussed above should be *measured initially at cost*. You should now read **Example 9.1**.

EXAMPLE 9.1: MEETING RECOGNITION CRITERIA

An entity is developing a new production process. During 2011, expenditure incurred was €1,000, of which €900 was incurred before 1 December 2011 and €100 was incurred in December 2011. At 1 December 2011, the production process met the criteria for recognition as an intangible asset. At the end of 2011 an intangible asset of €100 should be recorded, with €900 being expensed (i.e. incurred before recognition criteria met).

During 2012, further expenditure incurred amounted to €2,000. At the end of 2012 the recoverable amount of the know-how is estimated to be €1,900.

Therefore, at the end of 2012 the cost of the production process is €2,100 (€100 + €2,000). An impairment loss of €200 needs to be recorded, which may be reversed in a subsequent period if the requirements in IAS 36 are met (see **Chapter 10**).

To summarise at this point, in order for expenditure on intangibles to be capitalised, it must meet each and all of the three criteria (identifiability, control over a resource and the existence of future economic benefits) specified in IAS 38. Otherwise it should be expensed immediately in the SPLOCI. With respect to expenditure that *does* meet the three criteria, it should be measured initially in the statement of financial position at cost. The practical application of these three criteria is illustrated in **Example 9.3**.

If an entity acquires an intangible asset from a third party, it clearly meets the three criteria and should be measured initially in the statement of financial position at cost. However, an entity may also incur expenditure with the aim of developing an intangible asset internally (rather than through external acquisition). In broad terms, this type of expenditure may lead to either **internally generated goodwill** or an **internally generated intangible asset**. Each of these is now discussed below.

Internally Generated Goodwill

Goodwill is an accounting concept meaning the value of an entity over and above the value of its assets. Some expenditure, while it may be incurred with the aim of generating future revenues, does not result in an intangible asset being recognised in the financial statements. For example, though money spent by a company on developing customer relationships may help generate its future revenues, it will not result in an *identifiable* asset that could be sold separately from the business activities. Consequently, as it does not meet the identifiability criterion as discussed above, it cannot be recognised as an intangible asset under IAS 38. This expenditure is often referred to as contributing to **internally generated goodwill**.

IAS 38 states that internally generated goodwill should ***not*** be recognised as an asset. This is principally because of the difficulty, or impossibility, of separately identifying the events or transactions that contribute to the overall goodwill of the entity. Even if these were identifiable, the extent to which they generate future benefits and the value of such benefits are not usually capable of being measured reliably. Internally generated goodwill that is not recognised as an asset will either go completely unrecognised (if no expenditure was incurred) or will be recognised as an expense in the period incurred.

Internally Generated Intangible Assets – Development Costs

Development costs are the main internally generated intangible asset considered in IAS 38, with a distinction being made between expenditure incurred in either the *research* or *development* phases. If the enterprise is unable to distinguish between the research and development phases, then the entire expenditure must be recorded as a research phase expense.

Particularly from an examination perspective, as they are common examples, it is important to note that, for example, internally generated brands, mastheads, publishing titles and customer lists are *not* recognised as assets because they cannot be distinguished from the cost of developing the business as a whole. Consequently, expenditure on these items should be expensed in the SPLOCI in the period incurred.

Research Phase

IAS 38 states that **no intangible asset can arise in the research phase and the expenditure incurred during this phase must be written off as an expense since it is not possible to demonstrate that future economic benefits exist**. Examples of research phase expenditure include:
• activities aimed at obtaining new knowledge;
• the search for, evaluation and final selection of applications of research findings;

- the search for alternatives for materials, devices, products, processes, systems or services; and
- the formulation, design, evaluation and final selection of possible alternatives for new or improved materials, products, devices, processes, systems or devices.

The overriding feature of expenditure during this phase is that it tends to be exploratory and without a clearly defined outcome. Thus, expenditure on research should be recognised as an expense in the SPLOCI when it is incurred.

Development Phase

Expenditure incurred during the development phase must be recognised in the statement of financial position if, and only if, an enterprise can demonstrate *all* of the following criteria:
1. the technical feasibility of completing the intangible asset so that it will be available for use or sale;
2. the enterprise's intention to complete the intangible asset and use or sell it;
3. its ability to use or sell the intangible asset;
4. how the intangible asset will generate probable future economic benefits. The company should demonstrate the existence of a market for the output generated by the intangible asset or, if used internally, its usefulness;
5. the availability of adequate technical, financial and other resources to complete the development and to use or sell the intangible asset; and
6. the enterprise's ability to reliably measure the expenditure attributable to the intangible asset during its development.

The existence of these criteria could be verified by an internal business plan or by evidence of a lender's willingness to provide external finance for the project. Internal costing systems can often measure reliably the cost of generating an intangible asset internally, such as salary and other expenditure in securing copyrights or licences or developing computer software. Examples of development activities are the:
- design, construction and testing of pre-production or pre-use prototypes and models;
- design of tools, jigs, moulds and dies involving new technology;
- design, construction and operation of a pilot plant that is not of a scale economically feasible for commercial production; and
- design, construction and testing of a chosen alternative for new or improved materials, devices, products, processes, systems or services.

Once expenditure has been identified as relating to the development phase, the next decision is what elements of that expenditure should be capitalised/initially recognised at cost. This is now explained.

Cost of an Internally Generated Intangible Asset

The cost of an internally generated intangible asset comprises all expenditure that can be directly attributable and is necessary to creating, producing and preparing the asset so that it is capable of operating in the manner intended by management. The cost includes, if applicable:
- expenditure on materials and services used or consumed in generating the intangible asset;

- the salaries, wages and other employment-related costs of personnel directly engaged in generating the asset; and
- any expenditure directly attributable to generating the asset, such as fees to register a legal right and the amortisation of patents and licences.

The following are *not* included:
- selling, administration and other general overheads, unless directly attributable to the asset;
- clearly identified inefficiencies and initial operating losses; and
- expenditure on training staff to operate the asset.

Expenditure initially expensed in previous years may *not* be reinstated as part of an asset at a later date.

Subsequent Expenditure

Consistent with the principles contained in the *Conceptual Framework for Financial Reporting 2010* (see **Chapter 1**), subsequent expenditure should be expensed when incurred, *unless*:
(a) it is probable that the expenditure will increase future economic benefits beyond that originally assessed prior to the expenditure taking place; and
(b) the expenditure can be attributed to the asset and be measured reliably.

If both conditions (a) and (b) above are met, the subsequent expenditure should be added to the cost of the intangible asset.

Subsequent expenditure on development costs should be evaluated in accordance with the 'research' and 'development' phase principles outlined above. This effectively means that subsequent expenditure should be: expensed if it is in the nature of research expenditure; expensed if development expenditure but fails to satisfy the recognition criteria as an intangible asset; and added to the cost of the intangible asset if it satisfies the recognition criteria.

As noted above, subsequent expenditure on items such as brands, mastheads, customer lists, etc. should always be expensed to avoid the recognition of internally generated goodwill.

Measurement after Initial Recognition

As explained above, expenditure that meets the three criteria for capitalisation should be *measured initially at cost*. However, like other non-current assets (e.g. investment property (**Chapter 5**) and property, plant and equipment (**Chapter 6**)), after initial recognition there is a **choice as to how this expenditure can be recorded in the financial statements**. Under IAS 38, an entity may choose *either* **the cost model** *or* **the revaluation model**. Each of these models in now explained.

The Cost Model

Under the cost model, the intangible asset is carried at cost less accumulated **amortisation** (which is the equivalent to depreciation for tangible assets) and impairment losses (see **Chapter 10**).

The Revaluation Model

Under the revaluation model, the intangible asset is carried at a revalued amount, being its **fair value** at the date of the revaluation less any subsequent accumulated amortisation and impairment losses. Fair value should refer to an active market for the intangible asset. Revaluations should be carried out with sufficient regularity so that the **carrying value** is not materially different from the fair value at the statement of financial position date. The frequency of revaluations depends on the volatility of the fair values and, if they are significant, an annual valuation may be necessary. If there is no active market, then the class of asset *must* be carried at cost less accumulated amortisation and impairment losses. Furthermore, if the fair value can no longer be determined by reference to an active market, the carrying amount of the asset should be its revalued amount at the date of the last revaluation less accumulated amortisation and impairment losses. The fact that there is no active market should also trigger an impairment review (see **Chapter 10**).

Consistent with the treatment of tangible assets in accordance with IAS 16 (see **Chapter 6**), if an intangible asset is revalued, all the other assets in that class should also be revalued unless there is no active market for those assets. This is to prevent selective revaluation and reporting of a mixture of costs and values as at different dates.

Decreases in Fair Value The normal treatment for a decrease in the carrying amount as a result of a revaluation is to recognise it in arriving at profit/loss in the statement of profit or loss and other comprehensive income. The exception to this is where it reverses a surplus on the same asset, in which case it should be debited to the revaluation reserve in the equity section of the statement of financial position (and shown as a 'loss' under 'other comprehensive income') to the extent of a previous surplus on the same asset. This is the same accounting treatment as used for property, plant and equipment (IAS 16 – see **Chapter 6**, **Examples 6.12** and **6.13**).

Increases in Fair Value If the carrying amount of an intangible asset is increased as a result of a revaluation, the increase should be credited directly to 'equity' (and shown in 'other comprehensive income') *unless* it reverses a revaluation decrease (of the same asset) previously recognised in arriving at profit/loss, in which case the increase should also be recognised in arriving at profit/loss. Again, this is the same accounting treatment as used for property, plant and equipment (IAS 16 – see **Chapter 6**, **Examples 6.12** and **6.13**).

Again, similar to the treatment of tangible assets in accordance with IAS 16 (see **Chapter 6**, **Example 6.15**), if an intangible asset is revalued, any accumulated amortisation at the date of revaluation is either:
• restated proportionately with change in the gross carrying amount of the asset so that the carrying amount of the asset after revaluation equals its revalued amount; or
• eliminated against the gross carrying amount of the asset and the net amount restated to the revalued amount of the asset.

The cumulative revaluation surplus included in equity can be transferred directly to retained earnings when the surplus is realised (i.e. on retirement or disposal of the asset).

Useful Life of an Intangible Asset

IAS 38 requires that all the intangible assets be assessed to determine if their useful life is **indefinite** or **finite**. An *indefinite life* is one where there is no foreseeable limit to the period over which the asset is expected to generate net cash inflows for the entity. However, the term 'indefinite' does not mean infinite. A conclusion that the useful life is indefinite should *not* depend on planned future expenditure in excess of that required to maintain the asset at that standard of performance. An intangible asset with a *finite life* should be amortised, while an intangible asset with an indefinite life should not.

Many factors must be considered in determining the useful life of an intangible asset, including:
- the expected usage of the asset and whether it can be managed efficiently;
- typical product lifecycles;
- technical, technological, commercial or other types of obsolescence. For example, computer software is susceptible to changes in technology and should be written off over a short useful life. While the useful life may be very long, uncertainty justifies estimating the useful life on a prudent basis, although it does not justify an unrealistically short life;
- the stability of the industry in which the asset operates and changes in market demand;
- expected actions by competitors;
- the level of maintenance expenditure required to obtain future benefits;
- the period of control over the asset; and
- whether the useful life is dependent on the useful life of other assets in the entity.

The useful life of an intangible asset that arises from contractual or other legal rights should not exceed the period of the legal or contractual rights and may be shorter. The useful life may include a renewal period, but only if there is evidence to support renewal by the entity without significant cost. If there are both legal and economic factors influencing the useful life of an intangible asset, then the economic factors determine the period over which benefits will be received, but the legal factors may restrict the period over which the entity controls access to those benefits (i.e. the length of the contract is shorter than the economic life). The useful life is the shorter of the periods determined by these factors.

Useful life should be reviewed each period to determine whether events and circumstances support an indefinite useful life. If not, the change should be treated as a change in accounting estimate by amortising the asset over its remaining useful life in accordance with IAS 8 *Accounting Policies, Changes in Accounting Estimates and Errors* (see **Chapter 21**). Again, this is consistent with the treatment of tangible non-current assets (see **Chapter 6**, **Example 6.10**). It is important to note that a reassessment of useful life is a sign that the asset should be tested for impairment and any excess of the carrying amount over the recoverable amount should be treated as an impairment loss (see **Chapter 10**).

Issues associated with determining the useful life of an intangible asset are explained in the different scenarios presented in **Example 9.2**.

EXAMPLES 9.2: HOW TO DETERMINE 'USEFUL LIFE'

(a) An Acquired Customer List – if a direct mail company acquires a customer list and expects to derive benefit for at least one year, but not more than three years, the customer list should be amortised over the best estimate of useful life (for example, 18 months).

Even the intention to add customer names to the list must be ignored as the asset relates only to the list of customers that existed at the date it was acquired. (It should also be reviewed for impairment under IAS 36 *Impairment of Assets* – see **Chapter 10**.)

(b) An Acquired Patent that Expires in 15 Years – if there is a commitment to sell the patent after five years to a third party for 60% of the fair value of the patent at the date it was acquired, the patent should be amortised over five years with a **residual value** of 60% of the present value of the patent's fair value at the date it was acquired. (It should also be reviewed for impairment under IAS 36 *Impairment of Assets* – see **Chapter 10**.)

(c) An Acquired Copyright that has a Remaining Legal Life of 50 Years – if an analysis of consumer habits subsequently provides evidence that there are only 30 years left of future benefits, the asset must now be amortised over the new expected remaining estimated useful life of 30 years, as well as reviewing the asset for impairment.

(d) An Acquired Broadcast Licence that Expires in Five Years – assume the licence is renewable every 10 years, can be renewed indefinitely at little cost, the entity intends to renew the licence and the technology is not expected to be replaced in the foreseeable future. The licence would therefore be treated as having an indefinite useful life and thus the licence would not be amortised until its useful life is determined to be finite. The licence would be tested for impairment at the end of each annual reporting period and whenever there is an indication of impairment.

(e) The Broadcast Licence is Revoked – assume the licensing authority will no longer renew licences but decides to auction them and that there are three years before the licence expires. The useful life is no longer indefinite and must be amortised over the remaining useful life of three years, as well as being tested for impairment.

(f) An Acquired Airline Route Authority between Two Major Cities Expires in Three Years – the route authority must be renewed every five years and this is routinely granted at minimal cost and, historically, this route authority has been renewed. The acquiring entity expects to service the route indefinitely and cash flow analysis supports that view. The intangible asset therefore has an indefinite life and should not be amortised until its useful life is determined to be finite. It must, however, be tested annually for impairment and whenever there is an indication of an impairment.

(g) An Acquired Trademark Used to Identify and Distinguish a Leading Consumer Product that has been a Market Leader for the Past Eight Years – a trademark has a legal life of five years, but is renewable every 10 years at little cost and the entity intends to renew. This asset has an indefinite life and should not be amortised until its useful life is determined to be definite. It should also be tested for impairment annually or when there is an indication of impairment.

(h) A Trademark Acquired 10 Years Ago that Distinguishes a Leading Consumer Product – unexpected competition has emerged that will reduce future sales by 20%, but management expects that the 80% will continue indefinitely. An impairment must be recognised immediately to reduce the trademark to the recoverable amount. It would continue to be subject to annual impairment, although not amortised.

(i) A Trademark for a Line of Products Acquired Several Years Ago in a Business Combination – this is a well-established product on the market for 35 years. There is an expectation that there was no limit to the period of time it would contribute to cash flows, thus it has not been amortised. Management has recently decided that the product line will be discontinued over the next four years. It must now be tested for impairment and subsequently amortised over the next four years.

Amortisation Period and Method

Having discussed above how to determine the useful life of an intangible asset, it is now logical to discuss the amortisation of the intangible asset over its estimated useful life.

Under IAS 38, the carrying value of an intangible asset should be allocated over its useful life. As with tangible assets, the most difficult decision for management is determining the useful life of the asset. The useful life of an intangible asset should take account of such things as the:
• expected usage of the asset;
• possible obsolescence and expected actions of competitors;
• stability of the industry; and
• market demand for the products and services that the asset is generating.

Amortisation of the intangible asset should be allocated on a systematic basis over its useful life from the day it is available for use. This means that the basis should reflect the pattern of economic benefits being consumed – though the straight-line method should be adopted if the pattern of economic benefits cannot be determined reliably. IAS 38 requires the amortisation charge to be expensed unless permitted by another standard to be capitalised (e.g. IAS 2 *Inventory* – see **Chapter 11**). Though the method selected should be applied consistently, it would be rare for persuasive evidence to support a method that would result in lower amortisation than that achieved by straight-line, i.e. it is likely that the appropriate method will be straight-line.

The amortisation period and method should be reviewed at the end of each annual reporting period. If the expected useful life is different from previous estimates, the amortisation period should be changed. If there is a change in the expected pattern of consumption of future benefits, the amortisation period should be accounted for as a change in accounting estimates as per IAS 8 *Accounting Policies, Changes in Accounting Estimates and Errors* (e.g. it may become apparent that the reducing balance method is more appropriate than straight-line).

An intangible asset with an indefinite useful life should *not* be amortised. However, it is required to be tested annually for impairment and whenever there is an indication of impairment.

Derecognition, Retirement and Disposal

The discussion so far has focused upon the initial recognition and subsequent amortisation of intangible assets. At some point, however, it is likely that it will be necessary to cease to recognise (i.e. **derecognise**) an intangible asset in the statement of financial position. This situation is now addressed.

An intangible asset should be derecognised when:
(a) it is disposed of; or
(b) there are no future economic benefits expected from its use or disposal.

Gains or losses should be calculated as the difference between the net disposal proceeds and the carrying amount of the asset and should be recognised as income/expenses in the SPLOCI in the period in which the retirement or disposal occurs. The date of disposal should be determined by applying IAS 18 and the consideration should be valued initially at fair value. If the latter is deferred, then it should be recognised at the cash price equivalent. The difference between the nominal amount of the consideration and the cash price equivalent is recognised as interest revenue under IAS 18, according to the effective yield on the receivable.

Amortisation should not cease on temporary idleness of the intangible asset, unless it has already fully depreciated.

This section has covered a substantial volume of material and it is likely that it will have to be read (and re-read) on a number of occasions in order to fully grasp all of the issues covered. The following example draws together a number of the issues covered so far in relation to IAS 38.

EXAMPLE 9.3: SUMMARY OF BASIC PRINCIPLES

Aspire plc develops and manufactures drugs for the pharmaceutical industry. The following information relates to the company's activities in research and development for the year ended 31 December 2012.

	Project				
	1	2	3	4	5
	€000	€000	€000	€000	€000
Deferred development expenditure at 1 January 2012	400	-	570	-	-
Development expenditure incurred during 2012:					
Salaries and wages	40	33	-	60	20
Fees to register legal rights	-	2	-	2	4
Materials and services	5	15	-	12	5
Patents and licences	2	2	-	-	-
Market research costs	-	20	-	4	-

Additional Information:

Project 1: this project was originally expected to be highly profitable, but this is now in doubt as the high-profile scientist in charge of the project has left Aspire plc to join a competitor.

Project 2: €400,000 development expenditure on this project has already been written off in previous years. The directors now believe, on the best advice, that the project will earn revenue considerably in excess of all development costs and therefore now wish to reinstate the expenditure previously written off.

Project 3: commercial production started during the year. Sales were 30,000 units in 2012, and future sales are expected to be: 2013 – 60,000 units; 2014 – 40,000 units; 2015 – 10,000 units. No sales are expected after 2015.

Project 4: the costs related to the development of a new compound which meets the criteria for deferral of expenditure, and the development is expected to take three years.

Project 5: this is another new project, involving the development of a 'loss leader', expected to raise the level of future sales.

During 2012, Aspire plc spent €150,000 in order to exhibit its product range at a major overseas trade fair. This was the first time that Aspire plc had attended such an event. No orders have been received as a direct result of the fair, although the sales director has argued that contacts were made that will generate sales over the next few years. The company also spent €300,000 on staff training and development during the year. The company expects to achieve cost savings of €120,000 over the next three years.

Aspire plc's accounting policy for research and development is in accordance with the requirements of IAS 38 *Intangible Assets*. In applying this policy, Aspire writes off development expenditure in relation to estimated sales of its products (in units).

Requirement
(a) Explain, with supporting calculations, how the above projects should be treated in the financial statements of Aspire plc for the year ended 31 December 2012.
(b) Explain how the costs associated with the trade fair and staff development should be treated in Aspire plc's financial statements.

Solution

(a)
Project 1: expenditure, including that relating to the previous year, should be written off in 2012 as there is now considerable doubt about the outcome of the project.

Project 2: expenditure for 2012 can be deferred, but previous expenditure cannot be reinstated (per IAS 38).

Project 3: since commercial production has started, previous expenditure deferred should now be amortised. This will be done as a percentage of sales (units) of product.

Project 4: the development costs will be deferred.

Project 5: since the project is not expected to be profitable, its development costs should not be deferred.

Disclosure:
Non-current Assets
Intangible Assets   €574,000

Accounting policy note

Research and development expenditure is written off as incurred, except that development expenditure meeting specific criteria outlined in IAS 38 *Intangible Assets,* incurred on an individual project, is carried forward when its future recovery can be foreseen with reasonable assurance. Any expenditure deferred is amortised in proportion to estimated sales of products (in units).

Development costs:

	€000	€000
Balance b/f		970
Development expenditure incurred during the year	202	
Development expenditure written off during the year	598	(396)
		574

WORKINGS:

	Project					
	1	2	3	4	5	Total
	€000	€000	€000	€000	€000	€000
Deferred development expenditure at 1 January 2012	400	–	570	–	–	970
Development expenditure incurred during 2012:						
Salaries and wages	40	33	–	60	20	153
Fees to register legal rights	–	2	–	2	4	8
Materials and services	5	15	–	12	5	37
Patents and licences	2	2	–	–	–	4
	47	52	–	74	29	202
Total	447	52	570	74	29	1,172
Amortised in 2012	–	–	(122*)	–	–	(122)
Expensed in 2012**	(447)	–	–	–	(29)	(476)
Deferred at 31 December 2012	–	52	448	74	–	574

* 30/140 × €570,00 = €122,000

** Market research costs of €24,000 (Projects 2 and 4) also expensed in 2012.

(b)

There are no accounting rules that specifically address how the costs associated with the trade fair should be accounted for. However, it is unlikely that the company could justify doing anything other than writing off the cost because there is no particular reason to believe that the costs will be recovered. Although it might be a different matter if Aspire plc had obtained a number of orders from the fair. In relation to the staff development programme, no asset will be recognised because staff are not under the control of Aspire plc and when they leave, the benefits of the training, whatever they may be, also leave. The full €300,000 must be recognised in the SPLOCI in 2012.

9.3 DISCLOSURE

Most entities have different types of tangible non-current asset, such as property, plant, machinery and computers; assets which typically have established market values and are relatively easy to quantify and include on financial reports. However, many entities also possess valuable intangible assets, which have real value but are much harder to measure and quantify. Examples of such intangibles include organisational ability, research and development, customer databases, exclusivity within a particular market or geographic area, software and customer satisfaction. Intangible assets are important to the future success of a business and although they may not be as visible as tangible assets, it is important for businesses to capture, preserve and report on such assets.

The recognition and disclosure of information on intangible assets is of interest to users of financial statements and IAS 38 seeks to enhance the information provided. IAS 38 has extensive disclosure requirements with respect to intangible assets. These include:

General

The following should be disclosed for *each class* of intangible assets (see below for examples of classes of intangible asset), analysed between internally generated and other intangible assets:
- whether the useful lives are indefinite or finite and, if the latter, their useful lives or the amortisation rates used;
- the amortisation methods adopted;
- the gross carrying amount and accumulated amortisation at the start and end of the period;
- the line item of the SPLOCI in which the amortisation charge is included;
- a reconciliation of the carrying amount at the start and end of the period, showing: additions, split between internal, acquired and via business combinations;
  - retirements and disposals;
  - revaluations;
  - impairment losses;
  - impairment losses reversed;
  - amortisation during the period;
  - net exchange differences; and
  - other changes in carrying amount.

A class of intangible assets may include:
- brand names;
- mastheads and publishing rights;
- computer software;
- licences and franchises;
- copyrights, patents and other industrial property rights;
- recipes, formulae, models, designs and prototypes; and
- intangible assets under development.

The financial statements should also disclose:
(a) if an intangible asset has an indefinite useful life, the carrying amount and the reasons supporting the assessment of that life. The significant factors should be described;
(b) a description, the carrying amount and remaining amortisation period of any individual intangible asset that is material to the entity as a whole;
(c) for acquired intangibles via grant – the initial fair value, their carrying amount and whether carried under the benchmark or allowed alternative treatment for subsequent measurement;
(d) the existence and carrying amounts of intangibles whose title is restricted or pledged for security; and
(e) the amount of contractual commitments for acquisition of intangibles.

Intangible Assets Carried under the Allowed Alternative Treatment

The following should be disclosed in respect of intangible assets carried at valuation:
(a) by class of intangible assets:
   (i) the effective date of the revaluation,
   (ii) the carrying amount,
   (iii) the carrying amount had the benchmark treatment been adopted (historical cost);
(b) the amount of the revaluation surplus at the start and end of the period, indicating any changes and any restrictions on distribution; and
(c) the methods and significant assumptions applied in estimating the asset's fair values.

Research and Development Expenditure

With respect to research and development expenditure, the aggregate amount of research and development expenditure expensed during the period should be disclosed.

Other Information

In addition to the above, IAS 38 encourages the following disclosures:
(a) a description of any fully amortised intangible asset that is still in use; and
(b) a brief description of significant intangible assets controlled by the entity but not recognised as assets because they failed to meet the recognition criteria in IAS 38 or were generated prior to IAS 38 being made effective.

9.4 OTHER GUIDANCE

One issue that has risen to the fore in recent years is how to account for expenditure incurred in relation to website development. When accounting for internal expenditure on the development and operation of an entity's own website for internal or external access, important issues include:
• is the website an internally generated intangible asset that is subject to the requirements of IAS 38; and
• how is such expenditure accounted for?

These matters are addressed in SIC 32 *Intangible Assets – Web site Costs* which states that an entity's own website that arises from development and is for internal or external access is an internally developed intangible asset that is subject to the requirements of IAS 38. SIC 32 states that a website arising from internal development should be recognised as an intangible asset if it meets the three criteria in IAS 38. SIC 32 states that the nature of each activity for which expenditure is incurred and the website's stage of development or post-development should be evaluated to determine the appropriate accounting treatment. All expenditure on developing a website solely or primarily for promoting and advertising an entity's own products and services should be recognised as an expense when incurred. However, if an entity is able to demonstrate that a website is capable of generating future economic benefits (for example, direct revenues), then the related costs can be capitalised.

9.5 CONCLUSION

This chapter has addressed the following areas:
1. the accounting treatment for intangible assets that are *not* specifically covered by other standards;
2. the criteria necessary for the recognition of intangible assets;
3. how to measure the carrying amount of intangible assets; and
4. the disclosure requirements for intangible assets.

IAS 38 is an important accounting standard that impacts upon, and is impacted by, a number of issues in financial reporting, including accounting for business combinations (see **Part V**) and impairment (see **Chapter 10**). Consequently, it is important to have a clear understanding of the definition of an intangible asset and how such expenditure should be recognised and initially measured, in particular research and development expenditure.

SUMMARY OF LEARNING OBJECTIVES

After having studied this chapter, you should be able to:

Learning Objective 1 Define an intangible asset.

An *intangible asset* is an identifiable non-monetary asset without physical substance.

Learning Objective 2 Explain when expenditure on an intangible asset can be capitalised and demonstrate how such expenditure should be recognised and measured.

An intangible asset should be recognised if it is probable that the future economic benefits attributable to the asset will flow to the entity and the cost of the asset can be measured reliably. An intangible asset should be measured initially at cost. After initial recognition, an entity may choose either the cost model or the revaluation model. Under the cost model, the intangible asset is carried at cost less accumulated amortisation and impairment losses. Under the revaluation model, the intangible asset is carried at a revalued amount, being its fair value at the date of the revaluation less any subsequent accumulated amortisation and impairment losses.

Learning Objective 3 Discuss how to account for internally generated goodwill.

Internally generated goodwill should *not* be recognised as an asset as it is not an identifiable resource controlled by the entity that can be measured reliably at cost.

Learning Objective 4 Explain what conditions must be satisfied before development expenditure can be capitalised.

Development expenditure is capitalised only after technical and commercial feasibility of the asset for sale or use have been established. This means that the entity must intend and be able to complete the intangible asset and either use it or sell it and be able to demonstrate how the asset will generate future economic benefits.

Learning Objective 5 Apply the main disclosure requirements of IAS 38 *Intangible Assets*.

Disclosures must be provided for each class of intangible assets, analysed between internally generated and other intangible assets.

QUESTIONS

Self-test Questions

1. Under IAS 38 *Intangible Assets*, what are the categories of internally generated intangible assets that may never be recognised?
2. What criteria must be satisfied before development expenditure may be capitalised?
3. If all the conditions in the previous question are met, is it a requirement that development costs must be capitalised?

Review Questions

(See **Appendix One** for Suggested Solutions to Review Questions.)

Question 9.1

Sea Pharmaceuticals plc has negotiated a special government grant to provide 40% of the research costs of finding a suitable drug for the treatment of the virus disease that has seriously affected the seal population. The grant will also extend to a similar proportion of the costs of developing the drug for the treatment of infected seals. Payment of the grant will be made every quarter, on production of an audited statement of costs. The grant will be available for a minimum period of two years.

Requirement Draft a letter to the managing director of Sea Pharmaceuticals plc advising him of the accounting treatment you recommend in relation to the above project in accordance with IAS 38 *Intangible Assets* and IAS 20 *Accounting for Government Grants and Disclosure of Government Assistance* (see **Chapter 16**).

Challenging Questions

(Suggested Solutions to Challenging Questions are available to lecturers.)

Question 9.1

Nov Laboratories Limited has been involved in pharmaceuticals research projects for 15 years. The managing director has expressed concern that the variability in the level of research and development expenditure has distorted the reported profits for the company over the past five years. The following information is available:

1. Research and development expenditure over the past five years has been analysed as follows:

Year ended 31 December	Property, Plant and Equipment Acquired €	Research Costs €	Development Costs €
2008	50,000	445,000	125,000
2009	150,000	77,000	150,000
2010	210,000	40,000	215,000
2011	–	125,000	160,000
2012	–	88,000	145,000

2. The company depreciates all property, plant and equipment on the straight-line basis over 10 years, but writes off all other expenditure as incurred. The only non-current asset acquired prior to 2008 was plant, costing €200,000 and purchased in 2005.
3. The company is planning to acquire €300,000 of new property, plant and equipment in connection with its research and development activities over the next two years. In addition, it is anticipated that research and development expenditure will average €400,000 p.a. over the next five years. Approximately 70% of this expenditure will be classified as development expenditure.

Requirement As financial director of Nov Laboratories Limited, prepare a memorandum addressed to the managing director on the current accounting policy of the company, any possible changes that could be implemented and their impact on the company's reported results. (Assume any development costs that are to be capitalised are amortised over five years.)

Question 9.2

Grotto Limited makes up its accounts to 31 December each year. Its research and development expenditure for the years ending 31 December is as follows:

	Research €	Development €	Total €
Year ending 31 December 2008	30,000	60,000	90,000
Year ending 31 December 2009	38,000	54,000	92,000
Year ending 31 December 2010	48,000	75,000	123,000
Year ending 31 December 2011	55,000	80,000	135,000
Year ending 31 December 2012	64,000	94,000	158,000

	2008 €	2009 €	2010 €	2011 €	2012 €
Product C	60,000	19,000			
Product D		35,000	18,000	6,000	
Product E			42,000	26,000	
Product F			15,000	48,000	21,000
Product G					73,000

The accounting policy for research and development expenditure has been in accordance with the requirements of IAS 38 *Intangible Assets*. Development expenditure is recognised as an intangible asset when the conditions of IAS 38 are met. In applying this policy, the directors write off the development expenditure in relation to estimated sales of the product (in units). Arising from this policy, in the accounts for the four years to 31 December 2011, research expenditure in the amount of €171,000 has been written off. Development expenditure has been written off as follows.

- Product C: €60,000 has been written off. Sales of this product are at a standstill and are not expected to recover.
- Product D: all the development expenditure on this product has been written off because it was not considered to be commercially viable. Sales of only 20,000 units were made in 2011 and prospects of further sales appeared slight. However, it now appears that sales of this product are picking up – sales of 48,000 units are expected for 2012 and further sales of approximately 250,000 units are anticipated in later years.
- Product E: in 2011, 60,000 units of product E were sold. It was then estimated that approximately 180,000 further units would be sold over the next four years and that the sales would occur fairly evenly over that period. Arising from this, €16,000 of the expenditure was written off in 2011. Sales in 2012 should amount to approximately 30,000 units. Estimated further sales in the next two years are expected to total 80,000 units, approximately. No further sales are expected in the years after this.
- Product F: it is considered that approximately 500,000 units of this product will be sold in total, of which approximately 80,000 units will be sold in 2012.
- Product G: this product is still in the course of development. However, since there have been consumer association objections to a similar product in the USA, certain revisions are being considered to this product. It is not yet known how successful or how costly these revisions will prove to be.

Requirement
(a) Outline the accounting concepts you would have considered in accounting for research and development expenditure before any accounting standard was issued on the topic.

(b) Estimate the charge for research and development expenditure in the accounts of Grotto Limited for the year ended 31 December 2012 and illustrate the disclosure of that expenditure in accordance with IAS 38 *Intangible Assets*.

Question 9.3

Tram Limited's statement of profit or loss and other comprehensive income for the year ended 31 December 2012 shows a charge of €450,000 for research and development. An analysis of this expenditure reveals the following.

	€000
Cost of constructing warehouse and testing facility (four-year life)	90
Project High Speed	275
General research	85
	450

Project High Speed is concerned with the development of a new, emergency braking system and has been well received by the market. Tram Limited has sold ten new systems in 2012, and customer enquiries suggest approximately 20 systems per annum should be sold over the next two years.

Requirement Show and explain how this expenditure should be treated in the 2012 financial statements of Tram Limited.

IMPAIRMENT

LEARNING OBJECTIVES

After studying this chapter, you should be able to:
1. define the terms 'cash generating unit' and 'impairment loss';
2. list the factors which suggest that an asset may have been impaired;
3. explain, and apply, how the recoverable amount of an asset is determined;
4. calculate whether an impairment has occurred;
5. allocate an impairment loss amongst the assets of a cash generating unit; and
6. apply the main disclosure requirements of IAS 36 *Impairment of Assets*.

KEY TERMS AND DEFINITIONS FOR THIS CHAPTER

In order to aid your understanding of the concepts and issues covered in this chapter, it is important to understand and be familiar with the following key terms and definitions. As you study this chapter, you should refer back to them.

Arm's Length Transaction This is a transaction when all parties to the transaction are independent and on an equal footing.

Carrying Amount This is the amount at which an item is recognised (in the statement of financial position). In the case of non-current assets, it is after deducting accumulated depreciation (amortisation) and any accumulated impairment losses. It is sometimes referred to as the 'net book value' or 'written down value'.

Cash Generating Unit (CGU) This is the smallest identifiable group of assets that generates cash flows that are largely independent of cash inflows from other assets or groups of assets.

Costs of Disposal These are incremental costs directly attributable to the disposal of an asset, but excluding finance costs and income tax.

Fair Value less Costs of Disposal This is the amount obtainable from the sale of an asset or CGU in an arm's length transaction less costs of disposal. Colloquially it may also be referred to as the net realisable value (NRV).

Impairment Loss This is the amount by which the carrying amount of an asset or CGU exceeds its recoverable amount.

Net Book Value (NBV) See 'carrying amount'.

Non-current Asset This is an asset acquired for use within the business, with a view to earning profits from its use. A non-current asset is not acquired for resale and includes property, plant and equipment. Non-current assets are usually held and used by a business for a number of years.

Recoverable Amount This is the higher of an asset's fair value less costs to sell and its value in use (VIU).

Value in Use (VIU) This is the present value of future cash flows expected to be derived from the asset or CGU.

Written Down Value See 'Carrying Amount'.

10.1 INTRODUCTION

The recent, arguably current, global financial crisis has increased attention on accounting and whether the figures included in company financial statements are realistic. As these figures (for example, asset values and earnings) play a significant role in business valuation and lending decisions, it is important that users of financial statements believe they are reasonable and have not become impaired.

Impairment is a sudden diminution in the value of an individual **non-current asset** or **cash-generating unit** (CGU) over and above the normal wear and tear or reduction in value recognised by depreciation. Impairment occurs because something happens to the non-current asset or CGU itself or to the environment in which it operates. For example, a decline in property values during an economic downturn or a fall in demand for a product manufactured by particular plant and equipment due to a change in technology.

Key to this Chapter

IAS 36 prescribes the procedures that an entity applies to ensure that its non-current assets or CGUs are carried at no more than their recoverable amount. If a non-current asset or CGU is stated at a figure above its future use or sale value, then it is said to be impaired and an impairment loss should be recognised immediately (i.e. as an expense) in the statement of profit or loss and other comprehensive income – profit or loss (SPLOCI–P/L).

This chapter begins by describing the fundamental principles underlying impairment testing. It then develops these by explaining in more detail the scope of IAS 36, how to identify an asset that may be impaired, when impairment tests should be carried out, how to measure the recoverable amount and how to recognise an impairment loss for an individual asset and CGU. The reversal of impairment losses is also explained, as well as the required IAS 36 disclosures.

10.2 IAS 36 *IMPAIRMENT OF ASSETS*

Fundamental Principles

This section describes the fundamental principles with respect to testing for impairment. A sound understanding of these principles is essential in order to fully grasp the more complex aspects of this topic, which are explained in subsequent sections.

The aim of IAS 36 *Impairment of Assets* is to ensure that non-current assets or CGUs are carried at no more than their **recoverable amount**. The recoverable amount of a non-current asset or a CGU is the higher of its **fair value less costs of disposal** (also referred to as **net realisable value (NRV)**) and its **value in use (VIU)** (which is calculated by discounting the future cash flows that the non-current asset or CGU is expected to generate). If the **carrying value** exceeds the recoverable amount, then the non-current asset or CGU is impaired and IAS 36 requires a provision to be made for the **impairment loss**.

Figure 10.1 below illustrates how to assess if a non-current asset or CGU has been impaired, and it is strongly recommended that this diagram is studied carefully and applied when dealing with impairment issues.

> ***Note:*** for simplicity, the term '**asset**' will generally be used throughout the remainder of this chapter to refer to an individual 'non-current asset' or 'CGU'.

FIGURE 10.1: THE IMPAIRMENT DECISION

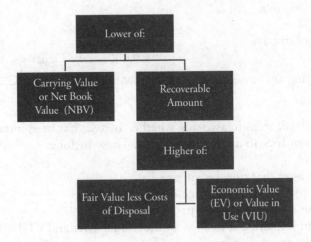

> ***Note:*** the terms 'carrying value' and 'net book value' (NBV), and 'economic value' (EV) and 'value in use' (VIU), are interchangeable, and probably used with equal regularity. It is therefore important to be familiar with each term (and its abbreviation). Each will be used throughout this chapter so that the reader becomes familiar with them, especially as alternative terms may be used in examination questions.

The first step in testing for impairment is to compare the asset's NRV and its VIU, and select the higher of these two figures (which is referred to as the recoverable amount). The recoverable amount should then be compared with the amount at which the asset is carried/recorded in the financial statements. If the carrying value is higher than the recoverable amount, then the asset is impaired, with the impairment amount being the difference between the carrying amount and the recoverable amount. Impairment losses are usually recognised as an expense in the statement of profit or loss and other comprehensive income. However, if an asset is carried at a revalued amount, impairment losses are treated in the same way as IAS 16 revaluation losses (see **Chapter 6**).

Examples 10.1 and **10.2** illustrate the impairment decision.

EXAMPLE 10.1: THE IMPAIRMENT DECISION (1)

Take an asset at 31 December 2012:
Carrying amount   €10,000
Fair value less costs of disposal   €12,000
Value in use   €13,000 – take higher }

There is no impairment because carrying amount is less than the recoverable amount.

EXAMPLE 10.2: THE IMPAIRMENT DECISION (2)

Take an asset at 31 December 2012:
Carrying amount   €10,000
Fair value less costs of disposal   €8,000
Value in use   €9,000 – take higher }

Impairment = carrying amount less recoverable amount = €10,000 − €9,000 = €1,000.

Having looked at the basic steps in assessing whether an asset has been impaired, some of the more detailed aspects of IAS 36 are now examined. These include:
- the scope of IAS 36;
- how to identify an asset that may be impaired;
- when impairment tests should be carried out;
- how to measure the recoverable amount;
- how to recognise an impairment loss for an individual asset and CGU; and
- how to deal with the reversal of impairment losses.

Scope of IAS 36

IAS 36 applies to accounting for impairment of all assets *except for*:
- inventories, as these are recorded at the lower of cost and NRV (IAS 2 *Inventories* – see **Chapter 11**);
- assets arising from construction contracts (IAS 11 *Construction Contracts* – see **Chapter 12**);

- deferred tax assets (IAS 12 *Income Taxes* – see **Chapter 13**);
- assets arising from employee benefits (IAS 19 *Employee Benefits* – see **Chapter 17**);
- financial assets within the scope of IAS 39 *Financial Instruments: Recognition and Measurement* (see **Chapter 25**);
- investment property measured at fair value (IAS 40 *Investment Property* – see **Chapter 5**);
- biological assets related to agricultural activity that are measured at fair value less estimated point-of-sale costs (IAS 41 *Agriculture* – see **Chapter 34**);
- deferred acquisition costs and intangible assets, arising from insurance contracts within the scope of IFRS 4 *Insurance Contracts* (see **Chapter 34**); and
- non-current assets (or disposal groups) classified as held for sale in accordance with IFRS 5 *Non-current Assets Held for Sale and Discontinued Operations* (see **Chapter 20**).

Identifying an Asset that may be Impaired

As illustrated in **Figure 10.1** above, an asset is impaired when the carrying amount of an asset exceeds its recoverable amount. At the end of each reporting period, an entity should assess whether or not there are indications of impairment losses. In making an assessment of whether or not there are indications of impairment, an entity, as a minimum, should consider evidence from both external and internal sources, *such as*:

External Sources of Evidence

- A significant decline in an asset's market value.
- Significant changes, with an adverse effect on the entity, that have taken place during the period or are set to take place in the near future (e.g. in the technological, economic or legal environments).
- Market interest rates have increased during the period, which has affected the discount rate.
- The carrying amount of the net assets in the entity is more than its market capitalisation.

Internal Sources of Evidence

- Evidence of obsolescence or physical damage.
- Plans to discontinue or restructure the operation to which the asset belongs or plans to dispose of the asset or reassess its useful life.
- Evidence that economic performance is worse than expected.
- Cash flows for operating and maintaining the asset are considerably higher than budgeted.
- A significant decline in budgeted cash flows or operating profit.

The above lists of external and internal evidence that might suggest an asset has been impaired is not intended to be exhaustive and there may be other indications that are equally important. Testing for impairment is not an exact science and a wide range of factors may need to be considered. Moreover, there may be significant judgement required when estimating factors such as discount rates and future cash flows.

If an asset is impaired, depreciation should also be reviewed and adjusted as the remaining useful life may be considerably shorter.

Timing of Impairment Tests

The annual impairment test for a CGU to which goodwill has been allocated may be carried out at any time during the year, provided that, for consistency, it is at the same time every year (e.g. to allow for seasonal demand/usage factors). Different CGUs may be tested for impairment at different times. However, if some of the goodwill was acquired in a business combination during the year, that CGU should be tested for impairment before the end of the current reporting period. This is because goodwill is an intangible asset and assumed to be most likely to suffer impairment before other assets (see **Chapter 26, Section 26.4**). If other assets or smaller CGUs are tested at the same time as the larger unit, these should be tested for impairment before the larger unit.

The most recent detailed impairment calculation made in a preceding reporting period of the recoverable amount of a CGU to which goodwill has been allocated may be adopted for the impairment test, provided that *all* of the following criteria are met:
- the assets and liabilities have not changed significantly since the most recent recoverable amount calculation;
- the most recent recoverable amount calculation resulted in an amount substantially in excess of the CGU's carrying amount; and
- based on an analysis of events and changed circumstances, the likelihood that a current recoverable amount determinable would be less than the current carrying amount of the CGU is remote. Although, for example, it may not have been reasonable to make this assumption in the aftermath of the 2007–08 property crash and thus another impairment test would be required.

Measuring Recoverable Amount

As explained above, under '**Fundamental Principles**', recoverable amount is the *higher* of the fair value less costs of disposal and value in use. Both fair value less costs of disposal and value in use need not necessarily be determined if either exceeds the carrying amount (i.e. NBV) since the asset is therefore not impaired (see **Figure 10.1**).

Recoverable amount should be determined for individual assets, unless the asset does not generate cash flows that are largely independent of those from a group of assets. If this latter situation applies, then recoverable amount is determined for the CGU to which the asset belongs, unless either:
- the asset's fair value less costs of disposal is higher than its NBV; or
- the asset's value in use can be determined to be close to its fair value less costs of disposal.

Some additional considerations with respect to fair value less costs of disposal and value in use are outlined below.

Fair Value less Costs of Disposal

The best evidence of fair value less costs of disposal is a binding sale agreement at arm's length, adjusted for costs directly attributable to disposal of the asset.

If there is no binding sale agreement, but the asset is traded on an active market, fair value less costs of disposal is the asset's market price less costs of disposal.

If no active market exists for the asset, fair value less costs of disposal should be based on the best information available to reflect what would be received between willing parties at arm's length, though it should not be based on a forced sale, as it is likely that the selling price of an asset would be reduced in the event of a forced sale.

Costs of disposal referred to above include legal costs, stamp duty and other direct incremental costs (but not reorganisation costs or termination benefits as these costs are outside the scope of IAS 36 (see **Scope** above)).

Value in Use

The following elements should be reflected in the calculation of value in use:
- an estimate of future cash flows to be derived from using the asset in the business;
- expectations about possible variations in the amount or timing of such flows;
- the time value of money (i.e. €1 received tomorrow is worth less than €1 received today);
- the price for bearing the uncertainty inherent in the asset (i.e. risk); and
- other factors, including illiquidity, that market participants would reflect in pricing expected future cash flows.

The calculation of value in use requires *estimating future cash flows* (see below) to be derived from continuing to use the asset and from ultimate disposal as well as applying the appropriate *discount rate* (see below) to those flows. Either the cash flows or the discount rate can be adjusted to reflect the elements listed above.

Basis for Estimates of Future Cash Flows Cash flows should be based on reasonable and supportable assumptions that represent management's best estimate of a range of economic conditions that exist over the life of the asset and take into account past ability of management to accurately forecast cash flows. Greater weight should be given to external evidence and cash flows should be based on the most recent financial forecasts approved by management covering, normally, a maximum period of five years (see **Example 10.11**). If a longer period is justified, budgets/forecasts should be extrapolated using a steady or declining growth rate that should not exceed the long-term average growth rate for the products, industries or countries in which the entity operates, unless a higher rate is justified (see **Example 10.10**). If appropriate, the growth rate should be zero or negative.

Discount Rate The discount rate used in calculating value in use (i.e. present value of future cash flows) should be a pre-tax rate that reflects both the time value of money and the specific risks attached to the asset (see **Example 10.10**). The latter is the return that investors would require if they were to choose an investment that would generate cash flows equivalent to those expected to be derived from the asset. Where an asset-specific rate is not directly available, then surrogates may be adopted.

Recognising an Impairment Loss for an Individual Asset

As stated in **Section 10.1**, impairment is a sudden diminution in the value of either an individual non-current asset or CGU over and above the normal wear and tear or reduction in value recognised by depreciation. We will now examine the impairment of an individual asset, and then focus on the recognition of an impairment loss in CGUs.

It is important to remember that after testing for impairment, an asset should be reduced to its recoverable amount **only if** the recoverable amount is less than its NBV. This reduction is known as an **impairment loss** and should be expensed in the statement of profit or loss and other comprehensive income in arriving at profit/loss for the year, unless the asset is carried at valuation. A revaluation decrease should be charged as an expense in the statement of profit or loss and other comprehensive income in arriving at profit/loss for the year to the extent that the impairment exceeds the amount held in the revaluation reserve for the same asset (otherwise the decrease/loss would be included under 'other comprehensive income').

Where the impairment loss is greater than the NBV, a liability should be recognised only if required by another international accounting standard. After recognition of the impairment loss, depreciation should be adjusted in future periods to allocate the asset's revised book value over the asset's remaining useful life. Any related deferred tax assets or liabilities are determined under IAS 12 by comparing the revised NBV of the asset with its tax base (see **Chapter 13**).

Recognising an Impairment Loss for a Cash Generating Unit

In this section, having introduced impairment and CGUs, we will address:
- goodwill and CGUs;
- the recoverable amount and the carrying amount of a CGU;
- corporate assets; and
- impairment losses and CGUs.

Remember: a **CGU** is the smallest identifiable group of assets that generates cash flows that are largely independent of cash inflows from other assets or groups of assets.

If there is any indication that an asset may be impaired, the recoverable amount (i.e. higher of net realisable value and value in use) should be estimated for that individual asset. If it is not possible to estimate the recoverable amount of the individual asset, then the entity should determine the recoverable amount of the CGU to which the asset belongs (i.e. the next level of identifiable assets). This occurs when an asset's *value in use* cannot be estimated to be close to its *fair value less costs to sell* and the asset does not generate cash inflows from continuing use that are largely independent of those from other assets (see **Example 10.3**). In such cases, the *value in use* and thus the *recoverable amount* must be determined only for the asset's CGU.

EXAMPLE 10.3: INDEPENDENT CASH FLOWS

A mine owns a private railway to support its mining activities. It could only be sold for scrap and does not generate independent cash flows from those of the mine. The CGU, in this case is, therefore, the mine as a whole, including the railway as the railway's value in use cannot be independently determined and would be very different from its scrap value.

Identification of an asset's CGU involves judgement and should be the lowest aggregation of assets that generate largely independent cash inflows from continuing use. This is illustrated in **Example 10.4**.

EXAMPLE 10.4: LOWEST AGGREGATION OF ASSETS

A bus company has a contract to provide a minimum service on five separate routes. Cash flows can be separately identified for each route. Even if one route is operating at a loss, the entity has no option to curtail any one route and the lowest independent level is the group of five routes together. The CGU is the bus company itself.

When estimating the cash inflows of a CGU, these should be from outside/third parties only and should consider various factors, including how management monitors the entity's operations. If an active market exists for the asset's or group of assets' output, then they should be identified as a CGU, even if some of the output is used internally. If this is the case, management's best estimate of future market prices should be used in determining the value in use of:
- the CGU when estimating the future cash inflows relating to internal use; and
- other CGUs of the entity when estimating future cash outflows that relate to internal use of the output.

CGUs should be identified consistently from period to period, unless a change is justified. IAS 36 *Impairment of Assets* provides a number of examples to illustrate the identification of CGUs, and these are shown under **Example 10.5** below.

EXAMPLE 10.5: IDENTIFYING CASH-GENERATING UNITS

Example 10.5(A) – Retail Store Chain

Store X belongs to retail chain M. X makes all purchases through M and pricing, marketing, advertising and human resource policies are decided by M, which also owns five other stores in the same city as X and 20 other stores in other cities. All are managed in the same way as X, and X was purchased with four other stores five years ago.

As X generates independent cash inflows and the stores are in different neighbourhoods, it appears X is a CGU.

Example 10.5(B) – Plant for an Intermediate Step in a Production Process

A significant raw material used for Y's final production is an intermediate product bought from X. X sells to Y at a transfer price that passes all margins to X. 80% of X's output is sold to Y and 20% to outside customers.

Case 1: X could sell to Y in the active market, and internal prices are higher than market prices.
Case 2: There is no active market for the products that X sells to Y.

Case 1: It is likely that X is a separate CGU and Y is also. However, internal transfer prices do not reflect the market price for X's output. Thus, in determining value in use for both X and Y, the entity should adjust financial forecasts/budgets to reflect management's best estimate of future market prices for those of X's products.

Case 2: It is likely that the recoverable amount of each plant cannot be assessed independently as the majority of X's production is used internally and could not be sold in an active market and the two plants are managed together. X and Y is the smallest group of assets that are largely independent.

Example 10.5(C) – Single Product Entity

Entity M produces a single product and owns plants A, B and C in different continents. A produces a component that is assembled in either B or C, but the combined capacity of B and C is not fully utilised. M's products are sold worldwide from either B or C and utilisation levels depend on the allocation of sales between the two sites.

Case 1: There is an active market for A's products.
Case 2: There is no active market for A's products.

Case 1: It is likely that A is a separate CGU, but B and C cannot be determined individually, thus B plus C is the smallest identifiable group of assets that are largely independent. M must adjust its financial budgets/forecasts to reflect its best estimate of future market prices for A's products.

Case 2: There are no independent CGUs as there is no active market for A's products. B and C are not independent as the cash flows for B and C depend on the allocation of production across the two sites. A, B and C represent the smallest identifiable CGU.

Example 10.5(D) – Magazine Titles

A publisher owns 150 titles (70 purchased and 80 self-created). The purchased titles are capitalised as intangible assets and the costs of self-created titles are expensed in accordance with IAS 38 *Intangible Assets* (see **Chapter 9**). Cash inflows are identifiable for each title and these are managed by customer segments. Old titles are abandoned for new titles in the same customer segments.

A CGU would be individual titles, as cash inflows are largely independent.

Example 10.5(E) – Building Half Rented to Others and Half Occupied for Own Use

M is a manufacturing company that owns a headquarters building that used to be fully occupied for internal use. After downsizing, 50% of the building is now used internally and 50% rented to third parties on a five-year lease. It is primarily a corporate asset thus the building cannot be considered to generate cash inflows that are largely independent of the cash inflows of the entity as a whole.

The CGU is, therefore, M as a whole.

(Source: IAS 36 *Impairment of Assets* – Illustrative Examples)

Having explained the identification of CGUs, we will now consider the implications of goodwill for CGUs.

CGUs and Goodwill

Goodwill does not generate cash flows independently; its benefits are not capable of being individually identified and separately recognised, and goodwill often contributes to multiple CGUs. IAS 36 states that goodwill should be allocated to each CGU that is expected to benefit from the goodwill on a reasonable and consistent basis. The CGU(s) to which goodwill is allocated should represent the lowest level within the entity at which the goodwill is monitored. If provisional values for goodwill are adopted, these must be finalised within 12 months.

If a CGU is disposed of, which includes goodwill previously allocated, the goodwill associated with the disposal should be:
* included in the NBV of the operation when determining gain or loss on disposal; and
* measured on the basis of relative values of the operation disposed of at the date of disposal and the portion of the CGU retained, unless the entity can demonstrate that another method better reflects the goodwill associated with the operation disposed of.

This is illustrated in **Example 10.6**.

EXAMPLE IO.6: GOODWILL AND DISPOSAL OF CASH GENERATING UNIT

An entity sells for €100 an operation that was part of a CGU to which goodwill was allocated. The goodwill allocated to the unit cannot be identified or associated with an asset group at a level lower than that unit, except arbitrarily. The recoverable amount of the portion of the CGU retained is €300. Because the goodwill allocated to the CGU cannot be identified, it is measured on the basis of the relative values disposed of and retained. Therefore, 25% of the goodwill allocated (€100/€400), is included in the NBV of the operation that is sold.

If an entity reorganises so that there are changes in the composition of one or more CGUs (to which goodwill has been allocated), the goodwill should be reallocated to units affected by adopting a relative value approach, similar to that used when an entity disposes of an operation within a CGU. This is illustrated in **Example 10.7**.

EXAMPLE IO.7: REORGANISATION OF CASH GENERATING UNIT

Goodwill was previously allocated to CGU A. The goodwill allocated to A cannot be identified with an asset group at a level lower than A, except arbitrarily. A is to be divided and integrated into three other CGUs: B, C and D. Therefore the goodwill allocated to A is reallocated to B, C and D based on the relative values of the three portions of A before those portions are integrated with B, C and D. If A is to be allocated 20:30:50 to B, C and D, respectively, then the goodwill previously allocated to A would be allocated to B, C and D in these proportions.

Any CGU containing goodwill should be tested for impairment annually. However, the way entities choose to measure the goodwill and **non-controlling interests** (NCI) affects the impairment test and the amount of impairment loss recognised.

> *Note:* if you are not familiar with the proportionate share and fair value methods of calculating goodwill (also referred to as the 'old' and 'new' methods, respectively), as explained in **Chapter 26**, you should review that now before continuing.

Under the proportionate share method (see **Chapter 26**), a notional gross-up of the entity's goodwill balance is required to ensure the carrying value of the CGU includes the goodwill attributable to the NCI. This grossed-up amount is compared to the recoverable amount of the CGU, which includes the entire cash flows or fair value attributable to the CGU, as well as the cash flows attributable to the controlling interest (CI). This is illustrated in **Example 10.8**.

EXAMPLE 10.8: GOODWILL AND NON-CONTROLLING INTERESTS

Assume that you have been provided with the following information in respect of a CGU and the related goodwill.

	Proportionate method €	Fair value method €
Identifiable net assets	1,000	1,000
Goodwill	400	450
Gross-up (€400 × 20%/80%)	100	–
Total carrying amount of CGU	1,500	1,450
Less recoverable amount	(1,100)	(1,100)
Impairment	400	350
Impairment included in SPLOCI – PL	320	350[1]

[1] The allocation of the impairment loss between CI and NCI:

Under the proportionate share method, only the CI's share of the impairment loss is recognised in the SPLOCI–P/L because only the CI's share of goodwill is recognised. Under the fair value method, the impairment loss is recognised in full in the SPLOCI–P/L. The headline loss is, therefore, higher for the entity that elects to adopt the fair value method.

With respect to allocating goodwill impairment losses between the CI and the NCI, the accounting is usually straightforward if the subsidiary with the NCI represents a CGU or group of CGUs for goodwill impairment-testing purposes (i.e. the allocation is done on the same basis as the allocation of profit).

Based on the example above, if profit is allocated on the basis of ownership interests, 20% of the impairment loss is allocated to the NCI. Therefore, under the proportionate share method, €80 of the €400 impairment loss is allocated to the NCI; however, it is not accounted for in the SPLOCI because only the CI's share of goodwill is recognised. The full impairment loss of €350 is recognised when the goodwill has been recognised on the fair value method, but €70 (20%) is allocated to the NCI.

The allocation of impairment losses between the CI and the NCI becomes more complex if the subsidiary is part of a larger CGU or group of CGUs for goodwill impairment-testing purposes.

Recoverable Amount and Carrying Amount of a CGU

Continuing with issues relating to impairment losses and CGUs, as explained previously, the recoverable amount of a CGU is the higher of its *fair value less costs to sell* and *value in use*. The carrying amount should be determined consistently with the way the recoverable amount is determined. The carrying amount of a CGU includes those assets that can be attributed directly or allocated on a reasonable and consistent basis to the CGU and does not include the carrying amount of any recognised liability, unless the recoverable amount of the CGU cannot be determined without its consideration.

The CGU should exclude cash flows relating to assets that are not part of a CGU. However, all assets that generate cash flows for the CGU should be included. In some cases (for example, goodwill and head office assets – see '**Corporate Assets**' below), future cash flows cannot be allocated to the CGU on a reasonable and consistent basis. Also certain liabilities may have to be considered (for example, on disposal of a CGU), if a buyer is forced to take over a liability. In that case, the liability must be included, as illustrated in **Example 10.9** below.

EXAMPLE IO.9: LIABILITIES AND CASH GENERATING UNITS

A company must restore a mine by law, and it has provided €500 for the cost of restoration which is equal to the present value of restoration costs. The CGU is the mine as a whole. Offers of €800 have been received to buy the mine and disposal costs are negligible. If the mine is sold, the buyer will assume responsibility for the restoration costs. The value in use is €1,200, excluding restoration costs, and the carrying amount is €1,000.

Fair value less costs of disposal	€800	
Value in use	€700	(€1,200 less €500)
Carrying amount of CGU	€500	(€1,000 less €500)

The recoverable amount of €800 exceeds its carrying amount of €500 by €300 and there is no impairment.

Corporate Assets

A CGU may contain corporate assets, which include head-office buildings and research centres. Their key characteristics are that they do not generate independent cash flows, thus their recoverable amount cannot be determined. Consequently, if there is an indication that a corporate asset may be impaired, the recoverable amount is determined for the CGU to which the corporate asset belongs and then this is compared with the carrying amount of this CGU to determine if an impairment loss arises.

If a portion of the carrying amount of a corporate asset:

1. can be allocated on a reasonable and consistent basis, then the entity should compare the carrying amount of the CGU (including corporate asset) with its recoverable amount and recognise any losses;
2. cannot be allocated on a reasonable and consistent basis, then the entity should:
    (a) compare the carrying amount of the CGU, excluding the corporate asset, with its recoverable amount and recognise any impairment loss,
    (b) identify the smallest CGU to which a portion of the corporate asset can be allocated on a reasonable and consistent basis, and
    (c) compare the carrying amount of the larger CGU, including a portion of the corporate asset, with its recoverable amount and recognise any impairment loss.

Example 10.10 below explains how to account for corporate assets within CGUs for the purposes of impairment testing.

EXAMPLE 10.10: CASH GENERATING UNITS AND CORPORATE ASSETS

Background

Entity M has three CGUs: A, B and C, none of which includes any goodwill. At the end of 2012 the carrying amounts are €100, €150 and €200. Corporate assets have a carrying amount of €200 (building €150, research centre €50). The remaining useful life of CGU A is 10 years and of CGUs B and C is 20 years each. The entity adopts a straight-line basis for depreciation. There is no basis to calculate the fair value less costs of disposal for each CGU, thus recoverable value is based on value in use using a 15% pre-tax discount rate.

On the basis of the above information, the impairment test and allocation of impairment losses would be carried out as follows.

Step 1: Identification of corporate assets
The carrying amount of headquarter buildings can be allocated on a reasonable and consistent basis. The research centre cannot be allocated in such a manner.

Allocation of corporate assets:

End of 2012	A	B	C	Total
Carrying amount	€100	€150	€200	€450
Useful life	10 years	20 years	20 years	
Weighting based on useful life	1	2	2	
Carrying amount after weighting	€100	€300	€400	€800
Pro rata allocation of building (1:3:4)	12.5%	37.5%	50%	100%
Allocation of CV of building (€150)	€19	€56	€75	€150
Carrying amount after allocation	€119	€206	€275	€600

Step 2: Determination of Recoverable Amount and Calculation of Impairment Losses

The recoverable amount of each individual CGU must be compared with its carrying amount, including the portion of the headquarters, and any impairment loss recognised. IAS 36 then requires the recoverable amount of M as a whole to be compared with its carrying amount, including the headquarters and the research centre. The calculation of A, B, C and M's value in use at the end of 2012 is shown in Working 1 (W1) and summarised below:

A – Future cash flows for 10 years discounted at 15% = €199
B – Future cash flows for 20 years discounted at 15% = €164
C – Future cash flows for 20 years discounted at 15% = €271
M – Future cash flows for 20 years discounted at 15% = €720

Step 3: Impairment-testing A, B and C

End of 2012	A	B	C
	€	€	€
Carrying amount after allocation of building	119	206	275
Recoverable amount	199	164	271
Impairment loss	0	(42)	(4)

Step 4: Allocation of impairment losses for CGUs B and C

		B	C	
		€	€	
To headquarters building	(42 × 56/206)	(12)	(1)	(4 × 75/275)
To assets in CGU	(42 × 150/206)	(30)	(3)	(4 × 200/275)
		(42)	(4)	

Because the research centre could not be allocated on a reasonable and consistent basis to A, B and C's CGUs, M compares the carrying amount of the smallest CGU to which the carrying amount of the research centre can be allocated (i.e. M as a whole) to its recoverable amount.

Step 5: Impairment-testing the 'larger' CGU (i.e. M as a whole)

End of 2012	A	B	C	Building	Research Centre	M
	€	€	€	€	€	€
CV	100	150	200	150	50	650
Impairment loss (first step)	–	(30)	(3)	(13)	–	(46)
CV (after first step)	100	120	197	137	50	(604)
Recoverable amount (W1)						720
Impairment loss for the larger CGU						0

Thus, no additional impairment loss results from the application of the impairment test to the 'larger' CGU. Only €46 uncovered in Step 1 is recognised.

W1 Year	A Future cash flows	A Discount at 15%	B Future cash flows	B Discount at 15%	C Future cash flows	C Discount at 15%	M Future cash flows	M Discount at 15%
	CU	CU	CU	CU	CU	CU	CU	CU
1	18	16	9	8	10	9	39	34
2	31	23	16	12	20	15	72	54
3	37	24	24	16	34	22	105	69
4	42	24	29	17	44	25	128	73
5	47	24	32	16	51	25	143	71
6	52	22	33	14	56	24	155	67
7	55	21	34	13	60	22	162	61
8	55	18	35	11	63	21	166	54
9	53	15	35	10	65	18	167	48
10	48	12	35	9	66	16	169	42
11			36	8	66	14	132	28
12			35	7	66	12	131	25
13			35	6	66	11	131	21
14			33	5	65	9	128	18
15			30	4	62	8	122	15
16			26	3	60	6	115	12
17			22	2	57	5	108	10
18			18	1	51	4	97	8
19			14	1	43	3	85	6
20			10	1	35	2	71	4
VIU		199		164		271		720*

* It is assumed that the research centre generates additional future cash flows for entity M as a whole. Therefore, the sum of the value in use of each individual CGU is less than the value in use of the entity as a whole. The additional cash flows are not attributable to the corporate assets.

Impairment Losses and CGUs

Remember, by definition a CGU is not an individual asset; it is a group of assets. Therefore, if an impairment loss arises (i.e. the recoverable amount is less than its carrying amount), it has to be allocated across the assets that make up the CGU. The impairment loss should be allocated to reduce the carrying amount of the assets:
* first, against goodwill to its implied value; and
* secondly, to other assets on a pro rata basis, based on the carrying amount of each asset in the unit.

These are treated as impairment losses on individual assets.

Example 10.11 combines a number of the issues explained so far. It addresses testing for impairment in two CGUs, illustrates how an impairment loss should be allocated across the assets in a CGU and identifies the journal entries necessary to reflect this in the financial statements. It is important to work through this example slowly and carefully.

Example 10.11: Allocating an Impairment Loss (1)

Beta Limited prepares its financial statements to 31 December each year. The company has been experiencing trading difficulties in recent years as a consequence of the economic recession. For internal reporting purposes, Beta Limited is divided into two cash generating units: Supply Division and Service Division. The historical cost carrying value of the non-current assets of the two cash generating units at 31 December 2012 is as follows:

	Supply Division €	Service Division €
Property, plant and equipment	885,000	816,000
Patent – cost	25,000	–
Goodwill	–	48,000
	910,000	864,000

The directors of Beta Limited believe that the fair value less costs of disposal of the Supply Division and Service Division cash generating units at 31 December 2012 is €751,000 and €738,000, respectively. With respect to the fair value less costs of disposal of the Supply Division cash generating unit, the directors estimate that the patent could be sold separately for €15,000.

Projections prepared for the company's bankers indicate the following projected net cash flows:

	Supply Division €	Service Division €
2013	210,000	207,000
2014	205,000	240,000
2015	275,000	275,000
2016	260,000	294,000

Cash flows for 2016 include the expected fair values less costs of disposal at that point in respect of each division. The required rate of return for both cash generating units is 10%.

Requirement Calculate the extent of any impairment loss in the Supply Division and Service Division cash generating units and show clearly the necessary journal entries required to reflect any impairment loss in the financial statements of Beta Limited for the year ended 31 December 2012.

Solution

Supply Division

Value in Use

	Cash Flow €	Discount factor	Present Value €
2013	210,000	0.909	190,890
2014	205,000	0.826	169,330
2015	275,000	0.751	206,525
2016	260,000	0.683	177,580
			744,325
Net Realisable Value			751,000

Recoverable Amount = €751,000
Impairment Loss = €159,000 (€910,000 − €751,000) (apportioned pro rata)

31 December 2012
DR   SPLOCI – P/L   €159,000
CR   Property, plant and equipment   €154,632
CR   Patent   €4,368

Service Division
Value in Use

	Cash Flow €	Discount factor	Present Value €
2013	207,000	0.909	188,163
2014	240,000	0.826	198,240
2015	275,000	0.751	206,525
2016	294,000	0.683	200,802
			793,730

Net Realisable Value   738,000

Recoverable Amount = €793,730

Impairment Loss €70,270 (€864,000 − €793,730) (write off against goodwill first)

31 December 2012
DR   SPLOCI – P/L   €70,270
CR   Property, plant and equipment   €22,270
CR   Goodwill   €48,000

Following on from **Example 10.11**, and the order for allocating an impairment loss over a group of assets in a CGU, it is important to note that an asset in a CGU should not be reduced below the highest of:
(a) its fair value less costs of disposal (if determinable);
(b) its value in use (if determinable); and
(c) zero.

The amount of the loss that would otherwise have been allocated to the asset should be allocated to the other assets on a pro rata basis. This is illustrated in **Example 10.12** below.

EXAMPLE 10.12: ALLOCATING AN IMPAIRMENT LOSS (2)

Isybisy Limited has identified an impairment loss of €60 million in one of its cash-generating units (CGU). The CGU showed a carrying amount of €160 million and a recoverable amount of €100 million at 31 August 2012.

Details of the carrying amount:	€m
Goodwill	20
Property	60
Machinery	40
Motor vehicles	20
Other non-current assets	20
	160

The fair value less costs to sell of the unit's assets do not differ significantly from their carrying values, except for the property, which had a market value of €70m at 31 August 2012.

Requirement Allocate the impairment loss arising in accordance with IAS 36 *Impairment of Assets.*

Solution

Allocation of Impairment Loss:

	Goodwill €m	Property €m	Machinery €m	Motor €m	Other €m
Carrying amount	20	60	40	20	20
Impairment loss (€60m)	(a) 20	(b) –	(c) 20	(c) 10	(c) 10
Revised carrying value	–	60	20	10	10

Notes:
(a) The loss is first allocated to the goodwill, i.e. €20 million.
(b) No impairment can be allocated to the property because its fair value less costs of disposal is greater than its carrying amount.
(c) The remainder of the loss, i.e. €40 million, is apportioned between the remaining assets pro rata to their carrying amounts, i.e. 40: 20: 20.

Machinery	€40m × 40/80 = €20m
Motor vehicles	€40m × 20/80 = €10m
Other non-current assets	€40m × 20/80 = €10m

Continuing with the discussion about CGUs and impairment, it is important to note that the allocation of an impairment loss is not an exact science and is often subjective. If the recoverable amount of each individual asset in a CGU cannot be estimated without undue cost or effort, IAS 36 requires an arbitrary allocation between assets of the CGU other than goodwill. If the recoverable amount of an individual asset cannot be determined:
• an impairment loss is recognised for the asset if its carrying value is greater than the higher of its fair value less costs to sell and the results of procedures described above;
• no impairment loss is recognised if the related CGU is not impaired, even if its fair value less costs to sell is less than its carrying amount.

This is illustrated in **Example 10.13**.

EXAMPLE 10.13: UNDUE COST OR EFFORT

A machine has suffered physical damage but is still working, although not as well as before it was damaged. The machine's fair value less costs of disposal is less than its carrying amount. The machine does not generate independent cash inflows. The smallest identifiable group of assets that includes the machine and generates cash inflows that are largely independent of the cash inflows from other assets is the production line to which the machine belongs. The recoverable amount of the production line shows that the production line taken as a whole is not impaired.

Assumption 1: Budgets/forecasts approved by management reflect no commitment of management to replace the machine.

Conclusion:
The recoverable amount of the machine alone cannot be estimated because the machine's value in use:
(a) may differ from its fair value less costs of disposal; and
(b) can be determined only for the CGU to which the machine belongs (i.e. the production line).

The production line is not impaired. Therefore, no impairment loss is recognised for the machine. Nevertheless, the entity may need to reassess the depreciation period or the depreciation method for the machine. Perhaps a shorter depreciation period (i.e. a faster depreciation method) is required to reflect the expected remaining useful life of the machine or the pattern in which economic benefits are expected to be consumed by the entity.

Assumption 2: Budgets/forecasts approved by management reflect a commitment of management to replace the machine and sell it in the near future. Cash flows from continuing use of the machine until its disposal are estimated to be negligible.

Conclusion:
The machine's value in use can be estimated to be close to its fair value less costs of disposal. Therefore, the recoverable amount of the machine can be determined and no consideration is given to the CGU to which the machine belongs (i.e. the production line). Because the machine's fair value less costs of disposal is less than its carrying amount, an impairment loss is recognised for the machine.

Reversal of an Impairment Loss

The discussion so far has focused on how to account for an impairment loss when it arises. However, it might also be the case that there is evidence that the conditions that gave rise to an impairment loss in previous accounting periods no longer exist, and therefore the decision is whether this needs to be reflected in the financial statements.

An entity should assess at the end of each reporting period whether there is any indication that an impairment loss recognised in prior periods, other than goodwill, may no longer exist or may have decreased. If any such indication exists, the entity should estimate the recoverable amount of that asset. In assessing whether or not there is a reversal of an impairment loss, the entity should, at a minimum, consider the following **external** and **internal sources of evidence**.

External Sources of Evidence

(a) The asset's market value has increased significantly during the period.
(b) Significant changes with a favourable impact in the technological, market, economic or legal environment in which the entity operates.
(c) Market interest rates have decreased and are likely to affect the discount rate and the recoverable amount.

Internal Sources of Evidence

(a) Significant changes with a favourable effect during the period or in the near future. It includes capital expenditure that enhances an asset's standard of performance; and
(b) Evidence indicates that economic performance is better than expected.

An impairment loss in prior periods, for assets other than goodwill (see below), should be reversed only if there is a change in estimate used to determine the asset's recoverable amount since the loss was recognised. Examples of changes in estimate include:

- a change in the basis for recoverable amount;
- if the recoverable amount was based on value in use – a change in the amount or timing of cash flows or in the discount rate; and
- if the recoverable amount was based on fair value less costs to sell – a change in the components of fair value less costs to sell.

However, an impairment loss is not reversed just because of the passage of time.

The issue is now explained in more detail in the context of an individual asset, a CGU and then goodwill.

Reversal of an Impairment Loss for an Individual Asset

The increased carrying value of an asset, other than goodwill (see below), due to a reversal should not exceed the carrying amount that would have existed had the asset not been impaired in prior years. Any increase in the carrying amount above the carrying amount had no impairment taken place would have been a revaluation.

A reversal should be recognised immediately in the SPLOCI–P/L unless the asset is carried at a revalued amount under another standard. Any reversal of an impairment loss on a revalued asset should be treated as a revaluation reserve increase and credited directly to equity. However, to the extent a loss was previously recognised as an expense in the SPLOCI–P/L, a reversal is also recognised in the SPLOCI–P/L.

After a reversal, the depreciation charge should be adjusted in future periods to allocate its revised carrying amount over its remaining useful life:

$$\frac{\textbf{Revised Carrying Amount} - \textbf{Residual Value}}{\textbf{Remaining Useful Life}}$$

Reversal of an Impairment Loss for a CGU

A reversal of an impairment loss for a CGU should be allocated to the assets in the unit, except for goodwill (see below), on a pro rata basis with the carrying amount of those assets. In allocating a reversal for a CGU, the carrying amount of an asset should not be increased above the lower of:

(a) its recoverable amount (if determinable);
(b) the carrying amount that would be determined had no impairment taken place.

The amount of the reversal of the impairment loss that would otherwise have been allocated to the asset should be allocated on a pro rata basis to the other assets of the CGU, except for goodwill.

Reversal of an Impairment Loss for Goodwill

An impairment loss recognised for goodwill should *not* be reversed in subsequent periods as IAS 38 (see **Chapter 9**) expressly forbids the creation of internally generated goodwill.

10.3 DISCLOSURE

Financial reporting is the communication of financial information and the annual report and financial statements are generally recognised as the key documents in the discharge of financial accountability to external users. Such reports communicate economic measurements of, and information about, the resources and performance of the reporting entity useful to those having reasonable rights to such information. Moreover, in the context of the *Conceptual Framework for Financial Reporting 2010* (see **Chapter 1**), the annual report and financial statements are the primary means by which the management of an entity is able to fulfil its reporting responsibility. Consequently, it is imperative that figures included in company financial statements are as realistic as possible, especially in light of the current global financial crisis and the use made of such figures in making economic decisions. For example, asset values and earnings play a significant role in business valuation and lending decisions. Moreover, it is important that users of financial statements believe the information presented is reasonable and that, for example, assets have not become impaired.

In order to facilitate this, IAS 36 states that an entity should disclose the following for each class of assets:
- the amount of impairment losses recognised in arriving at profit or loss in the statement of profit or loss and other comprehensive income during the period;
- the amount of reversals of impairment losses recognised in the SPLOCI–P/L during the period;
- the amount of impairment losses recognised directly in equity during the period; and
- the amount of reversals of impairment losses recognised directly in equity during the period.

This information may be included in a reconciliation of the carrying amount of property, plant and equipment, as required by IAS 16 (see **Chapter 6**).

The following should be disclosed for each material impairment loss recognised or reversed during the period for an individual asset, including goodwill, or a CGU:

(a) the events and circumstances that led to the recognition or reversal of the impairment;

(b) the amount of the impairment loss recognised or reversed;

(c) for an individual asset:
  (i) the nature of the asset,
  (ii) the reportable segment to which the asset belongs, if applicable;

(d) for a CGU:
  (i) a description of the CGU,
  (ii) the amount of the impairment loss recognised or reversed by class of asset and, if applicable, by reportable segment under IAS 14/IFRS 7,
  (iii) if the aggregation of assets for identifying the CGU has changed since the previous estimate of the CGU's recoverable amount, a description of the current and former way of aggregating assets and the reasons for changing the way the CGU is identified;

(e) whether the recoverable amount of the asset is its fair value less costs to sell or its value in use;

(f) if the recoverable amount is fair value less costs to sell, the basis used to determine fair value less costs to sell; and

(g) if the recoverable amount is value in use, the discount rate used in the current and previous estimates of value in use.

An entity is encouraged to disclose key assumptions used to determine the recoverable amount of assets (CGUs) during the period, but required to do so when goodwill or intangible assets with indefinite useful lives are included in a CGU. If goodwill has not been allocated to a CGU, the amount should be disclosed together with reasons for non-allocation. If an entity recognises the best estimate of a probable impairment loss for goodwill, the following should be disclosed:

(a) the fact that the impairment loss recognised for goodwill is an estimate, not yet finalised; and

(b) the reasons why the impairment loss has not been finalised.

In the immediate succeeding period, the nature and amount of any adjustments should be disclosed.

10.4 CONCLUSION

Impairment-testing must be carried out annually at the same time of the year for goodwill and intangible assets with an indefinite useful life. Other assets should be tested if there are indications of impairment. An impairment loss occurs when the carrying value of an asset or CGU is greater than its recoverable amount, i.e.

impairment loss = carrying amount − recoverable amount

where

recoverable amount is the higher of the asset's or CGU's **fair value less costs of disposal** and its **value in use**; *and*

value in use is calculated by discounting the future cash flows the asset or CGU is expected to generate.

Impairment losses are usually recognised as an expense in the statement of profit or loss and other comprehensive income. However, if an asset is carried at a revalued amount, impairment losses are treated in the same way as IAS 16 revaluation losses.

SUMMARY OF LEARNING OBJECTIVES

After having studied this chapter, you should be able to:

Learning Objective 1 Define the terms 'cash generating unit' and 'impairment loss'.

A 'cash generating unit' (CGU) is the smallest identifiable group of assets that generates cash flows that are largely independent of cash inflows from other assets or groups of assets. An impairment loss is the amount by which the carrying amount of an asset or CGU exceeds its recoverable amount.

Learning Objective 2 List the factors which suggest that an asset may have been impaired.

When making an assessment of whether or not there are indications of impairment, an entity should consider both external and internal sources. The former includes whether there has been a significant decline in an asset's market value, while the latter includes evidence of obsolescence or plans to discontinue or restructure the operation to which the asset belongs.

Learning Objective 3 Explain, and apply, how the recoverable amount of an asset is determined.

The recoverable amount is the higher of an asset's or CGU's fair value less costs of disposal and its value in use. Value in use is calculated by discounting the future cash flows the asset or CGU is expected to generate.

Learning Objective 4 Calculate whether an impairment has occurred.

For example, if the carrying amount of an asset is €100, its fair value less costs of disposal is €75 and its value in use €88, then the impairment is €12.

Learning Objective 5 Allocate an impairment loss amongst the assets of a cash generating unit.

An impairment loss should be recognised only if its recoverable amount is less than its carrying amount. The impairment is allocated to reduce the carrying amount of the assets first against goodwill to its implied value and then to other assets on a pro rata basis based on the carrying amount of each asset in the CGU.

Learning Objective 6 Apply the main disclosure requirements of IAS 36 *Impairment of Assets*.

Inter alia, an entity should disclose the amount of impairment losses/reversal recognised in arriving at profit or loss in the statement of profit or loss and other comprehensive income during the period, together with details of the events and circumstances that led to the recognition or reversal of the impairment.

QUESTIONS

Self-test Questions

1. Define the term 'impairment loss'.
2. Define the term 'cash generating unit'.
3. List the factors which suggest that an asset may have been impaired.
4. Explain how the recoverable amount of an asset is determined.

Review Questions

(See **Appendix One** for Suggested Solutions to Review Questions.)

Question 10.1

Keano Limited has identified an impairment loss of €60 million in one of its cash generating units (CGUs). The CGU showed a carrying amount of €160 million and a recoverable amount of €100 million at 31 December 2012.

Details of the carrying amount:	€m
Goodwill	20
Property	60
Machinery	40
Motor vehicles	20
Other non-current assets	20
	160

The fair value less costs to sell of the CGU's assets is less than their carrying values, except for the property, which had a market value of €70 million at 31 December 2012.

Requirement Allocate the impairment loss arising in accordance with IAS 36 *Impairment of Assets.*

Question 10.2 (*Based on Chartered Accountants Ireland, P3 Summer 2003, Question 4*)

BLUES Limited (BLUES) prepares its financial statements to 31 December each year. The company manufactures paint, and its operations are divided into two cash-generating units: domestic and commercial. The following issue needs to be resolved before the financial statements for the year ended 31 December 2012 can be finalised. The following information is available in relation to the two cash-generating units.

	Domestic €000	Commercial €000
Goodwill	–	1,200
Other intangible assets	1,500	300
Property	2,400	6,400
Plant and equipment	3,300	1,400
Historic cost-based carrying value	7,200	9,300

Fair value less costs of disposal	7,500	4,200

Future net cash inflows:

2013	1,200	1,200
2014	900	1,300
2015	2,700	1,600
2016	1,500	1,500
2017	1,600	900
2018	1,800	1,800

Discount rate appropriate to activities of cash generating units	10%	12%

Requirement

(a) Calculate whether an impairment loss arises for either of the two cash-generating units, domestic and commercial.

(b) Allocate any impairment loss arising in accordance with IAS 36 *Impairment of Assets*.

Present value factors:

Rate/Period	1	2	3	4	5	6
10%	0.909	0.826	0.751	0.683	0.620	0.564
12%	0.893	0.797	0.712	0.636	0.567	0.507

Challenging Questions

(Suggested Solutions to Challenging Questions are available to lecturers.)

Question 10.1

You are the financial controller of VERTIGO Limited (VERTIGO), an Irish company that prepares its financial statements to 31 December each year. The following issue needs to be resolved before the financial statements for the year ended 31 December 2012 can be finalised. On 1 January 2012, VERTIGO purchased all the shares of SAN JUAN Limited (SAN JÚAN) for €12,000,000. The fair value of the identifiable net assets of SAN JUAN at that date was €10,800,000. During the year ended 31 December 2012, SAN JUAN traded at a loss and the fair value of its net assets at 31 December 2012 was as follows:

	€000
Non-current assets – property, plant and equipment	7,800
Non-current assets – capitalised development costs	1,200
Net current assets	1,500
	10,500

An impairment review at 31 December 2012 indicated that the value in use of SAN JUAN at that date was €9,000,000 and that its fair value less costs of disposal was €8,500,000.

Requirement

(a) Calculate the impairment loss that would arise in the consolidated financial statements of the VERTIGO Group for the year ended 31 December 2012 as a result of the impairment review of SAN JUAN.

(b) Show how the impairment loss calculated in (a) would affect the carrying values of the various net assets in the consolidated statement of financial position of the VERTIGO Group as at 31 December 2012.

Question 10.2 *(Based on Chartered Accountants Ireland, CAP 2 Autumn 2010, Question 3)*

> *Note:* this question covers a number of related issues, some of which are covered more fully in other chapters. Consequently, before attempting this question, you should also study **Chapter 6** and **Chapter 17**.

Before you can leave for the weekend, the following issues need to be resolved.

Issue One:

BUSH Limited ("BUSH") prepares its financial statements to 31 December each year. The company purchased a freehold property with an estimated useful economic life of 40 years at a cost of €1,150,000 on 3 September 2007, and on 31 December 2010 the freehold property was professionally valued at €1,350,000, with an estimated useful economic life of 36 years on that date. On 14 June 2012, BUSH sold the property for €1,550,000.

It is company policy to: (i) depreciate freehold properties on a straight-line basis over their estimated useful economic life, with a full year's depreciation in the year of acquisition and none in the year of disposal; (ii) eliminate accumulated depreciation on revaluations; and (iii) transfer an amount from revaluation reserve to retained earnings (through the statement of changes in equity) each year equal to the difference between the depreciation on the revalued carrying value and the original cost.

Requirement Show clearly the journal entries required to record the sale of the property on 14 June 2012.

Issue Two:

MUMFORD Limited ("MUMFORD") prepares its financial statements to 31 December each year. The company has been experiencing trading difficulties in recent years as a consequence of the economic recession.

For internal reporting purposes, MUMFORD is divided into two cash generating units based on the nature of the customer: Private Sector and Public Sector. The historic cost carrying value of the non-current assets of the two cash generating units at 31 December 2012 is as follows:

	Private Sector €	Public Sector €
Property, plant and equipment	754,000	716,000
Patent – cost	20,000	-
Goodwill	-	28,000
	774,000	744,000

In addition, the historic cost carrying value of MUMFORD's head-office administrative property, plant and equipment at 31 December 2012 is €206,000. It is estimated that head office services the two cash generating units on an equal basis.

The directors of MUMFORD believe that the net realisable value of the Private Sector and Public Sector cash generating units at 31 December 2012 is €651,000 and €538,000, respectively. With respect to the net realisable value of the Private Sector cash generating unit, the directors estimate that the patent could be sold separately for €15,000.

Projections prepared for the company's bankers indicate the following projected net cash flows:

	Private Sector	Public Sector
	€	€
2013	170,000	212,000
2014	175,000	215,000
2015	245,000	240,000
2016	230,000	269,000

The required rate of return for both cash generating units is 10%.

Requirement Calculate the extent of any impairment loss in the Private Sector and Public Sector cash generating units and show clearly the necessary journal entries required to reflect any impairment loss in the financial statements of MUMFORD for the year ended 31 December 2012.

Issue Three:

Given the current economic climate, and in order to retain staff, FLEETFOX Limited ("FLEETFOX") offered a two-year interest-free loan of €10,000 to each of its employees on 1 January 2012. One hundred employees accepted the offer on this date. Under the terms of the agreement, the loan has to be repaid in full on 31 December 2013. If an employee who has availed of the loan offer leaves the company during the two-year period, then the loan must be repaid immediately. None of the employees who accepted the loan offer left the company during 2012. The market rate of interest for a two-year loan is 10% per annum. FLEETFOX wishes to disclose the loans as 'Loans and Receivables'.

Requirement Illustrate and explain clearly how the loans should be recorded in the financial statements of FLEETFOX for the year ended 31 December 2012.

Present Value Factors:

Rate/Period	1	2	3	4	5
10%	0.909	0.826	0.751	0.683	0.621

Question 10.3

Kravitz Limited has identified an impairment loss of €100m in one of its cash-generating units (CGU). The CGU showed a carrying amount of €460m and a recoverable amount of €360m at 31 December 2012. The loss of €100m is charged to the SPLOCI–P/L for the year ended 31 December 2012.

Details of the CGU carrying value

	€m
Goodwill	20
Property	160
Machinery	140
Motor vehicles	30
Other non-current assets	110

The fair value less costs to sell of the unit's assets do not differ significantly from the carrying values, except for the property, which had a market value of €170m at 31 December 2012.

Requirement

(a) Show how the impairment loss would be allocated to the CGU assets for the year ended 31 December 2012.

(b) At the end of December 2013, a review showed that the conditions which led to the impairment charge in 2012 no longer exist. What is the amount of reversal of impairment charge that could be included in the SPLOCI–P/L for the year ended 31 December 2013? (Assume the remaining useful life is five years for each of the motor vehicles, machinery and other non-current assets at August 2012.)

11

INVENTORIES

Learning Objectives

After having studied this chapter, you should be able to:
1. define the term 'inventory';
2. calculate the cost of inventory;
3. measure the net realisable value of inventory in accordance with IAS 2 *Inventories*;
4. apply cost formulae such as 'FIFO' and weighted average; and
5. apply the main disclosure requirements of IAS 2.

In order to aid your understanding of the concepts and issues covered in this chapter, it is important to understand and be familiar with the following key terms and definitions. As you study this chapter, you should refer back to the key terms and definitions listed below.

Key Terms and Definitions for this Chapter

Cost The cost of inventories consists of: cost of purchase; cost of conversion; and any other costs incurred in bringing the inventories to their present location and condition.

Inventory This refers to: raw materials; work-in-progress (WIP); finished goods produced; and goods purchased and held for resale by a business.

Net Realisable Value (NRV) This is defined as the estimated selling price in the ordinary course of business less the estimated costs of completion and less the estimated costs necessary to make the sale.

Normal Capacity This is the expected achievable production based on the average over several periods; it includes capacity lost through planned maintenance.

11.1 INTRODUCTION

The term **inventory** refers to:
- raw materials;
- work-in-progress (WIP);
- finished goods produced; and
- goods purchased and held for resale by a business.

Inventory that is not in current use is an idle resource and is costing the organisation money. Therefore, an organisation must have good reason to hold it. There are many reasons an organisation will hold inventory, but some of the most important are:

1. *Time* – time lags at stages in the supply chain, from supplier to user, usually means that it is essential to maintain a certain level of inventory to use in this 'lead time'. Therefore inventory may be held to ensure production is not disrupted;

2. *Uncertainty* – inventory may be held as a buffer to meet uncertainties in demand, supply and movements of goods. Therefore, inventory may be held to meet ongoing demand from customers and/or to meet an expected rise in demand; and

3. *Economies of scale* – the notion of 'one unit at a time at a place where the user needs it when he needs it' is unrealistic and would incur significant costs in terms of logistics. Bulk buying, movement and storing can bring economies of scale. Furthermore, inventory may be held to qualify for bulk order discounts/special promotions from suppliers and/or to meet a supplier's requirement for minimum order sizes.

These reasons are applicable at any stage of the production process.

However, there are costs associated with inventory. For example:
- holding costs (e.g. warehousing and insurance);
- ordering costs (e.g. delivery);
- shortage costs (e.g. the loss of sales revenue, the loss of customer goodwill and the cost of paying labour even when there are no raw materials to work with); and
- the purchase price.

Key to this Chapter

While, from an overall business perspective, there are myriad issues surrounding inventory, this chapter focuses on the *accounting treatment* of inventory and, in particular, the amount of cost to be recognised as an asset, in accordance with IAS 2 *Inventories,* and carried forward until the related revenues are recognised. **Section 11.2** begins by stating that under IAS 2, inventory should be measured at the *lower* of *cost* and *net realisable value* (NRV) in the financial statements. After this, the different components of cost are explained, followed by the definition of net realisable value (NRV). Finally, how to apply cost formulae such as, 'First In First Out' (FIFO) and weighted average is explained and the main IAS 2 disclosure requirements are outlined.

11.2 IAS 2 *INVENTORIES*

The Scope of IAS 2

IAS 2 prescribes the accounting treatment for all inventories, *except for:*
- work-in-progress (WIP) arising under construction contracts (IAS 11 *Construction Contracts* – see **Chapter 12**);
- financial instruments (IAS 39 *Financial Instruments: Recognition and Measurement* – see **Chapter 25**); and

- biological assets related to agricultural activity and agricultural produce at the point of harvest (IAS 41 *Agriculture* – see **Chapter 34**).

Measurement

Under IAS 2, **inventory should be measured** (i.e. recorded or valued in the financial statements) **at the *lower* of *cost* and *net realisable value*** (NRV).

> *Note:* it is imperative that students know this rule, together with the definitions of *cost* and *NRV.*

This text will now define cost, and its components, and then progress to explain net realisable value.

Cost

The *cost* of inventories consists of:
- cost of purchase;
- cost of conversion; and
- any other costs incurred in bringing the inventories to their present location and condition.

Cost of purchase is the total of:
- purchase price less trade discounts and rebates;
- import duties and other taxes not recoverable; and
- transport and handling costs.

Cost of conversion comprises:
- costs directly related to the units of production (e.g. direct materials, direct labour and direct expenses); and
- allocated fixed and variable production overheads. Fixed production overheads remain relatively constant regardless of the volume of production (e.g. depreciation and maintenance of factory buildings and equipment, and the cost of factory management and administration).

Other costs can only be included in the cost of inventories if they are incurred in bringing them to their present location and condition (e.g. the cost of designing products for specific customers). The following costs *cannot* be included in the cost of inventories; they must be written off as expenses immediately:
- abnormal amounts of wasted materials;
- storage costs – except where they are necessary in the production process before a further stage of production;
- administrative overheads that do not contribute to bringing products to their present location; and
- selling costs.

Example 11.1 is a basic illustration of the application of the decision rule that inventory should be valued at the lower of cost and NRV.

EXAMPLE II.I: VALUING INVENTORY (I)

DEF plc manufactures mechanical parrots, which trade under the name 'Parker'. In the year ended 31 December 2012, 10,000 'Parkers' are manufactured and the related costs were:

	€
Materials	3,000
Labour	4,000
Depreciation of machinery	2,000
Factory rates	1,000
Sundry factory expenses	2,000
Production storage costs	1,000
Selling expenses	2,000
Expenses at head office	4,000
	19,000

Requirement At 31 December 2012, there were 1,000 Parkers in inventory. Assuming that these have a resale value of €4 each, what value should be placed on the closing inventory?

Solution

		€
Cost:	Materials	3,000
	Labour	4,000
	Depreciation of machinery	2,000
	Factory rates	1,000
	Sundry factory expenses	2,000
	Production storage costs	1,000
		13,000

Number of Parkers produced	10,000
Therefore cost per item	€1.30
Number in inventory at year-end	1,000
Therefore cost of closing inventory	€1,300
Net realisable value = 1,000 × €4	€4,000

Therefore, inventory should be valued in the statement of financial position at €1,300.

Continuing with the costs of conversion, and in particular **overheads**, IAS 2 requires that *fixed production overheads* must be allocated to items of inventory on the basis of **normal capacity** of the production facilities. The key factors to be considered when applying this are:
- **normal capacity** is the expected achievable production based on the average over several periods – this includes capacity lost through planned maintenance;
- low production or idle plant will not result in a higher fixed overhead allocation to each unit (because the allocation should be based on normal capacity);
- unallocated overheads must be written off as an expense in the year in which they are incurred; and
- when production is abnormally high, the fixed production overhead allocated to each unit is decreased so that inventories are not valued above cost.

Example 11.2 includes fixed production overheads in the valuation of inventory.

EXAMPLE 11.2: VALUING INVENTORY (2)

The following information related to Unipoly plc, a manufacturer of can-openers, for the year ended 31 December 2012.

	€
Direct materials cost of can-opener per unit	1
Direct labour cost of can-opener per unit	1
Direct expenses cost of can-opener per unit	1
Production overheads per year	600,000
Administration overheads per year	200,000
Selling overheads per year	300,000
Interest payments per year	100,000

There was no finished goods inventory at the start of the year and no work-in-progress. There were 250,000 units in finished goods at the year-end. The normal annual level of production is 750,000 can-openers. However, in the year ended 31 December 2012, only 450,000 were produced because of a labour dispute.

Requirement Calculate the cost of finished goods at 31 December 2012 in accordance with IAS 2 *Inventories*.

Solution
Cost per unit:

		€
	Material	1.00
	Labour	1.00
	Other expenses	1.00
	Production overheads (€600,000/750,000 units)	0.80
		3.80

Valuation of finished goods inventory:
250,000 units × €3.80 =

	950,000

Continuing with **overheads**, IAS 2 states that variable production overheads are those indirect costs of production that vary directly or nearly directly with the volume of production (e.g. indirect material and indirect labour). Variable production overheads are allocated to each unit of production on the basis of the actual use of the production facilities.

Remember: under IAS 2, inventory should be measured at the *lower* of *cost* and *net realisable value* (NRV). Having discussed the definition of cost, NRV is now addressed.

Net Realisable Value (NRV)

NRV is defined as the:

Estimated selling price in the ordinary course of business
less the estimated costs of completion
less the estimated costs necessary to make the sale.

Where the cost of inventories may not be recoverable (for example, they are damaged or obsolete or selling prices have declined), they should not be carried in excess of the amounts expected to be realised from their sale (i.e. they must be valued at NRV).

Comparison of Cost and NRV

For each item of inventory (or group of items in the same product line), it is necessary to compare the cost of the inventory with its NRV. That item, or group of items, should then be measured (i.e. recorded in the financial statements) at the lower of cost and NRV. The application of this is illustrated in **Examples 11.3** and **11.4**.

EXAMPLE 11.3: LOWER OF COST AND NRV (1)

Finished goods of dissimilar items at 31 December 2012:

Item	Cost €	NRV €
1	1,000	1,400
2	800	700
3	2,500	2,800
4	1,800	1,700
5	200	300
6	300	250
	6,600	7,150

Inventory should be recorded in the financial statements at 31 December 2012 at:

Item	€
1	1,000
2	700
3	2,500
4	1,700
5	200
6	250
	6,350

EXAMPLE 11.4: LOWER OF COST AND NRV (2)

Patches Limited values inventory at the lower of cost and net realisable value in accordance with IAS 2 *Inventories*, and at 31 December 2012 the company's entire inventory is valued at cost in the draft financial statements for the year ended 31 December 2012. One of Patches Limited's products, 'Poang', is manufactured in two stages and there is a market for the unfinished stage one product. Details relating to Poang are as follows:

	No. of Units in Inventory at 31 December 2012	Cost per Unit €	Selling Price per Unit €
Poang – stage one	10,000	500	600
Additional costs		250	
Poang – finished	24,000	750	800

The selling costs associated with both the stage one and finished products are €20 per unit. Following the introduction of a similar product on to the market in November 2012 by a foreign competitor, Patches Limited has had to reduce the selling price of both the stage one and finished products to €475 and €700 per unit, respectively, from January 2013.

Requirement Calculate the value of the closing inventory of Poang at 31 December 2012 and show any adjustment required.

Solution

In accordance with IAS 2 *Inventories*, the decline in selling price of both the stage one and finished products should be accounted for at 31 December 2012 as the change in selling price confirms the conditions that existed at the end of the reporting period. The NRV is based on the selling price of the finished product.

	€	Cost per Unit €
Selling price – finished product	700	
Less selling costs	(20)	
NRV – finished product	680	750
Less additional costs	(250)	
NRV – stage one	430	500

Write down:	€
Finished – 24,000 × €70 (€750 – €680)	1,680,000
Stage one – 10,000 × €70 (€500 – €430)	700,000
	2,380,000

DR Cost of sales (and ultimately Retained Earnings)	€2,380,000	
CR Inventory		€2,380,000

In practice, the assessment of NRV may not be straightforward. IAS 2 states that it should take place *at the same time* as estimates are made of selling price and that a new assessment of NRV should be made in each subsequent accounting period. If the circumstances that previously caused inventories to be written down below cost no longer exist, or if there is clear evidence of an increase in NRV because of changed economic circumstances, the amount of the write down should be reversed (i.e. the reversal is limited to the amount of the original write down) so that the new carrying amount is the lower of the cost and the NRV. This might occur, for example, when an item of inventory that is carried at NRV, because its selling price has declined, is still on hand in a subsequent period and its selling price has increased.

Techniques for the Measurement of Cost

IAS 2 states that techniques for the measurement of cost, such as standard cost or the retail method, may be used for convenience if the results approximate to actual cost. With respect to these two techniques, IAS 2 states that:

Standard cost takes into account normal levels of materials and supplies, labour, efficiency and capacity utilisation. Standard costs *must* be reviewed regularly and revised, if necessary.

The retail method is calculated on the basis of sales value *less* gross margin percentage. This method is used in the retail industry for valuing inventories of large numbers of rapidly changing items with similar margins where other costing methods are impractical.

Cost Formulae

As stated above, IAS 2 requires that the application of the 'lower of cost and NRV' rule should be applied on an item-by-item basis (or group of similar items). Moreover, as described above, IAS 2 defines what is meant by 'cost'. In many circumstances, however, similar items that are purchased at different times, or even in different quantities, may have a different 'cost'. Consequently, IAS 2 allows either of two cost formulae to be used when inventories consist of a large number of interchangeable (i.e. identical or very similar) items. In these circumstances, specific identification of costs is not appropriate and costs should be assigned using either:
- *First In First Out (FIFO)*, which assumes that items purchased or manufactured first are subsequently sold first, resulting in the value of inventory at the reporting date being closer to current market prices; or
- *Weighted Average*, which is determined from the weighted average cost of items at the beginning of the period and the cost of similar items purchased or produced during the period.

The key features of the **FIFO method of pricing inventory issues** are that:
- it is an actual cost system (i.e. not a weighted average);
- it is a good representation of sound storekeeping;
- inventory valuation should approximate to current market value;
- it is acceptable under IAS 2;
- cost of sales will lag behind current cost because it is based on older costs and the replacement cost of items sold is likely to be higher; and
- cost comparison can be difficult if prices are volatile.

The key features of the **weighted average method of pricing inventory issues** are that:
- it is not an actual buying price;
- it is acceptable under IAS 2;
- it eases job comparison; and
- it smoothes out price fluctuations.

The application of these two methods is illustrated in **Examples 11.5** and **11.6**.

EXAMPLE 11.5: FIFO AND WEIGHTED AVERAGE (1)

A toy shop buys two batches of dolls during its accounting period:
Batch 1 purchased in Month 1: 5 @ €10 each; and
Batch 2 purchased in Month 2: 5 @ €12 each.
During Month 3, three dolls were sold @ €25 each.

Requirement Calculate the cost of closing inventory at the end of Month 3 using both FIFO and the weighted average methods for calculating the cost of inventory.

Solution

FIFO:		€
2 @ €10 =		20
5 @ €12 =		60
		80

Weighted average:		€
5 @ €10 =		50
5 @ €12 =		60
10 @ €11 =		110

Closing inventory 7 @ €11	77

EXAMPLE 11.6: FIFO AND WEIGHTED AVERAGE (2)

RED Limited purchases and re-sells a single product called a widget. Details of the purchases and sales of product widget during March 2013 are as follows:

1 March	Opening balance		Nil
	Purchases	100 units	@ €5.00 each
2 March	Sales	50 units	
10 March	Purchases	50 units	@ €5.50 each
20 March	Sales	60 units	
27 March	Purchases	100 units	@ €5.60 each

Requirement Prepare a table showing the changes in the level of inventory of product widget, the valuation per unit and the total value of inventory held during March 2013, using the :
  (i) First In, First Out (FIFO) method;
 (ii) Last In, First Out (LIFO) method; and
(iii) Weighted average method.

Solution

(i) First In, First Out (FIFO)

Date March	Qty	Receipts price	€	Qty	Issues price	€	Qty	Balance price	€
1							Nil		Nil
1	100	5.00	500				100	5.00	500
2				50	5.00	250	50	5.00	250
10	50	5.50	275				50	5.00	250
							50	5.50	275
							100		525
20				50	5.00	250			
				10	5.50	55			
				60		305	40	5.50	220

Date March	Qty	Receipts price	€	Qty	Issues price	€	Qty	Balance price	€
27	100	5.60	560				40	5.50	220
							100	5.60	560
							140		780

(ii) Last In, First Out (LIFO)

Date March	Qty	Receipts price	€	Qty	Issues price	€	Qty	Balance price	€
1							Nil		Nil
1	100	5.00	500				100	5.00	500
2				50	5.00	250	50	5.00	250
10	50	5.50	275				50	5.00	250
							50	5.50	275
							100		525
20				50	5.50	275			
				10	5.00	50			
				60		325	40	5.00	200
27	100	5.60	560				40	5.00	200
							100	5.60	560
							140		760

(iii) Weighted Average

Date March	Qty	Receipts price	€	Qty	Issues price	€	Qty	Balance price	€
1							Nil		Nil
1	100	5.00	500				100	5.00	500
2				50	5.00	250	50	5.00	250
10	50	5.50	275				100	5.25	525
20				60	5.25	315	40	5.25	210
27	100	5.60	560				140	5.50	770

Note: the option of using the Last In First Out (LIFO) method of measuring the cost of inventory is not available under IAS 2.

Recognition as an Expense

When inventories are sold, the carrying amount of those inventories should be recognised as an expense in the period when the related revenue is recognised, with any write downs or

246 INTERNATIONAL FINANCIAL ACCOUNTING AND REPORTING

reversals being recorded in the period they occur. If any inventories are used in the construction of non-current assets (e.g. property, plant and equipment), they should be capitalised and expended over the useful life of the non-current asset created.

Examples of costs excluded from the cost of inventories and recognised as expenses in the period in which they are incurred are:
• abnormal amounts of wasted materials, labour or other production costs;
• storage costs, unless those costs are necessary in the production process before a further production stage;
• administrative overheads that do not contribute to bringing inventories to their present location and condition; and
• selling costs.

Disclosure

Given that a wide variety of policies and practices are acceptable under IAS 2, particularly with respect to how the value of inventory is measured, it is important that adequate information is disclosed to enable users of financial statements to understand the impact of inventory valuation on reported performance. Consequently, IAS 2 states that the following disclosures should be included in the financial statements in respect of inventories:
• the accounting policy adopted in measuring inventories, including cost formulae;
• the total carrying amount of inventories analysed under major headings (for example, raw materials, WIP and finished goods);
• the carrying amount of inventories at fair value less costs to sell;
• the amount expended in the period;
• the amount of any write downs of inventories;
• the amount of any reversal of write downs;
• the cause of write downs; and
• the carrying amount of inventories pledged as security for liabilities.

11.3 CONCLUSION

In accordance with IAS 2, inventories should be measured at the lower of cost and NRV, which is the estimated selling price in the ordinary course of business less the estimated costs of completion and less the estimated costs necessary to make the sale. Cost includes all costs of purchase, costs of conversion and other costs incurred in bringing the inventories to their present location and condition. The cost of inventories, other than those for which specific identification of costs are appropriate, is assigned by using the FIFO or weighted average cost formula.

When inventories are sold, the carrying amount of those inventories is recognised as an expense in the same period as the revenue. The amount of any write down of inventories to NRV is recognised as an expense in the period the write down or loss occurs. The amount of any reversal of a write down of inventories is recognised as a reduction in the amount of inventories recognised as an expense in the period in which the reversal occurs.

Summary of Learning Objectives

Having studied this chapter, you should be able to:

Learning Objective 1 Define the term 'inventory'.

The term **'inventory'** refers to raw materials, work in progress, finished goods produced and goods purchased and held for resale by a business.

Learning Objective 2 How to calculate the cost of inventory.

The cost of inventories consists of the cost of purchase, cost of conversion and any other costs incurred in bringing the inventories to their present location and condition – see **Examples 11.1** and **11.2**.

Learning Objective 3 Measure the net realisable value (NRV) of inventory in accordance with IAS 2.

NRV is the estimated selling price in the ordinary course of business *less* the estimated costs of completion and *less* the estimated costs necessary to make the sale.

Learning Objective 4 How to apply cost formulae, such as FIFO and weighted average.

See **Examples 11.5** and **11.6**.

Learning Objective 5 Apply the main disclosure requirements of IAS 2.

The accounting policy adopted in measuring inventories, including cost formulae, together with the total carrying amount of inventories, analysed under major headings, must be disclosed.

QUESTIONS

Self-test Questions

1. How should inventory be measured in accordance with IAS 2?
2. What does the cost of inventory comprise?
3. Name and describe two methods identified in IAS 2 for the measurement of cost.

Review Questions

(See **Appendix One** for Suggested Solutions to Review Questions.)

Question 11.1

You are the accounting consultant to a public holding company that has four trading subsidiaries: Screws Limited, Brackets Limited, Frames Limited and Concrete Blocks Limited.

All the subsidiaries tend to be of roughly equal value. The accounts of the company are made up annually to 31 December.

Two weeks before the year-end, the Group Chief Accountant brings the following matters to your attention.

(a) The Group Chief Accountant has suggested to the management of Screws Limited, a manufacturing company, that their finished goods inventory must be accurately costed this year. However, the management of Screws Limited insist that their usual basis of selling price less 20% is convenient and also consistent since the same percentage is used each year.

(b) Brackets Limited, which manufactures a range of brass sockets, is currently facing a price war with its main competitor. It is anticipated that the company's trading results for the last quarter of the year will be as follows:

	Units (Tonnes)	€000
Sales	700	300
Brass consumed	700	(200)
Conversion costs		(120)
Selling costs		(30)
Loss		(50)

On 31 December, inventories consist only of 200 tonnes of completed brass sockets. The last consignment was purchased on 1 December at €500 per tonne and the published market price on 31 December is expected to be €520 per tonne. The Group Chief Accountant is uncertain how the brass inventory should be valued. The note on the group accounts will read: 'Inventories are valued at cost (in the case of finished goods, factory cost) or net realisable value if lower'.

(c) Frames Limited imported a shipment of windows from America on 15 November and the cost at the rate of exchange on that date was €100,000. The goods were not paid for until 10 December and the payment amounted to €120,000 due to an appreciation in the value of the US dollar during the three-week period. It is thought that only 5% of the consignment will have been sold by 31 December and the management of Frames Limited wishes to value the windows on that date at €114,000.

(d) Concrete Blocks Limited have hitherto included fixed costs and variable costs (in particular, fixed factory overheads) when valuing its inventory of finished goods. It now wishes to move over to a variable-cost-only basis of valuation, which it claims will give a truer picture of performance.

Requirement Prepare a memorandum for the attention of the Group Chief Accountant that addresses each of the points above.

Question 11.2

Techniques for the measurement of the cost of inventories, such as the 'retail method', may be used for convenience if the results approximate cost. The cost of the inventory is determined by reducing the sales value by the appropriate percentage gross margin.

Requirement

(a) Discuss when it might be appropriate to use the method referred to above.

(b) If a company traditionally applied a policy of calculating actual cost by item but changed to the above method, would a prior year adjustment (as defined by IAS 8 *Accounting Policies, Changes in Accounting Estimates and Errors*) be required? (See **Chapter 21**.)

(c) You are the audit senior of a company that uses the above method of inventory valuation. What factors would you consider in the audit of inventory?

Challenging Questions

(Suggested Solutions to Challenging Questions are available to lecturers.)

Question 11.1

Details of inventories of five separate products are as follows:

Product:	A	B	C	D	E
	€	€	€	€	€
Materials	1,000	2,000	1,500	6,000	1,200
Labour	500	500	600	600	600
Production overheads	400	400	500	500	500
Marketing overheads (yet to be incurred)	350	350	400	400	300
Selling overheads (yet to be incurred)	200	200	200	200	200
Administration costs	150	300	100	900	110
	2,600	3,750	3,300	8,600	2,910
Selling Price	2,800	3,700	3,000	7,200	2,900

Requirement Assuming that none of the above items has been sold at the year-end, value the inventory on the basis of IAS 2 *Inventories*.

Question 11.2

Micro Limited processes and sells a single product. Purchases of raw materials during the year were made at a regular rate of 1,000 tonnes at the beginning of each week. The price was €200 per tonne on 1 January 2012 and was increased to €300 per tonne on 1 July 2012 and remained constant from then on until the end of the year, 31 December 2012. In addition to this price a customs duty of €20 per tonne was paid throughout the year and transport from the docks to the factory cost €40 per tonne.

Variable costs of processing were €50 per tonne. There was capacity to process 1,000 tonnes per week and the fixed production costs for all levels of activity up to this capacity level were €60,000 per week. One tonne of raw materials is processed into one tonne of finished products and sold, at a delivery price of €480 per tonne, by a sales force whose cost was fixed at €6,000 per week. Average delivery costs to customers were €15 per tonne.

At the beginning of the year there was no inventory and at the end of the year there were 5,000 tonnes of raw material and 2,000 tonnes of finished product. It is expected that the costs and prices current at 31 December 2012 will continue during 2013.

Requirement Draft the accounting policy on inventory for the company to include in its financial statements.

(a) Calculate the value of inventory at 31 December 2012 on a basis acceptable under IAS 2 *Inventories*.

(b) Comment on the relative merits of FIFO and any other basis recognised under IAS 2 for valuing inventory.

Notes:

• You should assume that inventories of raw material can only be used to produce finished goods and cannot be re-sold as raw material at a realistic price.

• Assume a 52-week productive year, with production and sales spread evenly throughout the year.

12

CONSTRUCTION CONTRACTS

LEARNING OBJECTIVES

Having studied this chapter, you should be able to:
1. define a construction contract;
2. explain when profits and losses on construction contracts are to be recognised;
3. discuss how the recognition of a profit on a construction contract differs from the recognition of a loss;
4. account for profits and losses on construction contracts depending upon the expected outcome and the stage of completion; and
5. apply the main disclosure requirements for construction contracts.

KEY TERMS AND DEFINITIONS FOR THIS CHAPTER

Construction Contract A construction contract is specifically negotiated for the construction of an asset or a combination of assets that are closely interrelated or interdependent in terms of their design, technology and function or their ultimate purpose or use.

Contract Revenue This comprises of:
(a) the initial amount of revenue agreed in the contract; and
(b) variations in contract work, claims and incentive payments to the extent that it is probable that they will result in revenue and they are capable of being measured reliably. The revenue is measured at the fair value received or receivable. Uncertainties that may affect the measurement of contract revenue include:
  • agreed variations between contractor and customer in a subsequent period;
  • cost escalation clauses in a fixed-price contract; and
  • penalties imposed on the contractor because of delays.
A variation is included in contract revenue when:
  • it is probable that the customer will approve the variation; and
  • the revenue can be measured reliably.

Contract Costs These comprise:
  • costs that relate directly to the specific contract (see below);

- costs that are attributable to contract activity in general (see below) and can be allocated to the contract; and
- such other costs as are specifically chargeable to the customer under the terms of the contract.

Costs that relate *directly* to a specific contract include:
- site labour costs, including site supervision;
- cost of materials used in construction;
- depreciation of plant and equipment used on the contract;
- cost of moving plant, equipment and materials to and from the contract site;
- cost of hiring plant and equipment;
- cost of design and technical assistance that is directly related to the contract;
- the estimated cost of rectification and guarantee work, including expected warranty cost; and
- claims from third parties.

Costs that *may be* attributable to contract activity in general that can be allocated to specific contracts include:
- insurance;
- costs of design and technical assistance that are not directly related to a specific contract; and
- construction overheads.

Cost-plus Contract A cost-plus contract is a contract where a contractor is paid for all of its allowed expenses to a set limit *plus* additional payment to allow for a profit.

Fixed-price Contract A fixed-price contract requires the contractor to deliver a clearly defined piece of work to the customer at a predetermined price. A fixed-price contract shifts most or all risks from the customer to the contractor.

Please note that, as explained in **Chapter 2**, the IASB issued amendments to IAS 1 *Presentation of Financial Statements* in June 2011. These included a *proposal* that the title 'Statement of Profit or Loss and Other Comprehensive Income' (SPLOCI) be adopted (rather than, for example, 'statement of comprehensive income') and a *requirement* to revise the presentation of other comprehensive income (OCI) within the SPLOCI. These amendments are explained in detail in **Chapter 2, Section 2.3**.

12.1 INTRODUCTION

For most entities, revenue and expenses are relatively easily allocated to each accounting period (which is typically one year). However, for some entities, especially those whose work involves long-term contracts or span more than one accounting period, this is more difficult. For example, a building contractor who is building a new multistorey office block may commence the work in 2012 and complete it in 2016. If this type of contract was accounted for in a similar manner to the 'normal' sale of goods, then revenue and profit would not be recognised in the financial statements until the office block was completed, which is four years after it was started. While this approach is arguably consistent with the prudence concept, whereby profits are not anticipated until realised, it can also be argued that recognising the revenue and profit at the end of the project does not faithfully reflect the situation under the contract since, in reality, the revenue and profits have been earned over the four-year period and not just when the office block is finished (i.e. the accruals or matching concept – see **Chapter 1**). Consequently, there is arguably a conflict between the prudence and the accruals/matching concepts, with the accruals/matching concept winning.

This is because IAS 11 *Construction Contracts* requires that, in order for the financial statements to show a fair presentation of the activities of the enterprise and provide useful and relevant information to users, an appropriate part of **contract revenue** and profits should be included in the period in which the activity has taken place. The key issues in accounting for contracts that span more than one accounting period include:
- How much revenue should be included in the statement of profit or loss and other comprehensive income?
- How much should be charged for related costs?
- How much profit should be recognised in the period in respect of this contract?

Key to this Chapter

This chapter focuses on the accounting treatment of revenue and costs associated with **construction contracts** in accordance with IAS 11. **Section 12.2** outlines three important categories of contract, namely:
- when the outcome of a construction contract can be estimated reliably;
- when a contract's outcome cannot be estimated reliably; and
- when it is probable that a contract will incur losses.

Section 12.3 focuses on further issues associated with the application of these principles including the measurement of contract sales revenue and profit, together with the calculation of gross amounts due from/to customers. The IAS 11 disclosures are then illustrated in **Section 12.4**.

12.2 IAS 11 *CONSTRUCTION CONTRACTS* – THE BASICS

Scope of IAS 11

IAS 11 applies to the accounting treatment of construction contracts in the financial statements of contractors. As noted previously, due to the nature of the activity undertaken in construction contracts, the date at which the contract activity is entered into and the date when the activity is completed usually fall into different accounting periods. Therefore, the primary issue in accounting for construction contracts is the allocation of contract revenue and contract costs to the accounting periods in which construction work is performed.

IAS 11 requires that each contract must be accounted for separately and then the totals aggregated and included in the financial statements. The standard outlines three important **categories of contract**:

Category 1 – When the outcome of a construction contract can be estimated reliably.

Category 2 – When a contract's outcome cannot be estimated reliably.

Category 3 – When it is probable that total contract costs will exceed total contract revenue and therefore that the contract will incur losses.

Each of these contract categories is explained further below.

Category 1 – When a Contract's Outcome can be Estimated Reliably

When the outcome of a profitable construction contract can be estimated reliably, contract revenue and contract costs should be recognised as revenue and expenses, respectively, by reference to the stage of completion of the contract activity. The outcome can be estimated reliably when the contract revenue, contract costs to date and to completion, and the stage of completion can be measured reliably. This is illustrated in **Example 12.1** below.

EXAMPLE 12.1: CONTRACT OUTCOME ESTIMATED RELIABLY

Contract X at 31 December 2012:
Commencement date	1 January 2012
Completion date	31 December 2013
Contract price	€3,000,000
Cost to date	€1,000,000
Cost to complete	€1,000,000

Requirement Calculate the profit to be recognised in the statement of profit or loss and other comprehensive income for the year ended 31 December 2012 in respect of Contract X.

Suggested Approach

Step 1: Calculate the outcome for the contract

	€	€
Price		3,000,000
Costs:		
To date	1,000,000	
To complete	1,000,000	
Total cost		(2,000,000)
Profit		1,000,000

Step 2: Determine the stage of completion
For example, on the basis of Cost to Date / Total Cost (see **Section 12.3**)
€1,000,000 / €2,000,000 = 50%

Step 3: Statement of Profit or Loss and Other Comprehensive Income – Profit or Loss

	€
Revenue (€3,000,000 × 50%)	1,500,000
Cost of Sales (€2,000,000 × 50%)	(1,000,000)
Profit	500,000

The journal entries required to account for this are:

Revenue:	DR	Contract account	€1, 500,000	
	CR	Revenue		€1, 500,000
Cost of sales:	DR	Cost of sales	€1, 000,000	
	CR	Contract account		€1, 000,000

Category 2 – When a Contract's Outcome cannot be Estimated Reliably

When the outcome of a construction contract cannot be estimated reliably, revenue should be recognised only to the extent where it is probable that contract costs incurred are recoverable. Contract costs are recognised as expenses when incurred. If the outcome of the contract subsequently can be estimated reliably, the **percentage of completion method** is used for recognition of revenue and expenses (see Category 1).

This situation arises during the early stages of a contract when it is difficult to reliably estimate the outcome. See **Example 12.2**.

EXAMPLE 12.2: OUTCOME CANNOT BE ESTIMATED RELIABLY

Contract Y at 31 December 2012:

Commencement date	1 November 2012
Completion date	31 March 2014
Contract price	€5,000,000
Cost to date	€400,000
Cost to complete	€3,600,000

All costs are fully recoverable and the stage of completion is to be determined by reference to costs to date and total costs.

Requirement Calculate the profit to be recognised in the statement of profit or loss and other comprehensive income for the year ended 31 December 2012 in respect of Contract Y.

Suggested Approach

Step 1: Calculate the outcome for the contract

	€	€
Price		5,000,000
Costs:		
To date	400,000	
To complete	3,600,000	
Total cost		(4,000,000)
Profit		1,000,000

Step 2: Determine the stage of completion
Cost to Date / Total Cost
€400,000 / €4,000,000 = 10%
→Prudence dictates that it is too early to recognise any profit as the contract has only started.

Step 3: Statement of Profit or Loss and Other Comprehensive Income – Profit or Loss

	€
Revenue	400,000
Cost of Sales	(400,000)
Profit	0

The amount taken to revenue is the same as the cost of sales. In this instance, cost of sales is equal to costs to date (which coincidentally is also equal to 10% of total costs).

The journal entries required to account for this are:

Revenue:	DR	Contract account	€400,000	
	CR	Revenue		€400,000
Cost of sales:	DR	Cost of sales	€400,000	
	CR	Contract account		€400,000

Category 3 – When a Contract is Expected to Incur Losses

When it is probable that total contract costs will exceed total contract revenue, the expected loss should be recognised as an expense immediately. The whole loss to completion should be recognised. The amount of such a loss is determined irrespective of whether work has commenced on the contract and the stage of completion of contract activity. This is illustrated in **Example 12.3** below.

EXAMPLE 12.3: CONTRACT LOSS EXPECTED

Contract Z at 31 December 2012:

Commencement date	1 September 2012
Completion date	30 April 2014
Cost to date	€440,000
Cost to complete	€1,760,000
Contract price	€2,000,000
% completion	20

The stage of completion is to be determined by reference to costs to date and total costs.

Requirement Calculate the profit/loss to be recognised in the statement of profit or loss and other comprehensive income for the year ended 31 December 2012 in respect of Contract Z.

Suggested Approach

Step 1: Calculate the outcome for the contract

	€	€
Price		2,000,000
Costs:		
To date	440,000	
To complete	1,760,000	
Total cost		(2,200,000)
Loss		(200,000)

Step 2: Determine the stage of completion

Cost to Date / Total Cost
€440,000 / €2,200,000 = 20%

Step 3: Statement of Profit or Loss and Other Comprehensive Income – Profit or Loss

	€
Revenue (€2 million × 20%)	400,000
Cost of Sales (€2.2 million × 20%)	(440,000)
Loss	(40,000)
Provision for foreseeable loss (€160,000)	(160,000)
Total expected loss	(200,000)

When a contract is loss-making, irrespective of the stage of completion the full amount of the contract loss must be recognised.

The journal entries required to account for this are:

Revenue:	DR	Contract account	€400,000	
	CR	Revenue		€400,000
Cost of sales:	DR	Cost of sales	€400,000	
	CR	Contract account		€400,000

12.3 IAS 11 *CONSTRUCTION CONTRACTS* – FURTHER ISSUES

Having introduced the basic principles underlying IAS 11 in **Section 12.2**, further issues associated with the application of these principles are now explained. These are:
- When can the outcome of a contract be estimated reliably?
- How is the stage of completion of a contract measured?
- How is contract sales revenue measured?
- How is contract profit recognised?
- If the outcome of a contract is uncertain, what profit should be recognised?
- How are expected contract losses recognised?
- Gross amounts due from/to customers.

When Can the Outcome of a Contract be Estimated Reliably?

In broad terms, there are two types of construction contract:
- **fixed-price contracts**, and
- **cost-plus contracts**,

and the circumstances when the outcome of each of these types can be estimated reliably is discussed below.

Fixed-Price Contracts

In a fixed-price contract, the outcome can be estimated reliably when:
1. total revenue can be measured reliably;
2. it is probable that the economic benefits associated with the contract will flow into the entity;

3. both the contract costs to complete and the stage of completion at the end of the reporting period can be measured reliably; and
4. the contract costs attributable to the contract can be clearly identified and measured.

Cost-Plus Contracts

In a cost-plus contract, the outcome can be estimated reliably when the following two conditions are met:
1. it is probable that the economic benefits associated with the contract will flow to the entity; and
2. the contract costs attributable to the contract can be identified and measured.

How is the Stage of Completion of a Contract Measured?

Notwithstanding that, in practice, the stage of completion will be measured in a number of ways, including physical inspection, from an examination question perspective the stage of completion is *usually* calculated using ONE of the following formulae:

$$\frac{\textbf{Costs incurred to date}}{\textbf{Estimated total costs}} \qquad \textit{or} \qquad \frac{\textbf{Value of Work Certified}*}{\textbf{Contract price}}$$

* In construction contracts, the contractor normally receives payment against the value of the work completed at specific intervals. That part of the work done is usually certified in relation to the contract price, and not the cost of the contract, by an appointed architect.

How is Contract Sales Revenue Measured?

In order to estimate an appropriate part of contract revenue to be included in the statement of profit or loss and other comprehensive income – profit or loss (SPLOCI – P/L), the stage of completion of *each* contract must be established separately. There is no set rule on how to determine contract revenue, but the two main methods in practice are:
1. by reference to the proportion of work done, established either by certification of work by the surveyor, or by comparing the costs incurred to date to the total contract costs anticipated to give an estimate of work completed so far; and
2. by identifying specific points in the contract where the work completed has separately ascertainable sales values. For example, a contract for residential property development could have a sales value for the building of the house, and separate values for the construction of the garage, swimming pool, stables, etc.

Contract revenue should be recognised based on the activity on the contract in the period, regardless of the profit that is likely. Items that are included in the SPLOCI – P/L are recorded only once. Therefore, for a contract that spans, say, three years, any contract revenues recognised in previous years must be deducted. For example:
- Year 1: (total contract revenue × % stage of completion) = sales revenue for Year 1;
- Year 2: (total contract revenue × % stage of completion) less revenue recognised in Year 1 = sales revenue for Year 2;
- Year 3: (total contract revenue × % stage of completion) less revenue recognised in Years 1 and 2 = sales revenue for Year 3.

This is illustrated in **Example 12.4** below and also **Example 12.6**.

EXAMPLE 12.4: RECOGNISING CONTRACT REVENUE

Moby Limited has the following contract details for a contract that started in 2010:

	2010	2011	2012
Total contract sales value	€10 million	€11 million	€11.5 million
Estimated % completion	40%	75%	100%

Note: as the total contract value has changed over the duration of the contract, this can only be included in the revenue calculation if these amendments have been agreed with the customer. This is a common occurrence as the costs associated with labour and materials during the course of the contract may change, an unforeseen obstacle may occur that is beyond the control of the contractor or the customer's specifications may change.

Requirement Calculate the revenue to be recognised in the SPLOCI – P/L in each of the three years.

Solution

The revenue to be recognised is as follows:

	2010	2011	2012
Revenues recognisable to date:	€m	€m	€m
2010: 40% × €10 million	4.00		
2011: 75% × €11 million		8.25	
2012: 100% × €11.5 million			11.50
Less revenues recognised in prior periods	___	(4.00)	(8.25)
Revenue for the period	4.00	4.25	3.25

How is Contract Profit Recognised?

Similar to sales revenue, the recognition of contract profit is also usually based on the percentage of work completed on the contract. Usually, the amount of revenue and profit to be included will be decided based on work done, and cost of sales will be the balancing figure. As explained in **Section 12.1**, this is different from the normal basis for income recognition in the statement of profit or loss and other comprehensive income, which is transaction-led (i.e. make a sale, match the costs and the result is the profit). This is illustrated in **Examples 12.5** and **12.6** below.

EXAMPLE 12.5: RECOGNISING CONTRACT PROFIT

ABC Limited commenced Contract A in 2011 and has the following details for the year ended 31 December 2012:

Total contract value	€80 million
Costs incurred to date	€50 million
Estimated costs to complete	€7 million

Completion	80%	
Profit recognised in 2011	€11 million	

Requirement Calculate the profit to be recognised in the statement of profit or loss and other comprehensive income for the year ended 31 December 2012 in respect of Contract A.

Solution
Step 1
The first step is to calculate the total estimated profit on the contract:

	€m	€m
Total sales value of the contract		80
Less contract costs incurred to date	(50)	
Less estimated costs to completion	(7)	
Total estimated contract costs		(57)
		23

Step 2
Establish the stage of completion of the contract and calculate the profit recognisable to date:
Total estimated contract profit × % completion of the contract = recognisable profit to date
€23 million × 80% completion = €18.4 million.

Step 3
The third step is to calculate the profit reportable for this accounting period:

	€m
Recognisable profit to date	18.4
Less cumulative profit recognised in prior periods	(11.0)
Profit recognisable in 2012	7.4

In this case, €7.4 million will be included as part of profit in the SPLOCI–P/L for the year ended 31 December 2012.

EXAMPLE 12.6: RECOGNISING CONTRACT REVENUE, EXPENSES AND PROFIT

A contractor has a fixed-price contract for €9,000,000 to build a bridge. The initial amount of revenue agreed in the contract is €9,000,000. The contractor's initial estimate of contract costs is €8,000,000. It will take three years to build the bridge. By the end of Year 1, the contractor's estimate of contract costs has increased to €8,050,000. In Year 2, the customer approves a variation resulting in an increase in contract revenue of €200,000 and estimated additional contract costs of €150,000. At the end of Year 2, costs incurred include €100,000 for standard materials stored at the site to be used in Year 3 to complete the project.

The contractor determines the stage of completion of the contract by comparing the proportion of contract costs incurred for work performed to date with the latest estimated total contract costs. In accordance with IAS 11, the company recognises profit on construction contracts when the stage of completion is greater than 20%. A summary of the financial data during the construction period is as follows:

	Year 1 €000	Year 2 €000	Year 3 €000
Initial amount of revenue agreed in contract	9,000	9,000	9,000
Variation	–	200	200
Total contract revenue	9,000	9,200	9,200
Contract costs incurred to date	2,093	6,170	8,200
Contract costs to complete	5,957	2,030	–
Total estimated contract costs	8,050	8,200	8,200
Estimated profit	950	1,000	1,000
Stage of completion	26%	74%	100%

The stage of completion for Year 2 (74%) is determined by excluding from contract costs incurred for work performed to date the €100,000 of standard materials stored for use in Year 3.

The amounts of revenue, expenses and profit recognised in the SPLOCI–P/L in the three years are as follows:

		To date €000	Recognised in prior years €000	Recognised in current year €000
	€000			
Year 1	Revenue (9,000 × 0.26)	2,340		2,340
	Expenses (8,050 × 0.26)	2,093		2,093
	Profit	247		247
Year 2	Revenue (9,200 × 0.74)	6,808	2,340	4,468
	Expenses (8,200 × 0.74)	6,068	2,093	3,975
	Profit	740	247	493
Year 3	Revenue (9,200 × 1.00)	9,200	6,808	2,392
	Expenses (8,200 × 1.00)	8,200	6,068	2,132
	Profit	1,000	740	260

If the Outcome of a Contract is Uncertain, what Profit should be Recognised?

As explained with respect to Category 2 contracts (see above), if the outcome of the contract cannot be estimated with reasonable certainty, then no profit should be recognised. However, the statement of profit or loss and other comprehensive income must still reflect the activity in the period and so an appropriate part of revenue must still be recognised (and matched with the equivalent costs). This is illustrated in **Example 12.7** below.

EXAMPLE 12.7: CONTRACT OUTCOME UNCERTAIN

ABC Limited commenced Contract C in 2012 and has the following details for the year ended 31 December 2012:

	€m
Total contract value	40
Costs incurred to date	3
Estimated costs to complete	30
Completion	10%

Requirement Calculate the profit/loss to be recognised in the statement of profit or loss and other comprehensive income for the year ended 31 December 2012 in respect of Contract C, assuming that costs incurred to date are recoverable.

Solution

ABC Limited has only just commenced work on this contract (10% complete) and, while the contract is expected to be profit-making, the outcome cannot be measured with reasonable certainty. In this case, prudence dictates that no profit should be recognised in the year ended 31 December 2012.

Revenue would normally include 10% of revenue and cost of sales would be made to match the revenue to create a nil profit:

Statement of Profit or Loss and Other Comprehensive Income (Extract)	€m
Sales revenue (10% × €40 million)	4
Cost of sales	(4)
Profit/loss on contract	—

Required Accounting Treatment

However, in this case €4 million cannot be transferred to cost of sales as the costs incurred are €3 million to date. Where costs to date are less than the required cost of sales charge, the revenue figure is restricted to the level of costs incurred to date. The statement of profit or loss and other comprehensive income for 2011 would therefore include the following for contract C:

Statement of Profit or Loss and Other Comprehensive Income (Extract)	€m
Sales revenue	3
Cost of sales	(3)
Profit/loss on contract	—

How are Expected Contract Losses Recognised?

As explained with respect to Category 3 contract (see above), whenever an overall contract loss is expected, the loss *must* be recognised as soon as it is anticipated. The first step – calculating the overall profit or loss on the contract – would still be performed. However, if the overall contract is loss-making, the full amount of the loss will be recognised immediately. This is illustrated in **Example 12.8**.

EXAMPLE 12.8: RECOGNISING CONTRACT LOSSES

ABC Limited commenced Contract B during 2012 and will complete it in 2013. It has the following details for the year ended 31 December 2012:

Total contract value	€70m
Costs incurred to date	€40m
Estimated costs to complete	€39m
Completion	50%

Requirement Calculate the profit/loss to be recognised in the statement of profit or loss and other comprehensive income for the year ended 31 December 2012 and 2013 in respect of Contract B.

Solution

The first step is to calculate the overall outcome for this contract:

	€m	€m
Total sales value of the contract		70
Less contract costs incurred to date	(40)	
Less estimated costs to completion	(39)	
Total estimated contract costs		(79)
Total estimated contract loss		(9)

Contract B is 50% complete and revenue recognised must reflect this activity in the period, so the fact that the contract is loss-making does not remove the need to recognise sales revenue. What it does mean, however, is that cost of sales must be charged with an amount that results in the full-time contract loss of €9 million being recognised immediately.

Year 1 Statement of profit or loss and other comprehensive income (extract)	€m
Sales revenue (50% × €70m)	35
Cost of sales	(44)
Loss on contract	(9)

Cost of sales must be charged with €44 million to ensure that the full contract loss of €9 million is recognised in the first year (i.e. as soon as it is anticipated).

In this case, the cost of sales charge is made up of two elements:
1. 50% of total contract costs of €79 million = €39.5 million; and
2. the remaining amount of the loss that is expected to occur next year (2013), which is €4.5 million.

While the revenues and costs will occur as follows:

Statement of profit or loss and other comprehensive income (extract):	2012 €m	2013 €m
Sales revenue (50% in each of the two years)	35.0	35.0
Cost of sales	(39.5)	(39.5)
Loss on contract	(4.5)	(4.5)

Required Accounting Treatment

IAS 11 and prudence require that the whole of the loss is recognised as soon as it is anticipated and so the €4.5 million loss expected to occur in 2013 is pulled back and charged to 2012's statement of profit or loss and other comprehensive income through cost of sales. The statement of profit or loss and other comprehensive income extract now shows:

	2012 €m	2013 €m
Sales revenue (50% in each of the two years)	35	35
Cost of sales (€39.5 million + €4.5 million)	(44)	(35)
Profit/Loss on contract	(9)	–

Up until this point, the focus has largely been on accounting for construction contracts in the context of the statement of profit or loss and other comprehensive income. With respect to the statement of financial position, IAS 11 requires that an entity present the *gross amount due from/to customers* for construction contract work as an asset/liability. This is now explained.

Gross Amount Due From/To Customers

At the end of each reporting period, there may be two balances remaining in relation to construction contracts:
1. trade receivable (i.e. progress billings invoiced less progress billings received); and
2. balance on the contract account.

If the balance on the contract account is a debit, i.e. an asset, this should be presented as 'gross amount due from customers'. This comprises:

	€
Costs incurred (i.e. the customer owes the contractor for costs incurred on their behalf)	X
Plus recognised profits (i.e. the mark-up charged to the customer)	X
Less recognised losses (i.e. the contractor cannot recover all costs)	(X)
Less progress billings invoiced (i.e. when the contractor invoices the customer, the amount owed on the contract is reduced and it becomes a receivable)	X

This will be the case for construction contracts in progress for which costs incurred, plus recognised profits (less recognised losses), exceed progress billings. In this instance, the customer owes the contractor for costs incurred/construction contract work completed but not invoiced (i.e. it is therefore an asset). This is illustrated in **Example 12.9**.

EXAMPLE 12.9: GROSS AMOUNT DUE FROM CUSTOMER

Using ABC Limited's Contract A from **Example 12.5** and assuming that progress payments (invoiced and received) amount to €65 million.

ABC Limited commenced Contract A in 2011 and has the following details for the year ended 31 December 2012:

Total contract value	€80 million
Costs incurred to date	€50 million
Estimated costs to complete	€7 million
Completion	80%
Profit recognised in 2011	€11 million

Requirement Calculate the gross amount due from the customer to be included in the statement of financial position of ABC Limited at 31 December 2012 in respect of Contract A.

Solution	€m
Costs incurred	50.0
Plus recognised profits	18.4
Less recognised lossess	–
Less progress billings invoiced	(65.0)
Gross amount due from customer	3.4

If the balance on the contract account is a credit, i.e. a liability, this should be presented as 'gross amount due to customers'. This will be the case for construction contracts in progress for which progress billings exceed costs incurred plus recognised profits (less recognised losses). In this instance, the customer has been invoiced too much and is owed money back and/or the contractor is unable to recover all of the costs incurred (i.e. it is therefore a liability). This is illustrated in **Example 12.10**.

EXAMPLE 12.10: GROSS AMOUNT DUE TO CUSTOMER

ABC Limited commenced Contract D in 2011 and has the following details for the year ended 31 December 2012:

Total contract value	€70 million
Costs incurred to date	€60 million
Estimated costs to complete	€15 million
Completion	60%
Progress billings invoiced and received	€60 million

The overall contract is loss-making:	€m
Total contract value	70
Less total contract costs (€60 million + €15 million)	(75)
Overall anticipated contract loss	(5)

	€m
Costs incurred	60.0
Plus recognised profits	–
Less recognised losses	(5.0)
Less progress billings invoiced	(60.0)
Gross amount due from customer	(5.0)

This section has developed a number of the basic principles underlying IAS 11 that were introduced in **Section 12.2**. The issues covered in this section, **Section 12.3**, have included:

• When can the outcome of a contract be estimated reliably?
• How is the stage of completion of a contract measured?
• How is contract sales revenue measured?
• How is contract profit recognised?
• If the outcome of a contract is uncertain, what profit should be recognised?
• How are expected contract losses recognised?
• Gross amounts due from/to customers.

Before examining a number of the issues addressed so far in this chapter by way of a comprehensive example, the main journal entries required to account for construction contracts are summarised below.

During the accounting period, the costs associated with each contract are recorded in a separate contract account, with the typical entry to record these costs being:

DR   Contract account
CR   Current liabilities (or Bank if paid)

Then at the end of the accounting period, some or all of these costs are transferred to cost of sales as follows:

DR   Cost of sales
CR   Contract account

The revenue recognised in the accounting period is recorded as follows:

DR   Contract account
CR   Revenue

As the contract progresses, the progress billings invoiced to the customer are recorded as follows:

DR   Trade receivables
CR   Contract account

Then, when the customer pays the invoice:

DR   Bank
CR   Trade receivables

Note: each construction contract is accounted for separately so some contracts may have work in progress and some may not. Each contract is calculated and then the total from each contract is aggregated in the statement of financial position.

Example 12.11 combines a number of these issues in one comprehensive example.

EXAMPLE 12.11 – TESTING YOUR UNDERSTANDING

Crave Limited has three contracts in progress during the year and the following details are available for the year ended 31 December 2012:

Contract	Alpha	Beta	Gamma
Commenced	June 2011	January 2012	November 2012
Total contract value	€90m	€60m	€100m
Costs incurred to date	€70m	€45m	€15m
Estimated costs to complete	€10m	€23m	€70m
Completion	80%	60%	10%
Progress billings invoiced and received	€65m	€32m	€20m

Additional Information:

1. Contract Alpha commenced during 2011 and at 31 December 2011 was 50% complete; accordingly, appropriate amounts for revenue and profit were included in the 2011 statement of profit or loss and other comprehensive income.

2. Crave Limited has a policy of recognising *profit* on contracts once the contracts have reached a minimum of 30% completion. However, if, during the early stages of a contract, it is probable that contract costs incurred will be recovered, then contract revenue is recognised to the extent of costs incurred that are expected to be recoverable.

3. The directors of Crave Limited believe that costs incurred in respect of Gamma are fully recoverable.

Requirement How should Crave Limited reflect the contracts in its financial statements for the year ended 31 December 2012?

Solution

Sales Revenue:

	Alpha €m	Beta €m	Gamma €m
Revenues recognisable to date:			
Alpha (80% × €90 million)	72		
Beta (60% × €60 million)		36	
Gamma (see Note below)			15
Revenues previously recognised:			
Alpha (50% × €90 million)	(45)		
Revenues recognisable in the period	27	36	15

Total sales revenue that is recognisable and will be included in the statement of profit or loss and other comprehensive income for the year ended 31 December 2012 is €78 million (27 + 36 + 15).

Contract Profits and Losses:

	Alpha €m	Beta €m	Gamma €m
Overall contract position:			
Total contract value	90	60	100
Total contract costs (incurred to date plus cost to complete)	(80)	(68)	(85)
Contract profit/(loss)	10	(8)	15

Profits/(loss) recognisable to date:

Alpha (80% × €10 million)	8		
Beta (100% × (loss of €8 million))		(8)	
Gamma (nil – only 10% complete)			–
Amounts previously recognised:			
Alpha (50% × €10 million)	(5)		
Profits/(losses) in the period	3	(8)	–

Using the revenues and profits calculated above, the draft statement of profit or loss and other comprehensive income extract for Crave Limited for the year ended 31 December 2012 can be prepared.

	Alpha €m	Beta €m	Gamma €m	Total €m
Sales revenue	27	36	10	73
Cost of sales (balancing figure)	(24)	(44)	(10)	78
Contract profits/(losses)	3	(8)	–	(5)

Notes:
- Alpha – it is important to remember to deduct the revenues and therefore profits previously recognised;
- Beta – the overall contract is expected to make a loss of €8 million and therefore the entire loss must be recognised immediately. The cost of sales figure therefore, includes cost of sales for 2012 of €40.8 million (60% × total contract costs of €45 million incurred and €23 million to complete) plus anticipated loss for 2012 of €3.2 million (40% × €8 million); and
- Gamma – the costs incurred to date are recognised as cost of sales and matched with revenue.

Gross amount due from/(to) customers:	Alpha €m	Beta €m	Gamma €m	Total €m
Costs incurred	70	45	15	130
Plus recognised profits	8	–	–	8
Less recognised losses	–	(8)	–	(8)
Less progress billings invoiced	(65)	(32)	(20)	(117)
Gross amount due from/(to) customers	13	5	(5)	13

12.4 DISCLOSURES

Given that a wide variety of policies and practices are acceptable under IAS 11, particularly with respect to estimating the stage of completion and the recognition of profits, it is important that adequate information is disclosed to enable users of financial statements to understand the financial statements and make informed comparisons with other organisations if appropriate. Consequently, in accordance with IAS 11, an entity should disclose the following for construction contracts:

1. the amount recognised as revenue in the period;
2. the method used to determine the revenue recognised;

3. the method used to determine stage of completion;
4. for each contract in progress
    (a) Cost incurred to date and recognised profits (less losses),
    (b) The amount of advances received (i.e. payments from customers before the related work is performed),
    (c) The amount of retentions (i.e. progress billings not paid until satisfaction of conditions in contract or until defects are rectified);
5. the gross amount due from/to customers for contract work as an asset/liability (see **Examples 12.9–12.12**). The gross amount *due from* customers for contract work is equal to:

Cost incurred
plus recognised profits
less the sum of recognised losses and progress billings

for all contract work-in-progress for which costs incurred plus recognised profits less recognised losses exceeds progress billings.

The gross amount *due to* customers for contract work is equal to:

Cost incurred
plus recognised profits
less the sum of recognised losses and progress billings

for all contract work-in-progress for which progress billings exceed costs incurred plus recognised profits less recognised losses.

These disclosures, together with their calculation, are illustrated in **Example 12.12**.

EXAMPLE 12.12 – DISCLOSURES

A contractor has reached the end of its first year of operation. All its contract costs incurred have been paid for in cash and all its progress billings and advances have been received in cash. Contract costs incurred for contracts B, C and E include the costs of materials that have been purchased for the contract, but which have not been used in contract performance to date. For contracts B, C and E the customers have made advances to the contractor for work not yet performed. The status of its five contracts in progress at the end of Year 1 is as follows:

Contract	A	B	C	D	E	Total
	€000	€000	€000	€000	€000	€000
Contract revenue recognised	145	520	380	200	55	1,300
Contract expenses recognised	110	450	350	250	55	1,215
Expected losses recognised	–	–	–	40	30	70
Recognised profits less recognised losses	35	70	30	(90)	(30)	15
Contract costs incurred in the period	110	510	450	250	100	1,420
Contract costs incurred recognised as contract expenses	110	450	350	250	55	1,215

Contract work-in-progress	–	60	100	–	45	205
Contract revenue (see above)	145	520	380	200	55	1,300
Progress billings received	100	520	380	180	55	1,235
Unbilled contract revenue	45	–	–	20	–	65
Advances	–	80	20	–	25	125

The amounts to be disclosed in accordance with IAS 11 are as follows:

	€000
Contract revenue recognised as revenue in the period	1,300
Contract costs incurred and recognised profits (less recognised losses) to date	1,435
Advances received	125
Gross amount due from customers for contract work – presented as a current asset	220
Gross amount due to customers for contract work – presented as a current liability	(20)

The amounts to be disclosed are calculated as follows:

Contract	A €000	B €000	C €000	D €000	E €000	Total €000
Contract costs incurred in the period	110	510	450	250	100	1,420
Recognised profits less recognised losses	35	70	30	(90)	(30)	15
	145	580	480	160	70	1,435
Progress billings received	(100)	(520)	(380)	(180)	(55)	(1,235)
Amounts due from customers	45	60	100		15	220
Amounts due to customers				(20)		(20)

12.5 CONCLUSION

This chapter focuses on the accounting treatment of revenue and costs associated with construction contracts in accordance with IAS 11, the key points of which are:

- When the outcome of a construction contract can be estimated reliably, contract revenue and contract costs should be recognised as revenue and expenses, respectively, by reference to the stage of completion of the contract activity (percentage of completion method). The outcome can be estimated reliably when the contract revenue, contract costs to date and to completion, and the stage of completion can be measured reliably;
- When the outcome of a construction contract cannot be estimated reliably, revenue should be recognised only to the extent where it is probable that contract costs incurred are recoverable. Contract costs are recognised as expenses when incurred. If the outcome of the contract subsequently can be estimated reliably, the percentage of completion method is used for recognition of revenue and expenses; and
- Any expected loss on a construction contract should be recognised as an expense immediately.

SUMMARY OF LEARNING OBJECTIVES

After having studied this chapter, you should be able to:

Learning Objective 1 Define a construction contract.

A construction contract for the construction of a single asset, or a combination of assets that are related, usually spans more than one accounting period and thus creates some unusual accounting problems.

Learning Objective 2 Explain when profits and losses on construction contracts are to be recognised.

When the outcome of a profitable construction contract can be estimated reliably, contract revenue and costs should be recognised, as revenue and expenses respectively, by reference to the stage of completion of the contract at the end of the reporting period.

Learning Objective 3 Discuss how the recognition of a profit on a construction contract differs from the recognition of a loss.

While profits are recognised with reference to the stage of completion, when it is probable that total contract costs will exceed total contract revenue, the expected loss should be recognised as an expense immediately.

Learning Objective 4 Account for profits and losses on construction contracts depending on the expected outcome and the stage of completion.

IAS 11 identifies three important categories of contracts and each of these is explained in **Section 12.2**.

Learning Objective 5 Apply the main disclosure requirements for construction contracts.

The main disclosure requirements include the amount recognised as revenue in the period, the method used to determine the revenue recognised and the method used to determine stage of completion.

QUESTIONS

Self-test Questions

1. How would you define a construction contract?
2. When may profits and losses on construction contracts first be recognised?
3. How does the recognition of a profit on a construction contract differ from the recognition of a loss?

Review Questions

(See **Appendix One** for Suggested Solutions to Review Questions.)

Question 12.1

During the course of examining the draft accounts of BRIGADE plc for the year ended 31 December 2012, you have noted the following matter.

At 31 December 2012, the company was engaged in a construction contract with CONTOUR Limited, which had commenced in February 2012 and was expected to take a further two years to complete. The following data was used at 31 December 2012, in order to prepare the draft accounts in accordance with IAS 11 *Construction Contracts*.

	€000
Fixed contract price	3,000
Total costs incurred to date	1,420
Estimated further costs to completion	1,350
Progress billings invoiced and received to date	1,200

Profits are taken to arise evenly over the life of the contract, which at 31 December 2012 was estimated to be 45% complete.

On 1 April 2013, due to technical difficulties, it was found that the estimated further costs to complete the contract had increased over those which existed at 31 December 2012 by an additional €500,000. None of these additional costs can be passed on to the customer or claimed from any third party.

Requirement show how this contract will be reflected in the financial statements of CONTOUR Limited for the year ended 31 December 2012.

Question 12.2

Builders Limited, a medium-sized firm of building contractors, was engaged in the construction of a shopping centre in Bray. Details of the contract, which extended over three accounting periods, are:

	31 July 2010 €000	31 July 2011 €000	31 July 2012 €000
Contract price	950	1,000	1,100
Cost to date	230	520	820
Estimated total cost (updated)	750	780	820
Progress billings invoiced (cumulative)	270	680	1,100
Progress billings received (cumulative)	250	500	1,100
% completion	30	65	100

It is company policy to recognise profit on contracts once they have reached a minimum of 40% completion.

Note: assume that Attributable profit = % completion × estimated total profit.

Requirement
(a) Show the accounting entries for each of the three years ending 31 July 2010, 2011 and 2012.
(b) Show the extracts from the financial statements of Builders Limited for the year ending 31 July 2011.

Challenging Questions

(Suggested Solutions to Challenging Questions are available to lecturers.)

Question 12.1

You are the Financial Controller of DRY Limited, a firm of building contractors. The following details relate to three incomplete contracts in the company's books at 30 June 2010:

	Contract No. 1 €000	Contract No. 2 €000	Contract No. 3 €000
Cost of work to 30 June 2012 as certified (note 2)	205	385	150
Value of work to 30 June 2012 as certified	241	425	140
Progress billings invoiced to 30 June 2012	200	400	125
Progress billings received by 30 June 2012	190	380	120
Estimated costs to completion	135	470	700
Fixed contract price	400	935	850
Starting date	1 July 2011	1 July 2011	1 October 2011
Agreed completion date	31 December 2012	30 June 2013	30 June 2013

Additional Information:
1. The cost of work to 30 June 2012 has been determined after crediting unused materials and the written down value of plant in use.
2. Each contract provides for penalty payments for delays in completion at the following weekly rates:

Contract	€
No. 1	5,000
No. 2	10,000
No. 3	10,000

3. Due to an unofficial strike of bricklayers at the Contract No. 3 site, it is estimated that the completion date of this contract will be four weeks later than anticipated.
4. It has been decided that attributable profit is to be recognised on a basis of costs incurred to date as a proportion of total estimated costs.

Requirement You are required to show the information that would appear in the statement of profit or loss and other comprehensive income and statement of financial position for the year ended 30 June 2012.

Question 12.2

Expert Builders Limited is involved in three different construction contracts at 31 December 2012:

Contracts	1	2	3
Contract price	€4,000,000	€2,000,000	€900,000
Cost incurred to date	€2,560,000	€450,000	€100,000
Estimated cost to complete	€640,000	€1,350,000	€850,000
Value of work certified	€2,400,000	€200,000	€90,000
Progress billings to 31 December 2012	€2,200,000	€200,000	€80,000
Cash receipts to 31 December 2012	€2,000,000	€180,000	€70,000

This company determines stage of completion by reference to value of work certified as a proportion of total contract revenue.

Requirement Show how the above contracts would be included in the financial statements and notes of Expert Builders Limited for the year ended 31 December 2012.

Question 12.3 (Based on Chartered Accountants Ireland, CAP 2 Summer 2009, Question 4)

ZEPPELIN plc ("ZEPPELIN") is an Irish company involved in the manufacture of aeroplanes for both private and commercial use. For internal reporting purposes, the company is divided into two cash generating units (CGUs): Private and Commercial. During the year ended 31 December 2012, the Private CGU negotiated three separate fixed-price contracts to build a private jet for three wealthy football club owners.

	Contract 1 €000	Contract 2 €000	Contract 3 €000
Contract price	10,000	12,000	14,000
Costs incurred to 31 December 2012	5,600	6,000	5,040
Estimated costs to complete contract	5,600	4,000	7,560
Progress billings to 31 December 2012	4,800	6,500	5,000
Estimated percentage of contract complete at 31 December 2012	50%	60%	40%

Requirement Illustrate how each of the contracts negotiated by the Private CGU should be reflected in ZEPPELIN's statement of profit or loss and other comprehensive income and statement of financial position for the year ended 31 December 2012.

Question 12.4

Cohen Limited has three contracts in progress during the year and the following details are available for the year ended 31 December 2012.

Contract	Mary	Mungo	Midge
Commencement date	June 2011	January 2012	November 2012
Total contract value	€90m	€60m	€100m
Costs incurred to date	€70m	€45m	€15m
Estimated costs to complete	€10m	€23m	€70m
% completed at 31 December 2012	80%	60%	10%
Progress payments received	€65m	€32m	€20m

Additional Information:

1. Contract Mary commenced during 2011 and at 31 December 2011 was 50% complete; accordingly, appropriate amounts for revenue and profit were included in the 2011 statement of profit or loss and other comprehensive income.

2. Cohen Limited has a policy of recognising profit on contracts once the contracts have reached a minimum of 30% completion, to ensure that their outcome can be assessed with reasonable certainty.

Requirement

(a) Illustrate how Cohen Limited should reflect the contracts in its financial statements for the year ended 31 December 2012.

(b) The *Conceptual Framework for Financial Reporting (2010)* (*IFRS Framework*) effectively defines losses on individual transactions in such a way that they are associated with increases in liabilities or decreases in assets. A liability is defined as 'a present obligation of the enterprise arising from past events, the settlement of which is expected to result in an outflow from the enterprise of resources embodying economic benefits'.

Explain how the definition of losses contained in the *IFRS Framework* could be used to justify the requirement of lAS 11 *Construction Contracts* to recognise losses in full on construction contracts as soon as they can be foreseen.

Question 12.5

Bull Limited is currently engaged in three construction contracts, details of which are set out below:

Contract	20D	21D	22D
Contract commencement date	1 August 2011	1 November 2011	1 January 2012
	€	€	€
Contract value	500,000	300,000	400,000
Direct costs to date	180,000	150,000	120,000
Indirect costs to date	27,000	22,500	18,000
Estimated direct costs to complete	220,000	160,000	330,000
Estimated indirect costs to complete	33,000	24,000	49,500
Cash received to date	200,000	100,000	40,000
Progress billings to date	220,000	100,000	70,000
Estimated date of completion	31 July 2013	30 June 2013	30 September 2013

The company includes all expenses directly incurred by specific contracts under direct costs. Indirect costs are charged against each contract at 15% of direct costs.

Note: assume that degree of completion $= \dfrac{\text{Costs to date}}{\text{Total estimated costs}}$

Requirement Show the information that would appear in the statement of profit or loss and other comprehensive income and statement of financial position for the year ended 30 June 2012.

INCOME TAXES

LEARNING OBJECTIVES

After studying this chapter, you should be able to:
1. define, and explain the difference between, the terms 'current tax', 'deferred tax', 'permanent differences' and 'temporary differences';
2. explain the concept of the tax base of an asset or liability;
3. explain how temporary differences between accounting profits and taxable profits would affect the tax expense if deferred tax were not taken into account;
4. apply and discuss the recognition and measurement of deferred tax liabilities and deferred tax assets including the exceptions to recognition;
5. calculate the deferred tax asset/liability; and
6. apply the main disclosure requirements.

KEY TERMS AND DEFINITIONS FOR THIS CHAPTER

In order to aid your understanding of the concepts and issues covered in this chapter, it is important to understand and be familiar with the following key terms and definitions. As you study this chapter, you should refer back to them.

Carrying Amount This is the amount at which an item is recognised in the statement of financial position. In the case of non-current assets, it is after deducting accumulated depreciation and impairment losses. It is sometimes referred to as the 'net book value' (NBV) or 'written down value'.

Current Tax This is the amount of income taxes payable in respect of the **taxable profit** for a period.

Deferred Tax Assets These are amounts of income taxes recoverable in future periods in respect of:
(a) **deductible temporary differences**;
(b) carried forward unused tax losses; and
(c) carried forward unused tax credits.

Deferred Tax Liabilities These are amounts of income taxes payable in future periods in respect of taxable **temporary differences**.

Taxable Profit This is the profit for a period determined in accordance with the rules established by the taxation authorities, upon which income taxes are payable.

Tax Base The tax base of an *asset* is the amount attributed to it for tax purposes. The tax base of a *liability* is its carrying amount less any amount that will be deductible for tax purposes in respect of that liability in future periods.

Tax Expense This is the aggregate amount included in the determination of profit for the period in respect of current and deferred tax.

Temporary Differences These are differences between the carrying amount of an asset or liability in the statement of financial position and its **tax base**. Temporary differences may be either:

(a) **Taxable Temporary Differences** these are temporary differences that will result in taxable amounts in determining **taxable profit** (loss) of future periods when the carrying amount of the asset or liability is recovered or settled; or

(b) **Deductible Temporary Differences** these are temporary differences that will result in amounts that are deductible in determining taxable profit of future periods when the carrying amount of an asset or liability is recovered or settled.

13.1 INTRODUCTION

This chapter addresses the accounting treatment of both **current tax** and deferred tax in accordance with IAS 12 *Income Taxes*. It is important to appreciate that IAS 12 deals with the **accounting treatment** (and **not** the actual calculation of tax liabilities) of the income tax effects of transactions and other events recognised in an entity's financial statements during a period, both current and future. Moreover, despite its title, IAS 12 deals with *any taxes payable on company profits* regardless of what they are called (e.g. 'corporation tax'). Given the different national tax systems, this chapter assumes that the tax calculations have been completed and that the issue is therefore how to account for the taxation in the financial statements.

As the accounting recognition criteria are different from those that are normally set out in tax law, certain income and expenditure in financial statements will not be allowed for taxation purposes, thus causing **temporary differences**. IAS 12 accounts for the temporary differences between the accounting and **tax bases** of assets and liabilities rather than accounting for the timing differences between the accounting and tax consequences of revenue and expenses. IAS 12 uses a liability method and adopts a statement of financial position approach to accounting for taxation. It adopts a full provision statement of financial position approach to accounting for tax, assuming that the recovery of all assets and the settlement of all liabilities have tax consequences and that these consequences can be estimated reliably and cannot be avoided.

Key to this Chapter

In very simple terms, 'income tax' in the context of IAS 12 consists of two elements:

1. **current tax** – which is the amount of income taxes payable (i.e. primarily corporation tax) in respect of the taxable profit for a period; and

2. 'deferred tax' – the general principle in IAS 12 is that deferred tax liabilities should be recognised for all taxable temporary differences and that a deferred tax asset should be recognised for deductible temporary differences.

Income tax should be recognised as a liability to the extent that it has not yet been settled, and as an asset to the extent that the amounts already paid exceed the amount due.

This chapter begins by defining and explaining current tax (Section 13.2). After that, deferred tax is defined and the distinction between permanent and temporary differences explained, together with how temporary differences between accounting profits and taxable profits would affect the tax expense if deferred tax were not taken into account (Section 13.3). This section also discusses the recognition of deferred tax liabilities and deferred tax assets and explains the concept of the tax base of an asset or liability. Section 13.3 addresses the calculation and measurement of deferred tax assets and liabilities, with the main disclosure requirements being outlined in Section 13.4.

13.2 CURRENT TAX

Current tax is the amount of income tax payable/recoverable in respect of taxable profit/loss for the period. IAS 12 states that current tax for the current and prior periods should be recognised as a liability to the extent that it has not yet been settled, and as an asset to the extent that the amounts already paid exceed the amount due.

The benefit of a tax loss that can be carried back to recover current tax of a prior period should be recognised as an asset. Current tax assets and liabilities should be measured at the amount expected to be paid to (or recovered from) taxation authorities, using the rates/laws that have been enacted or substantially enacted by the reporting date.

Current tax assets and liabilities should only be offset if there is a legally enforceable right to offset the amounts concerned and the entity intends to do so. Any adjustments necessary to reflect under-/overestimates of current tax in previous periods should be included in the tax charge/credit for the current period in the statement of profit or loss and other comprehensive income – profit or loss.

These points are illustrated in Example 13.1.

EXAMPLE 13.1: CURRENT TAX

Aquaria Limited prepares its financial statements to 31 December each year. The following information is relevant for the year ended 31 December 2012:
• the current tax due is €1,000,000. This figure takes into account proposed new tax rates announced in September 2012, which are fully expected to be enacted in 2013. If the old rates are applied, the amount due would be €900,000;
• during 2012, payments on account amounted to €450,000 in respect of the 2012 current tax; and
• current tax for 2011 was underestimated by €75,000.

Requirement Calculate the current tax expense that should be shown in Aquaria Limited's statement of profit or loss and other comprehensive income for the year ended 31 December 2012 and the current tax balance that should be included in the statement of financial position as at that date.

Solution

As the new tax rates can be treated as 'substantially enacted', the current tax for 2012 is €1,000,000. In addition, the 2011 underestimate must also be taken into account, resulting in a 2012 tax charge of €1,075,000.

The current tax liability at 31 December 2012 is €550,000 (€1,000,000 − payments on account of €450,000).

Tax Consequences of Dividends

There are certain tax consequences of dividends. In some countries income taxes are payable at different rates if part of the net profit is paid out as dividends. Possible dividend distributions or tax refunds must be taken into account in measuring deferred tax assets and liabilities.

While IAS 10 *Events after the Reporting Period* (see **Chapter 15**) prohibits the accrual of a dividend that is proposed or declared after the end of the reporting period but before the financial statements were authorised for issue, IAS 12 requires disclosure of the tax consequences of such dividends as well as disclosure of the nature and amounts of the potential income tax consequences of dividends.

13.3 DEFERRED TAX

The amount of current tax due for a reporting period depends on the taxable profit for that period. However, it is likely that the taxable profit will be different from the reported accounting profit because of *permanent differences* and *temporary differences*. This section begins by explaining the distinction between permanent and temporary differences, together with how temporary differences between accounting profits and taxable profits would affect the tax expense if deferred tax were not taken into account. The concept of the tax base of an asset or liability is explained, followed by a discussion of when deferred tax liabilities and deferred tax assets should be recognised in the financial statements. The section then concludes by highlighting some measurement issues associated with the recognition of deferred tax assets and liabilities.

Permanent Differences

Some income and expenses may not be chargeable/deductible for tax and, consequently, there will be a permanent difference (i.e. one that will not reverse in the future) between the accounting and taxable profit. For example, many companies incur entertainment expenses in relation to business activities, which are subsequently written off against annual profits. Generally, these expenses cannot be claimed as allowable deductions for taxation purposes.

Temporary Differences

Some income and expenses included in the financial statements in one accounting period may be dealt with for tax purposes in a different accounting period. For example, revenue from the sale of goods is included in accounting profit when goods are delivered, but is included in taxable profit when cash is collected. While permanent differences cause no accounting problems and can be ignored, temporary differences can distort the reported figure for profit after tax. IAS 12 assumes that each asset and liability has a value for tax purposes and this is called a **tax base** (see below). Deferred tax relates to differences between the carrying amount of assets and liabilities in the statement of financial position, and the tax base of assets and liabilities. The differences between the **carrying amount** of an asset and liability and its tax base are **temporary differences**. There are two kinds of temporary differences, *taxable* and *deductible*, and these are explained below.

A Taxable Temporary Difference

> **Note:** it is important to remember that the general principle in IAS 12 is that deferred tax *liabilities* should be recognised for all taxable temporary differences.

A taxable temporary difference results in the payment of tax when the carrying amount of the asset or liability is settled. This means that a deferred tax liability will arise when the carrying amount of the asset is greater than its tax base, or the carrying value of the liability is less than its tax base. **Examples of taxable temporary differences** include:
- interest that is received in arrears and included in accounting profit on a time basis but taxed on a cash basis;
- accelerated depreciation for tax purposes (often because certain assets are subject to special tax treatment at a particular time); and
- capitalised development costs that are amortised in the statement of profit or loss and other comprehensive income in future periods but deducted in determining taxable profit in the year in which the expenditure is incurred.

Examples 13.2 and 13.3 below illustrate taxable temporary differences.

EXAMPLE 13.2: ASSET REVALUATION

Aquinas revalues a non-current asset from €1,000 to €1,200. As the tax base of the asset is €1,000, a taxable temporary difference of €200 therefore exists and gives rise to a deferred tax liability.

As Aquinas recovers the benefits embodied in the asset, the entity will only be able to claim tax deductions of €1,000. The temporary difference will therefore reverse and Aquinas will have to pay tax on the 'excess' of €200.

EXAMPLE 13.3: ACCELERATED DEPRECIATION

A company purchased a machine at a cost of €100,000 during Year 1. The machine's useful economic life is 4 years and the company received 100% capital allowances in Year 1. The tax rate is 40%.

| | Year 1 | Year 2 | Year 3 | Year 4 |
	€	€	€	€
Depreciation	25,000	25,000	25,000	25,000
Capital allowances	100,000	Nil	Nil	Nil
Difference	75,000	(25,000)	(25,000)	(25,000)
	Originating difference	*Reverse*	*Reverse*	*Reverse*
@ 40%	(30,000)	10,000	10,000	10,000
DR	SPLOCI – P/L	SFP – Deferred Tax	SFP – Deferred Tax	SFP – Deferred Tax
CR	SFP – Deferred Tax	SPLOCI – P/L	SPLOCI – P/L	SPLOCI – P/L

A Deductible Temporary Difference

> **Note:** it is important to remember that the general principle in IAS 12 is that a deferred tax *asset* should be recognised for deductible temporary differences.

A deductible temporary difference results in amounts being deductible in determining taxable profit or loss in future periods when the carrying value of the asset or liability is recovered or settled. When the carrying value of the liability is greater than its tax base or the carrying value of the asset is less than its tax base, then a deferred tax asset may arise. Examples of deductible temporary differences include:
- when accumulated depreciation in the financial statements is greater than the cumulative capital allowances up to the reporting period end;
- when research costs are written off to the statement of profit or loss and other comprehensive income when incurred, but are not allowed as a deduction in determining taxable profit until later;
- when benefit costs are deducted in determining accounting profit as the employee provides the service but are not deducted in determining taxable profit until the entity pays either retirement benefits or makes contributions to the benefit fund.

EXAMPLE 13.4: DEDUCTIBLE TEMPORARY DIFFERENCE

An entity recognises an accounting liability of €1,000, but the tax base of the liability is zero. A deductible temporary difference of €1,000 therefore exists, giving rise to a deferred tax asset.

As the entity settles the liability in future periods, the payments will be deductible for tax purposes. The temporary difference will therefore reverse and the entity will 'recover' tax relating to the €1,000 deduction.

Tax Base

It was stated above that IAS 12 assumes that each asset and liability has a value for tax purposes and this is called a 'tax base'. This is now explained further.

Normally, the tax base will be the amount that is attributed by the taxation authorities to it for tax purposes. While the notion is a simple one, the determination of a tax base in any given situation can be complex. However, some items of income and expenditure may not be taxable or tax deductible and they will never enter into the computation of taxable profit (see permanent differences above). Generally speaking, these items will have the same tax base as their carrying amount and no temporary difference will arise. For example, if an entity has in its statement of financial position interest receivable of €2 million, which is not taxable, then its tax base will be the same as its carrying value (i.e. €2 million). There is no temporary difference in this case and, therefore, no deferred taxation will arise.

The tax base of an asset and liability is illustrated in **Examples 13.5–13.7**.

EXAMPLE 13.5: TAX BASE – ASSET (A)

Amach Limited purchased equipment at a cost of €650,000 during the year ended 31 December 2010. For tax purposes, the total amount of capital allowances claimed as at 31 December 2012 amounted to €200,000. Amach Limited expects to claim the remaining amounts in future periods.

Requirement What is the tax base of the equipment at 31 December 2012?

Solution

The tax base of the equipment at 31 December 2012 is €450,000.

The tax base of a *liability* is its carrying amount less any amount that will be deductible for tax purposes in respect of that liability in future periods.

EXAMPLE 13.6: TAX BASE – ASSET (B)

RVP Limited has an item of plant with a carrying amount in the financial statements amounting to €10,000. The same item of plant has a tax base (a tax written down value) of €5,000. RVP Limited pays tax at 30%.

Requirement Calculate the deferred tax liability.

Solution

A temporary difference of €5,000 arises (€10,000 – €5,000). As RVP Limited pays tax at 30%, the deferred tax liability that should be recognised by RVP Limited amounts to €1,500 (€5,000 × 30%). To recognise this liability, RVP Limited should:

DR	SPLOCI – P/L	€1,500
CR	SFP – Non-current Liability – deferred tax	€1,500

Note:
If it is assumed that RVP Limited already had a deferred tax provision brought forward amounting to €500, then from the perspective of the SFP, the difference is taken to the SPLOCI as follows:

Deferred Tax	€
Opening balance	500
Movement in deferred tax*	1,000
Closing balance	1,500

*It is only the movement between the opening and closing provision for deferred tax that gets charged or (credited) to the SPLOCI.

DR SPLOCI – P/L	€1,000
CR SFP – Non-Current Liability – deferred tax	€1,000

EXAMPLE 13.7: TAX BASE – LIABILITY

At 31 December 2012, Isteach Limited had an accrued expense of €100,000 included in current liabilities. The expense is eligible for deduction for tax purposes on a cash basis.

Requirement What is the tax base of the accrued expense at 31 December 2012?

Solution

The tax base of the accrued expense at 31 December 2012 is €nil (being the carrying value of €100,000 less the amount deductible in the future of €100,000).

Recognition of Deferred Tax Liabilities

Thus, summarising the discussion so far with respect to deferred tax, IAS 12 requires deferred tax to be provided on temporary differences and, subject to the exceptions noted below, IAS 12 requires the entity to recognise a deferred tax liability in full in its financial statements.

The three **exceptions** to the requirement to recognise a deferred tax liability on all temporary differences are liabilities arising from:
- goodwill, for which impairment is not deductible for tax purposes. IAS 12 does not allow a deferred tax liability for goodwill on initial recognition or where any reduction in the value of goodwill is not allowed for tax purposes. Because **goodwill** is the residual amount after recognising assets and liabilities at fair value, recognising a deferred tax liability in respect of goodwill would simply increase the value of goodwill and, therefore, the recognition of a deferred tax liability in this regard is not allowed;
- the initial recognition of an asset/liability other than in a business combination that, at the time of the transaction, does not affect either the accounting or the taxable profit; and
- undistributed profits from investments where the enterprise is able to control the timing of the reversal of the difference and it is probable that the reversal will not occur in the foreseeable future.

It is important to note that deferred tax is required on **all revaluation gains** (e.g. upward revaluations of property in accordance with the IAS 16 revaluation model – see **Chapter 6**), i.e. rather than only when there is an agreement to sell a revalued asset, and on the unremitted earnings of associates (rather than only to the extent that distribution of earnings has been agreed). The calculation of a deferred tax provision is illustrated in **Example 13.8**.

EXAMPLE 13.8: DEFERRED TAX PROVISION

An entity has the following assets and liabilities recorded in its statement of financial position at 31 December 2012:

	Carrying Value €m	Tax Base €m
Property	20	14
Plant and equipment	10	8
Inventory	8	12
Trade receivables	6	8
Trade payables	12	12
Cash	4	4

The entity had made a provision for inventory obsolescence of €4 million that is not allowable for tax purposes until the inventory is sold, and an impairment charge against trade receivables of €2 million that will not be allowed in the current year for tax purposes but will be in the future. The tax rate is 30%.

Requirement Calculate the deferred tax provision at 31 December 2012.

Solution

	Carrying Value €m	Tax Base €m	Temporary Difference €m
Property	20	14	6
Plant and equipment	10	8	2
Inventory	8	12	(4)
Trade receivables	6	8	(2)
Trade payables	12	12	–
Cash	4	4	–
			2

The deferred tax provision should be €2 million × 30% = €600,000. The provision against inventory and the impairment charge for trade receivables will cause the tax base to be higher than the carrying value by the respective amounts.

Example 13.9 builds on the previous examples by illustrating the calculation of the deferred taxation provision together with the related tax charge in the statement of profit or loss and other comprehensive income over a number of years.

EXAMPLE 13.9: DEFERRED TAX PROVISION AND TAX CHARGE

MUFC Limited purchased a machine on 1 January 2012 for €48,000, which is estimated to have a useful economic life of seven years and a residual value at the end of its useful life of €6,000. MUFC Limited pays tax at 30% and MUFC Limited's tax authority grants capital allowances at a rate of 25% on a reducing balance basis (rounded up to the nearest thousand). MUFC Limited's profit before tax for each of the years 2012 to 2018 is estimated to be €80,000.

Requirement Calculate the provision for deferred taxation and the tax charge to be included in MUFC Limited's SPLOCI for each of the years 2012 to 2018.

Solution

Depreciation is €6,000 per annum ((€48,000 – €6,000) / 7).

The temporary differences are calculated as follows:

	2012	2013	2014	2015	2016	2017	2018
Financial Statements – Machine:	€	€	€	€	€	€	€
Net book value b/f	48,000	42,000	36,000	30,000	24,000	18,000	12,000
Depreciation	6,000	6,000	6,000	6,000	6,000	6,000	6,000
Net book value c/f	42,000	36,000	30,000	24,000	18,000	12,000	6,000
Tax Computation – Machine:							
Tax base b/f	48,000	36,000	27,000	20,000	15,000	11,000	8,000
Capital allowances at 25%	12,000	9,000	7,000	5,000	4,000	3,000	2,000
Tax base c/f	36,000	27,000	20,000	15,000	11,000	8,000	6,000
Temporary differences:							
Net book value	42,000	36,000	30,000	24,000	18,000	12,000	6,000
Tax base	36,000	27,000	20,000	15,000	11,000	8,000	6,000
Temporary difference	6,000	9,000	10,000	9,000	7,000	4,000	0
SFP – Deferred tax provision:							
Temporary difference at 30%	1,800	2,700	3,000	2,700	2,100	1,200	0

MUFC Limited's SPLOCI – P/L will show the following:

	2012	2013	2014	2015	2016	2017	2018
	€	€	€	€	€	€	€
Profit before taxation	80,000	80,000	80,000	80,000	80,000	80,000	80,000
Current tax at 30%	22,200	23,100	23,700	24,300	24,600	24,900	25,200
Deferred tax*	1,800	900	300	(300)	(600)	(900)	(1,200)
Profit after taxation	56,000	56,000	56,000	56,000	56,000	56,000	56,000

*The deferred tax charge/(credit) in the SPLOCI – P/L is only the movement in the deferred tax provision from one period to the next.

Recognition of Deferred Tax Assets

As noted above, deductible temporary differences give rise to deferred tax assets. However, a deferred tax asset should be recognised only to the extent that it is probable that a tax benefit will be realised in the future. Examples include tax losses carried forward or temporary differences arising on provisions that are not allowable for taxation until the future. Notwithstanding that the existence of current tax losses is probably evidence that future taxable profit will not be available, deferred tax assets can be recognised if it is probable that the deferred tax asset will be realised. Its realisation will depend on whether or not there are sufficient taxable profits available in the future.

Sufficient taxable profits can arise from three different sources:
1. Existing taxable temporary differences: in principle these differences should reverse in the same accounting period as the reversal of the deductible temporary difference, or in the period in which a tax loss is expected to be used;
2. If there are insufficient taxable temporary differences, the entity may recognise the deferred tax asset where it feels that there will be future taxable profits, other than that arising from taxable temporary differences. These profits should relate to the same taxable authority and entity; and
3. The entity may be able to prove that it can create tax-planning opportunities whereby the deductible temporary differences can be utilised. Wherever tax-planning opportunities are considered, management must have the capability and ability to implement them.

A deferred tax asset should be recognised for deductible temporary differences, unused tax losses and unused tax credits to the extent that it is probable that taxable profit will be available against which the deductible temporary differences can be utilised in the future.

Deferred tax assets for deductible temporary differences arising from investments in subsidiaries, associates, branches and joint ventures should be recognised to the extent that it is probable that the temporary difference will reverse in the foreseeable future and that taxable profit will be available against which the temporary difference will be utilised.

The carrying amount of deferred tax assets should be reviewed at the end of each reporting period and reduced to the extent that it is no longer probable that sufficient taxable profit will be available to allow the benefit of part, or all, of the deferred tax asset to be utilised. Any such reduction should be subsequently reversed to the extent that it becomes probable that sufficient taxable profit will be available.

Measurement of Deferred Tax Assets and Liabilities

In the previous two sections we discussed the recognition of deferred tax liabilities and assets. Some issues relating to the measurement of deferred tax assets and liabilities are now explained.
1. IAS 12 states that deferred tax assets and liabilities should be measured at the tax rates that are expected to apply to the period when the asset is realised or the liability is settled (this is often referred to as the 'liability method'), based on tax rates/laws that have been enacted or substantially enacted by the end of the reporting period. The measurement should reflect the entity's expectations, at the reporting date, as to the manner in which the carrying amount of its assets and liabilities will be recovered or settled. IAS 12 requires an entity to measure the deferred tax relating to an *asset* depending on whether the entity expects to recover the carrying amount of the asset through use or sale. However, it can be difficult and subjective to assess whether recovery will be through use or through sale when the asset is measured using the fair value model in IAS 40 *Investment Property* (see **Chapter 5**). Consequently, IAS 12 was amended in December 2010 to provide a practical solution to this problem by introducing the presumption that recovery of the carrying amount of the assets will normally be through sale.

2. IAS 12 stipulates that deferred tax assets and liabilities should *not* be discounted (because it is difficult to accurately predict the timing of the reversal of each temporary difference).

Group Financial Statements

Finally in this section, the implications of deferred tax for group financial statements are highlighted (see **Part V**, in particular **Chapters 27** and **28**).

This section begins by illustrating the allocation of purchase proceeds in a business combination (see **Example 13.10**).

EXAMPLE 13.10: ALLOCATION OF PURCHASE PROCEEDS IN A BUSINESS COMBINATION

River Limited is involved in the acquisition of Promise Limited and the following information is available:
- River Limited pays tax at the rate of 40%;
- the cost of acquiring Promise Limited was €500,000;
- the fair value of Promise Limited's net assets acquired is €750,000;
- the tax base of the assets acquired is €600,000;
- the fair value and the tax base of the liabilities acquired is €250,000; and
- the difference between the tax and fair values of the assets acquired is €150,000, which is made up of taxable temporary differences of €200,000 and deductible temporary differences of €50,000. The directors are confident that the deductible temporary differences are recoverable.

Requirement Show how the purchase price will be allocated.

The cost of acquiring Promise Limited of €500,000 is allocated as follows:

	€	€
Consideration		500,000
Allocation to identifiable assets/liabilities:		
Assets (excluding the goodwill/deferred tax asset)	750,000	
Deferred tax asset (€50,000 × 40%)	20,000	
Liabilities (excluding deferred tax liability)	(250,000)	
Deferred tax liability (€200,000 × 40%)	(80,000)	440,000
Difference goes to goodwill		60,000

If the goodwill is tax deductible in River Limited's jurisdiction, the amortisation period will cause the carrying amount for tax purposes to differ from that of the financial statements. Under IFRS 3 *Business Combinations* (see **Chapter 26**), goodwill is not amortised over its expected useful life, hence a temporary difference will develop with book values being greater than the tax base. If impairment charges are taken into consideration, then the carrying amounts may be lower than the corresponding tax basis.

If a gain on a bargain purchase arises on a business acquisition, i.e. 'negative goodwill' (see **Chapter 26**), IAS 12 states that the acquirer should reassess the values placed on the net assets and liabilities. If this does not lead to the elimination of the gain on bargain purchase, then that amount is reported as income in the current period. This is likely to result in a difference between the tax and carrying values for the negative goodwill, which is also a timing difference to be considered in computing the deferred tax balance.

In **Example 13.10** the directors of River Limited are confident that the deferred tax assets are recoverable. However, there are circumstances when there is substantial doubt about the ability to recover deferred tax assets and hence it is *not* probable that such an asset will be recovered. Under IAS 12, the deferred tax asset would not be recognised at the date of acquisition. If the directors of River Limited were *not* confident that the deferred tax asset would be recovered, the allocation of the purchase price would have to reflect that fact and more of the purchase cost would be allocated to goodwill than would have otherwise been the case in **Example 13.10**.

Temporary differences can also arise from adjustments on consolidation. The tax base of an item is often determined by the value in the entity's financial statements (i.e. the financial statements of a subsidiary). Deferred tax is determined on the basis of the consolidated financial statements and not the individual entity accounts. Therefore, the carrying value of an item in the consolidated accounts can be different from that in the individual entity accounts, thus giving rise to a temporary difference. An example of this is the consolidation adjustment that is required to eliminate unrealised profits and losses on the intragroup transfer of inventory (see **Example 13.11**). Such an adjustment will give rise to a temporary difference, which will reverse when the inventory is sold outside the group.

EXAMPLE 13.11: INTER-COMPANY SALES

A 100% subsidiary sold goods costing €30 million to its holding company for €33 million and all of these goods are still held in inventory at the year-end.

The unrealised profit of €3 million will have to be eliminated from the consolidated statement of profit or loss and other comprehensive income and from the consolidated statement of financial position in group inventory. The sale of the inventory is a taxable event and it causes a change in the tax base of the inventory. The carrying amount in the consolidated financial statements of the inventory will be €30,000,000 but the tax base is €33,000,000. This gives rise to a deferred tax asset of €3,000,000 at the tax rate of 30%, which is €900,000 (this is assuming that both the holding company and subsidiary are resident in the same tax jurisdiction).

IAS 12 does not specifically address how intragroup profits and losses should be measured for tax purposes, simply stating that the expected manner of recovery or settlement of tax should be taken into account. This would generally mean that the receiving company's tax rate should be used when calculating the provision for deferred tax, as the receiving company would be taxed when the asset or liability is realised.

13.4 DISCLOSURE

This section outlines the main disclosure issues associated with deferred tax.

Current tax assets and current tax liabilities should be offset on the statement of financial position *only* if the enterprise has the legal right and the intention to settle on a net basis.

Deferred tax assets and deferred tax liabilities should be offset on the statement of financial position *only* if the enterprise has the legal right to settle on a net basis and it is levied by the same taxing authority on the same entity or different entities that intend to realise the asset and settle the liability at the same time.

IAS 1 *Presentation of Financial Statements* **requires:**
* disclosure of the tax charge/credit on the face of the statement of profit or loss and other comprehensive income; and
* disclosures on the face of the statement of financial position about current tax assets, current tax liabilities, deferred tax assets and deferred tax liabilities.

In addition to the disclosures required by IAS 1, **IAS 12 requires** disclosure of the:
* tax charge/credit relating to ordinary activities on the face of the statement of profit or loss and other comprehensive income;
* major components of tax expense/tax income, including:
  ◦ current tax charge/credit,
  ◦ any adjustments of taxes of prior periods,
  ◦ amount of deferred tax charge/credit relating to the origination and reversal of temporary differences,
  ◦ amount of deferred tax charge/credit relating to changes in tax rates or the imposition of new taxes,
  ◦ amount of the benefit arising from a previously unrecognised tax loss, tax credit or temporary difference of a prior period,
  ◦ write down, or reversal of a previous write down, of a deferred tax asset, and
  ◦ amount of tax charge/credit relating to changes in accounting policies and corrections of errors;
* aggregate current and deferred tax relating to items reported directly in equity;
* tax relating to each component of other comprehensive income;
* relationship between tax charge/credit and the tax that would be expected by applying the current tax rate to accounting profit or loss (this can be presented as a reconciliation of amounts of tax or a reconciliation of the rate of tax);
* changes in tax rates;
* amounts and other details of deductible temporary differences, unused tax losses and unused tax credits;
* temporary differences associated with investments in subsidiaries, associates, branches and joint ventures;
* amount of deferred tax assets or liabilities recognised in the statement of financial position and the amount of deferred tax income or expense recognised in the statement of profit or loss and other comprehensive income for each type of temporary difference and unused tax loss and credit;

- tax relating to discontinued operations;
- tax consequences of dividends declared after the end of the reporting period;
- details of deferred tax assets; and
- tax consequences of future dividend payments.

13.5 OTHER RELATED GUIDANCE

Two other related pieces of guidance with implications for the accounting treatment of deferred tax are explained briefly below.

SIC 21 *Income Taxes – Recovery of Revalued Non-Depreciable Assets*

SIC 21 applies to instances where a non-depreciable asset (for example, freehold land) is carried at revaluation under IAS 16 (see **Chapter 6**). As such assets are assumed to have a finite useful life and not depreciated, therefore no part of the carrying amount of such an asset is considered to be recovered through its use. Therefore, SIC 21 concludes that the deferred tax liability or asset that arises from revaluation must be measured based on the tax consequences that would follow from the sale of the asset rather than through use. In some jurisdictions, this will result in the use of a capital gains tax rate rather than the rate applicable to corporate profits.

SIC 25 *Income Taxes – Changes in the Tax Status of an Enterprise or its Shareholders*

A change in the tax status of an entity or of its shareholders may have consequences for an entity by increasing or decreasing its tax liabilities or assets. This may, for example, occur upon the public listing of an entity's equity instruments or upon the restructuring of an entity's equity. It may also occur upon a controlling shareholder's move to a foreign country. As a result of such an event, an entity may be taxed differently (for example, it may gain or lose tax incentives or become subject to a different rate of tax in the future).

SIC 25 states that a change in the tax status of an enterprise or its shareholders does not give rise to increases or decreases in the pre-tax amounts recognised directly in equity (i.e. outside profit or loss). Therefore, SIC 25 concludes that the current and deferred tax consequences of the change in tax status should be included in net profit or loss for the period. However, where a transaction or event does result in a direct credit or charge to equity, for example the revaluation of property, plant or equipment under IAS 16, the related tax consequence would still be recognised in other comprehensive income.

13.6 CONCLUSION

As the accounting recognition criteria are different from those which are normally set out in tax law, certain income and expenditure in financial statements will not be allowed for taxation purposes, thus causing temporary differences. IAS 12 accounts for the temporary differences between the accounting and tax bases of assets and liabilities rather than accounting for the timing differences between the accounting and tax consequences of revenue and expenses. IAS 12 uses a liability method and adopts a statement of financial position approach to accounting for taxation. It adopts a full provision statement of financial position approach to accounting for tax, assuming that the recovery of all assets and the settlement of all liabilities have tax consequences and that these consequences can be estimated reliably and cannot be avoided.

IAS 12 requires that the tax consequences of transactions and events should be recognised in the same financial statement as the transaction or event. This means that current and deferred taxes are:

- recognised in equity if the items to which they relate are credited/charged to equity;
- recognised as identifiable assets or liabilities at the acquisition date if they arise as part of a business combination in accordance with IFRS 3 *Business Combinations* (see **Chapter 26**); and
- otherwise recognised as a tax charge or credit. There will usually be a single tax figure made up of both current and (where applicable) deferred tax.

In summary, the **process of accounting for deferred tax** is as follows:
1. determine the tax base of the assets and liabilities in the statement of financial position;
2. compare the carrying amounts in the statement of financial position with the *tax bas*e. Any differences will normally affect the deferred taxation calculation;
3. identify the temporary differences that have not been recognised due to exceptions in IAS 12;
4. apply the tax rates to the temporary differences;
5. determine the movement between opening and closing deferred *tax balances;*
6. decide whether the offset of deferred tax assets and liabilities between different companies is acceptable in the consolidated financial statements;
7. recognise the net change in deferred taxation.

In broad terms, if temporary differences cause:
- taxable profit to be *lower* than accounting profit *then* the tax charge in the statement of profit or loss and other comprehensive income should be increased (credit deferred tax account in the statement of financial position); or
- taxable profit to be *higher* than accounting profit *then* the tax charge in the statement of profit or loss and other comprehensive income should be reduced (debit deferred tax account in the statement of financial position).

Summary of Learning Objectives

Having studied this chapter, you should be able to:

Learning Objective 1 Define, and explain the difference between, the terms 'current tax', 'deferred tax', 'permanent differences' and 'temporary differences'.

'Current tax' is the amount of income taxes payable (recoverable) in respect of taxable profit (tax loss) for the period. 'Deferred tax' is an accounting concept relating to a future tax liability or asset, resulting from temporary differences or timing differences between the accounting value of assets and liabilities and their value for tax purposes. 'Permanent differences' arise because some income and expenses may not be chargeable/deductible for tax. 'Temporary differences' are differences between the carrying amount of an asset or liability recognised in the statements of financial position and the amount attributed to that asset or liability for tax purposes.

Learning Objective 2 Explain the concept of the tax base of an asset or liability.

The 'tax base' of an asset or liability is the amount attributed to that asset or liability for tax purposes.

Learning Objective 3 Explain how temporary differences between accounting profits and taxable profits would affect the tax expense unless deferred tax was taken into account.

Some income and expenses included in the financial statements in one accounting period may be dealt with for tax purposes in a different accounting period. These temporary differences can distort the reported figure for profit after tax. The differences between the carrying amount of an asset and liability and its tax base are temporary differences, of which there are two kinds: taxable and deductible.

Learning Objective 4 Apply and discuss the recognition and measurement of deferred tax liabilities and deferred tax assets, including the exceptions to recognition.

Deferred tax liabilities should be recognised for all taxable temporary differences, whereas a deferred tax asset should be recognised only to the extent that it is probable that a tax benefit will be realised in the future. Deferred tax assets and liabilities should be measured at the tax rates that are expected to apply to the period when the asset is realised or the liability is settled.

Learning Objective 5 Calculate the deferred tax asset/liability.

See **Examples 13.8 and 13.9** above.

Learning Objective 6 Apply the main disclosure requirements.

In broad terms the tax expense (tax credit) should be disclosed on the face of the statement of profit or loss and other comprehensive income, with details of current tax assets, current tax liabilities, deferred tax assets and deferred tax liabilities being disclosed on the face of the statement of financial position.

QUESTIONS

Self-test Questions

1. Explain the difference between current tax and deferred tax.
2. Explain the difference between permanent differences and temporary differences.
3. Explain the concept of the tax base of an asset or liability, and how this concept helps to identify situations in which deferred tax adjustments are required.
4. Explain how temporary differences between accounting profits and taxable profits would affect the tax expense unless deferred tax was taken into account.

Review Questions

(See **Appendix One** for Suggested Solutions to Review Questions.)

Question 13.1 (Based on Chartered Accountants Ireland, P3 Summer 2005, Question 4)

GATEWAY Limited (GATEWAY), a company that prepares its financial statements to 31 December each year, has been trading at a loss for the last 3–4 years. However, the directors expect the company to return to profitability in the near future. GATEWAY pays corporation tax at 25%, and the following information has been extracted from GATEWAY's books and records in respect of the year ended 31 December 2012:

1. Depreciation charged in the SPLOCI–P/L amounted to €3,250,000, while capital allowances of €4,750,000 were included in the tax computation;
2. The estimated tax loss for the year ended 31 December 2012 is €250,000 and, because prior year losses have been fully utilised, the tax loss for the year ended 31 December 2012 will have to be carried forward to future years;
3. The net book value of non-current assets qualifying for capital allowances at 31 December 2011 was €13,000,000 against a tax written down value of €12,000,000. This gave rise to a deferred tax provision at 31 December 2011 of €250,000. No other temporary differences existed at 31 December 2011; and
4. Although €500,000 was charged to the statement of profit or loss and other comprehensive income in the year ended 31 December 2012 in respect of royalties, the amount actually paid was €550,000.

Requirement

(a) Calculate the deferred tax charge to be included in the statement of profit or loss and other comprehensive income of GATEWAY for the year ended 31 December 2012, and the deferred tax provision required as at that date, in accordance with IAS 12 *Income Taxes*.
(b) Included in GATEWAY's non-current assets at 31 December 2012 is property recorded at €1,400,000. The property cost €2,000,000 when purchased, and depreciation totalling €600,000 has been charged up to 31 December 2012. GATEWAY has claimed total tax allowances of €800,000 on the property up to 31 December 2012, and is considering recording the property at its valuation of €1,800,000 in the financial statements for the year ended 31 December 2012. GATEWAY does not intend to sell the property.

Explain whether:
 (i) GATEWAY is permitted to record the property at valuation in the financial statements for the year ended 31 December 2012;
 (ii) Recording the property at its valuation of €1,800,000 will create an unavoidable incremental tax liability; and
 (iii) GATEWAY is permitted to discount any deferred tax asset or liability that may arise.

Challenging Questions

(Suggested Solutions to Challenging Questions are available to lecturers.)

Question 13.1 *(Based on Chartered Accountants Ireland, P3 Summer 2008, Question 6)*

BRUCE plc (BRUCE), an Irish-listed company that prepares its financial statements to 31 December each year, sells products to those involved in magic and illusion.

BRUCE
STATEMENT OF FINANCIAL POSITION
as at 31 December 2012

	Notes	Book Value €000	Tax Value €000
ASSETS			
Non-current Assets			
Property	(1)	40,000	10,000
Plant and equipment	(1)	20,000	8,000
Development costs	(2)	4,000	–
		64,000	18,000
Current Assets			
Inventory		8,000	8,000
Trade receivables		6,000	6,000
Bank and cash		2,000	2,000
		80,000	34,000
EQUITY AND LIABILITIES			
Capital and Reserves			
€1 ordinary shares		10,000	10,000
Retained earnings		41,000	1,000
		51,000	11,000
Non-current Liabilities			
Loan	(3)	8,000	9,000
Deferred income	(4)	4,000	–
Employee retirement benefit scheme	(5)	2,000	–
Deferred taxation	(6)	10,000	10,000
Current Liabilities			
Trade payables		4,000	4,000
Deferred income	(4)	1,000	–
		80,000	34,000

Additional Information:
1. The directors of BRUCE have decided to record the company's property, plant and equipment at fair value rather than depreciated historical cost. The fair value of the property at 31 December 2012 is deemed to be €50,000,000, while the fair value of plant and equipment on the same date is €25,000,000.
2. Development costs are capitalised and amortised over future periods in determining accounting profit but deducted in determining taxable profit in the period in which they are incurred.
3. During the year ended 31 December 2012, BRUCE negotiated a new loan with repayments commencing in 2014. For accounting purposes, the loan has been recorded net of

the associated transaction costs paid in 2012. These costs are allowable for tax in the year in which they are paid.

4. The deferred income relates to a non-taxable government grant received by BRUCE.
5. Employee retirement benefit costs are deducted in determining accounting profit when the service is provided by the employees, but deducted in determining taxable profit when contributions or retirement benefits are paid by BRUCE.
6. This represents the deferred taxation liability at 31 December 2011. During the year ended 31 December 2012, the taxation rate changed from 25% to 20%.
7. BRUCE's employee retirement benefit scheme is managed by the same investment bank that negotiated the new loan raised during 2012 (see Note 3). Furthermore, one of the investment managers in the investment bank is also a non-executive director of BRUCE. During the year ended 31 December 2012, BRUCE paid €7,000,000 into the employee retirement benefit scheme and paid fees amounting to €300,000 to the investment bank in relation to the administration of the employee retirement benefit scheme. In addition, during 2012 the investment manager received €20,000 from BRUCE for his services as a non-executive director. This fee was paid to all non-executive directors.

Requirement

(a) Calculate the deferred taxation expense to be included in the statement of profit or loss and other comprehensive income of BRUCE for the year ended 31 December 2012 and the deferred taxation liability as at that date.
(b) Discuss whether BRUCE's relationship and transactions with the investment bank should be disclosed in the financial statements for the year ended 31 December 2012.

PROVISIONS, CONTINGENT LIABILITIES AND CONTINGENT ASSETS

LEARNING OBJECTIVES

After having studied this chapter, you should be able to:
1. define the terms 'provision', 'contingent liability' and 'contingent asset';
2. explain when a provision should be recognised and how it should be measured and accounted for;
3. apply the accounting treatment for contingent liabilities and contingent assets; and
4. apply the main disclosure requirements.

KEY TERMS AND DEFINITIONS FOR THIS CHAPTER

In order to aid your understanding of the concepts and issues covered in this chapter, it is important to understand and be familiar with the following key terms and definitions. As you study this chapter, you should refer back to them.

Constructive Obligation An obligation that derives from the reporting entity's actions where:
(a) past practice, published policies or current statement would indicate that the entity will accept certain responsibilities; and
(b) the entity has created a valid expectation that it will discharge those responsibilities.

Contingent Asset A possible asset arising from past events whose existence will be confirmed only by the occurrence or non-occurrence of one or more uncertain future events not wholly within the entity's control.

Contingent Liability This is a:

(a) possible obligation arising from past events whose existence will only be confirmed by the occurrence, or non-occurrence, of one or more uncertain future events not wholly within the entity's control; *or*

(b) present obligation arising from past events but is not recognised because it is not probable that a transfer of economic benefits will be required to settle the obligation, or the amount of the obligation cannot be measured with sufficient reliability.

Legal Obligation An obligation that derives from a contract, legislation or other operation of law.

Liability This is a present obligation of a reporting entity arising from past events, the settlement of which is expected to result in an outflow from the entity of economic benefits.

Obligating Event This is an event that creates a legal or constructive obligation where an entity has no realistic alternative but to settle that obligation.

Provision A **liability** of uncertain timing or amount.

Restructuring The following are examples of events that may fall under the definition of *restructuring*: sale or termination of a line of business; closure of business locations in a country or region or the relocation of business activities from one country or region to another; changes in management structure, e.g. eliminating a layer of management; and fundamental reorganisations that have a material effect on the nature and focus of the entity's operations.

14.1 INTRODUCTION

In 'simple' terms, a **provision** is an amount to be deducted from current period profits in respect of a known liability because of something that has happened in the past that will be paid for in the future, albeit that the specific amount of the **liability** may not be known at present. The accruals concept (or matching principle – see **Chapter 1**) refers to the matching of the expenses with the revenues generated from those expenses for a specific period of time. It is one of the fundamental concepts of accruals accounting and it means that revenues and expenses must be recognised when they occur and not when payment is made or received. As a result, it is necessary to consider whether provisions are required when preparing financial statements in accordance with International Accounting Standards (IASs)/International Financial Reporting Standards (IFRSs).

However, a number of problems have arisen in the past with respect to provisions. For example:

• There has been no consistency in the accounting treatment. Some provisions are very popular (e.g. **restructuring** and **warranties**), whereas others are rarely adopted in practice (e.g. environmental).

• Some companies have deliberately manipulated their statement of profit or loss and other comprehensive income to smooth out earnings by the adoption of 'big bath' accounting provisions, which have no real substance. This is the practice of aggregating present

liabilities with expected liabilities of future years, including items related to ongoing operations, in one large provision. The effect of 'big bath' provisions was not only to report excessive liabilities at the outset but also to boost profitability in later years.
• Some provisions have been created that will never occur in practice. They are mere intentions rather than firm obligations of the reporting entity. Consequently, profits are often boosted in later years when the provisions are reversed.
• There has been a lack of detailed disclosure about provisions in general, thus making financial statements less useful and informative.

Consequently, guidance is essential on when provisions can and cannot be made in order to enhance the reliability of financial statements by preventing profit-smoothing (i.e. through the use of general provisions since no obligation exists) and ensuring that long-term provisions are recognised as soon as the obligation arises (i.e. irrespective of when actually paid).

The guidance comes in the form of IAS 37 *Provisions, Contingent Liabilities and Contingent Assets*, which sets out the principles of accounting for provisions, **contingent liabilities** and **contingent assets**. Its objective is to ensure that appropriate criteria and measurement bases are applied to these aspects of accounting and that sufficient information is disclosed in the notes to the financial statements to enable the reader to understand their nature, timing and amounts recorded.

IAS 37 does **not** apply to provisions, contingent liabilities and contingent assets that are:
• as a result of executory contracts (i.e. one where the conditions or terms have not yet been performed), except where the contract is onerous; and
• covered by another standard, including:
  ○ contingent liabilities assumed in business combinations (IFRS 3 *Business Combinations* – see **Chapter 26**);
  ○ provisions with regard to construction contracts (IAS 11 *Construction Contracts* – see **Chapter 12**); income taxes (IAS 12 *Income Taxes* – see **Chapter 13**); leases (IAS 17 *Leases* – see **Chapter 18**); employee benefits (IAS 19 *Employee Benefits* – see **Chapter 17**); and insurance contracts (IFRS 4 *Insurance Contracts* – see **Chapter 34**).

IAS 37 also does **not** apply to financial instruments (including guarantees) within the scope of IAS 39 *Financial Instruments: Recognition and Measurement* / IFRS 9 *Financial Instruments* (see **Chapter 25**).

Key to this Chapter

As stated, IAS 37 deals with *provisions, contingent liabilities* and *contingent assets*. The first issue to be resolved is whether a provision, contingent liability or contingent asset actually exists. Then, if one does, the issue is whether it should be recognised (i.e. recorded or reflected) in the financial statements. Consequently, **Section 14.2** of this chapter begins by defining the terms '*provision*', '*contingent liability*' and '*contingent asset*' and explains when each should be recognised in the financial statements. If recognition is necessary, then the next stage is to determine how it should be measured and accounted for. This is dealt with in **Section 14.3**. Finally, the main disclosure requirements are outlined in **Section 14.4**.

14.2 RECOGNITION

As noted above, the first issue to be resolved in the context of IAS 37 is whether a provision, contingent liability or contingent asset actually exists; then, if one does, whether it should be recognised (i.e. recorded or reflected) in the financial statements. This section begins by dealing with provisions, followed by contingent liabilities and then contingent assets.

Provisions

IAS 37 states that a provision exists, and should be recognised in the financial statements, when all of the following four criteria are met:
- there is a **present obligation** (**legal** or **constructive**), and
- as a result of a **past event**, and
- it is **probable** that a **transfer of economic benefits** will occur, and
- it can be **reliably measured**.

Using examples, the application of these four criteria is now discussed.

Note: unless stated otherwise, all of the entities in the examples have 31 December year-ends, and in all cases it is assumed that any expected outflows can be reliably measured. Furthermore, in some of the examples, the circumstances described may indicate possible impairment of the assets (see **Chapter 10**); this can be ignored for the purpose of determining whether a provision is required. Also, it can be assumed that, where the effect of the time value of money is material, any references to 'best estimate' are to the present value amount.

Present Obligation

A present obligation is one that exists at the reporting date as a result of a past event. This is illustrated in **Examples 14.1–14.3**.

EXAMPLE 14.1: SELF INSURANCE

An entity expects to pay €100,000 in damages based on previous experience.

As there is no present obligation/obligating event until an accident occurs, no provision is recognised. Although it could be argued that there is a constructive obligation due to past experience.

EXAMPLE 14.2: REFURBISHMENT COSTS (NO LEGISLATIVE REQUIREMENT)

A furnace has a lining that needs to be replaced every five years for technical reasons. At the reporting date, the lining has been in use for three years.

Is there a present obligation as a result of a past obligating event? – There is no present obligation.

Conclusion

No provision is recognised. The cost of replacing the lining is not recognised because, at the reporting date, no obligation to replace the lining exists independently of the company's future actions – even the intention to incur the expenditure depends on the company deciding to continue operating the furnace or to replace the lining. Instead of a provision being recognised, the depreciation of the lining takes account of its consumption, i.e. it is depreciated over five years. The re-lining costs then incurred are capitalised, with the consumption of each new lining shown by depreciation over the subsequent five years.

EXAMPLE 14.3: REFURBISHMENT COSTS (LEGISLATIVE REQUIREMENT)

An airline is required by law to overhaul its aircraft once every three years.

Is there a present obligation as a result of a past obligating event? – There is no present obligation.

Conclusion

No provision is recognised. The costs of overhauling aircraft are not recognised as a provision for the same reasons as the cost of replacing the lining is not recognised as a provision in the previous example. Even a legal requirement to overhaul does not make the costs of overhaul a liability, because no obligation exists to overhaul the aircraft independently of the entity's future actions. The entity could avoid the future expenditure by its future actions, for example by selling the aircraft. Instead of a provision being recognised, the depreciation of the aircraft takes account of the future incidence of maintenance costs (i.e. an amount equivalent to the expected maintenance costs is depreciated over three years).

There are two types of present obligation: legal and constructive. These are illustrated in **Example 14.4** and **Example 14.5**, respectively.

EXAMPLE 14.4: LEGAL PRESENT OBLIGATION – PROVISION FOR WARRANTIES

A manufacturer gives warranties at the time of sale to purchasers of its product. Under the terms of the contract for sale the manufacturer undertakes to make good, by repair or replacement, manufacturing defects that become apparent within three years from the date of sale. On past experience, it is probable (i.e. more likely than not) that there will be some claims under the warranties.

Is there a present obligation as a result of a past obligating event? – Yes, the obligating event is the sale of the product with a warranty, which gives rise to a legal obligation.

Is there a probable transfer of economic benefits? – Yes, probable for the warranties as a whole.

Conclusion

A provision is recognised for the best estimate of the costs of making good, under the warranty, products sold before the reporting date.

Example 14.5: Constructive Present Obligation – Refunds Policy

A retail store has a policy of refunding purchases for dissatisfied customers, even though it is under no legal obligation to do so. Its policy of making refunds is generally known.

Is there a present obligation as a result of a past obligating event? – The obligating event is the sale of the product, which gives rise to a constructive obligation because the conduct of the store has created a valid expectation on the part of its customers that the store will refund purchases.

Is there a probable transfer of economic benefits? – Yes, probable that a proportion of goods are returned for refund.

Conclusion
A provision is recognised for the best estimate of the costs of refunds.

Past Event

For an event to be considered 'past', it must have happened/taken place at the reporting date. A 'past event' must cause an obligation 'now', not at a later date (e.g. due to a change in legislation or because of a specific public statement). If a new law has still to be finalised at the reporting date, an obligation would only arise if the legislation was virtually certain (see **Example 14.6**).

Example 14.6: Contaminated Land (Legislation Virtually Certain to be Enacted)

An entity in the oil industry causes contamination, but cleans up only when required to do so under the laws of the particular country in which it operates. One country in which it operates has had no legislation requiring cleaning up and the entity has been contaminating land in that country for several years. At 31 December 2012, it is virtually certain that a draft law requiring a clean-up of land already contaminated will be enacted shortly after the year-end.

Is there a present obligation as a result of a past obligating event? – The obligating event is the contamination of the land because of the virtual certainty of legislation requiring cleaning up.

Is there a probable transfer of economic benefits? – Yes, probable.

Conclusion
A provision is recognised for the best estimate of the costs of the clean-up.

So far in this section on the recognition of provisions, the meaning of the terms 'present obligation' and 'past event' has been examined. The practical application of these terms is particularly relevant with respect to 'restructurings'. IAS 37 defines a restructuring as:
• a sale or termination of a line of business;
• closure of business locations or relocation of business activities;

- changes in management structure (for example, eliminating a layer of management); or
- a fundamental reorganisation of the company.

In accordance with IAS 37, restructuring provisions should be recognised as follows.
- **Sale of operations:** recognise a provision only after a binding sale agreement. If the binding sale agreement is after the reporting date, disclose but do not recognise the provision;
- **Closure or reorganisation of a business operation:** recognise a provision only after a detailed formal plan is adopted and announced publicly. A board decision is not enough (see **Example 14.7** and **Example 14.8**);
- **Future operating losses:** provisions should *not* be recognised for future operating losses, even in a restructuring, as they do not meet the definition of a liability. However, an expectation of future operating losses is an indication that certain assets of the operation may be impaired, and these assets should be tested for impairment in accordance with IAS 36 *Impairment of Assets* (see **Chapter 10**); and
- **Restructuring provision on acquisition:** recognise a provision only if there is an obligation at acquisition date.

Restructuring provisions should include only direct expenditures caused by the restructuring, not costs associated with the ongoing activities of the entity.

Probable Transfer of Economic Benefits

A transfer of economic benefits (i.e. cash or other resources) is only probable if an outflow is more likely than not to occur. If there are a number of similar obligations (e.g. warranties), the probability should be determined by considering the class as a whole (e.g. by using expected values). This is illustrated in **Examples 14.4–14.6**.

Reliable Estimate of the Obligation

A reliable estimate can usually be determined by examining the range of possible outcomes and making an estimate of obligation that is sufficiently reliable to use. If no reliable estimate can be made, a liability cannot be recognised and therefore it should be treated as a contingent liability.

Examples 14.7–14.9 further illustrate the issues raised above regarding the recognition of provisions. The details in **Examples 14.7** and **14.8** should be carefully compared as, despite their apparent similarity, their outcomes are very different.

EXAMPLE 14.7: CLOSURE OF A DIVISION (NO COMMUNICATION)

On 12 December 2012 the board of an entity decided to close down a division. Before the reporting date (31 December 2012) the decision was *not* communicated to any of those affected and no other steps were taken to implement the decision.

Is there a present obligation as a result of a past obligating event? – As there has been no obligating event (i.e. the communication of the decision before the end of the reporting period), there is no obligation.

Conclusion
No provision should be recognised at 31 December 2012 as the decision to close the division had not been communicated, and therefore not implemented, before the end of the reporting period.

EXAMPLE 14.8: CLOSURE OF A DIVISION (WITH COMMUNICATION)

On 12 December 2012, the board of an entity decided to close down a division making a particular product. On 20 December 2012 a detailed plan for closing down the division was agreed by the board. Letters were sent to customers warning them to seek an alternative source of supply and redundancy notices were sent to the staff of the division.

Is there a present obligation as a result of a past obligating event? – Yes, the obligating event is the communication of the decision to the customers and employees, which gives rise to a constructive obligation from that date because it creates a valid expectation that the division will be closed.

Is there an outflow of resources embodying economic benefits in settlement? – Yes, probable.

Conclusion
A provision is recognised at 31 December 2012 for the best estimate of the costs of closing the division as the decision to close the division had been implemented before the end of the reporting period. (*Note:* a decision only has to be implemented or commenced, not completed. Implementation can include the development of a detailed plan, together with the communication of the plan to trade unions, employees, the public and/or shareholders.)

The following example (**14.9**) introduces legal obligations into the decision on whether a provision is required. The decision at 31 December 2012 should be studied carefully.

EXAMPLE 14.9: LEGAL OBLIGATION

Under new legislation, an entity is required to fit smoke filters to its factories by 30 June 2012. The entity has not yet fitted the smoke filters.

(a) At the reporting date of 31 December 2011
Is there a present obligation as a result of a past obligating event? – There is no obligation because there is no obligating event either for the costs of fitting smoke filters or for fines under the legislation on this date.

Conclusion
(a) No provision is recognised for the cost of fitting the smoke filters.

(b) At the reporting date of 31 December 2012

Is there a present obligation as a result of a past obligating event? – There is still no obligation for the *costs* of fitting smoke filters because no obligating event has occurred (i.e. the fitting of the filters). However, an obligation might arise to pay fines or penalties under the legislation because the obligating event has occurred (i.e. the non-compliant operation of the factory).

Is there an outflow of resources embodying economic benefits in settlement? – The assessment of the probability of incurring fines and penalties through non-compliant operation depends on the details of the legislation and the stringency of the enforcement regime.

Conclusion

No provision is recognised for the costs of fitting smoke filters at 31 December 2011 and 2012. However, a provision should be recognised for the best estimate of any fines and penalties that are more likely than not to be imposed at 31 December 2012.

Changes in Provisions

The examples above address the situation where a decision is made as to whether or not to establish a provision for the first time. Once a provision is established, it should be reviewed at the end of each subsequent reporting date and adjusted to reflect the current best estimate. If it is no longer probable that a transfer of economic benefits will occur, the provision must be reversed. Where discounting is adopted (see **Example 14.14, Issue 5**), the subsequent unwinding of that discount should be treated as an interest expense (i.e. finance cost) in the statement of profit or loss and other comprehensive income, but separately disclosed. A provision should only be used for the expenditures for which it was originally recognised.

Reimbursement

An issue that can potentially complicate provisions is where a provision is likely to be reimbursed by a third party. For example, while Company A may sub-contract work to Company B, the customer would seek compensation from Company A for any faults or damages as the customer's contract is with Company A. However, Company A may be able to claim against Company B if its work is found to be negligent. Any potential reimbursement should only be recognised if it is *virtually certain* that it will be received. The reimbursement should be treated as a separate asset and not netted against any claim. Furthermore, it must not be recorded at a value higher than the amount of the provision. In the statement of profit or loss and other comprehensive income any expenses relating to the provision may be presented net of any amounts recognised for reimbursement.

Table 14.1 below summarises the position where some or all of the expenditure required to settle a provision (by Company A) is expected to be reimbursed by another party (Company B).

TABLE 14.1: REIMBURSEMENTS

Scenario	Company A has no obligation for the part of the expenditure to be reimbursed by Company B.	The obligation for the amount expected to be reimbursed by Company B remains with Company A and it is virtually certain that reimbursement by Company B will be received if Company A settles the provision.	The obligation for the amount expected to be reimbursed remains with Company A and the reimbursement is not virtually certain from Company B, even if Company A settles the provision.
Outcome	Company A has no liability for the amount to be reimbursed.	The reimbursement is recognised as a separate asset by Company A in its statement of financial position and may be offset against the expense in its statement of profit or loss and other comprehensive income.	The expected reimbursement is not recognised as an asset by Company A.
Disclosure	No disclosure is required by Company A.	The reimbursement is disclosed, together with the amount recognised for the reimbursement, in the financial statements of Company A.	The expected reimbursement is only disclosed by Company A (not recognised).

Onerous Contracts

An **onerous contract** is one in which the unavoidable costs of meeting the contract's obligations exceed the economic benefits expected to be received. As such, an onerous contract can give rise to a provision for the future cost of performing an uneconomic/unprofitable contract. In such circumstances, the present obligation under the contract (i.e. the signing of which is the past event) should be recognised and provided for. This is illustrated in **Example 14.10.**

EXAMPLE 14.10: AN ONEROUS CONTRACT

An entity operates profitably from a factory that it has leased under an operating lease. During December 2012 the entity relocates its operations to a new factory. The lease on the old factory continues for the next four years, it cannot be cancelled and the factory cannot be re-let to another user.

Is there a present obligation as a result of a past obligating event? – The obligating event is the signing of the lease contract, which gives rise to a legal obligation.

Is there an outflow of resources embodying economic benefits in settlement? – When the lease becomes onerous, an outflow of resources embodying economic benefits is probable. (Until the lease becomes onerous, the entity accounts for the lease under IAS 17 *Leases* (see **Chapter 8**).)

Conclusion

A provision is recognised at 31 December 2012 for the best estimate of the unavoidable lease payments.

Contingent Liabilities

As stated earlier, IAS 37 addresses the accounting treatment of provisions, contingent liabilities and contingent assets. This section commenced by examining when provisions should be recognised in the financial statements; contingent liabilities are now discussed.

A **contingent liability** is:
(a) a possible obligation arising from past events whose existence will only be confirmed by the occurrence, or non-occurrence, of one or more uncertain future events not wholly within the entity's control; *or*
(b) a present obligation arising from past events but is not recognised because it is not probable that a transfer of economic benefits will be required to settle the obligation, or the amount of the obligation cannot be measured with sufficient reliability.

Contingent liabilities should not be recognised but should be disclosed, unless the transfer of economic benefits is likely to be remote. If the likelihood of occurrence is remote, then disclosure is not required. Contingent liabilities are not recognised as liabilities because they are either only possible or they are present obligations that do not meet the recognition criteria as they are either probably unlikely to be settled or a sufficiently reliable estimate cannot be made of the obligation. If there is joint and several liability, then the entity should only provide for its own share and disclose the other parties' shares as contingent liabilities. Contingent liabilities need to be monitored regularly and if they become probable, then they will need to be disclosed as provisions in the year they became probable. These issues are included in **Example 14.11**.

EXAMPLE 14.11: A COURT CASE

After a wedding in 2011, 10 people died, possibly as a result of food-poisoning from products sold by the entity. Legal proceedings are started seeking damages from the entity, but it disputes liability. Up to the date of authorisation of the financial statements for the year to 31 December 2011 for issue, the entity's lawyers advise that it is probable that the entity will not be found liable. However, when the entity prepares the financial statements for the year to 31 December 2012, its lawyers advise that, owing to developments in the case, it is probable that the entity *will* be found liable.

(a) At 31 December 2011

Is there a present obligation as a result of a past obligating event? – On the basis of the evidence available when the financial statements were approved, there is no obligation as a result of past events.

Conclusion

No provision is recognised. The matter is disclosed as a contingent liability unless the probability of any outflow is regarded as remote.

(b) At 31 December 2012

Is there a present obligation as a result of a past obligating event? – On the basis of the evidence available, there is a present obligation.

Is there an outflow of resources embodying economic benefits in settlement? – Yes, probable.

Conclusion

A provision is recognised for the best estimate of the amount to settle the obligation.

Contingent Assets

Finally, the third element addressed in IAS 37 is contingent assets.

A **contingent asset** is a possible asset arising from past events whose existence will be confirmed only by the occurrence or non-occurrence of one or more uncertain future events not wholly within the entity's control.

An entity should not recognise a contingent asset as it would probably include an unrealised profit. However, if realisation is certain, then it should be recorded as an asset. A contingent asset, if probable, should be disclosed. A contingent asset should be continually assessed and if it becomes certain, then an asset should be recognised in the year that this occurs.

14.3 MEASUREMENT

If recognition is deemed necessary (see **Section 14.2**), then the next stage is to determine how it should be measured and accounted for. In particular, this involves obtaining a *best estimate* of the amount to be recognised, considering the *risks and uncertainties* associated with obtaining a best estimate and assessing whether amounts should be stated at their *present value*. These issues are discussed below.

> *Note:* in order to illustrate the issues discussed in **Section 14.3** and provide realistic examples, some of the issues dealt with in this section have unavoidably already been alluded to in **Section 14.2**.

Best Estimate

The amount recognised should be the best estimate (on a pre-tax basis) of the expenditure required to settle the present obligation at the reporting date (see **Example 14.10**).

EXAMPLE 14.12: OFFSHORE OILFIELD

An entity operates an offshore oilfield where its licensing agreement requires it to remove the oil-rig at the end of production and restore the seabed. Ninety percent of the eventual costs relate to the removal of the oil-rig and restoration of damage caused by building it, and 10% arise through the extraction of oil. At the reporting date, the rig has been constructed but no oil has been extracted.

Is there a present obligation as a result of a past obligating event? – The construction of the oil-rig creates a legal obligation under the terms of the licence to remove the rig and restore the seabed and is, thus, an obligating event. At the reporting date, however, there is no obligation to rectify the damage that will be caused by extraction of the oil.

Is there an outflow of resources embodying economic benefits in settlement? – Yes, probable.

Conclusion
A provision is recognised for the best estimate of 90% of the eventual costs that relate to the removal of the oil-rig and restoration of damage caused by building it. These costs are included as part of the cost of the oil-rig. The 10% of costs that arise through the extraction of oil are recognised as a liability when the oil is extracted.

Risks and Uncertainties

Risks and uncertainties should be taken into account in reaching the best estimate, but care must be taken to avoid an overstatement of the provision.

EXAMPLE 14.13: RISK AND UNCERTAINTY

Parker plc sells goods with a warranty under which customers are covered for the cost of repairs of any manufacturing defect that becomes apparent within the first six months of purchase. The company's past experience and future expectations indicate the following pattern of likely repairs.

Percentage of Goods Sold	Defects	Cost of Repairs € million
75%	None	–
20%	Minor	1.0
5%	Major	4.0

Requirement Calculate the expected cost of repairs.

Solution

The cost is found using 'expected values' (75% × €nil) + (20% × €1.0m) × (5% × €4.0m) = €400,000.

Present Value

If the time value of money is material, a provision should be discounted on a pre-tax basis and on a current market assessment of the specific risks attached to the liability (see **Example 14.14, Issue 5**).

Future Events

Future events should only be included in the measurement process if there is objective evidence that they will occur (e.g. new legislation is virtually certain).

Expected Disposal of Assets

Any gains on the expected disposal of assets should be ignored when measuring a provision.

Example 14.14 pulls together many of the issues covered in this chapter in the form of an exam-style question.

EXAMPLE 14.14: VARIED PROVISIONS

Diamond Limited (Diamond), a company that prepares its financial statements to 31 December each year, is involved in mining and exploration. Before the financial statements for the year ended 31 December 2012 can be finalised, a number of outstanding issues need to be resolved.

Issue 1
In order to provide funds for exploration work, bills receivable amounting to €4 million were discounted on 1 December 2012. These are due for maturity on 1 November 2013. The directors of Diamond are uncertain whether it is necessary to disclose this in the financial statements for the year ended 31 December 2012.

Issue 2
In February 2013, a customer commenced legal action against Diamond, alleging that drilling work completed in September 2012 had not been carried out in accordance with the terms of the contract. The directors of Diamond intend to defend the allegations vigorously and Diamond's legal advisors estimate that the company has a 75% chance of successfully defending the claim. If the customer is successful, penalties and legal fees are expected to amount to €1 million. If Diamond wins the case, non-recoverable legal fees of €25,000 will have been incurred. The directors of Diamond are proposing to omit reference to the legal action in the financial statements for the year ended 31 December 2012 as the writ was not issued until February 2013.

Issue 3
Diamond carried out a joint contract with Forever Limited (Forever). Under the terms of the contract, Diamond is liable for penalties if certain restoration work is not completed satisfactorily. Diamond has a separate agreement with Forever that enables the company to recover 50% of any penalties incurred from Forever. At 31 December 2012 the directors of Diamond estimate that penalties of €5 million will become payable, but are uncertain how this should be reflected in the financial statements for the year ended 31 December 2012.

Issue 4

Diamond purchased a private jet on 1 January 2012 at a cost of €24 million. The jet is to be used for transporting company executives to and from the various locations where the company is conducting mining and exploration work. Air regulations require the jet to be overhauled every three years, and it is estimated that each overhaul will cost €1.5 million. Diamond is proposing to charge depreciation on a straight-line basis over the jet's useful economic life of 12 years. Furthermore, it is proposed to create an annual provision of €500,000 to meet the overhaul costs every three years.

Issue 5

On 1 January 2012, Diamond was granted a licence to commence mining for silver. As a condition of being granted the licence, Diamond is obliged to restore the mountainside to its original state when the mining licence expires in six years' time. The directors of Diamond estimate that the total cost of restoration will be €120 million, of which 80% will be incurred when mining ceases and the remainder during mining. Mining commenced on 1 January 2012. Diamond's cost of capital is 10% and the risk-free rate is 4%. The directors of Diamond are proposing to provide for the restoration costs over the next six years based on projected production at the mine.

Requirement Prepare a Memorandum addressed to the finance director of Diamond explaining how each of the issues should be treated in the financial statements for the year ended 31 December 2012.

Present value factors:

Years	4%	10%
1	0.962	0.909
2	0.925	0.826
3	0.889	0.751
4	0.855	0.683
5	0.822	0.621
6	0.790	0.564

Solution

MEMORANDUM

DATE:
TO:
FROM:
SUBJECT:

Issue 1

Assuming the bills were discounted with recourse and therefore there is a risk that, if the bills are dishonoured, DIAMOND will have to settle the liability. Under IAS 37 *Provisions, Contingent Liabilities and Contingent Assets*, the contingent liability of €4 million should be disclosed in the notes to the financial statements.

Issue 2

The work was completed during the year ended 31 December 2012 and therefore it is relevant to the financial statements for the year ended 31 December 2012. As the legal fees of €25,000 are non-recoverable, these should be provided for. As a successful outcome is put at 75%, it is reasonable to treat the claim as a contingent liability and disclose by way of note, explaining the background to the claim and the expectations for a successful outcome.

Issue 3

IAS 37 *Provisions, Contingent Liabilities and Contingent Assets* deals with recoveries from third parties. Diamond is liable for 100% to the customer and therefore must provide for the full amount. If Diamond is virtually certain that Forever will honour their 50% and reimburse €2.5 million, the amount due may be shown as an asset.

Issue 4

The depreciation policy appears reasonable so long as the estimate of the useful economic life of 12 years is appropriate and the aircraft will have no residual value. But it is also necessary to consider industry practice.

With respect to the overhaul provision, there is no 'present obligation' to carry out the overhaul since it could be avoided by selling the jet when three years have elapsed. Therefore, no provision can be recognised. The depreciation takes account of future incidence of maintenance.

Issue 5

Under IAS 37 *Provisions, Contingent Liabilities and Contingent Assets*, a present obligation exists as a result of gaining the licence. There is the probable transfer of economic benefits and the amount of outflow can be reasonably estimated. Therefore it is necessary to create a provision for the full amount and capitalise the obligation as it meets the definition of an asset since it provides future economic benefits. Basing a provision on projected output is no longer allowed. The €120 million should be provided for now, taking account of the time value of money. IAS 37 states that the discount rate should be a pre-tax rate that reflects the time value of money and the risks specific to the liability. In this instance the risk-free rate should be applied as the funds can be set aside and reinvested at the risk-free rate.

6 years @ 4%:   Present value = 0.790 × €120 million = €94,800,000
Therefore, discount = €25,200,000
At 1/1/12:

DR	Non-current assets	€94,800,000	
CR	Provisions		€94,800,000

Depreciation each year:

DR	SPLOCI – P/L	€15,800,000	
CR	Non-current assets		€15,800,000

Unwinding the discount:

		€
2012	4% × €94,800,000	3,792,000
2013	4% × €98,592,000	3,943,680

2014	4% × €102,535,680	4,101,427
2015	4% × €106,637,107	4,265,484
2016	4% × €110,902,591	4,436,104
2017	4% × €115,338,695	4,613,548
	(Rounding difference €47,757)	25,152,243

The interest charge becomes progressively higher as it reflects the compounding of earnings of funds set aside earlier. The interest may be classified as exceptional if material. However, it might be possible to divide the asset into 'different component parts' with different lives and depreciate each accordingly. But it is necessary to consider whether each 'part' is separately distinguishable.

14.4 DISCLOSURES

IAS 37 disclosures can be divided into three types, i.e. those relating to provisions, contingent liabilities and contingent assets. The required disclosures for each of these are summarised below.

In broad terms, a provision requires adjustment and disclosure, whereas contingent liabilities and assets do not involve adjusting the financial statements and simply require disclosure. This is on the basis that the likelihood of a provision occurring is deemed to be probable, whereas a contingent liability is only possible. A contingent asset is not recognised on the grounds of prudence.

1. **Provisions** (for each class):
   - opening balance;
   - additional or adjustment to provisions;
   - amounts used;
   - amounts reversed; and
   - change in discounted amount (for example, unwinding or change in discount rate).

   In addition, a brief description of the nature of the provision should be provided, together with expected timing of outflows. An indication of the uncertainties re. the amount and timing of outflows and the amount of any reimbursement and associate asset recognised.

2. **Contingent Liabilities:**
   Unless remote, for each class of contingent liability, the following should be disclosed:
   - brief description of the nature of the contingency;
   - an estimate of its financial effect and an indication of the uncertainties; and
   - the possibility of any reimbursement.

3. **Contingent Assets:**
   If probable, a brief description of their nature and financial effect, if practicable.

14.5 CONCLUSION

The main requirements of IAS 37 are summarised below in **Tables 14.2** and **14.3**, together with **Figure 14.1**. **Table 14.2** and **Figure 14.1** deal with provisions and contingent liabilities.

TABLE 14.2: PROVISIONS AND CONTINGENT LIABILITIES

Where, as a result of past events, there may be an outflow of economic benefits in settlement of: (a) a present obligation; or (b) a possible obligation whose existence will be confirmed only by the occurrence or non-occurrence of one or more uncertain future events not wholly within the control of the entity, then:

If there is a present obligation, that probably requires an outflow of resources.	**If there is a possible obligation or present obligation that may, but probably will not, require an outflow of resources.**	**If there is a possible obligation or a present obligation where the likelihood of an outflow of resources is remote.**
A provision is recognised.	No provision is recognised.	No provision is recognised.
Disclosures are required for the provision.	Disclosures are required for the contingent liability.	No disclosure is required.

A contingent liability also arises in the extremely rare case where there is a liability that cannot be recognised because it cannot be measured reliably. Disclosures are required for the contingent liability.

Table 14.3 summarises the position with respect to contingent assets.

TABLE 14.3: CONTINGENT ASSETS

Where, as a result of past events, there is a possible asset whose existence will be confirmed only by the occurrence or non-occurrence of one or more uncertain future events not wholly within the control of the entity, then:

If the inflow of economic benefits is virtually certain.	**If the inflow of economic benefits is probable, but not virtually certain.**	**If the inflow is not probable.**
The asset is not contingent.	No asset is recognised.	No asset is recognised.
	Disclosures are required.	No disclosure is required.

The decision-making process with respect to provisions and contingent liabilities is condensed in **Figure 14.1**.

FIGURE 14.1: PROVISIONS AND CONTINGENT LIABILITIES

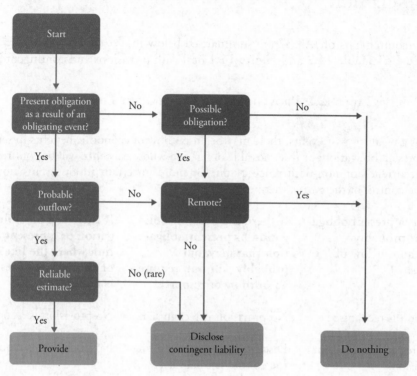

SUMMARY OF LEARNING OBJECTIVES

After having studied this chapter, you should be able to:

Learning Objective 1 Define the terms 'provision', 'contingent liability' and 'contingent asset'.

A provision is a liability of uncertain timing or amount; a contingent liability is a possible obligation arising from past events that is not recognised because it is not probable that a transfer of economic benefits will be required to settle the obligation, or the amount of the obligation cannot be measured with sufficient reliability. A contingent asset is a possible asset arising from past events whose existence will be confirmed only by the occurrence or non-occurrence of one or more uncertain future events not wholly within the entity's control.

Learning Objective 2 Explain when a provision should be recognised and how it should be measured and accounted for.

The recognition of a provision is summarised in **Table 14.2** and **Figure 14.1**. A provision should be measured at the best estimate of the amount (on a pre-tax basis) required to settle the present obligation at the reporting date. If the time value of money is material, a provision should be discounted on a pre-tax basis and on a current market assessment of the specific risks attached to the liability.

Learning Objective 3 Apply the accounting treatment for contingent liabilities and contingent assets.

See **Table 14.2** and **Table 14.3**.

Learning Objective 4 Apply the main disclosure requirements.

These are explained in **Section 14.4**. In broad terms, a provision requires adjustment and disclosure, whereas contingent liabilities and assets do not involve adjusting the financial statements and simply require disclosure.

QUESTIONS

Self-test Questions

1. How does IAS 37 define a provision?
2. According to IAS 37, when, and only when, can a provision be recognised?
3. Can a provision ever be made for future operating losses?
4. How does IAS 37 define a contingent liability?
5. When should a contingent liability be recognised?

Review Questions

(See **Appendix One** for Suggested Solutions to Review Questions.)

Question 14.1

During 2011 Bad Limited gives a guarantee of certain borrowings of Girls Limited, whose financial condition at that time is sound. During 2012 the financial condition of Girls Limited deteriorates and at 30 June 2012, Girls Limited files for protection from its creditors.

Requirement What accounting treatment is required at:
(a) 31 December 2011; and
(b) 31 December 2012?

Question 14.2

King Limited gives warranties at the time of sale to purchasers of its products. Under the terms of the warranty the manufacturer undertakes to make good, by repair or replacement, manufacturing defects that become apparent within a period of three years from the date of the sale.

Requirement Explain whether a provision should be recognised.

Question 14.3

In which of the following circumstances might a provision be recognised?
(a) On 13 December 2012 the board of an entity decided to close down a division. The accounting date of the company is 31 December. Before 31 December 2012, the decision was not communicated to any of those affected and no other steps were taken to implement the decision.
(b) The board agreed a detailed closure plan on 20 December 2012 and details were given to customers and employees.
(c) A company is obliged to incur clean-up costs for environmental damage (that has already been caused).
(d) A company intends to carry out future expenditure to operate in a particular way in the future.

Challenging Questions

(Suggested Solutions to Challenging Questions are available to lecturers.)

Question 14.1 (Based on Chartered Accountants Ireland, P2 Autumn 1997, Question 1)

Pelican Limited advised its solicitors to commence an action against its major supplier, claiming damages of €500,000 in respect of losses sustained as a result of the supply of faulty goods. According to legal advice, Pelican Limited stands a very good chance of winning its case.

Requirement Indicate how this situation should be dealt with in order to comply with standard accounting practice. (Assume a financial year-end of 31 December 2012 and that the issue is material.)

Question 14.2 (Based on Chartered Accountants Ireland, P2 Summer 1996, Question 1)

Highgrove plc is a manufacturing and distribution company. You are acting as auditor to Highgrove plc and you have been asked by the Board of Directors of the company to explain how the following items should be treated in the published accounts of the company for the year ended 31 December 2012.

In June 2012, Highgrove plc engaged a firm of building contractors to build an extension to the factory. In December 2012, just as the building was due to be completed, the structure collapsed and destroyed the canteen, which was directly underneath.

The company is suing the builder for compensation. Highgrove plc is claiming €150,000. The insurers of the building contractor have offered an out-of-court settlement of €80,000. Highgrove plc's lawyer believes that the offer made by the building contractor is unreasonable and that when the case comes to court in March 2013, Highgrove plc stands a very good chance of winning the full €150,000.

Requirement Prepare a Memorandum to the Board of Directors of Highgrove plc in which you state how the above should be reflected in the company's published financial statements for the year ended 31 December 2012. (Assume all transactions are material, and ignore taxation.)

Question 14.3 *(Based on Chartered Accountants Ireland, P2 Summer 2000, Question 4)*

(a) In accordance with IAS 37 *Provisions, Contingent Liabilities and Contingent Assets*, define a provision and explain briefly when a provision should be recognised in financial statements.

(b) JEANS AND JUMPERS plc is a well-known, high-street retail outlet with branches all over Ireland. The year-end of the company is 31 December 2012. The following information is available.

 (i) As part of its customer service, the company has a policy of refunding purchases to dissatisfied customers, even though there is no legal obligation to do so. In the past, approximately 10% of goods sold were returned and refunds given.

 (ii) During November 2012 a decision was taken in principle to close the company's Cork branch. However, no formalised plan in connection with the closure had been devised, the decision had not been communicated to the employees of the company at the date of the statement of financial position and no other steps had been taken to implement this decision at that date.

 (iii) The company is famous for its in-store 'tea rooms', where tired shoppers can avail of light refreshments. During the year ended 31 December 2012, 200 people became ill after eating the JEANS AND JUMPERS plc 'special super deluxe gateau'. Ten of these people died. Legal proceedings have been started against the company for compensation. However, the company denies liability, stating that, at the time of the food-poisoning outbreak, the local council was working on the water mains, fixing burst pipes, and it firmly believes that the water became contaminated during the repair process. The company's lawyers indicated, up to the date of approval of the financial statements, that the company would probably be found not liable.

 (iv) The company had a lease on an old warehouse in Galway. As part of a centralisation programme, all merchandise is now being stored in Dublin warehouses. JEANS AND JUMPERS plc has tried to cancel the Galway lease, three which still has three years to run. However, due to the terms of the lease contract, it has been unable to do so.

Requirement In respect of the financial statements of JEANS AND JUMPERS plc for the year ended 31 December 2012, outline each of the following in accordance with IAS 37 *Provisions, Contingent Liabilities and Contingent Assets*:
(a) the accounting treatment for each of the above items; and
(b) where appropriate, the disclosure requirements for each of the items.

(Assume all issues are material, and ignore taxation.)

Question 14.4

BLUES Limited (BLUES) prepares its financial statements to 31 December each year. The company manufactures paint, and its operations are divided into two cash-generating units: domestic and commercial. The following issue needs to be resolved before the financial statements for the year ended 31 December 2012 can be finalised.

In December 2012, BLUES announced publicly its intention to reduce the level of additives in all of the company's domestic and commercial paints. This will involve modifying the company's plant and equipment at an estimated cost of €12,000,000, payable in equal annual instalments over the next six years, commencing in December 2013. Plant and equipment at 31 December 2012 had an average remaining useful economic life of six years. The changes were prompted by market pressures and evaluated using discounted cash flow techniques. The discount rate used was 10%.

Requirement Explain how this should be accounted for, and show the amounts to be included in the financial statements for the year ended 31 December 2012.

Present value factors:

Rate/Period	1	2	3	4	5	6
10%	0.909	0.826	0.751	0.683	0.620	0.564
12%	0.893	0.797	0.712	0.636	0.567	0.507

Question 14.5

Pearl Limited gives warranties at the time of sale to purchasers of its products. Under the terms of the warranty the manufacturer undertakes to make good, by repair or replacement, manufacturing defects that become apparent within a period of three years from the date of the sale.

Requirement Should a provision be recognised?

Question 14.6

S & M Limited is a well-known, high-street retail outlet with branches all over UK and RoI. As part of its customer service, the company has a policy of refunding purchases to dissatisfied customers, even though there is no legal obligation to do so. In the past, approximately 10% of goods sold were returned and refunds given.

Requirement Outline the accounting treatment for this policy and the appropriate disclosures.

15

EVENTS AFTER THE REPORTING PERIOD

LEARNING OBJECTIVES

Having studied this chapter, you should be able to:
1. define events after the end of the reporting period;
2. distinguish between an adjusting and a non-adjusting event;
3. account for adjusting and non-adjusting events;
4. explain the IAS 10 *Events after the Reporting Period* requirements regarding proposed dividends; and
5. apply the main IAS 10 disclosure requirements.

KEY TERMS AND DEFINITIONS FOR THIS CHAPTER

In order to aid your understanding of the concepts and issues covered in this chapter, it is important to understand and be familiar with the following key terms and definitions. As you study this chapter, you should refer back to them.

Adjusting Event after the Reporting Period This is an event after the reporting period that provides further evidence of conditions that existed at the end of the reporting period, including an event that indicates that the **going concern assumption** in relation to the whole or part of the enterprise is not appropriate.

Event after the Reporting Period This is an event, which could be favourable or unfavourable, that occurs between the end of the reporting period and the date that the financial statements are authorised for issue. IAS 10 differentiates between an **adjusting event after the reporting period** and a **non-adjusting event after the reporting period**.

Going Concern Assumption Financial statements are prepared on the assumption that the entity will continue to operate without the threat of liquidation for the foreseeable future, usually regarded as at least one year.

Non-adjusting Event after the Reporting Period This is an event after the reporting period that is indicative of a condition that arose after the end of the reporting period.

15.1 INTRODUCTION

It is a fundamental principle of accounting that regard must be given to all available information when preparing financial statements. This must include relevant events occurring after the date of the statement of financial position and up to the date on which the financial statements are authorised for issue. The purpose of IAS 10 *Events after the Reporting Period* is to define the extent to which different types of event after the end of the reporting period are reflected in the financial statements.

Key to this Chapter

After defining what is meant by the term 'events after the end of the reporting period', this chapter explains the distinction between adjusting and non-adjusting events and illustrates how these events are accounted for in accordance with IAS 10 (**Section 15.2**). The main IAS 10 disclosure requirements are also outlined (**Section 15.3**).

15.2 IAS 10 EVENTS AFTER THE REPORTING PERIOD

An '**event after the reporting period**' is an event, which could be *favourable* or *unfavourable*, that occurs between the end of the reporting period and the date that the financial statements are approved by the board of directors. IAS 10 differentiates between an **adjusting event after the reporting period** and a **non-adjusting event after the reporting period**. Each of these two types of event is now explained. (*Note:* It can be assumed that the amounts included in the examples in this chapter would be considered material – see **Chapter 2**.)

Adjusting Events after the Reporting Period

An adjusting event after the reporting period is an event after the reporting period that provides further evidence of conditions that existed at the end of the reporting period, including an event that indicates that the **going concern** assumption in relation to the whole or part of the enterprise is not appropriate.

Examples of adjusting events after the reporting period include the:
• subsequent determination of the purchase price or of sale proceeds of assets purchased or sold before the year end (i.e. an agreement to buy or sell an asset was reached *before* the end of the reporting period, but the purchase or sale price was agreed *after* the end of the reporting period);
• valuation of a property that provides evidence of a permanent diminution in value (i.e. evidence comes to light *after* the end of the reporting period that indicates that conditions existed *before* the end of the reporting period that show property prices have suffered a permanent decline);
• sale of inventories after the date of the statement of financial position, which gives evidence about their net realisable value at the date of the statement of financial position (e.g. inventory recorded at its cost of €100,000 at the reporting date of 31 December 2012 was sold for €85,000 in January 2013);

- renegotiation of amounts owing by debtors or the insolvency of a debtor;
- bankruptcy of a debtor after the date of the statement of financial position that confirms that a loss existed at the date of the statement of financial position on trade receivables;
- amounts received or receivable in respect of insurance claims that were in the course of negotiation at the date of the statement of financial position; and
- discovery of errors or frauds that show the financial statements were incorrect.

IAS 10 states that, where there is an adjusting event, the financial statements must be changed to reflect this event.

Example 15.1 illustrates some of the adjusting events referred to above.

EXAMPLE 15.1: ADJUSTING EVENTS

Punjab plc (Punjab) is a producer and distributor of tea. The company's year-end is 31 December. The directors of Punjab are due to sign the company's financial statements for the year ended 31 December 2012 on 5 March 2013. The following information is available.

1. Flavoured tea is included in year-end inventory at its original cost of €120,000. Audit work carried out in February 2013 indicated that the tea was sold for €100,000 in January 2013 due to a fall in demand for such products during 2012.
2. During 2012 there had been industrial unrest amongst Punjab's production workers following the automation of one of the manufacturing processes. Management had sought to make 20% of the workforce redundant. In February 2013, following protracted negotiations, it was agreed that 15% of the workforce would be made redundant at a cost of €400,000.
3. On 31 January 2013, €250,000 was paid to Trevor Baggins as compensation for his removal as Marketing Director. Mr Baggins had been dismissed by the Chairman at the December 2012 Board meeting as a result of a serious disagreement over marketing strategy for 2013.
4. It was discovered in January 2013 that a long-serving employee had systematically stolen €250,000 over the previous four years. Material errors had thus been made in the financial statements over those years and there is now no chance of recovery.

Requirement Explain briefly how each of the above transactions should be treated in the financial statements of Punjab for the year ended 31 December 2012.

Solution

1. Inventory should be valued at the lower of cost and net realisable value, in accordance with IAS 2 *Inventories* (see **Chapter 11**). Demand fell during 2012 and the sale in January 2013 is evidence of conditions that existed at 31 December 2012. This is an adjusting event and the inventory at 31 December 2012 should therefore be written down by €20,000.
2. This is an adjusting event. The redundancy conditions existed at the end of the reporting period and the final agreement merely settled the terms. The cost of €400,000 being a 'one off' and not expected to occur with regularity should be considered for separate disclosure in the financial statements as an exceptional item under the normal statutory heading within which such costs are normally disclosed.

3. The dismissal of Mr Baggins took effect before the end of the financial year. As a consequence, the compensation payment of €250,000 will be an adjusting event and will be charged in the financial statements for the year ended 31 December 2012.
4. IAS 10 states that the discovery of errors/fraud that existed/occurred prior to the end of the reporting period is an adjusting event.

Non-adjusting Events after the Reporting Period

A non-adjusting event after the reporting period is an event after the reporting period that is indicative of a condition that arose after the end of the reporting period. Examples include:
- closing a significant part of the trading activities, if not anticipated at the year-end;
- the acquisition or disposal of a subsidiary after the date of the statement of financial position;
- major purchases and disposals of assets after the end of the reporting period;
- a fire after the end of the reporting period, which results in the destruction of a major production plant;
- a decline in the value of property and investments held as non-current assets, if it can be demonstrated that the decline occurred after the year-end;
- a decline in market value of investments between the date of the statement of financial position and the date when the financial statements are authorised for issue;
- announcing a plan to discontinue an operation; and
- commencing major litigation arising solely out of events that occurred after the date of the statement of financial position.

Non-adjusting events after the reporting date do *not* result in *changes in the amounts* in the financial statements. They may, however, be of such materiality that their *disclosure* is required by way of a note to ensure that the financial statements are not misleading. For material non-adjusting events after the end of the reporting period, the following disclosure is required:
- the nature of the event;
- an estimate of the financial effect, or a statement that it is not practicable to make such an estimate; and
- the estimate of the financial effect should be disclosed before taking account of taxation; and the taxation implications should be explained, where necessary, for a proper understanding of the financial position.

Example 15.2 illustrates some of the non-adjusting events referred to above.

EXAMPLE 15.2: NON-ADJUSTING EVENTS

Pinewood Limited is a furniture manufacturing company. The company was informed on 1 February 2013 that one of its major customers, Cushion Limited, had gone into liquidation. The liquidator indicated that no payments would be made to unsecured creditors. The amount owed by Cushion Limited on 1 February 2013 amounted to €55,000, of which

€30,000 related to goods invoiced on 10 December 2012 and €25,000 to goods invoiced on 15 January 2013.

Requirement Explain how the above item should be dealt with in the financial statements of Pinewood Limited for the year ended 31 December 2012.

Solution

The liquidation of Cushion Limited and its resultant consequence occurred after the end of the reporting period and will be dealt with in accordance with IAS 10 *Events after the Reporting Period*. As far as the total loss of €55,000 is concerned, at the end of the reporting period the relevant loss was €30,000. Since the balance of €25,000 represented a loss on goods sold after the end of the reporting period it was therefore a condition which did not exist at that date.

The liquidation and confirmation of insolvency of Cushion Limited is an event that provides evidence as to the recoverability of the debt of €30,000 due by Cushion Limited at 31 December 2012. The €30,000 will be written off as an irrecoverable debt and as, in the context of the scale of the company's trading, it is of material significance, it should be referred to in a note to the financial statements.

The further irrecoverable debt of €25,000 is not a charge against the profits in the statement of profit or loss and other comprehensive income for the year to 31 December 2012, but because it is of material significance to an understanding of the company's financial position, it should be reported by way of a note to the financial statements as a non-adjusting event.

Going Concern Issues Arising after the End of the Reporting Period

IAS 10 states that an entity should not prepare its financial statements on a going concern basis if management determines after the end of the reporting period either that it intends to liquidate the entity or to cease trading, or that it has no realistic alternative but to do so.

Proposed Dividends

Proposed dividends should *not* be recognised as a liability until approved by shareholders at the Annual General Meeting (AGM). This is illustrated in **Example 15.3**.

EXAMPLE 15.3: PROPOSED DIVIDENDS

(a) The shareholders of MLC Limited, a company that prepares its financial statements to 31 December each year, approved a dividend of 6 cent per share on 28 December 2012, but this was not paid until 23 January 2013.

(b) The Board of Directors of JBSM Limited, a company that prepares its financial statements to 31 December each year, proposed a dividend of 5 cent per share on 15 December 2012. The AGM is scheduled for 13 January 2013.

Requirement Explain the appropriate accounting treatment for (a) and (b) in respect of their financial statements for the year ended 31 December 2012.

Solution

IAS 10 states that companies should *only* accrue for dividends when approved by the shareholders at the AGM *before* the reporting date.

(a) The dividend was approved by the shareholders before the end of the reporting period and should be accrued for in the financial statements for the year ended 31 December 2012.

(b) As the dividend was *not* approved by the shareholders before the end of the reporting period, it should *not* be accrued for in the financial statements for the year ended 31 December 2012. However, the proposed dividends would be disclosed in the notes to the financial statements (as a non-adjusting event).

15.3 DISCLOSURE

As indicated above, non-adjusting events should be disclosed if they are of such importance that non-disclosure would affect the ability of users to make proper evaluations and decisions. The required disclosure is:

(a) the nature of the event; and

(b) an estimate of its financial effect or a statement that a reasonable estimate of the effect cannot be made.

For example: 'A fire occurred on 23 January 2013 and destroyed the company's factory. The best estimate is that it will cost €5 million to rebuild the factory and replace the machinery and inventory destroyed in the fire. The company is insured, but due to unusually high levels of inventory it is believed that it will only be possible to recover €4.6 million from the insurance company.'

Companies must disclose the date when the financial statements were authorised for issue and who gave that authorisation. If the enterprise's owners or others have the power to amend the financial statements after issuance, the enterprise must disclose that fact.

15.4 CONCLUSION

In summary, the key aspects of IAS 10 are:

- adjust the financial statements for adjusting events, i.e. events after the reporting period that provide further evidence of conditions that existed at the end of the reporting period, including events that indicate that the going concern assumption in relation to the whole or part of the enterprise is not appropriate;
- do not adjust for non-adjusting events, i.e. events or conditions that arose after the end of the reporting period; and
- if an entity declares dividends after the reporting period, the entity should not recognise those dividends as a liability at the end of the reporting period. That is a non-adjusting event.

SUMMARY OF LEARNING OBJECTIVES

After having studied this chapter, you should be able to:

Learning Objective 1 Define events after the end of the reporting period.

These are events occurring after the date of the statement of financial position and up to the date on which the financial statements are authorised for issue.

Learning Objective 2 Distinguish between an adjusting and a non-adjusting event.

An adjusting event is an event after the reporting period that provides further evidence of conditions that existed at the end of the reporting period, including an event that indicates that the going concern assumption in relation to the whole or part of the enterprise is not appropriate. A non-adjusting event is an event after the reporting period that is indicative of a condition that arose after the end of the reporting period.

Learning Objective 3 Account for adjusting and non-adjusting events.

The financial statements are adjusted for adjusting events, but not for non-adjusting events (these are disclosed if material).

Learning Objective 4 Explain the IAS 10 *Events after the Reporting Period* requirements regarding proposed dividends.

Proposed dividends should not be recognised as a liability until approved by shareholders at the AGM.

Learning Objective 5 Apply the main IAS 10 disclosure requirements.

For a non-adjusting event, the nature of the event and an estimate of its financial effect or a statement that a reasonable estimate of the effect cannot be made should be disclosed.

QUESTIONS

Self-test Questions

1. What is an event after the end of the reporting period?
2. What is an adjusting event?
3. Give three examples of an adjusting event.
4. Give three examples of a non-adjusting event.
5. In what circumstances will a non-adjusting event require changes in the amounts to be disclosed in the financial statements?

Review Questions

(See **Appendix One** for Suggested Solutions to Review Questions.) (Assume all transactions are material and ignore taxation.)

Question 15.1

The following events, which are considered to be material, occurred after the date of the statement of financial position of Bellamy Limited but before the authorisation of its financial statements.

(a) Cronser Limited, owing €20,000 to Bellamy Limited at the date of the statement of financial position, went into liquidation and available information suggests that there is little prospect of a dividend for unsecured creditors. The debt had increased to €30,000 at the date of the winding-up order.

(b) The liquidator of Bogmore Limited announced his intention to pay a dividend of 50 cent in the € to unsecured creditors. Three years previously, Bellamy Limited had provided for the full debt owing by Bogmore Limited at that time.

(c) A fire in one of Bellamy Limited's warehouses caused €50,000 worth of damage to inventory that had cost €80,000. This damage had not been covered by insurance. Of the damaged inventory, approximately 75% was in inventory at the date of the statement of financial position, the remaining 25% having been purchased after the date of the statement of financial position.

Requirement Indicate to what extent the foregoing events should affect the accounts of Bellamy Limited. State the reasons that support your conclusions.

Question 15.2

Fabricators Limited, an engineering company, makes up its financial statements to 31 March in each year. The financial statements for the year ended 31 March 2013 showed a turnover of €3 million and trading profit of €400,000. Before approval of the financial statements by the board of directors on 30 June 2013, the following events took place.

(a) The financial statements of Patchup Limited for the year ended 28 February 2013 were received, which indicated a permanent decline in that company's financial position. Fabricators Limited had bought shares in Patchup Limited some years ago and this purchase was included in unquoted investments at its cost of €100,000. The financial statements received indicated that the investment was now worth only €50,000.

(b) There was a fire at the company's warehouse on 30 April 2013 and inventory to the value of €500,000 was destroyed. It transpired that the inventory in the warehouse was underinsured by some 50%.

(c) On 31 March 2013 a provision had been made of €60,000 in respect of any remedial work required on plant supplied and installed at a customer's premises on 26 March 2013. No remedial work had been carried out and on 1 May 2013 the customer had confirmed acceptance of the plant. Accordingly, no further liability would be involved.

Requirement Explain, giving reasons as to how the above events should be dealt with in the company's financial statements for the year ended 31 March 2013.

Challenging Questions

(Suggested Solutions to Challenging Questions are available to lecturers.)

(Assume all transactions are material and ignore taxation.)

Question 15.1 *(Based on Chartered Accountants Ireland, P2 Summer 1997, Question 1)*

Blade Limited is a furniture manufacturing company. The company was informed on 1 February 2013 that one of its major customers, Greenwood Limited, had gone into liquidation. The liquidator indicated that no payments would be made to unsecured creditors. The amount owed by Greenwood Limited on 1 February 2013 amounted to €55,000, of which €30,000 related to goods invoiced on 10 December 2012 and €25,000 to goods invoiced on 15 January 2013.

Requirement Prepare a Memorandum for the Board of Directors in which you, acting as auditor, explain how the above item should be dealt with in the financial statements of Blade Limited for the year ended 31 December 2012.

Question 15.2 *(Based on Chartered Accountants Ireland, P2 Autumn 1997, Question 1)*

Sword Limited had inventory amounting to €120,000 in its statement of financial position at 31 December 2012. On 3 January 2013, a fire in the company's warehouse severely damaged this inventory. The inventory will now realise only €50,000.

Requirement Indicate how this situation should be dealt with in order to comply with standard accounting practice. (Assume a financial year-end of 31 December 2012.)

Question 15.3 *(Based on Chartered Accountants Ireland, P2 Summer 1996, Question 1)*

Highgrove plc is a manufacturing and distribution company. You are acting as auditor to Highgrove plc and you have been asked by the Board of Directors of the company to explain how the following items should be treated in the published accounts of the company for the year ended 31 December 2012:

(a) On 11 February 2013 Highgrove plc raised additional share capital of €100,000 by way of an issue of shares at full market price. This action had been planned and approved in October 2012; and

(b) On 19 December 2012 Highgrove plc sold an old warehouse that was surplus to requirements. The profit on sale was recorded in the accounts at €100,000. On 20 January 2013 the purchaser discovered that the roof of the warehouse was defective. Under the terms of the sale agreement, Highgrove plc was responsible for rectifying the problem. On 3 March 2013 Highgrove plc received a bill for €30,000 in connection with this rectification work.

Requirement You are required to prepare a memorandum to the Board of Directors of Highgrove plc in which you state how each of the above items should be reflected in the company's published financial statements for the year ended 31 December 2012.

Question 15.4 *(Based on Chartered Accountants Ireland, P2 Autumn 1998, Question 1)*

TOFFEE plc ('TOFFEE') is a manufacturer and distributor of confectionery goods. The company's year-end is 31 December. The directors of TOFFEE are due to sign the company's financial statements for the year ended 31 December 2012 on 5 March 2013. The company accountant collapsed in early January 2013, leaving the assistant accountant to prepare the year-end financial statements. Due to lack of experience, the assistant accountant was unsure of the accounting treatment of the following items and thus ignored them when drafting the year-end accounts:

(a) On 13 February 2013, TOFFEE terminated a contract with CRISP Inc., a US company based in Dallas, Texas. The contract had been in place for a number of years. In early January 2013, CRISP Inc. had been the subject of a federal investigation carried out by the public health agency. Under the terms of the contract, TOFFEE is obliged to pay €500,000 for early termination of the contract.

(b) Caramel used in the production of chocolate bars was included in year-end inventory at its cost of €120,000. Audit work carried out in February 2013 indicated that the caramel could have been purchased for €80,000 in January 2013, due to a fall in world commodity prices.

(c) During 2012 there had been industrial unrest amongst TOFFEE production workers following the automation of one of the manufacturing processes. Management had sought to make 20% of the workforce redundant. In February 2013, following protracted negotiations, it was agreed that 15% of the workforce would be made redundant at a cost of €400,000.

(d) On 31 January 2013, €250,000 was paid to Tony Raisin as compensation for his removal as Marketing Director. Mr Raisin had been dismissed by the Chairman at the December 2012 Board meeting as a result of a serious disagreement over marketing strategy for 2013.

Requirement

(a) Define an event after the end of the reporting period and distinguish between an adjusting event after the end of the reporting period and a non-adjusting event after the end of the reporting period.

(b) Explain briefly how each of the above transactions should be treated in the financial statements of TOFFEE for the year ended 31 December 2012, in accordance with the relevant accounting standard.

Question 15.5 (Based on Chartered Accountants Ireland, P2 Summer 1999, Question 1)

TOBACCO Limited ('TOBACCO') manufactures cigars. The following information is available for the company for the year ended 31 December 2012. The financial statements are due to be signed by the directors at the forthcoming board meeting in May 2013:

(a) TOBACCO's revenue for the financial year ended 31 December 2012 includes €300,000 relating to the sale, in October 2012, of a consignment of special cigars to the Moravian Government to celebrate the Silver Jubilee of its ruler. Following a coup in December 2012, the ruler was deposed and the Silver Jubilee celebrations were cancelled. TOBACCO does not now expect to receive payment of this debt.

(b) In January 2013 one of TOBACCO's French subsidiaries, LUM-METTE Limited, declared a dividend of €80,000 for the year ended 31 December 2012. TOBACCO holds a 75% interest in LUM-METTE Limited.

(c) At the December 2012 Board meeting of TOBACCO, a decision was taken in principle to dispose of SMOKE Limited, a subsidiary company based in Cork. This investment was valued in the statement of financial position of TOBACCO, at 31 December 2012, at €1,300,000. On 20 January 2013 the management of SMOKE Limited decided to buy the company for €2,000,000.

(d) TOBACCO Limited owned 60% of PIPE Limited, which it had acquired two years earlier at a cost of €1,500,000. The financial statements of PIPE Limited for the year ended 31 December 2012 were received by TOBACCO on 10 January 2013 and showed a permanent decline in the company's financial position. The cost of PIPE Limited (€1,500,000) was included under unquoted investments in the statement of financial position of TOBACCO. A review of the financial statements of PIPE Limited indicated that the investment was now worth only €700,000.

Requirement Indicate how each of the above items should be dealt with in the financial statements of TOBACCO Limited for the year ended 31 December 2012.

16

ACCOUNTING FOR GOVERNMENT GRANTS AND DISCLOSURE OF GOVERNMENT ASSISTANCE

LEARNING OBJECTIVES

Having studied this chapter, you should be able to:
1. distinguish between grants related to income and grants related to assets;
2. account for grants related to income;
3. apply the two allowable methods of accounting for grants related to assets; and
4. apply the main disclosure requirements.

KEY TERMS AND DEFINITIONS FOR THIS CHAPTER

In order to aid your understanding of the concepts and issues covered in this chapter, it is important to understand and be familiar with the following key terms and definitions. As you study this chapter, you should refer back to them.

Capital Expenditure This refers to expenditure to acquire **non-current assets** that are expected to provide future economic benefits (through their use in the business to generate income). Capital expenditure is recorded as an asset in the statement of financial position. Examples of capital expenditure are property, machinery and computers.

Depreciation This is the systematic allocation of the depreciable amount of an asset over its estimated useful economic life.

Government Assistance Action by government designed to provide an economic benefit specific to an entity or range of entities qualifying under certain criteria. Most assistance is in the form of grants to assist with **capital expenditure,** but some grants relate to **revenue expenditure**.

Government Grants Includes all forms of assistance from central government, government agencies and similar bodies, whether they are local, national or international.

Non-current Asset An asset acquired for use within the business, with a view to earning profits from its use. A non-current asset is not acquired for resale and includes property, plant and equipment. Non-current assets are usually held and used by a business for a number of years.

Revenue Expenditure This refers to those expenses incurred to acquire goods or services that are also essential in terms of the day-to-day operations of a business. However, the benefits that revenue expenditure gives are of a short-term nature and do not provide future economic benefits (i.e. the benefits are consumed over a short period of time, with less than one year being the period that is generally used). Revenue expenditure is recorded as an expense in the statement of profit or loss and other comprehensive income. Examples of revenue expenditure include office rent, heat and light, printing and stationery and repairs and maintenance.

16.1 INTRODUCTION

In broad terms, government grants are monies and other forms of assistance that do not need to be paid back as long as the recipient complies with the terms and conditions on which they were awarded. A grant proposal will typically resemble a business plan, showing how the grant will be used and how it will benefit the company, and even the wider community. Government grants are usually available to provide assistance to companies to start up a new business or expand an existing business. Traditionally, in the UK and in Ireland there has been a significant amount of 'government money' available for businesses to:

• help with **capital expenditure**;
• stimulate business growth through technological innovation;
• support the export of goods and services; and
• recruit and train new and current employees.

It is important to note that while grants may not have to be paid back, until the recipient complies with the conditions of receiving them there is a potential obligation to return all or part of the grant received.

Key to this Chapter

This chapter addresses the accounting treatment and disclosure of government grants in accordance with IAS 20 *Accounting for Government Grants and Disclosure of Government Assistance*. In the context of IAS 20, **government grants** include all forms of assistance from central government, government agencies and similar bodies, whether they are local, national or international. While most assistance is in the form of grants to help with **capital expenditure**, some grants relate to **revenue expenditure**.

IAS 20 distinguishes between grants related to income (revenue expenditure) and grants related to assets (capital expenditure). This chapter begins by explaining the relatively more straightforward accounting treatment for grants related to income before focusing on the application of the two allowable methods of accounting for grants related to assets (**Section 16.2**). Other guidance relating to government assistance (**Section 16.3**), together with the main IAS 20 disclosure requirements (**Section 16.4**), are also explained.

16.2 IAS 20 *ACCOUNTING FOR GOVERNMENT GRANTS AND DISCLOSURE OF GOVERNMENT ASSISTANCE*

IAS 20 *Accounting for Government Grants and Disclosure of Government Assistance* prescribes the accounting treatment for, and disclosure of, government grants and the disclosure of other forms of government assistance. It is important to remember IAS 20 does **not** deal with:
* government assistance that is provided in the form of benefits that are available in determining taxable income;
* government participation in the ownership of an entity; and
* government grants covered by IAS 41 *Agriculture* (see **Chapter 34**).

IAS 20 *Accounting for Government Grants and Disclosure of Government Assistance* requires that government grants should *not* be recognised in the statement of profit or loss and other comprehensive income *until* the conditions for receipt have been complied with and there is reasonable assurance that the grant will be received (prudence). Subject to this condition, the general principle is that all grants should be recognised in the statement of profit or loss and other comprehensive income to correspond with the expenditure to which they contribute *once* any conditions for the receipt of the grant have been met. Grants must *not* be credited directly to shareholders' interests (i.e. equity section of statement of financial position).

In broad terms, there are two types of grant:
* those related to income; and
* those related to assets.

Each of these is now discussed.

Grants Related to Income

Grants related to income cover the costs of certain categories of revenue expenditure (e.g. training costs). IAS 20 allows two possible methods for accounting for this type of grant:

Method 1 – under this method, the grant is presented as a credit in the statement of profit or loss and other comprehensive income, either separately or under a general heading, such as 'other income', by debiting bank and crediting income; or

Method 2 – under this method, the grant is deducted from the related expense by debiting bank and crediting the expense in the statement of profit or loss and other comprehensive income.

The application of these two methods is illustrated in **Example 16.1**.

EXAMPLE 16.1: GRANTS RELATED TO INCOME

In 2012 a company incurred training expenses of €500,000 and received a grant towards 10% of this cost.

Requirement How should the grant be accounted for under the two methods allowed in IAS 20?

Solution

	€
Method 1 – Showing Separately as Income:	
Gross Profit	X
plus: Other Income	50,000
	X
less: Expenses	
Training Expenses	(500,000)
Net Profit	X
Method 2 – Netting Against the Expense:	€
Gross Profit	X
less: Expenses	
Training Expenses (€500,000 – €50,000)	450,000
Net Profit	X

Whichever method is chosen, disclosure of the grant may be necessary for a proper understanding of the financial statements.

Grants Related to Assets

Grants related to assets cover the costs of certain categories of capital expenditure (e.g. property, plant and equipment, fixtures and fittings). The accounting treatment, in accordance with IAS 20, is to credit the amount of the grant to revenue in the statement of profit or loss and other comprehensive income over the useful life of the asset to which it relates by either:

Method 1 – under this method, the cost of the asset is reduced by the amount of the grant and the 'net' cost is depreciated; or

Method 2 – under this method, the amount of the grant is treated as a deferred credit in the statement of financial position, a portion of which is transferred to revenue in the statement of profit or loss and other comprehensive income annually over the life of the asset.

IAS 20 permits the use of either method, and these are illustrated in **Example 16.2** below.

EXAMPLE 16.2: GRANTS RELATED TO ASSETS

Company A purchases a machine for €120,000. It received a grant towards 20% of the cost of the machine. The machine has an expected life of three years, with an expected nil residual value. Profit for each year is €100,000 (before depreciation).

Requirement Account for the capital grant under the two methods allowed in IAS 20.

Solution
Method 1 – Reducing the Cost of Asset:

Statement of profit or loss and other comprehensive income	Year 1	Year 2	Year 3
	€	€	€
Profit before depreciation	100,000	100,000	100,000
Depreciation	*(32,000)	(32,000)	(32,000)
Profit	68,000	68,000	68,000

*(€120,000 − €24,000) ÷ 3

Statement of financial position	Year 1	Year 2	Year 3
	€	€	€
Non-current Asset at Cost (€120,000 − €24,000)	96,000	96,000	96,000
Accumulated Depreciation	32,000	64,000	96,000
Net Book Value	64,000	32,000	–

Method 2 – Treating the Grant as a Deferred Credit:

Statement of profit or loss and other comprehensive income	Year 1	Year 2	Year 3
	€	€	€
Profit before grant and depreciation	100,000	100,000	100,000
Depreciation (€120,000 ÷ 3 years)	(40,000)	(40,000)	(40,000)
Grant (€24,000 ÷ 3 years)	8,000	8,000	8,000
Profit	68,000	68,000	68,000

Statement of financial position	Year 1	Year 2	Year 3
	€	€	€
Non-current asset (cost)	120,000	120,000	120,000
Accumulated depreciation	40,000	80,000	120,000
Net book value	80,000	40,000	–
	€	€	€
Non-current liabilities			
Deferred income – Govt grants	8,000	0	0
Current liabilities			
Deferred income – Govt grants	8,000	8,000	Nil
Closing balance	16,000	8000	–

The main argument in favour of Method 1 (reducing the cost of the asset) is its simplicity. By crediting the grant to the cost of the asset, the resulting **depreciation** charge automatically

credits the amount of grant to revenue over the life of the asset. The arguments in favour of Method 2 (treating the grant as a deferred credit) are:
- it shows non-current assets at their true cost value;
- the depreciation charge is consistent with that for which no grant was received;
- netting off (i.e. Method 1) is potentially at odds with the offsetting principle (see **Chapter 2**); and
- it leads to better comparability from year to year and between companies.

Example 16.3 illustrates the accounting adjustments required if a decision is taken to change from Method 1 (Reducing the cost of the assets) to Method 2 (treating the grant as a deferred credit).

EXAMPLE 16.3: CHANGING METHOD

Cuisine Limited acquired certain items of equipment at a cost of €100,000 during the year ended 31 December 2012 for which the company received a government grant of 20%. The new accountant has recorded these items in property, plant and equipment at the net cost to Cuisine. The equipment has a useful life of four years.

Requirement Illustrate the alternative method for recording the equipment in accordance with IAS 20.

	Current Treatment €	Alternative Treatment €	Adjustment €
Equipment	80,000	100,000	20,000
Depreciation (1/4)	(20,000)	(25,000)	5,000
	60,000	75,000	

Grant received: 20% × €100,000 = €20,000

	DR €	CR €
DR Equipment (SFP)	20,000	
DR Depreciation (SPLOCI – P/L)	5,000	
CR Deferred income (SFP)		20,000
CR Equipment – accumulated depreciation (SFP)		5,000
DR Deferred income (SFP)	5,000	
CR SPLOCI – P/L		5,000

Repayment of Grants

A grant that becomes repayable should be treated as a revision of an accounting estimate. If the grant (relating to an expense item) has been fully credited to income, the repayment would normally be charged against profits in the year.

If the grant (relating to an expense item) has not been fully amortised, the repayment should first be offset against the unamortised balance, with any excess being charged as an expense.

The repayment of a grant relating to an asset should be accounted for by either increasing the carrying amount of the asset or reducing the deferred income balance. The cumulative additional depreciation that would have been recognised to date (in the absence of the grant) should be charged immediately as an expense.

Government Assistance

Government assistance, such as the provision of free technical or marketing advice, does not need to be reflected in the financial statements, but disclosure of the nature of the assistance may be necessary so that the financial statements are not misleading.

16.3 OTHER GUIDANCE

In some countries government assistance to entities can be aimed at the encouragement or long-term support of business activities either in certain regions or industry sectors. Often the conditions to receive such assistance may not be specifically related to the operating activities of the entity and therefore the issue is whether this type of assistance falls within the scope of IAS 20.

SIC 10 *Government Assistance – No Specific Relation to Operating Activities* states that this type of government assistance to entities does meet the definition of government grants in IAS 20, even if there are no conditions specifically relating to the operating activities of the entity other than the requirement to operate in certain regions or industry sectors. Such grants are therefore not credited directly to equity and should be accounted for as described above, in accordance with IAS 20, depending on whether they relate to income or assets.

16.4 DISCLOSURE

IAS 20 states that the following information should be disclosed, where applicable.
1. The accounting policy adopted, including the methods of presentation adopted in the financial statements for both grants related to income and grants related to assets. This is important as IAS 20 has two allowable methods of accounting for grants related to assets.
2. The nature and extent of government grants recognised in the financial statements and an indication of other forms of government assistance from which the entity has directly benefited; and
3. Unfulfilled conditions and other contingencies attaching to government assistance that has been recognised.

16.5 CONCLUSION

A government grant is not recognised until there is reasonable assurance that:
• the entity will comply with the conditions attached to it; and
• the grant will be received.

A government grant is recognised as income on a systematic basis over the periods necessary to match the grant income with the related costs that it is intended to compensate. If the related costs have already been incurred, the grant is recognised as income in the period in which it becomes receivable. A government grant is not credited directly to equity, with those related to assets being presented in the statement of financial position either as deferred income or as a deduction in determining the carrying amount of the asset.

A government grant that becomes repayable is accounted for as a revision to an accounting estimate (IAS 8 *Accounting Policies, Changes in Accounting Estimates and Errors* – see **Chapter 21**).

SUMMARY OF LEARNING OBJECTIVES

After having studied this chapter, you should be able to:

Learning Objective 1 Distinguish between grants related to income and grants related to assets.

In broad terms, there are two types of grant, those related to income and those related to assets. The former cover the costs of certain categories of revenue expenditure, while the latter cover the costs of certain categories of capital expenditure.

Learning Objective 2 Account for grants related to income.

IAS 20 allows two possible treatments: to present the grant as a credit in the statement of profit or loss and other comprehensive income; or deduct the grant from the related expense.

Learning Objective 3 Apply the two allowable methods of accounting for grants related to assets.

The accounting treatment is to credit the amount of the grant to revenue in the statement of profit or loss and other comprehensive income over the useful life of the asset to which it relates by either:
- reducing the cost of the asset by the amount of the grant and depreciating the 'net' cost; or
- treating the amount of the grant as a deferred credit in the statement of financial position, a portion of which is transferred to revenue in the statement of profit or loss and other comprehensive income annually over the life of the asset.

Learning Objective 4 Apply the main disclosure requirements.

The main disclosure requirements include: the accounting policy adopted, the nature and extent of government grants recognised in the financial statements, and details of any unfulfilled conditions and other contingencies attaching to government assistance that has been recognised.

QUESTIONS

Self-test Questions

1. How should grants related to income be accounted for?
2. What are the two allowable methods of accounting for grants related to assets?

3. What are the disclosure requirements listed in IAS 20?
4. When and how should potential liabilities to repay grants be accounted for?

Review Questions

(See **Appendix One** for Suggested Solutions to Review Questions.)

Question 16.1

Electronic Manufacturers Limited is installing a new production plant at a cost of €1 million, in respect of which government grants have been approved as follows:

       Capital costs: 40%
       Training costs: 100%

The company depreciated its plant and equipment on the basis of 20% on original cost. The directors are aware that the accounting treatment for grants is dealt with in IAS 20 *Accounting for Government Grants and Disclosure of Government Assistance*, and they have asked you to advise them on the accounting options available and the effect which they would have on the company's financial statements.

Requirement You are required to draft a report to the directors that:
(a) outlines the accounting treatment of the foregoing grants under IAS 20;
(b) recommends (with reasons) the treatment which you believe would be the most suitable in the case of Electronic Manufacturers Limited; and
(c) indicates the form of accounting policy or other notes which should be included in the annual financial statements of the company.

Question 16.2

An item of plant and equipment was purchased for €25,000 on 1 May 2012. It is expected that its useful life will be four years and that its residual value will be €1,000 at the end of its life. A government grant of €6,000 was received to assist with the cost of purchase, and a further grant of €500 was received to subsidise the wages of the skilled employees who will operate the plant and equipment during the first year of its use.

Requirement The Chief Accountant wishes to have your opinion as to how this should be reflected in the company's published financial statements for the year ended 30 April 2013. Your answer should include reference to appropriate International Accounting Standards.

Challenging Questions

(Suggested Solutions to Challenging Questions are available to lecturers.)

Question 16.1 *(Based on Chartered Accountants Ireland, P2 Summer 1997, Question 1)*

Blade Limited is a furniture manufacturing company. You are acting as auditor to the company and have been asked by the board of directors to indicate how the following item should be dealt with in the financial statements for the year ended 31 December 2012. During 2012, Blade Limited received a grant from the European Union of €500,000 towards the cost of a new machine that would be used in the production of wooden cabinets. The equipment has a useful economic life of five years.

Requirement Prepare a memorandum for the board of directors in which you explain how each of the above should be dealt with in the financial statements of Blade Limited for the year ended 31 December 2012.

Question 16.2 *(Based on Chartered Accountants Ireland, P2 Summer 2001, Question 4)*

ABC NEWSPAPER Limited has received a grant for €120,000 over four years in respect of providing employment in a deprived area.

Requirement Explain briefly the treatment of this grant in the company's financial statements.

Question 16.3 *(Based on Chartered Accountants Ireland, P2 Summer 2002, Question 2)*

Camcon Limited ('Camcon') operates a successful light engineering business with workshops in Belfast, Dublin and Galway. Camcon is to prepare accounts for the year ended 31 December 2012, and these have yet to be finalised and signed off. You have been provided with the following information regarding the company.

1. **Sale of Belfast Workshop** The Belfast workshop was sold to Eclipse plc on 1 November 2012 for €500,000, and the sale agreement stated that a further €80,000 relating to the sale of the Belfast workshop would be receivable by Camcon if a major new contract with Blackwell Bakery was to be secured. Negotiations for this new contract with Blackwell Bakery had commenced in late October 2012, but were still ongoing at 31 December 2012. At that time the directors of Camcon stated that the negotiations appeared to be going well and that it was probable that the contract would be signed within three months, but that it was still too early to suggest that the final outcome was virtually certain. In early February 2013, negotiations with Blackwell Bakery concluded successfully and a contract was subsequently agreed and signed on 12 February 2013. Camcon then received the extra €80,000 from the sale of the Belfast workshop from Eclipse plc on 20 February 2013.

2. **Irrecoverable Debts** On 11 January 2013 a major customer, Macbeth & Duncan, went into liquidation. In April 2013, Camcon received only 30% of the balance owing from Macbeth & Duncan as at 31 December 2012. No further monies are expected to be received from Macbeth & Duncan.

3. **Fire at Galway Workshop** A fire in the storeroom of the Galway workshop on 19 January 2013 destroyed €18,000 of inventory.

4. **Government Grants** During the year ended 31 December 2012, a package of government grant assistance was negotiated in respect of the Dublin and Galway workshops, the terms of which are as follows:

Grant Available	€
	Qualifying Expenditure
Graphic design for marketing brochure	1,000
Purchase of plant and machinery	5,000
Total	6,000

Scrutiny of the accounting records revealed the following:

(a) A marketing brochure was designed in November 2012 and final copies were printed and distributed in December 2012 at a cost of €10,000. The printer's invoice was received in November 2012. Due to a dispute over the colours used in the brochure, Camcon paid 75% of the printer's invoice in December 2012. The balance was paid in January 2013.

(b) New plant and machinery costing €20,000 was ordered from a German manufacturer in November 2012, but was only delivered, installed and paid for in February 2013. There have been no other additions to non-current assets since 1 January 2012.

(c) The company submitted a claim form in respect of these grants in March 2013 and lodged the resultant cheque for €6,000 in April 2013.

(d) The company's accounting policy is to depreciate plant and machinery over five years on a straight-line basis, charging a full year's depreciation in the year of purchase.

Requirement Write a letter to the financial controller of Camcon, outlining how each of the above matters should be treated in the company's accounts for the year ended 31 December 2012 and detailing, if appropriate, their financial effect and specific disclosure requirements.

Question 16.4

Kennedy Limited prepares its financial statements to 31 December each year and the following has to be resolved before the financial statements for the year ended 31 December 2012 can be finalised.

Issue:

During the year ended 31 December 2012, Kennedy Limited received a government grant to partially finance the purchase of plant and machinery that was required for an expansion of its manufacturing activities. Total expenditure of up to €1,500,000 on plant and machinery was approved by the relevant government department, with the grant being 60% of the total expenditure. The full amount of the grant was received by Kennedy Limited in 2012.

The conditions on which the grant was approved were that the expenditure would relate to the purchase of specific items of plant and machinery and that an additional 10 members of staff would be hired by Kennedy Limited. At 31 December 2012, Kennedy Limited had hired 12 additional staff and had purchased €1,200,000 of the specified plant and machinery. It is the intention of the directors, if cash flow permits, to purchase a further €600,000 worth of plant and machinery during the year ended 31 December 2013. It is company policy to depreciate plant and machinery at 8% per annum on a straight-line basis, and to provide a full year's depreciation in the year of purchase and none in the year of disposal.

The directors of Kennedy Limited believe that it is important to separately disclose grant assistance received in the financial statements. At 31 December 2012, the only accounting entry in relation to the grant received has been to record it as a separate item within deferred income in the company's draft financial statements for the year ended 31 December 2012.

Requirement Explain the correct accounting treatment and show any relevant journal entries for the government grant received by Kennedy Limited during the year ended 31 December 2012.

EMPLOYEE BENEFITS

LEARNING OBJECTIVES

Having studied this chapter, you should be able to:
1. define each of the main categories of employee benefits identified in IAS 19 *Employee Benefits*;
2. distinguish between a defined contribution pension plan and a defined benefit pension plan; and
3. apply and discuss the accounting treatment of defined contribution and defined benefit plans.

Note: the measurement of defined benefit obligations and the assessment of actuarial assumptions are outside the scope of this textbook.

KEY TERMS AND DEFINITIONS FOR THIS CHAPTER

In order to aid your understanding of the concepts and issues covered in this chapter, it is important to understand and be familiar with the following key terms and definitions. As you study this chapter, you should refer back to the key terms and definitions listed below. Other terms and definitions are also provided in the main body of the chapter.

Defined Benefit Pension Plans These are post-employment plans other than defined contribution plans. As the employer effectively agrees to a promised level of benefits, this exposes the enterprise to actuarial and investment risks.

Defined Contribution Pension Plans These are pension plans under which an enterprise pays fixed contributions into a separate entity (a fund) and has no legal or constructive obligation to pay further contributions if the fund does not hold sufficient assets to pay all employee benefits relating to employee service in the current and prior periods.

Employee Benefits This includes all forms of consideration given by an entity in exchange for services rendered by employees or for the termination of employment. Examples include wages, salaries, paid holidays, sick leave entitlement, bonuses, medical benefits, pension benefits and redundancy entitlements.

Fair Value This is the amount for which an asset could be exchanged between knowledgeable and willing parties in an arm's length transaction.

> **Post-employment Benefits Plans** Retirement benefits, such as pensions, and other post-employment benefits, such as post-employment medical care. The most common examples are defined contribution and defined benefit pension plans.
>
> **Short-term Benefits** All forms of consideration in exchange for service rendered by employees, including wages, salaries, holiday pay, sick leave, bonuses payable within 12 months of the reporting period and social security contributions payable in respect of employee benefits. They also include compensation in the form of financial assets, goods and services and equity instruments of the employer that are payable within 12 months after service is rendered.

17.1 INTRODUCTION

Most companies have both permanent and temporary employees, and employee costs constitute a significant portion of their business costs. While accounting for wages, salaries and other short-term benefits is, for the most part, relatively straightforward, post-employment benefits can be more troublesome. All benefits provided to employees, both short- and long-term, should be accounted for to ensure that an entity's financial statements reflect a liability when employees have worked in exchange for future benefits.

IAS 19 *Employee Benefits* prescribes the accounting for, and disclosure of, **employee benefits** by employers (that is, all forms of consideration given by an enterprise in exchange for service rendered by employees), *except* those to which IFRS 2 *Share-based Payment* applies (see **Chapter 34**). Furthermore, IAS 19 does *not* deal with reporting by employee benefit plans (see IAS 26 *Accounting and Reporting by Retirement Benefit Plans* – see **Chapter 34**).

The following are examples of employee benefits as defined by IAS 19 *Employee Benefits*:
- **short-term benefits** – wages, salaries, holiday pay, sick leave, bonuses payable within 12 months of the reporting period and social security contributions payable in respect of employee benefits;
- **post-employment benefits** – retirement benefits, pensions and post-retirement medical insurance;
- **long-term benefits** – long-term incentive plans, long-service awards and bonuses payable more than 12 months after the reporting period; and
- **termination benefits** – redundancy payments.

In addition to the benefits noted above, IAS 19 also applies to:
- profit-sharing plans;
- medical and life insurance benefits during employment;
- housing benefits;
- free or subsidised goods or services given to employees;
- post-employment life insurance benefits;
- long-service or sabbatical leave; and
- deferred compensation programmes (for example, pensions).

Accounting for post-employment benefits (i.e. retirement benefits, pensions and post-retirement medical insurance) is an important financial reporting issue. IAS 19 may not only have a significant impact on the statement of financial position and statement of profit or loss and other comprehensive income, it may also require the company to work closely with external specialists, such as actuaries, in order to assess potential pension deficits or surpluses. It has been suggested that many users of financial statements do not fully understand the information entities provide about post-employment benefits. Both users and preparers of financial statements have criticised the accounting requirements for failing to provide high-quality, transparent information about post-employment benefits. While recognising that accounting for post-employment benefits can be a complex area, this chapter seeks to explain the fundamental principles in as straightforward a manner as possible.

Key to this Chapter

It is important to remember that IAS 19 requires an entity to recognise a liability in the statement of financial position when an employee has provided a service in exchange for employee benefits to be paid in the future and an expense in the statement of profit or loss and other comprehensive income when the economic benefits arising from the service provided in exchange for the employee benefits are consumed. In simple terms, the principle underlying IAS 19 is that the cost of providing employee benefits should be recognised in the period in which the benefit is earned by the employee, rather than when it is paid or payable. In this chapter, employee benefits are classified and explained under the following headings in **Section 17.2**: short-term employee benefits; post-employment benefit plans; other long-term benefits; and termination benefits.

17.2 IAS 19 *EMPLOYEE BENEFITS*

IAS 19 *Employee Benefits*, which was originally issued in February 1998, was revised in June 2011, with the changes being applicable to annual reporting periods beginning on or after 1 January 2013. Early adoption is permitted. While the changes impact primarily on the accounting treatment of defined benefit pension plans (see **Post-employment Benefit Plans** below), the amendments also affect (for example) the classification of short-term employee benefits and the timing of the recognition of termination benefits. The accounting treatment for employee benefits outlined in this chapter is based on the revised IAS 19.

As stated above, in this section we will examine the accounting treatment of:
- short-term employee benefits (for example, salaries, wages, paid annual leave, sick leave entitlement and profit-sharing and bonus payments expected to be settled within 12 months of the period during which the service is provided);
- post-employment benefit plans (for example, defined contribution and benefit plans);
- other long-term benefits (for example, long-term paid sabbatical leave and disability benefits); and
- termination benefits (for example, redundancy payments).

While each of these is now explained in turn, greatest attention is devoted to post-employment benefit plans (**defined contribution pension plans** and **defined benefit pension plans**) as these are the most complicated and also tend to dominate examination questions on employee benefits.

Short-term Employee Benefits

For short-term employee benefits (i.e. those payable within 12 months after service is rendered, such as wages, paid vacation and sick leave, bonuses, and non-monetary benefits such as medical care and housing), the undiscounted amount of the benefits expected to be paid in respect of service rendered by employees in a period should be recognised in that period on an accruals basis.

For accumulating paid absences (for example, holiday leave entitlement), the expected cost should be recognised as the employees render service that increases their entitlement. This is illustrated in **Example 17.1**.

EXAMPLE 17.1: PAID ANNUAL LEAVE ENTITLEMENT

Belfast Limited has 1,000 employees and each employee is entitled to 30 days' paid annual leave each year. The holiday year commences on 1 July each year and, at the company's financial year-end of 31 December 2012, employees had on average each taken 10 days leave in the six months to 31 December 2012.

Requirement Assuming an annual salary of €30,000 and a working year of 250 days, calculate the provision to be made in the financial statements at 31 December 2012.

Solution

As employees are entitled to holiday leave of 15 days each at 31 December 2012 (6/12 months × 30 days), it is necessary to accrue for an additional 5 days (15 days − 10 days).

1,000 employees × 5 days × €120 per day = €600,000 (before any associated employer-related taxes).

The expected cost of short-term, non-accumulating, compensated absences (for example, maternity pay) should be recognised where the absences occur.

As noted previously, profit-sharing and bonus payments that are expected to be settled within 12 months of the period in which the service is provided fall within the definition of short-term employee benefits. In such cases, an enterprise should recognise the expected cost of profit-sharing and bonus payments when, and only when, it has a legal or constructive obligation to make such payments as a result of past events and a reliable estimate of the expected cost can be made (i.e. in accordance with IAS 37 *Provisions, Contingent Liabilities and Contingent Assets* – **Chapter 14**). This is illustrated in **Example 17.2**.

EXAMPLE 17.2: PROFIT-SHARING PLAN

Derry Limited, a company that prepares its financial statements to 31 December each year, agreed a profit-sharing plan with its employees on 1 January 2012. Under the terms of the plan, the company agreed to pay 10% of its profit after tax on a pro rata basis to staff who had been employed throughout the whole year. While on 1 January 2012 Derry Limited had 500 employees, only 300 of these employees were still employed by the company on 31 December 2012. Derry Limit's profit after tax for year ended 31 December 2012 was €1,000,000.

Requirement How should Derry Limited recognise the profit-sharing plan at 31 December 2012?

Solution

Derry Limited should recognise a liability and an expense of €60,000 (i.e. 10% × 60% employees remaining × €1,000,000).

Post-employment Benefit Plans

The most common type of post-employment benefit is a pension. As IAS 19 requires the cost of providing employee benefits to be recognised in the period in which the benefits are earned, the accounting treatment for a post-employment benefit plan will be determined according to whether the plan is a *defined contribution* or a *defined benefit* plan. Each of these types of pension plan is explained further below.

Defined Contribution Pension Plans

Under defined contribution pension plans, the level of benefits depends on the value of contributions paid in by each member and the investment performance achieved on those contributions. Therefore, the employer's liability is limited to the contributions it has agreed to pay and it has no legal or constructive obligation (see IAS 37 *Provisions, Contingent Liabilities and Contingent Assets* – **Chapter 14**) to pay further contributions if the fund does not have sufficient assets to pay employee benefits relating to employee service in the current and prior periods.

Therefore, for defined contribution plans, the cost to be recognised in the period is the contribution *payable* (not paid) in exchange for service rendered by employees during the period. For defined contribution plans the contribution *payable* (not paid) to the fund is expensed and the pension liability equals any unpaid contributions for past service. If contributions to a defined contribution plan do not fall due within 12 months after the end of the period in which the employee renders the service, they should be discounted to their present value.

EXAMPLE 17.3: DEFINED CONTRIBUTION PENSION PLANS

Bryson Limited operates a defined contribution pension plan for its employees. The company's contribution rate to the pension fund is 5% of gross salaries. During the year ended 31 December 2012, gross salaries amounted to €6,000,000. For convenience, a regular amount of €20,000 was transferred monthly into the pension fund by the company, with the balance due being paid by the company in January 2013.

Requirement Calculate the amounts to be included in the statement of profit or loss and other comprehensive income of Bryson Limited for the year ended 31 December 2012 and the statement of financial position as at that date.

Solution

The statement of profit or loss and other comprehensive income expense for the year ended 31 December 2012 is:

5% × €6,000,000 = €300,000. This is an expense in arriving at profit or loss unless it (or part thereof) may be capitalised as part of the cost of an asset where required or permitted by another accounting standard (for example, IAS 2 *Inventories* or IAS 16 *Property, Plant and Equipment*).

As payments of €240,000 (12 months × €20,000) were made during the year ended 31 December 2012 by Bryson Limited, an accrual of €60,000 is required in the statement of financial position at 31 December 2012.

While this is due to be paid in January 2013, if it was not due to be paid within 12 months of the end of the reporting period, the outstanding contributions should be discounted to their present values.

Actuarial and investment risks of defined contribution plans are assumed either by the employee or the third party. Pension plans not defined as defined contribution plans are classed as defined benefit plans. If an employer is unable to show that all actuarial and invest-ment risk has been transferred to another party and that its obligations are limited to contri-butions made during the period, then a pension plan is defined benefit.

In other words, under IAS 19, when a pension plan is *not* a defined contribution plan, it is by definition a defined benefit plan.

Defined Benefit Pension Plans

As stated above, a defined benefit plan is a post-employment benefit plan other than a defined contribution plan. For defined benefit pension plans, the pension plan rules (i.e. terms and conditions) specify the benefits to be paid and they are financed accordingly. The benefits are typically based on factors such as age, length of service and compensation. The employer retains the actuarial and investment risks of the plan.

For example, under the terms of a particular pension plan, a company contributes 6% of an employee's salary. The employee is guaranteed a return of the contributions plus interest of 4% a year. The plan would be classified as a defined benefit plan as the employer has guar-anteed a fixed rate of return and, as a result, carries the investment risk.

With respect to the accounting treatment of defined benefit pension plans, the key elements to be considered are the:
- statement of financial position;
- current service cost;
- past service cost;
- remeasurements; and
- statement of profit or loss and other comprehensive income.

Each of these elements is now explained.

Statement of Financial Position (Pension Plan Assets and Liabilities)   In simple terms, a pension plan will have 'assets' (i.e. money paid into the scheme and invested) and 'liabili-ties' (i.e. obligations under the scheme). IAS 19 approaches accounting for defined benefit plans from a statement of financial position perspective by describing how the pension plan assets and liabilities should be recognised and measured in the financial statements. To achieve this, the plan assets and liabilities are measured at each reporting date on an actuarial basis and discounted to present value. An actuary will make assumptions about items such as the discount rate, future salaries, future returns and medical costs.

In broad terms, the amount recognised in the statement of financial position, which could be either a net asset or a net liability, will arise as follows:

1. Opening statement of financial position – this will show a net defined benefit pension asset or obligation.
2. Current and past service costs – these increase the liability, with the corresponding expense being recognised in the statement of profit or loss and other comprehensive income – profit or loss (SPLOCI–P/L). As explained below (see **Past Service Cost**), past service costs are recognised in the period of the plan amendment.
3. Net interest expense/income – a discount rate, based on market yields at the end of the reporting period on high-quality corporate bonds (or government bonds when no deep market for corporate bonds exists), is applied to the defined benefit pension obligation at the beginning of the reporting period. The same interest rate is also applied to the carrying value of the defined benefit pension plan assets at the beginning of the reporting period to identify an amount of interest income (if any). The net interest expense or income is recognised in the SPLOCI–P/L.
4. Remeasurement – this is the net difference between the actual return on the defined benefit pension plan assets and obligations and the expected (see **3**. above). It is recognised through other comprehensive income (OCI).
5. Closing statement of financial position – this will show either a net defined benefit pension asset or obligation, depending upon each of the above.

Items **2.**, **3**. and **4**. are addressed in more detail below.

Over the life of the plan, changes in benefits under the plan will result in increases or decreases in the enterprise's obligation. Plan assets and plan liabilities from the different plans are normally presented separately in the statement of financial position.

Pension plan assets (i.e. money paid into the plan and invested in, for example, shares and/ or property) are measured at **fair value**, which is normally market value. Fair value can be estimated by discounting expected future cash flows. The rate used to discount estimated cash flows should be determined by reference to market yields at the reporting date on high-quality corporate bonds. IAS 19 is not specific on what it considers to be a high-quality bond and, therefore, this can lead to variation in the discount rates used. Valuations of plan assets should be carried out with sufficient regularity so that the amounts recognised in the financial statements do not differ materially from those that would be determined at the reporting date. A volatile economic environment will require frequent valuations – at least annually. The assumptions used for the purposes of such valuations should be unbiased and mutually compatible, and will include demographic assumptions, such as mortality, turnover and retirement age, and financial assumptions, such as discount rates, salary and benefit levels.

The pension plan liability (which is also referred to as the *defined benefit obligation*) will include both legal obligations and any constructive obligation arising from the employer's usual business practices, such as an established pattern of past practice (see IAS 37 *Provisions, Contingent Liabilities and Contingent Assets* – **Chapter 14**). IAS 19 encourages the involvement of a qualified actuary in measuring defined benefit obligations, and while IAS 19 does not require an annual actuarial valuation of the defined benefit obligation, the employer is required to determine the *present value of the defined benefit obligation*. IAS 19 states that the Projected Unit Credit Method should be used to determine the present value of the defined benefit obligation, the related *current service cost* (see below) and *past service cost* (see below). The **Projected Unit Credit Method** looks at each period of service that gives rise to additional units of benefit and measures each unit separately to build up the final obligation (see **Note** below). The whole of the post-employment benefit obligation is then discounted.

Note: from an examination perspective, due to its specialised nature, students would not be required to calculate the Projected Unit Credit Method, but simply to apply the figures given.

Current Service Cost   This is the increase in the present value of the defined benefit obligation that occurs as a result of employee service in the current period. In simple terms, this is the amount of pension entitlement that employees have earned in the accounting period. Therefore, it will increase the pension liability in the statement of financial position and be expensed in the statement of profit or loss and other comprehensive income.

Past Service Cost   This is the term used to describe the change in the obligation for employee service in prior periods arising as a result of changes to plan arrangements in the current period. Past service costs change the present value of the pension obligation and they arise from amendments to the terms and conditions of a defined benefit plan. For example, additional costs arise where new benefits are introduced or existing benefits improved, while costs are reduced where existing benefits are decreased. Under the revised IAS 19 (2011), past service costs should be recognised in the period of the plan amendment; unvested benefits are no longer spread over future periods. The pension liability in the statement of financial position will increase or decrease and the statement of profit or loss and other comprehensive income will be affected accordingly. This is illustrated in **Example 17.4**.

EXAMPLE 17.4: PAST SERVICE COSTS

Cork Limited, a company that prepares its financial statements to 31 December each year, operates a defined benefit pension plan that provides company employees with a pension of 3% of their final salary for each year of service with the company. The benefit becomes vested after five years' service. On 1 January 2012 Cork Limited improved the terms to 4% of final salary for each year of service, starting from 1 January 2009. At the date of improvement (1 January 2012) the present value of the additional benefits for service was:

Employees with less than five years of service on 1 January 2012,
with the average period until vesting being three years: €300,000
Employees with more than five years' service on 1 January 2012:   €500,000

Based on the information provided, the change in terms would result in a charge (expense) in the 2012 statement of profit or loss and other comprehensive income of Cork Limited of €800,000.

Remeasurements   As explained above, the fair value and present value of pension plan assets and liabilities respectively are estimated using actuarial assumptions. These assumptions (for example, about employee turnover, mortality, future increases in salaries and medical costs) are required in order to calculate the likely future cost of post-employment benefits and they can change from period to period. As a consequence, they influence the cost of the employee benefits. Since it is very unlikely that the actual outcome will match the estimated outcome, this gives rise to actuarial gains and losses.

As explained above with respect to the **Statement of Financial Position**, IAS 19 requires that the changes between the opening and closing plan assets and liabilities be disaggregated into three components: current and past service cost; net interest income/expense, and remeasurements. Service cost and net interest income/expense are presented in arriving at profit or loss. As Patricia McConnell writes, remeasurements are the remaining changes in the plan assets and liabilities and are included in other comprehensive income. "They represent period-to-period fluctuations in the long-term value of the net pension asset or liability. Remeasurements include actuarial gains and losses and the net return on plan assets." The net return on plan assets is calculated as the actual return on plan assets less the amount of imputed interest income on the plan assets that is included in net interest income/expense. "Unlike some components of OCI, pension remeasurements should never be recycled to profit or loss in subsequent periods."[1]

Prior to the revision of IAS 19 in June 2011, IAS 19 permitted choices on how to account for actuarial gains and losses, including immediate recognition in profit or loss and the 'corridor approach' which resulted in the deferral of gains and losses. However, delays in the recognition of gains and losses can give rise to misleading figures in the statement of financial position and multiple options for recognising gains and losses can lead to poor comparability. Consequently, the revised IAS 19 eliminates the previous choices and stipulates that all gains and losses on pension remeasurements are recognised immediately through 'other comprehensive income'. It is important to note that as actuarial gains and losses are no longer deferred using the corridor approach or recognised in profit or loss, this is likely to increase volatility in the statement of financial position and other comprehensive income.

Statement of Profit or Loss and Other Comprehensive Income As indicated above, the figure to be recognised in arriving at profit or loss is made up of the following components:
• current and past service costs; and
• net interest expense/income.

The net interest expense/income on the net pension liability or asset represents the financing cost/income of deferring payment or pre-paying employee services. It is calculated by multiplying the net pension liability or the net pension asset at the start of the period by the discount rate used to measure the pension liability (that is, the market yield at the end of the period on high quality corporate bonds.). In other words, the net interest income or expense will be the difference between the interest expense on the pension liability, calculated using its discount rate, and interest income imputed on the plan assets using the same rate. If the interest on the pension liability exceeds the imputed interest on the plan assets, it will be net interest expense. If the imputed interest on the plan assets exceeds the interest on the pension liability, it will be net interest income.

---

[1] McConnell, P "Benefits of the IASB's Recent Revisions to Pension Accounting" (2011) August, www.ifrs.org/investor-resources/2011-perspectives/August-2011/

Why is the net interest expense/income calculated using the 'same' discount rate?

While it is perhaps understandable why the rate used to discount the pension liability is also used to calculate interest expense on the pension liability, it is less apparent why this same rate is used to impute a return on plan assets. This is done on the basis that using the discount rate for both, rather than a different rate for the expected return on plan assets, avoids the problems that have been associated with the use of an expected return in the past. As McConnell writes, for example, it will improve comparability and it may also remove the (possible) temptation (or appearance) for management to use over-optimistic assumptions for the expected return on plan assets. McConnell observes that:

"Like the previous version of IAS 19, the revised IAS 19 does not specify where the individual components of net pension cost should be displayed, beyond specifying that service cost and net interest income or expense should go to profit or loss, while remeasurements [go through other comprehensive income] *unless* another IFRS permits or requires their inclusion in the cost of an asset. For example, service cost, or some portion of it, may qualify for capitalisation as a cost of inventory under IAS 2 *Inventories*. Consequently, a portion may remain in inventory at period end, while a portion may be in cost of sales. The portion, if any, that did not qualify for capitalisation should be included in arriving at profit or loss as well. It should be included in the same line item in which the company's related compensation expenses are presented" (for example, within selling expenses or administrative costs).

Note:

Remember, remeasurements are included in other comprehensive income.

The accounting treatment of defined benefit pension plans is illustrated in **Examples 17.5** and **17.6**. Please read through each carefully as they combine the various elements discussed above in relation to defined benefit pension plans.

Example 17.5: Accounting for Defined Benefit Pension Plans (1)

The following information is provided with respect to the defined benefit pension plan of Rush Limited for the year ended 31 December 2012.

	€000
Fair value of plan assets at 1 January 2012	1,800
Present value of obligation at 1 January 2012	2,000
Service cost	250
Benefits paid	300
Contributions paid	200
Fair value of plan assets at 31 December 2012	2,200
Present value of obligation at 31 December 2012	2,800

The yield on blue chip corporate bonds at 1 January 2012 was 10% and all the benefits and contributions were paid on 31 December 2012.

Requirement Show how the defined benefit pension plan would be accounted for in the financial statements of Rush Limited for the year ended 31 December 2012.

Solution

			Asset €000	Obligation €000	SPLOCI – P/L €000	SPLOCI – OCI €000
At 1 January 2012	Opening Balances – A & O		1,800	2,000		
	Debit	Credit				
Service cost	SPLOCI – P/L	Obligation		250	(250)	
Benefits paid	Obligation	Asset	(300)	(300)		
Contributions paid	Asset	Bank	200			
Net interest expense:						
		P/L – finance				
Asset	Asset	cost	180		180	
	P/L – finance					
Obligation	cost	Obligation	___	200	(200)	
			1,880	2,150		
Remeasurement – fair value gain on asset	Asset	OCI	320			320
Remeasurement – actuarial loss on obligation	OCI	Obligation	___	650	___	(650)
At 31 December 2012	Closing Balances – A & O		2,200	2,800	(270)	(330)

	€000
The net obligation in the statement of financial position at 31 December 2012 is:	600

Before dealing with **Example 17.6**, the accounting treatment of defined benefit pension plans (which is explained above in detail) in the statement of financial position and statement of profit or loss and other comprehensive income is summarised.

As explained above, the amount recognised in the statement of financial position in respect of a defined benefit pension plan will be as follows:
(i)   Opening statement of financial position – this will show a net defined benefit pension asset or obligation.
(ii) Current and past service costs – these increase the liability, with the corresponding expense being recognised in the SPLOCI–P/L. Past service costs are recognised in the period of the plan amendment.
(iii) Net interest expense/income – a discount rate, based on market yields at the end of the reporting period on high-quality corporate bonds (or government bonds when no deep market for corporate bonds exists), is applied to the defined benefit pension obligation at the beginning of the reporting period. The same interest rate is also applied to the carrying value of the defined benefit pension plan assets at the beginning of the reporting period to identify an amount of interest income (if any). The net interest expense or income is recognised in the SPLOCI–P/L.

(iv) Remeasurement – this is the net difference between the actual return on the defined benefit pension plan assets and obligations and the expected (see (iii) above). It is recognised through other comprehensive income (OCI).

(v) Closing statement of financial position – this will show either a net defined benefit pension asset or obligation, depending on each of the above.

As indicated above, the figure to be recognised in arriving at profit or loss is made up of the following components:
- current and past service costs; and
- net interest expense/income.

Remeasurements are the remaining changes in the plan assets and liabilities and are included in other comprehensive income.

Now read **Example 17.6**.

EXAMPLE 17.6: ACCOUNTING FOR DEFINED BENEFIT PENSION PLANS (2)

At 31 December 2011 the present value of the defined benefit obligation and the fair value of the pension plan's assets were each €800,000. The following information relates to the company's defined benefit pension plan during the year ended 31 December 2012:
  (i) the present value of the current service cost for the year ended 31 December 2012 was €160,000;
 (ii) contributions of €150,000 were paid into the plan;
(iii) the pension plan paid out benefits of €75,000; and
(iv) the present value of the pension plan's obligations and the fair value of the plan's assets were €1,100,000 and €1,050,000, respectively, at 31 December 2012. The yield on blue chip corporate bonds at 1 January 2012 was 10% and all the benefits and contributions were paid on 31 December 2012.

Requirement With respect to the financial statements for the year ended 31 December 2012, calculate the defined benefit pension plan:
(a) asset or liability;
(b) expense; and
(c) explain the movement in the defined benefit plan liability between 31 December 2011 and 31 December 2012.

Solution

(a)

	€
Fair value of plan assets at 31 December 2012	1,050,000
Present value of plan obligation at 31 December 2012	(1,100,000)
Net pension plan liability	(50,000)

(b)

	€
The defined benefit expense is:	
Present value of current service cost for 2012	160,000
Interest cost	160,000

(c)

The net opening position of 'nil' has become a liability of €50,000. This has arisen because the contributions (€150,000) are less than the expense (€160,000), and because of the net remeasurement loss of € 40,000 (which is taken through OCI).

WORKINGS

			Asset	Obligation	SPLOCI – P/L	SPLOCI – OCI
			€000	€000	€000	€000
At 1 January 2012	Opening Balances – A & O		800	800		
	Debit	Credit				
Service cost	SPLOCI – P/L	Obligation		160	(160)	
Benefits paid	Obligation	Asset	(75)	(75)		
Contributions paid	Asset	Bank	150			
Net interest expense:						
Asset	Asset	P/L – finance cost	80		80	
Obligation	P/L – finance cost	Obligation		80	(80)	
			955	965		
Remeasurement – fair value gain on asset	Asset	OCI	95			95
Remeasurement – actuarial loss on obligation	OCI	Obligation		135		(135)
At 31 December 2012	Closing Balances – A & O		1050	1,100	(160)	(40)

Other Long-term Benefits

Other long-term benefits include long-service leave, sabbatical leave, disability benefits and also profit-sharing or bonuses if paid more than 12 months after the end of the accounting period.

IAS 19 requires such benefits to be accounted for as follows:
• the asset that is available to settle the obligation should be measured at fair value;
• the obligation should be measured at the present value of expected outflow; and
• the expense to be recognised in the SPLOCI–P/L should comprise the service cost, the net interest expense/income and any re-measurements. There is no recognition of any remeasurements through other comprehensive income.

Consequently, the accounting treatment for other long-term benefits is similar to that for defined benefit pension plans, albeit that, in practice, it is a little more straightforward.

Termination Benefits

Termination benefits are a separate category of employee benefits because the event that gives rise to the entity's obligation is 'termination' rather than 'service'. They typically include lump sum payments on either compulsory or voluntary redundancy; examples are redundancy payments and salary until the end of a period in which the employee renders no further service. As any benefit that has a future-service obligation is not a termination benefit, this may reduce the number of arrangements that meet the definition of termination benefits.

IAS 19 specifies that termination benefits should be recognised when, and only when, the entity is demonstrably committed to either:
- terminating the employment of an employee or group of employees before the normal retirement date; or
- providing termination benefits as a result of an offer made in order to encourage voluntary redundancy.

An entity is demonstrably committed to a termination when, and only when, it has a detailed formal plan for the termination and it is unlikely to be withdrawn. Consequently, this might delay the recognition of voluntary termination benefits. Where termination benefits fall due after more than 12 months after the reporting date, they should be discounted to present value.

17.3 CONCLUSION

The objective of IAS 19 is to prescribe the accounting and disclosure for employee benefits and recognise when a liability arises for an entity in respect of service of an employee, which will result in benefits payable in the future. The main employee benefits that are addressed in IAS 19 are:
- short-term employee benefits;
- post-employment benefit plans;
- other long-term benefits; and
- termination benefits.

While each of these is explained in **Section 17.2**, the focus is on post-employment benefit plans (defined contribution and, in particular, defined benefit pension plans) as these are the most complicated and also tend to dominate examination questions on employee benefits. While pro-forma layouts and summaries are no substitute for detailed studying and understanding, the pro-forma layout for accounting for defined benefit pension plans provided in **Figure 17.1** may be useful.

FIGURE 17.1: ACCOUNTING FOR DEFINED BENEFIT PENSION PLANS
(Please note that this is only a 'rough guide' and the figures are for illustration purposes only.)

Pension Obligation	€
Present value of obligation at start of period	800,000
Interest cost at (say) 10%* (DR SPLOCI – P/L and CR Plan obligation (PO))	80,000
Present value of service cost for period (DR SPLOCI – P/L and CR PO)	160,000
Benefits paid during period (DR PO and CR Plan asset (PA))	(75,000)
	965,000
Present value of obligation at end of period	1,100,000
Remeasurement – actuarial loss on obligation	135,000

Plan Assets

	€
Fair value of plan assets at start of year	700,000
Return on plan assets* (DR PA and CR SPLOCI – P/L)	70,000
Contributions (DR PA and CR Bank)	200,000
Benefits paid during period (DR PO and CR PA)	(75,000)
	895,000
Fair value of plan assets at end of year	1,050,000
Remeasurement – fair value gain on asset	155,000

Statement of Financial Position

	€
Fair value of scheme assets at end of period (see PA)	1,050,000
Present value of scheme obligation at end of period (see PO)	(1,100,000)
Net pension scheme liability	(50,000)

Statement of Profit or Loss and Other Comprehensive Income

	€
Present value of current service cost for period	160,000
Net interest cost (€80,000 – €70,000)	10,000
	170,000

Remeasurements (through OCI)

	€
PA gain	155,000
PO Loss	(135,000)
	20,000

* The yield on blue chip corporate bonds at start of period.

Summary of Learning Objectives

After having studied this chapter, you should be able to:

Learning Objective 1 Define each of the main categories of employee benefits identified in IAS 19 *Employee Benefits*.

These include: short-term benefits (wages, salaries, holiday pay and sick leave); long-term benefits (long-term incentive plans and long-service awards); termination benefits (redundancy); and post-employment benefits (retirement benefits, pensions and post-retirement medical insurance).

Learning Objective 2 Distinguish between a defined contribution pension plan and a defined benefit pension plan.

Under defined contribution pension plans, the level of benefits depends on the value of contributions paid in by each member and the investment performance achieved on those contributions. Therefore, the employer's liability is limited to the contributions it has agreed to pay. For defined benefit pension plans the rules specify the benefits to be paid and they are financed accordingly, with the benefits being typically based on such factors as age, length of service and compensation.

Learning Objective 3 Apply and discuss the accounting treatment of defined contribution and defined benefit plans.

See **Section 17.2**.

QUESTIONS

Self-test Questions

1. List and briefly explain the four main categories of employee benefits identified by IAS 19.
2. Define the following key terms:
   (a) defined contribution pension plan;
   (b) defined benefit pension plan;
   (c) current service cost;
   (d) past service cost;
   (e) net interest expense / income; and
   (f) remeasurement.

Review Questions

(See **Appendix One** for Suggested Solutions to Review Questions.)

Question 17.1

Floyd Limited prepares its financial statements to 31 December each year. The company has 250 employees, each of whom is entitled to 30 days paid annual leave. The company's holiday year commences on 1 April and at 31 December 2012 the company's employees have, on average, each taken 15 days annual leave during the current financial year.

Requirement Assuming an average employee cost of €30,000 per annum and a five-day working week, calculate the provision for outstanding holiday entitlements that should be recognised in the financial statements of Floyd Limited for the year ended 31 December 2012 in respect of the current holiday year.

Question 17.2

The following information is provided with respect to the defined benefit pension plan of Christy Limited for the year ended 31 December 2012.

	€000
Fair value of plan assets at 1 January 2012	3,000
Present value of obligation at 1 January 2012	3,700
Current service cost	480
Benefits paid	575
Contributions paid	410
Fair value of plan assets at 31 December 2012	4,380
Present value of obligation at 31 December 2012	5,575

The yield on blue chip corporate bonds at 1 January 2012 was 5% and all the benefits and contributions were paid on 31 December 2012.

On 1 January 2012 the pension plan was amended to provide additional benefits, with effect from that date. The present value of the additional benefits at 1 January 2012 amounted to €350,000.

Requirement Show how the defined benefit pension plan would be accounted for in the financial statements of Rush Limited for the year ended 31 December 2012.

Challenging Questions

(Suggested Solutions to Challenging Questions are available to lecturers.)

Question 17.1

APF plc prepares its financial statements to 31 December each year. The company has a defined benefit pension plan. On 31 December 2011 the present value of the defined benefit obligation was €22,500,000 and the fair value of the plan's assets was €21,900,000. The following information is available in relation to the year ended 31 December 2012:
(a) the yield on blue chip corporate bonds at 1 January 2012 was 8%;
(b) APF plc made contributions of €3,800,000 into the plan, with employees contributing a further €1,500,000;
(c) the plan paid out benefits of €1,900,000 to past employees;
(d) the present value of the current service cost for the year ended 31 December 2012, before deducting employee contributions, was €3,700,000; and
(e) at 31 December 2012 the present value of the defined benefit obligation was €27,400,000 and the fair value of plan assets was €28,200,000.

Requirement With respect to the financial statements for the year ended 31 December 2012, calculate the:
(a) defined benefit expense; and
(b) defined benefit liability or asset.

Question 17.2 (Based on Chartered Accountants Ireland, CAP 2 Summer 2010, Question 4)

> **Please note** that this question covers a number of related issues, some of which are covered more fully in other chapters. Consequently, before attempting this question, you should also study **Chapter 13**.

RODENT Limited ("RODENT"), a small Irish company that prepares its financial statements to 31 December each year, is engaged in medical research.

RODENT
STATEMENT OF FINANCIAL POSITION
as at 31 December 2012

	Notes	Book Value €000	Tax Value €000
ASSETS			
Non-current Assets			
Property, plant and equipment	1	1,200	800
Capitalised development costs	2	4,100	-
Current Assets			
Cash in hand and at bank		80	80
		5,380	880
EQUITY AND LIABILITIES			
Equity Attributable to Owners			
€1 ordinary shares		100	100
Retained earnings		2,580	80
Non-current Liabilities			
Government grant	3	2,000	-
Deferred tax	4	680	680
Defined benefit pension scheme	5	-	-
Current Liabilities			
Payables and accruals		20	20
		5,380	880

Additional Information

1. The directors of RODENT have decided to record the company's property at market value rather than depreciated historic cost, with effect from 31 December 2012. The market value of the property, which equates to fair value, on this date is €500,000 higher than the depreciated historical cost figure of €1,200,000 recorded in the statement of financial position at 31 December 2012.
2. For accounting purposes, development costs are capitalised and amortised over future periods in accordance with IAS 38 *Intangible Assets*. These costs are allowable for tax purposes in the period incurred.
3. The government grant, which relates to research and development activities, is non-taxable.
4. This amount represents the deferred taxation liability at 31 December **2011**. The taxation rate has been 25% for a number of years and it is not expected to change.

5. This represents the balance at 31 December **2011** when the present value of the defined benefit obligation and the fair value of the scheme's assets were each €800,000. Pension costs are charged in arriving at accounting profit when the service is provided by the employees and deducted in arriving at taxable profit when contributions or retirement benefits are actually paid. The following information relates to the company's defined benefit scheme during the year ended 31 December 2012:

  (i) the present value of the current service cost for the year ended 31 December 2012 was €160,000 before deducting employee contributions;

  (ii) contributions paid into the scheme amounted to €150,000;

  (iii) the scheme paid out benefits of €75,000;

  (iv) the yield on blue chip corporate bonds at 1 January 2012 was 10%; and

  (v) the present value of the pension scheme obligations and the fair value of the scheme's assets were €1,100,000 and €1,050,000 respectively at 31 December 2012.

Requirement With respect to the financial statements of RODENT for the year ended 31 December 2012:

(a) Calculate the defined benefit pension scheme:

  (i) asset or liability; and

  (ii) expense.

(b) Calculate the deferred taxation expense and the deferred taxation asset or liability.

Present Value Factors:

	1%	2%	3%	4%	5%
4 years	0.9610	0.9238	0.8885	0.8548	0.8227
	6%	7%	8%	9%	10%
4 years	0.7921	0.7629	0.7350	0.7084	0.6830

DISTRIBUTION OF PROFITS AND ASSETS

LEARNING OBJECTIVES

Having studied this chapter on the distribution of profits and assets, you should understand:
1. the general rule governing the distribution of profits;
2. the distinction between public and private companies as regards distributable profits;
3. the distinction between realised and unrealised profits; and
4. how to deal with revaluation surpluses and deficits.

KEY TERMS AND DEFINITIONS FOR THIS CHAPTER

In order to aid your understanding of the concepts and issues covered in this chapter, it is important to understand and be familiar with the following key terms and definitions. As you study this chapter, you should refer back to them.

Distributable Profits These consist of accumulated realised profits less accumulated realised losses.

Distribution This is defined as any distribution of a company's assets to members (shareholders) of the company, whether in cash or otherwise, with the *exception* of:
- an issue of bonus shares;
- the redemption or purchase of the company's own shares out of capital (including the proceeds of a new issue) or out of unrealised profits;
- the reduction of share capital by reducing the liability on shares in respect of share capital not fully paid up and/or paying off paid-up share capital; and
- a distribution of assets to shareholders in a winding-up of the company.

Undistributable reserves of a public limited company These are defined as:

- the share premium account;
- the capital redemption reserve fund;
- the excess of accumulated unrealised profits, not previously capitalised, over accumulated unrealised losses not previously written off by a reduction or reorganisation of capital; and
- any other reserve that the company is prohibited from distributing by any enactment, or by its Memorandum or Articles of Association.

18.1 INTRODUCTION

Broadly, creditors are faced with two risks with respect to not being paid the monies that they are owed: first, the business risk that the company will not trade profitably and, secondly, that the company will be profitable but will pay shareholders rather than creditors. Therefore, excluding ordinary business risks, rules are required to protect creditors against ordinary shareholders being paid excessive dividends and depleting the capital of the business. The principle of **capital maintenance** is fundamental to the protection of creditors of limited liability companies since shareholders may deplete the equity or capital of a company by withdrawing excessive dividends (see **Chapter 1**). In simple terms, an entity has maintained its capital if it has as much capital at the end of the period as it had at the beginning of the period. The key in capital maintenance is deciding which concept is being adopted: the **financial concept** or the **physical concept**, because this then defines the basis on which profit is calculated (see **Chapter 1**). The choice of model will depend on the different degrees of relevance and reliability available, and management must seek an appropriate balance between the two.

Perhaps one of the most common concerns amongst preparers and users of financial statements with respect to the move to International Financial Reporting Standards (IFRS) is the impact on profits available for distribution (see below). The rules regarding the distribution of profits are set out in companies legislation and are unchanged by the transition to IFRS. However, the 'relevant accounts'[1] referred to in company law are now IFRS-based accounts and not the previous UK- and Irish-based GAAP (Generally Accepted Accounting Principles) accounts. Company law accounting rules, which are similar in the UK and Ireland, generally state that only *realised* profits may be included in the statement of profit or loss and other comprehensive income of company legislation accounts. IFRS, however, permits *unrealised* gains to be included in the statement of profit or loss and other comprehensive income of IFRS accounts in certain circumstances (see **Chapter 2**). However, regardless of the wider IFRS definition, the profits available for distribution comprise only realised profits less realised losses. In addition, the meaning of 'realised' has not been changed following the transition

---

[1] Relevant accounts are normally audited annual financial statements prepared in accordance with company legislation to give a true and fair view. In the case of a qualified audit report, the auditor is required to prepare a written statement stating whether such a qualification is material in determining the entity's distributable profits.

to IFRS and, in essence, an item is only realised when it has passed out of a company's control and the company has received cash or cash equivalents in return for it. Consequently, it will be important in future for companies to track the extent to which profits recognised in their IFRS accounts (or company law accounts) are in fact realised.

Key to this Chapter

This chapter explains the extent to which companies are able to distribute their profits to shareholders. While reading the chapter, it is important to bear in mind that the primary concern is to protect creditors of limited liability companies against shareholders depleting the equity or capital of a company by withdrawing excessive dividends. Consequently, the chapter focuses on what is meant by the term '**distribution**' and, in particular, on what are **distributable profits**.

18.2 DISTRIBUTIONS

After defining what is meant by the term '**distribution**', this section explains the principle of **distributable profits** and the meaning of realised and unrealised profits and losses.

A **distribution** is defined as any distribution of a company's assets to members (shareholders) of the company, whether in cash or otherwise, with the *exception* of:
- an issue of bonus shares;
- the redemption or purchase of the company's own shares out of capital (including the proceeds of a new issue) or out of unrealised profits;
- the reduction of share capital by reducing the liability on shares in respect of share capital not fully paid up and/or paying off paid-up share capital; and
- a distribution of assets to shareholders in a winding-up of the company.

Distributable Profits

All companies are prohibited under companies legislation from paying dividends except out of profits available for that purpose. The general principle is that **distributable profits** consist of accumulated realised profits less accumulated realised losses. While this definition permits the distribution of a capital profit as dividends (i.e. a surplus over book value realised on the sale of a non-current asset), the key words in the definition are:
- **accumulated** – which means that the balance of profit or loss from previous years must be brought into account in the current period; and
- **realised** – which prohibits the inclusion of unrealised profits arising from, for example, the revaluation of non-current assets retained by the company.

Therefore, while unrealised profits cannot be distributed, there is no difference between realised profits from normal trading and realised capital profits (for example, from the sale of a non-current asset). Interim dividends are allowed to be paid, provided they can be justified on the basis of the latest audited financial statements.

There is a further requirement for public limited companies (plc) that the total of the net assets of such must be equal to or more than the aggregate of the called-up share capital plus

undistributable reserves both at the date of, and immediately after, the distribution. **Undistributable reserves of a public limited company** are defined as:
- the share premium account;
- the capital redemption reserve fund;
- the excess of accumulated unrealised profits, not previously capitalised, over accumulated unrealised losses not previously written off by a reduction or reorganisation of capital; and
- any other reserve that the company is prohibited from distributing by any enactment, or by its Memorandum and Articles of Association.

This means that when dealing with a public limited company the distributable profits have to be reduced by any net unrealised loss. The difference in the definition of distributable profits between private and public limited companies is illustrated in **Example 18.1**.

EXAMPLE 18.1: DISTRIBUTABLE PROFITS – PUBLIC AND PRIVATE COMPANIES

Calculate the distributable profits of both Companies A and B, assuming that each is a:
(a) private company; and
(b) public company.

	A		B	
	€000	€000	€000	€000
Share capital		1,000		1,000
Unrealised profits	200		200	
Unrealised losses	-	200	(300)	(100)
Realised profits	300		800	
Realised losses	-	300	(200)	600
Share capital and reserves		1,500		1,500

Solution

A:
(a) Private Company
Realised profits – Realised losses = €300,000

(b) Public Company
Net realised profits less Net unrealised losses = €300,000

B:
(a) Private Company
€800,000 – €200,000 = €600,000

(b) Public Company
€600,000 – €100,000 = €500,000

As explained in **Chapter 6**, under IAS 16 *Property, Plant and Equipment*, companies are allowed to record non-current assets at valuation in the statement of financial position rather than depreciated historical cost. Assuming the valuation is higher than the depreciated historical cost, this will lead to a higher depreciation charge in the financial statements and therefore lower profits (relative to historical cost-based financial statements). Consequently, any excess depreciation on a revalued non-current asset above the amount of depreciation that would have been charged on its historical cost can be treated as a realised profit for the purpose of distributions. This is to avoid penalising companies that make an unrealised profit on the revaluation of an asset, and then charge depreciation on the revalued amount. This is illustrated in **Example 18.2**.

EXAMPLE 18.2: EXCESS DEPRECIATION ON REVALUED ASSETS

Assume a company buys an asset for €20,000, which has a life of four years and a nil residual value. If it is immediately revalued to €30,000, an unrealised profit of €10,000 would be credited to the revaluation reserve. Annual depreciation must be based on the revalued amount, in this case, 25% of €30,000 or €7,500. This exceeds depreciation, which would have been charged on the asset's cost (€5,000 p.a.) by €2,500 per annum. This €2,500 can be treated as a distributable profit.

Realised and Unrealised Profits and Losses

Company law typically does not specifically define realised profits or unrealised profits; instead it states that any determination of whether a profit or loss is realised must be made in light of best accounting practice (subject to decisions of the law courts in cases of dispute). The following are the rules contained in company law with respect to determining whether a profit or loss is realised or unrealised:
- a provision made in the accounts is a realised loss;
- a revaluation surplus is an unrealised profit;
- when a surplus arises on the revaluation of a non-current asset, and this is shown in the accounts, a higher depreciation charge will arise. The difference between the depreciation charge based on the revalued amount and the depreciation charge based on the book cost should be regarded as a realised profit;
- on the disposal of a revalued asset, any unrealised surplus or loss on valuation immediately becomes realised;
- if there is no available record of the original cost of an asset, its cost may be taken as the value put on it in the earliest available record; and
- if it is impossible to establish whether a profit or loss brought forward was realised or unrealised, any such profit may be treated as realised and any such loss as unrealised.

The application of the above rules is now considered in the context of revaluation deficits, revaluation surpluses and development expenditure.

Revaluation Deficits

The general rule is that any provision (including one for depreciation or diminution in value as well as provisions for liabilities, charges or losses) is treated as a realised loss. However, an exception to this general rule is if a 'revaluation provision' arises on a revaluation of *all* non-current assets (or on a revaluation of all non-current assets *other than* goodwill), then the revaluation deficit is an unrealised loss. Consequently, where a company undertakes a partial revaluation of non-current assets, a deficit on one asset is a realised loss and cannot therefore be offset against a surplus on another asset (an unrealised profit) for the purposes of arriving at distributable profits. A partial remedy to this problem is contained in company law. This is illustrated in **Example 18.3**.

Deficits arising on an asset where there has been a partial revaluation of the assets are to be treated as unrealised losses, provided that:
- the directors have 'considered' the aggregate value of the non-current assets, which have not been revalued at the date of the partial revaluation;
- the directors are satisfied that the aggregate value is not less than the aggregate book value; and
- a note to the accounts states the above two facts.

EXAMPLE 18.3: REVALUATION OF ASSETS

X Limited has the following statement of financial position:

	€000
Net Assets	320
Share capital	100
Share premium	50
Revaluation reserve	90
Retained earnings	80
	320

Two of the company's assets were revalued for the first time during the year, one giving rise to a surplus of €100,000, the other a deficit of €30,000.

Requirement What are the profits available for distribution and how would the figure differ if all the company's assets had been revalued?

Solution

Profits available for distribution:

	€000
Retained earnings	80

(*Note:* the revaluation deficit of €30,000 would be charged in arriving at profit or loss in the SPLOCI – P/L in accordance with IAS 16 (see **Chapter 6**).)

If all the company's assets had been revalued (or the directors had 'considered' the value of the assets not revalued), then the revalued deficit would be unrealised and therefore the profits available for distribution would be €110,000.

Revaluation Surpluses

Revaluation surpluses are unrealised profits in the accounting period in which the revaluation takes place and therefore not available for distribution. The only exception to this rule is where the same asset was:

- previously revalued giving rise to a deficit; and
- the deficit was treated as a realised loss.

In such a case, the revaluation surplus will be a realised profit to the extent that it makes good the realised loss. It should also be remembered that revaluation surpluses can eventually become realised profits when the asset is either depreciated or sold.

Development Expenditure

Deferred development expenditure is treated as an unrealised loss if the expenditure is carried forward under the provision of IAS 38 *Intangible Assets* (see **Chapter 9**). A note to the accounts is required stating this fact. It should also be noted that, if the expenditure is not treated as a realised loss in the year of expenditure, it will be a realised loss when written off in future years.

18.3 CONCLUSION

Accountants (and company directors) over the years have faced the problem of:
- What is meant by '*distributable profits*'?
- Can unrealised gains be distributed (i.e. paid out as dividend)?
- Must account be taken of unrealised losses before a distribution is paid?
- What is meant by '*realised*'?

While company law has attempted to rationalise the whole area of what constitutes distributable profits, like many areas of accounting, there remain areas of debate and judgement. However, regardless of this, it is important to remember that the underlying principle is the protection of creditors of limited liability companies against shareholders depleting the equity or capital of a company by withdrawing excessive dividends.

SUMMARY OF LEARNING OBJECTIVES

Having studied this chapter on the distribution of profits and assets, you should now understand:

Learning Objective 1 The general rule governing the distribution of profits.

The general principle is that distributable profits consist of accumulated realised profits less accumulated realised losses; therefore, unrealised profits cannot be distributed.

Learning Objective 2 The distinction between public and private companies as regards distributable profits.

In the case of public limited companies, the total of the net assets of a public limited company must be equal to or more than the aggregate of the called-up share capital plus undistributable reserves both at the date of, and immediately after, the distribution.

This means that when dealing with a public company the distributable profits have to be reduced by any net unrealised loss.

Learning Objective 3 The distinction between realised and unrealised profits.

In essence, an item is only realised when it has passed out of a company's control and the company has received cash or cash equivalents in return for it.

Learning Objective 4 How to deal with revaluation surpluses and deficits.

In broad terms, revaluation surpluses are unrealised profits in the accounting period in which the revaluation takes place and therefore not available for distribution.

QUESTIONS

Self-test Questions

1. What is the general rule as to which profits are available for distribution?
2. With a public company, how is this general rule amended?
3. Is there a strict legal definition of what is meant by 'realised profits'?
4. Is the profit attributable to construction contracts a realised or an unrealised profit?

Review Questions

(See **Appendix One** for Suggested Solutions to Review Questions.)

Question 18.1

John Sykes is an ordinary shareholder in Prosperous plc and has recently received the consolidated accounts of the Prosperous Group for the year ended 31 December 2012. He has been discussing the accounts with his accountants, Know Most & Co., and mentioned that he was not clear as to the amount of distributable reserves available for the payment of dividends.

Requirement
(a) Define profits available for distribution by a public company and the disclosure requirements for the company and the group.
(b) Explain the implications of the following items to profits available for distribution:
    (i) Research and development activities;
    (ii) Excess depreciation.

Question 18.2

Below are extracts from the statements of financial position of three companies as at 31 December 2012:

	Hay plc €000	Bee plc €000	Sea Limited €000
ASSETS			
Tangible Non-current Assets	1,200	700	300
Current Assets	600	400	300
	1,800	1,100	600
EQUITY AND LIABILITIES			
Capital and Reserves			
Issued share capital	300	300	300
Reserves:			
Revaluation	200	200	100
Profit on sale of non-current assets	200	100	–
Retained earnings start of year	600	(200)	(200)
Statement of profit or loss and other comprehensive income – profit or loss for the year	300	600	300
	1,600	1,000	500
Current Liabilities	200	100	100
	1,800	1,100	600

Bee's tangible non-current assets were revalued on 1 January 2012 from a cost price of €300,000 to a revalued amount of €500,000. All of Bee's tangible non-current assets have been purchased since 2007. They are depreciated over 10 years, using the straight-line method.

Sea's tangible non-current assets were revalued on 31 December 2012 from a cost price of €200,000 to a revalued amount of €300,000. However, in Sea's statement of profit or loss and other comprehensive income for 2012 the depreciation charge was based on the cost price figure.

Requirement Calculate the maximum distribution which Hay, Bee and Sea can each make.

Challenging Questions

(Suggested Solutions to Challenging Questions are available to lecturers.)

Question 18.1 (Based on Chartered Accountants Ireland, P2 Summer 1997, Question 1)

The following information is available for Halogen Limited:

Draft Statement of Profit or Loss and Other Comprehensive Income (Extract) for the Year Ended 31 December 2012

	€000
Profit before taxation	500
Taxation	(50)
Profit after taxation	450

Draft Statement of Changes in Equity (Extract) for the Year Ended 31 December 2012

	Note	€000
Profit for the financial year (as per draft above)		450
Unrealised surplus on revaluation of Property X	(1)	60

Unrealised loss on trade investments	(270)
Total recognised gains and losses since last annual report	240

Additional Information

1. Property X was revalued for the first time in 2012.
2. The company is entirely equity-financed, as follows:

	€000
Share capital (€1 ordinary shares)	200
Share premium	50
Capital redemption reserve fund	40

3. Retained profits were €90,000 at 1 January 2012.
4. Just before the year-end, the company sold some land at a profit of €70,000. This profit is not reflected in the draft profit figure above. The tax charge associated with this profit is €30,000 and this also has not been included in the draft taxation charge shown above.
5. A fire in part of the company's warehouse just before the year-end destroyed inventory worth €50,000. No adjustment has been made to reflect this fact in the draft profit figure.
6. Taxation is at a rate of 10%.

Requirement

(a) What profits are statutorily available for distribution? What additional restrictions are placed on public limited companies?
(b) What is the maximum distribution that Halogen Limited, as a private limited company, can make?
(c) If Halogen Limited was a public limited company, what would be the maximum distribution it could make?

Question 18.2 (Based on Chartered Accountants Ireland, P2 Autumn 1995, Question 1)

Demo Limited is a private company with a 31 December year-end. The following is the summarised statement of financial position for Demo Limited as at 31 December 2012:

Summarised Draft Statement of Financial Position as at 31 December 2012

	€000	€000
Net assets		400
Share capital		350
Share premium		40
Unrealised losses on asset revaluations	(20)	
Realised profits	60	
Realised losses	(30)	10
		400

Requirement

(a) As a private company, what is the maximum distribution of profits that Demo Limited can make?

(b) If Demo Limited were a public limited company, what would be the maximum distribution of profits the company could make?

Question 18.3 *(Based on Chartered Accountants Ireland, P2 Autumn 1999, Question 2)*

(a) Outline what profits are available for distribution by each of the following:
   (i) A private limited company; and
   (ii) A public limited company.
(b) You are given the following extracts from the draft statement of profit or loss and other comprehensive income of MORGAN ENTERPRISES for the year ended 31 December 2012:

Draft Statement of Profit or Loss and Other Comprehensive Income (Extracts) for the Year Ended 31 December 2012

	€000
Profit before taxation	1,000
Taxation	(200)
Profit after taxation	800

The following additional information is also available:
1. During 2012 two of the company's assets were revalued as follows:

   Property A – surplus of €200,000; and
   Land   – deficit of €110,000.

2. With respect to Property A, the depreciation charge for 2012 had been based on the revalued amount of the asset. The depreciation charge for 2012 was €30,000 more than would have been charged on a historical cost basis.
3. A flood occurred in the main warehouse of MORGAN ENTERPRISES just before the year-end and inventory worth €70,000 was destroyed. No adjustment has been made for this in the draft statement of profit or loss and other comprehensive income.
4. Just before the year-end, two employees were made redundant at a total cost of €20,000. No adjustment has been made for this in the draft statement of profit or loss and other comprehensive income.
5. Deferred development expenditure in the statement of financial position of MORGAN ENTERPRISES at 31 December 2012 amounted to €1,000,000.
6. An increase in trade investments before the year-end, amounting to €150,000, had not been reflected in the financial statements.
7. A portion of the company car park was sold before the year-end, yielding an after-tax profit of €900,000. No adjustment has been made for this in the draft statement of profit or loss and other comprehensive income.
8. The company is financed by equity capital as follows:

	€000
Share capital – ordinary shares €1 each fully paid	2,000
Share premium	400

9. Retained profits at 1 January 2012 were €2,800,000.
10. The tax rate is 20%.

Requirement

(a) Assuming that MORGAN ENTERPRISES is a private limited company, show what profits are available for distribution.

(b) Assuming that MORGAN ENTERPRISES is a public limited company, show what profits are available for distribution.

(c) Would your answers in (a) and (b) above have been any different if all of the company's non-current assets had been revalued during the year?

Question 18.4

(a) What is the general rule for determining distributable profits?

(b) State whether each of the following is an realised or an unrealised profit or loss and briefly explain the reason for your answer:

　(i) a charge to the statement of profit or loss and other comprehensive income as an allowance for irrecoverable debts;

　(ii) the final dividend receivable from a subsidiary in respect of an accounting period ending before the end of the parent company's financial year; and

　(iii) surpluses arising on revaluation of assets (before sale).

(c) The summarised statement of financial position at 30 September 2012 of Global Sports Limited is set out below:

	€000
Authorised Share Capital	
250,000 ordinary shares of €1 each	250
Called-up Share Capital	
200,000 ordinary shares of €1 each	200
Share Premium Account	175
Revaluation Reserve	150
Other Reserves:	
Capital Redemption Reserve Fund	125
General Reserve	100
Retained Earnings	200
	950
Non-current Assets	400
Net Current Assets	550
	950

The deficit on the revaluation reserve arose as a result of a revaluation of all the non-current assets, and the articles of association state that the general reserve is non-distributable.

Requirement

What are the legally distributable profits of Global Sports if:

　(i) it is a private company?

　(ii) it is a public company?

PART III

PREPARATION OF STATEMENT OF CASH FLOWS

STATEMENT OF CASH FLOWS – SINGLE COMPANY

LEARNING OBJECTIVES

Having studied this chapter on IAS 7 *Statement of Cash Flows*, you should be able to:
1. demonstrate a knowledge of the standard headings under which IAS 7 requires cash flows to be classified;
2. define cash and cash equivalents in accordance with IAS 7;
3. prepare a single company statement of cash flows in accordance with IAS 7 using both the direct and indirect methods; and
4. discuss the advantages of cash flow reporting.

KEY TERMS AND DEFINITIONS FOR THIS CHAPTER

In order to aid your understanding of the concepts and issues covered in this chapter, it is important to understand and be familiar with the following key terms and definitions. As you study this chapter, you should refer back to them.

Cash This refers to cash-in-hand and deposits repayable on demand.

Cash Equivalents Short-term, highly liquid investments that are readily convertible to known amounts of cash and that are subject to an insignificant risk of changes in value. Cash equivalents are not held for investment or other long-term purposes, but rather to meet short-term cash commitments. Therefore, their maturity date should normally be not more than three months from their acquisition date. Loans and other borrowings are 'investing' activities. Bank overdrafts, since repayable on demand, are included under cash and cash equivalents.

Cash Flow This refers to inflows and outflows of cash and cash equivalents.

Financing Activities Activities that result in changes in the size and composition of the equity capital and borrowings of the entity.

Investing Activities These relate to the acquisition and disposal of non-current assets and other investments not included in cash equivalents.

Operating Activities The principal revenue-producing activities of the entity, and other activities that are not investing or financing.

19.1 INTRODUCTION

The fundamental purpose of being in business is to generate profit, and it is profit that increases the owners' wealth. However, profitability is arguably a long-term objective. In the short term, business viability is determined by its ability to generate cash. Ultimately, profit, particularly profit determined under the broad variations possible under Generally Accepted Accounting Principles (GAAP), is of little value if it cannot be translated into cash. Consequently, cash flow is important. Even profitable companies will collapse if they do not have access to sufficient cash resources when it becomes necessary to settle their bills. Very few businesses could survive a prolonged period of net outflow of cash. It is a fact that most businesses fail purely and simply because they run out of cash and are unable to pay their bills as they fall due. Take, for example, the high-profile bankruptcy of Lehman Brothers in 2008. This was one of the most successful and oldest investment banks in the world and it failed not because it ran out of clients or sales but because it did not have enough cash to settle its debts (despite having $600 billion in assets).

Information about cash flows is therefore needed in order to help users of financial statements form an opinion on a company's liquidity, viability and financial adaptability. The statement of financial position provides information about the entity's financial position at a particular point in time, including assets, liabilities and equity and their relationship with each other at the reporting period date. The statement of financial position is often used to obtain information on liquidity, but the information is incomplete for this purpose as the statement of financial position is drawn up at a particular point in time. Consequently, the statement of cash flows, together with the statement of financial position and the statement of profit or loss and other comprehensive income, provides information about past cash flows and should therefore assist users in assessing future cash flows. The statement of cash flows is one of the primary financial statements and it provides users with information to enable them to assess the entity's liquidity, solvency and the quality of an entity's earnings. The statement of cash flows is intended to answer questions such as:

- Did the entity's profits generate sufficient funds for its continued operations? For example, profits are calculated on an accruals basis (not cash). Therefore, revenue shown in the statement of profit or loss and other comprehensive income may not yet have been received, and indeed (in the extreme) may never be received if the customer defaults or goes bankrupt.
- Is the entity capable of generating funds, as opposed to profit from its trading activities?
- Why has the bank overdraft increased, despite the company having had a profitable year? For example, an entity may deliberately build up its inventory at the end of the reporting

period; however, while the inventory will have to be paid for, there will be no impact on profit until the inventory is sold.

- How has the entity financed its increased non-current assets? Did it finance them from long-term sources or from **operating activities**? For example, while the purchase of non-current assets has an immediate cash impact if purchased for cash, the impact on the statement of profit or loss and other comprehensive income will be gradual in the form of depreciation charges.
- What was done with the loan that was taken out during the year?
- How did the entity meet its dividend and interest payments? Was it from operating activities, from increased borrowing or from sales of non-current assets?

This chapter focuses on the preparation of a statement of cash flows for a *single entity* in accordance with IAS 7 *Statement of Cash Flows*. Issues relating specifically to the preparation of a *consolidated* statement of cash flows are dealt with in **Part V**, **Chapter 33**.

19.2 IAS 7 *STATEMENT OF CASH FLOWS*

A statement of cash flows is one of the four *primary* financial statements and should therefore be presented with equal prominence to the statement of profit or loss and other comprehensive income, statement of financial position and statement of changes in equity. Financial statements should provide information that is useful to users and the statement of cash flows is an important part of the overall package of information provided to users, which includes the four primary financial statements and notes to the financial statements. As all types of entity can provide useful information about cash flows, whatever the nature of their revenue-producing activities, all entities are required to prepare a statement of cash flows. The objective of IAS 7 *Statement of Cash Flows* is to provide information to users of financial statements about the cash flows of an entity and its ability to generate **cash** and **cash equivalents**, together with indicating the cash needs of the entity.

Format of Statement of Cash Flows

IAS 7 requires the **cash flows** to be classified into three separate sections (operating, investing and financing), with the net movement totalled and added to the cash and cash equivalents at the start of the period to arrive at the cash and cash equivalents at the end of the period. Before explaining the content of each of these three sections (operating, investing and financing), the format of a statement of cash flows is summarised in **Figure 19.1**.

FIGURE 19.1: SUMMARISED STATEMENT OF CASH FLOWS

	€000
Cash flows from operating activities	X
Cash flows from investing activities	X
Cash flows from financing activities	X
Net increase/(decrease) in cash and cash equivalents during period	X
Cash and cash equivalents at beginning of period	X
Cash and cash equivalents at end of period	X

The form and content of each of the three main sections (operating, investing and financing) are now explained in more detail.

Note: the preparation of a statement of cash flows is not necessarily difficult and students may find it advantageous to prepare and learn a detailed pro-forma statement of cash flows at an early stage in their studies of this topic.

---

1. Cash Flows from Operating Activities

The first section of the statement of cash flows recognises that, although an enterprise may have generated a profit during the year and increased its assets, it may not necessarily have readily accessible cash as the money could be tied up in, for example, inventory and receivables. Also, in arriving at profit a number of non-cash deductions and additions have been included (e.g. depreciation, profit/loss on disposal). These need to be taken into account when calculating the actual cash generated. Cash flows from operating activities are in general the cash effects of transactions and other events relating to operating or trading activities normally shown in the statement of profit or loss and other comprehensive income in arriving at operating profit. This section of the statement of cash flows indicates whether, and to what extent, companies can generate cash from their operations. In simple terms, it seeks to convert an entity's reported operating profit into a cash figure. Examples of cash flows from operating activities are:
- cash receipts from the sale of goods and the rendering of services;
- cash receipts from royalties, fees, commissions and other revenue;
- cash payments to suppliers for goods and services;
- cash payments to and on behalf of employees;
- cash receipts and cash payments of an insurance entity for premiums and claims, annuities and other policy benefits;
- cash payments or refunds of income taxes unless they can be specifically identified with financing and **investing activities**; and
- cash receipts and payments from contracts held for dealing or trading purposes.

IAS 7 permits two methods of calculating operating cash flows:
(a) the *direct method;* and
(b) the *indirect method.*

Both methods lead to the same figure.

(a) Direct Method   This method shows operating cash receipts and payments (e.g. cash paid to suppliers and employees and cash received from customers). This is useful to users as it shows the actual sources and uses of cash. A specimen of this is shown in **Figure 19.2**.

FIGURE 19.2: DIRECT METHOD OF PRESENTING OPERATING CASH FLOWS

	€000
Cash received from customers	X
− Cash payments to suppliers	(X)
− Cash paid to and on behalf of employees	(X)

− Other cash payments	(X)
= Cash generated from operations	X
+ Interest received[1]	X
− Interest paid[1]	(X)
− Tax paid	(X)
− Dividends paid[1]	(X)
= Net cash inflow from operating activities	X

[1] Cash flows from interest and dividends received/paid should be disclosed separately. Each should be classified consistently from period to period as operating, investing or financing activities; however, IAS 7 is not prescriptive about where they are disclosed.

The use of the direct method is encouraged, where the necessary information is not too costly to obtain, as it discloses information not available elsewhere in the financial statements. However, many enterprises will not generate this information as a matter of course, so it may prove expensive to produce. IAS 7 does not require the direct method to be used and actually favours the indirect method. In practice, many entities opt not to disclose the information using the direct method.

(b) **Indirect Method**   This method requires the profit to be reconciled to the cash flow being generated by operations (i.e. it converts operating profit into a cash figure). The indirect method starts with profit before tax (as stated in the statement of profit or loss and other comprehensive income) and adjusts for non-cash charges and credits to arrive at the net cash flow from operating activities. A specimen is shown in **Figure 19.3**.

FIGURE 19.3: INDIRECT METHOD OF PRESENTING OPERATING CASH FLOWS

	€000
Profit before tax	X
+ Depreciation charges[1]	X
− Profit on disposal of equipment[2]	(X)
+ Interest expense	X
− Increase in inventories[3]	(X)
− Increase in receivables[4]	(X)
+ Increase in payables[5]	X
= cash generated from operations	X
+ Interest received[6]	X
− Interest paid[6]	(X)
− Tax paid	(X)
− Dividends paid[6]	(X)
= Net cash inflow from operating activities	X

Explanatory notes:
[1] Depreciation is a charge in arriving at profit before tax, but as it is not a cash flow, it is added back.

[2] A profit on disposal increases profit before tax, but as it does not represent the cash received (see 'investing' section), it is deducted (and vice versa for a loss on disposal).

[3] If inventories increase from one period to the next, then, all other things being equal, this reduces cash since they have to be paid for (and vice versa for a decrease in inventories).

[4] If receivables increase from one period to the next, then, all other things being equal, this reduces cash since in net terms less cash has been received in the period (and vice versa for a decrease in receivables).

[5] If payables increase from one period to the next, then, all other things being equal, this increases cash since in net terms suppliers have not been paid as much in the period as they were in the previous period (and vice versa for a decrease in payables).

[6] Cash flows from interest and dividends received/paid should be disclosed separately. Each should be classified consistently from period to period as operating, investing or financing; however, IAS 7 is not prescriptive about where they are disclosed.

The principal advantage claimed for this method is that it highlights the differences between profit before tax and net cash flow from operating activities. As some investors and creditors assess future cash flows by estimating future income and then allowing for accruals adjustments, knowledge of past accruals adjustments may be useful for this purpose.

If dividends paid are included as part of cash flows from operating activities, users can assess the entity's ability to pay dividends out of cash flows; if included as part of cash flows from **financing activities**, then it indicates the cost of obtaining financial resources. Tax cash flows should be disclosed separately and classified as operating activities, unless specifically identified with financing or investing activities. The preparation of the net cash flow from operating activities using the indirect method is illustrated in **Example 19.1**.

EXAMPLE 19.1: NET CASH FLOW FROM OPERATING ACTIVITIES (INDIRECT METHOD)

The following financial information relates to ABC Limited for the year ended 31 December 2012:

STATEMENT OF PROFIT OR LOSS AND OTHER COMPREHENSIVE INCOME
for the Year Ended 31 December 2012

	€000
Revenue	222
Operating expenses	(156)
Profit from operations	66
Finance costs	(9)
Profit before tax	57
Income tax expense	(21)
Profit for year	36

The following operating expenses were incurred in the year:

	€000
Wages	(36)
Auditor's remuneration	(6)

Depreciation	(42)
Cost of material used	(111)
Gain on sale of non-current assets	30
Rental income	9
	(156)

The following information is also available:

	31 December 2012	31 December 2011
	€000	€000
Inventories	21	12
Trade receivable	24	21
Trade payables	(15)	(9)

Requirement Calculate the net cash flow from operating activities using the indirect method.

Solution

	€000	€000
Profit before tax		57
Adjustment for non-cash items:		
Depreciation	42	
Finance cost	9	
Gain on sale of non-current assets	(30)	21
Movements in working capital:		
Increase in receivables	(3)	
Increase in payables	6	
Increase in inventories	(9)	(6)
Net cash inflow from operations		72

2. Cash Flows from Investing Activities

This second section in the statement of cash flows includes purchases and sales of non-current assets, and the purchase and sales of investments not qualifying as cash equivalents are included. While interest and dividends received may be classified under this heading, they may also be included under operating activities or financing. The illustration provided in IAS 7 includes them as investing. The separate disclosure of cash flows arising from investing activities is important because the cash flows represent the extent to which expenditures have been made for resources intended to generate future income and cash flows.

Examples of cash flows arising from investing activities are:
- cash payments to acquire property, plant and equipment, intangibles and other non-current assets;
- cash receipts from sales of property, plant and equipment, intangibles and other non-current assets;
- cash payments to acquire equity or debt instruments of other entities and interests in joint ventures;

- cash advances and loans made to other parties;
- cash receipts from sales of equity or debt instruments of other entities and interests in joint ventures;
- cash receipts from the repayment of advances and loans made to other parties;
- cash payments for futures contracts, forward contracts, option contracts and swap contracts, except when the contracts are held for dealing or trading purposes, or the payments are classified as financing activities; and
- cash receipts from futures contracts, forward contracts, option contracts and swap contracts, except when the contracts are held for dealing or trading purposes or the receipts are classified as financial activities.

Figure 19.4: Cash Flows from Investing Activities

	€000
Cash paid to acquire property, plant and equipment	(X)
Cash receipts from the sales of property, plant and equipment	X
Cash paid/received for shares and debentures in other entities	(X)
Loans received/repaid	X
Dividends received	X
Interest received	X
Net cash inflows from investing activities	X

3. Cash Flows from Financing Activities

The separate disclosure of cash flows arising from financing activities is important because it is useful in predicting claims by providers of capital to the entity on future cash flows. Examples of cash flows arising from financing activities include:
- cash proceeds from issuing shares or other equity instruments;
- cash payments to owners to acquire or redeem the entity's shares;
- cash proceeds from issuing debentures, loans, notes, bonds, mortgages and other short- or long-term borrowings;
- cash repayments of amounts borrowed; and
- cash payments by a lessee for the reduction of the outstanding liability relating to a finance lease.

The presentation of these items is illustrated in **Figure 19.5**.

(**Note:** finance leases are accounted for by the lessee capitalising the fair value of the related asset, or the present value of the minimum lease payments, if lower (see **Chapter 8**). A liability and a corresponding asset are produced, which do not reflect cash flows in the accounting period. The statement of cash flows records the cash flow (i.e. the rentals paid), with the reduction in liability shown under financing.)

Figure 19.5: Cash Flows from Financing Activities

	€000
Proceeds from share issue	X
Cash paid to acquire/redeem own shares	(X)

Cash proceeds from issuing debentures and loans	X
Capital repayments of finance leases	(X)
Dividends paid	(X)
Net cash inflows from financing activities	X

As illustrated in **Figure 19.1**, the statement of cash flows is completed as follows:

	€000
The sum of operating, investing and financing sections represents the net increase/decrease in cash and cash equivalents during the period	X
+ cash and cash equivalents at the start of the year	X
= cash and cash equivalents at the end of the year	X

Note: so far in this section we have examined the main components of a statement of cash flows and the key principles underlying its preparation. However, there are some other points that should be borne in mind as, while arguably not that common in practice, they have a tendency to feature to some extent in examination questions. These are discussed below.

Other Points

1. **Material Items in the Statement of Profit or Loss and Other Comprehensive Income** Where cash flows relate to items that are classified as material in the statement of profit or loss and other comprehensive income, they should be shown under the appropriate statutory headings, according to the nature of each item. The cash flows relating to material items should be identified in the statement cash flows, or a note to it, and the relationship between the cash flows and the originating material item should be explained.

2. **Material Cash Flows** Where cash flows are material because of their size and incidence but are not related to items that are treated as material in the statement of profit or loss and other comprehensive income, sufficient disclosure should be given to explain their cause and nature. For a cash flow to be material on the grounds of its size alone, it must be material in relation to cash flows of a similar nature.

3. **Discontinued Operations** Cash flows relating to discontinued operations should be shown separately, either on the face of the statement of cash flows or by note.

4. **Major Non-cash Transactions** Material transactions not resulting in movements of cash of the reporting entity should be disclosed in the notes to the statement of cash flows if disclosure is necessary for an understanding of the underlying transactions. Consideration for transactions may be in a form other than cash. The purpose of a statement of cash flows is to report cash flow; non-cash transactions should, therefore, not be reported in a statement of cash flows. However, to obtain a full picture of the alterations in financial position caused by the transactions for the period, separate disclosure of material non-cash

transactions is also necessary. Examples of non-cash transactions are finance leases and the conversion of debt to equity.

5. Foreign Currency Cash Flows Individual company cash flows arising from transactions in a foreign currency should be recorded in the entity's functional currency at the exchange rate at the date of the cash flow. The cash flows of a foreign subsidiary must be translated at the exchange rates between the functional currency and the foreign currency at the dates of the cash flows. (For further information on foreign subsidiaries and the preparation of a consolidated statement of cash flows, see **Chapter 33**.)

Example 19.2 below brings together the issues covered so far in this section in the form of an examination-style question. Before working through this example, it is important to learn the format of a statement of cash flows and, in particular, the sections (operating, investing and financing) where the different items 'go'.

EXAMPLE 19.2: STATEMENT OF CASH FLOWS

This example is based on the illustration in the Appendix to IAS 7. It applies the IAS 7 layout and shows both the indirect and direct methods of calculating operating cash flows. As the purpose of this example is primarily to illustrate the preparation of a single company statement of cash flows, the draft financial statements provided do not strictly comply with IAS 1 (see **Chapter 2**).

The draft financial statements of CCE Limited for the year ended 31 December 2012 are as follows:

STATEMENT OF PROFIT OR LOSS AND OTHER COMPREHENSIVE INCOME
for the Year Ended 31 December 2012

	€
Sales revenue	30,650
Cost of sales	(26,000)
Gross profit	4,650
Depreciation	(450)
Administrative and selling expenses	(950)
Interest expense (see Note 1)	(400)
Investment income (see Note 1)	500
Profit before tax	3,350
Income tax expense (see Note 4)	(120)
Profit for the year	3,230

STATEMENT OF FINANCIAL POSITION
as at 31 December 2012

	2012		2011	
	€	€	€	€
ASSETS				
Non-Current Assets				
Property, plant and equipment at cost	3,730		1,910	
Accumulated depreciation	(1,450)	2,280	(1,060)	850
Long-term investments		2,500		2,500

Current Assets		
Inventory	1,000	1,950
Accounts receivable (see Note 8)	1,900	1,200
Cash and cash equivalents (see below)	410	160
Total assets	8,090	6,660

EQUITY AND LIABILITIES
Capital and Reserves

Share capital	1,500	1,250
Retained earnings	3,410	1,380
Total shareholders' equity	4,910	2,630

Non-current Liabilities

Long-term debt (including finance leases)	2,300	1,040

Current Liabilities

Trade payables	250	1,890
Interest payable	230	100
Income taxes payable (see Note 3)	400	1,000
Total equity and liabilities	8,090	6,660

Cash and cash equivalents at 31 December are made up as follows:

	31 December	
	2012	2011
	€	€
Cash	40	25
Short-term investments	370	135
	410	160

Notes to draft financial statements:
1. Interest expense was €400, of which €170 was paid during the period. €100 relating to interest expense of the prior period was also paid during the period. €200 of interest was received during the period.
2. Dividends paid were €1,200.
3. The liability for tax at the beginning and end of the period was €1,000 and €400, respectively.
4. During the period, a further €15 tax was provided for. Withholding tax on dividends received amounted to €105, thus leading to the total tax expense of €120.
5. During the period, CCE Limited acquired property, plant and equipment with an aggregate cost of €1,900, of which €900 was acquired by means of finance leases. Cash payments of €1,000 were made to purchase property, plant and equipment.
6. €90 of capital repayment was paid under the finance leases.
7. Plant with an original cost of €80 and accumulated depreciation of €60 was sold for €20.

8. Accounts receivable as at the end of 2012 include €100 of interest receivable.
9. €250 was raised from the issue of share capital and a further €450 was raised from long-term borrowings.

Requirement

(a) Prepare a statement of cash flows for the year ended 31 December 2012 using the indirect method in accordance with the illustrative format in IAS 7 *Statement of Cash Flows*.

(b) Show the calculation of cash flows from operating activities using the direct method.

Suggested Approach

Figures for the statement of cash flows are derived from the differences between the opening and closing statement of financial position figures, using the information in the notes and in the statement of profit or loss and other comprehensive income to make necessary calculations. One approach to developing the answer is to adopt a standard procedure. Here is a suggested procedure for the indirect method (the more usual exam requirement).

Step 1: Set up a pro-forma statement of cash flows (main headings only), leaving plenty of space to insert detail. A whole page should be used.

Step 2: Study the additional information and mark with a cross those items affecting statement of financial position amounts.

Step 3: Begin the statement of cash flows by using the statement of profit or loss and other comprehensive income to work down to operating profit before working capital changes.

Step 4: Proceed line by line through the statement of financial position. If an item is not marked with a cross, the difference between the two figures may be entered direct to the statement of cash flows; if it is marked, a working is required. Use working ledger accounts to calculate missing figures. Insert the opening and closing balances from the statement of financial position into the working accounts, and then add information from the notes to complete the relevant ledger account. Balancing figures on the working accounts are then transferred to the statement of cash flows.

(a) Statement of Cash Flows for the Year Ended 31 December 2012

	Workings	€	€
Cash flows from operating activities			
Profit before tax		3,350	
Adjustments for:			
Depreciation		450	
Investment income		(500)	
Interest expense		400	
Operating profit before working capital changes		3,700	
Increase in trade receivables	1	(600)	
Decrease in inventories		950	
Decrease in trade payables		(1,640)	
Cash generated from operations		2,410	
Interest paid (see Note 6, **Figure 19.3**)	3	(270)	
Income taxes paid	4	(720)	
Net cash from operating activities			1,420

Cash flows from investing activities

Purchases of property, plant and equipment	5	(1,000)
Proceeds of sale of equipment	7	20
Interest received (see Note 6, **Figure 19.3**)	2	200
Dividends received (see Note 6, **Figure 19.3**)	2	200
Net cash used in investing activities		(580)

Cash flows from financing activities

Proceeds from issue of shares		250
Proceeds from long-term borrowings		450
Payment of finance lease liabilities		(90)
Dividends paid (see Note 6, **Figure 19.3**)		(1,200)
Net cash used in financing activities		(590)
Net increase in cash and cash equivalents		250
Cash and cash equivalents at beginning of period		160
Cash and cash equivalents at end of period		410

(b) Operating cash flow – direct method

	Workings	€
Cash receipts from customers	10	30,050
Cash paid to suppliers and employees	11	(27,640)
Cash generated from operations (as in part (a))		2,410
Interest paid		(270)
Income taxes paid		(720)
Net cash from operating activities (as in part (a))		1,420

Example of Notes to the Statement of Cash Flows

(These Notes are for illustration purposes only and some of the details are not provided in the question. For example, the undrawn borrowing facilities in Note 2 and the segment information in note 3.)

1. During 2012 cash payments of €1,000 were made to purchase property, plant and equipment.
2. Cash and cash equivalents consist of cash on hand and balances with banks and investments in money market instruments. Cash and cash equivalents included in the statement of cash flows comprise the following statement of financial position amounts:

Analysis of Cash and Cash Equivalents at 31 December

	2012 €	2011 €
Cash on hand and balances with banks	40	25
Short-term investments	370	135
Cash and cash equivalents	410	160

CCE Limited has undrawn borrowing facilities of €2,000,000, of which €700,000 may be used only for future expansion.

3. Segment Information (see **Chapter 24**)

Cash flows from:	Segment A €	Segment B €	Total €
Operating activities	1,700	(280)	1,420
Investing activities	(740)	160	(580)
Financing activities	(370)	(220)	(590)
	490	(200)	250

WORKINGS

(W1) Trade receivables

	€		€
Opening balance	1,200	Closing balance	
		(€1,900–€100*) (see Note 8)	1,800
Cash received (bal fig) (Statement of cash flows)	600		
	1,800		1,800

* €100 relates to interest and is not a trade receivable. Interest receivable included in W3.

(W2) Interest and dividends receivable

	€		€
Statement of profit or loss and other comprehensive income	500	Interest receivable c/f (see Note 8)	100
		Dividend received (bal fig) (Statement of cash flows)	200
		Interest received (see Note 1) (Statement of cash flows)	200
	500		500

(W3) Interest paid

	€		€
		Opening balance (see Note 1)	100
Cash paid (bal fig) (see Note 1) (Statement of cash flows)	270		
Closing balance	230	Statement of profit or loss and other comprehensive income	400
	500		500

(W4) Income taxes

	€		€
Cash paid (bal fig) (Statement of cash flows)	720	Opening balance	1,000
		Statement of profit or loss and other comprehensive income (€15 + €105)	
Closing balance	400	(see Note 4)	120
	1,120		1,120

(W5) Property, plant and equipment – cost

	€		€
Opening balance	1,910	Transfer disposal (see Note 7)	80
Leases (see Note 5)	900	Closing balance	3,730
Cash paid for additions (bal fig)			
(Statement of cash flows)	1,000		
	3,810		3,810

(W6) Property, plant and equipment – depreciation

	€		€
Transfer disposal	60	Opening balance	1,060
Closing balance	1,450	Statement of profit or loss and other	
		comprehensive income	450
	1,510		1,510

(W7) Property, plant and equipment – disposal

	€		€
Cost	80	Depreciation	60
		Cash received (Statement of cash	
		flows)	20
	80		80

(As there is no profit or loss on disposal, there is no adjustment to the reconciliation of operating profits.)

(W8) Long-term debt *(to reconcile balances)*

	€		€
Payments under finance leases (see		Opening balance	1,040
Note 6) (Statement of cash flows)	90	Finance leases (see Note 5)	900
Closing balance	2,300	Long-term borrowing	450
	2,390		2,390

(W9) Retained earnings *(to reconcile balances)*

	€		€
Dividend paid (Statement of cash flows)		Opening balance	1,380
		Statement of profit or loss and other	
	1,200	comprehensive income	3,230
Closing balance	3,410		
	4,610		4,610

(W10) Cash receipts from customers

	€
Opening trade receivables	1,200
Sales	30,650
	31,850
Less: closing trade receivables (€1,900 − €100)	1,800
	30,050

(W11) Cash paid to suppliers and employees	€
Opening trade payables	1,890
Purchases (€26,000 − €1,950 + €1,000)	25,050
	26,940
Less: closing trade payables	250
	26,690
Administrative and selling expenses	950
	27,640

19.3 CONCLUSION

This chapter focuses on the preparation of a statement of cash flows for a single entity in accordance with IAS 7 *Statement of Cash Flows*. Issues relating specifically to the preparation of a consolidated statement of cash flows are dealt with in **Part V, Chapter 33**.

Accounting profit is unlikely to be a reliable indicator of an entity's cash position. A statement of cash flows can provide valuable information on cash inflows and outflows during the accounting period and can be used to assess an entity's ability to generate cash from its operations. Analysts and other users of financial information often, formally and informally, develop models to assess and compare the present value of the future cash flows of entities. Historical cash flow information could be useful to check the accuracy of past assessments. It should be stressed, however, that a historical statement of cash flows does not provide complete information for assessing future cash flows. Statements of cash flows should normally be used in conjunction with statements of profit or loss and other comprehensive income and statements of financial position when making an assessment of future cash flows.

SUMMARY OF LEARNING OBJECTIVES

Having studied this chapter on IAS 7 *Statement of Cash Flows*, you should be able to:

Learning Objective 1 Demonstrate a knowledge of the standard headings under which IAS 7 requires cash flows to be classified.

IAS 7 requires the cash flows to be classified into three separate sections: operating; investing; and financing. These are shown in **Figure 19.1** and explained in **Section 19.2**.

Learning Objective 2 Define cash and cash equivalents in accordance with IAS 7.

Cash refers to cash-in-hand and deposits repayable on demand, while cash equivalents are short-term, highly liquid investments that are readily convertible to known amounts of cash and that are subject to an insignificant risk of changes in value. The maturity date of cash equivalents should normally be three months from their acquisition date.

Learning Objective 3 Prepare a single company statement of cash flows in accordance with IAS 7 using both the direct and indirect methods.

This is illustrated in **Section 19.3**.

Learning Objective 4 Discuss the advantages of cash flow reporting.

In the short term, business viability is determined by its ability to generate cash. Ultimately profit is of little value if it cannot be translated into cash. Even profitable companies will fail if they do not have access to sufficient cash resources. Consequently information about cash flows is essential in order to help users form an opinion on a company's liquidity, viability and financial adaptability.

QUESTIONS

Self-test Questions

1. What are the standard headings under which IAS 7 requires cash flows to be classified?
2. How does IAS 7 define cash and cash equivalents?
3. What does the direct method of reporting net cash flows from operating activities show?
4. What are the advantages of a statement of cash flows?

Review Questions

Question 19.1

BEN Limited

STATEMENT OF PROFIT OR LOSS AND OTHER COMPREHENSIVE INCOME
for the Year Ended 31 December 2012

	€000
Revenue	2,553
Cost of sales	(1,814)
Gross profit	739
Distribution costs	(125)
Administrative expenses	(264)
Operating profit	350
Interest received	25
Interest paid	(75)
Profit before taxation	300
Taxation	(140)
Profit for year	160

BEN Limited
STATEMENT OF FINANCIAL POSITION
as at 31 December

	2012 €000	2011 €000
ASSETS		
Non-current assets		
Property, plant and equipment	380	305
Intangible assets	250	200
Investments	–	25
Current assets		
Inventories	150	102
Receivables	390	315
Short-term investments	50	–
Cash in hand	2	1
Total assets	1,222	948
EQUITY AND LIABILITIES		
Equity		
Share capital (€1 ordinary shares)	200	150
Share premium account	160	150
Revaluation reserve	100	91
Retained earnings	160	100
	620	491
Non-current liabilities		
Long-term loan	170	50
Current liabilities		
Trade payables	127	119
Bank overdraft	85	98
Taxation	120	110
Dividends proposed	100	80
	432	407
Total equity and liabilities	1,222	948

Additional Information:
(a) The proceeds of the sale of non-current asset investments amounted to €30,000.
(b) Fixtures and fittings, with an original cost of €85,000 and a net book value of €45,000, were sold for €32,000 during the year.
(c) The following information relates to tangible non-current assets:

	31 December 2012 €000	31 December 2011 €000
Cost	720	595
Accumulated depreciation	340	290
Net book value	380	305

(d) 50,000 €1 ordinary shares were issued during the year at a premium of 20c per share.

(e) Wages charged in the statement of profit or loss and other comprehensive income amounted to €90,000, of which €5,000 was unpaid at the year-end.

(f) During the year ended 31 December 2012, dividends amounting to €100,000 were debited to equity. Dividends proposed, which are included in current liabilities, were approved by the shareholders prior to the relevant reporting period date.

Requirement Prepare a statement of cash flows for the year ended 31 December 2012 for Ben Limited using both direct and indirect methods in accordance with IAS 7 *Statement of Cash Flows*.

Question 19.2

The statement of profit or loss and other comprehensive income of HANSOL plc for the year ended 31 December 2012 and the statement of financial position as at that date are shown below.

HANSOL plc
STATEMENT OF PROFIT OR LOSS AND OTHER COMPREHENSIVE INCOME
for the Year Ended 31 December 2012

	€000
Revenue	37,182
Cost of sales	(28,340)
Gross profit	8,842
Operating expenses (including gain on sale of property, plant and equipment of €194,000)	(4,259)
Operating profit	4,583
Interest receivable	308
Finance costs	(224)
Profit before taxation	4,667
Income tax expense	(1,540)
Profit for the year	3,127

HANSOL plc
STATEMENT OF FINANCIAL POSITION
as at 31 December 2012

	Note	2012 €000	2011 €000
ASSETS			
Non-current Assets			
Property, plant and equipment	2	10,877	9,970
Intangible assets	1	162	270
		11,039	10,240
Current Assets			
Inventory		2,080	886
Trade receivables		6,006	4,542

Cash-in-hand and at bank		3,070	1,840
		11,156	7,268
Total assets		22,195	17,508

EQUITY AND LIABILITIES

Capital and Reserves

Called-up share capital	5	1,300	1,200
Share premium account	5	2,950	2,800
Other reserves		300	300
Retained earnings		5,848	4,921
		10,398	9,221
Non-current Liabilities	4	4,704	2,008
Current Liabilities	3	7,093	6,279
Total equity and liabilities		22,195	17,508

During the year ended 31 December 2012, dividends amounting to €2,200,000 were debited to equity.

Additional Information:
1. Intangible assets represent patents held by the company. These are amortised over the shorter of the anticipated period of profitable exploitation and the period to the expiry of the right. The company registered no new patents during 2012.
2. Property, plant and equipment

	Land and property €000	Plant and equipment €000	Total €000
Cost or valuation:			
At 1 January 2012	3,242	11,223	14,465
Additions	900	1,689	2,589
Disposals	–	(546)	(546)
	4,142	12,366	16,508
Accumulated depreciation:			
At 1 January 2012	1,291	3,204	4,495
Charge for year	410	1,116	1,526
On disposal	–	(390)	(390)
	1,701	3,930	5,631
Net book value:			
At 31 December 2012	2,441	8,436	10,877
At 31 December 2011	1,951	8,019	9,970

3. Current liabilities

	2012 €000	2011 €000
Bank overdraft	52	–
Trade payables	4,108	3,520

Fixed asset payable	1,196	1,178
Finance lease creditor	70	101
Income tax	1,258	1,178
Dividends	382	296
Accruals and deferred income	27	6
	7,093	6,279

Accruals and deferred income comprise interest payable on:

	2012	2011
	€000	€000
Finance leases	3	3
Bank overdraft	24	3
	27	6

4. Non-current liabilities

	2012	2011
	€000	€000
Medium-term bank loans	1,726	–
Finance lease obligations	238	358
Deferred taxation	2,740	1,650
	4,704	2,008

5. Called-up share capital and share premium account

	€1 Ordinary shares €000	Share premium €000
At 1 January 2012	1,200	2,800
Shares issued on acquisition	100	200
Expenses connected with share issue	–	(50)
At 31 December 2012	1,300	2,950

Requirement In accordance with IAS 7 *Statement of Cash Flows*, prepare a statement of cash flows using the indirect method for HANSOL plc in respect of the year ended 31 December 2012.

Challenging Questions

(Suggested Solutions to Challenging Questions are available to lecturers.)

Question 19.1 (Based on Chartered Accountants Ireland, P3 Autumn 1998, Question 6)

The following information is provided for SAPIENT Limited in respect of the year ended 31 December 2012:

SAPIENT Limited
STATEMENT OF PROFIT OR LOSS AND OTHER COMPREHENSIVE INCOME
for the Year Ended 31 December 2012

	€000
Revenue	4,020
Cost of sales	(2,060)
Gross profit	1,960
Distribution costs	(816)
Administrative expenses (includes profit on sale of plant of €100,000 and loss on sale of equipment of €20,000)	(214)
Operating profit	930
Interest receivable and similar income	108
Interest payable and similar charges	(128)
Profit on ordinary activities before taxation	910
Tax on profit on ordinary activities	(70)
Profit for year	840

SAPIENT Limited
STATEMENT OF FINANCIAL POSITION
as at 31 December 2012

	2012	2012	2011	2011
	€000	€000	€000	€000
ASSETS				
Non-current Assets				
Plant at cost	2,860		2,060	
Accumulated depreciation	(860)	2,000	(660)	1,400
Equipment at cost	1,260		1,140	
Accumulated depreciation	(660)	600	(620)	520
		2,600		1,920
Current Assets				
Inventory	370		410	
Trade receivables	590		290	
Investments	1,000		–	
Bank and cash	610	2,570	300	1,000
		5,170		2,920
EQUITY AND LIABILITIES				
Capital and Reserves				
Called-up share capital		2,300		2,000
Share premium account		100		–
Retained earnings		1,250		450
		3,650		2,450
Non-current Liabilities				
12% debentures		1,200		–
Current Liabilities				
Bank overdraft		–		100
Trade payables		205		305
Taxation		85		55

Dividends	30	320	10	470
		5,170		2,920

Additional Information:
1. Depreciation of non-current assets has been charged to distribution costs.
2. Included in administration expenses is €30,000 paid in connection with the share issue.
3. Plant with a net book value of €600,000, which had originally cost €1,000,000, was sold during the year.
4. Equipment with a net book value of €60,000, which had originally cost €200,000, was sold during the year.
5. All non-current asset additions during the year were paid for in cash.
6. Investments included within current assets relate to a nine-month term deposit that matures on 1 February 2013. If the deposit is withdrawn before the maturity date, all rights to interest in the month of withdrawal are forfeited.
7. Dividends of €40,000 were debited to equity during the year ended 31 December 2012.

Requirement Using both the direct and indirect methods, prepare a statement of cash flows for SAPIENT Limited for the year ended 31 December 2012 in accordance with IAS 7 *Statement of Cash Flows*.

Question 19.2 (Chartered Accountants Ireland, P3 Summer 2005, Question 5)

The statement of profit or loss and other comprehensive income for the year ended 31 December 2012 of Clinic Limited (Clinic) and a statement of financial position as at that date, together with comparative figures, are as follows.

Clinic Limited
STATEMENT OF PROFIT OR LOSS AND OTHER COMPREHENSIVE INCOME
for the Year Ended 31 December

	2012	2011
	€000	€000
Revenue	11,250	9,900
Cost of sales	(7,890)	(6,750)
Gross profit	3,360	3,150
Other operating expenses	(2,670)	(2,610)
Operating profit	690	540
Interest payable and similar charges	(540)	(270)
Profit before taxation	150	270
Income tax expense	(30)	(60)
Profit after taxation	120	210

Clinic Limited
STATEMENT OF FINANCIAL POSITION AS AT 31 DECEMBER

	2012	2011
ASSETS	€000	€000
Non-current Assets	1,440	1,320
Current Assets		
Inventory	1,890	1,530

Trade receivables	2,850	2,130
Bank and cash	30	30
	6,210	5,010

EQUITY AND LIABILITIES

Share Capital and Reserves

€1 ordinary shares	600	570
Share premium account	30	–
Retained earnings	210	180
	840	750

Non-current Liabilities

Bank loans	2,190	1,800
10% debentures	1,140	900
	3,330	2,700

Current Liabilities

Bank overdraft	30	–
Current instalments due on loans	540	540
10% debentures	300	–
Trade payables	1,080	870
Taxation	30	90
Dividends payable	60	60
	2,040	1,560
	6,210	5,010

Additional Information:

1. On 1 July 2012, Clinic issued 60,000 €1 ordinary shares at €2 per share. Additionally, CLINIC purchased and cancelled 30,000 of its own €1 ordinary shares on 1 October 2012 at €2 per share.
2. During the year ended 31 December 2012, Clinic sold non-current assets with a net book value of €90,000, which had originally cost €750,000, for cash. Included in trade payables at 31 December 2012 is an amount of €450,000 in respect of non-current assets purchased during the year ended 31 December 2012.
3. Depreciation of €600,000 was charged during the year ended 31 December 2012. This amount is included in 'other operating expenses', together with a profit on disposal on non-current assets of €60,000. Also included in other operating expenses is €30,000 paid in connection with the issue and purchase of ordinary shares during the year.
4. The following dividends were debited to equity:

	2012	2011
	€000	€000
Ordinary dividends	90	90

Requirement Prepare a statement of cash flows for Clinic for the year ended 31 December 2012 in accordance with IAS 7 *Statement of Cash Flows*.

Note: you are not required to prepare notes to the statement of cash flows.

PART IV

DISCLOSURES

20

NON-CURRENT ASSETS HELD FOR SALE AND DISCONTINUED OPERATIONS

LEARNING OBJECTIVES

Having studied this chapter on non-current assets held for sale and discontinued operations, you should be able to:
1. identify, measure and disclose non-current assets held for sale;
2. explain the concept of a disposal group;
3. define a discontinued operation;
4. account for a discontinued operation; and
5. apply the disclosure requirements relating to non-current assets held for sale and discontinued operations.

KEY TERMS AND DEFINITIONS FOR THIS CHAPTER

In order to aid your understanding of the concepts and issues covered in this chapter, it is important to understand and be familiar with the following key terms and definitions. As you study this chapter, you should refer back to them.

Arm's Length Transaction This is a transaction when all parties to the transaction are independent and on an equal footing.

Cash Generating Unit (CGU) The smallest identifiable group of assets that generate cash inflows that are largely independent of the cash inflows from other assets or groups of assets.

Costs to Sell The incremental costs directly attributable to the disposal of an asset or disposal of a group of assets, excluding finance costs and tax expense.

Discontinued Operation This is a component of an entity that either has been disposed of or is classified as held for sale and which: represents a separate major line of business or geographical area of operations; is part of a single co-ordinated plan to dispose of a separate major line of business or geographical area of operations; or is a subsidiary acquired exclusively with a view to resale.

Disposal Group A group of assets to be disposed of, by sale or otherwise, as a group in a single transaction, together with the liabilities directly associated with those assets that will be transferred in the transaction. A disposal group could be a group of **CGU**s or part of a CGU.

Fair Value The amount for which an asset could be exchanged or liability settled in an arm's length transaction.

Firm Purchase Commitment This is an agreement with an unrelated party binding on both parties and legally enforceable that: (1) specifies all significant terms; and (2) includes a disincentive for non-performance that is likely to make performance highly probable.

Net Realisable Value (NRV) This is the amount obtainable from the sale of an asset in an **arm's length transaction** less costs of disposal. It is also referred to as the fair value less **costs to sell**.

Non-current Asset This is an asset acquired for use within the business, with a view to earning profits from its use. A non-current asset is not acquired for resale and includes property, plant and equipment. Non-current assets are usually held and used by a business for a number of years.

20.1 INTRODUCTION

This chapter addresses two main issues: non-current assets held for sale and **discontinued operations**, both of which are dealt with by IFRS 5 *Non-current Assets Held for Sale and Discontinued Operations*.

Non-current assets, which typically include property, plant and equipment, are normally held for use in the day-to-day operations of the business rather than for sale. The 'cost' of using such assets is usually reflected in the financial statements through depreciation and, notwithstanding issues of impairment (see **Chapter 10**), the **net realisable value (NRV)** of these assets is generally of little interest to users of the financial statements. However, if non-current assets are held for sale rather than for continued use, then concepts of useful economic life and depreciation are no longer relevant and NRV becomes more important. As a result, given that the intention is not to continue to use the asset in the business, many of the accounting principles contained in IAS 16 *Property, Plant and Equipment* (see **Chapter 6**) are largely inappropriate (e.g. allocating the cost of the asset over its estimated useful economic life through depreciation). Moreover, as non-current assets that are held for sale are often used in operations that have been discontinued, it is logical that one accounting standard should address these (often) related issues.

This chapter explains how an entity should account for, and disclose, non-current assets held for sale and discontinued operations in accordance with IFRS 5 *Non-current Assets Held for*

Sale and Discontinued Operations. If a non-current asset is held for sale, the economic benefit of that asset is obtained through the asset's sale rather than through its continuous use in the business (future economic benefit). Such assets cease to be depreciated, as they are no longer being consumed by the business. Moreover, an asset held for sale is valued at the lower of either the asset's carrying value or the asset's **fair value** less the cost of selling this asset. For a non-current asset to be classified as **held for sale**, *all* of the following conditions must be satisfied:

- the asset must be available for immediate sale in its present condition and location;
- the asset's sale is expected to be completed within 12 months of classification as held for sale;
- there must be no expectation that the plan for selling the asset will be withdrawn or changed significantly; and
- the successful sale of the asset must be highly probable, signified by both:
  ○ the management's commitment to the asset-selling plan; and
  ○ the existence of active marketing to support the sale of the asset.

A **discontinued operation** is a component of an enterprise that has either been disposed of or is classified as held for sale, and which:

- represents a separate major line of business or geographical area of operations; and
- is part of a single, co-ordinated plan to dispose of this separate major line of business or geographical area of operations; or
- is a subsidiary acquired exclusively with a view to resale.

Key to this Chapter

IFRS 5 addresses two main issues:
- non-current assets held for sale; and
- discontinued operations.

After outlining the objective and scope of IFRS 5 in the next section, these two issues are explained in detail in **Sections 20.3** and **20.4**, respectively.

20.2 IFRS 5 *NON-CURRENT ASSETS HELD FOR SALE AND DISCONTINUED OPERATIONS*

Objective of IFRS 5

The objective of IFRS 5 is to improve the information about assets and **disposal groups** that are about to be disposed of and to improve the information about discontinued operations. It does this by specifying the:

- requirements for the classification, measurement and presentation of non-current assets held for sale, in particular requiring that such assets should be presented separately on the face of the statement of financial position (see **Section 20.3**, and **Example 20.10**); and
- rules for the presentation of discontinued operations, in particular requiring that the results of discontinued operations should be presented separately in the statement of profit or loss and other comprehensive income (see **Section 20.4**, and **Example 20.11**).

Scope of IFRS 5

The measurement provisions of IFRS 5 apply to all non-current assets and disposal groups, **except for**:

- deferred tax assets (IAS 12 *Income Taxes* – see **Chapter 13**);
- assets arising from employee benefits (IAS 19 *Employee Benefits* – see **Chapter 17**);
- financial assets within the scope of IAS 39 *Financial Instruments: Recognition and Measurement*/ IFRS 9 *Financial Instruments* (see **Chapter 25**);
- non-current assets that are accounted for in accordance with the fair value model in IAS 40 *Investment Property* (see **Chapter 5**);
- non-current assets that are measured at fair value less estimated point-of-sale costs in accordance with IAS 41 *Agriculture* (see **Chapter 34**); and
- contractual rights under insurance contracts as defined in IFRS 4 *Insurance Contracts* (see **Chapter 34**).

As stated above, IFRS 5 addresses two main issues: non-current assets held for sale and discontinued operations. These are dealt with in **Section 20.3** and **Section 20.4**, respectively.

20.3 NON-CURRENT ASSETS HELD FOR SALE

This section focuses on non-current assets held for sale. It begins by examining the classification and measurement of non-current assets held for sale, before examining changes to a plan of sale, non-current assets to be abandoned, impairment losses and changes in fair value. The section concludes by outlining the main presentation and disclosure requirements.

Classification and Measurement

The key points regarding the classification and measurement of non-current assets held for sale are:

- An entity must classify a non-current asset (or disposal group) as *held for sale* if its carrying amount will be recovered principally through a sale transaction rather than through continuing use. This means that the asset or disposal group must be available for *immediate sale* in its present condition and the sale must be *highly probable*, i.e. management must be committed to the disposal. If the period to complete the sale extends beyond one year due to circumstances outside the entity's control (see **Example 20.7**), this does not preclude the asset or disposal group from being treated in accordance with IFRS 5.
- An entity must measure a non-current asset (or disposal group) as held for resale at the lower of the carrying amount *and* fair value *less* **costs to sell**. When the sale is expected to occur after one year, costs to sell must be measured at their present value.
- An entity should not depreciate or amortise a non-current asset while it is classified as held for resale since the intention is to cease using the asset in the business and depreciation/ amortisation is the allocation of the cost of an asset over its estimated useful economic life. However, expenses and interest that relate to liabilities in a disposal group should be recognised as these are likely to be incurred.

- If a newly acquired asset meets the criteria as held for sale, it should be measured initially at fair value less costs to sell; and
- An entity must recognise an impairment loss for any initial or subsequent write down of an asset (or disposal group) from carrying amount to fair value less costs to sell.

Changes to a Plan of Sale

If an entity has classified an asset (or disposal group) as held for sale, in its statement of financial position, but the criteria no longer apply, it must reclassify it at the lower of:
- the carrying value at the date it was classified as held for sale adjusted by relevant depreciation; and
- the recoverable amount at the date of the decision not to sell.

The entity should include, in income from continuing operations, any required adjustments to the carrying value of a non-current asset that ceases to be classified as held for sale.

Non-current Assets to be Abandoned

These are *not* included as held for sale as their carrying amount will be recovered through use. However, if the **disposal group** to be abandoned is a component of an entity, the entity should present the results and cash flows of the disposal group as discontinued on the date it ceases to be used. **Example 20.1** illustrates when assets should be treated as abandoned (this should be contrasted with **Example 20.2**).

EXAMPLE 20.1: ABANDONED

In October 2012 an entity decides to abandon all of its cotton mills (major line of business). All work stops during 2013.

For 2012 the results and cash flows should be treated as continuing operations, but in 2013 the entity discloses the information for discontinued operations, including a restatement of any comparative figures.

A non-current asset that has been temporarily taken out of use as if abandoned should *not* be accounted for as abandoned. This is illustrated in **Example 20.2**.

EXAMPLE 20.2: NOT ABANDONED

An entity ceases to use a manufacturing plant because demand has declined. However, the plant is maintained in workable condition and it is expected to be brought back into use if demand picks up.

It is not, therefore, abandoned and the entity may not, for example, stop charging depreciation on the plant or treat it as a discontinued operation.

Classification of a Non-current Asset or Disposal Group as Held for Sale

An entity should classify a non-current asset (or disposal group) as held for sale in the reporting period in which *all* of the following criteria are met:

1. management is committed and has the authority to approve the action to sell;
2. the asset or disposal group is available for immediate sale in its present condition, subject to usual terms;
3. an active programme to locate a buyer is initiated;
4. the sale is highly probable and is expected to qualify for recognition as a completed sale within one year from the date of classification as held for sale;
5. the asset or disposal group is being actively marketed for sale at a reasonable price in relation to its fair value; and
6. actions required to complete the plan indicate that it is unlikely that significant changes to the plan will be made or the plan withdrawn.

A number of examples are now provided to illustrate the application of these criteria.

Example 20.3 considers what is considered a 'normal' time to vacate property so that it can be considered as available for immediate sale, even when there is a plan to sell in place.

EXAMPLE 20.3: PLAN TO SELL – TIME TO VACATE

An entity is committed to a plan to sell its HQ and has initiated action to find a buyer.

Situation 1
The entity intends to transfer the building to a buyer after it vacates the building. The time to vacate is normal. The criterion is met at the plan commitment date.

Situation 2
The entity will continue to use the building until a new HQ is built. The building will not be transferred until construction is completed. The delay demonstrates that the building is not available for immediate sale and thus the criterion is not met, even if a **firm purchase commitment** has already been entered into.

Example 20.4 addresses what is meant by 'available for immediate sale', even when active steps are being taken to find a buyer.

EXAMPLE 20.4: PLAN TO SELL – BACKLOG OF CUSTOMERS

An entity is committed to a plan to sell a manufacturing facility and has initiated action to locate a buyer, but there is a backlog of customer orders.

Situation 1
The entity intends to sell the manufacturing facility with its operations and any uncompleted orders will transfer to the buyer. The criterion will be met at the plan commitment date.

Situation 2

The entity intends to sell the manufacturing facility but without its operations and it does not intend to transfer it until it eliminates the backlog of orders. The delay means that the facility is not available for immediate sale and thus the criterion is not met until the operations cease, even if a firm purchase commitment were obtained before operations ceased.

When an entity acquires a non-current asset exclusively with a view to subsequent disposal, it should classify the non-current asset as held for sale at the acquisition date only if the one-year rule is met and it is highly probable that any other criteria that are not met at the acquisition date will be met within a short period following the acquisition. **Example 20.5** below emphasises that (mere) intentions to sell are *not* sufficient for non-current assets to be classified as 'available for immediate sale' in accordance with IFRS 5.

EXAMPLE 20.5: PLAN TO SELL – FUTURE WORK REQUIRED

An entity acquires a property via foreclosure comprising land and buildings that it intends to sell.

Situation 1

If the entity does not intend to sell until it completes renovations, the delay means the property is not available for immediate sale until the renovations are completed.

Situation 2

If, after renovations are completed and the property is classified as held for sale, the entity becomes aware of environmental damage, the property cannot be sold until remediation takes place. The property is thus not available for immediate sale and the criterion would not be met. It would have to be reclassified.

IFRS 5 states that a sale must be highly probable and expected to qualify for recognition as a completed sale within one year from the date of classification as held for sale. The application of this is illustrated in **Example 20.6**.

EXAMPLE 20.6: PROBABILITY OF SALE UNLIKELY

To qualify as held for sale, the sale of a non-current asset must be highly probable and be expected to qualify as a sale within one year. The criterion would *not* be met if, for example:

Situation 1

An entity that is a commercial leasing company is holding for sale or lease equipment that has recently ceased to be leased and the ultimate form of a future transaction has not yet been determined; or

Situation 2

An entity is committed to sell a property that is in use and the transfer will be accounted for as a sale and leaseback.

However, if the delay to complete the sale within one year is caused by events beyond the entity's control and there is sufficient evidence that the entity remains committed to its plan to sell the asset, the asset or disposal group can still be classified as held for sale in the following situations:

(a) at the date an entity commits itself to a plan to sell, it reasonably expects that others will impose conditions on the transfer of the asset that will extend the period beyond one year and:
   (i) actions cannot be initiated until after a firm purchase commitment is obtained, and
   (ii) a firm purchase commitment is highly probable within one year;
(b) an entity obtains a firm purchase commitment and a buyer unexpectedly imposes conditions to extend the period beyond one year and:
   (i) timely actions necessary to respond have been taken, and
   (ii) a favourable resolution of the delaying factors is expected;
(c) during the initial one-year period, circumstances arise that were previously considered unlikely and:
   (i) during the initial one year the entity took action to respond to the change in circumstances,
   (ii) the non-current asset is being actively marketed given the change in circumstances, and
   (iii) all of the six criteria referred to earlier are met.

The application of these situations is illustrated in **Examples 20.7–20.9.**

EXAMPLE 20.7: SALE PERIOD BEYOND ONE YEAR (A)

An entity in the power-generation industry is strongly committed to a plan to sell a disposal group that represents a significant portion of its regulated operations. The sale requires regulatory approval that could extend beyond one year. However, while it is highly probable that a buyer will be found, actions to obtain approval from the regulator cannot be initiated until a buyer is located and a firm purchase commitment obtained.

As the sale is highly probable, it may be classified as held for sale even though it extends beyond one year.

EXAMPLE 20.8: SALE PERIOD BEYOND ONE YEAR (B)

An entity is committed to sell a manufacturing facility but, after a firm purchase commitment is obtained, the buyer's inspection identifies environmental damage that must be made good and this will extend beyond one year. However, the entity has initiated appropriate procedures to repair the environmental damage and the sale remains highly probable.

Thus, it can be classified as held for sale.

EXAMPLE 20.9: SALE PERIOD BEYOND ONE YEAR (C)

An entity is committed to sell a non-current asset and classifies the asset as held for sale at that date.

Situation 1

If, during the initial one-year period: (1) market conditions deteriorate; (2) the asset is not sold; (3) no reasonable offers are received; and (4) the asset continues to be actively marketed, then at the end of the first year the asset would continue to be classified as held for sale.

Situation 2

If, during the following year: (1) market conditions deteriorate further; (2) the asset is not sold; and (3) the sale price has not been reduced, then as a result, in the absence of a price reduction, the asset is not available for immediate sale and therefore the criterion is not met. The asset will no longer be classified as held for sale and will need to be reclassified.

In accordance with IAS 10 *Events after the Reporting Period* (see **Chapter 15**), if the criteria are met after the end of the reporting period but before the financial statements are authorised, then an entity should not classify a non-current asset as held for sale. However, the entity should disclose the information in the Notes.

Impairment Losses and Subsequent Increases in Fair Values less Costs to Sell of Assets that were Previously Revalued

Any asset carried at a revalued amount under another IFRS should be revalued under that IFRS immediately before it is classified as held for sale under IFRS 5. For example, a non-current asset recorded at fair value in accordance with the IAS 16 revaluation model (see **Chapter 6, Section 6.2**). Any impairment loss that arises on reclassification of the asset should be recognised in the statement of profit or loss and other comprehensive income in accordance with IAS 16 (see **Chapter 6**) and IAS 36 *Impairment of Assets* (see **Chapter 10**).

Subsequent Impairment Losses

Any subsequent increases in costs to sell should be recognised in the statement of profit or loss and other comprehensive income. After classification as held for sale, any subsequent impairment must be accounted for in accordance with IFRS 5 and recognised in arriving at profit or loss, even for assets carried at revalued amounts.

Subsequent Gains

Any subsequent decreases in costs to sell (i.e. following revaluation) should be recognised in the statement of profit or loss and other comprehensive income in arriving at profit or loss. A gain for any subsequent increase in fair value less costs to sell should be recognised in arriving at profit or loss, but not in excess of the cumulative impairment loss recognised in accordance with IFRS 5.

Gains or Losses Relating to Continuing Operations

Any gain/loss on the remeasurement of a non-current asset classified as held for sale that does not meet the definition of a discontinued operation should be included in the profit/loss from continuing operations reported in the statement of profit or loss and other comprehensive income.

Presentation and Disclosure

Information should be presented to enable users to evaluate the financial effects of discontinued operations and disposals of non-current assets.

Presentation of a Non-current Asset or Disposal Group Classified as Held for Sale

These should be disclosed separately from other assets. The liabilities of a disposal group classified as held for sale should be presented separately from other liabilities. These assets and liabilities should not be offset but disclosed separately on the face of the statement of financial position. This is illustrated in **Example 20.10**.

EXAMPLE 20.10: DISCLOSURE – HELD FOR SALE

At the end of 2012, an entity decides to dispose of part of its assets together with the liabilities directly associated with those assets. This disposal, which meets the criteria as held for sale, takes the form of two disposal groups, as follows:

NBV after classification as held for sale:

	Disposal group 1 €	Disposal group 2 €
Property, plant and equipment	4,900	1,700
Asset for sale – financial asset	1,400*	-
Liabilities	(2,400)	(900)
NBV of disposal group	3,900	800

* An amount of €400 relating to these assets has been recognised directly in equity.

The presentation in the entity's statement of financial position of the disposal groups classified as held for sale can be shown as follows:

	2012 €	2011 €
Assets		
Non-current assets		
AAA	X	X
BBB	X	X
CCC	X	X

	X	X
Current assets		
DDD	X	X
EEE	X	X
	X	X
Non-current assets classified as held for sale (€4,900 + €1,400 + €1,700)	8,000	–
	X	X
Total assets	X	X
Equity and Liabilities		
Equity attributable to equity-holders of the parent		
FFF	X	X
GGG	X	X
Amounts recognised directly in equity relating to non-current assets held for sale	400	–
	X	X
Non-controlling interests	X	X
Total equity	X	X
Non-current liabilities		
HHH	X	X
III	X	X
JJJ	X	X
	X	X
Current liabilities		
KKK	X	X
LLL	X	X
MMM	X	X
Liabilities directly associated with non-current assets classified as held for sale (€2,400 + €900)	3,300	–
	X	X
Total liabilities	X	X
Total equity and liabilities	X	X

Additional Disclosures

The following should be disclosed in the Notes:
- a description of the non-current asset (or disposal group);
- a description of the facts and circumstances leading to the expected disposal and manner and timing of that disposal;
- the gain or loss on impairment or subsequent increase in fair value for assets previously not revalued; and
- if applicable, the segment in which the non-current asset is presented under IFRS 8 *Operating Segments*.

Any changes to a plan should be described and the facts and circumstances leading to the decision to change the plan provided.

20.4 DISCONTINUED OPERATIONS

This chapter addresses two main issues: non-current assets held for sale and discontinued operations, both of which are dealt with by IFRS 5. **Section 20.3** dealt with non-current assets held for sale and this section focuses on discontinued operations.

A **discontinued operation** may be a subsidiary, or a major line of business or geographical area. It will have been a **CGU** (or group of CGUs) as defined in IAS 36 *Impairment of Assets* (see **Chapter 10**). A component of an entity comprises operations and cash flows that can clearly be distinguished from the rest of the entity. A discontinued operation is a component of an entity that has either been disposed of or is classified as held for sale and that:
- represents a separate major line of business or geographical area of operations; or
- is part of a single co-ordinated plan to dispose of a separate major line of business or geographical area of operations; or
- is a subsidiary acquired exclusively with a view to resale.

Presentation and Disclosure

An entity should disclose for all periods presented (i.e. current and prior periods/comparatives):
(a) as a *single amount* on the face of the statement of profit or loss and other comprehensive income *comprising*:
    (i) post-tax profit/loss of discontinued operations, and
    (ii) post-tax gains/losses on measurement to fair value or on disposal of discontinued operations;
(b) an analysis of (a) into:
    (i) revenue, expenses and pre-tax profits/losses of discontinued operations,
    (ii) related tax expense,
    (iii) gains/losses on measurement to fair value or on disposal of discontinued operations, and
    (iv) related tax expense; and
(c) the net cash flows attributable to the operating, investing and financing activities of discontinued operations.

The disclosures required by (a) must be on the face of the statement of profit or loss and other comprehensive income, but the others may be presented in the Notes or on the face of the statement of profit or loss and other comprehensive income. Prior periods for disclosures (a) to (c) are also required. Adjustments to previous discontinued operations of prior periods should be classified separately, e.g. resolution of uncertainties.

As explained in **Chapter 1**, IAS 1 *Presentation of Financial Statements* permits the preparation of a statement of profit or loss and other comprehensive income on either the 'function of expenditure' (or cost of sales format) or the 'nature of expenditure' format, the choice between the two being made according to which most fairly presents the elements of the entity's performance. An example of how discontinued operations might be presented using the 'function of expenditure' format is shown in **Figure 20.1**.

FIGURE 20.1: X LIMITED – STATEMENT OF PROFIT OR LOSS AND OTHER
COMPREHENSIVE INCOME
for the Year Ended 31 December 2012
(Single Statement including Discontinued Operations)

	2012 €000	2011 €000
Continuing Operations		
Revenue	360,000	355,000
Cost of sales	(230,000)	(230,000)
Gross profit	130,000	125,000
Other operating income	20,667	11,300
Distribution costs	(9,000)	(8,700)
Administrative expenses	(20,000)	(21,000)
Other expenses	(2,100)	(1,200)
Finance costs	(8,000)	(7,500)
Share of profit/(loss) of associates	35,100	30,100
Profit/(loss) before tax	146,667	128,000
Income tax expense	(40,417)	(32,000)
Profit/(loss) for the year for continuing operations	106,250	96,000
Discontinued Operations		
Profit/(loss) for the year for discontinued operations*	15,000	-
Profit/(loss) for the year	121,250	96,000
Other comprehensive income:		
Items that may be reclassified into profit or loss	5,334	10,667
Exchange differences on translating foreign operations		
Items that will not be reclassified into profit or loss	933	(3,300)
Gain/(loss) on property revaluation		
Remeasurement of net defined benefit pension liability	7,000	(4,000)
Other comprehensive income for the year	13,267	3,367
Total comprehensive income for the year	134,517	99,367
Profit/(loss) attributable to:		
Owners of the parent	121,250	99,367
Non-controlling interests *(Group financial statements only)*	-	-
	121,250	99,367
Total comprehensive income/(loss) attributable to:		
Owners of the parent	134,517	99,367
Non-controlling interests *(Group financial statements only)*	-	-
	134,517	99,367
Earnings per share (see **Chapter 23**)	23.1c	14.6c

*Alternatively, profit from discontinued operations could be analysed in a separate column in the statement of profit or loss and other comprehensive income.

Presentation in the Statement of Cash Flows

An enterprise must disclose, either in the notes or on the face of the statement of cash flows, the net cash flows attributable to the operating, investing and financing activities of discontinued operations.

Example 20.11 below brings together a number of the issues covered in **Section 20.3** and **Section 20.4** in the form of an examination-style question. All of the issues included in this example have been explained and illustrated previously in this chapter.

EXAMPLE 20.11: NON-CURRENT ASSETS HELD FOR SALE AND
DISCONTINUED OPERATIONS

Marathon Limited (Marathon) has three divisions: a chocolate manufacturing division, a packaging division and a sweets manufacturing division. On 1 April 2012, the directors of Marathon decided to sell the sweets division as it was not in line with the core activities of the company. The decision was announced to the employees and the public on 1 June 2012. The net assets of the sweets division as at 31 December 2012 were €16 million (€20 million assets and €4 million liabilities).

On 10 May 2013, the board signed an agreement with Spangles Limited to sell the sweets division for €20 million. The net assets of the sweets division at this date were €18 million (€23 million assets and €5 million liabilities). Marathon incurred redundancy costs of €1 million, which had been expected from the date the decision to sell the division was made. The redundancies are not reflected in the statement of profit or loss and other comprehensive income below. The sale was completed on 1 July 2013 and the sweets division did not trade between 10 May 2013 and 1 July 2013.

The results of the sweets manufacturing division for 2012 and 2013 are:

	2012	2013 (to 1 July)
	€000	€000
Turnover	65,000	40,000
Expenses	(50,000)	(32,000)
Operating profit	15,000	8,000
Tax charge	(5,000)	(3,000)

Requirement Prepare extracts from the financial statements of Marathon (including Notes) for the year ended 31 December 2013 (including 2012 comparatives) in accordance with IFRS 5.

Suggested Solution

Marathon Limited
2012 FINANCIAL STATEMENTS
Note to the accounts

On 1 June 2012 the board of directors announced a plan to dispose of the sweets manufacturing segment as this segment is not in line with the core activities of the company. The company is actively seeking a buyer and hopes to have completed the sale by the end of 2013. At 31 December 2012 the carrying amount of the sweets segment assets was €20 million and the liabilities were €4 million. The sweets division had revenue of €65 million, incurred expenses of €50 million, had an operating profit of €14 million and a tax charge of €5 million on the profits for the year ended 31 December 2012. A provision of €1 million has been made in respect of redundancy costs expected when the division is sold.

Marathon Limited
2013 Financial Statements

Statement of Profit or Loss and Other Comprehensive Income (Extract)
for Year Ended 31 December 2013

	2013	2012
Continuing operations:	€000	€000
Revenue	X	X
Cost of sales, etc.	X	X
Profit for the period from continuing operations	X	X
	X	X
Discontinuing operations:		
Profit for the period from discontinued operations (note*)	X	X
Profit for the period	X	X

*Note on discontinued activities

	Discontinued Activities	
	2013	2012
	€000	€000
Revenue	40,000	65,000
Expenses	(32,000)	(50,000)
Redundancy costs	(1,000)	
Provision for redundancy costs	1,000	(1,000)
Operating profit	8,000	14,000
Profit on disposal of division	2,000	
Taxation	(3,000)	(5,000)

Please note that 2012 has been restated to present the results as discontinuing activities.

Statement of Financial Position (Extract)
as at 31 December 2013

	2013	2012
	€m	€m
Assets		
Non-current assets		
Property, plant and equip.	X	X
..		

Current assets		
..		
Non-current assets classified as held for sale*	$\overline{X}$	$\overline{X}$
		20
Total assets	X	X
	$\underline{\overline{X}}$	$\underline{\overline{X}}$
Equity and liabilities		
Capital and reserves		
OSC	X	X
..		
Non-current liabilities		
Trade and other payables	X	X
..		
	$\overline{X}$	$\overline{X}$
Liabilities directly associated with non-current assets classified as held for sale (4+1)**		
		5
Total liabilities	X	$\overline{X}$
Total equity and liabilities	$\underline{\overline{X}}$	$\underline{\overline{X}}$

* Assumed all the sweets assets are non-current (details disclosed here if material).
** Under IFRS 5 items meeting the classification as discontinued activities should be valued at fair value less costs to sell – provide for the redundancy costs.

In 2013 the assets and liabilities are removed.

Note to the accounts On 10 May 2013 the board signed an agreement to sell the sweets division for €20 million. This plan had been announced on 1 June 2012. The company decided to dispose of the division because its activities were inconsistent with the core activities of Marathon Limited. Marathon Limited recognised a provision of €1 million in 2012 for the costs of redundancy of employees, and this provision was released in 2013. Actual redundancy costs of €1 million were paid. The process of selling the company was completed on 1 July 2013 and the assets of the division at this date were €23 million and liabilities were €5 million. A pre-tax profit of €2 million was made on the disposal.

20.5 CONCLUSION

This chapter addresses two main issues: non-current assets held for sale and discontinued operations, both of which are dealt with in IFRS 5.

Assets held for sale A non-current asset (or disposal group) is classified as held for sale if its carrying amount will be recovered principally through a sale transaction rather than through continuing use. That is, the asset (or disposal group) is available for immediate sale and its sale is highly probable. A non-current asset (or disposal group) classified as held for sale is measured at the lower of fair value less costs to sell and its carrying amount. Once classified as held for sale, the asset is not depreciated. Any impairment loss on write down of the asset (or disposal group) to fair value less costs to sell is recognised in arriving at profit or loss in the statement of profit or loss and other comprehensive income. Any gain on subsequent increase in fair value less costs to sell is also recognised in profit or loss in the statement of profit of loss and other comprehensive income, but not in excess of the cumulative impairment loss already recognised on the asset either in accordance with IFRS 5 or IAS 36 *Impairment of Assets*.

Discontinued Operations A discontinued operation is a component of an entity that either has been disposed of or is held for sale. It may be a subsidiary, or a major line of business or geographical area. It will have been a cash-generating unit (or group of cash-generating units) as defined in IAS 36 *Impairment of Assets* (see **Chapter 10**).

SUMMARY OF LEARNING OBJECTIVES

Having studied this chapter on non-current assets held for sale and discontinued operations, you should be able to:

Learning Objective 1 Identify, measure and disclose non-current assets held for sale.

Once a non-current asset is classified as held for sale, it should cease to be depreciated and be valued at the lower of either the asset's carrying cost or the asset's fair value less the cost of selling this asset. For a non-current asset to be classified as held for sale, *all* of the following conditions must be satisfied:
- the asset must be available for immediate sale in its present condition and location;
- the asset's sale is expected to be completed within 12 months of classification as held for sale;
- there must be no expectation that the plan for selling the asset will be withdrawn or changed significantly; and
- the successful sale of the asset must be highly probable.

Learning Objective 2 Explain the concept of a disposal group.

A *disposal group* is a group of assets to be disposed of, by sale or otherwise, as a group in a single transaction, together with the liabilities directly associated with those assets that will be transferred in the transaction. A disposal group could be a group of CGUs or part of a CGU.

Learning Objective 3 Define a discontinued operation.

A *discontinued operation* is a component of an entity that either has been disposed of or is classified as held for sale and: represents a separate major line of business or geographical area of operations; is part of a single co-ordinated plan to dispose of a separate major line of business or geographical area of operations; or is a subsidiary acquired exclusively with a view to resale.

Learning Objective 4 Account for a discontinued operation.

An entity should disclose, for all periods presented, a single amount on the face of the statement of profit or loss and other comprehensive income comprising: 1. post-tax profit/loss of discontinued operations and 2. post-tax gains/losses on measurement to fair value or on disposal of discontinued operations.

Learning Objective 5 Apply the disclosure requirements relating to non-current assets held for sale and discontinued operations.

Information should be presented to enable users to evaluate the financial effects of discontinued operations and disposals of non-current assets (see **Sections 20.3** and **20.4**).

QUESTIONS

Self-test Questions

1. What is a discontinued operation?
2. What information must be disclosed in the financial statements for discontinued operations?

Review Questions

(See **Appendix One** for Suggested Solutions to Review Questions.)

Question 20.1

APF Limited is a divisionalised Irish company that trades from a number of retail outlets throughout Ireland. The company, which commenced trading approximately five years ago, prepares its financial statements to 31 December each year. During the last quarter of 2011, and the first half of 2012, APF Limited experienced severe trading difficulties and liquidity problems for the first time. Consequently, following a review of the business by the directors, it was decided to run down the non-core activities and focus on the 'premium' end of the company's market.

Issue 1 During 2012, APF Limited sold, for €1,000,000 cash, a division of the company. The sale proceeds represent the profit on the sale of the business and the directors wish to classify the proceeds as an extraordinary item in the company's statement of profit or loss and other comprehensive income for the year ended 31 December 2012. The directors believe that, while withdrawal from this market will have a material effect on the nature and focus of the company's operations, the company will benefit in the long-term because this market was too specialised and the division's customer base was entirely different from that of the company's core business. Up to the point of sale, this division had contributed the following:

	€000
Revenue	2,500
Cost of sales	1,500
Administrative expenses	500

Issue 2 In December 2012 the directors of APF Limited decided to close all of the company's retail outlets that sell less expensive, less exclusive items. The directors estimate that it

will take nine months to wind down these operations and that the net loss from these retail operations during this period will be €800,000. No provision has yet been made in the draft 2012 financial statements for this loss. The directors believe that any assets relating to these retail outlets are stated at their recoverable amount at 31 December 2012.

Requirement Explain how each of the above issues should be reflected in APF Limited's financial statements for the year ended 31 December 2012.

Challenging Questions

(Suggested Solutions to Challenging Questions are available to lecturers.)

Question 20.1 (Based on Chartered Accountants Ireland, P3 Autumn 2007, Question 4)

IT Global Limited (GLOBAL), a divisional company that prepares its financial statements to 31 December each year, is involved in the assembly of bespoke PC systems for home use (Assembly division), together with the retailing of computer hardware, software and related accessories (Retail division). Due to the deteriorating performance of the Assembly division as a result of strong price competition and changes in customer buying patterns, the directors of GLOBAL decided to significantly change the nature of the company's business focus.

Consequently, the directors approved the closure of the Assembly division, despite it typically generating approximately 25% of the company's revenue. Although details of the closure plan were announced publicly on 1 November 2012, including the cessation of advertising and promotion and the notification of suppliers, the Assembly division did not formally close until 31 March 2013.

GLOBAL
DRAFT TRIAL BALANCE
as at 31 December 2012

	DR €000	CR €000
Revenue – Assembly division		2,500
Revenue – Retail division		7,500
Purchases – Assembly division	1,500	
Purchases – Retail division	4,500	
Administrative expenses – Assembly division	300	
Administrative expenses – Retail division	1,200	
Selling and distribution costs – Assembly division	150	
Selling and distribution costs – Retail division	850	
Finance costs – Retail division	200	
Income tax expense – Assembly division	50	
Income tax expense – Retail division	150	
Property – cost	20,000	
Property – accumulated depreciation at 31 December 2012		4,000
Plant and equipment – cost	11,000	

Plant and equipment – accumulated depreciation at 31 December 2012		3,000
Inventory – Assembly division at 1 January 2012	500	
Inventory – Retail division at 1 January 2012	2,000	
Trade receivables/Trade payables	2,500	2,400
Other receivables/Other payables	500	400
Bank and cash	800	
€1 ordinary shares		1,000
Retained earnings at 1 January 2012		25,400
	46,200	46,200

Additional Information:

1. Property, plant and equipment shown in the trial balance above have been depreciated in accordance with company policy and relevant accounting standards in respect of the year ended 31 December 2012, with the depreciation charge being included in the appropriate expense category.

2. Inventory at 31 December 2012 consists of:

	€000
Assembly division	200
Retail division	1,900
	2,100

Included in the inventory of the Retail division at 31 December 2012 are items that originally cost €240,500. However, the items, which were not insured, were accidentally damaged while being moved in GLOBAL's warehouse and it will cost €90,000 to repair them. The normal selling price of the items is €375,000. GLOBAL has arranged to sell the items as refurbished goods through an agent, once the repair work has been completed, at a discount of 25% on the normal selling price. The agent will receive a commission of 12% of the reduced selling price.

3. The directors of GLOBAL would like to make a provision of €2,000,000 at 31 December 2012 for the costs of closing the Assembly division. This amount is net of €1,500,000 for the estimated profit on the disposal of property belonging to the division. During November and December 2012, GLOBAL pursued an active policy to locate a buyer for the property, which has a carrying value at 31 December 2012 of €2,500,000 and a fair value of €4,000,000. The contract for the sale of the property was signed on 17 March 2013 and completed on 11 April 2013 for €4,250,000.

4. The plant and equipment shown in the trial balance includes items relating to the Assembly division, which are being carried at a value of €1,000,000 at 31 December 2012. The directors anticipate that the plant and equipment will generate cash flows of €700,000 in the three months to 31 March 2013 and that its net selling price at 31 December 2012 was €800,000. The plant and equipment was sold on 31 March 2013 for €600,000.

5. It is anticipated that during the period 1 January 2013 to 31 March 2013 the Assembly division will incur operating losses of €250,000 before it closes. Furthermore, it is estimated that the company will incur retraining costs of €150,000 during this period.

Requirement Prepare the statement of profit or loss and other comprehensive income of GLOBAL for the year ended 31 December 2012 and the statement of financial position as at that date.

(Notes to the financial statements are not required, and the tax effects of any adjustments can be ignored.)

Question 20.2

IFRS 5 *Non-current Assets Held for Sale and Discontinued Operations* requires organisations to provide disclosures to help users understand the performance of the organisation in order to improve the decisions taken by users on the basis of the financial statements.

Requirement Describe how the disclosures relating to discontinued operations may help investors and lenders make decisions based on the financial statements.

ACCOUNTING POLICIES, CHANGES IN ACCOUNTING ESTIMATES AND ERRORS

LEARNING OBJECTIVES

Having studied this chapter you should be able to:
1. explain the criteria for selecting and changing accounting policies; and
2. account for and disclose changes in accounting policies, changes in accounting estimates and corrections of errors.

KEY TERMS AND DEFINITIONS FOR THIS CHAPTER

In order to aid your understanding of the concepts and issues covered in this chapter, it is important to understand and be familiar with the following key terms and definitions. As you study this chapter, you should refer back to them.

Accounting Policies The specific principles, basic conventions, rules and practices applied by the reporting entity in preparing and presenting its financial statements.

Carrying Amount This is the amount at which an asset is recognised in the statement of financial position.

Change in Accounting Estimate This is an adjustment of the carrying amount of an asset or liability, or the periodic consumption of an asset, that results from the assessment of the present status of and expected future benefits and obligations associated with assets and liabilities. Changes in accounting estimates are *not* corrections of errors.

Prior Period Errors Omissions from, and misstatements in, the entity's financial statements for one or more prior periods arising from a failure to use, or misuse of, reliable information that:

- was available when financial statements for those periods were authorised for issue; and
- could reasonably be expected to have been obtained and taken into account in the preparation and presentation of those financial statements.

Retrospective Change in Accounting Policy This is the application of a new accounting policy to transactions and events as if that policy had always been applied.

21.1 INTRODUCTION

While not an accounting standard, the *Conceptual Framework for Financial Reporting 2010 (IFRS Framework)* (see **Chapter 1, Section 1.3**) serves as a guide to resolving accounting issues that are not addressed directly in an accounting standard by setting out the principles that underlie the preparation and presentation of financial statements for external users. IAS 8 *Accounting Policies, Changes in Accounting Estimates and Errors* requires that, in the absence of an accounting standard or an interpretation that specifically applies to a transaction, an entity must use its judgement in developing and applying an **accounting policy** that results in information that is relevant and reliable. In making that judgement, IAS 8 requires management of the entity to consider the definitions, recognition criteria and measurement concepts for assets, liabilities, income and expenses in the *IFRS Framework*.

IAS 1 *Presentation of Financial Statements* (see **Chapter 2**) addresses issues associated with the presentation of financial statements. After IAS 1, the accounting standard that has most direct relevance to the presentation of financial statements is IAS 8 *Accounting Policies, Changes in Accounting Estimates and Errors*.

Key to this Chapter

As indicated by its title, IAS 8 deals with three issues: *accounting policies*, *changes in accounting estimates* and *errors*. Each of these is discussed in **Section 21.2**.

21.2 IAS 8 *ACCOUNTING POLICIES, CHANGES IN ACCOUNTING ESTIMATES AND ERRORS*

Objective and Scope of IAS 8

The objective of IAS 8 is to prescribe the criteria for selecting and changing **accounting policies**, together with the accounting treatment and disclosure of changes in accounting policies, **changes in accounting estimates** and correction of errors. IAS 8 applies to all financial statements prepared and presented in accordance with International Accounting Standards (IASs) and International Financial Reporting Standards (IFRSs).

As indicated by the title of IAS 8, the standard deals with three issues: *accounting policies*, *changes in accounting estimates* and *errors*. Each of these is discussed below, beginning with accounting policies and retrospective changes in them.

Accounting Policies

As explained in **Chapter 1**, one of the six qualitative characteristics of useful financial information is comparability, which involves consistency in the application of accounting concepts and policies.

Accounting policies are the specific principles, bases, conventions, rules and practices applied by an entity in preparing and presenting its financial statements. The key principles when selecting and applying accounting policies are:
- accounting policies should comply with IASs/IFRSs;
- where there is no specific IAS/IFRS, management should develop policies to ensure that the financial statements provide information that is:
  - relevant,
  - reliable,
  - reflects the substance of transactions,
  - neutral, i.e. free from bias,
  - prudent, and
  - complete in all material respects; and
- accounting policies should be selected and applied consistently for similar transactions.

Accounting policies are normally kept the same from period to period to ensure comparability of financial statements over time. However, there are three important situations where this principle of consistency should *not* be followed:
1. a change in accounting policy that results from the initial application of an IAS/IFRS (or 'Interpretation') should be accounted for using the specific transitional provisions of that standard (if any);
2. when a change in accounting policy results from the initial application of an IAS/IFRS (or Interpretation) which does not contain specific transitional provisions, the effect of the change in policy must be applied *retrospectively* (i.e. prior period adjustment) (see **Retrospective Changes in Accounting Policies** below); and
3. IAS 8 requires retrospective application of voluntary changes in accounting policies unless it is impracticable to determine the cumulative effect of the change. In such cases *prospective* application is allowed.

Retrospective Changes in Accounting Policies

When a **retrospective change in accounting policy** is required, the reporting entity must adjust the opening balance of each affected component of equity for the earliest prior period presented and any other relevant comparative amounts as if the new accounting policy had always been applied. This means that there will be a prior period adjustment to the balance of retained earnings brought forward in the statement of changes in equity. The total prior period adjustment is the cumulative effect on opening reserves as if the new policy had always been applied.

Comparative information should be restated unless it is impracticable to do so. If the adjustment to opening retained earnings cannot be reasonably determined, the change should be adjusted prospectively, i.e. included in the current period's statement of profit or loss and other comprehensive income.

When a change in accounting policy has a material effect on the current period, or any prior period presented, or may have a material effect in subsequent periods, the following disclosures should be made:
- the reasons for the change;
- the amount of the adjustment recognised in the current period; and
- the amount of the adjustment included in each period prior to those included in the financial statements.

A retrospective change in accounting policy is illustrated in **Examples 21.1** and **21.2**.

EXAMPLE 21.1: RETROSPECTIVE CHANGE IN ACCOUNTING POLICY (1)

Raven Limited has traditionally valued its inventory using the weighted average method of valuation (see **Chapter 11**, **Section 11.2**). During the year ended 31 December 2012, the directors of Raven Limited decided to change the method of inventory valuation to the First In First Out (FIFO) method in order to give a fairer presentation of the company's results and financial position.

The reported retained earnings of Raven Limited at 31 December 2010 were €2,500,000 and extracts from the company's financial statements for each of the last three years, on the basis of inventory being valued on a weighted average basis, are provided below.

	2010 €	2011 €	2012 €
Cost of sales	830,000	904,000	968,000
Profit after tax	50,000	80,000	105,000
Inventory valuation:			
Weighted average basis	275,000	257,000	304,000
FIFO basis	296,000	294,000	365,000

Requirement Based on the information provided above, show how the change in inventory valuation method will be reflected in the financial statements of Raven Limited for the year ended 31 December 2012.

Solution

	2012 €	2011 €
Statement of Profit or Loss and Other Comprehensive Income		
Cost of sales	944,000	888,000

Profit after tax	129,000	96,000
Statement of Financial Position		
Inventory	365,000	294,000

Statement of Changes in Equity

At start of period (€2,500,000 + €80,000)	2,580,000
Change in accounting policy (€21,000 + €16,000 (W1))	37,000
	2,617,000
Profit for year (€105,000 + €24,000 (W2))	129,000
	2,746,000

WORKINGS

(W1)

	€
Inventory movement (increase) – 2010	21,000
Inventory movement (increase) – 2011	37,000
Cost of sales impact (decrease) – 2011	16,000

(W2)

Inventory movement (increase) – 2011	37,000
Inventory movement (increase) – 2012	61,000
Cost of sales impact (decrease) – 2012	24,000

EXAMPLE 21.2: RETROSPECTIVE CHANGE IN ACCOUNTING POLICY (2)

Extract from the Notes to the Financial Statements

Voluntary change in accounting policy

These financial statements have been prepared on the basis of a retrospective application of a voluntary change in accounting policy relating to exploration and evaluation expenditure. The new exploration and evaluation expenditure accounting policy is to capitalise and carry forward exploration and evaluation expenditure as an asset when rights to tenure of the area of interest are current and costs are expected to be recouped through successful development and exploitation of the area of interest, or alternatively by its sale. The previous accounting policy was to charge exploration and evaluation expenditure as an expense in arriving at profit or loss as incurred.

The new accounting policy was adopted on 31 October 2012 and has been applied retrospectively. Management judges that the change in policy will result in the financial statements providing more relevant and no less reliable information because it will lead to a more transparent treatment of exploration and evaluation expenditure that meets the definition of an asset, and is consistent with the treatment of other assets controlled by the Group when it is probable that future economic benefits will flow to the Group and the asset has a cost that can be measured reliably. IFRS 6 *Exploration for and Evaluation of Mineral Resources* (see **Chapter 34**) allows both the previous and new accounting policies of the Group.

The impact of the change in accounting policy on the consolidated statement of profit or loss and other comprehensive income, consolidated statement of financial position and consolidated statements of cash flows is set out below:

Consolidated statement of profit or loss and other comprehensive income

Exploration and evaluation expenditure related to qualifying areas of interest has been capitalised in accordance with the accounting policy subject to an impairment review. This has resulted in a decrease in exploration and evaluation expenditure of €17.1 million and a net decrease in non-controlling interests of €1.1 million (2011: Nil) for the year to 31 December 2012. Net loss before and after tax before non-controlling interests has decreased by €17.1 million for the year to 31 December 2012 (2011: €7.3 million).

Basic and diluted loss per share has also been restated. This has resulted in a reduction of 2.3 cent in the loss per share for the year ended 31 December 2012 (2011: reduction of 1.1 cent per share).

Consolidated statement of financial position

The carried forward exploration and evaluation asset at 31 December 2012 has increased by €35.5 million. This adjustment represents a decrease in accumulated losses of €32.5 million, an increase in the Functional Currency Translation Reserve of €4.0 million and a decrease in non-controlling interests of €1.0 million.

The carried forward exploration and evaluation asset at 31 December 2011 has increased by €15.1 million. This adjustment represents a decrease in accumulated losses of €14.5 million and a net movement in deferred tax assets and liabilities of €0.6 million.

Cumulative capitalised exploration and evaluation expenditure at 1 January 2011 has increased by €7.4 million.

Consolidated statement of cash flows

Exploration and evaluation expenditure that is capitalised is included as part of cash flows from investing activities whereas exploration and evaluation expenditure that is expensed is included as part of cash flows from operating activities. This has resulted in additional cash outflows from investing activities being reflected for capitalised exploration expenditure of €17.6 million for the year to 31 December 2012 (2011: €7.4 million). This has also resulted in a corresponding reduction being reflected in the net cash outflow from operating activities for the equivalent periods.

(***Note:*** Under IFRS 6 *Exploration for and Evaluation of Mineral Resources* (see **Chapter 34**) an entity may change its accounting policies for exploration and evaluation expenditures if the change makes the financial statements more relevant to the economic decision-making needs of users and no less reliable, or more reliable and no less relevant to those needs. An entity should judge relevance and reliability using the criteria in IAS 8.)

Rather than change how certain figures are calculated (i.e. change in accounting policy), entities may decide to change the statutory heading under which certain amounts are disclosed (e.g. including the depreciation expense in cost of sales rather than administration expenses). This is referred to as a 'change in presentation' and, consistent with the principles outlined above with respect to accounting policies, the change in presentation has to be justified on the basis of giving a fairer presentation, with comparative figures adjusted accordingly (see **Example 21.3** and **Example 21.6**).

EXAMPLE 21.3: CHANGE IN PRESENTATION

The directors of Texas Limited have decided to include the depreciation charge for the year ended 31 December 2012 in cost of sales rather than administrative expenses, as was previously the policy.

In the financial statements for the year ended 31 December 2012, while no changes are required to the figures, additional disclosures are required. For example, comparative information should be re-stated (unless it is impracticable to do so), together with an explanation as to why the new policy will provide reliable and more relevant information.

Accounting Estimates

The second element in the title of IAS 8 is *changes in accounting estimates*. Accounting estimates and dealing with subsequent changes are now discussed.

As a result of the uncertainties inherent in business activities, many items in financial statements cannot be measured with precision but can only be estimated. Estimation involves judgements based on the latest available, reliable information. For example, estimates may be required of:
* irrecoverable debts;
* warranty obligations;
* inventory obsolescence; and
* useful lives of depreciable assets.

Changes in Accounting Estimates

An estimate may need revision if changes occur in the circumstances on which the estimate was based or as a result of new information or more experience. By its nature, the revision of an estimate does *not* relate to prior periods and is not the correction of an error.

The effect of a change in an accounting estimate should be recognised *prospectively* by including it in arriving at profit or loss in the statement or profit or loss and other comprehensive income in:
* the period of the change, if the change affects that period only (e.g. irrecoverable debts estimate); or
* the period of the change and future periods, if the change affects both (e.g. revising the useful life of a non-current asset).

To the extent that a change in an accounting estimate gives rise to changes in assets and liabilities, or relates to an item of equity, it should be recognised by adjusting the **carrying amount** of the related asset, liability or equity item in the period of the change.

A change in accounting estimate is illustrated in **Examples 21.4** and **21.5**.

EXAMPLE 21.4: CHANGE IN ACCOUNTING ESTIMATE (1)

Previously, Blackbird Limited depreciated plant and equipment using the reducing balance method at 20% per annum. The company is proposing to depreciate plant and equipment using the straight-line method over five years.

This decision involves a change in estimate (*not* accounting policy as the policy is still to write off the cost of the plant and equipment over its useful economic life).

EXAMPLE 21.5: CHANGE IN ACCOUNTING ESTIMATE (2)

Apple Limited reviews its depreciation policies annually. At the most recent review for the year ended 31 December 2012, the directors decided that the remaining useful economic life of machinery at 1 January 2012 was three years. Additional information in relation to machinery is as follows:

Machinery – cost at date of acquisition on 1 January 2009	€3,600,000
Estimated useful economic life at 1 January 2009	10 Years
Estimated residual value at 1 January 2009	€nil

Requirement Explain how to account for this change in the useful economic life of machinery in the financial statements of Apple Limited for the year ended 31 December 2012.

Solution

	€
Cost as at 1 January 2009	3,600,000
Depreciation y/e 31 December 2009	(360,000)
Depreciation y/e 31 December 2010	(360,000)
Depreciation y/e 31 December 2011	(360,000)
Net book value at 31 December 2011	2,520,000
Revised remaining useful economic life – 3 years	
Depreciation for year ended 31 December 2012	840,000

The change in the useful economic life of machinery is a change in accounting estimate and should be applied prospectively (with no changes made to prior period financial statements).

Note: as explained in **Chapter 1**, IASs/IFRSs apply only to material items. While materiality is a subjective concept, material items can be defined as those things that could make a major difference to an organisation's performance. Material information provides the basis for stakeholders and management to make sound judgements about the things that matter to them, and take actions that influence the organisation's performance. Hence, if the effect of the change in accounting estimate is *material*, its nature and amount must be disclosed.

A change in the measurement basis applied (see **Chapter 2, Section 2.3**), for example, a change from carrying non-current assets at historical cost to fair value, is a change in accounting policy and is *not* a change in accounting estimate. However, while the initial application of a policy to revalue assets in accordance with IAS 16 *Property, Plant and Equipment* or IAS 38 *Intangible Assets* is a change in accounting policy, it is dealt with as a revaluation in accordance with IAS 16 (see **Chapter 6**) or IAS 38 (see **Chapter 9**). This is illustrated in **Example 21.6** in the context of IAS 16.

EXAMPLE 21.6: CHANGE IN MEASUREMENT AND PRESENTATION

Murray Limited records plant and equipment at depreciated historical cost and has traditionally charged depreciation on plant and equipment at a rate of 20% per annum using the reducing balance method. On 1 January 2012, following a review of depreciation methods by the directors, it was decided to charge depreciation at a rate of 20% per annum on a straight-line basis as it more accurately reflects the pattern of usage of plant and equipment. In addition, the directors have decided that from 1 January 2012 it would be more appropriate to include the depreciation charge on plant and equipment in cost of sales rather than administrative expenses as was previously the case.

Requirement Advise management on the appropriate accounting treatment.

Solution

IAS 16 requires that depreciation methods, useful lives and residual values are reviewed annually. Any change to the depreciation method is clearly identified in IAS 16 as a change in accounting estimate, which is applied to the period in which the review is made and not retrospectively. It is *not* a change in accounting policy. Note that if the directors of Murray Limited had decided to change from carrying plant and equipment at depreciated historical cost to fair value (see **Chapter 6**), this would represent a change in the measurement basis and therefore a change in accounting policy. Note that this should be dealt with as a revaluation in accordance with IAS 16 (see **Chapter 6**) and not IAS 8 as illustrated in **Examples 21.1** and **21.2**.

IAS 1 requires that information is presented consistently from period to period. If a change is made in the presentation such as suggested above, then Murray Limited is required to make additional disclosure so users of financial statements understand the impact of the changes in presentation of an item. The disclosures required include: the nature of the reclassification; the amount of each item or class of items that is reclassified; and the reason for the classification.

If Murray Limited is unable to reclassify comparative figures, then the company must disclose the reason for not reclassifying amounts and the nature of the adjustments that would have been made if the amounts had been reclassified.

The final element in the title of IAS 8 is *errors*. Given that any errors made and discovered in the 'current' accounting period can be corrected immediately, the focus of IAS 8 is on errors made in one accounting period and not discovered until a later accounting period (i.e. after the financial statements containing the error have been published). These are referred to as prior period errors and are discussed below.

Prior Period Errors

Prior period errors are omissions from, and misstatements in, the entity's financial statements for one or more prior periods, arising from a failure to use, or misuse of, reliable information that:
1. was available when financial statements for those periods were authorised for issue; and
2. could reasonably be expected to have been obtained and taken into account in the preparation and presentation of those financial statements.

Such errors include the effects of mathematical mistakes, mistakes in applying accounting policies, oversights or misinterpretations of facts and fraud. While current period errors can be corrected before the financial statements are authorised for issue, sometimes material errors are not discovered until a later period and these should be corrected retrospectively in the first set of financial statements authorised for issue after the discovery. The total prior period adjustment is the cumulative error to the start of the period when the error is discovered, net of any attributable tax. This is explained in **Example 21.7** below.

An entity should correct material prior period errors retrospectively in the first set of financial statements authorised for issue after their discovery by:
• restating the opening balance of assets, liabilities and equity as if the error had never occurred, and presenting the necessary adjustment to the opening balance of accumulated profits in the statement of changes in equity; and
• restating the comparative figures presented as if the error had never occurred.

In applying these rules, the entity should disclose in the Notes:
- the nature of the prior period error;
- the amount of the correction to each financial statement line item presented for the prior periods; and
- the amount of the correction at the beginning of the earliest prior period presented.

EXAMPLE 21.7: PRIOR PERIOD ERROR

Angel plc has a retained profit of €32,781 for the year ended 31 December 2012 and its balance on its retained earnings stood at €709,311 on 1 January 2012.

It has been discovered, while producing the 2012 financial statements, that the closing inventory figure as at 31 December 2011 was overstated by €48,099, thus overstating the profit for the year ended 31 December 2011 by €48,099 (the retained profit figure for the year ended 31 December 2012 has been determined by using the correct inventory figure as at 1 January 2012).

The retained profit for the year ended 31 December 2011 was originally stated at €90,342, using the incorrect closing inventory figure.

In the statement of changes in equity, under movements on reserves, this adjustment would be shown as follows:

Angel plc
STATEMENT OF CHANGES IN EQUITY (EXTRACT)

	€
Balance at 31 December 2011	
As previously reported	709,311
Prior period adjustment (note x)	(48,099)
Restated	661,212
Retained profit for year	32,781
Balance at 31 December 2012	693,993

Note: the prior period adjustment represents an overstatement of the closing inventory figure as at 31 December 2011.

Note: only when it is impracticable to determine the cumulative effect of an error on prior periods can an entity correct an error prospectively.

21.3 DISCLOSURE REQUIREMENTS

Like the title of the accounting standard, the disclosure requirements in IAS 8 can be broken down into three components.
1. Changes in Accounting Policies (see **Examples 21.1** and **21.2**):
    (a) reason for change;
    (b) amount of the adjustment on the current period and for each period presented; and
    (c) the fact that comparative figures have been restated or that it was not practicable to do so.
2. Correction of Errors (see **Example 21.7**):
    (a) the nature of the prior period error;
    (b) the amount of the correction for each period presented;
    (c) the amount of the correction at the start of the earlier prior period presented; and

(d) if retrospective correction is not practicable, a description of how and when the error was corrected.
3. Changes in Accounting Estimates (see **Examples 21.4** and **21.5**):
    (a) the nature of the change;
    (b) the effect on the current periods financial statements; and
    (c) the effect in future periods, if this is practicable.

21.4 CONCLUSION

When an IAS/IFRS specifically applies to a transaction, event or condition, the accounting policy applied to that item is determined by applying the IAS/IFRS and, in the case of a new or revised accounting standard, considering any relevant implementation guidance for the IAS/IFRS. Accounting policies need not be applied when the effect of applying them is immaterial, as defined in IAS 1 *Presentation of Financial Statements*. In the absence of an IAS/IFRS that specifically applies to a transaction, event or condition, management should use its judgement in selecting and applying an accounting policy that results in relevant and reliable financial information.

IAS 8 specifies the following hierarchy of guidance for management to use when selecting accounting policies in such circumstances:
• requirements of IASs/IFRSs and Interpretations dealing with similar matters;
• the definitions, recognition criteria and measurement concepts for assets, liabilities, income and expenses in the *IFRS Framework*; and
• the most recent pronouncements of other standard-setting bodies that use a similar conceptual framework, other accounting literature and accepted industry practices, to the extent that these do not conflict with IASs/IFRSs and the *IFRS Framework*.

An entity should apply its accounting policies consistently for similar transactions, other events and conditions, unless an IAS/IFRS specifically requires or permits categorisation of items for which different policies may be appropriate. An entity should only change an accounting policy if the change is required by an IAS/IFRS, or results in the financial statements providing more relevant and reliable information about the entity's financial position, financial performance or cash flows. A change in accounting policy, resulting from the initial application of an IAS/IFRS, is accounted for in accordance with any specific transitional provisions of that IAS/IFRS. Otherwise a change in accounting policy is applied retrospectively to all periods presented in the financial statements as if the new accounting policy had always been applied.

The effect of a change in an accounting estimate is recognised prospectively in arriving at profit or loss in the period of the change, and also in profit or loss in future periods if the change affects both periods. Any corresponding changes in assets and liabilities, or to an item of equity, are recognised by adjusting the carrying amount of the asset, liability or equity item in the period of the change.

IAS 8 eliminates the distinction between fundamental errors and other material errors. All material errors should be corrected by restating the financial statements as if the error had never occurred. IAS 8 specifies the accounting treatment when it is impracticable to account for a change in accounting policy or a correction of a prior period error using retrospective restatement in accordance with the Standard. IAS 8 also specifies disclosures about accounting policies, changes in accounting estimates and errors.

SUMMARY OF LEARNING OBJECTIVES

After having studied this chapter you should be able to:

Learning Objective 1 Explain the criteria for selecting and changing accounting policies.

In the absence of an IAS/IFRS that specifically applies to a transaction, event or condition, management should use its judgement in selecting and applying an accounting policy that results in relevant and reliable financial information. An entity should only change an accounting policy if the change is required by an IAS/IFRS, or results in the financial statements providing more relevant and reliable information about the entity's financial position, financial performance or cash flows.

Learning Objective 2 Account for and disclose changes in accounting policies, changes in accounting estimates and corrections of errors.

A change in accounting policy, resulting from the initial application of an IAS/IFRS, is accounted for in accordance with any specific transitional provisions of that IAS/IFRS. Otherwise a change in accounting policy is applied *retrospectively* to all periods presented in the financial statements as if the new accounting policy had always been applied. The effect of a change in an accounting estimate is recognised *prospectively* in arriving at profit or loss in the period of the change, and also in profit or loss in future periods if the change affects both periods. Any corresponding changes in assets and liabilities, or to an item of equity, are recognised by adjusting the carrying amount of the asset, liability or equity item in the period of the change.

QUESTIONS

Self-test Questions

1. On what basis should accounting policies be selected?
2. In what circumstances may an entity change one of its accounting policies?
3. How are changes in accounting estimates accounted for?
4. How are prior period errors accounted for?
5. What are the disclosures if an accounting policy is changed?

Review Questions

(See **Appendix One** for Suggested Solutions to Review Questions.)

Question 21.1

Keano Limited adopted an accounting policy of capitalising exploration and evaluation expenditure and amortising it to the statement of profit or loss and other comprehensive income over four years. During 2012 the Directors decided that for 2012 and future years all exploration and evaluation expenditure should be written off as incurred. This decision has not resulted from any change in the expected outcome of projects on hand, but rather from a desire to give a fairer presentation of results and financial position.

Movements on Exploration and Evaluation Expenditure Account:

Year	Expenditure Incurred €000	Amortised to SPLOCI – P/L €000
2009	400	100
2010	600	250
2011	300	325
2012	500	500

The 2011 financial statements showed:

	€000
Retained earnings 1 January 2011	2,860
Retained earnings for the year	1,580
Retained earnings 31 December 2011	4,440

The retained earnings for the year ended 31 December 2012 were €1,820,000. This was arrived at after charging exploration and evaluation expenditure of €500,000.

Requirement Show how the change in accounting policy would be reflected in the financial statements of Keano Limited.

Question 21.2

The following are the draft summarised statements of profit or loss and other comprehensive income of Top Limited for the year ended 31 May 2013:

	2013 €	2012 €
Profit before tax	820,000	640,000
Income tax expenses	(328,000)	(256,000)
Profit after tax	492,000	384,000
Retained profit brought forward	1,174,000	890,000
Retained profit carried forward	1,666,000	1,274,000

During the audit of the financial statements for the year ended 31 May 2013, it was discovered that advertising expenditure was omitted from financial statements as follows:

	€
31 May 2013	110,000
31 May 2012	80,000
31 May 2011	60,000

The correction of these errors is not included in the above draft statements of profit or loss and other comprehensive income. The company's profits are taxable at 40%.

Requirement Redraft the statement of profit or loss and other comprehensive income of Top Limited for the year ended 31 May 2013.

Challenging Questions

(Suggested Solutions to Challenging Questions are available to lecturers.)

Question 21.1 (Based on Chartered Accountants Ireland, P3 Autumn 2005, Question 4)

Following the retirement of her father, the new Chief Executive of GOLD is proposing to change how certain items have been accounted for in GOLD's draft financial statements for the year ended 31 December 2012.

Proposal 1 Inventory, which is currently considered in aggregate on a FIFO basis, will be measured on a weighted average basis so that all items of inventory are measured on a similar basis.

Proposal 2 Plant and machinery, which is currently depreciated using the reducing balance method at 20% per annum, will be depreciated straight-line over five years and the depreciation will be charged to net operating expenses rather than cost of sales, as is currently the case.

Proposal 3 Interest incurred in connection with the construction of plant and machinery, which was previously written off to the statement of profit or loss and other comprehensive income, will be added to the cost of the plant and machinery.

Proposal 4 Following a discussion with an art dealer in December 2012, the new Chief Executive of GOLD discovered a painting that had hung in her father's office for many years could fetch at least €1,000,000 at auction. It is intended to sell the painting at auction as soon as possible and recognise the €1,000,000 gain in the financial statements for the year ended 31 December 2012.

Proposal 5 GOLD received a letter in January 2013 from BLING Limited (BLING), a company that had used GOLD's precious metals in the manufacture of jewellery during 2010. However, the innovative design of the jewellery has not proved popular and sales have been poor. BLING has threatened to sue GOLD for loss of earnings of €1,000,000 on the grounds that the precious metals are 'useless'. The Chief Executive of GOLD proposes to net the gain on the sale of the painting against the threatened claim for loss of earnings.

Requirement Prepare a memorandum to the new Chief Executive of GOLD explaining the accounting implications of each of the proposals.

22

RELATED PARTY DISCLOSURES

LEARNING OBJECTIVES

> Having studied this chapter on related parties, you should be able to:
> 1. explain the term 'related party';
> 2. identify an entity's related party relationships; and
> 3. describe the disclosures required when a related party relationship exists.

KEY TERMS AND DEFINITIONS FOR THIS CHAPTER

In order to aid your understanding of the concepts and issues covered in this chapter, it is important to understand and be familiar with the following key terms and definitions. As you study this chapter, you should refer back to them.

> **Arm's Length Transaction** This is a transaction when all parties to the transaction are independent and on an equal footing.
> **Related Party** IAS 24 *Related Party Disclosures* defines a related party as a *person* or *entity* that is related to the entity that is preparing its financial statements. This definition is expanded in **Section 22.2**.

22.1 INTRODUCTION

As explained in **Chapter 1**, financial reporting is the communication of financial information, and the fundamental objective of financial reporting is to communicate information about the resources and performance of the reporting entity useful to those having reasonable rights to such information. The *Conceptual Framework for Financial Reporting 2010* (*IFRS Framework*) (see **Chapter 1**) acknowledges that the primary users of general-purpose financial statements are present and potential investors, lenders and other creditors who use the information to make decisions about buying, selling or holding equity or debt instruments, and providing or settling loans or other forms of credit. The *IFRS Framework* also states that one of the qualitative characteristics of financial information is *relevance*. Information is relevant when it influences the economic decisions of users by helping them to evaluate past, present or future economic events, or confirming or correcting their past evaluations. An example of this could be where the financial performance of an entity is influenced by the relationship and transactions between the reporting entity and other parties that are in some way connected or related to the reporting entity.

In the absence of information to the contrary, it is assumed that a reporting entity has independent discretionary power over its transactions and resources and that it pursues its activities independently of the interests of its owners and management. The entity's transactions are presumed to have been undertaken at **arm's length** and users of general-purpose financial reports may require additional information in order to more fully understand a reporting entity's economic resources, claims and changes in resources and claims (see **Chapter 1**, **Section 1.3**). However, these assumptions may not be justified when **related party** relationships exist. The objective of IAS 24 *Related Party Disclosures* is to ensure that an entity's financial statements contain the disclosures necessary to draw attention to the possibility that its financial position and profit or loss may have been affected by the existence of related parties and by transactions and outstanding balances with such parties.

Key to this Chapter

IAS 24 is a disclosure standard; it does not address how transactions should be accounted for; merely whether, and how, they should be disclosed in the financial statements. This chapter begins by explaining what is meant by the term **related party**, before outlining why the disclosure of such relationships is necessary and providing indicators that a related party relationship may exist. The chapter concludes by summarising the disclosures required in accordance with IAS 24.

22.2 WHAT IS A RELATED PARTY?

IAS 24 defines a **related party** as a *person* or *entity* that is related to the entity that is preparing its financial statements. In practice, the following persons and entities are deemed to be related parties in accordance with IAS 24 (*Note:* from an examination perspective, the list simply has to be learnt).
1. A *person* or a close member of that person's family is *related* to a reporting entity if that person:
   (a) has control or joint control over the reporting entity;
   (b) has significant influence over the reporting entity; or
   (c) is a member of the key management personnel of the reporting entity or of a parent of the reporting entity.
2. An *entity* is *related* to a reporting entity if any of the following conditions applies:
   (a) the entity and the reporting entity are members of the same group (which means that each parent, subsidiary and fellow subsidiary is related to the others);
   (b) one entity is an associate or joint venture of the other entity (or an associate or joint venture of a member of a group of which the other entity is a member);
   (c) both entities are joint ventures of the same third party;

(d) one entity is a joint venture of a third entity and the other entity is an associate of the third entity;

(e) the entity is a post-employment defined benefit plan for the benefit of employees of either the reporting entity or an entity related to the reporting entity. If the reporting entity is itself such a plan, the sponsoring employers are also related to the reporting entity;

(f) the entity is controlled or jointly controlled by a person identified in 1. above; or

(g) a person identified in 1.(a) has significant influence over the entity or is a member of the key management personnel of the entity (or of a parent of the entity).

The following are examples of transactions that require disclosure if with a related party:
- purchases/sales of goods;
- purchases/sales of non-current tangible assets;
- rendering/receiving services;
- leases; and
- provisions of guarantees.

The application of the related party definition, together with the associated disclosure note, is illustrated in **Example 22.1**.

EXAMPLE 22.1: RELATED PARTIES

Mr Grant is a director and major shareholder of MORTAR. His son, Fergus, is an independent tax consultant and he advised MORTAR on certain issues associated with the acquisition of both PESTLE and POWDER, for which he was paid €100,000 during 2012, with a further €20,000 due to him at 31 December 2012. Both these amounts are included in MORTAR's draft financial statements for the year ended 31 December 2012. Mr Grant's daughter, Emer, is employed in MORTAR's Personnel Department, receiving an annual salary of €30,000. She does not have management responsibilities.

Requirement Illustrate the disclosures required in MORTAR's group financial statements in accordance with IAS 24 *Related Party Disclosures*.

Solution

With reference to MORTAR, under IAS 24 *Related Party Disclosures*, a party is related to an entity if it:
- directly or indirectly controls, is controlled by, or is under common control with the entity;
- has significant influence over the entity;
- is an associate of the entity;
- is a member of the key management personnel of the entity or its parent; or
- is a close member of the family of any of the aforementioned key management personnel.

Fergus and Emer Grant, through their relationship with their father (who is a director and therefore considered to be 'key management'), Mr Grant, are also related parties of MORTAR.

Fergus is not an employee of MORTAR and therefore amounts paid to him of €100,000, together with the amount outstanding at 31 December 2012 of €20,000, should

be disclosed in the 2012 financial statements. The following information should be provided:
- description of the relationship;
- details of the transaction;
- amounts involved; and
- amounts due at 31 December 2012.

Emer is an employee of MORTAR but is not key management and therefore is not expected to influence or be influenced by Mr Grant, therefore there is no requirement to disclose the emoluments paid to her.

Disclosure Note

Mr Grant is a director and major shareholder of MORTAR. His son, Fergus, is an independent tax consultant and he advised MORTAR on certain issues associated with the acquisition of both PESTLE and POWDER, for which he was paid €100,000 during 2012, with a further €20,000 due to him at 31 December 2012. Both these amounts are included in MORTAR's financial statements for the year ended 31 December 2012. Mr Grant's daughter, Emer, is employed in MORTAR's Personnel Department.

Parties Deemed not to be Related

The following are deemed *not* to be related:
- two entities simply because they have a director or key manager in common;
- two venturers who share joint control over a joint venture;
- providers of finance, trade unions, public utilities, and departments and agencies of a government that does not control, jointly control or significantly influence the reporting entity, simply by virtue of their normal dealings with an entity (even though they may affect the freedom of action of an entity or participate in its decision-making process); and
- a single customer, supplier, franchiser, distributor, or general agent with whom an entity transacts a significant volume of business merely by virtue of the resulting economic dependence.

Having explained what is meant by the term **related party**, **Section 22.3** now outlines why the disclosure of such relationships is considered important.

22.3 WHY ARE RELATED PARTY DISCLOSURES NECESSARY?

A related party relationship could affect a reporting entity's performance and financial position. For example, transactions between related parties may not be made at the same amounts as between unrelated parties, and knowledge of this is likely to be important to users of the financial statements.

Reasons why related party disclosures are necessary include:
- knowledge of related-party transactions may affect a user's assessment of the reporting entity's operations, or risks and opportunities facing the entity;

- a related party relationship could have an effect on the reporting entity's results; and
- transactions between related parties may not be made at arm's length.

While such relationships are a normal feature of business, IAS 24 requires certain information to be disclosed for the benefit of users of financial statements.

22.4 POTENTIAL RELATED PARTY INDICATORS

While IAS 24 defines what is meant by the term *related party* and also provides examples of related-party transactions, the identification of related parties in practice is fraught with difficulty. It might be expected that (some) companies may not wish to disclose the existence of related-party relationships, not because of fraudulent transactions taking place but simply due to a desire for privacy. Given the volume of transactions that may occur during a reporting period and the numerous parties that an entity may engage with, the existence of related-party relationships and transactions could easily go unnoticed.

Given that auditors are responsible for expressing an opinion on whether the financial statements give a true and fair view, they should be alert to indicators of potential related-party issues that may require special attention when performing the audit. Difficult economic times increase the possibility that the economic substance of certain transactions may be other than their legal form, or that the transactions may lack economic substance. **Example 22.2** below presents a range of scenarios that, if present, may indicate the existence of related-party relationships or transactions.

EXAMPLE 22.2: POTENTIAL RELATED-PARTY INDICATORS

(a) Agreements Whereby One Party Pays Expenses on Behalf of Another Party

One party is to pay certain expenses on behalf of a company and then recharge the expenses back to that company. Under this type of arrangement, the recharge and expense recognition by the company may never occur, resulting in understated expenses in the company's financial statements, particularly when the company is struggling financially.

(b) Circular Arrangements between Parties

Sales arrangements in which the seller of goods or services has concurrent obligations to the buyer to purchase goods or services or provide other benefits should be examined closely. In addition, collectability and liquidity should be closely examined in cases in which a party's ability to repay a loan is dependent on continued cash funding or sales from a related party.

(c) Engaging in Business Deals (such as Leases) at more or less than Market Value

A company may enter into a lease agreement with another party, owned in part by a member of an officer's family, at less than market rates. This relationship and the related transactions should be appropriately disclosed in the company's financial statements.

(d) Payments for Services at Inflated Prices

An officer, director or management representative of a company may be also employed by another organisation (for example, as a consultant) utilised by the company. This could lead to the organisation charging inflated fees for services rendered.

(e) Sale of Land with Arranged Financing

If a principal owner of a company sold land at fair market value and obtained financing for the buyer who was a marginal credit risk, the transaction would require related-party disclosure by the company if the financing were obtained from a lender who agreed to the transaction primarily to preserve a significant business relationship with the company.

(f) Sale of Securities

The sale of marketable securities by a principal owner of a company at a significant discount from quoted market prices to a large customer of the company would be a related-party transaction. As the transaction has no apparent business purpose, the facts may require disclosure of the transaction to reflect a fair presentation of financial position and results of operations of the company. However, it should be noted that, if the owner had sold the securities to the same party at fair market value, there would be no presumption of a related-party transaction.

(g) Unusual Material Transactions, particularly Close to Quarter- or Year-end

A company may recognise revenue on large, unusual transactions with another party conducted close to the end of the reporting period. Consideration should be given to whether or not the two parties might be related in some way. These transactions may not always be individually significant, but rather may involve several small sales transactions that in total are material. Repetitive period-end transactions with the same party should also be investigated for potential related-party relationships.

22.5 DISCLOSURE REQUIREMENTS

The following disclosures are required in accordance with IAS 24.
1. If there have been transactions between the reporting entity and related parties the following disclosure must be made:
   (a) the nature of the relationship;
   (b) the amount of the transactions (but items of a similar nature may be disclosed in aggregate);
   (c) outstanding balances, including details of any securities or guarantees;
   (d) provisions for doubtful debts on outstanding balances; and
   (e) any irrecoverable debts written off during a period on amounts due from related parties.

2. Key management compensation (all benefits) must be disclosed in total and for each of the following categories:
   (a) Short-term employee benefits (for example, wages and salaries);

(b) Post-employment benefits (for example, pensions);
(c) Other long-term benefits (for example, long-service leave);
(d) Termination benefits; and
(e) Share-based payments.

3. In the separate financial statements of an entity that is part of a consolidated group, it is necessary to disclose intragroup transactions and comply with other requirements of IAS 24.

4. Relationships between parent and subsidiaries:
   (a) these must be disclosed irrespective of whether there have been transactions between those related parties; and
   (b) an entity must disclose the name of its parent or its ultimate controlling party.

Note: items 3. and 4. above relate to group/consolidated financial statements. This is covered in **Part V**.

22.6 CONCLUSION

This chapter describes the disclosures required by IAS 24 *Related Party Disclosures* to draw attention to the possibility that the financial position and profit or loss of an entity may have been affected by the existence of related parties and by transactions and outstanding balances with such parties. IAS 24 should be applied when:
• identifying related-party relationships;
• identifying related-party transactions;
• identifying outstanding balances between an entity and its related parties;
• identifying the circumstances when disclosures are necessary; and
• determining the disclosures when required.

Summary of Learning Objectives

After having studied this chapter on related parties, you should be able to:

Learning Objective 1 Explain the term 'related party'.

A related party is a person or entity that is related to the entity that is preparing its financial statements. Further details are provided in **Section 22.2**.

Learning Objective 2 Identify an entity's related-party relationships.

Section 22.4 presents a range of scenarios that, if present, may indicate the existence of related-party relationships or transactions.

Learning Objective 3 Describe the disclosures required when a related-party relationship exists.

Details of the relationships and transactions to be disclosed are provided in **Section 22.5**.

QUESTIONS

Self-test Questions

1. In the context of IAS 24, what are the main parties to which a company may be related?
2. What are the disclosures required by IAS 24 with respect to related parties?

Review Questions

(See **Appendix One** for Suggested Solutions to Review Questions.)

Question 22.1

Groups of companies are considered to be related parties:
  (a) Sometimes.
  (b) Never.
  (c) Always.

Question 22.2

Intragroup transactions and balances appear in:
  (a) Consolidated financial statements.
  (b) Financial statements of individual statements.
  (c) Neither.

Question 22.3

A parent company can control or influence its subsidiary's:
  (a) Financial policies.
  (b) Operating policies.
  (c) Both.

Question 22.4

If no transactions occur between the related parties, can the profits and financial position of either party be affected by the other?
  (a) Yes.
  (b) No.

Question 22.5

What is the likely response of users of financial statements to the knowledge of related parties, their transactions and balances?
  (a) Ignore them.
  (b) Adjust their assessments of the risks and opportunities facing the undertaking.
  (c) Refuse to deal with the undertaking on principle.

Question 22.6

Which of the following are related parties?
  (a) Major shareholders.
  (b) Group companies.
  (c) Key managers.
  (d) Pension funds.
  (e) All suppliers.
  (f) All government departments.
  (g) Relatives of any member of staff.

Question 22.7

A major shareholder can avoid the consequences of related-party transactions by transacting other business through his wife, or her husband, when the undertaking in which he, or she, has invested is involved.
  (a) True.
  (b) False.
  (c) Sometimes.

Question 22.8

If services are provided without charge between group companies, does this qualify as a related-party transaction?
  (a) Yes.
  (b) No.

Question 22.9

Close family members of a related party: does a brother of the related party qualify as a related party in his own right?
  (a) Never.
  (b) Always.
  (c) Only if he is expected to influence, or be influenced by, the first related party in dealings with the undertaking.

Question 22.10

Close family members are included as related parties to:
  (a) Avoid related parties disguising their activities.
  (b) Help related parties disguise their activities.

Question 22.11

Classify each of the following transactions as either:
  (a) Short-term employment benefits.
  (b) Post-employment benefits.

(c) Long-term employment benefits.
(d) Equity compensation benefits.

Transactions:
(i) Share option schemes.
(ii) Pensions.
(iii) Paid sick leave.
(iv) Sabbatical leave.
(v) Subsidised goods or services provided to employees.

Question 22.12

Compensation relating to a director that is paid to the director's firm, rather than to the director directly:
(a) Can be ignored.
(b) Should be reported without mentioning the director's firm.
(c) Should be reported with a note detailing to whom it is paid.

Question 22.13

Significant influence in an undertaking is:
(a) Control of an undertaking.
(b) Power to participate in the financial and operating policy decisions.
(c) Holding 10% of the shares, without board representation.

Question 22.14

In considering any related-party relationship, attention should be directed primarily to:
(a) The legal form of the relationship.
(b) The substance of the relationship.
(c) Neither of these.

Question 22.15

Two venturers who share a joint venture are:
(a) Always related parties.
(b) Never related parties.
(c) Not necessarily related parties.

Question 22.16

Related party relationships need not be disclosed, if no transactions have taken place.
(a) True.
(b) False.

Challenging Questions

(Suggested Solutions to Challenging Questions are available to lecturers.)

Question 22.1

A bank is financing a construction company with a loan that provides 90% of the construction company's capital requirements. The construction company is owned by a friend of the Chief Executive Officer of the bank. The loan is secured on the assets of the construction company.

Requirement Is the construction company a related party?

Question 22.2

Company T trades with Company K. They are not in the same group of companies, but both of their parent companies have the same person as majority shareholder.

Requirement Are Company T and Company K related parties?

Question 22.3

Company M bought a franchise to run a Mexican food restaurant in Dublin.

Requirement Is Company M a related party to the company that sold it the franchise?

(*Note:* see also **Chapter 13**, Challenging Question 1, BRUCE plc (b).)

EARNINGS PER SHARE

LEARNING OBJECTIVES

Having studied this chapter on earnings per share, you should be able to:
1. define what is meant by the term 'earnings quality';
2. understand the concept of pro-forma earnings;
3. define basic and diluted earnings per share (EPS); and
4. apply the principles for the determination and presentation of basic and diluted EPS in an entity's financial statements in accordance with IAS 33 *Earnings per Share*.

KEY TERMS AND DEFINITIONS FOR THIS CHAPTER

In order to aid your understanding of the concepts and issues covered in this chapter, it is important to understand and be familiar with the following key terms and definitions. As you study this chapter, you should refer back to them.

Antidilution An increase in EPS or a reduction in loss per share resulting from the assumption that convertible instruments are converted, that options or warrants are exercised, or that **ordinary shares** are issued upon the satisfaction of specified conditions.

Bonus Issue This is a capitalisation of reserves and will have *no effect* on the earning capacity of the company. There is *no* inflow of funds.

Contingently Issuable Shares Shares issued for little or no cash or other consideration after certain conditions have been met (e.g. sales or profit targets).

Dilution A reduction in EPS or an increase in loss per share resulting from the assumption that convertible instruments are converted, that options or warrants are exercised, or that ordinary shares are issued upon the satisfaction of specified conditions.

Ordinary Share An equity instrument that is subordinate to all other classes of equity instruments.

Potential Ordinary Share (POS) A financial instrument or other contract that may entitle its holder to ordinary shares.

> **Rights Issue** An issue of shares for cash to existing shareholders at a price (usually) below the current market price. It is equivalent to a cash issue at full market price combined with a subsequent **bonus issue**.
>
> **Share Options and Warrants** These are financial instruments that give the holder the right to purchase ordinary shares at a fixed price, sometime in the future.

23.1 INTRODUCTION

Earnings are the profits of a company, and typically refer to profit after interest and tax as this, in broad terms, represents the profits of the year that are available for distribution to shareholders or for reinvestment in the business. Ultimately, a business's earnings are the main determinant of its share price because earnings, and the circumstances relating to them (see below with respect to 'earnings' quality'), can indicate whether the business will be profitable and successful in the long run. Investors and analysts look to earnings to determine the attractiveness of a particular share. Companies with poor earnings' prospects will typically have lower share prices than those with good prospects, since a company's ability to generate profit in the future plays a very important role in determining a share's price. A business's interim and annual earnings are typically compared to analyst estimates, as well as guidance provided by the business itself. In most situations, when earnings do not meet either of those estimates, a business's share price will tend to drop. On the other hand, when actual earnings beat estimates by a significant amount, the share price will likely surge.

Key to this Chapter

This chapter begins by explaining earnings' quality (**Section 23.2**), pro-forma earnings (**Section 23.3**) and earnings' management (**Section 23.4**) in order to provide a basis for explaining the calculation and disclosure of basic and diluted EPS in accordance with IAS 33 *Earnings per Share*, which is the focus of the chapter and is dealt with in **Sections 23.5–23.7**.

23.2 EARNINGS – QUALITY

There is no debating that shares with high-quality earnings are more likely than others to 'beat the market'. High-quality earnings can be characterised as repeatable, controllable and bankable. So how do you know quality when you see it? This is now considered further.

Quantity versus Quality

Earnings' quantity (not quality) tends to get the lion's share of attention during interim reporting seasons. Investors focus on actual EPS delivered, resulting either in share prices going up when companies exceed their forecasted profit targets, or falling when numbers come in below projection. At first glance, at least, when it comes to earnings, size matters most to investors. Savvy investors, however, take time to look at the *quality* of those earnings.

The quality rather than quantity of corporate earnings is a much better gauge of future earnings performance. Firms with high-quality earnings typically generate above-average price–earnings multiples (see **Chapter 35** – the price–earnings ratio is the most widely referred -to stock market ratio, and it represents the market's consensus of the future prospects of that share). Such firms also tend to outperform the market for a longer time. More reliable than other earnings, high-quality earnings give investors a good reason to pay more for the shares of companies that generate quality earnings.

Defining Quality

When analysing interim reports, investors should ask themselves three simple questions:
- Are the company's earnings repeatable?
- Are the company's earnings controllable?
- Are the company's earnings bankable?

Repeatable Earnings

Consider a company that posts earnings well ahead of stock market expectations, especially against the background of a slowing economy. This would be expected to result in a rise in share price. However, if, for example, the increased earnings come by way of job cuts and/or the sale of investments, it is likely that the share price will drop as the market realises that earnings' quality is questionable: the sale of assets is never repeatable. Once sold, assets cannot be sold again to produce more earnings. Sales growth and cost-cutting are the best routes to high-quality earnings. Both are repeatable. Sales growth in one quarter is normally (albeit not always) followed by sales growth in the next quarter. Similarly, costs, once cut, typically stay that way. Repeatable and fairly predictable earnings that come from sales and cost reductions are what investors prefer.

Controllable Earnings

There are many factors affecting earnings that companies cannot control. Consider the effects of exchange rates. For example, if a US company must convert its European profits back into the US dollar, a dollar that is falling against the Euro will boost the company's earnings. But management has nothing to do with those extra earnings or with repeating them in the future. On the other hand, if the dollar moves upwards, earnings growth could come in lower.

There are other uncontrollable factors that can raise earnings. Inflation, for instance, can give companies a brief profits boost when products in inventory are sold at prices increased by inflation. The price of inputs is another uncontrollable factor: falling jet fuel prices, for example, can improve airline industry profits. Even changes in the weather can boost earnings growth. Think of the extra profits from electrical utilities when temperatures are unusually hot or cold.

In reality, the highest-quality earnings go straight to the bank. Indeed, cash sales – which the company does control – are the source of the highest-quality earnings. Investors should seek firms with earnings figures that closely resemble cash that is left after expenses are subtracted from revenues.

Bankable Earnings

Most companies, however, must wait before they can deposit revenues in the bank. Cash payments often arrive later than receivables, so most companies, at times, enter sales as revenues, even though no money has exchanged hands. The fact that customers can cancel or refuse to pay creates large uncertainties, which in turn lower earnings' quality. At the same time, GAAP gives room for choices about what counts as reliable revenues and earnings. Smart investors should see surges in accounts receivable as a warning sign, a good reason to take the time to examine earnings' quality in detail.

Conclusion

High earnings are not as important as high-quality earnings, i.e. those that are repeatable, controllable and bankable. Earnings that surge because of a one-time, uncontrollable event are not earnings that are inherent to the activities of the business. These earnings are the result of luck, which is never a reason to invest. Those businesses that generate revenue but not cash are not engaging in activities that generate quality earnings. Quality earnings are taken to the bank.

23.3 PRO-FORMA EARNINGS

Pro-forma earnings describe earnings calculated by the preparation of financial statements that have hypothetical amounts, or estimates, built into the data to give a 'picture' of a company's profits if certain non-recurring items were excluded. Pro-forma earnings are not computed using standard GAAP, and usually leave out one-time expenses that are not part of normal company operations, such as restructuring costs following a merger. Essentially, a pro-forma financial statement can exclude anything a company believes obscures the accuracy of its financial outlook, and can be a useful piece of information to help assess a company's future prospects. While investors should stress GAAP net income, a look at pro-forma earnings can also be an informative exercise.

For example, net income does not tell the whole story when a company has one-time charges that are irrelevant to future profitability. Some companies, therefore, strip out certain costs that get in the way. This kind of earnings information can be very useful to investors who want an accurate view of a company's normal earnings outlook but, by omitting items that reduce reported earnings, this process can make a company appear profitable even when it is losing money.

Pro-forma earnings are designed to give investors a clearer view of a company's operations and, by their nature, exclude unique expenses and charges. The problem, however, is that there is not nearly as much regulation of pro-forma earnings as there is of financial statements falling under GAAP rules, so sometimes companies abuse the rules to make earnings appear better than they really are. Because traders and brokers focus so closely on whether or not the company beats or meets analyst expectations, the headlines that follow their earnings' announcements can mean everything. And if a company missed non-pro-forma expectations but stated that it beat the pro-forma expectations, its share price will not suffer as badly, and it might even go up – at least in the short term.

Problems with Pro-Forma Earnings

Companies all too often release positive earnings reports that exclude things like share-based employees' compensation and acquisition-related expenses. Such companies are expecting people to forget that these expenses are real and need to be included. Sometimes companies even take unsold inventory off their statements of financial position when reporting pro-forma earnings. But does producing that inventory cost money? Of course it does, so why should the company simply be able to write it off? It is bad management to produce goods that can't be sold, and a company's poor decisions shouldn't be erased from the financial statements.

This is not to say companies are always dishonest with pro-forma earnings – pro-forma does not mean the numbers are automatically being manipulated. To evaluate the legitimacy of pro-forma earnings, it is important to consider what the excluded costs are and decide whether or not these costs are real. For example, one-off or occasional write-downs or impairment of assets might be reasonable, but if this is happening on a regular basis, it might raise doubts over the reliability of the estimated earnings figure.

Benefits of Pro-Forma Analysis

Pro-forma figures are supposed to give investors a clearer view of company operations. For some companies, pro-forma earnings provide a much more accurate view of their financial performance and outlook because of the nature of their businesses. Companies in certain industries tend to utilise pro-forma reporting more than others, as the impetus to report pro-forma numbers is usually a result of industry characteristics. For example, some cable and telephone companies almost never make a net operating profit because they are constantly writing down large depreciation costs. In cases where pro-forma earnings do not include non-cash charges, investors can see what the actual cash profit is.

When a company undergoes substantial restructuring or completes a merger, significant one-time charges can occur as a result. These types of expenses do not compose part of the ongoing cost structure of the business, and therefore can unfairly weigh on short-term profit numbers.

Pro-forma financial statements are also prepared and used by corporate managers and investment banks to assess the operating prospects for their own businesses in the future and to assist in the valuation of potential takeover targets. They are useful tools to help identify a company's core value drivers and analyse changing trends within company operations.

Conclusion

Pro-forma earnings are informative when official earnings are blurred by large amounts of asset depreciation and impairment of goodwill. But it is important to question why a company might be excluding these amounts from its pro-forma earnings since, while they do not represent an actual 'cash expense, such write-downs are indicative of declines in value of the related assets. Moreover, it is important to remember that pro-forma figures have not undergone the same level of scrutiny as GAAP earnings and are not subject to the same level of regulation.

23.4 EARNINGS MANAGEMENT

Earnings management is a strategy used by the management of a company to deliberately manipulate the company's earnings so that the figures match a pre-determined target. This practice is carried out for the purpose of income smoothing. Thus, rather than having some years of exceptionally good or bad earnings, companies will try to keep the figures relatively stable by adding and removing profits from reserve accounts (known colloquially as 'cookie jar' accounts), whereby a company uses generous reserves from good years against losses that might be incurred in bad years. This gives the sense of 'income smoothing', because earnings are understated in good years and overstated in bad years.

Abusive earnings management is deemed by the Securities and Exchange Commission (SEC), the agency that is responsible for regulating the stock exchange in the United States, to be 'a material and intentional misrepresentation of results'. When income smoothing becomes excessive, the SEC may issue fines. Similar sanctions are available to the UK Financial Services Authority and the Central Bank of Ireland. Unfortunately, there is not much individual investors can do. Accounting laws for large corporations are extremely complex, which makes it very difficult for regular investors to pick up on accounting scandals before they happen. Although the different methods used by managers to smooth earnings can be very complex and confusing, the important thing to remember is that the driving force behind managing earnings is to meet a pre-specified target (often an analyst's consensus on earnings). However, as Warren Buffett stated, "managers that always promise to 'make the numbers' will at some point be tempted to make up the numbers".

According to Healy and Wahlen (1999),[1] earnings management occurs when managers use judgement in financial reporting and in structuring transactions to alter financial reports to either mislead some stakeholders about the underlying economic performance of a company or to influence contractual outcomes that depend on reported accounting numbers. Earnings management usually involves the artificial increase (or decrease) of revenues, profits or EPS figures through aggressive accounting tactics. Aggressive earnings management is a form of fraud and differs from reporting error (see **Chapter 21** – IAS 8 *Accounting Policies, Changes in Accounting Estimates and Errors*).

Management wishing to show a certain level of earnings or following a certain pattern seek loopholes in financial reporting standards that allow them to adjust the numbers as far as is practicable to achieve their desired aim or to satisfy projections by financial analysts. These adjustments amount to fraudulent financial reporting when they fall outside the bounds of acceptable accounting practice. Drivers for such behaviour include market expectations, personal realisation of a bonus and maintenance of position within a market sector. In most cases conformance to acceptable accounting practices is a matter of personal integrity. However, regardless of the motivations for such practices, the result is reported earnings that are unreliable. Aggressive earnings management becomes more probable when a company is affected by a downturn in business.

---

[1] Healy, P.M. and Wahlen, J.M. (1999). 'A Review of the Earnings Management Literature and its Implications for Standard Setting', *Accounting Horizons*, Vol. 13, No. 4, pp. 365–383.

Earnings management is seen as a pressing issue in current accounting practice. Part of the difficulty lies in the accepted recognition that there is no such thing as a single 'right' earnings figure and that it is possible for legitimate business practices to develop into unacceptable financial reporting. It is relatively easy for an auditor to detect error, but earnings management can involve sophisticated fraud that is covert. The requirement for management to assert that the accounts have been prepared properly offers no protection where those managers have already entered into conscious deceit and fraud. Auditors need to distinguish fraud from error by identifying the presence of intention.

The main forms of earnings management are as follows:
- unsuitable revenue recognition (e.g. early recognition of sales at the year-end to boost reported profits for that year);
- inappropriate accruals and estimates of liabilities (e.g. ignoring or being over-optimistic about the outcome of a legal case);
- excessive provisions and generous reserve accounting (e.g. excessive provisions in 'good' years that can be reversed or released to dampen the impact of 'bad' years); and
- intentional minor breaches of financial reporting requirements that aggregate to a material breach. For example, non-compliance with a number of accounting standards that individually is immaterial but material when considered in aggregate.

The previous sections have explained earnings' quality, pro-forma earnings and earnings management in order to provide a basis for explaining the calculation and disclosure of basic and diluted EPS in accordance with IAS 33, which is the focus of this chapter and dealt with in **Sections 23.5–23.7**.

23.5 IAS 33 *EARNINGS PER SHARE*

Objective of IAS 33

The remainder of this chapter addresses the principles for the determination and presentation of EPS in an entity's financial statements in accordance with IAS 33.

EPS is widely used by investors as a measure of a company's performance and is of particular importance in:
1. comparing the results of a company over a period of time; and
2. comparing the performance of one company's equity shares against the performance of another company's equity, and also against the returns obtainable from loan stock and other forms of investment.

Moreover, EPS is a key component of the price–earnings ratio, which expresses the relationship between the market price of a share and the EPS (see **Chapter 35**).

The purpose of any earnings yardstick is to achieve, as far as possible, clarity of meaning, comparability between one company and another, one year and another, and attribution of profits to the equity shares. IAS 33 goes some way to ensuring that all these aims are achieved. IAS 33 prescribes principles for the determination and presentation of EPS, so as to improve performance comparisons between different reporting organisations in the same reporting period and between different reporting periods for the same entity.

Scope of IAS 33

IAS 33 applies to organisations whose **ordinary shares** or **potential ordinary shares (POS)** are publicly traded and by organisations that are in the process of issuing ordinary shares or POS in public markets. EPS need only be presented on the basis of consolidated data. If an entity is not publicly traded but wishes voluntarily to disclose EPS, then it should be prepared on the same basis as IAS 33. While IAS 33 prescribes the principles for the determination and presentation of EPS, the focus is primarily on ensuring consistency in the calculation of the denominator (i.e. the 'bottom line' number of shares).

In simple terms, there are two types of EPS, basic and diluted, and their calculation is dealt with in **Section 23.6** and **Section 23.7**, respectively. However, before looking at these two sections, it is important to understand and be familiar with the **Key Terms and Definitions** included at the beginning of this chapter as this will aid your understanding of issues covered in **Section 23.6** and **Section 23.7**. As you study these sections, you should refer back to these terms and definitions.

While studying **Section 23.6** and **Section 23.7**, it is important to bear in mind the following points.

1. Dividends should not be shown on the face of the statement of profit or loss and other comprehensive income, but should be debited directly to equity and disclosed in the statement of changes in equity. However, in the interests of clarity (and brevity), they are often presented at the foot of the statement of profit or loss and other comprehensive income in some of the examples and questions presented in this chapter.

2. In the interests of brevity, the abbreviation 'SPLOCI' is used on occasion to refer to the 'Statement of Profit or Loss and Other Comprehensive Income'. The SPLOCI is divided into two components: a statement of profit or loss; and other comprehensive income (OCI) (see **Chapter 2**, **Section 2.3**). Where relevant, these two components are distinguished as follows: Statement of Profit or Loss and Other Comprehensive Income – Profit or Loss (SPLOCI – P/L); Statement of Profit or Loss and Other Comprehensive Income – Other Comprehensive Income (SPLOCI – OCI).

3. The presentation of shares in financial statements can be problematic. As a broad generalisation, an ordinary share, where the shareholder has no contractual right to any form of regular payment of dividends, is classified as equity. However, a preference share, where there is a contractual right to set dividend payments or if shares are redeemable at the option of the holder, will generally be treated as a liability. The grey area is the classification of the 'in-between shares', which may have both equity and liability components, since these shares should be treated as compound financial instruments with both an equity and liability component (with the value of the equity component being the residual amount after deducting the separately determined liability component from the fair value of the instrument as a whole – see **Chapter 25**). The presentation of such shares normally results in substantially all of their carrying value being allocated to the liability component, and the 'preference dividend' being treated as a finance cost in arriving at profit/loss for the period in the SPLOCI–P/L. Again, in the interests of clarity, and in recognition that this chapter focuses on the calculation of EPS rather than the presentation of preference shares, 'preference dividends' have usually *not* been charged in arriving at profit before tax in many of the examples and questions presented in this chapter (albeit that the preference shares are likely to be classified as non-current liabilities and therefore the 'dividend' would be classified as a finance cost).

23.6 BASIC EPS

As noted above, there are two types of EPS: basic and diluted. This section deals with basic EPS, with diluted EPS being explained in **Section 23.7**. We will begin by illustrating how basic EPS is calculated when there have been no changes in the ordinary share capital of the company during the accounting period, before focusing on dealing with the circumstances when the number of ordinary shares in issue has changed during the period.

Definition

An entity must calculate basic EPS for profit or loss attributable to ordinary equity-holders and, if presented, profit or loss from continuing operations attributable to their equity-holders. EPS should be reported in *cent* attributable to each equity share. The basic EPS calculation is:

$$\frac{\text{Profit/Loss attributable to Ordinary Shareholders, i.e. Earnings}}{\text{Weighted average number of ordinary shares outstanding during the period}}$$

Note: an ordinary share is an equity instrument that is subordinate to all other classes of equity instrument.

Examples 23.1–23.3 illustrate the calculation of basic EPS in circumstances where there have been no changes in the ordinary share capital during the accounting period, with each example becoming progressively more detailed.

EXAMPLE 23.1: BASIC EPS – NO CHANGES IN PERIOD (1)

A company has profits (or earnings) for the year of €100,000 and has 200,000 ordinary shares.

$$\text{EPS} = \frac{€100,000 \times 100}{200,000} = 50 \text{ cent per share}$$

The problem is defining what is meant by 'earnings' and what is meant by 'number of ordinary shares':
- earnings are the net profits after tax, interest, non-controlling interests (in the case of a group) and dividends on other classes of shares (e.g. preference dividends); and
- issued ordinary shares are all ordinary shares in circulation during the year. The weighted average approach is taken to calculate this amount.

Example 23.2 now introduces preference shares and preference dividends.

EXAMPLE 23.2: BASIC EPS – NO CHANGES IN PERIOD (2)

A company has the following issued share capital throughout the year:
- 200,000 ordinary shares of €1; and
- 50,000 10% preference shares of €1.

Extracts from the company's financial statements for the year ending 31 December 2012 showed:

	€	€
Net profit before taxation		60,000
Taxation		20,000
Net profit after taxation		40,000
Preference dividend (not charged in arriving at profit after tax – see note at end of **Section 23.5** above)	5,000	
Ordinary dividend	9,000	(14,000)
Retained profit for the year		26,000

Requirement Calculate the basic EPS for 2012.

Solution

$$EPS = \frac{Net\ Profit \times 100}{Number\ of\ Ordinary\ Shares}$$

$$EPS = \frac{€35,000}{200,000} \times 100 = 17.5\ cent$$

Example 23.3 is similar to the previous example, albeit more information is provided, which means a decision has to be made as to what is relevant for the purposes of calculating basic EPS.

EXAMPLE 23.3: BASIC EPS – NO CHANGES IN PERIOD (3)

BEANO plc
STATEMENT OF PROFIT OR LOSS AND OTHER COMPREHENSIVE INCOME
for the year ended 31 December 2012

	€	€
Revenue		6,400,000
Cost of sales		(4,480,000)
Gross profit		1,920,000
Other income		60,000
Distribution costs		(168,000)
Administrative expenses		(280,000)
Other expenses		(112,000)
Finance costs		(197,000)
Profit before tax		1,223,000
Tax		(366,900)
Profit after tax		856,100
Dividends:		
Preference (not charged in arriving at profit after tax – see note at end of **Section 23.5**)	100,000	
Ordinary	200,000	(300,000)
		556,100

Additional Information
1. At 1 January 2012 and 31 December 2012 the company had in issue:
   - 2,000,000 ordinary shares of 50 cent each; and
   - 1,000,000 10% preference shares of €1 each.
2. During the year ended 31 December 2012, BEANO plc paid the following dividends:

	€
Preference	100,000
Ordinary	200,000
	300,000

Requirement Calculate BEANO plc's basic EPS for the year ended 31 December 2012.

Solution

Calculation of Earnings:

	€
Profit after tax	856,100
Preference dividend	(100,000)
Profit attributable to ordinary shareholders	756,100

Calculation of Number of Ordinary Shares:
The general principle is that the number of ordinary shares is the weighted average number outstanding during the reporting period. If there are no ordinary shares issued during a reporting period, the number of shares for the basic EPS calculation is the number of shares in issue at the reporting period date. Therefore, the number of shares (denominator) for BEANO plc is 2,000,000.

$$\text{BEANO plc's EPS is}: \quad \frac{€756,100}{2,000,000} = 37.81 \text{ cent}$$

Note: if ordinary shares are issued during a period, the weighted average number outstanding during the period must be calculated.

Losses

If the earnings figure is a negative figure, then the EPS should be calculated in the normal way but shown as a loss per share.

Changes in Ordinary Share Capital and its Effect on Basic EPS

If new shares are issued during the accounting period, the denominator in the calculation of basic EPS will have to be changed. There are four ways in which the capital structure may change which will affect the calculation of basic EPS:
1. issue at full market price;
2. **bonus issue**, share split and share consolidation;
3. **rights issues**; and
4. shares issued as part of the purchase consideration for a business combination.

Each of these is dealt with further below.

> **Note:** when dealing with each of the four potential changes in capital structure, it is important to always consider: is the share issue time-apportioned depending on when it was issued during the accounting period and is there an impact on the prior year figures? The answer to these two questions influences how the basic EPS is calculated.

1. Issue at Full Market Price

Where new ordinary shares have been issued, either for cash at full market price or as consideration for the acquisition of an asset, the earnings should be apportioned over the average number of shares ranking for dividend during the period *weighted on a time basis*. There is no retrospective effect, therefore time apportion the issue but do not adjust prior year figures.

Examples 23.4 and **23.5** illustrate the calculation of basic EPS when there has been an issue of ordinary shares during the accounting period at full market price.

EXAMPLE 23.4: ISSUE AT FULL MARKET PRICE (I)

At 31 December 2011 the issued ordinary share capital of Top plc was 4 million shares of 50 cent each. On 1 October 2012 the company issued 1 million shares at market value €1.50. Earnings were:
- year ended 31 December 2011 – €400,000; and
- year ended 31 December 2012 – €500,000.

Requirement Calculate the basic EPS for 2011 and 2012.

Solution

2012:
No. of Shares
$(4,000,000 \times 9/12) + (5,000,000 \times 3/12) = 4,250,000$ shares

$$\frac{€500,000}{4,250,000} = 11.8 \text{ cent}$$

Do not adjust the 2011 comparative figure in the 2012 accounts.

$$\frac{€400,000}{4,000,000} = 10 \text{ cent}$$

Example 23.5 below develops the background information provided and introduces preference shares and preference dividends.

EXAMPLE 23.5: ISSUE AT FULL MARKET PRICE (2)

RP plc prepares its financial statements to 31 December each year and has a capital structure consisting of:
- 100,000 10% preference shares of €1 each; and
- 100,000 €1 ordinary shares.

In 2011 and 2012, RP plc had profits after tax of €50,000 and €60,000, respectively. On 30 September 2012, RP plc made an issue at full market price of 50,000 €1 ordinary shares. Preference dividends are not charged in arriving at profit after tax (see note at end of **Section 23.5** above).

Requirement Calculate the basic EPS for 2012 and the corresponding figure for 2011.

Solution

	2012	2011
	€	€
Profit after taxation	60,000	50,000
Less: Preference dividend	(10,000)	(10,000)
	50,000	40,000
Shares at 1 January	100,000	100,000
Issue at full market price:		
Before the year-end (50,000 × 3/12)	12,500	-
	112,500	100,000
EPS:		
$\dfrac{€50,000}{112,500}$	44 cent	
$\dfrac{€40,000}{100,000}$		40 cent

2. Bonus Issue, Share Split and Share Consolidation

Bonus Issue A bonus issue is a capitalisation of reserves and will have *no effect* on the earning capacity of the company. There is *no* inflow of funds. Where new equity shares have been issued by way of a bonus issue during the period, the earnings should be apportioned over the number of shares ranking for dividend after the capitalisation. Therefore, for comparative purposes, the corresponding figures for earlier periods should be adjusted accordingly since, although the 'bottom line' has increased, there has been no inflow of additional funds that could be used to increase earnings.

Examples 23.6 and **23.7** illustrate the calculation of basic EPS when there has been a bonus issue of ordinary shares during the accounting period.

EXAMPLE 23.6: BONUS ISSUE (1)

The background information is as per **Example 23.5** (RP plc). On 30 September 2012, a bonus issue of 100,000 ordinary shares was made by RP plc. (Remember, preference dividends are not charged in arriving at profit after tax (see note at end of **Section 23.5**).)

Requirement Calculate the basic EPS for 2012 and the corresponding figure for 2011.

Solution

	2012	2011
	€	€
Profit after Taxation	60,000	50,000
Less: Preference dividend	(10,000)	(10,000)
	50,000	40,000
Shares at 1 January	100,000	100,000
Bonus Issue	100,000	100,000
	200,000	200,000
EPS	25 cent	20 cent

Example 23.7 is similar to the previous example, albeit the wording of the terms of the bonus issue is slightly different and, therefore, requires a little more thought.

EXAMPLE 23.7: BONUS ISSUE (2)

At 31 December 2011, Ben plc had 4 million ordinary 25 cent shares in issue and 500,000 10% preference shares of €1 each. On 1 October 2012, the company made a one for four bonus issue out of reserves. The profit after tax for the year ended 31 December 2012 was €550,000, and for the year ended 31 December 2011 was €450,000. Preference dividends are not charged in arriving at profit after tax (see note at end of **Section 23.5**).

Requirement Calculate the basic EPS for 2011 and 2012.

EPS for 2012:
Earnings

	€
Profit after tax	550,000
Preference dividend	(50,000)
	500,000

EPS $\dfrac{€500,000}{5 \text{ million}}$ 10 cent

Comparative figure for 2011 in the 2012 financial statements must be adjusted:

either:

$$\frac{€400,000}{5 \text{ million}} = 8 \text{ cent}$$

or:

$$\frac{400,000}{4 \text{ million}} \times 4/5 = 8 \text{ cent}$$

Share Splits and Share Consolidations Similar considerations apply where equity shares are split into shares of smaller nominal value, i.e. a share of €1 nominal value is divided into five shares of 20 cent each or consolidated into shares of a higher nominal value, i.e. four shares of 25 cent each are consolidated into one share of €1. In both cases the number of shares outstanding before the event is adjusted for the proportionate change. The comparative figure must be adjusted. **Example 23.8** illustrates a share split.

EXAMPLE 23.8: SHARE SPLIT

Oak plc has 100,000 €1 ordinary shares in issue on 1 January 2012. On 1 October 2012, the company divides its shares into 400,000 ordinary shares of 25 cent each.

Therefore when calculating the EPS for 31 December 2012, divide by 400,000 shares.

3. Rights Issues

A **rights issue** is an issue of shares for cash to existing shareholders at a price (usually) below the current market price. It is equivalent to a cash issue at full market price combined with a subsequent bonus issue. This means that, while in practice all the shares in the rights issue are issued at a discount, IAS 33 treats this as being some at full market price and some for €nil consideration (i.e. for free), depending on the terms of the rights issue. When a company makes a rights issue at less than full market price, this will result in there being a new market price (after the rights issue), which will be less than that which existed when the rights issue took place. The new market price is known as the *theoretical ex rights price* (TERP). To arrive at figures for EPS when a rights issue is made, it is necessary to first calculate the TERP.

Examples 23.9 and **23.10** illustrate the calculation of basic EPS when there has been a rights issue during the accounting period.

EXAMPLE 23.9: RIGHTS ISSUE (I)

ABC has the following capital structure: 200,000 10% €1 preference shares and 200,000 €1 ordinary shares.

On 1 October 2012, ABC plc made a one for five rights issue at a price of €1.20. The market value on the last day of quotation-cum-rights[1] was €1.50. The calculation of the theoretical ex rights price (TERP) can be made in several ways. In this example, the calculation of the new market price is made from the point of view of the shareholder who, before the rights issue, has 5 ordinary shares and €1.20 in cash.

	€
Wealth of Shareholder with 5 ordinary shares prior to rights issue:	
5 × €1.50	7.50
Cost of taking up the right to buy one ordinary share:	
1 × €1.20	1.20
	8.70
Number of shares in issue:	6
Therefore TERP (€8.70/6):	€1.45

The procedure for calculating the EPS for the current year and the corresponding figure for the previous year is shown below.

The EPS for the corresponding previous period should be multiplied by the fraction:

$$\frac{\text{TERP}}{\text{Market price on last day of quotation (cum-rights)}}$$

To obtain the EPS for the current year:
1. multiply the number of shares before the rights issue by the fraction of the year before the date of issue and by the fraction:

$$\frac{\text{Market price on the last day of quotation (cum-rights)}}{\text{TERP}}$$

2. multiply the number of shares after the rights issue by the fraction of the year after the date of issue and add to the figure arrived at in (1).

Notes:
[1] Cum-rights – this is a situation in which the shareholders are entitled to any rights declared by a company. Shares that are trading cum-rights can be sold to another individual with the rights attached. The price of shares with cum-rights is normally higher than that of a stock with ex-rights.

Ex-rights – Shares that are trading ex rights no longer have rights attached because they have either expired, been transferred to another investor or been exercised.

Example 23.10 is similar to the previous example, albeit that it deals with the impact of a rights issue on different accounting periods.

EXAMPLE 23.10: RIGHTS ISSUE (2)

	2010	2011	2012
Net profit as at 31 December	€24,000	€30,400	€36,000
Shares before the rights issue	100,000		

The rights issue is to be one share for every five currently held (giving 20,000 new shares). Exercise price €1.00. The last date to exercise rights is 1 April 2011. The fair value of an ordinary share before the issue is €2.20.

Requirement Calculate the basic EPS for 2010, 2011 and 2012.

Solution

2010:

$$EPS = \frac{€24,000}{100,000} = 24 \text{ cent}$$

2011:
Rights issue takes place.
Calculate the theoretical ex-rights price

5 shares at €2.20	=	€11.00
1 share at €1.00	=	€1.00
6 shares	=	€12.00
Therefore, TERP	=	€2.00

Adjust 2010 EPS in 2011 financial statements

$$24c \times \frac{€2.00}{€2.20} = 21.82 \text{ cent}$$

EPS for 2011

100,000 × 3/12 × €2.20/€2.00	=	27,500
120,000 × 9/12		90,000
Number of shares to be used		117,500
$EPS = \dfrac{€30,400}{117,500}$	=	25.87 cent

2012

$$EPS = \frac{€36,000}{120,000} \qquad = \qquad 30 \text{ cent}$$

As noted above, there are four ways in which the capital structure of a company may change which will affect the calculation of basic EPS. These are:
1. issue at full market price;
2. bonus issue, share split and share consolidation;
3. rights issues; and
4. shares issued as part of the purchase consideration for a business combination.

The first three of these have been discussed above and the final one is now explained.

4. Shares Issued as Part of the Purchase Consideration for a Business Combination

The shares issued as part of the purchase consideration for a business combination are included in the weighted average number of shares as at the date of acquisition. Why? As the results of the new subsidiary are included in the consolidated financial statements from that date only, this is consistent with the treatment of pre- and post-acquisition earnings.

Dealing with shares issued as part of the purchase consideration for a business combination is shown in **Example 23.11**.

EXAMPLE 23.11: SHARES ISSUED AS PART OF THE PURCHASE CONSIDERATION

Pete plc has 1 million shares in issue on 1 January 2012. On 1 July 2012, Pete plc acquired 80% of the ordinary shares of Sue plc. As part of the consideration, Pete plc issued 400,000 ordinary shares at a market value of €2.50.

For the year ended 31 December 2012, the number of shares for the EPS calculation is:
(1 million × 6/12) + (1.4 million × 6/12) = 1.2 million

Alternative EPS Figures

While IAS 33 aims to ensure that the EPS is calculated in a uniform, consistent and comparable manner, users of financial statements ought to be cautious in interpreting the results. Quoted companies are simply too complex to make it possible to sum up a whole year's performance in a single ratio. Companies may attempt to help readers in this regard by disclosing alternative versions of EPS. IAS 33 permits the disclosure of additional EPS figures, calculated on another level of earnings. This additional EPS data should, however, be calculated using the same weighted average number of ordinary shares as for the basic EPS calculated according to IAS 33.

Disclosure Requirements for Basic EPS

IAS 33 requires that the following information be disclosed in relation to basic EPS.
- A reporting entity is required to present on the face of the statement of profit or loss and other comprehensive income the basic EPS for profit/loss both in total (i.e. including discontinued operations) and from continuing operations attributable to the ordinary equity-holders, including comparative figures (see **Chapter 2,** for example, **Figure 2.4**).
- Disclosure is still required when the basic EPS is negative, i.e. a loss per share.
- The amount used as the numerator in calculating the basic EPS must be disclosed (in the Notes) and a reconciliation of that amount to the net profit/loss for the period.
- The weighted average number of ordinary shares used in the calculation must also be disclosed.

23.7 DILUTED EPS

As mentioned previously, there are two types of EPS: basic and diluted. The calculation of the former is dealt with in **Section 23.6**, with this section explaining the latter.

At the end of a reporting period a company may have securities that do not have a claim to equity earnings *now*, but they may do in the *future*. These include:

1. options or warrants – these securities have the potential effect of increasing the number of equity shares ranking for dividend and so diluting, or 'watering down', the EPS. These securities may be dilutive potential ordinary shares (POS);
2. rights granted under employee or other share purchase plan;
3. contingently issuable shares;
4. convertible loan stock or convertible preference shares, which enable their holders to exchange their securities at a later date for ordinary shares at a predetermined rate; and
5. separate classes of equity share not yet entitled to a share of equity earnings, but becoming so at a future date (i.e. could increase the number of ordinary shares in the future and therefore dilute, or 'water down', EPS).

Each of these is dealt with further below.

The diluted EPS gives users of the financial statements a view on the POS of the entity. There is the potential to forecast the future EPS from the amounts given since it is based on what may happen to earnings and the number of ordinary shares in the future. The calculation of diluted EPS is consistent with that for basic EPS whilst giving effect to all dilutive POS. For the purpose of calculating diluted EPS, an entity should adjust profit or loss attributable to ordinary equity-holders of the entity, as calculated by the after-tax effects of:

• any dividends or other items related to dilutive POS deducted in arriving at profit or loss attributable to ordinary equity-holders of the entity;
• any interest recognised in the period related to dilutive POS; and
• any other changes in income or expense that would result from the conversion of the dilutive POS.

Note:
(a) When calculating diluted EPS (DEPS), always begin with both the earnings and number of shares used in the basic EPS. The following are the simple pro-forma calculations for the three main sets of securities.
(b) In considering whether POS are dilutive or antidilutive, each issue of POS is considered separately.
(c) In order to maximise the dilution of the basic EPS, each issue of POS is considered in sequence from the most dilutive to the least dilutive.
(d) POS should be treated as dilutive when conversion would decrease the net profit per share (or increase the net loss per share) from continuing operations.

Each of the five circumstances, referred to above, in which a company may have securities that do not have a claim to equity earnings *now*, but may do in the *future*, is explained below.

1. Share Options and Warrants

A **share option** allows the purchase of shares at a favourable amount, which is less than the fair value (see **Chapter 1**, **Section 1.4**) of existing shares. The assumed proceeds are deemed to be a mixture of:
1. an issue at fair (market) value; and
2. an issue for no consideration.

The calculation of diluted EPS includes shares deemed as issued for no consideration. (Shares issued at market value are deemed to be non-dilutive.) The principle is that the cash received for those shares deemed to be issued at full price can be used to increase earnings, whereas the 'free shares' increase the bottom-line number of shares but do not provide additional funds that can be used to increase earnings and therefore cause dilution. For this purpose, the following calculation is used:

$$\frac{\textbf{Shares under option} \times \textbf{exercise price}}{\textbf{Fair value of ordinary shares}}$$

This gives the number of shares that are to be excluded from the EPS calculation. This will become clearer in the following example.

EXAMPLE 23.12: SHARE OPTIONS

Net profit for 2012	€1,000,000
Weighted average number of ordinary shares for 2012	10 million
Average fair value of one ordinary share	€2.40
Weighted average number of shares under option during 2012	3 million
Exercise price for shares under option in 2012	€2.00

Requirement Calculate the basic and diluted EPS for 2012.

Solution

	Shares	Net profit	EPS
Net profit for 2012		€1,000,000	
Weighted average shares for 2012	10m		
Basic EPS			10 cent
Number of shares on option	3m		
Number of shares that would have been issued at fair value: $\frac{3m \times €2}{€2.40}$	(2.5m)		
Issued at no consideration	0.5m		
Diluted EPS	10.5m	€1,000,000	9.5 cent

Note: the net profit has not been increased, but the number of shares has. This is because the calculation only includes shares deemed to be issued for no consideration.

2. Employee Share Option Schemes

A share option is the right to buy a certain number of shares at a fixed price, sometime in the future, within a company. Employee share option schemes are typically used as an incentive for employees, who can generally exercise their options (i.e. buy the shares) after a specified period, known as the vesting period. Such schemes have become increasingly popular as an incentive scheme in organisations. Many schemes relate to performance criteria, which means that they are contingent on certain conditions being met (such as sales or profit targets). The section on contingently issuable shares (see below) explains how these schemes should be treated when calculating diluted EPS. Certain schemes do not have performance incentives. As with the share option approach, only those shares deemed as issued for no consideration are included (i.e. 'free shares'). The following example shows how these schemes should be treated.

EXAMPLE 23.13: NON-PERFORMANCE-RELATED EMPLOYEE SHARE OPTION SCHEME

A company runs a share option scheme based on the employee's period of service with the company. As at 31 December 2012 the provisions of the scheme were:

Date of grant	1 January 2012
Market price at grant date	€2.24
Exercise price of option	€1.80
Date of vesting	31 December 2014
Number of shares under option	3 million
Net profit for the year 2012	€1,000,000
Weighted average number of ordinary shares	10 million
Average fair value of an ordinary share	€2.70

Requirement Calculate the basic and diluted EPS for 2012.

Solution

	Shares	Net profit	EPS
Net profit for 2012		€1,000,000	
Weighted average shares for 2012	10m		
Basic EPS			10 cent
Number of shares on option	3m		
Number of shares that would have been issued at fair value: (3m × €1.80)/€2.70	(2.0m)		
Issued for no consideration	1.0m		
Diluted EPS	11.0m	€1,000,000	9.1 cent

Note: the net profit has not been increased, but the number of shares has. This is because the calculation only includes shares deemed to be issued for no consideration.

Note: IFRS 2 *Share-based Payment* (see **Chapter 34**) requires an entity to reflect in its statement of profit or loss and other comprehensive income and statement of financial position the effects of share-based payment transactions, including expenses associated with share options granted to employees.

3. Contingently Issuable Shares

Contingently issuable shares are shares that are to be issued after certain conditions have been met (for example, sales or profit targets). The shares are treated as outstanding (i.e. authorised and issued) if the conditions are satisfied and they are included in the calculation from the start of the period or the date of the agreement, if later. If the conditions are not met, the number included is based on the number of shares that would be issuable if the end of the period was the end of the contingency period. For the purposes of the diluted EPS calculation, these shares are included in full.

The following example (**Example 23.14**) gives two contingent events arising after the acquisition of a business. Most contingent events will be based on target sales or profit. The example includes the opening of new branches. This is also a measure of the entity's successful expansion. Note that many employee share option schemes operate in this manner.

EXAMPLE 23.14: CONTINGENTLY ISSUABLE SHARES

A company has 500,000 ordinary shares in issue at 1 January 2010. A recent business acquisition has given rise to the following contingently issuable shares:
- 10,000 ordinary shares for every new branch opened in the three years 2010–2012; and
- 1,000 ordinary shares for every €2,000 of net profit in excess of €900,000 over the three years ended 31 December 2012.

Shares related to the opening of a new branch are issued when the branch is opened, while shares related to the net profit contingency are issued on 1 January following the period in which a condition is met. A new branch was opened on 1 July 2010, another on 31 March 2011 and another on 1 October 2012. Reported net profits over the three years were €350,000, €400,000 and €600,000, respectively.

Requirement Calculate the basic and diluted EPS for 2010, 2011 and 2012.

Solution

Basic EPS

	2010	2011	2012
	€	€	€
Numerator	350,000	400,000	600,000
Denominator:			
Ordinary shares	500,000	510,000	520,000
Branch contingency	5,000 (i)	7,500 (i)	2,500 (i)
Earnings contingency	- (ii)	- (ii)	- (ii)
Total shares	505,000	517,500	522,500
Basic EPS	69.3 cent	77.3 cent	114.8 cent

Diluted EPS

	2010	2011	2012
	€	€	€
Numerator per basic EPS	350,000	400,000	600,000

Denominator:			
Ordinary shares in basic EPS	505,000	517,500	522,500
Additional shares:			
Branch contingency	5,000 (iii)	2,500 (iii)	7,500 (iii)
Earnings contingency	-	-	225,000 (iv)
Total shares	510,000	520,000	755,000
Diluted EPS	68.6 cent	76.9 cent	79.5 cent

Explanatory notes:
 (i) This figure is simply the shares due for opening a branch pro-rated over the year.
 (ii) It is not certain the net profit condition has been satisfied until after the three-year period. The effect is negligible for the fourth quarter and full year calculations since it is not certain the condition has been met until the end of the period.
 (iii) The contingently issuable shares are included from the start of the period in which they arise, so these figures are increasing the denominator by the full 10,000 shares.
 (iv) This is (€1,350,000 − €900,000)/€2,000 × 1,000. This figure will be included in the basic EPS figure in the following year (2013). Note that the €900,000 criterion was not exceeded in the prior year.

4. Convertibles

Convertible loan stock or **convertible preference shares** enable their holders to exchange their securities for ordinary shares at a specific date and at a predetermined rate. In cases where the issue of shares will affect earnings, the numerator should be adjusted accordingly. For example, this occurs when bonds (i.e. debt) or preference shares are converted. Interest is paid on the bond or preference dividends on the preference shares and when conversion takes place, this interest/preference dividend is no longer payable.

> *Note:* as interest on debt is allowable for tax purposes, only the after-tax cost of the interest is 'saved'. However, preference dividends are not allowable for tax purposes and therefore the full amount of the dividend is 'saved'.

This is illustrated with reference to convertible debt in **Example 23.15**.

EXAMPLE 23.15: CONVERTIBLE DEBT

Net profit	€500
Ordinary shares in issue	1,000
Basic EPS	50 cent
Convertible 15% bonds	200

Each block of five bonds is convertible to eight ordinary shares. The tax rate (including any deferred tax) is 40%.

Requirement Calculate the basic and diluted EPS.

Solution

Basic EPS = €500/1,000 = 50 cent

	€
Diluted EPS	
Earnings per basic EPS	500
Add interest saved net of tax 200 × 15% × 60%	18
	518
Shares per basic EPS	1,000
Add maximum shares on conversion 200 × 8/5	320
	1,320

DEPS = €518/1,320 = 39.2 cent
Earnings should be adjusted for savings or expenses occurring as a result of conversion.

Each of the four circumstances referred to above where a company may have securities that do not have a claim to equity earnings *now*, but may do in the *future*, have now been explained. In terms of calculating diluted EPS, the procedure is to calculate the potential dilution for each of the circumstances present (for example, given in the question) and rank them from the most dilutive to the least dilutive. This process is now explained.

5. Ranking Dilutive Securities

The approach prescribed by IAS 33 involves including only dilutive POS. Antidilutive shares are not to be included. This is a *prudent* approach, which recognises a potential reduction of earnings but not increases. **Example 23.16** and **Example 23.17** show how dilutive POS are identified and included in the calculation of EPS. The standard also states that the dilutive shares should be ranked and taken into account from the most dilutive down to the least dilutive. POS likely to have a dilutive effect on EPS include options, convertible bonds and convertible preference shares.

It should be noted that the numerator, for the purposes of ranking the dilutive shares, is net profit from *continuing operations* only (since dilution is concerned with what may happen in the future and this is the best estimate of future earnings). This is net profit after preference share dividends, but excluding discontinued operations. This is in contrast to the EPS calculation, which includes the full amount of net profit attributable to ordinary shareholders.

EXAMPLE 23.16: RANKING DILUTIVE SECURITIES (I)

Ranking Dilutive Securities for the Calculation of Weighted Average Number of Shares

Net profit attributable to ordinary shareholders	€20 million
Net profit from discontinued activities	€5 million
Ordinary shares outstanding	50 million
Average fair value of one ordinary share	€5.00

Potential ordinary shares:
- Convertible preference shares – 500,000 entitled to a cumulative dividend of €5. Each is convertible to 3 shares.
- 3% convertible bond – nominal amount €50 million. Each €1,000 bond is convertible to 50 shares. There is no amortisation of premium or discounting affecting the interest expense.
- Options – 10 million with exercise price of €4.

Tax rate – 30%

Requirement Calculate the basic and diluted EPS.

Solution

The effect on earnings on conversion of POS:

	Increase in Earnings €	Increase in Ordinary Shares Number	Effect on Earnings per Incremental Share €
Convertible preference shares			
Increase in net profit (€5 × 500,000)	2,500,000		
Incremental shares (3 × 500,000)		1,500,000	1.67
3% convertible bonds			
Increase in net profit			
50,000,000 × 0.03 × 70%	1,050,000		
Incremental shares (50,000 × 50)		2,500,000	0.42
Options			
Increase in earnings:	nil		
Incremental shares			
10 million × (€5 – €4)/€5		2,000,000 (W1)	nil

Therefore, options are the most dilutive as the increase in shares does not lead to any increase in EPS; this is followed by the 3% convertible bonds and finally the convertible preference shares in terms of their dilutive potential.

(W1)
Number of shares that would be issued at market value = 10m × 4/5 = 8m
Number of shares at no consideration = 2m

Identifying the dilutive shares to include in the diluted EPS:

	Net profit from continuing operations €	Ordinary shares Number	Per share €
Reported	15,000,000	50,000,000	0.300
Options	-	2,000,000	
	15,000,000	52,000,000	0.288 dilutive
3% convertible bonds	1,050,000	2,500,000	
	16,050,000	54,500,000	0.294 antidilutive
Convertible preference shares	2,500,000	1,500,000	
	18,550,000	56,000,000	0.331 antidilutive

To maximise the dilution of basic EPS, each issue of POS is considered in sequence from the most dilutive to the least dilutive, i.e. dilutive POS with the lowest 'Earnings per Incremental Share' are included in the DEPS calculation before those with the higher 'Earnings per Incremental Share'.

Note:
• The potential share issues are considered from the most dilutive to the least dilutive.
• Remember, POS should be treated as dilutive only when their conversion to ordinary shares would decrease net profit or increase net loss per share from continuing operations.
• The diluted EPS is increased by both the bonds and the preference shares. These are therefore ignored in the diluted EPS calculation.

	Including Discontinued Operations	Excluding Discontinued Operations
Basic EPS		
Net profit	€20 million	€15 million
Weighted average number of shares	50 million	50 million
Basic EPS	40 cent	30 cent
Diluted EPS		
Net profit (remains at)	€20 million	€15 million
Weighted average number of shares	52 million	52 million
Diluted EPS	38.5 cent	28.8 cent

Note:
• The cumulative dividend on the preference shares is not taken into consideration. Only the dividend for the year is included in the increase in earnings.
• It is important to remember the tax element in the bond interest.

The next example is based on the previous example, except that the convertible bonds are 1.5% bonds (which results in them being dilutive).

EXAMPLE 23.17: RANKING DILUTIVE SECURITIES (2)

Solution

Effect on earnings on conversion of POS:

	Increase in earnings €	Increase in number of ordinary shares	Earnings per share €
1.5% Convertible bonds			
Increase in net profit:			
$(50,000,000 \times 0.015 \times (1 - 0.3))$	525,000		
Incremental shares $(50,000 \times 50)$		2,500,000	0.21

Identifying the dilutive shares to include in the diluted EPS:

	Net profit from continuing operations €	Number of Ordinary shares Number	Earnings per share €
Reported	15,000,000	50,000,000	0.30
Options	-	2,000,000	
	15,000,000	52,000,000	0.29 Dilutive
1.5% convertible bonds	525,000	2,500,000	
	15,525,000	54,500,000	0.28 Dilutive

The convertible preference shares will remain antidilutive and basic EPS will remain at 40 cent.

	Including Discontinued Operations	Excluding Discontinued Operations
Diluted EPS:		
Net profit (€20,000,000 + €525,000) bond interest	€20,525,000	€15,525,000
Weighted average number of shares	54.5 million	54.5 million
Diluted EPS	37.7 cent	28.5 cent

Disclosure Requirements

IAS 33 requires that the following information be disclosed in relation to diluted EPS.
- IAS 33 requires that the diluted EPS is disclosed on the face of the statement of profit or loss and other comprehensive income, even if the amounts are negative. Comparative figures are also required.
- The amounts used as numerators in calculating the diluted EPS, reconciled to actual net profit (loss) for the period.

Example 23.18 brings together many of the issues covered in **Section 23.6** and **Section 23.7** in the form of an examination-style question. All of the issues included in this example are explained and illustrated previously in this chapter.

EXAMPLE 23.18: BASIC AND DILUTED EPS

The following information has been extracted from the financial statements of Diamond plc in respect of the year ended 31 December 2012:

Earnings	€
Net profit attributable to continuing operations	16,400,000
Less preference dividends	(6,400,000)
Profit from continuing operations attributable to ordinary shareholders	10,000,000
Loss from discontinued operations	(4,000,000)
Net profit attributable to ordinary shareholders	6,000,000
Ordinary shares outstanding	2,000,000
Average market price of one ordinary share during 2012	€75

The tax rate (including any deferred tax) is 40%.

POS:

- 100,000 options with exercise price of €60.
- 800,000 8% €100 convertible cumulative preference shares, with each preference share held convertible into two ordinary shares.
- 100,000,000 5% €1 convertible bonds, with each 1,000 block convertible into 20 ordinary shares.

Requirement Calculate the basic and diluted EPS for 2012.

Solution

Increase in earnings attributable to ordinary shareholders on conversion of POS.

	Increase in earnings	Increase in shares	Earnings per incremental share
Options			
Increase in earnings	Nil		
Incremental shares (100,000 × (€75 − €60)/€75)		20,000[a]	Nil
Convertible preference shares			
Increase in earnings (€8 × 800,000)	6,400,000		
Incremental shares (2 × 800,000)		1,600,000	4
5% Convertible bonds			
Increase in earnings (100,000,000 × 5% × 0.6)	3,000,000		
Incremental shares		2,000,000	1.50

Therefore, based on the above, the POS should be ranked as follows: (1) options (2) convertible bonds (3) convertible preference shares.

[a] Total options 100,000 − (100,000 × €60/€75) = 20,000 free shares.

Computation of diluted EPS:

	Earnings	Ordinary shares	EPS
As reported	10,000,000	2,000,000	5.00
Options	-	20,000	
	10,000,000	2,020,000	4.95 dilutive
5% Convertible bonds	3,000,000	2,000,000	
	13,000,000	4,020,000	3.23 dilutive
Convertible preference shares	6,400,000	1,600,000	
	19,400,000	5,620,000	3.45 antidilutive

The convertible preference shares are ignored in calculating the diluted EPS as they are antidilutive.

Computation of EPS:	Basic EPS	Diluted EPS
From continuing operations	5.00	3.23
From discontinued operations	(2.00)[b]	(0.99)[c]
Profit attributable to ordinary shareholders	3.00	2.24

[b] (€4,000,000 ÷ 2,000,000) = (2.00)
[c] (€4,000,000 ÷ 4,020,000) = (0.99)

23.8 CONCLUSION

EPS is an important, and often confusing, topic. An entity should present on the face of the statement of profit or loss and other comprehensive income its basic and diluted EPS for each class of ordinary shares that has a different right to share in profit for the period. An entity should calculate basic and diluted EPS for profit or loss from continuing operations attributable to the ordinary equity-holders of the parent entity. If an entity reports a discontinued operation, it also discloses basic and diluted EPS for the discontinued operation.

Basic Earnings per Share Basic EPS is calculated by dividing profit or loss attributable to ordinary equity-holders of the parent entity (the numerator) by the weighted average number of ordinary shares outstanding (the denominator) during the period. The profit or loss attributable to the parent entity is adjusted for the after-tax amounts of preference dividends, differences arising on the settlement of preference shares, and other similar effects of preference shares classified as equity. The weighted average number of ordinary shares outstanding during the period and for all periods presented is adjusted for events, other than the conversion of POS, that have changed the number of ordinary shares outstanding without a corresponding change in resources (for example, a bonus issue, a share split).

Diluted Earnings per Share Diluted EPS is calculated by adjusting the profit or loss attributable to ordinary equity-holders of the parent entity, and the weighted average number of ordinary shares outstanding, for the effects of all dilutive POS. The profit or loss attributable to ordinary equity-holders of the parent entity, as calculated for basic EPS, is adjusted for the after-tax effects of:

- any dividends or other items related to dilutive POS deducted in arriving at profit or loss attributable to ordinary equity-holders;
- any interest recognised in the period related to dilutive POS; and
- any other changes in income or expense that would result from the conversion of the dilutive POS.

The number of ordinary shares is the weighted average number of ordinary shares outstanding, as calculated for basic EPS, plus the weighted average number of ordinary shares that would be issued on the conversion of all the dilutive POS into ordinary shares. POS are treated as dilutive when their conversion to ordinary shares would decrease EPS or increase loss per share from continuing operations (for example, options and warrants, convertible instruments and contingently issuable shares).

IAS 33 requires that basic and diluted EPS be disclosed on the face of the SPLOCI both for net profit or loss for the period and also for profit or loss from continuing operations. Basic and diluted EPS for discontinued operations (if reported) may be reported either on the face of the SPLOCI or in a note. Additional per share amounts cannot be disclosed on the face of the SPLOCI; they can only be disclosed by way of Note.

Summary of Learning Objectives

After having studied this chapter on earnings per share, you should be able to:

Learning Objective 1 Define what is meant by the term 'earnings quality'.

High-quality earnings can be characterised as repeatable, controllable and bankable.

Learning Objective 2 Understand the concept of pro-forma earnings.

Pro-forma earnings are calculated by preparing Pro-forma financial statements. Pro-forma financial statements describe financial statements that have hypothetical amounts, or estimates, built into the data to give a 'picture' of a company's profits if certain non-recurring items were excluded.

Learning Objective 3 Define basic and diluted EPS.

Basic EPS is calculated by dividing profit or loss attributable to ordinary equity-holders of the parent entity (the numerator) by the weighted average number of ordinary shares outstanding (the denominator) during the period. Diluted EPS is calculated by adjusting the profit or loss attributable to ordinary equity-holders of the parent entity, and the weighted average number of ordinary shares outstanding, for the effects of all dilutive POS.

Learning Objective 4 Apply the principles for the determination and presentation of basic and diluted EPS in an entity's financial statements in accordance with IAS 33.

An entity should present, on the face of the statement of profit or loss and other comprehensive income, its basic and diluted EPS for each class of ordinary shares that has a different right to share in profit for the period.

QUESTIONS

Self-test Questions

1. To what companies does IAS 33 *Earnings per Share* apply?
2. Define basic and diluted EPS.
3. Following a rights issue, by what fraction should the EPS for the corresponding previous period be multiplied?
4. Summarise the disclosure requirements of IAS 33.

Review Questions

(See **Appendix One** for Suggested Solutions to Review Questions.)

Question 23.1

Extracts from the draft financial statements of Plum Plc for year ended 31 December 2012 show the following:

	€	€
Profit before tax		2,323,000
Less Taxation		
Corporation Tax	1,035,000	
Under provision for 2011	23,000	
		(1,058,000)
Profit after tax		1,265,000
From statement of changes in equity		
Transfer to reserves	115,000	
Dividends:		
Paid preference interim dividend	138,000	
Paid ordinary interim dividend	184,000	
Proposed preference final dividend	138,000	
Proposed ordinary final dividend	230,000	
		(805,000)
Retained profit		460,000

On 1 January 2012 the issued share capital of Plum Plc was 4,600,000 6% preference shares of €1 each and 4,140,000 ordinary shares of €1 each. The proposed dividends were approved by the shareholders during the year ended 31 December 2012. The preference dividends have *not* been charged in arriving at profit after tax in the statement of profit of loss and other comprehensive income.

Requirement Calculate the EPS (on basic and fully diluted basis) in respect of the year ended 31 December 2012 for each of the following circumstances (each of the four circumstances (a) to (d) is to be dealt with separately):

(a) On the basis that there was no change in the issued share capital of the company during the year ended 31 December 2012.

(b) On the basis that the company made a bonus issue on 1 October 2012 of one ordinary share for every four shares in issue at 30 September 2012.

(c) On the basis that the company made a rights issue of €1 ordinary shares on 1 October 2012 in the proportion of 1 for every 5 shares held, at a price of €1.20. The middle market price for the shares on the last day of quotation cum rights was €1.80 per share.

(d) On the basis that the company made no new issue of shares during the year ended 31 December 2012 but on that date it had in issue €1,150,000 10% convertible loan stock 2016–2019. This loan stock will be convertible into ordinary €1 shares as follows:
2016: 90 €1 shares for €100 nominal value loan stock;
2017: 85 €1 shares for €100 nominal value loan stock;
2018: 80 €1 shares for €100 nominal value loan stock;
2019: 75 €1 shares for €100 nominal value loan stock.
Assume tax at 50%.

Question 23.2

The following information has been extracted from the financial statements of Earno plc for the year ended 31 December.

	2012 €000	2011 €000
Revenue	2,000	1,600
Profit before tax	800	600
Taxation	(300)	(200)
Profit after taxation	500	400
Dividends:		
Paid		
14% Non-cumulative Preference	–	(20)
Proposed		
10% Cumulative Preference	(30)	(30)
14% Non-cumulative Preference	(60)	(40)
Ordinary	(10)	(10)
Transfer to Capital Reserves	(90)	–
Profit for year retained	310	300

The 14% preference dividend paid in 2011 is in respect of previous years. The proposed dividends in 2011 and 2012 were approved by shareholders of Earno plc during the year ended 31 December 2011 and 2012 respectively. Earno plc has issued ordinary share capital of 100,000 @ €1 each. The preference dividends have *not* been charged in arriving at profit after tax.

Requirement Each of the following questions should be considered independently of one another.

(a) Basic EPS.

Calculate the basic EPS for both years.

(b) Issue at Full Market Price.

Assuming that Earno plc had issued 5,000 ordinary shares on 31 March 2012 at full market price, calculate the basic EPS for both years.

(c) Capitalisation/Bonus/Scrip Issue.

Assuming that on 31 May 2012 Earno plc issued 1 ordinary share for every 5 already held, calculate the basic EPS for both years.

(d) Share Exchange.

Assuming that on 30 April 2012 Earno plc issued 10,000 ordinary shares as consideration for the acquisition of a subsidiary company, calculate the basic EPS for both years.

(e) Rights Issue for less than Full Market Price.

Assuming that on 30 June 2012 (market price of share €4), Earno plc invited its shareholders to subscribe to a 1 for 5 rights issue at €2 per share, calculate the basic EPS for both years.

(f) Diluted EPS.

(i) Another class of equity ranking for dividend in the future.

Assuming that on 1 January 2012, Earno plc had issued 10,000 'A' ordinary shares, which though not ranking for dividend in the current period would do so subsequently, calculate the diluted EPS.

(ii) Convertible Securities.

Assume that on 31 March 2012, Earno plc issued €5,000 10% convertible debentures. These were convertible into ordinary shares as follows:

2012:   40   Ordinary Shares for €100 Convertible Debentures;
2013:   30   Ordinary Shares for €100 Convertible Debentures;
2014:   20   Ordinary Shares for €100 Convertible Debentures;
2015:   15   Ordinary Shares for €100 Convertible Debentures.

None of the debentures had been converted at 31 December 2012.

Calculate the diluted EPS (assume corporation tax @ 50%).

Challenging Questions

(Suggested Solutions to Challenging Questions are available to lecturers.)

Question 23.1 *(Based on Chartered Accountants Ireland, P3 Summer 2003, Question 6)*

CLASSICAL plc (CLASSICAL) had one million ordinary €1 shares in issue on 1 January 2012. On 1 July 2012, CLASSICAL made a rights issue of one ordinary share for every two previously held, at a price of €6 per share. The fair value of one ordinary share was €9 throughout the year ended 31 December 2012. During the year ended 31 December 2012, the following POS were outstanding:

(a) 3,000,000 share options with an exercise price of €6 per share;

(b) 50,000 convertible preference shares entitled to a dividend of €5 per share. Each preference share is convertible into two ordinary shares; and

(c) 6,000,000 nominal 2% convertible bonds, convertible into 300 shares per each 6,000 bond held.

The reported basic EPS in 2011 was 36 cent. After deducting dividends and other appropriations of profit in respect of non-equity shares, CLASSICAL reported a net profit of €500,000 for the year ended 31 December 2012. CLASSICAL pays corporation tax at 25%.

Requirement
(a) Compute the basic EPS figure, including comparatives, to be reported in the financial statements of CLASSICAL for the year ended 31 December 2012 in accordance with IAS 33 *Earnings per Share*.
(b) Compute the diluted EPS of CLASSICAL for the year ended 31 December 2012 in accordance with IAS 33 *Earnings per Share*. (Comparative figures are not required.)

Question 23.2 (Based on Chartered Accountants Ireland, P3 Autumn 2004, Question 4)

The issued ordinary share capital of WELLER plc (WELLER) at 1 January *2011* was 6,000,000 ordinary shares of €0.50 each. On 30 June *2012*, WELLER made a fully subscribed 1 for 3 rights issue at €1 per share, when the average price of one ordinary share was €1.50. There were no other changes to WELLER's ordinary share capital in *2011* and *2012*. The average market price of one ordinary share in WELLER during *2011* and *2012* was €1.20 and €1.60, respectively. At 31 December *2011* and *2012*, WELLER had a 5% loan of €1,000,000, which was convertible into 500,000 ordinary shares of €0.50 each. WELLER pays corporation tax at 25%.

The following information is available from the statement of profit or loss and other comprehensive income and statement of changes in equity of WELLER for the years ended 31 December *2011* and *2012*.

| | | Year ended 31 December | | |
| | 2012 | | 2011 | |
	€000	€000	€000	€000
Operating profit		1,900		1,300
Gain/(loss) – litigation settlement		(200)		100
Interest payable		(60)		(50)
Profit before tax		1,640		1,350
Taxation		(410)		(340)
Profit after tax		1,230		1,010
Non-controlling interests		(246)		(202)
		984		808
Preference dividends paid (Note 1)		(102)		(102)
Ordinary dividends paid		(132)		(106)
Retained profit for the year		750		600
Retained profit at				
start of year as previously stated	1,900		1,300	
Prior period adjustment (Note 2)	(100)		–	
Retained profit at start of year as restated		1,800		1,300
Retained profit at end of year		2,550		1,900

Note 1: the preference dividends have *not* been charged in arriving at profit after tax in the SPLOCI.

Note 2: the prior period adjustment relates to the discovery of a fundamental error in *2012*, which would have affected WELLER's operating profit for the year ended 31 December *2011*.

Requirement

(a) Calculate, in accordance with IAS 33 Earnings per Share:
   (i)   WELLER's basic EPS for the year ended 31 December *2011*;
   (ii) WELLER's diluted EPS for the year ended 31 December *2011*;
   (iii) WELLER's basic EPS for the year ended 31 December *2012*;
   (iv) WELLER's adjusted EPS for the year ended 31 December 2011 to be included as a comparative figure in WELLER's financial statements for the year ended 31 December *2012*.

(b) Outline why it is considered important to measure EPS.

Question 23.3 *(Based on Chartered Accountants Ireland, P3 Summer 2006, Question 5)*

On 1 January 2012, BELLS plc (BELLS) had 1,000,000 €1 ordinary shares and 500,000 6% €1 convertible preference shares in issue. Preference dividends are paid half-yearly on 31 March and 30 September each year. The preference dividends have *not* been charged in arriving at profit after tax in the SPLOCI and BELLS' profit after tax for the year ended 31 December 2010 was:

	€000
Profit after tax:	
Continuing operations	3,000
Discontinued operations	500
	3,500

On 1 April 2012, BELLS issued a further 500,000 €1 ordinary shares at full market price. Warrants to purchase 450,000 €1 ordinary shares were issued on 31 May 2012 at €3 per share. While the warrants were due to expire on 31 May 2013, all were exercised on 28 February 2013. Convertible loan stock of €800,000 at an interest rate of 6% per annum was issued at par on 30 June 2011. Each €100 of loan stock is convertible into 10 €1 ordinary shares at any time at the option of the holder. Interest is paid half-yearly on 31 December and 30 June each year. On 1 July 2012, €300,000 of loan stock was converted when the market price was €4 per share. The preference shares are convertible into ordinary shares at the option of the holder on the basis of one €1 ordinary share for every four convertible preference shares held. Holders of 200,000 preference shares converted them into ordinary shares on 1 October 2012. The average market price of BELLS' ordinary shares during the year ended 31 December 2012 was €5 per share, and the tax rate is 25%.

BELLS' financial statements were approved on 31 March 2013.

Requirement Calculate the basic and diluted EPS for BELLS for the year ended 31 December 2012 in accordance with IAS 33 *Earnings per Share*.

Question 23.4

Accounting regulators believe that undue emphasis is placed on earnings per share (EPS) and that this leads to simplistic interpretation of financial performance. Many chief executives believe that their share price does not reflect the value of their company and yet are preoccupied with earnings-based ratios. It appears that if chief executives shared the views of the regulators, then they may disclose more meaningful information than EPS to the market, which may then reduce the 'reporting gap' and lead to higher share valuations. The 'reporting gap' can be said to be the difference between the information required by the stock market in order to evaluate the performance of a company and the actual information disclosed.

Requirement Discuss the potential problems of placing undue emphasis on the EPS figure.

OPERATING SEGMENTS

LEARNING OBJECTIVES

After having studied this chapter on operating segments, you should be able to:
1. explain the objectives of segment reporting and why the users of financial statements may find segment reporting useful;
2. identify an organisation's reportable and operating segments; and
3. apply the main disclosure requirements of IFRS 8 *Operating Segments*.

KEY TERMS AND DEFINITIONS FOR THIS CHAPTER

In order to aid your understanding of the concepts and issues covered in this chapter, it is important to understand and be familiar with the following key terms and definitions. As you study this chapter, you should refer back to them.

Chief Operating Decision Maker The term chief operating decision maker is not specifically defined in IFRS 8 as it refers to a function rather than a title. In some organisations the function could be fulfilled by a group of directors rather than an individual.

Operating Segment This is a component of an organisation:
- that engages in business activities from which it may earn revenues and incur expenses (including revenues and expenses relating to transactions with other components of the same organisation);
- whose operating results are reviewed regularly by the organisation's chief operating decision maker to make decisions about resources to be allocated to the segment and to assess its performance; and
- for which discrete financial information is available.

Reportable Segments These are operating segments (see below) or aggregations of operating segments that meet specified criteria outlined in **Section 24.2**.

24.1 INTRODUCTION

As explained in **Chapter 1**, financial reporting is an information system and the fundamental objective of financial reporting is to communicate information about the resources and performance of the reporting entity useful to those having reasonable rights to such information. It is recognised in the *Conceptual Framework for Financial Reporting 2010* (*IFRS Framework*) that the primary users of general purpose financial statements are present and potential investors, lenders and other creditors who use the information to inform their decisions on investing, lending or providing other forms of credit to the company. Relevance is one of the qualitative characteristics of financial information identified in the *IFRS Framework*, and information is relevant when it assists users in assessing past, present or future economic events or confirming or correcting their past evaluations. An example of this could be where the financial performance of an entity is influenced by the economic conditions of a particular geographical region in which it operates.

Many organisations provide a range of products or services and/or operate in different geographical areas. Each product/service or geographical area may be subject to different influences that result in different risks and rewards, which may not be obvious when the figures are aggregated in the entity's financial statements. Consequently, organisations are required to separately analyse their results by product/service and geographical area so that users can:
- better understand the organisation's past performance;
- better assess the organisation's risks and returns; and
- make more informed judgements about the organisation as a whole.

This chapter discusses the principles for reporting financial information by segment to help users of financial statements in accordance with IFRS 8 *Operating Segments*.

Key to this Chapter

IFRS 8 is a disclosure standard; it does not address how transactions should be accounted for, merely whether, and how, they should be disclosed in the financial statements. This chapter begins by explaining the objective and scope of IFRS 8, before defining the terms 'reportable segment' and 'operating segment', together with providing some examples to illustrate the application of these terms. The chapter concludes by summarising and illustrating the IFRS 8 disclosures.

24.2 IFRS 8 *OPERATING SEGMENTS*

Objective and Scope

IFRS 8 applies to the financial statements of any organisation whose debt or equity instruments are traded in a public market and to organisations that are in the process of issuing equity or debt in a public market. Other organisations that choose to disclose segment information in financial statements that comply with international financial reporting standards should make the disclosures in line with IFRS 8, if they describe such disclosures as 'segment information'. When both separate and consolidated financial statements are presented in a single financial report, segment information need only be presented in respect of the consolidated financial statements.

IFRS 8's core principle is that an organisation should disclose information to enable users of its financial statements to evaluate the nature and financial effects of the types of business activities in which it engages and the economic environments in which it operates. It requires operating segments to be identified on the basis of internal reports about components of the organisation that are regularly reviewed by the **chief operating decision-maker** in order to allocate resources to the segment and to assess its performance. The terms 'chief operating decision-maker' is not specifically defined in IFRS 8 as it refers to a function rather than a title. In some organisations the function could be fulfilled by a group of directors rather than an individual. As a result, IFRS 8 has been criticised for leaving segment identification too much to the discretion of the organisation and, therefore, hindering comparability between financial statements of different organisations.

Operating Segments

An **operating segment** is a component of an organisation:
- that engages in business activities from which it may earn revenues and incur expenses (including revenues and expenses relating to transactions with other components of the same organisation);
- the operating results of which are reviewed regularly by the organisation's chief operating decision-maker to make decisions about resources to be allocated to the segment and to assess its performance; and
- for which discrete financial information is available.

Reportable Segments

IFRS 8 requires an organisation to report financial and descriptive information about its *reportable segments*. **Reportable segments** are operating segments (see above) or aggregations of *operating segments* that meet specified criteria:
- its reported revenue, from both external customers and inter-segment sales or transfers, is 10% or more of the combined revenue, internal and external, of all operating segments; or
- the absolute measure of its reported profit or loss is 10% or more of the greater, in absolute amount, of (1) the combined reported profit of all operating segments that did not report a loss and (2) the combined reported loss of all operating segments that reported a loss; or
- its assets are 10% or more of the combined assets of all operating segments.

The application of these criteria is illustrated in **Example 24.1**.

If the total external revenue reported by operating segments constitutes less than 75% of the organisation's revenue, additional operating segments must be identified as reportable segments (even if they do not meet the quantitative thresholds set out above), until at least 75% of the organisation's revenue is included in reportable segments. IFRS 8 has detailed guidance about when operating segments may be combined to create a reportable segment.

This is also illustrated in **Example 24.1** below.

IFRS 8 does not define segment revenue, segment expense, segment result, segment assets or segment liabilities; although it does require an explanation of how segment profit or loss, segment assets and segment liabilities are measured for each operating segment. As a consequence, entities have some discretion in determining what is included in segment profit or loss under IFRS 8, albeit limited by their internal reporting practices. IFRS 8 states that a component of an organisation that sells primarily or exclusively to other operating segments of the organisation will meet the definition of an operating segment if the organisation is managed that way.

EXAMPLE 24.1: REPORTABLE SEGMENTS

An organisation has identified the following business components:

Component	Revenue External	Revenue Internal	Profit	Assets
	€000	€000	€000	€000
1	80,000	Nil	10,000	50,000
2	Nil	45,000	5,000	30,000
3	10,000	Nil	1,000	4,000
4	8,000	Nil	500	3,000
Total	98,000	45,000	16,500	87,000

Requirement Identify which of the segments should be classified as reportable in accordance with IFRS 8.

Solution

Components 1 and 2 would be separately reportable since they meet all three size criteria. Components 3 and 4 do not meet any of the size criteria and on the face of it are not separately reportable. The external revenue of component 1 is 82% of the total external revenue so the '75% threshold' is comfortably achieved. However, if Components 3 and 4 had similar economic characteristics, then, when aggregated, they would be over the 10% threshold for revenue and so could be reported as a combined segment.

IFRS 8 requires that current period and comparative segment information be reported consistently. This means that if a segment is identified as reportable in the current period but was not in the previous period, then equivalent comparative information should be presented, unless it would be prohibitively costly to obtain. IFRS 8 gives organisations discretion to report information regarding segments that do not meet the size criteria. Organisations can report on such segments where, in the opinion of management, information about the segments would be useful to users of the financial statements.

Not all operations of an organisation will necessarily be an operating segment (nor part of one). For example, the corporate headquarters or some functional departments may not earn revenues or they may earn revenues that are only incidental to the activities of the organisation. These would not be operating segments. In addition, IFRS 8 states specifically that an organisation's post-retirement benefit plans are not operating segments.

Example 24.2 addresses the principles underlying IFRS 8, and applies the standard to a more complex scenario than that presented in **Example 24.1**.

EXAMPLE 24.2: UNDERLYING PRINCIPLES AND DISCLOSURE

You are the financial accountant of Global Network plc, an environmental lobbying company that was established in Dublin in 1990. In recent years, Global Network plc has developed into an international group and it reports internally on the basis of the geographical region in which its lobbying activities take place, with the directors allocating resources and assessing performance on this basis. Global Network plc's results on a regional basis for the year ended 31 December 2012 can be summarised as follows:

	Revenue €000	Profit €000	Assets €000	Liabilities €000
United Kingdom and Ireland	522,000	74,000	802,000	220,000
Mainland Europe	180,000	31,000	631,000	193,000
North America	624,000	129,000	866,000	268,000
Other Geographical Regions	676,000	116,000	1,270,000	415,000
	2,002,000	350,000	3,569,000	1,096,000

The other geographical regions include Africa, Asia and South America. Given the competitive nature of Global Network plc's activities, the directors are sensitive about the extent of disclosures made by the company.

Requirement Prepare a memorandum addressed to the directors of Global Network plc that clearly:
1. explains how the principles of IFRS 8 *Operating Segments* apply to Global Network plc; and
2. illustrates the disclosures required by Global Network plc for the year ended 31 December 2012 in accordance with IFRS 8 *Operating Segments*.

Solution

MEMORANDUM

Date:	dd/mm/yy
To:	Directors of Global Network plc
From:	Financial Accountant of Global Network plc
Subject:	IFRS 8 *Operating Segments*

As requested...

(a) How the principles of IFRS 8 *Operating Segments* apply to Global Network plc

IFRS 8's core principle is that an organisation should disclose information to enable users of its financial statements to evaluate the nature and financial effects of the types of business activities in which it engages and the economic environments in which it operates. IFRS 8 requires an organisation to report financial and descriptive information about its *reportable segments*. Reportable segments are *operating segments* or aggregations of operating segments that meet specified criteria:

- its reported revenue, from both external customers and intersegment sales or transfers, is 10% or more of the combined revenue, internal and external, of all operating segments; or
- the absolute measure of its reported profit or loss is 10% or more of the greater, in absolute amount, of (1) the combined reported profit of all operating segments that did not report a loss and (2) the combined reported loss of all operating segments that reported a loss; or
- its assets are 10% or more of the combined assets of all operating segments.

If the total external revenue reported by operating segments constitutes less than 75% of the organisation's revenue, additional operating segments must be identified as reportable segments (even if they do not meet the quantitative thresholds set out above), until at least 75% of the organisation's revenue is included in reportable segments.

An operating segment is a component of an organisation:

- that engages in business activities from which it may earn revenues and incur expenses (including transactions with other components of the same organisation);
- whose operating results are reviewed regularly by the organisation's chief operating decision-maker to make decisions about resources to be allocated to the segment and assess its performance; and
- for which discrete financial information is available.

(b) Disclosures required by Global Network plc for the year ended 31 December 2012 in accordance with IFRS 8 *Operating Segments*

(The following should be read in conjunction with the disclosure requirements outlined in **Section 24.3**.)

The required disclosures include:

- how Global Network plc has identified its operating segments and the types of product and service from which each operating segment derives its revenues;
- information about the reported segment profit or loss, including certain specified revenues and expenses included in segment profit or loss, segment assets and segment liabilities and the basis of measurement;
- a reconciliation of the totals of segment revenues, reported segment profit or loss, segment assets, segment liabilities and other material items to corresponding items in Global Network plc's financial statements;
- information about each product and service or groups of products and services, even if Global Network plc has only one reportable segment;
- an analysis of revenues and certain non-current assets by geographical area, together with details of revenues/assets by individual foreign country (if material), irrespective of the identification of operating segments. However this need not be done if not used by the chief operating decision-maker, as the information is not readily available and the cost of obtaining it is too great; and
- information about transactions with major customers.

If the total revenues of the segments identified (with more than 10% each) do not come to at least 75% of Global Network plc's turnover, then management must include other operating segments, which will bring the total to over 75%.

Applying IFRS 8 to the information provided for Global Network plc:

	Revenue %	Profit %	Assets %	Liabilities %
United Kingdom and Ireland	26.0	21.1	22.5	20.1
Mainland Europe	9.0	8.9	17.7	17.6
North America	31.2	36.9	24.3	24.5
Other Geographical Regions	33.8	33.1	35.5	37.8

The key points arising are:
1. All regions, with the exception of Mainland Europe, pass the 'revenue' test, i.e. > 10%.
2. However, the currently reported three regions represent < 75% of total revenue (66.2%) and therefore additional regional segments must be identified and reported separately until 75% of Global Network plc's revenue is included in reportable segments.
3. Similarly, all regions, with the exception of Mainland Europe, pass the 10% profit/loss test.
4. However, Mainland Europe's assets are > 10% of the combined assets of all segments.

Note: IFRS 8 does not define segment revenue, profit/loss, assets or liabilities, but does require explanation of how these are measured. Therefore, there is a certain degree of flexibility, albeit disclosure is ultimately determined by internal reporting practices.

Finally in this section, it is worth noting that the requirements of IAS 36 *Impairment of Assets* (see **Chapter 10**) impact upon IFRS 8. As explained in **Chapter 10**, IAS 36 requires goodwill to be tested for impairment as part of the impairment-testing of the cash generating unit to which it relates. In identifying the units (or groups of units) to which goodwill is allocated for the purpose of impairment-testing, IAS 36 limits the size of such units or groups of units by reference to the organisation's reported segments.

While **Examples 24.1** and **24.2** illustrate the disclosures required in accordance with IFRS 8, these are discussed further in **Section 24.3**.

24.3 DISCLOSURE

As discussed previously, the disclosure principle in IFRS 8 is that an organisation should disclose 'information to enable users of its financial statements to evaluate the nature and financial effects of the types of business activities in which it engages and the economic environments in which it operates'.

In meeting this principle, an organisation must disclose:
• general information about how the organisation identified its operating segments and the types of product and service from which each operating segment derives its revenues;

- information about the reported segment profit or loss, including certain specified revenues and expenses included in segment profit or loss, segment assets and segment liabilities, and the basis of measurement;
- reconciliations of the totals of segment revenues, reported segment profit or loss, segment assets, segment liabilities and other material items to corresponding items in the organisation's financial statements;
- organisation-wide disclosures, even when an organisation has only one reportable segment. These include information about each product and service or groups of products and services;
- an analysis of revenues and certain non-current assets by geographical area is required – with an expanded requirement to disclose revenues/assets by individual foreign country (if material), irrespective of the identification of operating segments. If the information necesary for these analyses is not available and the cost to develop it would be excessive, that fact must be disclosed; and
- information about transactions with major customers. If revenues from transactions with a single external customer amount to 10% or more of the organisation's revenues, the total amount of revenue from each such customer and the segment or segments in which those revenues are reported must be disclosed. The organisation need not disclose the identity of a major customer nor the amount of revenues that each segment reports from that customer. For this purpose, a group of organisations known to the reporting organisation to be under common control will be considered a single customer, and a government and organisations known to the reporting organisation to be under the control of that government will be considered to be a single customer.

IFRS 8 requires that current period and comparative segment information be reported consistently. This means that if a segment is identified as reportable in the current period but was not in the previous period, then equivalent comparative information should be presented, unless it would be prohibitively costly to obtain. IFRS 8 gives organisations discretion to report information regarding segments that do not meet the size criteria. Organisations can report on such segments where, in the opinion of management, information about the segment would be useful to users of the financial statements.

Compared with the previous two examples, **Example 24.3** provides a more comprehensive illustration of the disclosures required in accordance with IFRS 8.

EXAMPLE 24.3: IFRS 8 DISCLOSURE

Note X: Segmental information

The Group has adopted IFRS 8 *Operating Segments* with effect from 29 March 2009. IFRS 8 requires operating segments to be identified on the basis of internal reporting about components of the Group that are regularly reviewed by the chief operating decision-maker to allocate resources to the segments and to assess their performance. In contrast, the predecessor Standard (IAS 14 *Segment Reporting*) required the Group to identify two sets of segments (business and geographical), using a risks and rewards approach, with the Group's system of internal financial reporting to key management personnel serving only as the starting-point for the identification of such segments.

The chief operating decision-maker has been identified as the executive directors. The executive directors review the Group's internal reporting in order to assess performance and allocate resources. The operating segments are Ireland/UK and International, which are reported in a manner consistent with the internal reporting to the executive directors. The Ireland/UK segment consists of the Group's retail business and franchise operations in these jurisdictions. The International segment consists of the Group's owned businesses in mainland Europe and Asia, together with international franchise operations.

The executive directors assess the performance of the operating segments based on a measure of operating profit. This measurement basis excludes the effects of exceptional items from the operating segments as well as gains or losses on the disposal of assets. Central costs are all classified as Ireland/UK costs and presented within Ireland/UK operating profit. The executive directors also monitor revenue within the segments. To increase transparency, the Group has decided to include an additional voluntary disclosure, analysing revenue within the reportable segments.

The following is an analysis of the Group's revenue and results by reportable segment:

	2012 Management €m	2012 Adjust-ment[1] €m	2012 Statutory €m	2011 Management €m	2011 Adjust-ment[1] €m	2011 Statutory €m
General Merchandise	4,186.2	(34.2)	4,152.0	3,944.4	(26.1)	3,918.3
Food	4,455.5	(39.6)	4,415.9	4,282.3	(36.3)	4,246.0
Ireland/UK revenue	8,641.7	(73.8)	8,567.9	8,226.7	(62.4)	8,164.3
Wholesale	297.7	–	297.7	272.3	–	272.3
Retail	673.1	(2.1)	671.0	627.2	(1.7)	625.5
International revenue	970.8	(2.1)	968.7	899.5	(1.7)	897.8
Group revenue	9,612.5	(75.9)	9,536.6	9,126.2	(64.1)	9,062.1
Ireland/UK operating profit	701.2	–	701.2	652.8	–	652.8
International operating profit	142.7	–	142.7	116.1	–	116.1
Group operating profit	843.9	–	843.9	768.9	–	768.9
Profit on property disposals			8.1			6.4
Exceptional costs			–			(135.9)
Exceptional pension credit			–			231.3
Group operating profit			852.0			870.7
Finance income			12.9			50.0
Finance costs			(162.2)			(214.5)
Profit before tax			702.7			706.2

[1] Adjustments relate to revenue items recognised in cost of sales for management accounting purposes.

Other segmental information:

	2012 Ireland/ UK €m	2012 Interna- tional €m	2012 Total €m	2011 Ireland/ UK €m	2011 Interna- tional €m	2011 Total €m
Additions to tangible and intangible assets (excluding goodwill)	360.0	29.3	389.3	611.8	40.2	652.0
Depreciation and amortization	398.7	29.2	427.9	384.4	24.6	409.0
Assets	6,242.7	910.5	7,153.2	6,530.8	727.3	7,258.1

Before concluding this section on IFRS 8 disclosures, it is worth noting that IFRS 8 significantly expands the requirements for segment information at interim reporting dates (see IAS 34 *Interim Financial Reporting* (see **Chapter 34**)).

24.5 CONCLUSION

Segment disclosures are widely regarded as some of the most useful disclosures in financial reports because of the extent to which they disaggregate financial information into meaningful, and often revealing, groupings. Disaggregation into meaningful and often revealing groupings assists users to better understand the entity's past performance; better assess the entity's risks and returns; and make more informed judgements about the entity as a whole. For example, an entity may appear profitable on a consolidated basis, but the segment disclosures reveal that one part of the business is performing poorly while another part is performing well. Over time, the poorly performing part may affect the entire entity's performance. This affects the entity's share price because analysts frequently look at predicted future cash flows in making their share price determinations.

Finally, to conclude this chapter, it is worth noting that the Financial Reporting Review Panel (FRRP) has raised concerns over the application of IFRS 8 *Operating Segments* and has asked a number of UK companies to provide more information. This is particularly in cases where only one operating segment is reported, but it appears that:
* the company/group has other businesses and operations in different countries;
* the operating analysis detailed in the narrative report varies from the operating segments provided in the financial statements;
* the responsibilities and titles of the executive management team hint at an organisational structure that is not reflected in its operating segments; and
* there is a contradiction between the commentary in the narrative report.

The FRRP has encouraged organisations to test their initial conclusions about their segmental reporting by considering the following nine questions.

1. What are the key operating decisions made in running the business?
2. Who makes these key operating decisions?
3. Who are the segment managers (as defined in IFRS 8) and who do they report to?
4. How are the organisation's activities reported in the information used by management to review performance and make resource allocation decisions between segments?
5. Is any proposed aggregation of operating segments into one reportable segment supported by the aggregation criteria in the standard, including consistency with the core principle?
6. Is the information about reportable segments based on IFRS measures or on an alternative basis?
7. Have the reported segment amounts been reconciled to the IFRS aggregate amounts?
8. Do the accounts describe the factors used to identify the reportable segments, including the basis on which the organisation is organised?
9. As a final question, management should ask themselves whether the reported segments appear consistent with their internal reporting and, if not, why not.

The FRRP draws attention to the fact that no exemption is given from any aspect of IFRS 8 on the grounds that disclosure would be commercially prejudicial.

SUMMARY OF LEARNING OBJECTIVES

After having studied this chapter on operating segments, you should be able to:

Learning Objective 1 Explain the objectives of segment reporting and why the users of financial statements may find segmental reporting useful.

IFRS 8's core principle is that an organisation should disclose information to enable users of its financial statements to evaluate the nature and financial effects of the types of business activities in which it engages and the economic environments in which it operates. Many organisations provide a range of products or services and/or operate in different geographical areas. Each product/service or geographical area may be subject to different influences that result in different risks and rewards that may not be obvious when the figures are aggregated in the entity's financial statements. Consequently, organisations are required to separately analyse their results by product/ service and geographical area so that users may better understand the organisation's past performance, better assess the organisation's risks and returns and make more informed judgements about the organisation as a whole.

Learning Objective 2 Identify an organisation's reportable and operating segments.

Reportable segments are operating segments or aggregations of *operating segments* that meet specified criteria with respect to revenue, profit and assets.

Learning Objective 3 Apply the main disclosure requirements of IFRS 8.

The disclosure principle in IFRS 8 is that an organisation should disclose information to enable users of its financial statements to evaluate the nature and financial effects of the types of business activities in which it engages and the economic environments in which it operates.

QUESTIONS

Self-test Questions

1. Explain the objectives of segment reporting and why the users of financial statements may find segment reporting useful.
2. Identify an organisation's reportable and operating segments in accordance with IFRS 8.
3. Outline the main disclosure requirements of IFRS 8.

Review Questions (Multiple Choice)

(See **Appendix One** for Suggested Solutions to Review Questions.)

Question 24.1

Operating segment information should:
  (i) increase the number of reported segments and provide more information;
  (ii) enable users to see an undertaking through the eyes of management;
  (iii) enable an undertaking to provide timely segment information for external interim reporting with relatively low incremental cost;
  (iv) enhance consistency with the management discussion and analysis or other annual report disclosures;
  (v) provide various measures of segment performance;
  (vi) reduce staff.

  (a) (i) and (ii).
  (b) (i) to (iii).
  (c) (i) to (iv).
  (d) (i) to (v).
  (e) (i) to (vi).

Question 24.2

Segments based on the structure of an undertaking's internal organisation have other significant advantages:
  (i) An ability to see an undertaking 'through the eyes of management' enhances a user's ability to predict actions or reactions of management, which can significantly affect the undertaking's prospects for future cash flows.
  (ii) As information about those segments is generated for management's use, the incremental cost of providing information for external reporting should be relatively low.
  (iii) Practice has demonstrated that the term 'industry' is subjective. Segments based on an existing internal structure should be less subjective.
  (iv) Earnings per share (EPS) calculations can be compared between segments.

(a) (i) and (ii).
(b) (i) to (iii).
(c) (i) to (iv).

Question 24.3

An operating segment is a component of an undertaking:
  (i) that engages in business activities from which it may earn revenues and incur expenses (including revenues and expenses relating to transactions with other components of the same undertaking);
 (ii) the operating results of which are regularly reviewed by the undertaking's chief operating decision-maker to make decisions about resources to be allocated to the segment and assess its performance;
(iii) for which discrete financial information is available;
(iv) that is taxed separately from other components.

(a) (i) and (ii).
(b) (i) to (iii).
(c) (i) to (iv).

Question 24.4

IFRS 8 requires an undertaking to report information about:
  (i) the revenues derived from its products or services (or groups of similar products and services);
 (ii) about the countries in which it earns revenues and holds assets;
(iii) about major clients;
(iv) about transactions with governments.

(a) (i) and (ii).
(b) (i) to (iii).
(c) (i) to (iv).

Question 24.5

IFRS 8 requires an undertaking to give descriptive information about:
  (i) the way the operating segments were determined;
 (ii) the products and services provided by the segments;
(iii) differences between the measurements used in reporting segment information and those used in the undertaking's financial statements;
(iv) changes in the measurement of segment amounts from period to period;
 (v) the impact of staff development policies on the segment.

(a) (i) and (ii).
(b) (i) to (iii).
(c) (i) to (iv).
(d) (i) to (v).

Question 24.6

A component of an undertaking that sells primarily or exclusively to other operating segments of the undertaking:
   (a) must be classed as an operating segment;
   (b) must be excluded from being an operating segment;
   (c) is included as an operating segment if the undertaking is managed that way.

Question 24.7

IFRS 8 requires the following information:
   (i) factors used to identify the undertaking's operating segments, including the basis of organisation (for example, whether management organises the undertaking around differences in products and services, geographical areas, regulatory environments, or a combination of factors, and whether segments have been aggregated);
   (ii) types of product and service from which each reportable segment derives its revenues;
   (iii) the economic environment of each segment;
   (iv) the legal structure of each segment.

   (a) (i) and (ii).
   (b) (i) to (iii).
   (c) (i) to (iv).

Question 24.8

With respect to 'interest':
   (a) net interest revenue must be shown;
   (b) neither interest revenue nor interest expense is required to be shown;
   (c) both interest revenue and interest expense are required to be shown;
   (d) both interest revenue and interest expense are required to be shown, unless a majority of the segment's revenues are from interest and the chief operating decision maker relies primarily on net interest revenue to assess the performance of the segment.

Question 24.9

IFRS 8 shall apply to:
   (i) listed companies;
   (ii) any company reporting under IFRS that wishes to provide the information;
   (iii) all other companies reporting under IFRS.

   (a) (i) and (ii).
   (b) (i) to (iii).

Question 24.10

If information is not presented to the directors in sectors:
   (a) look to the next lower level of internal segmentation that reports information along product and service lines or geographical lines;

(b) construct segments solely for external reporting purposes;
(c) segment information is not required for published financial statements.

Question 24.11

If a financial report contains both the consolidated financial statements of a parent, as well as the parent's separate financial statements, segment information is required:
(a) only in the consolidated financial statements;
(b) only in the parent's separate financial statements;
(c) in both sets of financial statements.

Challenging Questions (Multiple Choice)

(Suggested Solutions to Challenging Questions are available to lecturers.)

Question 24.1

An operating segment may engage in business activities for which it has yet to earn revenues, for example, start-up operations:
(a) will be operating segments before earning revenues;
(b) may be operating segments before earning revenues;
(c) will not be operating segments before earning revenues.

Question 24.2

Head-office expenses:
(a) can be allocated to segments on a reasonable basis;
(b) must not be allocated to segments;
(c) must be allocated to segments based on their turnover.

Question 24.3

An undertaking's pension plans:
(a) will be operating segments;
(b) may be operating segments;
(c) will not be operating segments.

Question 24.4

Two or more operating segments may be aggregated into a single operating segment if aggregation is consistent with the core principle of IFRS 8, the segments have similar economic characteristics and the segments are similar in each of the following respects:
(i) the nature of the products and services;
(ii) the nature of the production processes;

(iii) the type or class of client for their products and services;
(iv) the methods used to distribute their products or provide their services;
(v) if applicable, the nature of the regulatory environment, for example, banking, insurance or public utilities;
(vi) staff numbers.

(a) (i) and (ii).
(b) (i) to (iii).
(c) (i) to (iv).
(d) (i) to (v).
(e) (i) to (vi).

Question 24.5

As a percentage of sales, profits or assets, a segment should be at least:
(a) 5%;
(b) 7.5%;
(c) 10%;
(d) 15%;
(e) 20%.

Question 24.6

The total amount of revenue that should be covered by reportable segments is at least:
(a) 50%;
(b) 60%;
(c) 70%;
(d) 75%;
(e) 80%;
(f) 100%.

Question 24.7

Operating segments that do not meet any of the quantitative thresholds:
(a) may be considered reportable, and separately disclosed;
(b) must be combined and disclosed in 'all other segments';
(c) must be ignored.

Question 24.8

If an operating segment is identified as a reportable segment in the current period, segment data for a prior period:
(a) is not required;
(b) is optional;
(c) is required unless the necessary information is not available and the cost to develop it would be excessive.

Question 24.9

IFRS 8 requires reconciliations of segment totals to total undertaking amounts:
- (i) of segment revenues;
- (ii) reported segment profit or loss;
- (iii) segment assets;
- (iv) segment liabilities;
- (v) other material segment items;
- (vi) staff numbers.

- (a) (i) and (ii).
- (b) (i) to (iii).
- (c) (i) to (iv).
- (d) (i) to (v).
- (e) (i) to (vi).

Question 24.10

Information about the segments should include:
- (i) revenues from external clients;
- (ii) revenues from transactions with other operating segments of the same undertaking;
- (iii) interest revenue;
- (iv) interest expense;
- (v) depreciation and amortisation;
- (vi) material items of income and expense;
- (vii) the undertaking's interest in the profit or loss of associates and joint ventures accounted for by the equity method;
- (viii) income tax expense or income; and
- (ix) material non-cash items other than depreciation and amortisation.

- (a) (i) and (ii).
- (b) (i) to (iii).
- (c) (i) to (iv).
- (d) (i) to (v).
- (e) (i) to (vi).
- (f) (i) to (vii).
- (g) (i) to (viii).
- (h) (i) to (ix).

Question 24.11

An undertaking shall report the following geographical information:
- (i) Revenues from external clients attributed to the undertaking's country of domicile and attributed to all foreign countries in total from which the undertaking derives revenues;
- (ii) Non-current assets other than financial instruments, deferred tax assets, post-employment benefit assets, and rights arising under insurance contracts located in the

undertaking's country of domicile and located in all foreign countries in total in which the undertaking holds assets;

(iii) Non-current liabilities other than financial instruments, deferred tax liabilities, post-employment benefit liabilities, and rights arising under insurance contracts located in the undertaking's country of domicile and located in all foreign countries in total in which the undertaking has liabilities.

(a) (i) and (ii).
(b) (i) to (iii).

FINANCIAL INSTRUMENTS

LEARNING OBJECTIVES

The area of financial instruments is part of an ongoing project designed to improve and converge financial reporting standards. At present the following accounting standards govern the recognition, measurement and disclosure of financial instruments in financial statements:

- IAS 32 *Financial Instruments: Presentation;*
- IAS 39 *Financial Instruments: Recognition and Measurement* (however IAS 39 is gradually being replaced by IFRS 9);
- IFRS 7 *Financial Instruments: Disclosures*; and
- IFRS 9 *Financial Instruments* (which is gradually replacing IAS 39).

Taken together, their objective is to enhance financial-statement users' understanding of the significance of financial instruments to an entity's financial position, performance and cash flows.

After having studied this chapter, with respect to the above accounting standards, you should be able to:

1. define the terms 'financial instrument', 'financial asset', 'financial liability' and 'equity instrument' and 'derivative', and classify a financial instrument as either a financial asset, a financial liability or an equity instrument;
2. explain how a financial asset should be recognised and measured in an entity's financial statements;
3. explain how a financial liability should be recognised and measured in an entity's financial statements;
4. apply the more universal aspects of IAS 39, rather than the more specialised areas, with respect to hedge accounting; and
5. provide the appropriate disclosures (both qualitative and quantitative) for those items examinable under IAS 32, IAS 39 and IFRS 9. This includes information about: the significance of the financial instruments; and the nature and extent of the risks (credit, liquidity and market) arising from financial instruments.

KEY TERMS AND DEFINITIONS FOR THIS CHAPTER

In order to aid your understanding of the concepts and issues covered in this chapter, it is very important to understand and be familiar with the following key terms and definitions. This is a complex chapter and a significant part of the difficulty actually arises from not being familiar with the terms used. Consequently, as you study this chapter, you should refer back to the key terms and definitions listed below.

Derivative This is a financial instrument:
- whose value changes in response to the change in an underlying variable such as an interest rate, commodity or security price, or index;
- that requires no initial investment, or one that is smaller than would be required for a contract with similar response to changes in market factors; and
- that is settled at a future date.

Derecognition This means removing an item from the statement of financial position.

Equity Instrument Any contract that evidences a residual interest in the assets of an entity after deducting all of its liabilities.

Fair Value The amount for which an asset could be exchanged, or a liability settled, between knowledgeable, willing parties in an arm's length transaction.

Financial Asset This is any asset that is:
- cash;
- an equity instrument of another entity;
- a contractual right:
  - to receive cash or another financial asset from another entity; or
  - to exchange financial assets or financial liabilities with another entity under conditions that are potentially favourable to the entity; or
- a contract that will or may be settled in the entity's own equity instruments and may be either:
  - a non-derivative for which the entity is, or may be, obliged to receive a variable number of the entity's own equity instruments; or
  - a derivative that will or may be settled other than by the exchange of a fixed amount of cash or another financial asset for a fixed number of the entity's own equity instruments. For this purpose the entity's own equity instruments do not include instruments that are themselves contracts for the future receipt or delivery of the entity's own equity instruments.

Financial Instrument A contract that gives rise to a financial asset of one entity and a financial liability or equity instrument of another entity.

Financial Liability Any liability that is:
- a contractual obligation:
  - to deliver cash or another financial asset to another entity; or
  - to exchange financial assets or financial liabilities with another entity under conditions that are potentially unfavourable to the entity; or
- a contract that will or may be settled in the entity's own equity instruments.

25.1 INTRODUCTION

The *Conceptual Framework for Financial Reporting 2010* emphasises that the objective of general purpose financial reports is to provide information about a reporting entity's economic resources, claims and changes in those resources and claims (see **Chapter 1**). This includes information that assists users to assess an entity's financial strengths and weaknesses, including the resources that the entity controls, its financial structure, liquidity and solvency. Financial statements should portray the financial effects of transactions and other events, and, in the context of financial instruments, it is vital that they are properly recognised, measured and disclosed.

The issue of financial instruments is arguably one of the most complex subjects in financial accounting and reporting, particularly as it is subject to ongoing change. In a sense, it is a discipline in itself. In general terms, a financial instrument is a means of raising finance and, at a very basic level, includes 'everyday' loans. In practice, financial instruments are wide-ranging, extremely complex financial arrangements.

Perhaps the fact that there are separate international accounting standards that deal with how financial instruments should be presented, classified, measured and disclosed in an entity's statements is indicative of the potential complexity, and even controversial nature, of this topic. The relevant accounting standards are:
* IAS 32 *Financial Instruments: Presentation*;
* IAS 39 *Financial Instruments: Recognition and Measurement* (however IAS 39 is gradually being replaced by IFRS 9);
* IFRS 7 *Financial Instruments: Disclosures*; and
* IFRS 9 *Financial Instruments* (which is gradually replacing IAS 39).

IFRS 9 *Financial Instruments* is part of an ongoing project to replace IAS 39 *Financial Instruments: Recognition and Measurement*, and it represents the outcome of work undertaken by the International Accounting Standards Board (IASB) in conjunction with the Financial Accounting Standards Board in the US to improve and converge financial reporting standards.

IFRS 9 was originally issued in November 2009. This version of IFRS 9 introduced new requirements for classifying and measuring financial assets and was effective for annual periods beginning on or after 1 January 2013, with early adoption being permitted. However, in October 2010, the IASB reissued IFRS 9, with the updated standard including revised requirements for financial liabilities and carrying over the existing derecognition requirements from IAS 39. In December 2011 the effective date of IFRS 9 was amended to annual periods beginning on or after 1 January 2015 and the relief from restating comparative periods and the associated disclosures in IFRS 7 was modified. However, while IFRS 9 (2010) superseded IFRS 9 (2009), for annual reporting periods beginning before 1 January 2015 an entity may adopt IFRS 9 (2009) rather than IFRS 9 (2010).

Note: whilst it is acknowledged that the accounting requirements for financial instruments are currently in a state of flux with, for example, IAS 39 and two versions of IFRS 9 still being applicable, this chapter focuses primarily on IFRS 9 (2010), albeit reference is made to IFRS 39 where relevant for clarity and to place the changes introduced by IFRS 9 in context.

In general, IAS 32, IAS 39, IFRS 7 and IFRS 9 apply to all types of financial instrument **except**:

- those interests in subsidiaries, associates and joint ventures that are accounted for in accordance with IFRS 10 *Consolidated Financial Statements*, IAS 27 *Separate Financial Statements* or IAS 28 *Investments in Associates and Joint Ventures*. However, IAS 32 and IAS 39 apply in cases where under IAS 27 and IAS 28 such interests are to be accounted for under IAS 39 – for example, derivatives on an interest in a subsidiary, associate, or joint venture;
- employers' rights and obligations under employee benefit plans (IAS 19 *Employee Benefits* – see **Chapter 17**);
- rights and obligations under insurance contracts (with the exception that IAS 39 does apply to financial instruments that take the form of an insurance (or reinsurance) contract but that principally involve the transfer of financial risks and derivatives embedded in insurance contracts);
- financial instruments that meet the definition of an equity investment under IAS 32.

In broad terms, financial instruments can be categorised on the basis of either their 'form' or 'asset class'. Form depends on whether they are:

1. **cash instruments** – these are financial instruments whose value is determined directly by markets. They can be divided into **securities**, which are readily transferable, and **other cash instruments**, such as loans and deposits, where both borrower and lender have to agree on a transfer; or
2. **derivative instruments** – these are financial instruments that derive their value from the value and characteristics of one or more underlying assets. Usually, a derivative's value changes in response to changes in interest rates, the market value of one or more of the underlying assets or foreign exchange rates. Derivatives typically require little or no initial outlay and are settled at a future date. They can be divided into exchange-traded derivatives and over-the-counter (OTC) derivatives. **Examples of derivatives** include:
   - **Forwards** – contracts to purchase or sell a specific quantity of a financial instrument, a commodity or a foreign currency at a specified price determined at the outset, with delivery or settlement at a specified future date. Settlement is at maturity by actual delivery of the item specified in the contract, or by a cash settlement. For example, Company X agrees to buy US dollars from a bank at a set rate on a particular date in the future (Company X agrees to purchase US$500,000 from a bank at a rate of US$1.80 on 14 June 2014).
   - **Interest Rate Swaps** and **Forward Rate Agreements** – contracts to exchange cash flows as of a specified date or a series of specified dates based on a notional amount and fixed and floating rates. For example, a company that has a variable rate loan may enter into an agreement to swap the variable interest rate for a fixed rate with the same or a different lender. (Company X has a loan with a bank on which it pays a variable rate of interest of Euribor plus 2%. If the company wishes to fix the interest that it pays for (say) five years, it can enter into a 'swap' agreement by selling the variable rate and buying a fixed rate instrument with either the same or another bank.)
   - **Futures** – these are contracts similar to forwards, but with the following differences: futures are generic exchange-traded, whereas forwards are individually tailored. Futures

are generally settled through an offsetting (reversing) trade, whereas forwards are generally settled by delivery of the underlying item or cash settlement.

- **Options** – contracts between two parties for a future transaction on an asset at a reference (agreed) price. The buyer of the option gains the right, but not the obligation, to engage in that transaction, while the seller incurs the corresponding obligation to fulfil the transaction. The price of an option derives from the difference between the reference price and the value of the underlying asset (e.g. shares, bonds, currency) plus a premium based on the time remaining until the expiration of the option. An option that conveys the right to buy something is called a **call**; an option that conveys the right to sell is called a **put**. The reference price at which the underlying may be traded is called the **strike price** or **exercise price**. The process of activating an option and thereby trading the underlying asset at the agreed-upon price is referred to as exercising it. Most options have an expiration date. If the option is not exercised by the expiration date, it becomes void and worthless. In return for granting the option, called **writing the option**, the originator of the option collects a payment, the premium, from the buyer. The writer of an option must make good on delivering (or receiving) the underlying asset or its cash equivalent, if the option is exercised. An option can usually be sold by its original buyer to another party. Many options are created in standardised form and traded on an anonymous options exchange among the general public, while other over-the-counter options are customised ad hoc to the desires of the buyer, usually by an investment bank.
- **Caps** and **Floors** – these are contracts sometimes referred to as **interest rate options**. An **interest rate cap** will compensate the purchaser of the cap if interest rates rise above a predetermined rate (strike rate), while an **interest rate floor** will compensate the purchaser if rates fall below a predetermined rate.

Alternatively, financial instruments can be categorised by '*asset class*' depending on whether they are:

1. **Equity** – these reflect ownership of the issuing entity;
2. **Liability** – these reflect a loan the investor has made to the issuing entity. If it is debt, it can be further categorised into current (less than one year) and non-current (over one year); or
3. **Foreign exchange instruments and transactions** are neither a liability nor equity and belong in their own category.

While acknowledging the intricate and multifaceted nature of financial instruments, examples of each of the above categories ('form' and 'asset class') are illustrated in **Table 25.1**.

TABLE 25.1: EXAMPLES OF FINANCIAL INSTRUMENTS

Asset Class	Cash		Derivatives	
	Securities	Other Cash	Exchange-Traded	Over-the-Counter
Equity	Stock	N/A	Stock options, equity futures	Stock options

Liability: non-current	Bonds	Loans	Bond futures, Options on bond futures	Interest rate caps and floors, Interest rate options
Liability: current	Bills	Deposits	Short-term interest rate futures	Forward rate agreements
Foreign exchange	N/A	Spot foreign exchange	Currency futures	Foreign exchange options, Foreign exchange swaps, Currency swaps

Key to this Chapter

As noted above, that there are separate accounting standards dealing with how financial instruments should be presented, classified, measured and disclosed in an entity's statements is indicative of the potential complexity of this topic.

Notwithstanding this, the objective of these standards is to enhance financial statement users' understanding of the significance of financial instruments to an entity's financial position, performance and cash flows.

This chapter begins by considering some different aspects of the *definition of financial instruments* (**Section 25.2**), before focusing on the *measurement of financial assets* (**Section 25.3**) and the *measurement of financial liabilities* (**Section 25.4**). The chapter concludes with a review of *hedge accounting* (**Section 25.5**) and the *disclosure requirements* for financial instruments (**Section 25.6**).

25.2 FINANCIAL INSTRUMENTS: DEFINITIONS

Financial Instrument

First read the definition of a financial instrument, together with those for an equity instrument, financial asset and financial liability included in the **Key Terms and Definitions** section above. In addition, it is important to note that an entity must recognise a financial asset or a financial liability when, and only when, it becomes a party to the contractual provisions of the instrument. Now answer **Example 25.1**.

EXAMPLE 25.1: DEFINITION OF A FINANCIAL INSTRUMENT

Explain whether each of the following meet the definition of a financial instrument:
(a) issue of ordinary share capital;
(b) issue of debt;

(c) sale of goods on credit; and

(d) purchase of goods on credit.

Solution

(a) Issue of ordinary share capital represents an *equity instrument* since the shareholders own a financial asset and the company has an equity instrument in the form of new share capital.

(b) Issue of debt creates a *contractual obligation* between the company and the lender for the debt to be repaid in the future. Therefore the company has a financial liability and the lender has a financial asset.

(c) Sale of goods on credit creates a *contractual obligation* between the customer and the company. The customer has a financial liability and the company has a financial asset.

(d) Purchase of goods on credit creates a *contractual obligation* on the part of the company to pay for the goods. Therefore, the company has a financial liability and the supplier has a financial asset.

Equity Instrument or Financial Liability

Consistent with the *Conceptual Framework for Financial Reporting 2010* (see **Chapter 1**), a financial instrument should be classified as either an *equity instrument* or a *financial liability* according to the substance of the contract, not its legal form. An entity must make this decision at the time the instrument is initially recognised, and the classification cannot be subsequently revised based on changed circumstances.

A financial instrument is *an equity instrument* only if:
- the instrument includes *no contractual obligation* to deliver cash or another financial asset to another entity; and
- if the instrument will or may be settled in the issuer's own equity instruments, it is either:
   ○ a non-derivative that includes no contractual obligation for the issuer to deliver a variable number of its own equity instruments; or
   ○ a derivative that will be settled only by the issuer exchanging a fixed amount of cash or another financial asset for a fixed number of its own equity instruments.

The key issue in the above definition is whether a *contractual obligation* exists. **Example 25.2** and **Example 25.3** illustrate the application of this in practice. **Example 25.2** deals with probably the most common instance of this, i.e. preference shares.

EXAMPLE 25.2: CONTRACTUAL OBLIGATION – LIABILITY OR EQUITY

If an enterprise issues preference shares that pay a fixed rate of dividend and that have a mandatory redemption feature (for example, must be repaid on a specified date and at a specified amount in the future), the substance is that they are a *contractual obligation* to deliver cash and, therefore, should be recognised as a *liability*. For example:

- X Limited has 200,000 10% €1 preference shares in issue. The shares are redeemable in five years at a premium of 25 cent;
- Top Limited entered into a zero-coupon loan (i.e. interest and principal repayments deferred until maturity) for €400,000. No interest is payable during the term of the loan, but the loan is repayable after 5 years at €440,000.

In contrast, if the preference shares do not have a fixed maturity date, and the issuer does *not* have a contractual obligation to make any payment, then the preference shares would be treated as part of equity.

A contractual right or obligation to receive or deliver a number of its own shares or other equity instruments that varies so that the fair value of the entity's own equity instruments to be received or delivered equals the fixed monetary amount of the contractual right or obligation is a financial liability. This is illustrated in **Example 25.3**.

EXAMPLE 25.3: CONTRACTUAL OBLIGATION – FIXED MONETARY AMOUNT

For example, Company Y plc has a ***contractual obligation*** to pay Company Z €1,000,000 on 31 December 2013 by issuing its own shares. Therefore, the number of shares that Company Y plc has to issue on 31 December 2013 will depend on its share price on that date.

Compound Financial Instrument

When distinguishing between an equity instrument and a liability, the decision is not always an either/or one as the financial instrument may contain elements of both an equity instrument and a financial liability.

A compound financial instrument has both a liability and an equity component from the issuer's perspective. These component parts must be accounted for and presented separately according to their substance, based on the definitions of an equity instrument and a financial liability. The split is made at issuance and cannot be revised for subsequent changes in market interest rates, share prices or other events that changes the likelihood that the conversion option will be exercised. **Example 25.4** and **Example 25.5** address the issue of compound financial instruments.

Example 25.4 highlights the key points to look out for 'in words'.

EXAMPLE 25.4: COMPOUND FINANCIAL INSTRUMENT (1)

A convertible bond contains ***two components***. One is a ***financial liability***, namely the issuer's contractual obligation to pay cash, and the other is an ***equity instrument***, namely the holder's option to convert into common shares.

When the initial carrying amount of a compound financial instrument is required to be allocated between its equity and liability components, the **equity component** is assigned the residual amount after deducting from the fair value of the instrument as a whole the amount separately determined for the liability component.

Interest, dividends, gains and losses relating to an instrument classified as a liability should be reported in the statement of profit or loss and other comprehensive income in arriving at profit or loss. ***This means that dividend payments on preferred shares classified as liabilities are treated as expenses.*** On the other hand, distributions (such as dividends) to holders of a financial instrument classified as equity should be charged directly against equity, not against earnings. The transaction costs of an equity instrument (for example, share issue costs) should be deducted from equity.

Example 25.5 now adds some numbers to the illustration of a compound financial instrument.

EXAMPLE 25.5: COMPOUND FINANCIAL INSTRUMENT (2)

Tilt plc issued the following compound financial instrument at par on 31 December 2012: two million 50 cent 3% convertible bonds 2018. The value of two million 50 cent 3% convertible bonds 2018 without the conversion rights was estimated to be €960,000 on 31 December 2012.

Requirement Show the amounts that should be included in the financial statements of Tilt plc for the year ended 31 December 2012 in respect of the above transaction.

Solution

	€
Total amount raised at issue (2 million × 50 cent)	1,000,000
Allocated to liability (fair value of bond without rights)	(960,000)
Allocated to equity	40,000

The classification of the liability element is made at issuance (i.e. 31 December 2012) and not revised for subsequent changes in market interest rates, share prices or other events that change the likelihood of the conversion option being exercised.

Note: the purchase and issue of debt is also illustrated in **Example 25.8** and **Example 25.9**.

This section focused on definitional issues associated with financial instruments. The next two sections address the measurement of financial assets (**Section 25.3**) and financial liabilities (**Section 25.4**).

25.3 MEASUREMENT OF FINANCIAL ASSETS

> ***Note:*** as noted above, there are currently two applicable/extant accounting standards that deal with the measurement of financial instruments: IAS 39 and IFRS 9. However, again as noted previously, IFRS 9 is gradually replacing IAS 39 and has already done so with respect to the measurement of financial assets and liabilities. This chapter focuses primarily on IFRS 9, albeit reference is made to IAS 39 where relevant for clarity and to place the changes introduced by IFRS 9 in context.

To refresh your memory, please begin this section by reading the definitions of a financial instrument and a financial asset included in the **Key Terms and Definitions** section above.

In accordance with IFRS 9, financial assets may be classified under the following three headings:
1. financial assets measured at fair value through profit or loss (FVTPL);
2. financial assets measured at fair value through other comprehensive income (FVTOCI); and
3. financial assets measured at amortised cost.

Classification is made at the time the financial asset is initially recognised, namely when the entity becomes a party to the contractual provisions of the instrument.

Each of these classifications is now discussed in turn.

1. Financial Assets Measured at FVTPL

This is the default classification for financial assets and it applies to all financial assets unless they are designated to be measured and accounted for in another way. Financial assets classified as FVTPL are initially measured at fair value, with transaction costs being expensed as incurred in arriving at profit or loss in the period. The existence of a published price quoted in an active market is considered to be the best evidence of fair value. For assets (or liabilities) that are not quoted in an active market, fair value is determined using valuation techniques, such as discounted cash flow models or option-pricing models.

> ***Note:*** IFRS 9 contains guidance on when cost may be the best estimate of fair value and also when it might not be representative of fair value.

Financial assets measured at FVTPL include:
• financial assets held for trading purposes;
• derivatives, unless they are part of a properly designated hedging arrangement (see **Derivatives** below); and

- debt instruments, unless they have been correctly designated to be measured at amortised cost (see **Financial Assets Measured at Amortised Cost** below).

Using the example of a financial asset that is 'held for trading', the initial measurement of a financial asset classified as FVTPL is illustrated in **Example 25.6**.

EXAMPLE 25.6: INITIAL MEASUREMENT – 'HELD FOR TRADING'

A **debt security** that is **held for trading** is purchased for €8,000. Transaction costs are €600. The initial carrying amount is €8,000 *and the transaction costs of €600 are expensed.* This treatment applies because the debt security is classified as held for trading and, therefore, measured at fair value with changes in fair value recognised in profit or loss (i.e. measured at FVTPL).

Remeasurement to fair value takes place at each reporting date, with any movement in fair value taken to profit or loss in the year (i.e. measured at FVTPL), which effectively incorporates an annual impairment review (see **Impairment** below). The initial measurement, together with the movement in fair value at the reporting date, of a financial asset measured at FVTPL is shown in **Example 25.7**.

EXAMPLE 25.7: FINANCIAL ASSETS AT FAIR VALUE THROUGH PROFIT OR LOSS (FVTPL)

An entity acquires for cash 1,000 shares at €10 per share and can designate them as at fair value through profit or loss. At the year-end 31 December 2012, the quoted price increases to €16. The entity sells the shares €16,400 on 31 January 2013.

Initial recognition:
DR Financial assets at FVTPL	€10,000	
CR Cash		€10,000

31 December 2012:
DR Financial assets at FVTPL	€6,000	
CR SPLOCI – P/L		€6,000

31 January 2013:
DR Cash	€16,400	
CR Financial assets at FVTPL		€16,000
CR SPLOCI – P/L		€400

One problem that may arise in relation to financial assets measured at fair value is whether a reliable fair value can be determined at the reporting date. For financial assets that are traded on an exchange (for example, equity shares in a listed entity), this may be a relatively straightforward process. If, however, the financial assets in question are not traded on an exchange, there may be no definitive method to determine fair value at a particular date. This could result in the exercise of judgement or discretion, which could undermine the reliability or relevance of any amounts accounted for as a fair value.

Derivatives As noted above, all derivatives, including those linked to unquoted equity investments, are measured at fair value, with value changes being recognised in arriving at profit or loss unless the entity has elected to treat the derivative as a hedging instrument (see below) in accordance with IAS 39, in which case the requirements of IAS 39 apply.

Embedded Derivatives These are derivatives embedded within a host contract (for example, a construction contract in foreign currency), with the effect that some of the cash flows of the combined instrument vary in a way similar to a stand-alone derivative. If the host contract is not a financial asset, then the derivative should be separated from host contract and accounted for as a derivative when the conditions are met. The host contract should be accounted for as normal (for example, under IAS 11). If the host contract is an IFRS 9 financial asset, then it should be accounted for as a hybrid contract in accordance with IFRS 9.

2. Financial Assets Measured at FVTOCI

As noted above, the default position is that all equity investments within the scope of IFRS 9 are to be measured at fair value in the statement of financial position, with value changes being recognised in arriving at profit or loss in the period (i.e. FVTPL). There is no 'cost exception' for unquoted equities. However, at initial recognition, an entity may make an irrevocable election to report value changes in other comprehensive income (OCI); only dividend income is recognised in arriving at profit or loss in the period. This classification applies to *equity instruments only*. It will typically be applicable for equity interests that an entity intends to retain ownership of (i.e. those that are *not* held for trading). Initial recognition at fair value normally includes the associated transaction costs of purchase. The accounting treatment automatically incorporates an impairment review (see **Impairment** below), with any change in fair value taken through OCI in the period (i.e. measured at FVTOCI).

Upon derecognition (see **Derecognition of Financial Assets** below), any gain or loss is based on the carrying value at the date of disposal. It is important to note that there is no recycling of any amounts previously taken to equity in earlier accounting periods. Instead, at derecognition, an entity may choose to make an equity transfer from other components of equity to retained earnings as any amounts previously taken to equity can now be regarded as having been realised.

3. Financial Assets Measured at Amortised Cost

Amortised cost is the cost of an asset or liability adjusted to achieve a constant effective interest rate over the life of the asset or liability (see **Example 25.8** and **Example 25.9**). Amortised cost is calculated using the effective interest method. The effective interest rate is the rate that exactly discounts estimated future cash payments or receipts through the expected life of the financial instrument to the net carrying amount of the financial asset or liability. Financial assets that are *not* carried at FVTPL (for example, those carried at amortised cost) are subject to an annual impairment test (see **Impairment** below). Any impairment identified must be charged in full in arriving at profit or loss in the period.

The 'financial assets measured at amortised cost' classification applies *only to debt instruments* and must be designated upon initial recognition. In this instance, the financial assets initially measured at fair value plus transaction costs. A debt instrument that meets the following two tests *may* be measured at amortised cost (net of any write-down for impairment):

- **the business model test** – to pass this test, the entity must be holding the financial asset to collect the contractual cash flows associated with that financial asset. If this is not the case, for example, if the financial asset is being held and then traded to take advantage of changes in fair value prior to its contractual maturity, then the test is failed and the financial asset reverts to the default classification (i.e. measured at FVTPL); and
- **the cash flow characteristics test** – to pass this test, the contractual cash flows must consist solely of payment of interest and capital. If this is not the case, the test is failed and the financial asset reverts to the default classification (i.e. measured at FVTPL).

EXAMPLE 25.8: AMORTISED COST (1)

A debt security has a stated principal amount of €50,000, which will be repaid in five years at an interest rate of 6% per year payable annually at the end of each year. The entity purchases the security on 1 January 2012, at a discount, for €46,700. The effective interest rate of the investment in the debt security is approximately 7.65%. This is the discount rate that will give a present value of the future cash flows that equals the purchase price.

Based on the effective interest rate of 7.65%, the following can be computed.

Year ended 31 December	1 January (amortised cost)	Interest cash inflows at 6%	Interest income (A × 7.65%, rounded to nearest zero)	Amortisation of debt	31 December (amortised cost)
	(A)	(B)	(C)	(C-B)	(A+(C-B))
	€	€	€	€	€
2012	46,700	3,000	3,570	570	47,270
2013	47,270	3,000	3,620	620	47,890
2014	47,890	3,000	3,660	660	48,550
2015	48,550	3,000	3,710	710	49,260
2016	49,260	3,000	3,740 (rounded down)	740	0 (after repayment of principal)

At 31 December 2012, the entity A makes the following entry:

DR Cash	€3,000	
DR Debt security	€570	
CR SPLOCI – P/L – Interest income		€3,570

Example 25.9 is similar to the previous one, with the exception that the initial value of the loan stock has to be calculated (in **Example 25.8** this was given).

EXAMPLE 25.9: AMORTISED COST (2)

Simple Minds Limited, a company that prepares its financial statements to 31 December each year, issued €750,000 of 3% loan stock on 1 January 2012 at a discount of 5%. Issue costs amounted to €13,175, and interest is payable on 31 December each year. The loan stock is redeemable on 31 December 2015 at a premium of 10%. The effective rate of interest is 7.25%.

Requirement
(a) At what amount should the loan stock be measured on 1 January 2012?
(b) Calculate the amounts at which the loan stock should be recorded in the company's statement of financial position on 31 December 2012, 2013, 2014 and 2015.

Solution

(a)

			€
Proceeds	(€750,000 × 95%)		712,500
Issue costs			(13,175)
			699,325

(b)

Year	Balance on 1 January	Interest @ 7.25%	Paid	Balance on 31 December
	€	€	€	€
2012	699,325	50,701	(22,500)	727,526
2013	727,526	52,746	(22,500)	757,772
2014	757,772	54,938	(22,500)	790,210
2015	790,210	57,290	(847,500)	0
		215,675		

Even if a debt instrument meets the two amortised-cost tests (see above), IFRS 9 contains an option to designate a financial asset as measured at FVTPL if doing so eliminates or significantly reduces a measurement or recognition inconsistency (sometimes referred to as an 'accounting mismatch') that would otherwise arise from measuring assets or liabilities or recognising the gains and losses on them on different bases.

Debt instruments that fail one or both of these tests, or are not designated initially as being measured at amortised cost, must be measured at FVTPL.

One example of a financial asset that would *fail* is a convertible bond. While there is receipt of the nominal rate of interest payable by the bond issuer, and the bond will be converted into shares or cash at a later date, the cash flows are affected by the fact that the bondholder has a choice to make at some later date – either to receive shares or cash at the time the bond is redeemed. The nominal rate of interest received will be lower than for an equivalent financial asset without conversion rights to reflect the right of choice the bondholder will make at some later date.

Before considering other issues related to the measurement of financial assets, **Example 25.10** compares the accounting treatment of a financial asset on the basis that it is classified as FVTPL and at amortised cost.

EXAMPLE 25.10: MEASUREMENT OF A FINANCIAL ASSET AT FVTPL AND AMORTISED COST

Aquaria Limited purchased a five-year bond on 1 January 2012 at a cost of €5m with annual interest of 5%, which is also the effective rate, payable on 31 December annually. At the reporting date of 31 December 2012 interest has been received as expected and the market rate of interest is now 6%.

Requirement Account for the financial asset on the basis that it is classified:
(a) as FVTPL; and
(b) to be measured at amortised cost, on the assumption it passes the necessary tests and has been properly designated at initial recognition.

Solution
(a) If classified as FVTPL

This requires that the fair value of the bond is measured based on expected future cash flows discounted at the current market rate of interest of 6% as follows:

Year	Expected cash flows	6% discount factor	Present value €m
31 December 2013	€5m × 5% = €0.25m	0.9434	0.2358
31 December 2014	€0.25m	0.8900	0.2225
31 December 2015	€0.25m	0.8396	0.2099
31 December 2016	€0.25m + €5m	0.7921	4.1585
			4.8267

Therefore, at the reporting date of 31 December 2012, the financial asset will be stated at a fair value of €4.8267m, with the fall in fair value, amounting to €0.1733m, taken to profit or loss in the year. Interest received, amounting to €0.25m, will be taken to profit or loss for the year.

(b) If classified to be measured at amortised cost

This requires that the fair value of the bond is measured based on expected future cash flows discounted at the original effective rate of 5%. This will continue to be at €5m, as illustrated below:

Year	Expected cash flows	5% discount factor	Present value €m
31 December 2013	€5m × 5% = €0.25m	0.9524	0.2381
31 December 2014	€0.25m	0.9070	0.2267
31 December 2015	€0.25m	0.8638	0.2160
31 December 2016	€0.25m + €5m	0.8227	4.3192
			5.0000

In addition, interest received during the year of €0.25m will be taken to profit or loss for the year.

Note: with respect to financial assets, the available-for-sale and held-to-maturity categories currently in IAS 39 are not included in IFRS 9.

Reclassification of Financial Assets

For financial assets, reclassification is required between FVTPL and amortised cost, or vice versa, if, and only if, the entity's business model objective (see test above) for its financial assets changes so that its previous model assessment no longer applies. If reclassification is appropriate, it must be done prospectively from the reclassification date. An entity does not restate any previously recognised gains, losses or interest.

IFRS 9 does not allow reclassification where the:
• OCI option has been exercised for a financial asset; or
• fair value option has been exercised in any circumstance for a financial asset or financial liability.

Impairment of Financial Assets

Just like other non-current assets, once financial assets have been recognised in the financial statements, they can become impaired and are subject to annual impairment tests (see **Chapter 10**). However, IFRS 9 effectively incorporates an impairment review for financial assets that are measured at fair value, as any fall in fair value is taken to profit or loss or OCI in the period, depending on the classification of the financial asset (see above). For financial assets designated to be measured at amortised cost, an entity must make an assessment at each reporting date whether there is evidence of possible impairment; if there is, an impairment review should be performed. If impairment is identified, it is charged in arriving at profit or loss immediately. Quantification of the recoverable amount would normally be based on the present value of the expected future cash flows, estimated at the date of the impairment review and discounted to their present value, based on the original effective rate of return at the date the financial asset was issued.

Dealing with impairment is illustrated in **Example 25.11**.

EXAMPLE 25.11: IMPAIRMENT OF FINANCIAL ASSETS MEASURED AT AMORTISED COST

Using the information contained in **Example 25.10**, where the carrying value of the financial asset at 31 December 2012 was €5m. If, in early 2013, it was identified that the bond issuer was beginning to experience financial difficulties and that there was doubt regarding full recovery of the amounts due to Aquaria Limited, an impairment review would be required. The expected future cash flows now expected by Aquaria Limited from the bond issuer are as follows:

31 December 2013	€0.20m
31 December 2014	€0.20m
31 December 2015	€0.20m
31 December 2016	€0.20m + €4.4m

Requirement Calculate the extent of impairment of the financial asset to be included in the financial statements of Aquaria Limited for the year ending 31 December 2013.

Solution
The future expected cash flows are discounted to present value based on the original effective rate associated with the financial asset of 5%, as follows:

Year	Expected cash flows	5% discount factor	Present value €m
31 December 2013	€0.20m	0.9524	0.1905
31 December 2014	€0.20m	0.9070	0.1814
31 December 2015	€0.20m	0.8638	0.1727
31 December 2016	€0.205m + €4.4m	0.8227	3.7844
			4.3290

Therefore, impairment amounting to the change in carrying value of (€5.0m – €4.329m) €0.671m will be recognised as an impairment charge in the year to 31 December 2013. Additionally, there will also be recognition of interest receivable in the SPLOCI – P/L for the year amounting to (€4.329m × 5%) €0.2165m.

Derecognition of a Financial Asset

The basic premise for the **derecognition** model in IFRS 9 (carried over from IAS 39) is to determine whether the asset under consideration for derecognition is:
- an asset in its entirety;
- specifically identified cash flows from an asset (or a group of similar financial assets);
- a fully proportionate share of the cash flows from an asset; or
- a fully proportionate share of specifically identified cash flows from a financial asset.

Once the value of the asset under consideration for derecognition has been determined, an assessment is made as to whether the asset has been transferred and, if so, whether the transfer of that asset is subsequently eligible for derecognition. An asset is transferred if either the entity has transferred the contractual rights to receive the cash flows, or the entity has retained the contractual rights to receive the cash flows from the asset, but has assumed a contractual obligation to pass those cash flows on under an arrangement that meets the following three conditions:

- the entity has no obligation to pay amounts to the eventual recipient unless it collects equivalent amounts on the original asset;
- the entity is prohibited from selling or pledging the original asset (other than as security to the eventual recipient); and
- the entity has an obligation to remit those cash flows without material delay.

Once an entity has determined that the asset has been transferred, it then determines whether or not it has transferred substantially all of the risks and rewards of ownership of the asset. If substantially all the risks and rewards have been transferred, the asset is derecognised. If substantially all the risks and rewards have been retained, derecognition of the asset is precluded.

If the entity has neither retained nor transferred substantially all of the risks and rewards of the asset, then the entity must assess whether it has relinquished control of the asset or not. If the entity does not control the asset, then derecognition is appropriate. However, if the entity has retained control of the asset, then the entity continues to recognise the asset to the extent to which it has a continuing involvement in the asset. Derecognition of a financial asset is illustrated in **Example 25.12**, and the various derecognition steps are summarised in **Figure 25.1** below.

EXAMPLE 25.12: DERECOGNITION OF A FINANCIAL ASSET

(a) If a company sells an investment in shares, but retains the right to repurchase the shares at any time at a price equal to their current fair value, then it should derecognise the asset.

(b) If a company sells an investment in shares and enters into an agreement whereby the buyer will return any increases in value to the company and the company will pay the buyer interest plus compensation for any decrease in the value of the investment, then the company should not derecognise the investment as it has retained substantially all the risks and rewards.

FIGURE 25.1: DERECOGNITION OF A FINANCIAL ASSET

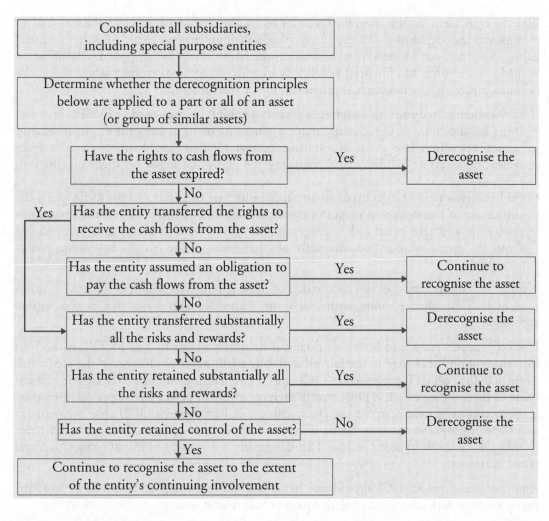

25.4 MEASUREMENT OF FINANCIAL LIABILITIES

Having examined the measurement of financial assets, including their impairment and derecognition, this section focuses on financial liabilities.

To refresh your memory, please read the definitions of a financial instrument and a financial liability included in the **Key Terms and Definitions** above.

As explained in the introduction to this chapter (**Section 25.1**), IFRS 9 was updated in October 2010 to include the recognition and measurement of financial liabilities. Essentially, the requirements of IAS 39 in relation to financial liabilities are now contained in IFRS 9 and require that financial liabilities should be accounted for as follows:
1. financial liabilities measured at FVTPL; and
2. financial liabilities at amortised cost.

1. Financial Liabilities Measured at FVTPL

Like the equivalent classification for financial assets, this includes financial liabilities *held for trading* and also derivatives that are not part of a hedging arrangement. All other financial liabilities are measured at amortised cost unless the fair value option is applied. Classification is made at the time the financial liability is initially recognised, namely when the entity becomes a party to the contractual provisions of the instrument.

IFRS 9 contains an option to designate a financial liability as measured at FVTPL if:
- doing so eliminates or significantly reduces a measurement or recognition inconsistency (sometimes referred to as an 'accounting mismatch') that would otherwise arise from measuring assets or liabilities or recognising the gains and losses on them on different bases; or
- the liability is part or a group of financial liabilities or financial assets and financial liabilities that is managed and its performance is evaluated on a fair value basis, in accordance with a documented risk-management or investment strategy, and information about the group is provided internally on that basis to the entity's key management personnel.

A financial liability that does not meet either of these criteria may still be designated as measured at FVTPL when it contains one or more embedded derivatives that would require separation.

IFRS 9 requires gains and losses on financial liabilities designated as FVTPL to be split into the amount of change in the fair value that is attributable to changes in the credit risk of the liability, which is presented in OCI, and the remaining amount of change in the fair value of the liability which is presented in arriving at profit or loss in the period. However, if this accounting treatment for the credit risk (i.e. taken through OCI) creates or enlarges an accounting mismatch in profit or loss, then the gain or loss relating to credit risk should also be taken to profit or loss. This determination is made at initial recognition and is not reassessed.

Amounts presented in OCI should not be subsequently transferred to profit or loss; the entity may only transfer the cumulative gain or loss within equity.

2. Financial Liabilities Measured at Amortised Cost

If financial liabilities are not measured at FVTPL, they are measured at amortised cost. This is illustrated in **Example 25.13**.

EXAMPLE 25.13: FINANCIAL LIABILITIES MEASURED AT AMORTISED COST
(DEEP DISCOUNT BONDS)

Coffee Limited issued debt with a nominal value of €400,000 on 1 January 2012, receiving proceeds of €315,526. The debt will be redeemed on 31 December 2016. The interest rate on the debt is 4% and the internal rate of return is 9.5%.

Based on the information provided, the debt should be accounted for as follows:

At inception:

DR	Cash	€315,526
CR	Liability	€315,526

Annual interest payments:

	€
4% × €400,000 × 5 years	80,000
Deep discount (€400,000 – €315,526)	84,474
	164,474

Year	SPLOCI – P/L Charge €*	Interest Paid €	Winding up interest charged to SPLOCI – P/L** €	SFP – Liability €
2012	29,975	16,000	13,975	329,501
2013	31,303	16,000	15,303	344,804
2014	32,756	16,000	16,756	361,560
2015	34,348	16,000	18,348	379,908
2016	36,092	16,000	20,092	400,000
		80,000	84,474	

*Opening SFP liability × 9.5% [for example, 2012: €315,526 × 9.5%]
**This is included in the SPLOCI–P/L charge. It represents the allocation/unwinding of the deep discount over the period of the debt.

Note: IFRS 9 retains the option for some liabilities, which would normally be measured at amortised cost, to be measured at FVTPL if, in doing so, it eliminates or reduces an 'accounting mismatch'.

Offsetting

As explained in **Chapter 2**, IAS 1 *Presentation of Financial Statements* states that assets and liabilities, and income and expenses, should not be offset (i.e. netted against each other) unless required or permitted by a standard. IAS 32 prescribes rules for the offsetting of financial assets and financial liabilities. It specifies that a financial asset and a financial liability should be offset and the net amount reported when an enterprise:
- currently has a legally enforceable right of set-off; and
- intends either to settle on a net basis, or to realise the asset and settle the liability simultaneously.

In December 2011, the IASB issued an amendment to IAS 32 relating to the offsetting of assets and liabilities (applicable to annual periods beginning on or after 1 January 2014). This amendment, which sought to clarify certain aspects of IAS 32 because of diversity in application of the requirements on offsetting, focuses on four main areas:
- the meaning of 'currently has a legally enforceable right of set-off';
- the application of simultaneous realisation and settlement;

- the offsetting of collateral amounts; and
- the unit of account for applying the offsetting requirements.

Derecognition of a Financial Liability

A financial liability should be removed from the statement of financial position when, and only when, it is extinguished, i.e. when the obligation specified in the contract is either discharged, cancelled or expired. Where there has been an exchange between an existing borrower and lender of debt instruments with substantially different terms, or there has been a substantial modification of the terms of an existing financial liability, this transaction is accounted for as an extinguishment of the original financial liability and the recognition of a new financial liability. A gain or loss from extinguishment of the original financial liability is recognised in arriving at profit or loss in the statement of profit or loss and other comprehensive income.

25.5 HEDGE ACCOUNTING

Financial assets and liabilities that are designated as a hedged item or hedging instrument are subject to measurement under the *hedge accounting requirements* of IAS 39; although hedge accounting is one of the IASB projects likely to form part of future changes to IFRS 9. Those requirements are now explained.

Hedge accounting is permitted under certain circumstances, provided that the hedging relationship is:
- formally designated and documented, including the entity's risk-management objective and strategy for undertaking the hedge, identification of the hedging instrument, the hedged item, the nature of the risk being hedged, and how the entity will assess the hedging instrument's effectiveness; and
- expected to be highly effective in achieving offsetting changes in fair value or cash flows attributable to the hedged risk as designated and documented, and effectiveness can be measured reliably.

Hedging Instruments

All derivative contracts with an external counterpart may be designated as **hedging instruments**, with the exception for some written options. An external non-derivative financial asset or liability may not be designated as a hedging instrument, except as a hedge of foreign currency risk. A proportion of the derivative may be designated as the hedging instrument. Generally, specific cash flows inherent in a derivative cannot be designated in a hedge relationship while other cash flows are excluded. However, the intrinsic value and the time value of an option contract may be separated, with only the intrinsic value being designated. Similarly, the interest element and the spot price of a forward can also be separated, with the spot price being the designated risk.

Hedged Items

A hedged item can be a:
- single recognised asset or liability, a firm commitment, a highly probable transaction or a net investment in a foreign operation;
- group of assets, liabilities, firm commitments, highly probable forecast transactions or net investments in foreign operations with similar risk characteristics;
- held-to-maturity investment for foreign currency or credit risk (but not for interest risk or prepayment risk);
- portion of the cash flows or fair value of a financial asset or financial liability; or
- non-financial item for foreign currency risk only or the risk of changes in fair value of the entire item.

Main Categories of Hedges

The main categories of hedges are as follows:
1. A **fair value hedge** is a hedge of the exposure to changes in fair value of a recognised asset or liability or a previously unrecognised firm commitment to buy or sell an asset at a fixed price or an identified portion of such an asset, liability or firm commitment, that is attributable to a particular risk and could affect profit or loss. The gain or loss from the change in fair value of the hedging instrument is recognised immediately in arriving at profit or loss in the statement of profit or loss and other comprehensive income. At the same time, the carrying amount of the hedged item is adjusted for the corresponding gain or loss with respect to the hedged risk, which is also recognised immediately in net profit or loss in the statement of profit or loss and other comprehensive income. A fair value hedge is illustrated in **Example 25.14.**

EXAMPLE 25.14: FAIR VALUE HEDGE

Duvet Limited is an Irish company that prepares its financial statements to 31 December each year. On 1 January 2011 Duvet Limited purchased an investment in an equity investment for €100. The company has decided to account for the investment at fair value through other comprehensive income. The fair value of the equity investment on 31 December 2011 and 2012 was €110 and €105 respectively. On 31 December 2011 Duvet Limited purchased a derivative asset, and its fair value had increased by €4 on 31 December 2012. Assuming that the derivative asset is designated as a hedge from 1 January 2012, the accounting treatment would be as follows:

Year ended 31 December 2011:
The increase in fair value of the investment will be taken to equity through other comprehensive income and it will be recorded at its fair value of €110 in the statement of financial position at 31 December 2011.

Year ended 31 December 2012:
The decline in value of €5 on the equity instrument will be charged in arriving at profit or loss in the statement of profit or loss and other comprehensive income and hedged by the increase in the derivative of €4. At 31 December 2012, the statement of financial position will show an equity investment at €105, a derivative at €4, with the net effect on the statement of profit or loss and other comprehensive income being €1.

2. A **cash flow hedge** is a hedge of the exposure to variability in cash flows that:
   (a) is attributable to a particular risk associated with a recognised asset or liability (such as all or some future interest payments on variable rate debt) or a highly probable forecast transaction; and
   (b) could affect profit or loss.

A cash flow hedge is illustrated in **Example 25.15**.

EXAMPLE 25.15: CASH FLOW HEDGE

A company expects to purchase a piece of machinery for $10 million in a year's time (31 July 2014). In order to offset the risk of increases in the euro rate, the company enters into a forward contract to purchase $10 million in 1 year for a fixed amount (€6,500,000). The forward contract is designated as a cash flow hedge and has an initial fair value of zero.

At the year-end (31 October 2013), the dollar ($) has appreciated and the value of $10 million is €6,660,000. The machine will still cost $10 million so the company concludes that the hedge is 100% effective. Thus the entire change in the fair value of the hedging instrument is recognised directly in reserves.

DR	Forward contract	€160,000	
CR	Other components of equity – cash flow hedge reserve		€160,000

The effect of the cash flow hedge is to lock in the price of $10 million for the machine. The gain in equity at the time of the purchase of the machine will either be released from equity as the machine is depreciated or be deducted from the initial carrying amount of the machine.

The portion of the gain or loss on the hedging instrument that is determined to be an effective hedge is recognised directly in equity and recycled to the statement of profit or loss and other comprehensive income when the hedged cash transaction affects profit or loss.

If a hedge of a forecast transaction subsequently results in the recognition of a financial asset or a financial liability, any gain or loss on the hedging instrument that was previously recognised directly in equity is 'recycled' into profit or loss in the same period(s) in which the financial asset or liability affects profit or loss.

If a hedge of a forecast transaction subsequently results in the recognition of a non-financial asset or non-financial liability, then the entity has an accounting policy *option* that must be applied to all such hedges of forecast transactions:
- **same accounting as for recognition of a financial asset or financial liability** – any gain or loss on the hedging instrument that was previously recognised directly in equity is 'recycled' into profit or loss in the same period(s) in which the non-financial asset or liability affects profit or loss; or
- **'basis adjustment' of the acquired non-financial asset or liability** – the gain or loss on the hedging instrument that was previously recognised directly in equity is removed from equity and is included in the initial cost or other carrying amount of the acquired non-financial asset or liability.

Discontinuation of Hedge Accounting

The term **derecognition** means removing an item from the statement of financial position.

Chapter 1 explains when an asset or liability should be *recognised* in accordance with the *Conceptual Framework for Financial Reporting 2010*. In broad terms:
* *assets* should be recognised in the statement of financial position when it is probable that future economic benefits will flow to the entity (i.e. they will help to generate positive cash flows) and the asset has a cost or value that can be reliably measured (e.g. its purchase price or market value); and
* *liabilities* should be recognised in the statement of financial position when it is probable that an outflow of resources will result from the settlement of a present obligation and the amount can be measured reliably (e.g. a claim against the company is likely to be success-ful and the amount of damages can be reasonably estimated).

Therefore, assets and liabilities should be derecognised when these conditions no longer apply.

Hedge accounting must be discontinued prospectively (i.e. going forward and not as a prior period adjustment in accordance with IAS 8 *Accounting Policies, Changes in Accounting Estimates and Errors* – see **Chapter 21**) if:
* the hedging instrument expires or is sold, terminated, or exercised;
* the hedge no longer meets the hedge accounting criteria – for example, it is no longer effective;
* for cash flow hedges the forecast transaction is no longer expected to occur; or
* the entity revokes the hedge designation.

For the purpose of measuring the carrying amount of the hedged item when fair value hedge accounting ceases, a revised effective interest rate is calculated.

If hedge accounting ceases for a cash flow hedge relationship because the forecast transaction is no longer expected to occur, gains and losses deferred in equity must be taken to the state-ment of profit or loss and other comprehensive income immediately. If the transaction is still expected to occur and the hedge relationship ceases, the amounts accumulated in equity will be retained in equity until the hedged item affects profit or loss.

If a hedged financial instrument that is measured at amortised cost has been adjusted for the gain or loss attributable to the hedged risk in a fair value hedge, this adjustment is amortised in arriving at profit or loss in the statement of profit or loss and other comprehensive income based on a recalculated effective interest rate on this date such that the adjustment is fully amortised by the maturity of the instrument. Amortisation may begin as soon as an adjust-ment exists and must begin no later than when the hedged item ceases to be adjusted for changes in its fair value attributable to the risks being hedged.

25.6 DISCLOSURE REQUIREMENTS

As indicated in **Section 25.1**, there are separate accounting standards that deal with how financial instruments should be recognised, measured and disclosed in an entity's financial statements. This section focuses on how financial instruments should be disclosed in accord-ance with IFRS 7 *Financial Instruments: Disclosures*.

An entity must group its financial instruments into classes of similar instruments and, when disclosures are required, make disclosures by class. The two main categories of disclosures required by IFRS 7 are information about the:
1. significance of financial instruments; and
2. nature and extent of risks arising from financial instruments.

The disclosures in respect of each of these two categories are outlined below

1. Significance of Financial Instruments

These disclosures are classified under the headings of: statement of financial position; statement of profit or loss and other comprehensive income; and other disclosures. Each is described below.

Statement of Financial Position   The following information must be disclosed with respect to items included in the statement of financial position:
- disclosure of the significance of financial instruments for an entity's financial position and performance;
- special disclosures about financial assets and financial liabilities designated to be measured at fair value through profit or loss, including disclosures about credit risk and market risk and changes in fair values;
- reclassifications of financial instruments from fair value to amortised cost or vice versa;
- disclosures about derecognitions, including transfers of financial assets for which derecognition accounting is not permitted;
- information about financial assets pledged as collateral and about financial or non-financial assets held as collateral;
- reconciliation of the allowance account for credit losses (irrecoverable debts);
- information about compound financial instruments with multiple embedded derivatives; and
- breaches of terms of loan agreements.

Statement of Profit or Loss and Other Comprehensive Income and Equity   The following information must be disclosed with respect to items included in the statement of profit or loss and other comprehensive income and equity:
- items of income, expense, gains and losses, with separate disclosure of gains and losses from:
  - financial assets measured at fair value through profit or loss, showing separately those held for trading and those designated at initial recognition, and
  - fee income and expense;
- amount of impairment losses on financial assets; and
- interest income on impaired financial assets.

Other Disclosures

- accounting policies for financial instruments;
- information about hedge accounting, including:
  - a description of each hedge, hedging instrument and fair values of those instruments, and nature of risks being hedged,

- for cash flow hedges, the periods in which the cash flows are expected to occur, when they are expected to enter into the determination of profit or loss, and a description of any forecast transaction for which hedge accounting had previously been used but which is no longer expected to occur,
- if a gain or loss on a hedging instrument in a cash flow hedge has been recognised directly in equity, an entity should disclose the following:
  - the amount that was so recognised in equity during the period,
  - the amount that was removed from equity and included in profit or loss for the period, and
  - the amount that was removed from equity during the period and included in the initial measurement of the acquisition cost or other carrying amount of a non-financial asset or non-financial liability in a hedged highly probable forecast transaction,
- for fair value hedges, information about the fair value changes of the hedging instrument and the hedged item, and
- hedge ineffectiveness recognised in profit or loss (separately for cash flow hedges and hedges of a net investment in a foreign operation);
- information about the fair values of each class of financial asset and financial liability, along with:
  - comparable carrying amounts,
  - a description of how fair value was determined, and
  - detailed information if fair value cannot be measured reliably.

2. Nature and Extent of Exposure to Risks Arising from Financial Instruments

Qualitative Disclosures   These describe:
- risk exposures for each type of financial instrument;
- management's objectives, policies, and processes for managing those risks; and
- changes from the prior period.

Quantitative Disclosures   These provide information about the extent to which the entity is exposed to risk, based on information provided internally to the entity's key management personnel, and include:
- summary quantitative data about exposure to each risk at the reporting date;
- disclosures about *credit risk*, *liquidity risk* and *market risk* (see below); and
- concentrations of risk.

Credit Risk   This includes the maximum amount of exposure (before deducting the value of collateral), description of collateral, information about the credit quality of financial assets that are neither past due nor impaired, and information about credit quality of financial assets whose terms have been renegotiated:
- for financial assets that are past due or impaired, analytical disclosures are required; and
- information about collateral or other credit enhancements obtained or called.

Liquidity Risk   Liquidity risk is the risk that an entity will have difficulties in paying its financial liabilities. Disclosures include:
- a maturity analysis of financial liabilities; and
- description of approach to risk management.

Market Risk This is the risk that the fair value or cash flows of a financial instrument will fluctuate due to changes in market prices. Market risk reflects interest rate risk, currency risk and other price risks. Disclosures about market risk include:

- a sensitivity analysis of each type of market risk to which the entity is exposed; and
- IFRS 7 provides that if an entity prepares a sensitivity analysis for management purposes that reflects interdependencies of more than one component of market risk (for instance, interest risk and foreign currency risk combined), it may disclose that analysis instead of a separate sensitivity analysis for each type of market risk.

In December 2011, in order to help financial statement users to evaluate the effect or potential effect of netting arrangements on an entity's financial position, the disclosure requirements in IFRS 7 were amended to require information about all recognised financial instruments that are offset and financial instruments subject to enforceable master netting arrangements even if they are not offset. (A master netting arrangement is an agreement that provides for a single net settlement of all financial instruments covered by the agreement in the event of default on, or termination of, any one contract. These arrangements are commonly used by financial institutions to provide protection against loss in the event of bankruptcy or other circumstances that result in a counterparty being unable to meet its obligations.)

Finally in the section, **Example 25.16** illustrates how a number of the items discussed in this chapter might be reflected in the financial statements. You should pay particular attention to Notes 3 and 4, and the cross-references to the other notes therein

EXAMPLE 25.16: PRESENTATION AND DISCLOSURE OF FINANCIAL INSTRUMENTS

Nantes
CONSOLIDATED STATEMENT OF FINANCIAL POSITION
AS AT 31 DECEMBER

	Notes	2012 €000	2011 €000
ASSETS			
Non-current Assets			
Property, plant and equipment		17,200	12,500
Goodwill		735	-
Current Assets			
Inventory		1,920	1,800
Trade receivables		3,980	3,710
Cash-in-hand and at bank		5,135	5,020
		28,970	23,030
EQUITY AND LIABILITIES			
Equity Attributable to Owners			
€1 ordinary shares		2,400	1,200

Share premium		833	-
Retained earnings		12,219	11,671
Other components of equity	3	280	150
Non-controlling interests – equity		834	1,610
Non-current Liabilities	4	5,380	3,890
Current Liabilities	5	7,024	4,509
		28,970	23,030

Notes to the Financial Statements (extract)

3. Other Components of Equity

	€000
At 31 December 2011	150
Share options (see Note 7)	55
8% Convertible bonds (see Notes 9 and 10)	75
At 31 December 2012	280

4. Non-current Liabilities

	2012 €000	2011 €000
1,000,000 10% €1 convertible cumulative redeemable preference shares (see Note 8)	850	850
1,000,000 8% €1 convertible bonds (see Note 9)	925	-
Bank loan	1,050	-
Finance lease obligations	2,555	3,040
	5,380	3,890

5. Current Liabilities

	2012 €000	2011 €000
Bank overdraft	384	10
Trade payable	5,580	3,650
Property, plant and equipment payable	475	110
Finance lease obligations	290	405
Income tax	240	290
Finance lease interest	24	24
Bank interest	31	20
	7,024	4,509

6. On 1 July 2012, Nantes issued 1,000,000 €1 ordinary shares at €1.50 per share, with the cash proceeds being received immediately. Subsequently, on 1 October 2012, Nantes purchased and cancelled 250,000 of its own €1 ordinary shares at par. On 14 February 2013, prior to the finalisation of the 2010 consolidated financial statements, Nantes made a bonus issue of one for five €1 ordinary shares. Each of the above transactions is reflected appropriately in the company's 2012 consolidated financial statements.

7. At 1 January 2010, Nantes had two share option schemes in operation, and the options outstanding on this date were as follows:
   - 450,000 €1 ordinary shares at €1.74; and
   - 750,000 €1 ordinary shares at €1.85.

   On 1 April 2012, options for a further 1,000,000 €1 ordinary shares at €1.95 were granted. Under each of the share option schemes, the options are exercisable before 31 December 2017. On 1 December 2012, the options relating to the 450,000 €1 ordinary shares at €1.74 were exercised, with Nantes receiving the proceeds immediately. The average market price of one €1 ordinary share in Nantes during the year ended 31 December 2012 was €2. Nantes charges to operating expenses the fair value of equity instruments at their grant date over their vesting period in accordance with IFRS 2 *Share-based Payment* (see Note 3). Each of the above share option transactions is reflected appropriately in the company's 2012 consolidated financial statements.

8. The 1,000,000 10% €1 convertible cumulative redeemable preference shares shown in Nantes' consolidated statement of financial position as at 31 December 2011 and 2012 were issued in 2006 and are convertible at the option of the preference shareholders of Nantes on 31 December 2017 and 2018 on the basis of one €1 ordinary share for every four €1 convertible cumulative redeemable preference shares held. The 10% €1 convertible cumulative redeemable preference shares are redeemable at the option of the preference shareholders on 31 December 2017 and 2018 at €1.70 per €1 convertible cumulative redeemable preference share. None of the preference dividends was outstanding at 31 December 2011 and 2012, being paid on 31 December in each of the years respectively. Each of the above transactions with respect to the 1,000,000 10% €1 convertible cumulative redeemable preference shares is reflected appropriately in the company's 2012 consolidated financial statements.

9. Nantes issued 1,000,000 8% €1 convertible bonds on 1 January 2012 at par. Each €1 bond is convertible into three €1 ordinary shares at the option of the bondholder on 31 December 2020. The issue of the bonds, together with the related interest, which was paid on 31 December 2012, is reflected appropriately in the company's 2010 consolidated financial statements.

10. Nantes regards the 10% €1 convertible cumulative redeemable preference shares (see Note 8) and 8% €1 convertible bonds (see Note 9) as compound financial instruments consisting of a liability component and an equity component. The fair value of the liability component at the date of issue is estimated using the prevailing market interest rate for similar non-convertible instruments. The difference between the issue proceeds and the fair value of the liability component is assumed to represent the embedded option to convert the liability into ordinary shares and is included in equity (see Note 3). The interest expense of the liability component is calculated by applying the market interest rate for similar non-convertible instruments at the date of issue to the liability component of the instrument. The difference between this amount and the dividend or interest paid is added to the carrying amount of the liability component and is included in finance costs, together with the dividend or interest payable, in the statement of profit or loss and other comprehensive income.

25.7 CONCLUSION

The area of financial instruments is an important and complex subject in financial accounting and reporting. A financial instrument is a means of raising finance. While at a very basic level it includes 'everyday' loans, many financial instruments are wide-ranging, extremely complicated arrangements. This chapter is complex and, indeed, some would argue that the area of financial instruments is a discipline in itself. Moreover, the area of financial instruments is continually changing and, consequently, it is important to keep track of developments in this area (e.g. through the website of the IFRS foundation and the IASB: www.ifrs.org).

To the extent that IFRS 9 does not yet deal with a particular issue, the requirements of IAS 39 continue to apply. Further changes are likely with respect to derivatives and hedging. However, as things stand (31 December 2012), the main requirements of IFRS 9 may be summarised as follows:

Recognition

An entity should recognise the financial instrument in the statement of financial position when it becomes a party to the contractual provisions of the instrument.

Financial assets are classified as:
- FVTPL;
- FVTOCI; or
- amortised cost on the basis of the business model for managing the asset and its contractual cash flow characteristics.

Financial liabilities are classified as:
- FVTPL if held for trading or designated as such; or
- amortised cost.

Debt instruments are reclassified when an entity changes its business model for managing financial instruments.

IFRS 9 prohibits the reclassification of financial liabilities.

A financial asset should be derecognised when:
- contractual rights to cash flows expire; or
- substantially all the risks and rewards of ownership are transferred to another party.

A financial liability should be derecognised when the liability is extinguished.

Measurement

	Initial Measurement	*Subsequent Measurement*	*Related Income/ Expense*
Financial assets at FV	FV of consideration given	Remeasured to FV at each reporting date	Changes in FV are recognised in: P/L; or OCI if the asset is an equity instrument not held for trading and an election is made
Financial assets at amortised cost	FV of consideration given plus transactions costs	Initial measurement less principal repayments plus/minus cumulative amortisation less impairment	Interest income (received & winding up) in P/L
Financial liabilities at FVTPL	FV of consideration received	Remeasured to FV at each reporting date	Changes in FV of financial liabilities held for trading are recognised in P/L
Financial liabilities *designated* at FVTPL		The change is split into two elements: • Gain/loss from credit risk is recognised in OCI; and • Other gain/loss is recognised in P/L.	
Financial liabilities at amortised cost	FV of consideration received less transactions costs	Initial measurement less principal repayments plus/minus cumulative amortisation less impairment	Interest expense (paid and winding up) in P/L

Summary of Learning Objectives

This chapter deals with the area of financial instruments, which is part of an ongoing project designed to improve and converge financial reporting standards. At present the relevant accounting standards are:
• IAS 32 *Financial Instruments: Presentation*;
• IAS 39 *Financial Instruments: Recognition and Measurement* (however IAS 39 is gradually being replaced by IFRS 9);
• IFRS 7 *Financial Instruments: Disclosures*; and
• IFRS 9 *Financial Instruments* (which is gradually replacing IAS 39).

Taken together, their objective is to enhance financial statement users' understanding of the significance of financial instruments to an entity's financial position, performance and cash flows.

Learning Objective 1 Define the terms 'financial instrument', 'financial asset', 'financial liability' and 'equity instrument' and 'derivative', and classify a financial instrument as either a financial asset, a financial liability or an equity instrument.

See **Section 25.2**.

Learning Objective 2 Explain how a financial asset should be recognised and measured in an entity's financial statements.

See **Section 25.3**.

Learning Objective 3 Explain how a financial liability should be recognised and measured in an entity's financial statements.

See **Section 25.4**.

Learning Objective 4 Apply the more universal aspects of IAS 39, rather than the more specialised areas, with respect to hedge accounting

See **Section 25.5**.

Learning Objective 5 Provide the appropriate disclosures (both qualitative and quantitative) for those items within the scope of this textbook under IAS 32, IAS 39 and IFRS 9. This includes information about: the significance of the financial instruments; and the nature and extent of the risks (credit, liquidity and market) arising from financial instruments.

See **Section 25.6**.

QUESTIONS

Self-test Questions

1. Define the terms 'financial instrument', 'financial asset', 'financial liability', 'equity instrument' and 'derivative'.
2. Explain the difference between financial liabilities and equity.
3. Explain how preference shares should be accounted for.
4. Identify and explain the three classifications of financial asset outlined in IFRS 9.
5. Explain the terms 'credit risk', 'liquidity risk' and 'market risk' in the context of IFRS 7, and outline the main disclosure required in relation to each of these risks.

Review Questions

(See **Appendix One** for Suggested Solutions to Review Questions.)

Question 25.1

On 1 January 2008, VERTIGO issued 30,000,000 €1 preference shares at par, incurring issue costs of €300,000. The dividend payable on the preference shares was 4% per annum, payable on 31 December each year. The redemption date for the preference shares was 31 December 2012 at a price of €1.35 per share. The effective interest cost of the preference shares is 10%. The statement of financial position of VERTIGO on 30 December 2012, the day prior to the redemption of the preferences shares, was as follows:

	€000
€1 ordinary share capital	300,000
Redeemable preference shares	40,500
Share premium account	77,000
Retained earnings	182,500
	600,000

Requirement
(a) Calculate the finance cost in respect of the preference shares for EACH of the five years ended 31 December 2008 to 2012.
(b) Assuming the redemption occurred, prepare the capital and reserves section of the statement of financial position of the VERTIGO Group as at 31 December 2012.

Question 25.2

On 1 January 2012, after discussions with your firm, MIRROR issued 9,000,000 6% debentures of €1 each at an issue price of 95 cent for every €1 debenture. The direct costs associated with the issue amounted to €76,400. MIRROR will redeem the debentures on 31 December 2015 at a premium of 10 cent for every €1 debenture purchased. The effective rate of interest on the debenture issue is 10%.

Requirement With respect to the debenture issue, calculate the interest to be charged in the statement of profit or loss and other comprehensive income of MIRROR for each of the four years ending 31 December 2012 to 2015 and the amount to be shown in the statement of financial position at each of the above reporting dates.

Challenging Questions

(Suggested Solutions to Challenging Questions are available to lecturers.)

Question 25.1

On 1 January 2012, BEROL Limited (BEROL) raised 500,000 €1 non-equity shares at a premium of €0.10 per share, incurring issue costs of €10,000. The shares have a fixed cumulative dividend of 5% per annum payable half-yearly, and are redeemable on 31 December 2016 at a premium of 20%. The implicit rate of interest is 6.544%.

Requirement Calculate the finance cost to be charged in the statement of profit or loss and other comprehensive income of BEROL in each of the five years to 31 December 2016, and the carrying value at the end of each of the five years.

Question 25.2

You are a trainee chartered accountant with STAND & DELIVER. The Financial Accountant of HOOD Limited (HOOD), an audit client of your firm, has requested your advice on a number of issues prior to the commencement of the audit of the financial statements for the year ended 31 December 2012.

Issue 1 On 1 December 2012, HOOD purchased equipment for $140,000, when the exchange rate was €1 equals $5. At 31 December 2012 the exchange rate was €1 equals $4.8. The account was settled on 28 February 2013 when €1 equals $5.4.

Issue 2 In September 2012, HOOD signed an agreement with TUCK Limited (TUCK), a finance company, to factor its trade receivables. Under the terms of the agreement, TUCK assumes legal title and responsibility for the collection of all HOOD's trade receivables. At the end of each month, HOOD sells 90% of its trade receivables to TUCK, with the remaining 10%, less a deduction for finance and administration costs, being paid to HOOD only when the cash is received. Any trade receivables that do not pay TUCK within 10 weeks of the debt being sold are transferred back to HOOD and HOOD refunds the cash advanced by TUCK.

Issue 3 During 2012, one of the directors of HOOD, Mr Sherwood, purchased additional shares in HOOD in the market. Another director, Mr Forest, who was also a partner in a firm of chartered surveyors, was paid €100,000 for property valuation work carried out by the surveying company.

Issue 4 On 1 January 2012, HOOD issued four million €1 bonds at par, redeemable on 31 December 2020 at €2 per €1 bond. No interest is payable during the nine years from 1 January 2012 to 31 December 2020. The implicit rate of interest in the bond is 8%. Bondholders can elect to convert their bondholdings on 31 December 2020 into €1 ordinary shares on the basis of one €1 ordinary share for every one €1 bond held. The market price of each €1 ordinary share in HOOD was €1.50 on 1 January 2012 and the share price is expected to increase by approximately 10 cent per annum.

Requirement Prepare a memorandum that explains how the above issues should be accounted for in the financial statements of HOOD for the year ended 31 December 2012.

PART V

ACCOUNTING FOR BUSINESS COMBINATIONS

CHAPTER

26

BUSINESS COMBINATIONS AND CONSOLIDATED FINANCIAL STATEMENTS

LEARNING OBJECTIVES

After having studied this chapter, you should:
1. understand and be able to apply the criteria to identify a subsidiary;
2. be able to calculate and account for positive goodwill and a gain from a bargain purchase;
3. be able to calculate and account for non-controlling interests at the acquisition date; and
4. be able to apply the main disclosure requirements.

KEY TERMS AND DEFINITIONS FOR THIS CHAPTER

In order to aid your understanding of the concepts and issues covered in this chapter, it is important to understand and be familiar with the following key terms and definitions. This is a complex chapter and a significant part of the difficulty actually arises from not being familiar with the terms used. Consequently, as you study this chapter, you should refer back to the key terms and definitions listed below.

Associate This is an entity over which the investor has significant influence.
Consolidated Financial Statements These are the financial statements of a group in which the assets, liabilities, equity, income, expenses and cash flows of the parent and its subsidiaries are presented as those of a single economic entity.
Control An investor controls an investee when the investor is exposed to, or has rights to, variable returns from its involvement with the investee and has the ability to affect those returns through its power over the investee.

Equity Method This is a method of accounting whereby the investment is initially recognised at cost and adjusted thereafter for the post-acquisition change in the investor's share of the investee's net assets. The investor's profit or loss includes its share of the investee's profit or loss and the investor's other comprehensive income includes its share of the investee's other comprehensive income.

Interest in another Entity This refers to contractual and non-contractual involvement that exposes an entity to variability of returns from the performance of the other entity. An interest in another entity can be evidenced by, but is not limited to, the holding of equity or debt instruments as well as other forms of involvement such as the provision of funding, liquidity support, credit enhancement and guarantees. It includes the means by which an entity has control or joint control of, or significant influence over, another entity. An entity does not necessarily have an interest in another entity solely because of a typical customer-supplier relationship.

Joint Arrangement This is an arrangement of which two or more parties have joint control.

Joint Control This is the contractually agreed sharing of control of an arrangement, which exists only when decisions about the relevant activities require the unanimous consent of the parties sharing control.

Non-controlling Interest (NCI) This is the portion of the net results and net assets of a subsidiary attributable to interests not owned directly or indirectly by the parent.

Parent This is an entity that controls one or more entities.

Power This is existing rights that give the current ability to direct the relevant activities.

Protective Rights These are rights designed to protect the interest of the party holding those rights without giving that party power over the entity to which those rights relate.

Relevant Activities These are activities of the investee that significantly affect the investee's returns.

Separate Financial Statements These are financial statements presented by a parent (i.e. an investor with control of a subsidiary), an investor with joint control of, or significant influence over, an investee, in which the investments are accounted for at cost or in accordance with IFRS 9 *Financial Instruments* (see **Chapter 25**).

Significant Influence This is the power to participate in the financial and operating policy decisions of the investee, but is not control or joint control of those policies.

Separate Vehicle This is a separately identifiable financial structure, including separate legal entities or entities recognised by statute, regardless of whether those entities have a legal personality.

Structured Entity This is an entity that has been designed so that voting or similar rights are not the dominant factor in deciding who controls the entity, such as when any voting rights relate to administrative tasks only and the relevant activities are directed by means of contractual arrangements.

26.1 INTRODUCTION

For a variety of legal, tax and other reasons, undertakings often choose to conduct their business activities not through a single legal entity but through several undertakings under the ultimate **control** of the **parent** of the group. For this reason, the accounts of an individual parent company by themselves do not present a full picture of its economic activities or financial position.

In broad terms, control is the power to govern accounting and financial policies and a parent is an entity that has one or more **subsidiaries**, with a subsidiary being an entity that is controlled by another (i.e. the parent). **Consolidated financial statements**, which can be defined as the financial statements of a group presented as those of a single economic entity, are therefore required in order to reflect the extended business unit that conducts the activities under the control of the parent.

In June 2003, the International Accounting Standards Board (IASB) began a project to address diversity in practice related to consolidation, with the aim being to produce a single consolidation model that clarified the definition of control and provided additional guidance on the application of the model. In May 2011, the IASB:

- amended IAS 27 *Consolidated and Separate Financial Statements*, and replaced it with IAS 27 *Separate Financial Statements*;
- amended IAS 28 *Investments in Associates*, and replaced it with IAS 28 *Investments in Associates and Joint Ventures*;
- issued IFRS 10 *Consolidated Financial Statements*;
- issued IFRS 11 *Joint Arrangements*; and
- issued IFRS 12 *Disclosure of Interests in Other Entities*.

All of the above new or amended standards apply to annual reporting periods beginning on or after 1 January 2013, with early application permitted.

Table 26.1 indicates the five new or amended accounting standards and their respective scopes.

TABLE 26.1: RESPECTIVE SCOPE OF CONSOLIDATION STANDARDS

	Accounting	Disclosure	Separate Financial Statements
Subsidiaries	IFRS 10		
Associates	IAS 28 (2011)		IAS 27 (2011)
Joint Arrangements	IAS 28 (2011) and IFRS 11	IFRS 12	IFRS 11
Unconsolidated Entities	IFRS 9		IFRS 12

Consequently, with respect to the preparation of consolidated financial statements, the key accounting standards are:

- IAS 27 *Separate Financial Statements* (2011) (discussed in this chapter, see **Section 26.2**);
- IFRS 10 *Consolidated Financial Statements* (discussed in this chapter, see **Section 26.3**);

- IFRS 12 *Disclosure of Interests in Other Entities* (discussed in this chapter, see **Section 26.3**);
- IFRS 3 *Business Combinations* (discussed in this chapter, see **Section 26.4**);
- IAS 28 *Investments in Associates and Joint Ventures* (see **Chapter 29**); and
- IFRS 11 *Joint Arrangements* (see **Chapter 30**).

The interaction between IFRSs 10, 11 and 12 and IAS 28 is illustrated in **Figure 26.1**.

FIGURE 26.1: INTERACTION BETWEEN IFRSs 10, 11 AND 12 AND IAS 28

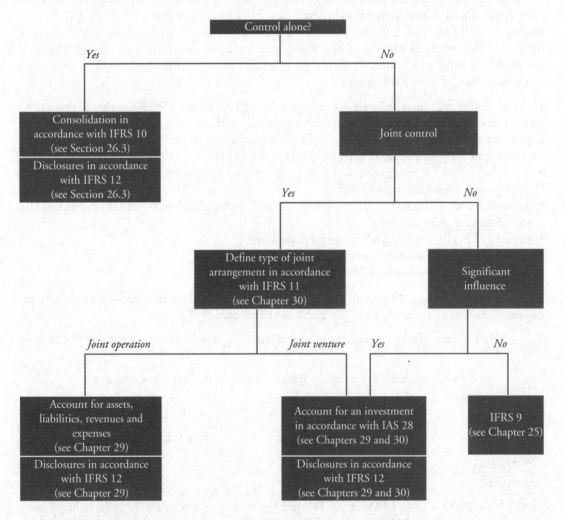

Other relevant accounting standards in the context of the study of consolidated financial statements include:
- IFRS 5 *Non-current Assets Held for Sale and Discontinued Operations* (see **Chapter 20**);
- IAS 7 *Statement of Cash Flows* (see **Chapter 19** and **Chapter 33**);
- IAS 21 *The Effects of Changes in Foreign Exchange Rates* (see **Chapter 31**);
- IAS 29 *Financial Reporting in Hyperinflationary Economies* (see **Chapter 31**);

- IAS 36 *Impairment of Assets* (see **Chapter 10**); and
- IAS 38 *Intangible Assets* (see **Chapter 9**).

In broad terms, the study of consolidated financial statements involves the following:

1. The preparation of a consolidated statement of financial position (see **Chapter 27**).
2. The preparation of a consolidated statement of profit or loss and other comprehensive income (see **Chapter 28**).
3. Accounting for associates (**Chapter 29**).
4. Accounting for joint arrangements (**Chapter 30**).
5. Dealing with foreign companies (**Chapter 31**).
6. The disposal of subsidiaries (**Chapter 32**).
7. The preparation of a consolidated statement of cash flows (**Chapter 33**).

The purpose of this chapter is to describe the main features of IFRS 3, IFRS 10 and IFRS 12. This is important, as a sound understanding of IFRS 3 and IFRS 10 in particular, is necessary to fully appreciate the rationale for the practical consolidated accounting procedures explained in **Chapters 27** and **28**. Therefore, this chapter, together with **Chapters 27 and 28**, focuses on accounting for *subsidiaries*, with *associates* and *joint arrangements* being covered primarily in **Chapter 29** and **Chapter 30** respectively.

Generally speaking, with respect to accounting for subsidiaries, the company owning the shares is referred to as the 'parent' (P) and the 'group' represents the parent and any subsidiaries. (***Note:*** for ownership purposes, preference shares are not relevant.)

Key to this Chapter

This chapter begins by outlining the different types of interest that one entity may have in other entities. For example, a subsidiary interest, associate interest, joint arrangement and investment interest (see **Section 26.2**). Drawing upon the requirements of IFRS 10 *Consolidated Financial Statements* and IFRS 12 *Disclosure of Interests in Other Entities*, this is followed by a discussion of the key factors to be considered when preparing and presenting consolidated financial statements (see **Section 26.3**). The chapter concludes by reviewing the key elements of IFRS 3 *Business Combinations*, in particular the calculation of goodwill and non-controlling interests (see **Section 26.4**).

26.2 TYPES OF INTERESTS IN OTHER ENTITIES

The method of preparing group financial statements depends on how an *interest* in an entity has been defined. As a rough rule of thumb, a company can have four basic types of interest in another company, which are described below and the key characteristics of which are then summarised in **Table 26.2**.

1. Subsidiary Interest

In simple terms, when a company has a subsidiary interest in another entity it owns, or controls, 50% or more of the ordinary share capital of that entity. (The issue of control is developed in **Section 26.3**.)

Imagine that you and a friend are purchasing a car and, for reasons best known to yourselves, your friend buys the tyres and you purchase the rest. If somebody asked you who owned the car, you would probably reply that you do; but, as a quiet aside, you would mention that your friend owns the tyres.

Similarly, if P owns (say) 95% of the shares in a company, then we prepare a set of consolidated financial statements as if the ownership is actually 100%, and show a separate amount to reflect the other 5% that P does not own, known as non-controlling interests.

The reason for this approach is that, while P effectively has full control over the company (subsidiary), it does not have full legal title to 100% of the shares. The 5% shareholders are known as the non-controlling interest.

Accounting Treatment for Subsidiaries

In the individual financial statements of the parent (i.e. their 'separate financial statements'), the investment in a subsidiary is accounted for at cost or in accordance with IFRS 9 *Financial Instruments* (see **Chapter 25**). Investments carried at cost should be measured at the lower of their carrying amount and fair value less costs to sell. Investments that are accounted for at cost and classified as held for sale in accordance with IFRS 5 *Non-current Assets Held for Sale and Discontinued Operations* should be accounted for in accordance with that IFRS (see **Chapter 20**).

In the consolidated financial statements of the parent, the assets, liabilities, equity, income, expenses and cash flows of the parent and its subsidiaries are presented as those of a single economic entity. This is explained in more detail in **Section 26.3** and **Section 26.4**.

2. Associate Interest

Broadly, an associate is an entity over which the investor has significant influence, with significant influence being the power to participate in (but not control) the financial and operating policy decisions of the investee. In basic terms, this is often assumed to be a share holding of between 20%–49%. This is discussed in detail in **Chapter 29**.

For example, if an entity owns only 30% of the equity shares of another company, it does not have effective control of the company. Then, only 30% of the results of an associate company are reflected in that entity's financial statements.

Accounting Treatment for Associates

In the individual financial statements of the entity (i.e. their 'separate financial statements'), the investment in an associate is accounted for at cost or in accordance with IFRS 9 *Financial Instruments* (see **Chapter 25**). Investments carried at cost should be measured at the lower of their carrying amount and fair value less costs to sell. Investments that are accounted for at cost and classified as held for sale in accordance with IFRS 5 *Non-current Assets Held for Sale and Discontinued Operations* should be accounted for in accordance with that IFRS (see **Chapter 20**).

In its consolidated financial statements, an investor uses the equity method of accounting for investments in associates. This is explained in detail in **Chapter 29**.

3. Joint Arrangement

Prior to May 2011, the accounting treatment of joint ventures was governed by IAS 31 and SIC 13. In May 2011, the IASB issued IFRS 11, which classifies **joint arrangements** as being either a **joint operation** or a **joint venture**. IFRS 11 supersedes IAS 31 and SIC 13, and is effective from 1 January 2013, with early application permitted. Under IFRS 11:

- A **joint operation** is a joint arrangement whereby the parties that have joint control of the arrangement have rights to the assets, and obligations for the liabilities, relating to the arrangement. Those parties are called joint operators.
- A **joint venture** is a joint arrangement whereby the parties that have joint control of the arrangement have rights to the net assets of the arrangement. Those parties are called joint venturers.

Accounting Treatment for Joint Arrangements

With respect to joint operations, an investor should recognise its own assets, liabilities and transactions in both its separate and consolidated financial statements.

In the case of a joint venture, the investment should be accounted for at cost or in accordance with IFRS 9 *Financial Instruments* (see **Chapter 25**) in the entity's separate financial statements. Investments carried at cost should be measured at the lower of their carrying amount and fair value less costs to sell. Investments that are accounted for at cost and classified as held for sale in accordance with IFRS 5 *Non-current Assets Held for Sale and Discontinued Operations* should be accounted for in accordance with that IFRS (see **Chapter 20**). In its consolidated financial statements, an investor must adopt the equity method of accounting for under IFRS 11. This is explained in detail in **Chapter 30**.

4. Investment Interest

This is generally considered to be an interest of less than 20% in the equity shares of another entity.

Accounting Treatment for an Investment Interest

Given the ownership interest is less than 20%, the investor is usually deemed not to have control (see subsidiary interest above) or significant influence (see associate interest above). Consequently, the investment is accounted for at fair value. Investments that are accounted for at cost and classified as held for sale in accordance with IFRS 5 *Non-current Assets Held for Sale and Discontinued Operations* should be accounted for in accordance with that IFRS (see **Chapter 20**).

The different types of interest in other entities discussed above are summarised in **Table 26.2**.

TABLE 26.2: TYPES OF INTEREST IN OTHER ENTITIES

	Subsidiary Interest	Associate Interest	Joint Arrangement	Investment Interest
Ownership	≥ 50%	20%–49%	Joint	< 20%
Accounting Standards	IFRS 3	IAS 28	IFRS 11	IFRS 9
Accounting Treatment	Consolidation.	Equity method.	Joint operation – in accordance with relevant IFRSs; and Joint venture – equity method.	At fair value. Separate consolidated financial statements are not required for such an interest.

26.3 PREPARATION AND PRESENTATION OF CONSOLIDATED FINANCIAL STATEMENTS

Introduction

As noted above with respect to the preparation and presentation of consolidated financial statements, in May 2011, the IASB:

- amended IAS 27 *Consolidated and Separate Financial Statements*, and replaced it with IAS 27 *Separate Financial Statements*;
- issued IFRS 10 *Consolidated Financial Statements*;
- issued IFRS 12 *Disclosure of Interests in Other Entities*.

The above new or amended standards apply to annual reporting periods beginning on or after 1 January 2013 and early adoption is permitted.

The publication of IFRS 10 and IFRS 12 completes two important projects included in the IASB's Memorandum of Understanding with the US national standard-setter, the Financial Accounting Standards Board, to create a common set of high-quality global accounting standards.

While the IASB believed that the global financial crisis illustrated that the existing consolidation guidance was not fundamentally flawed, it was accepted that there was a need for new disclosure requirements to provide users with better information. In particular, the IASB believed that perceived inconsistencies between the consolidation guidance in IAS 27 and SIC-12 *Consolidation – Special Purpose Entities*, resulted in diversity in practice in a number of areas:

- **Applying the definition of control:** the perceived conflict of emphasis between IAS 27 (power to govern financial and operating policies) and SIC-12 (risks and rewards) led to inconsistent application of the definition of control for different types of entity.

- **Control without a majority of voting rights:** because IAS 27 did not provide explicit guidance in this area, similar relationships between entities were being accounted for differently.
- **Agency relationships:** the lack of guidance for these relationships meant that similar transactions (for example, those involving funds or investment conduits) were being accounted for differently.

The IASB believes that a control model that is built on principles (i.e. power, returns and the link between those elements) will result in accounting that better reflects the economic substance of the underlying relationships between entities. It is hoped that by introducing a single control model (in IFRS 10) that applies to all entities, and by providing additional application guidance, this will increase consistent application in these areas.

The remainder of this section considers the principles underlying the preparation of consolidated financial statements in accordance with IFRS 10 and outlines the disclosure requirements in IFRS 12. However, in order to place this discussion in context, **Table 26.3** summarises the main changes resulting from the amendments to IAS 27 and SIC-12 and the publication of IFRS 10 and IFRS 12.

TABLE 26.3: MAIN CHANGES FROM IAS 27 AND SIC-12 TO IFRS 10 AND IFRS 12

IAS 27 and SIC-12	IFRS 10 and IFRS 12
Control as the basis for consolidation: IAS 27 identifies control as the basis for consolidation and focuses on the power to govern the financial and operating policies for assessing control of typical operating entities. In contrast, SIC-12 focuses on risks and rewards for assessing control of special purpose entities.	**IFRS 10 identifies control as the single basis for consolidation for all types of entity:** There is no separate guidance with a different consolidation model for special purposes entities; this guidance is incorporated into the single consolidation model in IFRS 10. The new control definition reflects that an investor can achieve power over an investee in many ways, not just through governing financial and operating policies. The investor must assess whether it has rights to direct the relevant activities. Although exposure to risks and rewards is an indicator of control, it is not the sole focus for consolidation for any type of entity.
Control without a majority of voting rights: Although the idea that an investor could control an investee while holding less than 50% of the voting rights was implicit in IAS 27, it was not explicitly stated.	**IFRS 10 states that an investor can control an investee with less than 50% of the voting rights of the investee:** IFRS 10 provides specific application guidance for assessing control in such cases.

Potential voting rights:
Only *currently exercisable* potential voting rights are considered when assessing control.

Potential voting rights need to be considered in assessing control, but only if they are *substantive*:
Potential voting rights are substantive when the holder has the practical ability to exercise its rights and when those rights are exercisable when decisions about the direction of the relevant activities need to be made. Deciding whether potential voting rights are substantive requires judgement. Potential voting rights may need to be considered even if they are not currently exercisable.

Agency relationships:
IAS 27 has no specific guidance regarding situations when power is delegated by a principal to an agent.

IFRS 10 contains specific application guidance for agency relationships:
When decision-making authority has been delegated by a principal to an agent, an agent in such a relationship does not control the entity. The principal that has delegated the decision-making authority would consolidate the entity.

Disclosures:
IAS 27 and SIC-12 contain limited disclosure requirements for consolidated entities and no disclosure requirements for unconsolidated structured entities.

IFRS 12 expands the disclosures for both consolidated entities and unconsolidated structured entities:
The disclosure objectives in IFRS 12 give preparers flexibility to tailor their individual disclosures to meet these objectives. IFRS 12 presents a single disclosure standard for reporting entities with special relationships with other entities, including subsidiaries, joint ventures, associates and unconsolidated structured entities.

IFRS 10 *Consolidated Financial Statements*

This subsection summarises the key features of IFRS 10.

IFRS 10 provides a single consolidation model that identifies **control as the basis for consolidation** for all types of entity.

IFRS 10:
- requires a parent entity (i.e. an entity that controls one or more other entities) to present consolidated financial statements;
- defines the principle of control, and establishes control as the basis for consolidation;
- sets out how to apply the principle of control to identify whether an investor controls an investee and therefore must consolidate the investee; and
- sets out the accounting requirements for the preparation of consolidated financial statements.

IFRS 10 states that an investor **controls** an investee if and only if the investor has *all* of the following elements:
- power over the investee – this arises from rights, and such rights can be straightforward (for example, through voting rights) or complex (for example, embedded in contractual arrangements);
- exposure, or rights, to variable returns from its involvement with the investee – such returns must have the potential to vary as a result of the investee's performance and can be positive, negative, or both; and
- the ability to use its power over the investee to affect the amount of the investor's returns.

If an investor controls an investee, it is *required to prepare consolidated financial statements*, *except* if it meets *all* of the following conditions:
- it is a wholly-owned subsidiary or is a partially-owned subsidiary of another entity and its other owners, including those not otherwise entitled to vote, have been informed about, and do not object to, the parent not presenting consolidated financial statements;
- its debt or equity instruments are not traded in a domestic or foreign public market (i.e. stock exchange);
- it did not file, nor is it in the process of filing, its financial statements with a securities commission or other regulatory organisation for the purpose of issuing any class of instruments in a public market; and
- its ultimate or any intermediate parent of the parent produces consolidated financial statements available for public use that comply with IFRSs.

Where consolidated financial statements are prepared, the *consolidation procedures* involve:
- combining like items of assets, liabilities, equity, income, expenses and cash flows of the parent with those of its subsidiaries from the date it gains control until the date when the reporting entity ceases to control the subsidiary;
- offsetting (i.e. eliminating) the carrying amount of the parent's investment in each subsidiary and the parent's portion of equity of each subsidiary (**Section 26.4** explains how to account for any related goodwill in accordance with IFRS 3 *Business Combinations*); and
- eliminating in full intragroup assets and liabilities, equity, income, expenses and cash flows relating to transactions between entities of the group, together with any profits or losses resulting from intragroup transactions that are recognised in assets, such as inventory and non-current.

The parent and subsidiary are required to have the *same reporting dates*, unless impracticable. Where impracticable, the most recent financial statements of the subsidiary should be used, adjusted for the effects of significant transactions or events between the reporting dates of the subsidiary and consolidated financial statements. The difference between the date of the subsidiary's financial statements and that of the consolidated financial statements should be no more than three months.

With respect to *non-controlling interests*, these should be presented in the consolidated statement of financial position within equity, separately from the equity of the owners of the parent (see **Chapter 2**, **Figure 2.1**). Profit or loss for the period, together with each component of other comprehensive income, should be attributed to the owners of the parent and to the non-controlling interests. In addition, total comprehensive income should be attributed between the owners of the parent and non-controlling interests, even if this results in the non-controlling interests having a deficit balance (see **Chapter 2**, **Figure 2.2**).

Changes in ownership of a subsidiary that *do not* result in a loss of control are equity transactions (i.e. transactions with owners in their capacity as owners). If a parent *loses control* of a subsidiary, the parent should:
- derecognise the assets and liabilities of the former subsidiary from the consolidated statement of financial position;
- recognise any investment retained in the former subsidiary at its fair value when control is lost and subsequently account for it in accordance with relevant IFRSs (for example, IAS 28 or IFRS 11). That fair value is regarded as the fair value on initial recognition of a financial asset in accordance with IFRS 9 *Financial Instruments* or, when appropriate, the cost on initial recognition of an investment in an associate or joint venture;
- recognise the gain or loss associated with the loss of control attributable to the former controlling interest (see **Chapter 32**).

The accounting treatment for changes in ownership is explained and illustrated in **Chapter 32**.

IFRS 12 *Disclosure of Interests in Other Entities*

There are no disclosures specified in IFRS 10. Instead, IFRS 12 *Disclosure of Interests in Other Entities* outlines the disclosures required.

IFRS 12 combines the disclosure requirements for subsidiaries, joint arrangements, associates and unconsolidated structured entities. Consistent with the *Conceptual Framework for Financial Reporting 2010* (see **Chapter 1**), it requires a reporting entity to disclose information that helps users to assess the nature and financial effects of the reporting entity's relationship with other entities. IFRS 12 establishes disclosure objectives that require an entity to disclose information that helps users:
- understand the judgements and assumptions made by a reporting entity when deciding how to classify its involvement with another entity;
- understand the interest that non-controlling interests have in consolidated entities; and
- assess the nature of the risks associated with interests in other entities.

In summary, IFRS 12 specifies the following disclosures.

For Interests in Subsidiaries
An entity should disclose information that enables users of its consolidated financial statements to:
- understand the composition of the group;
- understand the interest that non-controlling interests have in the group's activities and cash flows;
- evaluate the nature and extent of significant restrictions on its ability to access or use assets, and settle liabilities, of the group;
- evaluate the nature of, and changes in, the risks associated with its interests in consolidated structured entities;
- evaluate the consequences of changes in its ownership interest in a subsidiary that do not result in a loss of control; and
- evaluate the consequences of losing control of a subsidiary during the reporting period.

Interests in Associates and Joint Arrangements (see **Chapter 29** and **Chapter 30** respectively)
An entity should disclose information that enables users of its financial statements to evaluate:

- the nature, extent and financial effects of its interests in joint arrangements and associates, including the nature and effects of its contractual relationship with the other investors with joint control of, or significant influence over, joint arrangements and associates;
- the nature of, and changes in, the risks associated with its interests in joint ventures and associates.

Interests in Unconsolidated Structured Entities
An entity should disclose information that enables users of its financial statements to understand the nature and extent of its interests in unconsolidated structured entities and evaluate the nature of, and changes in, the risks associated with its interests in unconsolidated structured entities.

26.4 IFRS 3 *BUSINESS COMBINATIONS*

The previous section focused on the preparation and presentation of consolidated financial statements in the context of IFRS 10, together with the disclosure requirements of IFRS 12. IFRS 10 is a conceptual or principles-based standard that addresses primarily the issue of control, and therefore whether a subsidiary relationship exists. This section concentrates on IFRS 3, which might be classed as a more 'nuts and bolts' or technical accounting standard.

Scope of IFRS 3

IFRS 3 deals with the accounting for business combinations and the ongoing accounting for goodwill acquired in business combinations. A **business combination** is a transaction or event in which an acquirer obtains control of one or more businesses. In simple terms, a business combination is the bringing together of separate entities into one reporting entity. The agreement may be structured in a number of ways for legal, taxation or other reasons, and may result in the creation of a parent–subsidiary relationship in which the acquirer is the parent and the acquiree the subsidiary.

IFRS 3 does *not* apply to:

- business combinations in which separate entities or businesses are brought together to form a **joint arrangement**;
- business combinations involving entities or businesses under **common control**; and
- business combinations in which separate entities or businesses are brought together to form a reporting entity by contract alone without the obtaining of an ownership interest.

Accounting for Business Combinations

All business combinations should be accounted for under the **acquisition method**. This method recognises that the acquirer acquires the net assets and that the measurement of the acquirer's own net assets is not affected by the transaction. The following steps should be undertaken in applying the acquisition method:

1. identify the acquirer;
2. determine the acquisition date;
3. recognise and measure the identifiable net assets acquired;
4. recognise and measure any non-controlling interest; and
5. recognise and measure goodwill or gain from a bargain purchase.

Each of these steps is now discussed in turn.

1. Identify the Acquirer

An acquirer should be identified for all business combinations. The **acquirer** is the entity that obtains control of the other combining entity. The acquisition method assumes an acquirer. **Control** is the power to govern the financial and operating policies of an entity in order to obtain benefits. Normally, this requires more than 50% of an entity's voting rights. Even if this is not the case the following could result in an acquirer:

(a) power over more than 50% of voting rights via agreement with other investors; or
(b) power to govern the financial and operating policies of the other entity under statute or an agreement; or
(c) power to appoint or remove the majority of the board of directors; or
(d) power to cast a majority of votes at meetings of the board of directors.

Although it may be difficult to identify an acquirer there are usually indications that one exists. Examples of such indicators include:

- if the fair value of one of the combining entities is significantly greater than the other;
- if there is an exchange of voting ordinary shares for cash; and
- if the management of one dominates the selection of the management team of the combined entity.

Note: in a **business combination via exchange of equity**, the entity that issues the equity shares is usually the acquirer. However, all pertinent facts should be considered in determining which of the combining entities has the power to govern the operating and financial policies of the other entity.

2. Determine the Acquisition Date

This is the date on which the acquirer obtains control of the acquiree.

3. Recognise and Measure the Identifiable Net Assets Acquired

The acquirer, at acquisition date, should allocate the cost of a business combination by recognising the acquiree's identifiable net assets at their acquisition-date fair value. Any difference between the cost of the combination and the acquirer's interest in the net fair value of identifiable net assets should be accounted for as goodwill (see **Example 26.4**). However, non-current assets held for sale and discontinued operations are valued at fair value less costs to sell (as per IFRS 5 – see **Chapter 20**).

The acquirer's statement of profit or loss and other comprehensive income should incorporate the acquiree's post-acquisition profits and losses in the statement of profit or loss and other comprehensive income. Expenses should be based on the cost of the business combination (for example, depreciation should be based on fair values of those depreciable assets at the acquisition date) (i.e. based on their cost to the acquirer).

4. Recognise and Measure any Non-controlling Interest

IFRS 3 has an explicit option, available on a transaction-by-transaction basis, to measure any non-controlling interest in the entity acquired either at **fair value** (the new method – see **Examples 26.2** and **26.3**) or at the **non-controlling interest's proportionate share of the net identifiable assets of the entity acquired** (the old method – see **Examples 26.1** and **26.3**). For the purpose of measuring non-controlling interest at *fair value*, it may be possible to determine the acquisition-date fair value on the basis of market prices for the equity shares not held by the acquirer. When a market price for the equity shares is not available because the shares are not publicly traded, the acquirer must measure the fair value of the non-controlling interest using other valuation techniques.

It has long been argued (mainly by academics) that the traditional (old) method of calculating goodwill only recognises the goodwill acquired by the parent, and is based on the parent's ownership interest rather than the goodwill controlled by the parent. In other words, any goodwill attributable to the non-controlling interest is not recognised. Consequently, the new method has been introduced. However, the problem with the new method is that goodwill (or what is subsumed within it) is a very complex item. If asked to describe goodwill, traditional aspects such as product reputation, skilled workforce, site location, market share and so on, all spring to mind. These are perfectly valid, but in an acquisition, goodwill may contain other factors, such as a premium to acquire control and the value of synergies (cost savings or higher profits) when the subsidiary is integrated within the rest of the group. While the non-controlling interest can legitimately lay claim to its share of the more traditional aspects of goodwill, it is unlikely to benefit from the other aspects, as they relate to the ability to control the subsidiary.

Thus, it may not be appropriate to value the non-controlling interest's share of goodwill proportionately with that of the parent. IFRS 3 seeks to resolve this problem (under the new method – see **Examples 26.2** and **26.3**) by requiring the non-controlling interest to be measured at its 'fair value', rather than at 'its proportionate share of the fair value of the acquiree's identifiable net assets'. The difference between these two values is, effectively, the non-controlling interest's share of goodwill which may or may not be proportionate to the parent's share of goodwill. IFRS 3 recognises that there may be many ways of calculating the fair value of the non-controlling interest but does not go into detail on this matter; however it does acknowledge that the market price of the subsidiary's shares prior to the acquisition may be a reasonable basis on which to value the shareholding of the non-controlling interest.

Example 26.1 illustrates the calculation of non-controlling interests using the old 'proportionate share' method.

Example 26.1: Non-controlling Interests (Old Method)

Parent pays €100 million for 80% of Subsidiary which has net assets with a fair value of €75 million. Goodwill of €40m (€100m – (80% × €75m)) would be recognised, and the non-controlling interests would be €15m (20% × €75m).

		€m
Cost of acquisition		100
Fair value of net assets	€75m	
Group share of net assets	80%	(60)
Goodwill		40

Hypothetically, if we assume that purchasing 100% of Subsidiary would have cost proportionately more, the consideration would have been €125m (€100m/80%) and goodwill would then be €50m (€125m – €75m) and there would be no non-controlling interests. This demonstrates that, where a non-controlling interest exists, the traditional consolidation method only records the parent's share of the goodwill, and the non-controlling interest is carried at its proportionate share of the fair value of the subsidiary's net assets (which excludes any attributable goodwill). The argument goes that as we consolidate the whole of a subsidiary's other assets (and liabilities), why should goodwill be any different? After all, it is an asset!

Based on the same information contained in **Example 26.1**, the calculation of non-controlling interests using the new 'fair value' method is shown in **Example 26.2**.

Example 26.2: Non-controlling Interests (New Method)

Developing the above example, and assuming that the value of the goodwill of the non-controlling interest is proportionate to that of the parent, therefore consolidated goodwill of €50m would be recognised (this includes both the controlling (€40m) and the non-controlling interest (€10m) in goodwill) and the non-controlling interest would be €25m (€15m + €10m attributed goodwill). In effect, consolidated goodwill and the non-controlling interest are 'grossed up' by the non-controlling interest's share of goodwill (€10m in this case). Although this may seem new, it is in fact an extension of the methodology in IAS 36 *Impairment of Assets* when calculating the impairment of goodwill of a cash-generating unit where there is a non-controlling interest (see **Chapter 10**).

A further illustration of the old and new methods is provided in **Example 26.3**.

Example 26.3: Non-controlling Interests (Old and New Methods)

P pays €800 million to purchase 80% of the shares of S. The fair value of 100% of S's identifiable net assets is €600 million.

If P elects to measure non-controlling interests at their proportionate interest in net assets of S of €120 million (20% × €600m), the consolidated financial statements show goodwill of €320 (€800m + €120m – €600m).

If P elects to measure non-controlling interests at fair value and determines that fair value to be €185 million, then goodwill of €385 million is recognised (€800m + €185m – €600m). The fair value of the 20% non-controlling interest in S will not necessarily be proportionate to the price paid by P for its 80%, primarily due to control premium or discount.

Additional examples relating to the calculation of goodwill are provided in **Chapter 27**.

5. Recognise and Measure Goodwill or Gain from a Bargain Purchase

Goodwill represents future economic benefits that are not capable of being individually identified and separately recognised. It is, essentially, the residual cost after allocating fair value to identifiable net assets taken over.

Goodwill is measured as the *difference between*:
- the aggregate of:
  - the acquisition-date fair value of the consideration transferred;
  - the amount of any non-controlling interest in the entity acquired (see above for two measurement options); and
  - in a business combination achieved in stages, the acquisition-date fair value of the acquirer's previously-held equity interest in the entity acquired; and
- the net of the acquisition-date amounts of the identifiable assets acquired and the liabilities assumed, both measured in accordance with IFRS 3.

If the difference above is **positive**, the acquirer should recognise the goodwill as an **asset**.

If the difference above is **negative**, the resulting gain is recognised as a bargain purchase in **profit or loss**.

After initial recognition, the acquirer should measure goodwill at cost less accumulated impairment losses. It should *not* be amortised, but instead tested annually for impairment, or more frequently, if events indicate that it might be impaired, in accordance with IAS 36 (see **Chapter 10**).

The debate over whether goodwill should be arbitrarily amortised or tested for impairment annually is a contentious one. The following arguments are often put forward in support of amortising goodwill:
- Amortisation is a method of allocating the cost of goodwill over the periods it is consumed, and is consistent with the approach taken to other intangible and tangible non-current assets that do not have indefinite useful lives.
- Acquired goodwill is an asset that is consumed over time and replaced with internally generated goodwill. Amortisation therefore ensures that the acquired goodwill is written off and no internally generated goodwill is recognised in its place. This is consistent with the general prohibition on recognising goodwill generated internally by an entity.
- The useful life of acquired goodwill cannot be predicted with a satisfactory level of reliability, nor can the pattern in which that goodwill is consumed be known. Therefore, amortisation over an arbitrary period of time is the only practical solution to an intractable problem.

However, the useful life of acquired goodwill and the pattern in which it diminishes generally are not possible to predict, yet its amortisation depends on such predictions. As a result, the amount amortised in any given period can at best be described as an arbitrary estimate of the consumption of acquired goodwill during that period. In addition, both anecdotal and research evidence supports the view that the amortisation charge for goodwill has little, if any, information value for most users of financial statements, and that an impairment-only model provides users with more useful information. Critics have argued that goodwill may not decline in value and that, even if it does, the arbitrary amounts recorded periodically as goodwill amortisation are unlikely to reflect that decline. In this view, goodwill amortisation simply adds noise to earnings, thereby reducing their usefulness to investors. Accounting standard-setters, in contrast, have until recently maintained that goodwill is likely to be a wasting asset in most circumstances and that recording goodwill amortisation makes reported earnings more useful to investors by reflecting its decline in value.

Empirical studies have examined the extent to which variation in inventory prices is explained by earnings before goodwill amortisation and by reported earnings, which includes goodwill amortisation. These studies find evidence consistent with the criticisms of the previous accounting rules for goodwill, i.e. earnings before goodwill amortisation explain more of the variation in share prices than reported earnings and, for each year, the difference in explanatory power is statistically significant. Moreover, the findings strongly suggest that goodwill amortisation merely adds noise to reported earnings. Overall, the results indicate that the recently adopted reporting rules for purchased goodwill are likely to increase the usefulness of earnings as a summary indicator of share value.

Costs of a Business Combination

The acquirer should measure the cost of a business combination as the aggregate of the fair values of assets given, liabilities incurred and equity issued by the acquirer in exchange for control of the acquiree (see **Examples 26.1–26.4**). The published price at the date of exchange of a quoted equity provides the best evidence of the instrument's fair value. The acquisition date is the date when the acquirer effectively obtains control of the acquiree. When this is achieved through a single transaction, the date of exchange coincides with the acquisition date. However, if acquired in stages:
(a) the cost is the aggregate of individual transactions; and
(b) the date of exchange is the date of each exchange transaction, whereas the acquisition date is the date on which the acquirer obtains control.

When settlement of any part of the cost is deferred, the fair value is determined by discounting the amounts payable to their present value at the date of exchange.

The consideration for an acquisition includes the acquisition-date fair value of contingent consideration. If the amount of contingent consideration changes as a result of a post-acquisition event (such as meeting an earnings target), accounting for the change in consideration depends on whether the additional consideration is an equity instrument or cash or other assets paid or owed. If it is equity, the original amount is not re-measured. If the additional consideration is cash or other assets paid or owed, the changed amount is recognised in arriving at profit or loss in the statement of profit or loss and other comprehensive income. If the amount of consideration changes because of new information about the fair value of the amount of consideration at acquisition date (rather than because of a post-acquisition event), then retrospective restatement is required. Changes to contingent consideration resulting from events after the acquisition date must be recognised in arriving at profit or loss in the statement of profit or loss and other comprehensive income.

The cost of a combination includes liabilities incurred by the acquirer in exchange for control of the acquiree. Future losses should *not* be included as part of the cost. The costs of issuing debt instruments are accounted for under IFRS 9, and costs of issuing equity instruments are accounted for under IAS 32. All other costs associated with the acquisition *must be expensed*, including reimbursements to the acquiree for bearing some of the acquisition costs. Examples of costs to be expensed include finder's fees; advisory, legal, accounting, valuation, and other professional or consulting fees; and general administrative costs, including the costs of maintaining an internal acquisitions department.

Provisional Accounting

Fair values need to be assigned to the acquiree's identifiable net assets initially. If these can only be determined provisionally at the end of the reporting period then these values may be adopted. However the acquirer should recognise any adjustments, after finalising the initial accounting, to those provisional values within 12 months of the acquisition date. Also, any adjustments should be recognised from the acquisition date.

Disclosures

An acquirer should disclose information that enables users of its financial statements to evaluate the nature and financial effect of business combinations that occur either during the reporting period or after the end of the reporting period but before the financial statements are authorised for issue. To achieve this, the following information should be provided for each business combination affected during the reporting period:
(a) the names and descriptions of the combining entities;
(b) the acquisition date;
(c) the percentage of voting equity instruments acquired;
(d) primary reasons for the business combination;
(e) the cost of the combination and a description of the components of that cost. When equity instruments are issued the following should also be disclosed:
  (i)   the number of equity instruments issued, and
  (ii) the fair value of those instruments and the basis for determining that fair value;
(f) details of operations that the entity has decided to dispose of;
(g) the amounts recognised for each class of the acquiree's net assets at acquisition date together with their carrying amounts immediately prior to the combination;
(h) the amount of any excess recognised in profit or loss in the statement of profit or loss and other comprehensive income arising from a gain on a bargain purchase;
(i) a description of the factors contributing to the recognition of goodwill; and
(j) the amount of the acquiree's profit or loss since the acquisition date included in the acquirer's profit or loss for the period, unless impracticable. If impracticable, that fact must be disclosed.

The information above may be disclosed in aggregate for business combinations that are individually immaterial.

The following should also be provided, unless it would be impracticable to do so:
(a) the revenue of the combined entity for the period as though the acquisition date was at the start of the reporting period; and
(b) the profit or loss of the combined entity for the period as though the acquisition date was at the start of the reporting period.

If it is impracticable to disclose this information, then that fact must be disclosed.

An acquirer should disclose information that enables users to evaluate the financial effects of gains, losses, error corrections and other adjustments recognised in the current period that relate to business combinations that were effected in the current or in previous periods. In that regard the following should be disclosed:
(a) the amount and explanation of any gain/loss recognised in the current reporting period;
(b) if the initial accounting is provisional, the amounts and explanations of adjustments made to provisional values during the reporting period; and
(c) information about error corrections required to be disclosed under IAS 8 (see **Chapter 21**).

An entity should disclose information that enables users to evaluate changes in the carrying amount of goodwill during the reporting period. That requires a reconciliation of goodwill between the start and end of the reporting period.

From a technical accounting perspective, IFRS 3, which is the focus of this section, is concerned largely with the calculation of goodwill and non-controlling interests. The calculation of these two items is combined in **Example 26.4**.

EXAMPLE 26.4: GOODWILL AND NON-CONTROLLING INTERESTS

On 1 January 2012 Bruce plc (Bruce) acquired 3,000,000 equity shares in Clarence Limited (Clarence) by an exchange of one share in Bruce for every two shares in Clarence, plus €1.25 per acquired Clarence share in cash. The market price of each Bruce share at the date of acquisition was €6, and the market price of each Clarence share at the date of acquisition was €3.25.

Bruce has a policy of valuing non-controlling interests at fair value at the date of acquisition. For this purpose, the share price of Clarence at this date should be used.

An extract from the draft statement of financial position of Clarence at 31 December 2012 showed:

	€
€1 Equity shares	4,000,000
Retained earnings	
– at 31 December 2011	6,000,000
– for year ended 31 December 2012	2,900,000
	12,900,000

Requirement Based on the information provided, calculate the:
(i) goodwill arising on the acquisition of Clarence; and
(ii) non-controlling interests to be included in Bruce's consolidated statement of financial position at 31 December 2012.

Solution

Bruce purchased 3,000,000/4,000,000 shares in Clarence (i.e. 75%), for consideration of €12,750,000 ((1,500,000 shares × €6) + (3,000,000 shares × €1.25)).

(i) Goodwill in Clarence

	€000	€000
Investment at cost:		
Shares issued (3,000,000/2 × €6)		9,000
Cash (3,000,000 × €1.25)		3,750
Total consideration		12,750
Equity shares of Clarence	4,000	
Pre-acquisition reserves	6,000	
	75% × 10,000	(7,500)
Bruce's share of goodwill		5,250
Fair value of non-controlling interest at date of acquisition – 1,000,000 shares at €3.25		3,250
Non-controlling interest's share of Clarence's net assets at date of acquisition (€10,000,000 × 25%)		(2,500)
Non-controlling interest's share of goodwill		750
Total goodwill is therefore (€5,250,000 + €750,000)		6,000

This applies the old methodology for calculating the goodwill with the non-controlling interest's goodwill calculated separately. Although it should be noted that under the old method the reported goodwill figure would be €5,250,000 (i.e. excluding NCI share). Applying the new method of calculating goodwill gives the same total figure, but it is a little simpler:

	€000
Consideration paid by the parent (as before)	12,750
Fair value of the non-controlling interest (as before)	3,250
	16,000
Fair value of subsidiary's net assets (based on equity as before)	(10,000)
Total goodwill	6,000

(ii) Non-controlling interest

	€000
Equity at 31 December 2012	12,900
The non-controlling interest's share of net identifiable assets (× 25%)	3,225
Non-controlling interest share of goodwill (see (i) above)	750
	3,975

Note: subsequent to the date of acquisition, a non-controlling interest is valued at its proportionate share of the carrying value of the subsidiary's net identifiable assets (equal to its equity) plus its attributed goodwill (less any impairment). The non-controlling interest is only valued at fair value at the date of acquisition.

SOLUTION NOTES

(a) There are a number of ways of presenting the information to test the new method for calculating the non-controlling interest at the date of acquisition. As above, the subsidiary's share price just before the acquisition could be given and then used to value the non-controlling interest. It is then a matter of multiplying the share price by the number of shares held by the non-controlling interest:

e.g. 1,000,000 × €3.25 = €3,250,000 (see (i) above).

In practice the parent is likely to have paid more than the subsidiary's pre-acquisition share price in order to gain control.

The question could simply state that the directors valued the non-controlling interest at the date of acquisition at €3,250,000.

An alternative approach would be to give in the question the value of the goodwill attributable to the non-controlling interest. In this case, the non-controlling interest's goodwill would be added to the parent's goodwill (calculated by the old method) and to the carrying amount of the non-controlling interest itself (e.g. €750,000 (see (i) above)).

(b) The consideration given by Bruce for the shares of Clarence works out at €4.25 per share, i.e. consideration of €12,750,000 for 3,000,000 shares. This is considerably higher than the market price of Clarence's shares (€3.25) before the acquisition. This probably reflects the cost of gaining control of Clarence. This is also why it is probably appropriate to value the non-controlling interest in Clarence shares at €3.25 each, because (by definition) the non-controlling interest does not have any control. This also explains why Bruce's share of Clarence's goodwill at 87.5% (i.e. €5,250,000/€6,000,000) is much higher than its proportionate shareholding in Clarence (which is 75%).

(c) The 1,500,000 shares issued by Bruce in the share exchange, at a value of €6 each, would be recorded as €1 per share as capital and €5 per share as premium, giving an increase in share capital of €1,500,000 and a share premium of €7,500,000.

(d) If goodwill had been impaired by €1,000,000. IAS 36 requires a subsidiary's goodwill impairment to be allocated between the parent and the non-controlling interest on the same basis as the subsidiary's profits and losses are allocated. Thus, of the impairment of €1,000,000, €750,000 would be allocated to the parent and €250,000 would be allocated to the non-controlling interest, writing it down to €3,725,000 (€3,975,000 – €250,000). It could be argued that this requirement represents an anomaly: of the recognised goodwill (before the impairment) of €6,000,000 only €750,000 (i.e. 12½%) relates to the non-controlling interest, but it suffers 25% (its proportionate shareholding in Clarence) of the goodwill impairment.

26.5 CONCLUSION

Many companies comprise different entities acquired at different times throughout their corporate life. Whilst, after the acquisition of a subsidiary by a parent, the subsidiary continues to maintain separate accounting records, in reality the parent company controls the subsidiary and so the subsidiary no longer operates completely independently. Since the parent controls the subsidiary, in accordance with various accounting standards, the parent must present the subsidiary's and its own financial operations in a combined manner (even though the two companies are separate legal entities). The parent company does so by preparing consolidated financial statements that combine the assets, liabilities, revenue and expenses of the parent as well as those of its subsidiaries.

In preparing consolidated financial statements, the parent must eliminate numerous transactions between itself and the subsidiary. For example, the parent must eliminate transactions for accounts receivable and accounts payable to avoid counting revenue twice and giving the user of the consolidated financial statements the impression that the consolidated entity has more profits or owes more money than it actually does.

Part V of this text deals with various aspects of accounting for business combinations. This chapter focused on the preparation and presentation of consolidated financial statements in the context of IFRS 10 and IFRS 3, together with the disclosure requirements of IFRS 12. IFRS 10 is concerned primarily with the issue of control, and therefore whether a subsidiary relationship exists. IFRS 3 is more of a technical accounting standard and is concerned primarily with the calculation of goodwill and non-controlling interests. The remaining chapters in this Part of the text address:

- **Chapter 27** Consolidated Statement of Financial Position;
- **Chapter 28** Consolidated Statement of Profit or Loss and Other Comprehensive Income;
- **Chapter 29** Associates;
- **Chapter 30** Joint Arrangements;
- **Chapter 31** Foreign Currency Transactions and Translation of Foreign Operations;
- **Chapter 32** Disposal of Subsidiaries; and
- **Chapter 33** Consolidated Statement of Cash Flows.

SUMMARY OF LEARNING OBJECTIVES

After having studied this chapter, you should:

Learning Objective 1 Understand and be able to apply the criteria to identify a subsidiary.

Subsidiary recognition is based upon the concept of control. In accordance with IFRS 10, an investor is deemed to control an investor when the investor is exposed to, or has rights to, variable returns from its involvement with the investee and has the ability to affect those returns through its power over the investee (see **Section 26.3**).

Learning Objective 2 Be able to calculate and account for positive goodwill and a gain from a bargain purchase.

Goodwill represents future economic benefits that are not capable of being individually identified and separately recognised. It is measured as the difference between:

- the aggregate of:
  - the acquisition-date fair value of the consideration transferred;
  - the amount of any non-controlling interest in the entity acquired; and

○ in a business combination achieved in stages, the acquisition-date fair value of the acquirer's previously held equity interest in the entity acquired; and

- the net of the acquisition-date amounts of the identifiable assets acquired and the liabilities assumed, both measured in accordance with IFRS 3.

If the difference is positive, the acquirer should recognise the goodwill as an asset; whereas if the difference is negative, the resulting gain is recognised as a bargain purchase in profit or loss (see **Section 26.4**).

Learning Objective 3 Be able to calculate and account for non-controlling interests at the acquisition date.

IFRS 3 has an explicit option, available on a transaction-by-transaction basis, to measure any non-controlling interest in the entity acquired either at fair value (new method) or at the non-controlling interest's proportionate share of the net identifiable assets of the entity acquired (old method) (see **Section 26.4**).

Learning Objective 4 Apply the main disclosure requirements.

IFRS 12 *Disclosure of Interests in Other Entities* outlines the disclosures requirements for subsidiaries, joint arrangements, associates and unconsolidated structured entities (see **Section 26.3**).

QUESTIONS

Self-test Questions

1. Summarise the main features of IFRS 10.
2. Summarise the main features of IFRS 3.
3. Explain how goodwill should be calculated in accordance with IFRS 3.
4. Describe the two ways in which non-controlling interests may be calculated under IFRS 3.

Note: There are additional examples and questions dealing with the calculation of goodwill and non-controlling interests in **Chapters 27** and **28**.

Review Questions

(See **Appendix One** for Suggested Solutions to Review Questions.)

Question 26.1

Parent owns 80% of Subsidiary. The consolidated statement of financial position contains the following amounts relating to Subsidiary (a CGU) at 31 December 2012:

	€
Identifiable net assets of Subsidiary	500
Consolidated goodwill (Parent share only – old method)	160
	660
NCI (20% × €500)	100

An impairment review of Subsidiary was conducted at 31 December 2012.

Requirement Calculate the impairment loss and show how it would be allocated if the recoverable amount of Subsidiary at 31 December 2012 was €450.

Challenging Questions

(Suggested Solutions to Challenging Questions are available to lecturers.)

Question 26.1

Parent owns 80% of Subsidiary. The consolidated statement of financial position contains the following amounts relating to Subsidiary (a CGU) at 31 December 2012:

	€
Identifiable net assets of Subsidiary	500
Consolidated goodwill (Parent share only – old method)	160
	660
NCI (20% × €500)	100

Requirement Calculate the impairment loss and show how it would be allocated if the recoverable amount of Subsidiary at 31 December 2012 was €550.

Question 26.2

The statements of financial position of two companies, Blues Limited and Soul Limited, at 31 December 2012 are shown below:

	Blues Limited €000	Soul Limited €000
Property, plant and equipment	90	110
Investment in Soul Limited at cost	110	-
Current assets	50	20
	250	130
Equity and liabilities		
Ordinary share capital €1	100	100
Retained earnings	120	15
	220	115
Current liabilities	30	15
	250	30

Blues Limited acquired 80% of the ordinary shares of Soul Limited on 1 January 2012, when the retained earnings of Soul Limited were €10,000. No impairment of goodwill has occurred to date. On the date of acquisition, the fair value of the non-controlling interests in Soul Limited was €25,000. Blues Limited has a cost of capital of 10%.

Requirement

(a) Prepare a consolidated statement of financial position as at 31 December 2012 assuming that Blues Limited values non-controlling interests using the proportion of net assets method (i.e. old method).

(b) Calculate the goodwill and the non-controlling interest assuming that Blues Limited measures the non-controlling interest at fair value.

(c) Blues Limited financed the acquisition of Soul Limited by offering a share for share exchange of two shares for every four acquired in Soul Limited and a cash payment of €1 per share payable three years later. The market value of shares in Blues Limited was €2. Calculate the cost of investment and show the journals to record it in the financial statements of Blues Limited.

27

CONSOLIDATED STATEMENT OF FINANCIAL POSITION

LEARNING OBJECTIVES

This chapter deals with the preparation of a consolidated statement of financial position. After having studied this chapter, you should be able to:
1. ascertain the structure of the group;
2. calculate goodwill;
3. calculate non-controlling interests at both the acquisition and reporting dates;
4. calculate consolidated retained earnings; and
5. prepare a consolidated statement of financial position.

KEY TERMS AND DEFINITIONS FOR THIS CHAPTER

In order to aid your understanding of the concepts and issues covered in this chapter, it is important to understand and be familiar with the following key terms and definitions. As you study this chapter, you should refer back to them.

> **Consolidated Financial Statements** The financial statements of a group in which the assets, liabilities, equity, income, expenses and cash flows of the parent and its subsidiaries are presented as those of a single economic entity.
>
> **Control of an Investee** An investor controls an investee when the investor is exposed to, or has rights to, variable returns from its involvement with the investee and has the ability to affect those returns through its power over the investee.
>
> **Goodwill** This represents future economic benefits that are not capable of being individually identified and separately recognised. It is essentially the residual cost after allocating fair value to identifiable net assets taken over. Goodwill is measured as the difference between:

- the aggregate of:
  - the acquisition-date fair value of the consideration transferred;
  - the amount of any non-controlling interest in the entity acquired (see **Chapter 26** for two measurement options); and
  - in a business combination achieved in stages, the acquisition-date fair value of the acquirer's previously held equity interest in the entity acquired; and
- the net of the acquisition-date amounts of the identifiable assets acquired and the liabilities assumed, both measured in accordance with IFRS 3.

If the difference above is positive, the acquirer should recognise the goodwill as an asset. If the difference above is negative, the resulting gain is recognised as a bargain purchase in profit or loss.

Non-controlling interest (NCI) This is the portion of the net results and net assets of a subsidiary attributable to interests not owned directly or indirectly by the parent.

Parent An entity that controls one or more entities.

Power Existing rights that give the current ability to direct the relevant activities.

Protective rights Rights designed to protect the interest of the party holding those rights without giving that party power over the entity to which those rights relate.

Relevant activities Activities of the investee that significantly affect the investee's returns.

Note: in order to aid understanding, 'guidance notes' are enclosed in square brackets […] throughout the text.

27.1 INTRODUCTION

Companies frequently acquire controlling interests in other companies. In these circumstances, the acquiring (or investing) company reflects the purchase of the subsidiary as an investment in its accounts. However, although the parent company has control over the assets and liabilities of the subsidiary, the members of the parent company are not given any indication of the underlying net assets or earnings attributable to their company's investment, i.e. they do not clearly see the value which the subsidiary is contributing to the net assets of the group. For this reason, all holding companies are generally required to submit both a separate company statement of financial position and a consolidated statement of financial position.

By preparing a consolidated statement of financial position, the group is regarded as one business and the consolidated financial statements attempt to show the position and earnings of the group in a manner as near as possible to the way in which such information would have been disclosed if the parent company had acquired the various individual assets and liabilities of the subsidiary [as opposed to acquiring the shares of the subsidiary]. However, it is important to remember that consolidation is an accounting technique or convention designed to present a group of entities under common ownership as a single entity; legally this 'single entity' does not exist.

Key to this Chapter

This chapter addresses the preparation of a consolidated statement of financial position. In terms of its format, after describing how to ascertain the group structure (see **Section 27.2**), the main adjustments or issues usually encountered in preparing a consolidated statement of financial position are explained. To facilitate an understanding of how to prepare a consolidated statement of financial position, these adjustments are discussed in the following, arguably progressively more difficult, order:

- Calculating the premium/discount on acquisition (see **Section 27.3**).
- Distinguishing between pre- and post-acquisition profits (see **Section 27.4**).
- Dealing with non-controlling interests (see **Section 27.5**).
- Accounting for proposed dividends (see **Section 27.6**).
- Adjusting for dividends out of pre-acquisition profits (see **Section 27.7**).
- Reconciling inter-company balances (see **Section 27.8**).
- Eliminating unrealised profit on intragroup transfer of assets (see **Section 27.9**).
- Revaluing tangible non-current assets (see **Section 27.10**).

After explaining the above adjustments individually, the chapter concludes by combining a number of them in a single comprehensive example (see **Section 27.11**).

27.2 IDENTIFYING THE GROUP STRUCTURE

Throughout this chapter, 'P Limited' refers to the parent company and 'S Limited' to the subsidiary. Before any work is commenced on the consolidation process, the group structure must be established:

1. first, identify the parent company (P); then
2. calculate the percentage holding.

The group structure is determined by the number of *ordinary shares* held. This is illustrated in **Example 27.1**.

EXAMPLE 27.1: GROUP STRUCTURE

P Limited purchased 60,000 shares in S Limited for €20,000. The ordinary share capital of S Limited is 100,000 shares at €1 each.

Requirement How should S Limited be treated by P Limited? [Consider your answer before reading below.]

Solution

1. In the absence of any other information, P is the parent company.
2. Percentage holding:

	S Limited
Group (60,000/100,000 shares)	60%
Non-controlling interests	40%
	100%

As P Limited has > 50% of the shareholding of S Limited, S Limited is treated as a subsidiary.

While the previous example considered the group structure simply in terms of the acquisition of shares, the next example builds on this by providing more information on both the 'parent' and the 'subsidiary'. While this is still a relatively simple example, understanding the underlying principles that are illustrated is fundamental to being able to grasp the more difficult consolidation issues covered in this and other chapters. Please read through it carefully and more than once.

EXAMPLE 27.2: MY FIRST CONSOLIDATED STATEMENT OF FINANCIAL POSITION

P Limited [the parent] is a trading company selling widgets. It imports these widgets from European countries for distribution on the Irish market. Its statement of financial position at 31 December 2012 is as follows:

	€
Property, plant and equipment	100,000
Current assets	40,000
	140,000
Ordinary share capital	50,000
Retained earnings	60,000
Current liabilities	30,000
	140,000

On 31 December 2012, P Limited decides to establish a manufacturing operation and sets up a subsidiary company, S Limited, for this purpose. [Therefore, there are no retained earnings at 31 December 2012 as S Limited was formed on this date. However, if alternatively S Limited was acquired on this date then all retained earned earnings at 31 December 2012 would be classified as pre-acquisition retained earnings.] P Limited injected capital of €40,000 financed by way of loan [i.e. P borrowed €40,000 to purchase the shares.] S Limited purchases property, plant and equipment at a cost of €30,000 on that day. The remaining €10,000 is left in the bank. The statement of financial position of S Limited [the subsidiary] is now as follows:

	€
Property, plant and equipment	30,000
Current assets (bank)	10,000
	40,000
Ordinary share capital	40,000

Since P Limited has raised a loan of €40,000 to contribute the initial capital of S Limited, the statement of financial position of P Limited reflects the changes as:
1. an investment of €40,000 in S Limited; and
2. a loan of €40,000.

[This would be recorded as follows:
In P's books – DR Investment in S €40,000 and CR Loan €40,000;
In S's books – DR Bank €40,000 and CR Ordinary share capital €40,000; then DR PPE €30,000 and CR Bank €30,000.]

We can now show the statements of financial position of P Limited and S Limited as at 31 December 2012:

	P Limited €	S Limited €
Property, plant and equipment	100,000	30,000
Investment in S Limited [i.e. at cost]	40,000	-
Current assets	40,000	10,000
	180,000	40,000
Ordinary share capital	50,000	40,000
Retained earnings [S Limited's reserves are €nil at incorporation.]	60,000	-
Current liabilities [including loan of €40,000]	70,000	-
	180,000	40,000

When you consider the scenario in group terms, the group has raised a loan of €40,000, it has purchased property, plant and equipment at a cost of €30,000 and now has €10,000 in a bank account as working capital for the new venture.

You should *always* prepare a cost of control account to ascertain if any goodwill arises on the acquisition.

Cost of Control Account

	€		€
Cost of investment in S Limited	40,000	S Limited – share capital	40,000
		S Limited – retained earnings	-
		Goodwill	-
	40,000		40,000

The group statement of financial position may now be prepared.

P Limited
Consolidated Statement of Financial Position

	P Limited €	S Limited €	Consolidation Adjustments €	Group SFP €
Property plant and equipment	100,000	30,000	-	130,000
Investment in S Limited	40,000	-	(40,000)	-

Current assets	40,000	10,000	-	50,000
	180,000	40,000	(40,000)	180,000
Ordinary share capital	50,000	40,000	(40,000) [P only]	50,000
Retained earnings	60,000	-	-	60,000
Current liabilities	70,000	-	-	70,000
	180,000	40,000	(40,000)	180,000

[Obviously, it is only the far right column that is published.]

Considering the final group statement of financial position, it shows:
(a) additional property, plant and equipment of €30,000;
(b) additional current assets of €10,000; and
(c) additional current liabilities of €40,000.

This is the exact way the statement of financial position would have looked if S Limited had *not* been formed and if the establishment of the manufacturing venture had simply taken place in P Limited. In this fashion, the consolidated statement of financial position shows the group as one business entity. The net assets of S Limited [€40,000 in this example] have been substituted for the cost of investment in S Limited. The share capital of S Limited is then cancelled out because the net assets of S Limited are included in the consolidated statement of financial position.

From the point of view of the group as a whole, the ordinary share capital of the group is the original €50,000 invested by the members of the holding company. The capital of the subsidiary [€40,000] is cancelled out on consolidation.

In the above example, P Limited founded a subsidiary, S Limited, and held 100% of the share capital of that subsidiary. [Therefore there were no pre-/post-acquisition retained earnings and no non-controlling interests. How these are dealt with is addressed later.] The same principles apply where a parent company purchases the shares of another company that is already trading [which then becomes a subsidiary]. However, in this scenario, the issue of pre-/post-acquisition retained earnings will arise (see **Section 27.4**), together with non-controlling interests if less than 100% of the shares are acquired (see **Section 27.5**). Before dealing with these issues, the next section introduces premium/discount on acquisition.

27.3 PREMIUM/DISCOUNT ON ACQUISITION

An investing company may pay more (or less) for a company than the underlying value of its net assets. Where the purchase price *exceeds* the value of the underlying net assets, the difference is known as a 'premium on acquisition', or 'goodwill on consolidation'. It is also referred to as 'purchased goodwill' or 'positive goodwill'. If the purchase price is *less than* the underlying value of the net assets, then negative goodwill, a gain from a bargain purchase or a discount on acquisition will arise (**note:** these three terms mean the same thing and are often used interchangeably). IFRS 3 *Business Combinations* requires the immediate recognition of a gain from a bargain purchase (sometimes referred to as negative goodwill) as a gain in the

consolidated statement of profit or loss and other comprehensive income. Goodwill is measured as the difference between:
- the aggregate of:
  - (i) the acquisition-date fair value of the consideration transferred;
  - (ii) the amount of any non-controlling interest in the entity acquired*; and
  - (iii) in a business combination achieved in stages, the acquisition-date fair value of the acquirer's previously held equity interest in the entity acquired; and
- the net of the acquisition-date amounts of the identifiable assets acquired and the liabilities assumed, both measured in accordance with IFRS 3.

*Note: As explained in **Chapter 26**, the non-controlling interest [which, in simple terms, arises when P acquires less than 100% (but more than 50%) of the ordinary share capital of S (see **Section 26. 3**, **Chapter 26**)] may be valued at its proportionate share of the subsidiary's net identifiable assets, in which case consolidated goodwill would be that relating to the parent only [the 'old' method]. Alternatively, the non-controlling interest may be at its fair value [the 'new' method], in which case the consolidated goodwill represents that of both the parent and the non-controlling interest. It is important to realise that the 'new approach' only applies *at the date of acquisition*. Subsequent to acquisition, both the non-controlling interest and the fair value of the subsidiary's net assets will have changed. IFRS 3 recognises that there may be many ways of calculating the fair value of the non-controlling interest and does not go into detail on this matter, but it recognises that the market price of the subsidiary's shares prior to the acquisition may be a reasonable basis on which to value the shareholding of the non-controlling interest.

In simple terms, **goodwill = consideration paid by parent + non-controlling interest − fair value of the subsidiary's net identifiable assets**. If the difference is positive, the acquirer should recognise the goodwill as an asset; whereas if the difference is negative, the resulting gain is recognised as a bargain purchase in profit or loss (i.e. credited to the consolidated statement of profit or loss and other comprehensive income).

Example 27.3 illustrates the calculation and presentation of positive goodwill (negative goodwill is dealt with in **Example 27.6**).

EXAMPLE 27.3: POSITIVE GOODWILL

P Limited acquired all the shares in S Limited [therefore no non-controlling interest] for €50,000 at the date of incorporation [therefore no pre-acquisition retained earnings] of S Limited. At 31 December 2012 the statements of financial position were as follows:

	P Limited €	S Limited €
ASSETS		
Sundry *net* assets [abbreviated format for simplicity]	110,000	200,000
Investment in S Limited [i.e. the cost]	50,000	-
	160,000	200,000
EQUITY		
Ordinary share capital	80,000	40,000
Retained earnings	80,000	160,000
	160,000	200,000

In preparing the consolidated statement of financial position as at 31 December 2012:
(a) net assets of S Limited at the date of acquisition were represented by share capital of
€40,000 and the retained earnings of €Nil*;
(b) cost of investment was €50,000.
[*Note: that the reserves at the date of acquisition were €Nil because the shares were purchased at the date of incorporation of S Limited.]

Goodwill:	€
Consideration paid by parent	50,000
+ non-controlling interest [n/a – 100% acquisition]	-
− fair value of the subsidiary's net identifiable assets	(40,000)
Premium on acquisition [positive goodwill]	10,000

The consolidated statement of financial position as at 31 December 2012 is as follows:

	P Limited €	S Limited €	Consolidated Adjustments €	Group SFP €
Sundry *net* assets	110,000	200,000	-	310,000
Investment in S Limited	50,000	-	(50,000)	-
Goodwill	-	-	10,000	10,000
	160,000	200,000	(40,000)	320,000
Ordinary share capital	80,000	40,000	(40,000)	[P only] 80,000
Retained earnings	80,000	160,000		**240,000
	160,000	200,000	(40,000)	320,000

[**This represents the retained earnings of P plus P's share of the post-acquisition retained earnings of S.]

It should be clear that the principle of the cost of investment in S Limited being cancelled against the share capital of S Limited still applies. [For the moment, remember that all of S's retained earnings are post acquisition and therefore none is included in the cost of control account.] However, the difference between the two amounts [€10,000 in **Example 27.3**] is represented as goodwill [being premium of cost over net assets acquired]. To surmount the difficulty of computing the goodwill or discount on acquisition, a cost of control account is used. In **Example 27.3**, this account would appear as follows:

Cost of Control Account			
	€		€
Cost of investment	50,000	S Limited – share capital	40,000
	-	Balance c/d	10,000
	50,000		50,000
Balance b/d	10,000		
[representing goodwill on consolidation]			

The entries in the cost of control account are effectively the same as those in the 'Consolidation Adjustments' column in **Example 27.3**.

Example 27.2 and **Example 27.3** adopt a 'consolidation adjustments column' approach. An alternative approach is to use 'T accounts'. While some may find using T accounts more time-consuming in an examination, others may prefer it. However, even if a 'consolidation adjustments column' approach is used, it is essential to *always* think in double-entry terms.

The main steps for using T accounts are:
1. Open a T account for every heading on the statements of financial position and enter opening balances per the question.
2. Post to the T accounts any journal adjustments necessary [every exam question will involve these].
3. Do the consolidation adjustments [remember for every debit there is a credit!].
4. Close off the T accounts.
5. Prepare the consolidated statement of financial position.

The following illustrates a T account approach to **Example 27.3**.

Sundry Net Assets

	€		€
P	110,000	Consolidated statement	310,000
S	200,000	of financial position	
		(CSFP)	
	310,000		310,000

Generally the tangible non-current assets, current assets and current liabilities of P Limited and S Limited are totalled for the consolidated statement of financial position [subject to any adjustments in the question].

Investment in S Limited

	€		€
P	50,000	Cost of control	50,000

All the cost of the investment in S Limited is transferred to cost of control account in order to value any goodwill.

Ordinary Shares

	€		€
Cost of control	40,000	P	80,000
(100% × €40,000)		S	40,000
CSFP	80,000		
	120,000		120,000

The capital of S Limited must be dealt with in the workings. The capital of P is the capital of the group.

Consolidated Retained Earnings

	€		€
Cost of control (100% × zero)	Nil	P	80,000
CSFP	240,000	S	160,000
	240,000		240,000

[Remember, the cost of control account is used to ascertain the goodwill (positive or negative) arising on the acquisition of a subsidiary. The group's share of the reserves of S Limited at the date of acquisition [i.e. pre-acquisition] is transferred to cost of control [i.e. to measure goodwill]. Remember too, in this example, pre-acquisition reserves are nil since S Limited was acquired on the same day as it was incorporated.]

Cost of Control

	€		€
Investment in S	50,000	Ordinary shares	40,000
		Retained earnings	Nil
		CSFP – Goodwill	10,000
	50,000		50,000

[Remember, positive goodwill is not amortised; it is tested for impairment annually.]

P Limited
CONSOLIDATED STATEMENT OF FINANCIAL POSITION
as at 31 December 2012

	€
Assets	
Sundry *net* assets	310,000
Goodwill	10,000
	320,000
Equity	
Ordinary share capital	80,000
Retained earnings	240,000
	320,000

If P Limited had paid only €30,000 for the net assets (€40,000) of S Limited at the date of acquisition, a gain from a bargain purchase (i.e. negative goodwill) of €10,000 would have arisen. IFRS 3 requires the immediate recognition of negative goodwill as a gain in the consolidated statement of profit or loss and other comprehensive income (CSPLOCI).

27.4 PRE-ACQUISITION PROFITS

In each of the previous two sections, together with the related examples, P Limited acquired its interest at the date of incorporation of S Limited and accordingly the net assets of S Limited at the date of acquisition were represented by the share capital of S Limited since no reserves exist at date of incorporation. This is now developed by introducing pre-acquisition reserves. In **Example 27.4** the parent acquires its interest in the subsidiary after incorporation.

EXAMPLE 27.4: PRE-ACQUISITION PROFITS

P Limited acquired all [i.e. still ignoring non-controlling interests] the shares of S Limited after one year's trading when its reserves were €20,000 [i.e. pre-acquisition]. The statements of financial position of the two companies at 31 December 2012 were as follows:

	P Limited €		S Limited €
Assets			
Sundry *net* assets	90,000		200,000
Investment in S Limited	70,000		-
	160,000		200,000
Equity			
Ordinary share capital	80,000		40,000
Retained earnings	80,000	[includes pre- and post-acquisition reserves]	160,000
	160,000		200,000

In this situation, the net assets of S Limited at the date of acquisition were represented by the share capital plus reserves of S Limited at that date. It is both these amounts [i.e. share capital plus reserves at date of acquisition] that are cancelled against the cost of investment in preparing the consolidated statement of financial position.

First, calculate the goodwill/discount on acquisition:

Goodwill:	€
Consideration paid by parent	70,000
+ non-controlling interest [n/a as 100% acquisition]	-
− fair value of the subsidiary's net identifiable assets [share capital + reserves]	(60,000)
Premium on acquisition [positive goodwill]	10,000

Alternatively, this could be calculated as follows:

Cost of Control Account

	€		€
Consideration paid	70,000	Fair value of net assets	60,000
		Goodwill	10,000
	70,000		70,000

CONSOLIDATED STATEMENT OF FINANCIAL POSITION
as at 31 December 2012

	P Limited €	S Limited €	Consolidation Adjustments €	Group SFP €
Sundry *net* assets	90,000	200,000	-	290,000
Investment in S Limited	70,000	-	(70,000)	-
Goodwill	-	-	10,000	10,000
	160,000	200,000	(60,000)	300,000
Ordinary share capital	80,000	40,000	(40,000)	[P only] 80,000
Retained earnings	80,000	160,000	(20,000)	220,000
	160,000	200,000	(60,000)	300,000

The effect of P Limited acquiring a controlling interest in S Limited is to freeze and capitalise the pre-acquisition profits. Therefore, the pre-acquisition profits are *not* available for distribution by P Limited. The consolidated retained earnings figure of €220,000 is made up of P Limited's retained earnings [€80,000] plus P's share [100%] of S Limited's post-acquisition retained earnings [€140,000].

The cost of control account and the consolidated revenue reserves account are shown below to aid understanding of the adjustments required. In the cost of control account you will always credit the account with 'what you got for your purchase price' [i.e. the group's share of the capital and all reserves of S Limited at the date of acquisition].

Cost of Control Account

	€		€
Investment in S Limited	70,000	S Limited share capital	40,000
		S Limited – pre-acquisition profits	20,000
		Balance c/d	10,000
	70,000		70,000
Balance b/d	10,000		

[representing goodwill on consolidation]

Consolidated Retained Earnings

	€		€
Cost of control	20,000	P Limited	80,000
Balance c/d	220,000	S Limited	160,000
	240,000		240,000
		Balance b/d	220,000

[representing retained earnings in consolidated statement of financial position]

27.5 NON-CONTROLLING INTERESTS

Up until this point in the chapter the parent has always acquired 100% of the subsidiary's shares. This assumption is now relaxed. Where the parent company acquires less than a 100% interest in a subsidiary company, the percentage of the subsidiary that is not owned by the parent is known as the non-controlling interest [NCI] [prior to the revision of IAS 27 and IFRS 3 in January 2008 this was referred to as the minority interest]. In preparing the consolidated statement of financial position, the group and non-controlling interest are reflected by showing the combined net assets of the parent and subsidiary companies, and then separately disclosing the non-controlling interest in the net assets of the subsidiary company at the reporting date.

As explained in **Chapter 26, Section 26.4**, IFRS 3 has an explicit option, available on a transaction-by-transaction basis, to measure any *non-controlling interest* in the entity acquired *at the* *date of acquisition* either at fair value [new method] or at the non-controlling interest's proportionate share of the net identifiable assets of the entity acquired [old method]. This latter treatment corresponds to the measurement basis prescribed in IFRS 3 before it was revised in 2008 and hence it is often referred to as the 'old method'. For the purpose of measuring non-controlling interest at fair value, it may be possible to determine the acquisition-date fair value on the basis of market prices for the equity shares not held by the acquirer. When a market price for the equity shares is not available because the shares are not publicly-traded, the acquirer must measure the fair value of the non-controlling interest using other valuation techniques.

Note: if the non-controlling interest is valued at its proportionate share of the subsidiary's net identifiable assets [the 'old' method], goodwill relates to the parent's share only. Alternatively, if the non-controlling interest is valued at its fair value [the 'new' method], goodwill represents that of both the parent and the non-controlling interest. It is important to realise that the new 'formula' only applies at the date of acquisition. Subsequent to acquisition, both the non-controlling interest and the fair value of the subsidiary's net assets will have changed.

The consolidated retained earnings of the subsidiary at date of acquisition are represented by a portion of the net assets. Any distribution of these assets would effectively represent a return of P Limited's investment in S Limited. The effect of P Limited acquiring control of S Limited is to capitalise the subsidiary's reserves at the date of acquisition. These pre-acquisition profits cannot be regarded as distributable by P Limited under company legislation. In the consolidated retained earnings account, the amounts per the statements of financial position of P Limited and S Limited are introduced on the credit side. The reserves of S Limited are then allocated as follows:

1. the non-controlling interest in S Limited get their share of all of S Limited's reserves [at the reporting date] regardless of the date of P Limited's acquisition [this is irrelevant as far as the NCI is concerned]; and
2. P Limited's interest in the reserves of S Limited at the date of acquisition is transferred to the cost of control account.

Of the reserves of S Limited, all that remains in the consolidated reserves account is P Limited's share of the post-acquisition profits of S Limited. This amount, together with the reserves of P Limited, comprises the balance of consolidated reserves in the consolidated statement of financial position.

Example 27.5 builds upon the previous examples by including pre-acquisition reserves and non-controlling interests.

EXAMPLE 27.5: NON-CONTROLLING INTERESTS

Now assume that P Limited acquired 80% [therefore NCI = 20%] of the ordinary share capital of S Limited for €56,000 [see 'Investment in S Limited' below] when S Limited reserves were €20,000 [i.e. pre-acquisition]. The statements of financial position at 31 December 2012 were as follows:

	P Limited €	S Limited €
ASSETS		
Sundry *net* assets	104,000	200,000

Investment in S Limited	56,000	-
	160,000	200,000

EQUITY

Ordinary share capital	80,000	40,000
Retained earnings	80,000	160,000
	160,000	200,000

Before any work is commenced on the consolidated financial statements, the group structure must be established.

	S Limited
Group	80%
Non-controlling interest (NCI)	20%
	100%

For the purposes of this example, it is assumed that the proportionate share method equates to the fair value method when measuring the non-controlling interest *at the date of acquisition*:

i.e. 20% of (€40,000 + €20,000) = €12,000 *at the date of acquisition*.

The non-controlling interest in S Limited at 31 December 2012:

i.e. 20% of €200,000 = €40,000 *at the reporting date*. [The pre- and post-acquisition reserves distinction does not apply to NCI.]

The goodwill/discount on acquisition is:

	€
Goodwill:	
Consideration paid by parent	56,000
+ non-controlling interest	12,000
− fair value of the subsidiary's net identifiable assets	(60,000)
Premium on acquisition [positive goodwill]	8,000

CONSOLIDATED STATEMENT OF FINANCIAL POSITION
as at 31 December 2012

	P Limited	S Limited	Consolidation Adjustments	Group SFP
	€	€	€	€
Sundry *net* assets	104,000	200,000	-	304,000
Investment in S Limited	56,000	-	(56,000)	-
Goodwill	-	-	8,000	8,000
	160,000	200,000	(48,000)	312,000
Ordinary share capital	80,000	40,000	(40,000)	[P only] 80,000
Retained earnings	80,000	160,000	(48,000)	[see below] 192,000
Non-controlling interest	-	-	40,000	40,000
	160,000	200,000	(48,000)	312,000

Cost of Control Account

	€		€
Investment in S Limited	56,000	S Limited share capital	
NCI at acquisition date	12,000	[at date of acquisition]	40,000
		S Limited retained earnings	
		[at date of acquisition]	20,000
		Goodwill c/d	8,000
	68,000		68,000
Goodwill b/d	8,000		

The cost of investment in S Limited of €56,000 is cancelled, goodwill of €8,000 arises on consolidation and the ordinary share capital of S Limited (€40,000) is cancelled out in preparing the consolidated statement of financial position.

Consolidated Retained Earnings

	€		€
Non-controlling interest			
[at reporting date]			
(€160,000 × 20%)	32,000	P Limited	80,000
		S Limited	160,000
Cost of control account			
(pre-acquisition profits)			
(€20,000 × 80%)	16,000		
Balance c/d	192,000		
	240,000		240,000
		Balance b/d	192,000

This balance represents:

	€
(a) 100% of P Limited retained earnings	80,000
(b) 80% of S Limited post-acquisition profits (€160,000 − €20,000) × 80%	112,000
	192,000

Non-controlling Interest Account *(at reporting date)*

	€		€
Balance c/d	40,000	S Limited share capital	
		(€40,000 × 20%)	8,000
		S Limited retained earnings	
		(€160,000 × 20%)	32,000
	40,000		40,000
		Balance b/d	40,000

This non-controlling interest account reflects the interest of the non-controlling shareholders in the shareholders' funds of S Limited at the reporting date. In this case, the non-controlling interest is 20% and the non-controlling interest account has been credited with its share of the capital and retained earnings of S Limited at the reporting date. As can be seen from the credit side of the T account, the non-controlling interest balance represents:

	€
1. 20% of S Limited's ordinary share capital	8,000
2. 20% of S Limited's reserves	32,000
	40,000

Consolidated retained earnings at the reporting date are the retained earnings of the holding company *plus* the group's share of the post-acquisition retained earnings of the subsidiary company at the reporting date. Applying this to the consolidated retained earnings in **Example 27.5**:

	€
Retained earnings of P Limited	80,000
Retained earnings of S Limited	160,000
	240,000
Less non-controlling interest in retained earnings of S Limited (20% × €160,000)	(32,000)
Less holding company share of pre-acquisition retained earnings (80% × €20,000)	(16,000)
	192,000

If a T account approach is adopted, the following working accounts complete this:

Sundry Net Assets

	€		€
P	104,000	Consolidated statement	
S	200,000	of financial position	304,000
	304,000		304,000

Investment in S Limited

	€		€
P	56,000	Cost of control	56,000

Ordinary Shares

	€		€
Cost of control (80% × €40,000)	32,000	P	80,000
Non-controlling interest		S	40,000
(20% × €40,000)	8,000		
Consolidated statement of			
financial position	80,000		
	120,000		120,000

Note: a good proportion of the marks in a consolidated statement of financial position question is normally attributed to the calculation of: goodwill; consolidated retained earnings reserves; and non-controlling interest. It is vital, therefore, that clear workings for these accounts are always presented to the examiner.

Example 27.6 continues to develop the issues addressed in previous examples, with the point being the inclusion of a gain from a bargain purchase (i.e. negative goodwill) (see **Section 27.3**).

EXAMPLE 27.6: GAIN FROM A BARGAIN PURCHASE

CONSOLIDATED STATEMENT OF FINANCIAL POSITION
as at 31 December 2012

	P Limited €	S Limited €
Assets		
Sundry net assets	102,000	74,000
Investment in S Limited	43,000	-
	145,000	74,000
Equity		
Share capital (€1 shares)	100,000	50,000
Retained earnings	45,000	24,000
	145,000	74,000

P Limited acquired 37,500 shares [37,500/50,000 = 75%, therefore NCI = 25%] in S Limited at a cost of €43,000 [see 'Investment in S Limited' above] when S Limited's retained earnings were €10,000 [i.e. pre-acquisition].

Requirement Prepare the consolidated statement of financial position as at 31 December 2012.

Solution

CONSOLIDATED STATEMENT OF FINANCIAL POSITION
as at 31 December 2012

	P Limited €	S Limited €		Consolidation Adjustments €	Group SFP €
Sundry net assets	102,000	74,000		-	176,000
Shares in S Limited			[see cost of		
	43,000	-	control account]	(43,000)	
	145,000	74,000		(43,000)	176,000
Ordinary share capital	100,000	50,000	[P only]	(50,000)	100,000
Retained earnings	45,000	24,000		(11,500)	57,500
Non-controlling interest	-	-	[€74,000 × 25%]	18,500	18,500
	145,000	74,000		(43,000)	176,000

WORKINGS:

Group structure	S Limited
Group	75%
NCI	25%
	100%

For the purposes of this example, it is assumed that the proportionate share method equates to the fair value method. This is explained in **Chapter 26**, **Section 26.4**.

Cost of Control Account

	€		€
Cost of shares held	43,000	Share capital – S Limited	50,000
NCI (at acquisition date)	15,000		
Goodwill	2,000	Retained earnings – S Limited	10,000
	60,000		60,000

The gain on the bargain purchase of €2,000 arising on the acquisition of S Limited has been credited to revenue reserves in accordance with IFRS 3.

Non-controlling Interest Account *(at reporting date)*

	€		€
Balance c/d	18,500	Share capital – S Limited	12,500
		Retained earnings – S Limited	
		(25% × €24,000)	6,000
	-		
	18,500		18,500

Consolidated Retained Earnings Account

	€		€
Cost of control account		P Limited	45,000
(75% × € 10,000)	7,500	S Limited	24,000
Non-controlling interest	6,000	Gain on bargain purchase	2,000
Balance c/d	57,500		
	71,000		71,000
		Balance b/d	57,500

27.6 PROPOSED DIVIDENDS

Continuing with the process of developing the issues involved in preparing a consolidated statement of financial position, the matter of dividends is now introduced. This section deals with the treatment of dividends that may (or may not) have been approved at the reporting date, while the next section tackles dividends that are paid out of pre-acquisition profits.

There is no entitlement to ordinary dividends until they are approved at the Annual General Meeting by the shareholders. Consequently, dividends declared after the reporting date should not be recognised as liabilities unless there 'is a legal obligation' to receive the dividend (IAS 10 *Events after the Reporting Date*) (see **Chapter 15, Example 15.3**).

Where S Limited, has (incorrectly) accrued a proposed dividend in its financial statements and P Limited has *not* taken credit for its share of that dividend, then the appropriate adjustment is:

> DR   Current liabilities – S
> CR   Retained earnings – S

Where S Limited has (incorrectly) accrued a proposed dividend in its financial statements and P Limited *has* taken credit for its share of that dividend, then the appropriate adjustment is:

> DR   Current liabilities – S
> DR   Investment income – P
> CR   Retained earnings – S
> CR   Receivables – P

However, in the case of proposed dividends that have been (legitimately) accrued, steps must be made to ensure that the:

1. parent's share of the proposed dividend of the subsidiary is not included in the group statement of financial position as it represents an inter-company liability and only the amount due to the non-controlling interest is accrued;
2. correct reserves figure of the subsidiary is used for the purposes of calculating the non-controlling interest.

If a subsidiary has legitimately accrued proposed dividends at the year-end, it is important to ascertain whether the parent has taken credit for its share or not. This is illustrated in **Example 27.7** and **Example 27.8**.

EXAMPLE 27.7: PARENT HAS TAKEN CREDIT

P Limited owns 80% of the ordinary shares of S Limited, a company that has legitimately accrued a proposed dividend at the reporting date. P Limited *has* taken credit for its share of that dividend.

EXTRACTS FROM STATEMENTS OF FINANCIAL POSITION
as at 31 December 2012:

	P Limited €	S Limited €
Current Assets		
Dividends receivable	40,000	-
Current Liabilities		
Proposed ordinary dividends	100,000	50,000

The proposed dividends were approved by the shareholders prior to 31 December 2012.

Solution

80% of S Limited's dividend (€40,000) is owed to P Limited and should be eliminated on consolidation. The remainder of S Limited's dividend is due to the non-controlling interest (€10,000) and should be disclosed in the consolidated statement of financial position under current liabilities along with the proposed dividend of P Limited.

Journal Adjustment:

		€	€
Jnl 1	DR Proposed dividends	40,000	
	CR Dividends receivable		40,000
	To cancel the intragroup dividend		

Using T accounts:

Proposed Dividends

	€		€
Jnl 1	40,000	P	100,000
CSFP P Limited	100,000	S	50,000
Non-controlling interest	10,000		-
	150,000		150,000

Dividends Receivable

	€		€
P	40,000	Jnl 1	40,000

EXTRACT FROM THE CONSOLIDATED STATEMENT OF FINANCIAL POSITION
as at 31 December 2012:

Current Liabilities	€
Proposed dividends	110,000

While in the previous example the parent had taken credit for its share of the proposed dividend, this is not the case in **Example 27.8**.

EXAMPLE 27.8: PARENT HAS NOT TAKEN CREDIT

P Limited owns 80% of the ordinary shares of S Limited, a company that has legitimately accrued a proposed dividend at the reporting date. However, P Limited has *not* taken credit for its share of that dividend.

EXTRACTS FROM STATEMENTS OF FINANCIAL POSITION
as at 31 December 2012:

	P Limited	S Limited
Current Liabilities	€	€
Proposed ordinary dividends	100,000	50,000

The proposed dividends were approved by the shareholders prior to 31 December 2012.

Solution

- Bring in the dividend receivable into P Limited's accounts;
- cancel the intragroup dividend; and
- the remainder of S Limited's dividend is due to the non-controlling interest.

Journal Adjustments:		€	€
Jnl 1	DR Dividends receivable	40,000	
	CR P Limited statement of profit or loss and		
	other comprehensive income		40,000
Jnl 2	DR Proposed dividends	40,000	
	CR Dividends receivable		40,000

Using T accounts:

Proposed Dividends

	€			€
Jnl 2	40,000	P		100,000
CSFP P Limited	100,000	S		50,000
Non-controlling interest	10,000			
	150,000			150,000

Dividends Receivable

	€		€
Jnl 1	40,000	Jnl 2	40,000

EXTRACT FROM THE CONSOLIDATED STATEMENT OF FINANCIAL POSITION
as at 31 December 2012:

Current Liabilities	€
Proposed dividends	110,000

Examples 27.7 and **27.8** have an identical effect on the consolidated statement of financial position but the adjustments differ. Pay careful attention when answering questions as to whether P Limited *has* taken credit for its share or P Limited has *not* taken credit.

27.7 DIVIDENDS OUT OF PRE-ACQUISITION PROFITS

After having discussed proposed dividends in the previous section, the treatment of dividends paid out of pre-acquisition profits is now considered from both a company law and IAS/IFRS perspective.

When a parent company purchases a subsidiary, company law dictates that the reserves of the subsidiary at the date of acquisition are 'frozen'. The effect of this is that, if a dividend is paid by the subsidiary out of pre-acquisition profits, it cannot be recognised as income in the books of the parent company. Traditionally, under accounting standards this was also the case, with the parent reducing the cost of the investment in the subsidiary by the dividend received (i.e. the dividend was deemed to be a refund of part of the investment).

However, IAS 27 *Separate Financial Statements* states that an entity shall recognise a dividend from a subsidiary, jointly controlled entity or associate in arriving at profit or loss in its separate financial statements when its right to receive the dividend is established. This is consistent with IAS 18 *Revenue* (see **Chapter 4**). Therefore, from a IAS/IFRS perspective, this effectively removes the pre-/post-acquisition distinction with respect to dividends paid by a subsidiary as IAS 27 allows an entity to recognise a dividend paid from pre-acquisition profits from a subsidiary in arriving at profit or loss in its separate financial statements (albeit this is at variance with company law).

Example 27.9 illustrates the treatment of dividends paid out of pre-acquisition profits from both a company law and IAS/IFRS perspective.

EXAMPLE 27.9: DIVIDENDS PAID OUT OF PRE-ACQUISITION PROFITS

On a September 2012 Christy Limited purchased 75% of the ordinary share capital of Voyage Limited for €1,635,000 when the issued ordinary share capital of Voyage Limited was €750,000 and the retained earnings were €1,200,000. At the date of acquisition, the fair value of the net assets of Voyage Limited was the same as their book value. In December 2012, Voyage Limited paid a dividend of €75,000 out of profits in existence at 3 September 2012.

Requirement Show the calculation of goodwill under company law and extant IASs/ IFRSs.

Under Company Law:

The dividend is treated as a partial return of the cost of the investment in Voyage Limited. The investment in Voyage Limited is created with the dividend received and the retained earnings of Voyage Limited at the date of acquisition are reduced by the total dividend paid.

	€	€
Cost of investment		1,635,000
Less pre-acquisition dividend received (€75,000 × 75%)		(56,250)
		1,578,750
Fair value of net asset at acquisition date:		
Ordinary share capital	750,000	
Retained earnings	1,200,000	
Less pre-acquisition dividend	(75,000)	
	1,875,000	

| Christy Limited's share at 75% | 1,406,250 |
| Goodwill | 172,500 |

Under Extant IASs/IFRSs:
Christy Limited can include the dividend paid out of pre-acquisition profits in arriving at profit or loss in its statement of profit or loss and other comprehensive income, with the goodwill being calculated as if it was paid out of post-acquisition retained earnings.

	€	€
Cost of investment		1,635,000
Fair value of net asset at acquisition date:		
Ordinary share capital	750,000	
Retained earnings	1,200,000	
	1,950,000	
Christy Limited's share at 75%		1,462,500
Goodwill		172,500

In order to ensure that the investment is not overstated, an impairment test is required in accordance with IAS 36 *Impairment of Assets* where a dividend is paid from a subsidiary, associate or jointly controlled entity to the parent and:
- the amount of the dividend exceeds the total comprehensive income of the subsidiary, associate or jointly controlled entity in the period in which the dividend is declared; or
- the carrying amount of the investment in the separate financial statements exceeds the carrying amount in the consolidated financial statements of the investee's net assets (including goodwill).

This is Illustrated in **Example 27.10**.

EXAMPLE 27.10: DIVIDENDS PAID OUT OF PRE-ACQUISITION PROFITS AND IMPAIRMENT

Bruce Limited acquired 100% of the ordinary share capital of Clarence Limited for €300 cash. The statements of financial position of Bruce Limited and Clarence Limited immediately prior to the acquisition showed the following:

Bruce Limited
Statement of Financial Position (Pre-acquisition)

Assets	€	Equity and Liabilities	€
Property, plant and equipment	100	Shareholders' Funds	500
Investments	200	Retained Earnings	100
Accounts receivable	1,000	Accounts payable	800
Cash	400	Accruals	300
	1,700		1,700

Clarence Limited
Statement of Financial Position (Pre-acquisition)

Assets	€	Equity and Liabilities	€
Property, plant and equipment	50	Shareholders' Funds	270
Investments	100	Retained Earnings	30
Accounts receivable	400	Accounts payable	300
Cash	50	Accruals	–
	600		600

The statement of financial position of Bruce Limited immediately after the acquisition is as follows:

Bruce Limited
Statement of Financial Position (Post-acquisition)

Assets	€	Equity and Liabilities	€
Property, plant and equipment	100	Shareholders' Funds	500
Investments	200	Retained Earnings	100
Investments in S	300	Accounts payable	800
Accounts receivable	1,000	Accruals	300
Cash	100		
	1,700		1,700

Shortly after the acquisition by Bruce Limited, Clarence Limited paid a dividend of €30 out of pre-acquisition profits which Bruce Limited recorded in its own separate financial statements accounts as investment income. However, by this time, the value of Clarence Limited fell to €270, indicating that the investment in Clarence Limited had been impaired by €30. The impairment is recorded in the statement of profit or loss and other comprehensive income of Bruce Limited, eliminating benefit of the dividend.

Therefore, in Bruce Limited's statement of financial position, the net cost of the investment in Clarence Limited is reduced from €300 to €270 (€300 – €30), and cash increased from €100 to €130.

The statements of financial position of Bruce Limited and Clarence Limited immediately after the dividend are as follows:

Bruce Limited
Statement of Financial Position (After dividend received)

Assets	€	Equity and Liabilities	€
Property, plant and equipment	100	Shareholders' Funds	500
Investments	200	Retained Earnings**	100
Investments in S*	270	Accounts payable	800
Accounts receivable	1,000	Accruals	300
Cash	130		
	1,700		1,700

* After recording an impairment of €30(€300 – €30)
** €100 + €30 dividends received – €30 impairment charge = €100

Clarence Limited
Statement of Financial Position (After dividend payment)

Assets	€	Equity and Liabilities	€
Property, plant and equipment	50	Shareholders' Funds	270
Investments	100	Retained Earnings	–
Accounts receivable	400	Accounts payable	300
Cash	20	Accruals	–
	570		570

The consolidated statement of financial position of Bruce Group is:

Bruce Group
Consolidated Statement of Financial Position

Assets	€	Equity and Liabilities	€
Property, plant and equipment (50 + 100)	150	Shareholders' Funds	500
Investments (100 + 200)	300	Retained Earnings	100
Accounts receivable (400 + 1,000)	1,400	Accounts payable (300 + 800)	1,100
Cash (20 + 130)	150	Accruals	300
	2,000		2,000

27.8 INTER-COMPANY BALANCES

Continuing with the theme of this chapter of explaining the different issues that are commonly encountered when preparing a consolidated statement of financial position, inter-company balances are now addressed. Consolidated financial statements should present the financial statements of the parent and its subsidiaries as if they were the financial statements of a single entity. Particular items that often require cancellation as part of this process are now explained. These include: loans; current accounts; debentures; and bills of exchange. Each is now considered in turn.

Loans

In cancelling loans the credit balance of one company is offset against the debit balance of the other company, thus eliminating both balances from the consolidated statement of financial position.

Current Accounts

In situations where the current accounts as between the companies in the group are in agreement, i.e. the creditor company shows the same balance in its books in respect of the indebtedness as the debtor company, the cancellation procedure is exactly the same as with loans above. However, frequently the current accounts are not in agreement. This lack of agreement normally stems from cash and/or goods being in transit from one company to the other. Before cancelling inter-company current accounts, they must be brought into agreement. This is done as follows:

- for items in transit between parent and subsidiary companies, adjust the accounts of the parent company regardless of which way the cash or goods are going; and
- for items in transit between fellow subsidiaries, adjust the accounts of the company to which goods or cash are in transit.

The elimination of current accounts is shown in **Example 27.11**.

EXAMPLE 27.11: ELIMINATING CURRENT ACCOUNTS

Current accounts in the books of:

P Limited – with S Limited – €1,490 (debit)

S Limited – with P Limited – €740 (credit)

At year-end there were in transit:

Goods – from P Limited to S Limited – €500

Cash – from S Limited to P Limited – €250

Current Account in Books of P Limited

	€		€
Balance b/d	1,490	Goods in transit	500
		Cash in transit	250
		Balance c/d	740
	1,490		1,490

The goods and cash in transit will be incorporated in the consolidated statement of financial position. The current account balance of €740 will be cancelled on consolidation against the equivalent balance in S.

Debentures and Other Loans

For consolidated statement of financial position purposes, the inter-company indebtedness of loans and interest payable and receivable should cancel. Loans and interest payable to holders outside the group should remain on the consolidated statement of financial position, being disclosed under group liabilities. Debentures and other loans of subsidiaries held outside the group should be disclosed in the consolidated statement of financial position as part of group debentures and loans. They must never be disclosed as part of non-controlling interest as they do not form part of their equity interest in the subsidiary. This is illustrated in **Example 27.12**.

EXAMPLE 27.12: INTER-COMPANY BALANCES

S Limited has €15,000 of 5% debentures, of which P Limited holds €10,000 and outsiders hold €5,000. The payables of S Limited amount to €25,000, of which €900 represents debenture interest payable, while receivables of P Limited amount to €30,000 of which €600 represents debenture interest receivable. In addition, the receivables of S Limited amount to €35,000 and payables of P Limited amount to €27,000.

Requirement Show the balances that should appear in the consolidated statement of financial position in respect of:
(a) 6% debentures.
(b) Receivables.
(c) Payables.

Solution

	P Limited	S Limited	Consolidation Adjustment	Consolidated SFP
	€	€	€	€
	DR/(CR)	DR/(CR)	DR/(CR)	DR/(CR)
Invest in debentures	10,000	-	(10,000)	–
6% debentures	-	(15,000)	(10,000)	(5,000)
Payables	(27,000)	(25,000)	(600)	(51,400)
Receivables	30,000	35,000	(600)	64,400
			-	

In T account Form:

Investment in Debentures

	€		€
P	10,000	Cost of control	10,000

Debentures

	€		€
Cost of control	10,000	S	15,000
CSFP	5,000		
	15,000		15,000

Payables

	€		€
Jnl (intragroup deb. interest)	600	P	27,000
CSFP	51,400	S	25,000
	52,000		52,000

Receivables			
	€		€
P	30,000	Jnl (intragroup deb. interest)	600
S	35,000	CSFP	64,400
	65,000		65,000

Cost of Control			
	€		€
Investment in debentures	10,000	Debentures	10,000

Bills of Exchange

Bills of exchange are the final item discussed in this section on different types of inter-company balances. Bills receivable and bills payable between group companies must be cancelled in the same way as other inter-company balances. The cancellation process may be complicated where bills payable by one company (the accepting company) to another company within the same group (the drawing company) have been discounted by that company before the reporting date. In such cases, the discounted bills cannot be regarded as an inter-company liability because the payment will not be to the drawing company but to the person who discounted them.

Furthermore, the amount disclosed by way of note to the accounts of the drawing company in respect of the contingent liability for bills discounted must be adjusted in the consolidated statement of financial position to exclude the contingent liability that relates to bills payable by another member of the same group. The elimination of bills receivable and payable between group companies is shown in **Example 27.13**.

EXAMPLE 27.13: BILLS OF EXCHANGE

		P Limited	S Limited
		€	€
Bills receivable:	from S Limited	12,000	--
	from others	30,000	6,000
		42,000	6,000
Bills payable:	to P Limited	--	15,000
	to others	9,000	27,000
		9,000	42,000
Note to Statement of Financial Position:			
Contingent liability for bills discounted		8,400	4,800

S Limited owes €15,000 of bills to P Limited, but P Limited has only €12,000 of bills receivable on its books. Therefore, P Limited must have discounted €3,000 worth of these bills. The €3,000 of bills discounted by P Limited will therefore be payable by S Limited to the discounter, i.e. outside the group.

If P Limited has a contingent liability at the reporting date of €8,400 on the bills it has discounted, only €5,400 of that is a contingent liability which arises from outside the group.

Amounts to be included in consolidated financial statements:

Bills receivable		€
	P Limited (€30,000)	
	S Limited (€6,000)	36,000
Bills payable		
	P Limited (€9,000)	
	S Limited (€27,000 + €3,000)	39,000

Note to the Consolidated Statement of Financial Position:
Contingent liability for bills discounted

P Limited €5,400	
S Limited €4,800	10,200

Using T accounts:

Bills Receivable

	€			€
P	42,000	Jnl (intragroup)		12,000
S	6,000	CSFP		36,000
	48,000			48,000

Bills Payable

	€			€
JNL	12,000	P		9,000
CSFP	39,000	S		42,000
	51,000			51,000

27.9 UNREALISED PROFIT ON THE INTRAGROUP TRANSFER OF ASSETS

This section deals with unrealised profit in respect of two different types of asset: inventory; and non-current assets.

Inventory and Unrealised Profit

Where unrealised profit arises from trading between group companies, an adjustment must be made for the unrealised profit. It must first be established in which company's books the unrealised profit has been recorded, with the adjustment being made in the accounts of the selling company. If the unrealised profit has arisen as a result of P Limited selling goods to S Limited at a profit, but S Limited has not sold those goods at the year-end, the adjustment is straightforward:

DR   Consolidated reserves (retained profits of P Limited)
CR   Inventory

However, if the unrealised profit arose in the books of S Limited (for example, S Limited sold goods to P Limited and P Limited still has these goods included in inventory at the year-end), then allowance must be made for the non-controlling interest share in the unrealised profit:

DR   Consolidated reserves (group share)
DR   Non-controlling interest (non-controlling interest share)
CR   Inventory

The elimination of unrealised profit in inventory is shown in **Example 27.14**.

EXAMPLE 27.14: INVENTORY PROFIT

At the reporting date, S Limited's inventory includes €3,200 of goods at invoice price bought from P Limited. P Limited adds $33^{1}/_{3}\%$ to cost. P Limited owns 80% of S Limited.

Therefore, S Limited's inventory should be recorded at its original cost plus $33^{1}/_{3}\%$.

The unrealised profit is $€3,200 \times \dfrac{33^{1}/_{3}}{133^{1}/_{3}} = €800$

Inventory Account		
		€
	Unrealised profit	800

Consolidated Reserves		
	€	
Unrealised profit	800	

The elimination of unrealised profit on the inter-company sale of non-current assets is now explained.

Non-current Assets (Property, Plant and Equipment) and Unrealised Profit

When one company in the group sells to another member of the group an asset that is regarded as non-current, provision must be made for any profit taken by the seller. As with the unrealised profits arising on inventory, the following should be applied:

1. the whole of the unrealised profit should be eliminated;
2. a part should be borne by the non-controlling interest if the unrealised profit has been included in the accounts of a subsidiary; and
3. correct the resulting over-depreciation.

In the separate accounts of the purchasing company, depreciation will be provided on the purchase price to that company of the tangible non-current asset. In the consolidated financial statements, depreciation should be provided on the cost to the group of the tangible non-current asset. The effect of this is that, for consolidation purposes, adjustment should be made eliminating the excess depreciation. This is illustrated in **Example 27.15** and **Example 27.16**, with the first example dealing with a sale from the parent to the subsidiary.

Example 27.15: From Parent to Subsidiary

During the year P Limited (which owns 80% of the ordinary share capital of S Limited) sold to S Limited a tangible non-current asset for €30,000. The asset had been bought by P Limited on the first day of the current year for €24,000 and had thus not been depreciated by P Limited. Depreciation is provided within the group at 10% per annum on a straight-line basis. The journal adjustments would be as follows:

	€	€
DR Consolidated Reserves	6,000	
CR Tangible non-current assets		6,000

Being the elimination of unrealised profit on intragroup transfer of non-current assets.

	€	€
DR Tangible non-current assets – Accumulated depreciation	600	
CR Reserves S		600

Being the correction of accumulated depreciation on assets transferred to group companies (10% × 6,000).

Example 27.16 deals with the sale of a non-current asset from the subsidiary to the parent.

Example 27.16: From Subsidiary to Parent

On 1 January 2010, S Limited sold a tangible non-current asset for €100,000 to P Limited. The asset cost S Limited €50,000 on 1 January 2008. Depreciation is charged by the group at 10% per annum on a straight-line basis. P Limited owns 75% of S Limited. The current year-end is 31 December 2012.

			€
Cost to the group	1 January 2008		50,000
Depreciation	2008		(5,000)
	2009		(5,000)
NBV at date of transfer	1 January 2010		40,000
Value transferred	1 January 2010		100,000
Unrealised profit			60,000

DR Consolidated reserves (group share) (€60,000 × 75%)   €45,000
DR Non-controlling interest (NCI share) (€60,000 × 25%)   €15,000
CR Tangible non-current asset – cost   €60,000
Being the elimination of the unrealised tangible non-current asset profit.

An adjustment is also required to correct three years of over-depreciation in the books of P Limited.

	€
€100,000 × 10% × 3 years	30,000
Correct depreciation, i.e. based on cost to the group	
50,000 × 10% × 3 years	15,000
	15,000

DR Tangible Non-current asset – Depreciation   €15,000
CR Consolidated Reserves   €15,000
As there has been over-depreciation charged by P, tangible non-current assets are valued too low.

To summarise the accounting adjustments following an intragroup sale of non-current assets:
- If P sells a non-current asset to S, then remove the profit/loss from P and adjust S's books for the over-/under-depreciation of the asset. This over-/under-depreciation charge is ultimately split between the parent and non-controlling interests.
- If S sells a non-current asset to P, then remove the profit/loss from S and adjust P's books for the over-/under-depreciation of the asset.

27.10 REVALUATION OF TANGIBLE NON-CURRENT ASSETS

Finally in this chapter, before drawing together the different issues in a comprehensive example (**Section 27.11**), the revaluation of tangible non-current assets is explained.

In most cases, on acquisition of a subsidiary, the assets of the subsidiary would have been revalued for the purpose of determining the purchase price. This revaluation should be preferably recorded by the subsidiary in its own separate accounts. Failing this, the revaluation should be made as a consolidation adjustment as follows:

    DR   Non-current assets
    CR   Cost of control account (group's share)
    CR   Non-controlling interest (their share)

Where a consolidation adjustment is made, depreciation should also be adjusted appropriately if the net assets revalued include any tangible non-current assets. This adjustment should be debited to the subsidiary company's reserves. The non-controlling interest should then be charged with their share of the adjustment, while the remainder should be charged against post-acquisition reserves. This is illustrated in **Example 27.17**.

EXAMPLE 27.17: ASSET REVALUATION

Assume that P Limited acquired 80% of the ordinary share capital of S Limited two years ago (31 December 2010). The tangible non-current assets of S Limited (book value €160,000) were revalued at €180,000 at the date of acquisition. This revaluation has *not* been recorded in the books of S Limited. Depreciation has been provided by S Limited at the rate of 10% per annum on the reducing balanced basis since the acquisition. At the reporting date (31 December 2012), the net book value of these tangible non-current assets in S Limited's books was €129,600.

Requirement Prepare the necessary journal entries, giving effect to the revaluation and any necessary depreciation adjustment.

Solution

	€	€
1. DR Tangible non-current assets	20,000	
CR Cost of control account		16,000
CR Non-controlling interests account		4,000
2. DR Consolidated reserves account	3,040	
DR Non-controlling interests account	760	
CR Accumulated depreciation account		3,800

	S Limited	Consolidation	
	€	€	€
Net book amount 31 December 2010	160,000		
Valuation 31 December 2010		180,000	
Depreciation 2011 10%	(16,000)	(18,000)	2,000
	144,000	162,000	
Depreciation 2012 10%	(14,400)	(16,200)	1,800
	129,600	145,800	
Extra depreciation			3,800

27.11 STEPS FOR PREPARING A CONSOLIDATED STATEMENT OF FINANCIAL POSITION

Having studied the basic techniques of consolidated financial statements in the previous sections, the following steps can be followed when preparing a consolidated statement of financial position. While these steps do not have to be followed in the order listed, they are a useful checklist of procedures to be considered in most questions. It is only by practising questions (as many as possible and as often as possible) that an appropriate examination technique can be developed.
1. Establish and record the group structure.
2. Open 'T' accounts.

3. Transfer the relevant balances from the statement of financial position of the parent and the subsidiary to the 'T' accounts.
4. Put through any journal adjustments required by the question.
5. Give the non-controlling interest their share of all reserves by:

      DR   Relevant reserves accounts

      CR   Non-controlling interest

with the non-controlling interest's percentage of the reserves (at the reporting date).

Pay particular attention to the option selected for dealing with non-controlling interests at the acquisition date [either at fair value (new method) or at the non-controlling interest's proportionate share of the net identifiable assets of the entity acquired (old method)].

6. Give the non-controlling interest their share of the share capital by:

      DR   Share capital

      CR   Non-controlling interest

with the share capital that was not acquired by the parent.

7. Transfer to the cost of control account the parent company's share of the subsidiary's reserves and share capital at acquisition date:

      DR   Share capital

      DR   Relevant reserves account

      CR   Cost of control

8. Transfer to the cost of control account the cost of the investment in the subsidiary:

      DR   Cost of control

      CR   Investment

Remember, consolidated goodwill is calculated as follows: consideration paid by parent + non-controlling interest − fair value of the subsidiary's net identifiable assets. Furthermore, it is important to remember that the non-controlling interest in the above formula may be valued at its proportionate share of the subsidiary's net identifiable assets, in which case consolidated goodwill would be that relating to the parent only [old method]. Alternatively, the non-controlling interest may be at its fair value [new method], in which case the consolidated goodwill represents that of both the parent and the non-controlling interest.

9. Calculate inter-company profits:

These arise most frequently in the areas of inventory and tangible non-current assets. Accounts should be opened for items in respect of which there have been inter-company profits:

      DR Retained profits

      CR Relevant asset account

with full amount of the unrealised profit.

10. Extract balances from the accounts referred to in Step 2 above, inserting them into the consolidated statement of financial position.
11. Aggregate the remaining balances in the statements of financial position, inserting them into the consolidated statement of financial position.

The following example includes many of the issues explained and illustrated in **Sections 27.2–27.10**. You should read through the background information carefully and then attempt to answer the question without looking at the solution. When completed, compare your answer with the suggested solution.

COMPREHENSIVE EXAMPLE 27.18: CONSOLIDATED STATEMENT OF FINANCIAL POSITION

On 1 January 2012 Toffer acquired the following non-current investment:

• Three million equity shares in KTE by an exchange of one share in Toffer for every two shares in KTE, plus €1.25 per acquired KTE share in cash. The market price of each Toffer share at the date of acquisition was €6.00, and the market price of each KTE share at the date of acquisition was €3.25.

Only the cash consideration of the above investment has been recorded by Toffer. In addition, €500,000 of professional costs relating to the acquisition of KTE is included in the cost of the investment.

The summarised draft statements of financial position of Toffer and KTE at 31 December 2012 are:

	Toffer €000	KTE €000
ASSETS		
Non-current Assets		
Property, plant and equipment	18,400	10,400
Investment in KTE	4,250	nil
Financial asset held for trading	6,500	nil
	29,150	10,400
Current Assets		
Inventory	6,900	6,200
Trade receivables	12,200	1,500
Total assets	48,250	18,100
EQUITY AND LIABILITIES		
€1 Equity shares	10,000	4,000
Retained earnings		
– at 31 December 2011	16,000	6,000
– for year ended 31 December 2012	9,250	2,900
	35,250	12,900
Non-current Liabilities		
7% Loan notes	5,000	1,000
Current Liabilities	8,000	4,200
Total equity and liabilities	48,250	18,100

Additional Information:

1. At the date of acquisition, KTE had five years remaining of an agreement to supply goods to one of its major customers. KTE believes it is highly likely that the agreement will be renewed when it expires. This customer agreement is not recognised in KTE's financial statements above. The directors of Toffer estimate that the value of this customer-based contract has a fair value of €1 million, an indefinite life, and has not suffered any impairment.

2. On 1 January 2012, Toffer sold an item of plant to KTE at its agreed fair value of €2.5 million. Its carrying amount prior to the sale was €2 million. The estimated remaining life of the plant at the date of sale was five years (straight-line depreciation).
3. During the year ended 31 December 2012, KTE sold goods to Toffer for €2.7 million. KTE had marked up these goods by 50% on cost. Toffer had a third of the goods still in its inventory at 31 December 2012. There were no intragroup payables/receivables at 31 December 2012.
4. Toffer has a policy of valuing non-controlling interests at fair value at the date of acquisition. For this purpose, the share price of KTE at this date should be used. Impairment tests on 31 December 2012 concluded that the goodwill arising on the acquisition of KTE had not been impaired.
5. The financial asset held for trading is included in Toffer's statement of financial position (above) at its fair value on 1 January 2012, but it has a fair value of €9 million at 31 December 2012.
6. No dividends were paid during the year by either of the companies.

Requirement Prepare the consolidated statement of financial position for Toffer as at 31 December 2012.

Solution

Note:
Toffer purchased 3,000,000/4,000,000 shares in KTE (i.e. 75%), paying €12.75m ((1.5m shares × €6) + (3m shares × €1.25)).

Note: there are a number of ways of presenting the information to test the new method for calculating the non-controlling interest at the date of acquisition. As above, the subsidiary's share price just before the acquisition could be given and then used to value the non-controlling interest. It is then a matter of multiplying the share price by the number of shares held by the non-controlling interest. For example, 1 million × €3.25 = €3.25 million (see (W2) below). Alternatively, the question could simply state that the directors valued the non-controlling interest at the date of acquisition at €3.25 million (for example, in note 4). In practice the parent is likely to have paid more than the subsidiary's pre-acquisition share price in order to gain control.

An alternative approach would be to give in the question the value of the goodwill attributable to the non-controlling interest. In this case, the non-controlling interest's goodwill would be added to the parent's goodwill (calculated by the old method) and to the carrying amount of the non-controlling interest itself (for example, €500,000 (see W2 below)).

Toffer
CONSOLIDATED STATEMENT OF FINANCIAL POSITION
as at 31 December 2012

ASSETS	€000	€000
Non-current Assets		
PPE (€18,400 + €10,400 − €2,500 + €2,000 + €100 (W1))		28,400
Goodwill (W2)		5,000
Customer-based intangible asset		1,000

Investments:

Financial asset held for trading		9,000
		43,400

Current Assets

Inventory (€6,900 + €6,200 − €300 (W3))	12,800	
Trade receivables (€12,200 + €1,500)	13,700	26,500
Total assets		69,900

EQUITY AND LIABILITIES

€1 Equity shares (W4)		11,500
Share premium (W4)	7,500	
Retained earnings (W5)	28,775	36,275
		47,775
Non-controlling interests (W6)		3,925
		51,700

Non-current Liabilities

7% Loan notes (€5,000 + €1,000)		6,000
Current Liabilities (€8,000 + €4,200)		12,200
Total equity and liabilities		69,900

WORKINGS

(W1) Property, plant and equipment
The transfer of the plant creates an initial unrealised profit (URP) of €500,000 which must be cancelled on consolidation:

DR Consolidated reserves	€500,000	
CR Non-current assets		€500,000

Given that the plant is now recorded at its cost to the group, it is necessary to adjust the depreciation charge in KTE's books in order to reflect this 'lower' cost (i.e. €500,000/5 = €100,000 for each year (straight-line depreciation over five years) in the post-acquisition period):

DR Non-current assets	€100,000	
CR KTE retained earnings		€100,000

(W2) Goodwill in KTE

	€000	€000
Investment at cost:		
Shares issued (3,000/2 × €6)		9,000
Cash (3,000 × €1.25)		3,750
Total consideration		12,750
Equity shares of KTE	4,000	
Pre-acquisition reserves	6,000	

Customer-based contract	1,000	
	75% × 11,000	(8,250)
Parent's share of goodwill		4,500
Fair value of non-controlling interest at date of acquisition – 1 million shares at €3.25		3,250
Non-controlling interest's share of KTE's net assets at acquisition date (€11,000 × 25%)		(2,750)
Non-controlling interest's share of goodwill		500
Total goodwill is therefore (€4,500 + €500)		5,000

Note: this applies the old methodology for calculating the goodwill with the non-controlling interest's goodwill calculated separately. Applying the new method of calculating goodwill gives the same total figure, but it is a little simpler:

	€000
Consideration paid by the parent (as before)	12,750
Fair value of the non-controlling interest (as before)	3,250
	16,000
Fair value of subsidiary's net assets (based on equity as before)	(11,000)
Total goodwill	5,000

Note: the consideration given by Toffer for the shares of KTE works out at €4.25 per share, i.e. consideration of €12.75 million for three million shares. This is considerably higher than the market price of KTE's shares (€3.25) before the acquisition. This probably reflects the cost of gaining control of KTE. This is also why it is probably appropriate to value the non-controlling interest in KTE shares at €3.25 each, because (by definition) the non-controlling interest does not have any control. This also explains why Toffer's share of KTE's goodwill at 90% (i.e. 4,500/5,000) is much higher than its proportionate shareholding in KTE (which is 75%).

(W3) The unrealised profit (URP) in inventory

Intragroup sales are €2.7m on which KTE made a profit of €900,000 (€2,700 × 50/150). One-third of these are still in the inventory of Toffer, thus there is an unrealised profit of €300,000.

(W4) Share issues

The 1.5 million shares issued by Toffer in the share exchange, at a value of €6 each, would be recorded as €1 per share as capital and €5 per share as premium, giving an increase in share capital of €1.5m and a share premium of €7.5m.

(W5) Consolidated retained earnings

	€000
Toffer's retained earnings	25,250
Professional costs of acquisition must be expensed	(500)

KTE's post-acquisition profits (€2,900 − €300 URP + €100 (see W(1))) × 75%	2,025
URP in plant (see (W1))	(500)
Gain on available-for-sale investment (€9,000 − €6,500) (see below)	2,500
The gain on available-for-sale investments must be recognised directly in equity.	28,775

(W6) Non-controlling interest

	€000
Equity at 31 December 2012 (€12,900 + €100) (W1)	13,000
Customer-based contract	1,000
URP in inventory	(300)
	13,700

The non-controlling interest's share of net identifiable assets (× 25%)	3,425
Non-controlling interest share of goodwill (W2)	500
	3,925

Note: subsequent to the date of acquisition, a non-controlling interest is valued at its proportionate share of the carrying value of the subsidiary's net identifiable assets (equal to its equity) plus its attributed goodwill (less any impairment). The non-controlling interest is only valued at fair value at the date of acquisition.

Note: if goodwill had been impaired by €1million, IAS 36 requires a subsidiary's goodwill impairment to be allocated between the parent and the non-controlling interest on the same basis as the subsidiary's profits and losses are allocated. Thus, of the impairment of €1 million, €750,000 would be allocated to the parent (and debited to group retained earnings reducing them to €29.525 million (€30,275,000 − €750,000)) and €250,000 would be allocated to the non-controlling interest, writing it down to €3.675 million (€3,925,000 − €250,000). It could be argued that this requirement represents an anomaly: of the recognised goodwill (before the impairment) of €5 million, only €500,000 (i.e. 10%) relates to the non-controlling interest, but it suffers 25% (its proportionate shareholding in KTE) of the goodwill impairment.

27.12 CONCLUSION

Consolidated financial statements combine the financial statements of separate legal entities controlled by a parent company into one set of financial statements for the entire group of companies. They are a representation of how the combined entities are performing as a group. The consolidated financial statements should provide a true and fair view of the financial and operating conditions of the group. In preparing consolidated financial statements, the parent company must eliminate transactions between the parent and its subsidiaries before presenting the consolidated financial statements to the public to avoid double counting, thus giving the reader the impression that the consolidated entity has more profits or owes more money than it actually does.

For example, let's assume that ABC acquires all of the shares of DEF. Both ABC and DEF continue as separate legal entities. ABC is the parent company and DEF is the subsidiary company. Each of these companies continues to operate their respective business and each will publish their own financial statements. However, both existing and potential investors in ABC will find it helpful to see the financial results and the financial position of the economic entity (the combination of ABC and DEF) that they control. Therefore the consolidated statement of profit or loss and other comprehensive income of ABC reports all of the revenues that the economic entity earned from outside customers. The consolidated statement of profit or loss and other comprehensive income also reports all of the expenses that were incurred outside of the economic entity. The consolidated statement of financial position of ABC will report all of the assets and liabilities of the economic entity (amounts owed and receivable between ABC and DEF are eliminated on consolidation).

SUMMARY OF LEARNING OBJECTIVES

This chapter deals with the preparation of a consolidated statement of financial position. After having studied this chapter, you should be able to:

Learning Objective 1 Ascertain the structure of the group.

The structure of a group is determined by the number of *ordinary shares* held by the parent in the subsidiary.

Learning Objective 2 Calculate goodwill.

In simple terms, **goodwill = consideration paid by parent + non-controlling interest − fair value of the subsidiary's net identifiable assets**. If the difference is positive, the acquirer should recognise the goodwill as an asset; whereas if the difference is negative, the resulting gain is recognised as a bargain purchase in arriving at profit or loss in the consolidated statement of profit or loss and other comprehensive income.

Learning Objective 3 Calculate non-controlling interests at both the acquisition and reporting dates.

Where the parent company acquires less than a 100% interest in a subsidiary company, the percentage of the subsidiary that is not owned by the parent is known as the non-controlling interest. IFRS 3 has an explicit option, available on an acquisition-by-acquisition basis, to measure any non-controlling interest in the entity acquired *at the date of acquisition* either at fair value [new method] or at the non-controlling interest's proportionate share of the net identifiable assets of the entity acquired [old method].

When preparing the consolidated statement of financial position at the reporting date, non-controlling interest is reflected by showing their interest in the net assets of the subsidiary company at the reporting date.

Learning Objective 4 Calculate consolidated retained earnings.

At the reporting date retained earnings are represented by the reserves of the holding company *plus* the group's share of the post-acquisition reserves of the subsidiary company at the reporting date.

Learning Objective 5 Prepare a consolidated statement of financial position.

This chapter explains the main issues likely to be encountered when preparing a consolidated statement of financial position, and while all of these may not need to be addressed in every question, they are a useful checklist of procedures to be considered in most questions. It is only by practising questions [as many as possible and as often as possible] that an appropriate examination technique can be developed.

QUESTIONS

Self-test Questions

1. Explain how the investment in a subsidiary is reported in the parent's own financial statements.
2. Explain the difference between pre-acquisition and post-acquisition profits of a subsidiary.
3. Explain how inter-company balances should be treated in the consolidated statement of financial position.
4. Explain how a gain on a bargain purchase (i.e. negative goodwill) may arise and its accounting treatment.
5. Discuss briefly the main reasons for the preparation of consolidated financial statements.

Review Questions

(See **Appendix One** for Suggested Solutions to Review Questions.)

Question 27.1

Llewellyn Limited paid €68,000 for its interest in Roberts Limited on 1 July 2012. The following is the draft consolidated statement of financial position of Llewellyn Limited and its subsidiary Roberts Limited at 30 June 2013.

	€	€
Assets		
Non-current assets		
Property (cost)		30,000

Plant (book value)			80,000
Goodwill			16,000
			126,000
Current assets			
Inventory			32,000
Receivables			24,000
Cash			4,000
			60,000
Total Assets			186,000
Equity and Liabilities			
Equity			
Share Capital €1			100,000
Retained earnings	– Llewellyn Limited	20,000	
	– Roberts (since acquisition)	12,000	32,000
Total Equity			132,000
Current Liabilities			
Sundry Payables			54,000
Total Liabilities			54,000
Total Equity and Liabilities			186,000

Additional Information:

1. Llewellyn Limited acquired only 80% of the ordinary share capital of Roberts Limited, whereas it was assumed by the Assistant Accountant who drew up the draft consolidated statement of financial position that the whole of it had been acquired.
2. Inventory shown in the statement of financial position of Roberts Limited was under-valued by €1,000 at 30 June 2012 and by €1,600 at 30 June 2013.
3. Plant shown in the statement of financial position of Roberts Limited at 30 June 2012 was overvalued by €2,000 (rate of depreciation – 10% per annum).
4. Inventory held by Roberts Limited at 30 June 2013 includes €800 transferred from Llewellyn Limited which cost the latter €600.
5. Roberts Limited has no preference capital, no reserves other than the retained profit account balance and had paid no dividends since the acquisition of the shares by Llewellyn Limited.
6. With respect to the measurement of non-controlling interests at the date of acquisition, the proportionate share method equates to the fair value method. The directors of Llewellyn Limited are confident that any goodwill arising on the acquisition of Roberts Limited has not suffered any impairment.

Requirement

(a) Present working papers in the form of ledger accounts showing the adjustments necessary to correct the Consolidated Statement of Financial Position.
(b) Present the revised Consolidated Statement of Financial Position as at 30 June 2013.

(Ignore taxation.)

Question 27.2

The following is a summary of the balances in the books of Black Limited as at 31 March 2013:

	Black Limited €	Bird Limited €
Assets		
Non-current Assets		
Property, plant and equipment	190,000	190,000
Investment in Bird:		
75,000 ordinary shares	165,000	-
60,000 preference shares	60,000	-
5,000 debentures	5,000	
	420,000	190,000
Current Assets	145,500	143,400
Total Assets	565,500	333,400
Equity and Liabilities		
Equity		
Ordinary shares (€1)	300,000	100,000
7% preference shares (€1)	-	80,000
General reserve	50,000	40,000
Retained earnings	98,500	44,400
	448,500	264,400
Non-current liabilities		
6% Debentures	-	20,000
Current liabilities		
Trade payables	87,000	32,200
Proposed dividends: Ordinary	30,000	10,000
Preference	-	5,600
Debenture interest accrued	-	1,200
Total current liabilities	117,000	49,000
Total Equity and Liabilities	565,500	333,400

Additional Information:
(a) Black Limited acquired the shares of Bird Limited, cum dividend, on 31 March 2012. With respect to the preference shares, there is no contractual right to the dividend and its payment is solely at the discretion of the directors of Bird Limited; they have been classified as equity rather than debt.
(b) The general reserve of Bird Limited was the same on 31 March 2012 as on 31 March 2013. The balance on the retained earnings of Bird Limited is made up as follows:

	€
Balance on 31 March 2012	28,000
Net profit for the year ended 31 March 2013	32,000
	60,000
Less provision for proposed dividends	15,600
	44,400

(c) The inventory of Bird Limited on 31 March 2013 included €16,000 in respect of goods purchased from Black Limited. These goods had been sold by Black Limited to Bird Limited at such a price as to give Black Limited a profit of 20% on the invoice price.

(d) The retained earnings of Bird Limited on 31 March 2012 is after providing for the preference dividend of €5,600 and a proposed ordinary dividend of €5,000, both of which were subsequently paid, but had been incorrectly credited to the statement of profit or loss and other comprehensive income of Black Limited.

(e) No entries had been made in the books of Black Limited in respect of the debenture interest due from, or the proposed dividend of, Bird Limited for the year ended 31 March 2013.

(f) The proposed dividends included in current liabilities at 31 May 2013 were approved during the year ended 31 March 2013 by the shareholders of the respective companies.

(g) With respect to the measurement of non-controlling interests at the date of acquisition, the proportionate share method equates to the fair value method. The directors of Black Limited are confident that any goodwill arising on the acquisition of Bird Limited has not suffered any impairment.

Requirement You are required to prepare the consolidated statement of financial position of Black Limited, and its subsidiary company, Bird Limited, as at 31 March 2013.

Challenging Questions

(Suggested Solutions to Challenging Questions are available to lecturers.)

Question 27.1 (Based on Chartered Accountants Ireland, P3 Autumn 1997, Question 3)

MORN Limited, NOON Limited and NIGHT Limited are three companies involved in the production of television programmes, primarily dealing with news and current affairs. A number of the management team of MORN Limited are also key figures on the management teams of NOON Limited and NIGHT Limited, and MORN Limited has always been able to exercise a dominant influence over the policies and programming decisions of the other two companies.

On 1 January 2012, MORN Limited purchased 96,000 €1 ordinary shares in NOON Limited and 40,500 €1 ordinary shares in NIGHT Limited at a cost of €135,000 and €54,000 respectively. On the same date, NOON Limited purchased 36,000 €1 ordinary shares in NIGHT Limited at a cost of €47,250. The draft statements of financial position of the three companies at 31 December 2012 are shown below.

	MORN Limited €	NOON Limited €	NIGHT Limited €
ASSETS			
Non-current Assets			
Property, plant and equipment	214,500	90,000	50,000
Investments	189,000	47,250	-
	403,500	137,250	50,000
Current Assets			
Inventory	77,200	34,300	32,600
Receivables	189,800	158,050	143,600
Cash	11,000	8,600	4,100
	278,000	200,950	180,300
	681,500	338,200	230,300
EQUITY and LIABILITIES			
Capital and Reserves			
Called up share capital	300,000	120,000	90,000
Retained earnings	75,000	54,000	37,500
	375,000	174,000	127,500
Non-current Liabilities	185,100	77,100	60,100
Current Liabilities	121,400	87,100	42,700
	681,500	338,200	230,300

Additional Information:

1. On 1 January 2012, the retained earnings of NOON Limited and NIGHT Limited were €20,000 and €12,000 respectively.

2. In arriving at the consideration for the shares in NOON Limited, property, plant and equipment was revalued at €115,000 and receivables amounting to €3,000 were deemed irrecoverable. No entry has been made in the books in respect of these valuations and there were no purchases or sales of property, plant and equipment by any of the companies during the year. The directors wish to give effect to the revaluations in the consolidated financial statements. With respect to the measurement of non-controlling interests at the date of acquisition, the proportionate share method equated to the fair value method. There is no evidence to suggest that the goodwill arising on the acquisition of NOON and NIGHT has been impaired.

3. Property, plant and equipment represent filming equipment owned by the companies. Depreciation is to be provided at 10% per annum on a straight-line basis.

4. During the year ended 31 December 2012, NOON Limited sold to NIGHT Limited blank films and tapes for use in programme production for €50,000 cash on delivery. NOON Limited had originally purchased the inventory for €36,000 direct from the manufacturer. At the reporting date, one half of the films and tapes still remained in inventory.

5. Receivables of NIGHT Limited include €5,000 owed by MORN Limited.

6. Included in the current liabilities of MORN Limited is €4,100 owed by the company to NIGHT Limited.

7. A cheque for €900 was sent by MORN Limited on 30 December 2012 to NIGHT Limited but was not received until 2 January 2013.

Requirement Prepare the consolidated statement of financial position of MORN Limited as at 31 December 2012.

Question 27.2 (Based on Chartered Accountants Ireland, P3 Summer 1998, Question 4)

XTRA plc was incorporated in 1985 and makes up its accounts to 31 December each year. Its main business is the hire and retail of videos, records, compact discs and computer games. The company had traded very profitably throughout Ireland until the late 1990s when its results deteriorated dramatically as a result of fierce competition from larger retailers based in Great Britain entering the Irish market. In reaction to the falling profit margins and share price, the directors decided to try to halt the decline through a policy of acquisition and merger. The company has negotiated debt financing of up to €5 million at a fixed rate of 10% per annum with Allied North West Bank should it be required.

(a) During the second half of 2012 the directors of XTRA plc and VDO plc had discussions with a view to a combination of the two companies. As a result of these negotiations it was agreed that:

- on 31 December 2012 XTRA plc should acquire 1,440,000 of the issued ordinary shares of VDO plc;
- XTRA plc should pay cash of 12 cent for each VDO plc share, plus a one for one share exchange. At the date of the offer the market price of a share in XTRA plc was €1.20 per share and the market price of a share in VDO plc was €1.15 per share. XTRA plc shares had remained relatively stable at approximately €1.20 per share during 2012, whereas VDO plc shares had ranged from €1.10 to €1.35 per share. Before the offer neither company owned any shares in the other;
- the consideration would be increased by 144,000 shares if a contingent liability in VDO plc in respect of a claim for wrongful dismissal by a former director did not crystallise.

The summarised statements of financial position at 31 December 2012 of XTRA plc and VDO plc before the proposed combination were:

	XTRA plc €m	VDO plc €m
ASSETS		
Non-current Assets		
Land	1.20	0.86
Property, plant and equipment	2.51	1.67
	3.71	2.53
Current Assets		
Inventory	0.60	0.23
Receivables	0.49	0.19
Cash-in-hand and at bank	0.15	0.34
	1.24	0.76
	4.95	3.29

EQUITY AND LIABILITIES
Capital and Reserves

€1 ordinary shares	2.00	1.50
Revaluation	0.49	-
Retained earnings	1.90	1.00
	4.39	2.50
Current Liabilities	0.56	0.79
	4.95	3.29

Additional Information:
1. The fair value of the assets of VDO plc at 31 December 2012 was:

Land	€1.3m
Property, plant and equipment	€1.6m
Inventory	€0.2m
Receivables	€0.16m

2. With respect to the measurement of non-controlling interests at the date of acquisition, the proportionate share method equated to the fair value method.

Requirement
(a) Prepare the consolidated statement of financial position of XTRA plc and VDO plc.
(b) On 31 December 2012, XTRA plc acquired 90% of the ordinary shares of DAT Limited, a company involved in digital audio technology. While DAT Limited has suffered trading losses in recent years, the directors of XTRA plc are confident that, after incurring reorganisation costs of €250,000 and future trading losses of €150,000, DAT Limited will return to profit.

The purchase consideration comprised deferred consideration of €3,000,000, payable in equal instalments on 31 December 2013, 2014 and 2015. The book value of the net assets of DAT Limited was €2.2m. This included land with a book value of €800,000 but a market value of €1.1m.

XTRA plc incurred accountancy fees of €60,000 and legal fees of €40,000 in connection with the acquisition, and €40,000 in respect of time spent by directors of XTRA plc.

Requirement
(i) Calculate the goodwill to be dealt with in the consolidated financial statements of XTRA plc for the year ended 31 December 2012.
(ii) Explain clearly the treatment of the deferred consideration in the statement of profit or loss and other comprehensive income of XTRA plc for the year ended 31 December 2012 and the statement of financial position at that date.

Note: the following annuity table (extract) should be used where appropriate:

Period	10%
1	0.9090
2	0.8264
3	0.7513

Question 27.3 *(Based on Chartered Accountants Ireland, P3 Autumn 1999, Question 5)*

On 1 January 2010 HUMPTY Limited purchased 320,000 €1 ordinary shares in DUMPTY Limited. On this date the fair value of DUMPTY Limited's separable net assets differed from their book values as follows:

	Statement of financial position value at 1 January 2010 €000	Fair value at 1 January 2010 €000
Property, plant and equipment	500	750
Inventory	100	125
Trade receivables	60	55

However, DUMPTY did not incorporate these fair values into its books of account. With respect to the measurement of non-controlling interests at the date of acquisition, the proportionate share method equated to the fair value method. The directors of HUMPTY believe that the goodwill arising on the acquisition of DUMPTY was impaired for the first time by €345,000 during the year ended 31 December 2012.

On 1 January 2010, the property, plant and equipment of DUMPTY Limited had a remaining useful life of five years and retained earnings stood at €150,000. During 2010 HUMPTY Limited incurred reorganisation costs of €200,000 in order to successfully incorporate DUMPTY Limited into the group. None of the property, plant and equipment of DUMPTY Limited purchased on 1 January 2010 has been sold at 31 December 2012, but the inventory purchased was sold at a profit during 2010.

During 2012 DUMPTY Limited sold goods costing €160,000 to HUMPTY Limited for €200,000. At 31 December 2012 the inventory of HUMPTY Limited includes €50,000 (at cost to HUMPTY Limited) of the goods purchased from DUMPTY Limited.

The individual company statements of financial position of HUMPTY Limited and DUMPTY Limited at 31 December 2012 are as follows:

STATEMENT OF FINANCIAL POSITION
as at 31 December 2012

	HUMPTY Limited €000	DUMPTY Limited €000
ASSETS		
Non-current Assets		
Property, plant and equipment	900	700
Investment in DUMPTY Limited	1,231	-
	2,131	700
Current Assets		
Inventory	164	86
Trade receivables	196	-
Bank and cash	68	81
	428	167
	2,559	867

EQUITY AND LIABILITIES
Capital and Reserves

€1 ordinary shares	1,000	400
Retained earnings	1,217	370
	2,217	770
Non-current Liabilities	200	40
Current Liabilities	142	57
	2,559	867

Requirement

(a) Prepare the consolidated statement of financial position for the HUMPTY group as at 31 December 2012.

(b) The remaining ordinary share capital of DUMPTY Limited is owned by EGG Limited, a company that is wholly owned by a director of DUMPTY Limited. During 2010 EGG Limited purchased property from DUMPTY Limited. The sale price was set by an independent property surveyor. Discuss the implications of this transaction for the year ended 31 December 2012 with regard to IAS 24 *Related Party Disclosures*.

Question 27.4 *(Based on Chartered Accountants Ireland, P3 Autumn 2001, Question 6)*

The draft statements of financial position of NIP Limited and TUCK Limited as at 31 December 2012 are as follows:

	NIP €000	TUCK €000
ASSETS		
Non-current Assets		
Property	5,000	2,000
Plant and equipment	3,500	2,500
	8,500	4,500
Current Assets		
Inventory	2,500	3,000
Receivables – TUCK	1,100	-
Receivables – others	400	1,000
Bills receivable from TUCK	900	
Bank	100	100
	5,000	4,100
	13,500	8,600
EQUITY AND LIABILITIES		
Capital and Reserves		
€1 ordinary shares	1,000	1,000
Retained earnings	10,000	4,000
	11,000	5,000
Current Liabilities		
Payables	2,500	2,700
Bills payable to NIP	-	900

2,500	3,600
13,500	8,600

Additional Information:

1. On 1 January 2012, NIP issued 900,000 €1 ordinary shares with a market value of €5 per share in return for 900,000 €1 ordinary shares in TUCK when the balance on TUCK's retained earnings was €3,000,000. On that date, the book value and fair value of net assets were the same, except that the property that had a book value of €2,200,000 was valued at €2,700,000. The revaluation has not been incorporated into the books of TUCK. Depreciation is 10% per annum on book value. The investment in TUCK has not yet been incorporated into the books of NIP. With respect to the measurement of non-controlling interests at the date of acquisition, the proportionate share method equates to the fair value method.
2. The inventory of TUCK includes items purchased from NIP for €1,250,000. NIP had made a profit of 25% on cost in respect of these items.
3. One of the products manufactured by NIP has been sold below its cost during the year ended 31 December 2012. Consequently, the directors believe that the plant and equipment used to manufacture this product have suffered a permanent diminution in value. The carrying value, at historical cost, of the plant and equipment at 31 December 2012 is €400,000 and the net realisable value is estimated to be €200,000. The anticipated net cash inflows from this product are expected to be €100,000 per annum for the next four years. (A market discount rate of 10% per annum should be used in any present value computations.)
4. During the year ended 31 December 2011, three people died using machinery manufactured by NIP. Legal proceedings were started in 2011, but NIP did not provide for potential damages at 31 December 2011 on their lawyers' advice that it was unlikely NIP would be found liable. However, by 31 December 2012, NIP's lawyers believe that, owing to developments in the case, it is probable that NIP will be found liable for damages of approximately €2,000,000.

Requirement Prepare the consolidated statement of financial position of NIP Group as at 31 December 2012.

Present value factors:	Years	10%	Cumulative	Years	10%	Cumulative
	1	0.909	0.909	3	0.751	2.487
	2	0.827	1.736	4	0.683	3.170

Question 27.5 *(Based on Chartered Accountants Ireland, P3 Summer 2003, Question 5)*

The statements of financial position of ROCK plc (ROCK) and ROLL plc (ROLL) as at 31 December 2012 are presented below.

	ROCK	ROLL
	€000	€000
ASSETS		
Non-current Assets		
Property, plant and equipment	5,760	4,000

Investment in ROLL	3,330	-
Current Assets	1,260	864
	10,350	4,864
EQUITY AND LIABILITIES		
Capital and Reserves		
€0.50 ordinary shares	2,700	1,600
€1 8% preference shares	-	800
Share premium	810	160
Retained earnings	3,960	904
	7,470	3,464
Non-current Liabilities		
10% debentures 2016	1,800	800
Current Liabilities	1,080	600
	10,350	4,864

Additional Information:

1. On 1 January 2010, ROCK purchased the following shares and debentures in ROLL:
   - 2,400,000 €0.50 ordinary shares;
   - 400,000 8% €1 preference shares;
   - 10% debentures with a nominal value of €320,000.

   The nominal value of ROLL's share capital and debentures has not changed since 1 January 2010. On that date, the share premium account and the retained earnings of ROLL stood at €160,000 credit and €560,000 debit respectively. With respect to the preference shares, there is no contractual right to the dividend and its payment is solely at the discretion of the directors. Consequently, the preference shares are classified as equity rather than debt. With respect to the measurement of non-controlling interests at the date of acquisition, the proportionate share method equated to the fair value method.

2. On 1 January 2010, the property, plant and equipment of ROLL had a fair value of €800,000 in excess of their book values, and a remaining useful economic life of 20 years on this date. This has not yet been reflected in the books of ROLL.

3. During the year ended 31 December 2012, ROCK sold equipment to ROLL for €1,000,000 at a profit of 25% of selling price. ROLL charges a full year's depreciation in the year of acquisition, charging €200,000 depreciation in the year ended 31 December 2012 on the basis that the equipment had a useful economic life of five years.

4. During the year ended 31 December 2012, ROLL paid an interim dividend to its preference and ordinary shareholders of €32,000 and €50,000 respectively. Dividends proposed, but not yet approved, at 31 December 2012 to ROLL's preference and ordinary shareholders amount to €32,000 and €160,000 respectively. At 31 December 2012, ROLL has accrued the debenture interest payable for the period 1 July 2012 to 31 December 2012. ROCK does not accrue dividends or interest receivable.

5. The directors of ROCK believe that the goodwill arising on the acquisition of ROLL was impaired for the first time by €333,000 during the year ended 31 December 2012.

Requirement Prepare the consolidated statement of financial position for the ROCK Group as at 31 December 2012.

CONSOLIDATED STATEMENT OF PROFIT OR LOSS AND OTHER COMPREHENSIVE INCOME

LEARNING OBJECTIVES

This chapter deals with the preparation of a consolidated statement of profit or loss and other comprehensive income. Having studied this chapter, you should be able to:
1. apply the more common consolidation adjustments such as intragroup sales, charges and non-controlling interests;
2. deal with the implications of adjustments in respect of issues such as the revaluation of assets, the acquisition of a subsidiary during the accounting period and the intergroup transfer of tangible non-current assets; and
3. prepare a consolidated statement of profit or loss and other comprehensive income.

KEY TERMS AND DEFINITIONS FOR THIS CHAPTER

In order to aid your understanding of the concepts and issues covered in this chapter, it is important to understand and be familiar with the following key terms and definitions. As you study this chapter, you should refer back to them.

> **Consolidated Financial Statements** The financial statements of a group in which the assets, liabilities, equity, income, expenses and cash flows of the parent and its subsidiaries are presented as those of a single economic entity.

Control of an Investee An investor controls an investee when the investor is exposed to, or has rights to, variable returns from its involvement with the investee and has the ability to affect those returns through its power over the investee.

Intragroup Inventory This is inventory on hand at the reporting date which has been purchased from another group company.

Non-controlling Interest (NCI) This is the portion of the net results and net assets of a subsidiary attributable to interests not owned directly or indirectly by the parent.

Parent An entity that controls one or more entities.

Power Existing rights that give the current ability to direct the relevant activities.

Protective Rights Rights designed to protect the interest of the party holding those rights without giving that party power over the entity to which those rights relate.

Relevant Activities Activities of the investee that significantly affect the investee's returns.

Please note that, as explained in **Chapter 2**, the IASB issued amendments to IAS 1 *Presentation of Financial Statements* in June 2011. These included a *proposal* that the title 'Statement of Profit or Loss and Other Comprehensive Income' (SPLOCI) be adopted (rather than, for example, 'statement of comprehensive income') and a *requirement* to revise the presentation of other comprehensive income (OCI) within the SPLOCI. These amendments are explained in detail in **Chapter 2**, **Section 2.3**.

28.1 INTRODUCTION

Chapters 26 and **27** introduced the key principles associated with the preparation of consolidated financial statements and, in particular, the consolidated statement of financial position. This chapter, while focusing on the preparation of a consolidated statement of profit or loss and other comprehensive income (CSPLOCI), develops these principles further.

Key to this Chapter

While **Chapter 27** focused on the consolidated statement of financial position, this chapter addresses the preparation of a consolidated statement of profit or loss and other comprehensive income. In terms of the format of this chapter, the next section explains how to deal with a number of the most common adjustments which are required when preparing a consolidated statement of profit or loss and other comprehensive income. To facilitate an understanding of how to prepare a consolidated statement of profit or loss and other comprehensive

income, these adjustments are discussed in the following, arguably progressively more difficult, order:
- intragroup sales;
- intragroup inventory;
- intragroup charges;
- non-controlling interests;
- dividends; and
- retained profit brought forward.

Having addressed these adjustments individually, a single comprehensive example illustrates how they might be combined in an examination-type question (**Example 28.5**).

After explaining the 'basics' in **Section 28.2**, a number of more complicated adjustments are described and illustrated in **Section 28.3**. These are:
- revaluation of assets;
- acquisition of a subsidiary during the accounting period;
- unrealised profit in opening inventory;
- pre-acquisition reserves; and
- intragroup transfer of tangible non-current assets.

28.2 COMMON CONSOLIDATION ADJUSTMENTS

It is important to remember that many consolidation adjustments are made *only* for the purposes of preparing consolidated financial statements and often the subsidiary undertaking (for example) will not adjust their own individual financial statements. In this section we will outline the most common adjustments that are required in preparing a consolidated statement of profit or loss and other comprehensive income. These are:
- intragroup sales;
- intragroup inventory;
- intragroup charges;
- non-controlling interest (NCI);
- dividends; and
- retained profit brought forward.

Note: this is not an exhaustive list, and care needs to be taken to identify any other potential adjustments.

Intragroup Sales

It is important to remember that consolidated financial statements report transactions and balances with parties outside the group. However, often companies within a group will sell goods/services to one another. Therefore, when preparing group accounts it is important to remember that these in fact are not sales made by the group as they remain internal. As such, intragroup sales (and purchases and, ultimately, cost of sales) should be eliminated from the consolidated financial statements. **Remember**: as one company's sales are another company's cost of sales, both amounts should be excluded. The elimination of intragroup sales is shown in **Example 28.1**.

EXAMPLE 28.1: INTRAGROUP SALES

A parent company has a 70% interest in a subsidiary. Items in the statements of profit or loss and other comprehensive income of each company included the following:

	Parent €	Subsidiary €
Revenue	800,000	600,000
Cost of Sales	480,000	350,000

These figures include sales from the subsidiary to the parent company of €100,000.

Requirement How much should be included in the consolidated statement of profit or loss and other comprehensive income in respect of the following:
1. Revenue?
2. Cost of Sales?

Solution

The sales from the subsidiary to the parent company are only internal to the group and as such should not be included in revenue in the consolidated statement of profit or loss and other comprehensive income. Consequently, the sales have been recorded as purchases by the parent and these, too, need to be eliminated.

1. Revenue (€800,000 + €600,000 − €100,000) = €1,300,000
2. Cost of Sales (€480,000 + €350,000 − €100,000) = €730,000

Intragroup Inventory

Where **intragroup inventory** (i.e. inventory on hand at the reporting date, which has been purchased from another group company) is held by a group company at the reporting date, any profit element must be excluded. It is necessary to adjust the books of the company that made the unrealised inventory profits, i.e. the selling company. Care must be taken to identify which company made the sale. If the parent company made the sale, then all of the unrealised profit is charged to the parent's books. In contrast, if the subsidiary made the sale, then the unrealised profit is charged between the parent and the subsidiary in their ownership ratio. The issue of intragroup inventory is also discussed in relation to the statement of financial position in **Chapter 27**, **Section 27.9**. **Example 28.2** illustrates the elimination of unrealised inventory profits when the sale is from the parent to the subsidiary.

EXAMPLE 28.2: PARENT TO SUBSIDIARY

In October 2012, Parent Limited sold goods to Subsidiary Limited with an invoice value of €400,000, on which Parent Limited made a mark-up of 25%. One half of these goods remained in Subsidiary Limited's inventory at 31 December 2012. There was no other trading between the two companies during 2012.

Requirement Prepare the adjustments required.

Solution

Inter-company transactions	€000	€000
(a) Sales		
DR Revenue	400	
CR Cost of sales		400
(b) Inventory profit		
DR Cost of sales	40	
CR Inventory		40

Being inventory profit €400,000 × 50% × 25/125

In contrast to the previous example, **Example 28.3** addresses the elimination of unrealised inventory profit when the sale is from the subsidiary to the parent.

EXAMPLE 28.3: SUBSIDIARY TO PARENT

Company A is the parent company of Company B, owning 80%. The year-end is 31 December 2012 and consolidated accounts are to be prepared. The following information is available:

	Company A €	Company B €
Revenue	100,000	80,000
Cost of Sales	60,000	30,000
Inventory on hand 31 December 2012	50,000	30,000

Company B sold to Company A €20,000 of goods during 2012, at a mark-up of 10%. At 31 December 2012, Company A had remaining in inventory €8,000 of these goods.

Requirement Prepare the adjustments required.

Solution

Company B is selling to A at a profit, however this profit is only realised to the group once company A sells the inventory externally. As such, any profit element which is still in inventory needs to be eliminated.

Adjustments:

1. Exclude €20,000 from company B's revenue and company A's purchases, being intragroup sales (DR Sales €20,000 and CR Cost of sales €20,000).
2. Inventory on hand at 31 December 2012 includes €8,000 which was the cost from company B to company A. However, the cost to the group was €8,000 × 100/110 = €7,273. Therefore the profit on the inventory is €727. This is to be eliminated from the group inventory, with consolidated cost of sales being increased by €727 (DR Cost of sales €727, CR Inventory €727). As the sale is from the subsidiary to the parent, the non-controlling interest is charged with their share of the inventory profit i.e. €727 × 20% = €145.40 (DR Cost of sales €727, CR Inventory €727). Therefore group inventory in the consolidated statement of financial position at 31 December 2012 will be stated at €79,273 (i.e. €50,000 + €30,000 − €727).

Intragroup Charges

Continuing with the more common adjustments involved in preparing a consolidated statement of profit or loss and other comprehensive income, the issue of intragroup charges is now highlighted. As all intragroup transactions, together with any resulting profit, should be eliminated, it is necessary to ensure that intragroup management charges, interest on loans, debenture interest and dividends are all cancelled out of group expenses and group income. This is illustrated in **Example 28.5**.

Non-controlling Interests

Non-controlling interests were discussed in detail in **Chapter 27**, **Section 27.5** in relation to the consolidated statement of financial position. The underlying principles are the same in respect of the consolidated statement of profit or loss and other comprehensive income. After 'profit after taxation', it is necessary to calculate the portion of profit of subsidiaries that relates to non-controlling interests (i.e. minority shareholders). The **non-controlling interest** (NCI) in the profit of subsidiary companies is based on the profits after tax of the subsidiaries, after any adjustments required in the particular circumstances that impact on subsidiary profits. For example, unrealised profit on intragroup inventory (see **Example 28.3**).

Ordinary Dividends

It is evident from a number of the issues discussed above (for example, intragroup sales, intragroup inventory, intragroup charges and non-controlling interests) that many of the adjustments often required when preparing a consolidated statement of financial position (see **Chapter 27**) also have implications for the consolidated statement of profit or loss and other comprehensive income. Consistent with this, the matter of ordinary dividends, which was also addressed in **Chapter 27**, **Section 27.6** and **Section 27.7**, is now discussed.

Ordinary dividends are an appropriation of profit and, therefore, should be taken through reserves. Furthermore, proposed ordinary dividends cannot be accrued until approved by shareholders at the annual general meeting (AGM) (see **Chapter 15** and IAS 10 *Events after the Reporting Period*). Dividends declared after the reporting date should only be recognised as liabilities at the reporting date if there is a legal obligation to receive them. Consequently, proposed ordinary dividends may need to be reversed.

With respect to ordinary dividends paid by the subsidiary (S), most is paid to the Parent (P) and is therefore cancelled or eliminated on consolidation. The remainder of S's dividend is paid to the non-controlling interest and is included in the non-controlling interest calculation referred to in the Non-controlling Interest section above.

Note: the presentation of shares (and related dividends) in financial statements can be problematic. As a broad generalisation, an ordinary share, where the shareholder has no contractual right to any form of regular payment of dividends, is classified as equity and any ordinary dividends are presented as a movement through reserves in the statement of changes in equity. However, a preference share, where there is a contractual right to set dividend payments or if shares are redeemable at the option of the

---

holder, will generally be treated as a liability. A grey area is the classification of the 'in-between shares', which may have both equity and liability components. Under IFRS 9 *Financial Instruments* (see **Chapter 25**), these shares should be treated as compound financial instruments with both an equity and liability component and the value of the equity component being the residual amount after deducting the separately determined liability component from the fair value of the instrument as a whole. Presentation in accordance with IFRS 9, therefore, results in substantially all of the **carrying value** of these shares being allocated to the liability component and the 'preference dividend' being treated as a finance cost in arriving at profit/loss for the period in the statement of profit or loss and other comprehensive income.

Retained Earnings Brought Forward

Finally, before combining the various issues discussed so far in a single comprehensive example (see **Example 28.5** below), the issue of consolidated retained earnings is revisited (see **Chapter 27**, **Section 27.4**).

While this figure is not included as part of the consolidated statement of profit or loss and other comprehensive income, it is important to be able to calculate retained earnings brought forward when preparing the consolidated statement of financial position and consolidated statement of changes in equity.

The definition of **retained earnings brought forward** is:
• the retained earnings of the parent at the start of the period; *plus*
• the group's share of the *post-acquisition* earnings of the subsidiary to the start of the period.

This is shown in **Example 28.4**.

EXAMPLE 28.4: RETAINED EARNINGS

Company A acquired 80% of the ordinary shares of Company B on 1 January 2011 when the retained earnings of Company B were €100,000 credit. At 1 January 2012, the retained earnings of the companies were:

A Limited	€800,000
B Limited	€250,000

Requirement Calculate the consolidated retained earnings brought forward in the consolidated statement of changes in equity for the year ended 31 December 2012 at 1 January 2012.

Solution

Company A Limited	€800,000
Company B Limited (80% × (€250,000 − €100,000))	€120,000
	€920,000

After discussing a number of common issues often encountered when preparing a consolidated statement of profit or loss and other comprehensive income, these are combined and presented in a single comprehensive example.

Example 28.5 involves a more detailed question on consolidated statement of profit or loss and other comprehensive income. Read through it carefully and slowly. Remember that *all* intragroup transactions should be eliminated from the consolidated financial statements.

EXAMPLE 28.5: CONSOLIDATED STATEMENT OF PROFIT OR LOSS AND OTHER COMPREHENSIVE INCOME

The draft statements of profit or loss and other comprehensive income of Apple, Pear and Plum Limited for the year ended 31 December 2012 are shown below.

	Apple Limited €	Pear Limited €	Plum Limited €
Revenue	620,000	310,000	280,000
Less: Cost of Sales	492,000	218,000	178,000
Gross Profit	128,000	92,000	102,000
Less: Expenses			
Admin. expenses	37,200	20,000	22,000
Depreciation	10,200	7,800	6,000
Interest on loans	–	1,400	2,000
Debenture interest	–	10,000	–
Selling expenses	53,000	21,000	16,000
	100,400	60,200	46,000
Add: Sundry Income	15,100	2,600	200
Profit before tax	42,700	34,400	56,200
Income tax expense	15,100	12,000	25,000
Profit after tax	27,600	22,400	31,200

Additional Information:

1. Apple Limited purchased the following shares in 2009:
   90,000 ordinary shares €1 each in Pear (total issued: 100,000)
   180,000 ordinary shares €1 each in Plum (total issued: 200,000)
   Apple controls any operating and policy decisions in both Pear and Plum. The retained earnings at the dates of acquisition were:
   Pear   €1,600   Debit
   Plum   €5,800   Credit

2. During 2012, Apple sold goods to Plum for €48,000. Of these, Plum holds goods costing €2,700 at the year-end. Apple makes a 20% gross profit based on cost.

3. The retained earnings of Apple, Pear and Plum are as follows:

	Apple €	Pear €	Plum €
Profit after tax for year ended 31 December 2012	27,600	22,400	31,200
Ordinary dividends paid during year ended 31 December 2012	(10,000)	(2,000)	(3,000)
Retained earnings at 1 January 2012	48,000	16,000	21,000
Retained earnings at 31 December 2012	65,600	36,400	49,200

Dividends received from subsidiaries have been included in the holding company's sundry income.

Requirement Prepare the consolidated statement of profit or loss and other comprehensive income of Apple group for the year ended 31 December 2012.

Solution

1. Group Structure

   Always begin every consolidated account question by drafting a group structure and establishing the type of interest held. In this example, Apple Limited owns 90% of the ordinary shares in both Pear and Plum.

	Pear Ordinary	Plum Ordinary
Group	90%	90%
NCI	10%	10%
	100%	100%
	=> Subsidiary	=> Subsidiary

2. Revenue (Sales)

   It is stated that during 2012 Apple sold goods of €48,000 to Plum. Consequently, the group (as a single entity) has sold goods to itself and has included these in both its sales and cost of sales. Any intragroup revenue therefore must be excluded from both group sales and group cost of sales, thus cancelling the transactions in the consolidated statement of profit or loss and other comprehensive income:

	Apple €	Pear €	Plum €	Adjustment €	Consolidated €
Revenue	620,000	310,000	280,000	(48,000)	1,162,000
Cost of Sales	(492,000)	(218,000)	(178,000)	48,000	(840,000)
Gross Profit	128,000	92,000	102,000	–	322,000

   Note that this adjustment has no profit effect.

3. Unrealised profit in inventory

   It is stated that, of the sales from Apple to Plum, €2,700 are still in Plum's inventory at the year-end. Apple makes 20% profit on cost of all sales. Consequently, the group closing inventory includes a profit element on goods which the group (as a single entity) has not sold.

   The unrealised profit is: €2,700 $\times \dfrac{20}{120}$ = €450

   Closing inventory in the statement of financial position and closing inventory in cost of sales must be reduced in the books of the consolidated accounts to eliminate any unrealised profits included in inventory.

   DR Cost of Sales   €450
   CR Inventory   €450

   This adjustment of €450 is made in the column of the company whose individual statement of profit or loss and other comprehensive income includes the unrealised profit (i.e. the selling company). In this case, the goods were sold by Apple to Plum. Apple has made a 'notional' or unrealised profit from a group point of view as a result of this transaction and, consequently, it is in Apple's column that the adjustment is made.

	Apple €	Pear €	Plum €	Adjustment €	Consolidated €
Revenue	620,000	310,000	280,000	(48,000)	1,162,000
Draft Cost of Sales	(492,000)	(218,000)	(178,000)		
Inventory adjustment	(450)	–	–	–	–
	(492,450)	(218,000)	(178,000)	48,000	(840,450)
Gross Profit	127,550	92,000	102,000	–	321,550

Note: the group's gross profit has been reduced by €450. The other side of this entry is statement of financial position inventory being reduced by €450.

4. Intragroup dividends
Apple has received its share of the subsidiary dividends:

		€
Pear	90% × €2,000	1,800
Plum	90% × €3,000	2,700
		4,500

These dividends have to be excluded from the holding company's income in the consolidated statement of profit or loss and other comprehensive income.

	€
Sundry income per Apple accounts	15,100
Less: dividends from subsidiaries	(4,500)
Sundry income for consolidations	10,600

	Apple €	Pear €	Plum €	Adjustment €	Consolidated €
Gross profit	127,550	92,000	102,000	–	321,550
Less expenses	(100,400)	(60,200)	(46,000)	–	(206,600)
Add income	10,600	2,600	200	–	13,400
Profit before tax	37,750	34,400	56,200	–	128,350
Income tax expense	(15,100)	(12,000)	(25,000)	–	(52,100)
Profit after tax	22,650	22,400	31,200	–	76,250

5. Non-controlling interests
At this stage, it is necessary to recognise the fact that, although Apple has control over the activities of the companies in the group, it does *not* have legal title to 100% of the shares and consequently to all the profits. It is necessary, therefore, to calculate and show the amount of the 'Profit after tax' which is attributable to the non-controlling interest.

(a) Pear: Profit after tax   €22,400
                                    × 10%
         Non-controlling interest   €2,240

(b) Plum: Profit after tax   €31,200
                                      × 10%
         Non-controlling interest   €3,120

	Apple €	Pear €	Plum €	Adjustment €	Total €
Profit after tax	22,650	22,400	31,200	–	76,250
Non-controlling interest	–	(2,240)	(3,120)	–	(5,360)
Group profit	22,650	20,160	28,080		70,890

6. Dividend shuffle
Remember dividends paid are debited directly to equity. As can be seen from the question, the group embarked on a policy of transferring profits from the subsidiaries to the holding company by paying dividends. This must be reflected in the consolidated retained earnings by 'shuffling' the dividend from one company to another.

	Apple €	Pear €	Plum €	Consolidated €
Profit attributable to the group	22,650	20,160	28,080	70,890
Pear – ordinary dividend	1,800	(1,800)	–	–
Plum – ordinary dividend	2,700	–	(2,700)	–
	27,150	18,360	25,380	70,890

Note: this must come out to be zero, i.e. it makes no difference to the total profit attributable to the group.

7. Parent company dividend
Again, remember that the parent company's dividend should be shown as a movement in retained earnings and should be subtracted after the dividend shuffle has been completed.

8. Reserves brought forward
The reserves in the subsidiaries, when Apple purchased the shares, were:
Pear   €1,600   Debit
Plum   €5,800   Credit

Two points must be noted here:
(a) pre-acquisition reserves must be excluded from the consolidated accounts; and
(b) only the group share is included.

	Pear €	Plum €
Reserves b/f	16,000	21,000
Pre-acquisition reserves	1,600	(5,800)
Post-acquisition reserves	17,600	15,200
	× 90%	× 90%
Group share only	15,840	13,680

The consolidated retained earnings can now be completed:

	Apple €	Pear €	Plum €	Consolidated €
Profit attributable to the group	22,650	20,160	28,080	70,890
Intragroup dividend	4,500	(1,800)	(2,700)	–

Parent dividend	(10,000)			(10,000)
	17,150	18,360	25,380	60,890
Reserves b/f	48,000	15,840	13,680	77,520
Reserves c/f	65,150	34,200	39,060	138,410

Your final consolidated statement of profit or loss and other comprehensive income workings should look like this:

	Apple €	Pear €	Plum €	Adj. €	Consol. €
Revenue	620,000	310,000	280,000	(48,000)	1,162,000
Draft Cost of sales	492,000	218,000	178,000		
Inventory adjustment	450				
	(492,450)	(218,000)	(178,000)	(48,000)	(840,450)
Gross profit	127,550	92,000	102,000	–	321,550
Administration expenses	37,200	20,000	22,000		79,200
Depreciation	10,200	7,800	6,000		24,000
Interest on loans		1,400	2,000		3,400
Debenture Interest					10,000
Selling expenses	53,000	21,000	16,000		90,000
	(100,400)	(60,200)	(46,000)	–	(206,600)
Sundry income	10,600	2,600	200		13,400
Profit before tax	37,750	34,400	56,200		128,350
Income tax expense	(15,100)	(12,000)	(25,000)		(52,100)
Profit after tax	22,650	22,400	31,200		76,250
Non-controlling interest	–	(2,240)	(3,120)		(5,360)
Group profit	22,650	20,160	28,080		69,990
Reserves b/f	48,000	15,840	13,680		77,520
Intragroup dividends	4,500	(1,800)	(2,700)		–
Dividends – Apple	(10,000)	–	–		(10,000)
Reserves c/f	65,150	34,200	39,060		138,410

The final solution, albeit not in a form suitable for publication, will look as follows:

Apple Limited
ABBREVIATED CONSOLIDATED STATEMENT OF PROFIT OR LOSS AND OTHER
COMPREHENSIVE INCOME
For Year Ended 31 December 2012

	Notes	€
Revenue	(x)	1,162,000
Profit before tax	(3)	128,350
Income tax expense	(x)	(52,100)
Profit on ordinary activities after tax		76,250

Non-controlling interest		(5,360)
Profit attributable to the group	(5)	70,890
Reserves brought forward		77,520
Dividends paid		(10,000)
Reserves carried forward		138,410

Note: for ease of illustration, reserves brought forward and dividends paid are shown at the foot of the consolidated statement of profit or loss and other comprehensive income. These figures are presented in the consolidated statement of changes in equity.

(3) Profit on ordinary activities is arrived at after charging:

	€
Directors' remuneration (say, for example)	7,000
Depreciation	24,000
Interest on loans	3,400
Debenture interest	10,000

(5) Of this amount, €27,600 is dealt with in the books of the holding company.

28.3 OTHER ADJUSTMENTS

Section 28.2 focused on the more common adjustments encountered when preparing a consolidated statement of profit or loss and other comprehensive income. However, it may be necessary to deal with the implications of adjustments, other than those outlined in **Section 28.2**, when preparing a consolidated statement of profit or loss and other comprehensive income. These include:
- revaluation of assets;
- acquisition of a subsidiary during the accounting period;
- unrealised profit in opening inventory;
- pre-acquisition reserves; and
- intragroup transfer of tangible non-current assets.

Revaluation of Assets

When a holding company purchases the shares of a subsidiary, the net assets of the subsidiary must be included in the consolidated statement of financial position at their fair value at the date of acquisition. This revaluation to fair value is a consolidation adjustment only, i.e. the subsidiary does not (although it may) record the necessary revaluation journal in its own books and records. Consequently, the revaluation of the net assets to their fair values can be accounted for in either:
- the books of the subsidiary (before consolidation takes place); or
- as a consolidation adjustment.

If the revaluation is accounted for in the books of the subsidiary, then no further consolidation adjustment is required.

If, however, no entries have been posted to the subsidiary's books (as is usually the case in questions), the revaluations will need to be incorporated into the consolidated financial statements. This may have an effect on the consolidated statement of profit or loss and other comprehensive income. For example, in respect of non-current assets, the depreciation charge in the subsidiary's accounts will be based on the carrying value in the subsidiary's books. Since these non-current assets will require a revaluation adjustment, a revised depreciation charge (either upwards or downwards) will have to be computed based on the revalued amount.

Acquisition of a Subsidiary during the Accounting Period

Where a subsidiary is acquired during an accounting period, the pre-acquisition profits of that subsidiary must be excluded from the consolidated statement of profit or loss and other comprehensive income. This effectively requires the calculation of the proportion of each item in the statement of profit or loss and other comprehensive income of the subsidiary for the current year that accrued before and after the date of acquisition. Only items after the date of acquisition should be included in the consolidated statement of profit or loss and other comprehensive income.

The pre- and post-acquisition elements are generally calculated on:
• a time-apportioned basis (e.g. revenue);
• an actual basis (e.g. exceptional items); or
• a combination of the two.

> *Note:* unless the basis to be applied in the exam is stated, a time-apportioned basis will be appropriate for all items. For an acquisition during an accounting period, the statement of profit or loss and other comprehensive income should be time-apportioned (but not the statement of financial position – **remember** this is the position at the end of the accounting period).

Accounting for the acquisition of a subsidiary during the accounting period in the consolidated statement of profit or loss and other comprehensive income is shown in **Example 28.6**.

EXAMPLE 28.6: ACQUISITION DURING THE ACCOUNTING PERIOD

STATEMENT OF PROFIT OR LOSS AND OTHER COMPREHENSIVE INCOME
for the Year Ended 31 December 2012

	P Limited €	S Limited €
Profit before taxation	100,000	60,000
Income tax expense	45,000	27,000
Profit after taxation	55,000	33,000

P Limited acquired 80% of S Limited on 30 April 2012.

Additional information on specific items in the newly acquired subsidiary's statement of profit or loss and other comprehensive income is as follows:

1. Revenue and expenses
   The amount will include only the subsidiary's post-acquisition revenue and expenses (generally time-apportioned).

2. Profit before taxation
   This will include only the post-acquisition results of the subsidiary (generally time-apportioned):

   $$= €60,000 \times \frac{8}{12} = €40,000.$$

3. Disclosure items relating to profit before taxation
   In relation to depreciation, auditors' remuneration and interest payable, they should be apportioned on a time basis and only the post-acquisition element should be included in the consolidated statement of profit or loss and other comprehensive income.

4. Income tax expense
   The taxation charge will include only the subsidiary's post-acquisition taxation charge (generally time-apportioned):

   $$= €27,000 \times \frac{8}{12} = €18,000.$$

Requirement Prepare the consolidated statement of profit or loss and other comprehensive income for the year ended 31 December 2012.

Solution

	P Limited €	S Limited €	Consolidated €
Profit before taxation	100,000	40,000	140,000
Income tax expense	45,000	18,000	63,000
Profit after taxation	55,000	22,000	77,000
Non-controlling interests	–	4,400	4,400
	55,000	17,600	72,600

1. Non-controlling interests
   The non-controlling interest share will be based on the (already calculated) post-acquisition profit after tax figure. Attention is brought to the fact that this profit figure has already been time-apportioned, thus further time-apportioning of the non-controlling interest figure itself would not be appropriate.
2. Subsidiary dividends
   Subsidiary dividends in the year of acquisition must be time-apportioned to ensure that only the post-acquisition element is included in the dividend shuffle. The remaining element (i.e. the pre-acquisition dividend) is excluded from the dividend shuffle (see **Chapter 27**).
3. Retained profits brought forward
   Since the subsidiary was acquired during the year, all the retained profits brought forward in relation to the subsidiary must be eliminated since they are all pre-acquisition. This will be reflected in the consolidated statement of changes in equity.

Unrealised Profit in Opening Inventory

An adjustment may be required to reduce opening inventory where, at the beginning of the year, one company's inventory included goods purchased from another company in the group. In this case, the adjustment required will reduce opening inventory in cost of sales and will reduce opening reserves carried forward, by the unrealised profit element. Remember that the adjustment should be made in the appropriate company's column (i.e. the company carrying the profit). The issue of unrealised profit in opening inventory is presented in **Example 28.7**.

EXAMPLE 28.7: UNREALISED PROFIT IN OPENING INVENTORY

The following are the statements of profit or loss and other comprehensive income for each of the companies in PKF Group Limited for the year ended 31 December 2012.

	P Limited €	K Limited €	F Limited €
Revenue	100,000	50,000	20,000
Cost of sales	75,000	43,000	9,000
Gross profit	25,000	7,000	11,000
Administration expenses	5,000	6,000	3,000
Net profit	20,000	1,000	8,000
Balance at 1 January 2012	30,000	8,500	2,500
	50,000	9,500	10,500

1. P Limited sold F Limited €10,000 worth of goods during the year at a mark-up on cost of 25%.
2. F Limited had inventory goods purchased from P Limited:

	€
1 January 2012	2,000
31 December 2012	3,500

3. P Limited purchased 100% of F Limited and 80% of K Limited some years ago, when the balances of their retained profits were as follows:

	€
K Limited	Debit 2,000
F Limited	Credit 1,000

Requirement Prepare the consolidated statement of profit or loss and other comprehensive income workings for PKF Group Limited for the year ended 31 December 2012.

Solution

WORKINGS
1. Group Structure

	K Limited	F Limited
Group	80%	100%
NCI	20%	-
	100%	100%

2. Inventory adjustments

Opening group inventory and opening group reserves are overstated by the profit element of €2,000 × 25/125 = €400.

Closing group inventory and closing group reserves are overstated by the profit element €3,500 × 25/125 = €700.

3. Profit brought forward

	P Limited €	K Limited €	F Limited €
Reserves brought forward	30,000	8,500	2,500
Pre-acquisition reserves	-	2,000	(1,000)
Post-acquisition reserves	30,000	10,500	1,500
		× 80%	× 100%
Group share only	30,000	8,400	1,500
Less: Unrealised profit in opening inventory	(400)	–	–
	29,600	8,400	1,500

4. Consolidation workings

	P Limited €	K Limited €	F Limited €	Adjustment €	Consol. €
Revenue	100,000	50,000	20,000	(10,000)	160,000
Draft cost of sales	75,000	43,000	9,000	(10,000)	117,000
Less: Op. inventory adj.	(400)				(400)
Add: Cl. inventory adj.	700				700
Cost of sales	75,300	43,000	9,000	(10,000)	117,300
Gross profit	24,700	7,000	11,000		42,700
Administrative exp.	5,000	6,000	3,000	–	14,000
Net profit	19,700	1,000	8,000	–	28,700
Non-controlling interest	–	(200)	–	–	(200)
Profit att. to the Group	19,700	800	8,000	–	28,500
Reserves b/f	29,600	8,400	1,500		39,500
Reserves c/f	49,300	9,200	9,500	–	68,000

Pre-acquisition Reserves

A fundamental principle that must always be remembered in consolidated accounts is that any reserves a subsidiary owned prior to the acquisition of the shares by the parent are not part of the group reserves and thus must be excluded from the reserves of the group in the consolidated accounts. Effectively, this means that the pre-acquisition reserves of a subsidiary are 'frozen'.

However, as explained in **Chapter 27 (Section 27.7)**, IAS 27 *Separate Financial Statements* states that an entity shall recognise a dividend from a subsidiary, jointly controlled entity or associate in arriving at profit or loss in its separate financial statements when its right to receive the dividend is established. Therefore, this effectively removes the pre-/post-acquisition distinction with respect to dividends paid by a subsidiary, as IAS 27 allows an entity to recognise a dividend paid from pre-acquisition profits from a subsidiary in arriving at profit or loss in its separate financial statements (albeit this is at variance with company law).

Intragroup Transfer of Tangible Non-current Assets (Property, plant and equipment)

In Apple Limited (see **Section 28.3**), it is illustrated that where inventory has been transferred (at cost plus profit) from one group company to another, and a portion of these goods is still included in the year-end inventory of the receiving company, then the unrealised profit element on these inventory must be excluded from the consolidated accounts. Consequently, an adjustment was made to reduce the value of closing inventory included in the consolidated statement of profit or loss and other comprehensive income and consolidated statement of financial position by the unrealised profit element. Note that this adjustment was made in the column of the company whose individual statement of profit or loss and other comprehensive income included the unrealised profit.

Similar treatment should be applied to a situation where a group company transfers tangible non-current assets to another company at a profit. An adjustment is required to cancel any unrealised profit on such assets held at the year-end:

DR Profit on sale of non-current assets	Statement of profit or loss and other comprehensive income	X
CR Non-current assets	Statement of financial position	X

An additional problem arises, however, in the area of tangible non-current assets, in that depreciation charges to the statement of profit or loss and other comprehensive income would be based on the 'incorrect' inflated non-current asset value. Consequently, an additional journal entry is required to reduce the depreciation charge to its correct amount so that it is based on original cost to the group:

DR Accumulation depreciation	Statement of financial position	X
CR Depreciation charge	Statement of profit or loss and other comprehensive income	X

As in the case of unrealised profits in inventory, any adjustments correcting unrealised tangible non-current asset profits are made in the column of the company whose individual statement of profit or loss and other comprehensive income included the unrealised profit, i.e. the seller of the asset. However, any depreciation adjustment must be made in the column of the company now charging the depreciation, i.e. the buyer of the asset.

Prior to posting the correcting consolidated journals, it is vital to establish when the transfer of the tangible non-current assets took place:
- in the current period; or
- in a previous period.

If the transfer took place in the current year, then the current year's consolidated statement of profit or loss and other comprehensive income will require adjustment with respect to:
- the profit on sale of tangible current assets; and
- the depreciation charges.

If the transfer took place in a previous period, then reserves brought forward will require adjustment with respect to:
- the profit on sale of tangible non-current assets; and
- the depreciation charges of previous periods since the transfer.

Additionally, in such a case, note again the company column in which to make each adjustment:
- elimination of profit – seller;
- correction of depreciation – buyer.

In such a case the current year's consolidated statement of profit or loss and other comprehensive income will require an adjustment with respect to the current year depreciation charge.

28.4 CONCLUSION

The preparation of a consolidated statement of profit or loss and other comprehensive income is summarised in **Table 28.1** below, where the following abbreviations are used:

P   =   Parent
S   =   Subsidiary
IG =   Intragroup items

TABLE 28.1: PRO FORMA CONSOLIDATED STATEMENT OF PROFIT OR LOSS AND OTHER COMPREHENSIVE INCOME

Item	Computation
1. Revenue	P + S minus IG
2. Cost of sales	P + S minus IG + unrealised inventory profit
3. All expenses	P + S ± any adjustments in question, such as extra or over-depreciation
4. Investment income	Only dividends received from outside the group
5. Income tax expenses	P + S
6. Non-controlling interest	S profit after taxation as adjusted.
7. Transfers to reserve	P + group's share of S
8. Retained profit brought forward	P + group's share of S's post-acquisition profits

Remember ordinary dividends are an appropriation of profits and should be taken through reserves.

SUMMARY OF LEARNING OBJECTIVES

This chapter deals with the preparation of a consolidated statement of profit or loss and other comprehensive income. Having studied this chapter, you should be able to:

Learning Objective 1 Apply the more common consolidation adjustments such as intragroup sales, charges and non-controlling interests.

Adjustments in respect of intragroup sales, intragroup inventory, intragroup charges, non-controlling interests, dividends and retained profit brought forward are explained individually in **Section 28.2**, and then illustrated in a single comprehensive example (**Example 28.5**).

Learning Objective 2 Deal with the implications of adjustments in respect of issues such as the revaluation of assets, the acquisition of a subsidiary during the accounting period and the intragroup transfer of tangible non-current assets.

A number of more complicated adjustments are described and illustrated in **Section 28.3**. These include: revaluation of assets; acquisition of a subsidiary during the accounting period; unrealised profit in opening inventory; pre-acquisition reserves; and intragroup transfer of tangible non-current assets.

Learning Objective 3 Prepare a consolidated statement of profit or loss and other comprehensive income.

An understanding of the different adjustments addressed in Learning Objectives 1 and 2 facilitates the preparation of a consolidated statement of profit or loss and other comprehensive income.

QUESTIONS

Self-test Questions

1. List and explain six of the most common adjustments typically encountered in the preparation of a consolidated statement of profit or loss and other comprehensive income.
2. Explain how the following issues should be dealt with when preparing a consolidated statement of profit or loss and other comprehensive income:
   (a) Revaluation of assets;
   (b) Acquisition of a subsidiary during the accounting period;
   (c) Opening unrealised inventory profit;
   (d) Pre-acquisition reserves; and
   (e) Intragroup transfer of tangible non-current assets.

Note: for ease of illustration, dividends and retained earnings are often shown at the foot of the statement of profit or loss and other comprehensive income in questions. These figures would normally be included in the statement of changes in equity.

Review Questions

(See **Appendix One** for Suggested Solutions to Review Questions.)

Question 28.1

X Limited owns 90% of the ordinary share capital of Y Limited. The statements of profit or loss and other comprehensive income for X Limited and Y Limited are as follows for the year ended 31 December 2012:

	X Limited €	Y Limited €
Revenue	10,000	7,000
Cost of sales	(6,000)	(1,000)

Gross profit	4,000	6,000
Administration expenses	(500)	(600)
Depreciation	(1,000)	(1,200)
Profit before tax	2,500	4,200
Income tax expense	(400)	(100)
Profit after tax	2,100	4,100
Reserves brought forward	10,000	7,000
Reserves carried forward	12,100	11,100

Additional Information:

1. X Limited purchased the shares in Y Limited on 1 January 2008, at which time Y Limited's statement of financial position contained:

		€
Retained earnings		3,000
Property, plant and equipment	Cost	12,000
	Fair value	15,000

With respect to the measurement of non-controlling interests at the date of acquisition, the proportionate share method equated to the fair value method.

2. Property, plant and equipment are depreciated at 10% straight-line. The assets in Y Limited were not revalued to fair value at the date of acquisition by X Limited.

Requirement Draft the consolidated statement of profit or loss and other comprehensive income for the year ended 31 December 2012.

Question 28.2

The statements of profit or loss and other comprehensive income of C Limited and A Limited are as follows for the year ended 31 December 2012.

	C	A
	€	€
Net profit	10,000	5,000
Income tax expense	1,000	1,000
Profit after tax	9,000	4,000
Balance brought forward	15,000	6,000
Balance carried forward	24,000	10,000

Additional Information:

1. C Limited purchased 60% of the ordinary share capital of A Limited on 1 January 2009 when the retained profit was a debit balance of €3,000.
2. Included in the net assets of A Limited taken over were tangible non-current assets with a book value of €12,000. At 1 January 2009, the fair value of these assets was €15,000.
3. A Limited depreciates all its tangible non-current assets on a 20% reducing balance basis, and carries all assets at cost.
4. With respect to the measurement of non-controlling interests at the date of acquisition, the proportionate share method equated to the fair value method.

Requirement Draft the consolidated workings for the CA Group for the year ended 31 December 2012.

Question 28.3

The statements of profit or loss and other comprehensive income of X Limited and Y Limited are as follows for the year ended 31 December 2012:

	X Limited	Y Limited
	€	€
Revenue	10,000	7,000
Cost of sales	(6,000)	(1,000)
Gross profit	4,000	6,000
Administration expenses	(1,000)	(500)
Distribution costs	–	(700)
Profit before tax	3,000	4,800
Income tax expense	(500)	(300)
Profit after tax	2,500	4,500

Additional Information:

1. X Limited purchased 9,000 of the 10,000 €1 ordinary shares in issue of Y Limited on 28 February 2012. With respect to the measurement of non-controlling interests at the date of acquisition, the proportionate share method equated to the fair value method.
2. The distribution costs in the statement of profit or loss and other comprehensive income of Y Limited were incurred in November 2012.
3. During the year ended 31 December 2012, X Limited and Y Limited proposed, approved and paid ordinary dividends of €200 and €4,000 respectively. X Limited has not yet accounted for ordinary dividends received from Y Limited.
4. Retained earnings of X Limited and Y Limited are as follows:

	X Limited	Y Limited
	€	€
Profit after tax	2,500	4,500
Retained earnings b/f	10,000	8,000
Ordinary dividends	(200)	(4,000)
Retained earnings at 31 December 2012	12,300	8,500

Requirement Prepare the consolidated statement of profit or loss and other comprehensive income for the year ended 31 December 2012.

Question 28.4

Extracts from the statements of profit or loss and other comprehensive income for the year ended 31 December 2012 of P Limited and S Limited show the following:

	€	€
	P Limited	S Limited
Gross profit	10,000	6,000
Administration expenses	(1,000)	(2,000)

Profit on sale of tangible non-current assets	2,000	–
Depreciation	(4,000)	(375)
Profit before tax	7,000	3,625
Income tax expense	(1,000)	(1,500)
Profit after tax	6,000	2,125

Additional Information:
1. P Limited owns 75% of the equity share capital of S Limited.
2. The profit on sale of tangible non-current assets in P Limited arose as a result of a transfer of a part of its plant and machinery to S Limited on 30 June 2012.

	€
Cost to P Limited	10,000
Accumulated depreciation 30 June 2012	4,500
Net book value	5,500
Value transferred to S Limited	7,500
Profit on transfer	2,000

S Limited had no non-current assets prior to 30 June 2012 and has not acquired/disposed of any since. The group's policy is to depreciate plant at 10% on cost on a month-by-month basis. S Limited has, however, been calculating depreciation on the transferred asset at 10% of the transfer value on a month-by-month basis.

Requirement Draft the consolidated statement of profit or loss and other comprehensive income for the year ended 31 December 2012.

Challenging Questions

(Suggested Solutions to Challenging Questions are available to lecturers.)

Question 28.1 (Based on Chartered Accountants Ireland, P3 Autumn 2002, Question 4)

The draft statements of profit or loss and other comprehensive income of ARK Limited (ARK), BOAT Limited (BOAT) and CANOE Limited (CANOE) for the year ended 31 December 2012 are as follows:

	ARK €m	BOAT €m	CANOE €m
Turnover	2,100	1,260	1,680
Cost of sales	(840)	(504)	(630)
Gross profit	1,260	756	1,050
Other operating expenses	(630)	(378)	(546)
Operating profit	630	378	504
Investment income	126	–	–
Interest payable and similar charges	(252)	(126)	(168)
Profit before tax	504	252	336
Taxation	(168)	(62)	(118)
Profit after tax	336	190	218
Dividends paid	(210)	(106)	(168)

Retained profit for the year	126	84	50
Retained profit at 1 January 2012	1,050	690	195
Retained profit at 31 December 2012	1,176	774	245

Additional Information:

1. On 1 January 2006, ARK purchased 160 million €1 ordinary shares in BOAT for €500 million. The net assets of BOAT at 1 January 2006 comprised:

	€m
€1 ordinary shares	200
Retained earnings	325
	525

There was no difference between the book value of BOAT's net assets and their fair value at 1 January 2006.

2. On 1 July 2012, ARK purchased 180 million €1 ordinary shares in CANOE for €458 million. The net assets of CANOE at 1 January 2012 comprised:

	€m
€1 ordinary shares	240
Retained earnings	195
	435

There was no difference between the book value of CANOE's net assets and their fair value at 1 July 2012.

3. On 1 July 2012, ARK sold its entire investment in BOAT for €950 million in cash, incurring a tax liability of €50 million in connection with the sale. ARK has not yet accounted for the effects of the sale. On 1 July 2012, the goodwill arising on the acquisition of BOAT was carried at €32 million. (*Note:* the disposal of subsidiaries is dealt with in **Chapter 32**.)

4. In December 2012, ARK sold raw materials to CANOE for €30 million, making a profit of €10 million. These raw materials are included at invoice value in the inventory of CANOE at 31 December 2012.

5. It is group policy to charge all of any profit or loss arising on intragroup sales against group reserves.

Requirement Prepare the consolidated statement of profit or loss and other comprehensive income of ARK Group for the year ended 31 December 2012, **starting with profit before tax and ending with retained profit at 31 December 2012**, having regard to the fact that ARK does not propose to publish its own statement of profit or loss and other comprehensive income.

Note: you may assume that transactions accrue evenly throughout the year.

Question 28.2 (Based on Chartered Accountants Ireland, P3 Autumn 2004, Question 1)

You are the financial accountant of WORK plc (WORK), a company that prepares its financial statements to 31 December each year. WORK has investments in two companies, REST Limited (REST) and PLAY Limited (PLAY). The draft statements of profit or loss and other comprehensive income of these three companies for the year ended 31 December 2012 are as follows:

	WORK €000	REST €000	PLAY €000
Revenue	75,000	64,000	14,000
Cost of sales	(37,500)	(32,000)	(7,000)
Gross profit	37,500	32,000	7,000
Other operating expenses	(20,000)	(16,000)	(3,000)
Operating profit	17,500	16,000	4,000
Investment income	2,000	–	–
Interest payable	(2,500)	(1,000)	(500)
Profit before taxation	17,000	15,000	3,500
Taxation	(4,250)	(3,500)	(875)
Profit after taxation	12,750	11,500	2,625
Dividends paid	(2,750)	–	(2,000)
Retained profit for the year	10,000	11,500	625
Retained profit at start of year	20,000	15,500	14,375
Retained profit at end of year	30,000	27,000	15,000

Additional Information:

1. On 1 January 2007, WORK purchased 80% of the ordinary share capital of REST for €7,500,000. The fair value of the net assets of REST was the same as their book value on that date. The statement of financial position of REST on 1 January 2007 showed:

	€000
€1 ordinary share capital	1,000
Retained earnings	4,000
	5,000

2. On 1 January 2012, WORK purchased 100% of the ordinary share capital of PLAY for €10,500,000. The statement of financial position of PLAY on that date showed:

	€000		€000
Property, plant and equipment	6,000	€1 ordinary share capital	1,625
Inventory	10,000	Retained earnings	14,375
	16,000		16,000

The fair value of the net assets of PLAY was the same as their book value on the acquisition date. Property, plant and equipment are depreciated over six years. During 2012, 50% of the inventory was sold outside the Group on normal trading terms, with the remaining inventory to be sold in 2013.

3. On 30 September 2012, WORK disposed of the whole of its investment in REST for €30,000,000. The taxation payable in connection with the disposal is €1,000,000. The effect of the disposal has not yet been incorporated into the statement of profit or loss and other comprehensive income of WORK. The activities of REST are similar to

WORK and the directors of WORK believe that the performance of the Group will not be materially affected following the disposal of REST. (***Note:*** the disposal of subsidiaries is dealt with in **Chapter 32**.)

4. During the year ended 31 December 2012, PLAY sold raw materials to WORK at original cost plus a mark-up of 25%. At 31 December 2012, half of the raw materials sold to WORK, at a cost of €120,000, remained in WORK's inventory.

5. WORK charges PLAY a management fee of €50,000 per annum. The charge is included in the revenue of WORK and the other operating expenses of PLAY.

6. There is no evidence that any goodwill arising on the acquisition of REST and PLAY has ever been impaired.

Requirement Prepare the consolidated statement of profit or loss and other comprehensive income of the WORK Group for the year ended 31 December 2012.

Question 28.3 *(Based on Chartered Accountants Ireland, P3 Autumn 2005, Question 6)*

MARBLE plc (MARBLE) purchased 36,000,000 of the 45,000,000 €1 ordinary shares in FALLS Limited (FALLS) on 1 April 2012 for €200,000,000. The statements of profit or loss and other comprehensive income of both companies for the year ended 31 December 2012 are as follows:

STATEMENT OF PROFIT OR LOSS AND OTHER COMPREHENSIVE INCOME
for the Year Ended 31 December 2012

	MARBLE	FALLS
	€000	€000
Revenue	900,000	250,000
Cost of sales	(720,000)	(180,000)
Gross profit	180,000	70,000
Other operating expenses	(30,000)	(20,000)
Operating profit	150,000	50,000
Interest payable and similar charges	(10,000)	(4,000)
Profit on ordinary activities before taxation	140,000	46,000
Income tax expense	(35,000)	(12,000)
Profit on ordinary activities after taxation	105,000	34,000
Retained profit at start of year	210,000	80,000
Retained profit at end of year	315,000	114,000

Additional Information:

1. The only fair value adjustment that is required in respect of the acquisition of FALLS relates to a building, the details of which are as follows:

	€000
Cost	100,000
Accumulated depreciation at 1 January 2012	(8,000)
Net book value at 1 January 2012	92,000

The building, which had a useful economic life of 25 years on 1 January 2010, is in a prime commercial location and has increased dramatically in value since it was purchased

by FALLS on 1 January 2010. The replacement cost of a similar building, with a similar remaining useful economic life at 1 April 2012, is €161,000,000.
2. The activities of both companies occur evenly throughout the year. In June 2012, MARBLE sold goods to FALLS for €30,000,000, and one-third of these goods remained unsold at 31 December 2012. MARBLE marks up the cost of goods sold by 25%.
3. Both MARBLE and FALLS charge depreciation on a time-apportionment basis to net operating expenses. The directors of MARBLE believe that the goodwill arising on the acquisition of FALLS has been impaired by €2,910,000 at 31 December 2012.

Requirement Prepare the consolidated statement of profit or loss and other comprehensive income of MARBLE Group for the year ended 31 December 2012.

Question 28.4

The statements of profit or loss and other comprehensive income of P Limited and its subsidiaries, S Limited and T Limited, for the year ending 31 December 2012 are as follows:

	P Limited €	S Limited €	T Limited €
Profit before items set out hereunder	298,500	120,000	90,000
Income from quoted investment	1,200	1,500	–
Dividends receivable			
From S Limited	19,200	–	–
From T Limited	13,500	–	–
	332,400	121,500	90,000
Administrative expenses	(45,000)	(16,500)	(21,000)
Profit before tax	287,400)	105,000	69,000
Income tax expense	105,000	48,000	30,000
Profit after taxation	182,400	57,000	39,000

Additional Information:
1. P Limited owns 80% of the ordinary shares of S Limited and 75% of the ordinary shares of T Limited. With respect to the measurement of non-controlling interests at the date of acquisition, the proportionate share method equated to the fair value method.
2. At the date of acquisition of the shares by P Limited the balances of retained profits were:
   (i) S Limited €4,500 credit; and
   (ii) T Limited €1,830 debit.
3. Included in P Limited's profit is €15,000 from sale of goods to S Limited. Of these goods, S Limited still has in inventory on 31 December 2012 goods invoiced at €3,000. All goods sold by P Limited produce a profit of 25% on the selling price.
4. During the year ended 31 December 2012, P Limited, S Limited and T Limited paid dividends of €60,000, €24,000 and €18,000 respectively.
5. Retained earnings at 31 December 2011 were as follows:

P Limited €	S Limited €	T Limited €
25,950	12,600	11,250

Requirement Prepare the consolidated statement of profit or loss and other comprehensive income of P Limited for the year ending 31 December 2012 in a form suitable for publication.

Question 28.5

BACK plc (BACK) prepares its financial statements to 31 December each year. On 1 January 2012, BACK acquired 90% of the ordinary share capital of FRONT Limited (FRONT) at a cost of €3,808,000. The draft statements of profit or loss and other comprehensive income of BACK and FRONT for the year ended 31 December 2012 are as follows:

	BACK	FRONT
	€000	€000
Revenue	90,000	7,800
Cost of sales	(60,000)	(4,900)
Gross profit	30,000	2,900
Operating expenses	(9,900)	(760)
Operating profit	20,100	2,140
Finance costs	(160)	(40)
Interest receivable	80	20
Profit before tax	20,020	2,120
Income tax expense	(6,420)	(400)
Profit after tax	13,600	1,720

Additional Information:
1. The net assets of FRONT on 1 January 2012 were as follows:

	Carrying value	Fair value
	€000	€000
Property, plant and equipment	2,400	2,240
Inventory	1,200	1,040
Other net assets	640	640
	4,240	3,920

The difference between the carrying value and the fair value of property, plant and equipment is due to a revaluation of property, while the reduction in inventory relates to a fair value adjustment in order to bring FRONT's inventory into line with those of BACK. Otherwise the accounting policies adopted by FRONT are similar to those of BACK. The required change in the closing inventory value of FRONT to ensure uniform accounting policies is a decrease of €120,000. The fair values shown above have not yet been incorporated into FRONT's financial statements.

2. Following the acquisition of shares in FRONT, the directors of BACK decided to run down certain parts of BACK's business activities. These were finally discontinued in December 2012. The combined contribution to the business of these activities in 2012 was:

	€000
Turnover	10,000
Cost of sales	9,910
Gross profit	90

Operating expenses   (50)

Operating profit   40

3. The directors of BACK estimate that the goodwill arising on the acquisition of FRONT was impaired by €28,000 at 31 December 2012.

4. BACK and FRONT follow a policy of depreciating all fixed assets at 10% per annum on their carrying value. Depreciation is charged to cost of sales in the statement of profit or loss and other comprehensive income.

5. FRONT purchases raw materials from BACK. During the year ended 31 December 2012, purchases of these raw materials by FRONT from BACK amounted to €10,000,000. At 31 December 2012, the inventory of FRONT included raw materials purchased from BACK at a cost of €3,000,000. BACK supplies raw materials at cost plus 25%.

Requirement Prepare the consolidated statement of profit or loss and other comprehensive income of BACK Group plc for the year ended 31 December 2012 in a form suitable for publication.

29

ASSOCIATES

LEARNING OBJECTIVES

This chapter addresses the accounting treatment for investments in associates. After having studied this chapter, you should be able to:
1. explain the terms 'associate' and 'significant influence';
2. understand and apply the criteria to identify an associate;
3. explain the equity method of accounting and how it differs from the consolidation approach used for subsidiaries;
4. apply the equity method of accounting for an associate; and
5. apply the main disclosure requirements.

KEY TERMS AND DEFINITIONS FOR THIS CHAPTER

In order to aid your understanding of the concepts and issues covered in this chapter, it is important to understand and be familiar with the following key terms and definitions. As you study this chapter, you should refer back to them.

Associate This an entity in which the investor has significant influence and which is neither a subsidiary nor a joint arrangement.

Cost Method The investment is recorded at cost. The statement of profit or loss and other comprehensive income reflects income only to the extent that the investor receives distributions from the investee subsequent to the date of acquisition.

Equity Method A method of accounting whereby the investment is initially recorded at cost and adjusted thereafter to reflect the investor's share of the post-acquisition net profit or loss of the investee/associate. The statement of profit or loss and other comprehensive income reflects the investor's share of the results of operations of the investee. Distributions received from the investee reduce the carrying amount of the investment. Adjustments to the carrying amount may also be required arising from changes in the investee's equity that have not been included in the income statement (e.g. revaluations).

Joint Arrangement This is an arrangement of which two or more parties have joint control.

Joint Control The contractually agreed sharing of control of an arrangement, which exists only when decisions about the relevant activities require the unanimous consent of the parties sharing control.

Significant Influence The power to participate in the financial and operating policy decisions of the investee but not control those policies. If an investor holds, directly or indirectly, 20% or more of the voting power of the investee, it is presumed that it has significant influence, unless it can be clearly demonstrated that this is not the case. Conversely, if less than 20%, the presumption is that the investor does not have significant influence. A majority shareholding by another investor does not preclude an investor having significant influence. Its existence is usually evidenced in one or more of the following ways:

- representation on the board of directors;
- participation in policy-making processes;
- material transactions between the investor and the investee;
- interchange of managerial personnel; or
- provision of essential technical information.

29.1 INTRODUCTION

Before moving on to consider how to account for associates, it is worthwhile briefly recapping some of the principles addressed so far in the consolidation part of the book (see **Part V**). **Chapters 26–28** focused on the concept that consolidated financial statements are legally required where a parent undertaking has subsidiaries at the start, during and/or at the end of its financial period. The rationale for the preparation of consolidated financial statements is that the financial statements of the parent undertaking (which typically record the investment in the subsidiary at cost in the statement of financial position and show dividend income from the subsidiary in the statement of profit or loss and other comprehensive income) do not give users of financial statements (see **Chapter 1**) sufficient information about an undertaking which the parent is able to control. Therefore, the consolidated statement of financial position replaces the investment in the subsidiary with its underlying net assets (and non-controlling interests, if applicable) and the consolidated statement of profit or loss and other comprehensive income replaces dividend income from the subsidiary with its underlying profits and losses (less non-controlling interests, if applicable). In a nutshell, this is at **the heart of consolidated accounting**.

The notion that historical cost information about investments and investment income is inadequate for providing users of financial information with sufficient information is equally applicable in situations where the investor does not have control, but has a degree of influence over the operations of the investee. However, full consolidation may be inappropriate given the investor does not have control (and therefore, by definition, someone else may). Such a scenario applies to associates (discussed in this chapter) and **joint arrangements** (see **Chapter 30**) whereby the objective of the accounting treatment is to reflect the effect on an investor's financial position and performance of its interest in these two special kinds of investment. In both cases, the investor is partly accountable for the activities of the investment because of the degree of influence it can exercise over the affairs of the investment. In these circumstances a modified form of consolidation is deemed to be most appropriate.

As indicated above, this chapter deals with the accounting treatment of **associates**. As explained in **Chapter 26**, prior to May 2011, the relevant accounting standard for associates was IAS 28 *Investments in Associates* (with a separate standard, IAS 31 *Interests in Joint Ventures*, dealing with joint arrangements). In May 2011, the International Accounting Standards Board (IASB) combined these two standards into an amended IAS 28 *Investments in Associates and Joint Ventures*, which applies to annual reporting periods beginning on or after 1 January 2013, with early application permitted. There are no disclosures specified in the amended IAS 28; instead, the disclosure requirements have been placed in IFRS 12 *Disclosure of Interests in Other Entities* (see **Section 29.3**).

With respect to associates, the accounting treatment is similar under both versions of IAS 28; although this is not the case with respect to joint arrangements which are dealt with separately in **Chapter 30**. However, the accounting requirements outlined with respect to associates (this **Chapter**) and joint arrangements (**Chapter 30**) are in accordance with IAS 28 *Investments in Associates and Joint Ventures*.

Key to this Chapter

This chapter deals with associates. The next section discusses how associates should be accounted for in the financial statements of a company that does, and does not, publish consolidated financial statements. **Section 29.3** then explains the application of the equity method of accounting, together with the disclosure requirements, and illustrates this in two detailed examples (**Example 29.1** and **Example 29.2**).

29.2 ACCOUNTING FOR ASSOCIATES

In broad terms, there are two categories of company that have an investment in an associate: those that *do not* publish consolidated financial statements and those that *do*. The accounting treatment of each of these categories is outlined below.

Category 1: When an investor *does not* publish consolidated financial statements

An investment in an associate, for an entity *not publishing* consolidated financial statements, should be either:
1. carried at cost (or in accordance with IFRS 5 *Non-Current Assets Held for Sale and Discontinued Operations*, if applicable (see **Chapter 20**)); or
2. accounted for under IFRS 9 *Financial Instruments* (see **Chapter 25**).

In essence, an investor should provide the same information about its investments in associates as those entities that issue consolidated financial statements.

Category 2: When an investor *does* publish consolidated financial statements

An investment in an associate, for an entity *publishing* consolidated financial statements, should be accounted for as follows:

In the Separate Financial Statements of the Investor

1. At cost (or in accordance with IFRS 5, if applicable (see **Chapter 20**)); or
2. in accordance with IFRS 9 (see **Chapter 25**).

In the Consolidated Financial Statements of the Investor

An investor should use the equity method of accounting for associates, other than in the following circumstances. An entity is exempt from applying the equity method if the investment meets one of the following conditions:

- The entity is a parent that is exempt from preparing consolidated financial statements under IFRS 10 *Consolidated Financial Statements* (see **Chapter 26**), or if all of the following four conditions are met (in which case the entity need not apply the equity method):
    1. the entity is a wholly-owned subsidiary, or is a partially-owned subsidiary of another entity and its other owners, including those not otherwise entitled to vote, have been informed about, and do not object to, the investor not applying the equity method;
    2. the investor's debt or equity instruments are not traded in a public market;
    3. the entity did not file, nor is it in the process of filing, its financial statements with a securities commission or other regulatory organisation for the purpose of issuing any class of instruments in a public market; and
    4. the ultimate or any intermediate parent of the entity produces consolidated financial statements available for public use that comply with International Financial Reporting Standards.
- When an investment in an associate is held by, or is held indirectly through, an entity that is a venture capital organisation, or a mutual fund, unit trust and similar entities including investment-linked insurance funds, the entity may elect to measure investments in those associates and joint ventures at fair value through profit or loss in accordance with IFRS 9 *Financial Instruments* (see **Chapter 25**).
- When the investment, or portion of an investment, meets the criteria to be classified as held for sale, the portion so classified is accounted for in accordance with IFRS 5 *Non-current Assets Held for Sale and Discontinued Operations* (see **Chapter 20**). Any remaining portion is accounted for using the equity method until the time of disposal, at which time the retained investment is accounted for under IFRS 9, unless the retained interest continues to be an associate or joint venture.

With the exception of the circumstances above, investments in associates *must be* accounted for using the *equity method* irrespective of whether the investor also has investments in subsidiaries or prepares group financial statements. The application of the equity method is explained in **Section 29.3**.

An investor should discontinue the use of the equity method from the date that significant influence ceases. For example, if the investment becomes a subsidiary, the entity accounts for its investment in accordance with IFRS 3 *Business Combinations* and IFRS 10 (see **Chapter 26**).

If an investment in an associate becomes an investment in a joint venture (or vice versa), the entity continues to apply the equity method and does not remeasure the retained interest.

29.3 APPLYING THE EQUITY METHOD

After explaining the general principles with respect to the application of the equity method, this section now illustrates how it is applied in the statement of financial position and statement of profit or loss and other comprehensive income.

General Principles

In its consolidated financial statements, an investor uses the equity method of accounting for investments in associates. Many of the procedures that are appropriate for the application of the equity method are similar to the consolidation procedures described in **Chapter 26**. Furthermore, the concepts underlying the procedures used in accounting for the acquisition of a subsidiary are also adopted in accounting for the acquisition of an investment in an associate. For example, on acquisition, any difference between the cost of acquisition and the investor's share of the fair values of the net identifiable assets is accounted for under IFRS 3 (see **Chapter 26**). Appropriate adjustments to post-acquisition share of profits are made to account for:
1. depreciation based on fair values; and
2. impairment of goodwill.

The most recent available financial statements of the associate should be used by the investor in applying the equity method and they should (usually) be drawn up to the same date as the investor's financial statements. When the dates differ, the associate often prepares statements specifically for the investor to the same date, but if this is impracticable, then a different date may be used. However, the length of the reporting periods should be consistent from period to period. Any difference between the reporting date of the investor and its associate must not be more than three months. When different dates have to be adopted, any adjustments for significant events occurring between the date of the associate's statements and the date of the investor's financial statements must be made.

If an investor's share of losses of an associate (i.e. rather than profits) equals or exceeds its 'interest in the associate' (i.e. as stated in the statement of financial position), the investor should discontinue recognising its share of further losses. The 'interest in an associate' is the carrying amount of the investment in the associate under the equity method together with any long-term interests that, in substance, form part of the investor's net investment in the associate. After the investor's interest is reduced to zero, additional losses should be recognised by a provision (liability) only to the extent that the investor has incurred legal or constructive obligations or made payments on behalf of the associate. If the associate subsequently reports profits, the investor should resume recognising its share of those profits only after its share of the profits equals the share of losses not recognised.

Many of the procedures that are appropriate for the application of the equity method are similar to the consolidation procedures described in **Chapter 28**. For example, if an associate is accounted for using the equity method, unrealised profits and losses resulting from upstream (for example, sales *from* the associate *to* the investor) and downstream (for example, sales *from* the investor *to* the associate) transactions should be eliminated to the extent of the investor's interest in the associate. However, unrealised losses should not be eliminated to the extent that the transaction provides evidence of an impairment of the asset transferred.

Uniform accounting policies should be adopted and appropriate adjustments made to the associate's statements, but if this is not practicable that fact must be disclosed.

Statement of Financial Position

None of the individual assets and liabilities of the associate are 'consolidated' with those of the parent and subsidiaries (if there are any). Instead, under equity accounting, the investment in an associate is carried to the (consolidated) statement of financial position at a valuation. The carrying amount of an investment in an associate in a (consolidated) statement of financial position can be arrived at by using one of two methods of calculation, both of which are illustrated in **Figure 29.1**.

FIGURE 29.1: CARRYING AMOUNT OF AN ASSOCIATE

Method 1	€000
Cost of investment	X
Plus	
Share of post-acquisition retained profits and reserves of Associate (to reporting date)	X
Less	
Any premium written off (because of impairment)	(X)
Carrying amount of investment	X
Method 2	
Group's share of net asset of Associate (at reporting date)	X
Plus	
Premium on acquisition not written off since acquisition date	X
Carrying amount of investment	X

It is important to remember that a premium on acquisition (goodwill) should be tested for impairment annually, in accordance with IAS 36 *Impairment of Assets,* and written down if there is impairment (see **Chapter 10**). The recoverable amount of an investment should be assessed for each individual associate unless that associate does not generate independent cash flows. In determining value in use, an entity should estimate:

1. its share of the present value of estimated future cash flows expected to be generated by the investee as a whole, including the proceeds on ultimate disposal; or
2. the present value of estimated future cash flows expected to arise from dividends and from ultimate disposal.

Both methods give the same result under appropriate assumptions. Any impairment loss is allocated first to goodwill, in accordance with IAS 36.

Statement of Profit or Loss and Other Comprehensive Income

The investing group should take credit for its share of the earnings of the associate, whether or not the associate has distributed those earnings by way of dividends. Under equity accounting the associate's revenue, cost of sales, expenses and tax are *not* consolidated with those of the investing group. The consolidated statement of profit or loss and other comprehensive income only includes the group's share of the associate's (post-acquisition) profit after tax. While IAS 28 does not prescribe how the investor's share of its associate's profits should be presented in the statement of profit or loss and other comprehensive income, the example in IAS 1 *Presentation of Financial Statements* discloses this **single figure** just before 'profit before tax'. (This is illustrated in **Figure 2.3**, **Chapter 2**). The following example illustrates the application of equity accounting.

EXAMPLE 29.1: DEALING WITH AN ASSOCIATE IN CONSOLIDATED
FINANCIAL STATEMENTS USING EQUITY ACCOUNTING

Parent Limited purchased 90,000 ordinary shares in Apple Limited on 1 January 2011 when the retained earnings of Apple Limited were €100,000. The cost of the investment was €140,000.

DRAFT STATEMENTS OF FINANCIAL POSITION
as at 31 December 2012

	Parent Limited and Subsidiaries €000	Apple Limited €000
Assets		
Tangible non-current assets	3,260	580
Investment in Apple	140	–
Current assets	1,250	290
	4,650	870
Equity and Liabilities		
Ordinary €1 shares	1,000	300
Retained earnings	2,720	400
	3,720	700
Current liabilities	930	170
	4,650	870

STATEMENTS OF PROFIT OR LOSS AND OTHER COMPREHENSIVE INCOME
for the year ended 31 December 2012

	Parent Limited and Subsidiaries €000	Apple Limited €000
Revenue	9,800	2,630
Cost of sales	(6,858)	(1,840)
Gross profit	2,942	790
Dividends from Apple Limited	9	–
Distribution costs	(391)	(120)
Administrative expenses	(670)	(200)
Finance costs	(410)	(120)
Profit before tax	1,480	350
Income tax expense	(440)	(110)
Profit after tax	1,040	240

Additional Information:

1. The premium on acquisition (goodwill) of Apple Limited has been impaired for the first time by €5,000 during the year under review.
2. During year ended 31 December 2012, Parent Limited and Apple Limited debited €100,000 and €30,000 respectively to equity in respect of dividends paid.

Requirement Prepare the consolidated statement of profit or loss and other comprehensive income for the year ended 31 December 2012, together with the statement of financial position as at that date, for Parent Limited.

Solution

Under equity accounting none of the assets and liabilities (net assets) of the associate is consolidated. The associate can be dealt with by means of two journal entries:

	€000	€000
DR Investment in Apple Limited	90	
CR Reserves		90

Being the group's share of the post-acquisition retained profits and reserves of Apple as at the reporting date (30% × (€400,000 − €100,000)).

DR Retained profits	5	
CR Investment in Apple		5

Being the cumulative impairment of goodwill to the reporting date.

Tangible Non-current Assets

	€000		€000
Group	3,260	CSFP	3,260

Investment in Apple

	€000		€000
Group	140	Journal 2	5
Journal 1	90	CSFP	225
	230		230

Current Assets

	€000		€000
Group	1,250	CSFP	1,250

Current Liabilities

	€000		€000
CSFP	930	Group	930

Ordinary Shares

	€000		€000
CSFP	1,000	Group	1,000

Retained Earnings

	€000		€000
Journal 2	5	Group	2,720
CSFP	2,805	Journal 1	90
	2,810		2,810

The individual assets and liabilities of Apple (net assets) are not included in the consolidated statement of financial position under equity accounting.

CONSOLIDATED STATEMENT OF FINANCIAL POSITION
as at 31 December 2012

	€000
Assets	
Tangible non-current assets	3,260
Investment in associated company (W1)	225
Current assets	1,250
	4,735
Equity and Liabilities	
Ordinary €1 shares	1,000
Retained earnings (W2)	2,805
	3,805
Current liabilities	930
	4,735

(W1)	€000
Investment at cost	140
Share of post-acquisition profits	90

| Premium on acquisition written off | (5) |
| | 225 |

The carrying amount of the investment in Apple Limited could also be calculated as follows:

	€000
Share of net assets (€700 × 30%)	210
Premium not written off	15
	225

Calculation of Premium	
Cost of investment	140
Acquired (30% × (€300 + €100))	120
Premium on acquisition	20
Premium	20
Written off – Impairment	5
Balance remaining	15

(W2)	€000
Parent Limited and Subsidiaries	2,720
Apple Limited ((€400 − €100) × 30%)	90
Impairment of goodwill	(5)
	2,805

CONSOLIDATED STATEMENT OF PROFIT OR LOSS AND OTHER COMPREHENSIVE INCOME
for the Year Ended 31 December 2012

	€000
Revenue	9,800
Cost of sales	(6,858)
Gross profit	2,942
Distribution costs	(391)
Administrative expenses	(670)
Finance costs	(410)
Share of profit of associate	
((30% × €240) − €5)	67
Net profit	1,538
Income tax expense	(440)
Profit after tax	1,098

Note: under equity accounting, the associated company's revenue, cost of sales, expenses and tax are not consolidated with those of the group; instead the group's share of Apple's profit after tax is included as a single figure. The retained earnings of the associate are included in the group's retained profits from the date of acquisition (i.e. consistent with normal consolidation principles).

Apple declared a dividend of €30,000, of which the Parent is entitled to €9,000 (€30,000 × 30%) of this. The Parent has included this as investment income in its own statement of profit or loss and other comprehensive income. This is not shown separately in the consolidated statement of profit or loss and other comprehensive income.

After illustrating how to account for an associate in consolidated financial statements by applying the equity method of accounting in **Example 29.1**, the next subsection outlines the disclosures required in relation to associates.

Disclosure

Following the revision to IAS 28 in May 2011 (see **Section 29.1**), the disclosure requirements for associates have been placed in IFRS 12 *Disclosure of Interests in Other Entities*. IFRS 12 is a comprehensive disclosure standard for subsidiaries, joint arrangements, associates and unconsolidated structured entities.

In order for users of financial statements to better understand the relationship between an investor and its associates, the information disclosed should enable users of its financial statements to evaluate:
- the nature, extent and financial effects of interests in associates, including the nature and effects of contractual relationships; and
- the nature of, and changes in, the risks associated with interests in associates.

For example, this might include:
(a) an appropriate listing and description of significant associates, including the proportion of ownership interest and, if different, the proportion of voting power held; and
(b) the methods used to account for such investments.

Investments in associates should be classified as non-current assets and disclosed separately in the statement of financial position. The investor's share of profits/losses should be disclosed separately in the statement of profit or loss and other comprehensive income.

Other disclosures include:
- the fair value of investments in associates (if published);
- summarised financial information of associates (for example, amounts of assets, liabilities, revenue and profit/loss);
- why significant influence is present if the holding is less than 20%;
- if an associate is not accounted for under equity accounting;
- the unrecognised share of losses of an associate; and
- the reporting date of the associate if different from the investor.

The following example develops the issues explained so far in this chapter, and illustrates how to account for an associate on a step-by-step basis.

EXAMPLE 29.2: DEALING WITH ASSOCIATES STEP-BY-STEP

AROMA plc (AROMA) purchased 30% of THERAPY Limited (THERAPY) on 1 July 2009. At all times, AROMA participates fully in THERAPY's financial and operating policy decisions. At the date of acquisition, THERAPY's statement of financial position was as follows:

Capital and Reserves	€000
€1 ordinary shares	1,000
Revaluation reserve	100
Retained earnings	450
	1,550

The statements of financial position of AROMA and THERAPY as at 30 June 2013 are as follows:

	AROMA		THERAPY	
	€000	€000	€000	€000
ASSETS				
Non-current Assets				
Property, plant and equipment		4,000		3,500
Investment in THERAPY		1,000		-
		5,000		3,500
Current Assets				
Inventory	670		430	
Receivables	500		395	
Bank and cash	130	1,300	215	1,040
		6,300		4,540
EQUITY AND LIABILITIES				
Capital and Reserves				
€1 ordinary shares		2,000		1,000
Revaluation reserve		1,000		500
Retained earnings		2,550		2,470
		5,550		3,970
Current Liabilities		750		570
		6,300		4,540

In addition, the draft statements of profit or loss and other comprehensive income of the two companies for the year ended 30 June 2013 are as follows:

	AROMA	THERAPY
	€000	€000
Revenue	5,000	3,000
Cost of sales	(3,000)	(1,500)
Gross profit	2,000	1,500
Operating expenses	(750)	(440)

Trading profit	1,250	1,060
Interest	(50)	(10)
Profit before taxation	1,200	1,050
Income tax expense	(400)	(350)
Profit after taxation	800	700
Ordinary dividends proposed (but not approved)	(300)	(50)
Retained profit for the year	500	650

Requirement Prepare the consolidated statement of profit or loss and other comprehensive income of AROMA Group for the year ended 30 June 2013, and statement of financial position as at that date.

Solution

WORKINGS:

Step One
Calculate the goodwill in the investment in THERAPY.

	€000	€000
Cost of investment		1,000
Share capital	1,000	
Revaluation reserve	100	
Retained earnings	450	
	1,550	
× 30%		(465)
		535

There is no evidence of impairment, therefore record at €535,000.

Step Two
Complete the top half of the statement of financial position.

	€000
Investment in THERAPY's net assets:	
(30% × (€3,970,000 + Proposed dividend €50,000)	1,206
Goodwill (Step 1)	535
	1,741

Step Three
Calculate statement of financial position reserves.

	€000	€000
Revaluation Reserve		
AROMA		1,000
THERAPY		
– at reporting date	500	
– at acquisition	(100)	

	400	
	× 30%	120
		1,120

Retained Earnings

AROMA (€2,550,000 + Proposed dividend €300,000)		2,850
THERAPY		
– at reporting date (€2,470,000 + Proposed dividend €50,000)	2,520	
– at acquisition	(450)	
	2,070	
	× 30%	621
		3,471

Step Four
Calculate the figures to be included in the consolidated statement of profit or loss and other comprehensive income.

	€000
Profit after interest and tax	700
Group share 30%	210

Step Five
Prepare the consolidated statement of profit or loss and other comprehensive income and statement of financial position.

AROMA Group
CONSOLIDATED STATEMENT OF PROFIT OR LOSS AND OTHER COMPREHENSIVE INCOME
for the Year Ended 30 June 2013

	€000
Revenue	5,000
Cost of sales	(3,000)
Gross profit	2,000
Operating expenses	(750)
Operating profit	1,250
Interest payable	(50)
Share of profit of associate	210
Profit before tax	1,410
Income tax expense	(400)
Profit after tax	1,010

AROMA Group
CONSOLIDATED STATEMENT OF FINANCIAL POSITION
as at 30 June 2013

	€000	€000
ASSETS		
Non-current Assets		
Property, plant and equipment		4,000
Investments – investment in associate		1,741
		5,741

Current Assets		
Inventory	670	
Receivables	500	
Bank and cash	130	1,300
		7,041
EQUITY AND LIABILITIES		
Capital and Reserves		
Share capital		2,000
Revaluation reserve		1,120
Retained earnings		3,471
		6,591
Current Liabilities (€750,000 − Proposed dividend €300,000)		450
		7,041

The following example develops **Example 27.18** (see **Chapter 27**), which illustrates the consolidation of a subsidiary company (KTE) only, by adding an associate company to the information. As much of the core information remains unchanged from **Example 27.18**, this example therefore provides an opportunity to directly compare the difference(s) between accounting for a subsidiary and a subsidiary together with an associate. If you have already studied **Chapter 27**, this example also enables you to test your knowledge of the earlier chapter before attempting the **Review Questions** and **Challenging Questions** at the end of this chapter.

COMPREHENSIVE EXAMPLE 29.3: SUBSIDIARY AND ASSOCIATE

On 1 January 2012 Toffer acquired the following non-current investments:
- three million equity shares in KTE by an exchange of one share in Toffer for every two shares in KTE, plus €1.25 per acquired KTE share in cash. The market price of each Toffer share at the date of acquisition was €6, and the market price of each KTE share at the date of acquisition was €3.25; and
- thirty percent of the equity shares of LN at a cost of €7.50 per share in cash.

Only the cash consideration of the above investments has been recorded by Toffer. In addition, €500,000 of professional costs relating to the acquisition of KTE is included in the cost of the investment.

The summarised draft statements of financial position of the three companies at 31 December 2012 are:

	Toffer €000	KTE €000	LN €000
ASSETS			
Non-current Assets			
Property, plant and equipment	18,400	10,400	18,000

Investments in KTE and LN	13,250	nil	nil
Financial asset held for trading	6,500	nil	nil
	38,150	10,400	18,000
Current Assets			
Inventory	6,900	6,200	3,600
Trade receivables	3,200	1,500	2,400
Total assets	48,250	18,100	24,000
EQUITY AND LIABILITIES			
€1 Equity shares	10,000	4,000	4,000
Retained earnings			
– at 31 December 2011	16,000	6,000	11,000
– for year ended 31 December 2012	9,250	2,900	5,000
	35,250	12,900	20,000
Non-current Liabilities			
7% Loan notes	5,000	1,000	1,000
Current Liabilities	8,000	4,200	3,000
Total equity and liabilities	48,250	18,100	24,000

Additional Information:

(i) At the date of acquisition, KTE had five years remaining of an agreement to supply goods to one of its major customers. KTE believes it is highly likely that the agreement will be renewed when it expires. The directors of Toffer estimate that the value of this customer-based contract has a fair value of €1m, an indefinite life, and has not suffered any impairment.

(ii) On 1 January 2012, Toffer sold an item of plant to KTE at its agreed fair value of €2.5m. Its carrying amount prior to the sale was €2m. The estimated remaining life of the plant at the date of sale was five years (straight-line depreciation).

(iii) During the year ended 31 December 2012, KTE sold goods to Toffer for €2.7m. KTE had marked-up these goods by 50% on cost. Toffer had a third of the goods still in its inventory at 31 December 2012. There were no intragroup payables/receivables at 31 December 2012.

(iv) Toffer has a policy of valuing non-controlling interests at fair value at the date of acquisition. For this purpose, the share price of KTE at this date should be used. Impairment tests on 31 December 2012 concluded that neither the goodwill arising on the acquisition of KTE nor the value of the investment in LN have been impaired.

(v) The financial asset held for trading is included in Toffer's statement of financial position (above) at its fair value on 1 January 2012, but it has a fair value of €9m at 31 December 2012.

(vi) No dividends were paid during the year by any of the companies.

Requirement Prepare the consolidated statement of financial position for Toffer as at 31 December 2012.

Solution
Note:
- Toffer purchased 3,000,000/4,000,000 shares in KTE (i.e. 75%), paying €12.75m ((1.5m shares × €6) + (3m shares × €1.25)).
- Toffer purchased 1,200,000 shares in LN at €7.50 each = €9,000,000.

Note: there are a number of ways of presenting the information to test the new method for calculating the non-controlling interest at the date of acquisition. As above, the subsidiary's share price just before the acquisition could be given and then used to value the non-controlling interest. It is then a matter of multiplying the share price by the number of shares held by the non-controlling interest. For example, 1 million × €3.25 = €3.25m (see W(ii) below). Alternatively, the question could simply state that the directors valued the non-controlling interest at the date of acquisition at €3.25m (for example in note (iv)). In practice the parent is likely to have paid more than the subsidiary's pre-acquisition share price in order to gain control.

An alternative approach would be for the question to give the value of the goodwill attributable to the non-controlling interest. In this case, the non-controlling interest's goodwill would be added to the parent's goodwill (calculated by the old method) and to the carrying amount of the non-controlling interest itself (for example, €500,000 (see W(ii) below)).

Toffer
CONSOLIDATED STATEMENT OF FINANCIAL POSITION
as at 31 December 2012

	€000	€000
ASSETS		
Non-current Assets		
PPE (€18,400 + €10,400 − €2,500 + €2,000 + €100 (W(i)))		28,400
Goodwill (W(ii))		5,000
Customer-based intangible asset		1,000
Investments:		
− Associate (W(iii))		10,500
− Financial asset held for trading		9,000
		53,900
Current Assets		
Inventory (€6,900 + €6,200 − €300 (W(iv)))	12,800	
Trade receivables (€3,200 + €1,500)	4,700	17,500
Total assets		71,400
EQUITY AND LIABILITIES		
€1 Equity shares (W(v))		11,500
Share premium (W(v))	7,500	
Retained earnings (W(vi))	30,275	37,775
		49,275
Non-controlling interests (W(vii))		3,925
		53,200

Non-current Liabilities	
7% Loan notes (€5,000 + €1,000)	6,000
Current Liabilities (€8,000 + €4,200)	12,000
Total equity and liabilities	71,400

WORKINGS

W(i) Property, plant and equipment

The transfer of the plant creates an initial unrealised profit (URP) of €500,000 which must be cancelled on consolidation:

DR Consolidated reserves	€500,000	
CR Non-current assets		€500,000

Given that the plant is now recorded at its cost to the group, it is necessary to adjust the depreciation charge in KTE's books in order to reflect this 'lower' cost (i.e. €500,000/5 = €100,000 for each year (straight-line depreciation over five years) in the post-acquisition period):

DR Non-current assets	€100,000	
CR KTE retained earnings		€100,000

W(ii) Goodwill in KTE

	€000	€000
Investment at cost:		
Shares issued (3,000/2 × €6)		9,000
Cash (3,000 × €1.25)		3,750
Total consideration		12,750
Equity shares of KTE	4,000	
Pre-acquisition reserves	6,000	
Customer-based contract	1,000	
	75% × 11,000	(8,250)
Parent's share of goodwill		4,500

Fair value of non-controlling interest at date of acquisition – 1 million shares at €3.25	3,250
Non-controlling interest's share of KTE's net assets at acquisition date (€11,000 × 25%)	(2,750)
Non-controlling interest's share of goodwill	500
Total goodwill is therefore (€4,500 + €500)	5,000

Note: this applies the old methodology for calculating the goodwill with the non-controlling interest's goodwill calculated separately. Applying the new method of calculating goodwill gives the same total figure, but it is a little simpler:

	€000
Consideration paid by the parent (as before)	12,750
Fair value of the non-controlling interest (as before)	3,250
	16,000

Fair value of subsidiary's net assets (based on equity as before)	(11,000)
Total goodwill	5,000

Note: the consideration given by Toffer for the shares of KTE works out at €4.25 per share, i.e. consideration of €12.75m for three million shares. This is considerably higher than the market price of KTE's shares (€3.25) before the acquisition. This probably reflects the cost of gaining control of KTE. This is also why it is probably appropriate to value the non-controlling interest in KTE shares at €3.25 each, because (by definition) the non-controlling interest does not have any control. This also explains why Toffer's share of KTE's goodwill at 90% (i.e. 4,500/5,000) is much higher than its proportionate shareholding in KTE (which is 75%).

W(iii) Carrying amount of LN at 31 December 2008

	€000
Cost (4,000 × 30% × €7.50)	9,000
Share post acquisition profit (€5,000 × 30%)	1,500
	10,500

W(iv) The unrealised profit (URP) in inventory
Intra-group sales are €2.7m on which KTE made a profit of €900,000 (€2,700 x 50/150). One third of these are still in the inventory of Toffer, thus there is an unrealised profit of €300,000.

W(v) Share issues
The 1.5 million shares issued by Toffer in the share exchange, at a value of €6 each, would be recorded as €1 per share as capital and €5 per share as premium, giving an increase in share capital of €1.5m and a share premium of €7.5m.

W(vi) Consolidated retained earnings

	€000
Toffer's retained earnings	25,250
Professional costs of acquisition must be expensed	(500)
KTE's post acquisition profits (€2,900 – €300 URP + €100 (W(i))) × 75%	2,025
LN's post acquisition profits (€5,000 × 30%)	1,500
URP in plant (see W(i))	(500)
Gain on available-for-sale investment (€9,000 – €6,500) (see below)	2,500
	30,275

The gain on available-for-sale investments must be recognised directly in equity.

W(vii) Non-controlling interest

	€000
Equity at 31 December 2012 (€12,900 + €100 (W(i))	13,000
Customer-based contract	1,000
URP in inventory	(300)
	13,700
The non-controlling interest's share of net identifiable assets (x 25%)	3,425
Non-controlling interest share of goodwill (W(ii))	500
	3,925

Note: subsequent to the date of acquisition, a non-controlling interest is valued at its proportionate share of the carrying value of the subsidiary's net identifiable assets (equal to its equity) plus its attributed goodwill (less any impairment). The non-controlling interest is only valued at fair value at the date of acquisition.

Note: if goodwill had been impaired by €1m, IAS 36 requires a subsidiary's goodwill impairment to be allocated between the parent and the non-controlling interest on the same basis as the subsidiary's profits and losses are allocated. Thus, of the impairment of €1m, €750,000 would be allocated to the parent (and debited to group retained earnings, reducing them to €29.525m (€30,275,000 – €750,000)) and €250,000 would be allocated to the non-controlling interest, writing it down to €3.675m (€3,925,000 – €250,000). It could be argued that this requirement represents an anomaly: of the recognised goodwill (before the impairment) of €5m, only €500,000 (i.e. 10%) relates to the non-controlling interest, but it suffers 25% (its proportionate shareholding in KTE) of the goodwill impairment.

29.4 CONCLUSION

An associate is an entity in which the investor has significant influence and which is neither a subsidiary nor a joint venture of the investor. Significant influence is the power to participate in the financial and operating policy decisions of the investee, but is not control over those policies. If an investor holds, directly or indirectly, 20% or more of the voting power of the investee, it is presumed that it has significant influence unless it can be clearly demonstrated that this is not the case.

In the consolidated financial statements of the investor, IAS 28 requires the use of the equity method of accounting for associates (with some exceptions). Under this method of accounting the investment is initially recorded at cost and adjusted thereafter to reflect the investor's post-acquisition share of the net profit or loss of the investee/associate. The statement of profit or loss and other comprehensive income reflects the investor's share of the results of operations of the investee. While IAS 28 does not prescribe how the investor's share of its associate's profits should be presented in the statement of profit or loss and other comprehensive income, the example in IAS 1 defines this as the share of associate's profit attributable to equity holders of the associates (i.e. share of profit after interest and tax of the associate). This is disclosed just before 'profit before tax'.

SUMMARY OF LEARNING OBJECTIVES

This chapter addresses the accounting treatment for investments in associates. After having studied this chapter, you should be able to:

Learning Objective 1 Explain the terms associate and significant influence.

An associate is an entity in which the investor has significant influence and which is neither a subsidiary nor a joint venture of the investor. Significant influence is deemed to be the power to participate in the financial and operating policy decisions of the investee but not control those policies. Broadly, if an investor holds, directly or indirectly, 20% or more of the voting power of the investee, it is presumed that it has significant influence.

Learning Objective 2 Understand and apply the criteria to identify an associate.

The existence (or not) of significant influence is fundamental to the identification of an associate, and its existence is usually evidenced in one or more of the following ways: representation on the board of directors; participation in policy-making processes; material transactions between the investor and the investee; interchange of managerial personnel; or the provision of essential technical information.

Learning Objective 3 Explain the equity method of accounting and how it differs from the consolidation approach used for subsidiaries.

Under 'full' consolidation, the assets and liabilities and revenue and costs of the investee (together with non-controlling interests, if applicable) are included on a line-by-line basis in the consolidated statement of financial position and consolidated statement of profit or loss and other comprehensive income. However, this approach is considered inappropriate where the investor does not have control (and therefore, by definition, someone else may) of the investee. Equity accounting is essentially a modified form of consolidation whereby the investment in the statement of financial position is initially recorded at cost and adjusted thereafter to reflect the investor's post-acquisition share of the net profit or loss. The statement of profit or loss and other comprehensive income reflects the investor's share of the profit after tax of the investee on a single line.

Learning Objective 4 Apply the equity method of accounting for an associate.

The equity method is a method of accounting whereby the investment is initially recorded at cost and adjusted thereafter to reflect the investor's share of the post-acquisition net profit or loss of the investee/associate. The statement of profit or loss and other comprehensive income reflects the investor's share of the results of operations of the investee. Distributions received from the investee reduce the carrying amount of the investment. Adjustments to the carrying amount may also be required if arising from changes in the investee's equity that have not been included in the income statement (for example, revaluations).

The equity method of accounting is explained in **Section 29.3** and its application illustrated in **Example 29.1** and **Example 29.2**.

Learning Objective 5 Apply the main disclosure requirements.

Investments in associates should be classified as non-current assets and disclosed separately in the statement of financial position. The investor's share of profits/losses should be disclosed **separately** in the statement of profit or loss and other comprehensive income.

QUESTIONS

Self-test Questions

1. Explain the terms associate and significant influence.
2. Explain the equity method of accounting and how it differs from the consolidation approach used for subsidiaries.

> **Note:** for ease of illustration, dividends and retained earnings are often shown at the foot of the statement of profit or loss and other comprehensive income in questions. These figures would normally be included in the statement of changes in equity.

Review Questions

(See **Appendix One** for Suggested Solutions to Review Questions.)

Question 29.1

The draft consolidated statement of profit or loss and other comprehensive income of Parker Limited and its subsidiary companies, together with the draft statement of profit or loss and other comprehensive income of Duke Limited, for the year ended 30 September 2013 are set out below.

	Parker Limited Group €000	Duke Limited €000
Revenue	31,980	12,200
Gross profit	2,312	879
Dividends from Duke Limited	24	–
	2,336	879
Administrative expenses	(541)	(199)
Finance costs	(4)	–
Profit before tax	1,791	680
Income tax expense	1,108	380
Profit after tax	683	300
Non-controlling interest in subsidiaries	(41)	–
	642	300

Additional Information:

1. Parker Limited acquired a 30% holding in Duke Limited on 1 October 2012.
2. The retained earnings of the Parker Limited Group and Duke Limited at 30 September 2013 are as follows:

	Parker Limited Group €000	Duke Limited €000
Profit after tax and non-controlling interests	642	300
Retained earnings at 30 September 2012	345	89
Dividends paid during year ended 30 September 2013	(100)	(80)
Retained earnings at 30 September 2013	887	309

Requirement You are required to prepare the consolidated statement of profit or loss and other comprehensive income of Parker Limited for the year ended 30 September 2013.

Question 29.2

Golf Limited is a trading company, which has recently sought to diversify its interests by purchasing shares in other companies. It has been its policy to insist on appointing a director to the board of any company, so as to take an active part in the management, where its investment comprises more than 20% of the equity share capital. The following investments have been made:
1. on 1 January 2012, 15% of the ordinary share capital of Club Limited;
2. on 1 July 2012, 30% of the ordinary share capital of Ball Limited; and
3. on 1 November 2012, 75% of the ordinary share capital of Tee Limited. For the purposes of measuring non-controlling interests at the date of acquisition, the proportionate share method equates to the fair value method.

The draft statements of profit or loss and other comprehensive income of the four companies for the year ended 30 June 2013 show:

	Golf Limited €	Club Limited €	Ball Limited €	Tee Limited €
Revenue	2,100,000	3,900,000	1,900,000	1,200,000
Trading profit	250,000	400,000	210,000	126,000
Dividends	46,500	–	–	–
	296,500	400,000	210,000	126,000
Income tax expense	90,000	170,000	85,000	51,000
	206,500	230,000	125,000	75,000

Additional Information:
1. Included in the inventory of Tee Limited was €24,000 for goods purchased from Golf Limited, subsequent to 1 November 2012. Golf Limited realised its usual 25% gross profit, based on selling price when it sold these goods.
2. Retained earnings

	Golf Limited €	Club Limited €	Ball Limited €	Tee Limited €
Profit after tax	206,500	230,000	125,000	75,000
Retained earnings b/f	450,000	306,000	235,000	200,000
Ordinary dividends paid	(132,000)	(100,000)	(60,000)	(32,000)
Retained earnings	524,500	436,000	300,000	243,000

3. There has been no change in the fair value of the investment in Club Limited since acquisition. The dividend received from Club Limited has not yet been incorporated in the draft statement of profit or loss and other comprehensive income of Golf Limited. All other dividends have been accounted for by Golf Limited.

Requirement Prepare the consolidated statement of profit or loss and other comprehensive income of Golf Limited for the year ended 30 June 2013 in a form suitable for publication.

Question 29.3

The summarised statements of financial position of Gold Limited, Silver Limited and Bronze Limited as on 30 November 2012 were as follows:

	Gold Limited €	Silver Limited €	Bronze Limited €
Assets			
Non-current assets			
Property, plant and equipment	100,000	70,000	50,050
Investment in Silver	100,000	–	–
Investment in Bronze	30,500	–	–
	230,500	70,000	50,050
Current assets			
Inventory	26,500	36,000	10,000
Receivables	83,750	125,000	36,300
Cash at bank	2,000	25,000	–
Cash on hand	100	–	–
Current accounts: Gold Limited	–	–	2,500
Silver Limited	1,000	–	–
Bronze Limited	–	650	–
	113,350	186,650	48,800
Total Assets	343,850	256,650	98,850
Equity and Liabilities			
Equity			
Ordinary share capital (50 cent)	50,000	100,000	25,000
Share premium account	10,000	–	–
Capital reserve	61,500	59,250	5,000
Other reserves	35,000	5,000	10,000
Retained profits	26,450	45,300	15,000
Total equity	182,950	209,550	55,000
Current liabilities			
Payables	120,900	31,600	21,200
Bank overdraft	27,500	–	15,000
Taxation	10,000	15,000	7,000
Current accounts: Gold Limited	–	500	–
Silver Limited	–	–	650
Bronze Limited	2,500	–	–
Total Liabilities	160,900	47,100	43,850
Total Equity and Liabilities	343,850	256,650	98,850

Additional Information:

1. Shares acquired by Gold Limited in Silver Limited: 150,000 ordinary shares on 30 November 2010 at a cost of €100,000. Shares acquired by Gold Limited in Bronze Limited: 20,000 ordinary shares on 30 November 2011 at a cost of €30,500.

2. State of affairs relevant to the acquisition dates:

	Silver Limited	Bronze Limited
	€	€
Issued share capital	100,000	25,000
Capital reserve	19,250	–
Retained profits	4,300	5,000
Contingency reserve	5,000	10,000
	128,550	40,000

3. The current account difference arises from a cheque being in transit as on 30 November 2012.

4. All the property of Silver Limited was disposed of on 31 May 2012 and the profit on sale credited to capital reserve.

5. One-eighth of the inventory of Silver Limited as on 30 November 2012 has been invoiced to that company by Gold Limited at cost plus 20%.

6. With respect to the measurement of non-controlling interests at the date of acquisition, the proportionate share method equates to the fair value method. The directors of Gold Limited are confident that any goodwill arising on the acquisitions of Silver Limited and Bronze Limited has not suffered any impairment.

Requirement You are required to prepare the consolidated statement of financial position of Gold Limited and its subsidiary and associated companies on 30 November 2012.

Challenging Questions

(Suggested Solutions to Challenging Questions are available to lecturers.)

Question 29.1 (Based on Chartered Accountants Ireland, P3 Summer 2004, Question 6)

You are the accountant for COCKTAIL Group, which consists of three companies: COCKTAIL plc (COCKTAIL), UMBRELLA Limited (UMBRELLA), and CHERRY Limited (CHERRY). The individual company statements of financial position as at 31 December 2012 are presented below.

	COCKTAIL € million	UMBRELLA € million	CHERRY € million
ASSETS			
Non-current Assets			
Property, plant and equipment	324	168	180
Investment in UMBRELLA			
and CHERRY	450	–	–
	774	168	180

Current Assets			
Inventory	144	108	90
Receivables	72	102	96
Current account with			
UMBRELLA	25	–	–
Bank and cash	288	6	6
	1,303	384	372
EQUITY AND LIABILITIES			
Capital and reserves:			
€1 ordinary shares	360	120	100
Retained earnings	822	186	212
	1,182	306	312
Current Liabilities			
Trade payables	61	33	40
Current account with			
COCKTAIL	–	5	–
Other payables	60	40	20
	1,303	384	372

Additional Information:

1. On 1 January 2008, COCKTAIL purchased 96 million €1 ordinary shares in UMBRELLA for €330 million. The retained earnings of UMBRELLA stood at €120 million on this date and property, plant and equipment with a remaining useful life of 10 years were recorded at €20 million less than their fair value. With respect to the measurement of non-controlling interests at the date of acquisition, the proportionate share method equates to the fair value method.

2. On 1 January 2012, COCKTAIL purchased 30 million €1 ordinary shares in CHERRY for €120 million. The retained earnings of CHERRY stood at €190 million on this date. The net assets of CHERRY had a fair value that was the same as their book value.

3. During 2012 UMBRELLA sold raw materials to COCKTAIL for €2 million, making a profit of 25% on cost. COCKTAIL paid for the raw materials on delivery, and had €500,000 of these in inventory at 31 December 2012.

4. On 30 December 2012, UMBRELLA sent a cheque for €20,000,000 to COCKTAIL that was not received until 2 January 2013.

5. Dividends proposed at 31 December 2012, which are included in other payables, are as follows:

	€ million
COCKTAIL	30
UMBRELLA	20

Dividends receivable by COCKTAIL from UMBRELLA are included in receivables.

6. The directors of COCKTAIL estimate that the goodwill arising on the acquisition of UMBRELLA was impaired for the first time during the year ended 31 December 2012 by €61,000,000. It is group policy to charge a full year's depreciation in the year of acquisition.

Requirement Prepare the consolidated statement of financial position for COCKTAIL Group as at 31 December 2012.

Note:

1. The answer does NOT require a consolidated statement of profit or loss and other comprehensive income and statement of financial position in a form suitable for publication. These statements may be presented by way of a consolidation schedule.
2. Notes to the financial statements are NOT required, nor is a statement indicating the amount of profit dealt with in the holding company's statement of profit or loss and other comprehensive income.
3. All workings should be clearly shown.

Question 29.2 (Based on Chartered Accountants Ireland, P3 Summer 2000, Question 1)

You are the accountant for EARTH plc group, reporting directly to the Finance Director. EARTH plc group consists of three companies: EARTH plc, WIND Limited and WATER Limited. The individual company statements of profit or loss and other comprehensive income for the year ended 31 December 2012 and statements of financial position as at that date are presented below.

STATEMENTS OF PROFIT OR LOSS AND OTHER COMPREHENSIVE INCOME
for the Year Ended 31 December 2012

	EARTH plc € million	WIND Limited € million	WATER Limited € million
Revenue	460	250	300
Cost of sales	(180)	(70)	(100)
Gross profit	280	180	200
Net operating expenses	(70)	(30)	(20)
Operating profit	210	150	180
Investment income	61	–	–
Interest payable	(30)	(10)	(10)
Profit on ordinary activities before tax	241	140	170
Tax on ordinary activities	(50)	(40)	(50)
Profit on ordinary activities after tax	191	100	120
Dividends proposed	(80)	(50)	(70)
Retained profit for the year	111	50	50

STATEMENTS OF FINANCIAL POSITION
as at 31 December 2012

	EARTH plc € million	WIND Limited € million	WATER Limited € million
ASSETS			
Non-current Assets			
Property, plant and equipment	540	280	300
Investments	750	–	–
	1,290	280	300

Current Assets			
Inventory	240	180	150
Receivables	120	170	160
Bank and cash	480	10	10
	2,130	640	620
EQUITY AND LIABILITIES			
Capital and Reserves			
€1 ordinary shares	600	200	160
Retained earnings	1,370	310	360
	1,970	510	520
Current Liabilities	160	130	100
	2,130	640	620

Additional Information:

1. On 1 January 2008 EARTH plc purchased 160 million €1 ordinary shares in WIND Limited for €550 million. The statement of profit or loss and other comprehensive income of WIND Limited stood at €210 million on this date and property, plant and equipment with a remaining useful life of 10 years were recorded at €40 million less than their fair value. For the purposes of measuring non-controlling interests at the date of acquisition, the proportionate share method equated to the fair value method. The directors of EARTH plc estimate that the goodwill arising on the acquisition of WIND Limited was impaired for the first time during the year ended 31 December 2012 by €95 million.

2. On 1 January 2012 EARTH plc purchased 48 million €1 ordinary shares in WATER Limited for €200 million. The statement of profit or loss and other comprehensive income of WATER Limited stood at €310 million on this date. The net assets of WATER Limited had a fair value that was the same as their book value. The goodwill arising on the acquisition of WATER Limited has not been impaired at 31 December 2012.

3. During 2012 WIND Limited sold raw materials to EARTH plc for €2 million, making a profit of 25% on cost. EARTH plc paid for the raw materials on delivery, and had €500,000 of these in inventory at 31 December 2012.

4. The profits of EARTH plc, WIND Limited and WATER Limited accrue evenly throughout the year. It is group policy to charge a full year's depreciation in the year of acquisition. Depreciation charges are included in net operating expenses.

5. EARTH plc's investment income, which is included in receivables, represents dividends receivable from WIND Limited and WATER Limited. Dividends proposed are included in current liabilities at 31 December 2012.

Requirement

(a) Prepare the consolidated statement of profit or loss and other comprehensive income of EARTH plc group for the year ended 31 December 2012.

(b) Prepare the consolidated statement of financial position for EARTH plc group as at 31 December 2012.

Note:

1. The answer does NOT require a consolidated statement of profit or loss and other comprehensive income and statement of financial position in a form suitable for publication. These statements may be presented by way of a consolidation schedule.

2. Notes to the financial statements are NOT required, nor is a statement indicating the amount of profit dealt with in the holding company's statement of profit or loss and other comprehensive income.
3. All workings should be clearly shown.

Question 29.3 (Based on Chartered Accountants Ireland, P3 Autumn 2001, Question 1)

OPUS Limited (OPUS), a company which prepares its financial statements to 31 December each year, carries on business as a distributor of musical instruments. On 1 January 2012, OPUS acquired 90% of the ordinary share capital of SONATA Limited (SONATA) at a cost of €942,000. On the same day, OPUS also acquired 30% of the ordinary share capital of PRELUDE Limited (PRELUDE) at a cost of €220,000.

The draft statements of profit or loss and other comprehensive income of OPUS, SONATA and PRELUDE for the year ended 31 December 2012 are as follows:

	OPUS	SONATA	PRELUDE
	€000	€000	€000
Revenue	22,500	1,950	1,500
Cost of sales	(15,000)	(1,225)	(1,000)
Gross profit	7,500	725	500
Distribution costs	(2,200)	(175)	(90)
Administrative expenses	(275)	(15)	(10)
Operating profit	5,025	535	400
Interest payable and similar charges	(40)	(10)	(20)
Interest receivable	20	5	10
Profit on ordinary activities before tax	5,005	530	390
Tax on profit on ordinary activities	(1,605)	(100)	(80)
Profit on ordinary activities after tax	3,400	430	310
Dividends paid	(250)	–	–
Retained profit for the year	3,150	430	310

Additional Information:
1. The net assets of SONATA on 1 January 2012 were as follows:

	Carrying value	Fair value
	€000	€000
Property, plant and equipment	600	560
Inventory	300	260
Other net assets	160	160
	1,060	980

The difference between the carrying value and the fair value of property, plant and equipment is due to a revaluation of property, while the reduction in inventory relates to a change in the accounting policy for inventory in order to bring SONATA's inventory into line with those of OPUS. Otherwise the accounting policies adopted by SONATA are similar to those of OPUS. The required change in the closing inventory of SONATA to ensure uniform accounting policies is a decrease of €30,000. The fair values shown above have not yet been incorporated into SONATA's financial statements. With respect to the measurement of non-controlling interests at the date of acquisition, the proportionate share method equates to the fair value method. The directors of OPUS believe that the goodwill arising on the acquisition of SONATA was impaired by €12,000 at 31 December 2012.

2. The fair value of the net assets of PRELUDE was the same as their book value on 1 January 2012. The statement of financial position of PRELUDE showed the following on this date:

	€000
Share capital	200
Retained earnings	450
	650

The directors of OPUS estimate that the goodwill arising on the acquisition of PRELUDE has not been impaired at 31 December 2012.

3. Following the acquisition of shares in SONATA and PRELUDE, the directors of OPUS decided to run down certain parts of OPUS's business activities. These were finally discontinued in December 2012. The contribution to the business of these activities in 2012 was:

	€000
Turnover	2,500
Cost of sales	2,000
Gross profit	500
Distribution costs	(290)
Administrative expenses	(200)
Operating profit	10

4. It is Group policy to charge any impairment of goodwill to cost of sales.
5. OPUS, SONATA and PRELUDE each follow a policy of depreciating all fixed assets at 10% per annum on their carrying value. Depreciation is charged to cost of sales in the statement of profit or loss and other comprehensive income.
6. There were no inter-company sales between OPUS, SONATA and PRELUDE, and the directors of OPUS are not directors of SONATA or PRELUDE.

Requirement Assuming that SONATA is to be accounted for as a subsidiary and PRELUDE as an associate, prepare the consolidated statement of profit or loss and other comprehensive income of OPUS Group for the year ended 31 December 2012 in a form suitable for publication.

Note:
1. A statement detailing the amount of the consolidated profit dealt with in OPUS's financial statements is not required.
2. Notes to the consolidated statement of profit or loss and other comprehensive income are not required.

Question 29.4 *(Based on Chartered Accountants Ireland, CAP 2 Autumn 2009, Question 3)*

DYLAN plc (DYLAN) acquired 40,000,000 of the €1 ordinary share capital of MARLEY Limited (MARLEY) on 1 January 2012. On the same day, DYLAN also purchased 3,000,000 of the €1 ordinary shares of YOUNG Limited. On 1 January 2012, the fair value of the net assets of MARLEY and YOUNG was the same as their book value, and neither company has issued ordinary shares in recent years.

DYLAN, MARLEY and YOUNG prepare their financial statements to 31 December each year, and their statements of profit or loss and other comprehensive income for the year ended 31 December 2012 and statements of financial position as at that date are as follows:

Statements of Profit or Loss and Other Comprehensive Income
for the Year Ended 31 December 2012

	DYLAN	MARLEY	YOUNG
	€000	€000	€000
Revenue	800,000	750,000	300,000
Cost of sales	(450,000)	(375,000)	(400,000)
Gross profit	350,000	375,000	(100,000)
Net operating expenses	(150,000)	(185,000)	(160,000)
Profit from operations	200,000	190,000	(260,000)
Income tax expense	(50,000)	(47,500)	–
Net profit/(loss) from operations	150,000	142,500	(260,000)

Statements of Financial Position
as at 31 December 2012

	DYLAN	MARLEY	YOUNG
	€000	€000	€000
Non-current Assets			
Property, plant and equipment	200,000	250,000	10,000
Investment in MARLEY	55,000	–	–
Investment in YOUNG	75,000	–	–
Current Assets			
Inventory	54,000	35,000	25,000
Trade receivables	41,000	85,000	9,000
Current account with MARLEY	50,000	–	–
Bank and cash	20,000	15,000	6,000
	495,000	385,000	50,000
EQUITY AND LIABILITIES			
Capital and Reserves			
€1 ordinary shares	80,000	50,000	10,000
Retained earnings	310,000	190,000	(30,000)
Non-current Liabilities			
Loans	75,000	50,000	15,000
Current Liabilities			
Trade payables	30,000	60,000	55,000
Current account with DYLAN	–	35,000	–
	495,000	385,000	50,000

Additional Information:

1. On 30 December 2012, MARLEY transferred €15,000,000 to Dylan. However, this was not received by DYLAN until 3 January 2013.

2. During 2012, YOUNG encountered significant problems with the quality of the raw materials used in manufacturing its main product. The company's directors are confident that these problems were satisfactorily resolved by 31 December 2012 and that the company will return to profitability in 2013. DYLAN has not incurred or guaranteed any obligations on behalf of YOUNG.

3. In November 2012, DYLAN purchased goods from YOUNG on which YOUNG earned a profit of €1,000,000. DYLAN's inventory at 31 December 2012 included 60% of the items purchased from YOUNG.

4. WILLIAMS Limited (WILLIAMS), a customer of DYLAN, owed DYLAN €2,000,000 on 31 December 2012 and this amount is included in DYLAN's trade receivables on this date. WILLIAMS went into receivership in March 2013 with €800,000 of the debt still owing. The receiver has indicated that they expect to be able to pay 25 cent in the euro on all debts owed.

Requirement Prepare the consolidated statement of profit or loss and other comprehensive income of DYLAN for the year ended 31 December 2012 and the consolidated statement of financial position as at that date.

Question 29.5 (Based on Chartered Accountants Ireland, CAP 2 Summer 2010, Question 2)

SUMO plc ("SUMO"), an Irish company that prepares its financial statements to 31 December each year, is involved in the manufacture of kit cars. On 1 January 2012, SUMO purchased 800,000 of the €1 ordinary shares in COBRA Limited ("COBRA") for cash, a company that specialises in the manufacture of chassis. The fair value of COBRA's net assets was the same as their book value except for plant and equipment which was understated by €400,000. COBRA has not reflected this in its financial statements at 31 December 2012.

On 1 July 2012, SUMO purchased 300,000 of the €1 ordinary shares in VIPER Limited ("VIPER") for cash, a company that manufactures customised exhaust systems. On this date, the fair value of VIPER's net assets was the same as their book value.

STATEMENTS OF PROFIT OR LOSS AND OTHER COMPREHENSIVE INCOME
for the Year Ended 31 December 2012

	SUMO €000	COBRA €000	VIPER €000
Revenue	15,000	2,500	1,000
Cost of sales	(9,000)	(1,250)	(350)
Gross profit	6,000	1,250	650
Operating expenses	(2,200)	(250)	(150)
Operating profit	3,800	1,000	500
Investment income	160	–	–
Profit before tax	3,960	1,000	500
Income tax expense	(1,200)	(300)	(120)
Profit after tax	2,760	700	380

STATEMENTS OF FINANCIAL POSITION
as at 31 December 2012

	SUMO €000	COBRA €000	VIPER €000
ASSETS			
Non-current Assets			
Plant and equipment	12,000	2,500	2,000
Investment in COBRA	2,250	–	–
Investment in VIPER	750	–	–
Current Assets			
Inventory	1,800	250	100
Receivables	1,200	150	60
Bank and cash	200	50	30
	18,200	2,950	2,190
EQUITY AND LIABILITIES			
Equity Attributable to Owners			
€1 ordinary shares	10,000	1,000	1,000
Share premium	1,000	200	100
Retained earnings	5,200	1,460	980
Current Liabilities			
Trade payables	1,100	50	60
Dividends payable	500	200	–
Other payables	400	40	50
	18,200	2,950	2,190

Additional Information:
1. In October 2012, COBRA sold goods to SUMO with an invoice value of €400,000 on which COBRA made a mark-up of 25%. One half of these goods remained in SUMO's inventory at 31 December 2012. There was no other trading between SUMO, COBRA and VIPER during 2012.
2. None of the three companies has issued or cancelled shares since incorporation. Each of the companies depreciates plant and equipment on a straight-line basis at 25% per annum, with depreciation being reflected in operating expenses.
3. With respect to the measurement of non-controlling interests at the date of acquisition of COBRA, the proportionate share method equates to the fair value method. The directors of SUMO are confident that any goodwill arising on the acquisition of COBRA and VIPER had not been impaired at 31 December 2012.
4. The shareholders of SUMO and COBRA approved the proposed dividends in December 2012. These were paid in 2013.
5. The activities and profits of the three companies accrue evenly throughout the year.

Requirement Prepare the consolidated statement of profit or loss and other comprehensive income for the year ended 31 December 2012 of SUMO and the consolidated statement of financial position as at that date.

30

JOINT ARRANGEMENTS

LEARNING OBJECTIVES

This chapter focuses on the accounting treatment of joint ventures. Having studied this chapter, you should be able to:
1. explain the terms 'joint control' and 'joint arrangement';
2. distinguish between a joint operation and a joint venture;
3. account for the different forms of joint arrangement in accordance with IFRS 11 *Joint Arrangements*; and
4. apply the main disclosure requirements of IFRS 11.

KEY TERMS AND DEFINITIONS FOR THIS CHAPTER

In order to aid your understanding of the concepts and issues covered in this chapter, it is important to understand and be familiar with the following key terms and definitions. As you study this chapter, you should refer back to them.

Equity Method A method of accounting whereby the investment is initially recognised at cost and adjusted thereafter for the post-acquisition change in the investor's share of the investee's net assets. The investor's profit or loss includes its share of the investee's profit or loss and the investor's other comprehensive income includes its share of the investee's other comprehensive income. This is explained and illustrated in detail in **Chapter 29**.

Joint Arrangement This is an arrangement of which two or more parties have joint control.

Joint Control This is the contractually agreed sharing of control of an arrangement, which exists only when decisions about the relevant activities require the unanimous consent of the parties sharing control.

Joint Operation This is a joint arrangement whereby the parties that have joint control of the arrangement have rights to the assets, and obligations for the liabilities, relating to the arrangement.

Joint Venture This is a joint arrangement whereby the parties that have joint control of the arrangement have rights to the net assets of the arrangement.

Joint Venturer This is a party to a joint venture that has joint control of that joint venture.

Party to a Joint Arrangement This is an entity that participates in a joint arrangement, regardless of whether that entity has joint control of the arrangement.

Separate Vehicle This is a separately identifiable financial structure, including separate legal entities or entities recognised by statute, regardless of whether those entities have a legal personality.

30.1 INTRODUCTION

A joint arrangement is a strategic alliance between two or more individuals or entities to engage in a specific project or undertaking. One of the most well-known joint arrangement arrangements is Sony–Ericsson, a joint venture between Japanese consumer electronics company Sony Corporation and the Swedish telecommunications company Ericsson to make mobile phones. The stated reason for this venture is to combine Sony's consumer electronics expertise with Ericsson's technological leadership in the communications sector.

There are many good business and accounting reasons to participate in a joint arrangement. For example, it:
- provides companies with the opportunity to gain new capacity and expertise;
- allows companies to enter related areas of businesses or new geographic markets or gain new technological knowledge;
- gives access to greater resources, including specialised staff and technology;
- shares risks with a venture partner;
- can be flexible. For example, a joint venture can have a limited life span and only cover part of what you do, thus limiting both your commitment and the business' exposure; and
- can allow companies to gradually separate a business from the rest of the organisation, and eventually, sell it to the other parent company. Evidence suggests that approximately 80% of all joint ventures end in a sale by one partner to the other.

However, joint arrangements are not without their difficulties. It takes time and effort to build the right relationship and partnering with another business can be challenging. Problems are likely to arise if:
- the objectives of the arrangement are not 100% clear and communicated to everyone involved;
- there is an imbalance in levels of expertise, investment or assets brought into the arrangement by the different partners;
- different cultures and management styles result in poor integration and co-operation;
- the partners do not provide enough leadership and support in the early stages;
- there is inadequate research and analysis – success in a joint venture depends on thorough research and analysis of the objectives.

Prior to May 2011, the accounting treatment of **joint arrangements** (previously referred to collectively as joint ventures) was governed by IAS 31 *Interests in Joint Ventures* and SIC 13 *Jointly Controlled Entities – Non-Monetary Contributions by Venturers*. In May 2011, the International Accounting Standards Board (IASB) issued IFRS 11 *Joint Arrangements*. This standard establishes principles for the financial reporting by parties to a **joint arrangement**, which is classified as being either a **joint operation** or a **joint venture** (this latter classification should not be confused with the broad use of the term 'joint venture' in IAS 31). IFRS 11 supersedes IAS 31 and SIC 13, and is effective from 1 January 2013, with early application permitted.

When revising IAS 31, the IASB was mainly concerned with remedying two aspects of IAS 31 that were considered impediments to high-quality reporting of joint arrangements:

1. The accounting requirements in IAS 31 may not have always reflected the rights and obligations of the parties arising from the arrangements in which they were involved.
2. IAS 31 gave entities a choice to apply either proportionate consolidation or the equity method to all of their jointly controlled entities.

The IASB argued that these two aspects of IAS 31 could create situations where:

• arrangements that entitle the parties to similar rights and obligations are accounted for differently; and, conversely
• arrangements that entitle the parties to different rights and obligations are accounted for similarly.

The accounting requirements discussed in this chapter with respect to joint arrangements are based on IFRS 11.

Key to this Chapter

This chapter explains the accounting treatment of joint arrangements in accordance with IFRS 11. **Section 30.2** concentrates on the classification of and treatment accounting for a joint operation and a joint venture. The disclosure requirements of IFRS 11 are presented in **Section 30.3**.

30.2 IFRS 11 *JOINT ARRANGEMENTS*

As mentioned previously, in May 2011 the IASB issued IFRS 11, which supersedes IAS 31 and SIC 13 and is effective from 1 January 2013, with early application permitted.

Consistent with the *Conceptual Framework for Financial Reporting 2010* (see **Chapter 1**), IFRS 11 introduces a principle-based approach to accounting for joint arrangements by requiring a party to a joint arrangement to recognise its rights and obligations arising from the arrangement. The application of this principle:

• enhances *verifiability* and *understandability* because the accounting reflects more faithfully the economic phenomena that it purports to represent (i.e. a party's rights and obligations arising from the arrangements);
• enhances *consistency* because it provides the same accounting outcome for each type of joint arrangement; and
• increases *comparability* among financial statements because it will enable users to identify and understand similarities in, and differences between, similar arrangements.

Under IFRS 11, a **joint arrangement** is an arrangement in which two or more parties have **joint control**. Joint control is the contractually agreed sharing of control of an arrangement, which exists only when decisions about the relevant activities require the unanimous consent of the parties sharing control. An entity that is a party to an arrangement shall assess whether the contractual arrangement gives all the parties, or a group of the parties, control of the arrangement collectively. The assessment of joint control is illustrated in **Figure 30.1** and **Example 30.1**.

FIGURE 30.1: ASSESSING JOINT CONTROL

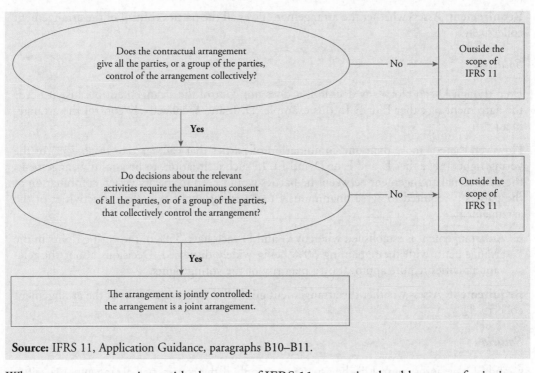

Source: IFRS 11, Application Guidance, paragraphs B10–B11.

When an arrangement is outside the scope of IFRS 11, an entity should account for its interest in the arrangement in accordance with relevant IFRSs (for example, IFRS 9 (see **Chapter 25**), IFRS 10 (see **Chapter 26**) or IAS 28 (see **Chapter 29**)).

EXAMPLE 30.1: ASSESSING JOINT CONTROL

1. Three parties (A, B and C) establish an arrangement whereby: A has 50% of the voting rights in the arrangement; B has 30%; and C has 20%. The contractual arrangement between A, B and C specifies that at least 75% of the voting rights are required to make decisions about the relevant activities of the arrangement.

Requirement Assess whether the arrangement gives all the parties control of the arrangement collectively.

Solution

Even though A can block any decision, it does not control the arrangement because it needs the agreement of B. The terms of the contractual arrangement (i.e. at least 75% of the voting rights are required to make decisions about the relevant activities) imply that A and B have joint control of the arrangement because decisions about the relevant activities of the arrangement cannot be made without both A and B agreeing.

2. Three parties (D, E and F) establish an arrangement whereby: D has 50% of the voting rights in the arrangement; and E and F each have 25%. The contractual arrangement between D, E and F specifies that at least 75% of the voting rights are required to make decisions about the relevant activities of the arrangement.

Requirement Assess whether the arrangement gives all the parties control of the arrangement collectively.

Solution

Even though D can block any decision, it does not control the arrangement because it needs the agreement of either E or F. In this example, D, E and F collectively control the arrangement.

However, there is more than one combination of parties that can agree to reach 75% of the voting rights (i.e. either D and E or D and F). In such a situation, to be a joint arrangement, the contractual arrangement between the parties would need to specify which combination of the parties is required to agree unanimously to decisions about the relevant activities of the arrangement.

3. An arrangement is established whereby G and H each have 35% of the voting rights in the arrangement, with the remaining 30% being widely dispersed. Decisions about the relevant activities require approval by a majority of the voting rights.

Requirement Assess whether the arrangement gives all the parties control of the arrangement collectively.

Solution

G and H have joint control of the arrangement only if the contractual arrangement specifies that decisions about the relevant activities of the arrangement require both G and H agreeing.

Source: IFRS 11, Application Guidance.

A joint arrangement is classified as either a **joint operation** or a **joint venture**.
- A **joint operation** is a joint arrangement whereby the parties that have joint control of the arrangement have rights to the assets, and obligations for the liabilities, relating to the arrangement. Those parties are called joint operators, and they are required to account for assets, liabilities and corresponding revenues and expenses from the arrangement.
- A **joint venture** is a joint arrangement whereby the parties that have joint control of the arrangement have rights to the net assets of the arrangement. Those parties are called joint venturers and they are required to account for the arrangement using the **equity method**.

The classification of a joint arrangement is illustrated in **Figure 30.2** and **Figure 30.3**.

FIGURE 30.2: CLASSIFICATION OF A JOINT ARRANGEMENT (1)

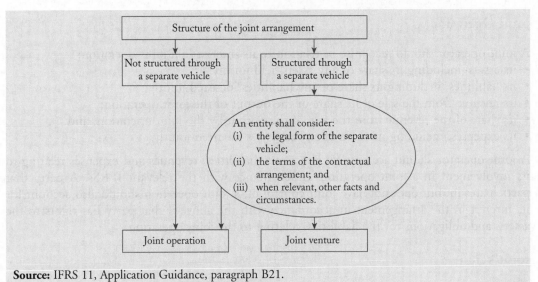

Source: IFRS 11, Application Guidance, paragraph B21.

FIGURE 30.3: CLASSIFICATION OF A JOINT ARRANGEMENT (2)

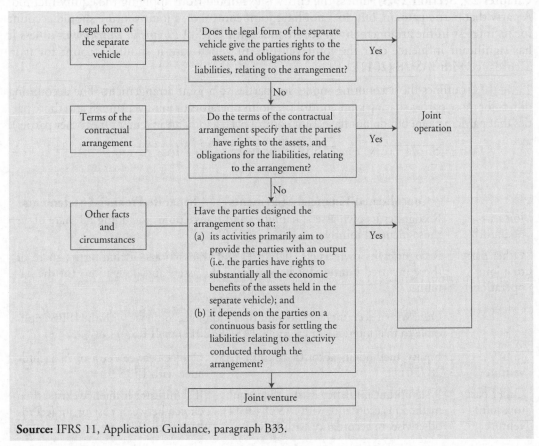

Source: IFRS 11, Application Guidance, paragraph B33.

The accounting treatment for a joint operation and joint venture is explained below.

Joint Operation

A joint operator should recognise in relation to its interest in a joint operation:
- its assets, including its share of any assets held jointly;
- its liabilities, including its share of any liabilities incurred jointly;
- its revenue from the sale of its share of the output of the joint operation;
- its share of the revenue from the sale of the output by the joint operation; and
- its expenses, including its share of any expenses incurred jointly.

A joint operator should account for the assets, liabilities, revenues and expenses relating to its involvement in a joint operation in accordance with the relevant IFRSs. A party that participates in, but does not have joint control of, a joint operation should also account for its interest in the arrangement in accordance with the above if that party has rights to the assets, and obligations for the liabilities, relating to the joint operation.

Joint Venture

A joint venturer should recognise its interest in a joint venture as an investment and shall account for that investment using the equity method in accordance with IAS 28 (2011) (see **Chapter 29**, **Section 29.3**), unless the entity is exempted from applying the equity method. A party that participates in, but does not have joint control of, a joint venture should account for its interest in the arrangement in accordance with IFRS 9 *Financial Instruments* unless it has significant influence over the joint venture, in which case it should account for it in accordance with IAS 28 (2011).

Table 30.1 outlines the accounting model for parties to a joint arrangement. The accounting differs for those parties sharing joint control (i.e. joint operators or joint venturers) and those parties that participate in, but do not have joint control over, a joint arrangement (i.e. other parties).

TABLE 30.1: ACCOUNTING MODEL FOR PARTIES TO A JOINT ARRANGEMENT

	Consolidated Financial Statements	Separate Financial Statements
Joint operator	Recognises its own assets, liabilities and transactions, including its share of those incurred jointly.	
Other party to a joint operation	Recognises its own assets, liabilities and transactions, including its share of those incurred jointly, if it has rights to the assets and obligations for the liabilities. Otherwise it accounts for the joint operation in accordance with the IFRS applicable to that interest (for example, IAS 28 (2011) or IFRS 9).	
Joint venture	Equity method in accordance with IAS 28 (2011).	Choice between cost or in accordance with IFRS 9.
Other party to a joint venture	If significant influence exists, then equity method in accordance with IAS 28 (2011); otherwise, in accordance with IFRS 9.	If significant influence exists, then choice between cost or in accordance with IFRS 9.

30.3 DISCLOSURE

There are no disclosures specified in IFRS 11. Instead, the disclosure requirements for joint arrangements have been placed in IFRS 12 *Disclosure of Interests in Other Entities*. IFRS 12 is a comprehensive disclosure standard for subsidiaries, joint arrangements, associates and unconsolidated structured entities. The IASB issued IFRS 11 at the same time as IFRS 10 *Consolidated Financial Statements*, IFRS 12 and the amended IAS 27 *Separate Financial Statements* and IAS 28 *Investments in Associates and Joint Ventures*.

The disclosure requirements for joint arrangements in IFRS 12 aim to include information that helps users of financial statements to evaluate the nature, extent and financial effects of an entity's interests in joint arrangements, and the nature of the risks associated with those interests. The following disclosure requirements aim to fulfil this objective:
- a list of joint arrangements that are material for the entity, including a description of the nature of the entity's relationship with its joint arrangements; and
- summarised financial information on an individual basis for those joint ventures that are material to the entity. This disclosure requirement will enable users to understand the net debt position of the joint ventures and will give them information to help them value the entity's investments in joint ventures.

30.4 CONCLUSION

A joint arrangement is a contractual agreement whereby two or more parties undertake an economic activity that is subject to joint control. The venture can be for one specific project or a continuing business relationship. A joint arrangement may be a limited company, a partnership or other legal structure depending on a number of considerations such as tax and tort liability. Joint arrangements are often between a local and foreign company, and are often seen as a viable business alternative where companies can complement their skill sets or gain a geographic presence.

Prior to May 2011, the accounting treatment of joint ventures was governed by IAS 31 and SIC 13. In May 2011, the IASB issued IFRS 11, which classifies **joint arrangements** as being either a **joint operation** or a **joint venture**. IFRS 11 supersedes IAS 31 and SIC 13 and is effective from 1 January 2013, with early application permitted. IFRS 11 does two main things:
1. Arrangements that are similar to jointly controlled assets or jointly controlled operations under IAS 31 are now called **joint operations**.
2. IAS 31 jointly controlled entities, which are now called **joint ventures**, are no longer allowed to use proportionate consolidation; they must use the equity method.

SUMMARY OF LEARNING OBJECTIVES

This chapter focuses on the accounting treatment of joint arrangements. After having studied this chapter, you should be able to:

Learning Objective 1 Explain the term 'joint arrangement'.

This is a contractual agreement whereby two or more parties undertake an economic activity that is subject to joint control.

Learning Objective 2 Distinguish between a joint operation and a joint venture.

A **joint operation** is a joint arrangement whereby the parties that have joint control of the arrangement have rights to the assets, and obligations for the liabilities, relating to the arrangement. A **joint venture** is a joint arrangement whereby the parties that have joint control of the arrangement have rights to the net assets of the arrangement.

Learning Objective 3 Account for the different forms of joint arrangement in accordance with IFRS 11.

Table 30.1 outlines the accounting model for parties to a joint arrangement. The accounting differs for those parties sharing joint control (i.e. joint operators or joint venturers) and those parties that participate in, but do not have joint control over, a joint arrangement (i.e. other parties).

A **joint operation** is a joint arrangement whereby the parties that have joint control of the arrangement have rights to the assets, and obligations for the liabilities, relating to the arrangement. Those parties are called joint operators and they should account for the assets, liabilities, revenues and expenses relating to their involvement in a joint operation in accordance with the relevant IFRSs. A party that participates in, but does not have joint control of, a joint operation should also account for its interest in the arrangement in accordance with the above if that party has rights to the assets, and obligations for the liabilities, relating to the joint operation.

A **joint venture** is a joint arrangement whereby the parties that have joint control of the arrangement have rights to the net assets of the arrangement. Those parties are called joint venturers and they should recognise their interest in a joint venture as an investment and shall account for that investment using the equity method in accordance with IAS 28 (2011) (see **Chapter 29, Section 29.3**).

Learning Objective 4 Apply the main disclosure requirements of IFRS 11.

See **Section 30.3**.

QUESTIONS

Self-test Questions

1. Explain the term 'joint arrangement'.
2. Distinguish between joint operations and joint ventures.

> **Note:** for ease of illustration, dividends and retained earnings are often shown at the foot of the statement of profit or loss and other comprehensive income in questions. These figures would normally be included in the statement of changes in equity.

Review Questions

(See **Appendix One** for Suggested Solutions to Review Questions.)

Review Questions 30.1 and 30.2 deal with subsidiaries and/or associates and are presented as revision of the consolidation principles covered in **Chapters 26–29**. Moreover, as associates are accounted for using the equity method, this is therefore relevant for joint arrangements.

Question 30.1 *(Based on Chartered Accountants Ireland, P3 Autumn 1998, Question 2)*

TRUE plc acquired 675,000 shares in FAIR Limited on 1 January 2010. The reserves of FAIR Limited at the date of acquisition comprised retained earnings of €100,000 and capital reserve of €50,000. With respect to the measurement of non-controlling interests at the date of acquisition, the proportionate share method equated to the fair value method. The draft statements of financial position of both these companies as at 31 December 2012 are given below.

	TRUE plc		FAIR Limited	
	€	€	€	€
ASSETS				
Non-current Assets				
Property, plant and equipment		1,750,000		1,050,000
Investments – shares in Fair				
Limited at cost		950,000		
		2,700,000		
Current assets				
Inventory	415,000		210,000	
Receivables	510,000		240,000	
Current account with				
FAIR Limited	25,000		–	
Bank and cash	200,000	1,150,000	60,000	510,000
		3,850,000		1,560,000
EQUITY AND LIABILITIES				
Capital and Reserves				
€1 ordinary shares		2,000,000		750,000
Retained earnings		950,000		495,000
Capital reserve		300,000		75,000
		3,250,000		1,320,000
Current Liabilities				
Trade payables	450,000		185,000	
Current account with				
TRUE Limited	–		5,000	
Proposed dividend	150,000	600,000	50,000	240,000
		3,850,000		1,560,000

In addition, the draft statements of profit or loss and other comprehensive income of the two companies for the year ended 31 December 2012 are as follows:

	TRUE plc €	FAIR Limited €
Revenue	4,050,000	990,000
Cost of sales	(2,088,000)	(558,000)
Gross profit	1,962,000	432,000
Operating expenses	(1,260,000)	(198,000)
Trading profit	702,000	234,000
Investment income	45,000	–
Profit before taxation	747,000	234,000
Taxation	(180,000)	(72,000)
Profit after taxation	567,000	162,000
Ordinary dividends paid	(255,000)	(50,000)
Ordinary dividends proposed	(150,000)	(50,000)
Retained profit for the year	162,000	62,000

Additional Information:

1. TRUE plc has not yet accounted for its share of the proposed dividend by FAIR Limited.
2. On 30 December 2012 FAIR Limited sent a cheque for €20,000 to TRUE plc which was not received until 2 January 2013.
3. TRUE plc sold goods to FAIR Limited during the year at an invoice price of €225,000. The goods were invoiced at cost plus 25%. One half of these goods was still in FAIR Limited's inventory at 31 December 2012.
4. On 7 January 2013 a power failure at one of the refrigerated storage units owned by FAIR Limited destroyed inventory with a book value at the year-end of €42,000. The company has negotiated a settlement of €35,000 with the insurance company.
5. On 13 January 2013 SHAKEY Limited, a customer of TRUE plc, went into receivership. There had been no movement on this customer's account since the year-end, at which time SHAKEY Limited owed €30,000 to TRUE plc. Unaware of the difficulties that SHAKEY Limited was facing, no provision had been made against this account nor did any reservation of title clauses exist.
6. The directors of TRUE estimate that the goodwill arising on the acquisition of FAIR was impaired for the first time during the year ended 31 December 2012 by €84,000.

Requirement Prepare the consolidated statement of profit or loss and other comprehensive income of TRUE plc for the year ended 31 December 2012 and the consolidated statement of financial position as at that date.

Question 30.2 (Based on Chartered Accountants Ireland, P3 Summer 1999, Question 4)

Archer PLC owns a number of subsidiaries, and prepares its consolidated financial statements to 31 December each year. During 2012 ARCHER plc purchased interests in BOW Limited and ARROW Limited. Draft statements of profit or loss and other comprehensive income for the year ended 31 December 2012 and statements of financial position as at that date for ARCHER Group (excluding BOW Limited and ARROW Limited), and for BOW Limited and ARROW Limited are presented below.

STATEMENTS OF PROFIT OR LOSS AND OTHER COMPREHENSIVE INCOME
for the Year Ended 31 December 2012

	ARCHER Group €m	BOW Limited €m	ARROW Limited €m
Revenue	3,000	200	1,800
Cost of sales	(1,800)	(125)	(900)
Gross profit	1,200	75	900
Operating expenses	(500)	(25)	(260)
Operating profit	700	50	640
Interest payable	(20)	(5)	(10)
Profit before tax	680	45	630
Tax	(200)	(10)	(190)
Profit after tax	480	35	440
Dividends paid	(180)	–	(40)
Retained profit for year	300	35	400

STATEMENTS OF FINANCIAL POSITION
as at 31 December 2012

	ARCHER Group €m	BOW Limited €m	ARROW Limited €m
ASSETS			
Non-current Assets			
Property, plant and equipment	2,200	40	2,100
Investment in BOW Limited	200	–	–
Investment in ARROW Limited	800	–	–
	3,200	40	2,100
Current Assets			
Inventory	400	125	250
Receivables	300	–	240
Bank and cash	80	200	110
	3,980	365	2,700
EQUITY AND LIABILITIES			
Capital and Reserves			
€1 ordinary shares (equity)	1,200	100	600
Revaluation reserve	600	–	300
Retained earnings	1,700	235	1,500
	3,500	335	2,400
Current Liabilities	480	30	300
	3,980	365	2,700

Additional Information:

1. On 1 January 2012 ARCHER plc purchased 100% of the ordinary share capital of BOW Limited. The details were as follows:

	€m
Cost of investment	200
Fair value of net assets acquired:	
– property, plant and equipment	50
– inventory	250

Property, plant and equipment are to be depreciated over five years. During 2012, 50% of the inventory was sold outside the group on normal trading terms, with the remaining inventory expected to be sold in 2013. The acquisition of BOW Limited has not yet been incorporated into the ARCHER Group financial statements shown above.

2. On 1 January 2012 ARCHER plc purchased 30% of ARROW Limited. ARCHER plc contributes to ARROW plc's activities and is actively involved in ARROW Limited's financial and operating policy decisions. ARROW Limited's statement of financial position at 1 January 2012 showed:

	€m
Share capital	600
Revaluation reserve	300
Retained earnings	1,100
	2,000

Apart from recording the cost of the investment, the acquisition of ARROW Limited has not yet been incorporated into the ARCHER Group financial statements shown above.

Requirement Prepare the consolidated statement of profit or loss and other comprehensive income for the year ended 31 December 2012 and the statement of financial position as at that date for ARCHER Group.

Challenging Questions

(Suggested Solutions to Challenging Questions are available to lecturers.)

Question 30.1 (Based on Chartered Accountants Ireland, P3 Summer 2006, Questions 1 and 2)

You are the Finance Director of THOMPSON Group plc (THOMPSON), a group of companies that imports, blends and packs high quality tea for sale to the retail trade. THOMPSON prepares its financial statements to 31 December each year, and you have just extracted the following trial balance as at 31 December 2012 from the group's books and records:

TRIAL BALANCE
as at 31 December 2012

	Note	DR €000	CR €000
€1 ordinary shares			1,000
Retained earnings at 31 December 2011			600

Cost of investment in ROSS Limited	1	250	
Cost of investment in DAVID Limited	2	150	
Property – cost at 31 December 2011	3	600	
Property – accumulated depreciation at 31 December 2011	4		108
Plant and equipment – cost at 31 December 2011		1,800	
Plant and equipment – accumulated depreciation at 31 December 2011	4		292
Development costs		100	
Inventory at 31 December 2011	5	260	
Trade receivables		35	
Prepayments		15	
Bank overdraft			25
Trade payables			40
Accruals			12
10% debentures	6		600
Revenue			9,500
Purchases		4,200	
Selling and distribution costs		1,750	
Administrative expenses		1,972	
Debenture interest paid		45	
Dividends paid		1,000	
		12,177	12,177

Additional Information:
1. On 1 January 2012, THOMPSON purchased 60,000 €1 ordinary shares in ROSS Limited (ROSS), a company that is involved in the tea trade but whose focus is on the price of the product rather than the quality. The retained earnings of ROSS stood at €170,000 on 1 January 2012, and the net assets of ROSS had a fair value that was the same as their book value. The statement of profit or loss and other comprehensive income of ROSS for the year ended 31 December 2012, and the statement of financial position as at that date, are shown below:

STATEMENT OF PROFIT OR LOSS AND OTHER COMPREHENSIVE INCOME
for the Year Ended 31 December 2012

	€000
Revenue	500
Cost of sales	(200)
Gross profit	300
Administrative expenses	(100)
Profit before tax	200
Income tax	(50)
Profit after tax	150

STATEMENT OF FINANCIAL POSITION
as at 31 December 2012

	€000
ASSETS	
Non-current Assets	
Plant and equipment	500
Current Assets	
Inventory	30
Receivables	40
Bank and cash	10
	580
EQUITY AND LIABILITIES	
Capital and Reserves	
€1 ordinary shares	200
Retained earnings	320
Current Liabilities	
Trade payables	60
	580

Only the cost of the investment in ROSS is included in THOMPSON's trial balance as at 31 December 2012. The directors of THOMPSON estimate that the goodwill arising on the acquisition of ROSS was impaired by €39,000 during the year ended 31 December 2012.

2. During the year ended 31 December 2012, THOMPSON became involved in a joint arrangement with GRAEME Incorporated (GRAEME) with a view to expanding their operations to other countries. THOMPSON and GRAEME each purchased 50% of the ordinary share capital in a new entity, DAVID Limited (DAVID). Under the terms of the joint arrangement, THOMPSON and GRAEME have rights to the net assets of the arrangement. Neither THOMPSON nor GRAEME is able to control DAVID without the support of the other, and all decisions on financial and operating policy, economic performance and financial position require the consent of both THOMPSON and GRAEME. The following information is available with respect to DAVID's activities during the year ended 31 December 2012.

STATEMENT OF PROFIT OR LOSS AND OTHER COMPREHENSIVE INCOME
for the Period Ended 31 December 2012

	€000
Revenue	300
Cost of sales	(100)
Gross profit	200
Administrative expenses	(50)
Profit before tax	150

	€000
Income tax	(30)
Profit after tax	120

STATEMENT OF FINANCIAL POSITION
as at 31 December 2012

	€000
ASSETS	
Non-current Assets	
Plant and equipment	290
Current Assets	
Inventory	20
Receivables	10
Bank and cash	5
	325
EQUITY AND LIABILITIES	
Capital and Reserves	
€1 ordinary shares	200
Retained earnings	120
Current Liabilities	
Trade payables	5
	325

Only the cost of the investment in DAVID is included in THOMPSON's trial balance as at 31 December 2012. The directors of THOMPSON are confident that any goodwill arising on the acquisition of DAVID has not been impaired at 31 December 2012.

3. The property shown in the trial balance was acquired a number of years ago and the estimated useful economic life was 50 years at the time of purchase. As at 31 December 2012, the property is to be revalued to €1,000,000.

4. It is group policy to provide a full year's depreciation in the year of acquisition and none in the year of disposal. All depreciation is charged to administrative expenses and is calculated as follows:
   Property   – straight-line over estimated useful economic life;
   Plant and equipment   – 10% straight-line.

5. THOMPSON's inventory at 31 December 2012 is valued by the directors at €275,000. Included in this figure is speciality tea valued at its original cost of €60,000. The replacement cost of the tea is €30,000 and its market value, based upon sales in January and February 2013, is €50,000 before selling and distribution costs of €5,000.

6. The 10% debentures were issued on 1 January 2012 and are redeemable on 31 December 2016. Interest is paid quarterly in arrears and the first payment was due on 1 April 2012.

7. In February 2013, THOMPSON received a claim from a former employee for €25,000 alleging discrimination at work and unfair dismissal in October 2012. While the directors refute the claim, they believe the courts are likely to uphold it. As the claim was received in 2013, the directors have decided not to account for it in 2012 and wait until the outcome of the case is known with certainty. The directors believe the case will not be resolved until 2014.

8. There is no trading between THOMPSON, ROSS, GRAEME and DAVID, and there was no change in the share capital of the companies during 2012.

9. THOMPSON's tax charge for 2012, which takes into account all relevant items, is €325,250.

Requirement

Prepare the consolidated statement of profit or loss and other comprehensive income for THOMPSON for the year ended 31 December 2012 and the consolidated statement of financial position as at that date.

31

FOREIGN CURRENCY TRANSACTIONS AND TRANSLATION OF FOREIGN OPERATIONS

LEARNING OBJECTIVES

This chapter deals with foreign currency transactions and the translation of the financial statements of foreign operations into a presentation currency. Having studied this chapter, you should be able to:

1. include foreign currency transactions in the financial statements of a reporting entity;
2. translate the financial statements of a foreign entity into a presentation currency and include them in the financial statements of a reporting entity; and
3. account for entities reporting in the currency of a hyperinflationary economy.

KEY TERMS AND DEFINITIONS FOR THIS CHAPTER

In order to aid your understanding of the concepts and issues covered in this chapter, it is important to understand and be familiar with the following key terms and definitions. This is a complex chapter and a significant part of the difficulty actually arises from not being familiar with the terms used. Consequently, as you study this chapter, you should refer back to the key terms and definitions listed below.

Closing Rate The spot exchange rate at the reporting date.

Currency Options In finance, a foreign exchange option (commonly shortened to just FX option or currency option) is a **derivative** financial instrument where the owner has the right, but not the obligation, to exchange money denominated in one currency into another currency at a pre-agreed exchange rate on a specified date.

Derivative This is a financial instrument:
- whose value changes in response to the change in an underlying variable such as an interest rate, commodity or security price, or index;
- that requires no initial investment, or one that is smaller than would be required for a contract with similar response to changes in market factors; and
- that is settled at a future date.

Exchange Difference The difference resulting from translating one currency into another currency at different exchange rates.

Exchange Rate The ratio of exchange for two currencies.

Foreign Currency A currency other than the functional currency of the entity.

Foreign Currency Accounts Foreign currency accounts can be a good option for importers and exporters as they allow you to 'net' receivables and payables in the same currency. These accounts allow the receipt of inward payments, cheques/cash and also allow the issue of international money transfers and drafts. They are offered by most of the UK clearing banks.

Foreign Operation This is a subsidiary, associate, joint venture or branch whose activities are based in a country or currency other than those of the reporting entity.

Forward Foreign Exchange Contracts One way to hedge against **exchange rate** movements is to arrange a forward foreign exchange contract. This is an agreement initiated by you to buy or sell a specific amount of **foreign currency** at a certain rate, on or before a certain date.

Functional Currency This is the currency of the primary economic environment in which the entity operates and is the currency used for measurement in the financial statements.

Hedge Accounting This is a practice in which a risky trading position and its hedge are treated as one item so that the gains in one automatically offset the losses in the other.

Monetary Items These are money and assets/liabilities held to be received/paid in fixed or determinable amounts. Examples include deferred tax, pensions and provisions. The feature of a non-monetary item is the absence of a right to receive a fixed or determinable amount of money (this includes prepayments, goodwill, intangible assets, inventory and property).

Net Investment in a Foreign Operation The amount of the interest in the net assets of that operation. This includes long-term receivables or loans, but does not include trade receivables or trade payables.

Presentation Currency The currency in which the financial statements are presented.

Spot Rate The **exchange rate** for immediate delivery.

Please note that, as explained in **Chapter 2**, the IASB issued amendments to IAS 1 *Presentation of Financial Statements* in June 2011. These included a *proposal* that the title 'Statement of Profit or Loss and Other Comprehensive Income' (SPLOCI) be adopted (rather than, for example, 'statement of comprehensive income') and a *requirement* to revise the presentation of other comprehensive income (OCI) within the SPLOCI. These amendments are explained in detail in **Chapter 2**, **Section 2.3**.

31.1 INTRODUCTION

Exchange rates can have an effect on a business's competitiveness. For example, changing **foreign currency** exchange rates affect the cost of imported and exported goods and services, and hence the profitability of companies that conduct aspects of their business in different currencies. In simple terms:

- if the Euro gets weaker, then companies based in the Eurozone have to trade more Euros in order to get another currency. Therefore, importing goods becomes more expensive; although exporting goods is easier as 'your' goods are 'cheaper' abroad.
- in contrast, if the Euro gets stronger, the 'other people' have to trade more of their currency to get the same amount of Euros. Thus, this makes it more difficult for companies based in the Eurozone to export, because their goods are now more expensive to the rest of the world. However, importing goods becomes less expensive.

To a large extent, there is no one best situation – it largely depends on the nature of your business. Indeed, it could be argued that it is the volatility and uncertainty that causes problems for business not necessarily the relative strength of one currency vis-à-vis another.

Consequently, it can be seen that when a business deals in a foreign currency it is exposed to certain risks:

- it might find that after agreeing a price for exported or imported goods the exchange rate changes before delivery. Clearly, this can work both for and against the business, depending on whether it is importing or exporting; and
- some countries' currencies are more volatile than others because of their inflationary or unstable economies. This makes their exchange rates more liable to extreme movements.

Carrying out business transactions in a foreign currency will have an effect on normal accountancy procedures since it is necessary to convert foreign currency payments and deposits into the entity's domestic currency. In addition, holding assets and liabilities in a foreign currency will have an impact on the statement of financial position since, owing to exchange rate movements, their value might differ radically from one year to the next.

Of course, because exchange rates can go both up and down, a business could gamble that this will work out in their favour. However, this is extremely risky and could result in significant financial loss. It is safer to reduce the risk by using one of the forms of hedging. Hedging simply means insuring against the price of an item – in this case, currency – moving against the business in the future (e.g. **forward foreign exchange contracts**, opening **foreign currency accounts** and buying **currency options**). A business in the Eurozone could also consider trading overseas in Euro – effectively transferring the foreign exchange risk to the business it is dealing with. Whether this is an appropriate solution will probably depend on the product in question and the relative bargaining strength of the two businesses.

Key to this Chapter

The accounting treatment of issues associated with foreign currency is guided primarily by two accounting standards: IAS 21 *The Effects of Changes in Foreign Exchange Rates* and IAS 29 *Financial Reporting in Hyperinflationary Economies*.

The purpose of IAS 21 is to set out how to account for transactions in foreign currencies and **foreign operations**. IAS 21 shows how to translate financial statements into a **presentation currency**, which is the currency in which the financial statements are presented. This contrasts with the **functional currency**, which is the currency of the primary economic environment in which the (foreign) entity operates. Key issues are the exchange rates, that should be used, and how the effects of changes in exchange rates are recorded in the financial statements.

With respect to IAS 21, **Section 31.2** explains how to account for non-consolidation-related transactions denominated in a foreign currency (i.e. sales or purchases of goods, services and non-current assets denominated in a foreign currency), while the translation of foreign entities is addressed in **Section 31.3**.

Accounting for entities reporting in the currency of a hyperinflationary economy in accordance with IAS 29 is explained in **Section 31.4**.

IFRS 9 applies to many foreign currency derivatives and, accordingly, these are excluded from the scope of IAS 21 (see **Chapter 25**). Those foreign currency derivatives that are not within the scope of IFRS 9 (for example, some foreign currency derivatives that are embedded in other contracts) are within the scope of IAS 21. In addition, IAS 21 applies when an entity translates amounts relating to derivatives from its functional currency to its presentation currency. Furthermore, IAS 21 does not apply to hedge accounting for foreign currency items, including the hedging of a net investment in a foreign operation; IAS 39 addresses hedge accounting (see **Chapter 25**). IAS 21 does not apply to the presentation in a statement of cash flows of the cash flows arising from transactions in a foreign currency, or to the translation of cash flows of a foreign operation (see IAS 7 *Statement of Cash Flows* – **Chapter 33**).

31.2 FOREIGN CURRENCY TRANSACTIONS

This section deals with non-consolidation-related transactions denominated in a foreign currency. In simple terms, this is the sale or purchase of goods, services and non-current assets denominated in a foreign currency. The key issues in the accounting process are:
- how to initially recognise (i.e. account for) the transaction when it occurs;
- then how to account for the transaction at the end of subsequent reporting periods; and
- finally, how to account for any changes in foreign currency exchange rates.

Each of these is now discussed in turn.

Initial Recognition

A foreign currency transaction is a transaction that is either denominated or requires settlement in a foreign currency, including:
1. buying or selling of goods or services whose price is denominated in a foreign currency;

2. borrowing or lending of funds in a foreign currency; or
3. acquisition or disposal of assets denominated in a foreign currency.

A foreign currency transaction should be recorded initially by applying the **spot rate** at the date of the transaction. For practical reasons, an average rate (e.g. an average rate for week or month as deemed most appropriate by the reporting entity) for a period may be adopted unless the rate fluctuates significantly (see **Example 31.1**).

Reporting at Subsequent Reporting Dates

At each reporting date:
1. **monetary items** should be translated at the **closing rate** (e.g. trade receivables and payables – see **Example 31.2**);
2. non-monetary items measured at historical cost are translated at the exchange rate at the date of the transaction (for example, tangible non-current assets and inventory – see **Example 31.3**); and
3. non-monetary items are measured at fair value at the exchange rate when value was determined.

The carrying amount is determined in conjunction with other standards (e.g. IAS 2 *Inventories*, IAS 16 *Property, Plant and Equipment* and, where impairment exists, by IAS 36 *Impairment of Assets*).

Recognition of Exchange Differences

With respect to non-consolidated-related transactions denominated in a foreign currency, **exchange differences** arising on settlement of *monetary items* should be expensed in arriving at profit or loss in the statement of profit or loss and other comprehensive income in the period they arise.

Where a gain/loss on a *non-monetary item* is recognised directly in equity, any exchange component of that gain/loss should be recognised directly in equity. Conversely, when a gain/loss on a *non-monetary item* is recognised in profit or loss, any exchange component of that gain/loss should be recognised in arriving at profit or loss in the statement of profit or loss and other comprehensive income.

Now, having explained each of the three key issues in the accounting process (i.e. initial recognition, reporting at subsequent reporting dates and exchange differences), these are illustrated below.

If a transaction is settled before the end of a reporting period (see **Example 31.1**), then:
(i) record the foreign currency transaction in the functional currency at the spot exchange rate at the date of the transaction (an average rate for a period may be used if exchange rates do not fluctuate significantly);
(ii) record the settlement at the exchange rate at the date of settlement; and
(iii) recognise the exchange difference (i.e. (i) minus (ii) in arriving at profit or loss in the statement of profit or loss and other comprehensive income).

EXAMPLE 31.1: TRANSACTION SETTLED AT THE REPORTING DATE

Blue Limited, whose year-end is 31 December, buys goods from a foreign company for 180,000 Ricos on 31 July 2013. The transaction is settled on 31 October 2013.

Exchange Rates
31 July 2013	€1 =	1.5 Ricos
31 October 2013	€1 =	1.6 Ricos

		€	€
DR	SPLOCI – P/L – Purchases	120,000	
CR	Trade payables		120,000

Being initial recognition of purchase of goods on credit (€180,000 ÷ 1.5)

DR	Trade payables	112,500	
CR	Cash		112,500

Being payment for goods (€180,000 ÷ 1.6)

DR	Trade payables	7,500	
CR	SPLOCI – P/L (e.g. cost of sales)		7,500

Being the exchange difference arising between original purchase and settlement of liability.

Note: the same principles as illustrated in **Example 31.1** would apply to the purchase of a non-current tangible asset if the transaction has been settled at the reporting date (see **Example 31.3** if not settled).

If a transaction is *not* settled before the end of a reporting period (see **Example 31.2**), then:
  (i)   record the transaction (in the functional currency) at the spot exchange rate at the date of the transaction;
 (ii)   retranslate any monetary items; and
(iii)   recognise any exchange difference in arriving at operating profit in the statement of profit or loss and other comprehensive income.

EXAMPLE 31.2: TRANSACTION NOT SETTLED AT THE REPORTING DATE

Top Limited buys goods from a foreign company for 500,000 Zicos on 31 October 2012. The transaction was not settled at 31 December 2012, the company's year-end.

Exchange Rates
31 October 2012	€1 =	1.6 Zicos
31 December 2012	€1 =	1.75 Zicos

		€	€
DR	SPLOCI – P/L – Purchases	312,500	
CR	Trade payables		312,500

Being initial recognition of purchase of goods on credit (€500,000 ÷ 1.6).

At the 31 December 2012, the trade payables must be translated at the closing rate (1.75):

DR	Trade payables	26,786	
CR	SPLOCI – P/L		26,786

Being translation of trade payable at the closing rate (€500,000 ÷ 1.75 = €285,714) and recognition of subsequent exchange difference.

Examples **31.1** and **31.2** deal with the purchase of goods in a foreign currency (i.e. monetary items). The accounting treatment for a transaction involving a non-monetary item that has not been settled at the end of the reporting period is illustrated in **Example 31.3**. As noted above, when a non-monetary item (e.g. property, plant and equipment) has been purchased in a foreign currency, it is recorded at the spot rate at the date of the transaction (historical cost) and it is not subsequently retranslated.

EXAMPLE 31.3: PURCHASE OF A NON-MONETARY ITEM

A company purchased a property on 1 January 2013 for 20,000 DM (when €1 = 4DM), with the account being settled on 1 March 2013 when the exchange rate was 20,000 DM = €5,500. If the company's year-end is after 1 March 2013, then this transaction should be recorded as follows:

At 1 January 2013:

DR	Property	€5,000	
CR	Payables		€5,000

Being initial recognition of property.

At 1 March 2013:

DR	Payables	€5,000	
DR	SPLOCI – P/L – exchange loss	€500	
CR	Bank		€5,500

Being settlement of liability and recognition of exchange difference.

However, if the company's year-end is 31 January 2013, and at 31 January 2013 20,000 DM = €4,900, then:

At 31 January 2013:

DR	Payables	€100	
CR	SPLOCI – P/L – exchange gain		€100

Being retranslation of liability (i.e. monetary item) at the reporting date and recognition of exchange difference.

At 1 March 2013:		
DR Payables	€4,900	
DR SPLOCI – P/L – exchange loss	€600	
CR Bank		€5,500
Being settlement of liability and recognition of exchange difference.		

Having explained how to account for non-consolidation-related transactions denominated in a foreign currency (i.e. sales or purchases of goods, services and non-current assets denominated in a foreign currency), the next section deals with the translation of foreign entities.

Before reading the next section, just to refresh your memory, please (re)read the **Key Terms and Definitions** section above.

31.3 FOREIGN CURRENCY TRANSLATION

This section explains how to account for the translation of foreign entities in accordance with IAS 21. The incorporation of a foreign operation should follow normal consolidation procedures (e.g. elimination of intercompany balances – see **Chapters 26–28**). However, an intragroup monetary asset/liability cannot be eliminated against a corresponding intragroup asset/liability without showing the results of currency fluctuations in the consolidated accounts. Such exchange differences should continue to be recognised as income/expenses or in equity, as appropriate. IFRS 10 permits the use of different reporting dates as long as they are no more than three months apart and adjustments are made for the effects of any significant transactions between those dates. In such cases, the exchange rate to adopt is that at the reporting date of the foreign operation. The same approach should be applied to the equity method of accounting for associates and joint ventures.

IAS 21 shows how to translate financial statements into a presentation currency, which is the currency in which the financial statements are presented. This contrasts with the functional currency, which is the currency of the primary economic environment in which the (foreign) entity operates. Depending on the relationship between the parent and the subsidiary companies, the presentation currency and the functional currency may or may not be the same. We will now examine how to identify an entity's functional currency.

Functional Currency

Regardless of whether an entity is 'foreign' or not, its functional currency is the currency of the primary economic environment in which the entity operates. An entity's functional currency reflects the underlying transactions, events and conditions that are relevant to it. In most cases, the functional currency of a reporting entity is the currency of the country in which it is situated and in which it carries out most of its transactions. A reporting entity (regardless of whether it is 'foreign') should consider certain factors when determining its functional currency, including the currency:
• that mainly influences sales prices for goods and services (i.e. the currency in which prices are denominated and settled);

- of the country whose competitive forces and regulations mainly determine the selling prices of its goods and services;
- that mainly influences labour, material and other costs of providing goods/services;
- in which funds from financing activities are generated; and
- in which receipts from operating activities are usually retained.

When the entity *is a foreign operation* the following additional factors are considered:
- whether the activities of the foreign operation are an extension of the reporting entity;
- whether transactions with the foreign entity are a high or low proportion of the foreign operation's activities;
- whether cash flows of the foreign operation directly affect those of the reporting entity; and
- whether cash flows of the foreign operation are sufficient to service existing and expected debt obligations.

Where the indicators are mixed, management must exercise its judgement as to the functional currency to adopt that best reflects the underlying transactions.

The next section explains how to consolidate a foreign entity when the presentation currency (i.e. the currency in which the financial statements are presented) is the same as the functional currency (i.e. the currency that best reflects the underlying transactions, events and conditions that are relevant to it).

Presentation Currency = Functional Currency

The results (i.e. statement of profit or loss and other comprehensive income) and position (i.e. statement of financial position) of an entity whose functional currency is the same as the presentation currency should be translated as follows:
1. monetary items at the closing rate;
2. non-monetary items, which are measured at historical cost, at the exchange rate at the date of the transaction;
3. income and expenses at the exchange rates at the dates of the transactions. For practical reasons, which includes most examination questions, an average rate may be adopted unless exchange rates fluctuate significantly; and
4. exchange differences should be recognised as part of profit or loss (in the SPLOCI – P/L) for the period.

This situation typically applies where the foreign entity effectively acts as a selling agent for the parent company (i.e. the business or trade of the foreign subsidiary is largely driven by, or dependent upon, the parent). For example, the foreign subsidiary is responsible for selling the parent's goods overseas or the foreign subsidiary manufactures a component solely for use by the parent company.

The importance of the four points above is easily missed; however, it is vital they are learnt. Their application is illustrated in **Example 31.4** below.

Presentation Currency ≠ Functional Currency (Presentation Currency Method)

If the presentation currency of the foreign entity differs from its functional currency, its results and financial position need to be translated into the presentation currency. The group, in particular, needs a common currency. The results and position of an entity whose functional currency is not the currency of a hyperinflationary economy should be translated into the presentation currency as follows:

1. assets and liabilities at the closing rate;
2. income and expenses at the exchange rates at the dates of the transactions. For practical reasons (including most examination questions), an average rate may be adopted unless exchange rates fluctuate significantly. However, actual rates should be used for opening and closing inventory and depreciation; and
3. all exchange differences should be recognised in equity as a separate component (through other comprehensive income). These exchange differences are not recognised as income or expenses (in the SPLOCI – P/L) as they have little or no direct effect on present and future cash flows from operations.

This method is known as the presentation currency method; it is often referred to as the closing rate method since, as indicated in Point 1 above, the closing exchange rate is used to translate all assets and liabilities in the statement of financial position. It typically applies where the parent company is primarily interested in the net worth of the foreign entity or retains its interest as a long-term investment (i.e. the subsidiary operates independently of the parent and is not dependent on the parent for business).

Again, while the importance of the three points above can be missed, it is very important that they are learnt. Their application is illustrated in **Example 31.4**.

Foreign Exchange Differences

In Presentation Currency = Functional Currency and Presentation Currency ≠ Functional Currency (Presentation Currency Method), we referred to the treatment of exchange differences.

Presentation Currency = Functional Currency:
- exchange differences should be recognised as part of profit or loss for the period (in the SPLOCI – P/L).

Presentation Currency ≠ Functional Currency (Presentation Currency Method):
- all exchange differences should be recognised in equity as a separate component (through other comprehensive income) (in the SPLOCI – P/L). These exchange differences are not recognised as income or expenses as they have little or no direct effect on present and future cash flows from operations. They are recognised in profit or loss if the foreign operation is disposed of.

Foreign exchange differences arise from:
1. translating income and expenses at the transaction rate and assets/liabilities at the closing rate;
2. translating opening net assets at an exchange rate different from that previously reported; and
3. as any goodwill and fair value adjustments should be treated as assets and liabilities of the foreign operation, they therefore must be expressed in the functional currency of the foreign operation and translated at the closing rate.

If a foreign operation is *not* 100% owned by the parent company, then exchange differences should be allocated to non-controlling interests.

As described in **Chapter 26**, IFRS 3 has an explicit option, available on a transaction-by-transaction basis (i.e. the same option does not have to be applied to all acquisitions, entities can pick and choose), to measure any non-controlling interest in the entity acquired either at fair value (new method) or at the non-controlling interest's proportionate share of the net identifiable assets of the entity acquired (old method). The valuation of the goodwill to be included in the consolidated statement of financial position will be affected by the method used. If the old method is adopted, then goodwill represents the parent's share only and any exchange differences in respect of goodwill relate to the parent only. However, if the new method is adopted, then goodwill includes both the parent's and non-controlling interest's share, and consequently any resultant exchange differences should be allocated in proportion to their shareholdings between both parties.

Recognition of Exchange Differences

Having outlined how exchange differences may arise, this section now explains how to account for them.

Exchange differences on settlement of *monetary items* should be expensed in arriving at profit or loss in the statement of profit or loss and other comprehensive income in the period they arise, with the exception of IAS 21 paragraph 32 differences (see below). Where a gain/loss on a *non-monetary item* is recognised directly in equity, any exchange difference component of that gain/loss should also be recognised in equity through other comprehensive income. Conversely, when a gain/loss on a *non-monetary item* is recognised in profit or loss, any exchange difference component of that gain/loss should also be recognised in profit or loss (i.e. in the SPLOCI – P/L).

IAS 21 paragraph 32 states that exchange differences on a monetary item that forms part of an entity's **net investment in a foreign operation** be recognised as income/expense in the separate financial statements of the reporting entity or foreign operation, as appropriate. They should be recorded initially in a separate component of equity and recognised in profit/loss on disposal of the net investment.

However, when a monetary item that forms part of an entity's net investment in a foreign operation is denominated in the functional currency of the reporting entity, an exchange difference should be recorded in equity. In addition, a monetary item that forms part of the net investment in a foreign operation may be denominated in a currency other than the functional currency. Exchange differences should be recognised in equity.

When an entity keeps its books in a currency other than its functional currency (perhaps because it is required to do so by the parent company), all amounts are re-measured in the functional currency (i.e. monetary items at closing rate and non-monetary at date of transaction).

Tax Effects of All Exchange Differences

Gains and losses on foreign currency transactions may have associated tax effects and these should be accounted for under IAS 12 *Income Taxes* (see **Chapter 13**).

Using the same information, **Example 31.4** illustrates how to translate the financial statements of a foreign subsidiary under the two scenarios discussed above. This is when the:
• Presentation Currency = Functional Currency (remember, exchange differences should be recognised as part of profit or loss for the period); and

- Presentation Currency ≠ Functional Currency (remember, all exchange differences should be recognised in equity as a separate component (through other comprehensive income)).

Before studying this example, please ensure that you understand the material covered so far in **Section 31.3**. In addition, you should work through the example slowly, ensuring that you understand how the steps outlined in the two subsections above (**Presentation Currency = Functional Currency** and **Presentation Currency ≠ Functional Currency**) have been applied.

EXAMPLE 31.4: TRANSLATION OF A FOREIGN SUBSIDIARY

You are given the following information in relation to Quickbuck Limited:
1. Quickbuck Limited is a US subsidiary of an Irish company, Prosperous Limited.
2. You are informed that the rates of exchange between the US dollar and the Euro were as follows:

Through 2011 and on 31 December 2011	$3 to €1
31 December 2012	$5 to €1
Average in 2012	$4 to €1
Average at date of acquisition of Quickbuck inventory held 31 December 2012	$4.8 to €1

3. Property, plant and equipment of Quickbuck Limited were bought in Ireland, shipped to and erected for Quickbuck Limited at a cost of €120,000.

   The net book value of property, plant and equipment of Quickbuck Limited at 31 December 2012 was arrived at as follows:

	$
Cost	300,000
Depreciation	30,000
	270,000
Depreciation for 2012	30,000

4. All of the shares in Quickbuck Limited were acquired by Prosperous Limited when Quickbuck Limited was formed for €25,000.
5. When the dividends were paid from Quickbuck Limited to Prosperous Limited the rate of exchange was $4 to €1.
6. The statement of profit or loss and other comprehensive income of Quickbuck Limited for the year ended 31 December 2012 was as follows:

	$	$
Revenue		544,275
Opening inventory	41,000	
Purchases	152,525	
Closing inventory	(48,525)	145,000
Gross profit		399,275
Depreciation	30,000	
Other expenses	271,050	301,050
Profit before taxation		98,225
Income tax expense		24,275
Profit after taxation		73,950

Dividends paid and proposed during the year ended 31 December 2012 by Quickbuck Limited were as follows:

Paid $10,000
Proposed $10,000

The proposed dividends were approved by shareholders of Quickbuck Limited prior to 31 December 2012.

7. The Statement of Financial Position of Quickbuck Limited as at 31 December 2012 was as follows:

	$
Assets	
Non-current Assets:	
Property, plant and equipment	270,000
Current Assets:	
Balance at bank	9,475
Receivables	45,500
Inventory	48,525
	103,500
Total Assets	373,500
Equity and Liabilities	
Equity:	
Ordinary Share Capital	75,000
Retained earnings	70,450
	145,450
Non-current liabilities:	
Loan	90,000
Current liabilities:	
Payables	103,775
Taxation	24,275
Dividends	10,000
	138,050
Total equity and liabilities	373,500

Requirement You are required to translate the accounts of Quickbuck Limited into € where:
(a) Quickbuck Limited has a different functional currency than Prosperous Limited; and
(b) Quickbuck Limited has the same functional currency as Prosperous Limited.

Solution

Note: remember Quickbuck Limited was acquired on its date of incorporation.

Abbreviations Used:

A&L = Assets and Liabilities; AR = Average Rate; CR = Closing Rate; ER = Exchange Rate; HR = Historical Rate; NA = Net Assets; SPLOCI = Statement of Profit or Loss and Other Comprehensive Income; SFP = Statement of Financial Position.

Note: in order to aid understanding, guidance notes are enclosed in square brackets [....].

(a) PRESENTATION CURRENCY

1. Translate Opening Net Assets

	$	Rate	€
Ordinary Share Capital	75,000	3	25,000
Reserves	16,500	3	5,500 *(bal)
	91,500		30,500

* Proof of opening Reserves:			
At opening rate plus	16,500	3	5,500
Ordinary Share Capital at opening rate	75,000	3	25,000
Ordinary Share Capital at acquisition rate	75,000	3	(25,000)
			5,500

2. Translate retained earnings for year

	$	Rate	€
Profit after Tax	73,950	4	18,488
Dividends Paid	(10,000)	4	(2,500)
Dividends Proposed	(10,000)	5	(2,000)
Retained Profit	53,950		13,988

3. Calculate exchange difference

	$	ER	€
(a) Opening net assets at opening rate *[Prior year CR]*			
Ordinary share capital [No change]	75,000	3	25,000
Retained earnings [$70,450 − $53,950]	16,500	*(Balance)*	5,500
	91,500	3	30,500
Opening NA at CR	91,500	5	18,300
			12,200
(b) Translate retained earnings (SPLOCI – P/L at AR v SFP at CR)			
Profit after tax [See SPLOCI – P/L]	73,950	4	18,488
Dividends paid [Per question]	(10,000)	4	(2,500)
Dividends proposed	(10,000)	5	(2,000)
Retained earnings per SPLOCI – P/L [mainly at AR]	53,950		13,988
Retained earnings per SFP [at CR]	53,950	5	(10,790)
			3,198
(c) Total exchange loss			15,398

4. Prepare Movement on Reserves

		€
Balance at 1 January 2012	(W1)	5,500
Retained Profit	(W2)	13,988
Exchange Losses (should be presented separately)	(W3)	(15,398)
Balance at 31 December 2012		4,090

5. Translate Statement of Financial Position

	$	Rate	€
Ordinary Share Capital	75,000	3	25,000
Reserves	70,450		4,090
	145,450		29,090
Loan	90,000	5	18,000
	235,450		47,090
Total Net Assets	235,450	5	47,090

Quickbuck Limited
STATEMENT OF PROFIT OR LOSS AND OTHER COMPREHENSIVE INCOME
for the Year Ended 31 December 2012

	$	ER	€
Revenue	544,275	4	136,069
Cost of sales	(145,000)	4	(36,250)
Gross profit	399,275		99,819
Depreciation	(30,000)	4	(7,500)
Other expenses	(271,050)	4	(67,762)
Profit before tax	98,225		24,557
Income tax expense	(24,275)	4	(6,069)
Profit after tax	73,950		18,488
Other Comprehensive Income:			
Foreign exchange losses			(3,198)
			15,290

Quickbuck Limited
STATEMENT OF FINANCIAL POSITION
as at 31 December 2012

	$	ER	€
Property, plant and equipment	270,000	5	54,000
Inventory	48,525	5	9,705
Receivables	45,500	5	9,100
Bank and cash	9,475	5	1,895
	373,500		74,700
Ordinary share capital	75,000	3	25,000
Retained earnings	70,450		19,488
Foreign currency translation reserve			(15,398)
Loan	90,000	5	18,000
Payables	103,775	5	20,755
Taxation	24,275	5	4,855
Proposed dividends	10,000	5	2,000
	373,500		74,700

(b) FUNCTIONAL CURRENCY METHOD

1. Translate Opening Statement of Financial Position

	$	Rate	€
Ordinary Share Capital	75,000	3	25,000
Reserves	16,500		25,500
	91,500		50,500
Property, plant and equipment	300,000	2.5	120,000
Inventory	41,000	3	13,667
Monetary Liabilities (to balance)	*(249,500)	3	(83,167)
	91,500		50,500

2. Translate Statement of Financial Position
[Non-monetary at HR and Monetary A&L at CR]

	$	ER	€
Property, plant and equipment	270,000	2.5	108,000

Inventory	48,525	4.8	10,109
Receivables	45,500	5	9,100
Bank and cash	9,475	5	1,895
	373,500		129,104
Ordinary share capital	75,000	3	25,000
Retained earnings	70,450	(Balance)	58,494
Loan	90,000	5	18,000
Payables	103,775	5	20,755
Taxation	24,275	5	4,855
Proposed dividends	10,000	5	2,000
	373,500		129,104

3. Translate Statement of Profit or Loss and Other Comprehensive Income

	$	Rate	€
Revenue	544,275	4	136,069
Opening Inventory	41,000	3	13,667
Purchases	152,525	4	38,131
Closing Inventory	(48,525)	4.8	(10,109)
	145,000		41,689
Gross Profit	399,275		94,380
Depreciation	(30,000)	2.5	(12,000)
Other Expenses	(271,050)	4	(67,762)
Exchange Gain/(Loss) (see below)	-		28,945
Profit before Tax	98,225		43,563
Income tax expense	24,275	4	6,069
Profit after Tax	73,950		37,494

Note: the difference between opening and closing net assets of Quickbuck Limited is the retained profit for the year in Euros:

	€
Closing net assets	83,494
Opening net assets	50,500
	32,994

The exchange difference (i.e. €28,945) is the balancing figure in the translated statement of profit or loss and other comprehensive income. This is shown below.

	$	ER	€
(a) Translate opening SFP			
Ordinary share capital	75,000	3	25,000
Retained earnings [$70,450 − $53,950]	16,500	(Balance)	25,500
	91,500		50,500
Property, plant and equipment	300,000	2.5	120,000
Inventory	41,000	3	13,667
Net monetary liabilities (to balance)	(249,500)	3	(83,167)
	91,500		50,500

(b)

Opening retained earnings (see above)	25,500
+ profit for year (Profit after tax €8,549 − dividends paid €2,500 − dividends proposed €2,000)	4,049
Closing retained earnings	(58,494)
Exchange gain (include in SPLOCI − P/L)	28,945

Before concluding this section on the translation of the financial statements of a foreign entity, some further points are discussed.

Change in Functional Currency

When there is a change in the functional currency (for example, the relationship between a parent and foreign subsidiary changes from being one of a 'selling agent' to one where the subsidiary acts independently and is no longer reliant on the parent for its business), the translation procedures applicable to the new functional currency should be applied from the date of the change. A change should only be made if there is a change to those underlying transactions. The effect is accounted for prospectively. All items are translated using the new functional exchange rate at the date of the change. These are then treated as their historical cost. Exchange differences previously recognised in equity are not recognised as income or expenses until the disposal of the operation.

Disposal of a Foreign Operation

Any cumulative exchange differences in equity should be recognised as income or expenses when the gain or loss on disposal is recognised.

Disclosure

An entity should disclose:
1. the amount of exchange differences included in arriving at profit or loss in the statement of profit or loss and other comprehensive income, except those arising from IFRS 9;
2. net exchange differences classified as a component of equity and a reconciliation of opening and closing equity at start and end of the year;
3. when the presentation currency is different from the functional currency, that fact should be disclosed as well as disclosure of the functional currency and the reason for using a different presentation currency;
4. when there is a change in the functional currency of either the reporting entity or a significant foreign operation, that fact and reason for the change should be disclosed;
5. when an entity presents its financial statements in a currency different from its functional currency, it should describe the statements as complying with IFRSs only if they comply with all of the requirements of each applicable standard and SIC.

Where the requirements listed at item (5) above are not met, an entity should:
1. clearly identify the information as supplementary;
2. disclose the currency in which the supplementary information is displayed; and

3. disclose the entity's functional currency and method of translation used to determine the supplementary information.

(With respect to the disclosures above, all references are to the functional currency of the parent, if referring to a group.)

31.4 IAS 29 *FINANCIAL REPORTING IN HYPERINFLATIONARY ECONOMIES*

In accordance with IAS 21, in **Section 31.2** we examine how to account for non-consolidation-related transactions denominated in a foreign currency (i.e. sales or purchases of goods, services and non-current assets denominated in a foreign currency), while the translation of foreign entities is addressed in **Section 31.3**.

This section deals with accounting for entities reporting in the currency of a hyperinflationary economy in accordance with IAS 29 *Financial Reporting in Hyperinflationary Economies*.

Objective of IAS 29

The objective of IAS 29 *Financial Reporting in Hyperinflationary Economies* is to establish specific standards for entities reporting in the currency of a hyperinflationary economy, so that the financial information provided is meaningful.

Scope of IAS 29

IAS 29 applies to the primary financial statements, including consolidated financial statements, of any entity whose functional currency is the currency of a hyperinflationary economy. In a hyperinflationary economy, reporting in local currency is not useful as money loses purchasing power and therefore the financial statements become misleading. IAS 29 does not establish an absolute rate at which hyperinflation is deemed to exist. It is a matter of judgement when the standard becomes necessary but the following characteristics should be reviewed:
1. the general population prefers to invest in non-monetary assets or in a relatively stable currency;
2. the general population regards monetary amounts, not in terms of local currency, but in terms of a relatively stable currency;
3. credit sales and purchases take place at prices adjusted for the expected loss in purchasing power, even if the credit period is short;
4. interest rates, wages and prices are linked to a price index; and
5. the cumulative inflation rate over three years is approaching or exceeds 100% (i.e. prices double in a three-year period).

IAS 29 states that it is preferable that all enterprises in the same hyperinflationary economy apply the standard from the same date; although this is likely to be very difficult to achieve in practice. IAS 29 applies from the start of the reporting period in which hyperinflation is identified.

The Restatement of Financial Statements

Prices change over time due to changes in supply and demand as well as general forces (for example, changes in energy and labour costs) pushing up the general level of prices.

In most countries, the primary financial statements are prepared on an historical cost basis, except for the revaluation of property, etc. Some enterprises, however, adopt a current cost approach using specific price increases. The adjustments that are required, depending on which of these two bases is used to prepare the primary financial statements, are outlined below.

In a hyperinflationary economy, financial statements must be expressed in terms of an up-to-date measuring unit if they are to be useful. The financial statements of an entity whose functional currency is that of a hyperinflationary economy, whether historical or current cost methods are used, must be restated in current measuring unit terms. The corresponding figures for the previous period must also be restated in current measuring unit terms. The gain/loss on the net monetary position should be included within income and separately disclosed.

The restatement of financial statements in accordance with IAS 29 requires the application of certain procedures and judgement. IAS 29 states that the consistent application of these procedures and judgements from period to period is more important than the precise accuracy of the amounts included in the restated financial statements.

Historical Cost Financial Statements

If an entity prepares its financial statements using the historical cost basis, then the following adjustments are required in order to restate them in current measuring unit terms.

Statement of Financial Position

Statement of financial position amounts should be restated by applying a general price index (i.e. a measure of the change in the general price of goods and services). Monetary items are not restated, as they are already stated in current monetary terms; index-linked bonds and loans are adjusted in accordance with the relevant agreements. All other non-monetary assets should be restated unless already carried at net realisable value or market value. Most non-monetary assets require the application of a general price index to their historical costs and accumulated depreciation from the date of acquisition to the reporting date. Inventory (raw materials, work-in-progress and finished goods) should be restated from the dates on which the costs of purchase and of conversion were incurred.

If detailed records of acquisition dates are not available or capable of estimation then, in rare circumstances, an independent professional assessment may form the basis for their restatement. If a general price index is not available, then an estimate should be based on movements in the exchange rate between the functional and a relatively stable foreign currency. Where non-monetary assets are revalued, these should be restated from the date of revaluation. Where non-current assets are impaired they must be reduced to their recoverable amounts and inventory to net realisable value.

An investee that is accounted for under the equity method may report in the currency of a hyperinflationary economy. The statement of financial position and statement of profit or loss and other comprehensive income are restated in accordance with this standard in order to calculate the investor's share of its net assets and results. If expressed in a foreign currency they are translated at closing rates.

It is not appropriate both to restate the capital expenditure financed by borrowing and to capitalise that part of the borrowing costs that compensates for inflation during the same period. The borrowing costs should be expensed. Also, if undue effort or cost is needed to impute interest, such assets are restated from the payment date, not the date of purchase.

On first application of the standard, owners' equity must be restated by applying a general price index from the dates that different components of equity arose. Any revaluation surplus that arose in previous periods is eliminated. At the end of the first period and subsequently, all components of owners' equity are restated by applying a general price index from the start of the period to date of contribution.

Statement of Profit or Loss and Other Comprehensive Income

All items must be expressed in terms of current measuring units at the reporting date (i.e. by being restated from the dates when initially recorded by the general price index).

Gain or Loss on Net Monetary Position

Any excess of monetary assets over monetary liabilities loses purchasing power and vice versa. The gain/loss is the difference resulting from the restatement of non-monetary assets, owners' equity and statement of profit or loss and other comprehensive income items and the adjustment of index-linked assets and liabilities. The gain/loss may be estimated by applying the change in a general price index to the weighted average for the period of the difference between monetary assets and monetary liabilities. The gain or loss is included in net income. Other statement of profit or loss and other comprehensive income items (e.g. interest, foreign exchange differences) are also associated with the monetary position. They should be presented together with the gain or loss on the net monetary position in the statement of profit or loss and other comprehensive income.

Current Cost Financial Statements

If an entity prepares its financial statements using the current cost basis, then the following adjustments are required in order to restate them in current measuring unit terms.

Statement of Financial Position

Items stated at current cost are not restated as they are already in current measurement units. Any other items should be expressed in terms of current measuring units at the reporting date (i.e. by being restated from the dates when initially recorded by the general price index).

Gain or Loss on Net Monetary Position

This is accounted for in accordance with the historical cost approach (see above).

Taxes

The restatement of financial statements may give rise to differences between the carrying amount of individual assets and liabilities in the statement of financial position and their tax bases. These should be accounted for in accordance with IAS 12 *Income Taxes* (see **Chapter 13**).

Statement of Cash Flows

All items in the statement of cash flows should be expressed in current measuring units at the reporting date.

Statement of Profit or Loss and Other Comprehensive Income

All amounts need to be restated from their current cost at date of transactions to the reporting date by applying a general price index.

Corresponding Figures

These are restated by applying a general price index so that comparative financial statements are presented in terms of current measuring units at the end of the reporting period.

Consolidated Financial Statements

Subsidiaries reporting in the hyperinflationary economy must be restated by applying a general price index and, if that is a foreign subsidiary, then its restated financial statements should be translated at closing rates.

Selection and Use of the General Price Index

All enterprises that report in the currency of the same economy should use the same index.

Economies Ceasing to be Hyperinflationary

When an economy ceases to be hyperinflationary and an entity discontinues using this standard, it should treat the amounts expressed at the end of the previous period as the basis for its subsequent financial statements.

Disclosures

IAS 29 requires that the following disclosures be made in order to make clear the basis of dealing with the effects of inflation in the financial statements:
1. the fact that the financial statements and the corresponding periods have been restated for changes in general purchasing power and are restated in terms of current measurement units at the reporting date;
2. whether the financial statements are based on historical cost or current cost; and
3. the identity and level of the price index at the reporting date and the movement in the index during the current and previous reporting period.

31.5 CONCLUSION

Foreign Currency Transactions

A foreign currency transaction is recorded initially in the reporting entity's functional currency, by applying to the foreign currency amount the spot exchange rate between the functional currency and the foreign currency at the date of the transaction. For practical reasons, a rate that approximates the actual rate at the date of the transaction is often used (e.g. an average weekly or monthly rate). The functional currency is the currency of the primary economic environment in which the entity operates.

At each reporting date:
* foreign currency monetary items are translated using the closing rate;
* non-monetary items that are measured in terms of historical cost in a foreign currency are translated using the exchange rate at the date of the transaction; and
* non-monetary items that are measured at fair value in a foreign currency are translated using the exchange rates at the date when the fair value was determined.

Foreign Operations

Assuming that you understand the detailed material contained in **Section 31.3**, the following summarises the procedures to be followed when answering a question that requires the consolidation of a foreign entity.
* If the foreign subsidiary's activities are an extension of the parent's (i.e. acts as selling agent) (same functional currency):
  (a) statement of profit or loss and other comprehensive income – translate at actual/average rate (historical rate for non-monetary items) (dividends paid at actual rate; 'approved' proposed dividends at closing rate);
  (b) statement of financial position – translate non-monetary items at historical rate, monetary items at closing rate and shareholders' funds to balance; and
  (c) exchange difference – include as part of profit/loss for period.

* If the foreign subsidiary operates in a semi-autonomous manner (translation to presentation currency):
  (a) statement of profit or loss and other comprehensive income – translate at average rate (dividends paid at actual rate; 'approved' proposed dividends at closing rate);
  (b) statement of financial position – translate assets and liabilities at closing rate; and
  (c) exchange differences – taken to equity through other comprehensive income.

Foreign exchange differences arise from:
1. translating income and expenses at the transaction rate and assets/liabilities at the closing rate;
2. translating opening net assets at an exchange rate different from that previously reported; and
3. the fact that any goodwill and fair value adjustments should be treated as assets and liabilities of the foreign operation and they therefore must be expressed in the functional currency of the foreign operation and translated at the closing rate.

If a foreign operation is not 100% owned by the parent company, then exchange differences should be allocated to non-controlling interests. This also applies to goodwill if appropriate.

Summary of Learning Objectives

This chapter deals with foreign currency transactions and the translation of the financial statements of foreign operations into a presentation currency. After having studied this chapter, you should be able to:

Learning Objective 1 Include foreign currency transactions in the financial statements of a reporting entity.

See **Section 31.2**, but in summary at each reporting date:
- foreign currency monetary items are translated using the closing rate;
- non-monetary items that are measured in terms of historical cost in a foreign currency are translated using the exchange rate at the date of the transaction; and
- non-monetary items that are measured at fair value in a foreign currency are translated using the exchange rates at the date when the fair value was determined.

Learning Objective 2 Translate the financial statements of an foreign entity into a presentation currency and include them in the financial statements of a reporting entity.

See **Section 31.3**. In summary:

- if the foreign subsidiary's activities are an extension of the parent's (i.e. acts as selling agent) (same functional currency):
  - (a) statement of profit or loss and other comprehensive income – translate at actual/average rate (historical rate for non-monetary items) (dividends paid at actual rate; 'approved' proposed dividends at closing rate);
  - (b) statement of financial position – translate non-monetary items at historical rate, monetary items at closing rate and shareholders' funds to balance; and
  - (c) exchange difference – include as part of profit/loss for period.

- if the foreign subsidiary operates in a semi-autonomous manner (translation to presentation currency):
  - (a) statement of profit or loss and other comprehensive income – translate at average rate (dividends paid at actual rate; 'approved' proposed dividends at closing rate);
  - (b) statement of financial position – translate assets and liabilities at closing rate; and
  - (c) exchange differences – taken to equity through other comprehensive income.

Learning Objective 3 Account for entities reporting in the currency of a hyperinflationary economy.

See **Section 31.4**. To summarise, in a hyperinflationary economy, financial statements must be expressed in terms of an up-to-date measuring unit if they are to be useful. The financial statements of an entity whose functional currency is that of a hyperinflationary economy, whether historical or current cost methods are used, must be restated in current measuring unit terms.

Note: for ease of illustration, dividends and retained earnings are often shown at the foot of the statement of profit or loss and other comprehensive income in questions. These figures would normally be included in the statement of changes in equity.

QUESTIONS

Self-test Questions (Multiple Choice)

Question 31.1

IAS 21 *The Effects of Changes in Foreign Exchange Rates*, defines the functional currency as the currency:
(a) in which the foreign operation measures and records its transactions.
(b) of the primary economic environment in which the entity operates.
(c) in which the financial statements are presented.
(d) of the country in which the subsidiary is located.

Question 31.2

According to IAS 21 *The Effects of Changes in Foreign Exchange Rates,* the following statement 'the currency that affects the economic wealth of the entity' provides a definition of:
(a) functional currency.
(b) local currency.
(c) presentation currency.
(d) foreign currency.

Question 31.3

According to IAS 21 *The Effects of Changes in Foreign Exchange Rates* the currency in which an entity primarily generates and expends cash is considered to be the:
(a) economic currency.
(b) domestic currency.
(c) presentation currency.
(d) functional currency.

Question 31.4

Indicators pointing towards the local overseas currency as the functional currency include:
(i) Parent's cash flows are directly affected on a current basis.

(ii) Cash flows are primarily in the local currency and do not affect the parent's cash flows.
(iii) Sales prices are primarily responsive to exchange rate changes in the short-term.
(iv) Production costs are determined primarily by local conditions.

(a) (i) and (iii) only;
(b) (ii) and (iv) only;
(c) (i), (iii) and (iv) only;
(d) (i), (ii) and (iv) only.

Question 31.5

When translating the revenue and expenses in the statement of profit or loss and other comprehensive income, theoretically each item of revenue and expense should be translated using the spot exchange rate between the:
(a) functional currency and the foreign currency on the reporting date.
(b) presentation currency and the functional currency on the reporting date.
(c) functional currency and the foreign currency on the date the transaction occurred.
(d) presentation currency and the local currency on the transaction date.

Question 31.6

By applying the definition provided in IAS 21 *The Effects of Changes in Foreign Exchange Rates* the following items will be regarded as a monetary item:
(a) Property, plant and equipment.
(b) Land and buildings.
(c) Inventory.
(d) Accounts receivable.

Question 31.7

The general rule for translating liabilities denominated in a foreign currency into the functional currency is to:
(a) translate all liabilities using the current rate existing at the reporting date.
(b) first classify the liabilities into current and non-current.
(c) first classify the liabilities as monetary or non-monetary.
(d) translate all liabilities using the rate current on entering into the transaction.

Suggested Solutions to Self-test Questions

Question	1	2	3	4	5	6	7
Part	(b)	(a)	(d)	(b)	(c)	(d)	(c)

Review Questions

(See **Appendix One** for Suggested Solutions to Review Questions.)

Question 31.1

MANCO Limited has entered into the following transactions involving foreign currencies during the year ended 31 March 2013.

1. A 20-year loan of US$1,000,000 was obtained from an American bank on 1 August 2012. The proceeds of the loan were remitted when the exchange rate was US$1.75 = €1.
2. A special machine was purchased from a South American supplier, FRTZ, on 1 October 2012 for DM55,000 when the exchange rate was DM3.15 = €1. This machine is estimated to have an effective useful life of five years, and the company's policy is to use the straight-line method of depreciation commencing on the date of acquisition. Payment for this machine was made in full on 15 December 2012, when the exchange rate was DM3.00 = €1.
3. Goods for resale were purchased from a Brazilian supplier, ETIEN, on 12 February 2013, for BFr600,000 when the exchange rate was BFr68.00 = €1. This amount was still unpaid at 31 March 2013.

The accountant at MANCO Limited, who has never before had to deal with transactions involving foreign currencies, kept the above notes but has made no entries whatsoever in the books in respect of these transactions. The relevant exchange rates at 31 March 2013 were as follows:

$$US\$1.80 = €1.00 \qquad DM3.20 = €1.00 \qquad BFr69.50 = €1.00$$

Requirement

(a) Prepare journal entries (including *cash*) to show the accountant of MANCO Limited how each of the transactions (1) to (3) above, in respect of the year ended 31 March 2013, should be entered into the books of MANCO Limited;
(b) Show how each of the transactions (1) to (3) above would be included in the accounts of MANCO Limited for the year ended 31 March 2013 by preparing appropriate extracts from the accounts for each transaction. (It is sufficient to indicate the amounts which should be included under the appropriate heading in the statement of financial position and statement of profit or loss and other comprehensive income.)

Question 31.2

Ray International Limited is a manufacturing company, with a wholly owned subsidiary M Distribution BV operating in the Netherlands. The draft financial statements of the parent company in €s and of the subsidiary in Dutch Guilders (DFL) for the year ended 31 December 2012 are as follows:

STATEMENTS OF PROFIT OR LOSS AND OTHER COMPREHENSIVE INCOME
for the Year Ended 31 December 2012

	M Distribution BV DFL000	RAY International Limited €000
Revenue	12,600	10,871
Profit before taxation	1,750	2,600
Income tax expense	(210)	(1,300)
Profit for year	1,540	1,300
Balance at beginning of year	–	480
Dividends paid during year	(500)	–
Balance at end of year	1,040	1,780

STATEMENTS OF FINANCIAL POSITION
as at 31 December 2012

	DFL000	€000
Assets		
Non-current assets		
Property, plant and equipment	600	3,240
Investment in M Distribution	–	400
	600	3,640
Current Assets		
Inventory	2,020	2,390
Other	1,164	1,472
	3,184	3,862
Total assets	3,784	7,502
Equity and liabilities		
Equity		
Share capital	1,200	2,000
Retained profits	1,040	1,780
	2,240	3,780
Non-current liabilities		
Long-term loan	–	294
Current liabilities	1,544	3,428
Total equity and liabilities	3,784	7,502

Additional Information:
1. M Distribution BV was incorporated and commenced trading on 1 January 2012. All property, plant and equipment was purchased on that date.
2. The relevant Dutch Guilder exchange rates are as follows:
   (a) 1 January 2012   3.0 DFL to €1
   (b) 31 December 2012   4.0 DFL to €1
   (c) Average for 2012   3.5 DFL to €1
3. The profit before taxation figure of the parent company includes dividend income from the subsidiary of €125,000.
4. The current assets of the parent company include a balance due from the subsidiary in respect of sales invoiced to the subsidiary in €s, of €382,000. The corresponding liability in the books of the subsidiary is recorded at 1,381,000 Dutch Guilders.
5. The revenue figure of the parent company includes sales to the subsidiary of €2,450,000. There are no inter-company profits in inventory.

Requirement You are required to prepare the consolidated statement of profit or loss and other comprehensive income and the consolidated statement of financial position of RAY International Limited and its subsidiary for the year ended 31 December 2012 assuming that the functional currency of M Distribution BV is different from the functional currency of Ray International Limited.

Question 31.3

BELVOIR plc (BELVOIR) purchased 35,000 ordinary shares in an Australian company, PERTH Limited (PERTH), on the 30 April 2012. For the purposes of measuring non-controlling interests at the date of acquisition, the proportionate share method equated to the fair value method. The summarised statements of financial position of the two companies at 31 December 2012 are as follows:

	BELVOIR €000	PERTH A$000
ASSETS		
Non-current Assets		
Property, plant and equipment	50,000	150,000
Investment in PERTH	11,667	-
	61,667	150,000
Current Assets		
Inventory	75,000	200,000
Receivables	175,000	250,000
Cash	5,000	25,000
	255,000	475,000
	316,667	625,000
EQUITY AND LIABILITIES		
Capital and Reserves		
€1/A$1 ordinary shares	50,000	50,000
Capital reserve	25,000	60,000
Retained earnings	55,000	65,000
	130,000	175,000
Non-current Liabilities	26,667	75,000
Current Liabilities	160,000	375,000
	316,667	625,000

Additional Information:

1. Included in the current liabilities of PERTH is A$75,000 in respect of proposed dividends. These were approved by the shareholders in March 2013.
2. BELVOIR accounts for dividends when received.
3. The summarised statements of profit or loss and other comprehensive income of BELVOIR and PERTH for the year ended 31 December 2012 are as follows:

12 months to 31 December 2012

	BELVOIR €000	PERTH A$000
Profit before tax	35,000	70,000
Taxation	(5,000)	(20,000)
Profit after tax	30,000	50,000

4. Rates of exchange

1 January 2012	€1 : A$12.5
Average for 2012	€1 : A$14.0
30 April 2012	€1 : A$13.0
31 December 2012	€1 : A$15.0

Requirement Prepare the consolidated statement of financial position of BELVOIR Group at 31 December 2012, assuming that the functional currency of PERTH is different from that of BELVOIR.

Challenging Questions

(Suggested Solutions to Challenging Questions are available to lecturers.)

Question 31.1 (Based on Chartered Accountants Ireland, P3 Summer 1997, Question 4)

The year-end of STUNT Limited (STUNT) is 31 December.
(a) On 1 December 2012, STUNT purchased raw materials from DENVER Limited, its US supplier, for $84,000 with payment due on 31 January 2013. The prevailing exchange rates were as follows:

1 December 2012	€1 = $1.58
31 December 2012	€1 = $1.56
31 January 2013	€1 = $1.60
2012 average rate	€1 = $1.59

Requirement
  (i) Show the value at which the invoice should be recorded in trade payables and inventory on 1 December 2012.
 (ii) Show the value at which the invoice should be recorded in trade payables and inventory on the 31 December 2012.
(iii) Show the settlement value of the invoice.
(iv) Show the accounting treatment for any exchange gain or loss arising.

(b) On 1 December 2012, STUNT sold finished goods to a Swiss company for €600,000 when the exchange rate ruling was €1 = Sf10.8. No cash was received from the Swiss company until 31 January 2013 when the exchange rate was €1 = Sf12.8. The exchange rate at 31 December 2012 was €1 = Sf9.6.

Requirement How would the transaction be recorded at 1 December 2012, 31 December 2012 and 31 January 2013?

(c) Draft a suitable foreign currencies accounting policy note for STUNT Limited.

Question 31.2 (Based on Chartered Accountants Ireland, P3 Summer 1996, Question 4)

On 1 January 2003 HOME Limited purchased 80% of the shares of AWAY Limited, a company incorporated and operating in Maru, a country whose currency is Maruvian dollars

(M$). The reserves of AWAY Limited amounted to M$100,000 on 1 January 2003. For the purposes of measuring non-controlling interests at the date of acquisition, the proportionate share method equated to the fair value method. Goodwill is only reduced by impairment. Impairment of €5,000 occurred during the year under review.

The statements of financial position of HOME Limited and AWAY Limited at 31 December 2012 are as follows:

	HOME Limited €000	AWAY Limited M$000
Assets		
Non-current assets		
Property, plant and equipment	740	815
Investment in AWAY Limited at cost	95	–
	835	815
Current assets		
Inventory	85	60
Receivables	215	80
Cash in hand and at bank	87	20
	387	160
Total assets	1,222	975
Equity and liabilities		
Equity		
Called up share capital	300	500
Reserves	615	355
	915	855
Current liabilities	307	120
Total equity and liabilities	1,222	975

Additional Information:

1. The financial statements for the year ended 31 December 2012 included the following:

	HOME €000	AWAY M$000
Operating profit	370	297
Dividend received from AWAY Limited	9	–
Taxation charge	(160)	(77)
Dividend paid	–	(60)
Profit retained for the financial year	219	160

No other dividends were paid or proposed by either company.

2. The following exchange rates have been ascertained:

1 January 2003	M$10 = €1
31 December 2011	M$ 6 = €1

31 December 2012   M$ 5 = €1
Average rate for the year ended 31 December 2012   M$5.5 = €1

3. The functional currency of Away Limited is the M$, while the functional currency of Home Limited is the Euro.

4. Consolidated reserves at 31 December 2011 amounted to €441,000.

Requirement Prepare the consolidated statement of financial position of HOME Limited as at 31 December 2012, and a statement of movements on reserves during the year ended on that date.

Question 31.3 (Based on Chartered Accountants Ireland, CAP 2 Autumn 2009, Question 2)

On 1 January 2010, CITIZEN plc (CITIZEN) acquired all of the ordinary share capital of an Australian company, KANE Limited (KANE). CITIZEN's presentation currency is the Euro (€). KANE operates independently of CITIZEN and its functional currency is the Australian dollar (A$). At the date of acquisition the retained earnings of KANE were A$45,000,000. The statements of profit or loss and other comprehensive income of CITIZEN and KANE for the year ended 31 December 2012 and their statements of financial position as that date are as follows:

STATEMENT OF PROFIT OR LOSS AND OTHER COMPREHENSIVE INCOME
for the Year Ended 31 December 2012

	CITIZEN	CITIZEN	KANE	KANE
	€000	€000	A$000	A$000
Revenue		520,000		360,000
Opening inventory	80,000		50,000	
Purchases	300,000		202,500	
Closing inventory	(40,000)	340,000	(22,500)	230,000
Gross profit		180,000		130,000
Distribution costs		(30,000)		(20,000)
Administrative expenses		(20,000)		(9,000)
Depreciation		(10,000)		(11,000)
Profit from operations		120,000		90,000
Income tax expense		(48,000)		(36,000)
Profit for year		72,000		54,000
Other Comprehensive Income:				
Surplus on revaluation of property		–		11,000
		72,000		65,000

STATEMENT OF FINANCIAL POSITION
as at 31 December 2012

	CITIZEN	KANE
	€000	A$000
Non-current Assets		
Property, plant and equipment	300,000	200,000
Investment in KANE	35,000	–

Current Assets		
Inventory	40,000	22,500
Receivables	55,000	47,500
Current account with KANE	4,000	–
Bank and cash	26,000	10,000
	460,000	280,000

EQUITY AND LIABILITIES

Capital and Reserves		
€1 ordinary shares	10,000	20,000
Revaluation reserve	–	11,000
Retained earnings	310,000	163,000
Non-current Liabilities		
Loans	60,000	20,000
Current Liabilities		
Payables	70,000	40,000
Current account with CITIZEN	–	20,000
Loans	10,000	6,000
	460,000	280,000

Additional Information:

1. All of KANE's property, plant and equipment were acquired on or before 1 January 2010. The revaluation reserve relates to the revaluation of property on 1 January 2010 in accordance with group policy.
2. KANE's opening and closing inventory was purchased on 1 December 2011 and 1 December 2012 respectively.
3. Exchange rates were as follows:

	€1 = A$
1 January 2010	2
1 December 2011	2.5
31 December 2011	2.75
1 December 2012	4.5
31 December 2012	5
Average 2012	4

4. During 2012, goodwill arising on the acquisition of KANE was impaired for the first time by A$400,000.

Requirement

(a) Prepare the consolidated statement of profit or loss and other comprehensive income of CITIZEN for the year ended 31 December 2012 and the consolidated statement of financial position as at that date.

(b) Show how the profit/loss on exchange differences arose in CITIZEN's consolidated financial statements for the year ended 31 December 2012.

DISPOSAL OF SUBSIDIARIES

LEARNING OBJECTIVES

Having studied this chapter, you should be able to account for the disposal of a subsidiary under the following circumstances:
1. disposal of an entire holding in a subsidiary;
2. partial disposal of an interest in a subsidiary leading to reduced subsidiary interest;
3. disposal of an interest in a subsidiary leading to an investment in an associate; and
4. disposal of an interest in a subsidiary leading to an investment interest.

KEY TERMS AND DEFINITIONS FOR THIS CHAPTER

Associate An entity in which the investor has significant influence and which is neither a subsidiary nor a joint venture of the investor.

Carrying Amount This is the amount at which an asset is recognised in the statement of financial position.

Cost Method The investment is recorded at cost. The statement of profit or loss and other comprehensive income reflects income only to the extent that the investor receives distributions from the investee subsequent to the date of acquisition.

Equity Method A method of accounting whereby the investment is initially recorded at cost and adjusted thereafter to reflect the investor's share of the post-acquisition net profit or loss of the investee/associate. The statement of profit or loss and other comprehensive income reflects the investor's share of the results of operations of the investee. Distributions received from the investee reduce the carrying amount of the investment. Adjustments to the carrying amount may also be required arising from changes in the investee's equity that have not been included in the statement of profit or loss and other comprehensive income (for example, revaluations).

Equity Transactions These are transactions with owners in their capacity as owners.

Fair Value This is the amount for which an asset could be exchanged between knowledgeable and willing parties in an arm's length transaction.

Non-Controlling Interest This is an ownership interest in an entity where the held position gives the investor no influence on how the company is run. In simple terms, any position that holds less than 50% of the outstanding voting shares is deemed to be a non-controlling interest.

Significant Influence This is the power to participate in the financial and operating policy decisions of the investee but not to control those policies. If an investor holds, directly or indirectly, 20% or more of the voting power of the investee, it is presumed that it has significant influence, unless it can be clearly demonstrated that this is not the case. Conversely, if less than 20%, the presumption is that the investor does not have significant influence. A majority shareholding by another investor does not preclude an investor having significant influence. Its existence is usually evidenced in one or more of the following ways:

- representation on the board of directors;
- participation in policy-making processes;
- material transactions between the investor and the investee;
- interchange of managerial personnel; or
- provision of essential technical information.

Subsidiary An entity in which the investor has dominant influence and therefore controls. In simple terms, control is presumed to exist when the parent owns over 50% of the voting power of an enterprise unless, in exceptional circumstances, it can be clearly demonstrated that such ownership does not constitute control.

Please note that, as explained in **Chapter 2**, the IASB issued amendments to IAS 1 *Presentation of Financial Statements* in June 2011. These included a *proposal* that the title 'Statement of Profit or Loss and Other Comprehensive Income' (SPLOCI) be adopted (rather than, for example, 'statement of comprehensive income') and a *requirement* to revise the presentation of other comprehensive income (OCI) within the SPLOCI. These amendments are explained in detail in **Chapter 2**, **Section 2.3**.

32.1 INTRODUCTION

This chapter examines how to account for the disposal of an interest in a subsidiary. It is important to remember that when an undertaking ceases to be a subsidiary undertaking, the consolidated financial statements for the period should include the results of the subsidiary up to the date that it ceases to be a subsidiary. Furthermore, it is imperative that you are aware that the calculation of the profit/loss on disposal in the consolidated financial statements is different from that in the holding company's own accounts.

Key to this Chapter

IFRS 10 *Consolidated Financial Statements* deals with the disposal of subsidiaries.

This chapter considers the calculation of the profit/loss on the disposal of a subsidiary in the following circumstances:

- Disposal of an entire holding in a subsidiary (see **Section 32.3**).
- Partial disposal of an interest in a subsidiary leading to reduced subsidiary interest (see **Section 32.4**).
- Disposal of an interest in a subsidiary leading to an investment in an associate (see **Section 32.5**).
- Disposal of an interest in a subsidiary leading to an investment interest (see **Section 32.6**).

Before studying this topic, it is vital that you revise the calculation of goodwill arising on the acquisition of a subsidiary (see **Chapter 26**).

Note: all of the examples and questions in this chapter assume that, for the purposes of measuring non-controlling interests at the date of acquisition, the proportionate share method equates to the fair value method.

32.2 DISPOSAL OF SUBSIDIARIES

As stated previously, IFRS 10 *Consolidated Financial Statements* deals with the disposal of subsidiaries. In broad terms, there are two possible scenarios:

1. a change in a parent's ownership interest in a subsidiary that *does not* result in the loss of control; and
2. a change in a parent's ownership interest in a subsidiary that *does* result in the loss of control.

Each of these will impact on both the parent's individual financial statements and the consolidated financial statements.

No Loss of Control

Changes in a parent's ownership interest in a subsidiary that *do not* result in a loss of control are accounted for as **equity transactions** (i.e. transactions with owners in their capacity as owners). This is explained further in **Section 32.4**.

In such circumstances, the **carrying amounts** of the controlling and **non-controlling interests** should be adjusted to reflect the changes in their relative interests in the subsidiary. Any difference between the amount by which the non-controlling interests are adjusted and the **fair value** of the consideration paid or received should be recognised directly in equity and attributed to the owners of the parent.

Loss of Control

A parent could lose control of a subsidiary with or without a change in absolute or relative ownership levels. This could occur, for example, when a subsidiary becomes subject to the control of a government, court, administrator or regulator. It also could occur as a result of a contractual agreement.

If a parent loses control of a subsidiary, it should:

1. derecognise the assets (including any goodwill) and liabilities of the subsidiary at their carrying amounts at the date when control is lost;
2. derecognise the carrying amount of any non-controlling interests in the former subsidiary at the date when control is lost (including any components of other comprehensive income attributable to them);
3. recognise:
   (a) the fair value of the consideration received, if any, from the transaction, event or circumstances that resulted in the loss of control; and
   (b) if the transaction that resulted in the loss of control involves a distribution of shares of the subsidiary to owners in their capacity as owners, that distribution;
4. recognise any investment retained in the former subsidiary at its fair value at the date when control is lost;
5. reclassify to profit or loss, or transfer directly to retained earnings if required in accordance with other IFRSs, the amounts identified in the paragraph* below; and
6. recognise any resulting difference as a gain or loss in arriving at the profit or loss attributable to the parent.

The circumstances leading to the loss of control of a subsidiary are illustrated more fully in **Section 32.3**, **Section 32.5** and **Section 32.6**.

On the loss of control of a subsidiary, any investment retained in the former subsidiary and any amounts owed by or to the former subsidiary should be accounted for in accordance with other IFRSs from the date when control is lost.

* If a parent loses control of a subsidiary, the parent should account for all amounts recognised in other comprehensive income in relation to that subsidiary on the same basis as would be required if the parent had directly disposed of the related assets or liabilities. Therefore, if a gain or loss previously recognised in other comprehensive income would be reclassified to profit or loss on the disposal of the related assets or liabilities, the parent should reclassify the gain or loss from equity to profit or loss (as a reclassification adjustment) when it loses control of the subsidiary. For example, if a subsidiary has cumulative exchange differences relating to a foreign operation and the parent loses control of the subsidiary, the parent should reclassify to profit or loss the gain or loss previously recognised in other comprehensive income in relation to the foreign operation. Similarly, if a revaluation surplus previously recognised in other comprehensive income would be transferred directly to retained earnings on the disposal of the asset, the parent should transfer the revaluation surplus directly to retained earnings when it loses control of the subsidiary.

32.3 DISPOSAL OF AN ENTIRE HOLDING IN A SUBSIDIARY

As stated earlier, this chapter considers the calculation of the profit/loss on the disposal of a subsidiary under the following circumstances: disposal of an entire holding in a subsidiary; partial disposal of an interest in a subsidiary leading to reduced subsidiary interest; disposal of an interest in a subsidiary leading to an investment in an associate; and disposal of an interest in a subsidiary leading to an investment interest. This section deals with the first of those circumstances.

In addition, it is important to remember that when an undertaking ceases to be a subsidiary undertaking, the consolidated financial statements for the period should include the results of the subsidiary up to the date that it ceases to be a subsidiary. Furthermore, it is imperative that you are aware that the calculation of the profit/loss on disposal in the consolidated financial statements is different from that in the holding company's own accounts.

This section begins by considering the disposal of an entire holding in a subsidiary in the parent company's accounts and then the consolidated accounts.

Parent Company's Accounts

The cash received on disposal of the investment, and the profit/loss on that disposal, will be recorded in the parent company's own accounts. The profit/loss for a complete disposal is simply the difference between the sale proceeds and the carrying value of the investment. This is illustrated in **Example 32.1**.

EXAMPLE 32.1: DISPOSAL OF ENTIRE HOLDING IN PARENT'S ACCOUNTS

During the year ended 31 December 2012, Company A sold all of its shares in Subsidiary B for €18,900,000. Prior to the sale, Company A owned 75% of Subsidiary B, which it had acquired for €11,300,000. The sale gave rise to a tax liability of €1,300,000.

	€
Sale proceeds	18,900,000
Cost	(11,300,000)
	7,600,000
Tax	(1,300,000)
Profit on disposal	6,300,000

This would be recorded as follows:

DR	Bank	€18,900,000	
CR	Tax liability		€1,300,000
CR	Cost of investment		€11,300,000
CR	SPLOCI – P/L (appropriate statutory heading at the discretion of the company)		€6,300,000

Consolidated Accounts

In the consolidated accounts, the sale proceeds should be deducted from the share of the net assets of the subsidiary disposed of. The net assets include any goodwill arising on the acquisition of the subsidiary that has not been impaired. For example:

	€
Sale proceeds	X
Less reduction in carrying value of identifiable net assets relating to the disposal	(X)

Less unimpaired goodwill arising on acquisition	(X)
Profit/loss on disposal of subsidiary (before tax)	X

EXAMPLE 32.2: DISPOSAL OF ENTIRE HOLDING IN CONSOLIDATED ACCOUNTS

The following are the draft financial statements of P Limited and S Limited for the year ended 31 December 2012.

STATEMENT OF PROFIT OR LOSS AND OTHER COMPREHENSIVE INCOME

	P Limited	S Limited
	€	€
Profit before tax	60,000	40,000
Income tax expense	(24,000)	(16,000)
Profit after tax	36,000	24,000
Retained profit b/f	104,000	16,000
	140,000	40,000

Statement of Financial Position

	P	S
Assets	€	€
Investment in S	75,000	–
Sundry net assets	265,000	100,000
	340,000	100,000
Equity		
Ordinary €1 shares	200,000	60,000
Reserves	140,000	40,000
	340,000	100,000

P Limited acquired 75% of the ordinary shares of S Limited on 1 January 2011 when the reserves of S Limited were €10,000. The investment is sold for €115,000 on 31 December 2012. Goodwill, which is accounted for in accordance with IFRS 3, suffered impairment of €4,500 during the year ended 31 December 2011.

Requirement Calculate the profit on disposal of the shares to be included in P Limited's own and consolidated financial statements.

Solution

	€
Profit on disposal of shares	
1. In P Limited's own accounts:	
Sale proceeds	115,000
Cost of investment	(75,000)
	40,000
2. In consolidated accounts:	
Goodwill	
€75,000 − 75% (€60,000 + €10,000)	22,500
Written off y/e 31 December 2011 (impairment)	(4,500)

Remaining	<u>18,000</u>
Profit on disposal	
Sale proceeds	115,000
Share of net assets at date of disposal (€100,000 × 75%)	<u>(75,000)</u>
	40,000
Less attributable goodwill	<u>(18,000)</u>
	<u>22,000</u>

Note: S Limited is a subsidiary until 31 December 2012, therefore its results for the full year must be consolidated.

P Limited

CONSOLIDATED STATEMENT OF PROFIT OR LOSS AND OTHER COMPREHENSIVE INCOME
for the Year Ended 31 December 2012

	€
Profit on disposal of subsidiary	22,000
Operating profit	<u>100,000</u>
Profit before tax	122,000
Income tax expense	<u>(40,000)</u>
Profit after tax	82,000
Non-controlling interest (25% × €24,000)	<u>(6,000)</u>
	<u>76,000</u>
Retained earnings at start of period	104,000
Retained earnings at end of period	<u>180,000</u>

P Limited

STATEMENT OF FINANCIAL POSITION
as at 31 December 2012

		€
Assets		
Sundry net assets	(W2)	<u>380,000</u>
Equity		
Ordinary € 1 shares		200,000
Reserves	(W3)	<u>180,000</u>
		<u>380,000</u>

W1	
P Limited	104,000
S Limited 75% (€16,000 − €10,000)	4,500
Goodwill written off (because of impairment)	<u>(4,500)</u>
	<u>104,000</u>
W2	
P Limited	265,000
Proceeds from sale of investment	<u>115,000</u>
	<u>380,000</u>

W3
P Limited
Profit on sale (per P's own accounts)

140,000
40,000
180,000

The difference between the gain in the parent's statement of profit or loss and other comprehensive income and the gain reported in the consolidated statement of profit or loss and other comprehensive income is €18,000 (€40,000 − €22,000). This difference represents the share of the post-acquisition profits retained in the subsidiary of €22,500 ((€40,000 − €10,000) × 75%) that has been reported in the group statement of profit or loss and other comprehensive income less the goodwill impaired of €4,500.

32.4 PARTIAL DISPOSAL OF AN INTEREST IN A SUBSIDIARY LEADING TO REDUCED SUBSIDIARY INTEREST

As discussed earlier, a parent can dispose of part of its interest in a subsidiary but still retain control (i.e. in simple terms, maintain its ownership above 50%). This section addresses this situation.

Under IFRS 10, all entities are required to apply the economic entity model for transactions with non-controlling interests. Thus, changes in a parent's interest in a subsidiary that do not result in the loss of control are accounted for in equity. Any difference between the amount transferred to non-controlling interests (percentage held outside the group) and the proceeds received is recorded in the parent's equity. The amounts recognised in equity for the change in ownership that do not result in a change of control are *NOT* reclassified to profit or loss upon loss of control. The partial disposal of an interest in a subsidiary leading to reduced subsidiary interest is illustrated in **Example 32.3**, in both the parent's and consolidated accounts.

EXAMPLE 32.3: PARTIAL DISPOSAL WITH SUBSIDIARY INTEREST RETAINED

P Limited purchased a 100% interest in S Limited for €500,000 at the end of 2010 when the fair value of S Limited's net assets was €400,000. P Limited sold 40% of its investment in S Limited on 31 December 2012 for €450,000, retaining a 60% controlling interest in S Limited. The carrying value of S Limited's net assets at 31 December 2012 is €900,000 (including goodwill of €100,000).

Parent Company's Accounts:

	€
Sale proceeds	450,000
Less cost of investment in S Limited (€500,000 × 40%)	(200,000)
Gain on sale in P Limited's accounts	250,000

Consolidated Accounts:

Note: a change in ownership that does not result in loss of control is considered an equity transaction. The identifiable net assets (including goodwill) remain unchanged and any difference between the amount by which the non-controlling interest is recorded (including non-controlling interest share of goodwill) and the fair value of the consideration received is recognised directly in equity and attributed to the controlling interests. The change in non-controlling interest is recorded at its proportionate interest of the carrying value of the subsidiary.

Therefore, the gain on sale would *not* be recorded in the consolidated statement of profit or loss and other comprehensive income. The difference between the fair value of the consideration received and the amount by which the non-controlling interest is recorded is recognised directly in equity.

	€
Sale proceeds	450,000
Recognition of non-controlling interest (€900,000 × 40%)	(360,000)
Credit to equity	90,000

This would be recorded as follows:

DR	Bank	€450,000	
CR	Non-controlling interest		€360,000
CR	Equity – other components		€90,000

The difference between the gain in the parent's statement of profit or loss and other comprehensive income and the gain reported in the consolidated statement of profit or loss and other comprehensive income is €160,000. This difference represents the share of the post-acquisition profits retained in the subsidiary of €160,000 ((€900,000 − €500,000) × 40%) which have been reported in the group statement of profit or loss and other comprehensive income up to the date of sale.

The non-controlling interest immediately after the disposal will be 40% of the net carrying value of S Limited's net assets, including any goodwill in the consolidated statement of financial position of €900,000 (i.e. €360,000).

Following on from the previous example, **Example 32.4** and **Example 32.5** illustrate the impact in the consolidated accounts of a partial disposal with reduced subsidiary interest, depending on whether goodwill was impaired. These two examples use the same figures so as to more clearly highlight the impact.

EXAMPLE 32.4: GOODWILL NOT IMPAIRED

P Limited purchased a 100% interest in S Limited on 31 December 2010, with goodwill of €80,000 arising on the acquisition. On 31 December 2012, the net assets of S Limited, excluding goodwill, were €400,000 and P Limited disposed of 40% of its interest for €200,000 on this date. The goodwill arising on the acquisition of S Limited had not been impaired since 31 December 2010.

Consolidated Accounts:

	€
Sale proceeds	200,000
Less recognition of non-controlling interest in S Limited (€480,000 × 40%)	(192,000)
Credit to equity	8,000

EXAMPLE 32.5: GOODWILL IMPAIRED

P Limited purchased a 100% interest in S Limited on 31 December 2010, with goodwill of €80,000 arising on the acquisition. On 31 December 2012, the net assets of S Limited, excluding goodwill, were €400,000 and P Limited disposed of 40% of its interest for €200,000 on this date. The goodwill arising on the acquisition of S Limited had been impaired by €20,000 at 31 December 2012.

Consolidated Accounts:

	€
Sale proceeds	200,000
Less recognition of non-controlling interest in S Limited (€460,000 × 40%)	(184,000)
Credit to equity	16,000

32.5 DISPOSAL OF AN INTEREST IN A SUBSIDIARY LEADING TO AN INVESTMENT IN AN ASSOCIATE

An entity that has a subsidiary interest in another entity (i.e. greater than 50% ownership and therefore dominant influence presumed) may dispose of part of this interest so as to reduce its interest to between 20%–50% (i.e. presumed to lead to significant influence and associate status).

The consequences of the sale of an interest in a subsidiary that results in the parent losing control of the subsidiary, but retaining significant influence, is illustrated in **Example 32.6.**

EXAMPLE 32.6: ASSOCIATE STATUS

P Limited purchased a 100% interest in S Limited for €500,000 at the end of 2010 when the fair value of S Limited's net assets was €400,000. Therefore goodwill is €100,000. P Limited sold 60% of its investment in S Limited on 31 December 2012 for €675,000, retaining a 40% non-controlling interest in S Limited. The carrying value of S Limited's net assets at 31 December 2012 is €900,000 (including goodwill of €100,000).

Parent Company's Accounts:

	€
Sale proceeds	675,000
Less cost of investment in S Limited (€500,000 × 60%)	(300,000)
Gain on sale in P Limited's accounts	375,000

Consolidated Accounts:

Note: for simplicity, it is assumed that the fair value of the investment in S Limited retained is proportionate to the fair value of the 60% sold (i.e. €450,000). In the consolidated accounts, the carrying value of net assets (including goodwill) should be derecognised when control is lost. This is compared to the proceeds received and the fair value of the investment retained.

	€
Sale proceeds	675,000
Fair value of 40% interest retained	450,000
	1,125,000
Less net assets disposed (including goodwill)	(900,000)
Gain on sale	225,000

This gain on loss of control would be recorded in arriving at profit or loss. It includes the gain of €135,000 (€675,000 − (€900,000 × 60%)) on the portion sold. However, it also includes a gain on remeasurement of the 40% retained interest of €90,000 (€360,000 to €450,000). This fair value element of the gain should be disclosed separately in a note to the statement of profit or loss and other comprehensive income.

32.6 DISPOSAL OF AN INTEREST IN A SUBSIDIARY LEADING TO AN INVESTMENT INTEREST

The consequences of the sale of an interest in a subsidiary may be that the parent loses both control of the subsidiary and significant influence. A typical example of this would be if, after the disposal, the 'parent' retained less than 20% of the ordinary shares. The consequences of this are shown in **Example 32.7**.

EXAMPLE 32.7: INVESTMENT STATUS

P Limited purchased a 100% interest in S Limited for €500,000 at the end of 2010 when the fair value of S Limited's net assets was €400,000. Therefore, goodwill is €100,000. P Limited sold 90% of its investment in S Limited on 31 December 2012 for €855,000, retaining a 10% interest in S Limited. The carrying value of S Limited's net assets at 31 December 2012 is €900,000 (including goodwill of €100,000). The fair value of the remaining interest is €95,000 (assumed, for simplicity, to be pro rata to the fair value of the 90% sold).

Parent Company's Accounts:

	€
Sale proceeds	855,000
Less cost of investment in S Limited (€500,000 × 90%)	(450,000)
Gain on sale in P Limited's accounts	405,000

Consolidated Accounts:
Note: in the consolidated accounts, the carrying value of net assets (including goodwill) should be derecognised when control is lost. This is compared to the proceeds received and the fair value of the investment retained.

	€
Sale proceeds	855,000
Fair value of 10% interest retained	95,000
	950,000
Less net assets disposed (including goodwill)	(900,000)
Gain on sale	50,000

This gain on loss of control would be recorded in arriving at profit or loss. It includes the gain of €45,000 (€855,000 − (€900,000 × 90%)) on the 90% sold as well as €5,000 related to the gain on remeasurement of the 10% retained (€90,000 to €95,000).

32.7 CONCLUSION

While accounting for disposal of shares in a subsidiary is a complex area, IFRS 10 is very specific with regard to the treatment of such disposals. As can be seen from each of the scenarios presented above, the concept of 'control' or 'dominant influence' is fundamental to how the disposal of an interest in a subsidiary is accounted for. Changes to a parent's ownership interest in a subsidiary that do not result in a loss of control are accounted for as equity transactions and no profit or loss on disposal is reported in the consolidated statement of profit or loss and other comprehensive income. However, if a parent loses control then:

- the subsidiary's assets and liabilities must be derecognised from the consolidated statement of financial position as well as the non-controlling interests in those net assets;
- any gain or loss on disposal should be recognised in the consolidated statement of profit or loss and other comprehensive income; and
- any investment in the former subsidiary should be recognised at its fair value on the date when control is lost.

Summary of Learning Objectives

After having studied this chapter, you should be able to account for the disposal of a subsidiary under the following circumstances:

Learning Objective 1 Disposal of an entire holding in a subsidiary and therefore resulting in loss of control.

In the parent company's accounts, the profit/loss for a complete disposal is simply the difference between the sale proceeds and the carrying value of the investment. The cash received on disposal of the investment, and the profit/loss on that disposal, will be recorded in the parent company's own accounts. In the consolidated accounts, the sale proceeds should be deducted from the share of the net assets of the subsidiary disposed of. The net assets comprise any goodwill arising on the acquisition of the subsidiary that has not been impaired. (See **Section 32.3**.)

Learning Objective 2 Partial disposal of an interest in a subsidiary leading to reduced subsidiary interest, but not loss of control.

Changes in a parent's interest in a subsidiary that do not result in the loss of control are accounted for in equity. Any difference between the amount transferred to non-controlling interests and the proceeds received is recorded in the parent's equity. The amounts recognised in equity for the change in ownership that do not result in a change of control are *NOT* reclassified to profit or loss upon loss of control. (See **Section 32.4**.)

Learning Objective 3 Disposal of an interest in a subsidiary leading to an investment in an associate and resulting in loss of control, but retaining significant influence.

In the parent company's accounts, the proportion of the cost of the investment disposed of is deducted from the sale proceeds to arrive at the gain/loss on disposal. In the consolidated accounts, the carrying value of net assets (including goodwill) should be derecognised when control is lost. This is compared to the proceeds received and the fair value of the investment retained. (See **Section 32.5**.)

Learning Objective 4 Disposal of an interest in a subsidiary leading to an investment interest and loss of both control and significant influence.

In the parent company's accounts, the proportion of the cost of the investment disposed of is deducted from the sale proceeds to arrive at the gain/loss on disposal. In the consolidated accounts, the carrying value of net assets (including goodwill) should be derecognised when control is lost. This is compared to the proceeds received and the fair value of the investment retained. (See **Section 32.6**.)

QUESTIONS

Review Question

(See **Appendix One** for Suggested Solutions to Review Questions.)

Question 32.1

Smith Limited bought 80% of the share capital of Jones Limited for €324,000 on 1 October 2010. At that date Jones Limited's retained earnings stood at €180,000. The statements of financial position at 30 September 2013 and the summarised statements of profit or loss and other comprehensive income to that date are given below.

	Smith Limited €000	Jones Limited €000
Assets		
Tangible non-current assets	360	270
Investment in Jones Limited	324	–
Net current assets	270	270
	954	540
Equity		
€1 ordinary shares	540	180
Retained earnings	414	360
	954	540
Profit before tax	153	126
Income tax expense	(45)	(36)
Retained profit	108	90
Retained profit b/f	306	270
Retained profit c/f	414	360

No entries have been made in the accounts for any of the transactions below. Assume that profits accrue evenly throughout the year and that any goodwill is accounted for in accordance with IFRS 3.

(Ignore taxation.)

Requirement Prepare the consolidated statement of profit or loss and other comprehensive income for the year ended 30 September 2013, and the statement of financial position as at that date, under each of the following circumstances:

(a) Smith Limited sells its entire holding in Jones Limited for €650,000 on 30 September 2013.

(b) Smith Limited sells its entire holding in Jones Limited for €650,000 on 30 June 2013.

(Assume that no goodwill is written off due to impairment.)

Challenging Question

(Suggested Solutions to Challenging Questions are available to lecturers.)

Question 32.1

Using the information provided above for **Review Question 32.1**, Smith Limited.

Requirement Prepare the consolidated statement of profit or loss and other comprehensive income for the year ended 30 September 2013, and the statement of financial position as at that date, under each of the following circumstances:

(a) Smith Limited sells one quarter of its holding in Jones Limited for €160,000 on 30 June 2013.

(b) Smith Limited sells one half of its holding in Jones Limited for €340,000 on 30 June 2013, and the remaining holding is to be dealt with as an associate.

(Assume that no goodwill is written off due to impairment.)

33

STATEMENT OF CASH FLOWS – CONSOLIDATED

Learning Objectives

Having studied this chapter, you should be able to prepare a consolidated statement of cash flows in accordance with IAS 7 *Statement of Cash Flows*.

Key Terms and Definitions for this Chapter

Closing Rate This is the spot exchange rate at the reporting date.

Equity Method A method of accounting whereby the investment is initially recorded at cost and adjusted thereafter to reflect the investor's share of the post-acquisition net profit or loss of the investee/associate. The statement of profit or loss and other comprehensive income reflects the investor's share of the results of operations of the investee. Distributions received from the investee reduce the carrying amount of the investment. Adjustments to the carrying amount may also be required arising from changes in the investee's equity that have not been included in the statement of profit or loss and other comprehensive income (for example, revaluations).

Exchange Rate This is the ratio of exchange for two currencies.

Foreign Currency This is a currency other than the functional currency of the entity.

Functional Currency This is the currency of the primary economic environment in which the entity operates.

Foreign Operation This is a subsidiary, associate, joint venture or branch whose activities are based in a country or currency other than those of the reporting entity.

Jointly Controlled Entities This is a joint venture that involves the establishment of a separate legal entity.

Joint Venture This is a contractual agreement whereby two or more parties undertake an economic activity that is subject to joint control.

Non-Controlling Interest (NCI) This is an ownership interest in an entity where the held position gives the investor no influence on how the company is run. In simple terms, any position that holds less than 50% of the outstanding voting shares is deemed to be a non-controlling interest.

Presentation Currency This is the currency in which the financial statements are presented.

Proportionate Consolidation This is a method of accounting and reporting whereby a venturer's share of each of the assets, liabilities, income and expenses of a jointly controlled entity is combined on a line-by-line basis with similar items in the venturer's financial statements or reported as separate line items.

33.1 INTRODUCTION

Part V of this book (**Chapters 26–33**), which focuses on issues relating to accounting for business combinations, concludes in this chapter by dealing with the preparation of a consolidated statement of cash flows.

The preparation of a statement of cash flows for a single entity, together with the more general issues relating to the preparation of statements of cash flow, is dealt with in **Part III**, **Chapter 19**. With respect to the preparation of a consolidated statement of cash flows, some points worthy of note at this stage are:

- Consistent with the principles underlying the preparation of a consolidated statement of profit or loss and other comprehensive income (CSPLOCI) and consolidated statement of financial position, a consolidated statement of cash flows should exclude internal flows of cash within the group.
- The cash flows of any entity which is accounted for using the **equity method** (see **Chapter 29**) should only be included in the consolidated statement of cash flows to the extent of the actual cash flows between the group and entity concerned; for example, dividends received in cash and loans made or repaid.
- Dividends paid to the non-controlling interest should be included under the heading of 'cash flows from financing activities' in the consolidated statement of cash flows; and
- the amount shown in the consolidated statement of cash flows for subsidiaries purchased/disposed of is the amount paid/received net of cash and cash equivalents acquired/disposed of. This should be shown in the 'investing activities' section of the consolidated statement of cash flows.

Key to this Chapter

In terms of the format of this chapter, it begins by explaining four issues that are particularly relevant when preparing a consolidated statement of cash flows (see **Section 33.2**). These relate to: non-controlling interests; associates and joint ventures; the acquisition and disposal of a subsidiary; and foreign operations. Before concluding by outlining the main disclosure requirements (see **Section 33.3**), a comprehensive example is presented in order to illustrate the preparation of a consolidated statement of cash flows (see **Example 33.3**).

> ***Note:*** for ease of illustration, dividends and retained earnings are sometimes shown at the foot of the statement of profit or loss and other comprehensive income in examples and questions. These figures would normally be included in the statement of changes in equity. In addition, for similar reasons, non-controlling interests are presented immediately following profit after tax rather than in accordance with IAS 1 *Presentation of Financial Statements* (see **Chapter 2**).

33.2 SPECIAL ISSUES WHEN PREPARING A CONSOLIDATED STATEMENT OF CASH FLOWS

In general, the principles involved in the preparation of a consolidated statement of cash flows are the same as those for an individual company. However, the following issues are peculiar to groups:
- dealing with the non-controlling interests in subsidiaries;
- dealing with associates and joint ventures;
- acquisition and disposal of a subsidiary during an accounting period; and
- dealing with foreign operations.

Dealing with Non-controlling Interests

A subsidiary gets full consolidation and therefore all its assets and liabilities are included in the consolidated statement of financial position whether or not there is a non-controlling interest. This means that cash flows for subsidiaries relating to such items as operating activities, taxation, acquisition or disposal of non-current assets are combined with those of the parent undertaking. However, certain items need special attention:
- issue of shares for cash to non-controlling interests;
- redemption of shares owned by non-controlling interests; and
- dividends paid to non-controlling interests.

Cash flows relating to the first and second items would appear in the consolidated statement of cash flows under 'financing activities'. In the absence of the acquisition or disposal of a subsidiary (part of which is owned by the non-controlling interests) during the period, dividends paid to non-controlling interests can be ascertained from the T account as follows:

Non-controlling Interests			
	€		€
Cash (dividends paid) balancing figure	X	Bal b/d (per opening CSFP)	X
Bal c/d (closing CSFP)	X	Share of profit after tax (per CSPLOCI – P/L)	X
	X		X

Dividends paid to non-controlling interests would be included under cash flows from operating activities or cash flows from financing activities in the statement of cash flows.

Dealing with Associates and Joint Ventures

Investments in Associates

If an associate is accounted for in the consolidated accounts using the equity method of accounting, this means that the consolidated statement of profit or loss and other comprehensive income includes the group's share of the profit before tax of the associate plus the group's share of its tax charge. Neither of these entries involves cash flow, but the group cash flow is affected by the dividends received from associates. When an investment in an associate is accounted for by using the equity method (the normal treatment), the statement of cash flows of the investor must only include cash flows between itself and the associate, e.g. dividends received from the associate, advances to or from the associate. Dividends received from associates can be calculated as follows:

Investment in Associates			
	€		€
Bal b/d (from opening CSFP)	X	Dividends received from associate	X
Share of associate's profit after tax	X	Balance c/d (from closing CSFP)	X
	X		X

Dividends received from associated undertakings should be included under operating cash flows or investing activities.

Investments in Joint Ventures

Similar to associates (above) investments in joint ventures are accounted for using the **equity method** (see **Chapter 30**). In the statement of cash flows only actual cash flows from sales and purchases between the group and joint venture, and investments in and dividends from the entity should be included (**not** the share of profit included in the statement of profit or loss and other comprehensive income). Dividends should be included in operating cash flows or investing activities.

Acquisition of a Subsidiary during an Accounting Period

If a subsidiary joins the group during the accounting period, the statement of cash flows should include cash flows for the same period as that for which the group's statement of profit or loss and other comprehensive income includes the results of the subsidiary (i.e. from the date of acquisition to the end of the accounting period). In addition:
1. the net cash flow from the acquisition must be shown separately under investing activities;
2. the notes to the statement of cash flows must include the:
   (a) total purchase consideration,
   (b) portion of the purchase consideration discharged by either cash or cash equivalents, and
   (c) amount of cash and cash equivalents in the subsidiary acquired.

This should be dealt with in the consolidated statement of cash flows under 'investing activities'. Dealing with the acquisition of a subsidiary in a consolidated statement of cash flows is illustrated in **Example 33.1**. Any cash paid as part of the consideration would be included as a cash outflow, while any balances of cash and overdrafts transferred as part of the acquisition should be offset.

EXAMPLE 33.1: ACQUISITION OF A SUBSIDIARY

During the period under review, P Limited acquired 80% of the ordinary shares of S Limited.

	€000
Details of the acquisition:	
Fair value of net assets acquired	
Non-current assets	500
Inventory	180
Trade receivables	140
Cash	20
Trade payables	(120)
	720
Non-controlling interest @ 20%	(144)
Goodwill	24
	600
Discharged by:	
Issue of shares	200
Cash paid	400
	600

Extract from statement of cash flows:
Investing activities
Purchase of subsidiary (€400,000 − €20,000)   (380)

Note: while P Limited paid €400,000 in cash for S Limited, the actual net cash flow is €380,000 since S Limited held cash of €20,000 at the acquisition date.

With respect to **Example 33.1** it should be noted that the non-current assets (€500,000), inventory (€180,000), receivables (€140,000) and payables (€120,000) should be excluded from changes in these items in the consolidated statement of cash flows. A note to the statement of cash flows should show a summary of the effects of the acquisition (for example, see 'note' at end of **Example 33.1**).

Disposal of a Subsidiary during an Accounting Period

If a subsidiary leaves the group during the accounting period, the statement of cash flows should include cash flows for the same period as that for which the group's statement of profit or loss and other comprehensive income includes the results of the subsidiary (i.e. from the start of the period to the date of disposal). In addition:

1. the net cash flow from the disposal must be shown separately under investing activities;
2. the notes to the statement of cash flows must include the:
   (a) total disposal consideration, and
   (b) amount of cash and cash equivalents in the subsidiary sold.

This should be dealt with in the consolidated statement of cash flows under 'investing activities'. Any cash received as part of the disposal consideration would be included as a cash inflow while any balances of cash and overdrafts transferred as part of the disposal should be offset. **Example 33.2** illustrates how the disposal of a subsidiary is dealt with in a consolidated statement of cash flows.

EXAMPLE 33.2: DISPOSAL OF A SUBSIDIARY

During the accounting period Plug plc Limited sold 80% of its holding in AMP Limited for €140,000 cash. The statement of financial position of AMP Limited at the date of disposal was:

	€000
Tangible non-current assets	115
Inventory	55
Receivables	36
Cash	14
Payables	(60)
	160
Ordinary shares €1	50
Reserves	110
	160

Extract from consolidated statement of cash flows:

	€000
Investing Activities	
Sale of subsidiary (140 − 14)	126

A note should be given showing a summary of the effects of the disposal as follows:

Disposal of subsidiary undertaking

	€000
Net assets disposed of	
Tangible non-current assets	115
Inventory	55
Receivables	36
Cash	14
Payables	(60)
	160
Non-controlling interest @ 20%	(32)
Profit on disposal	12
	140
Satisfied by cash	140

Dealing with Foreign Operations

As accounting for foreign currency transactions and translations can be a complicated area, it may be useful to revise **Chapter 31** at this point.

The Individual Company

Cash flows arising from transactions in a **foreign currency** should be recorded in the entity's **functional currency** at the **exchange rate** at the date of the cash flows.

Foreign Subsidiaries

The cash flows of a foreign subsidiary must be translated at the exchange rates between the **functional currency** and the foreign currency at the dates of the cash flows – a weighted average rate for the period can be used.

If the **presentation currency** method is used to consolidate results, then the subsidiary's cash flows should be translated at an average rate (statement of profit or loss and other comprehensive income). But if the average rate is used, then merely using the statement of financial position figures would not be appropriate, as the statement of cash flows would not comply with IAS 7 (some items being translated at the **closing rate**). Therefore, the steps are:
* prepare the statement of cash flows for each subsidiary;
* translate each into 'Euro' using the average rate;
* consolidate each into the consolidated statement of cash flows; and
* foreign exchange differences on translation must be analysed into their constituent parts: non-current assets, receivables, cash, payables and non-controlling interests.

As mentioned previously, while this chapter focuses on the preparation of a consolidated statement of cash flows, many of the issues are similar to those encountered when preparing a statement of cash flows for a single entity. Consequently, before continuing with the remainder of this chapter, you should revise **Chapter 19** which addresses these 'common' issues in detail.

Example 33.3 illustrates the preparation of a consolidated statement of cash flows, combining many of the issues identified in **Chapter 19** and some the consolidation-specific issues discussed above.

EXAMPLE 33.3: CONSOLIDATED STATEMENT OF CASH FLOWS

Drumview plc prepares its financial statements to 31 December each year and extracts from the group's consolidated financial statements are shown below:

	Note	2012 €000	2011 €000
Consolidated Statement of Profit or Loss and Other Comprehensive Income:			
Gross profit		900	800
Net operating expenses	1	(300)	(250)
Profit from operations		600	550

Finance charges		(60)	(50)
Share of profit of associate		75	60
Profit before tax		615	560
Taxation		(150)	(140)
Profit after tax		465	420
Non-controlling interests		(93)	(84)
Group profit		372	336

Consolidated Statement of Financial Position:

ASSETS

Non-current Assets

Property	1	–	100
Plant and equipment	2	360	320
Goodwill	3	30	20
Investment in associate		120	45
		510	485

Current Assets

Inventory		200	170
Trade receivables		250	220
Bank and cash		30	25
		990	900

EQUITY AND LIABILITIES

Capital and Reserves

Ordinary share capital		100	100
Revaluation reserves		–	45
Retained earnings	4	445	100
Non-controlling interests		75	90
		620	335

Non-current Liabilities

Obligations under finance leases		100	80

Current Liabilities

Trade Payables		40	215
Taxation		100	120
Dividends payable to holding company		65	90
Dividends payable to non-controlling interests		15	20
Obligations under finance leases		50	40
		990	900

Additional Information:

1. Included in net operating expenses for the year ended 31 December 2012 is a gain of €50,000 arising on the sale of a property during the year. The property had been revalued a number of years previously, with the surplus being credited to revaluation reserves. It is group policy to charge a full year's depreciation in the year of acquisition and none in the year of disposal.

2. During the year ended 31 December 2012, Drumview plc entered into new finance lease agreements in respect of plant and equipment. The amounts debited to non-current assets in respect of such agreements during the year totalled €75,000. There were no other additions to property, plant and equipment during the year.

3. During the year ended 31 December 2012, Drumview plc purchased 75% of the ordinary share capital of Malvern Limited for €90,000 in cash. The fair value of the net assets of Malvern Limited at the date of acquisition was:

	€000
Plant and equipment	80
Inventory	15
Trade receivables	15
Bank and cash	2
Trade payables	(32)
	80

4. During the year ended 31 December 2012, dividends amounting to €72,000 were debited to equity.

Requirement

(a) Discuss the decision usefulness of the required classifications of cash flows under IAS 7 *Statement of Cash Flows*.

(b) Prepare the consolidated statement of cash flows of Drumview plc for the year ended 31 December 2012 in accordance with IAS 7 *Statement of Cash Flows*.

Solution

(a) Cash flows must be classified into cash flows from operating, investing and financing activities.

Operating cash flows are the principal revenue-producing activities of an entity and any other activities that do not fall within investing and financing activities. Such cash flows include receipts from customers, payments to suppliers and employees and income taxes. Operating cash flows may also include interest and dividends received (though these items may be classified as investing) and interest paid (though this item may be classified as financing).

Investing cash flows are the acquisition and disposal of long-term assets (such as property, plant and equipment, subsidiaries, businesses and intangibles) and other investments not included in cash equivalents (such as shares in other entities).

Financing activities are activities that result in changes in the size and composition of the equity capital and borrowing of an entity (such as the issue of new shares, buyback of shares, new borrowings, repayment of borrowings and the payment of dividends, though payment of dividends are sometimes classified as an operating activity).

(b)

Drumview plc
CONSOLIDATED STATEMENT OF CASH FLOWS
for the Year Ended 31 December 2012

	€000	€000
Cash Flows from Operating Activities		
Net cash from operating activities (W8)		218
Cash Flows from Investing Activities		
Cash received from sale of property (W1)	150	
Acquisition of subsidiary (W3(c))	(88)	62
		280
Cash Flows from Financing Activities		
Capital element of finance lease payments (W7)	(45)	
Dividends paid to non-controlling interests (W5(a))	(133)	
Dividends paid to holding company (W5(b))	(97)	(275)
Net increase in cash and cash equivalents during year		5
(See movement in bank and cash per Statement of Financial Position)		
Cash and cash equivalents at start of year		25
Cash and cash equivalents at end of year		30

WORKINGS

1. Sale of property	€000
Net book value at 31 December 2011 (see Statement of Financial Position)	100
Gain on disposal (see Note 1) (This increases accounting profit but is not a cash flow and should be deducted when reconciling cash flows from operating activities.)	50
Therefore proceeds/cash received [Investing Activities]	150

2. Depreciation of plant and equipment	€000
Opening balance (Net book value)	320
Acquired from Malvern Limited	80
Finance lease	75
Closing balance (Net book value)	(360)
Depreciation	115

Note:
(a) There is no property depreciation as all property was disposed of during 2012 and no depreciation is charged in the year of disposal.

(b) As Note 2 indicates that Drumview Limited entered into new finance lease agreements during 2012 in respect of plant and equipment, it is therefore necessary to calculate the amount paid in respect of these during 2012 (W7). There were no other additions.

3. Goodwill	€000
(a) On acquisition of Malvern Limited:	
Paid	90
Non-controlling Interests:	
Fair value of net assets at date of acquisition (Note 3) €80,000 × 25%	20
	110
Fair value of net assets acquired (Note 3)	
	(80)
Goodwill arising on the acquisition of Malvern Limited	30

(b) Impairment of goodwill:	
Opening balance	20
Goodwill arising on acquisition of Malvern Limited (W3(a))	30
Closing balance	(30)
Goodwill impaired during 2012 and charged in arriving at operating profit	20

(But as this is not a cash flow, it should be added back when reconciling cash flows from operating activities.)

(c) Acquisition of Malvern Limited:	
Purchase price (Note 3)	(90)
Bank and cash taken over	2
Net outflow [Investing Activities]	(88)

4. Dividends received from associate	€000
Opening balance	45
Statement of Profit or Loss and Other Comprehensive Income	75
Closing balance	(120)
Paid	-

5. Dividends paid	€000
(a) To non-controlling interests	
Opening balance (€90,000 + €20,000) (NCI + NCI dividends)	110
Statement of Profit or Loss and Other Comprehensive Income	93
Malvern Limited (NCI taken over during year) (€80,000 × 25%)	20
Closing balance (€75,000 + €15,000) (NCI + NCI dividends)	(90)
Paid [Financing Activities]	133

(b) To holding company	
Opening balance	90
Debited to equity during year (Note 4)	72
Closing balance	(65)
Paid to hold company shareholders [Financing Activities]	97

6. Taxation	€000
Opening balance	120
Statement of Profit or Loss and Other Comprehensive Income	150

Closing balance	(100)
Paid	170

7. Finance lease	€000
Opening balance (€80,000 + €40,000)	120
Additions during year (Note 2)	75
Closing balance (€100,000 + €50,000)	(150)
Paid [Financing Activities]	45

8. Reconciliation of operating profit	€000
Operating profit	600
Gain on disposal of property (W1)	(50)
Depreciation (W2)	115
Impairment of goodwill (W3)	20
Increase in inventory (€170,000 + €15,000 − €200,000)	(15)
Increase in trade receivables (€220,000 + €15,000 − €250,000)	(15)
Decrease in trade payables (€215,000 + €32,000 − €40,000)	(207)
Interest paid (As there is no interest prepayment or accrual, the figure per the statement of profit or loss and other comprehensive income represents the amount paid.)	(60)
Tax paid (W6)	(170)
Net cash from operating activities	218

33.3 DISCLOSURE

After having explained the preparation of a consolidated statement of cash flows in the previous section, this section outlines the disclosures required in accordance with IAS 7.

Notes to the Statement of Cash Flows (Direct and Indirect Method)

In the case of a subsidiary joining or leaving a group during a year, the cash flows of the subsidiary will be included in the consolidated statement of cash flows for the same period as the group's statement of profit or loss and other comprehensive income includes the subsidiary's results. In respect of both acquisitions and disposals, the following details should be disclosed:
- total purchase/disposal consideration;
- portion of purchase/disposal consideration discharged by means of cash and cash equivalents;
- amount of cash and cash equivalents in subsidiary disposed of; and
- amount of assets and liabilities, other than cash and cash equivalents in the subsidiary acquired, summarised by major headings.

Where the sale or purchase of a subsidiary has a material effect on the amounts reported under the standard headings in the statement of cash flows, a note should be appended showing these effects as far as practicable. The disclosure required in relation to the acquisition of a subsidiary during an accounting period is illustrated in **Example 33.4**. Similar information is required in respect of a disposed subsidiary.

EXAMPLE 33.4: DISCLOSURE OF ACQUIRED SUBSIDIARY

Acquisition of subsidiary:
During the period the group acquired subsidiary X. The fair value of assets acquired and liabilities assumed were as follows:

	€million
Cash	40
Inventory	100
Accounts receivable	100
Property, plant and equipment	650
Trade payables	(100)
Long-term debts	(200)
Total purchase price	590
Less: Cash of X	(40)
Cash flow on acquisition net of cash acquired	550

For other notes to the statement of cash flows, see **Part III**, **Chapter 19**.

33.4 CONCLUSION

While this chapter focuses on the preparation of a consolidated statement of cash flows, many of the issues are similar to those encountered when preparing a statement of cash flows for a single entity and these are addressed in detail in **Chapter 19**.

With respect to the preparation of a consolidated statement of cash flows in particular, the key issues to be aware of are (see **Section 33.2**): non-controlling interests; associates and joint ventures; the acquisition and disposal of a subsidiary; and foreign operations. In addition, IAS 7 also requires the disclosure of information relating to any subsidiaries acquired or disposed of during the accounting period (see **Section 33.3**).

SUMMARY OF LEARNING OBJECTIVES

Having studied this chapter, you should be able to:

Learning Objective 1 Prepare a consolidated statement of cash flows in accordance with IAS 7 *Statement of Cash Flows*.

IAS 7 requires cash flows to be classified as three separate sections: operating; investing; and financing. These sections are discussed in detail in **Chapter 19** (see **Figure 19.1** and **Section 19.2**), with the preparation of a consolidated statement of cash flows being illustrated in **Example 33.3** above.

In addition to the general disclosures required under IAS 7 (see **Section 19.2**), additional disclosures must be provided in relation to any subsidiaries acquired or disposed of during the accounting period (see **Section 33.3**).

QUESTIONS

Review Questions

(See **Appendix One** for Suggested Solutions to Review Questions.)

Question 33.1

Universal plc
CONSOLIDATED STATEMENT OF FINANCIAL POSITION
as at 30 October 2012

	2012 €000	2011 €000
Assets		
Non-current assets		
Property, plant and equipment	2,190	1,480
Goodwill	11	–
Investment in associate	830	740
	3,031	2,220
Current assets		
Inventory	910	868
Trade receivables	650	592
Cash	15	10
	1,575	1,470
Total assets	4,606	3,690
Equity and Liabilities		
Ordinary share capital	1,400	1,200
Share premium	200	100
Retained earnings	982	766
	2,582	2,066
Non-controlling interest	380	230
	2,962	2,296
Non-current liabilities		
10% debentures	360	280

Current liabilities

Trade payables	514	498
Bank overdraft	60	95
Corporate tax	450	328
Proposed dividends	240	180
Accruals	20	13
	1,284	1,114
Total equity and liabilities	4,606	3,690

Universal plc
Consolidated Statement of Profit or Loss and Other Comprehensive Income
for the Year Ended 31 October 2012

	€000
Group Operating Profit	986
Interest payable	(160)
	826
Share of profit of associate	130
	956
Taxation	(415)
Group profit after tax	541
Non-controlling interest	(126)
	415

Notes to the Financial Statements:

1. Group Profit before tax

The following have been included:	€000
Depreciation of property, plant and equipment	167
Profit on disposal of property, plant and equipment	10

2. Property, plant and equipment

	€000
Net book value 1 November 2011	1,480
Additions	987
Net book value of disposals	(110)
Depreciation charge for year	(167)
Net book value 31 October 2012	2,190

3. Called up share capital

€1 shares fully paid	€000
1 November 2011	1200
Issued for cash	200
31 October 2012	1400

4. Reserves

	Share Premium	Retained Earnings
	€000	€000
November 2011	100	766
Received on share issue	100	–

Profit for year	–	415
Dividends	–	(199)
31 October 2012	200	982

The dividends debited to retained earnings were approved by the shareholders prior to the reporting date.

5. Acquisition of Subsidiary: Star Limited
   Details of the acquisition are:

Net Assets Acquired	€000
Property, plant and equipment	160
Inventory	40
Cash	20
Payables	(50)
	170
Goodwill	11
Non-controlling Interest	(51)
	130
Discharged by	
Cash	130

Requirement Prepare the consolidated statement of cash flows of Universal plc for the year ended 31 October 2012 in accordance with IAS 7 *Statement of Cash Flows*.

Question 33.2 *(Based on Chartered Accountants Ireland, P3 Summer 1999, Question 5)*

SWEET plc was founded in the 1970s. During the 1980s SWEET plc relied on external acquisition to expand. For the last 7–8 years the group has focused on internal development. However, on 1 January 2012, SWEET plc acquired 75% of the ordinary share capital of GENTLE Limited. The purchase was financed by €365 million in cash and 50 million €1 ordinary shares with a market value of €75 million. The statement of financial position of GENTLE Limited at 1 January 2012 showed:

	€m
Property, plant and equipment	420
Inventory	300
Receivables	240
Bank deposit account	19
Bank overdraft	(275)
Trade payables	(160)
Taxation	(64)
	480

The directors of SWEET estimate that the goodwill arising on the acquisition of GENTLE had been impaired by €16 million at 31 December 2012. This has been charged to 'other operating expenses' in the consolidated statement of profit or loss and other comprehensive income for the year ended 31 December 2012.

SWEET plc
CONSOLIDATED STATEMENT OF PROFIT OR LOSS AND OTHER COMPREHENSIVE INCOME
for the Year Ended 31 December 2012

	Note	€m
Revenue		3,400
Cost of sales		(1,560)
Gross profit		1,840
Other operating expenses	2	(816)
Operating profit	1	1,024
Interest payable	3	(190)
Profit before tax		834
Income tax expense	4	(290)
Profit after tax		544
Non-controlling interests		(80)
Group profit		464

SWEET plc
CONSOLIDATED STATEMENT OF FINANCIAL POSITION
as at 31 December 2012

	2012		2011	
	€m	€m	€m	€m
ASSETS				
Non-current Assets				
Property, plant and equipment (note 5)		3,280		2,960
Intangible assets		64		–
		3,344		2,960
Current Assets				
Inventory	1,220		1,280	
Receivables	1,740	2,960	1,440	2,720
		6,304		5,680
EQUITY AND LIABILITIES				
Capital and Reserves				
€1 ordinary shares		1,010		960
Reserves		1,794		1,520
		2,804		2,480
Non-controlling interests (equity)		600		496
		3,404		2,976
Non-current Liabilities				
Obligations under finance leases		1,040		960
Deferred taxation		256		184
Current Liabilities				
Bank overdraft	24		164	
Trade payables	750		680	
Taxation	190		164	

Obligations under finance leases	400		360	
Proposed dividends	240	1,604	192	1,560
		6,304		5,680

Additional Information:

1. Depreciation charged in arriving at operating profit in the consolidated statement of profit or loss and other comprehensive income of SWEET plc for the year ended 31 December 2012 amounted to €750 million.

2. There is a loss on disposal of property, plant and equipment of €26 million included in other operating expenses. This relates to the scrapping of plant and equipment during the year with a net book value of €26 million. No proceeds were received.

3. Interest payable €m
   - on loans and overdrafts   40
   - on finance lease rental payments   150
        190

4. Taxation €m
   - corporation tax   245
   - deferred taxation   45
        290

5. Additions to property, plant and equipment during the year include plant and equipment purchased under finance lease contracts which would have cost €480 million if purchased outright. Also, property was revalued upwards by €25 million and SWEET plc capitalised interest paid during the year of €10 million relating to the construction of a new factory.

6. During the year ended 31 December 2012, dividends of €240 million were debited to equity.

Requirement Prepare the consolidated statement of cash flows of SWEET plc for the year ended 31 December 2012 in accordance with IAS 7 *Statement of Cash Flows*.
(You are not required to provide notes to the consolidated statement of cash flows.)

Challenging Questions

(Suggested Solutions to Challenging Questions are available to lecturers.)

Question 33.1 *(Based on Chartered Accountants Ireland, P3 Summer 1997, Question 2)*

The consolidated statement of profit or loss and other comprehensive income of VOYAGE plc for the year ended 31 December 2012 and the statement of financial position as at that date are shown below.

VOYAGE plc
CONSOLIDATED STATEMENT OF PROFIT OR LOSS AND OTHER COMPREHENSIVE INCOME
for the Year Ended 31 December 2012

	€000
Revenue	74,364
Cost of sales	(56,680)

Gross profit	17,684
Net operating expenses (including profit on sale of property, plant and equipment of €388,000)	(8,518)
Operating profit	9,166
Interest receivable and similar income	616
Interest payable and similar charges	(447)
Profit on ordinary activities before taxation	9,335
Tax on profit on ordinary activities	(3,081)
Profit on ordinary activities after taxation	6,254
Equity non-controlling interest	(83)
Profit for financial year	6,171

VOYAGE plc

CONSOLIDATED STATEMENT OF FINANCIAL POSITION
as at 31 December 2012

	Note	2012 €000	2011 €000
ASSETS			
Non-current Assets			
Property, plant and equipment	2	24,062	19,940
Intangible assets	1	324	540
		24,386	20,480
Current Assets			
Inventory		1,939	1,771
Trade receivables		9,792	9,085
Cash in hand and at bank		3,923	3,679
		15,654	14,535
		40,040	35,015
EQUITY AND LIABILITIES			
Capital and Reserves			
Called up share capital	5	2,479	2,319
Share premium account	5	5,889	5,569
Other reserves		555	555
Retained earnings		7,040	9,379
		15,963	17,822
Non-controlling interests (equity)		483	619
		16,446	18,441
Non-current Liabilities	4	9,408	4,016
Current Liabilities	3	14,186	12,558
		40,040	35,015

Additional Information:

1. Intangible fixed assets represent patents held by the company. These are amortised over the shorter of the anticipated period of profitable exploitation and the period to the expiry of the right. The company registered no new patents during 2012.
2. Property, plant and equipment

	Land and property €000	Plant and equipment €000	Total €000
Cost or valuation			
At 1 January 2012	6,483	22,446	28,929
Subsidiary acquired (note 6)	1,800	3,378	5,178
Additions	–	5,611	5,611
Disposals	–	(1,092)	(1,092)
	8,283	30,343	38,626
Accumulated depreciation			
At 1 January 2012	2,582	6,407	8,989
Charge for year	820	2,232	3,052
Subsidiary acquired (note 6)	1,280	2,023	3,303
On disposal	–	(780)	(780)
	4,682	9,882	14,564
Net book value			
At 31 December 2012	3,601	20,461	24,062
At 31 December 2011	3,901	16,039	19,940

	2012 €000	2011 €000
3. Current Liabilities		
Bank borrowings	104	–
Trade payables	8,217	7,039
Property, plant and equipment creditor	2,391	2,357
Finance lease creditor	141	202
Corporation tax	2,515	2,357
Dividends	764	592
Accruals and deferred income	54	11
	14,186	12,558

Accruals and deferred income comprise interest payable on:

– finance leases	5	6
– bank borrowings	49	5
	54	11

4. Non-current Liabilities		
Medium-term bank loans	3,453	–
Finance lease obligations	476	715
Deferred tax	5,479	3,301
	9,408	4,016

5. Called up share capital and share premium account

	€1 Ordinary shares €000	Share premium €000
At 1 January 2012	2,319	5,569

Shares issued on acquisition	160	440
Expenses connected with share issue	–	(120)
At 31 December 2012	2,479	5,889

6. Purchase of subsidiary undertaking
During 2012, VOYAGE plc purchased CHRISTY Limited, acquiring the following net assets:

	€000
Property, plant and equipment	1,875
Inventory	456
Trade receivables	1,170
Cash at bank and in hand	42
Bank overdraft	(73)
Trade payables	(705)
Medium-term loans	(967)
Deferred taxation	(908)
	890

Consideration was satisfied by:

Shares allotted	600
Cash	4,400
	5,000

The directors of VOYAGE plc are pleased with the positive effect CHRISTY Limited has had on turnover and operating profits.

7. During the year ended 31 December 2012, dividends of €4,400,000 were debited to equity.

Requirement In accordance with IAS 7 *Statement of Cash Flows*, prepare each of the following for VOYAGE plc in respect of the year ended 31 December 2012:
(a) A consolidated statement of cash flows.
(b) A reconciliation of operating profit to net cash flow from operating activities.

Question 33.2 (Based on Chartered Accountants Ireland, P3 Autumn 2000, Question 1)

A close friend became unemployed six months ago when the company she was working for was forced into liquidation due to severe cash flow problems. After months of applications and interviews, she has received two job offers, one of which is from CHOPPER Plc. Before making a decision your friend wishes to obtain as much information as possible about the two companies and has asked for your assistance. She has provided you with the following information in respect to CHOPPER Plc.

CHOPPER plc prepares its financial statements to 31 December each year. The company's consolidated statement of profit or loss and other comprehensive income for the years ended 31 December 2011 and 2012, together with the consolidated statement of financial position as at those dates, are presented below.

CHOPPER Plc
CONSOLIDATED STATEMENT OF PROFIT OR LOSS AND OTHER COMPREHENSIVE INCOME
for the Year Ended 31 December 2012

	2012 € million	2011 € million
Continuing Operations		
Turnover		
– continuing operations	2,100	1,850
Cost of sales	(1,670)	(1,400)
Gross profit	430	450
Other operating expenses (2012: includes loss on disposal of property, plant and equipment of €5 million)	(155)	(95)
Operating profit		
– continuing operations	275	355
Interest payable and similar charges	(15)	(10)
Profit before tax	260	345
Tax	(80)	(85)
Profit after tax	180	260
Discontinued Operations:		
Net profit for year for discontinued operations	10	25
	190	285
Non-controlling interests – equity	(38)	(57)
Group profit	152	228

CHOPPER Plc
CONSOLIDATED STATEMENT OF FINANCIAL POSITION
as at 31 December 2012

	2012 € million	2011 € million
ASSETS		
Non-current Assets		
Tangible assets	780	480
Goodwill	60	100
	840	580
Current Assets		
Inventory	210	190
Trade receivables	390	250
	600	440
	1,440	1,020
EQUITY AND LIABILITIES		
Capital and Reserves		
€1 ordinary shares	100	100
Retained earnings	327	200
	427	300

Non-controlling interests	73	150
	500	450
Non-current Liabilities		
Obligations under finance leases	290	60
Deferred tax	100	50
	390	110
Current Liabilities		
Bank overdraft	12	15
Trade payables	300	275
Proposed dividend	25	20
Corporation tax	80	85
Obligations under finance leases	130	60
Accrued interest and finance charges	3	5
	550	460
	1,440	1,020

Additional Information:

1. Property, plant and equipment €m

Cost:

	€m
At 1 January 2012	800
Additions	620
Disposals	(370)
At 31 December 2012	1,050

Accumulated depreciation:

At 1 January 2012	320
Charge for the year	150
On disposals	(200)
At 31 December 2012	270

Net book value:

At 31 December 2012	780
At 31 December 2011	480

Additions during 2012 include assets purchased under finance leases that would have cost €400 million if purchased outright. None of the assets disposed of during 2012 was held under finance lease contracts.

2. On 30 June 2012 CHOPPER plc disposed of all of its 75% interest in KINGPIN Limited for €160 million in cash. KINGPIN Limited's results are classified as discontinued in the consolidated statement of profit or loss and other comprehensive income. The net profit for the year for discontinued operations shown in the consolidated statement of profit or loss and other comprehensive income comprises:

	€m
Profit for the year from trading operations	20
Loss on disposal of discontinued operations	(10)
	10

The loss on disposal of discontinued operations is arrived at as follows:

	€m
Sale proceeds	160
Goodwill	(8)
Net assets disposed of (75% of €216 million)	(162)
	(10)

At 30 June 2012 the consolidated carrying values of the assets and liabilities of KINGPIN Limited were as follows:

ASSETS	€m	€m
Non-current Assets		
Cost	230	
Accumulated depreciation	(80)	150
Current Assets		
Trade receivables	60	
Cash at bank	56	116
		266
EQUITY AND LIABILITIES		
Capital and Reserves		
Share capital		100
Retained earnings		116
		216
Current Liabilities		
Trade payables		42
Corporation tax		8
		266

Apart from the sale of KINGPIN Limited, there were no other acquisitions or disposals of subsidiary undertakings during 2012. It is group policy to provide a full year's depreciation charge in the year of acquisition and none in the year of disposal.

3. During the year ended 31 December 2012, dividends of €25 million were debited to equity.

Requirement
(a) Prepare a consolidated statement of cash flows for the year ended 31 December 2012 for CHOPPER plc in accordance with IAS 7 *Statement of Cash Flows*.
(b) Prepare a reconciliation of operating profit to operating cash flows that clearly distinguishes between net cash flows from continuing and discontinued operations.

Question 33.3 *(Based on Chartered Accountants Ireland, P3 Autumn 2003, Questions 1 and 2)*

In recent years, TWIST plc (TWIST) has pursued an aggressive acquisition policy in order to expand its business. On 1 June 2012, TWIST purchased all of the ordinary share capital of SHOUT Limited (SHOUT), acquiring the following net assets:

	€ million
Property, plant and equipment	2,100
Inventory	950
Trade receivables	1,600
Cash at bank and in hand	10
Bank overdraft	(18)
Trade payables	(1,300)
Medium-term loans	(842)
	2,500

Consideration was satisfied by:	
Shares allotted	800
Cash	2,200
	3,000

The consolidated statement of profit or loss and other comprehensive income of TWIST for the year ended 31 December 2012 and the statement of financial position as at that date are shown below.

TWIST plc
CONSOLIDATED STATEMENT OF PROFIT OR LOSS AND OTHER COMPREHENSIVE INCOME
for the Year Ended 31 December 2012

	€m	€m
Revenue		
– continuing operations	1,060	
– acquisitions	430	
Total turnover		1,490
Cost of sales		(1,130)
Gross profit		360
Net operating expenses (including profit on sale of property, plant and equipment in continuing operations of €11 million)		(169)
Operating profit		
– continuing operations	141	
– acquisitions	50	
Total operating profit		191
Interest receivable and similar income		21
Interest payable and similar charges		(19)
Profit on ordinary activities before taxation		193
Tax on profit on ordinary activities		(58)
Profit on ordinary activities after taxation		135
Equity non-controlling interest		(5)
Profit for financial year		130

TWIST plc
CONSOLIDATED STATEMENT OF FINANCIAL POSITION
as at 31 December 2012

	Note	2012 € million	2011 € million
ASSETS			
Non-current Assets			
– Tangible assets	1	13,880	9,050
– Intangible assets	2	520	950
		14,400	10,000
Current Assets			
– Inventory		3,100	2,800
– Trade receivables		5,250	5,100
– Cash in hand and at bank		1,900	1,850
		10,250	9,750
		24,650	19,750
EQUITY AND LIABILITIES			
Capital and Reserves			
Called up share capital	5	3,200	3,000
Share premium account	5	2,690	2,100
Other reserves		900	900
Retained earnings		3,580	3,550
		10,370	9,550
Non-controlling interests (equity)		330	1,300
		10,700	10,850
Non-current Liabilities	3	4,800	2,100
Current Liabilities	4	9,150	6,800
		24,650	19,750

Since acquisition, SHOUT has contributed €600 million to the group's net operating cash flow, paid €7 million in respect of investing activities and used €15 million for financing activities.

Additional Information:

1. Property, Plant and Equipment

	€ million
Cost or valuation	
At 1 January 2012	11,200
Subsidiary acquired	3,000
Additions	4,100
Disposals	(450)
	17,850
Accumulated depreciation	
At 1 January 2012	2,150

Charge for year	1,120
Subsidiary acquired	900
On disposal	(200)
	3,970

Net book value	
At 31 December 2012	13,880
At 31 December 2011	9,050

2. Intangible Assets

	Goodwill € million	Patents € million	Total € million
At 1 January 2012	300	650	950
Additions	500	–	500
Impairment/amortisation during the year	(300)	(630)	(930)
At 31 December 2012	500	20	520

Goodwill was impaired by €300 million during the year ended 31 December 2012. Patents are amortised over the shorter of the anticipated period of profitable exploitation and the period to the expiry of the right.

	2012 € million	2011 € million
3. Non-current Liabilities		
Medium-term bank loans	3,400	–
Finance lease obligations	1,400	2,100
	4,800	2,100

	2012 € million	2011 € million
4. Current Liabilities		
Bank borrowings	100	–
Trade payables	4,105	2,530
Fixed asset payable	2,300	1,550
Finance lease payable	145	200
Corporation tax	1,900	2,000
Dividends	570	500
Accruals and deferred income	30	20
	9,150	6,800

Accruals and deferred income comprise interest payable on:

– finance leases	10	10
– bank borrowings	20	10
	30	20

5. Capital and Reserves

	€1 Ordinary shares € million	Share premium € million
At 1 January 2012	3,000	2,100
Shares issued on acquisition	200	600

Expenses connected with share issue	–	(10)
At 31 December 2012	3,200	2,690

During the year ended 31 December 2012, €100 million was debited to equity in respect of dividends.

Requirement In accordance with IAS 7 *Statement of Cash Flows*, prepare each of the following for TWIST plc in respect of the year ended 31 December 2012:

(a) A consolidated statement of cash flows.

(b) A reconciliation of operating profit to net cash flow from operating activities.

(c) Outline the disclosures that are required for the purchase of subsidiary undertakings, in accordance with IAS 7 *Statement of Cash Flows*, in respect of the acquisition of SHOUT by TWIST during the year ended 31 December 2012.

(d) Calculate the basic earnings per share for the year ended 31 December 2012 for TWIST in accordance with IAS 33 *Earnings per Share*.

PART VI

FURTHER ISSUES

34

OTHER ACCOUNTING STANDARDS

After having read this chapter, and with respect to the following standards, you should be able to:
1. IAS 41 *Agriculture* – demonstrate an understanding of the basic principles and features of IAS 41, appreciate the circumstances when they may be applicable and apply the main disclosure requirements;
2. IFRS 2 *Share-based Payment* – apply and discuss the recognition and measurement criteria for share-based payment transactions, account for modifications, cancellations and settlements of share-based payment transactions, and apply the main disclosure requirements;
3. IAS 34 *Interim Financial Reporting* – demonstrate an understanding of the basic principles and features of IAS 34, and apply the main disclosure requirements;
4. IFRS 4 *Insurance Contracts* – demonstrate an understanding of the basic principles and features of IFRS 4, and apply the main disclosure requirements;
5. IFRS 6 *Exploration for and Evaluation of Mineral Resources* – demonstrate an understanding of the basic principles and features of IFRS 6, and apply the main disclosure requirements; and
6. IAS 26 *Accounting and Reporting by Retirement Benefit Plans* – demonstrate an understanding of the basic principles and features of IAS 26, and apply the main disclosure requirements.

34.1 INTRODUCTION

The application and integration of the principles underpinning the more common or frequently applied accounting standards are covered in previous chapters. This chapter completes the analysis of extant International Accounting Standards (IASs) and International Financial Reporting Standards (IFRSs) by examining the remaining six standards not dealt with elsewhere in the text. While these standards are interesting and relevant, they arguably have a narrow and specialised appeal; consequently, they are not covered in the same level of detail as standards in other chapters. They are:

- IAS 41 *Agriculture* (see **Section 34.2**);
- IFRS 2 *Share-based Payment* (see **Section 34.3**);
- IAS 34 *Interim Financial Reporting* (see **Section 34.4**);
- IFRS 4 *Insurance Contracts* (see **Section 34.5**);
- IFRS 6 *Exploration for and Evaluation of Mineral Resources* (see **Section 34.6**); and
- IAS 26 *Accounting and Reporting by Retirement Benefit Plans* (see **Section 34.7**).

Each of these accounting standards, unrelated to each other, is now addressed in turn.

Please note that, as explained in **Chapter 2**, the IASB issued amendments to IAS 1 *Presentation of Financial Statements* in June 2011. These included a *proposal* that the title 'Statement of Profit or Loss and Other Comprehensive Income' (SPLOCI) be adopted (rather than, for example, 'statement of comprehensive income') and a *requirement* to revise the presentation of other comprehensive income (OCI) within the SPLOCI. These amendments are explained in detail in **Chapter 2**, **Section 2.3**.

34.2 IAS 41 *AGRICULTURE*

Introduction

IAS 41 *Agriculture* prescribes the accounting treatment, financial statement presentation and disclosures related to agricultural activity. IAS 41 does *not* apply to:

- land related to agricultural activity (IAS 16 *Property, Plant and Equipment* – see **Chapter 6**);
- intangible assets related to agricultural activity (IAS 38 *Intangible Assets* – see **Chapter 9**); and
- the processing of agricultural produce after harvest (IAS 2 *Inventories* – see **Chapter 11**).

IAS 41 has been published because of the economic importance of agriculture in both developed and developing countries. However, the main problem in developing such a standard is the great diversity in practice that exists in agriculture. It is also very difficult to apply traditional accounting methods to agricultural activities. Some of the contentious issues are:

1. When and how should entities account for critical events associated with biological transformation (growth, procreation, production and degeneration) which alter the substance of biological assets.
2. Statement of financial position classification is made difficult by the variety and characteristics of the living assets of agriculture (i.e. animals and plants).
3. The nature of management of agricultural activities means that the unit of measurement is difficult to determine For example, biological assets, and the produce derived from them, cannot be measured using cost-based concepts outlined in IAS 2 (see **Chapter 11**) and IAS 16 (see **Chapter 6**) since cattle, for example, are often not purchased but are born and develop.

KEY TERMS AND DEFINITIONS

Agricultural Activity The management by an enterprise of the biological transformation of biological assets for sale into agricultural produce or into additional biological assets.

Agricultural Produce The harvested product of an enterprise's biological assets (for example, milk and crops).

Biological Asset A living animal or plant (for example, sheep, cattle, trees, vines).

Biological Transformation The processes of growth, degeneration, production and procreation that cause qualitative and quantitative changes in a biological asset.

Group of Biological Assets An aggregation of similar living animals or plants.

Harvest The detachment of produce from a biological asset or the cessation of a biological asset's life processes.

Scope

IAS 41 applies to the three elements that form part of, or result from, agricultural activity. These are:
1. biological assets;
2. agricultural produce at the point of harvest; and
3. government grants.

Examples of agricultural activity are provided in **Table 34.1** and then illustrated in **Example 34.1**.

TABLE 34.1: AGRICULTURAL ACTIVITY

Biological assets	Agricultural produce	Products that are the result of processing after harvest
Sheep	Wool	Yarn, carpet
Trees in a plantation forest	Logs	Lumber
Plants	Cotton; harvested cane	Thread, clothing; sugar
Dairy cattle	Milk	Cheese
Pigs	Carcass	Sausages, cured hams
Bushes	Leaf	Tea; cured tobacco
Vines	Grapes	Wine
Fruit trees	Picked fruit	Processed fruit

EXAMPLE 34.1: MIXED BUSINESSES

1. Entity A raises cattle, slaughters them at its abattoirs and sells the carcasses to the local meat market. Which of these activities are within the scope of IAS 41?

    The cattle are biological assets while they are living. When they are slaughtered, biological transformation ceases and the carcasses meet the definition of agricultural produce. Hence, Entity A should account for the live cattle in accordance with IAS 41 and the carcasses as inventory in accordance with IAS 2 *Inventories* (see **Chapter 11**).

2. Entity B grows vines, harvests the grapes and produces wine. Which of these activities is within the scope of IAS 41?

The grapevines are biological assets that continually generate crops of grapes. When the entity harvests the grapes, their biological transformation ceases and they become agricultural produce. The grapevines continue to be living plants and should be recognised as biological assets. Assets such as wine, which are subject to a lengthy maturation period, are not biological assets. These processes are analogous to the conversion of raw materials to a finished product rather than biological transformation. Therefore, the entity should account for the grapevines in accordance with IAS 41, and the harvested grapes and the production of wine as inventory in accordance with IAS 2.

Each of the three elements of agricultural activity referred to above in **Table 34.1** is now explained in more detail. This is followed by a description of the related disclosures.

Biological Assets

These are the core income-producing assets of agricultural activity, held for their transformation abilities. **Biological transformation** leads to various different outcomes. For example:
1. Asset changes – growth (increase in quantity and/or quality) and degeneration (decrease in quantity and/or quality).
2. Creation of new assets – production (separable non-living products) and procreation (separable living animals).

Asset changes are critical to the flow of future economic benefits, both in and beyond the current accounting period, but their relative importance depends on the purpose of the agricultural activity.

IAS 41 distinguishes between two broad categories of **agricultural production**:
1. **Consumable** – animals/plants harvested (for example, livestock intended for the production of meat, livestock held for sale, trees grown for lumber); and
2. **Bearer** – animals/plants that bear produce for harvest (for example, livestock from which milk is produced, fruit trees, grapevines).

Biological assets (i.e. living animals or plants) are usually managed in groups of similar animal or plant classes with characteristics that permit sustainability in perpetuity (i.e. the biological assets are renewed at a rate equal to or greater than the rate at which they are consumed), and land often forms an integral part of the activity itself.

This section on biological assets concludes by considering when they should be recognised, together with how they should be measured and presented in the financial statements.

Recognition

The recognition criteria are consistent with those for other assets in that biological assets may not be recognised unless the following conditions are met:
1. the enterprise controls the asset as a result of past events;
2. it is probable that future economic benefits will flow to the enterprise; and
3. the fair value or cost can be measured reliably.

Measurement

IAS 41 requires that, at each reporting date, all biological assets should be measured at **fair value** less estimated point of sale costs on the basis that fair value has greater relevance, reliability, comparability and understandability as a measure of future economic benefits. The primary indicator of fair value should be **net market value** as this provides the best evidence of fair value when an active market exists. IAS 41 permits an alternative method of valuation if a fair value cannot be determined because market prices are not available. In such circumstances, which are expected to be rare since market values are usually available for biological assets and agricultural produce, cost less accumulated depreciation and impairment losses may be used. The alternative basis is only permitted on initial recognition.

The gain on initial recognition of biological assets at fair value less costs to sell, and changes in fair value less costs to sell of biological assets during a period, should be reported in arriving at net profit or loss for the period in the statement of profit or loss and other comprehensive income.

The change in fair value of biological assets may be part physical change (i.e. growth) and part price (i.e. fair value) change. IAS 41 encourages, but does not require, the separate disclosure of these two components on the basis that it assists with appraising current period performance and future prospects.

The recommended method of separating the above components is to calculate the change attributable to the differences in fair value by restating biological assets on hand at the date of the opening statement of financial position using end of period fair values and comparing this with the closing carrying amount. There are exceptions to this approach; for example where the production cycle is less than one year (broiler chickens, mushroom growing and cereal crops). In these cases the total change in carrying amount should be reported in the statement of profit or loss and other comprehensive income as a single item of income or expense in arriving at profit or loss. Any other events giving rise to a change in biological assets of such a size, nature or incidence that their disclosure is relevant to explain the entity's performance should be included in the change in biological assets recognised as income or expense. They should be recorded as a separate item in the reconciliation required to determine the change attributable to biological transformation.

Example 34.2 illustrates how to separate physical change and price change.

EXAMPLE 34.2: MEASUREMENT OF BIOLOGICAL ASSETS

A herd of 10 2-year-old animals was held at 1 January 2012. One animal, aged 2.5 years, was purchased on 1 July 2012 for €108, and one animal was born on 1 July 2012. No animals were sold or disposed of during the period. Per unit fair values less estimated point-of-sale costs were as follows:

	€
2-year-old animal at 1 January 2012	100
newborn animal at 1 July 2012	70
2.5-year-old animal at 1 July 2012	108
newborn animal at 31 December 2012	72
0.5-year-old animal at 31 December 2012	80
2-year-old animal at 31 December 2012	105
2.5-year-old animal at 31 December 2012	111
3-year-old animal at 31 December 2012	120

Before separating the physical change and the price change, it is useful to examine the overall movement in the valuation of the herd during 2012.

	€
Fair value less estimated point-of-sale costs of herd at 1 January 2012:	
(10 × €100)	1,000
Purchased on 1 July 2010:	
(1 × €108)	108
	1,108

	€
Fair value less estimated point-of-sale costs of herd at 31 December 2012:	
11 × €120	1,320
1 × €80	80
	1,400

Therefore the movement in valuation during the period is €292 (€1,400 – €1,108). This can be explained by:

Increase in fair value less estimated point-of-sale costs due to price change:

	€
10 × (€105 − €100)	50
1 × (€111 − €108)	3
1 × (€72 − €70)	2
	55

Increase in fair value less estimated point-of-sale costs due to physical change:

	€
10 × (€120 − €105)	150
1 × (€120 − €111)	9
1 × (€80 − €72)	8
1 × €70	70
	237

Presentation

In the statement of financial position, biological assets should be classified as a separate class of assets falling under neither current nor non-current classifications. Biological assets should also be sub-classified as follows:

1. class of animal or plant;
2. nature of activities (consumable or bearer); and
3. maturity or immaturity for intended purpose.

In the statement of profit or loss and other comprehensive income, an analysis of income and expenses based on their nature should be presented rather than the function/cost of sales method (see **Chapter 2, Section 23**). IAS 41 also requires detailed disclosures to include the measurement base used for fair value and the details of the reconciliation of the change in carrying value for the year. These disclosure requirements are illustrated in **Example 34.2**.

Agricultural Produce

As mentioned at the beginning of **Section 34.2**, IAS 41 applies to three elements that form part of agricultural activity: biological assets (see above); agricultural produce; and government grants. The second element, agricultural produce, should be recognised at the point of harvest (for example, detachment from the biological asset) and this should end once the produce enters trading activities or the production processes. Agricultural produce should be measured at fair value less estimated costs to sell at the point of harvest at each reporting date. The change in the carrying amount of agriculture produce held at two reporting dates should be recognised as income or expenses in the statement of profit or loss and other comprehensive income. However, this will be rare as such produce is usually sold or processed within a short time.

Agricultural produce that is harvested for trading or processing activities should be measured at fair value at the date of harvest. This amount is the deemed cost for the application of IAS 2 *Inventories* (see **Chapter 11**). Agricultural produce should be classified as inventory in the statement of financial position and disclosed separately either on the face of the statement of financial position or in the notes.

Government Grants

These are the third and final element of agricultural activity. An unconditional government grant related to a biological asset should be measured at fair value less estimated point-of-sale costs and recognised as income when, and only when, the grant becomes receivable. If a grant requires an enterprise not to engage in agricultural activity, the enterprise should only recognise the grant as income when the conditions are met. IAS 20 *Accounting for Government Grants and Disclosure of Government Assistance* does not apply to such grants. However, if a biological asset is measured at cost less accumulated depreciation and impairment losses then IAS 20 does apply (see **Chapter 16**).

Disclosure

IAS 41 requires extensive disclosures in relation to the three elements that form part of agricultural activity: biological assets; agricultural produce; and government grants. The more common disclosures in respect of these three elements are outlined below and illustrated in **Example 34.3**.

An enterprise should disclose the aggregate gain or loss arising during the current period on initial recognition of biological assets and agricultural produce and from the change in fair value less estimated point-of-sale costs of biological assets, as well as a description of each group of biological assets (see note 3, **Example 34.2**). If not disclosed elsewhere, the following should also be disclosed (see note 1, **Example 34.2**):
1. the nature of its activities involving each group of biological assets; and
2. non-financial measures or estimates of the physical quantities of:
    (a) each group of the enterprise's biological assets at the end of the period, and
    (b) output of agricultural produce during the period.

The methods and significant assumptions applied in determining the fair value of each group of agricultural produce at the point of harvest and each group of biological assets should be disclosed (see note 2, **Example 34.2**).

An enterprise should also disclose:

1. the existence and carrying amounts of biological assets whose title is restricted, and the carrying amounts of biological assets pledged as security for liabilities;
2. the amount of commitments for the development or acquisition of biological assets; and
3. financial risk-management strategies related to agricultural activity (for example, see note 4, Example 34.2).

A reconciliation should be provided of changes in the carrying amount of biological assets between the start and the end of the current period and this should include:

1. the gain or loss arising from changes in fair value less estimated point-of-sale costs;
2. increases due to purchases;
3. decreases due to sales;
4. decreases due to harvest;
5. increases resulting from business combinations;
6. net exchange differences arising from the translation of financial statements of a foreign entity; and
7. other changes.

The following example illustrates the practical application of some of the IAS 41 disclosures.

EXAMPLE 34.3: APPLYING IAS 41

XYZ Dairy Limited
STATEMENT OF FINANCIAL POSITION
as at 31 December

	2012 €	2012 €	2011 €	2011 €
ASSETS				
Non-current assets				
Dairy livestock – immature	52,060		47,730	
Dairy livestock – mature	372,990		411,840	
Biological assets (Note 3)		425,050		459,570
Property, plant and equipment		1,462,650		1,409,800
Total non-current assets		1,887,700		1,869,370
Current assets				
Inventories		82,950		70,650
Trade and other receivables		80,000		65,000
Cash		18,000		10,000
Total current assets		180,950		145,650
Total assets		2,068,650		2,015,020
EQUITY AND LIABILITIES				
Equity				
Issued capital		1,000,000		1,000,000

Accumulated profits	902,828	865,000
Total equity	1,902,828	1,865,000
Current liabilities		
Trade and other payables	165,822	150,020
Total current liabilities	165,822	150,020
Total equity and liabilities	2,068,650	2,015,020

STATEMENT OF PROFIT OR LOSS AND OTHER COMPREHENSIVE INCOME
for the Year Ended 31 December 2012

	€
Fair value of milk produced	518,240
Gains arising from changes in fair value less	
Estimated point-of-sale costs of dairy livestock (Note 3)	39,930
	558,170
Inventories used	(137,523)
Staff costs	(127,283)
Depreciation expense	(15,250)
Other operating expenses	(197,092)
	(477,148)
Profit from operations	81,022
Income tax expense	(43,194)
Net profit for the period	37,828

STATEMENT OF CHANGES IN EQUITY
for the Year Ended 31 December 2012

	Share capital €	Accumulated profits €	Year ended 31 December 2012 €
Balance at 1 January 2012	1,000,000	865,000	1,865,000
Net profit for the period		37,828	37,828
Balance at 31 December 2012	1,000,000	902,828	1,902,828

STATEMENT OF CASH FLOWS
for the Year Ended 31 December 2012

	€
Cash flows from operating activities:	
Cash receipts from sales of milk	506,027
Cash receipts from sales of livestock	97,913
Cash paid for supplies and to employee	(460,831)
Cash paid for purchases of livestock	(23,815)
	119,294
Income taxes paid	(43,194)
Net cash flow from operating activities	76,100

Cash flows from investing activities:	
Purchase of property, plant and equipment	(68,100)
Net cash used in investing activities	(68,100)
Net increase in cash	8,000
Cash at beginning of period	10,000
Cash at end of period	18,000

NOTES TO THE FINANCIAL STATEMENTS

1. Operations and Principal Activities: XYZ Dairy Limited ('the Company') is engaged in milk production for supply to various customers. At 31 December 2012, the Company held 419 cows able to produce milk (mature assets) and 137 heifers being raised to produce milk in the future (immature assets). The Company produced 157,584 litres of milk with a fair value less estimated point-of-sale costs of €518,240 (that is determined at the time of milking) in the year ended 31 December 2012.

2. Accounting Policies for Livestock and Milk: Livestock are measured at their fair value less estimated point-of-sale costs. The fair value of livestock is determined based on market prices of livestock of similar age, breed, and genetic merit. Milk is initially measured at its fair value less estimated point-of-sale costs at the time of milking. The fair value of milk is determined based on market prices in the local area.

3. Biological Assets

	€
Reconciliation of Carrying Amounts of Dairy livestock	
Carrying amount at 1 January 2012	459,570
Increases due to purchases	26,250
Gain arising from changes in fair value less estimated point-of-sale costs attributable to physical changes	15,350
Gain arising from changes in fair value less estimated point-of-sale costs attributable to price changes	24,580
Decreases due to sales	(100,700)
Carrying amount at 31 December 2012	425,050

4. Financial Risk-management Strategies: The Company is exposed to financial risks arising from changes in milk prices. The Company does not anticipate that milk prices will decline significantly in the foreseeable future and, therefore, has not entered into derivative or other contracts to manage the risk of a decline in milk prices. The Company reviews its outlook for milk prices regularly in considering the need for active risk-management.

34.3 IFRS 2 *SHARE-BASED PAYMENT*

Introduction

When senior employees negotiate an employment package, this will often comprise a salary and pension together with other benefits such as share of profits. However, until recently, these options were not expensed as there was no associated cash flow. This is a good example of the application of substance over form since, in the past, when a company granted share options to employees as part of their remuneration this cost was not charged in the statement of profit or loss and other comprehensive income. This distorted the financial position of the company and raised corporate governance concerns. IFRS 2 *Share-based Payment* changes this.

A **share-based payment** is a transaction in which an entity receives or acquires goods or services either as consideration for its equity instruments or by incurring liabilities for amounts based on the price of the entity's shares or other equity instruments of the entity. IFRS 2 prescribes the financial reporting by an entity when it undertakes a share-based payment transaction.

Equity granted to employees in their capacity as employees (for example, in return for continued service) are within the scope of IFRS 2, as are transfers of an entity's equity instruments by its shareholders to suppliers. However, a transaction with an employee in his/her capacity as a holder of equity of the entity is not a share-based payment transaction. Furthermore, IFRS 2 does not apply to a business combination (IFRS 3 *Business Combinations* – see **Chapter 26**). Hence, equity issued in a business combination in exchange for control of the acquiree is not within the scope of IFRS 2.

IFRS 2 sets out measurement principles and specific requirements for three types of share-based payment transaction:
1. equity-settled share-based payment transactions;
2. cash-settled share-based payment transactions; and
3. share-based payment transactions with cash alternatives.

After defining a number of key terms, each of the three types of share-based payment transactions is explained. The section concludes with a summary of the related disclosures.

Key Terms and Definitions

Cash-settled Share-based Payment Transaction A share-based payment transaction in which the entity acquires goods or services by incurring a liability to transfer cash or other assets to the supplier of those goods or services for amounts that are based on the price (or value) of the entity's shares or other equity instruments of the entity. In this instance, the entity pays cash based on the share price.

Employees and Others Providing Similar Services Individuals who render personal services to the entity and either the individuals are regarded as employees for legal or tax purposes or the individuals work for the entity under its direction in the same way as individuals who are regarded as employees for legal or tax purposes, or the services rendered are similar to those rendered by employees. For example, the term encompasses all management personnel, i.e. those persons having authority and responsibility for planning, directing and controlling the activities of the entity, including non-executive directors.

Equity Instrument A contract that evidences a residual interest in the assets of an entity after deducting all of its liabilities. The *IFRS Framework* (see **Chapter 1**) defines a liability as a present obligation of the entity arising from past events, the settlement of which is expected to result in an outflow from the entity of resources embodying economic benefits (i.e. an outflow of cash or other assets of the entity).

Equity-settled Share-based Payment Transaction A transaction in which the entity receives goods or services as consideration for equity instruments of the entity (including shares or share options), or acquires goods or services by incurring liabilities to the supplier of those goods or services for amounts that are based on the price of the entity's shares or other equity instruments of the entity. In this case, the entity issues shares (not cash).

Fair Value The amount for which an 'equity instrument granted' or an asset could be exchanged, or a liability settled, between knowledgeable, willing parties in an arm's length transaction.

Grant Date The date at which the entity and another party (including an employee) agree to a share-based payment arrangement, being when the entity and the counterparty have a shared understanding of the terms and conditions of the arrangement. At grant date the entity confers on the counterparty the right to cash, other assets, or equity instruments of the entity, provided the specified vesting conditions, if any, are met. If that agreement is subject to an approval process (for example, by shareholders), grant date is the date when that approval is obtained. The grant date is the key date with regards to determining when a liability should be recognised.

Intrinsic Value The difference between the fair value of the shares to which the counterparty has the (conditional or unconditional) right to subscribe or which it has the right to receive, and the price (if any) the counterparty is (or will be) required to pay for those shares. For example, a share option with an exercise price of €15 on a share with a fair value of €20 has an intrinsic value of €5.

Share-option A contract that gives the holder the right, but not the obligation (i.e. the holder does not have to purchase the shares) to subscribe to the entity's shares at a fixed or determinable price for a specified period of time.

Vesting Conditions The conditions that must be satisfied for the contractee to become entitled to receive cash, other assets or equity instruments of the entity, under a share-based payment arrangement. Vesting conditions include service conditions, which require the other party to complete a specified period of service, and performance conditions, which require specified performance targets to be met (such as a specified increase in the entity's profit over a specified period of time).

Vesting Period The period during which all the specified vesting conditions of a share-based payment arrangement are to be satisfied.

Equity-settled Share-based Payment Transactions

For equity-settled share-based payment transactions (for example, shares, options and warrants), the entity should measure the *goods* or *services* received, and the corresponding increase in equity (recognised through other comprehensive income), at the fair value of the goods or services received, unless that fair value cannot be estimated reliably. If the entity cannot estimate reliably the fair value of the goods or services received, the entity should measure their value, and the corresponding increase in equity, indirectly, by reference to the fair value of the equity instruments granted.

Example 34.4 explains how share options granted in exchange for goods (rather than services) should be accounted for.

EXAMPLE 34.4: SHARE OPTIONS FOR GOODS

A company issues share options in order to pay for the purchase of inventory. The share options were issued on 1 June 2010. The inventory was eventually sold on 31 December 2012. The value of the inventory on 1 June 2010 was €6 million and this value was unchanged up to the date of sale. The sale proceeds were €8 million. The shares issued have a market value of €6.3 million.

Requirement How will this transaction be dealt with in the financial statements?

Solution

IFRS 2 states that the fair value of the goods and services received should be used to value the share options unless the fair value of the goods cannot be measured reliably. Thus equity would be increased by €6 million and inventory increased by €6 million. The inventory value will be expensed on sale. In summary, the accounting treatment for equity-settled share-based payment transactions is: DR SPLOCI – P/L and CR Equity.

For transactions with employees and others providing similar services, the fair value of the services received are referred to the fair value of the equity granted, as it is not possible to estimate reliably the fair value of the services received. The fair value of equity should be measured at the grant date. Typically, share options are granted to employees as part of their remuneration package. Usually, it is not possible to measure directly the services received for particular components of the employee's remuneration package. It might also not be possible to measure the fair value of the total remuneration package independently without measuring directly the fair value of equity instruments granted. **Example 34.5** illustrates how share options granted in exchange for services (rather than goods) should be accounted for.

EXAMPLE 34.5: SHARE OPTIONS FOR EMPLOYEE SERVICES

A company granted a total of 100 share options to 10 members of its executive management team (10 options each) on 1 January 2012. These options vest at the end of a three-year period. The company has determined that each option has a fair value at the date of grant equal to €15. The company expects that all 100 options will vest and therefore records the following entry at 30 June 2012 (the end of its first six-month interim reporting period).

		€	€
DR	SPLOCI – P/L – salaries	250	
CR	Equity		250

[(100 × €15)/6 periods = €250 per period]

If all 100 shares vest, the above entry would be made at the end of each six-month reporting period. However, if one member of the executive management team leaves during the second half of 2012, therefore forfeiting the entire amount of 10 options, the following entry at 31 December 2012 would be made:

		€	€
DR	SPLOCI – P/L – salaries	150	
CR	Equity		150

[(90 × €15)/6 periods = €225 per period
(€225 × 4) − (€250 + €250 + €250) = €150]

Often the grant of equity instruments may contain conditions which must be met before there is entitlement to the shares. These are called **vesting conditions** and their accounting treatment is illustrated in **Example 34.6**. It is important to note that if the condition is specifically related to the market price of the company's shares then such conditions are ignored for the purposes of estimating the number of equity shares that will vest. The thinking behind this is that these conditions have already been taken into account when fair-valuing the shares. If the performance condition is based upon, for example, the growth in profit or earnings per share then it will have to be taken into account in estimating the fair value of the option at the grant date. By granting shares or share options, the entity is paying additional remuneration to obtain additional benefits. Estimating the fair value of those additional benefits is likely to be difficult. Because of the difficulty of measuring directly the fair value of the services received, the entity should measure the fair value of the employee services received by reference to the fair value of the equity instruments granted. If vesting conditions exist, the charge in the statement of profit or loss and other comprehensive income should be adjusted for the equity not yet granted. This is shown in **Example 34.6**.

EXAMPLE 34.6: SHARE OPTIONS WITH VESTING CONDITIONS

A company grants 2,000 share options to each of its three directors on 1 January 2012 subject to the directors being employed on 31 December 2014. The options vest on 31 December 2014. The fair value of each option on 1 January 2012 is €10 and it is anticipated that all of the share options will vest on 31 December 2014. The options will only vest if the company's share price reaches €14 per share. The price at 31 December 2012 was €8 and it is not anticipated that it will rise over the next two years. It is anticipated that there will only be two directors employed on 31 December 2014.

Requirement How will the share options be treated in the financial statements for the year ended 31 December 2012?

Solution

The market-based condition, i.e. the increase in the share price, can be ignored for the purpose of the calculation. However the employment condition must be taken into account. The options will be treated as follows:

2,000 options $\times$ 2 directors $\times$ €10 $\times$ 1 year/3 years = €13,333. Equity will be increased by this amount and an expense shown in the statement of profit or loss and other comprehensive income for the year ended 31 December 2012.

Note: there is no reversal of amounts recognised for services received from an employee even if the vested equity instruments are later forfeited or the share options are not exercised. However, the entity is able to make a transfer from one component of equity (for example, an options equity reserve) to another (for example, retained earnings).

For parties other than employees, there is a rebuttable presumption that the fair value of the goods or services received can be estimated reliably. It is measured at the date the entity obtains the goods or the counterparty renders service. In rare cases, if the entity rebuts this presumption because it cannot estimate reliably the fair value of the goods or services received, the entity should measure the goods or services received, and the corresponding increase in equity, indirectly, by reference to the fair value of the equity instruments granted, measured at the date the entity obtains the goods or the counterparty renders the service.

The terms of an existing share-based payment transaction may be modified; for example, by altering the exercise price of the share options, the number of share options granted or the vesting conditions. If this occurs, the entity must recognise at least the amount that would have been recognised had the terms not changed. If there is any incremental cost, this should be recognised over any remaining vesting period. This is illustrated in **Example 34.7**.

EXAMPLE 34.7: MODIFICATION OF TERMS AND CONDITIONS

On 1 January 2010, Twentitle Limited granted 100 share options to each of its 250 employees, with each of the share options being conditional upon the employee working for Twentitle Limited until 31 December 2012. At the grant date, the fair value of each share option was €12.00.

During 2010, 10 employees left Twentitle Limited and the company's directors estimated that a total of 10% of the 250 employees would leave during the three-year period 2010–12.

At the beginning of 2011, Twentitle Limited modified the terms and conditions of the share option by reducing the exercise price. This had the effect of increasing the fair value of a share option at the beginning of 2011 by €7.00.

During 2011, a further six employees left the company and the directors revised their estimate of the total number of the 250 employees to 8% that would leave the company during the three-year period 2010–12.

During 2012, a further five employees left the company.

Requirement Calculate the remuneration expense that should be recognised in Twentitle Limited's financial statements in respect of the share-based payment agreement for each of the three years 2010–12.

Solution
2010:
It is estimated that 25 employees would leave the company (10% × 250). Therefore 225 employees will be eligible under the scheme.

225 employees × €12   = €2,700
€2,700 / 3 years   = €900

| DR | SPLOCI – P/L | €900 | |
| CR | Equity – Share Options Reserve | | €900 |

2011:
It is estimated that 20 employees would leave the company (8% × 250). Therefore 230 employees will be eligible under the scheme.

	€	
230 employees × €12 = €2,760		
(€2,760 / 3 years) × 2 years	1,840	
230 employees × €7 = €1,610		
€1,610 / 2 years	805	
Less charged in 2010 in SPLOCI – P/L	(900)	
	1,745	

DR	SPLOCI – P/L	€1,745	
CR	Equity – Share Options Reserve		€1,745

2012:

In total over the three years, 21 employees left the company (10 + 6 + 5). Therefore 229 employees are eligible under the scheme.

	€
229 employees × €12	2,748
229 employees × €7	1,603
Less charged in 2010 and 2011 in SPLOCI – P/L (€900 + €1,745)	(2,645)
	1,706

DR	SPLOCI – P/L	€1,706	
CR	Equity – Share Options Reserve		€1,706

If equity-settled share-based transactions are cancelled or settled, then the entity must immediately recognise any amount that would otherwise have been recognised over a vesting period. Any payments up to the fair value of the equity instruments granted at cancellation or at settlement is a repurchase of an equity interest (i.e. debit equity). Any payment in excess of the fair value of equity instrument granted at cancellation or at settlement is recognised as an expense in arriving at profit or loss in the statement of profit or loss and other comprehensive income.

Cash-settled Share-based Payment Transactions

Cash-settled share-based payment transactions occur where goods or services are paid for at amounts that are based on the price of the company's equity instruments (for example, share appreciation rights). The expense for cash-settled transactions is the cash paid by the company. For cash-settled share-based payment transactions, the entity should measure the goods or services acquired and the liability incurred at the fair value of the liability. Until the liability is settled, the entity should re-measure the fair value of the liability at each reporting date and at the date of settlement, with any changes in fair value recognised in arriving at profit or loss for the period in the statement of profit or loss and other comprehensive income.

For example, an entity might grant share appreciation rights to employees as part of their remuneration package, whereby the employees will become entitled to a future cash payment (rather than an equity instrument), based on the increase in the entity's share price from a specified level over a specified period of time. Or an entity might grant to its employees a right to receive a future cash payment by granting to them a right to shares (including shares to be issued upon the exercise of share options) that are redeemable, either mandatorily (for example, upon cessation of employment) or at the employee's option. As the employees will receive cash (albeit based upon the share price), this is a cash-settled share-based payment transaction.

The entity should recognise the services received, and a liability to pay for those services, as the employees render service. For example, some share appreciation rights vest immediately, and the employees are therefore not required to complete a specified period of service to become entitled to the cash payment. In the absence of evidence to the contrary, the entity should presume that the services rendered by the employees, in exchange for the share appreciation rights, have been received. Thus, the entity should recognise immediately the services received and a liability to pay for them. If the share appreciation rights do not vest until the employees have completed a specified period of service, the entity should recognise the services received, and a liability to pay for them, as the employees render service during that period.

The liability should be measured, initially and at each reporting date, until settled at the fair value of the share appreciation rights, by applying an option pricing model, taking into account the terms and conditions on which the share appreciation rights were granted, and the extent to which the employees have rendered service to date. This is illustrated in **Example 34.8**.

EXAMPLE 34.8: SHARE APPRECIATION RIGHTS

Red plc granted 300 share appreciation rights to each of its 500 employees on 1 August 2012. Management believe that, as at 31 July 2013, Red plc's year-end, 80% of the awards will vest on 31 July 2014. The fair value of each share appreciation right on 31 July 2013 is €15.

Requirement What is the fair value of the liability to be recorded in the financial statements for the year ended 31 July 2013?

Solution

300 rights × 500 employees × 80% × €15 × 1 year/2 year = €900,000

To summarise: the accounting treatment for cash-settled share-based payment transactions is: DR SPLOCI – P/L and CR SFP – liability.

Share-based Payment Transactions with Cash Alternatives

For share-based payment transactions in which the terms of the arrangement provide either the entity or the counterparty with the choice of whether the entity settles the transaction in cash (or other assets) or by issuing equity instruments, the entity should account for that transaction, or the components of that transaction, as a cash-settled share-based payment transaction if, and to the extent that, the entity has incurred a liability to settle in cash or other assets, or as an equity-settled share-based payment transaction if, and to the extent that, no such liability has been incurred.

Disclosures

IFRS 2 requires extensive disclosure requirements under three main headings. First, information that enables users of financial statements to understand the nature and extent of the share-based payment transactions that existed during the period. Secondly, information that allows users to understand how the fair value of the goods or services received or the fair value of the equity instruments which have been granted during the period was determined. Thirdly information that allows users of financial statements to understand the effect of expenses which have arisen from share-based payment transactions in the entity's statement of profit or loss and other comprehensive income during the period.

34.4 IAS 34 *INTERIM FINANCIAL REPORTING*

Introduction

As explained in **Chapter 1**, the *Conceptual Framework for Financial Reporting 2010* states that financial information is more useful if it is frequent and timely. Many stakeholders, including regulators, increasingly require reports on a more frequent basis than annually. Indeed, the interest in such information has increased in light of recent corporate collapses and difficulties.

An interim financial report is a financial report containing either a complete set of financial statements or a set of condensed financial statements for a financial reporting period shorter than a full financial year, typically a quarter or half-year. IAS 34 *Interim Financial Reporting* prescribes the minimum content of an interim financial report and the principles for recognition and measurement in any interim financial statements. IAS 34 does not specify which entities must publish interim financial reports, how frequently or how soon after the end of an interim period. Those are matters that are usually specified by local law or regulation. However, entities that are required or choose to publish interim financial reports in accordance with IASs must apply IAS 34. IAS 34 is not mandatory, but instead strongly recommends to regulators that interim financial reporting should be a requirement for publicly traded securities. Specifically they are encouraged to:
- publish an interim report for at least the first six months of their financial year; and
- make the report available no later than 60 days after the end of the interim report.

Key Term and Definition

> **Interim Financial Report** This is a financial report containing either a complete set of financial statements or a set of condensed financial statements for a financial reporting period shorter than a full financial year, typically a quarter or half-year.

After outlining the content of an interim financial report, this section then explains the accounting periods to be covered by the financial statements contained in that report. Then the basis on which different items should be measured is discussed, followed by consideration of when estimates can be used.

Content of an Interim Financial Report

IAS 34 defines the minimum content of an interim report as follows:
1. Condensed statement of financial position.
2. Condensed statement of profit or loss and other comprehensive income.
3. Condensed statement of all changes in equity or changes in equity other than those arising from capital transactions with owners and distributions to owners.
4. Condensed statement of cash flows.
5. Selected explanatory notes.

The condensed statements should include each of the headings and subtotals that were included in its most recent annual financial statements. Additional line items should be included if their omission would make the condensed interim statements misleading.

Basic and diluted EPS should be presented on the face of a statement of profit or loss and other comprehensive income for an interim period (see **Chapter 23**). The notes to the interim report should include the following information (unless the information is contained elsewhere in the report):
1. A statement that the same accounting policies and methods of computation are followed in the interim statements as applied in the most recent annual statements or, if changed, a description of the nature and effect of the change.
2. Explanatory comments about the seasonality or cyclicality of interim operations.
3. The nature and amount of unusual items affecting assets, liabilities, incomes and expenses because of their nature, size or incidence.
4. The nature and amount of changes in estimates of amounts reported in prior interim periods of the current financial year or changes in estimates of amounts reported in prior financial years, i.e. those changes that have a material effect in the current interim period (please note that the use of estimates is discussed separately below).
5. The issue and/or repurchase of equity or debt securities.
6. Dividends paid, with amounts shown separately for ordinary and other shares.
7. Segmental results (if IFRS 8 *Operating Segments* applies). In May 2012, the IASB aligned the disclosure requirements of IAS 34 and IFRS 8 with respect to the reporting of segment assets so that the total assets for a reportable segment need to be disclosed only when the amounts are regularly provided to the chief operating decision maker and there has been a material change in the total assets for a segment from that previously disclosed in the last annual financial statements (see **Chapter 24**). The change is applicable to annual periods beginning on or after 1 January 2013, with permitted retrospective application.
8. Material events since the end of the interim period.
9. Effect of business combinations during the interim reporting period.
10. Changes in contingent liabilities or contingent assets since the last annual reporting date.
11. If the interim report is in compliance with IAS 34, that fact should be disclosed.

Periods Covered

After having explained the content of an interim financial report, this subsection now addresses the periods to be covered by the report. Based on the requirements of

IAS 34, the statements required to be presented in the half-yearly interim financial report by an entity with a 31 December year-end, that reports *half-yearly*, are shown in **Table 34.2**.

TABLE 34.2: STATEMENTS REQUIRED FOR ENTITIES THAT REPORT HALF-YEARLY

Statement	Current Reporting Period	Comparative
Statement of position at	30 June 2012	31 December 2011
Statement of profit or loss and other comprehensive income (and, where applicable, separate income statement) – 6 months ended	30 June 2012	30 June 2011
Statement of changes in equity – 6 months ended	30 June 2012	30 June 2011
Statement of cash flows – 6 months ended	30 June 2012	30 June 2011

Based on the requirements of IAS 34, the statements required to be presented in the half-yearly interim financial report by an entity with a 31 December year-end, that reports *quarterly*, are shown in **Table 34.3**:

TABLE 34.3: STATEMENTS REQUIRED FOR ENTITIES THAT REPORT QUARTERLY

Statement	Current Reporting Period	Comparative
Statement of financial position at	30 June 2012	31 December 2011
Statement of profit or loss and other comprehensive income (and, where applicable, separate income statement) – 6 months ended: 3 months ended	30 June 2012: 30 June 2012	30 June 2011: 30 June 2011
Statement of changes in equity – 6 months ended	30 June 2012	30 June 2011
Statement of cash flows – 6 months ended	30 June 2012	30 June 2011

Measurement

After having discussed the content of an interim financial report and the associated periods to be reflected in that report, this section considers the basis on which the reported figures are measured.

Measurements for interim reporting purposes should be on a year-to-date basis so that the frequency of the reporting does not affect the measurement of annual results. The issue of materiality is discussed in **Chapter 1**, particularly with respect to Chapters 3 and 4 of the *Conceptual Framework for Financial Reporting 2010*. In broad terms, information is material if its omission or misstatement could influence the decision-making of users. IAS 34 states that materiality should be assessed in relation to the interim period financial data and not forecast annual data. Several important measurement points are:

1. **Same accounting policies as those in annual financial statements** The same accounting policies should be adopted in the interim as are applied in the annual statements, except for accounting policy changes made after the date of the most recent annual financial statements that will be reflected in the next set of annual statements. The guiding principle for recognition and measurement is that an enterprise should use the same recognition and measurement principles in its interim statements as it does in its annual financial statements (for example, a cost would not be classified as an asset in the interim report if it would not be classified as such in the annual report).

2. **Revenues received occasionally, seasonally or cyclically** Revenue which is received occasionally or seasonally should not be anticipated or deferred in interim reports. The principles of revenue recognition should be applied consistently to interim and annual reports (see **Chapter 4**).

3. **Costs incurred unevenly during the financial year** These should only be anticipated or deferred if it would be appropriate to anticipate or defer the expense in the annual financial statements. It would be inappropriate to anticipate part of the cost of a major advertising campaign later in the year for which no expenses have yet been incurred.

Examples of the above measurement principles include:

- *Employer payroll taxes and insurance contributions* In some countries these are assessed on an annual basis but paid at an uneven rate during the year. It is therefore appropriate, in this situation, to adopt an estimated average annual tax rate for the year in an interim statement, not the actual tax paid. Taxes are an annual assessment, but payment is uneven.

- *Cost of a planned major periodic overhaul* The cost of such an event must not be anticipated unless there is a legal or constructive obligation to carry out the work. A mere intention to carry out work later in the year is not sufficient justification to create a liability.

- *Year-end bonus* This should not be provided in the interim report unless there is a constructive obligation to pay such a bonus and it can be reliably measured.

- *Intangible asset* IAS 34 must follow IAS 38 *Intangible assets* (see **Chapter 9**) and thus it would be inappropriate in an interim report to defer a cost in the expectation that it will eventually be part of a non-monetary *intangible asset* that has not yet been recognised.

- *Holiday pay* If holiday pay is an enforceable obligation on the employer, then any unpaid accumulated holiday pay should be accrued in the interim report.

- *Tax on income* An expense for tax should be included in the interim report and the tax rate should be the estimated average annual tax rate for the year (see **Example 34.9**).

EXAMPLE 34.9: TAX ON INCOME

1. Assume a quarterly reporting entity expects to earn €10,000 pre-tax each quarter and operates in a tax jurisdiction with a tax rate of 20% on the first €20,000 and 30% on all additional earnings. If actual earnings match expectations, the tax reported in each quarter is as follows:
   - Tax expense: €2,500; €2,500; €2,500; €2,500 = Total €10,000
   - Total earnings estimate: €40,000 (€20,000 × 20%) = €4,000 + €20,000 × 30% = €6,000 (i.e. €10,000/4 = €2,500)

2. Assume a quarterly reporting entity expects to earn €15,000 pre-tax in quarter 1 but incur losses of €5,000 in quarters 2–4. If the tax rate is 20%, the tax reported in each quarter is as follows:
   - Tax expense: €3,000; (€1,000); (€1,000); (€1,000) = Total €Nil

3. Assume a year-end of 30 June and a taxable year-end of 31 December, together with pre-tax earnings of €10,000 each quarter and an average tax rate of 30% in year 1 and 40% in year 2.
   - Tax expense: €3,000; €3,000; €4,000; €4,000 = Total €14,000

- *Inventory valuations* Inventory should be valued in the same way as for year-end accounts, but it will be necessary to rely more heavily on estimates for interim reports (see **Chapter 11**).
- *Depreciation* In the interim statement, depreciation should only be charged on assets that have been owned during the period. It should not be charged on assets that will be acquired later in the financial year.
- *Foreign currency translation gains and losses* These should be calculated using the same principles as those used at the end of the year in accordance with IAS 21 (see **Chapter 31**).

Use of Estimates

The *Conceptual Framework for Financial Reporting 2010* (see **Chapter 1**) recognises that many estimates are made in the preparation of financial statements (for example, inventory valuation, estimated useful lives of assets, recoverability of debts). Being cautious when exercising judgement in arriving at these estimates is known as prudence. While prudence is a generally accepted concept in the preparation of financial statements, the concept does not extend to including excess provisions, overstating liabilities or understating income or assets. This would bias the information and make it unreliable to users. However, while accounting information must be reliable and free from material error, it may be necessary to sacrifice some accuracy and reliability for the sake of timeliness and cost benefits.

This is particularly the case in interim reporting where estimates must be used to a greater extent in interim reporting. Some examples are:
1. **Inventories** There is no need for a full inventory count and it is sufficient to estimate inventory values using sales margins;
2. **Provisions** It is inappropriate to bear the cost of experts to advise on the appropriate amount of a provision or the value of non-current assets at the interim date; and
3. **Income taxes** It is sufficient to apply an estimated weighted average tax rate to income earned in all jurisdictions. There is no need to calculate the tax rate in each country separately.

34.5 IFRS 4 *INSURANCE CONTRACTS*

Introduction

IFRS 4 *Insurance Contracts* is the first guidance from the IASB on accounting for insurance contracts. IFRS 4, which provides guidance on accounting for insurance contracts issued by companies, was issued because the IASB believed that there was need for improved disclosures for insurance contracts, together with some improvements to recognition and measurement practices.

After defining a number of key terms, the scope of IFRS 4 is explained. Then, as IFRS 4 is concerned primarily with disclosure, the main accounting policies and disclosures required by the standard are presented.

KEY TERMS AND DEFINITIONS

Insurance Assets These are an insurer's net contractual rights under an insurance contract.

Insurance Contract This is a contract under which one party (the insurer) accepts significant insurance risk from another party (the policyholder) by agreeing to compensate the policyholder if a specified uncertain future event (the insured event) adversely affects the policyholder.

Insurance Liability This is an insurer's net contractual obligations under an insurance contract.

Scope

IFRS 4 applies to virtually all insurance contracts that an entity issues and holds. However, it does not apply to other assets and liabilities of an insurer, such as financial assets and financial liabilities within the scope of IFRS 9 *Financial Instruments* (see **Chapter 25**).

Accounting Policies

IFRS 4:
- prohibits provisions for possible claims under contracts that are not in existence at the reporting date (such as catastrophe provisions);
- requires a test for the adequacy of recognised insurance liabilities and an impairment test for insurance assets; and
- requires an insurer to keep insurance liabilities in its statement of financial position until they are discharged or cancelled, or expire, and prohibits offsetting insurance liabilities against related assets and income or expense from insurance contracts against the expense or income from the related insurance contract.

IFRS 4 permits an insurer to change its accounting policies for insurance contracts only if, as a result of the change, its financial statements present information that is more relevant and no less reliable, or more reliable and no less relevant. In particular, an insurer cannot introduce any of the following practices, although it may continue using accounting policies that involve them:
- measuring insurance liabilities on an undiscounted basis;
- measuring contractual rights to future investment management fees at an amount that exceeds their fair value as implied by a comparison with current market-based fees for similar services; and
- using non-uniform accounting policies for the insurance liabilities of subsidiaries.

IFRS 4 states that an insurer need not change its accounting policies for insurance contracts to eliminate excessive prudence. However, if an insurer already measures its insurance contracts with sufficient prudence, it should not introduce additional prudence.

Disclosures

IFRS 4 requires disclosure of:
- information that helps users understand the amounts in the insurer's financial statements that arise from insurance contracts. For example: accounting policies for insurance contracts and related assets, liabilities, income and expenses; information about the assumptions that have the greatest effect on the measurement of assets, liabilities, income and expenses including, if practicable, quantified disclosure of those assumptions; the effect of changes in assumptions; and reconciliations of changes in insurance liabilities;
- information that helps users to evaluate the nature and extent of risks arising from insurance contracts. For example: risk-management objectives and policies; the terms and conditions of insurance contracts that have a material effect on the amount, timing and uncertainty of the insurer's future cash flows; and information about insurance risk; and
- actual claims compared with previous estimates.

34.6 IFRS 6 *EXPLORATION FOR AND EVALUATION OF MINERAL RESOURCES*

Introduction

Under IFRS 6 *Exploration for and Evaluation of Mineral Resources*, **exploration for and evaluation of mineral resources** refers to the search for mineral resources, including minerals, oil and natural gas, once an entity has obtained legal rights to explore in a specific area, as well as the determination of the technical feasibility and commercial viability of extracting the mineral resource.

Exploration and evaluation expenditures are expenditures incurred in connection with the exploration and evaluation of mineral resources before the technical feasibility and commercial viability of extracting a mineral resource is demonstrable. Prior to IFRS 6, there was a lack of consistency with regards to the treatment of these costs, with some companies capitalising them and others expensing them immediately. However, while IFRS 6 seeks to provide guidance to companies, it does not aim to harmonise accounting practice.

After defining a number of key terms, the key issues associated with IFRS 6 are identified and explained. The section concludes by outlining the main disclosures required under IFRS 6.

KEY TERMS AND DEFINITIONS

Exploration and Evaluation Expenditures These are expenditures incurred in connection with the exploration and evaluation of mineral resources before the technical feasibility and commercial viability of extracting a mineral resource is demonstrable.

Exploration for and Evaluation of Mineral Resources This refers to the search for mineral resources, including minerals, oil and natural gas, once an entity has obtained legal rights to explore in a specific area, as well as the determination of the technical feasibility and commercial viability of extracting the mineral resource.

Key Issues

IFRS 6 permits an entity to develop an accounting policy for recognition of exploration and evaluation expenditures as assets without specifically considering the requirements of IAS 8 *Accounting Policies, Changes in Accounting Estimates and Errors* (see **Chapter 21**), so long as the information is relevant and reliable; albeit the policy may not be in full compliance with the definition of an asset in the *Conceptual Framework for Financial Reporting 2010* (see **Chapter 1**). This is illustrated in **Example 34.10**. Thus, an entity adopting IFRS 6 may continue to use the accounting policies applied immediately before adopting the IFRS. Consequently, IFRS 6 effectively allows an exemption from the *Conceptual Framework for Financial Reporting 2010*.

EXAMPLE 34.10: ADOPTING IFRS 6

Texas plc, a company involved in oil exploration that has always capitalised exploration costs, is adopting IFRS 6.

Texas plc can change its accounting policy but only if it brings the company more in line with the *Conceptual Framework for Financial Reporting 2010*. The change must result in a policy that is more reliable and no less relevant or more relevant and no less reliable than the previous policy. Texas plc may therefore have an asset on the statement of financial position that does not meet the definition in the *Conceptual Framework for Financial Reporting 2010*, i.e. the capitalisation criteria may not require the demonstration of future economic benefits and thus following IFRS 6 may result in earlier capitalisation than would be the case under the *Conceptual Framework for Financial Reporting 2010*.

Once recognised, exploration and evaluation assets can be classified as either tangible assets under IAS 16 *Property, Plant and Equipment* (see **Chapter 6**) or intangible assets under IAS 38 *Intangible Assets* (see **Chapter 9**). Initially, under both IAS 16 and IAS 38, the assets are recognised using the cost model. Subsequently, entities have the choice of using the cost model or applying the revaluation model as described in IAS 16 and IAS 38. It is not necessary to provide for depreciation since the economic benefits that the assets represent are not consumed until the production phase.

The exploration industry (primarily oil and gas) has faced particular difficulties following the adoption of IASs/IFRSs. The most problematic standard is IAS 36 *Impairment of Assets* (see **Chapter 10**) as it requires entities to consider cash generating units (CGUs) as their lowest possible level; therefore, in the extreme, an individual petrol station might be considered a separate CGU.

IFRS 6 requires entities recognising exploration and evaluation assets to perform an impairment test in accordance with IAS 36 on those assets when facts and circumstances suggest that the carrying amount of the assets may exceed their recoverable amount (see **Chapter 10**).

Once an entity has demonstrated the technical and commercial feasibility of extracting a mineral resource, the assets fall outside the scope of IFRS 6 and are reclassified according to other appropriate standards. An impairment test must be performed at this point, i.e. before reclassification.

Disclosures

IFRS 6 requires disclosure of information that identifies and explains the amounts recognised in its financial statements arising from the exploration for and evaluation of mineral resources, including:
- its accounting policies for exploration and evaluation expenditures, including the recognition of exploration and evaluation assets; and
- the amounts of assets, liabilities, income and expense and operating and investing cash flows arising from the exploration for and evaluation of mineral resources.

34.7 IAS 26 *ACCOUNTING AND REPORTING BY RETIREMENT BENEFIT PLANS*

Scope and Objective of IAS 26

IAS 26 *Accounting and Reporting by Retirement Benefit Plans* applies to the financial statements of **retirement benefit plans**. The accounting treatment of such plans in the financial statements of any entity that operates a retirement benefit plan is addressed in **Chapter 17**.

The objective of IAS 26 is to specify measurement and disclosure principles for the reports of retirement benefit plans. All plans should include in their reports a statement of changes in net assets available for benefits, a summary of significant accounting policies and a description of the plan and the effect of any changes in the plan during the period.

After defining a number of key terms, the content of the reports on retirement benefit plans are outlined. This is followed by a description of the disclosure requirements in accordance with IAS 26.

KEY TERMS AND DEFINITIONS

> **Defined Benefit Plan** This is a retirement benefit plan by which employees receive benefits based on a formula usually linked to employee earnings.
>
> **Defined Contribution Plan** This is a retirement benefit plan by which benefits to employees are based on the amount of funds contributed to the plan plus investment earnings thereon.
>
> **Retirement Benefit Plan** This is an arrangement by which an entity provides benefits (annual income or lump sum) to employees on or after they terminate from service when such benefits, or the contributions towards them, can be determined or estimated in advance of retirement from the provisions of a document or from the entity's practices.

The Reports of Retirement Benefit Plans

There are two types of retirement benefit plan, **defined contribution** and **defined benefit**, and the content of the reports on these plans is outlined below.

Defined Contribution Plans

The financial statements of a defined contribution plan contain a statement of net assets available for benefits and a description of the funding policy.

Defined Benefit Plans

The financial statements of a defined benefit plan contain either:
- a statement that shows:
  - the net assets available for benefits;
  - the actuarial present value of promised retirement benefits, distinguishing between vested and non-vested benefits; and
  - the resulting excess or deficit; or
- a statement of net assets available for benefits including either:
  - a note disclosing the actuarial present value of promised retirement benefits, distinguishing between vested and non-vested benefits; or
  - a reference to this information in an accompanying actuarial report.

If an actuarial valuation has not been prepared at the date of the report of a defined benefit plan, the most recent valuation should be used as a base and the date of the valuation disclosed.

The actuarial present value of promised retirement benefits is based on the benefits promised under the terms of the plan on service rendered to date, using either current salary levels or projected salary levels. Retirement benefit plan investments are carried at fair value.

Disclosure

IAS 26 specifies detailed disclosures in the financial statements of retirement benefit plans. The key elements are:
- Statement of net assets available for benefits.
- Statement of changes in net assets available for benefits.
- Description of funding policy.
- Summary of significant accounting policies.
- Description of the plan and of the effect of any changes in the plan during the period.
- For defined benefit plans, the actuarial present value of promised benefit obligations, a description of actuarial assumptions and a description of the method used to calculate the actuarial present value of promised benefit obligations.

34.8 CONCLUSION

This chapter completes the analysis of extant IASs/IFRSs by examining the remaining six standards not dealt with elsewhere in the text. Each of these standards is separate and none is related to another. The standards covered in this chapter are: IAS 41 *Agriculture*, IFRS 2

Share-based Payment, IAS 34 *Interim Financial Reporting*, IFRS 4 *Insurance Contracts*, IFRS 6 *Exploration for and Evaluation of Mineral Resources* and IAS 26 *Accounting and Reporting by Retirement Benefit Plans*.

In summary, the key points to be remembered with respect to each of these standards are:

- IAS 41 is a very specific accounting standard and as such is not examined frequently. However, when dealing with biological assets, it is important to remember that IAS 2 does not apply and that biological assets are not recorded at the lower of cost and net realisable value.
- The issue of share-based payments has become more high profile in recent years and consequently so has IFRS 2. As a result IFRS 2 is growing in importance from both a practical and examination perspective.
- While IAS 34 is arguably a relatively minor accounting standard, the issue of interim financial reporting and the importance of the publication of more timely financial information has gained prominence given the current global financial crisis and the growing number of companies in difficulty.
- IFRS 4 provides guidance on accounting for insurance contracts issued by companies. It was issued primarily because the IASB believed there was need for improved disclosures for insurance contracts.
- IFRS 6 permits an entity to develop an accounting policy for recognition of exploration and evaluation expenditures as assets without specifically considering the requirements of IAS 8 so long as the information is relevant and reliable; albeit the policy may not be in full compliance with the definition of an asset in the *Conceptual Framework for Financial Reporting 2010*. In addition, IFRS 6 requires entities recognising exploration and evaluation assets to perform an impairment test, in accordance with IAS 36, on those assets when facts and circumstances suggest that the carrying amount of the assets may exceed their recoverable amount.
- The objective of IAS 26 is to specify measurement and disclosure principles for the reports of retirement benefit plans, both defined contribution and defined benefit plans. All plans should include in their reports a statement of changes in net assets available for benefits, a summary of significant accounting policies and a description of the plan and the effect of any changes in the plan during the period.

SUMMARY OF LEARNING OBJECTIVES

As this chapter deals with six different standards, separate learning objectives are provided for each standard.

Learning Objective 1: IAS 41 *Agriculture* – demonstrate an understanding of the basic principles and features of IAS 41, appreciate the circumstances when they may be applicable and apply the main disclosure requirements.

See **Section 34.2**.

Learning Objective 2: IFRS 2 *Share-based Payment* – apply and discuss the recognition and measurement criteria for share-based payment transactions, account for modifications, cancellations and settlements of share-based payment transactions, and apply the main disclosure requirements.

See **Section 34.3**.

Learning Objective 3: IAS 34 *Interim Financial Reporting* – demonstrate an understanding of the basic principles and features of IAS 34, and apply the main disclosure requirements.

See **Section 34.4**.

Learning Objective 4: IFRS 4 *Insurance Contracts* – demonstrate an understanding of the basic principles and features of IFRS 4, and apply the main disclosure requirements.

See **Section 34.5**.

Learning Objective 5: IFRS 6 *Exploration for and Evaluation of Mineral Resources* – demonstrate an understanding of the basic principles and features of IFRS 6, and apply the main disclosure requirements.

See **Section 34.6**.

Learning Objective 6: IAS 26 *Accounting and Reporting by Retirement Benefit Plans* – demonstrate an understanding of the basic principles and features of IAS 26, and apply the main disclosure requirements.

See **Section 34.7**.

QUESTIONS

Review Questions

(See **Appendix One** for Suggested Solutions to Review Questions.)

Question 34.1

Three 2-year-old dairy cows were purchased during the year ended 31 December 2011 for €200 each. During the year ended 31 December 2012, a further three 2-year-old dairy cows were purchased for €220 each. Three calves were born on 31 December 2012. There were no sales of dairy cattle during 2011 or 2012.

The market prices of dairy cattle at 31 December 2011 and 2012 were as follows:

	2011 €	2012 €
Calf	70	95
2-year-old dairy cow	200	220
3-year-old dairy cow	230	250

The costs to sell are negligible.

Requirement

(a) Calculate the value of the dairy herd at 31 December 2011 and 31 December 2012.

(b) Show and explain the accounting entries required to recognise the change in the value of the dairy herd from 31 December 2011 to 31 December 2012.

Question 34.2

Christy Limited issued 1 million €1 ordinary shares on 1 June 2010 to pay for inventory. On this date the underlying ordinary shares had a market value of €4.5 million. The inventory was sold on 31 December 2012 for €6.2 million. The inventory, which could be measured reliably, was valued at €4.1 million on 1 June 2010 and its value did not change up to the date of sale on 31 December 2012.

Requirement Explain how this transaction should be recognised in the financial statements of Christy Limited.

Question 34.3

BCG Limited granted 5,000 share options to each of its four directors on 1 January 2012, subject to the directors still being employed by the company on 31 December 2014 and BCG Limited's share price exceeding €20 per share.

On *1 January 2012*, the fair value of each option was €15 and it was expected that the four directors would still be employed by BCG Limited on 31 December 2014.

On *31 December 2012*, the share price of BCG Limited was €14.50 and it was not expected to change significantly over the next two years. It was anticipated that only three of the directors would still be employed by BCG Limited on 31 December 2014.

Requirement Show and explain how to account for the share options in the financial statements of BCG Limited for the year ended 31 December 2012.

Challenging Questions

(Suggested Solutions to Challenging Questions are available to lecturers.)

Question 34.1

On 1 January 2011, Ifar Limited granted 250 cash share appreciation rights (SARs) to each of its 500 employees on condition that they continued to work for the company until 31 December 2013. During 2011, 50 employees left Ifar Limited and it was estimated that a further 100 employees in total would leave the company during 2012 and 2013.

During 2012, a further 30 employees left Ifar Limited and it was estimated that 50 employees would leave the company during 2013.

During 2013, 25 employees left Ifar Limited.

The fair value of each SAR on 31 December in each of the following years was:

Year	2011	2012	2013
Fair value of SAR	€10.00	€12.00	€14.00

Requirement Calculate the expense to be recognised in the statement of profit or loss and other comprehensive income of Ifar Limited for each of the three years ending 31 December 2011 – 2013, together with the corresponding liability in the statement of financial position on each of these dates.

ANALYSIS AND INTERPRETATION OF FINANCIAL INFORMATION

LEARNING OBJECTIVES

After having studied this chapter on the analysis and interpretation of financial information, you should be able to:

1. discuss who are the primary users of ratio analysis;
2. demonstrate an understanding of when ratio analysis should be used;
3. explain the limitations of ratio analysis;
4. select and calculate the main ratios and statistics commonly used in interpreting accounts;
5. identify and evaluate significant features and issues in financial statements, including financial balance and overtrading;
6. highlight inconsistencies in financial information through analysis and the application of ratios;
7. make inferences from the analysis of information, taking into account the limitations of the information, the analytical methods used and the business environment in which the entity operates; and
8. produce reports which critically analyse and interpret results over time or between activities, tailored to the technical understanding of the different user groups.

KEY TERMS AND DEFINITIONS FOR THIS CHAPTER

Efficiency Ratios These measure an entity's effective use of its assets.
Financial Balance This is the balance between the various forms of available finance relative to the requirements of the entity.

Liquidity Ratios These measure how accessible an entity's cash is.

Overtrading This arises where an entity expands its turnover fairly rapidly without securing additional long-term capital adequate for its needs.

Profitability Ratios These show the relationship between profitability and revenue.

Ratio This expresses the relationship between two or more figures.

Ratio Analysis This is a tool used to conduct a quantitative analysis of information in an entity's financial statements.

Window Dressing This is a strategy used near the end of the reporting period to improve the appearance of the financial statements. For example, a company that operates throughout the year with a negative balance in its bank account may not wish to report this publicly in its financial statements. Therefore, to avoid doing so, the company withholds payments close to the end of the reporting period (*say* between 20–31 December for a 31 December reporting period) so that the bank balance is positive. Then shortly after the end of the reporting period (*say* 5 January), the company pays those amounts that normally would have been paid at the end of December.

Note: the terms 'interest', 'interest cost', 'interest charge' and 'interest expense' are used interchangeably throughout this chapter. These terms equate to the 'finance cost' heading in the statement of profit or loss and other comprehensive income (see **Chapter 2**).

35.1 INTRODUCTION

Chapter 1 explains that, in accordance with the *Conceptual Framework for Financial Reporting 2010*, financial information is prepared to satisfy in some way the needs of different stakeholders in a business. Many of the subsequent chapters then concentrated on how financial statements are prepared, together with how to apply different accounting standards as part of this process and comply with disclosure requirements. In contrast, this chapter focuses on the significance of the figures contained in the financial statements and how they might be interpreted by different users of financial statements. For example, to assess whether a company is:
- performing well or badly; and
- financially strong or financially vulnerable.

Ratio analysis is a tool used to conduct a quantitative analysis of information in an entity's financial statements. Ratios are typically calculated from current year figures and are then compared to previous years, other business entities, the industry, or even the economy in order to assess the performance of the entity under review.

There are many ratios that can be calculated from the financial statements, and these ratios can be classified or divided into many different categories. In **Section 35.3**, ratios are presented under the following six headings: Profitability; Liquidity; Efficiency; Growth; Investment; and Cash Flow.

Key to this Chapter

In order to facilitate the achievement of the learning objectives, this chapter is structured as follows:
- Analysis of financial statements and the use of ratios (**Section 35.2**).
- Categories and calculation of ratios (**Section 35.3**).
- Financial balance and overtrading (**Section 35.4**).
- Accounting policies and the limitations of ratio analysis (**Section 35.5**).

35.2 ANALYSIS OF FINANCIAL STATEMENTS AND USE OF RATIOS

As explained above, ratio analysis is a tool used in the analysis and interpretation of financial statements. By definition, a **ratio** expresses the relationship between two or more figures. On this basis, ratios are only meaningful when:
- calculated correctly;
- compared with similar ratios on an:
  - internal basis (company statistics); and
  - external basis (industry statistics).

When comparing ratios it is important to compare 'like with like'. Therefore, any exceptional items or one-time charges need to be excluded from the calculations for comparison purposes. This is illustrated in **Example 35.1**.

EXAMPLE 35.1: COMPARING LIKE WITH LIKE

Company X began trading in 2006. Due to significant growth in the first three years, Company X engaged in an aggressive acquisition policy in 2012. This led to €100,000 of one-time charges and an overall profit before tax of €50,000. Shareholders' equity amounted to €1,500,000.

In this scenario, Return on Capital Employed (ROCE), which is calculated by dividing shareholders' equity into profit (see **Section 35.3**, efficiency ratios), before one-time charges would be 10%, whilst after would be 3.33%. When comparing 2012 ratios to past years or to industry averages, it is therefore important to compare ROCE before one-time charges as these are not standard costs.

Notwithstanding the fact that ratios are only meaningful when compared to similar calculations, ratio analysis can be a useful tool. For example:
- internally, ratios can be used to compare:
  - past performance; and
  - actual results versus budgets and forecasts.
- externally, ratios may be used to compare:
  - similar entities at the same stage of development; and
  - entities within the same industry.

What Information does a User Require?

Chapter 1 (Section 1.3) explains that the various users of financial statements require information for quite different purposes. Moreover, as mentioned above and shown in **Section 35.3**, many ratios can be calculated from the financial statements, and these ratios can be classified or divided into many different categories. However, not all ratios will be relevant to a particular situation. It is therefore important to determine the precise information needs of the user and the decisions that have to be taken after analysing the relevant information.

> Key Questions are: 'What decision is being made?' and 'What information is relevant to that decision?'

The managers of the company are likely to be concerned about all aspects of the company and therefore may want to know about all of the key ratios in each category. Shareholders or potential investors are concerned primarily with the investment ratios, although certain financial stability and profitability measures are also likely to be of interest. Creditors are most likely to be concerned about financial stability, although a bank, acting as a major source of finance, will usually also look at profitability.

Other Items of Information

Ratio analysis on its own is not sufficient for interpreting company financial statements. There are other items of information which should be looked at, such as:
- the Chairman's Report and Directors' Report, which may help to explain past performance and discuss future expectations;
- the age and nature of the company's assets which, for example, may indicate that certain assets will need to be replaced in the near future or that the company has adequate capacity to meet future sales demand;
- current and future developments in the company's markets, at home and overseas, including recent acquisitions or disposals of a subsidiary by the company. For example, such information may indicate that the company's future prospects are healthy (or not);
- any other noticeable features of the annual report and financial statements, such as events after the end of the reporting period, contingent liabilities, a qualified audit report and the company's taxation position. For example, a qualified audit report may indicate that there are doubts over certain figures in the financial statements (on which the ratios are based); and
- any relevant government legislation, both existing and intended. For example, proposed legislation with respect to emissions, minimum wage rates or tax rates may impact on future profits and performance.

Notwithstanding that, as discussed above, the analysis and interpretation of a company's performance should ideally be based on information drawn from a range of sources. The next section explains the main ratios that can be calculated from the financial statements.

35.3 CATEGORIES AND CALCULATION OF RATIOS

Main Categories of Ratios

As mentioned above, ratios can be classified or divided into many different categories; although not all ratios will be relevant to each situation. In this section, ratios are presented under the following six headings: Profitability; Liquidity; Efficiency; Growth; Investment; and Cash Flow.

1. Profitability

Profitability ratios need to be looked at in conjunction with liquidity ratios (see below). Profitability ratios show the relationship between profitability and revenue and relevant ratios include: Gross Profit on Revenue (also called gross margin); Net Profit on Revenue (also called net margin); and Contribution to Revenue.

Gross Profit on Revenue (also called Gross Margin) This ratio is shown as a percentage and is the margin that the company makes on its sales. It indicates the efficiency of the production department as well as the pricing policy of the business. The formula is:

$$\frac{\text{Gross Profit}}{\text{Revenue}} \times 100$$

The ratio is expected to remain reasonably constant. Since the ratio consists of a small number of components, a change may be traced to changes in:
(a) *selling prices* – normally deliberate although sometimes unavoidable, for example because of increased competition;
(b) *sales mix* – often deliberate;
(c) *purchase cost* – including carriage or discounts;
(d) *production cost* – materials, labour or production overheads; and
(e) *inventory* – errors in counting, valuing or cut-off; inventory shortages.

Inter-company comparison of margins can be very useful but it is especially important to look at businesses within the same sector. For example, food retailing is able to support low margins because of the high volume of sales. A manufacturing industry would usually have higher margins.

Low margins usually suggest poor performance, inefficiency of operations and/or a poor pricing policy, but may be due to one-off expansion costs (for example, in connection with launching a new product) or trying to increase market share, which are not expected to re-occur in the future. Lower margins than usual suggest scope for improvement. In addition, one has to take into account the type of business involved. In the supermarket trade one will find a high inventory turnover and low gross margins. By contrast, in the jewellery trade there would be low inventory turnover and high gross margins. If there are a number of products manufactured, it would be necessary to obtain different figures for the different products in order to assess individual product margins. Therefore when using ratios, it is important to always bear in mind the context in which they are being applied. As a rule of thumb, there is an inverse relationship between the gross profit percentage and the inventory turnover.

Above average margins are usually a sign of good management, although unusually high margins may make the competition keen to join in and enjoy the 'rich pickings'.

Net Profit on Revenue (also called Net Profit Margin) This ratio indicates the relative efficiency of the organisation with reference to trading overheads. It is calculated after deducting all expenses but usually before interest and taxation. The formula is:

$$\frac{\text{Profit Before Interest and Taxation}}{\text{Revenue}} \times 100$$

This ratio is affected by more factors than the gross profit margin, but it is equally useful, and if the company does not disclose a cost of sales it may be used on its own in lieu of the gross profit percentage (GP%).

One of the many factors affecting the trading profit margin is depreciation, which is open to considerable subjective judgement. Inter-company comparisons should be made after suitable adjustments to align accounting policies. The percentage will vary significantly from industry to industry and industry averages are important. A change in either the gross or net margins is a sign that a more detailed analysis should be undertaken of the possible causal factors. This might include an investigation of:

(a) material cost compared to revenue;
(b) direct labour cost compared to revenue;
(c) production overheads compared to revenue;
(d) administration cost compared to revenue; and
(e) selling and distribution cost compared to revenue.

Contribution to Revenue Contribution is defined as revenue (or sales) less variable costs. This ratio reveals the level of sales that must be achieved before an organisation can break even. The higher the ratio, the quicker a firm covers its fixed costs and is making profits. The formula is:

$$\frac{\text{Revenue less Variable Costs}}{\text{Revenue}}$$

A low ratio might indicate that a reduction in revenue could easily lead to a loss-making situation as fixed costs still have to be covered and hence a company would need to quickly examine costs of sales policy to prevent losses being incurred.

2. Liquidity

Liquidity is the measure of how accessible the company's cash is. The importance of liquidity to businesses cannot be overestimated. Both profitability and liquidity need to be examined individually and may often show a very weak relationship. Profitable organisations may suffer from liquidity problems that could be fatal; whilst less profitable businesses might survive or blossom because of better liquidity management. Profitability without liquidity is not enough to ensure survival.

Each of the four following key liquidity ratios is now considered in turn: Current or Working Capital Ratio; Acid Test or Quick Ratio; Receivables Ratio; and Payables Ratio.

Current Ratio (Working Capital Ratio) This ratio is calculated as follows:

$$\frac{\text{Current assets}}{\text{Current liabilities}}$$

The current ratio measures the adequacy of current assets to meet its short-term liabilities and it essentially shows the net liquid position of a company at the reporting date.

It reflects whether the company is in a position to meet its liabilities as they fall due. Traditionally a current ratio of 2 or higher was regarded as appropriate for most businesses to maintain creditworthiness; however, more recently a figure of 1.5 is regarded as the norm. However, it is important to note that these figures are only a guide and may differ from industry to industry. It is important for a company to have a relatively high current ratio as inventory is usually the biggest current asset and may not be easily convertible into cash. This is why the current ratio should always be calculated in conjunction with the acid test ratio (see below).

If a company is showing an excessive current ratio, the question may be asked whether too many liquid funds are tied up in assets, indicating poor financial management. A higher figure should be regarded with suspicion as it may be due to:
(a) high levels of inventory and receivables (check working capital management ratios); or
(b) high cash levels which could be put to better use (for example by investing in non-current assets).

The current ratio should be looked at in the light of what is normal for the business. For example, supermarkets tend to have low current ratios because:
(a) there are no trade receivables; and
(b) there is usually very tight cash control as there will be considerable investment in developing new sites and improving sites.

It is also worth considering:
(a) *Availability of further finance* – for example, is the overdraft at the limit? Very often this information is highly relevant but not disclosed in the accounts;
(b) *Seasonal nature of the business* – one way of determining whether a business is seasonal in nature is to compare the interest charges in the statement of profit or loss and other comprehensive income with the overdraft and other loans in the statement of financial position; if the interest rate appears abnormally high this is probably because the company has had higher levels of borrowings during the year;
(c) *Nature of the inventory* – as stated above, where inventory is slow-moving, the quick ratio probably provides a better indicator of short-term liquidity.

Acid Test or Quick Ratio This ratio is calculated as follows:

$$\frac{\text{Current assets} - \text{inventory}}{\text{Current liabilities}}$$

This ratio provides an indication of the immediate liquid position of a business, i.e. by eliminating inventory from current assets it provides the acid test of whether the company has sufficient resources (receivables and cash) to settle its liabilities. The generally accepted ratio is 1:1, or perhaps a little less depending on the type of business and the relationship of the business with its creditors. Norms for the quick ratio range from 1 to 0.7. Again, however, this is only a guide and should only be used as such. Like the current ratio it is relevant to consider the nature of the business (again, supermarkets have very low quick ratios). Considerable differences will be found amongst various types of business. This is because of the fact that the ratio is not a precise measure of liquidity and is liable to be influenced by debt collection and credit payment periods, which will vary considerably between industries. It is important to always calculate the current ratio in conjunction with the acid test ratio.

This is an effective tool to highlight any potential inventory problems. A high current ratio, but a low acid test ratio, could indicate excessive inventory holdings, which could lead to concerns of obsolescence and slow-moving inventory.

Sometimes the quick ratio is calculated on the basis of a six-week time frame (i.e. the quick assets are those which will turn into cash in six weeks; quick liabilities are those which fall due for payment within six weeks). This basis would usually include the following in quick assets:
• bank, cash and short-term investments; and
• trade receivables.

Quick liabilities would usually include:
• bank overdraft, which is usually repayable on demand;
• trade payables, tax and social security; and
• dividends approved but still unpaid.

Corporation tax may be excluded on the basis that it falls due for payment outside of the six-week time frame referred to above. However, it can also be argued that it should be included since it is arguably the one liability that a company has to meet.

When interpreting the quick ratio, care should be taken over the status of the bank overdraft. A company with a low quick ratio may actually have no problem in paying its payables if sufficient overall overdraft facilities are available.

Both the current and quick ratio may be distorted by **window dressing**; for example, if the current ratio is 1.4 and trade payables are paid just before the year-end out of positive cash balances, the ratios improve as shown below.

EXAMPLE 35.2: WINDOW DRESSING

	Before	Repayment of €400 trade payables	After
Current assets	€1,400	−€400	€1,000
Current liabilities	€1,000	−€400	€600
Current ratio	1.4		1.7

It is important to look at the limitations of the liquidity ratios:
(a) they do not take into account any unutilised credit facilities, which may be available to the company in times of cash shortage. Therefore, it is useful to look for any mention of an unused draw-down facility or bank overdraft limit. Whilst this does not come into the ratio calculation, it may be important for commentary purposes; and
(b) they are static ratios whereas liquidity is an ever-changing area. A firm whose liquidity ratio is less than 1 would probably like to know how quickly it could reinstate itself to an acceptable position without taking drastic action. An indication of this would be revealed by the following formula:

$$\frac{\textbf{Current Liabilities} - \textbf{Liquid Assets}}{\textbf{Cash Flow in Normal Trading Year}} \times \textbf{365}$$

In considering the liquidity ratio (and indeed the current ratio) it should also be borne in mind that these ratios should only account for short-term liquidity. Therefore:

(c) while a bank overdraft is legally repayable on demand, in substance it may be more in the nature of medium-term financing and could be excluded from the calculation of the liquidity ratio; and

(d) among the current assets there may be short-term investments which represent funds set aside for future capital investment in the organisation. It may be that these should not be looked upon as being applicable to the payment of current liabilities and, accordingly, perhaps should be excluded from the calculation of the acid test ratio.

Receivables Ratio (alternatively called average collection period or receivables days)
This may be expressed as a percentage or as a number of days and is calculated as follows:

$$\frac{\text{Trade Receivables}}{\text{Credit Sales (VAT inclusive)}} \times 100\%$$

$$\frac{\text{Trade Receivables}}{\text{Credit Sales (VAT inclusive)}} \times 365$$

The trade receivables used may be a year-end figure or the average for the year. Where an average is used to calculate a number of days the ratio is the average number of days' credit taken by customers. Similarly, where separate credit sales figures are not available, then it may be necessary to use the total revenue figure. Whichever approach is adopted, it is important that it is applied consistently.

Where sales are seasonal in nature, it may be misleading to use the receivables figure at the accounting date. A more appropriate figure to use may be the average of the balances at the end of each month of the trading period. Where there has been a significant increase in sales towards the end of the period, the average of the opening and closing receivables balances of the trading period would reflect more accurately the substance of the situation. Otherwise, the receivables balances at the accounting date would be misleadingly high when compared to revenue.

An excessive receivables ratio is indicative of poor credit control or even a sign of **overtrading**. Furthermore, it may indicate that an excessive amount of money is tied up in receivables; this consideration being particularly serious in an atmosphere of high interest rates. If the receivables ratio is considered excessive, the receivables should be 'aged' in order to gain a clear picture as to the true liquidity of the receivables. For example, receivables may be analysed between those less than 30 days old, those between 31 and 60 days old, those between 61 and 90 days old and those over 90 days. The ageing process highlights the specific areas for more detailed consideration. For example, past experience may indicate those receivables that remain uncollected after 90 days are unlikely to be received.

For cash-based businesses such as supermarkets, receivables days are unlikely to exceed 1 as there are no true credit sales. Although this may vary slightly if a significant portion of customers pay by debit or credit card as there maybe a short delay before the business receives payment. For other businesses the result should be compared with the stated credit policy. Periods of 30 days or 'at the end of the month following delivery' are common credit terms.

Increasing receivables days is usually a bad sign as it suggests lack of proper credit control. However, it may be due to:
(a) a deliberate policy to extend the stated credit period to attract more trade; and
(b) one major new customer being allowed different terms.

Falling receivables days is usually a good sign, though it could indicate that the company is suffering a cash shortage. The receivables ratio can be distorted by:
(a) using year-end figures that do not represent average receivables;
(b) debt factoring, which results in very low receivables; and
(c) other credit finance agreements such as hire purchase, where there is insufficient analysis of revenue (HP receivables should be shown separately) to calculate proper ratios.

Trade Payables Ratio (alternatively called average payment period or payables days)
This ratio expresses in days the average length of credit taken by the business in settling its debts with suppliers. The formula is:

$$\frac{\textbf{Trade Payables}}{\textbf{Credit Purchases of Raw Materials (VAT inclusive)}} \times \textbf{365}$$

As with the receivables ratio considered above, with a seasonal or growing business some average rather than the accounting date balances should perhaps be used. Also, due to lack of analysis, it may be necessary to use total payables and total purchases figures. An average of trade payables may also be used. Where purchases are not known, cost of sales could be used.

If the receiver's ratio is too high, it may possibly imply a potential loss of goodwill and withdrawal of credit facilities from suppliers. It might also be indicative of liquidity problems.

The ratio is always compared to previous years. Once again there are two main contrasting points:
(a) a long credit period may be good as it represents a source of free finance; or
(b) a long credit period may indicate that the company is unable to pay more quickly because of liquidity problems.

Note that if the credit period is long:
(a) the company may develop a poor reputation as a slow payer and may not be able to find new suppliers;
(b) existing suppliers may decide to discontinue supplies; and
(c) the company may be losing out on worthwhile cash discounts.

3. *Efficiency*

Efficiency is the overall measure of the company's effective use of assets. The ratios that indicate the level of efficiency of management in utilising its assets are as follows: Return on Capital Employed; Revenue to Non-current Assets; Revenue to Net Current Assets; Inventory Turnover; and Non-current Assets to Total Assets.

Return on Capital Employed (ROCE) (Primary Ratio) The absolute figure of profit earned is not, in itself, significant since the size of the business earning that profit may vary enormously. It is significant to consider the size of the profit figure relative to the size of the business, size being expressed in terms of the quantity of capital employed by that business.

The ratio shows how efficiently a business is using its resources and, in general, an adequate return on capital employed is why the shareholders invest in the business. ROCE is a key ratio in assessing financial achievement. It reflects the earning power of the business operations. If the return is very low, the business may be better off realising its assets and investing the proceeds in a high interest bank account! (This may sound extreme, but should be considered, particularly for a small, unprofitable business with valuable assets such as freehold property.) Furthermore a low return can easily become a loss if the business suffers a downturn.

The ratio in simple form is:

$$\frac{\text{Profit}}{\text{Capital employed}} \times 100\%$$

There are a number of varying definitions of capital and of the appropriate profit to use in measuring the return. It is important to use the correct capital calculation with the relevant profit calculation. In general, the calculation is defined as above, albeit with alternative definitions of 'profit' and 'capital employed' as illustrated in **Table 35.1**.

TABLE 35.1: ROCE DEFINITIONS

Profit	Capital Employed
Profit before tax and interest	Gross assets = Non-current assets and current assets
Profit before tax and interest	Net assets = Gross assets less current liabilities
Profit after tax	Shareholders' capital = Total share capital and reserves
Profit after tax and preference dividends	Shareholders' equity capital = Ordinary share capital plus reserves

Which definition is used depends on the objective of the ratio. The first two would be used where one is interested in assessing the overall profitability of the business. Profit may be before or after tax. Profit after tax is a more accurate reflection of profits (management should seek to legitimately minimise tax); however, as deferred tax provisions are likely to be subjective, profit before tax may be more objective. The final two provide an indication of the return to shareholders. For example, the last one is more relevant for existing or prospective shareholders than management.

While the return on capital employed ratio is effective in revealing levels of performance, it does not provide us with an indication as to the reasons for an increase or decline in profitability. This may be indicated by a sub-division of the ROCE ratio into two ratios as follows:

Operating Profit ÷ Revenue *and* **Revenue ÷ Operating Assets Employed**

A change in the return on capital employed may be the result of a change in the profit per €1 of revenue or a change in the amount of revenue achieved per €1 invested. If there has been a significant change in the assets, it may be necessary to use an average figure rather than a year-end figure. Once calculated, ROCE should be compared with:

(a) *Previous years' figures* – provided there have been no changes in accounting policies, or suitable adjustments have been made to facilitate comparison (note however that the effect of not replacing non-current assets is that their value will decrease and ROCE will increase).

(b) *Company's target ROCE* – where the company's management has determined a target return as part of its budget procedure, consistent failure by a part of the business to meet the target may make it a target for disposal.

(c) *Cost of borrowings* – if the cost of borrowing is, say, 10% and ROCE 7%, then further borrowings will reduce EPS unless the extra money can be used in areas where the ROCE is higher than the cost of borrowings.

(d) *Other companies in same industry* – care is required in interpretation, since there may be:
   (i) different accounting policies (for example, research and development expenditure, inventory valuation and depreciation);
   (ii) different ages of plant, where assets are written down to low book values the ROCE will appear high; and
   (iii) leased assets, which may not appear in the statement of financial position at all.

Revenue to Tangible Non-current Assets This is calculated as follows:

$$\frac{\text{Revenue}}{\text{Tangible non-current assets}}$$

This ratio indicates the amount of revenue achieved for each €1 invested in non-current assets. A high ratio reveals an efficient utilisation of non-current assets. A low ratio indicates the opposite; perhaps suggesting that there is spare capacity and that consideration needs to be given to the disposal of excess assets. It is important to examine the industry which the entity operates within as this ratio will vary significantly from industry to industry. In a high manufacturing industry, this ratio is particularly important and the expectation is that this ratio would be high, indicating effective use of the non-current assets such as plant and machinery. Conversely, in a retail organisation such as a jeweller, this ratio is not so important.

It is also important to look at the depreciation history of the non-current assets involved as, in a situation where there are old assets stated at historical cost and heavily depreciated, one might have an unrealistically high ratio. Furthermore, if there are occasional valuations carried out (as opposed to regular valuations), trends will be distorted when the valuations take place.

Revenue to Net Current Assets This is calculated as follows:

$$\frac{\text{Revenue}}{\text{Net current assets}}$$

This ratio reveals how effectively the working capital is being utilised. A high ratio is normally indicative of a high level of efficiency. However, it could indicate liquidity problems as a result of over-trading. To examine this scenario, one would need to look at the growth of the company and take a subjective view as to how adequately the company is coping with the growth. As with the previous ratio, this is highly dependent on the industry, since retail companies may have very low receivables and inventory levels, generating significant sales per Euro of working capital.

Inventory Turnover This ratio is typically expressed as follows:

$$\frac{\text{Inventory}}{\text{Materials Cost of Sales}} \times 365$$

This ratio expresses in days, the amount of inventory in relation to cost of sales. In extreme circumstances, where one cannot obtain a cost of sales, the revenue figure is used. This should not, however, weaken any trend analysis undertaken, provided the same ratio is used consistently over the years. A low number of days indicates that management is able to turn over inventory efficiently. A high ratio may indicate poor inventory control, resulting in excessive inventories and thus an excessive investment therein, and perhaps also damaged or obsolete inventories. To investigate this further, this ratio should perhaps be examined in conjunction with the current ratio and the acid test ratio. Where inventories have built up abnormally at the accounting date, then an average inventory figure should be used.

An alternative format for this ratio is:

$$\frac{\text{Cost of Sales}}{\text{Inventory}} = \text{times p.a.}$$

This yields a multiple expressed as, say, 10 times per annum. While both formats are acceptable, it is often argued that the first format shown is more easily understood as it expresses the ratio in terms of the number of days for which inventory is held before being sold. Sometimes an average (based on the average inventory) is calculated, which has a smoothing effect but may dampen the effect of a major change in the period.

An increasing number of days (or a diminished multiple) implies that inventory is turning over less quickly. This is usually regarded as a bad sign as it may:
(a) reflect lack of demand for the goods;
(b) reflect poor inventory control, with its associated costs such as storage and insurance; and
(c) ultimately lead to inventory obsolescence and related write offs.

However, it may not necessarily be bad where:
(a) management is buying inventory in larger quantities to take advantage of trade discounts;
(b) management has increased inventory levels to avoid stock-outs; and
(c) the increase is slight and due to distortion of the ratio caused by comparing a year-end inventory figure with cost of sales for the year and that year has been one of increasing growth.

Inventory turnover ratios vary enormously with the nature of the business. For example, a fishmonger would have an inventory turnover period of 1 to 2 days, whereas a building contractor may have an inventory turnover period of 200 days. Manufacturing companies may have an inventory turnover ratio of 60 to 100 days; this period is likely to increase as the goods made become larger and more complex.

For large and complex items (for example, rolling stock or aircraft) there may be sharp fluctuations in inventory turnover according to whether delivery took place just before or just after the year-end. A manufacturer should take into consideration:

(a) reliability of suppliers – if the supplier is unreliable it is prudent to hold more raw materials; and

(b) demand – if demand is erratic it is prudent to hold more finished goods.

Non-current Assets to Total Assets This is calculated as follows:

$$\frac{\text{Non-current Assets}}{\text{Total Assets}}$$

Non-current assets generate profits and in a manufacturing industry a high ratio is desirable. Before any interpretation is placed on the ratio, the following factors should be borne in mind:

(a) investment in non-current assets depends on the nature of the business; a service industry would have much smaller non-current asset needs than a heavy manufacturing or engineering industry;

(b) the policy of the business with regard to leasing (particularly where leased assets are not accounted for under substance over form) (see **Chapter 1**, **Section 1.3** and **Chapter 8**) and hiring might influence the statement of financial position movements; and

(c) non-current assets are purchased with a view to future revenues; in the early stages of the life of a business, one might find high amounts invested in non-current assets. Therefore, it is important to always look at the stage of development of the company.

4. Growth

A company is usually considered to be growing if its revenue, profits and/or cash flows are increasing at a faster rate than those of the industry in which it is based and/or the overall economy. A growing company tends to have profitable reinvestment opportunities for its own retained earnings. Thus, it may pay little to no dividends to shareholders, opting to reinvest its profits back into the business. 'Growth' companies, which are most often seen in the technology-based industries, are expected to increase profits markedly in the future and thus the market bids up their share prices. This contrasts with 'mature' companies, such as diversified utility companies or traditional manufacturing companies, which have stable earnings with minimal growth.

In interpreting the extent of a company's growth, the following areas should be examined:

• revenue;
• profit before tax;
• non-current assets; and
• total capital employed.

Movement in any of these areas needs to be considered in conjunction with all of the other areas. For example, an increase in revenue may explain the increase in current assets (receivables) and hence capital employed.

5. Investment

Various users of financial statements require information for quite different purposes, and it is important that appropriate ratios are computed to suit the particular situation (i.e. question requirement). The following ratios are those an actual or potential investor might use in assessing a company for investment purposes: Earnings per Share; Earnings Yield; Dividend Yield; Dividend Cover; Price Earnings Ratio; Gearing Ratio; Debt Ratio; and Interest to Earnings Ratio. Each of those ratios will now be considered in turn.

Earnings per Share The calculation of EPS was covered in **Part IV**, **Chapter 23**. The EPS is used primarily as a measure of profitability, thus an increasing EPS is seen as a good sign. The EPS is also used to calculate the price earnings ratio which is dealt with below. The limitations of EPS include:

(a) In times of rising prices EPS will increase as profits increase. Thus any improvement in EPS should be viewed in the context of the effect of price level changes on the company's profits.

(b) Where there is a new share issue, the shares are included for, say, half of the year on the grounds that earnings will also increase for half of the year. However, in practice a new project does not begin generating normal returns immediately, so a new share issue is often accompanied by a decrease in EPS.

(c) EPS is dependent on an earnings figure which is a subjective measure. Some elements of that earnings figure are particularly subjective, such as the movements on provisions.

(d) EPS cannot be used as a basis of comparison between companies as the number of shares in issue in any particular company is not related to the amount of capital employed. For example, two companies may have the same amount of capital employed but one company has 100,000 €1 shares in issue and reserves of €4,900,000. Another company may have 5 million 50 cent shares in issue and reserves of €2,500,000. If earnings are the same, EPS is different.

(e) EPS is an historical figure based on historical accounts. This is a disadvantage where it is used for a forward looking figure such as the price earnings ratio (considered below).

(f) The fully diluted EPS (FDEPS) is a theoretical measure of the effect of dilution on the basic EPS. There is no evidence to suggest that even the most sophisticated analysts use the FDEPS. This is because of its hypothetical nature. However, the FDEPS should serve as a warning to equity shareholders that their future earnings will be affected by diluting factors. Thus notes in the accounts relating to convertible loan stock, convertible preference shares and share options should all be analysed carefully.

Earnings Yield This shows the return on the market price of a share. It is calculated as follows:

$$\frac{\text{Earnings per Share}}{\text{Market Price per Share}} \times 100$$

It is the reciprocal of the price earnings ratio, which is discussed below in detail.

Dividend Yield This shows the income return on an investment expressed as a percentage. It is calculated as follows:

$$\frac{\text{Gross Dividend per Share}}{\text{Market Price per Share}} \times 100$$

It allows for comparison between the return on an investment and the available return on investments in other shares, or in other forms of investment. The yield indicates the risks involved in the investment as estimated by the stock market. Where risks are said to be high, the investors will seek a high dividend yield to compensate for the risks. A low dividend yield means that the market accepts the low current return on its investment in anticipation of future expansion and profit growth. Overall, however, the yields will vary with the overall state of the stock market. Where share market prices are low, dividend yield will be high and vice versa.

Dividend Cover This is the relationship between available profits and the dividends payable out of the profits, the dividends being calculated on a maximum distribution basis. The profit figure is often adjusted to exclude non-trading profits and losses on the basis that the cover should relate to trading activities. This ratio indicates the number of times the ordinary dividend is covered by profits attributable to the ordinary shareholders. The formula is:

<u>**Profit after Taxation and Preference Dividend**</u>
Ordinary Dividend

It indicates potential for increased dividends in the future, assuming that current profits are maintained. It also shows to what level profits can decline before a reduction in dividends is enforced. However, it should be noted that, in anticipating future dividends, other factors, such as cash flow, capital structure and capital expenditure should be taken into account.

Note that the numerator profit figure is that which is available to the ordinary shareholders as a dividend and thus would be stated after non-controlling interests have been accounted for.

Price Earnings (P/E) Ratio This is the most widely referred to stock market ratio, also commonly described as an earnings multiple. It is calculated as the 'purchase of a number of years' earnings', but it represents the market's consensus of the future prospects of that share. This is the relationship between the market price of a share and the earnings per share. The formula is:

<u>**Market Price per Share**</u>
Earnings per Share

The P/E ratio shows the number of times' earnings a shareholder is willing to pay in order to purchase the shares. A high P/E ratio is indicative that the market has expectations of large growth potential for that company. Correspondingly the lower the P/E ratio, the lower the expected future growth for that company. As with dividend yield, the general level of P/E ratios on the stock market will be a reflection of the confidence of investors. Using the price earnings ratio, it is possible to compare companies, industries and even countries. For example, *The Financial Times* publishes P/E ratios for individual companies listed on the London Stock Exchange and for industry sectors. This allows an investor to judge the market rating of his share with that of other shares in the same industry. Although two organisations may have the same earnings per share, they may have different price earnings ratios due to a difference in share prices. This difference in share prices could be the result of any of the following factors:

(a) *Investors' opinion of current earnings* – if current earnings are considered to be rising in one company and constant in another, then the former company will be more likely to have a higher share price.

(b) *Dividend policy* – while one school of thought is that dividend policy has no effect on share price, another is that it is relevant to the valuation of a business. This latter view believes that: dividends remove uncertainty about the level of earnings and hence higher dividends raise share prices; and investors are more interested in short-term income as it is more certain than potential future long-term earnings which result in capital gains. Although tax considerations are also relevant since investors in high tax bands might prefer a business to retain earnings since this would reduce their tax liability (at least in the short term).

(c) *Risk factor* – this varies with the different types of industries involved. This could be due to such things as the locations in which a company operates and the climate, politics, market situation.

(d) *Market in the shares* – this is particularly pertinent in Ireland; shares with a restricted market would tend to have lower share prices than shares in a more free market.

(e) *Gearing* – a company with a high gearing (see below) can expect to have a lower price earnings ratio than one with a low gearing.

Another aspect of interpreting the P/E ratio is that a published EPS exists for a year and therefore the P/E ratio given in a newspaper is generally based on an increasingly out-of-date EPS. To give an extreme but simple example:

EXAMPLE 35.3: INTERPRETING THE P/E RATIO

For the year ended 31 December 2011, X plc had:
  (i) EPS = 10 cent;
 (ii) overall market P/E ratio = 10;
(iii) P/E ratio = 20 (because market expects above average growth);
 (iv) market price at 30 April 2012 (date of publication of previous year's accounts) = €2;
  (v) during 2012, X plc does even better than expected and by 29 April 2013 the share price is up to €3, therefore giving a P/E ratio of 30 (based on EPS for year ended 31 December 2011);
 (vi) year ended 31 December 2012, EPS = 15 cent, announced on 30 April 2013.

This is in line with expectations so share price is unchanged and P/E ratio drops again to 20 (€3/15 cent).

Gearing   This is calculated as follows:

$$\frac{\text{Total Debt}}{\text{Ordinary shareholders' funds, i.e. Equity}}$$

Note: total debt is the sum of the preference share capital, loan capital and short-term loans, and sometimes Total Capital Employed is used as the denominator, i.e. equity plus non-current liabilities.

'Gearing' is the relationship between a company's equity capital (known as residual return capital) and reserves and its fixed return capital. A company is *highly geared* if it has a substantial proportion of its capital in the form of preference shares or debentures or loan stock. A company is said to have *low gearing* if only a small proportion of its capital is in the form of preference shares, debentures or loan stock. A company financed entirely by equity shares has *no gearing*.

The importance of gearing can be illustrated by an example.

EXAMPLE 35.4: GEARING AND EPS

Two companies, A plc and B plc, both have capital of €10,000. A plc has it all in the form of equity shares of €1 each, B plc has 5,000 €1 equity shares and €5,000 of 10% debentures. Both companies earn profits of €5,000 in year 1 and €2,000 in year 2.

Tax is assumed at 35% and the dividend paid is 10 cent per share.

The capital position is therefore as follows:

	A plc €	B plc €
Shares	10,000	5,000
Debentures	–	5,000
	10,000	10,000

Requirement What is the EPS in each year?

Solution

	A plc Year 1 €	A plc Year 2 €	B plc Year 1 €	B plc Year 2 €
Profit before tax and debenture interest	5,000	2,000	5,000	2,000
Debenture interest	–	–	500	500
	5,000	2,000	4,500	1,500
Taxation (35%)	1,750	700	1,575	525
Earnings	3,250	1,300	2,925	975
Dividend (10%)	1,000	1,000	500	500
Retained profits	2,250	300	2,425	475
Earnings per share	32.5c	13c	58.5c	19.5c

The effects of gearing can be seen to be as follows:

(a) Debenture interest is an allowable deduction *before taxation*, whereas dividends are paid out of profits *after taxation*; B Plc has consistently higher retained profits than A Plc.

(b) Earnings of a highly geared company are more sensitive to profit changes. This is illustrated as follows:

	A plc	B plc
Change in profit before interest and taxation	−60%	−60%
Change in earnings	−60%	−66 2/3%

The reason for the fluctuation is obviously the element of debenture interest which must be paid regardless of profit level. This more than proportionate change in earnings is important in relation to the share price of the companies. Many investors value their shares by applying a multiple (known as the P/E ratio) to the earnings per share. Applying a multiple of, say, 10 to the EPS disclosed above would indicate share valuations as follows:

	A plc		B plc	
Year	1	2	1	2
Share price	€3.25	€1.30	€5.85	€1.95

Thus the share price of a highly geared company will often be more volatile than that of a company with only a small amount of gearing.

Not all companies are suitable for a highly geared structure. A company must have two fundamental characteristics if it is to use gearing successfully. These are as follows:

(a) *Relatively stable profits* Debenture interest must be paid whether or not profits are earned. A company with erratic profits may, in a bad year, have insufficient funds to pay debenture interest. This would result in the appointment of a receiver and possibly the liquidation of the company.

(b) *Suitable assets for security* Most issues of loan capital are secured on some or all of the company's assets which must be suitable for the purpose. A company with most of its capital invested in fast depreciating assets or inventory subject to rapid changes in demand and price would not be suitable for high gearing.

The classic examples of companies that are suited to high gearing are those in property investment and the hotel/leisure services industry. These companies generally enjoy relatively stable profits and have assets that are highly suitable for charging. Note that, nonetheless, these are industries that could be described as cyclical. Companies not suited to high gearing would include those in the extractive industries and high-tech industries where constant changes occur. These companies could experience erratic profits and would generally have inadequate assets to pledge as security.

Debt Ratio The debt ratio or gearing ratio appropriate to a particular business depends on the stability in value and realisability of the assets concerned. It may be calculated simply as:

$$\frac{\text{Total Debt}}{\text{Total Assets}}$$

Other methods commonly used for expressing gearing include:
(a) debt/equity ratio, calculated by taking:

$$\frac{\textbf{Loans} + \textbf{redeemable preference share capital}}{\textbf{Ordinary share capital} + \textbf{reserves} + \textbf{non-controlling interests}}$$

This is more sensitive than:

(b) percentage of capital employed represented by borrowings:

Loans + redeemable preference share capital
$$\overline{\text{Total capital}}$$

where total capital is loans, redeemable preference share capital, ordinary share capital and non-controlling interests.

Interest to Earnings Ratio (Interest Cover) The formula is as follows:

Profit before Interest and Taxation
$$\overline{\text{Loan Interest Paid and Payable}}$$

This formula gives an indication of the amount of coverage of the fixed interest requirements. It indicates the margin a company has available in the event of a downturn in earnings before it is unable to cover its fixed interest requirements.

6. *Cash Flow*

The preparation of a statement of cash flows is covered in **Chapter 19** and **Chapter 33** (IAS 7 *Statement of Cash Flows*). It is, therefore, only necessary at this point to consider what information this statement offers to the analyst. The statement enables us to see what the management has done with the cash coming in under its control. The general principles one is looking for are:

(a) long-term acquisitions should be covered by long-term funds;

(b) conversely, long-term funds raised (for example, share issues and loans) should be used for productive purposes (for example, non-current assets and acquisitions) and not allowed to lie about as excessive working capital; and

(c) working capital levels should be maintained. Some increase in working capital is necessary as inflation or growth necessitates increases in inventory holding and receivables financing.

Two useful ratios are:

Trading Cash Flow Ratio: $\dfrac{\textbf{Funds generated by operating activities}}{\textbf{Inventory}}$

This ratio highlights the ability of the company to generate sufficient funds from trading to cover its working capital requirements, payment of tax, dividends and loan service costs, without recourse to other inflows.

Net Cash Flow Ratio: $\dfrac{\textbf{Net Cash inflow/outflow before financing}}{\textbf{Revenue}}$

This ratio highlights the ability of the company to generate sufficient funds to meet any loan repayments and to finance future developments.

Bear in mind that a published statement of cash flows covers a whole year and may not reveal critical points of cash shortage that may have arisen during the year, particularly for a company engaged in a seasonal trade. It is, therefore, appropriate for companies to prepare cash forecasts showing the movements of cash over shorter periods, perhaps months or even weeks.

35.4 FINANCIAL BALANCE AND OVERTRADING

The previous section explained the calculation of a number of key ratios. It is important that these ratios are not viewed in isolation and that the overall picture presented is taken into account. Two significant features that should be considered are financial balance and overtrading. These are now explained below.

Financial Balance

Financial balance is the balance between the various forms of available finance relative to the requirements of the business. A business must have a *sufficient level of long-term capital* to finance its long-term investment in non-current assets. Part of the investment in current assets would also be financed by relatively permanent capital with the balance being provided by trade credit and other short-term borrowings. Any expansion in activity will normally require a broadening of the long-term capital base, without which 'overtrading' may develop (see below). *Suitability of finance* is also a key factor. A permanent expansion of a company's activities should not be financed by temporary, short-term borrowings. A short-term increase in activity such as the 'January sales' in a retail trading company could ideally be financed by an overdraft.

A major addition to non-current assets, such as the construction of a new factory, would not normally be financed on a long-term basis by an overdraft. It might be found, however, that the expenditure was temporarily financed by short-term loans until construction was completed, when the overdraft would be 'funded' by a long-term borrowing secured on the completed building.

Overtrading

Overtrading arises where a company expands its turnover fairly rapidly without securing additional long-term capital adequate for its needs. The symptoms of overtrading are:
- inventory increasing, possibly more than proportionately to sales;
- receivables increasing, possibly more than proportionately to sales;
- cash and liquid assets declining at a fairly alarming rate; and
- payables increasing rapidly.

The above symptoms simply imply that the company has expanded without giving proper thought to the necessity to expand its capital base. It has consequently continued to rely on its payables, and probably its bank overdraft, to provide the additional finance required. It will reach a stage where payables will withhold further supplies and bankers will refuse to honour further cheques until borrowings are reduced. The problem is that borrowings cannot be reduced until sales revenue is earned, which in turn cannot be achieved until production is completed, which in turn is dependent upon materials being available and wages paid. The overall result is deadlock and rapid financial collapse!

This is a particularly difficult stage for any small- to medium-sized company. They have reached a stage in their life when conventional creditor and overdraft facilities are being stretched to the maximum, but they are probably too small to manage flotation. In many cases, by proper planning, the company can arrange fixed-term loan funding from the bank rather than relying exclusively on overdraft finance.

35.5 ACCOUNTING POLICIES AND THE LIMITATIONS OF RATIO ANALYSIS

Ratio analysis is not an exact science; while a useful analytical tool, it arguably does not provide 'answers' and only highlights areas that may require further investigation. When analysing and interpreting the financial statements of a business, it is important to bear in mind that different companies can legitimately adopt alternative accounting policies for similar items and the limitations of ratio analysis. These two issues are now discussed below.

The Effect of Choice of Accounting Policies

Where accounting standards allow alternative treatment of items in the accounts, the accounting policy note should declare which policy has been chosen (see **Chapter 8** – IAS 8 *Accounting Policies, Changes in Accounting Estimates and Errors*). The accounting policy should then be applied consistently.

Changing accounting policies can have a radical effect on the results of a company. A change in accounting policy is treated as a prior period adjustment (see **Chapter 8**). The problem with this situation is that the directors may be able to manipulate the results of a company through changes of accounting policy.

The effect of such a change is very short-term. Most analysts and sophisticated users will discount its effect immediately, except to the extent that it will affect any dividend (because of the possible effect on distributable profits).

Limitations of Ratio Analysis

(a) Unless ratios are calculated in a uniform manner, from uniform data, comparisons can be very misleading.

(b) The accounting periods covered by the financial statements may not reflect representative financial positions. It must be remembered that a 'balance sheet' is a statement of financial position. It indicates the state of affairs at a particular point in time. Abnormal accounting date figures will distort any ratios produced. Additionally, any 'window dressing' techniques will distort the statement of financial position. In such circumstances, a statement of financial position drawn up a short period before or after the accounting date might reveal a much different situation, particularly in the current area of the statement of financial position. Therefore, it is important to always look at events prior to and after the reporting date and, if necessary, use average figures to compute the ratios. Many businesses produce accounts to a date on which there are relatively low amounts of trading activity. Retail organisations often have an end of February accounting date (after the peak pre-Christmas trading and the January sales). As a result, the items on a statement of financial position are not representative of the items throughout the accounting period.

(c) Financial statements themselves have limitations as they contain arbitrary estimates and figures that are based on personal decisions.

(d) The application of accounting policies in the preparation of financial statements must be understood when attempting to interpret financial ratios. Ratios are only comparable when the figures used therein are computed in the same manner from year to year or from firm to firm. Therefore any changes in accounting policies by firms that are being compared will render the ratios incomparable.

(e) The earning power of a business may well be affected by factors that are not reflected in the financial statements. Thus, these do not necessarily represent a complete picture of a business but only a collection of those parts which can be translated into money terms; for example, the size of the order book is normally ignored in financial statements. Ratios are only a guide and should be used in conjunction with a subjective viewpoint:

• What are the future plans of the company?
• What is the lifecycle of the product?
• What customer profile does the company have?
• What is the market share the company occupies?
• Is the business a high-risk type or in a relatively stable industry?

(f) Ratios must not be used as the sole test of efficiency. Concentration on ratios may inhibit the incentive to grow and expand, to the detriment of the long-term interests of the company. Favourable trends in ratios may not be examined any further. However, this may well be a short-sighted view, and the current performance may be at the expense of long-term strategic performance. All movements in ratios need to be examined and all underlying reasons explained.

(g) A few simple ratios do not provide an automatic means of running a company. Business problems usually involve complex patterns that cannot be solved solely by the use of ratios. Ratios do not provide control; they merely indicate where controls are flawed and highlight areas for improvement. Therefore, it is important to analyse ratios carefully as it is only by investigation that the weak controls are identified.

Ratio analysis is susceptible to the same underlying weaknesses and economic factors as accounts themselves. For example, in times of high inflation, capital employed may be understated and cost of sales may be understated, resulting in overstated profits. Thus, one would be relating overstated profits to understated capital employed. The result could be a significant overstatement of return. On this basis, it is important to comment on any economic factors affecting the entity and highlight the impact they have on the ratios.

35.6 CONCLUSION

Ratio analysis is an important and interesting topic, particularly because it can help to reveal so much about the performance of a business. For example: how profitable a business is; whether a business has sufficient resources to pay its creditors; or whether a business is doing better or worse than its competitors. **Section 35.3** illustrates and explains a number of fundamental ratios. However, ratios are simply one number divided by another and as such they may or may not be informative. Moreover, of the myriad ratios that could be generated, some will be more meaningful than others. The key is the way in which ratios are analysed and applied, and being able to 'take a step back' from the individual numbers to form an overall picture of how the business is performing. It is not uncommon for ratios to be contradictory, with some indicators being positive and others less so. A good strategy is to compare the ratios to some sort of benchmark, such as a similar company (if available), industry averages or to how the company has performed in the past.

While a popular choice, students often do not score well on questions dealing with the analysis and interpretation of financial information. As a poor examination technique is a common issue, it may be helpful to approach such examination questions in the following manner:

1. Read the question and identify from what viewpoint the report has to be prepared (for example, existing or potential investor, bank manager, supplier etc.).
2. Prepare a schedule of ratios with two or three main ratios for each key area (calculations should be included in an appendix and not the main body of the report).
3. Address the ratios and link any trends (for example, low inventory turnover with low acid test ratio).
4. Write the commentary, considering the format and include a limitations caveat.
5. Include any assumptions made.

Common mistakes in analysis and interpretation questions include:
- too much time devoted to the calculations and too many ratios calculated;
- insufficient commentary as a result of time wasted on calculations;
- irrelevant ratios calculated and used;
- not reading question properly to identify the interested party (for example, bank manager, company management, investor);
- calculations and commentary mixed – calculations should be kept in supporting schedules/ appendices;
- the report merely restates the data rather than drawing conclusions from the ratios; and
- failure to deliver on the requirements of the question (for example, if asked for memorandum, do not write a letter).

SUMMARY OF LEARNING OBJECTIVES

After having studied this chapter on the analysis and interpretation of financial information, you should be able to:

Learning Objective 1 Discuss who are the primary users of ratio analysis.

These include: managers and directors of the company who are likely to be concerned about all aspects of the company; shareholders or potential investors who will be concerned primarily with the investment ratios, although certain financial stability and profitability measures are also likely to be of interest; and creditors who are most likely to be concerned about financial stability, although a bank, acting as a major source of finance, will usually also look at profitability.

Learning Objective 2 Demonstrate an understanding of when ratio analysis should be used.

Ratio analysis can be used to assess whether a company is performing well or badly, or financially strong or financially vulnerable. Internally, ratios can be used to compare past performance and actual results against budgets and forecasts. Externally, ratios may be used to compare similar entities at the same stage of development and entities within the same industry.

Learning Objective 3 Explain the limitations of ratio analysis.

This includes: consistency of accounting figures, policies and reporting dates; window dressing; lifecycle of the firm; and the age of assets.

Learning Objective 4 Select and calculate the main ratios and statistics commonly used in interpreting accounts.

Ratios can be classified or divided into many different categories. For example: Profitability; Liquidity; Efficiency; Growth; Investment; and Cash Flow.

Learning Objective 5 Identify and evaluate significant features and issues in financial statements, including financial balance and overtrading.

Financial balance is the balance between the various forms of available finance relative to the requirements of the business and overtrading arises where a company expands its turnover fairly rapidly without securing additional long-term capital adequate for its needs.

Learning Objective 6 Highlight inconsistencies in financial information through analysis and the application of ratios.

For example, this might be as a result of changes in accounting policy, including the way in which certain figures are calculated and presented.

Learning Objective 7 Make inferences from the analysis of information, taking into account the limitations of the information, the analytical methods used and the business environment in which the entity operates.

For example, whether a company is performing well or badly, or is financially strong or financially vulnerable.

Learning Objective 8 Produce reports that critically analyse and interpret results over time or between activities tailored to the technical understanding of the different user groups.

The various users of financial statements require information for quite different purposes. While **Section 35.3** outlines a number of ratios, not all will be relevant to every situation. It is therefore important to determine the precise information needs of the user and the decisions that have to be taken after analysing the relevant information. For example: shareholders or potential investors are likely to be concerned primarily with the investment ratios, although certain financial stability and profitability measures are also likely to be of interest; and creditors are most likely to be concerned about financial stability, although a bank, acting as a major source of finance, will usually also look at profitability.

QUESTIONS

Self-test Questions

1. When is ratio analysis used?
2. What are the limitations of ratio analysis?
3. Name the main categories of ratio analysis.
4. How should one-time charges be treated in ratio analysis?
5. Who are the primary users of ratio analysis?

Review Questions

(See **Appendix One** for Suggested Solutions to Review Questions.)

Question 35.1

DUL Limited is a small manufacturing company which commenced trading in 1986. The Managing Director, Mr Evans, is of the opinion that the company is performing extremely well in a period of high inflation and recession. However, the company's bankers are concerned at the high level of overdraft, and Mr Evans has engaged you, as Management Consultant, to report on the company's performance. The following information is made available to you:

SUMMARISED STATEMENTS OF PROFIT OR LOSS AND OTHER COMPREHENSIVE INCOME
for the Years Ended 30 June

	2010 €000	2011 €000	2012 €000
Revenue	100	140	196
Profit before interest	11	13	14
Interest	5	7	9
Profit before tax	6	6	5
Income tax expense	2	2	3
Retained profits	4	4	2

SUMMARISED STATEMENTS OF FINANCIAL POSITION
as at 30 June

	2010 €000	2011 €000	2012 €000
Assets			
Non-current assets	40	56	78
Current assets			
Inventories	20	28	39
Receivables	20	28	43
	40	56	82
Total assets	80	112	160

Equity and Liabilities
Equity

Share capital	15	15	15
Retained earnings	10	14	16
	25	29	31
Non-current liabilities			
Deferred taxation	3	5	8
Current liabilities			
Payables	10	28	57
Bank overdraft	42	50	64
	52	78	121
Total equity and liabilities	80	112	160

Requirement You are required, on the basis of the information supplied, to prepare a report for the Managing Director of DUL Limited, commenting upon the performance and financial position of the company.

Question 35.2

You are the Management Accountant of Fry plc. Laurie plc is a competitor in the same industry and it has been operating for two years. Summaries of Laurie plc's statements of profit or loss and other comprehensive income and statements of financial position for the previous three years are given below.

SUMMARISED STATEMENTS OF PROFIT OR LOSS AND OTHER COMPREHENSIVE INCOME
for the Years Ended 31 December

	2010	2011	2012
	€m	€m	€m
Revenue	840	981	913
Cost of sales	(554)	(645)	(590)
Gross profit	286	336	323
Selling, distribution and administration expenses	(186)	(214)	(219)
Profit before interest	100	122	104
Interest	(6)	(15)	(19)
Profit before taxation	94	107	85
Income tax expense	(45)	(52)	(45)
Profit after taxation	49	55	40

SUMMARISED STATEMENTS OF FINANCIAL POSITION
as at 31 December

	2010	2011	2012
	€m	€m	€m
Assets			
Non-current assets			
Property, plant and equipment at net book value	176	206	216
Intangible assets	36	40	48
	212	246	264

Current assets			
Inventories	237	303	294
Receivables	105	141	160
Bank	52	58	52
	394	502	506
Total Assets	606	748	770
Equity and Liabilities			
Equity			
Ordinary share capital	100	100	100
Retained profits	299	330	346
	399	430	446
Non-current liabilities			
Long-term loans	74	138	138
Current liabilities			
Trade payables	53	75	75
Other payables	80	105	111
	133	180	186
Total Equity and Liabilities	606	748	770

During each of the years ended 31 December 2010, 2011 and 2012, €24m was debited to equity in respect of dividends. You may assume that the index of retail prices has remained constant between 2010 and 2012.

Requirement Write a report for the Finance Director of Fry plc which analyses the performance of Laurie plc, showing any calculations in an appendix to the report.

Question 35.3

Limetree Limited was founded by Cindy and Eugene Lemmon in 2005. The company manufactures and distributes luxury soft furnishings to the retail trade in Ireland. In common with many start-ups, the company encountered some financial difficulty in the early years. However, with the support of its bank it has managed to grow and prosper. Its revenue and profitability levels have increased each year since 2006, helped by the demand for new houses. The company prepares its accounts to 30 June each year. Operating results and statements of financial position to 30 June 2012 and 2013 are shown in Appendix 1. The year to 30 June 2013 was the first year since start-up that the company experienced a fall in demand, caused by the slump in demand for houses during the year.

The company's bank manager has been receiving the monthly accounts since December 2012, when the overdraft limit of €400,000 was breached. He has asked to see the year's accounts to 30 June 2013 by the end of July in order to assess the overall financial position of the company.

You are given the following financial indicators for companies operating in the same industry as Limetree:

- Operating gearing   7.5 (the percentage of fixed costs relative to total costs)
- Debt/Equity   65%
- Return on Equity   14% (Profit after tax/Equity)
- Dividend Cover   2 (Profit after tax/Dividends)
- Interest Cover   3 (Operating profit/interest)

Requirement

(a) Calculate, in respect of Limetree, the same indicators as are set out above for the industry for the years to 30 June 2012 and 2013.
(b) Using the results of your answer at (a), and from a review of the information available in **Appendix I**:
   (i) identify matters that may be of concern to the bank manager, giving reasons for your answer;
   (ii) outline the points you would make to the bank manager in support of the company's financial performance and position.

Note: some issues to consider:

- What economic factors might impact upon the company's line of business?
- What is the company's future outlook, relationship with its bank and track record?

APPENDIX I
Limetree Limited
SUMMARISED OPERATING RESULTS

	30 June 2013 €000	30 June 2012 €000
Revenue	7,640	8,000
Cost of sales		
Materials	(1,240)	(1,380)
Labour	(2,530)	(2,550)
Overheads	(990)	(950)
	(4,760)	(4,880)
Gross Profit	2,880	3,120
Selling and Distribution	(685)	(640)
Administration	(1,880)	(1,910)
Operating Profit	315	570
Interest	(134)	(94)
Profit before tax	181	476
Income tax expense @ 40%	(72)	(190)
Profit after tax	109	286

Limetree Limited
STATEMENT OF FINANCIAL POSITION

	30 June 2013 €000	30 June 2012 €000
Assets		
Non-Current Assets	969	843
Current Assets		
Inventories	1,010	824
Receivables	1,210	1,180
	2,220	2,004
Total Assets	3,189	2,847
Equity and Liabilities		
Equity		
Share capital and premium	350	300
Retained earnings	749	650
	1,099	950
Non-Current Liabilities		
Long-term loan from bank	500	500
Current Liabilities		
Payables	1,064	847
Taxation	72	190
Bank overdraft	454	360
	1,590	1,397
Total Equity and Liabilities	3,189	2,847

During the years ended 30 June 2012 and 2013, €60,000 and €10,000 respectively was debited to equity in respect of dividends.

Question 35.4

The details given below are a summary of the statements of financial position of six public companies engaged in different industries.

	A	B	C	D	E	F
Assets						
Land and other buildings	10	2	26	24	57	5
Other non-current assets	17	1	34	-	13	73
Inventories and work-in-progress	44	-	22	55	16	1
Trade receivables	6	77	15	4	1	13
Other receivables	11	-	-	8	2	5
Cash and investments	12	20	3	9	11	3
	100	100	100	100	100	100
Equity and Liabilities						
Capital and reserves	37	5	62	58	55	50
Non-current Liabilities	12	5	4	13	6	25
Current Liabilities						

Trade payables	32	85	34	14	24	6
Other payables	16	5	-	14	15	11
Bank overdraft	3	-	-	1	-	8
	100	100	100	100	100	100

The activities of each company are as follows:
1. Operator of a chain of retail supermarkets.
2. Sea ferry operator.
3. Property investor and house builder. Apart from supplying managers, including site management, for the house building side of its operations this company completely subcontracts all building work.
4. A vertically integrated company in the food industry, which owns farms, flour mills, bakeries and retail outlets.
5. Commercial bank with a network of branches.
6. Contractor in the civil engineering industry.

Note: no company employs off-balance sheet finance such as leasing.

Requirement
(a) State which of the above activities relate to which set of statement of financial position details, giving a brief summary of your reasoning in each case. (No marks will be awarded for matching where no explanation is given.)
(b) What do you consider to be the major limitations of ratio analysis as a means of interpreting accounting information?

Challenging Questions

(Suggested Solutions to Challenging Questions are available to lecturers.)

Question 35.1 *(Based on Chartered Accountants Ireland, P3 Summer 1996, Question 3)*

The summarised statement of profit or loss and other comprehensive income of HOTPOT plc for the year ended 31 December 2012 and statement of financial position as at that date are as follows:

SUMMARISED STATEMENT OF PROFIT OR LOSS AND OTHER COMPREHENSIVE INCOME
for the Year Ended 31 December 2012

	Notes	€000
Revenue		4,020
Cost of sales	(1)	(2,110)
Gross profit		1,910
Distribution costs		(320)
Administrative expenses	(1)	(500)
Operating profit		1,090
Interest paid		(300)
Income tax expense		(360)
Net profit after taxation		430

STATEMENT OF FINANCIAL POSITION
as at 31 December

	Notes	2012 €000	2011 €000
Assets			
Non-current assets			
Property, plant and equipment	(2)	9,470	7,420
Current assets			
Inventory		850	750
Receivables		2,275	1,980
Cash in hand and at bank		175	580
		3,300	3,310
Total Assets		12,770	10,730
Equity and Liabilities			
Equity			
Called up share capital (€1 ordinary shares)	(4)	1,200	1,000
Share premium account		535	660
Retained profits		3,380	3,150
		5,115	4,810
Non-current liabilities	(5)	4000	2,000
		9,115	6,810
Current liabilities	(3)	3,655	3,920
Total Equity and Liabilities		12,770	10,730

Additional Information

(1) Cost of sales includes wages and salaries of €480,000. Administrative expenses include wages and salaries of €348,000 and unrecoverable debts of €62,000.

	2012 €000	€000	2011 €000	€000
(2) Property, plant and equipment				
Land and buildings at cost		4,840		3,070
Less: Accumulated depreciation		660		510
Plant, machinery and equipment at cost		4,180		2,560
Less: Accumulated depreciation	15,140		14,510	
	9,850	5,290	9,650	4,860
		9,470		7,420

During the year, plant which had originally cost €1,460,000, and on which accumulated depreciation of €712,000 had been provided, was sold for €700,000.

(3) Current liabilities

	2012 €000	2011 €000
Bank overdraft	2,000	1,300
Payables	1,214	1,382
Taxation	320	1,150

PAYE and PRSI/NIC	41	28
Dividends	80	60
	3,655	3,920

(4) The company made a rights issue of 1 for 20 at €1.50 per share payable in full on 1 January 2012. On 1 April 2012, a bonus issue of 1 for 7 was made.

(5) On 1 January 2012, the company issued a further €2,000,000 mortgage debentures. Interest was paid on all debentures on 30 June and 31 December 2012.

(6) During the year ended 31 December 2012, €200,000 was debited to equity in respect of dividends.

Requirement Using only the common information provided above:

(a) Calculate for HOTPOT plc for 2011 and 2012:
  (i) The current ratio and the acid test ratio; and
  (ii) TWO alternative gearing ratios.

(b) Explain the significance of the gearing ratio in analysing the accounts of a business, and set out your reasons for selecting the methods of calculation you have used in (a) above.

(c) Draft a brief report for the management of HOTPOT plc, commenting on the liquidity and gearing of the company at 31 December 2012 as compared with the previous year.

Question 35.2 (Based on Chartered Accountants Ireland, P3 Summer 1995, Question 1)

The following draft accounts have been prepared for DOLAN plc for the year ended 31 December 2012:

SUMMARISED STATEMENTS OF PROFIT OR LOSS AND OTHER COMPREHENSIVE INCOME
for the Years Ended 31 December

	2012 €000	2012 €000	2011 €000	2011 €000
Revenue		24,350	16,000	23,100
Purchases	16,100			
Inventory movement	350	16,450	(400)	15,600
Gross profit		7,900		7,500
Depreciation	100		85	
Other operating expenses	6,400		6,365	
Finance costs	300	6,800	250	6,700
Net profit before tax		1,100		800
Income tax expense		(300)		(200)
Net profit after tax		800		600

STATEMENTS OF FINANCIAL POSITION
as at 31 December

	2012 €000	2011 €000
Assets		
Non-current assets	5,750	4,300
Inventories	3,150	3,500

Trade receivables	3,600	3,200
Bank	650	-
	13,150	11,000
Equity and Liabilities		
Share capital	4,000	4,000
Revaluation reserve	1,000	-
Retained earnings	680	380
10% debentures	3,000	2,500
Bank overdraft	-	450
Trade payables	3,600	3,000
Taxation	370	270
Dividends	500	400
Total equity and liabilities	13,150	11,000

During the years ended 31 December 2011 and 2012, €400,000 and €500,000 were debited to equity in respect of dividends paid.

Requirement Prepare a *brief* report for the Board of DOLAN plc on the performance of the company during 2012 as compared with the previous year. You should include in your report a schedule of appropriate ratios.

Question 35.3 *(Based on Chartered Accountants Ireland, P3 Summer 1992, Question 2)*

SWIZZLE Limited produces a range of alcoholic and soft drinks and also owns a number of public houses and inns. The company's latest published accounts have been summarised as follows:

SUMMARISED STATEMENTS OF PROFIT OR LOSS AND OTHER COMPREHENSIVE INCOME
for the Years Ended 31 December

	2012	2011
	€000	€000
Revenue	10,800	8,600
Operating profit	1,405	1,032
Income from other non-current asset investments	43	31
Finance costs	(470)	(260)
Profit before taxation	978	803
Income tax expense	(298)	(203)
Profit for the year	680	600

STATEMENTS OF FINANCIAL POSITION
as at 31 December

	2012	2011
	€000	€000
Assets		
Non-current assets		
Property, plant and equipment	14,180	8,120
Investments	480	350

	14,660	8,470
Current assets	1,970	1,650
Total Assets	16,630	10,120
Equity and Liabilities		
Equity		
Ordinary Share Capital €1	1,200	800
Share premium	510	300
Revaluation reserve	3,500	-
Retained profits	4,970	4,540
	10,180	5,640
Non-current liabilities	4,220	2,360
Current liabilities	2,230	2,120
Total Equity and Liabilities	16,630	10,120

The notes to the accounts state that the company revalued its non-industrial properties on 31 December 2012. It is company policy not to provide depreciation on these properties, but to maintain them out of revenue expenditure to a standard that ensures their estimated aggregate realisable value exceeds their net book amounts. During year ended 31 December 2011 and 2012, €200,000 and €250,000 were debited to equity in respect of dividends.

Requirement Prepare a report for the Managing Director of SWIZZLE Limited on the financial performance of the company during 2012. Insofar as the information provided permits, your report should include appropriate ratios and be presented under the following main headings:
(a) Profitability;
(b) Assets utilisation;
(c) Solvency; and
(d) Gearing.

Question 35.4 (*Based on Chartered Accountants Ireland, CAP 2 Autumn 2009, Question 4*)

KING plc (KING) owns a number of subsidiaries, one of which is THRONE plc (THRONE) in which it has an 80% stake. In terms of KING's portfolio of investments, THRONE represents a relatively minor investment and the company operates independently, with little or no interference from KING.

As assistant to KING's finance director, you have been asked to analyse the performance of THRONE because each of KING's investments will be reviewed at the next meeting of the board of directors. THRONE has provided the following information with respect to its 2012 activities.

THRONE
STATEMENT OF PROFIT OR LOSS AND OTHER COMPREHENSIVE INCOME
for the Year Ended 31 December

	2012	2011
	€000	€000
Revenue	565	440
Cost of sales	(190)	(176)

Gross profit	375	264
Net operating expenses	(120)	(89)
Profit from operations	255	175
Interest expense	(16)	(10)
	239	165
Income tax expense	(46)	(34)
Net profit from operations	193	131

THRONE
STATEMENT OF FINANCIAL POSITION
as at 31 December

	2012	2011
	€000	€000
Non-current Assets		
Property, plant and equipment	765	750
Intangible assets	310	65
	1,075	815
Current Assets		
Inventory	55	30
Trade receivables	48	100
Bank and cash	38	90
	141	220
	1,216	1,035
EQUITY AND LIABILITIES		
Capital and Reserves		
€1 ordinary shares	375	375
Share premium	125	125
Revaluation reserve	40	40
Retained earnings	450	300
	990	840
Non-current Liabilities – Loans	146	100
Current Liabilities – Trade payables	80	95
	1,216	1,035

Additional Information:
1. All of THRONE's sales and purchases are on credit.
2. THRONE's share price at 31 December 2011 and 31 December 2012 was 110 cent and 165 cent respectively.
3. During the year ended 31 December 2011 and 31 December 2012, THRONE paid ordinary dividends of €20,000 and €40,000 respectively.

Requirement Prepare a *report* for KING's finance director which analyses the performance of THRONE during the year ended 31 December 2012 and identifies any further information required to complete the analysis.

Question 35.5 (Based on Chartered Accountants Ireland, CAP 2 Autumn 2010, Question 4)

The retail grocery trade in Ireland has undergone significant change in recent years with the growth in large grocery multiples and the decline of independent retailers. One of your firm's clients that is involved in the retail grocery trade in Ireland, GEORGE Limited ("GEORGE"), has requested that you evaluate the performance of two of its main competitors, JOHN Limited ("JOHN") and PAUL Limited ("PAUL").

Details of market share in the sector for 2012 are provided in **Table 1**.

TABLE 1: 2012 IRISH RETAIL GROCERY MARKET SHARE

	%
JOHN	28
PAUL	27
GEORGE	18
RINGO Limited	17
Other independent retailers	10
	100

Information on the growth profiles of JOHN and PAUL since 2000 is provided in **Table 2**.

TABLE 2: GROWTH PROFILES

	2000	2004	2008	2012
JOHN:				
Number of stores	210	260	285	315
Average store size (square metres)	12,850	15,100	19,300	24,400
PAUL:				
Number of stores	550	460	380	400
Average store size (square metres)	11,250	16,100	21,750	26,450

Summary financial information for JOHN and PAUL is provided in **Table 3** and **Table 4** respectively.

TABLE 3: JOHN – SUMMARY FINANCIAL INFORMATION

STATEMENT OF PROFIT OR LOSS AND OTHER COMPREHENSIVE INCOME for the Year Ended 31 December					
	2008	2009	2010	2011	2012
	€m	€m	€m	€m	€m
Sales	4,790	5,660	6,930	7,815	8,700
Cost of sales	(4,400)	(5,165)	(6,300)	(7,050)	(7,825)
Gross profit	390	495	630	765	875
Operating expenses	(112)	(125)	(160)	(210)	(250)
Operating profit	278	370	470	555	625

Interest received	50	60	80	80	120
Finance costs	(25)	(55)	(95)	(115)	(105)
Profit before tax	303	375	455	520	640
Income tax	(110)	(125)	(140)	(165)	(185)
Profit after tax	193	250	315	355	455

STATEMENT OF FINANCIAL POSITION
at 31 December

	2008	2009	2010	2011	2012
	€m	€m	€m	€m	€m
ASSETS					
Non-current Assets					
Property	1,290	1,800	2,120	2,490	3,000
Plant and equipment	455	540	615	725	835
Investments	65	30	20	20	30
	1,810	2,370	2,755	3,235	3,865
Current Assets					
Inventory	240	285	310	360	360
Trade receivables	30	75	90	115	80
Other receivables	10	35	50	25	220
Bank and cash	70	90	140	110	175
	2,160	2,855	3,345	3,845	4,700
EQUITY and LIABILITIES					
Equity	1,025	1,170	1,405	1,675	2,640
Non-current Liabilities					
Loans	430	835	965	850	815
Other	20	10	15	220	25
Current Liabilities					
Trade payables	380	440	480	555	580
Other	305	400	480	545	640
	2,160	2,855	3,345	3,845	4,700
Dividends paid	60	75	90	115	160

TABLE 4: PAUL – SUMMARY FINANCIAL INFORMATION

STATEMENT OF PROFIT OR LOSS AND OTHER COMPREHENSIVE INCOME
for the Year Ended 31 December

	2008	2009	2010	2011	2012
	€m	€m	€m	€m	€m
Sales	4,120	4,720	5,400	6,345	7,095
Cost of sales	(3,815)	(4,340)	(4,950)	(5,790)	(6,435)
Gross profit	305	380	450	555	660

Operating expenses	(95)	(105)	(100)	(140)	(180)
Operating profit	210	275	350	415	480
Interest received	35	40	55	70	125
Finance costs	(20)	(40)	(45)	(55)	(60)
Profit before tax	225	275	360	430	545
Income tax	(75)	(90)	(110)	(135)	(150)
Profit after tax	150	185	250	295	395

STATEMENT OF FINANCIAL POSITION
at 31 December

	2008 €m	2009 €m	2010 €m	2011 €m	2012 €m
ASSETS					
Non-current Assets					
Property	875	1,035	1,320	2,150	2,770
Plant and equipment	540	685	835	715	780
Investments	-	-	5	5	5
	1,415	1,720	2,160	2,870	3,555
Current Assets					
Inventory	180	190	215	230	220
Trade receivables	40	25	20	50	35
Other receivables	10	5	5	205	300
Bank and cash	25	80	25	300	40
	1,670	2,020	2,425	3,655	4,150
EQUITY and LIABILITIES					
Equity	865	1,030	1,255	2,160	2,445
Non-current Liabilities					
Loans	305	300	345	525	690
Other	60	75	90	20	55
Current Liabilities					
Trade payables	285	330	405	450	500
Other	155	285	330	500	460
	1,670	2,020	2,425	3,655	4,150
Dividends paid	40	55	65	95	120

Requirement Prepare a *report* for the directors of GEORGE that evaluates the performance of JOHN and PAUL.

Question 35.6

You are given the following summarised financial statements of Holly plc, which is a competitor of your company.

SUMMARISED STATEMENTS OF PROFIT OR LOSS AND OTHER COMPREHENSIVE INCOME
for the Years Ended 31 December

	2009 €m	2010 €m	2011 €m	2012 €m
Revenue	35,100	39,000	41,700	42,900
Cost of sales	(22,800)	(25,800)	(28,200)	(30,300)
Gross profit	12,300	13,200	13,500	12,600
Distribution costs	1,800	2,100	2,400	3,000
Administration costs	5,400	5,700	6,900	5,700
	(7,200)	(7,800)	(9,300)	(8,700)
Operating profit	5,100	5,400	4,200	3,900
Interest	(150)	(600)	(1,200)	1,500
Profit before taxation	4,950	4,800	3,000	2,400
Income tax expense	(750)	(150)	(300)	(450)
Profit after taxation	4,200	4,650	2,700	1,950

SUMMARISED STATEMENTS OF FINANCIAL POSITION
as at 31 December

	2009 €m	2010 €m	2011 €m	2012 €m
Assets				
Non-Current Assets	4,596	6,672	8,586	8,268
Current assets				
Inventories	4,800	5,400	5,100	4,500
Receivables	6,300	7,800	9,000	9,600
Bank	204	-	-	-
	11,304	13,200	14,100	14,100
Total Assets	15,900	19,872	22,686	22,368
Equity and Liabilities				
Equity				
Ordinary share capital	6,900	6,900	6,900	6,900
General reserve	2,910	2,910	2,910	2,910
Retained profits	1,320	2,070	2,370	2,820
	11,130	11,880	12,180	12,630
Non-current Liabilities				
Loans	-	1,500	3,000	3,300
Current Liabilities				
Trade payables	2,160	2,400	2,220	2,106
Other payables	2,610	2,190	2,010	1,584
Bank overdraft	-	1,902	3,276	2,748
	4,770	6,492	7,506	6,438
Total Equity and Liabilities	15,900	19,872	22,686	22,368

During the years ended 31 December 2009, 2010, 2011 and 2012, €3,600m, €3,900m, €2,400m and €1,500m was debited to equity in respect of dividends paid.

Requirement You are required to prepare a report for the board of Directors of your company interpreting the financial statements of Holly plc from 2009 to 2012, including an analysis of its profitability and financial position.

> *Note:* Some issues to consider:
> • Are the two companies the same size, operating in the same geographical region and at similar stages in their lifecycle?
> • Do the two companies have similar reputations, track records and objectives?

Question 35.7

Egg Limited Accountant, Mr Montague, has assembled the following data from the company's last five sets of historical cost accounts.

	2012	2011	2010	2009	2008
Net profit margin:					
$\dfrac{\text{Profit before tax and interest}}{\text{Revenue}}$	5.6%	5.4%	4.9%	5.1%	5.3%
Return on capital employed:					
$\dfrac{\text{Profit before tax and interest}}{\text{Total assets less current liabilities}}$	12.3%	13.5%	11.8%	14.3%	14.3%
Interest cover:					
$\dfrac{\text{Profit before interest and tax}}{\text{Interest}}$	2.4	5.2	5.5	6.0	2.9
Dividend cover:					
$\dfrac{\text{Earnings}}{\text{Ordinary dividend}}$	2.3	2.1	1.8	2.0	2.7
Gearing:					
$\dfrac{\text{Debt}}{\text{Equity}}$	60.7%	57.2%	44.5%	12.8%	34.6%
$\dfrac{\text{Debt}}{\text{Equity + non-controlling interests}}$	56.3%	54.0%	41.9%	11.1%	32.4%
Quick ratio:					
$\dfrac{\text{Current assets less inventory}}{\text{Current liabilities}}$	68.6%	68.2%	72.5%	109.4%	90.2%
Current ratio:					
$\dfrac{\text{Current assets}}{\text{Current liabilities}}$	141.8%	141.5%	147.2%	189.1%	180.6%

Asset turnover:

$\dfrac{\text{Revenue}}{\text{Total assets less current liabilities}}$	2.2	2.5	2.4	2.8	2.7

Working capital turnover:

$\dfrac{\text{Revenue}}{\text{Working capital}}$	7.8	7.2	6.3	6.7	5.5

Earnings per share:	Pre-tax	18.44c	15.75c	12.15c	14.35c	16.67c
	Net	11.96c	10.08c	8.12c	8.41c	10.79c

Ordinary dividend per share	5.2c	4.8c	4.5c	4.2c	4.0c

Net assets per share	94.7c	90.2c	86.2c	86.3c	81.8c

Requirement You are required to prepare a report for Mr Montague on the company's financial state and progress over the period based on the information in the report, and commenting on its possible limitations if there have been price changes in the period.

Note: Some issues to consider:
- What does each of the ratios mean?
- What are the trends?
- Is there a 'link' between certain ratios?

ACCOUNTING FOR PARTNERSHIPS

LEARNING OBJECTIVES

Having studied this chapter on accounting for partnerships, you should:
1. be aware of the key aspects of the Partnership Act 1890;
2. understand the basic accounting principles with respect to partnerships;
3. be able to account for simple partnership changes, partnership changes requiring adjustments to asset values, the dissolution of a partnership, amalgamations and the conversion of a partnership to a limited company.

KEY TERMS AND DEFINITIONS FOR THIS CHAPTER

In order to aid your understanding of the concepts and issues covered in this chapter, it is important to understand and be familiar with the following key terms and definitions. As you study this chapter, you should refer back to them.

Appropriation Account This is a ledger account that deals with the allocation of net profit between the partners.

Current Accounts These are used to deal with the regular transactions between the partners and the partnership.

Drawings This is the withdrawal of money by a partner as an allowance.

Fixed Capital Accounts These record the amount of capital introduced into the partnership by the partners. They are not used to record drawings or shares of profits but only major changes in the relations between partners. In particular, fixed capital accounts are used to deal with capital introduced or withdrawn by new or retiring partners and revaluation adjustments. In practice, the term is commonly abbreviated to 'capital account'.

Partnership In broad terms, this is an association of two or more persons engaged in a business enterprise in which the profits and losses are shared proportionately.

36.1 INTRODUCTION

This chapter deals with accounting for partnerships. In the previous chapters, the terminology used in IAS 1 *Presentation of Financial Statements* was adopted, not least because the focus was on the application of accounting standards in a corporate context. However, as explained in **Chapter 1**, given that International Accounting Standards (IASs) and International Financial Reporting Standards (IFRSs) are aimed primarily at companies and groups of companies, it is considered more appropriate to use the term 'income statement' in this chapter to refer to the 'statement of profit or loss and other comprehensive income'. Although it is accepted that limited liability partnerships are permitted to use IAS/IFRSs.

After outlining the key aspects of the Partnership Act 1890 in **Section 36.2**, this chapter explains the basic accounting principles with respect to partnerships (see **Section 36.3**). Following that, more complicated aspects of partnership accounting are addressed, including:
- partnership changes (see **Section 36.4**);
- partnership changes requiring adjustments to asset values (see **Section 36.5**);
- the dissolution of a partnership (see **Section 36.6**);
- amalgamations (see **Section 36.7**); and
- the conversion of a partnership to a limited company (see **Section 36.8**).

36.2 PARTNERSHIP ACT 1890

The Partnership Act 1890 ('the 1890 Act') defines a partnership as "the relation which subsists between persons carrying on business in common with a view of profit". The main substance of a partnership is that each partner is an agent of all the others for the purpose of the business. Each partner is therefore bound by the acts of the other partners and each partner can be sued in his own name for the whole or any partnership debts. Every partnership is set up by an agreement between the partners, either orally or in writing. If the agreement between the partners is silent on any matter affecting the relationship between the partners, then the relevant provisions of the 1890 Act apply.

The main section of the 1890 Act that is relevant from an accounting point of view is section 24, which states among other things that:
(a) no interest is paid on capital of the partners;
(b) no remuneration is paid to partners for acting in the business;
(c) profits and losses are to be shared equally between partners; and
(d) interest at the rate of 5% per annum is paid on loans made by partners to the partnership in excess of their agreed capitals.

It should be emphasised that the above rules **only apply in the absence of a different agreement between the partners**. Partnership agreements will typically cover such items as those mentioned above, in addition to setting out other rights and duties of partners which are important to the satisfactory running of the partnership.

36.3 BASIC PRINCIPLES

Before looking at the basic principles that are particular to partnership accounts, it should be emphasised that the basic book-keeping and accounting procedures adopted in relation to companies and explained in Parts I–IV of this text apply equally to partnerships. After describing the conventional methods of dividing profit and maintaining equity between partners, this section outlines the accounting distinctions between partnerships and sole traders. Then capital accounts and current accounts are explained, followed by how partners' shares of profit/losses and their drawings are recorded and presented in the partnership accounts. This subsection concludes by considering appropriation accounts, guaranteed minimum profit share and interest on drawings.

The Conventional Methods of Dividing Profit and Maintaining Equity between Partners

A partnership agreement (which need not necessarily be in written form) will govern the relationships between the partners. Important matters to be covered in such an agreement include:
(a) name of firm, the type of business and duration;
(b) capital to be introduced by partners;
(c) distribution of profits between partners;
(d) drawings by partners (i.e. the withdrawal of money by a partner as an allowance);
(e) arrangements for dissolution, or on the death or retirement of partners;
(f) settling of disputes; and
(g) preparation and audit of accounts.

The division of profit stated in the partnership agreement may be necessarily complex in order to reflect the expected differing efforts and contributions of the partners. For example, some or all of the partners may be entitled to a salary to reflect the differing management involvement in the business. Interest on capital may be provided to reflect the differing amounts of capital contributed. The profit shares may differ to reflect seniority or greater skills.

It is important to appreciate, however, that the different profit-sharing arrangements are a means of dividing the profits of the partnership and are not expenses of the business. A partnership salary is merely a device for calculating the division of profit; it is not a salary in the normal meaning of the term.

Accounting Distinctions between Partnerships and Sole Traders

While the accounting techniques developed for sole traders are generally applicable to partnerships, there are certain important differences, which are shown in **Table 36.1**.

TABLE 36.1: SOLE TRADER AND PARTNERSHIP BOOKS OF ACCOUNT

Item	Sole Trader's Books	Partnership's Books
Capital introduced	Capital account	Partners' fixed capital accounts
Drawings and share of the profit	Capital account	Partners' current accounts
Division of profits	Not applicable – one proprietor only	Appropriation account

As illustrated in **Table 36.1**, the main accounts in a partnership's books of account are the fixed capital account, current account and appropriation account. Each of these is now explained in detail.

Fixed Capital Accounts

At the commencement of a partnership, an agreement will have to be reached as to the amount of capital to be introduced. This could be in the form of cash or other assets. Whatever the form of assets introduced and debited to asset accounts, it is normal to make the credit entry to **fixed capital accounts** (in practice, this term is often abbreviated to 'capital account'). These are so-called because they are not then used to record drawings or shares of profits but only major changes in the relations between partners. In particular, fixed capital accounts are used to deal with:

1. capital introduced or withdrawn by new or retiring partners; and
2. revaluation adjustments.

The balances on fixed capital accounts do not necessarily bear any relation to the division of profits. However, to compensate partners who provide a larger share of the capital, it is common for notional interest on capital accounts to be paid to partners. This is dealt with through the current and appropriation accounts.

Current Accounts

Current accounts are used to deal with the regular transactions between the partners and the firm, i.e. matters other than those sufficiently fundamental to be dealt with through the capital accounts. Most commonly these are:

1. share of profits, interest on capital and partners' salaries (usually computed annually); and
2. monthly drawings against the annual share of profit.

Recording the Partners' Shares of Profit/Losses and their Drawings in the Ledger Accounts and Statement of Financial Position Presentation

After having explained the purpose of the capital account and the current account, this sub-section illustrates how partners' shares of profit/losses and their drawings are recorded in these accounts and presented in the partnership statement of financial position.

EXAMPLE 36.1: RECORDING PROFITS AND DRAWINGS

Nab and Crag commenced business in partnership on 1 January 2012, contributing as fixed capital €5,000 and €10,000 cash respectively. All profits and losses are shared equally. The profit for the year ended 31 December 2012 amounted to €10,000. Drawings for Nab and Crag amounted to €3,000 and €4,000 respectively.

Requirement Prepare the capital and current accounts and statement of financial position extracts.

Solution

Partners' Capital Accounts

		Nab €	Crag €				Nab €	Crag €
				2012				
				1 Jan	Cash		5,000	10,000

Partners' Current Accounts

		€	€				€	€
2012				2012				
1 Dec	Drawings	3,000	4,000	31 Dec	Share of profits	5,000	5,000
	Balance c/d	2,000	1,000					
		5,000	5,000				5,000	5,000
				2013				
				1 Jan	Balance b/d	2,000	1,000

The above accounts are presented in a columnar format. This is quite common in a partnership set of books as each partner will have similar transactions during the year. A columnar format allows two (or more) separate accounts to be shown using the same narrative. It is important to remember though, that each partner's account is separate from that of the other partner(s).

STATEMENT OF FINANCIAL POSITION (extract)
at 31 December 2012

	Capital accounts €	Current accounts €	Total €
Partners' account:			
Nab	5,000	2,000	7,000
Crag	10,000	1,000	11,000
	15,000	3,000	18,000

Note that the current account balances of €2,000 and €1,000 will be credited in the following year with profit shares and debited with drawings.

One of the main differences between the capital section of the statement of financial position of a sole trader and a partnership is that the partnership statement of financial position will often only give the closing balances, whereas in the sole trader's statement movements in capital are shown. The main reason for the difference is simply one of space. Movements in the capital and current accounts for a few partners cannot be easily accommodated on the face of the statement of financial position. In addition to dealing with an overdrawn current account, this is illustrated in **Example 36.2**.

EXAMPLE 36.2: OVERDRAWN CURRENT ACCOUNT

The information is the same as in **Example 36.1**, except that Nab's drawings are €5,300.

Solution

The current accounts now become:

Partners' Current Accounts

		Nab €	Crag €			Nab €	Crag €
2012				2012			
	Drawings	5,300	4,000		Share of profits	5,000	5,000
31 Dec	Balance c/d		1,000	31 Dec	Balance b/d	300	
		5,300	5,000			5,300	5,000
2013				2013			
1 Jan	Balance b/d	300		1 Jan	Balance b/d		1,000

As Nab's current account is overdrawn, how is this presented in the statement of financial position?

STATEMENT OF FINANCIAL POSITION (EXTRACT)
at 31 December 2012

	Capital accounts €	Current accounts €	€
Partners' account:			
Nab	5,000	(300)	4,700
Crag	10,000	1,000	11,000
	15,000	700	15,700

After having explained two of the main partnership accounts (i.e. fixed capital account and current account), the next subsection addresses the third: the appropriation account.

Appropriation Account

The appropriation account is a ledger account dealing with the allocation of net profit between the partners. In practice, it is often included as the final part of the income statement. An important point is that all allocations of profit to partners in their capacity as partners, and during the time they actually are partners, are made through the appropriation account. This applies even though such allocations may be described as partners' salaries, interest on capital or a share of profits. **Example 36.3** illustrates the allocation of partnership profits using the appropriation account.

Example 36.3: Allocation of Partnership Profits

Pike and Scar are in partnership and have the following profit-sharing arrangements:
1. interest on capital is to be provided at a rate of 8% p.a.;
2. Pike and Scar are to receive salaries of €6,000 and €8,000 p.a. respectively;
3. the balance of profit or loss is to be divided between Pike and Scar in the ratio 3 : 2.

Net profit for the year-end 31 December 2012 amounts to €20,000 and capital account balances on that date are: Pike, €12,000 and Scar, €9,000.

Requirement Prepare:
(a) a statement showing the allocation of profit between the partners; and
(b) relevant entries in the income statement and appropriation account.

Solution

(a) Allocation of net profit of €20,000

	Pike	Scar	Total
	€	€	€
Interest on capital	960	720	1,680
Salaries	6,000	8,000	14,000
Balance of profits			
(€20,000 – €15,680) in ratio 3 : 2	(3/5) 2,592	(2/5) 1,728	4,320
Totals	9,552	10,448	20,000

Note that this is only a calculation of the allocation of profit and not part of the double entry book-keeping system, merely providing the figures for the appropriation and current accounts.

Extract from Income Statement and Appropriation Account
for the year ended 31 December 2012

	€	€
Sales		X
Cost of sales		X
Gross profit		X
Expenses		X
Net profit		20,000
Allocated to:		
Pike	9,552	
Scar	10,448	20,000

The income statement appropriation account is closed by transferring the profit shares to the credit of the partners' current accounts. The double entry is therefore:

Debit	*Credit*	*With*
Income statement appropriation account	Pike's current account	€9,552
Income statement appropriation account	Scar's current account	€10,448

For the purposes of examinations (and in practice) parts (a) and (b) above can be amalgamated as follows:

EXTRACT FROM INCOME STATEMENT AND APPROPRIATION ACCOUNT
for the year ended 31 December 2012

	€
Sales	X
Cost of sales	X
Gross profit	X
Expenses	X
Net profit for year	X
	20,000

APPROPRIATION STATEMENT
for the year ended 31 December 2012

	Pike	Scar	Total
	€	€	€
Interest on capital	960	720	1,680
Salaries	6,000	8,000	14,000
Balance of profits (€20,000 − €15,680) in ratio 3 : 2	2,592 (3/5)	1,728 (2/5)	4,320
Totals	9,552	10,448	20,000

The debits actually being made are as before (€9,552 and €10,448).

Example 36.3 illustrates the allocation of partnership profits. Example 36.4 addresses the allocation of partnership losses once interest on capital and salaries have been dealt with.

EXAMPLE 36.4: ALLOCATION OF PARTNERSHIP LOSSES

The facts are the same as for Example 36.3, except that net profit is now only €3,680.

Requirement Show the allocation of profit between the partners.

Solution

Allocation of net profit of €3,680:

	Pike	Scar	Total
	€	€	€
Interest on capital	960	720	1,680
Salaries	6,000	8,000	14,000
Balance of loss €3,680 − €15,680 = (€12,000) to be shared in ratio 3 : 2	(7,200)	(4,800)	(12,000)
Totals	(240)	3,920	3,680

The double entry in this case is:

Debit	Credit	With
Income statement appropriation account	Scar's current account	€3,920
Pike's current account	Income statement appropriation account	€240

The relevant part of the income statement would show:

	€	€
Net profit		3,680
Allocated to:		
Scar	3,920	
Pike	(240)	
		3,680

One point that regularly causes difficulties is the partners' salaries. The key is to remember at the outset that a partner's salary is an appropriation of profit, whereas a salary paid to an employee is an expense. Accordingly, a salary to which a partner is entitled is included as part of the appropriation statement. Questions sometimes state that a partner has withdrawn his salary. In this case:

1. include the salary in the appropriation statement as usual; and
2. separately treat the withdrawal of the salary as drawings.

Debit	Credit	With
Partner's current account	Bank	Amount withdrawn

Guaranteed Minimum Profit Share

In certain partnership agreements a partner may be guaranteed a minimum share of profits. The appropriation of profit would proceed in the normal way. If the result is that the partner has less than this minimum, the deficit will be made good by the other partners (normally in profit-sharing ratio). This is illustrated in **Example 36.5**.

EXAMPLE 36.5: GUARANTEED MINIMUM PROFITS

Tessa, Laura and Jane are in partnership and have the following profit-sharing arrangements:
1. Tessa and Laura are to receive salaries of €20,000 and €30,000 respectively;
2. the balance of profit or loss is to be divided Tessa 1, Laura 2 and Jane 3; and
3. Tessa is guaranteed a minimum profit share of €25,000.

The net profit for the year ended 31 December 2012 is €68,000.

Requirement Prepare the appropriation account for the year ended 31 December 2012.

Solution

APPROPRIATION ACCOUNT
for the year ended ended 31 December 2012

	Tessa €	Laura €	Jane €	Total €
Net profit				68,000
Salaries	20,000	30,000	–	(50,000)
				18,000
Balance of profits (1 : 2 : 3)	3,000	6,000	9,000	(18,000)
	23,000	36,000	9,000	
Adjustment	2,000			
Laura 2/5 × 2,000		(800)		
Jane 3/5 × 2,000			(1,200)	
Total	25,000	35,200	7,800	68,000

Interest on Drawings

Occasionally there is a provision in a partnership agreement for a notional interest charge on the drawings by each partner. The interest charges are merely a negative profit share – they are a means by which total profits are allocated between the partners. The reason for an interest on drawings provision is that those partners who draw out more cash than their colleagues in the early part of an accounting period should suffer a cost. Interest on drawings is dealt with in **Example 36.6**.

EXAMPLE 36.6: INTEREST ON DRAWINGS

Dick and Dastardly are in partnership. The capital and current accounts as at 1 January 2012 show:

	€ Capital	€ Current
Dick	50,000	2,500
Dastardly	20,000	3,000

The partnership agreement provides for the following:
(a) profits and losses are shared between Dick and Dastardly in percentages 60 and 40;
(b) interest on capital at 10% per annum is allowed; and
(c) interest on drawings is charged at 12% per annum.

Drawings for the year to 31 December 2012 are:	Dick	Dastardly
	€	€
1 February 2012	5,000	2,000
30 September 2012	2,000	5,000

The profit for the year ended 31 December 2012 is €20,000.

Requirement Prepare the appropriation account and the current accounts for the year ended 31 December 2012.

Solution

APPROPRIATION ACCOUNT
for the year ended 31 December 2012

	Dick	Dastardly	
	€	€	€
Profit for the year			20,000
Add: Interest on drawings (see working)	(610)	(370)	980
			20,980
Less: Interest on capital:			
50,000 × 10%	5,000		
20,000 × 10%		2,000	(7,000)
Balance in profit-sharing ratio:			13,980
13,980 × 60%	8,388		
13,980 × 40%		5,592	(13,980)
Total allocation	12,778	7,222	20,000

Current Accounts

		Dick	Dastardly			Dick	Dastardly
		€	€			€	€
2012:				2012:			
1 Feb	Drawing	5,000	2,000		Balance b/d	2,500	3,000
30 Sep	Drawing	2,000	5,000	31 Dec	Share of		
	Balance c/d	8,278	3,222		Profits	12,778	7,222
		15,278	10,222			15,278	10,222

WORKINGS

		Dick	Dastardly
		€	€
Interest on drawings:			
1 February 2012	5,000 × 12% × 11/12	550	
	2,000 × 12% × 11/12		220
30 September 2012	2,000 × 12% × 3/12	60	
	5,000 × 12% × 3/12		150
		610	370

Example 36.7, which consolidates the material covered to date in the chapter, illustrates the preparation of full partnership accounts from the trial balance stage.

EXAMPLE 36.7: PREPARATION OF FULL PARTNERSHIP ACCOUNTS

You are provided with the following information regarding the partnership of Dacre, Hutton and Tod.

Trial balance at 31 December 2012:

	DR €	CR €
Sales		50,000
Inventory at 1 January 2012	6,000	
Purchases	29,250	
Carriage inwards	250	
Carriage outwards	400	
Payables		4,000
Cash at bank	3,900	
Current accounts:		
Dacre		900
Hutton		750
Tod		1,350
Capital accounts:		
Dacre		4,000
Hutton		5,000
Tod		6,000
Drawings:		
Dacre	2,000	
Hutton	3,000	
Tod	5,000	
Sundry expenses	2,800	
Receivables	13,000	
Shop fittings:		
Cost	8,000	
Accumulated depreciation		1,600
	73,600	73,600

Additional information:
(a) closing inventory is valued for accounts purposes at €5,500;
(b) depreciation of €800 is to be provided on the shop fittings; and
(c) the profit-sharing arrangements are as follows:
  (i) interest on capital is to be provided at a rate of 10% per annum;
  (ii) Dacre and Tod are to receive salaries of €3,000 and €4,000 per annum respectively; and
  (iii) the balance of profit or loss is to be divided between Dacre, Hutton and Tod in the ratio of 3 : 8 : 4.

Requirement Prepare final accounts together with current accounts of the partners at 31 December 2012.

Solution

Dacre, Hutton and Tod
INCOME STATEMENT
for the year ended 31 December 2012

	€	€
Sales		50,000
Opening inventory	6,000	
Purchases	29,250	
Carriage inwards	250	
	35,500	
Less: Closing inventory	5,500	30,000
Gross profit		20,000
Sundry expenses	2,800	
Carriage outwards	400	
Depreciation	800	4,000
Net profit		16,000
Allocated to:		
Dacre		4,900
Hutton		4,500
Tod		6,600
		16,000

STATEMENT OF FINANCIAL POSITION
as at 31 December 2012

	Cost €	Acc depn €	€
Non-current Assets			
Shop fittings	8,000	2,400	5,600
Current Assets			
Inventory		5,500	
Receivables		13,000	
Cash		3,900	22,400
			28,000

Partners' accounts

	Capital accounts €	Current accounts €	Total €
Dacre	4,000	3,800	7,800
Hutton	5,000	2,250	7,250
Tod	6,000	2,950	8,950
	15,000	9,000	24,000
Current Liabilities			
Payables			4,000
			28,000

Partners' Current Accounts

		Dacre €	Hutton €	Tod €				Dacre €	Hutton €	Tod €
2012					2012					
	Drawing	2,000	3,000	5,000	1 Jan	Bal b/d		900	750	1,350
31 Dec	Bal c/d	3,800	2,250	2,950		IS app.		4,900	4,500	6,600
		5,800	5,250	7,950				5,800	5,250	7,950
					2013					
					1 Jan	Bal b/d		3,800	2,250	2,950

WORKINGS

The adjustments for inventory and depreciation should by now be familiar. The new development is that, having calculated the profit for the period, it has to be appropriated between Dacre, Hutton and Tod. To calculate their respective shares an appropriation statement is used.

	Dacre €	Hutton €	Tod €	Total €
Interest on capital	400	500	600	1,500
Salaries	3,000	–	4,000	7,000
Balance of profit (€16,000 − €8,500) in ratio 3 : 8 : 4	1,500	4,000	2,000	7,500
	4,900	4,500	6,600	16,000

This gives us the figures for the double entry:
DR   Income statement appropriation
CR   Partners' current accounts

36.4 BASIC PARTNERSHIP CHANGES

Partnership changes may occur in three quite different situations:
1. when a partner leaves, dies or retires;
2. when a new partner enters the partnership; and
3. when existing partners change their profit-sharing arrangements.

From the accounting viewpoint there are two aspects:
1. dividing profits between old and new partners when the change occurs during the course of the financial period; and
2. the problem of valuing partnership assets, especially goodwill, at the time of the change (see below).

Division of Profits in a Partnership Change

There will be many occasions when a partnership change does not take place at a convenient date (such as the accounting year-end). For the purpose of dividing profits equitably between the partners concerned, it is necessary to apportion (or allocate) profits between those arising before the change, and those arising afterwards. In most cases where the trade is not of a seasonal nature, sales occur at an even rate during the year. It will then be reasonable to apportion sales on a time basis. Having apportioned the profit between the different parts of the year, it is then allocated between the partners according to their arrangements for sharing profits during those periods. This is demonstrated in **Example 36.8**.

EXAMPLE 36.8: ADMISSION OF A NEW PARTNER

Gavel and Kirk are in partnership, sharing profits in the ratio 3 : 2, after Gavel has received a salary of €2,000 per annum. The accounting year-end of the partnership is 31 December. On 30 June 2012, Blea is admitted to the partnership. The new profit-sharing arrangements provide for Gavel's salary of €2,000 per annum to be maintained, and for Blea to receive a salary of €3,000 per annum. The balance is to be shared between Gavel, Kirk and Blea in the ratio 2 : 2 : 1.

The net profit for the year to 31 December 2012 is €22,000.

Requirement Show the transfer to the partners' current accounts for the year ended 31 December 2012.

Solution

Assuming that the net profit of €22,000 accrues evenly over the year, it may be apportioned on a time basis as follows:

		€
1 January 2012 to 30 June 2012	6/12 × €22,000	11,000
1 July 2012 to 31 December 2012	6/12 × €22,000	11,000
		22,000

The net profit relating to each six-month period is allocated according to the profit-sharing arrangements operating during that period.

STATEMENT OF ALLOCATION OF PROFIT

	Gavel €	Kirk €	Blea €	Total €
Six months to 30 June 2012				
Salary:				
Gavel 6/12 × €2,000	1,000	–	–	1,000
Balance of profit (€11,000 − €1,000) in ratio 3 : 2	6,000	4,000	–	10,000
	7,000	4,000	–	11,000

	Gavel €	Kirk €	Blea €	Total €
Six months to 31 December 2012				
Salary:				
Gavel 6/12 × €2,000	1,000	–	–	1,000
Blea 6/12 × €3,000	–	–	1,500	1,500

Balance of profit (€11,000 − €2,500) in ratio 2 : 2 : 1	3,400	3,400	1,700	8,500
	4,400	3,400	3,200	11,000
Totals – 12 months	11,400	7,400	3,200	22,000

Remember that the salaries and interest on capital percentages are expressed at an annual rate.

PARTNERS' CURRENT ACCOUNTS EXTRACT

Gavel €	Kirk €	Blea €		Gavel €	Kirk €	Blea €
			Income statement appropriation:			
			To 30 June 2012	7,000	4,000	–
			To 31 Dec 2012	4,400	3,400	3,200

Apportionment of Profit: Some Complications

Unless otherwise instructed, it is acceptable to apportion profits on a time basis. Occasionally, a question may specify an alternative basis. This is illustrated in **Example 36.9**.

EXAMPLE 36.9: ALTERNATIVE APPORTIONMENT OF PROFIT

Assume that in the previous example the net profit of €22,000 was arrived at as follows:

	€	€
Sales (€96,000 in six months to 30 June 2012)		160,000
Cost of sales		(118,000)
Gross profit		42,000
Selling and distribution expenses	5,500	
Administrative expenses	12,500	
Financial expenses	2,000	
		20,000
Net profit		22,000

Requirement Show the apportionment of profit between the two parts of the year. (Assume that gross profit and selling expenses are to be apportioned on a turnover basis and all other items on a time basis. The allocation of profit between the partners is not required.)

Solution

	€
Turnover:	
Six months to 30 June 2012	96,000
Six months to 31 December 2012	64,000
	160,000

The ratio of turnover is therefore 96 : 64 or 3 : 2.

	Six months to 30 June 2012		Six months to 31 December 2012		Total	
	€	€	€	€	€	€
Gross profit (3 : 2)		25,200		16,800		42,000
Selling expenses (3 : 2)	3,300		2,200		5,500	
Administrative expenses (1 : 1)	6,250		6,250		12,500	
Financial expenses (1 : 1)	1,000		1,000		2,000	
		10,550		9,450		20,000
Net profit		14,650		7,350		22,000

The apportionment of net profit is therefore:

	€
Six months to 30 June 2012	14,650
Six months to 31 December 2012	7,350
	22,000

As can be seen, in a seasonal business, where sales fluctuate greatly from month to month, the apportionment of a net profit on a time basis may give a misleading picture.

Partnership Changes Involving No Adjustments to Asset Values: Recording Introductions and Withdrawals of Capital in the Ledger Accounts

This subsection develops issues associated with partnership changes by dealing with both the withdrawal of an existing partner and the admission of a new partner. However, for the sake of clarity two unrealistic assumptions will be made, namely that at the date of partnership changes:
1. all tangible assets (for example, non-current assets and inventory) are stated in the accounts at their current value; and
2. goodwill is ignored.

These two assumptions are relaxed in **Section 36.5**.

While these unrealistic assumptions are removed in **Section 36.5** (see below), first two possible causes of a change in the partnership are considered – the retirement of an existing partner and the admission of a new partner.

Retirement of an Existing Partner

When a partner retires it is important first of all to ensure that his current account is credited with his share of profits and debited with his drawings up to the date of retirement. The balances on his current and capital accounts are then transferred to a loan account and becomes a liability of the business. The manner and timing of the payment of this liability are likely to be regulated by the partnership agreement. In practice the amount will probably be paid in instalments, with allowance for interest on the unpaid balance. Since the former partner is no longer a partner of the business, the interest cannot be regarded as an appropriation of profit and must be regarded as an expense of the partnership (in the same way as interest on a bank overdraft).

EXAMPLE 36.10: RETIREMENT OF A PARTNER

Birk, How and Stile have been in partnership for many years. Birk retired from the partnership on 1 July 2012. At 30 June 2012 the summarised statement of financial position showed the following position:

	€
Sundry assets	27,296

Partners' accounts	Capital accounts	Current accounts	Total
	€	€	€
Birk	12,000	1,735	13,735
How	8,000	2,064	10,064
Stile	3,000	497	3,497
	23,000	4,296	27,296

The current account balances reflect profit shares and drawings up to 30 June 2012.

Requirement Prepare the partners' accounts at 1 July 2012 following the retirement of Birk.

Solution

On 1 July 2012 the balances on Birk's capital and current accounts should be transferred to a loan account and regarded as a liability of the partnership. The statement of financial position at 1 July 2012 would show:

	€
Sundry assets	27,296

Partners' accounts	Capital accounts	Current accounts	
	€	€	€
How	8,000	2,064	10,064
Stile	3,000	497	3,497
	11,000	2,561	13,561
Loan account – Birk			13,735
			27,296

Birk is now a creditor of the partnership as he is no longer a partner.

Admission of a New Partner

A new partner will often be required to bring in cash as a contribution to the fixed capital of the partnership. This cash is therefore credited to the partner's capital account. This is illustrated in **Example 36.11**.

EXAMPLE 36.11: ADMISSION OF A PARTNER

Following on from **Example 36.10**, Tarn is admitted to the partnership on 3 July 2012 and he introduces cash of €2,500 as his fixed capital.

Requirement Prepare the partners' capital accounts and statement of financial position following the admission of Tarn.

Solution

The partners' current accounts would not be affected, but the capital accounts would appear as follows:

Partners' capital accounts

	Birk €	How €	Stile €	Tarn €		Birk €	How €	Stile €	Tarn €
2 July 2012:					1 July 2012:				–
Loan account	12,000	–	–	–	Balance b/d	12,000	8,000	3,000	
					3 July 2012:				
					Cash	–	–	–	2,500

A summarised statement of financial position at 3 July 2012 would then show the following position:

			€
Sundry assets (€27,296 + €2,500)			29,796

Partners' accounts	Capital accounts €	Current accounts €	Total €
How	8,000	2,064	10,064
Stile	3,000	497	3,497
Tarn	2,500	–	2,500
	13,500	2,561	16,061
Loan account – Birk			13,735
			29,796

If Tarn had contributed his capital share in the form of an asset other than cash (for example, a car valued at €2,500), the double entry would have been:

Debit	Credit	With
Motor car account	Tarn's capital account	€2,500

The only effect on the statement of financial position would then be the make-up of the sundry assets figure of €27,296 as between non-current and current assets.

36.5 PARTNERSHIP CHANGES REQUIRING ADJUSTMENTS TO ASSET VALUES

As explained earlier, two simplistic assumptions have been made so far:

1. no notice has been taken of any difference between the current value of individual tangible assets and the amount at which they were stated in the books of account. On a change in partnership-sharing arrangements, such account must be taken as partners are entitled to share capital profits in the same ratio as they share revenue profits. Thus, just as profits are time-apportioned between periods before and after the change, it is necessary to take account of capital gains or losses at the date of change; and
2. goodwill has been ignored.

These issues are now addressed.

Why a Revaluation is Required on a Partnership Change

Any change in a partnership (and remember a change can be an admission of a new partner, the retirement of an old partner or a change in profit-sharing ratios) affects partners' rights to profits and assets. The entitlement to a one-third share in profits means an entitlement to a one-third share in any increase or decrease in the value of the assets which exist in the partnership as well. To the extent that the current worth of the assets is different from their book value, a profit or loss will have accrued on the asset from the date of acquisition of the asset to the date of the partnership change. This profit or loss will need to be allocated to each partner in the old profit-sharing ratio as the partnership change triggers off new profit-sharing ratios. The gain/loss is computed by revaluing the net assets at the date of change.

Adjustments in Respect of Tangible Assets

Wherever there is a change in profit-sharing arrangements, a partnership will take account of changes in the value of its tangible assets. In this instance, use will be made of a revaluation account to calculate the overall gain or loss on the revaluation; this will then be shared between the old partners in their old profit-sharing ratios. The initial book-keeping entries are as follows:

Debit	Credit	With
Assets	Revaluation	Increases in assets' values
Revaluation	Assets	Decreases in assets' values
Liabilities	Revaluation	Decreases in liability values
Revaluation	Liabilities	Increases in liability values

At this stage the balance on the revaluation account will represent the surplus or deficiency on the revaluation, which will be shared between the old partners in their old profit-sharing ratios as follows:

Debit	Credit	With
Revaluation	Partners' capital accounts	Surplus on revaluation
Partners' capital accounts	Revaluation	Deficit on revaluation

Asset revaluation is illustrated further in **Example 36.12**.

EXAMPLE 36.12: ASSET REVALUATION

Trooper, Tremlett and Arkle are in partnership, sharing profits in the ratio 4 : 3 : 3. As at 1 January 2012 Randall is to be admitted to the partnership, thereafter profits are to be shared equally. Randall is to introduce capital of €30,000.

The partnership's statement of financial position as at 31 December 2011 shows the following:

	€	€
Non-current assets:		
Property		70,000
Plant and machinery		30,000
Fixtures and fittings		25,000
		125,000
Current assets:		
Inventory	35,000	
Receivables	28,000	
Bank	17,000	80,000
		205,000

	Capital €	Current €	Total €
Partners' accounts:			
Trooper	50,000	2,000	52,000
Tremlett	53,750	4,000	57,750
Arkle	65,000	3,000	68,000
	168,750	9,000	177,750
Current liabilities:			27,250
Payables			205,000

For the purposes of the revaluation the assets of the partnership are to be revalued as follows:

	€
Property	80,000
Plant and machinery	27,500
Fixtures and fittings	32,100
Inventory	36,350
Receivables	27,750

Requirement Prepare the:
(a) revaluation account;
(b) partners' capital accounts; and
(c) statement of financial position of the partnership as at 1 January 2012.

Solution

(a)

Revaluation

	€	€		€
Plant and machinery		2,500	Property	10,000
Receivables		250	Fixtures	7,100
Profit on revaluation:			Inventory	1,350
Trooper (4)	6,280			
Tremlett (3)	4,710			
Arkle (3)	4,710			
	15,700			
	18,450			18,450

(b)

Partners' Capital Accounts

	Trooper	Tremlett	Arkle	Randall		Trooper	Tremlett	Arkle	Randall
	€	€	€	€		€	€	€	€
Balance c/d	56,280	58,460	69,710	30,000	Bal. b/d	50,000	53,750	65,000	
					Revaln	6,280	4,710	4,710	
					Bank				30,000
	56,280	58,460	69,710	30,000		56,280	58,460	69,710	30,000

(c)

Trooper, Tremlett, Arkle and Randall
STATEMENT OF FINANCIAL POSITION
as at 1 January 2012

Non-current assets:

	€	€
Property		80,000
Plant and machinery		27,500
Fixtures and fittings		32,100
		139,600

Current assets:

	€	€
Inventory	36,350	
Receivables	27,750	
Bank (€17,000 + €30,000)	47,000	111,100
		250,700

	Capital €	Current €	Total €
Partners' accounts:			
Trooper	56,280	2,000	58,280
Tremlett	58,460	4,000	62,460
Arkle	69,710	3,000	72,710
Randall	30,000	–	30,000
	214,450	9,000	223,450
Current liabilities:			
Payables			27,250
			250,700

Note: in **Example 36.12** the capital accounts were adjusted for the change in asset values as it is a capital transaction. In particular, the revaluation does not create realised profits (i.e. they are not in the form of cash) and thus partners cannot increase their drawings out of their current accounts.

Goodwill

Measurement of Goodwill

As discussed in **Chapter 26**, there can be no precise valuation of goodwill, which has to be essentially the result of an exercise of judgement of the worth of the business as a whole by the parties involved. In examination questions the examiner will either tell you the valuation to be placed on the goodwill, or give sufficient information to enable you to calculate the figure. The most likely possibilities are as follows:
1. goodwill is valued at €12,000;
2. X introduces €3,000 in payment for his share of one-quarter of the goodwill. If a quarter share is valued at €3,000, then the total value for goodwill is €12,000;
3. goodwill is to be valued at three times last year's profit of €4,000. Three times last year's profit is €12,000, giving the total value for goodwill; or
4. the business is worth €200,000 and the fair value of the tangible net assets is €160,000. Goodwill is therefore €40,000.

Adjustments in Respect of Goodwill

There are two main situations as regards goodwill:
1. the partners wish to include goodwill as an asset in their statement of financial position, which is the least likely situation in practice; or
2. the partners do not wish to include goodwill as an asset in their statement of financial position, but the effect of goodwill needs to be reflected in their capital accounts.

Goodwill included as an Asset in the Statement of Financial Position

In this situation use can be made of the revaluation account in the normal fashion:

Debit	Credit	With
Goodwill	Revaluation	Increase in the value of goodwill
Revaluation	Goodwill	Decrease in the value of goodwill

If goodwill has not previously been incorporated in the books, the entry is:

Debit	Credit	With
Goodwill	Revaluation	The agreed value of goodwill

This is illustrated in **Example 36.13**.

EXAMPLE 36.13: ASSET REVALUATION AND GOODWILL

Laid, Back and Gower are in partnership, sharing profits 5 : 3 : 2. As at 1 January 2013 Gooch is to be admitted to the partnership; thereafter profits are to be shared equally. Gooch is to introduce capital of €40,000, of which €10,000 represents a payment for his share of the goodwill, which is subsequently to be disclosed in the books.

The partnership's statement of financial position as at 31 December 2012 shows the following:

	€	€
Non-current assets:		
Property		42,500
Plant and machinery		16,750
Fixtures and fittings		12,800
		72,050
Current assets:		
Inventory	15,800	
Receivables	29,471	
Bank	18,623	
		63,894
		135,944
Partners' capital accounts:		
Laid		61,237
Back		18,476
Gower		31,518
		111,231
Current liabilities:		
Payables		24,713
		135,944

For the purposes of the revaluation the assets of the partnership are to be revalued as follows:

	€
Property	75,000
Plant and machinery	21,250
Fixtures and fittings	11,000

Requirement Prepare the:

(a) revaluation account;

(b) partners' capital accounts; and

(c) statement of financial position of the partnership as at 1 January 2013.

Solution

(a)

Revaluation Account

	€	€		€
Fixtures and fittings		1,800	Property	32,500
Profit on revaluation:			Plant and machinery	4,500
Laid (5)	37,600		Goodwill	40,000
Back (3)	22,560			
Gower (2)	15,040			
		75,200		
		77,000		77,000

If Gooch is introducing €10,000 for his share of the goodwill (one-quarter thereof), the total value of goodwill must be €40,000.

(b)

Partners' Capital Accounts

	Laid €	Back €	Gower €	Gooch €		Laid €	Back €	Gower €	Gooch €
Bal. c/d	98,837	41,036	46,558	40,000	Bal. b/d	61,237	18,476	31,518	
					Bank				40,000
					Revaln	37,600	22,560	15,040	
	98,837	41,036	46,558	40,000		98,837	41,036	46,558	40,000

(c)

Laid, Back, Gower and Gooch
STATEMENT OF FINANCIAL POSITION
as at 1 January 2013

	€	€
Non-current assets:		
Goodwill		40,000
Property		75,000
Plant and machinery		21,250
Fixtures and fittings		11,000
		147,250

Current assets:		
Inventory	15,800	
Receivables	29,471	
Bank (€18,623 + €40,000)	58,623	103,894
		251,144
Partners' capital accounts:		
Laid		98,837
Back		41,036
Gower		46,558
Gooch		40,000
		226,431
Current liabilities		
Payables		24,713
		251,144

Goodwill is the only Asset that Requires Revaluation

Quite often, it is only goodwill that requires to be revalued. The book value of the tangible assets may be fairly close to their market value and thus the time and expense involved in making valuations is too great compared to the benefits. If only goodwill is being revalued, the revaluation account need not be used. The revaluation increase (or decrease) can be transferred from the goodwill account to the partners' capital accounts as shown in **Example 36.14**.

EXAMPLE 36.14: REVALUATION OF GOODWILL

The Faldo, Woosnam partnership is to admit Newcomer into the partnership as at 1 July 2012. Faldo and Woosnam currently share profits 3 : 1 after annual salaries of €100,000 each. As from 1 July 2012 the profit-sharing ratio will be Faldo 3, Woosnam 2, Newcomer 2, after annual salaries of €120,000 each.

The partnership statement of financial position as at 30 June 2012 shows:

			€
Assets:			45,000

Partners' account:	Capital	Current	Total
	€	€	€
Faldo	20,000	8,000	28,000
Woosnam	12,000	5,000	17,000
	32,000	13,000	45,000

Goodwill, which does not currently appear on the statement of financial position, is estimated to be worth €280,000. Newcomer is to pay €90,000 capital into the business. Goodwill is to remain as an asset in the books.

Requirement Prepare the partnership statement of financial position as at 1 July 2012 after the admission of Newcomer.

Solution

Faldo, Woosnam and Newcomer
STATEMENT OF FINANCIAL POSITION
as at 1 July 2012

	€
Goodwill	280,000
Other assets (€45,000 + €90,000)	135,000
	415,000

Partners' accounts:	Capital	Current	Total
	€	€	€
Faldo	230,000	8,000	238,000
Woosnam	82,000	5,000	87,000
Newcomer	90,000	–	90,000
	402,000	13,000	415,000

WORKINGS

Goodwill

	€		€
Valuation to capital accounts	280,000		

Capital accounts

	Faldo	Woosnam	Newcomer		Faldo	Woosnam	Newcomer
	€	€	€		€	€	€
Balance c/d	230,000	82,000	90,000	Balance b/d	20,000	12,000	
				Goodwill 3 : 1	210,000	70,000	
				Cash			90,000
	230,000	82,000	90,000		230,000	82,000	90,000

Goodwill not included as an Asset in the Statement of Financial Position

In many cases, goodwill will not be shown in the statement of financial position after a partnership change despite the fact that a new partner, for example, has paid for a share. There are a number of reasons why partnerships do not wish to record goodwill in the statement of financial position:

Subjective Nature of Valuation The value attached to goodwill on a partnership change is either a matter of negotiation between the partners or derived from a formula in the partnership agreement. It only represents a value attached to the asset at the time of the change. In changing business conditions in the future its value may be very different.

Taxation For capital gains tax purposes, it is generally disadvantageous to record partnership goodwill as an asset.

Amortisation If goodwill is recorded as an asset, should it not be written down like any other non-current asset? Some would say 'yes' and some 'no'. The argument is, however, avoided if goodwill is not shown in the first place. This will not change the need to make entries to account for goodwill; the old partners by allowing another person into partnership are sharing their business with him. They are thus selling some of the past goodwill to him and this fact needs to be recorded in the capital accounts. The approach to be adopted in this instance is to open up temporarily an account for goodwill, using the following journal entries:

Debit	*Credit*	*With*
New partner's capital accounts – goodwill	Old partners' capital accounts – goodwill	Their share of the goodwill (using old profit-sharing ratio) Their share of the goodwill (using new profit-sharing ratio)

In simple terms this can be described as:
1. write up goodwill in the old profit-sharing ratios (OPSR); and
2. write it down in the new profit-sharing ratios (NPSR).

This process is demonstrated in **Example 36.15**.

EXAMPLE 36.15: NON-DISCLOSURE OF GOODWILL

Francis, Robson and Hateley are in partnership, sharing profits 7 : 2 : 1. As at 1 January 2013 Harford is to be admitted to the partnership; thereafter profits are to be shared 3 : 3 : 3 : 1. Harford is to introduce capital of €50,000, of which €12,000 represents a payment for his share of the goodwill, not to be disclosed in the books.

An extract from the partnership statement of financial position as at 31 December 2012 shows the following:

	€
Capital accounts:	
Francis	36,761
Robson	27,304
Hateley	29,287
	93,352

Requirement Assuming that there are no revaluations necessary to any other assets, prepare the:
(a) partners' capital accounts; and
(b) goodwill account.

Solution

(a)

Partners' capital accounts

	Francis €	Robson €	Hateley €	Harford €		Francis €	Robson €	Hateley €	Harford €
Gwill	36,000	36,000	36,000	12,000	Bal. b/d	36,761	27,304	29,287	
					Bank				50,000
Bal. c/d	84,761	15,304	5,287	38,000	Gwill	84,000	24,000	12,000	
	120,761	51,304	41,287	50,000		120,761	51,304	41,287	50,000

(b)

Goodwill

	€		€
Francis (7)	84,000	Francis (3)	36,000
Robson (2)	24,000	Robson (3)	36,000
Hateley (1)	12,000	Hateley (3)	36,000
		Harford (1)	12,000
	120,000		120,000

If Harford is introducing €12,000 for his share of the goodwill (one-tenth thereof), the total value of goodwill must be €120,000.

Conclusion

Goodwill invariably appears as a complication in questions involving partnerships. The key is to follow the requirements of the question. Confusion often arises in the case of goodwill not shown in the books in the sense that it appears unfair that, for instance, Harford (see Example 36.15), pays in €50,000 on admission to the partnership and yet ends up with only €38,000 on his capital account. However, the point to remember is that the statement of financial position does not include goodwill. If goodwill were subsequently to be included in the books, say on 2 January 2013, Harford's capital account would be credited with his share of the goodwill (1/10 × €120,000 = €12,000). Similarly, if the partnership were dissolved, Harford would be entitled to a one-tenth share in the profit on the disposal of the partnership, which would include the valuation placed on the goodwill.

In any event, the key is to follow the requirement in the question, which is likely to treat the partners fairly.

36.6 DISSOLUTION OF PARTNERSHIP

Objective of Dissolution

The objective of dissolution is to dispose of the partnership assets, pay off the liabilities and distribute the balance to the partners according to their entitlements. The amount each partner receives is the balance on his or her capital account plus his or her share of the profit arising on the disposal of the assets (or minus any share of loss). If the final result is that a partner's account is in deficit, he or she has to pay the money in to allow the other partners to draw out their full entitlement.

Reasons for Dissolution

While there are many reasons why a partnership may be dissolved, the more common reasons for dissolution are:
(a) death or retirement of a partner;
(b) disagreement among the partners;
(c) continuing trading losses; and
(d) completion of the purpose for which the partnership was formed.

Whatever the reason, the accounting treatment is the same.

The Realisation Account

The first book-keeping step in dealing with dissolution is to open a realisation account, sometimes called a dissolution account. All the assets' balances, except cash-in-hand and cash at bank, are transferred in to the debit of the realisation account. The proceeds of sale of these assets will be credited to the realisation account, the balance on which will then be the profit or loss on the dissolution, subject to some minor items. The assets could be sold separately or as a single going concern unit. In either case the proceeds are credited to the realisation account.

Dealing with Liabilities

The liabilities of the partnership have to be paid (debit the liability accounts and credit cash). It may be that liabilities are paid off for a little more or less than the book amounts, perhaps because of cash discounts or negotiated settlements. Any such difference is debited or credited to the realisation account as representing the loss or profit arising on the final settlement of the liabilities.

Expenses of Dissolution

The expenses of dissolution are simply debited to the realisation account when paid.

Assets Taken Over by the Partners

It may be that partners agree to take over certain partnership assets at dissolution. To record this, it is necessary to credit the realisation account and debit the capital account of the partner concerned.

Partners' Accounts

Partners may have both capital accounts and current accounts. The distinction between them ceases to have any meaning on dissolution and current account balances should be transferred to the capital accounts.

Sale of Business as a Going Concern – Goodwill

If the business is sold as a going concern, this means that a single sum is received for all or most of the assets. The value of unrecorded goodwill may be an element in the total consideration, but there is no need to record this specifically. The total consideration is credited to the realisation account (debit cash) and the value attributed to the goodwill merely added to the profit on the sale and is thus automatically credited to the partners in their profit-sharing ratios.

Sale of Business as a Going Concern – Liabilities Taken Over

A purchaser of the business may agree to take over all or some of the partnership's liabilities. The easiest way to deal with this is to credit the liabilities taken over to the realisation account, so that the profit or loss arising on the sale in the realisation account is the difference between the consideration and the *net assets* taken over.

Final Settlement with the Partners

When all the entries described above have been recorded, there will remain only the partners' capital accounts and the cash at bank. It only remains to draw cheques to pay the partners the balances due to them. Any partner with a debit balance on his or her capital account will pay in cash to clear the balance (see note below). It could happen that the dissolution is spread over a long period so that payments on account are made to the partners as the sale of the assets proceeds.

Note: if a partner's capital account shows a debit balance on dissolution, the partner has to pay the debit balance to the partnership to settle the account. However, if the partner becomes insolvent then he would be unable to pay back the amount owed by him to the partnership. The amount not paid is a loss to the partnership which under the *Garner vs Murray* rule is to be borne by the solvent partners. According to the *Garner vs Murray* rule, the loss on account of insolvency of a partner is a capital loss which should be borne by the solvent partners in the ratio of their capitals standing in the statement of financial position on the date of dissolution of the partnership. The capitals according to this rule are ascertained after making all adjustments regarding reserves, drawings, unrecorded assets on the date of the statement of financial position on the date of dissolution of the partnership.

Example 36.16 illustrates many of the procedures described above.

EXAMPLE 36.16: PARTNERSHIP DISSOLUTION

A, B and C share profits 4 : 3 : 3. They agree to dissolve their partnership at the end of the financial year, when the statement of financial position appeared as follows:

	€	€
Non-current assets, at cost less depreciation:		
Freehold		40,000
Plant and machinery		15,000
Motor vehicles (three cars)		16,000
		71,000

Current assets:

Inventory	50,000	
Receivables	25,000	
Cash	15,000	
		90,000
		161,000

Partners' accounts:

	A	B	C	Total
	€	€	€	€
Capital	40,000	30,000	20,000	90,000
Current	15,000	10,000	5,000	30,000
	55,000	40,000	25,000	120,000
Current liabilities				21,000
Loan account – D				20,000
				161,000

The following are sold for cash:

	€
Freehold	80,000
Plant and machinery	13,000
Inventory	43,000
	136,000

The payables are settled for €20,000.
C takes over the receivables at an agreed value of €22,000.
A takes over D's loan at its book value.
A, B and C take over the cars at the following valuations:

A	€6,000
B	€8,000
C	€4,000

Realisation expenses are €2,000.

Requirement Prepare the ledger accounts to show the closing of the partnership records.

Solution

Numbers in brackets refer to sequence of entries.

Realisation Account

	€		€
Book value of assets:		Sale or disposal proceeds:	
Realisation expenses		(1) Cash – sold	
To partners – profit on realisation		(2) Partners' accounts –	
in PSR:		assets taken over	

(1) Freehold account	40,000	(2) Cash – sale proceeds	136,000
(1) Plant and machinery account	15,000	(4) Discount received on payables	1,000
(1) Motor vehicles account	16,000		
		Partners' accounts – assets taken over:	
(1) Inventory account	50,000	(5) C receivables	22,000
(1) Receivables account	25,000	(5) A motor car	6,000
(7) Cash – realisation expenses	2,000	(5) B motor car	8,000
		(5) C motor car	4,000
Partners' accounts – profit on			
A 40% €11,600			
B 30% €8,700			
C 30% €8,700	29,000		
	177,000		177,000

Partners' Accounts

	A €	B €	C €		A €	B €	C €
(5) Receivables taken over			22,000	Balances b/d:			
(5) Motor cars taken over	6,000	8,000	4,000	Capital accounts	40,000	30,000	20,000
(8) Cash to settle	80,600	40,700	7,700	Current accounts	15,000	10,000	5,000
				(6) D's loan account	20,000		
				Realisation account:			
				Profit	11,600	8,700	8,700
	86,600	48,700	33,700		86,600	48,700	33,700

Payables' Account

	€		€
(3) Cash	20,000	Balance b/d	21,000
(4) Realisation account discount received on settlement	1,000		
	21,000		21,000

D's Loan Account

	€		€
(6) Partner's capital account – A	20,000	Balance b/d	20,000

Cash Account

		€			€
Balance b/d		15,000	(3) Payables		20,000
Sale proceeds to realisation account:			(7) Realisation expenses		2,000
			Partners' accounts to settle:		
(2) Freehold	80,000		(8) A	80,600	
(2) Plant/ machinery	13,000		(8) B	40,700	
(2) Inventory	43,000		(8) C	7,700	
		136,000			129,000
		151,000			151,000

36.7 AMALGAMATIONS

Individual traders and/or partnerships may decide to merge or amalgamate into a new single partnership. After outlining the procedures necessary to carry this out, the process is illustrated in **Example 36.17** and **Example 36.18**.

Procedure

Step 1 – Each trader/partner will record the capital profit or loss accruing to him at the date of the merger. Values will be placed on the tangible net assets and goodwill of each trader's/partner's business and these values can be incorporated into the trader's/partner's books by use of a revaluation account. The entries will be similar to the revaluation of assets on a partnership change. The balancing figure in the revaluation account will be transferred to the trader's capital account.

Step 2 – Any assets not being taken over by the new partnership are removed from the trader's/partner's books by transferring the book value of the assets to the debit of the trader's/partner's capital account.

Step 3 – The separate books can now be merged at the agreed values. The new partnership assets will be the sum of the assets of the two sole trader's/partner's and each person's capital account will be their opening balance of capital in the new partnership. If goodwill is not to appear as an asset in the statement of financial position, the combined amount needs to be written off against each partner's capital account in a new profit-sharing ratio.

EXAMPLE 36.17: PARTNERSHIP AMALGAMATIONS (I)

Partnership A agrees to amalgamate with partnership C to form X & Co.

The statements of financial position of the two partnerships at the date of the merger were as follows:

	A €	C €
Non-current assets:		
Freehold property	10,000	
Plant and machinery	4,000	7,000
Motor vehicle	3,000	
	17,000	7,000
Current assets:		
Inventory	4,000	3,000
Receivables	2,000	1,000
Cash at bank	2,000	4,000
	25,000	15,000
Capital accounts:		
A	18,000	
C		9,000
Loan from F	2,000	
Trade payables	5,000	6,000
	25,000	15,000

X & Co. was to take over all the assets and liabilities of the two partnerships except:

1. F's loan, for which A agreed to take over responsibility; and
2. A was to take over the car.

The following were the agreed values placed on the assets of the old partnerships.

	A €	C €
Goodwill	9,000	3,000
Freehold property	14,000	–
Plant and machinery	3,000	6,000
Inventory	4,000	2,000
Receivables	2,000	1,000

Trade payables were taken over at their book value.
Profit sharing in the new partnership is 3 : 1 between A and C.
Goodwill was not to appear in the new partnership's statement of financial position.

Requirement Prepare the:

(a) statement of financial position of X & Co. immediately following the amalgamation; and

(b) closing entries in the books of A and C to record the revaluation and the entries in their capital accounts.

Solution

(a)

X & Co.
STATEMENT OF FINANCIAL POSITION
after Amalgamation

	€	€
Non-current assets:		
Freehold property		14,000
Plant and machinery		
(€3,000 + €6,000)		9,000
		23,000
Current assets:		
Inventory (€4,000 + €2,000)	6,000	
Receivables (€2,000 + €1,000)	3,000	
Cash (€2,000 + €4,000)	6,000	15,000
		38,000
(b)		
Capital accounts (see below):		
A		20,000
C		7,000
		27,000
Current liabilities:		
Trade payables		
(€5,000 + €6,000)		11,000
		38,000

The closing entries for the books of A and C are:

Capital Accounts

	A	C		A	C
	€	€		€	€
Motor vehicle	3,000	-	Balance b/d	18,000	9,000
Goodwill	9,000	3,000	Loan	2,000	-
Receivables	-	2,000	Goodwill	9,000	3,000
Balance c/d	20,000	7,000	Receivables	3,000	-
	32,000	12,000		32,000	12,000

A further illustration of the amalgamation process is provided in **Example 36.18**.

EXAMPLE 36.18: PARTNERSHIP AMALGAMATION (2)

P and Q are in partnership in a similar business to R and S. It is agreed that the two partnerships should amalgamate into one firm called Letters. The profit-sharing ratios are as follows:

	P	Q	R	S
Old Firms	3	2	3	2
New Firm	8	5	4	3

At the date of amalgamation, the statements of financial position of the two firms were as follows:

	PQ €	RS €			PQ €	RS €
Assets	39,000	33,000	Capital P	P	20,000	
Bank	1,000	2,000		Q	15,000	
				R		16,000
				S		12,000
			Liabilities		5,000	7,000
	40,000	35,000			40,000	35,000

The agreement to amalgamate provides that the assets of PQ be valued at €45,000 and the assets of RS be valued at €29,000. Payables are to be taken over at net book value. The capital of Letters is to be €66,000 and is to be contributed by the partners in their new profit-sharing ratio.

Requirement Close the books of PQ and RS and prepare the opening statement of financial position of Letters.

Solution

	Total	P	Q	R	S
New Profit-sharing ratio	20	8	5	4	3
Capital to be contributed	€66,000	€26,400	€16,500	€13,200	€9,900

Realisation Accounts

	PQ €	RS €			PQ €		RS €
Assets	39,000	33,000	Payables		5,000		7,000
Profit on Realisation:			Assets to				
P: 3/5 €3,600			Letters 45,000			29,000	
Q: 2/5 €2,400	6,000		Less:				
			Payables 5,000	40,000		7,000	22,000
			Loss on Realisation:				
			R: 3/5			2,400	
			S: 2/5			1,600	4,000
	45,000	33,000			45,000		33,000

Bank Accounts

		PQ €	RS €			PQ €	RS €
Balance		1,000	2,000	Capital account	Q	900	
Capital account	P	2,800			R		400
					S		500
				Letters		2,900	1,100
		3,800	2,000			3,800	2,000

Capital Accounts

	P €	Q €	R €	S €		P €	Q €	R €	S €
Loss on					Balance	20,000	15,000	16,000	12,000
Realisation			2,400	1,600	Profit on				
Balance to					Realisation	3,600	2,400		
Letters	26,400	16,500	13,200	9,900					
Bank		900	400	500	Bank	2,800			
	26,400	17,400	16,000	12,000		26,400	17,400	16,000	12,000

Letters

	PQ €	RS €			PQ €	RS €
Assets (net)	40,000	22,000	Capital account	P	26,400	
Bank	2,900	1,100		Q	16,500	
				R		13,200
				S		9,900
	42,900	23,100			42,900	23,100

Letters
STATEMENT OF FINANCIAL POSITION
after Amalgamation

	€			€
Assets	74,000	Capital account P	€26,400	
Bank	4,000	Q	€16,500	
		R	€13,200	
		S	€ 9,900	
				66,000
		Liabilities		12,000
	78,000			78,000

36.8 CONVERSION TO A LIMITED COMPANY

While a detailed analysis of the advantages and disadvantages of operating as a sole trader, partnership or limited company are outside the scope of this book, the main reason for a sole trader or partnership wishing to convert to a limited company is to enable the sole trader or partners not to be personally liable for the debts of the business. As a sole trader or partnership does not have a separate legal identity, each has joint and several liability for the debts of the business. However, a shareholder in a limited company is not responsible for the debts of the company in the event of its insolvency. A shareholder's liability is limited to any amount still unpaid on the issue of the shares. If the shares were issued fully paid (as they normally are), then the shareholder has no further liability. In addition, a company may find it easier to attract new capital since investors become shareholders and not partners. Indeed, in the long term, companies can be floated on a stock exchange. However, before incorporating a business as a company, the tax implications need to be considered carefully.

Sometimes the assets and liabilities of a partnership are transferred to a limited company in exchange for shares and the partnership is dissolved. There are basically two stages involved in this process:
1. closing the partnership books; and
2. setting up the purchasing company's books.

The steps involved in each of these two stages are listed below.

Closing the Partnership Books

1. Transfer all assets (except cash) and liabilities to the realisation account at book value.
2. Clear the Current accounts to the Capital accounts.
3. The purchase consideration to be paid by the company should be credited to the realisation account and debited to a 'personal account' opened for the purchasing company.
4. Close off the realisation account transferring any balance to the Partners' accounts in their profit-sharing ratio.
5. Close off the Purchasing Company's personal account by crediting it with shares, debentures or cash as appropriate.
6. Close off the partners' accounts by debiting them with shares, debentures or cash in agreed proportions.

The Purchasing Company's Books

1. Record the acquisition by using a 'Purchase of Business Account';
2. In the Purchase of Business Account:
   • credit it with the assets taken over, debiting the individual ledger accounts;
   • debit it with the liabilities taken over, crediting the individual ledger accounts;
   • debit it with the purchase consideration, creating the appropriate accounts; and
   • any difference between the purchase consideration paid and the value of the assets acquired will be treated either as goodwill or a capital reserve.

Examples 36.19–36.21 illustrate the conversion of a partnership to a limited company, with each example becoming progressively more detailed. Example 36.19 requires the preparation of the ledger accounts but not the opening statement of financial position.

EXAMPLE 36.19: LEDGER ACCOUNTS FOR CONVERSION

Macbeth and Hamlet are in partnership selling draughty castles, sharing profits in the ratio 3 : 2. Their draft statement of financial position at 31 December 2012 is as follows:

Non-current assets	Cost	Depreciation	Net
	€	€	€
Freehold premises	30,000		30,000
Fixtures and fittings	5,000	4,000	1,000
Motor vehicles	4,000	1,000	3,000
	39,000	5,000	34,000
Current assets			
Sundry receivables			20,000
Cash at bank			600
			54,600
Partnership accounts			
Capital accounts			
Macbeth			20,000
Hamlet			2,500
			22,500
Current accounts			
Macbeth			3,000
Hamlet			500
			26,000
Non-current liabilities			
Loan – Macbeth			16,000
Current liabilities			
Sundry payables			12,600
			54,600

Lear Limited is incorporated for the purpose of taking over the business. It is to acquire the freehold premises at a valuation of €40,000 and the other assets (with the exception of cash and motor vehicles) at book value. These values are to be introduced into Lear Limited's books. The current liabilities are also taken over by the new company.

The purchase consideration of €60,000 is to be settled by 20,000 ordinary €1 shares in Lear Limited and cash of €30,000, obtained by a bank overdraft. Hamlet is to take over both cars at a valuation of €2,500 and the partners have agreed to divide the shares in their profit-sharing ratio. Macbeth's loan is to be repaid in cash by the partnership.

Requirement Show the ledger account transactions necessary to record the above for the partnership.

Solution

1.

Realisation Account

	€		€
Premises	30,000	Motor vehicles	2,500
Fixtures and fittings	1,000	Payables	12,600
Motor vehicles	3,000	Loan	16,000
Receivables	20,000	Purchase consideration	
Loan (bank)	16,000	(Lear Limited)	60,000
Partners:			
Hamlet	8,440		
Macbeth	12,660		
	91,100		91,100

2.

Capital Accounts

	Macbeth	Hamlet		Macbeth	Hamlet
	€	€		€	€
Cars		2,500	Balance b/d	20,000	2,500
Lear – Shares	18,000	12,000	Current A/c	3,000	500
Bank	17,660		Realisation A/c	12,660	8,440
			Bank		3,060
	35,660	14,500		35,660	14,500

3.

Lear Limited Account

	€		€
Realisation account	60,000	Partners' account: (Shares)	
		Macbeth	18,000
		Hamlet	12,000
			30,000
		Bank	30,000
	60,000		60,000

4.

Cash Account

	€		€
Balance b/d	600	Loan	16,000
Lear	30,000	Macbeth	17,660
Hamlet	3,060		
	33,660		33,660

5. Lear Limited

Purchase of Business Account

	€		€
Payables	12,600	Premises	40,000
Purchase Consideration:		Fixtures and fittings	1,000
Share capital	20,000	Receivables	20,000
Share premium	10,000		
Bank	30,000	∴ Goodwill	11,600
	72,600		72,600

Example 36.20 develops the previous example by including the preparation of the opening company statement of financial position.

EXAMPLE 36.20: LEDGER ACCOUNTS AND OPENING STATEMENT OF FINANCIAL POSITION

A, B and C are in partnership, sharing profits and losses 5/8, 2/8 and 1/8. They decide to form a limited company, ABC Limited, and transfer the net assets, other than cash thereto. The statement of financial position of the partnership at the date of transfer was as follows:

	€				€
Assets	35,000	Capital account:	A	€12,000	
Bank	5,000		B	€10,000	
			C	€8,000	30,000
		Payables			10,000
	40,000				40,000

The assets (excluding bank) are being taken over at a valuation of €50,000, payables at net book value. The purchase consideration is €45,000, made up of 160,000 ordinary shares of 25 cent each, to be divided amongst the partners (A: 1/2, B 1/4, C: 1/4) and €5,000 10% debentures to be divided in profit-sharing ratio.

Requirement Close the books of the partnership and show the opening statement of financial position of ABC Limited.

Solution

The first step is to prepare the realisation account, transferring the book value of the assets into the account and, if any liabilities are being taken over, the book value of the liabilities as a credit into the account. The purchase consideration is then credited into the account and debited to an account with the new company (ABC Limited) and the difference is the profit or loss on realisation. In this example, there is a profit of €20,000 which is divided between the partners in their profit-sharing ratio (see below).

Realisation Account

	€		€
Assets	35,000	Payables	10,000
Profit on realisation:		ABC Limited Net assets	45,000
Capital A/c A 5/8	€12,500		
B 2/8	€5,000		
C 1/8	€2,500		
	20,000		
	55,000		55,000

The next step is to set out the capital accounts of the partners in columnar form as set out below:

Capital Accounts

	A	B	C		A	B	C
	€	€	€		€	€	€
Ordinary shares				Balances	12,000	10,000	8,000
in ABC Limited	20,000	10,000	10,000	Profit on realisation	12,500	5,000	2,500
Debentures in				Bank account			125
ABC Limited	3,125	1,250	625				
Bank account	1,375	3,750					
	24,500	15,000	10,625		24,500	15,000	10,625

The capital accounts have opening balances of €12,000, €10,000 and €8,000 respectively. The profit on realisation is credited to their accounts from the realisation account. Their accounts are debited with the purchase consideration which is in the form of:
1. 160,000 ordinary shares of 25 cent each; and
2. €5,000 10% debentures.

The credits are to the accounts with the new company (ABC Limited).

The ordinary shares are to be divided amongst the partners as agreed in the ratios of A:1/2, B:1/4, C:1/4 therefore the 160,000 shares at 25 cent each, i.e. €40,000, will be divided as follows:

A €20,000 (80,000 shares);
B €10,000 (40,000 shares); and
C €10,000 (40,000 shares).

On the other hand, the debentures are to be divided as agreed in their profit-sharing ratio so they will be divided as follows:

A (5/8) €3,125
B (2/8) €1,250
C (1/8) €625

The balance remaining in the bank account is then distributed to the partners to pay off the remaining balances in their capital accounts. In the solution to this question it is assumed that C has sufficient funds to pay off the debit balance of €125 that arises on his account. If not, that balance would be borne by the other partners on the basis of their last agreed capitals in accordance with the *Garner v. Murray* rule.

Bank Account

	€			€
Balance	5,000	Capital account	A	1,375
Capital account C	125		B	3,750
	5,125			5,125

ABC Limited

	€		€
Realisation account	45,000	Capital account – Shares	40,000
		Debentures	5,000
	45,000		45,000

New Company – ABC Limited:
In addition to closing down the books of the partnership it is necessary to set up an opening statement of financial position of the new company. This statement of financial position will include the ordinary shares and debentures issued by the company which are offset by the assets less liabilities taken over. The statement of financial position of ABC Limited in this example will be as follows:

ABC Limited
STATEMENT OF FINANCIAL POSITION
at conversion date

	€		€
Assets	50,000	Ordinary shares	40,000
Goodwill (see note 3)	5,000	10% debentures	5,000
		Payables	10,000
	55,000		55,000

Notes
1. 160,000 shares of 25 cent each were issued, thus the ordinary share capital will be €40,000.
2. €5,000 of 10% debentures were also issued.
3. The assets taken over are brought in to the new statement of financial position at the valuation when taken over, i.e. €50,000, and the liabilities, in this case payables, at €10,000. This means that there are net assets taken over of €40,000 which cost the company €45,000, and therefore the company has paid for goodwill in the amount of €5,000 which must also be included in the opening statement of financial position to balance it.

The final example in this section builds on the previous example by providing more detailed information on both the partnership and the basis of the conversion.

EXAMPLE 36.21: CONVERSION TO A LIMITED COMPANY

Apple, Pear, Banana and Grape are in partnership, sharing profits and losses 7 : 4 : 2 : 2. At 31 December 2012 they decide to form a limited company called Fruit Limited. At that date the statement of financial position of the partnership was as follows:

	€				€
Goodwill	30,000	Capital account	Apple		80,000
Property	70,000		Pear		30,000
Plant	23,600		Banana		19,000
Motor Vehicles	12,900		Grape		17,000
					146,000
Inventory	32,300	Loan account –	Apple		9,000
Receivables	30,300	Payables			31,700
		Bank overdraft			12,400
	199,100				199,100

The company is to take over all assets and liabilities except the bank overdraft and Apple's loan which is to be settled by the other partners in their profit-sharing ratio. The costs of conversion, which amounted to €3,200, are to be paid by the partnership.

The payables are to be taken over at a discount of €1,900 and the assets at the following valuations.

	€
Goodwill	Nil
Property	85,000
Plant	22,000
Motor Vehicles	10,700
Inventory	27,600
Receivables	29,100

The purchase consideration is €140,000, made up of 125,000 ordinary shares of €1 each (€65,000 of which are payable to Apple, the balance to be divided among the other partners in their profit-sharing ratio) and €10,000 in cash.

Requirement Assuming all the above transactions have taken place, close the books of the partnership and prepare the opening statement of financial position of Fruit Limited at 31 December 2012.

Solution

Realisation Account					
	€				€
Assets at NBV	199,100	Payables			31,700
Bank Cost of Conversion	3,200	Fruit Limited Purchase consideration			140,000
		Loss on realisation			
		Apple	7/15	14,280	
		Pear	4/15	8,160	
		Banana	2/15	4,080	
		Grape	2/15	4,080	30,600
	202,300				202,300

Loan Account Apple

			€		€
Capital account	Pear	4/8	4,500	Balance	9,000
	Banana	2/8	2,250		
	Grape	2/8	2,250		
			9,000		9,000

Bank Account

		€		€
Fruit Limited		10,000	Balance	12,400
Capital account	Apple	1,880	Cost of conversion	3,200
	Pear	4,860	Capital account Banana	1,570
	Grape	430		
		17,170		17,170

Capital Accounts

	Apple €	Pear €	Banana €	Grape €		Apple €	Pear €	Banana €	Grape €
Loss on Realisation	14,280	8,160	4,080	4,080	Balance	80,000	30,000	19,000	17,000
Fruit Ord. Shares	65,000	30,000	15,000	15,000	Loan Apple		4,500	2,250	2,250
Share Premium	2,600	1,200	600	600	Bank	1,880	4,860	–	430
Bank		1,570							
	81,880	39,360	21,250	19,680		81,880	39,360	21,250	19,680

Fruit Limited

			€				€	€	€
Purchase consideration			140,000	Ordinary Shares:					
				Apple				65,000	
				Pear	4/8	30,000			
				Banana	2/8	15,000			
				Grape	2/8	15,000	60,000	125,000	
				Share Premium:					
				Apple	65/125		2,600		
				Pear	30/125		1,200		
				Banana	15/125		600		
				Grape	15/125		600	5,000	
				Cash				10,000	
			140,000					140,000	

Fruit Limited
STATEMENT OF FINANCIAL POSITION
at 31 December 2012

	€		€
Property	85,000	Ordinary shares of €1 each	125,000
Plant	22,000	Share Premium	5,000

Motor Vehicles	10,700	Capital reserve (see note)	4,600
Inventory	27,600		134,600
Receivables	29,100	Payables	29,800
		Bank overdraft	19,000
	174,400		174,400

This is to be divided amongst the partners in the ratio of the shares issued.

Capital reserve

	€	€
Asset Valuations:		
Property	85,000	
Plant	22,000	
Motor Vehicles	10,700	
Inventory	27,600	
Receivables	29,100	
	174,400	
Less: Payables	29,800	144,600
Purchase consideration		140,000
Capital Reserve		4,600

Capital reserve is effectively the opposite of goodwill.

36.9 CONCLUSION

The key points about partnership accounts are as follows:
- The initial capital put into the business by each partner is shown by means of a capital account for each partner.
- Each partner also has a current account.
- The net profit of the partnership is appropriated by the partners according to some previously agreed ratio.
- Partners may be charged interest on their drawings and may receive interest on capital.
- If a partner makes a loan to the business, he will receive interest on it in the normal way.
- On admission or retirement of a partner, one partnership ends and another begins. The goodwill of the old partnership must be valued and attributed to the old partners in the old profit-sharing ratio, as should any profit or loss on revaluation of assets. If goodwill (or revaluation profits and losses) are not to be retained in the books, they must be attributed to the new partners in the new profit-sharing ratio (debit capital accounts for goodwill and revaluation surplus, credit for revaluation deficit).
- The conversion of a partnership business to a limited company effectively involves the dissolution of the partnership. The assets are transferred to the company in exchange for an issue of shares and loan stock.

LEARNING OBJECTIVES

After having studied this chapter on accounting for partnerships, you should:

Learning Objective 1 Be aware of the key aspects of the Partnership Act 1890.

Every partnership is set up by an agreement between the partners, either orally or in writing. If the agreement between the partners is silent on any matter affecting relationship between the partners, then the relevant provisions of the Partnership Act 1890 apply.

Learning Objective 2 Understand the basic accounting principles with respect to partnerships.

The basic book-keeping and accounting procedures adopted in relation to companies apply equally to partnerships. However, differences arise in dealing with the ownership of the partnership and accounting for issues such as capital to be introduced by partners, the distribution of profits between partners and drawings by partners. (See **Section 36.3.**)

Learning Objective 3 Be able to account for simple partnership changes, partnership changes requiring adjustments to asset values, the dissolution of a partnership, amalgamations and the conversion of a partnership to a limited company.

Aspects of partnership accounting can be relatively complicated and, particularly from a student perspective, require considerable practice. These issues are explained and illustrated in **Sections 36.4–36.8.**

QUESTIONS

Self-test Questions

1. What is a Partnership?
2. What is the difference between a partner's capital account and a partner's current account?
3. How is profit shared between partners?
4. What are the entries required to introduce goodwill into a partnership and subsequently to eliminate it?
5. If tangible assets are revalued on admission of a partner, how is the profit or loss on revaluation treated?
6. What does a realisation account act as?
7. What is the entry for the purchase consideration from a company for the partnership assets?
8. Where does the balance on the realisation account go?
9. In the company's books, where does the balance on the Purchase of Business account go?

Review Questions

(See **Appendix One** for Suggested Solutions to Review Questions.)

Question 36.1 (Based on Chartered Accountants Ireland, P2 Summer 1997)

Murphy, Noonan and MacIntyre are in partnership, sharing profits and losses in the ratio 4 : 3 : 1. The following statement of financial position was available for the partnership for the year ended 31 December 2011:

	€000	€000
Non-current assets		
Premises		150,000
Fixtures and fittings		65,000
Motor vehicles		40,000
		255,000
Current assets		
Inventory	20,000	
Receivables	15,000	
Bank	25,000	
		60,000
		315,000
Capital accounts		
Murphy	120,000	
Noonan	90,000	
MacIntyre	40,000	250,000
Current accounts		
Murphy	7,500	
Noonan	4,200	
MacIntyre	3,300	15,000
Loan from MacIntyre		10,000
Current liabilities		
Payables		40,000
		315,000

The following additional information is available:
1. On 31 December 2011, MacIntyre decided to retire from the partnership, and on 1 January 2012, Riordan was admitted to the partnership. It was agreed that the new profit-sharing ratio would be Murphy, Noonan, Riordan 5 : 4 : 1.
2. On 31 December 2011, some of the assets and liabilities of the partnership were revalued as follows:

	€000
Premises	200
Fixtures and fittings	40
Inventory	15

All other assets and liabilities remained at their existing book values.

3. It was agreed that Riordan would introduce €40,000 into the partnership, this amount to include €6,000 in respect of Riordan's share of goodwill. A goodwill account is not to be maintained permanently in the accounts of the partnership.

4. On MacIntyre's retirement, it was agreed that he should take his car at its net book value in part payment of all that is owed to him by the partnership, excluding his loan. In relation to his loan of €10,000, MacIntyre agreed to an immediate repayment of half this amount, with the balance remaining as a loan to the partnership.

5. Profits for the year ended 31 December 2012 were €28,000.

6. Cash drawings in the year ended 31 December 2012 were as follows:

	€
Murphy	4,000
Noonan	2,000
Riordan	1,000

7. Following a major disagreement between the partners on 31 December 2012, it was decided that the partnership should be dissolved. The firm paid its payables in full, paid realisation expenses of €2,000, and repaid MacIntyre's loan of €5,000. The assets of the firm realised €270,000.

8. The statement of financial position extract for the partnership (before dissolution) at 31 December 2012 was as follows:

	€000
Premises	200
Fixtures and fittings	40
Motor vehicles	35
Inventory	23
Receivables	35
Bank	4.7
Payables	(40)
Loan from MacIntyre	(5)
	292.7

Requirement

(a) Prepare the revaluation account at 31 December 2011.

(b) Prepare the realisation account on the dissolution of the partnership.

(c) Prepare the partners' capital and current accounts to reflect all of the above transactions.

Question 36.2 (Based on Chartered Accountants Ireland, P2 Summer 1996)

North, South and East have been in partnership for many years, sharing profits in the ratio 5 : 3 : 2. On 1 January 2012 they formed a company, Direction Limited, to take over the assets and liabilities of the partnership at that date. The following information is available:

1. The statement of financial position of the partnership as at 31 December 2011, is as follows:

	€000
Non-current assets	85
Inventory	15
Trade receivables	35
Bank	5
	140
Capital accounts	
North	40
South	35
East	20
Current accounts	
North	8
South	4
East	3
Payables	30
	140

2. The agreement to take over the net assets of the partnership provides that the non-current assets would be taken over at a value of €130,000 and receivables at €30,000. All other assets and liabilities are to be taken over at book value.
3. The company is to issue €1 ordinary shares to the partners in proportion to the final balances remaining on their capital accounts (after the transfer of current account balances) at 31 December 2011.
4. The company was incorporated on 1 January 2012.
5. It is agreed that the three partners should become directors of the company and should each receive directors' fees of €2,000 per annum.
6. Direction Limited prepared the following trial balance at 31 December 2012:

	€000	€000
Non-current assets	230	
Receivables	60	
Inventory	25	
Bank	20	
Payables	–	40
Share capital and reserves	–	295
	335	335

Requirement
(a) Close the books of the partnership.
(b) Prepare the statement of financial position of Direction Limited for the year ended 31 December 2012.

Question 36.3 (Based on Chartered Accountants Ireland, P2 Summer 1999)

Redcar, Pontefract and Haydock are in partnership, sharing profits 5 : 3 : 2. The year-end of the partnership is 31 December. On 31 December 2012, Haydock retires from the partnership. The summarised statement of financial position of the partnership at that date is as follows:

Redcar, Pontefract & Haydock
STATEMENT OF FINANCIAL POSITION
as at 31 December 2012

	€000	€000
Non-current assets		120
Current assets	50	
Bank	10	
		60
		180
Capital accounts		
Redcar	80	
Pontefract	40	
Haydock	20	140
Current liabilities		40
		180

The following additional information is available:

1. On the same date that Haydock retired, it was agreed that Ludlow would be admitted as a partner. Ludlow would introduce €50,000 into the partnership; this amount was to include €5,000 in respect of his share of goodwill. A goodwill account is *not* to be maintained in the books of the partnership.
2. The new profit-sharing ratio would be: Redcar : Pontefract : Ludlow – 6 : 3 : 1.
3. At 31 December 2012, non-current assets were valued at €160,000 and current assets were valued at €45,000. The balance owing to Haydock on his retirement should be transferred to a loan account.

Requirement Assuming that the assets of the partnership are to be taken over at their revalued amounts, show:
(a) the revaluation account;
(b) the partners' capital accounts; and
(c) the amended statement of financial position of the partnership to reflect the above changes.

Challenging Questions

(Suggested Solutions to Challenging Questions are available to lecturers.)

Question 36.1 (Based on Chartered Accountants Ireland, P2 Autumn 2000)

Pop, Fizz and Bottle are in partnership as a soft drink distributor, sharing profits in the ratio 5 : 3 : 2. The summarised statement of financial position of the partnership as at 31 December 2012 is as follows:

SUMMARISED STATEMENT OF FINANCIAL POSITION
as at 31 December 2012

	€000	€000
Non-current assets		120
Current assets		
Inventory	32	

Receivables	68	
Cash at bank	125	
		225
		345
Capital accounts		
Pop	160	
Fizz	140	
Bottle	20	
		320
Current liabilities		
Payables		25
		345

The following additional information is available:

1. It was decided that the partnership would convert into a limited company trading as BUBBLES Limited on 1 April 2013.
2. On conversion, the non-current assets were valued at €170,000 and the partners decided that book debts were overstated as their customer, X Limited, had been declared bankrupt, whilst owing €8,000 to the partnership. Discussions with the receiver indicated they were only expecting to receive 25 cent for every €1 outstanding by X Limited to the partnership. Five percent of the remaining general debt was also deemed to be non-collectible and, accordingly, it was agreed to provide for this amount before the book debts were transferred.
3. Pop, Fizz and Bottle will be directors in the newly formed company, each receiving a salary of €10,000 per annum.
4. The partners' final capital accounts will not be repaid to them. These will be converted into loan accounts in the limited company.
5. The issued share capital of the company will be 200,000 €1 ordinary shares. The partners have agreed that, on incorporation, they will allocate their shareholding in the same proportion as their old profit-sharing ratio. These shares will be purchased through the directors' loan accounts.
6. The profits of the partnership for the last three months of trading ended 31 March 2013 (before adjusting for the allowance for the receivable) were €65,000 and it is assumed that these profits were all received in cash during the period. Profits are allocated to partners after charging interest on opening capital of 20% per annum, as agreed in the partnership agreement.

Requirement

(a) Close the books of the partnership by preparing the following accounts:
  (i) realisation account;
  (ii) partners' capital accounts as at 31 March 2013.
(b) Prepare the opening statement of financial position for BUBBLES Limited as at 1 April 2013.

Question 36.2 *(Based on Chartered Accountants Ireland, P2 Autumn 2001)*

Law and Order are partners in a solicitors' partnership, sharing profits in the ratio 3 : 2. The year-end of the partnership is 31 December. The summarised statement of financial position of the partnership as at 31 December 2011 is as follows:

Law and Order
STATEMENT OF FINANCIAL POSITION
as at 31 December 2011

	€000	€000
Non-current Assets		
Property	30	
Office equipment	20	
		50
Current assets	18	
Cash at bank	17	
		35
		85
Capital accounts		
Law	40	
Order	20	
		60
Current liabilities		25
		85

The following additional information is available:

1. On 1 July 2012 Law retired and on that date a new partner, Judge, was admitted. The new profit-sharing ratio is to be 1 : 1.
2. Set out below are relevant extracts from the partnership agreement:
   (i) on the retirement of a partner the assets of the partnership must be revalued and the partners' capital accounts adjusted accordingly; and
   (ii) profits are allocated in the partners' profit-sharing ratio after interest on capital and salaries have been deducted. Interest on capital of 10% per annum for Law and 5% per annum for Order is calculated on the partners' opening capital accounts. Judge is not entitled to interest on capital.

   Agreed partner salaries per annum are as follows:

	€
Law	17,000
Order	30,000
Judge	21,000

   (iii) partners are entitled to drawings of €1,000 per month, which will be credited to their capital account. This provision also applies to new partners.
3. On 1 July 2012 Judge paid €10,000 into the practice in respect of goodwill. No goodwill account is to be maintained in the accounts.
4. On 1 July 2012, the property held by the partnership was valued at €55,000. The book value of all the remaining assets and liabilities (except for the bank balance) remained the same.
5. On his retirement Law's capital account will be converted into a loan account.
6. Net profits of the partnership for the year ended 31 December 2012 were €112,000. Assume that all profits have been earned evenly during the year and have been received in cash at bank.

Requirement Prepare each of the following:
(a) Income statement appropriation account for the year ended 31 December 2012.
(b) Partners' capital accounts as at 31 December 2012.
(c) Statement of financial position of the partnership as at 31 December 2012.

Question 36.3 (Based on Chartered Accountants Ireland, P2 Summer 2002)

Shamrock, Thistle and Leek are a partnership, sharing profits in the ratio 5 : 3 : 2 respectively, and are involved in the design of Gaelic theme pubs. STOUT Limited ('STOUT') has decided to purchase the business at the end of its financial year (31 December 2012). The statement of financial position of the partnership as at that date is as follows:

	€	€
Non-current Assets (net of depreciation)		
Land and buildings		260,000
Plant and equipment		40,000
Motor vehicles (see Note (i))		32,000
		332,000
Current Assets		
Inventory (at cost)	61,000	
Receivables	130,000	
Cash at bank and in hand	2,500	
		193,500
		525,500
Capital Accounts		
Shamrock		140,000
Thistle		80,000
Leek		77,000
		297,000
Non-current liabilities (see Note (ii))		59,500
Building loan	67,000	
Other liabilities (see Note (i))	102,500	
		169,000
		525,500

Notes to the accounts:
(i) Other liabilities comprise:

	€
Trade payables	48,000
Accrued expenses	12,500
VAT and PAYE	23,000
Bank loans:	
Car 1	8,000
Car 2	11,000
	102,500

The net book values in respect of the above cars financed by way of bank loans are €18,000 for Car 1 and €14,000 for Car 2 respectively. There are no other motor vehicles in the business.

(ii) Long-term liabilities are made up as follows:

Bank Loans:

Car 1	€16,000
Car 2	€8,000
Building Loan	€35,000

The following additional details are also available:

1. Shamrock is to keep his car (Car 1) personally, and also pay off the bank loan thereon personally. (This asset and corresponding liability are not to be taken over by STOUT.)
2. All other non-current assets and the bank loan liabilities in respect of Car 2 only are being taken over by STOUT at an agreed price of €450,000.
3. Of the inventory, it has been agreed that 20% is actually worthless. Apart from this, STOUT is purchasing the remainder at cost less 5%.
4. Receivables, less a general provision of 7.5%, are to be taken over by STOUT.
5. Trade payables and accrued expenses are to be taken over by STOUT at a value of €55,000.
6. As well as the VAT and PAYE balances disclosed in the accounts, which STOUT Limited will pay in full, the auditors of STOUT have discovered an additional VAT liability of €16,000. They intend to disclose this to the authorities, and interest and penalties of 12% will accrue in respect of this additional liability. It has been agreed that the partners will pay for 50% of this additional VAT liability and 80% of penalties.
7. The building loan liability is not being taken over by STOUT. Instead, this loan should be allocated to the partners in proportion to their profit-sharing ratio.
8. Legal costs relating to the sale of the partnership amount to €15,000 and are to be paid by the partners.

Requirement Prepare a realisation account and the partners' capital accounts to show the closure of the partnership books.

Question 36.4 (Based on Chartered Accountants Ireland, P2 Autumn 2002)

Jones, Hopkins and Lewis are in partnership, sharing profits in the following ratio:

Jones	40%
Hopkins	30%
Lewis	30%

Interest on capital is charged on the opening capital accounts of Jones and Lewis at 3% and 5% respectively. Hopkins receives an annual salary of €15,000. The financial year-end of the partnership is 31 December each year.

On 1 July 2012 Clarke was introduced as a fourth partner in the business. The revised profit-sharing ratios are as follows.

Jones	30%
Hopkins	20%

Lewis	20%
Clarke	30%

The new partner (Clarke) is to receive an annual salary of €5,000 – interest on capital and salaries in respect of the other partners is to remain unchanged.

The following is the DRAFT TRIAL BALANCE of the partnership as at 31 December 2012:

	€	€
Sales		275,000
Opening inventory	60,000	
Purchases	125,000	
Motor expenses	15,000	
Salaries	30,000	
Telephone	6,000	
Heat and light	5,000	
General expenses	1,000	
Property – cost	50,000	
Property – additions	20,000	
Property accumulated depreciation		6,000
Equipment – cost	75,000	
Equipment – accumulated depreciation		36,600
Motor cars – cost	100,000	
Motor cars – accumulated depreciation		56,250
Trade receivables	15,000	
Cash at bank	6,500	
Cash on hand	200	
Bank overdraft		16,000
Loan account		15,000
Trade payables		23,000
Opening capital		
– Jones		120,150
– Hopkins		94,000
– Lewis		93,000
Drawings		
– Jones	80,000	
– Hopkins	70,000	
– Lewis	70,000	
– Clarke	6,300	
	735,000	735,000

On the advice of the partners, the following adjustments have to be made to the above draft trial balance:

1. Inventory – an inventory-count was conducted at the year-end. Inventory was valued at €82,000 based on cost. However, 15% of this inventory has a net realisable value of only €6,000. A further €8,000 of the total inventory is considered obsolete and should be written off.

2. Non-current Assets – no depreciation for the year ended 31 December 2012 has been included in the draft trial balance. Depreciation should be provided for as follows:

Property   4% per annum on a straight-line basis;
Equipment   20% per annum on a reducing-balance basis; and
Motor cars   25% per annum on a reducing-balance basis.

3. Receivables – a specific unrecoverable debt of €1,200 is to be provided for. An allowance for receivables should be provided for, based on 1.5% of all remaining receivables.
4. Accruals – year-end accruals have *not* been included in the draft trial balance. Accruals are to be provided as follows:

Accountancy   €1,500   Heat and light   €500   Telephone   €300

5. Capital Grant – at the year-end a capital grant of €12,000 was receivable in respect of the year's property additions. This is to be released to the income statement in line with depreciation. No entries have been included in the draft trial balance in respect of this capital grant.
6. Goodwill – at the time of Clarke's admission to the partnership goodwill was valued at €15,000. No goodwill account is to be maintained in the accounts.
7. Assume that the profits or losses accrue evenly over the course of the year.
8. No revaluation of non-current assets was required at any time during the year.

Requirement In order to account for the admission of Clarke to the partnership and, in light of the above adjustments, draft each of the following:
(a) The income statement for the year ended 31 December 2012.
(b) The statement of financial position as at 31 December 2012.
(c) The partners' individual capital accounts as at 31 December 2012.

Question 36.5 (Based on Chartered Accountants Ireland, P2 Summer 2003)

Bob, Chris and David are in partnership, sharing profits in the following ratios:

Bob   60%
Chris   30%
David   10%

On 31 December 2012 David retires from the partnership. The summarised statement of financial position of the partnership as at that date is as follows:

SUMMARISED STATEMENT OF FINANCIAL POSITION
as at 31 December 2012

	€000	€000
Non-current Assets		
Property	230	
Office equipment	85	
Motor vehicles	64	379
Current Assets	55	
Cash at bank	18	
		73
		452

Capital accounts	
Bob	168
Chris	140
David	120
	428
Current Liabilities	24
	452

The following additional information is available:

1. On 31 December 2012 Alan is admitted as a partner. Alan is to introduce cash of €60,000 into the partnership, including €5,000 for his share of the goodwill. A goodwill account is not to be maintained in the books of the partnership. The partners have also agreed that Alan can also introduce his own car into the partnership. The car has a value of €15,000.

2. After the change in partners, the new profit-sharing ratio is to be as follows:

Alan	10%
Bob	50%
Chris	40%

3. On 31 December 2012, the property was valued at €500,000. This revaluation is to be reflected in the accounts.

4. On leaving the partnership, David took his company car and computer. It was agreed that David could take these assets at their respective net book values. The assets were both purchased on 1 January 2009 for €30,000 and had been depreciated at 20% on a straight-line basis.

5. On retirement, any balance remaining on David's capital account will be converted into a loan.

Requirement Prepare each of the following:

(a) The partners' amended capital accounts as at 31 December 2012.

(b) The amended statement of financial position for the new partnership as at 31 December 2012.

Question 36.6 *(Based on Chartered Accountants Ireland, P2 Summer 2000)*

BECKHAM and ADAMS are in partnership, sharing profits in the ratio of 5 : 3. NOONAN and NORTON are in partnership in a similar business sharing profits in the ratio of 5 : 4. It is decided that the two partnerships should amalgamate to form one firm, A B & N. The following information is available:

1. The profit-sharing ratios in the new firm will be as follows: BECKHAM : ADAMS : NOONAN : NORTON – 10 : 7 : 8 : 5

2. The statements of financial position of the two firms at the date of the amalgamation were as follows:

	BECKHAM & ADAMS €000	NOONAN and NORTON €000
Non-current Assets	50	30
Current Assets		
Inventory	10	12

Receivables	20	13
Bank	15	5
	95	60
Capital Accounts		
Beckham	50	
Adams	25	
Noonan		35
Norton		15
Current		
Payables	15	10
Taxation payable	5	–
	95	60

3. Under the terms of the amalgamation, the following was agreed:
    (i) the non-current assets of BECKHAM and ADAMS would be valued at €70,000 while the non-current assets of NOONAN and NORTON would be valued at €20,000;
    (ii) the inventory of BECKHAM and ADAMS would be valued at €7,000 while the inventory of NOONAN and NORTON would be valued at €10,000;
    (iii) all other assets and all liabilities to be taken over at their book values;
4. The capital of A B & N is to be contributed by the partners in their profit-sharing ratios and is to amount in total to €130,000.

Requirement
(a) Close the books of the partnerships of BECKHAM and ADAMS, and NOONAN and NORTON by preparing the following accounts:
    (i) the partners' capital account;
    (ii) the realisation account;
    (iii) the bank account.
(b) Prepare the opening statement of financial position of A B & N.

Question 36.7 (Based on Chartered Accountants Ireland, P2 Autumn 2000)

Rod, Hook and Bait are in partnership sharing profits in the ratio 6 : 4 : 2. The statement of financial position of the partnership as at 31 December 2012 was as follows:

	€000	€000
Non-current assets		2,000
Current assets		
Inventory	300	
Receivables	900	
Bank	100	
		1,300
		3,300
Capital accounts		
Rod		1,300
Hook		800
Bait		400
		2,500

Current liabilities		
Payables	600	
Accruals	200	
		800
		3,300

The following additional information is available:

1. On 31 December 2012, Hook retired from the partnership. On the same date Line was admitted as a partner. It was agreed that Line should introduce €400,000 into the partnership, this amount to include €40,000 in respect of his share of goodwill. (A goodwill account is not to be maintained in the books of the partnership.) The new profit-sharing ratio will be Rod : Bait : Line – 7 : 3 : 2. The balance owing to Hook on his retirement is to be transferred to a loan account.

2. On 1 July 2013, the business was sold to FISH Limited. Under the terms of the sale agreement, the non-current assets were to be taken over at a value of €2,500,000, and inventory at €240,000. All other assets and liabilities were to be taken over at book value.

3. FISH Limited issued €1 ordinary shares to the partners in proportion to the final balances on their capital accounts at 30 June 2013. The profit available for appropriation for the six-month period ended 30 June 2013 was €100,000.

4. FISH Limited was incorporated and commenced trading on 1 July 2013.

Requirement

(a) Prepare the partners' capital accounts at 31 December 2012 to reflect the retirement of Hook and the entry of Line to the partnership.

(b) Close the books of the partnership by preparing the following accounts:
   (i) realisation account; and
   (ii) partners' capital accounts.

(Ignore depreciation.)

Appendix One

REVIEW QUESTIONS – SUGGESTED SOLUTIONS

Question Intro. 1

While on the one hand changing the residual values and useful lives of the company's non-current assets will provide investors and creditors with less useful information about ABC Limited's operating profit, on the other hand, Tim may feel he has an obligation to protect his fellow accounting staff.

However, a broader stakeholder analysis might suggest that misstating the depreciation expense could lead to lack of confidence in ABC Limited's financial statements that, if detected, could lead to a higher cost of capital and fines. In the long run, Tim and his accounting colleagues, together with other employees, could lose their jobs.

Question Intro. 2

The trade receivables should be reclassified from current to non-current trade receivables as current assets are defined as those that will be consumed or generate cash within one year. If the trade receivables are not reclassified, while the current ratio will remain high enough for the company to secure the additional debt finance, the lender may be misled about the financial state of the company and its potential to meet the loan conditions.

Since the accountant and the finance director recognise that the delay in the collection of the trade receivables has an impact on the conflicting interests of DEF Limited and the lender, the reclassification decision has ethical dimensions. If the finance director insists that the trade receivables should not be reclassified, the accountant will have to decide whether to accept the finance director's decision, speak with other directors in the company or take some other action. Other actions may include speaking to the audit committee or to the chairman of the board of directors.

Question Intro. 3

The finance director should not manipulate the company's profit before tax to meet the bonus arrangement. The economic interests of the directors and the potential for their bonus plans conflict with the shareholders' interest that the company's financial statements present a true and fair view. If the warranty expense is reduced and the original estimate transpires to be accurate, the shareholders are harmed because the company will have paid a bonus that the directors did not earn. The managing director is acting unethically and his action serves only his self-interest and has no clear basis in proper accounting procedures.

Question Intro. 4

There is no perfect or easy solution to a situation such as this. Where there is a high degree of estimation, as is the case with percentage of completion, there is also much room for discussion, disagreement and undue influence to be brought to light. Professional judgement and integrity are certainly challenged in situations of this nature.

There should be consistency in the approach adopted year-on-year to estimate the percentage of completion, together with an assessment of the experience, knowledge and skill of the individual project managers so as to obtain some confidence in the reliability of their estimates. The financial accountant has, however, a professional obligation to ensure that, in his professional judgement, the final results are presented fairly and in accordance with generally accepted accounting principles.

Question Intro. 5

This is an issue of potential conflict of interest. Would a reasonable and informed third party, having knowledge of all the relevant information, reasonably conclude that your independence was compromised? Have you actually been influenced in your professional judgement as a result of your client's offer?

It is necessary to establish the facts of the case. For example, is the client offering you a 'deal' greater than that currently being offered? For example, is it greater than the discount to which members of staff are entitled on a regular basis? Indeed, is it a 'good price' merely by reference to other retailers and is it in fact the 'normal' price?

Even if the offer made by the client is specific to you, the quantum of the benefit is likely to be relevant. For example, if the effective discount is 5%, whatever the price of the vehicle purchased, then it is unlikely that an informed third party would regard that your independence was compromised. In addition to the ethical guidance of Chartered Accountants Ireland, you should also refer to your employer's internal policies and contractual obligations. Moreover, common sense should dictate that it would be sensible to clarify your position with your employer.

Independence of mind is the state of mind that permits the provision of an opinion without being affected by influences that compromise professional judgement, allowing an individual to act with integrity and exercise objectivity and professional scepticism. Independence in appearance requires you to avoid facts and circumstances that are so significant that a reasonable and informed third party, having knowledge of all relevant information, including safeguards applied, would reasonably conclude that integrity, objectivity, and professional scepticism had been compromised. Thus, it can be seen that there are circumstances when your client's offer may not compromise your integrity, especially as you are a trainee accountant.

However, there are circumstances in which your integrity could be called into doubt, and the more senior your position in the firm, the greater the risk of this occurring. It may, however, be possible to ensure that safeguards are put in place to protect your independence. These might include an independent review of any work undertaken, the work to be undertaken by qualified staff within your firm who are not directly under your influence, rotation of the partner in charge and also the senior staff. The appropriate safeguards will depend on: your position within the firm; the size and circumstances of the practice and the client; and the perceived threat to your integrity.

Question 1.1

(a) *The Corporate Report* (Accounting Standards Steering Committee, 1975), which was the first major initiative in Britain and Ireland to examine the purpose of financial reporting, was a comprehensive treatise that reviewed users, purposes and measurement bases for financial reporting. *The Corporate Report*, identified seven groups who are potential users of financial reports. These are as follows:

(i) The *equity investor group* comprises both existing holders of equity interest in the business entity (e.g. ordinary shareholders in a limited company) and investors who might be interested in investing in the equity of business.

(ii) The *loan creditor group* includes both long-term loan creditors of the business (e.g. debenture holders) and short-term creditors (e.g. banks providing an overdraft facility).

(iii) The *employee group* includes both existing and prospective employees of the business, and possibly also its past employees (if they receive a pension from the business).

(iv) The *analyst adviser group* includes financial analysts and journalists, economists, trade unions, stockbrokers and credit-rating agencies. Members of this group use published accounts for their own research purposes or to provide analysis and advice for other groups such as investors, employees and the general public.

(v) The *business contact group* includes customers, trade creditors and suppliers of the business and, in a different sense, competitors, and also those interested in a business merger or takeover.

(vi) *Government departments* (both local and national) may have a varying interest in published accounts (e.g. tax authorities have a different interest from departments concerned with promoting or regulating trade and commerce).

(vii) *The public* includes taxpayers, rate-payers, political parties, consumer groups, environment protection societies and local pressure groups etc.

(b) The needs of each user of financial accounts will vary according to the group or groups to which the user belongs.

(i) Equity investors need information to help them reach share trading decisions, such as whether to buy or sell certain shares and whether or not to subscribe to a new share issue. Information might also be required to help them make voting decisions at general meetings. They need to make judgements about future share prices and future dividends. To help them, information about the past results of the business, the current situation and forecast future prospects are required.

(ii) Long-term loan creditors are interested in similar issues to those described in (i) above. For listed securities, investors want information to assist them in trading decisions. They are also concerned about the security of their loan, and information about the efficiency of management may be helpful, as well as about the economic stability and vulnerability of the borrower. If debenture trust deeds or articles of association restrict the borrowing capacity of the borrower, the long-term loan creditors may use published accounts to check that the terms of the deed or articles are being adhered to.

(iii) Short-term loan creditors (such as banks) are concerned with the short-term liquidity of the borrower and its ability to meet its debt payments when they fall due. Information about the liquidity of the borrower will affect the loan debenture of this group.

(iv) The employee group requires information to help make an assessment about the security and prospects of employment, and to help in reaching a judgement about the level of wages or salaries which they might justifiably expect to receive. Other information needs concern the ability of the business to continue paying wages, conditions (health and safety etc.) at work, the contributions made by employees to the business, training and career prospects.

(v) The analyst-adviser group acts as an agency for members of other user groups, and its information needs will therefore be the same as those of the user groups it advises. For example, stockholders need information similar to the requirements of equity investors and loan investors, whereas trade unions need information which is of interest to employees. Analysts and advisers will probably be capable of a more sophisticated analysis of information, and might therefore require more detailed information.

(vi) The business contact group's information needs are variable. Regular suppliers need to know about the long-term supply requirements and financial viability of the business; and trade creditors want to know about its ability to pay its debts on time and without default.

Customers are concerned about the continuing supply of goods from the business (including prices, quality and conditions of sale). Competitors attempt to make comparisons between the results of the reporting entity and their own performance. Those concerns interested in a merger or takeover will have the same information needs as the equity investor group.

(vii) The government as a debtor or creditor of a business may have the same information needs as members of the business contact group. As tax collectors, the government will demand tax returns from a business and may also be concerned about the ability of the business to pay additional levies from, say, a new tax. The central government may want returns in order to analyse the national balance of payments, gross national product and other such indicators of national economic performance.

(viii) In general, government departments and agencies need information to assess the likely effect of government policies in achieving the government's political or economic aims.

(ix) Members of the public require information to help them assess the effect of the business entity on the community as a whole. *The Corporate Report* noted that 'members of the community may wish to know about the role of economic entities as employers, cash flows, profitability and efficiency of enterprises, contributions to political organisations, pressure groups and charities, their impact on the balance of trade, transactions with home and overseas governments, compliance with law and voluntary actions and expenditure affecting society or the environment. Corporate reports cannot satisfy all the imaginable information needs to the public'.

(c) The purpose of financial statements is to present information to people who wish to know something of the performance and situation of the reporting business entity. Accountancy is largely an information system for management, owners of the business and others.

The government clearly considers that not only existing shareholders but also other users of accounts are entitled to information about certain business entities and, to this end, there have been a variety of enactments about the amount of accounting information to be published. In particular, the company legislation specifies minimum information which companies must publish and file, for public inspection, with the registrar. The government's assessment of user needs therefore influences financial reporting.

While individual business entities might decide voluntarily to provide extra information to users of accounts, it would appear that, in practice, information disclosure is kept to the minimum required by law or an accounting standard.

In theory, the needs of different user groups should be ascertained and the way in which they use financial information to reach decisions should be analysed. Financial statements can then be prepared which help them to make their decisions. If necessary, users should also be educated to understand properly what the accounting information is telling them.

The Corporate Report considered the needs of various user groups, and came to the conclusion that, although some 'missing' information needs could be met by additional disclosures in existing financial statements (e.g. in notes to the accounts), there was also a need for additional financial statements (such as a value-added statement, an employment report, a statement of money exchanges with government, a statement of future prospects etc.). The discussion paper recommended that financial statements should be consciously moulded and developed to meet the needs of users for decision-making.

The paper also acknowledged, however, that some users' needs are more important than the needs of others. For example, the information needs of the public are too broad to be accommodated and no concessions should be made to the needs of business competitors. It would seem reasonable to presume that the most important user groups are equity investors (existing or potential owners of the business) and employees, together with loan creditors and trade creditors.

The claim of shareholders (as owners of the business) to the greatest amount of information is perhaps acknowledged by the company legislation which allows small- and medium-sized companies to file modified accounts, although full accounts must be presented to shareholders.

The information needs of employees are not yet well catered for by financial statements, although some companies publish employment and/or employee reports voluntarily. Company legislation also calls for more disclosure of employment information than hitherto. Company legislation has also called for disclosure of information which may assist loan or creditor groups in making lending decisions to a company (e.g. information about guarantees and financial commitments, contingent liabilities etc.).

Published financial information is rarely adapted to suit the needs of the analyst-adviser group for more sophisticated information, although some businesses might agree voluntarily to supply economists or statisticians etc. with confidential information for their work.

It has also been suggested that financial statements should be simplified to help users who do not properly understand accounting information. Most notably, some companies simplify their results and present them in an employee report, to give their employees some useful understanding of the financial situation of their business. This type of report is voluntary and very few businesses provide them.

In summary, it may be concluded that the information needs of some users are more prominent than the needs of others. These needs are considered by government legislation, regulations in accounting standards and on a voluntary basis by individual business entities. To a certain extent, each of these attempts to ensure that a fixed minimum amount of information is provided to help user groups reach decisions concerning the reporting business entity, although more concern has been shown so far for company accounts than for the accounts of unincorporated entities.

Question 1.2

Investment decisions are largely based on financial information and analysis. Financial reports, which are prepared for shareholders, potential shareholders and other uses, are, however, based on principles and rules that vary from country to country. This makes comparability and transparency of financial information very difficult. Some multinationals may have to prepare reports on activities on several bases for use in different countries and this can create an unnecessary financial burden and can damage the credibility of financial reports.

The increasing levels of cross-border financing transactions and securities trading have highlighted the need for financial information to be based on a single set of rules and principles. An internationally accepted accounting framework is also beneficial to developing countries that cannot bear the cost of establishing a national standard-setting body.

Question 1.3

A conceptual framework provides guidance on the broad principles of financial reporting. It highlights how items should be recorded and how they should be measured and presented. The setting of broad principles could assist in the development of accounting standards, ensuring that the principles are followed consistently as standards and rules are developed.

A conceptual framework can provide guidance on how similar items are treated. By providing definitions and criteria that can be used in deciding the recognition and measurement of items, conceptual frameworks can act as a point of reference for those setting standards, those preparing and those using financial information.

The existence of a conceptual framework can remove the need to address the underlying issues over and over again. Where underlying principles have been established and the accounting standards are based on these principles, there is no need to deal with them fully in each of the standards. This will save the standard-setters time in developing standards and will again ensure consistent treatment of items.

Where a technical issue is raised but is not specifically addressed in an accounting standard, a conceptual framework can help provide guidance on how such items should be treated. Where a short-term technical solution is provided by the standard-setters, the existence of a conceptual framework will ensure that the treatment is consistent with the broad set of agreed principles.

Question 2.1

V Limited
STATEMENT OF PROFIT OR LOSS AND OTHER COMPREHENSIVE INCOME
for the Year Ended 30 September 2012

Notes		€000	€000
	Revenue		430
	Cost of sales		(188)
	Gross profit		242
	Distribution costs	(25)	
	Administrative expenses	(21)	(46)
1.	Profit from operations		196
	Income from investments		12
	Finance cost		(14)
	Profit before tax		194
2.	Income tax expense		(50)
	Profit for the year		144

V Limited
STATEMENT OF FINANCIAL POSITION
as at 30 September 2012

Notes		€000	€000
	ASSETS		
	Non-current assets		
4.	Tangible assets		498
	Investments		100
			598
	Current Assets		
	Inventory	13	
	Receivables	23	
	Bank	157	193
			791
	EQUITY AND LIABILITIES		
	Capital and reserves		
	Issued capital	100	
	Retained earnings	415	515

	Non-current Liabilities		
	Loan notes	140	
5.	Deferred tax	45	
	Deferred Income (W3)	24	209
	Current Liabilities		
	Trade Payables	7	
	Taxation (W2)	57	
	Deferred Income (W3)	3	67
			791

Notes

1. Profit from operations

	€000
Profit from operations is arrived at after charging:	
Depreciation	32
Staff costs	74

2. Taxation (statement of profit or loss and other
      comprehensive income)

	€000
Taxation estimated for this year	
Under provision for previous year	57
Decrease in deferred tax provision	10
Charge to statement of profit or loss and other comprehensive income	(17)
	50

3. Dividends proposed
    A final dividend of €50,000 is proposed for the year.

4. Tangible non-current assets

	Land and Buildings	Plant	Total
Cost	€000	€000	€000
At 1 October 2011	450	210	660
Additions	0	70	70
At 30 September 2012	450	280	730
Depreciation			
At 1 October 2011	40	160	200
Charge for year	4	28	32
At 30 September 2012	44	188	232
Carrying amount at 30 September 2012	406	92	498
Carrying amount at 1 October 2011	410	50	460

5.	Deferred Taxation	€000
	Opening balance	62
	Decrease in provision	(17)
		45

6. Statement of Changes in Equity (extract)

	Retained Earnings	€000
	Profit for the year	144
	Dividends paid (€48,000 + €72,000)	(120)
	Retained profit for the year	24
	Retained earnings at 30 September 2011	391
	Retained earnings at 30 September 2012	415

WORKINGS

1. Analysis of expenses

	Cost of Sales €000	Distribution Costs €000	Administrative Expenses €000
Opening inventory	10		
Purchases	102		
Advertising		15	
Administration salaries			14
Manufacturing wages	60		
Audit fee			7
Irrecoverable debts		10	
Government grant	(3)		
Depreciation:			
Building	4		
Plant	28		
Closing inventory	(13)		
	188	25	21

2.

	Taxation			
	€000			€000
Balance brought down	10	SPLOCI – P/L – under provision		10
Balance c/d	57	SPLOCI – P/L – charge for the year		57
	67			67
		Balance b/d		57

3. Government grant:
   The €30,000 government grant received is accounted for as follows:
   • €3,000 credited to cost of sales (see W1); and
   • balance of €27,000 analysed between current and non-current liabilities under the heading of 'deferred income'.

Question 2.2

Rose Limited
STATEMENT OF CHANGES IN EQUITY
for the Year Ended 31 December 2012

	Share Capital €	Share Premium €	Revaluation Reserve €	Retained Earnings €	Total Equity €
At 31 December 2011	300,000	50,000	80,000	1,280,000	1,710,000
Change in accounting Policy*	–	–	–	(35,000)	(35,000)
Restated balance	300,000	50,000	80,000	1,245,000	1,675,000
Changes in Equity for 2012					
Dividends	–		–	(25,000)	(25,000)
Total comprehensive income**	–	–	70,000	120,000	190,000
Bonus issue of share capital	30,000	(30,000)			
Rights issue	30,000	15,000	–	–	45,000
Total Changes in Equity in 2012	60,000	(15,000)	70,000	95,000	210,000
At 31 December 2012	360,000	35,000	150,000	1,340,000	1,885,000

* IAS 8 *Accounting Policies, Changes in Accounting Estimates and Errors* and IFRS 6 *Exploration for and Evaluation of Mineral Resources* are addressed in **Chapter 21** and **Chapter 34** respectively. Under IFRS 6 an entity may change its accounting policies for exploration and evaluation expenditures if the change makes the financial statements more relevant and no less reliable, or more reliable and no less relevant.

** Total Comprehensive Income	€
Profit for the year	120,000
Gain on revaluation of property	70,000
	190,000

Question 3.1

(a) The advantages of harmonising accounting standards

The users and preparers of financial statements should benefit from having one accounting language. For example:

- **Investors** – both individual and corporate, would be able to compare the financial results of different companies internationally as well as nationally in making investment decisions. There is a growing amount of investment across borders and differences in accounting practices inhibit cross-border analysis. Harmonisation of accounting practices would therefore be of benefit to such analysts;
- **Global/international companies** – management control would be improved because harmonisation would aid internal communication of financial information, and the consolidation of foreign subsidiaries and associated companies would be easier. In addition, in today's global capital and trading markets, the appraisal of foreign companies for takeovers and mergers would be more straightforward and, by making the accounts more easily understood by foreign investors, companies would have better access to

foreign investor funds. The reporting requirements of overseas inventory exchanges would be similar and a reduction in audit costs might be achieved;
- **Governments of developing countries** – would save time and money if they could adopt international standards and, if these were used internally, they could attempt to control the activities of foreign multi national companies in their own country. This would make it more difficult for companies to 'hide' behind different foreign accounting practices;
- **International accounting firms** – accounting and auditing would be much easier if similar accounting practices existed throughout the world; and
- **Tax authorities** – it would be easier to calculate the tax liability of investors, including multinationals that receive income from overseas sources.

(b) The reasons why harmonisation has not yet been achieved

The main factors are:
- **Different user groups** – there is no consensus on who the relevant user groups are and their respective importance. In the USA, investor and creditor groups are given prominence, while in Europe employees enjoy a higher profile;
- **Different purposes of financial reporting** – in some countries the purpose is solely for tax assessment, while in others it is for investor decision-making;
- **Different legal systems** – these prevent the development of certain accounting practices and restrict the options available;
- **Nationalism** – this has resulted in an unwillingness to accept another country's standards;
- **Different needs** – developing countries are behind in the standard-setting process and they need to develop the basic standards and principles already in place in most developed countries;
- **Cultural differences** – have resulted in objectives for accounting systems differing from country to country; and
- **Lack of strong accountancy bodies** – many countries do not have a strong independent accountancy profession to press for better standards and greater harmonisation.

Question 4.1

Issue 1 MASTERTICKETS should recognise €500 as revenue. The agency acts purely as an agent for the promoter and therefore its revenue arises from the rendering of services, i.e. earning commission by selling tickets. The ownership of the €4,500 belongs to the promoter.

Issue 2 LAGAN makes its money by promoting a service – the website – that brings together buyers and sellers of products. LAGAN is neither a buyer nor a seller and takes no risks related to the products. It earns a fee for making a market (through the website). LAGAN should only recognise revenue of €40,000.

Issue 3 The upfront fee should be spread over the service period, i.e. the customer is not buying 'activation', but is buying a mobile phone service. Therefore the upfront fee should be matched with the cost of providing the service over the life of the contract.

Issue 4

		€000
(a)	Total profit/loss	
	Contract price	15,000

Costs to date	(9,250)
Estimated to complete	(4,000)
Estimated contract profit/loss	1,750

(b)   Attributable profit/loss*

Stage of completion		11/17 = 64.7%	
Costs certified/Estimated total costs	€8,500/€13,250 = 64.2%		
Turnover	€9,500/€15,000 = 63.3%		
Cash received	€9,000/€15,000 = 60%		
Therefore attributable profit/loss	Take, say	(63%)	1,103

(c)   Revenue

Costs certified to date**	8,500
Attributable profit	1,103
	9,603

(d)   Gross amount due from customer

Costs incurred	9,250
Add recognised profits	1,103
Less progress billings invoiced	(9,500)
	853

Note:

* The calculation of attributable profit/loss is subjective and alternative assumptions may be equally valid.

** Costs certified to date are taken as cost of sales since this represents the 'cost' of the contract value completed. Then, as stated in the question, this figure is adjusted by attributable profit to arrive at contract revenue.

Question 5.1

RIGHT: is not an investment property as it is used and occupied by HELIX. Depreciate in accordance with IAS 16 *Property, Plant and Equipment*.

LEFT: is not an investment property as it is let to, and occupied by, another group company. Depreciate in accordance with IAS 16 *Property, Plant and Equipment*.

UP: is an investment property under IAS 40 *Investment Property* as it meets the definition of an investment property. It should be noted that, per IAS 28 *Investment in Associates and Joint Ventures*, which was issued in May 2011 and is effective from 1 January 2013, an associate company is not a group company. No depreciation to be charged.

DOWN: is an investment property under IAS 40 *Investment Property*. Depreciate over 12 years if the cost model is adopted.

Question 6.1

MEMORANDUM

Date:
To:
From:
Subject:

Review point 1 The company uses the properties and therefore they are not 'investment properties' under IAS 40 *Investment Property*. IAS 16 *Property, Plant and Equipment* does not allow companies to take a selective approach to the valuation of non-current assets within the same class. Therefore, if WELLER wishes to move to market value, both properties will have to be shown at market value. Also following revaluation, depreciation should be based on the revalued amount. The revaluation loss on the Derry property should be charged in arriving at profit or loss in the statement of profit or loss and other comprehensive income along with the depreciation charge.

The revaluation gain on the Cork property will be credited to the equity/revaluation reserve (and shown under 'other comprehensive income' in the statement of profit or loss and other comprehensive income), i.e. it is not included in arriving at the profit/loss for the year.

Review point 2 Previously IAS 23 *Borrowing Costs* allowed companies to choose whether or not to capitalise the €600,000 loan interest. However, in accordance with the revised IAS 23 (effective for accounting periods beginning on or after 1 January 2009 – see **Chapter 7**), WELLER must capitalise qualifying borrowing costs.

For:
• Greater comparability between the cost of purchased non-current assets and the cost of self-constructed non-current assets.
• Better matching of income and expenditure since depreciation will include the capitalised interest.

Against:
• Too arbitrary and therefore reduces the comparability of financial statements.

In many cases, borrowing will not be as specific as in this case. It is more likely to form part of the company's general financing. Although it is still possible to capitalise a percentage of the borrowing cost, determining the amount will be much more difficult. IAS 23 suggests using a capitalisation rate based upon a weighted average of the rates applicable to general borrowing. But this will be a very judgmental process.

Review point 3 Rental payments during a fitting-out period should not be capitalised as, under IAS 16 *Property, Plant and Equipment*, such payments are not costs that are directly attributable to bringing the fixtures and fittings into their intended use, nor are they finance costs.

IAS 17 *Leases* requires rentals under operating leases to be charged on a straight-line basis over the lease term and therefore it is not possible to defer the payments and spread them over the period when the property is in use.

Review point 4

Reasons	Problems
1. Different management intentions with respect to operational lives, intended use and renewal policy.	1. Appraisal of company financial performance and reported profit.
2. Use of estimates with respect to residual values and lives based upon management views, intentions, past experience and foresight.	2. Lack of consistency between companies.

3. Application of accounting concepts (prudence).

4. Maintenance and repair policies.

3. Results in different profit/loss on disposal being reported.

Review point 5 The primary justification for non-depreciation of freehold land is that land does not wear out in the same way as all other assets and therefore does not have a finite life span. Also, the usefulness of land does not erode with age. Generally, the value of land will rise through time and land requires little or no maintenance.

Question 6.2

	€
Basic list price	500,000
Less 10% discount	(50,000)
	450,000
Shipping and handling	20,000
Testing	10,000
Cabling and wiring	30,000
Own staff costs	16,000
	526,000

The early settlement discount is a 'finance' decision and therefore included as a 'revenue' item. The maintenance contract is also a 'revenue' item.

Question 7.1

The revised IAS 23 *Borrowing Costs* (effective for accounting periods beginning on or after 1 January 2009) states that qualifying borrowing costs *must be* capitalised. Therefore, based on the information provided, ROBINSON will be required to capitalise €600,000 loan interest (€10m × 6%) in 2012. The facility will therefore be stated in the statement of financial position at 31 December 2012 at €10,600,000. It is likely that depreciation will begin in 2013 when the facility becomes ready for use.

As all companies are now required to capitalise qualifying borrowing costs, this should result in:
• greater comparability between the cost of purchased non-current assets and the cost of self-constructed non-current assets;
• better matching of income and expenditure since depreciation will include the capitalised interest.

In many cases, borrowing will not be as specific as in this case. It is more likely to form part of the company's general financing. Although it is still possible to capitalise a percentage of the borrowing cost, determining the amount will be much more difficult. IAS 23 suggests using a capitalisation rate based upon a weighted average of the rates applicable to general borrowing. But this will be a very judgmental process.

Question 8.1

Statement of profit or loss and other comprehensive income: depreciation €16,000 (€64,000 ÷ 4) plus interest €6,400 = decrease profit by €22,400.

Non-current Assets: Cost €64,000 less depreciation €16,000 = increase non-current assets by €48,000.

Liabilities: €80,000 − €20,000 = €60,000 less interest suspense €9,600 = increase liabilities by €50,400.

Lease Schedule	Opening Bal.	Rental	Capital	10% Interest	Closing Bal.
	€	€	€	€	€
	64,000	20,000	13,600	6,400[1]	50,400

[1] When the rental payment is in arrears, the interest is calculated on the opening balance.

Question 8.2

(a) Effect on projected profits

	2013	2014	2015
	€	€	€
Depreciation charge	12,500	25,000	25,000
Finance charge (interest (W3))	7,823	13,393	8,549
Effect on profit before tax	20,323	38,393	33,549

Note: depreciation for non-current assets held under finance leases must be consistent with that for similar assets which are owned. If there is no reasonable certainty that the lessee will obtain ownership at the end of the lease, the asset should be depreciated over the shorter of the lease term or the life of the asset (IAS 17). Given the machine has an estimated useful life of six years and the secondary lease period is at €1 per annum, it is considered appropriate to depreciate the machine over six years (rather than four, being the shorter of the lease term).

(b)

STATEMENT OF FINANCIAL POSITION (Extracts)

	31 May 2013	31 May 2014	31 May 2015
Non-current Assets	€	€	€
Leased machinery	150,000	150,000	150,000
Accumulated depreciation	(12,500)	(37,500)	(62,500)
Net book value	137,500	112,500	87,500
Non-current liabilities			
Obligations under finance leases	74,266	39,716	–
	74,266	39,716	–
Current liabilities			
Obligations under finance leases	30,044	34,550	39,716
Accruals and deferred income	7,823	5,570	2,995
	37,867	40,120	42,711

Note: the lease commences on 30 November 2012 and the first accounting period ends 31 May 2013. Therefore, the first period includes the lease for 6 months only.

(W1)   Calculation of Finance Charges
Total lease payments ignoring secondary period:

	€
Minimum lease payments (4 × €45,690)	182,760
Less fair value of asset	(150,000)
Implicit finance charge	32,760

Note: we are told that the interest rate implicit in the lease is 15%. Therefore, we can spread the finance charges over the life of lease as set out in (W3).

(W2)   Opening Capital Amount

	€
Asset value	150,000
– Payment in advance	45,690
Opening amount	104,310

(W3)   Spreading the Finance Charge

Period	Opening Capital Balance €	Lease payment on 30/11 €	Interest* €	Date Interest Paid €	Capital Repaid €	Closing Capital Balance €	Total Annual Interest €
30/11/12 – 31/5/13	104,310^	–	7,823	30.11.00	–	104,310	7,823
31/5/13 – 30/11/13	104,310	45,690	7,823	30.11.00	30,044	74,266	N/A
30/11/13 – 31/5/14	74,266	–	5,570	30.11.01	–	74,266	13,393
31/5/14 – 30/11/14	74,266	45,690	5,570	30.11.01	34,550	39,716	N/A
30/11/14 – 31/5/15	39,716	–	2,979	30.11.02	–	39,716	8,549
31/5/15 – 30/11/15	39,716	45,690	2,979	30.11.02	39,732	(16)	2,979

*Interest is calculated at 15% on the outstanding capital balance for each half-year period.

	€
^Fair value	150,000
Less 1st payment in advance (deemed to be capital)	45,690
	104,310

Note: the first payment is in advance and is deemed to be all capital. Therefore, as the payment in the year to 31/5/13 was deemed to be a 'capital' advance, an accrual of €7,823 must be made in respect of the finance charge for this year in accordance with the matching concept. It is arguably equally valid to assume that the first payment (in advance) includes the repayment of both interest and capital. Although there would still be an interest expense in the statement of profit or loss and other comprehensive income for the year ended 31/5/13, there would be no interest accrual in the statement of financial position at the end of the period. This assumption would therefore result in a different CL/NCL split.

Question 8.3

(a) Operating Lease

Annual charge to statement of profit or loss and other comprehensive income is €2,500 × 4 = €10,000, i.e. the amount payable for the year.

(b) (i) Sum of Digits Approach

Finance Charge Computation	€
Total payments €2,500 × 12	30,000
Cost of Asset	25,000
Finance Charge	5,000

No. of payments (excluding advance payment) = 11
Sum of Digits = 11 + 10 + 9 + 8 + 7 + 6 + 5 + 4 + 3 + 2 + 1 = 66

Period		€		€	
1.	11/66 ×	5,000	=	833	
2.	10/66 ×	5,000	=	757	2,878
3.	9/66 ×	5,000	=	682	
4.	8/66 ×	5,000	=	606	
5.	7/66 ×	5,000	=	530	
6.	6/66 ×	5,000	=	455	1,667
7.	5/66 ×	5,000	=	379	
8.	4/66 ×	5,000	=	303	
9.	3/66 ×	5,000	=	227	
10.	2/66 ×	5,000	=	152	455
11.	1/66 ×	5,000	=	76	
				5,000	

Year	Finance Charge €	Depreciation €	Total Charge €
1.	2,878	4,167	7,045
2.	1,667	4,167	5,834
3.	455	4,167	4,622
4.	–	4,167	4,167
5.	–	4,166	4,167
6.	–	4,166	4,167

Note: leased assets are depreciated over the shorter of the lease term or its useful life when it is not reasonably certain that ownership will transfer to the lessee.

The lease term is the period for which the lessee has contracted to lease the asset *and* any further terms which the lessee has the option to continue to lease the asset, with or without further payment, which option it is reasonably certain at the inception of the lease that the lessee will exercise.

(b) (ii) Actuarial Approach

	€
Net cost to lessor	
Cost of asset	25,000
Advance lease payments	2,500
	22,500

Calculation of implicit rate of interest

$$\text{PV Factor} = \frac{\text{Net Cost}}{\text{Payments}} = \frac{22,500}{2,500} = 9$$

Interest rate equating a factor of 9 over 11 payments is 3.5%.

Division of rentals between finance charge element and capital element:

Period	Capital Sum at Start €	Rental €	Capital Sum during Period €	Finance Charge €	Capital Repayments €	Capital Sum at End €
1.	25,000	2,500	22,500			22,500
				787	1,713	
2.	22,500	2,500	20,787			20,787
				728	1,772	
3.	20,787	2,500	19,015			19,015
				666	1,834	
4.	19,015	2,500	17,181			17,181
				601	1,899	
5.	17,181	2,500	15,282			15,282
				535	1,965	
6.	15,282	2,500	13,317			13,317
				466	2,034	
7.	13,317	2,500	11,283			11,283
				395	2,105	
8.	11,283	2,500	9,178			9,178
				321	2,179	
9.	9,178	2,500	6,999			6,999
				245	2,255	
10.	6,999	2,500	4,744			4,744
				166	2,334	
11.	4,744	2,500	2,410			2,410
				84	2,416	
12.	2,410	2,500		6		

Charge to statement of profit or loss and other comprehensive income:

Year	Finance Charge €	Depreciation €	Total €
1.	2,782	4,167	6,949
2.	1,717	4,167	5,884
3.	501	4,167	4,668
4.		4,167	4,167
5.		4,166	4,167
6.		4,166	4,167

(c)

STATEMENT OF FINANCIAL POSITION (EXTRACTS)

	€
Non-current assets	
Assets purchased under finance lease	
Cost	25,000
Accumulated Depreciation	4,167
	20,833
Non-current Liabilities	
Leasehold obligations	9,178
Current Liabilities	
Finance charges accrued	601
Leasehold obligations (€17,181 – €9,178)	8,003

Question 9.1

Mr Denis Lyons	Barrett Wiltshire & Co.
Managing Director	Chartered Accountants
Sea Pharmaceuticals plc	10 High Street
Clonshaugh Industrial Estate	Kilkenny
Coolock	
Dublin	

14 June 2013

Dear Mr Lyons,

Further to our recent conversation, I wish to outline the suggested accounting treatment appropriate for your research and development expenditure and the related capital grants receivable.

Research and Development My understanding is that your project is to discover and develop a treatment drug for seal viruses. To determine the appropriate accounting treatment, we must refer to the guidance set out in IAS 38 *Intangible Assets*. The provisions of IAS 38 as applied to the facts of your case would suggest the following:

1. The cost of initial investigative work into seal viruses should be expensed to the statement of profit or loss and other comprehensive income as incurred, as it falls into the category of research.
2. The cost of development work (i.e. the application of research findings to the development of sea vaccines) should be:
   (a) expensed to statement of profit or loss and other comprehensive income as incurred, if it does not satisfy the conditions for recognition as an intangible asset; or
   (b) capitalised as an intangible asset in the statement of financial position if the following five conditions are satisfied:
     (i) technical feasibility of completing the intangible asset;
     (ii) intention by the entity to complete the asset and use or sell it;
     (iii) the ability of the entity to use or sell the asset;
     (vi) the likelihood of the asset ge nerating probable future economic benefits, e.g. existence of a market for the output of the asset; and
     (v) the ability to measure the expenditure attributable to the asset.

Government Grants The general rule, as outlined in IAS 20 *Accounting for Government Grants and Disclosure of Government Assistance,* for the treatment of government grants, is that they should be accounted for in a manner consistent with the related expenditure. The portion of the grants attributable to the original investigative work should be credited in arriving at profit or loss to the statement of profit or loss and other comprehensive income when received. If the development costs qualify for capitalisation as an intangible asset under the provisions of IAS 38 above, then the related grants can be treated on a similar basis, i.e. the entire grant relating to the development costs can be credited to a deferred income account and amortised to the statement of profit or loss and other comprehensive income in arriving at profit or loss over the period in which revenues are expected to be generated.

I trust that the above has addressed the main issues relevant to your case. If I can be of any further assistance, please call.

Yours faithfully,

Question 10.1

Allocation of Impairment Loss:

	Goodwill €million	Property €million	Machinery €million	Motor Vehicles €million	Other €million
Carrying amount	20	60	40	20	20
Impairment loss €60m	20	-	20	10	10
Revised carrying value	Nil	60	20	10	10

Explanation:
(a) The loss is firstly allocated to the goodwill, i.e. €20 million.
(b) No impairment can be allocated to the property because its fair value less cost to sell is greater than its carrying amount.
(c) The remainder of the loss, i.e. €40 million, is apportioned between the remaining assets pro rata to their carrying amounts: 40 : 20 : 20

Machinery   €40m × 40/80 = €20m
Motor vehicles   €40m × 20/80 = €10m
Other assets   €40m × 20/80 = €10m

Question 10.2

(a)

1. Present value of future cash flows:

	Domestic			*Commercial*		
	Cash flow €000	PV – 10%	PV €000	Cash flow €000	PV – 12%	PV €000
2013	1,200	0.909	1,090.8	1,200	0.893	1,071.6
2014	900	0.826	743.4	1,300	0.797	1,036.1
2015	2,700	0.751	2,027.7	1,600	0.712	1,139.2
2016	1,500	0.683	1,024.5	1,500	0.636	954
2017	1,600	0.620	992	900	0.567	510.3
2018	1,800	0.564	1,015.2	1,800	0.507	912.6
			6,893.6			5,623.8

2. Recoverable amount – higher of VIU and fair value less costs of disposal:

	€000	€000
VIU	6,893.6	5,623.8
FV less costs of disposal	7,500	4,200
	Therefore recoverable amount €7,500	Therefore recoverable amount €5,623.8

3. Impairment loss – lower of carrying value and recoverable amount:

	€000	€000
CV	7,200	9,300
RA	7,500	5,623.8
Impairment	-	3,676.2

(b) Allocated over the Commercial IGU

	n/a	Revised Carrying Value
	€000	€000
	3,676.2	–
Goodwill	(1,200)	–
Other IA (see note below)	(300)	–
	2,176.2	
Property [6,400 – (6,400/7,800 × 2,176.2)]		4,614.4
Plant and equipment [1,400 – (1,400/7,800 × 2,176.2)]		1,009.4
		5,623.8

Note: an impairment loss should be recognised only if its recoverable amount is less than its carrying amount. Where the impairment loss cannot be identified as relating to a specific asset, it should be apportioned within the CGU to reduce the most subjective values first, as follows:

(i) first against goodwill to its implied value (it could be argued that after reducing goodwill, the impairment loss should next be allocated against 'other intangible assets' on the basis that these are the next 'most subjective values'. Much will depend on the nature of these assets and the decision may often be a matter of judgement. Hence, in this solution, the impairment loss has been allocated against 'other intangibles' in full before applying (b) below).
(ii) then to other assets on a pro rata basis, based on the carrying amount of each asset in the unit.

This is discussed further in IAS 36, paragraph 104 and BCZ 178; albeit the proposal to include this approach within IAS 36 was withdrawn (BCZ 180).

These are treated as impairment losses on individual assets. In allocating the loss an asset should not be reduced below the higher of:
(i) its fair value less costs of disposal (if determinable);
(ii) its value in use (if determinable); and
(iii) zero.

The amount of the loss that would otherwise have been allocated to the asset shall be allocated to the other assets on a pro rata basis. If the recoverable amount of each individual asset in a CGU cannot be estimated without undue cost or effort, IAS 36 requires an arbitrary allocation between assets of the CGU other than goodwill. If the recoverable amount of an individual asset cannot be determined:

(i) an impairment loss is recognised for the asset if its carrying value is greater than the higher of its fair value less costs of disposal and the results of the procedures described above;

(ii) no impairment loss is recognised if the related CGU is not impaired, even if its fair value less costs of disposal is less than its carrying amount.

Question 11.1

MEMORANDUM

Date: dd/mm/yy
To: J. Jones, Group Chief Accountant
From: B. Williams, Accounting Consultant
Subject: Valuation of Subsidiary Company's Inventory

General Before considering the particular circumstance relating to each subsidiary, it is important to note that IFRS10 *Consolidated Financial Statements* requires that all companies in a group should prepare their financial statements using uniform accounting policies for like transactions and other events in similar circumstances. IAS 2 *Inventories* states that inventories should be valued at the lower of cost and net realisable value.

Screws Limited It is considered that the use of selling price less 20% as a basis of valuing inventories in a manufacturing company is not satisfactory in the light of IAS 2 *Inventories* as it is considered unlikely that such a method could give a reasonable approximation to actual cost; consistency and convenience are not valid reasons for valuing inventory at retail price less a margin.

The finished goods should be valued at the lower of cost or net realisable value. Cost should be taken as that expenditure which has been incurred in the normal course of business in bringing the goods to their present location and condition and should include, in addition to the cost of purchase, such costs of conversion as are appropriate to that location and condition.

The cost of conversion would comprise of:
(a) costs specifically attributable to the units of production;
(b) production overheads (based on the normal level of activity); and
(c) other overheads, if any, incurred in bringing the goods to their present location and condition.

Brackets Limited *Note:* when answering this part of the question, it has been assumed that the last consignment consisted of 200 tonnes or more. If the last consignment did not consist of 200 tonnes, then the cost of the brass would be determined by using the cost of the latest 200 tonnes purchased, i.e. on a FIFO basis.

	Cost per tonne at 31 December
	€
Brass purchase cost	500.00
Conversion cost (€120,000/700)	171.43
	671.43

	Net realisable value per tonne
	€
Market price	520.00
Less: selling costs (€30,000/700)	(42.86)
	477.14

Consequently, the inventory held at the year-end should be valued at €477.14 per tonne.

Frames Limited   IAS 21 *The Effects of Changes in Foreign Exchange Rates* states that a foreign currency transaction should be recorded by the reporting entity on initial recognition in the functional currency by applying the spot exchange rate between the functional currency and the foreign currency at the date of the transaction. The date of the transaction is defined as the date on which the transaction first qualifies for recognition under IFRS. Consequently, the inventory should be valued at the rate prevailing on 15 November. The exchange fluctuation between the date of purchase (15 November) and the date of payment (10 December) should be treated as an exchange loss in inventory in the current year's statement of profit or loss and other comprehensive income. Year-end inventories should, therefore, be valued at 95% of €100,000, i.e. €95,000.

Concrete Blocks   IAS 2 states that costs of conversion of inventories include costs directly related to the units of production such as direct labour. They also include a systematic allocation of fixed and variable production overheads that are incurred in converting materials into finished goods. The allocation of fixed production overheads is based on the normal capacity of the production facilities. It would seem that the use of the term 'based on normal level of activity' suggests that fixed overheads should be included in the valuation of inventory. It would appear, therefore, that in order to comply with the standard, it would be necessary to continue to include fixed factory overheads.

Question 11.2

(a) A retailer with:
 • a large range of low price commodities;
 • a strong management information system; and
 • reasonably consistent margins throughout the accounting period.

   Examples: Superquinn, HMV

   Examples of enterprises where such a method would NOT be appropriate would be:
 • hi-fi shop (individual items can be easily valued at actual cost);
 • an enterprise with weak information systems, i.e. details of departmental or product margins may be unavailable; and
 • manufacturing enterprise.

(b) No prior-period adjustment should be made. The company's accounting policy should be to value inventory at the lower of cost or Net Realisable Value (NRV). The previous calculations of measuring actual costs and the new calculations measuring selling price less an estimated profit margin are both *methods* to value inventory at cost. The change described is therefore a change in method not a change in accounting policy. Consequently, no prior-period adjustment is required.

(c) Factors to be considered include:
   (i) Are departmental or product gross-margin analyses sufficient? It would be inappropriate for Superquinn (for example) to use a blanket 10% gross margin for the 'food department' when meats and dairy products would presumably be sold at quite different gross margins.
   (ii) Is VAT properly deducted from the total selling prices?
   (iii) How are the estimated profit margins calculated? The margins must include all costs of purchase (as defined in IAS 2) but exclude all other costs, e.g. administration costs. (Costs of conversion would be irrelevant because if such costs were incurred, say by a manufacturing company, this method would be appropriate.)
   (iv) How do the estimated profit margins compare with actual profit margins?
   (v) How are 'special promotions' or 'sale prices' listed at the year-end (which would result in a lower sales price for certain goods) treated?

Question 12.1

1. Overall contract outcome:	€000	€000
Contact Price		3,000
Costs to date	1,420	
Estimated cost to completion	1,350	
Estimated total cost		(2,770)
Estimated total profit on completion		230
Additional costs		(500)
Expected loss		(270)

2. Statement of profit or loss and other comprehensive	€000
Revenue €3,000,000 x 45%	1,350
Cost of sales – costs incurred to date	(1,420)
	(70)
Provision for loss	(200)
	(270)

3. Gross amounts due to customer	€000
Costs incurred to date	1,420
Less recognised losses	(270)
Less progress billings invoiced	(1.200)
	(50)

Question 12.2

(a)

Y/e 31 July 2010

The decision when to take credit for attributable profit is often subjective. At 31 July **2010** the contract was 30% complete. While profit could often be taken at this point, none is taken in this instance as the question states that it is company policy to recognise profit once contracts have reached a minimum of 40% completion. However, the contract is expected to be profitable overall, so it is appropriate to show as turnover a proportion of the total contract value which will produce a zero profit – IAS 11 states that revenue can be recognised to the extent of contract costs incurred which are expected to be recoverable.

Therefore the costs to date (2010) of €230,000 will be recognised as cost of sales, with an equivalent amount as revenue.

Work in Progress				Revenue			
	€000		€000		€000		€000
Bank	230	Cost of Sales	230				
	230		230	SPLOCI – P/L	230	Rec - AROC	230

Receivables – Trade				Receivables – Amts recoverable on Contracts			
	€000		€000		€000		€000
		Bank	250	Revenue	230	Trade rec.	270
Amounts							
recoverable	270	Bal c/d	20	Bal. c/d	40		—
	270		270		270		270

Y/e 31 July 2011

	€000	€000
Estimated Total Profit (€1,000,000 – €780,000) =		220
Attributable Profit = €220,000 × 65%		143
Cost of Sales = €780,000 × 65% =	507	
Less Amount y/e 31/7/2010	(230)	
		277
Revenue = €143,000 + €277,000 =		420

Work in Progress				Revenue			
	€000		€000		€000		€000
Balance b/d	–	Cost of Sales	277	SPLOCI – P/L	420	Rec AROC	420
Bank	290	Balance c/d	13				
	290		290				

Receivables – Trade				Receivables – Amts recoverable on Contracts			
	€000		€000		€000		€000
Balance c/d	20	Bank	250	Revenue	420	Bal. b/d	40
Amts rec.	410	Balance c/d	180	Bal. c/d	30	Trade rec.	410
	430		430		450		450

Y/e 31 July 2012

	€000	€000
Estimated Total Profit		280
Attributable Profit (€280,000 × 100%)	280	
Less taken in previous periods	143	137
Cost of Sales (€820,000 × 100%)	820	
Less Amounts w/o in previous periods (€ 230,000 + €277,000)	(507)	
This period		313
Revenue = Cost of Sales + Attributable Profit = €313,000 + €137,000 =		450

Work in Progress				Revenue			
	€000		€000		€000		€000
Bal. b/d	13	CoS	313	SPLOCI – P/L	450	Rec - AROC	450
Bank	300						
	313		313				

Receivables – Trade				Receivables – Amts recoverable on Contracts			
	€000		€000		€000		€000
Balance c/d	180	Bank	600	Revenue	450	Bal. b/d	30
Amts rec.	420					Trade rec.	420
	270		270		450		450

(b)

Extracts from Financial Statements for Year Ended 31 July 2011

STATEMENT OF PROFIT OR LOSS AND OTHER COMPREHENSIVE INCOME

	€000
Revenue	420
Cost of Sales	(277)
Gross Profit	143

STATEMENT OF FINANCIAL POSITION

Trade Receivables	180
Current liabilities	
Gross amount due to customer (see below)	17

Notes to Financial Statement for Year Ended 31 July 2011

Gross amount due to customer	€000
Cost incurred to date	520
Recognised profit	143
Recognised losses	–
Progress billings	(680)
	(17)

Question 13.1

(a)

	€	€
Capital allowances (Note 1):		
Capital allowances	4,750,000	
Depreciation charged	(3,250,000)	
Net originating differences		1,500,000

Tax loss (Note 2):	DT asset offset against DT liability.	(250,000)
Royalties (Note 4):	SPLOCI – P/L charge less than amount allowable for tax, therefore provision needed.	50,000
		1,300,000
SPLOCI – P/L – charge:	@25%	325,000
SFP:	Opening balance	250,000
	SPLOCI – P/L charge	325,000
	Closing balance	575,000

(b)

(i) **Asset revaluations** – IAS 16 *Property, Plant and Equipment* permits the use of the 'cost' model and, the valuation model. IAS 16 requires residual values to be reviewed at each reporting date and that whichever model is adopted that it is applied consistently. All assets of a particular class must be revalued, but not necessarily all classes of asset. A class of asset is defined as a category of non-current asset having a similar nature, function or use in the business of the company.

Where a policy of revaluation is adopted, IAS 16 does not require an 'expert valuer' to conduct the valuations and valuations need only be conducted 'regularly'.

IAS 16 requires increases in an asset's residual value, based on current prices, to reduce the ongoing depreciation charge. If the residual value equals or exceeds the asset's carrying value, the depreciation charge is reduced to zero.

Revaluation losses may be reported differently. Under IAS 16, revaluation decreases are only charged to the statement of profit or loss and other comprehensive income to the extent that they exceed previous surpluses.

(ii) **IAS 12 *Income Taxes*** – the temporary difference prior to revaluation is €200,000 (€800,000 – €600,000). The tax payable (€50,000) is an unavoidable tax liability. If the asset is retained, future tax allowances will be €1,200,000 and future depreciation will be €1,400,000. The tax payable on net reversing temporary differences is €50,000. If the property is sold, then the tax written down value is €1,200,000 and €1,400,000 for accounts purposes. Therefore the unavoidable tax liability on the reversing temporary difference is €50,000.

Under IAS 12 revaluing the property to €1,800,000 will create an unavoidable incremental tax liability as deferred tax is required on all revaluation gains (rather than only when there is an agreement to sell a revalued asset). IAS 12 requires deferred tax to be provided on temporary differences rather than timing differences.

(iii) **Discounting** – IAS 12 does not allow deferred tax assets and liabilities to be discounted.

Question 14.1

(a) **At 31 December 2011** – there is a present obligation as a result of a past obligating event. The obligating event is the giving of the guarantee, which gives rise to a legal obligation. However, at 31 December 2011 no transfer of economic benefits is probable in settlement of the obligation.

No provision is recognised. The guarantee is disclosed as a contingent liability unless the probability of any transfer is regarded as remote.

(b) **At 31 December 2012** – as above, there is a present obligation as a result of a past obligating event, namely the giving of the guarantee.

At 31 December 2012 it is probable that a transfer of economic events will be required to settle the obligation. A provision is therefore recognised for the best estimate of the obligation.

Question 14.2

King Limited *cannot avoid* the cost of repairing or replacing all items of product that manifest manufacturing defects in respect of which warranties are given before the date of the statement of financial position, and a provision for the cost of this should therefore be made.

King Limited is obliged to repair or replace items that fail within the entire warranty period. Therefore, in respect *of this year's sales,* the obligation provided for at the date of the statement of financial position should be the cost of making good items for which defects have been notified but not yet processed, *plus* an estimate of costs in respect of the other items sold for which there is sufficient evidence that manufacturing defects will manifest themselves during their remaining periods of warranty cover.

Question 14.3

(a) On 13 December 2012 the board of an entity decided to close down a division. The accounting date of the company is 31 December. Before 31 December 2012, the decision was not communicated to any of those affected and no other steps were taken to implement the decision. No provision would be recognised as the decision has not been communicated (i.e. it is still an intention not an obligation).

(b) The board agreed a detailed closure plan on 20 December 2012 and details were given to customers and employees. A provision would be made in the 2012 financial statements.

(c) A company is obliged to incur clean-up costs for environmental damage (that has already been caused). A provision for such costs is appropriate.

(d) A company intends to carry out future expenditure to operate in a particular way in the future. No present obligation exists and under IAS 37 no provision would be appropriate. This is because the entity could avoid the future expenditure by its future actions, maybe by changing its method of operation.

Question 15.1

(a) This is an adjusting event, and an adjustment should be made to the accounts in respect of the €20,000 owing at the date of the statement of financial position, putting through a charge in the statement of profit or loss and other comprehensive income and writing off the debt in the statement of financial position. No adjustment should be made in respect of the further €10,000 arising after the date of the statement of financial position, as this is a non-adjusting event. However, if €10,000 is material in the context of the company's accounts, then a note should be attached to the financial statements stating that further debts incurred in respect of Cronser Limited after the date of the statement of financial position of €10,000 are unlikely to be recoverable.

(b) This is an adjusting event as it relates to the writing-off of the debt prior to the date of the statement of financial position, part of which is now recoverable. It is therefore appropriate to bring in a credit to the statement of profit or loss and other comprehensive income in respect of the recoverable part of the debt and to include it as an asset in the statement of financial position. However, the company should be very sure that the dividend is receivable before treating it as an adjusting event.

(c) This is a non-adjusting event as the fire occurred after the date of the statement of financial position. However, as the amount of the inventory lost is most likely material to the company, it will be necessary to disclose the item in a note to the accounts.

Question 15.2

IAS 10 *Events after the Reporting Period* deals with the treatment of 'those events, both favourable and unfavourable, which occur between the date of the statement of financial position and the date on which the financial statements were approved by the board of directors'. A distinction is then made between events after the end of the reporting period, which are:

(i) adjusting events that provide additional evidence of conditions that existed at the date of the statement of financial position and have a material effect on the amounts included in the accounts (e.g. receipt of money from a debtor who had been regarded as an unrecoverable debt);

(ii) non-adjusting events that create new conditions, which did not exist at the date of the statement of financial position (e.g. a new issue of shares).

IAS 10 requires that:

(i) financial statements should be prepared on the basis of conditions which existed at the date of the statement of financial position;

(ii) if there is an adjusting event after the end of the reporting period which materially affects the view of conditions existing at the date of the statement of financial position the amounts to be included in the financial statements should be amended to reflect the event;

(iii) if there is a non-adjusting event after the end of the reporting period which is of such material significance that not to report it would prevent users of the financial statements from reaching a proper understanding of the financial position, it should be disclosed by way of note to the accounts. The note should describe the nature of the event and an estimate of its financial effect (or a statement that it is not practicable to make such an estimate);

(iv) the financial statements should also disclose the date on which they were authorised for issue by the board of directors. This is a necessary requirement so those users can establish the duration of the period after the date of the statement of financial position.

The treatment of the events arising in the case of Fabricators Limited would be as follows:

(a) The fall in value of the investment in Patchup Limited has arisen over the previous year and that company's financial accounts for the year to 28 February 2013 provide additional evidence of conditions that existed at the date of the statement of financial position. The loss of €50,000 is material in terms of the trading profit figure and, as an adjusting event, should be reflected in the financial statements of Fabricators Limited. This will involve writing down the investment by €50,000, with the charge being reflected in arriving at profit or loss in the statement of profit or loss and other comprehensive income.

(b) The destruction of inventory by a fire on 30 April (one month after the date of the statement of financial position) must be considered to be a non-adjusting event (i.e. 'a new condition which did not exist at the date of the statement of financial position'). Since the loss is material, being €250,000, it should be disclosed by way of a note to the accounts. The note should describe the nature of the event and an estimate of its financial effect. Non-reporting of this event would prevent users of the financial statements from reaching a proper understanding of the financial position.

(c) The confirmation by the customer that no remedial work was required on the plant supplied and that no further liability would arise means that an overprovision has been made in the accounts to 31 March. Since this condition 'existed at the date of the statement of financial position' this event is an adjusting event and the provision of €60,000 should be written back in the year-end accounts. This will result in a credit to the statement of profit or loss and other comprehensive income of €60,000 in arriving at profit or loss.

Question 16.1

dd/mm/yy
The Directors
Electronic Manufacturers Limited
Dublin

Dear Sirs,

Accounting Treatment of Government Grants

The grants which have been approved for the new production facilities fall into two distinct classes:

1. the grant for training costs – revenue-based grant; and
2. the grant for plant – capital-based grant.

These grants are treated differently for accounting purposes. IAS 20 provides that:

(i) revenue-based grants are to be credited to the statement of profit or loss and other comprehensive income, either as other income or netted against the expense category, in the period in which the related revenue expenditure has been incurred and, where actual amounts are not known precisely, appropriate estimates must be made; and

(ii) capital-based grants are to be credited to the statement of profit or loss and other comprehensive income over the life of the appropriate tangible non-current assets by either:

   (i) reducing the costs of the assets by the full amount of the grants; or

   (ii) treating the amount of the grant as deferred credit, a portion of which is transferred to revenue annually. Where this method is used, the amount of the deferred credit should, if material, be shown separately in the statement of financial position and separate from the shareholders' funds.

Where there is a contingent liability to repay any grant received, this must be disclosed by way of a note to the accounts.

As far as the company is concerned, I recommend that the following accounting policies be adopted:

• training grants – these grants be credited to revenue as they accrue due; and

• grants on plant – these grants be treated as deferred credits and disclosed in the statement of financial position under the heading 'Government Grants' and allocated to the statement of profit or loss and other comprehensive income over the life of the individual items of plant at the same rates as depreciation is charged.

I consider that the foregoing treatment of grants on plant is the most suitable as it will enable more accurate management information to be compiled on such matters as the rate of return on capital employed, comparative costs with existing plant, and control over the actual ordering and installation costs of the plant. As grants can vary depending on government action, more reliable statistics can be compiled for future use.

Either accounting treatment of the capital-based grant will result in the same net profit figure because, while the depreciation charge in method (b)(i) will be lower than that in method (b)(ii), a compensatory amount will be transferred from the deferred credit account 'Government Grants' to credit the statement of profit or loss and other comprehensive income in method (b)(ii).

In the financial statements the following notes should be included:

Accounting Policies

1. Grants:
   Grants receivable on additions to tangible non-current assets are credited to the Government Grants Account and are allocated to the statement of profit or loss and other comprehensive income over the estimated effective lives of the assets concerned. Revenue-based grants are credited directly to the statement of profit or loss and other comprehensive income in the year in which they become due.

2. Government Grants:

	€
Balance at start of year	X
Receivable for year	X
Released to statement of profit or loss and other comprehensive income	(X)
Balance at end of year	X

3. Contingent Liabilities:
   Under various agreements between the company and the Industrial Development Authority, the company has received grants amounting to € _____ . There exists a contingent liability to repay in whole or in part the grants received if certain circumstances set out in the agreements occur before receipt of the final instalment of the grants or within ten years thereafter.

Question 16.2

Depreciation per year:

$$\frac{\text{Cost less residual value}}{\text{Useful Life}} \quad = \quad \frac{€25,000 - €1,000}{4} \quad = \quad €6,000 \text{ p.a.}$$

Amortisation of capital grant:

$$\frac{\text{Amount received}}{\text{Useful Life}} \quad = \quad \frac{€6,000}{4} \quad = \quad €1,500 \text{ p.a.}$$

Depreciation is charged to the statement of profit or loss and other comprehensive income based on the gross cost less any residual value of the plant. On the assumption that this cost is apportioned over the 4 years' useful life by means of the straight-line method of depreciation, the annual depreciation charge will be €6,000.

Capital grants on non-current assets are amortised to the statement of profit or loss and other comprehensive income over the useful life of the related assets in the same ratio as the related depreciation is written off. This means that there will be a credit of €1,500 to the statement of profit or loss and other comprehensive income each year.

The amount of the grant, €6,000, will be credited to a deferred income account (for example, capital grants received) and each year an amount of €1,500 will be debited thereto and credited to the statement of profit or loss and other comprehensive income. The €1,500 will be shown separately in the statement of profit or loss and other comprehensive income and not deducted from the depreciation. It will be described as capital grants released. The balance on the Capital Grants Received account will be shown separately in the statement of financial position under its own heading 'Deferred Income'; it will not be shown as part of the shareholders' funds.

The grant of €500 for wages will be credited to the statement of profit or loss and other comprehensive income in the year in which the expenditure to which it relates is incurred, i.e. the year 2012/13.

The purchase price of €25,000 of the plant and equipment will be shown in the statement of financial position as an addition to the previous year's gross cost of non-current assets (plant and machinery). The depreciation charge will be added to the total depreciation brought forward from the previous year.

There should be a note to the statement of financial position indicating the conditions precedent to the repayment of any of the grants, if applicable.

The accounting policy followed by the company in respect of grants should also be disclosed.

Question 17.1

Holiday entitlement per month (days)	2.5
Holiday entitlement earned in 9 months up to 31 December 2012 (days)	22.5
Average days taken	(15)
Average outstanding holiday entitlement at 31 December 2012 (days)	7.5

	€
Average annual salary	30,000
Therefore average cost per working day (260 working days per annum)	115.38
Cost of outstanding holiday entitlement per employee (7.5 days)	865.35
Therefore, total cost of outstanding holiday entitlements at 31 December 2012 (250 employees)	216,337.50

Question 17.2

		Asset	Obligation	P/L	OCI
		€000	€000	€000	€000
At 1 January 2012	Opening Balances – A & O	3,000	3,700		
	Debit	*Credit*			
Current service cost	SPLOCI – P/L	Obligation		480	(480)	
Past service cost	SPLOCI – P/L	Obligation		350	(350)	
Benefits paid	Obligation	Asset	(575)	(575)		
Contributions paid	Asset	Bank	410			
Net interest expense:						
Asset	Asset	P/L – finance cost	150		150	
Obligation	P/L – finance cost	Obligation		185	(185)	
		2,985	4,140		
Re-measurement- fair value gain on asset	Asset	OCI	1,395			1,395
Re-measurement - actuarial loss on obligation	OCI	Obligation		1,435		(1,435)
At 31 December 2012	Closing Balances – A & O	4,380	5,575	(865)	(40)

	€000
The net obligation in the statement of financial position at 31 December 2012 is:	1,195

Question 18.1

(a) Define profits available for distribution

Available profits are defined as:
- accumulated realised profits less accumulated realised losses;
- the total of the net assets must be equal or more than the aggregate of the called-up share capital plus undistributable reserves.

Undistributable reserves include:
- share premium account;
- capital redemption reserve;
- excess of accumulated unrealised profits over accumulated unrealised losses;
- any reserve that the company is prohibited from distributing.

Disclosure requirement:
There are no statutory requirements for companies to distinguish in their accounts between distributable and non-distributable reserves, although it might become necessary to make some disclosure in order to give a true and fair view. In the group accounts, there is a presumption that the holding company could arrange for the profits dealt with in the accounts of the subsidiary companies to be passed up to the holding company and be available for distribution to the shareholders of the holding company.

(b)

(i) Research and development activities

Only distributions to be made out of the company's net realised profits are permitted. In determining net realised profits, any amount shown in respect of development costs, which is included as an asset in the statement of financial position, is to be treated as a realised loss, unless the directors consider that there are special circumstances that justify a decision not to treat the development costs as a realised loss. If the directors decide that there is justification, the accounts must explain the circumstances that are being relied on. In general, if development costs are carried forward in accordance with the provisions of IAS 38 *Intangible Assets*, this will normally provide the directors with appropriate justification.

(ii) Excess depreciation

When a company has revalued a non-current asset to show an unrealised profit, it will be required to charge depreciation on the revalued amount in the statement of profit or loss and other comprehensive income. However, when determining the distributable profits, the excess depreciation is added back to the realised profit disclosed in the statement of profit or loss and other comprehensive income on the grounds that it is a part realisation of the revaluation surplus. It will be appropriate, therefore, to make a transfer annually from undistributable to distributable reserves, i.e. from the revaluation reserve to retained earnings.

Question 18.2

Hay plc: €1,000,000 (€200,000 + €600,000 + €300,000)
Bee plc: €520,000 (€100,000 + (€200,000) + €600,000 + €20,000*)
* = Depreciation adjustment

	€
Depreciation based on revalued figure	50,000
Depreciation based on historical figure	30,000
Difference	20,000

Sea Limited: €100,000 ((€200,000) + €300,000). Since Sea Limited is a private company, the unrealised profit (the revaluation reserve) is ignored.

Question 19.1

Ben Limited
STATEMENT OF CASH FLOWS
for the Year Ended 31 December 2012

	€000	€000
Net cash flows from operating activities		
Profit before tax	300	
Interest received	(25)	
Interest paid	75	
Depreciation charge	90	
Loss on sale of tangible non-current assets	13	
Profit on sale of non-current asset investments	(5)	
Increase in inventories	(48)	
Increase in receivables	(75)	
Increase in payables	8	
Cash generated from operations	333	
Interest received	25	

Interest paid	(75)	
Dividends paid	(80)	
Tax paid	(130)	
Net cash flows from operating activities		73
Cash flows from investing activities		
Payments to acquire tangible non-current assets	(201)	
Payments to acquire intangible non-current assets	(50)	
Receipts from sales of tangible non-current assets	32	
Receipts from sale of non-current asset investments	30	
Net cash flows from investing activities		(189)
Cash flows from financing activities		
Issue of share capital	60	
Long-term loan	120	
Net cash flows from financing		180
Increase in cash and cash equivalents (Note 1)		64
Cash and cash equivalents at 1/1/2012 (Note 1)		(97)
Cash and cash equivalents at 31/12/2012 (Note 1)		33

NOTES TO THE STATEMENT OF CASH FLOWS:

1. Analysis of the Balances of Cash and Cash Equivalents as shown in the Statement of Financial Position

	2012	2011	Change in Year
	€000	€000	€000
Cash in hand	2	1	1
Short-term investments	50	–	50
Bank overdraft	(85)	(98)	13
	(33)	(97)	64

WORKINGS

(W1)

Tangible Assets

	€000		€000
Balance b/d	595	Disposals	85
Revaluation reserve	9		
Therefore additions	201	Balance c/d	720
	805		805

(W2)

Depreciation

	€000		€000
Disposal	40	Balance b/d	290
Balance c/d	340	SPLOCI – P/L	90
	380		380

(W3)

Disposal a/c

	€000		€000
Tangible assets	85	Depreciation	40
		Cash	32
		SPLOCI – P/L	13
	85		85

(W4)

	Taxation		
	€000		€000
Cash	130	Balance b/d	110
Balance c/d	120	SPLOCI – P/L	140
	250		250

(W5)

	Dividends		
	€000		€000
Cash	80	Balance b/d	80
Balance c/d	100	Debited to equity	100
	180		180

WORKINGS (for Direct Method):

(W6)

Purchases	€000
Cost of sales	1,814
Closing stock	150
Opening stock	(102)
Purchases	1,862

(W7)

	Trade Payables		
	€000		€000
Cash	1,859	Balance b/d	119
Balance c/d (127 – 5)	122	Purchases (W6)	1,862
	1,981		1,981

(W8)

	Receivables		
	€000		€000
Balance c/d	315	Cash	2,478
SPLOCI – P/L – Revenue	2,553	Balance b/d	390
	2,868		2,868

Direct Method – Cash generated from Operating Activities

	€000
Cash received from customers	2,478
Cash paid to suppliers for goods and services*	(2,060)
Cash paid to and on behalf of employees (see question, note (e))	(85)
Cash generated from operations	333

	€000
*Trade payables	1,859
Distribution	125
Administrative	264
Depreciation	(90)
Wages	(90)
Net loss on disposals	(8)
	2,060

Question 19.2

STATEMENT OF CASH FLOWS
for Year Ended 31 December 2012

	€000	€000
Operating activities		
Net cash flows from operating activities (see below)		1,574
Investing activities		
Receipts from sales of property, plant and equipment (W4)	350	
Payments to acquire property, plant and equipment (W5)	(2,571)	
Net cash flows from investing activities		(2,221)
Financing activities		
Capital element of finance leases (W6)	(151)	
Issue of shares, including premium	300	
Share issue expenses	(50)	
Medium-term bank loans (W7)	1,726	
Net cash inflow from financing		1,825
Increase in cash and cash equivalents during the year*		1,178
Cash and cash equivalents at start of year		1,840
Cash and cash equivalents at end of year		3,018

* Proof:	
Movement bank and cash	1,230
Movement overdraft	(52)
	1,178

RECONCILIATION OF OPERATING PROFIT TO NET CASH FLOWS FROM OPERATING ACTIVITIES

	€000
Profit before tax	4,667
Interest receivable	(308)
Finance costs	224
Gain on sale of property, plant and equipment	(194)
Amortisation of patents (W8)	108
Depreciation	1,526
Increase in inventory (W9)	(1,194)
Increase in trade receivables (W10)	(1,464)
Increase in trade payables (W11)	588
	3,953
Interest received	308
Interest paid (W1)	(203)
Tax paid (W3)	(370)
Dividends paid (W2)	(2,114)
	1,574

WORKINGS

		€000
1.	Interest paid	
	Balance at beginning of year	6
	SPLOCI – P/L	224
	Balance at end of year	(27)
	Paid during the year	203

2.	Dividends paid	
	Balance at beginning of year	296
	Statement of changes in equity	2,200
	Balance at end of year	(382)
	Paid during the year	2,114

3.	Tax paid	
	Balance at beginning of year (€1,178,000 + €1,650,000)	2,828
	SPLOCI – P/L	1,540
		4,368
	Balance at end of year (€1,258,000 + €2,740,000)	(3,998)
	Paid during the year	370

4.	Cash from sale of non-current assets	
	Per SPLOCI – P/L	194
	NBV of assets disposed (€546,000 – €390,000)	156
	Cash received	350

5.	Purchase of property, plant and equipment	
	Balance at end of year (NBV)	10,877
	Net book value of disposals	156
	Depreciation charge	1,526
	Increase in non-current asset payable (€1,196,000 – €1,178,000)	(18)
		12,541
	Balance at start of year (NBV)	(9,970)
	Cash paid	2,571

6.	Capital element of finance leases	
	Balance at beginning of year (€101,000 + €358,000)	459
	Balance at end of year (€70,000 + €238,000)	(308)
		151

7.	Medium-term loans	
	Balance at end of year	1726
	Balance at beginning of year	–
		1,726

8. Amortisation of patents

Balance at beginning of year	270
Balance at end of year	(162)
Amortised during the year	108

9. Increase in inventory

Balance at end of year	2,080
Balance at beginning of year	(886)
Increase in inventory	1,194

10. Increase in trade receivables

Balance at end of year	6,006
Balance at beginning of year	(4,542)
Increase in trade receivables	1,464

11. Increase in trade payables

Balance at end of year	4,108
Balance at beginning of year	(3,520)
Increase in trade payables	588

Question 20.1

Issue 1 – Sale of division

(a) Per IFRS 5 *Non-current Assets Held for Sale and Discontinued Operations* this should be classified as relating to 'discontinued operations' since it represents withdrawal from the market (as indicated by different customer base) and changing the nature and focus of operations which is consistent with the company's long-term plans. Discontinued operations may be disclosed at the foot of the statement of profit or loss and other comprehensive income or, alternatively, profit from discontinued operations can be analysed in a separate column on the face of the statement of profit or loss and other comprehensive income. In this instance, the former treatment has been adopted resulting in a €500,000 profit for discontinued operations being disclosed at the foot of the company's statement of profit or loss and other comprehensive income.

(b) 'Extraordinary items' have been banned and it is a decision for the company to highlight/separately disclose 'exceptional' items. IAS 1 *Presentation of Financial Statements* makes no reference to 'super exceptional" items. The €1m profit could be included in 'administrative expenses'.

Issue 2 – Closure of retail outlets

APF Limited is not clearly demonstrably committed to the termination and therefore the operation is not discontinued under IFRS 5 *Non-current Assets Held for Sale and Discontinued Operations*. No provision should be made for the expected trading loss of €800,000. The assets are stated at their recoverable amount, therefore no adjustment is required.

Question 21.1

If Keano Limited had always adopted the new policy, the following additional amounts would have been written off in arriving at profit or loss for the period in the statement of profit or loss and other comprehensive income:

	€000	€000
2009	(400 − 100)	300
2010	(600 − 250)	350
2011	(300 − 325)	(25)
		625

This is the total prior-period adjustment in the 2012 financial statements, i.e. the total cumulative adjustment up to the end of the previous period as if the new policy had been previously used.

Note: This amount should be analysed between:
(a) the amount affecting the previous year, i.e. 2011 – €25,000 credit; and
(b) the amount affecting the retained profits at the start of the previous year, i.e. 1 January 2011 – €650,000 debit.

Statement of Changes in Equity

	2012		2011	
	€000	€000	€000	€000
Retained profit for the year		1,820		1,605 (1580 + 25)
Retained earnings brought forward as previously reported	4,440		2,860	
Prior-period adjustment	(625)		(650)	
As restated		3,815		2,210
Retained earnings carried forward		5,635		3,815

Accounting Entry in 2011 comparatives in
2012 financial statements.

	€000	€000
DR Retained earnings	625	
CR Exploration and evaluation expenditure		625

Note:
If Keano Limited (in the 2012 financial statements) had decided that the expenditure on the projects on hand should not be deferred to future periods because management was of the opinion that it may not be recovered (prudence) – this would not constitute a change in an accounting policy.

Question 21.2

The total prior period adjustment in the cumulative error up to 31 May 2012.

	€
31 May 2012	80,000
31 May 2011	60,000
	140,000
less attributable tax 40%	(56,000)
	84,000

Analyse the total into:
(a) The amount affecting the immediate past year, i.e. 31 May 2013   = €48,000
(b) The amount affecting the retained profit up to 31 May 2011   = €36,000

Revised Statements of Profit or Loss and Other Comprehensive Income:

	2013	2012
	€	€
Profit before tax (820–110) and (640–80)	710,000	560,000
Income tax expenses	(284,000)	(224,000)
Profit after tax	426,000	336,000

Statement of changes in equity:

	2013	2012
	€	€
Retained profit for the year	426,000	336,000
Retained profit brought forward		
As previously reported	1,174,000	890,000
Prior-period adjustment	(84,000)	(36,000)
As restated	1,090,000	854,000
Retained profit carried forward	1,516,000	1,190,000

Question	Answer
22.1	(c)
22.2	(b)
22.3	(c)
22.4	(a)
22.5	(b)
22.6	Yes – (a), (b), (c) and (d); No – (e), (f) and (g)
22.7	(b)
22.8	(a)
22.9	(c)
22.10	(a)
22.11	(a) (iii) and (v); (b) (ii); (c) (iv); (d) (i)
22.12	(c)
22.13	(b)
22.14	(b)
22.15	(c)
22.16	(b)

Question 23.1

(a)

	Earnings
	€
Profit before tax	2,323,000
Less Taxation	(1,058,000)
Profit after tax	1,265,000
Less: preference dividends	(276,000)
Earnings	989,000

Earnings per share

$$\frac{989,000}{4,140,000}$$

$$= 23.9 \text{ cent}$$

(b)

Shares in issue at 31 December 2012 = 4,140,000 + 4,140,000/4 = 5,175,000

EPS

$$\frac{€989,000}{5,175,000}$$

$$= 19.1 \text{ cent}$$

(c) The first step is to calculate the theoretical ex-rights price. Consider the holder of 5 shares:

	No.	€
Before rights issue	5 @ 1.80	9.00
Rights issue	1 @ 1.20	1.20
After rights issue	6	10.20

The theoretical ex-rights price is therefore €10.20/6 = €1.70
The number of shares in issue before the rights issue must be multiplied by the fraction:

Market price on last day of quotation cum rights	= €1.80
Theoretical ex-rights price	€1.70

Number of shares in issue during the year:

Proportion of year		Shares in issue	Fraction	Total
1/1/2012 – 1/10/2012	9/12 ×	4,140,000	× 1.8/1.7	3,287,647
	3/12 ×	4,968,000		1,242,000
				4,529,647

EPS

$$= \frac{€989,000}{4,529,647}$$

$$= 21.8 \text{ cent}$$

(d) The maximum number of shares into which the loan stock could be converted is 90% × 1,150,000 = 1,035,000. The calculation of fully diluted EPS should be based on the assumption that such a conversion actually took place on 1 January 2012. Shares in issue during the year would then have numbered 5,175,000 (4,140,000 + 1,035,000) and revised earnings would be as follows.

	€	€
Earnings from (a) above		989,000
Interest saved by conversion	115,000	
Less attributable taxation	(57,500)	57,500
		1,046,500

		1,046,500
EPS		5,175,000
		= 20.2 cent

Question 23.2

(a) Basic EPS

	2012	2011
	€000	€000
Profit after tax	500	400
14% Non-cumulative Pref. Div. Paid		(20)
10% Cumulative Pref. Div. Proposed	(30)	(30)
14% Non-cumulative Pref. Div. Proposed	(60)	(40)
	410	310

Earnings	€410,000	€310,000
Ordinary Shares	100,000	100,000
Basic EPS =	410 cent	310 cent

(b) Issue at Full Market Price
The denominator should be weighted in accordance with the portion of the year in which the additional shares were in issue.

	2012	2011
Earnings (€)	410,000	310,000
Ordinary Shares	100,000 + (5,000 × 9/12)	100,000
Basic EPS	= 395 cent	= 310 cent

Note: Earno plc should not be compared with Plum plc above. It has been assumed in Earno that the additional cash generated by the share has been a factor in increasing earnings from €310,000 in 2011 to €410,000 in the current year.

(c) Capitalisation Issue

	2012	2011
Earnings	€410,000	€310,000
Ordinary Shares	100,000 + 20,000	100,000
Basic EPS	342 cent	310 cent

As shares have been issued without any cash being generated, it is necessary to adjust the 2011 EPS figure so as to preserve comparability.

$$€3.1 \times \frac{100,000}{120,000} = €2.58$$

	2012	2011
Correct Basic EPS	342c	258c

(d) Share Exchange

$$EPS = \frac{€410,000}{100,000 + (10,000 \times 8/12)} = 384 \text{ cent}$$

The reason that the additional 10,000 shares are taken in for 8 months only is that any earnings of the subsidiary prior to 30 April would be pre-acquisition and, as such, should be excluded from group earnings. It has been assumed that the subsidiary's earnings have been a factor in increasing earnings since 2011.

(e) Rights issue for less than full market price
We could regard this issue as being partly a bonus issue and partly an issue at full market price. The bonus portion is then treated as in (c) above:

(i) the bonus shares being deemed in issue from 1 January 2012; and
(ii) the 2011 EPS figure being reduced as in (c) above.

Calculation of Theoretical Ex-Rights price:

i.e. the price to which the share should fall after the rights issue

100,000 @ €4 =	400,000
20,000 @ €2 =	40,000
120,000	€440,000

$$\text{Theoretical ex-rights price} = \frac{€440,000}{120,000} = €3.67$$

	2012	2011
Earnings	€410,000	€310,000
Ordinary Shares	$(100,000 \times 6/12 \times €4/€3.67) + (120,000 \times 6/12)$	100,000
Basic EPS	358 cent	310 cent

It is necessary, however, to adjust the EPS ratio of 2011, as shares have been issued during 2012 for which the full market price was not obtained.

	2012	2011
Basic EPS	358 cent	$310 \times (3.67/4)$
		= 284 cent

(f) Fully Diluted Earnings Per Share
(i) Another class of equity ranking for dividend in the future:

	2012
Earnings	€410,000
Ordinary Shares	100,000 + 10,000
FDEPS	= 373 cent

(ii) Convertible Securities

Earnings per basic EPS	€410,000
Interest saved if €5,000 of 10% debentures are converted into ordinary shares on 31 March 2012 $(5,000 \times 10\% \times 9/12 \times 50\%)$	187
	€410,187

	2012
Earnings	410,187
Number of shares	$100,000 + (5,000 \times 40/100 \times 9/12)$
FDEPS	= 404 cent

The DEPS is not calculated for 2011 as the same assumptions did not apply.

Questions	Answer
24.1	(d)
24.2	(b)
24.3	(b)
24.4	(b)

24.5	(c)
24.6	(c)
24.7	(a)
24.8	(d)
24.9	(a)
24.10	(a)
24.11	(a)

Question 25.1

(a)

	€000
Total proceeds	30,000
Issue costs	(300)
	29,700

Total payments
– dividends €30,000 × 0.04 × 5 years	(6,000)
– redemption 30,000 × €1.35	(40,500)
	(16,800)

Finance cost	O/bal	FC (10%)	Paid	C/bal
	€000	€000	€000	€000
2008	29,700	2,970	(1,200)	31,470
2009	31,470	3,147	(1,200)	33,417
2010	33,417	3,342	(1,200)	35,559
2011	35,559	3,556	(1,200)	37,915
2012	37,915	3,792	(41,700)	-
			(Rounding €7)	

(b)

STATEMENT OF FINANCIAL POSITION (Extract)
as at 31 December 2012

	€000
Capital and Reserves	
€1 ordinary shares	300,000
Capital redemption reserve	30,000
Share premium account	77,000
Retained earnings (€182.5m – €30m)	152,500
	559,500

Question 25.2

		€
Proceeds	9 million × €0.95	8,550,000
Issue costs		(76,400)
Net proceeds		8,473,600

O/bal	Amount borrowed	Interest @ 10%	Paid (6%)	C/bal
	€	€	€	€
2012	8,473,600	847,360	(540,000)	8,780,960
2013	8,780,960	878,096	(540,000)	9,119,056
2014	9,119,056	911,906	(540,000)	9,490,962
2015	9,490,962	949,096	(10,440,000)	Nil*

*€58 rounding difference

Example:

2012	DR	SPLOCI – P/L – finance cost	€847,360	
	CR	Bank		€540,000
	CR	Debentures		€307,360

Question 26.1

As the recoverable amount of the CGU as a whole is €450, some of this must relate to the (unrecognised) goodwill of the NCI. Therefore, IAS 36 requires a notional adjustment for the goodwill of the NCI, before being compared to the recoverable amount of €450.

	Goodwill	Net assets	Total
	€	€	€
Carrying amount – Parent	160	500	660
Notional adjustment – NCI	40	–	40
	200	500	700
Recoverable amount			(450)
Impairment loss			250

If the goodwill of Parent is €160 and this represents 80%, then the goodwill attributable to the NCI is €40 (€160 × 20%/80%). This impairment loss is first allocated to €200 goodwill of €200 (eliminating it) and the remaining €50 (€250 – €200) to the identifiable net assets, leaving a carrying amount of €450 (€500 – €50), which is now equal to the recoverable amount of the CGU.

Question 27.1

(a)

	€
1. Cost of Investment in Roberts	68,000
Goodwill	(16,000)
	52,000

2. Therefore 100% of Roberts' capital and reserves at acquisition date = €52,000
3. Plant @ acquisition over-valued by 2,000

DR Cost of Control 80%	1,600	
DR Non-controlling interest 20%	400	
CR Plant		2,000

4.

DR CSPLOCI – P/L	200	
CR Inventory		200

Being unrealised profit included in Roberts' inventory purchased for Llewellyn.

In the draft consolidated statement of financial position 100% of post-acquisition profits of Roberts = €12,000, and 20% of this must be transferred to non-controlling interest.

Cost of Control

	€		€
Cost	68,000	Capital and Reserves	52,000
	____	Goodwill c/d	16,000
	68,000		68,000
Balance b/d	16,000	Journal 2	800
Journal 1	10,400		
Journal 3	1,600	Balance c/d	27,200
	28,000		28,000

Consolidated Reserves

	€		€
Journal 4	200	Balance b/f	32,000
Journal 5	2,400	Journal 2	480
Balance c/d	30,040	Journal 3	160
	32,640		32,640

Non-controlling Interest

	€			€
JNL 3	400	JNL	1	10,400
			2	320
Bal c/d	12,760		3	40
			5	2,400
	13,160			13,160

JOURNAL ADJUSTMENTS

	DR	CR
	€	€

1. DR Cost of Control   10,400
   CR Non-controlling interest   10,400
   Being transfer of 20% of Roberts Capital and Reserves at acquisition date to non-controlling interest.

2. DR Inventory   1,600
   (a) CR Cost of Control   800
   (b) CR Consolidated Reserves   480
   (c) CR Non-controlling Interest   320
   (a) 80% × €1,000 (Pre-acq.)
   (b) 80% × (€1,600 – €1,000) (Post-acq.)
   (c) 20% × 1,600

   Being adjustment to opening and closing inventory to correct Assistant Accountant's assumption that Llewellyn had acquired 100% of Roberts.

3. (a) DR   Cost of Control (Pre-acq.)   1,600
        DR   Non-controlling Interest   400

CR	Plant		2,000	
(b) DR	Depreciation Provision	200		
CR	Consolidated Reserves (Post-acq.)		160	
CR	Non-controlling Interest		40	

Being adjustment to plant to reflect over-valuation and correct acquisition percentage.

4. DR Consolidated Reserves   200

  CR Inventory   200

  Being unrealised profit included in Roberts' inventory purchased from Llewellyn.

5. DR Consolidated Reserves   2,400

  CR Non-controlling Interest   2,400

  Being NCI's share of post-acquisition profits (20%) incorrectly
  credited to Llewellyn by Assistant Accountant.

(b)

REVISED CONSOLIDATED STATEMENT OF FINANCIAL POSITION
as at 30 June 2013

	€		€
Property	30,000	Ordinary Shares	100,000
Plant at book value	78,200	Retained profits	30,040
Goodwill	27,200	Non-controlling interest	12,760
Inventory	33,400	Payables	54,000
Receivables	24,000		
Cash	4,000		
	196,800		196,800

Question 27.2

Black Limited
CONSOLIDATED STATEMENT OF FINANCIAL POSITION
as at 31 March 2013

Assets	€
Non-current Assets	
Property, plant and equipment	380,000
Goodwill	31,050
	411,050
Current Assets	285,700
Total Assets	696,750
Equity and Liabilities	
Equity	
Ordinary share capital	300,000
General reserve	50,000
Retained earnings	111,650

	461,650
Non-controlling interest	66,100
	527,750
Non-current Liabilities 6% Debentures	15,000
Current Liabilities	
Trade payables	119,200
Proposed dividends (30,000 + 3,390)	33,900
Debenture interest accrued	900
	154,000
Total Equity and Liabilities	696,750

Correcting Entries in Books:

	€	€
(i) Incorrect credit of dividends received out of pre-acquisition profits to SPLOCI of BLACK Limited		
Retained earnings	7,950	
Cost of Control Account		7,950
(ii) Correction of the incorrect pre-acquisition reserve calculation		
Cost of Investment	7,950	
Retained earnings		7,950
(iii) Credit of debenture interest receivable by Black Limited from Bird Limited		
Debenture interest receivable	300	
Retained Profits		300
(iv) Reversal of dividends payable by Bird Limited from Black Limited		
Dividends Payable	15,600	
Retained earnings		15,600
(v) Correction of unrealised inventory profit		
Retained earnings	3,200	
Inventory (€16,000 × 20%)		3,200

Group Structure:

	Bird	
	Ord.	Pref.
Group	75%	75%
Non-controlling interest	25%	25%
	100%	100%

Cost of Control Account

	€		€
Cost of investment: Ord	165,000	OSC	75,000
Pref	60,000	PSC	60,000
Pre-acquisition Dividend	7,950	Retained Profits	28,950

	General Reserve	30,000
	Pre-acquisition Dividend	7,950
	Goodwill	31,050
232,950		232,950

Tutorial Notes to Cost of Control Account:

1. A dividend has been declared out of Bird Limited's pre-acquisition profits. The group share of the dividend is as follows:

	€
Ordinary 5,600 × 75% =	4,200
Preference 5,000 × 75% =	3,750
	7,950

The cost of investment has been reduced as this is effectively a refund of Black Limited's purchase consideration (see journal (ii) above). Black Limited has incorrectly recognised this amount as income in a previous statement of profit or loss and other comprehensive income. Thus, group reserves must also be reduced by €7,950.

2. Note that the profit figure used to calculate group share of pre-acquisition profits is that before the dividend has been deducted.

Profit after dividend at 31/3/2012	€28,000
Add back pre-acquisition dividend	€10,600
	€38,600

Pref.	Ord.
7% × €80,000	(bal)
€5,600	€33,000
× 75%	× 75%
€4,200	€24,750

€28,950

3. Note that the profit figure above used to calculate the pre-acquisition reserves was that before the pre-acquisition dividends. This is not strictly correct because, by their very nature, pre-acquisition dividends reduce the level of reserves that existed at the date of acquisition. Consequently, this is corrected by crediting back some of the already frozen reserves to the consolidated reserves account and debiting the cost of control (see journal (i) above). The amount of the correction is the group share of the pre-acquisition dividend.

Non-controlling Interest Account

	€		€
		OSC	25,000
Other payables	3,900	PSC	20,000
Balance carried down	66,100	SPLOCI	15,000
		General Reserve	10,000
	70,000		70,000

Tutorial Notes to Non-Controlling Interest Account:

1. Note that the profit before the deduction of the current year dividend has been used to calculate the non-controlling interest share of reserves.

Reserves before dividend

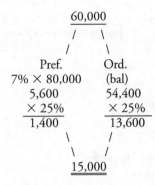

$$60,000$$

```
                Pref.         Ord.
           7% × 80,000       (bal)
              5,600          54,400
              × 25%          × 25%
              1,400          13,600

                   15,000
```

The non-controlling interest share of the dividends for the year is as follows:

	€
Ordinary 10,000 × 25% =	2,500
Preference 5,600 × 25% =	1,400
	3,900

This amount is to be reclassified as 'other payables'.

2. Debentures and debenture interest must not be posted to the non-controlling interest account.

Consolidated Earnings

	€			€
		Balance b/d	– Black	98,500
			– Bird	44,400
Cost of Control Account	28,950			
Non-controlling interest	15,000	Pre-acquisition dividend (i)		7,950
Inventory Adjustment	3,200	Debenture interest due		300
Pre-acquisition dividend (ii)	7,950	Dividend proposed		15,600
Balance carried down	111,650			
	166,750			166,750

Tutorial Notes on Consolidated Reserves:
1. The reserves of Black Limited above incorrectly include a dividend made by Bird out of pre-acquisition reserves, of €7,950. Such a dividend should be treated as a refund of capital not as income and thus the group reserves have been reduced by €7,950.
2. The dividends proposed by Bird Limited are reversed. No adjustment to reverse them out of Black is required as they were not recognised as receivable in the books of Black Limited.
3. Debenture interest payable by Bird Limited has not been recognised in the books of Black Limited. The group share of this interest, i.e. €1,200 × 25%, has been credited to group reserves.

General Reserves

	€			€
Cost of Control	30,000	Balance b/d	– Black	50,000
Non-controlling interest	10,000		– Bird	40,000
Balance carried down	50,000			
	90,000			90,000

WORKINGS (Alternative Presentation)

JOURNAL ADJUSTMENTS

		€	€
1.	DR Retained Profits Black	3,200	
	CR Inventory		3,200
	Being unrealised inventory profit		
2.	DR Retained Profits Black	7,950	
	CR Investment in Bird		7,950
	Being dividends from pre-acquisition profits		
3.	DR Debenture Interest Receivable	300	
	CR Retained Profits Black		300
	Being debenture interest receivable		
4.	DR Dividends receivable	11,700	
	CR Retained Profits Black		11,700
	Being dividends receivable from Bird		

i.e.   Pref. €5,600 × 75%   =   4,200
        Ord. €10,000 × 75%   =   7,500

		€	€
5.	DR Debenture Int. Accrued	300	
	CR Debenture Int. Receivable		300
	Being cancellation of intragroup balance		
6.	DR Proposed dividends	11,700	
	CR Dividends Receivable		11,700
	Being cancellation of intragroup balance		

Property Plant and Equipment

	€		€
Black	190,000	CSFP	380,000
Bird	190,000		
	380,000		380,000

Inv. in Bird

	€		€
Ordinary shares	165,000	Journal 2	7,950
Preference shares	60,000	Cost of Control	222,050
Debentures	5,000		
	230,000		230,000

Current Assets

	€		€
Black	145,500	Journal 1	3,200
Bird	143,400	CSFP	285,700
	288,900		288,900

Ord. Shares

	€		€
Cost of Control	75,000	Black	300,000
Non-controlling interest	25,000	Bird	100,000
CSFP	300,000		400,000
	400,000		400,000

Pref. Shares

	€		€
Cost of Control	60,000	Black	–
Non-controlling interest	20,000	Bird	80,000
	80,000		80,000

General Reserve

	€		€
Cost of Control	30,000	Black	50,000
(75% × €40,000)		Bird	40,000
Non-controlling Interest	10,000		
(25% × €40,000)	50,000		
CSFP	90,000		90,000

Retained Profit

	€		€
Journal 1 Black	3,200	Black	98,500
Journal 2 Black	7,950	Bird	44,400
Cost of Control	21,000	Journal 3 Black	300
(75% × €28,000)	11,100	Journal 4 Black	11,700
Non-controlling interest			
(25% × €44,400)			
CSFP	111,650		
	154,900		154,900

Trade Payables

	€		€
CSFP	119,200	Black	87,000
		Bird	32,200
	119,200		119,200

Proposed Dividends

	€		€
Journal 6	11,700	Black	30,000
CSFP Black	30,000	Bird Ord	10,000
NCI	3,900	Pref	5,600
	45,600		45,600

Debentures Int. Accrued

	€		€
Journal 5	300	Bird	1,200
CSFP	900		
	1,200		1,200

Debentures Int. Receivable

	€		€
Journal 3	300	Journal 5	300

Dividends Receivable

	€		€
Journal 4	11,700	Journal 6	11,700

Cost of Control

	€		€
Inv. in Bird	222,050	Ord. Shares	75,000
		Pref. Shares	60,000
		Debs.	5,000
		Gen. Reserve	30,000
		Retained Profit	21,000
		Goodwill – CSFP	31,050
	222,050		222,050

Non-controlling Interest

	€		€
CSFP	66,100	Ord. Shares	25,000
		Pref. Shares	20,000
		Gen. Reserve	10,000
		Retained Profit	11,100
	66,100		66,100

Question 28.1

	X Limited	Y Limited	Consolidated
	€	€	€
Revenue	10,000	7,000	17,000
Cost of sales	(6,000)	(1,000)	(7,000)
Gross profit	4,000	6,000	10,000
Administration expenses	(500)	(600)	(1,100)
Depreciation (W3)	(1,000)	(1,500)	(2,500)
Profit before tax	2,500	3,900	6,400
Income tax expense	(400)	(100)	(500)

Profit after tax	2,100	3,800	5,900
Non-controlling interest (W4)	--	(380)	(380)
Profit attributable to the group	2,100	3,420	5,520
Reserves brought forward (W5)	10,000	2,520	12,520
Reserves carried forward	12,100	5,940	18,040

WORKINGS

1. Group structure

	Y Limited
Group	90%
Non-controlling interest	10%
	100%

2. Tangible non-current assets

Tangible non-current assets included in Y Limited's statement of financial position are understated:

DR	Tangible non-current assets	€3,000
CR	Revaluation reserve	€3,000

This journal entry is a statement of financial position entry and thus does not affect the solution's statement of profit or loss and other comprehensive income.

3. Depreciation

Depreciation charges included in Y Limited statement of profit or loss and other comprehensive income are based on cost. For consolidation purposes, this must be amended to ensure that the depreciation charge is based on the revalued amount:

		Depreciation on		
		Cost	**Fair value**	**Difference**
		€	**€**	**€**
Year ended:	2008	1,200	1,500	300
	2009	1,200	1,500	300
	2010	1,200	1,500	300
	2011	1,200	1,500	300
	2012	1,200	1,500	300
		6,000	7,500	1,500

Depreciation in Y Limited is thus understated in:

	€
• the current year (2012)	300
• prior years since acquisition (2008–2011)	1,200
	1,500

This requires two adjustments:

(a) Increase the current year charge in Y Limited by €300:

DR	Depreciation (SPLOCI – P/L)	€300	
CR	Accumulation depreciation (SFP)		€300

(b) Increase prior year's charge in Y Limited by €1,200:

DR	Retained earnings	€1,200	
CR	Accumulation depreciation (SFP)		€1,200

4. Non-controlling interest

	€
Y Limited – Profit after Tax (as adjusted by extra depreciation for current year)	3,800
	× 10%
Non-controlling interest	380

5. Reserves brought forward

	€ Y Limited
Reserves b/fwd per individual accounts	7,000
Pre-acquisition reserves	(3,000)
Post-acquisition reserves	4,000
Depreciation adjustment (W3)	(1,200)
Post-acquisition reserves (as adjusted)	2,800
	× 90%
Group share only	2,520

Key points:
- The current year's depreciation adjustment is made in the subsidiary statement of profit or loss and other comprehensive income column.
- The accumulated depreciation adjustment is made to subsidiary reserves prior to calculating the group share only.
- In this way, only 90% of the relevant adjustment is included in the consolidated statement of profit or loss and other comprehensive income.

Question 28.2

1. Group structure:

	Group	60%
	NCI	40%
		100%
		= > Subsidiary

2. Tangible non-current assets

	Based on book value	Based on fair value	SCI diff.
	€	€	€
1 January 2009	12,000	15,000	
Depreciation	(2,400)	(3,000)	600
31 December 2009	9,600	12,000	
Depreciation	(1,920)	(2,400)	480
31 December 2010	7,680	9,600	
Depreciation	(1,536)	(1,920)	384
31 December 2011	6,144	7,680	
Depreciation	(1,229)	(1,536)	307
31 December 2012	4,915	6,144	

= > Reserves of A Limited for consolidation purposes at 31 December 2011 are overstated by:

		€
Depreciation	2009	600
	2010	480
	2011	384
		1,464

Profit for the year is overstated for 2012 by €307.

3. Calculation of reserves brought forward

	C	A
	€	€
Per individual accounts	15,000	6,000
Pre-acquisition reserves		3,000
Post-acquisition reserves	15,000	9,000
Depreciation adjustment		(1,464)
	15,000	7,536
		× 60%
Group share only	15,000	4,522

4. Workings (Consolidated statement of profit or loss and other comprehensive income)

	C	A	Consolidated
	€	€	€
Net profit (draft)	10,000	5,000	15,000
Depreciation adjustment		(307)	(307)
Net profit	10,000	4,693	14,693
Income tax expense	1,000	1,000	(2,000)
Profit after tax	9,000	3,693	12,693
Non-controlling interest (40%)	-	(1,477)	(1,477)

Profit attributable to the group	9,000	2,216	11,216
Balance brought forward	15,000	4,522	19,522
Balance carried forward	24,000	6,738	30,738

Question 28.3

	X Limited	Y Limited (10 months)	Consolidated
	€	€	€
Revenue	10,000	5,833	15,833
Cost of sales	(6,000)	(833)	(6,833)
Gross profit	4,000	5,000	9,000
Administration expenses	(1,000)	(417)	(1,417)
Distribution costs	-	(700)	(700)
Profit before tax	3,000	3,883	6,883
Income tax expense	(500)	(250)	(750)
Profit after tax	2,500	3,633	6,133
Non-controlling interest (W3)	-	(363)	(363)
PATTG	2,500	3,270	5,770

WORKINGS

1. Group Structure

	Y Limited
Group	90%
NCI	10%
	100%

2. Acquisition during the year

Time-apportion all items in Y Limited by 10/12, except the distribution costs, which arose entirely after 28 February 2012.

3. Non-controlling interest

Y Limited – Profit after tax	€
	3,633
	× 10%
	363

4. Subsidiary dividends

These must be time-apportioned, with only the post-acquisition element being included in the dividend shuffle in the calculation of consolidated retained earnings.

	Total	Post-acquisition	Group Share
	€	€	€
Y Limited: Ordinary dividends	4,000 × 10/12	3,333 × 90%	3,000

5. Consolidated retained earnings

	X Limited €	Y Limited €	Group €
PATTG	2,500	3,270	5,770
Retained earnings b/f	10,000	-	10,000
Subsidiary dividends (W4)	3,000	(3,000)	-
X Limited Dividends paid	(200)	-	(200)
Retained earnings c/f	15,300	270	15,570

Note: Y Limited had no post-acquisition reserves at 1 January 2012.

Question 28.4

	P Limited €	S Limited €	Consolidated €
Gross profit	10,000	6,000	16,000
Administration expenses	(1,000)	(2,000)	(3,000)
Depreciation	(4,000)	(500)	(4,500)
Profit before tax	5,000	3,500	8,500
Income tax expense	(1,000)	(1,500)	(2,500)
Profit after tax	4,000	2,000	6,000
Non-controlling interest (W4)	--	(500)	(500)
Profit attributable to group	4,000	1,500	5,500

1. Group Structure

	S Limited
Group	75%
Non-controlling interest	25%
	100% = > Subsidiary

2. Unrealised tangible non-current asset profit
   Cancel the unrealised non-current asset profit

DR Profit on sale of non-current asset P Limited	€2,000	
CR Tangible non-current assets		€2,000

3. Correct depreciation charge

	€
Charged by S Limited (€7,500 × 10% × 6/12)	375
Current charge in accordance with group policy	
(€10,000 × 10% × 6/12)	500
	125

DR Depreciation charge – SPLOCI – S Limited	€125	
CR Accumulated depreciation SFP		€125

4. Non-controlling interest

	€
Profit after tax S Limited (after depreciation adjustment)	2,000
	× 25%
Non-controlling interest	500

Note:
 (i) The adjustment correcting the unrealised profit is made in P Limited as this is the company whose statement of profit or loss and other comprehensive income included the unrealised profit, i.e. the selling company.
(ii) The adjustment correcting the depreciation is made in S Limited as this is the company where individual statement of profit or loss and other comprehensive income included the incorrect depreciation charge, i.e. the buying company.

Question 29.1

Parker Group

Consolidated Statement of Profit or Loss and Other Comprehensive Income
for the Year Ended 30 September 2013

	€000
Turnover	31,980
Group profit (Note 1)	1,767
Share of profits of associate	90
Profit before taxation	1,857
Taxation	1,108
Profit after taxation	749
Profit attributable to non-controlling interests in subsidiaries	(41)
Profit attributable to the group	708

	Parker Limited Group	Duke Limited
Group profit	€000	€000
Trading profits	2,312	879
Admin expenses	(541)	(199)
Finance cost	(4)	0
	1,767	680
	× 30%	204
Tax – associate (Duke €380,000 × 30%)		(114)
		90
Group retained earnings at beginning of year per draft accounts		345

Note: no retained earnings for Duke Limited can be included at 1 October 2012, as the investment by the group in that company was made during the year under review.

statement of changes in equity (extract)

	€000
Retained earnings at End of Year	
Profit for year ended 30 September 2013	708
Retained earnings b/f	345

Ordinary dividends paid year ended 30 September 2013	(100)
	953

Note: Duke Limited is accounted for using the equity method.

Question 29.2

Golf Limited
CONSOLIDATED STATEMENT OF PROFIT OR LOSS AND OTHER COMPREHENSIVE INCOME
for the Year Ended 30 June 2013

	€
Revenue	2,876,000
Group Profit	343,000
Share of profit of associate	37,500
Profit before taxation	380,500
Income tax expense	124,000
Profit after taxation	256,500
Profit attributable to non-controlling interests	(12,500)
Profit attributable to the group (Note 1)	244,000

Note 1: Profit attributable to the company
  Of this profit €209,000 is dealt with in the accounts of the parent company.
  (Note to students: €169,000 + €6,000 (inventory profit) + €34,000 = €209,000)

Note 2: Retained earnings at end of year
  This amount is dealt with in the accounts of:

	€
– the parent company	521,000
– the subsidiary company	21,500
– the associated company	19,500
	562,000

Note: IAS 28 *Investments in Associates and Joint Ventures* does not prescribe how the investor's share of its associates profit should be presented in the statement of profit or loss and other comprehensive income. The example in IAS 1 defines the share of profit of associates as the share of associates' profit attributable to equity holders of the associates, i.e. after tax and non-controlling interests in the associates. This is disclosed just before 'profit before tax'.

Group Structure:

	Club Ord.	Ball Ord.	Tee Ord.
Group	15%	30%	75%
Other interest	85%	70%	25%
	100%	100%	100%

Note:
(a) Club is a trade investment and is thus accounted for only to the extent of dividends receivable in accordance with IFRS 9. Note (3) to the question indicates that Golf has not yet accounted for the dividend received from Club. Hence, the following adjustment is required in Golf's books

DR	Bank	€15,000
CR	SPLOCI – P/L	€15,000

(b) Ball is an associated company to be accounted for under the provisions of IAS 28.

WORKINGS (CONSOLIDATED STATEMENT OF PROFIT OR LOSS AND OTHER COMPREHENSIVE INCOME)

	Golf	Tee	Ball	Adj.	Total
	€	(2/3) €	€	€	€
Revenue	2,100,000	800,000		(24,000)	2,876,000
Draft Profit	250,000	84,000			
Dividend from Club	15,000				
Inventory adjustment	(6,000)				
Group Profit	259,000	84,000			343,000
Associated company profit			37,500		37,500
Profit before tax					380,500
Taxation	(90,000)	(34,000)			(124,000)
Profit after tax	169,000	50,000	37,500		256,500
Non-controlling interest		(12,500)			(12,500)
Profit attributable to the group	169,000	37,500	37,500		244,000
Retained Earnings:					
Profit attributable to the group	169,000	37,500	37,500		244,000
Tee – Ordinary	16,000	(16,000)	---		----
Ball – Ordinary	18,000		(18,000)		
	203,000	21,500	19,500		244,000
Golf – Ordinary	(132,000)				(132,000)
Retained profit for year	71,000	21,500	19,500		112,000
Balance brought forward	450,000	-	-		450,000
Balance carried forward	521,000	21,500	19,500		562,000

Notes to workings:
1. €24,000 intragroup sales to be eliminated;
2. Tee acquired on 1/11/2012 – thus 2/3 of results to be taken in;
3. non-controlling interest: Tee – Profit after tax (2/3) €50,000 × 25% = €12,500; and
4. dividend shuffle.

Tee:	Ordinary
	€
Total dividend	32,000
	× 2/3
Post-acquisition dividends	21,333
	× 75%
Group share only	16,000

Ball: Ordinary dividend €60,000 × 30% = €18,000

WORKINGS (CONSOLIDATED STATEMENT OF PROFIT OR LOSS AND OTHER COMPREHENSIVE
INCOME – alternative approach)

Group Profit

	€
Golf:	250,000
Tee × 8 months (€126,000 × 2/3)	84,000
Unrealised inventory profit (€24,000 × 25%)	(6,000)
Dividends from Club (Note)	15,000
	343,000

The dividend from Club must be included as it is from a company outside the group.

Share of Profit of Associate

	€
Ball PBT €210,000 × 30%	63,000
Taxation €85,000 × 30%	(25,500)
	37,500

Income tax expenses

	€	€
Group: Golf	90,000	
Tee (8 months) €51,000 × 2/3	34,000	124,000

Non-controlling interest

Tee – Profit after tax (8 months – 2/3) €50,000 × 25% = €12,500

Retained Profit b/f

Both the subsidiary (Tee) and the associate Ball were bought during the year under review. Therefore, they cannot be included in the group retained profit b/f as there were no post-acquisition profits in those companies at 1 July 2012.

Golf only   €450,000

Question 29.3

Gold Limited
CONSOLIDATED STATEMENT OF FINANCIAL POSITION
as at 30 November 2012

	€
Assets	
Non-current assets	
Property, plant and equipment	170,000
Goodwill	3,587
Investment in associate (see Note 1)	36,500
	210,087
Current Assets	
Inventory	61,750
Receivables	208,750
Bank and cash	27,600

Current account with associate	650
	298,750
Total Assets	508,837

Equity and Liabilities	
Equity	
Ordinary share capital	50,000
Share premium	10,000
Capital reserve	93,500
Other reserves	35,000
Retained earnings	60,450
	248,950
Non-controlling interest	52,387
	301,337
Current Liabilities	
Payables	152,500
Bank overdraft	27,500
Taxation	25,000
Current account with associate	2,500
	207,500
Total Equity and Liabilities	508,837

Journal Adjustments

	€	€
1. DR Cash	500	
CR Current account with Silver		500

Being cash in transit at reporting date (adjusted in the accounts of the parent)

2. DR Retained earnings Gold	750	
CR Inventory		750

Being unrealised profit on inventory (€36,000 × 1/8 × 1/6)

3. DR Inventory in Associate	6,000	
CR Cap res (€5,000 × 40%)		2,000
CR Ret. earnings (€10,000 × 40%)		4,000

post-acquisition Being the group share of post-acquisition retained reserves in associate

Cost of Control Account

	€		€
Investment in Silver Limited	100,000	Ordinary Share Capital	75,000
		Capital Reserve	14,438
		Retained earnings	3,225
		Contingency Reserve	3,750
		Goodwill	3,587
	100,000		100,000

Alternatively:

		€
Cost of investment		100,000
Non-controlling Interest at Acquisition:	€	
Ordinary shares	100,000	
Capital reserves	19,250	
Retained earnings	4,300	
Contingency reserve	5,000	
	128,550	
	× 25%	32,137
Net assets acquired		(128,550)
Goodwill		3,587

Capital Reserve Account

	€		€
Cost of Control (€19,250 × 3/4)	14,438	Gold Limited	61,500
NCI (€59,250 × 1/4)	14,812	Silver Limited	59,250
Consolidated SFP	93,500	Investment in Associated	
		Company	2,000
	122,750		122,750

Retained Profits

	€		€
Cost of Control (€4,300 × 3/4)	3,225	Gold Limited	26,450
NCI (€45,300 × 1/4)	11,325	Silver Limited	45,300
Journal (2)	750	Investment in Associated	
Consolidated SFP	60,450	Company	4,000
	75,750		75,750

Other Reserves

	€		€
Cost of Control (€5,000 × 3/4)	3,750	Gold Limited	35,000
NCI (€5,000 × 1/4)	1,250	Silver Limited	5,000
Consolidated SFP	35,000		
	40,000		40,000

Non-controlling Interests

	€		€
Consolidated SFP	52,387	Ordinary Share Capital	25,000
		Capital Reserve	14,812
		Retained earnings	11,325
		Contingency Reserve	1,250
	52,387		52,387

Investment in Associated Company Account

	€		€
Cost of Investment	30,500	Consolidated SFP	36,500
Retained earnings – Associate			
(€15,000 – €5,000) × 40%	4,000		
Capital Reserve – Associate			
(€5,000 × 40%)	2,000		
	36,500		36,500

Current account with Silver

	€		€
Gold	1,000	Journal 1	500
		Contra	500
	1,000		1,000

Current account with Bronze

	€		€
CSFP	2,500	Gold	2,500
	2,500		2,500

Current account with Gold

	€		€
Contra	500	Silver	500
	500		500

Current account with Bronze

	€		€
Silver	650	CSFP	650
	650		650

The current account balances between Gold and Bronze, and Silver and Bronze will be transferred to the consolidated statement of financial position as they are not intragroup.

Inventory

	€		€
Gold	26,500	Journal 2	750
Silver	36,000	CSFP	61,750
	62,500		62,500

Cash

	€		€
Gold	100		
Journal 1	500	CSFP	600
	600		600

WORKINGS

1. Group structure

	Silver	Bronze
Group	75%	40%
NCI/other	25%	60%
	100%	100%

2. Group Share of Net Assets of Bronze:
   40% × €55,000 = €22,000

3. Premium on Acquisition:
   €30,500 – (40% × €40,000) = €14,500

Note 1: Investment in Associated Company

	€
Groups Share of Net Assets	22,000
Premium on Acquisition	14,500
	36,500

Note 2: Treatment of Associated Company
The associated company is stated at cost plus the group's share of retained post-acquisition profits/reserves. Thus, for example, for retained earnings:

	€
Balance at acquisition	5,000
Balance at 30/11/2012	15,000
Post-acquisition retained earnings	10,000
Group share (× 40%)	4,000

Entry required is:

DR	Investment in associated company	€4,000
CR	Consolidated retained earnings	€4,000

Question 30.1

True plc
CONSOLIDATED STATEMENT OF PROFIT OR LOSS AND OTHER COMPREHENSIVE INCOME
for the Year Ended 31 December 2012

	€
Revenue (W5)	4,815,000

Cost of sales (W5)		(2,443,500)
Gross profit (W5)		2,371,500
Operating expenses (W5)		(1,572,000)
Profit before taxation		799,500
Taxation (W5)		(252,000)
Profit after taxation		547,500
Non-controlling interests (W7)		(16,200)
Profit attributable to the owners		531,300

True plc
CONSOLIDATED STATEMENT OF FINANCIAL POSITION
as at 31 December 2012

	€	€
ASSETS		
Non-current Assets		
Property, plant and equipment		2,800,000
Goodwill		56,000
		2,856,000
Current Assets		
Inventory (W4)	602,500	
Receivables (€750,000 – €30,000)	720,000	
Bank and cash (incl. €20,000 in transit)	280,000	1,602,500
		4,458,500
EQUITY AND LIABILITIES		
Capital and Reserves		
€1 ordinary shares		2,000,000
Retained earnings (W2)		1,364,000
Capital reserve (W3)		322,500
		3,686,500
Non-controlling interest		137,000
		3,823,500
Current Liabilities		
Trade payables		635,000
		4,458,500

WORKINGS
1. Statement of financial position consolidation schedule
   (i) Dividends declared after the reporting date should not be recognised as liabilities unless there is a legal obligation to receive them (IAS 10 *Events after the Reporting Date*). There is no entitlement to ordinary dividends until they are approved at the Annual General Meeting by the shareholders, and therefore the proposed dividends should be reversed.

DR	Current liabilities	200,000	
CR	Retained earnings		200,000

The adjusted balance on TRUE and FAIR's retained earnings at 31 December 2012 is €1,100,000 and €545,000 respectively.

Furthermore, dividends paid should be debited directly to equity.

(ii) The inter-company accounts differ by €20,000, being cash in transit from FAIR Limited to TRUE plc. This will appear as a current asset in the consolidated statement of financial position.

(iii) Non-controlling interest (at reporting date):

	€
Share capital (10% × €750,000)	75,000
Retained earnings (10% × €545,000)	54,500
Capital reserve (10% × €75,000)	7,500
	137,000

(iv) Goodwill

	€	€
Cost of investment		950,000
NCI:		
Share capital	750,000	
Retained earnings	100,000	
Capital reserves	50,000	
	900,000 × 10%	90,000
NA acquired		(900,000)
Goodwill (W2)		140,000

The goodwill was impaired by €84,000 during the year ended 31 December 2012 and therefore the statement of financial position value at 31 December 2012 is €56,000.

2. Retained earnings

	€
TRUE plc	1,100,000
Share of FAIR Limited's post-acquisition reserves	
(€545,000 – 100,000) × 90%	400,500
	1,500,500
Goodwill impairment (W1(iv))	(84,000)
less unrealised profit in inventory (W4)	(22,500)
less allowance for receivables (incl. in TRUE op. expenses	(30,000)
(Per note 5))	1,364,000

3. Capital reserve

	€
TRUE plc	300,000
Share of FAIR Limited's post-acquisition reserves	
(€75,000 – €50,000) × 90%	22,500
	322,500

4. Unrealised profit in inventory
25/125 × €225,000 × 50% = €22,500

Therefore eliminate in full against the group retained earnings as TRUE plc originally recorded the profit.

5. Consolidation schedule

	TRUE	FAIR	Adjusted	Consolidated
	€	€	€	€
Revenue	4,050,000	990,000	(225,000)	4,815,000
Cost of sales	(2,088,000)	(558,000)	202,500	(2,443,500)
Gross profit	1,962,000	432,000	(W4) (22,500)	2,371,500
Op. exp.	(W8) (1,290,000)	(198,000)	(W1(iv)) (84,000)	(1,572,000)
Taxation	(180,000)	(72,000)		(252,000)

6. Dividends received by TRUE plc from FAIR Limited,
   i.e. paid dividends only since TRUE had not yet accounted for the proposed dividend
   90% × €50,000 = €45,000.

   Therefore all investment income recorded in TRUE plc's SPLOCI – P/L is intragroup.

7. Non-controlling interest based on profit after tax of FAIR Limited is €16,200 (€162,000 × 10%).

8. Power failure   = non-adjusting event after the reporting period.

   Irrecoverable debt   = provision required on the assumption that the conditions that led to receivership existed at the reporting date.

Question 30.2

ARCHER Group
CONSOLIDATED STATEMENT OF PROFIT OR LOSS AND OTHER COMPREHENSIVE INCOME
for the Year Ended 31 December 2012

	€million	€million
Revenue (€3,000m + €200m)		3,200
Cost of sales (€1,800m + €125m)		(1,925)
Gross profit (€1,200m + €75m)		1,275
Operating expenses (€500m + €25m – €100m (W1))		(425)
Operating profit		850
Finance costs (€20m + €5m)		(25)
Share of profit of associate (W2(v))		132
Profit before tax		957
Tax on profit – group (€200m + €10m)		(210)
Profit after tax		747

ARCHER Group
CONSOLIDATED STATEMENT OF FINANCIAL POSITION
as at 31 December 2012

	€million	€million
ASSETS		
Non-current Assets		
Property, plant and equipment (€2,200m + €40m)		2,240
Investments – investment in associate (ARROW Limited)		920
		3,160

Current Assets

Inventory (€400m + €125m)	525	
Receivables (€300m)	300	
Bank and cash (€80m + €200m + €12m)	292	1,117
		4,277

EQUITY AND LIABILITIES

Capital and Reserves

Share capital	1,200
Revaluation reserve	600
RE (€1,700m + negative goodwill €100m (W1) + sub. €35m + assoc. €120m (W2(iv)) + divs. €12m)	1,967
	3,767
Current Liabilities (€480m + €30m)	510
	4,277

WORKINGS

1. Acquisition of BOW Limited (Note 1)

   There is a gain from a bargain purchase (negative goodwill) of €100 million arising on the acquisition of BOW. In accordance with IFRS 3, this should be recognised in arriving at profit or loss in the statement of profit or loss and other comprehensive income.

2. Purchase of ARROW Limited (30%)

		€million	€million
(i) Goodwill			
Cost of investment			800
Share capital		600	
Revaluation reserve		300	
Retained earnings		1,100	
		2,000	
	@ 30%		600
Goodwill			200

   No evidence of impairment therefore carried at €200m

	€million
(ii) Investment in associate	
30% × €2,400	720
Unimpaired goodwill	200
	920

		€million
(iii) Revaluation reserve		
ARROW Limited	@ 31/12/12	300
@ acquisition date		(300)
		nil

		€million
(iv) Retained earnings		
ARROW Limited	@ 31/12/12	1,500
@ acquisition date		1,100
		400
@ 30%		120

	€million
(v) Share of operating profits in associate	
Operating profit – €640m × 30%	192
Interest payable – €10m × 30%	(3)
Tax on profits – €190m × 30%	(57)

While IAS 28 does not prescribe how the investor's share of its associate's profits should be presented in the statement of profit or loss and other comprehensive income, the example in IAS 1 *Presentation of Financial Statements* discloses this *single figure* just before 'profit before tax'. This is illustrated in **Figure 2.3**, **Chapter 2**.

3. Answer assumes that depreciation has already been charged in BOW Limited's accounts,

i.e.   Fair value @ 1/1/12   = €50 / 5 = €10m
        Book value @ 31/12/12   = €40m

4. Dividends paid are debited directly to equity.

Question 31.1

(a) JOURNAL ENTRIES:

	€	€

Transaction 1

J.1 DR Cash — 571,429
    CR Loan Account — — 571,429
    Being a loan of US$1m received at $1.75 = €1

J.2 DR Loan Account — 15,873
    CR SPLOCI – P/L — — 15,873
    Being retranslation of US$ loan at closing exchange rate of $1.80 = €1

Transaction 2

J.3 DR Property, plant and equipment — 17,460
    CR Trade Payables – Frtz — — 17,460
    Being purchase of assets of DM55,000 at DM 3.15 = €1

J.4 DR SPLOCI – P/L — 1,746
    CR Accumulated depreciation — — 1,746
    Being depreciation of non-current asset for half-year at 20%

J.5 DR Trade payables – Frtz — 17,460
    DR SPLOCI – P/L — 873
    CR Cash — — 18,333
    Being settlement of non-current asset Purchase at DM 3.0 = €1

Transaction 3

J.6 DR Purchases — 8,824
    CR Trade payables – Etien — — 8,824
    Being purchase of goods for resale at BFr 68.00 = €1

    DR Trade payables – Etien — 191
    CR SPLOCI – P/L — — 191
    Being gain on retranslation on BFr 600,000 at BFr 69.50 = €1

Include these items in closing inventory (if any still held at 31 March 2010) at the exchange rate of BFr 68.00 = €1

(b) EXTRACTS FROM ACCOUNTS

Transaction 1

SFP:	Current liabilities:	
	US Bank Loan (€571,429−€15,873)	€555,556
SPLOCI:	Exchange Gain	€15,873
	(included in arriving at profit or loss in SPLOCI)	

Transaction 2

SFP:	Non-current Assets	
	Cost	
	Property, plant and equipment	€17,460
	Accumulated Depreciation	
	Property, plant and equipment	€1,746
SPLOCI:	Included in arriving at profit or loss in SPLOCI	
	Depreciation	€1,746
	Exchange Loss	€873

Transaction 3

SFP:	Current liabilities	
	Trade Payables (€8,824−€191)	€8,633
SPLOCI:	Included in arriving at profit or loss in SPLOCI	
	Exchange gain	€191

Question 31.2

Ray International Limited and Subsidiary
CONSOLIDATED STATEMENT OF PROFIT OR LOSS AND OTHER COMPREHENSIVE INCOME
for the Year Ended 31 December 2012

	€000
	12,021
Revenue	2,933
Profit before tax	(1,360)
Income tax expense	1,573
Profit for year	

STATEMENT OF CHANGES IN EQUITY (EXTRACTS)	
	480
Retained earnings at start of year	(150)*
Foreign currency translation reserve movement (shown in OCI)	1,903
Retained earnings at end of year	

* Opening net investment of 1,200,000 Dfl

At opening rate of 3 Dfl to €	=	400
At closing rate of 4 Dfl to €	=	300

Profits for year of 1,393,000 Dfl

At average rate of 3.5 Dfl	(100)
	= 398
At closing rate of 4 Dfl	= 348
	(50)
	(150)

Ray International Limited and Subsidiary
CONSOLIDATED STATEMENT OF FINANCIAL POSITION
as at 31 December 2012

	€000
Assets	
Non-current assets	
Current assets	3,390
Inventory	
Other	2,895
	1,381
	4,276
Total assets	7,666
Equity and liabilities	
Equity	
Share capital	
Retained earnings	2,000
Foreign currency translation reserve	2,053
	(150)
Non-current liabilities	3,903
Long-term loan	
	294
Current liabilities	
Total equity and liabilities	3,469
	7,666

WORKINGS

STATEMENTS OF PROFIT OR LOSS AND OTHER COMPREHENSIVE INCOME AND RETAINED EARNINGS FOR YEAR

	M Distribution BV Dfl000	Rate	MD. BV €000	Ray Inter'l Limited €000	Adj.	Consolidated
Revenue	12,600	3.5	3,600	10,871	(2,450) a	12,021
Profit before tax	1,603 b	3.5	458	2,600	(125)	2,933
Income tax expense	(210)	3.5	(60)	(1,300)	–	(1,360)
Profit for year	1,393	3.5	398	1,300	(125)	1,573
Dividend	(500)	Actual	(125)	–	125 c	–
	893		273	1,300		1,573
Exchange Loss			(150)			(150)

	M BV	Rate	€000		
Balance at beginning of year	–			–	480	–	480
Balance at end of year	893	4		123	1,780	–	1,903

STATEMENTS OF FINANCIAL POSITION

	M BV	Rate	€000	M €000	Ray Inter'l	Adj.	Consol.
Non-current assets	600	4		150	3,240		3,390
Investment		4			400	(400)	
Current assets							
Inventory	2,020	4	505		2,390		2,895
Other	1,164	4	291		1,472	(382) d	1,381
	3,184		796		3,862		4,276
Current Liabilities	1,691b	4	423		3,428	(382)	(3,469)
	1,493		373		434		807
Total net assets	2,093			523	4,074	(400)	4,197
Share capital	1,200	actual		400	2,000	(400)	2,000
Retained profits	893			123	1,780		1,903
	2,093			523	3,780	(400)	3,903
Loan	–			-	294	-	294
	2,093			523	4,074	(400)	4,197

Adjustments:
(a) elimination of intercompany sales
(b) translation of intercompany balance at year-end in books of MI Distribution BV:

	Dfl
Receivable in Ray's books	
= €382,000 @ year-end rate =	1,528,000
Payable in MI's books	1,381,000
Difference on exchange	147,000
Profit before taxation	1,750,000
Currency adjustment	147,000
	1,603,000
Current liabilities	1,544,000
Currency adjustment	147,000
	1,691,000

(c) elimination of intercompany dividend   €125,000
(d) elimination of intercompany account   €382,000

Question 31.3

BELVOIR plc
CONSOLIDATED STATEMENT OF FINANCIAL POSITION
as at 31 December 2012

	BELVOIR €000	PERTH A$	PERTH €000	Adjustments €000	Consol. €000
ASSETS					
Non-current Assets					
Property, plant and equipment	50,000	150,000	10,000		60,000
Investment in PERTH	11,667	–	–	(11,667)	–
	61,667	150,000	10,000		60,000
Current Assets					
Inventory	75,000	200,000	13,333		88,333
Receivables	175,000	250,000	16,667		191,667
Cash	5,000	25,000	1,667		6,667
	255,000	475,000	31,667		286,667
	316,667	625,000	41,667		346,667
EQUITY AND LIABILITIES					
Capital and Reserves					
Ordinary shares	50,000	50,000	3,333	(3,333)	50,000
Capital reserves	25,000	60,000	4,000	(4,000)	25,000
Currency reserve	–	–	–	(W6)	(1,555)
Retained earnings	55,000	65,000	4,334	(W3)	56,555
	130,000	175,000	11,667		130,000
Non-controlling interests				(W2)	5,000
					135,000
Non-current Liabilities					
Provisions	26,667	75,000	5,000		31,667
Current Liabilities					
Payables	160,000	375,000	25,000	(W4) (5,000)	180,000
	316,667	625,000	41,667		346,667

WORKINGS

1. Cost of control

	DR €000	CR €000
Investment in PERTH	11,667	
NCI:		
Shares (50,000/13 × 30%)	1,154	
Capital reserve (60,000/13 × 30%)	1,384	
Retained earnings at 1/4/2012*	2,461	
Shares (50,000/13)		3,846
Capital reserve (60,000/13)		4,615
Retained earnings at 1/4/2012**		8,205
	16,666	16,666

Therefore goodwill is €nil.

*Profit for year	A$50,000
Time % (4/12)	A$16,667
Reserves at 1/1/2012	A$90,000
(65,000 + 75,000 − 50,000)	A$106,667 × 0.3 / 13

**Profit for year	A$50,000
Time % (4/12)	A$16,667
Reserves at 1/1/2012	A$90,000
(65,000 + 75,000 − 50,000)	A$106,667 / 13

2. Non-controlling interest

	DR €000	CR €000
Ordinary shares (15,000/15)		1,000
Capital reserve (60,000/15 @ 30%)		1,200
Closing retained earnings ((65,000 + 75,000)/15 @ 30%)		2,800
Balance	5,000	
	5,000	5,000

3. Consolidated retained earnings

	DR €000	CR €000
BELVOIR		55,000
PERTH ((65,000 + 75,000)/15)		9,333
Non-controlling interest account	2,800	
Cost of control (W1) (8,205 − 2,461)	5,744	
Currency difference on opening reserves (W5)		766
Balance	56,555	
	65,099	65,099

4. Proposed dividend – PERTH

	DR €000	CR €000
Should be reversed:		
DR Current liabilities (A$75,000/15)	5,000	
CR Retained earnings		5,000

5. Currency difference

	€000
A$106,667 @ 70% ÷ 13 = 74,667 ÷ 13 =	5,744
A$106,667 @ 70% ÷ 13 = 74,667 ÷ 15 =	4,978
	766

6. Currency reserve

PERTH share of NA at 30/4/2012	A$000	Xrate	€000
Retained earnings (106,667 × 70%)	74,667	13	5,744
Capital reserves (60,000 × 70%)	42,000	13	3,231
Share capital (50,000 × 70%)	35,000	13	2,692
	151,667		11,667
30/4/2012 NA at 31/12/2012 rate	151,667	15	10,112
			1,555

Question 32.1

(a)

CONSOLIDATED STATEMENT OF FINANCIAL POSITION
as at 30 September 2013

Assets	€000
Tangible non-current assets	360
Net current assets (€270,000 + €650,000)	920
	1,280

Equity	
€1 ordinary shares	540
Retained earnings (W5)	740
	1,280

CONSOLIDATED STATEMENT OF PROFIT OR LOSS AND OTHER COMPREHENSIVE INCOME
for the year ended 30 September 2013

	€000
Profit on disposal of subsidiary (W1)	182
Profit before tax (€153,000 + €126,000)	279
Income tax expense (€45,000 + €36,000)	(81)

	380
Non-controlling interest (20% × €90,000)	(18)
Profit attributable to members of Smith Limited	362

Retained profit brought forward (W4)	378
Retained profit carried forward	740

WORKINGS

1. Profit on disposal in Jones Limited	€000
Sales proceeds	650
Cost	(324)
Profit in Smith Limited	326

2. Group profit of disposal	€000
Sales proceeds	650
Share of net assets at date of disposal (€540,000 × 80%)	(432)
Goodwill at date of acquisition	(36)
	182

3. Goodwill	€000
Cost of investment	324
NCI at acquisition (€360,000 × 20%)	72
Net assets acquired	(360)
	36

4. Retained profit brought forward	€000
Smith	306
Jones: 80% × (€270,000 – €180,000)	72
	378

5. Retained profit carried forward	€000
Smith	414
Profit on disposal (W1)	326
	740

(b)

CONSOLIDATED STATEMENT OF FINANCIAL POSITION
as at 30 September 2013

	€000
Assets	
Non-current assets	360
Net current assets (€270,000 + €650,000)	920
	1,280
Equity	

Ordinary shares	540
Retained profits (W5)	740
	1280

Consolidated Statement of Profit or Loss and Other Comprehensive Income
for the year ended 30 September 2013

	€000
Profit before tax (€153,000 + (9/12 × €126,000))	247.5
Profit on sale of subsidiary	200.0
Tax €45,000 + (€36,000 × 9/12))	(72.0)
Profit after tax	375.5
Non-controlling interest	
(20% × €90,000 × 9/12)	13.5
Profit attributable to members of Smith Limited	362.0
Retained profit brought forward as before	378.0
Retained profit carried forward (W5)	740.0

Note: Jones Limited is a subsidiary for 9 months.

Workings

1. Profit on disposal in Smith Limited	€000
Sale proceeds	650
Cost	(324)
Profit in Smith Limited	326
2. Group profit of disposal	€000
Sales proceeds	650
Share of net assets at date of disposal (€517,500 (W3) × 80%)	(414)
Goodwill at date of acquisition	(36)
	200
3. Net assets at 30/6/2013	€000
At 1/10/2012	450.0
Retained profit to 30/6/2013 (€90,000 × 9/2013)	67.5
	517.5
4. Retained profit brought forward	€000
Smith	306
Jones: 80% × (€270,000 − €180,000)	72
	378
5. Retained profit carried forward	€000
Smith	414
Profit on disposal (W1)	326
	740

Question 33.1

Universal PLC
STATEMENT OF CASH FLOWS
for the Year Ended 31 October 2012

	€000	€000
Net cash flow from operating activities		
Operating profit	986	
Depreciation	167	
Profits on sale of tangible non-current assets	(10)	
Increase in inventory ((€910 − €40) − €868)	(2)	
Increase in trade receivables (€650 − €592)	(58)	
Decrease in trade payables and accruals ((€514 − €50) − €498 + (€20 − €13))	(27)	
Cash generated from operations		1,056
Interest paid		(160)
Dividends paid by Universal plc		(139)
Dividends paid to non-controlling interest		(27)
Dividends received from associate		40
Tax paid		(293)
Net cash flow from operating activities		477
Cash flows from investing activities		
Payments to acquire tangible non-current assets (€987 − €160)	(827)	
Receipts from sale of tangible non-current assets (€110 + €10)	120	
Purchase of subsidiary company (€130 − €20)	(110)	
Net cash flow from investing activities		(817)
Cash flows from financing activities		
Issue of share capital at a premium	300	
Issue of debentures	80	
Net cash flow from financing		380
Increase in cash and cash equivalents		40
Cash and cash equivalents at 1 November 2011		(85)
Cash and cash equivalents at 31 October 2012		(45)

WORKINGS

(W1)   Investment in Associate

	€000		€000
Bal b/d	740	therefore cash (dividend)	40
Share of profit	130	Bal c/d	830
	870		870

(W2)   Inventory

	€000
At 31 October 2012	910
At 1 November 2011	868
Increase	42
Less acquired with new subsidiary Star Limited	40
change	2

(W3)   Non-controlling Interest

	€000		€000
Therefore cash dividend	27	Bal b/d	230
Bal c/d	380	SPLOCI – P/L	126
		Acquisition during	
		year (Star Limited)	51
	407		407

(W4)   €000

Additions during year	987
Less acquired with Star Limited	160
Per statement of cash flows	827

(W5)   Taxation

	€000		€000
Therefore cash	293	Bal b/d	328
Bal c/d	450	SPLOCI – P/L	415
	743		743

(W6)   Dividends paid by U

	€000		€000
Cash	139	Balance b/d	180
Balance c/d	240	Equity	199
	379		379

Question 33.2 (Based on Chartered Accountants Ireland, P3 Summer 1999, Question 5)

SWEET plc
CONSOLIDATED STATEMENT OF CASH FLOWS
for the Year Ended 31 December 2012

	Working	€million	€million
Net cash flows from operating activities	2		1,378
Cash flows from investing activities			
Purchase of PPE	5	(161)	
Sale of PPE		-	
Purchase of GENTLE		(365)	
Net o/d of GENTLE (€275,000 – €19,000)		(256)	(782)
Cash flows from financing activities			
Dividends paid to non-controlling interests	(W3)	(96)	
Capital element of finance lease repaid	(W6)	(360)	(456)

Increase in cash and cash equivalents	140
Cash and cash equivalents at 1 January 2012	(164)
Cash and cash equivalents at 31 December 2012 (o/d)	(24)

WORKINGS

	€million
1. Goodwill	
NA acquired (75% × €480m)	360
Paid (€365m + €75m)	(440)
	80

	€16 million
Impairment	

	€million
2. Operating cash flows	
Net profit before tax and interest	1,024
Loss on disposal	26
Goodwill impairment	16
Depreciation	750
Inventory (€1,280 − (€1,220 − €300)	360
Receivables (€1,440 − (€1,740 − €240)	(60)
Payables (€680 − (€750 − €160)	(90)
	2,026
Interest paid (incl. interest capitalised)	(50)
Interest element of lease (N3)	(150)
Tax (W4)	(256)
Equity dividends paid (PY bal.)	(192)
	1,378

	€million
3. Non-controlling interests	
Opening balance	496
GENTLE – % NA (25% × €480)	120
SPLOCI – P/L	80
Closing balance	(600)
	96

	€million
4. Taxation	
Opening balance (€164m + €184m)	348
GENTLE liabilities	64
SPLOCI – P/L	290
Closing balance (€190m + €256m)	(446)
Paid	256

	€million
5. PPE	
Opening balance	2,960
Revaluation	25
GENTLE Limited	420
Depreciation	(750)
Loss on disposal	(26)
Closing balance	(3,280)

Inc. PPE	651
Finance lease PPE	(480)
Interest capitalised	(10)
Cash paid	161

6. Finance leases (capital)

	€million
Opening balance (€360m + €960m)	1,320
New during year	480
Closing balance (€400m + €1,040m)	(1,440)
Cash paid	360

7. Reserves

	€million
Opening balance	1,520
SPLOCI (€464m − €240m)	224
Revaluation	25
Share premium	25
	1,794

Question 34.1

(a)

	€
31 December 2011:	
3 × 2-year-old dairy cows x €200 each	600

	€
31 December 2012:	
3 × 3-year-old dairy cows x £250 each	750
3 × 2-year-old dairy cows x £220 each	660
3 × calves x €95 each	285
	1,695

(b)

	€
Opening balance at 1 January 2012	600
Cost of purchases	660
	1,260
Closing balance at 31 December 2012	1,695
Increase in fair value* – recognised in arriving at profit or loss	435

*The costs to sell are negligible.

The movement in fair value is recognised as follows:

	DR €	CR €
DR Biological asset	435	
CR SPLOCI – P/L		435

Being increase in fair value less costs to sell of dairy herd in 2012

Question 34.2

As the shares were issued as consideration for receipt of inventory, this transaction falls within the scope of IFRS 2 *Share-based Payment*.

Accordingly, the inventory should be recognised as an asset at the fair value of the goods received (€4.1 million) (as it could be measured reliably), with the credit being to share capital/share premium.

	DR €m	CR €m
DR SFP – Inventory	4.1	
CR Ordinary share capital		1.0
CR Share premium		3.1

The inventory is presented as an asset on the statement of financial position until sold, when the €4.1 million is included in cost of sales, the revenue of €6.2 million recorded and the €2.1 million recognised.

Note: in this question, the fair value of the inventory could be estimated reliably. If the fair value of the goods cannot be measured reliably, then the transaction would be measured at fair value of the equity instruments granted (i.e. €4.5 million).

Question 34.3

The €20 target share price is a market-based performance condition. As such, it is reflected in the fair value of the share option on the grant date. Failure to meet a market-based performance condition does not prevent recognition of the expense in respect of goods and services received as long as all the other vesting conditions are met.

The vesting date is 31 December 2014 (i.e. 3 years from date when the options were granted, and the cost of the options should be allocated over this period).

Number of options	5,000
Expected number of directors at vesting	3
Fair value	€15
Therefore the total cost is	€225,000
This should be recognised over 3 years at	€75,000 p.a.

In 2012:

	DR	CR
DR SPLOCI – P/L – salaries and wages	€75,000	
CR Equity – share options reserve		€75,000

Question 35.1

Belfast
31 July 2012

Mr Evans
Managing Director
DUL Limited
Belfast

Dear Mr Evans

Report on the performance of DUL Limited

As requested, I have examined the summarised statements of profit or loss and other comprehensive income of DUL Limited for each of the three years ended 30 June 2012, together with the statements of financial position as at 30 June 2010, 2011 and 2012.

My examination indicated that the company is 'overtrading', i.e. it has expanded its business to a level which is inconsistent with the amount of permanent funding and working capital available. In so doing the company now is in the position where, unless immediate remedial action is taken, it is in danger of 'going under'.

Before I list the characteristics of overtrading which I noted in your company, I will set out some symptoms that are generally regarded as characteristic of 'overtrading':

1. Undue dependence on other people's money, e.g. bank borrowings and trade payables.
2. High debt/equity ratio with the majority of borrowing being short-term.
3. Tight liquidity.
4. Low working capital to revenue for the type of business.
5. Growth in net profit not keeping pace with revenue.
6. Not operating within the normal credit terms for the type of business.
7. Over-optimism in the investment in non-current assets, especially where this is financed by payables money.

The more of the foregoing characteristics that are evidenced, the more critical is the financial condition of the company. It must be pointed out, however, that adverse trends in ratios are indicative, rather than absolute figures, since many companies have survived when their ratios were out of line with normal expectancies. Generally speaking, once an adverse and sharp change in direction takes place it can become almost irreversible if left unchecked for long.

While I have calculated a number of ratios based upon the figures in your accounts (see my comments below), I wish to advise you that I need access to more detailed information in order to make particular rather than generalised comments. These ratios would seem to indicate as follows:

(a) Revenue. The company is growing substantially in terms of the monetary value of sales, a compound growth of 40% per annum has been achieved, and the investment in non-current assets has also increased at the same rate. This is not unusual for a new company, especially a small company, although it would be unrealistic to expect this growth to continue, a tailing-off is probable.

(b) Profit margins are inexorably falling. The key margin of profit before interest and tax has fallen from 11% in 2010 to 9.29% in 2011 and 7.14% in 2012. This trend is indicative of sales being made without reference to their profitability with possibly a market share target in view.

(c) Interest charges have continually increased, reflecting the higher bank overdraft, and the 'cover' in terms of profit before interest is falling. In 2012 the increase in interest resulted in a fall in profit after interest in comparison with each of the preceding years. This is a very dangerous trend.

(d) Debt to equity (shareholders' funds) ratio. The ratio of debt (borrowings) to equity has increased from a base of 168% in 2010 to a high of 206% in 2012 and, as you have told me, the bank is very concerned about its size. One of the contributory causes of this is the insufficient profits being earned in order to build up the equity base.

(e) Liquidity and working capital. The working capital is the difference between the current assets and current liabilities and provides the buffer within which a business finances the peaks in its cash cycle of production, revenue, receivables less trade credit received. The working capital is also a measure of the equity interest in the current assets as distinguished from the non-current assets. The smaller the relation of working capital becomes to revenue, the lower is the tolerance point to fluctuations in the business. In DUL Limited there is a negative working capital which is worsening every year and this, combined with the increasing size of the bank overdraft, is extremely dangerous.

(f) Relationship between profits and revenue. If the growth in sales in not matched by profits retained in the business, the company will become more dependent on borrowings to finance the net assets required to support the revenue. The eventual outcome will be lower profits as margins become reduced through inability to meet interest charges. The revenue growth of DUL Limited has not been matched by a corresponding growth in profits before interest due to a fall in profit margins: the resulting effects of this situation as outlined are clearly evident in the company. It would seem that the company has concentrated on revenue growth or market share without consideration of profitability; alternatively, management information and/or internal controls may be weak.

(g) Credit from suppliers. The taking of extended credit from suppliers affects credit rating, eventually resulting in difficulty in obtaining credit and suppliers; it may even result in cash with order terms of supply. Eventually, profitability will suffer as productivity becomes disrupted. If a major supplier becomes disaffected, the company would be left very exposed. There may be a connection between the taking of extended credit from suppliers and the continual rise in the bank overdraft, endeavouring to allay the bank's concern through the expediency of not paying suppliers.

Conclusion

The company appears to have been undercapitalised from its inception and this defect has been compounded by the subsequent lack of profitability. To ensure the survival of the company it is essential that an immediate investigation is made into the profitability of each product line with the cutting out of unprofitable or least profitable lines, disposal of any resulting surplus non-current assets, a corresponding reduction in inventories and receivables, a reduction in overheads and an increase in productivity. An immediate look at your own credit control procedures is necessary since receivables have increased in 2012 to 80 days from a previous period of 73 days. As a corollary to this, it is necessary to gain the confidence of your bankers and I suggest that you see your bankers (before they ask you to see them) and place your proposals before them and get their support. The only alternative is the injection of substantial fresh capital.

If you require any additional information or assistance in the investigation I suggested, I will be glad to help.

Yours sincerely,

A. Wiseman

Question 35.2

To	Finance Director
From	Management Accountant
Subject	Performance of Laurie plc 2010 – 2012

As requested, please find below my analysis of the company's performance based on information provided.

1. Profitability
   The gross profit margin has remained relatively static over the three-year period, although it has risen by approximately 1% in 2012. ROCE, while improving very slightly in 2011 to 21.5% has dropped dramatically in 2012 to 17.8%. The net profit margin has also fallen in 2012, in spite of the improvement in the gross profit margin. This marks a rise in expenses, which suggests that they are not being well controlled. The utilisation of assets compared to the revenue generated has also declined, reflecting the drop in trading activity between 2011 and 2012.

2. Trading levels
   It is apparent that there was a dramatic increase in trading activity between 2010 and 2012, but then a significant fall in 2012. Revenue rose by 17% in 2011 but fell by 7% in 2012. The reason for this fluctuation is unclear. It may be the effect of some kind of one-off event, or it may be the effect of a change in product mix. Whatever the reason, it appears that improved credit terms granted to customers (receivables payment period up from 46 to 64 days) has not stopped the drop in revenue.

3. Working capital
   Both the current ratio and quick ratio demonstrate an adequate working capital situation, although the quick ratio has shown a slight decline. There has been an increased investment over the period in inventories and receivables, which has been only partly financed by longer payment periods to payables and a rise in other payables mainly between 2010 and 2011.

4. Capital Structure
   The level of gearing of the company increased when a further €64m was raised in long-term loans in 2011 to add to the €74m already in the statement of financial position. Although this does not seem to be a particularly high level of gearing, the debt/equity ratio did rise from 18.5% to 32.0% in 2011. The interest charge has risen to €19m from €6m in 2010. The 2011 charge was €15m, suggesting that either the interest rate on the loan is flexible, or that the full interest charge was not incurred in 2011. The new long-term loan appears to have funded the expansion in both non-current and current assets.

Question 35.3

(a) Calculation of Relevant Indicators
  (i) Operating Gearing = Contribution / Profit before interest and tax
       2012: 3,120/570 = 5.5
       2013: 2,880/315 = 9.1
       Industry = 7.5

  (ii) Debt/ Equity
       2012: (500 + 360o/d)/(300 + 650) = 90.5%
       2013: (500 + 454o/d)/(350 + 749) = 86.8%
       Industry = 65%

  (iii) Return on Equity
       2012: 286/950 = 30%
       2013: 109/1,099 = 9.9%
       Industry = 14%

  (iv) Dividend Cover
       2012: 286/60 = 4.8
       2013: 109/10 = 10.9
       Industry = 2

  (v) Interest Cover
       2012: 570 / 94 = 6.1
       2013: 315 / 134 = 2.4
       Industry = 3

(b) (i) The bank manager may be concerned at the company's financial performance and position for the following reasons:
    I The level of financial gearing is high by industry standards. The bank has an exposure of €954,000. Not all of this is secured.
    II The high level of operating gearing in 2013 is a worrying feature from the bank's point of view because it suggests that the level of business risk is high. The combination of high business risk and financial risk may not be satisfactory from the viewpoint of a provider of finance.
    III The interest cover has fallen significantly, caused by the fall in profits, increased overdraft and possibly higher interest rates during the year. The company's ability to repay borrowing may be questioned if this trend continues.
    IV The operating result discloses a fall in revenue but no overall fall in costs. This suggests, and is confirmed by the measure of operating gearing, that the fixed-cost base of the company is high. Further falls in revenue could therefore result in a corresponding drop in profit levels.
    V The bank manager may also seek explanations for the increase in inventory and receivable days despite the fall in revenue. While the increase was financed by taking more credit from suppliers, it would be a matter of concern if this source of credit was withdrawn and the company was forced to ask the bank for increased finance solely due to inefficient management of working capital.

(b) (ii) The following points in support of the company would be made:
    I This is the first year in many that has seen a fall in demand for the company's products. As this is related to the demand for houses, it is possible that the fall in revenue was for reasons outside the control of management, e.g. interest rate/ housing crisis. In the event, turnover fell only by 4.5%. The resolution of the interest rate/housing crisis could well result in a resumption of the company's growth.
    II The dividend for 2013 has been sharply reduced. This illustrates that the equity holders are willing to 'share the pain'.
    III The equity holders also invested €50,000 during the year, thereby contributing to a resolution of the cash crisis mid-year.
    IV While the company's debt/equity is higher than the industry average, it has fallen by 4% since 2012. In addition, the interest cover is only marginally lower than the industry average.

    V While a relatively high proportion of the company's costs are fixed, this is also true for the industry. Given the performance in 2012, where the company's operating gearing was 5.5 compared to the industry's 7.5, it is apparent that the company's difficulties are sales related, and not necessarily purely cost related.

    VI The company is backed by non-current assets of almost €1 million, which should be of comfort to the bank. This represents an increase of €126,000 since 2012.

    VII The company has been responsive to the Bank Manager's request for information, e.g. monthly accounts since December.

Question 35.4

Tutorial note: although some of the six statements of financial position have similarities in their asset structures, there are a few features that stand out and make identification easy. Once the obvious matches have been ticked off, a process of elimination leads gradually to a complete solution.

(a) Company 5, the bank, should be easy to identify. Most of a bank's assets and liabilities are monetary: loans and advances (receivables) and customer deposits (payables). Other assets and liabilities are small in comparison. This picture fits in with statement of financial position B.

Company 1, the retail supermarket chain, would be expected to have a high level of investment in shop premises (land and buildings). Inventories would also account for a significant proportion of assets. Most sales are on cash terms, so receivables are negligible while cash levels should be relatively high. This picture fits in with statement of financial position E.

The main assets of a sea ferry operator are the ferries themselves 'other non-current assets' in the statements of financial position given in the question. Each ferry owned would be a very major purchase and one would expect to see a significant amount of long-term external finance. This picture fits in with statement of financial position F.

Company 3 is engaged in two activities: property investment (high level of inventories) and house building (high level of investment in land). This picture fits in well with statement of financial position D.

The remaining two companies (the vertically integrated company in the food industry and the civil engineering contractor) might each be expected to have a fairly broad spectrum of assets. However, there are two features indicating that the contractor is represented by statement of financial position A:

  (i) Statement of financial position A shows that the company's major asset is inventories and work-in-progress.

  (ii) Statement of financial position C shows a big investment in land and buildings, as would be expected of a company owning farms, flour mills, bakeries and retail outlets.

Summary

Statement of financial position	Company
A	6. Civil engineering contractor
B	5. Commercial bank
C	4. Company in food industry
D	3. Property investor/house-builder
E	1. Retail supermarket chain
F	2. Sea ferry operator

(b) Limitations of Ratio Analysis

Accounts are not wholly comparable with each other in spite of adherence to IASs/IFRSs because there are sometimes several permissible methods of accounting and IASs/IFRSs do not always cover all areas on which a company needs to have an accounting policy. For example, different companies may apply different criteria to decide whether a contract should be accounted for as a long- or a short-term contract in accordance with IAS 11. Additionally, points of detail in applying IASs/IFRSs will differ; each company will have a different estimate of the economic lives of its non-current assets and so will depreciate them at different rates and on different bases.

Ratio analysis applied to historical cost accounts takes no account of inflation or current costs, especially as there is no requirement to revalue appreciating assets yearly. ROCE, for example, will appear to be higher for a company whose asset base is stated at historical cost and/or is fully depreciated than for a company whose assets are new and/or revalued and which makes the same profits. Ratio analysis is therefore of limited value in predicting future performance or in showing the rate of return in real terms.

Because the statement of financial position is stated as at a particular day, ratios derived from that day's figures may not reflect the company's usual circumstances. For example, it is common practice to run inventories down before the reporting date to minimise the disruption caused by a full inventory-take and to reduce inventories and payables, thus improving the company's apparent liquidity. In this case, calculating the current ratio and inventory and payables turnover periods from year-end figures will not produce meaningful results.

Ratios such as ROCE which produce measures expressed in percentage terms can be misleading because they necessarily take no account of absolute values. Thus, an investor told that company A's ROCE is 20% may think that it is a better investment vehicle than company B whose ROCE is only 15%. However, if told that company A has total net assets employed of €100,000 whereas company B has €5 million, then he may feel differently.

Question 36.1

(a)

REVALUATION ACCOUNT

		€			€
(a) 31/12/2011	To Fixtures		31/12/2011	By Premises a/c	50,000
	and Fittings a/c	25,000			
	Inventory a/c	5,000			
	Capital a/cs				
	Murphy – 1/2	10,000			
	Noonan – 3/8	7,500			
	MacIntyre – 1/8	2,500			
		50,000			50,000

(b)

REALISATION ACCOUNT

		€			€
(b) 31/12/2012	To Transfer –		31/12/2012	By Bank	
	Asset Accounts (W4)	333,000		Sale of Assets	270,000
	Bank – Realisation			Capital a/cs	
	Expenses	2,000		Less Divisible	

Murphy – 1/2	32,500
Noonan – 4/10	26,000
Riordan – 1/10	6,500
335,000	335,000

(c)

Capital Account

	M €	N €	Mac €	R €		M €	N €	Mac €	R €
Car	-	-	5,000	-	At 31/12/2011	120,000	90,000	40,000	-
On retirement	-	-	48,300	-	Revaluation	10,000	7,500	2,500	-
Goodwill	30,000	24,000	-	6,000	Goodwill	30,000	22,500	7,500	-
Realisation	32,500	26,000	÷	6,500	Capital	-	-	-	40,000
Paid	115,000	83,400	-	29,300	Profit – 2012	14,000	11,200	-	2,800
Current account	-	-	-	1,000	Current account	3,500	2,200	3,300	-
	177,500	133,400	53,300	42,800		177,500	133,400	53,300	42,800

Current Account

	M €	N €	Mac €	R €		M €	N €	Mac €	R €
Drawings	4,000	2,000	-	1,000	At 31/12/2011	7,500	4,200	3,300	-
To capital	3,500	2,200	3,300	-	To capital	-	-	-	1,000
	7,500	4,200	3,300	1,000		7,500	4,200	3,300	1,000

WORKINGS

1. MacIntyre Car
   Since there is no indication as to the net book value of MacIntyre's car, it is assumed that a fair value might be €5,000, being the total NBV of all the cars divided in profit ratio (MacIntyre 1/8). The quality of each partner's car would probably reflect each partner's share in the firm.

2. Goodwill
   Valuation:
   Riordan paid €6,000 for 1/10 share
   $\therefore$ value = 6,000 × 10   = €60,000

   Old Goodwill Divisible
   Murphy   4/8 × 60,000   = €30,000
   Noonan   3/8 × 60,000   = €22,500
   MacIntyre   1/8 × 60,000   = €7,500

   New Goodwill Divisible
   Murphy   5/10 × 60,000   = €30,000
   Noonan   4/10 × 60,000   = €24,000
   Riordan   1/10 × 60,000   = €6,000

3. Profits for 2012 Divisible
   Total Profit   €28,000
   Murphy   5/10   €14,000
   Noonan   4/10   €11,200

Riordan   1/10   €2,800

4. Assets Transferred to Realisation Account

	€
Premises	200
Fixtures	40
Motor Vehicles	35
Inventory	23
Receivables	35
	333

5. Memorandum Bank Account

	DR €	CR €
Balance 31/12/2012	4,700	
Proceeds of Realisation of Assets	270,000	
Payment of Loan to MacIntyre		5,000
Payment of Payables		40,000
Payment of Expenses		2,000
Payment of Capital a/c Balances		
Murphy		115,000
Noonan		83,400
Riordan		29,300
	274,700	274,700

Question 36.2

(a)

JOURNAL ENTRIES

		DR €000	CR €000
Jan 1	Realisation Account	140	
Jan 1	To Non-current Assets Account		85
	Inventory Account		15
	Receivables Account		35
	Bank		5

Transfer of balances on Asset Accounts to Realisation Account

Jan 1	Payables Account	30	
	To Realisation Account		30

Transfer of balance on Payables Accounts

Jan 1	Direction Limited	150	
	To Realisation Account		150

Agreed value of assets less liabilities taken over (130 + 15 + 30 + 5 − 30)

Jan 1	Realisation Account	40	
	To Partners' Capital Accounts		

North		20
South		12
East		8

Profit on takeover of assets less liabilities by Direction Limited, divided in profit ratios.

Jan 1	Partners' Capital Accounts		
	North	68	
	South	51	
	East	31	
	To Direction Limited		150

Allocation of Ordinary Shares to partners in proportion to the balances on Capital Accounts

Jan 1	Partners' Current Accounts	
	North	8
	South	4
	East	3
	To Partners' Capital Accounts	
	North	8
	South	4
	East	3

Transfer of Partners' Current Accounts Balances to Partners' Capital Accounts

PARTNERS' ACCOUNTS
CAPITAL

		€000 North	€000 South	€000 East
2012				
Jan 1	by Balance	40	35	20
	Transfer Current Accounts	8	4	3
	Realisation Account	20	12	8
		68	51	31
Jan 1	to Direction Limited	68	51	31
		68	51	31

CURRENT

Jan 1	by Balances	8	4	3
Jan 1	to Transfer to Capital Accounts	8	4	3

Realisation Account

2012		€000	2012		€000
Jan 1	to Asset Accounts	140	Jan 1	by Direction Limited	150
				Payables	30
	Profit on Realisation				
	Divisible				
	North 1/2	20			
	South 3/10	12			
	East 2/10	8			
		180			180

Direction Limited

2012		€000	2012		€000
Jan 1	to Asset Accounts	150	Jan 1	by Partners' Capital	
				Accounts	
				North	68
				South	51
				East	31
		150			150

(b)

Direction Limited
STATEMENT OF FINANCIAL POSITION
as at 31 December 2012

	€	€
NON-CURRENT ASSETS		
At 1 January 2012	130,000	
Additions during year	100,000	230,000
CURRENT ASSETS		
Inventory	25,000	
Receivables	60,000	
Bank	20,000	
		105,000
		335,000
REPRESENTED BY		
Issued Share Capital		
150,000 €1 ordinary shares, fully paid	150,000	
Retained earnings	145,000	
	295,000	
CURRENT LIABILITIES		
Payables falling due within 1 year		40,000
		335,000

WORKINGS

1. Retained Profit for year to 31 December 2012
    Share Capital and Reserves   295
    Less: Issued Share Capital   (150)
        Retained Profit for year   145

2. Division of Profit on Realisation
    The profit on realisation (40,000) is divisible in the ratio in which the
    partners share profit via
    North 1/2 (20,000), South 3/10 (12,000) and East 2/10 (8,000)

3. Increase in non-current assets
    The book value of non-current assets at 31 December 2012 was   230
    The valuation at 1 January 2012 was   130
    Therefore additions during year were   100

4. Net Assets at Takeover Valuation
    Non-current assets   130
    Inventory   15
    Receivables   30
    Bank   5
                                                                        180
    Less: Payables   30
    Satisfied by issue of 150,000   150
    Ordinary shares of €1 each

Question 36.3

(a)

Revaluation Account

	€000		€000
Current assets	5	Non-current assets	40
		Goodwill *	50
Revaluation surplus:			
Redcar	42.5		
Pontefract	25.5		
Haydock	17		
	90		90

*Goodwill €5,000 = 1/10 share, thus total goodwill = €50,000

(b)

Capital Accounts (Before re-transfer of revaluation surplus)

	Redcar	Pontefract	Haydock	Ludlow
	€000	€000	€000	€000
Opening balance	80	40	20	-
Revaluation surplus*	42.5	25.5	17	
Capital introduced				50
Transfer to loan account			(37)	
Closing balance	122.5	65.5	0	50

*Surplus credited to old partners in old profit-sharing ratios.

Capital Accounts (After re-transfer of revaluation surplus)

	Redcar €000	Pontefract €000	Haydock €000	Ludlow €000
Opening balance	80	40	20	-
Revaluation surplus*	42.5	25.5	17	
Revaluation surplus**	(51)	(25.5)	-	(8.5)
Capital introduced				50
Transfer to loan account			(37)	
Closing balance	71.5	40	0	41.5

*Surplus credited to old partners in old profit-sharing ratios.
** Surplus debited to new partners in new profit-sharing ratio 6 : 3 : 1.

(c)

STATEMENT OF FINANCIAL POSITION OF PARTNERSHIP
to reflect changes
(before re-transfer of revaluation surplus)

	€000
Goodwill	50
Non-current assets	160
Current assets	45
Bank (10,000 + 50,000)	60
	315
Capital Accounts	
Redcar	122.5
Pontefract	65.5
Ludlow	50
Loan due to Haydock	37
	275
Current liabilities	40
	315

(c)

STATEMENT OF FINANCIAL POSITION OF PARTNERSHIP
to reflect changes
(after re-transfer of revaluation surplus)

	€000
Non-current assets	120
Current assets	50
Bank (€10,000 + €50,000)	60
	230
Capital Accounts	
Redcar	71.5

Pontefract	40
Ludlow	41.5
Loan due to Haydock	37
Current liabilities	40
	230

Glossary of Terms and Definitions

Accounting Policies The specific principles, basic conventions, rules and practices applied by the reporting entity in preparing and presenting its financial statements.

Accruals Amounts charged against the profit for a particular period but not paid for until after the end of the period.

Accruals Accounting Under this basis of accounting, the effects of transactions are recognised when they occur and are recorded and reported in the accounting periods to which they relate, irrespective of cash flows arising from these transactions.

Accumulated Depreciation Non-current assets are recorded in the statement of financial position at their cost less accumulated depreciation, with accumulated depreciation being the depreciation charge made in the first year that the asset is owned and used, plus the depreciation charge made in subsequent years of ownership and use.

Adjusting Event after the Reporting Period An event after the reporting period that provides further evidence of conditions that existed at the end of the reporting period, including an event indicating that the going concern assumption in relation to the whole or part of the enterprise is not appropriate.

Agricultural Activity The management by an enterprise of the biological transformation of biological assets for sale into agricultural produce or into additional biological assets.

Agricultural Produce The harvested product of an enterprise's biological assets (e.g milk and crops).

Amortisation The systematic allocation of the depreciable amount of an intangible asset over its useful life.

Antidilution An increase in earnings per share (EPS) or a reduction in loss per share resulting from the assumption that convertible instruments are converted, that options or warrants are exercised, or that ordinary shares are issued upon the satisfaction of specified conditions.

Appropriation Account This is a partnership ledger account that deals with the allocation of net profit between the partners.

Arm's Length Transaction A transaction when all parties to the transaction are independent and on an equal footing.

Assets Rights or other access to future economic benefits controlled by an entity as a result of past transactions or events.

Associate An entity in which the investor has significant influence, which is deemed to be the power to participate in the financial and operating policy decisions of the investee but not control those policies. If an investor holds, directly or indirectly, 20% or more of the voting power of the investee, it is presumed that it has significant influence, unless it can be clearly demonstrated that this is not the case. Conversely, if less than 20%, the presumption is that the investor does not have significant influence. A majority shareholding by another investor does not preclude an investor having significant influence. Its existence is usually evidenced in one or more of the following ways:

- representation on the board of directors;
- participation in policy-making processes;
- material transactions between the investor and the investee;

- interchange of managerial personnel; or
- provision of essential technical information.

Biological Asset A living animal or plant (e.g. sheep, cattle, trees, vines).

Biological Transformation The processes of growth, degeneration, production and procreation that cause qualitative and quantitative changes in a biological asset.

Bonus Issue This is a capitalisation of reserves and will have *no effect* on the earning capacity of the company. There is *no* inflow of funds.

Borrowing Costs Interest and other costs incurred by an entity in connection with the borrowing of funds. Examples of borrowing costs include:

- interest on bank overdrafts and other short-term and long-term borrowings;
- amortisation of discounts and premiums on borrowings;
- finance charges in respect of finance leases (IAS 17 *Leases*); and
- exchange differences arising from foreign currency borrowings when they cause adjustments to interest costs.

Capital Expenditure This refers to expenditure to acquire non-current assets that are expected to provide future economic benefits (through their use in the business to generate income). Capital expenditure is recorded as an asset in the statement of financial position.

Carrying Amount/Value The amount at which an item is recognised (in the statement of financial position). In the case of non-current assets, it is after deducting accumulated depreciation (amortisation) and any accumulated impairment losses. It is sometimes referred to as the 'net book value' or 'written-down value'.

Cash This refers to cash-in-hand and deposits repayable on demand.

Cash Flow Inflows and outflows of cash and cash equivalents.

Cash Accounting A method of accounting that records cash payments and cash receipts as they occur within an accounting period.

Cash Equivalents These are short-term, highly liquid investments that are readily convertible to known amounts of cash and which are subject to an insignificant risk of changes in value. Cash equivalents are not held for investment or other long-term purposes, but rather to meet short-term cash commitments. Therefore, their maturity date should normally be no more than three months from their acquisition date.

Cash Generating Unit (CGU) The smallest identifiable group of assets that generates cash flows that are largely independent of cash inflows from other assets or groups of assets.

Cash-settled Share-based Payment Transaction A share-based payment transaction in which the entity acquires goods or services by incurring a liability to transfer cash or other assets to the supplier of those goods or services for amounts that are based on the price (or value) of the entity's shares or other equity instruments of the entity. In this instance, the entity pays cash based on the share price.

Change in Accounting Estimate An adjustment of the carrying amount of an asset or liability, or the periodic consumption of an asset, which results from the assessment of the present status of and expected future benefits and obligations associated with assets and liabilities. Changes in accounting estimates are *not* corrections of errors.

Chief Operating Decision-Maker The term chief operating decision-maker is not specifically defined in IFRS 8, as it refers to a function rather than a title. In some organisations, the function could be fulfilled by a group of directors rather than an individual.

Consolidated Financial Statements The financial statements of a group in which the assets, liabilities, equity, income, expenses and cash flows of the parent and its subsidiaries are presented as those of a single economic entity.

Consolidation The aggregation of the financial statements of more than one company into a single set of financial statements as if they were one separate entity.

Construction Contract A construction contract is specifically negotiated for the construction of an asset or a combination of assets that are closely interrelated or interdependent in terms of their design, technology and function, or their ultimate purpose or use.

Contract Costs These comprise:
- costs that relate directly to the specific contract;
- costs that are attributable to contract activity in general and can be allocated to the contract; and
- such other costs as are specifically chargeable to the customer under the terms of the contract.

Contract Revenue This comprises of:
(a) the initial amount of revenue agreed in the contract; and
(b) variations in contract work, claims and incentive payments to the extent that it is probable that they will result in revenue and they are capable of being reliably measured.

The revenue is measured at the fair value received or receivable. Uncertainties that may affect the measurement of contract revenue include:
- agreed variations between contractor and customer in a subsequent period;
- cost escalation clauses in a fixed price contract; and
- penalties imposed on the contractor because of delays.

A variation is included in contract revenue when:
- it is probable that the customer will approve the variation; and
- the revenue can be measured reliably.

Constructive Obligation An obligation that derives from the reporting entity's actions where:
(a) past practice, published policies or current statement would indicate that the entity will accept certain responsibilities; and
(b) the entity has created a valid expectation that it will discharge those responsibilities.

Contingent Asset A possible asset arising from past events whose existence will be confirmed only by the occurrence or non-occurrence of one or more uncertain future events not wholly within the entity's control.

Contingent Liability This is either:
(a) a possible obligation arising from past events whose existence will only be confirmed by the occurrence, or non-occurrence, of one or more uncertain future events not wholly within the entity's control; *or*
(b) a present obligation arising from past events but is not recognised because it is not probable that a transfer of economic benefits will be required to settle the obligation, or the amount of the obligation cannot be measured with sufficient reliability.

Contingently Issuable Shares Shares issued for little or no cash or other consideration after certain conditions have been met (e.g. sales or profit targets).

Control An investor controls an investee when the investor is exposed, or has rights, to variable returns from its involvement with the investee and has the ability to affect those returns through its power over the investee.

Cost The amount of cash or cash equivalents paid or the fair value of the other consideration given to acquire an asset at the time of its acquisition or construction or, where applicable, the amount attributed to that asset when initially recognised in accordance with the specific requirements of an IFRS (e.g. IFRS 2 *Share-based Payment*).

Cost of Inventories This consists of: cost of purchase; cost of conversion; and any other costs incurred in bringing the inventories to their present location and condition.

Cost or Valuation of Assets Assets are valued at the lower of cost or recoverable amount.

Cost-plus Contract A cost-plus contract is a contract where a contractor is paid for all of its allowed expenses to a set limit *plus* additional payment to allow for a profit.

Costs of Disposal These are incremental costs directly attributable to the disposal of an asset or disposal group of assets, excluding finance costs and income tax.

Cost Method The investment is recorded at cost. The statement of profit or loss and other comprehensive income – profit or loss reflects income only to the extent that the investor receives distributions from the investee subsequent to the date of acquisition.

Closing Rate The spot exchange rate at the reporting date.

Currency Options In finance, a foreign exchange option (commonly shortened to just FX option or currency option) is a derivative financial instrument where the owner has the right, but not the obligation, to exchange money denominated in one currency into another currency at a pre-agreed exchange rate on a specified date.

Current Accounts In the context of partnership accounting, these are used to deal with the regular transactions between the partners and the partnership.

Current Assets Current assets include cash or other assets, which can reasonably be expected to be converted to cash in the normal course of business (usually within 12 months), including inventories, receivables and prepayments.

Current Liabilities Liabilities incurred in the normal course of business that fall due within one year and include payables and accruals.

Current Tax This is the amount of income taxes payable in respect of the taxable profit for a period.

Deferred Tax Assets Amounts of income taxes recoverable in future periods in respect of:
  (a) deductible temporary differences;
  (b) carried forward unused tax losses; and
  (c) carried forward unused tax credits.

Deferred Tax Liabilities Amounts of income taxes payable in future periods in respect of taxable temporary differences.

Defined Benefit Pension Plans Post-employment plans other than defined contribution plans. As the employer effectively agrees to a promised level of benefits, this exposes the enterprise to actuarial and investment risks.

Defined Contribution Pension Plans Pension plans under which an enterprise pays fixed contributions into a separate entity (a fund) and has no legal or constructive obligation to pay further contributions if the fund does not hold sufficient assets to pay all employee benefits relating to employee service in the current and prior periods.

Defined Contribution Plan A retirement benefit plan by which benefits to employees are based on the amount of funds contributed to the plan plus investment earnings thereon.

Defined Benefit Plan A retirement benefit plan by which employees receive benefits based on a formula usually linked to employee earnings.

Depreciable Amount The cost of an asset, or other amount substituted for cost (e.g. market valuation), less the residual value of the asset.

Depreciation This is defined as a measure of the wearing out, consumption or other reduction in the useful life of a non-current asset, whether arising from use, passage of time or obsolescence through technological or market changes; the systematic allocation of the depreciable amount of an asset over its estimated useful economic life. For intangible assets, the term 'amortisation' is used instead of depreciation.

Derecognition This means removing an item from the statement of financial position.

Derivative This is a financial instrument:
  • whose value changes in response to the change in an underlying variable such as an interest rate, commodity or security price, or index;
  • that requires no initial investment, or one that is smaller than would be required for a contract with similar response to changes in market factors; and
  • that is settled at a future date.

Development The application of research findings or other knowledge to plan or design the production of new or substantially improved materials, devices, products, processes, systems or services prior to the commencement of commercial production or use.

Dilution A reduction in earnings per share (EPS) or an increase in loss per share resulting from the assumption that convertible instruments are converted, that options or warrants are exercised, or that ordinary shares are issued upon the satisfaction of specified conditions.

Discontinued Operation A component of an entity that either has been disposed of or is classified as held for sale, and that: represents a separate major line of business or geographical area of operations; is part of a single co-ordinated plan to dispose of a separate major line of business or geographical area of operations; or is a subsidiary acquired exclusively with a view to resale.

Disposal Group A group of assets to be disposed of, by sale or otherwise, as a group in a single transaction, together with the liabilities directly associated with those assets that will be transferred in the transaction. A disposal group could be a group of cash generating units (CGUs) or part of a CGU.

Distributable Profits These consist of accumulated realised profits less accumulated realised losses.

Distribution This is defined as any distribution of a company's assets to members (shareholders) of the company, whether in cash or otherwise, with the *exception* of:

- an issue of bonus shares;
- the redemption or purchase of the company's own shares out of capital (including the proceeds of a new issue) or out of unrealised profits;
- the reduction of share capital by reducing the liability on shares in respect of share capital not fully paid-up and/or paying off paid-up share capital; and
- a distribution of assets to shareholders in a winding up of the company.

Drawings The withdrawal of money by a partner as an allowance.

Efficiency Ratios These measure an entity's effective use of its assets.

Employees and Others Providing Similar Services Individuals who render personal services to the entity, and either the individuals are regarded as employees for legal or tax purposes or the individuals work for the entity under its direction in the same way as individuals who are regarded as employees for legal or tax purposes, or the services rendered are similar to those rendered by employees.

Equity Instrument A contract that evidences a residual interest in the assets of an entity after deducting all of its liabilities.

Equity Method A method of accounting whereby the investment is initially recorded at cost and adjusted thereafter to reflect the investor's share of the post-acquisition net profit or loss of the investee/associate. The statement of profit or loss and other comprehensive income reflects the investor's share of the results of operations of the investee. Distributions received from the investee reduce the carrying amount of the investment. Adjustments to the carrying amount may also be required arising from changes in the investee's equity that have not been included in arriving at profit or loss (e.g. revaluations).

Equity Transactions Transactions with owners in their capacity as owners.

Estimated Useful Economic Life Is the:

(a) period over which an asset is expected to be available for use by an entity; or
(b) number of production or similar units expected to be obtained from the asset by an entity.

Event After the Reporting Period This is an event, which could be favourable or unfavourable, that occurs between the end of the reporting period and the date that the financial statements are authorised for issue. IAS 10 differentiates between an adjusting event after the reporting period and a non-adjusting event after the reporting period.

Exchange Difference The difference resulting from translating one currency into another currency at different exchange rates.

Exchange Rate The ratio of exchange for two currencies.

Exploration and Evaluation Expenditures These are expenditures incurred in connection with the exploration and evaluation of mineral resources before the technical feasibility and commercial viability of extracting a mineral resource is demonstrable.

Exploration for and Evaluation of Mineral Resources The search for mineral resources, including minerals, oil and natural gas once an entity has obtained legal rights to explore in a specific area, as well as the determination of the technical feasibility and commercial viability of extracting the mineral resource.

Fair Value The amount for which an asset could be exchanged, or a liability settled, between knowledgeable, willing parties in an arm's length transaction (see IFRS 13).

Fair Value less Costs of Disposal This is the amount obtainable from the sale of an asset or cash generating unit (CGU) in an arm's length transaction less costs of disposal.

Finance Lease A finance lease is a lease that transfers substantially all the risks and rewards associated with the ownership of an asset to the lessee. A finance lease usually involves payment by a lessee to a lessor at the full cost of the asset together with a return on the finance provided by the lessor.

Financial Asset This is any asset that is:

- cash;
- an equity instrument of another entity;
- a contractual right:

- ° to receive cash or another financial asset from another entity; or
  - ° to exchange financial assets or financial liabilities with another entity under conditions that are potentially favourable to the entity; or
- a contract that will or may be settled in the entity's own equity instruments and is:
  - ° a non-derivative for which the entity is, or may be, obliged to receive a variable number of the entity's own equity instruments; or
  - ° a derivative that will or may be settled other than by the exchange of a fixed amount of cash or another financial asset for a fixed number of the entity's own equity instruments. For this purpose, the entity's own equity instruments do not include instruments that are themselves contracts for the future receipt or delivery of the entity's own equity instruments.

Financial Balance The balance between the various forms of available finance relative to the requirements of the entity.

Financial Instrument A contract that gives rise to a financial asset of one entity and a financial liability or equity instrument of another entity.

Financial Liability Any liability that is:
- a contractual obligation:
  - ° to deliver cash or another financial asset to another entity; or
  - ° to exchange financial assets or financial liabilities with another entity under conditions that are potentially unfavourable to the entity; or
- a contract that will or may be settled in the entity's own equity instruments.

Financing Activities Activities that result in changes in the size and composition of the equity capital and borrowings of the entity.

Firm Purchase Commitment This is an agreement with an unrelated party, binding on both parties and legally enforceable, that: (1) specifies all significant terms; and (2) includes a disincentive for non-performance that is likely to make performance highly probable.

Fixed Capital Accounts In the context of partnership accounting, these record the amount of capital introduced into the partnership by the partners. They are not used to record drawings or shares of profits but only major changes in the relations between partners. In particular, fixed capital accounts are used to deal with capital introduced or withdrawn by new or retiring partners and revaluation adjustments. In practice, the term is commonly abbreviated to 'capital account'.

Fixed-price Contract A fixed-price contract requires the contractor to deliver a clearly defined piece of work to the customer at a predetermined price. A fixed-price contract shifts most or all risks from the customer to the contractor.

Foreign Currency A currency other than the functional currency of the entity.

Foreign Currency Accounts Foreign currency accounts can be a good option for importers and exporters as they allow one to 'net' receivables and payables in the same currency. These accounts allow the receipt of inward payments, cheques/cash and also allow the issue of international money transfers and drafts. They are offered by most of the clearing banks.

Foreign Operation A subsidiary, associate, joint venture or branch whose activities are based in a country or currency other than those of the reporting entity.

Forward Foreign Exchange Contracts One way to hedge against exchange rate movements is to arrange a forward foreign exchange contract. This is an agreement initiated by you to buy or sell a specific amount of foreign currency at a certain rate, on or before a certain date.

Fraud The intentional misstatement or omission of amounts or disclosures designed to deceive financial statement users.

Functional Currency The currency of the primary economic environment in which the entity operates.

Generally Accepted Accounting Principles (GAAP) The accounting and disclosure requirements of company legislation and pronouncements by the International Accounting Standards Board (IASB), supplemented by accumulated professional judgement.

Going Concern Assumption/Basis Financial statements are prepared on the assumption that the entity will continue to operate without the threat of liquidation for the foreseeable future, usually regarded as at least one year.

Government Assistance Action by government designed to provide an economic benefit specific to an entity or range of entities qualifying under certain criteria. Most assistance is in the form of grants to assist with capital expenditure but some grants relate to revenue expenditure.

Government Grants Includes all forms of assistance from central government, government agencies and similar bodies, whether they are local, national or international.

Goodwill This represents future economic benefits that are not capable of being individually identified and separately recognised. It is essentially the residual cost after allocating fair value to identifiable net assets taken over. Goodwill is measured as the difference between:

- the aggregate of:
  - the acquisition-date fair value of the consideration transferred;
  - the amount of any non-controlling interest in the entity acquired; and
  - in a business combination achieved in stages, the acquisition-date fair value of the acquirer's previously held equity interest in the entity acquired; and
- the net of the acquisition-date amounts of the identifiable assets acquired and the liabilities assumed, both measured in accordance with IFRS 3 *Business Combinations*.

If the difference above is positive, the acquirer should recognise the goodwill as an asset. If the difference above is negative, the resulting gain is recognised as a bargain purchase in profit or loss.

Grant Date The date at which the entity and another party (including an employee) agree to a share-based payment arrangement, being when the entity and the counterparty have a shared understanding of the terms and conditions of the arrangement. At grant date, the entity confers on the counterparty the right to cash, other assets or equity instruments of the entity, provided the specified vesting conditions, if any, are met. If that agreement is subject to an approval process (e.g. by shareholders), the grant date is the date when that approval is obtained.

Group of Biological Assets An aggregation of similar living animals or plants.

Harvest The detachment of produce from a biological asset or the cessation of a biological asset's life processes.

Hedge Accounting This is a practice in which a risky trading position and its hedge are treated as one item so that the gains in one automatically offset the losses in the other.

Human Capital This is the stock of competences, knowledge and personality attributes embodied in the workforce of the business so as to produce economic value.

Impairment Loss The amount by which the carrying amount of an asset or cash generation unit (CGU) exceeds its recoverable amount. (Impairment should be recognised in accordance with IAS 36 *Impairment of Assets*.)

Insurance Assets An insurer's net contractual rights under an insurance contract.

Insurance Contract A contract under which one party (the insurer) accepts significant insurance risk from another party (the policyholder) by agreeing to compensate the policyholder if a specified uncertain future event (the insured event) adversely affects the policyholder.

Insurance Liability An insurer's net contractual obligations under an insurance contract.

Intangible Asset An intangible asset is an identifiable non-monetary asset without physical substance but which is identifiable and controlled by the entity and has an estimated useful life of more than one year. Examples of such assets include patents and copyrights, organisational ability, research and development, customer databases, exclusivity within a particular market or geographic area, software, customer satisfaction and the speed at which companies are able to bring new products and services to market.

Interest in Another Entity This refers to contractual and non-contractual involvement that exposes an entity to variability of returns from the performance of another entity. An interest in another entity can be evidenced by, but is not limited to, the holding of equity or debt instruments, as well as other forms of involvement such as the provision of funding, liquidity support, credit enhancement and guarantees. It includes the means by which an entity has control or joint control of, or significant influence over, another entity. An entity does not necessarily have an interest in another entity solely because of a typical customer-supplier relationship.

Interim Financial Report A financial report containing either a complete set of financial statements or a set of condensed financial statements for a financial reporting period shorter than a full financial year, typically a quarter or half-year.

Intragroup Inventory Inventory on hand at the reporting date which has been purchased from another group company.

Intrinsic Value The difference between the fair value of the shares to which the counterparty has the (conditional or unconditional) right to subscribe or which it has the right to receive, and the price (if any) the counterparty is (or will be) required to pay for those shares. For example, a share option with an exercise price of €15 on a share with a fair value of €20 has an intrinsic value of €5.

Inventory This includes: raw materials; work-in-progress (WIP); finished goods produced; consumable stores; goods or other assets purchased for use or resale by the business in the provision of its services.

Investing Activities These relate to the acquisition and disposal of non-current assets and other investments not included in cash equivalents.

Investment Property Property (land or a building, or part of a building, or both) held (by the owner or by the lessee under a finance lease) to earn rentals or for capital appreciation, or both. It excludes property that is held for:
- use in the production or supply of goods or services, or for administrative purposes; or
- sale in the ordinary course of business.

Joint Arrangement This is an arrangement of which two or more parties have joint control.

Joint Control The contractually agreed sharing of control of an arrangement, which exists only when decisions about the relevant activities require the unanimous consent of the parties sharing control.

Joint Operation A joint arrangement whereby the parties that have joint control of the arrangement have rights to the assets, and obligations for the liabilities, relating to the arrangement.

Joint Venture A contractual agreement whereby two or more parties undertake an economic activity that is subject to joint control.

Joint Venturer A party to a joint venture that has joint control of that joint venture.

Lease An agreement whereby the lessor conveys to the lessee, in return for a payment or series of payments, the right to use an asset for an agreed period of time. There are two types of lease: a finance lease; and an operating lease.

Lease Term The non-cancellable period for which the lessee has contracted to lease the asset together with any further terms for which the lessee has the option to continue to lease the asset, with or without further payment, when at the inception of the lease it is reasonably certain that the lessee will exercise the option.

Legal Obligation An obligation that derives from a contract, legislation or other operation of law.

Liability An obligation to transfer future economic benefits as a result of past transactions or events.

Liquidity Ratios These measure how accessible an entity's cash is.

Materiality This is an expression of the relative significance of a particular matter in the context of the financial statements as a whole. A matter is material if its omission or misstatement could reasonably be expected to influence the decisions of users of financial statements.

Minimum Lease Payments Payments over the lease term that the lessee is, or can be, required to make (excluding contingent rent, costs for services and taxes to be paid by and reimbursed to the lessor), together with any amounts guaranteed by the lessee or related party.

Monetary Items Money and assets/liabilities held to be received/paid in fixed or determinable amounts. Examples include deferred tax, pensions and provisions.

Net Investment in a Foreign Operation The amount of the interest in the net assets of that operation. This includes long-term receivables or loans, but does not include trade receivables or trade payables.

Non-controlling Interest (NCI) The portion of the net results and net assets of a subsidiary attributable to interests not owned directly or indirectly by the parent.

Non-current Assets Assets with an expected life of more than one year held for use on a continuous basis, e.g. land and buildings, patents, etc. Non-current assets usually comprise tangible and intangible non-current assets.

Net Realisable Value (NRV) This is defined as the estimated selling price in the ordinary course of business less the estimated costs of completion and less the estimated costs necessary to make the sale. It is the amount obtainable from the sale of an asset in an arm's length transaction less costs of disposal.

Non-adjusting Event after the Reporting Period An event after the reporting period that is indicative of a condition that arose after the end of the reporting period.

Normal Capacity The expected achievable production based on the average over several periods. It includes capacity lost through planned maintenance.

Obligating Event An event that creates a legal or constructive obligation where an entity has no realistic alternative but to settle that obligation.

Operating Activities The principal revenue-producing activities of the entity, and other activities that are not investing or financing.

Operating Lease This type of lease does *not* transfer all the risks and rewards incidental to ownership of an asset to the lessee; these are retained by the lessor. Indicators that a lease is an operating lease are that:
- at the inception of the lease, the present value of minimum lease payments *does not* amount to substantially all of the fair value of the leased asset; and
- the lease term is significantly less than the useful life of the asset.

Operating Segment A component of an organisation:
- that engages in business activities from which it may earn revenues and incur expenses (including revenues and expenses relating to transactions with other components of the same organisation);
- whose operating results are reviewed regularly by the organisation's chief operating decision-maker to make decisions about resources to be allocated to the segment and to assess its performance; and
- for which discrete financial information is available.

Ordinary Share An equity instrument that is subordinate to all other classes of equity instruments.

Overtrading This arises where an entity expands its turnover fairly rapidly without securing additional long-term capital adequate for its needs.

Parent In the context of consolidation, a parent is an entity that holds more than 50% of the equity of another entity and is therefore deemed to control that entity. Control in this context is defined as ability to direct policies and management. In this type of relationship, the controlling company is the parent and the controlled company is referred to as the subsidiary. The parent company prepares and publishes consolidated financial statements at the end of the year to reflect this relationship.

Partnership In broad terms, this is an association of two or more persons engaged in a business enterprise in which the profits and losses are shared proportionally.

Party to a Joint Arrangement An entity that participates in a joint arrangement, regardless of whether that entity has joint control of the arrangement.

Post-employment Benefits Plans Retirement benefits, such as pensions, and other post-employment benefits, such as post-employment medical care. The most common examples are defined contribution and defined benefit pension plans.

Potential Ordinary Share (POS) A financial instrument or other contract that may entitle its holder to ordinary shares.

Power Existing rights that give the current ability to direct the relevant activities.

Prepayments Amounts paid in a period which relate to charges of a subsequent period.

Presentation Currency This is the currency in which the financial statements are presented.

Prior Period Errors Omissions from, and misstatements in, the entity's financial statements for one or more prior periods arising from a failure to use, or misuse of, reliable information that:

- was available when financial statements for those periods were authorised for issue; and
- could reasonably be expected to have been obtained and taken into account in the preparation and presentation of those financial statements.

Profitability Ratios These show the relationship between profitability and revenue.

Property, Plant and Equipment Are tangible items that are:

(a) held for use in the production or supply of goods or services, for rental to others or for administrative purposes; and

(b) expected to be used during more than one accounting or financial period.

Protective Rights These are rights designed to protect the interest of the party holding those rights without giving that party power over the entity to which those rights relate.

Provision A liability of uncertain timing or amount. Examples of provisions are those for restructuring for early retirement and pension commitments.

Qualifying Asset An asset that necessarily takes a substantial period of time to get ready for its intended use or sale. For example, a property or bridge that has to be constructed.

Ratio This expresses the relationship between two or more figures.

Ratio Analysis A tool used to conduct a quantitative analysis of information in an entity's financial statements.

Recoverable Amount This is the higher of an asset's fair value less costs of disposal and its value in use (VIU).

Related Party IAS 24 *Related Party Disclosures* defines a related party as a *person* or *entity* that is related to the entity that is preparing its financial statements.

Relevant Activities Activities of the investee that significantly affect the investee's returns.

Reportable Segments Operating segments or aggregations of operating segments that meet specified criteria.

Research An original and planned investigation undertaken with the prospect of gaining new scientific or technical knowledge and understanding.

Residual Value of an Asset The estimated amount that an entity would currently obtain from the disposal or sale of the asset, after deducting the estimated costs of disposal, if the asset were already of the age and in the condition expected at the end of its estimated useful economic life.

Restructuring The following are examples of events that may fall under the definition of *restructuring*: sale or termination of a line of business; closure of business locations in a country or region or the relocation of business activities from one country or region to another; changes in management structure, e.g. eliminating a layer of management; and fundamental reorganisations that have a material effect on the nature and focus of the entity's operations.

Retirement Benefit Plan An arrangement by which an entity provides benefits (annual income or lump sum) to employees when or after they terminate from service, when such benefits, or the contributions towards them, can be determined or estimated in advance of retirement from the provisions of a document or from the entity's practices.

Retrospective Change in Accounting Policy This is the application of a new accounting policy to transactions and events as if that policy had always been applied.

Revenue IAS 18 *Revenue* defines revenue as the gross inflow of economic benefits (cash, receivables, other assets) arising from the ordinary operating activities of an entity such as sales of goods, sales of services, interest, royalties and dividends. Revenue should be measured at the fair value of the consideration receivable.

Revenue Expenditure This refers to those expenses incurred to acquire goods or services that are also essential in terms of the day-to-day operations of a business. However, the benefits that revenue expenditure gives are of a short-term nature and do not provide future economic benefits (i.e. the benefits are consumed over a short period of time, with less than one year being the period that is generally used). Revenue expenditure is recorded as an expense in arriving at profit or loss in the statement of profit or loss and other comprehensive income.

Rights Issue An issue of shares for cash to existing shareholders at a price (usually) below the current market price. It is equivalent to a cash issue at full market price combined with a subsequent bonus issue.

Separate Financial Statements Financial statements presented by a parent (i.e. an investor with control of a subsidiary), an investor with joint control of, or significant influence over, an investee, in which the investments are accounted for at cost or in accordance with IFRS 9 *Financial Instruments*.

Separate Vehicle A separately identifiable financial structure, including separate legal entities or entities recognised by statute, regardless of whether those entities have a legal personality.

Share-based Payment Transaction A transaction in which the entity receives goods or services as consideration for equity instruments of the entity (including shares or share options), or acquires goods or services by incurring liabilities to the supplier of those goods or services for amounts that are based on the price of the entity's shares or other equity instruments of the entity. In this case, the entity issues shares (not cash).

Share Option A contract that gives the holder the right, but not the obligation (i.e. the holder does not have to purchase the shares), to subscribe to the entity's shares at a fixed or determinable price for a specified period of time.

Share Options and Warrants These are financial instruments that give the holder the right to purchase ordinary shares at a fixed price, sometime in the future.

Short-term Benefits All forms of consideration in exchange for service rendered by employees including wages, salaries, holiday pay, sick leave, bonuses payable within 12 months of the reporting period and social security contributions payable in respect of employee benefits. They also include compensation in the form of financial assets, goods and services, and equity instruments of the employer that are payable within 12 months after service is rendered.

Short-term Investment This is an item in the current assets section of a statement of financial position and represents any investments that a company has made that will expire within one year. For the most part, these will consist of shares and bonds that can be liquidated fairly quickly.

Significant Influence The power to participate in the financial and operating policy decisions of the investee but not control those policies. If an investor holds, directly or indirectly, 20% or more of the voting power of the investee, it is presumed that it has significant influence, unless it can be clearly demonstrated that this is not the case. Conversely, if less than 20%, the presumption is that the investor does not have significant influence. A majority shareholding by another investor does not preclude an investor having significant influence. Its existence is usually evidenced in one or more of the following ways:
- representation on the board of directors;
- participation in policy-making processes;
- material transactions between the investor and the investee;
- interchange of managerial personnel; or
- provision of essential technical information.

Spot Rate The exchange rate for immediate delivery.

Statement of Cash Flows This statement reports on an entity's cash flow activities, particularly its operating, investing and financing activities.

Statement of Changes in Equity This statement illustrates the changes in an entity's equity throughout the reporting period.

Statement of Profit or Loss and Other Comprehensive Income (often referred to as an 'income statement' or 'profit and loss account') This statement shows the revenues from operations, expenses of operating and the resulting net profit or loss over a specific period of time. The term 'comprehensive income' for a period includes profit or loss for that period plus other comprehensive income recognised in that period. The components of other comprehensive income include: changes in revaluation surplus; actuarial gains and losses on defined benefit plans recognised in accordance with IAS 19; and gains and losses arising from translating the financial statements of a foreign operation (IAS 21). An entity has a choice of presenting: a single statement of profit or loss and other comprehensive income; or two statements, an income statement displaying components of profit or loss and a statement of other comprehensive income that begins with profit or loss (bottom line of the income statement) and displays components of other comprehensive income.

Statement of Financial Position (often referred to as a 'balance sheet') This financial statement reports an entity's assets, liabilities and equity at a given point in time.

Structured Entity An entity that has been designed so that voting or similar rights are not the dominant factor in deciding who controls the entity, such as when any voting rights relate to administrative tasks only and the relevant activities are directed by means of contractual arrangements.

Subsidiary An entity in which the investor has dominant influence and therefore controls. In simple terms, control is presumed to exist when the parent owns over 50% of the voting power of an enterprise unless, in exceptional circumstances, it can be clearly demonstrated that such ownership does not constitute control. Control in this context is defined as ability to direct policies and management.

Tangible Non-current Assets Assets that have a physical identity, such as buildings, furniture, plant and equipment, and which are used by the business to provide the infrastructure for the provision of its goods and services.

Taxable Profit The profit for a period determined in accordance with the rules established by the taxation authorities, upon which income taxes are payable.

Tax Base The tax base of an *asset* is the amount attributed to it for tax purposes. The tax base of a *liability* is its carrying amount less any amount that will be deductible for tax purposes in respect of that liability in future periods.

Tax Expense The aggregate amount included in the determination of profit for the period in respect of current and deferred tax.

Temporary Differences These are differences between the carrying amount of an asset or liability in the statement of financial position and its tax base. Temporary differences may be either taxable temporary differences or deductible temporary differences.

Trade and Other Payables Monies owed to another entity by the business as a result of the normal course of activities of a business.

Trade and Other Receivables Monies owed by another entity to the business as a result of the normal course of activities of a business.

Undistributable reserves of a public limited company These are defined as:
- the share premium account;
- the capital redemption reserve fund;
- the excess of accumulated unrealised profits, not previously capitalised, over accumulated unrealised losses not previously written off by a reduction or reorganisation of capital; and
- any other reserve that the company is prohibited from distributing by any enactment, or by its Memorandum or Articles of Association.

Useful Economic Life The useful economic life of a tangible non-current asset is the period over which the entity expects to derive economic benefits from the asset.

Value in Use (VIU) This is the present value of future cash flows expected to be derived from the asset or cash generating unit (CGU).

Vesting Conditions The conditions that must be satisfied for the contractee to become entitled to receive cash, other assets or equity instruments of the entity, under a share-based payment arrangement. Vesting conditions include service conditions, which require the other party to complete a specified period of service, and performance conditions, which require specified performance targets to be met (such as a specified increase in the entity's profit over a specified period of time).

Vesting Period The period during which all the specified vesting conditions of a share-based payment arrangement are to be satisfied.

Window Dressing This is a strategy used near the end of the reporting period to improve the appearance of the financial statements. For example, a company that operates throughout the year with a negative balance in its bank account may not wish to report this publicly in its financial statements. Therefore, to avoid doing so, the company withholds payments close to the end of the reporting period (*say* between 20–31 December for a 31 December reporting period) so that the bank balance is positive. Then shortly after the end of the reporting period (*say* 5 January), the company pays those amounts that normally would have been paid at the end of December.

Index